Journalizing and Posting

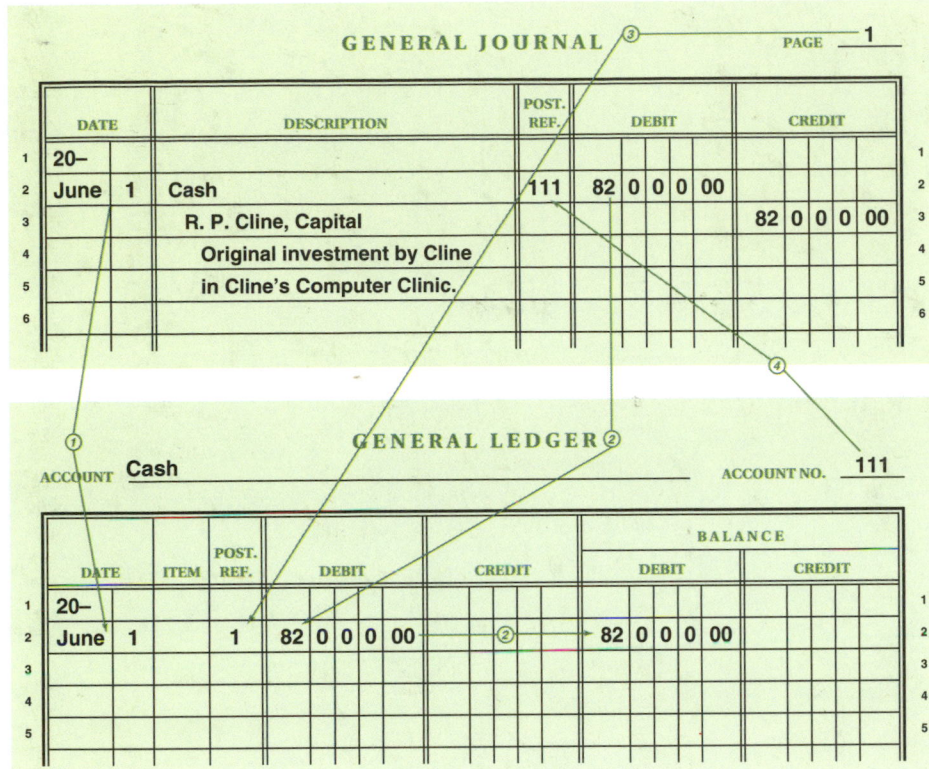

GENERAL JOURNAL ③ PAGE ___1___

	DATE		DESCRIPTION	POST. REF.	DEBIT	CREDIT	
1	20–						1
2	June	1	Cash	111	82 0 0 0 00		2
3			R. P. Cline, Capital			82 0 0 0 00	3
4			Original investment by Cline				4
5			in Cline's Computer Clinic.				5
6							6

① Date of transaction
② Amount of transaction
③ Page number of the journal
④ Ledger account number

GENERAL LEDGER ②

ACCOUNT **Cash** ACCOUNT NO. **111**

	DATE		ITEM	POST. REF.	DEBIT	CREDIT	BALANCE DEBIT	BALANCE CREDIT	
1	20–								1
2	June	1		1	82 0 0 0 00	②	82 0 0 0 00		2
3									3
4									4
5									5

The Work Sheet

Account Name	Trial Balance Debit	Trial Balance Credit	Adjustments Debit	Adjustments Credit	Adjusted Trial Balance Debit	Adjusted Trial Balance Credit	Income Statement Debit	Income Statement Credit	Balance Sheet Debit	Balance Sheet Credit
	Assets				Assets				Assets	
		Liabilities				Liabilities				Liabilities
		Capital				Capital				Capital
	Drawing				Drawing				Drawing	
		Revenue				Revenue		Revenue		
	Expenses				Expenses		Expenses			

Steps in the Closing Process

R Close the Revenue accounts into Income Summary.

E Close the Expenses accounts into Income Summary.

I Close the Income Summary Account into the Capital Account, transferring the net income or net loss to the Capital Account.

D Close the Drawing account into the Capital Account.

COLLEGE ACCOUNTING

NINTH EDITION

1-26

Douglas J. McQuaig
Wenatchee Valley College, Emeritus

Patricia A. Bille
Highline Community College

HOUGHTON MIFFLIN COMPANY   BOSTON   NEW YORK

This text is sincerely dedicated to the students who will use it.

Every possible effort has been made to produce an understandable, up-to-date, and accurate presentation of the fundamentals of accounting.

This text is intended to be an important element in your course, as well as an invaluable future reference for you in the preparation of your career in business.

Best wishes for your success.

Douglas J. McQuaig

Patricia A. Bille

Executive Publisher: George Hoffman
Senior Sponsoring Editor: Ann West
Senior Marketing Manager: Mike Schenk
Marketing Coordinator: Erin Lane
Senior Development Editor: Chere Bemelmans
Editorial Assistant: Diane Akerman
Project Editor: Paula Kmetz
Art and Design Manager: Gary Crespo
Cover Design Manager: Anne S. Katzeff
Senior Photo Editor: Jennifer Meyer Dare
Composition Buyer: Chuck Dutton
New Title Project Manager: James Lonergan

Cover Photo © Y. Takahashi/Getty Images

This book is written to provide accurate and authoritative information concerning the covered topics. It is not meant to take the place of professional advice. The companies and financial information in this book have been created for instructional purposes. No reference to any specific company or person is intended or should be inferred. Any similarity with an existing company or person is coincidental.

Printed in the U.S.A.

Library of Congress Control Number: 2006938443
ISBN-10: 0-618-82417-0
ISBN-13: 978-0-618-82417-5

123456789-DOW-11 10 09 08 07

Contents

PART THREE

THE ACCOUNTING CYCLE FOR A MERCHANDISING BUSINESS; USING SPECIAL JOURNALS

PART FOUR

ACCOUNTING FOR PROMISSORY NOTES

PART FIVE

ACCOUNTING FOR VALUATION OF RECEIVABLES, INVENTORY, AND PROPERTY AND EQUIPMENT

PART SIX

ACCOUNTING FOR PARTNERSHIPS AND CORPORATIONS

PART SEVEN
ACCOUNTING FOR DECISION MAKING AND MANUFACTURING

Preface

The study of accounting enables college students to achieve three important objectives: (1) to train for jobs in accounting; (2) to train for other careers such as technical, managerial, and executive positions; or (3) to prepare for advanced studies in accounting and business. We designed *College Accounting* to help students reach these goals by developing their practical accounting skills in an understandable basic accounting text. But today's students need more than just basic accounting skills; students need to feel comfortable with rapidly changing technology, understand how to make sound ethical and business decisions, and become successful problem solvers and communicators. In the ninth edition, we have revised *College Accounting* to increase its relevance in today's world and to provide additional technology to help students learn basic accounting skills and think and solve problems in the current business world.

EMPHASIS ON BUILDING STUDY SKILLS AND CAREER PATHS

The ninth edition of *College Accounting* continues to emphasize the importance of college accounting as a gateway to a variety of jobs and career paths, and the program provides numerous tools aimed at enabling students to build the skills, habits, and outlook that will help them succeed in school and beyond. The text itself contains a number of features that will help students see their studies in a real-world context. Ethics, problem solving, and communications are central to today's accounting needs, and we have focused on covering these issues in a variety of ways. Three text features in particular strengthen this outlook:

Internet Links to Accounting These chapter openers provide a hands-on look at many of today's well-known businesses that are active on the Internet. Each opener first introduces students to the company and then asks a series of questions about the company that relates directly to the chapter topics. We provide web addresses for further investigation of the company. These questions and addresses are designed to prompt discussion, written responses, or additional questions that focus on the chapter. The related end-of-chapter feature follows through to provide students with meaningful web activities. Students are exposed not only to web exploration but also to critical thinking, problem solving, and communication activities.

Careers in Your Future Prominent business people whose professional lives began with accounting are featured throughout the text. Our hope is that their words and stories will encourage and inspire students and provide good role models as they advance in their careers.

End-of-Chapter Cases We have provided a series of brief cases at the end of each chapter to help students keep the business perspective in mind. *Consider and Communicate, Critical Thinking, What's Wrong with This Picture?,* and

A Question of Ethics foster problem-solving and communication skills that students will need in today's business world. With each case, students have an opportunity to develop their problem-solving skills and employ their knowledge of accounting to complete a task. The cases may be appropriate for individual or team responses—discussion of these cases in class, particularly questions involving ethical issues, can be particularly useful.

The support materials and supplements for *College Accounting*, Ninth Edition, also reinforce the theme of study skills and career success. Described more fully below, the resources available in "Your Guide to an A" on the McQuaig/Bille Study Center website provide students with a wealth of opportunities to review and test their understanding of the text content. Videos outline important skills, such as organizational and writing skills, needed to succeed in school and work, and handy MP3 downloads give students the opportunity to integrate their learning into everyday life. A print supplement, *Guide to Success in College Accounting*, gives students some additional study support, such as math review, learning style assessment, and career planning.

THOROUGHLY REVISED AND RELEVANT TEXT

In addition to the new features described above, we have completely revised and updated the ninth edition to increase its relevance for today's complex and challenging world.

Major Content Changes

A complete list of content changes from the eighth to the ninth editions is available in the Transition Guide (located on the Online Learning Center website or in the *Instructor's Resource Manual with Solutions*), but a brief listing of the most important content changes follows:

- **Chapter 4: Adjusting Entries and the Work Sheet** The use of electronic spreadsheets for preparing work sheets is introduced in this chapter, and the work sheet is shown prepared manually and using Microsoft Excel. The tools used to prepare the Excel work sheet are also illustrated.

- **Chapter 5: Closing Entries and the Post-Closing Trial Balance** We describe in more detail the differences in accounting methods.

- **Chapter 7: Bank Accounts and Cash Funds** We have added a discussion of internal controls as a part of cash management as well as a discussion of electronic funds transfers.

- **Chapter 8: Employee Earnings and Deductions** We have updated the tax percentages and tax forms while including a section describing laws that affect payroll activities.

- **Appendixes C and D for Chapters 10 and 11: An Alternative to Special Journals** These new appendixes discuss and illustrate the basic general journal entries for a merchandising business. The appendixes are designed to be used in place of the coverage of special journals in Chapters 10 and 11 if a detailed discussion of special journals is not desired.

- **Chapter 18: Property and Equipment** Leasehold improvements are now introduced and discussed, and MACRS property class descriptions have been updated.

- **Chapter 19: Partnerships** Various types of partnerships, including general partnerships, limited partnerships, and limited liability partnerships, are now defined and discussed.
- **Chapter 20: Corporate Organization and Capital Stock** S corporations and limited liability companies (LLCs) are now defined and discussed.

Special Text Features and Enhancements

Along with a complete revision of text and end-of-chapter assignment material, several new pedagogical features have been added to the ninth edition:

Extended Text Examples Cline's Computer Clinic is integrated throughout Chapters 1 through 5 to illustrate the completion of the accounting cycle for a sole proprietorship service business using a general journal. Rainier Plumbing Supply is featured throughout Chapters 10 through 13 to illustrate the completion of the accounting cycle for a sole proprietorship merchandising business using special journals. Rainier Plumbing Supply is reintroduced at appropriate points in Chapters 14 through 18.

The Computer Clinic Designed to give students experience using computers to manage accounting transactions, this continuous general ledger problem featuring *All About You Spa*, a sole proprietorship service business, begins in Chapter 3 by asking students to open the accounting books for the business. Students are required to enter into general ledger software (Peachtree, QuickBooks, or Houghton Mifflin's Windows General Ledger) the company name, company type, and chart of accounts before journalizing and posting the first month's transactions and printing a trial balance. After Chapter 4, "Adjusting Entries and the Work Sheet," students continue with *All About You Spa* by completing the end-of-the-month adjustments and printing the financial statements. After Chapter 5, "Closing Entries and the Post-Closing Trial Balance," students again work with *All About You Spa* to close the books for the month and print a post-closing trial balance.

All About You Spa returns in Chapters 10 through 13, when the owner adds two lines of merchandise to the business. Special journals for sales, purchases, cash receipts, and cash payments are introduced, and procedures are completed to end the accounting period.

ACCESSIBLE AND USER-FRIENDLY CONTENT

Although the ninth edition of *College Accounting* has been updated and revised, some things have not changed. Drawing from more than sixty-seven years of combined teaching experience, we continue to provide students with a strong basic knowledge of accounting terms, concepts, and procedures. The text is logically organized, liberally illustrated, and paced in a manner that is easy for students to read and understand. Generous use of white space provides an uncluttered reading environment with ample area for student or instructor notes.

Proven Pedagogy

The ninth edition of this text is built on a solid pedagogical foundation appreciated by instructors and students through many editions. The careful pacing of new topics, consistent review, and thorough and meaningful assignment material all create a well-balanced presentation that helps guarantee student success.

Throughout each chapter:

- **Performance objectives** appear at the beginning of each chapter to help students focus on key learning outcomes. They are then highlighted in the margin alongside the related text discussion. A performance objective number serves as a reference to the objectives in the chapter summary, exercises, and problems.
- **Key terms** appear in red and are defined in the text and repeated in a glossary at the end of the chapter.
- **Remembers,** also in the margin, provide learning hints or summaries, often alerting students to common procedural pitfalls to help them complete their work successfully.
- **FYIs,** similarly, provide practical tips or information about accounting and business.

Each chapter ends with a Review of Performance Objectives and a Glossary that lists terms with definitions. Questions, exercises, cases, and problems follow and include:

- **Discussion Questions** Questions based on the main points in the text and appropriate for either class discussion or for homework are included at the end of each chapter.
- **Exercises** For practice in applying concepts, exercises are provided with each chapter. Each exercise is described briefly in the margin with a reference to the appropriate performance objective.
- **Cases** End-of-chapter cases develop problem-solving and communication skills that will help students succeed in today's business world.
- **Problems** Each chapter contains four A and four B problems. The A and B problems are parallel in content and level of difficulty. They are arranged in order of difficulty, with Problems 1A and 1B in each chapter being the simplest and the last problem in each series being the most comprehensive. Check Figures appear alongside every A and B problem's instructions in the text.

Problems that can be solved using the Houghton Mifflin Windows General Ledger program are designated by the first icon on the left.

Problems that can be worked using Spreadsheet Applications for College Accounting are identified by the second icon on the left.

- **Before a Test Check** This feature provides questions (true/false, multiple choice, matching, and completion) and brief application problems after every two to four chapters. These pretest activities let students check their understanding of what they have read and practiced in the preceding chapters prior to taking a test.
- **Accounting Cycle Review and Comprehensive Review Problem** These features give students the opportunity to apply accounting procedures to help them understand the process they have just studied in a series of chapters (1–5) and (7–13). Accounting Cycle Review Problems A and B involve the full accounting cycle, one for Splashdown and the other for Wind Riders,

both sole proprietorship service businesses. The Comprehensive Review Problem following Chapter 13 involves the full accounting cycle for Fine Fabrics, a sole proprietorship merchandising business.

Focus on the Fundamentals

College Accounting, Ninth Edition, presents the basics of accounting in a practical, easy-to-comprehend manner. Great emphasis is placed on developing a firm foundation of fundamental procedures. Appropriate repetition and extensive use of examples enable students to develop self-confidence and to make progress in gradual stages. Color photographs round out the text—and provide additional real-world insights.

Recording business transactions is directly related to the fundamental accounting equation. Each newly introduced transaction is fully illustrated and is supported with T account examples. Comprehensive reviews of T accounts, organized in relation to the fundamental accounting equation, appear in the *Working Papers with Study Guide,* student website, and *College Accounting Resources for Students* CD-ROM to assist as students review material and complete assignments.

College Accounting, Ninth Edition, is also a very readable text. We write in short sentences and use many illustrations to help students relate the words to the procedures. Each chapter of *College Accounting* has been reviewed by business instructors who teach courses in English as a Second Language and English for Special Purposes, as well as by students enrolled in these classes. With their assistance and advice, we have taken steps to ensure that the text is accessible to all readers.

Each chapter is limited to the presentation of one major concept, which is amply illustrated with business documents and report forms. As terms are introduced, they are defined thoroughly and are used in subsequent examples. Comprehension is also enhanced through the use of "Remember" and "FYI" statements, which offer a learning hint or a practical tip about a topic.

Emphasis on Accounting Terminology

We firmly believe that accounting is the language of business and that learning new terminology is an essential part of a first course. Each key term is printed in red and is explained when it is first introduced. The end-of-chapter glossary repeats the definitions of the terms presented in the chapter. In addition, page numbers are included for each glossary term, making it easy for students to refer to a term in the chapter. The glossary terms are included on electronic flash cards on the student website, providing yet another interactive opportunity for learning.

Proven Color-Coded Pedagogy

The ninth edition of *College Accounting* continues to implement a color-coded pedagogy that helps students recognize and remember key points. The pedagogical use of color also helps students understand the flow of accounting data and identify different types of documents and reports used in accounting. Finally, the use of color helps students identify the performance objectives for each chapter, recognize the performance objectives called for in each exercise, and review material efficiently and effectively.

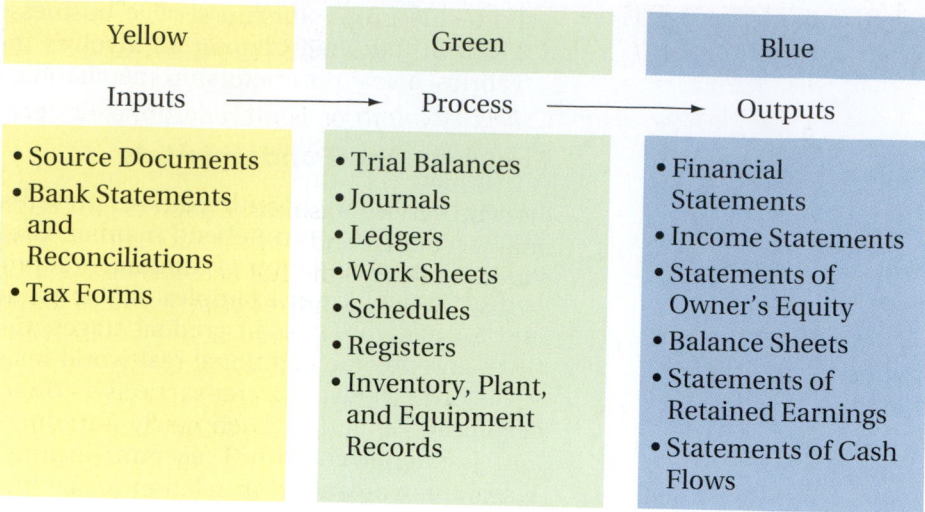

The ninth edition's consistent use of color extends to the treatment of accounting forms, financial statements, and documents in the text and end-of-chapter assignments.

- **Source documents,** such as invoices, bank statements, facsimiles, and other material that originates with outside sources, are shown in yellow.
- **Working papers, journals, ledgers, trial balances, and other forms and schedules** used as part of the internal accounting process are shown in green.
- **Financial statements,** including balances sheets, income statements, statements of owners' equity, and statements of cash flows, are shown in blue.

This distinctive treatment differentiates these elements and helps students see where each element belongs in the accounting cycle. Seeing these relationships helps students understand how accountants transform data into useful information.

GUARANTEE OF QUALITY MATERIAL

Successful use of an accounting text depends on more than the interesting and memorable presentation of material by the instructor and the text. The overall quality of the chapter-opening features, examples, illustrations, color photographs, end-of-chapter questions, exercises, cases, and problems, as well as ancillary materials, are critical to learning and retaining the facts and concepts that are covered in the course. Instructors and students must be assured that these materials are complete, consistent, and accurate.

Together with our publisher, we have taken a multistep approach to ensure quality materials for classroom use. The quality-control system begins with in-depth reviews of the original manuscript and concludes with accuracy reviews of page proof by instructors who are actively teaching the course.

FLEXIBLE CHAPTER COVERAGE

College Accounting, Ninth Edition, is designed primarily for use in a course extending two or three quarters or two semesters. The text is divided into parts: Chapters 1 through 5 cover the full accounting cycle for a sole proprietorship service business. Chapters 6 through 9 cover the combined journal, bank accounts, and payroll accounting. Chapters 10 through 13 cover special journals and the full accounting cycle for a merchandising firm. In this section, new appendixes covering sales and purchases on account as well as cash receipts and cash payments provide an alternative treatment for instructors who would prefer not to cover special journals in their course. Chapters 14 through 18 cover notes payable and receivable as well as the valuation of receivables, inventories, and property assets. Chapters 19 through 22 cover partnerships and corporations. Chapters 23 through 26 cover the statement of cash flows and financial statement analysis as well as departmental and manufacturing accounting.

The following appendixes expand content coverage and increase the instructor's options for structuring the course:

- **Appendix A: Methods of Depreciation (after Chapter 4)** This appendix describes methods of depreciation, including the Modified Accelerated Cost Recovery System.
- **Appendix B: Bad Debts (after Chapter 7)** This appendix covers the allowance and specific charge-off methods.
- **NEW! Appendix C: Sales and Purchases on Account: An Alternative to Special Journals (after Chapter 10)** This new appendix illustrates the basic general journal entries related to sales and purchases for a merchandising business. It is designed to be used in place of the coverage of special journals in Chapter 10 if a detailed discussion of special journals is not desired.
- **NEW! Appendix D: Cash Receipts and Cash Payments: An Alternative to Special Journals (after Chapter 11)** This new appendix illustrates the basic general journal entries related to cash receipts and cash payments for a merchandising business. It is designed to be used in place of the coverage of special journals in Chapter 11 if a detailed discussion of special journals is not desired.
- **Appendix E: Inventory Methods (after Chapter 13)** This appendix discusses methods used to determine the amount of the ending inventory for a merchandising business.
- **Appendix F: Financial Statement Analysis (after Chapter 13)** This appendix describes percentages and ratios used to interpret information in financial statements.
- **Appendix G: The Statement of Cash Flows (after Chapter 13)** This appendix discusses the indirect method of determining cash flows.
- **Appendix H: Estimating the Value of Inventories (after Chapter 17)** Appendix H examines the retail and gross profit methods.
- **Appendix I: The Voucher System of Accounting (after Chapter 18)** This appendix illustrates the use of the voucher system as a means of internal control, particularly of cash.
- **Appendix J: Statement of Cash Flows—Indirect Method (after Chapter 23)** This appendix illustrates the indirect method of determining cash flows.

Because many students take only one quarter or one semester of accounting, Appendixes A, B, E, F, and G offer an exposure to the basics of depreciation, the valuation of receivables and inventory, financial statement analysis, and the statement of cash flows.

These five appendixes are developed more fully and presented as chapters in the second half of the text, as follows:

- Appendix A, Methods of Depreciation, is expanded into Chapter 18, Property and Equipment.
- Appendix B, Bad Debts, is expanded into Chapter 16, Uncollectible Accounts.
- Appendix E, Inventory Methods, is expanded into Chapter 17, Ending Merchandise Inventory.
- Appendix F, Financial Statement Analysis, is expanded into Chapter 24, Comparative Financial Statements.
- Appendix G, The Statement of Cash Flows, is expanded into Chapter 23, The Statement of Cash Flows—Direct Method.

Appendixes H, I, and J, presented in the second half of the book, offer an exposure to estimating the value of inventories, the voucher system, and the statement of cash flows—indirect method.

SUPPLEMENTARY LEARNING AIDS FOR STUDENTS AND SUPPORT MATERIALS FOR INSTRUCTORS

For the ninth edition, we have assembled the most comprehensive package of student and instructor aids—both print and electronic—to complement a wide variety of teaching styles and course emphases. The complete *College Accounting* teaching and learning package is listed below. Detailed descriptions of each element of the support package are available in the *Instructor's Resource Manual with Solutions* and on the instructor website.

For Students

Working Papers with Study Guide (available in print and on CD-ROM)
Working Papers with Study Guide contains forms for students to use in completing all of the exercises and problems in the textbook along with study materials for every chapter. It also provides an introduction to working with spreadsheets and guidelines for working a practice set. It is available in the following volumes:

- *Working Papers with Study Guide 1–13*
- *Working Papers with Study Guide 14–26*
- *Electronic Working Papers with Study Guide 1–26*

General Ledger Software CD-ROM　This CD-ROM includes the thoroughly updated and enhanced Houghton Mifflin General Ledger Software, which can be used to solve selected problems (identified with the GLS icon) at the end of each text chapter. Houghton Mifflin Windows General Ledger Software offers complete coverage of accounting concepts and procedures in an extremely simple and user-friendly, computerized environment. The General Ledger Software CD-ROM is packaged with every *College Accounting* textbook.

Smarthinking Tutoring   In partnership with SMARTHINKING, we offer personalized, online tutoring during typical homework hours. Students can interact live online with an experienced SMARTHINKING "e-structor" (online tutor), submit questions and spreadsheets anytime for response by an e-structor within twenty-four hours, and review independent study resources—including interactive websites and Frequently Asked Questions posed to SMARTHINKING e-structors—around the clock.

Online Learning Center (college.hmco.com/PIC/mcquaig9)   The Online Learning Center, updated for the ninth edition, provides students with text-specific resources that reinforce key concepts in the *College Accounting* program. The Online Learning Center links students to ACE practice tests for self-quizzing, Flashcards and Crossword Puzzles to reinforce vocabulary, and suggested Internet research activities, business readings, and websites for companies featured in the text to provide real-world context. In addition, Excel spreadsheet files let students solve end-of-chapter problems using Excel spreadsheet software.

Your Guide to an A   In addition to the resources found in the Online Learning Center, every new text comes with a passkey that provides access to "Your Guide to an A," an additional set of online resources developed to reinforce chapter concepts for a variety of learning styles. These premium online study tools include MP3 downloads for audio chapter review and self-testing, an additional set of ACE practice quizzes (ACE+), online chapter study guides, and a series of skillbuilding video modules to help students develop and improve their study skills. Students who do not buy a new text will be able to purchase access to "Your Guide to an A" materials from the McQuaig/Bille website.

Peachtree Educator's Edition   This popular accounting software tool is now available to students. The educational version is the same as the professional version used by most businesses. At the option of the instructor, students can use this commercial package or the Houghton Mifflin Windows General Ledger Software to work selected problems in the text and accompanying practice sets. Instructors who prefer to use QuickBooks, another popular commercial software package, can do so by obtaining a site license or offering the option of QuickBooks on the Web; all text problems can be worked using the current version of either Peachtree or QuickBooks.

Practice Sets   A wealth of manual and computerized practice sets is available for use with *College Accounting*, Ninth Edition, with new sets being developed regularly. A complete listing and description of each practice set and its support package can be found in the *Instructor's Resource Manual with Solutions*, with new sets introduced and described on the Online Teaching Center. New to the ninth edition is the *Digi-Tec* practice case, a small merchandising corporation using either a periodic or perpetual inventory system. This practice case covers a one-month accounting period, enabling the student to acquire experience in dealing with the entire accounting cycle, and can be worked manually or electronically. The CD-ROM version gives the student the option of completing the practice case using Microsoft Excel, QuickBooks (2003 or newer), Peachtree Accounting (Educational version 8), or Houghton Mifflin General Ledger Software (version 3.3, provided).

Other available practice sets include:

- *Divesports* is a unique source document simulation that requires students to work through seven months of continuous business activity for a sole proprietorship service business; *Divesports* adds merchandising in Chapter 10. *Divesports* can be assigned between Chapters 3 and 13.

- *Sounds Abound,* Second Edition, is a computerized practice set that covers a month in the life of a sole proprietorship. Assigned after Chapter 5, *Sounds Abound* can be used with Houghton Mifflin's General Ledger Software program.

- *Balloon Adventures* is a source document simulation. *Balloon Adventures* is a sole proprietorship service business using a general journal and can be assigned after Chapter 9.

- *Oak Creek Canyon Jewelers* gives students experience in recording fourth-quarter payroll and preparing end-of-quarter and end-of-year reports for a sole proprietorship. Assigned after Chapter 9, *Oak Creek Canyon* can be worked using Peachtree.

- *Rug Bug* gives students experience with a wholesale business. Assigned after Chapter 13, *Rug Bug* can be worked using Peachtree.

- *Spa Magic* is a source document simulation. It is a sole proprietorship merchandising business featuring special journals and payroll, and can be assigned after Chapter 13; it can be worked using Peachtree, QuickBooks, or Houghton Mifflin's General Ledger Software program.

- *The Wax Works: A Cumulative Shoebox Practice Set with Business Papers* is a realistic exercise in which the student/bookkeeper is "hired" by a sole proprietorship retail candle shop. It can be assigned after Chapter 13.

- *Verde Audio and Video* is a sole proprietorship requiring students to complete all the store's transactions for the fourth quarter of the business year. Assigned after Chapter 15, it can be worked with Peachtree.

- *Camp Kits* requires students to take on the role of a staff accountant at a partnership merchandising business. Assigned after Chapter 19, students will gain experience with handling dishonored accounts receivable, write-offs, partner investments, and inventory tracking.

- *Eagle Tea, Inc.* covers three quarterly accounting cycles within a corporation using general journal entries. Specific coverage includes the issuance of par-value stock, issuance of stock for noncash assets, corporate income taxes, appropriations of retained earnings, declaration and payment of dividends, stock splits, and issuance and amortization of bonds. *Eagle Tea, Inc.* can be assigned after Chapter 20.

For Instructors

Course Management Systems   Because homework and practice are integral parts of accounting courses, and because grading homework and tests can present a challenge to instructors, we offer auto-graded homework in our Course Management Systems. The Eduspace® online learning tool pairs the widely recognized resources of Blackboard with quality, text-specific content from Houghton Mifflin, including automatically graded exercises based on the exercises at the end of each text chapter. SMARTHINKING online tutoring, MP3 files of chapter summaries, Skillbuilders videos, and other resources come ready to use. Premium Blackboard course cartridges and WebCT ePacks are also available.

Instructor's Resource Manual with Solutions The *Instructor's Resource Manual with Solutions* contains valuable resources to assist instructors in teaching accounting. The IRM contains Teaching Objectives, Key Points, and Lecture Outlines for every chapter, as well as Solutions for all questions, exercises, cases, and problems in the text. In addition it includes:

- Review of T Account Placement and Representative Transactions
- Suggested Homework Check Questions with Solutions, keyed to end-of-chapter assignments, provide students with the opportunity to practice the interpretive portion of the accounting process (with suggested answers)
- Difficulty and Time Chart for Practice Sets

The *Instructor's Resource Manual with Solutions* is available in the following volumes:

- *Instructor's Resource Manual with Solutions 1–13*
- *Instructor's Resource Manual with Solutions 14–26*

Online Teaching Center (college.hmco.com/PIC/mcquaig9) The Online Teaching Center provides instructors with text-specific resources that reinforce key concepts in the *College Accounting* program. The Online Teaching Center includes password-protected course materials, such as completely revised Premium PowerPoint slides with video and original content; Classroom Response System content; sample syllabi; and Electronic Solutions, which are fully functioning Excel spreadsheets for all exercises and problems in the text.

Printed Test Bank with Achievement Tests (A and B) and HMTesting Instructor CD-ROM HMTesting—now powered by *Diploma*®—contains the computerized version of the Test Bank. HMTesting provides instructors with all the tools they need to create, customize, and deliver multiple types of tests. Instructors can add their own questions or edit existing algorithmic questions within *Diploma*'s powerful electronic platform. Instructors can select, edit, and add questions, or generate randomly selected questions to produce a test master for easy duplication. Online Testing and Gradebook functions allow instructors to administer tests via their local area network or the Internet, set up classes, record grades from tests or assignments, analyze grades, and compile class and individual statistics. HMTesting can be used on both PCs and Macintosh computers.

PowerPoint Slides—Basic and Premium Basic slides include demonstration problems, examples, accounting forms, tables, and art from the textbook. Premium slides include additional original content, supplementary teaching examples, video, photographs, and discussion questions. Both sets of slides are available at the Online Teaching Center.

Teaching and Solutions Transparencies (downloadable from the Online Teaching Center website)

ACKNOWLEDGMENTS

We sincerely thank the editorial staff of Houghton Mifflin for their continuous support. Leslie Kauffman deserves special recognition for her tireless work on our manuscript. Also, we thank our many students at Highline Community College for their observations and evaluations. During the writing of the ninth edition, we consulted many users of the text throughout the country. Their constructive suggestions are reflected in the changes that we have made. Unfortunately, space does not permit mention of all those who have contributed to this volume. Those reviewers and advisors who have contributed to *College Accounting* through their reviews, class testing, market feedback, and accuracy checking are as follows:

Joe Adamo, *Cazenovia College;* Marjorie Ashton, *Truckee Meadows Community College;* Teresa Anderson, *Eastern New Mexico University;* Gregory D. Barnes, *Clarion University;* Charles M. Betts, *Delaware Technical and Community College;* Michelle Berube, *Corinthian Colleges,* Florida; Lee Cannell, *El Paso Community College;* Steven Christian, *Jackson Community College;* Jean Condon, *Mid-Plains Community College Area (Nebraska);* Mark Dawson, *Duquesne University;* Roger Dimick, *Lamar Institute of Technology;* Patricia A. Doherty, *Boston University School of Management;* Richard Dugger, *Kilgore College;* Donna Eakman, *Montana State University, Great Falls;* Talaat Elshazly, *College of Charleston;* Nancy Fallon, *Albertus Magnus College;* Michael J. Farina, *Cerritos College;* Mark Fronke, *Cerritos College;* Allen Ford, *Institute for the Deaf, Rochester Institute of Technology;* Michael Girvin, *Highline Community College;* David Groom, *University of Hawaii—Maui Community College;* Christine Uber Grosse, *Thunderbird, The American Graduate School of International Management;* Dennis A. Gutting, *Orange County Community College;* David Hall; Scott Hays, *Central Oregon Community College;* Thea Hosselrode, *Allegany College of Maryland;* Peggy Hughes, *Allegany College of Maryland;* Ray Ingram, *Southwest Georgia Technical College;* Lori Jacobson, *North Idaho College;* Ernie Keller, *Montana State University, Great Falls;* Cathy Xanthaky Larson, *Middlesex Community College;* Susan D. Looney, *Mohave Community College;* Nelson Martin, *Wenatchee Valley College;* George J. McGowan; Gail A. Mestas; Wanda Metzgar, *Selland College of Applied Technology;* Michael Monahan; Howard Mount, *Highline Community College;* Paul Muller, *Western Nevada Community College;* Jenine Muscove, *Bradford Hall Career Institute;* Kenneth Newton, *Cleveland State Community College;* Jon Nitschke, *Montana State University, Great Falls;* Therese H. Palacios, *San Antonio College;* Janet Pasterkamp, *Montana State University, Great Falls;* Cathy Pekarek; Joel Peralto, *University of Hawaii—Hawaii Community College;* Betty Pilchard, *Heartland Community College;* Bob Sanner, *Central Community College;* Robin Shurtz; Alice Sineath, *Forsyth Technical Community College;* Marion Taube, *University of Pittsburgh;* Josephine Vondras, *Orange County Community College;* Kay Westerfield, *University of Oregon;* Jack Wiehler, *San Joaquin Delta College;* and Sara Wilson.

As always, we would like to thank our families for their understanding and cooperation. Without their support, this text would never have been written. Heartfelt appreciation is extended to my wife, Beverlie McQuaig, for her detailed proofreading and good humor. Pertinent suggestions for updating the material were given by my children: Judy McQuaig Courshon, C.P.A., M.T., of Wellspring Group PS, CPAs; John McQuaig, C.P.A., C.M.C., of McQuaig and Welk PLLC; and Laurie McQuaig, D.C. We also express continued gratitude to Bruce Bille, Tracy Bille-Newkirk, and James Newkirk, C.P.A., for their encouragement and assistance, and to the memory of Ryan Bille and Wesley and Adeline Harris for their courage and inspiration.

Douglas J. McQuaig
Patricia A. Bille

COLLEGE ACCOUNTING

1–26

Introduction to Accounting

Performance Objectives

After you have completed this introduction to accounting, you will be able to do the following:

1. Define *accounting*.
2. Explain the importance of accounting information.
3. Describe the various career opportunities in accounting.
4. Define *ethics*.

Accounting is often called the language of business because, when confronted with events of a business nature, all people in society—owners, managers, creditors, employees, attorneys, engineers, and so forth—must use accounting terms and concepts to describe these events. Examples of accounting terms are *net, gross, yield, valuation, accrued, deferred*—the list could go on and on. So it is logical that anyone entering the business world should know enough of its "language" to communicate with others and to understand their communications.

As you acquire knowledge of accounting, you will gain an understanding of the way businesses operate and the reasoning involved in making business decisions. Even if you are not involved directly in accounting activities, you will certainly need to be sufficiently acquainted with the "language" to be able to understand the meaning of accounting information, how it is compiled, how it can be used, and its limitations.

You may be surprised to find that you are already familiar with many accounting terms. Recalling your personal business activities and relating them to your study of accounting will be very helpful to you. For example, when you purchased this textbook, you exchanged cash or a promise to pay cash for the book. As you will see, this exchange is an accounting event. You are going to recognize many activities and terms as you begin your study of accounting.

DEFINITION OF ACCOUNTING

OBJECTIVE 1
Define *accounting*.

Accounting is the process of analyzing, classifying, recording, summarizing, and interpreting business transactions in financial or monetary terms. A business **transaction** is an event that has a direct effect on the operation of an economic unit, is expressed in terms of money, and is recorded. Examples of business transactions are buying or selling goods, renting a building, paying employees, and buying insurance.

Accounting is an important part of all types of businesses. These cruise ships require the same extensive recordkeeping as any large destination resort. The ship is a large floating hotel with guests, employees, management, recreational activities, restaurants, and shops.

The primary purpose of accounting is to provide the financial information needed for the efficient operation of an economic unit. The term **economic unit** includes not only business enterprises but also not-for-profit entities, such as government bodies, churches and synagogues, clubs, and public charities. Business enterprises or organizations may be called firms or companies. All of these entities require some type of accounting records. An **accountant** is a person who keeps the financial history of the transactions of an economic unit in written form.

Because it is important that all those who receive accounting reports be able to interpret them, a set of rules or guidelines for the accounting process has been developed. These guidelines or rules are known as **generally accepted accounting principles (GAAP)**.

Bookkeeping and Accounting

There are distinctions between bookkeeping and accounting. The two processes are closely related, but there is no universally accepted line of separation. Generally, bookkeeping involves the systematic recording of business transactions in financial terms. Accounting functions at a higher level. An accountant sets up the system that a bookkeeper uses to record business transactions. An accountant may supervise the work of the bookkeeper and prepare financial statements and tax reports. Although the bookkeeper's work is more routine, it is hard to draw a line where the bookkeeper's work ends and the accountant's begins.

IMPORTANCE OF ACCOUNTING INFORMATION

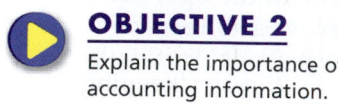

OBJECTIVE 2

Explain the importance of accounting information.

Anyone who aspires to a position of leadership in business or government needs knowledge of accounting. A study of accounting gives a person the necessary background and also gives him or her an understanding of the scope, functions, and policies of an organization. A person may not be doing the accounting work, but he or she will be continually dealing with accounting forms, language, and reports.

Users of Accounting Information

Owners Owners have invested their money or goods in a business organization. They desire information regarding the company's earnings, its prospects for future earnings, and its ability to pay its debts.

Managers Managers and supervisors have to prepare financial reports, understand accounting data contained in reports and budgets, and express future plans in financial terms. People who have management jobs must know how accounting information is developed in order to evaluate performance in meeting goals.

Creditors Creditors lend money or extend credit to the company for the purchase of goods and services. The company's creditors include suppliers, banks, and other lending institutions, such as loan companies. Creditors are interested in the firm's ability to pay its debts.

Government agencies Taxing authorities verify information submitted by companies concerning a variety of taxes, such as income taxes, sales taxes, and employment taxes. Public utilities, such as electric and gas companies, must provide financial information to regulatory agencies.

Accounting and Technology

Before the invention of calculators and computers, all business transactions were recorded by hand. Now computers perform routine recordkeeping operations and prepare financial reports. Computers are used today in all types of businesses, both large and small. One question often arises: "Is the computer taking over accountants' jobs?" Actually, with the introduction of computers, more jobs have been created to fulfill management's need for more information.

Regardless of whether a business uses a computer, the nature of accounting is the same. The computer is a powerful tool of the accountant. However, as a tool, the computer is only as useful as the ability of the operator. The operator must be skilled to key the correct information into the computer program. Otherwise, as the saying goes, "garbage in, garbage out."

CAREER OPPORTUNITIES IN ACCOUNTING

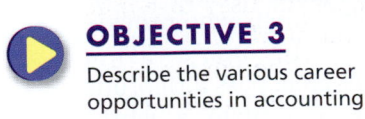

OBJECTIVE 3

Describe the various career opportunities in accounting.

To find job opportunities in accounting, all you need to do is read the newspapers' classified advertisements or browse the Internet. Although the jobs listed in these ads require varying amounts of education and experience, most of them are for positions as accounting clerks, general bookkeepers, or accountants. Let's take a look at the requirements and duties of these positions.

Accounting Clerk/Technician

An accounting clerk/technician does routine recording of financial information. The duties of accounting clerks vary with the size of the company. In small businesses, accounting clerks handle most of the recordkeeping functions. In large companies, clerks specialize in one part of the accounting system, such as payroll, accounts receivable, accounts payable, cash, inventory, or purchases. The minimum requirement for most accounting clerk positions is one term or semester of an accounting course.

General Bookkeeper

Many small- and medium-sized companies employ one person to oversee their bookkeeping operations. This person is called a general or full-charge bookkeeper. The general bookkeeper supervises the work of accounting clerks. Requirements for this job vary with the size of the company and the complexity of the accounting system. The minimum requirement for most general bookkeeper jobs is one or two years of accounting as well as experience as an accounting clerk.

Paraprofessional Accountant

To bridge a gap between the general bookkeeper and the professional accountant many firms are hiring **paraprofessional accountants**. They are able to manage the duties of the general bookkeeper as well as many of the duties of a professional accountant under that accountant's supervision. Qualifications generally include a two-year degree or certificate in accounting as well as appropriate prior experience.

Accountant

The term *accountant* describes a fairly broad range of jobs. The accountant may design and manage the entire accounting system for a business. The accountant may also prepare the financial statements and tax returns and perform audits. Many accountants enter the field with a four-year college degree in accounting; however, it is not unusual for accountants to start at entry-level positions and work their way up to management positions. Although accountants are employed in every kind of economic unit, they are classified into one of three categories: public accounting, managerial or private accounting, and not-for-profit accounting. We'll briefly look at these categories.

Accountants are employed in every kind of economic unit. Many start in entry-level positions and work their way up to management.

Public Accounting   Certified public accountants (CPAs) are independent professionals who provide services to clients for a fee. To become a CPA, a person must have a college degree, pass a rigorous examination, and generally complete a work-experience requirement. Public accountants design accounting systems, prepare tax returns, provide financial advice about business operations, and audit financial statements.

Managerial or Private Accounting   Most people who are accountants are employed by private business organizations. These accountants (not necessarily CPAs) manage the accounting system, prepare budgets, determine

Charitable organizations must be closely attuned to their cash situation as funds are donated and in turn shared with those in need. Those who manage charities must be able to report to the public and various government agencies where the money comes from, where it has gone, and how much was kept to run the charity.

costs of products, and provide financial information for managers and owners. Accountants have many opportunities to advance into top management positions. The Certified Management Accountant (CMA) exam has become an important partner to the CPA credentials.

Not-for-Profit Accounting Not-for-profit accounting is used for government agencies, hospitals, churches and synagogues, and schools. Accountants for these organizations prepare budgets and maintain records of revenues and expenses. It should be noted that some not-for-profit organizations do in fact make a profit; however, the profit is kept in the organization and not distributed. For example, a hospital makes a profit and then reinvests the profit in modern equipment. Local, state, and federal government bodies employ vast numbers of people in accounting positions.

ETHICS

OBJECTIVE 4

Define *ethics*.

Ethics is a philosophy or code or system of morality—that is, how we conduct ourselves from day to day in a variety of situations requiring a decision, usually of a right or wrong nature. Ethics, as it relates to accounting, would be the way accountants and other keepers of financial information conduct the business of accounting according to laws of the state and their own personal code or system of morality.

There are books and textbooks available on ethics, as well as classes on the subject. With mounting evidence of questionable ethics in business reported in print and portrayed through the visual media, it is apparent that some individuals are in need of additional schooling in and practice of ethical behavior at all levels.

CHAPTER REVIEW

Online Study Center
ACE the test!

Review of Performance Objectives

1. Define *accounting*.

   Accounting is the process of analyzing, classifying, recording, summarizing, and interpreting business transactions in financial or monetary terms. It is also an information system and the language of business.

2. Explain the importance of accounting information.

   A study of accounting gives a person the necessary background to understand the scope, functions, and policies of an organization.

3. Describe the various career opportunities in accounting.

   Accountants, paraprofessional accountants, bookkeepers, and accounting clerks will find employment opportunities in several areas—in the public sector, the private sector, or not-for-profit organizations.

4. Define *ethics*.

   Ethics is a philosophy or code or system of morality—that is, how we conduct ourselves from day to day in a variety of situations requiring a decision, usually of a right or wrong nature. Ethics, as it relates to accounting, would be the way accountants and other keepers of financial information conduct themselves according to laws of the state and their own personal code or system of morality.

Glossary

Accountant A person who keeps the financial history of the transactions of an economic unit in written form; sometimes mistakenly called a bookkeeper. (2)

Accounting The process of analyzing, classifying, recording, summarizing, and interpreting business transactions in financial or monetary terms; sometimes mistakenly called bookkeeping. (1)

Economic unit Includes both business enterprises and not-for-profit entities, such as government bodies, churches and synagogues, clubs, and public charities. (2)

Ethics A philosophy or code or system of morality—that is, how we conduct ourselves from day to day in a variety of situations requiring a decision, usually of a right or wrong nature. (5)

Generally accepted accounting principles (GAAP) The rules or guidelines used for carrying out the accounting process. (2)

Paraprofessional accountant A person who is qualified in accounting to assume the duties of a general bookkeeper as well as some of those of a professional accountant under that accountant's supervision. (4)

Transaction An event directly affecting an economic entity that can be expressed in terms of money and that must be recorded in the accounting records. (1)

Have you ever bought clothes from Gap? How about from Banana Republic or Old Navy? All three brands belong to Gap Inc., an international specialty retailer that sells clothing, accessories, and personal care items. When you buy a pair of jeans from Gap and pay cash, it's an expense to you and revenue to the store. You can also buy those jeans using your credit card, in which case it's a liability to you because you promise to pay the credit card company for your purchase at a later date. After completing this chapter, you will understand what accounting is and why it is important. Every business transaction that takes place in each of the stores mentioned above is recorded and then reported to the parent company, Gap Inc. You can go to Gap Inc.'s website to see its annual reports: **http://www.gapinc.com/ public/Investors/inv_fin_annual_reports_and_proxy.htm.** As you view the financial statements, which begin on page 37 of the 2005 Annual Report, think about the fundamental accounting equation, which you will learn about in this chapter. At the end of the chapter is further discussion with exercises about the accounting equation as it applies to Gap Inc.

Performance Objectives

After you have completed this chapter, you will be able to do the following:

1. Define and identify *asset, liability,* and *owner's equity* accounts.

2. Record a group of business transactions, in column form, involving changes in assets, liabilities, and owner's equity.

3. Define and identify *revenue* and *expense* accounts.

4. Record a group of business transactions, in column form, involving all five elements of the fundamental accounting equation.

A s we stated in the Introduction, accounting is the process of analyzing, classifying, recording, and summarizing business transactions. We now introduce the analyzing, classifying, and recording steps in the accounting process.

ASSETS, LIABILITIES, AND OWNER'S EQUITY

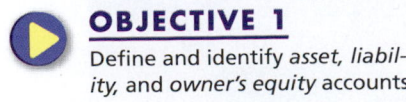

OBJECTIVE 1
Define and identify *asset, liability,* and *owner's equity* accounts.

The Fundamental Accounting Equation

Assets are properties or things of value, such as cash, equipment, copyrights, buildings, and land, owned and controlled by an economic unit or

FYI

Other terms for equity are *investment, net worth,* or *proprietorship.*

business entity. By the term **business entity**, we mean that the business is an economic unit in itself, and the assets or properties of the business are completely separate from the owner's personal assets. However, the owner has a claim on the assets of the business and generally has a responsibility for its debts. **The owner's right, claim, or financial interest is expressed by the word equity in the business.** Another term that could be used is **capital**. Whenever you see the term **owner's equity**, it means the owner's right to or investment in the business.

Assets	=	Owner's Equity
Properties or things of value owned by the business		Owner's *right* to or investment in the business

Suppose the total value of the assets is $60,000 and the business entity does not owe any amount against the assets. Then,

Assets	=	Owner's Equity
$60,000 =		$60,000

Or suppose the assets consist of a truck that costs $32,000. The owner has invested $11,000 for the truck, and the business entity has borrowed the remainder from the bank, which is a **creditor** (one to whom money is owed). This business transaction or event can be shown as follows:

Assets	=	Liabilities	+	Owner's Equity
Items owned		Amounts owed to creditors		Owner's investment
$32,000	=	$21,000	+	$11,000

We have now introduced a new classification, **liabilities**, which represent debts. They are the amounts that the business entity owes its creditors. The debts may originate because the business bought goods or services on credit,

When a company's liabilities are greater than its assets, it may be forced into bankruptcy. The money earned from a going-out-of-business sale is used to pay creditors. Accurate accounting practices, especially tracking cash, can help a company avoid bankruptcy.

borrowed money, or otherwise created an obligation to pay. The creditors' claims to the assets have priority over the claims of the owner.

An equation expressing the relationship of assets, liabilities, and owner's equity is called the **fundamental accounting equation (Assets = Liabilities + Owner's Equity).** We'll deal with this equation constantly from now on. If we know two parts of this equation, we can determine the third. Let's look at some examples.

Determine Assets   Ms. Acosta has $16,000 invested in her travel agency, and the agency owes creditors $4,000; that is, the agency has liabilities of $4,000. Then,

Assets	=	Liabilities	+	Owner's Equity
?	=	$4,000	+	$16,000

We can find the amount of the business's assets by adding the liabilities and the owner's equity:

$ 4,000 Liabilities
+ 16,000 Owner's Equity
$20,000 Assets

The completed equation now reads

Assets	=	Liabilities	+	Owner's Equity
$20,000	=	$4,000	+	$16,000

Like a balancing scale, the equation stays in balance by making equal or offsetting increases and decreases to one side or both sides.

Determine Owner's Equity   Mr. Ruiz owns an auto repair shop. His business has assets of $38,000, and it owes creditors $5,000; that is, it has liabilities of $5,000. Then,

Assets	=	Liabilities	+	Owner's Equity
$38,000	=	$5,000	+	?

We find the owner's equity by subtracting the liabilities from the assets:

$38,000 Assets
− 5,000 Liabilities
$33,000 Owner's Equity

The completed equation now reads

Assets	=	Liabilities	+	Owner's Equity
$38,000	=	$5,000	+	$33,000

Determine Liabilities   Mr. Vogel's insurance agency has assets of $68,000; his investment (his equity) amounts to $22,000. Then,

Assets	=	Liabilities	+	Owner's Equity
$68,000	=	?	+	$22,000

Assets owned by a business may be as small as a calculator or as large as a delivery truck or building.

To find the firm's total liabilities, we subtract the equity from the assets:

$68,000 Assets
−   22,000 Owner's Equity
―――――――――――
$46,000 Liabilities

The completed equation reads

Assets	=	Liabilities	+	Owner's Equity
$68,000	=	$46,000	+	$22,000

Recording Business Transactions

OBJECTIVE 2

Record a group of business transactions, in column form, involving changes in assets, liabilities, and owner's equity.

As you know, business transactions are events that have a direct effect on the operations of an economic unit or enterprise and are expressed in terms of money. Each business transaction must be recorded in the accounting records. As business transactions are recorded, the amounts listed under the headings Assets, Liabilities, and Owner's Equity change. However, **the total of one side of the fundamental accounting equation must always equal the total of the other side.** The categories under these three main headings are called **accounts.**

Let's look at a group of business transactions. These transactions are typical of those seen in a service or professional type of business. In these transactions, let's assume that R. P. Cline establishes her own business and calls it Cline's Computer Clinic. Cline's Computer Clinic is a **sole proprietorship**, or a one-owner business.

Transaction (a)   **Cline deposited $82,000 in a bank account in the name of the business.** Cline deposits $82,000 cash in a separate bank account in the name of Cline's Computer Clinic. This separate bank account will help Cline keep her business investment separate from her personal funds. This is an example of the **separate entity concept**, according to which a business is treated as a separate economic or accounting entity. The business is independent or stands by itself; it is separate from its owners, creditors, and customers.

The Cash account consists of bank deposits and money on hand. The business now has $82,000 more in cash than before, and Cline's investment has also increased by $82,000. The account denoted by the owner's name followed by the word *Capital* records the amount of the owner's investment, or equity, in the business. The effect of this transaction on the fundamental accounting equation is as follows:

Assets	=	Liabilities	+	Owner's Equity
Items owned		Amounts owed to creditors		Owner's investment
Cash	=			R. P. Cline, Capital
(a) +82,000	=			+82,000

Besides cash, an investment may be in the form of goods, such as equipment. The word *Capital* used under Owner's Equity therefore does not always mean that cash was invested.

Transaction (b) Company bought equipment, paying cash, $64,000. Cline's first task is to get her company ready for business; to do that, she needs the proper equipment. Accordingly, Cline's Computer Clinic buys equipment costing $64,000 and pays cash. **It is important to note at this point that Cline does not invest any new money. She simply exchanges part of the business's cash for equipment.** Because equipment is a new type of property for the firm, a new account, Equipment, is created. Equipment is included under Assets. As a result of this transaction, the accounting equation changes:

	Assets	=	Liabilities	+	Owner's Equity
	Items owned		Amounts owed to creditors		Owner's investment
	Cash + Equipment	=			R. P. Cline, Capital
Initial Investment	82,000	=			82,000
(b)	−64,000 +64,000				
New balances	18,000+ 64,000	=			82,000
	82,000				82,000

Transaction (c) Company bought equipment on account from Surgo Products, $10,000. Cline's Computer Clinic buys equipment costing $10,000 on credit from Surgo Products.

The Equipment account shows an increase because the business owns $10,000 more in equipment. There is also an increase in liabilities because the business now owes $10,000. The liability account **Accounts Payable** is used for short-term liabilities or charge accounts, usually due within thirty days. (The company to which money is owed is called a creditor.) There is now a total of $92,000 on each side of the equals sign. Because Cline's Computer Clinic owes money to Surgo Products, Surgo Products is called a creditor of Cline's Computer Clinic.

	Assets	=	Liabilities	+	Owner's Equity
	Items owned		Amounts owed to creditors		Owner's investment
	Cash + Equipment	=	Accounts Payable	+	R. P. Cline, Capital
Previous balances	18,000 + 64,000	=			82,000
(c)	+10,000		+10,000		
New balances	18,000 + 74,000	=	10,000	+	82,000
	92,000			92,000	

Observe that the recording of each transaction must yield an equation that is in balance. For example, transaction (b) resulted in a minus $64,000 and a plus $64,000 *on the same side,* with nothing recorded on the other side, and transaction (c) resulted in a $10,000 increase to both sides of the equation. It does not matter whether you change one side or both sides. **The important point is that whenever a transaction is properly recorded, the accounting equation remains in balance.**

Transaction (d)   Company paid Surgo Products, a creditor, on account, $6,000. Cline's Computer Clinic pays $6,000 to Surgo Products, to be applied against the firm's liability of $10,000.

   With this payment, cash is being reduced. At the same time, the firm *owes* less than before, so the transaction should be recorded as a reduction in liabilities.

	Assets		=	Liabilities	+	Owner's Equity
	Items owned			Amounts owed to creditors		Owner's investment
	Cash	+ Equipment	=	Accounts Payable	+	R. P. Cline, Capital
Previous balances	18,000 +	74,000	=	10,000	+	82,000
(d)	−6,000			−6,000		
New balances	12,000 +	74,000	=	4,000	+	82,000
	86,000				86,000	

Transaction (e)   Owner invested equipment in the business. Cline invested her own computer equipment in Cline's Computer Clinic having a **fair market value** of $6,200. **Fair market value is the present worth of an asset.** It is the amount that would be received if the asset were sold on the open market. Additional investments may be in the form of equipment, cash, tools, or real estate.

	Assets		=	Liabilities	+	Owner's Equity
	Items owned			Amounts owed to creditors		Owner's investment
	Cash	+ Equipment	=	Accounts Payable	+	R. P. Cline, Capital
Previous balances	12,000 +	74,000	=	4,000	+	82,000
(e)		+6,200				+6,200
New balances	12,000 +	80,200	=	4,000	+	88,200
	92,200				92,200	

   Accounting, as we said before, is the process of analyzing, classifying, recording, summarizing, and interpreting business transactions in terms of money. Look at the transactions thus far for Cline's Computer Clinic and see if you understand that we have gone through certain steps (in the form of questions). Let's illustrate these steps using transaction (e), owner invests equipment in the business.

1. **What accounts are involved?** Equipment and R. P. Cline, Capital are involved.
2. **What are the classifications of the accounts involved?** Equipment is an asset and R. P. Cline, Capital is an owner's equity account.

3. **Are the accounts increased or decreased?** Equipment is increased because Cline's Computer Clinic has more equipment than before. R. P. Cline, Capital is increased because Cline has a greater investment than before.
4. **Is the equation in balance after the transaction has been recorded?** Yes.

Next, we record the transaction. We will stress this step-by-step process throughout the text. This example serves as an introduction to **double-entry accounting**. The "double" element is demonstrated by the fact that each transaction must be recorded in at least two accounts, keeping the accounting equation in balance.

Summary of Transactions

Let's summarize the business transactions of Cline's Computer Clinic in column form, identifying each transaction by a letter of the alphabet. To test your understanding of the recording procedure, describe the nature of the transactions that have taken place.

	Assets		=	Liabilities	+	Owner's Equity
	Cash +	Equip.	=	Accounts + Payable		R. P. Cline, Capital
Transaction (a)	+82,000					+82,000
Transaction (b)	−64,000	+64,000				
Balance	18,000 +	64,000	=			82,000
Transaction (c)		+10,000		+10,000		
Balance	18,000 +	74,000	=	10,000	+	82,000
Transaction (d)	−6,000			−6,000		
Balance	12,000 +	74,000	=	4,000	+	82,000
Transaction (e)		+6,200				+6,200
Balance	12,000 +	80,200	=	4,000	+	88,200
	92,200				92,200	

The following observations apply to all types of business transactions:

1. Every transaction is recorded as an increase and/or decrease in two or more accounts.
2. One side of the equation is always equal to the other side of the equation.

In this chapter we are using a column arrangement as a practical device to show how transactions are recorded. This arrangement is useful for showing increases and decreases in various accounts as a result of the transactions. We also show new balances after recording each transaction.

REVENUE AND EXPENSE ACCOUNTS

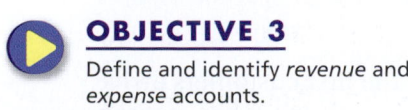

OBJECTIVE 3

Define and identify *revenue* and *expense* accounts.

Revenues are the amounts earned by a business. Examples of revenues are fees earned for performing services, income from selling merchandise, rent income for the use of property, and interest income for lending money. Revenues may be in the form of cash or credit card receipts. Revenues may also result from credit sales to charge customers, in which case cash will be received at a later time.

Expenses are the costs that relate to earning revenue (or the costs of doing business). Examples of expenses are wages expense for labor performed, rent expense for the use of property, interest expense for the use of money, and advertising expense for the use of various media (for example, newspapers, radio, and direct mail). Another example is supplies expense to include supplies used in the completion of a task performed by a service business, such as cleaning fluids used by a carpet cleaner company. Expenses may be paid in cash when incurred (that is, immediately) or at a later time. Expenses to be paid at a later time involve Accounts Payable.

Revenues and expenses directly affect owner's equity. **If a business earns revenue, an increase in owner's equity occurs. When a business incurs or pays expenses, owner's equity decreases.** For the present, think of it this way: If the company makes money, the owner's equity is increased. If the company has to pay out money for the costs of doing business, then the owner's equity is decreased. Revenues and expenses fall under the umbrella of owner's equity: Revenue increases owner's equity; expenses decrease owner's equity.

Chart of Accounts

The **chart of accounts** is the official list of accounts *tailor-made* for the business. All the company's transactions must be recorded using the official account titles.

We now present the chart of accounts for Cline's Computer Clinic. Some of the accounts are new to you, but they will be explained as we move along. When numbering account titles, the 100s are used for assets, the 200s are used for liabilities, the 300s are used for owner's equity accounts, the 400s are used for revenue accounts, and the 500s are used for expense accounts. You will encounter longer account numbers, but the first digit will usually be the same for any service business. In any case, use the exact account titles listed in the company's chart of accounts. Any changes must be approved by management.

FYI

When setting up and maintaining the chart of accounts on a computer, you may find that you must reserve the 500 accounts for cost accounts (used in a merchandising business). You may need to number expenses as 600s. Read the setup instructions in your software package.

Chart of Accounts

Assets

111 Cash
113 Accounts Receivable
117 Prepaid Insurance
124 Equipment

Liabilities

221 Accounts Payable

Owner's Equity

311 R. P. Cline, Capital
312 R. P. Cline, Drawing

Revenue (increase in Owner's Equity)

411 Income from Services

Expenses (decrease in Owner's Equity)

511 Wages Expense
512 Rent Expense
513 Supplies Expense
514 Advertising Expense
515 Utilities Expense

OBJECTIVE 4

Record a group of business transactions, in column form, involving all five elements of the fundamental accounting equation.

Recording Business Transactions

Soon after the opening of Cline's Computer Clinic, the first customers arrive, beginning a flow of revenue for the business. Let's examine more transactions of Cline's Computer Clinic for the first month of operations.

Transaction (f) **Company sold computer repair services for cash, $3,520.** Cline's Computer Clinic receives cash revenue of $3,520 in return for computer repair services performed for customers over two weeks. In other words, the company earns $3,520 for services performed for cash customers. Revenue has the effect of increasing owner's equity, but because the company wants to know how much revenue is earned, we set up a special column for revenue. The revenue account for Cline's Computer Clinic is called Income from Services. The accounting equation is affected as follows (PB stands for previous balance, and NB stands for new balance).

	Assets		= Liabilities +	Owner's Equity		
	Cash	+ Equipment	Accounts Payable	R. P. Cline, Capital	+ Revenue	
PB	12,000 +	80,200	= 4,000 +	88,200		
(f)	+3,520				+3,520 (Income from Services)	
NB	15,520 +	80,200	= 4,000 +	88,200 +	3,520	
		95,720			95,720	

Transaction (g) **Company paid rent for the month, $900.** Shortly after opening the business, Cline's Computer Clinic pays the month's rent of $900. Rent is payment for the privilege of occupying a building.

It seems logical that, if revenue is added to owner's equity, then expenses (the opposite of revenue) must be subtracted from owner's equity. To be consistent, a separate column is set up for expenses.

We want to have a running total of the amount of expenses to be subtracted from owner's equity. To keep up this running total, as each new expense is incurred (or comes into being), it must be added to the previous total.

	Assets		= Liabilities +	Owner's Equity			
	Cash	+ Equip.	Accounts Payable	R. P. Cline, Capital	+ Revenue	− Expenses	
PB	15,520 +	80,200 =	4,000 +	88,200 +	3,520		
(g)	−900					+900 (Rent Expense)	
NB	14,620 +	80,200 =	4,000 +	88,200	3,520	− 900	
		94,820			94,820		

Because the time period represented by the rent payment is one month or less, we record the $900 as an expense. If the payment covered a period longer than one month, we would record the amount under an asset called Prepaid Rent.

Let's review the mental process for formulating the entry by asking:

1. **What are the accounts involved?** In this transaction, they are Cash and Rent Expense.
2. **What are the classifications of the accounts involved?** Cash is an asset, and Rent Expense is an expense.
3. **Are the accounts increased or decreased?** Cash is decreased because after the payment we have less cash than we had before. Rent Expense is increased. Thus there is a $900 reduction in total owner's equity.
4. **Is the equation in balance after the transaction has been recorded?** Yes.

Banks and other financial institutions sell their services to other businesses as well as to individuals.

Transaction (h) **Company bought supplies on credit.** Cline's Computer Clinic buys CD-R recordable compact discs and holders, manuals, and invoice forms costing $870 on credit from Freeman Company. Compact discs and holders for storing troubleshooting programs and customer files during installations and repairs, as well as manuals and invoice forms, are considered to be supplies to be used up by Cline's Computer Clinic in the performance of computer repair work for clients and are recorded as an expense. For a service business, for tax purposes (IRS Notice 2001-76), supplies may now be originally recorded as an expense rather than being added to an inventory account.

	Assets	=	Liabilities +		Owner's Equity		
	Cash + Equip.		Accounts Payable	R. P. Cline, Capital	+ Revenue	− Expenses	
PB	14,620 + 80,200 =		4,000	88,200	+ 3,520	−	900
(h)			+870				+870
							(Supplies Expense)
NB	14,620 + 80,200 =		4,870	+ 88,200	+ 3,520	−	1,770
	94,820				94,820		

Transaction (i) **Company paid for insurance.** Cline's Computer Clinic paid $480 for a one-year liability insurance policy. At the time of payment, the company has not used up the insurance; thus, it is not yet an expense. As the insurance expires (is used), it will become an expense. **However, because it is paid in advance for a period longer than one month, it has value and is therefore recorded as an asset.**

	Assets		=	Liabilities +		Owner's Equity		
	Cash + Equip. + Ppd. Ins.			Accounts Payable	R. P. Cline, Capital	+ Revenue	− Expenses	
PB	14,620 + 80,200		=	4,870	+ 88,200	+ 3,520	− 1,770	
(i)	−480	+480						
NB	14,140 + 80,200 +	480 =		4,870	+ 88,200	+ 3,520	− 1,770	
	94,820				94,820			

At the end of the year or accounting period, an adjustment will have to be made to take out the expired portion (that is, coverage for the months that have been used up) and record it as an expense. We discuss this adjustment in a later chapter.

Observe that each time a transaction is recorded, the total amount on one side of the equation **remains equal** to the total amount on the other side. As proof of this equality, look at the following computation:

Cash	$14,140	**Accounts Payable**	$ 4,870
Equipment	80,200	**R. P. Cline, Capital**	88,200
Prepaid Insurance	480	**Revenue**	3,520
		Subtotal	$96,590
		Expenses	−1,770
	$94,820		$94,820

Steps in Analyzing Transactions

Now that we have recorded transactions in all five classifications of accounts, let's pause to go through the steps we have followed:

Step 1. Read the transaction to understand what is happening and how it affects the business. For example, the business has more revenue, or has more expenses, or has more cash, or owes less to creditors.

Step 2. Identify the accounts involved and decide whether the accounts are increased or decreased. Look for Cash first; you will quickly recognize if cash is coming in or going out.

Step 3. Decide on the classifications of the accounts involved. For example, Equipment is something the business owns, and it's an asset; Accounts Payable is an amount the business owes, and it's a liability; Rent is an expense.

Step 4. After recording the transaction, make sure the accounting equation is in balance.

Transaction (j)   Company received a bill for an expense. Cline's Computer Clinic receives a bill from the *Daily* for newspaper advertising, $340. Cline's Computer Clinic has simply received the bill for advertising; it has not paid any cash. Previously, we described an expense as money to be paid for the cost of doing business. An expense of $340 has now been incurred (or has taken place), and it should be recorded as an increase in expenses (Advertising Expense). Also, since the company owes $340 more than before and intends to pay at a later time, this amount should be recorded as an increase in Accounts Payable.

	Assets			= Liabilities +		Owner's Equity		
	Cash	+ Equip.	+ Ppd. Ins.	Accounts Payable	R. P. Cline, Capital	+ Revenue	−	Expenses
PB	14,140	+ 80,200	+ 480 =	4,870	+ 88,200	+ 3,520	−	1,770
(j)				**+340**				**+340** (Advertising Expense)
NB	14,140	+ 80,200	+ 480 =	5,210	+ 88,200	+ 3,520	−	2,110
		94,820				94,820		

Transaction (k)   Company sold services on account. Cline's Computer Clinic signs a contract with Computer Makeovers to refurbish some of the computers it receives on a credit basis. Cline's Computer Clinic completes a refurbishing job and bills Computer Makeovers $1,470 for services performed.

A company uses the **Accounts Receivable** account to record the amounts due from (legal claims against) charge customers. Since Cline's Computer Clinic's claim against Computer Makeovers is $1,470 more than before the transaction took place, it seems logical to add $1,470 to Accounts Receivable. Revenue is earned or recognized when the service is performed, even though the $1,470 has not been received in cash. We count the $1,470 as an increase in revenue and an increase in Accounts Receivable. Keep in mind that Accounts Receivable is an asset, or something that is owned. Cline's Computer Clinic owns a claim of $1,470 against Computer Makeovers.

	Cash	+ Equip.	+ Ppd. Ins.	+ Accts. Rec.	= Accounts Payable	+ R. P. Cline, Capital	+ Revenue	− Expenses
	Assets				**= Liabilities +**	**Owner's Equity**		
PB	14,140	+ 80,200	+ 480		= 5,210	+ 88,200	+ 3,520	− 2,110
(k)				+1,470			+1,470	
						(Income from Services)		
NB	14,140	+ 80,200	+ 480	+ 1,470	= 5,210	+ 88,200	+ 4,990	− 2,110
	96,290					96,290		

When Computer Makeovers pays the $1,470 bill in cash, Cline's Computer Clinic will record this transaction as an increase in Cash and a decrease in Accounts Receivable. At that time, Cline's Computer Clinic will not have to make an entry for the revenue account, because the revenue was earned and recorded when the service was performed.

Transaction (l)   Company paid creditor on account. Cline's Computer Clinic pays $1,800 to Surgo Products, its creditor (the party to whom it owes money), as part payment on account.

	Cash	+ Equip.	+ Ppd. Ins.	+ Accts. Rec.	= Accounts Payable	+ R. P. Cline, Capital	+ Revenue	− Expenses
	Assets				**= Liabilities +**	**Owner's Equity**		
PB	14,140	+ 80,200	+ 480	+ 1,470	= 5,210	+ 88,200	+ 4,990	− 2,110
(l)	−1,800				−1,800			
NB	12,340	+ 80,200	+ 480	+ 1,470	= 3,410	+ 88,200	+ 4,990	− 2,110
	94,490					94,490		

Transaction (m)   Company paid an expense in cash. Cline's Computer Clinic receives a bill from Regional Power, Inc. for $320. Because the bill was not previously recorded as a liability and is to be paid immediately, we record the amount directly as an expense.

	Cash	+ Equip.	+ Ppd. Ins.	+ Accts. Rec.	= Accounts Payable	+ R. P. Cline, Capital	+ Revenue	− Expenses
	Assets				**= Liabilities +**	**Owner's Equity**		
PB	12,340	+ 80,200	+ 480	+ 1,470	= 3,410	+ 88,200	+ 4,990	− 2,110
(m)	−320							+320
								(Utilities Expense)
NB	12,020	+ 80,200	+ 480	+ 1,470	= 3,410	+ 88,200	+ 4,990	− 2,430
	94,170					94,170		

Transaction (n) **Company paid creditor on account.** Cline's Computer Clinic pays $340 to the *Daily* for advertising. Recall that this bill had previously been recorded as a liability in transaction (j).

	Assets				=	Liabilities +		Owner's Equity		
	Cash	+ Equip.	+ Ppd. Ins.	+ Accts. Rec.	=	Accounts Payable	+	R. P. Cline, Capital	+ Revenue	− Expenses
PB	12,020	+ 80,200	+ 480	+ 1,470	=	3,410	+	88,200	+ 4,990	− 2,430
(n)	−340					−340				
NB	11,680	+ 80,200	+ 480	+ 1,470	=	3,070	+	88,200	+ 4,990	− 2,430
	93,830							93,830		

Transaction (o) **Company paid an expense in cash.** Cline's Computer Clinic pays wages of a part-time employee, $2,980.

	Assets				=	Liabilities +		Owner's Equity		
	Cash	+ Equip.	+ Ppd. Ins.	+ Accts. Rec.	=	Accounts Payable	+	R. P. Cline, Capital	+ Revenue	− Expenses
PB	11,680	+ 80,200	+ 480	+ 1,470	=	3,070	+	88,200	+ 4,990	− 2,430
(o)	−2,980									+2,980
										(Wages Expense)
NB	8,700	+ 80,200	+ 480	+ 1,470	=	3,070	+	88,200	+ 4,990	− 5,410
	90,850							90,850		

Transaction (p) **Company buys equipment on account and makes a cash down payment.** Cline's Computer Clinic buys additional equipment from Surgo Products for $3,520, paying $620 down, with the remaining $2,900 on account. Because buying an item *on account* is the same as buying it *on credit,* both terms are used to describe such transactions.

	Assets				=	Liabilities +		Owner's Equity		
	Cash	+ Equip.	+ Ppd. Ins.	+ Accts. Rec.	=	Accounts Payable	+	R. P. Cline, Capital	+ Revenue	− Expenses
PB	8,700	+ 80,200	+ 480	+ 1,470	=	3,070	+	88,200	+ 4,990	− 5,410
(p)	−620	+3,520				+2,900				
NB	8,080	+ 83,720	+ 480	+ 1,470	=	5,970	+	88,200	+ 4,990	− 5,410
	93,750							93,750		

Again, because the equipment is expected to last for years, Cline's Computer Clinic lists this $3,520 as an increase in the assets. Note that three accounts are involved in this transaction: Cash, because cash was paid out; Equipment, because the company has more equipment than before; and Accounts Payable, because the company owes more than before.

Transaction (q) **Company receives cash on account from credit customer.** Cline's Computer Clinic receives $850 from Computer Makeovers to apply against the amount billed in transaction (k). Computer Makeovers now owes Cline's Computer Clinic less than it did, and so Cline's Computer Clinic deducts the $850 from Accounts Receivable. An exchange of assets has no effect on the total of the equation.

	Assets				=	Liabilities +		Owner's Equity		
	Cash	+ Equip.	+ Ppd. Ins.	+ Accts. Rec.		Accounts Payable	R. P. Cline, Capital	+ Revenue	− Expenses	
PB	8,080	+ 83,720	+ 480	+ 1,470	=	5,970	+ 88,200	+ 4,990	− 5,410	
(q)	+850			−850						
NB	8,930	+ 83,720	+ 480	+ 620	=	5,970	+ 88,200	+ 4,990	− 5,410	
		93,750						93,750		

Cline's Computer Clinic previously listed the amount as revenue, so it should definitely not be recorded as revenue again. Think of paying income tax twice on the $850—once is enough.

Transaction (r)   Company sells services for cash. Cline's Computer Clinic receives revenue from cash customers for the rest of the month, $6,020.

	Assets				=	Liabilities +		Owner's Equity		
	Cash	+ Equip.	+ Ppd. Ins.	+ Accts. Rec.		Accounts Payable	R. P. Cline, Capital	+ Revenue	− Expenses	
PB	8,930	+ 83,720	+ 480	+ 620	=	5,970	+ 88,200	+ 4,990	− 5,410	
(r)	+6,020							+6,020		
								(Income from Services)		
NB	14,950	+ 83,720	+ 480	+ 620	=	5,970	+ 88,200	+ 11,010	− 5,410	
		99,770						99,770		

Transaction (s)   Owner makes a cash withdrawal. At the end of the month, Cline withdraws $3,000 in cash from the business for her personal living costs. A **withdrawal** may be considered the opposite of an investment in cash by the owner and is treated as a temporary decrease in owner's equity because it is made in anticipation of profits. Withdrawals are different from expenses. Expenses are paid to someone else for the cost of goods or services used in the business, whereas withdrawals are paid directly to the owner. A withdrawal may consist of cash or other assets.

Because the owner takes cash out of the business, there is a decrease of $3,000 in Cash. This also decreases Capital, because Cline has reduced her equity. We record $3,000 as a minus under Capital and label it as Drawing.

	Assets				=	Liabilities +		Owner's Equity		
	Cash	+ Equip.	+ Ppd. Ins.	+ Accts. Rec.		Accounts Payable	R. P. Cline, Capital	+ Revenue	− Expenses	
PB	14,950	+ 83,720	+ 480	+ 620	=	5,970	+ 88,200	+ 11,010	− 5,410	
(s)	−3,000						−3,000			
							(Drawing)			
NB	11,950	+ 83,720	+ 480	+ 620	=	5,970	+ 85,200	+ 11,010	− 5,410	
		96,770						96,770		

Summary of Transactions f Through s

Figure 1 summarizes business transactions (f) through (s) of Cline's Computer Clinic with the transactions identified by letter. To test your understanding of the recording procedure, describe the nature of the transactions.

	Assets			= Liabilities +		Owner's Equity		
	Cash + Equip. +	Ppd. Ins. +	Accts. Rec.	Accounts Payable	R. P. Cline, Capital	+ Revenue	− Expenses	

Bal.	12,000 + 80,200			=	4,000 +	88,200			
(f)	+3,520						+3,520		
							(Income from Services)		
Bal.	15,520 + 80,200			=	4,000 +	88,200 +	3,520		
(g)	−900							+900	
								(Rent Expense)	
Bal.	14,620 + 80,200			=	4,000 +	88,200 +	3,520 −	900	
(h)					+870			+870	
								(Supplies Expense)	
Bal.	14,620 + 80,200			=	4,870 +	88,200 +	3,520 −	1,770	
(i)	−480	+480							
Bal.	14,140 + 80,200 +		480	=	4,870 +	88,200 +	3,520 −	1,770	
(j)					+340			+340	
								(Advertising Expense)	
Bal.	14,140 + 80,200 +		480	=	5,210 +	88,200 +	3,520 −	2,110	
(k)			+1,470				+1,470		
							(Income from Services)		
Bal.	14,140 + 80,200 +		480 + 1,470 =		5,210 +	88,200 +	4,990 −	2,110	
(l)	−1,800				−1,800				
Bal.	12,340 + 80,200 +		480 + 1,470 =		3,410 +	88,200 +	4,990 −	2,110	
(m)	−320							+320	
								(Utilities Expense)	
Bal.	12,020 + 80,200 +		480 + 1,470 =		3,410 +	88,200 +	4,990 −	2,430	
(n)	−340				−340				
Bal.	11,680 + 80,200 +		480 + 1,470 =		3,070 +	88,200 +	4,990 −	2,430	
(o)	−2,980							+2,980	
								(Wages Expense)	
Bal.	8,700 + 80,200 +		480 + 1,470 =		3,070 +	88,200 +	4,990 −	5,410	
(p)	−620 +3,520				+2,900				
Bal.	8,080 + 83,720 +		480 + 1,470 =		5,970 +	88,200 +	4,990 −	5,410	
(q)	+850		−850						
Bal.	8,930 + 83,720 +		480 + 620 =		5,970 +	88,200 +	4,990 −	5,410	
(r)	+6,020						+6,020		
							(Income from Services)		
Bal.	14,950 + 83,720 +		480 + 620 =		5,970 +	88,200 +	11,010 −	5,410	
(s)	−3,000					−3,000			
						(Drawing)			
	11,950 + 83,720 +		480 + 620 =		5,970 +	85,200 +	11,010 −	5,410	

Left Side of Equals Sign		Right Side of Equals Sign	
Cash	$11,950	**Accounts Payable**	$ 5,970
Equipment	83,720	**R. P. Cline, Capital**	85,200
Prepaid Insurance	480	**Revenue**	11,010
Accounts Receivable	620	**Subtotal**	$102,180
		Expenses	−5,410
	$96,770		$ 96,770

FIGURE 1

CHAPTER REVIEW

Online Study Center
ACE the test!

Review of Performance Objectives

1. Define and identify *asset*, *liability*, and *owner's equity* accounts.

   Assets are cash, properties, or things of value owned by the business. *Liabilities* are amounts the business owes to creditors. *Owner's equity* is the owner's investment or net worth.

2. Record a group of business transactions, in column form, involving changes in assets, liabilities, and owner's equity.

   The accounting equation is stated as assets equals liabilities plus owner's equity. Under the appropriate classification, a separate column is set up for each account. Transactions are recorded by listing amounts as either additions to or deductions from the various accounts. The equation must always remain in balance.

3. Define and identify *revenue* and *expense* accounts.

   Revenue consists of amounts earned by a business, such as fees earned for performing services, income from selling merchandise, rent income for the use of property, or interest earned for lending money. *Expenses* are the costs of earning revenue—that is, of doing business—such as wages expense, rent expense, interest expense, and advertising expense.

4. Record a group of business transactions, in column form, involving all five elements of the fundamental accounting equation.

   The accounting equation has been expanded and appears as follows:

   Assets = Liabilities + Owner's Equity (Capital) + Revenue − Expenses

   Accounts are classified and listed under each heading. Transactions are recorded by listing amounts as either additions to or deductions from the various accounts. The equation must always remain in balance.

Glossary

Accounts The categories under the Assets, Liabilities, and Owner's Equity headings. (10)

Accounts Payable A liability account used for short-term liabilities or charge accounts, usually due within thirty days. (11)

Accounts Receivable An account used to record the amounts owed by (legal claims against) charge customers. (18)

Assets Cash, properties, and other things of value owned by an economic unit or business entity. (7)

Business entity A business enterprise, separate and distinct from the persons who supply the assets it uses. Property acquired by a business is an asset of the business. The owner is separate from the business and in fact has claims on it and a responsibility for its debts. (8)

Capital The owner's investment, or equity, in an enterprise. (8)

Chart of accounts The official list of account titles to be used to record the transactions of a business. (14)

Creditor One to whom money is owed. (8)

Double-entry accounting The system by which each business transaction is recorded in at least two accounts and the accounting equation is kept in balance. (13)

Equity The value of a right or claim to or financial interest in an asset or group of assets. (8)

Expenses The costs that relate to earning revenue (the costs of doing business); examples are wages, rent, interest, and advertising. They may be paid in cash immediately or at a future time (accounts payable). (14)

Fair market value The present worth of an asset or the amount that would be received if the asset were sold to an outsider on the open market. (12)

Fundamental accounting equation (Assets = Liabilities + Owner's Equity) An equation expressing the relationship of assets, liabilities, and owner's equity. (9)

Liabilities Debts or amounts owed to creditors. (8)

Owner's equity The owner's right to or investment in the business. (8)

Revenues The amounts a business earns; examples are fees earned for performing services, sales of merchandise, rent income, and interest income. They may be in the form of cash, credit card receipts, or accounts receivable (charge accounts). (13)

Separate entity concept The concept by which a business is treated as a separate economic or accounting entity. The business stands by itself, separate from its owners, creditors, and customers. (10)

Sole proprietorship A one-owner business. (10)

Withdrawal The taking of cash or other assets out of a business by the owner for his or her own use. (This is also referred to as *drawing*.) A withdrawal is treated as a temporary decrease in owner's equity. (20)

QUESTIONS, EXERCISES, AND CASES

Discussion Questions

1. Define assets, liabilities, owner's equity, revenues, and expenses.
2. Explain the separate entity concept.
3. How do Accounts Payable and Accounts Receivable differ?
4. Describe two ways to increase owner's equity and two ways to decrease owner's equity.
5. How will the fundamental accounting equation change if supplies are purchased on account? Explain how this purchase will or will not change the owner's equity.
6. When an owner withdraws cash or goods from the business, why is this considered an increase to the Drawing account and not an increase to the wages account?
7. Define *chart of accounts*, and identify the categories of accounts.
8. What account titles would you suggest for the chart of accounts for a jeep touring company owned by W. Sands? List the accounts by account category and include an appropriate account number for each.

Exercises

P.O. 1

Calculate missing amounts in the accounting equation.

Exercise 1-1 Complete the following equations:

a. Assets of $21,000 = Liabilities of $7,300 + Owner's Equity of $_____
b. Assets of $_____ − Liabilities of $15,000 = Owner's Equity of $25,000
c. Assets of $23,000 − Owner's Equity of $12,000 = Liabilities of $_____

P.O. 1

Calculate missing amounts in the accounting equation.

Exercise 1-2 Determine the following amounts:

a. The amount of the liabilities of a business that has $60,300 in assets and in which the owner has $35,000 equity.
b. The equity of the owner of a tour van that cost $38,000 who owes $18,400 on an installment loan payable to the bank.
c. The amount of the assets of a business that has $10,350 in liabilities and in which the owner has $24,180 equity.

P.O. 1

Formulate the accounting equation.

Exercise 1-3 Dr. L. M. Paydaar is an ophthalmologist. As of December 31, Dr. Paydaar owned the following property that related to his professional practice, Paydaar Eye Clinic:

Cash, $2,480
Professional Equipment, $58,000
Office Equipment, $10,460

On the same date, he owed the following business creditors:

Nichols Supply Company, $4,120
Rodriquez Equipment Sales, $3,970

Compute the following amounts in the accounting equation:

Assets $_____ = Liabilities $_____ + Owner's Equity $_____

P.O. 1,3

Describe transactions affecting the accounting equation.

Exercise 1-4 Describe a business transaction that will do the following:

a. Increase an asset and increase a liability
b. Decrease an asset and decrease a liability
c. Decrease an asset and increase an expense
d. Increase an asset and increase owner's equity
e. Increase an asset and decrease an asset
f. Increase an asset and increase revenue

P.O. 2

Describe various transactions.

Exercise 1-5 Describe a transaction that resulted in the following entries:

	Cash +	Office Equipment	+ Professional Equipment	=	Accounts Payable	+	B. Loren, Capital
(a)	+14,300						+14,300
(b)	−1,650		+1,650				
Bal.	12,650		+ 1,650	=			14,300
(c)		+550			+550		
Bal.	12,650 +	550	+ 1,650	=	550	+	14,300
(d)	−1,200		+6,000		+4,800		
Bal.	11,450 +	550	+ 7,650	=	5,350	+	14,300
(e)	−1,000				−1,000		
Bal.	10,450 +	550	+ 7,650	=	4,350	+	14,300

Column headers (spanning): **Assets** = **Liabilities** + **Owner's Equity**

P.O. 1,3

Classify accounts.

Exercise 1-6 Label the following accounts as asset (A), liability (L), owner's equity (OE), revenue (R), or expense (E):

  a. Office Supplies Expense
  b. Professional Fees
  c. Prepaid Insurance A
  d. R. Baca, Drawing
  e. Accounts Payable
  f. Service Income
  g. R. Baca, Capital
  h. Rent Expense
  i. Accounts Receivable
  j. Wages Expense

P.O. 4

Describe various transactions.

Exercise 1-7 Describe a transaction that resulted in the following changes in accounts:

  a. Rent Expense is increased by $950, and Cash is decreased by $950.
  b. Advertising Expense is increased by $841, and Accounts Payable is increased by $841.
  c. Accounts Receivable is increased by $285, and Service Income is increased by $285.
  d. Cash is decreased by $320, and C. Taylor, Drawing, is increased by $320.
  e. Equipment is increased by $850, Cash is decreased by $450, and Accounts Payable is increased by $400.
  f. Cash is increased by $630, and Accounts Receivable is decreased by $630.

P.O. 2,4

Describe various transactions.

Exercise 1-8 Describe the transactions that are recorded in the following equation.

	Assets			= Liabilities +		Owner's Equity		
	Cash +	Accounts Receivable	+Equipment	Accounts Payable	J. Ohno, + Capital	Revenue	–	Expenses
(a)	+22,000		+5,000		+27,000			
(b)	−1,050							+1,050 (Rent Expense)
Bal.	20,950	+	5,000 =		27,000		–	1,050
(c)		+1,800				+1,800 (Income from Services)		
Bal.	20,950 +	1,800	+ 5,000 =		27,000	1,800	–	1,050
(d)	−4,000		+15,000	+11,000				
Bal.	16,950 +	1,800	+ 20,000 =	11,000 +	27,000 +	1,800	–	1,050
(e)	−2,000				−2,000 (Drawing)			
Bal.	14,950 +	1,800	+ 20,000 =	11,000 +	25,000 +	1,800	–	1,050
		36,750				36,750		

Recall from Performance Objective 1 in the chapter that the fundamental accounting equation expresses the relationship of assets, liabilities, and owner's equity. This is what the balance sheet reports. Using information from Gap Inc.'s balance sheet, found on page 38 of the 2005 Annual Report, create a completed accounting equation (Assets = Liabilities + Stockholders' Equity). The term Stockholders' Equity is used for Gap Inc. because the company sells shares of its stock to the public. On January 28, 2006, Gap Inc.'s total assets equaled $8,821,000,000; total liabilities equaled $3,396,000,000 (current liabilities of $1,942,000,000 plus long-term liabilities of $1,454,000,000); and total stockholders' equity equaled $5,425,000,000. As you can see, when we place these amounts into the fundamental accounting equation, the total of one side of the equation equals the total of the other side of the equation.

Assets	=	Liabilities	+	Stockholders' Equity
$8,821,000,000	=	$3,396,000,000	+	$5,425,000,000

1. If you purchase a pair of jeans from Gap for $40 cash, how will the store record this transaction? (Ignore sales taxes.)
2. How would Gap record a $30,000 payment for its monthly rent for one of its stores?

CONSIDER AND COMMUNICATE

A friend of yours wants to start her own house, plant, and pet sitting business. She already has a business license that is required in her city. She has had a personal checking account for years. You have told her that she also needs to open a separate account for her business needs, but she does not understand why she needs to have two separate accounts. Explain to her why she should have a business account separate from her personal account. Use some of the language of business you have learned in your text's Introduction and in this chapter.

WHAT'S WRONG WITH THIS PICTURE?

Eddie Cabrera has just opened Cabrera's Golf Cart Service. He has calculated the following amounts and then placed them in the fundamental accounting equation as he remembers it from his accounting class five years ago. He asks that you review his figures and give your opinion because he wants to start out on a correct footing.

Money in the drawer	$2,395
What I owe people	484
What people owe me	995

$$\underline{\textbf{Assets}} = \underline{\textbf{Liabilities}} + \underline{\textbf{Owner's Equity}}$$

	Assets		Liabilities		Owner's Equity
	2,395		484		
	995				
Totals	3,390 =		484	+	?

Eddie's Proof: A − L = OE

2,395 − 995 = 1,400 OE

1. Do you agree with Eddie's calculations?
2. If not, show how you would explain it to Eddie using the classifications of the fundamental accounting equation.

CRITICAL THINKING

Please read the following memorandum and follow the instructions set forth.

MEMORANDUM

TO: Your Name   DATE: July 31, 20—
FROM: J. Lara,   SUBJECT: Calculations for Baxter Co.
       Supervisor

Please provide the following ASAP (as soon as possible).

1. The balance of cash in Baxter Company's checkbook shows $13,740. I need to know if this ties to or matches the Cash account balance. I do know that total assets amount to $44,670. Office Equipment amounts to $3,650. Other noncash assets are Equipment, $25,480 and Prepaid Insurance, $1,800.
2. D. Baxter, the owner, wants to know the amount of his owner's equity. I pulled the outstanding bills, which amount to $8,430.
3. Please put the information in a memo addressed to me.
4. Thank you for your prompt response

PROBLEM SET A

For additional help, see the demonstration problem at the beginning of each chapter in your Working Papers.

P.O. 1,2,3,4

Problem 1-1A In July of this year, J. L. Walters established a business called Walters Realty. The account headings are presented on the following page. Transactions completed during the month follow.

Assets	=	Liabilities +		Owner's Equity
Cash + Office Equipment		Accounts Payable	Capital	, + Revenue − Expenses

a. Walters deposited $14,000 in a bank account in the name of the business.
b. Paid the office rent for the current month, $400, Ck. No. 1000 (Rent Expense).
c. Bought office supplies, paying cash, $445, Ck. No. 1001 (Supplies Expense).
d. Bought office equipment on account from Bellos Computers, $7,200.
e. Received a bill from the *Weekly Crier* for advertising, $556 (Advertising Expense).
f. Paid on account to Bellos Computers, a creditor, $1,000, Ck. No. 1002.
g. Sold services for cash, $2,960 (Service Income).
h. Received and paid the bill for utilities, $238, Ck. No. 1003 (Utilities Expense).
i. Paid on account to the *Weekly Crier*, a creditor, $556, Ck. No. 1004.
j. Paid truck expenses, $356, Ck. No. 1005 (Truck Maintenance Expense).
k. Walters withdrew cash for personal use, $1,200, Ck. No. 1006 (J. L. Walters, Drawing).

Check Figure

Left side of equals sign total, $19,965

Instructions

1. In the equation, write the owner's name above the term *Capital*.
2. Record the transactions and the balance after each transaction. Identify the account affected when the transaction involves revenue, expenses, or a withdrawal.
3. Write the account totals from the left side of the equals sign and add them. Write the account totals from the right side of the equals sign and add them. If the two totals are not equal, first check the addition and subtraction. If you still cannot find the error, reanalyze each transaction.

P.O. 1,2,3,4

Problem 1-2A In March, T. Camus, M.D., established the Camus Sports Injury Clinic. The clinic's account headings are presented below. Transactions completed during the month of March follow.

Assets		=	Liabilities +		Owner's Equity
Cash + Office Equipment	+ Professional Equipment		Accounts Payable	Capital	, + Revenue − Expenses

a. Camus deposited $25,000 in a bank account in the name of the business.
b. Paid the rent for the month, $1,100, Ck. No. 1000 (Rent Expense).
c. Bought supplies on account from Herzog Co., $1,170 (Supplies Expense).
d. Bought professional equipment on account from Norman Company, $5,800.
e. Bought office equipment on account from Masterson Co., $864.
f. Sold professional services for cash, $4,820 (Professional Fees).
g. Paid on account to Norman Company, a creditor, $1,850, Ck. No. 1001.
h. Received and paid the bill for utilities, $382, Ck. No. 1002 (Utilities Expense).
i. Paid the salary of the assistant, $1,150, Ck. No. 1003 (Salary Expense).
j. Sold professional services for cash, $3,800 (Professional Fees).
k. Camus withdrew cash for personal use, $1,600, Ck. No. 1004 (T. Camus, Drawing).

Check Figure

Cash, $27,538

Instructions

1. In the equation, write the owner's name above the term *Capital*.
2. Record the transactions and the balance after each transaction. Identify the account affected when the transaction involves revenue, expenses, or a withdrawal.
3. Write the account totals from the left side of the equals sign and add them. Write the account totals from the right side of the equals sign and add them. If the two totals are not equal, first check the addition and subtraction. If you still cannot find the error, reanalyze each transaction.

P.O. 1,2,3,4

Problem 1-3A S. Strohm, Attorney at Law, opened his office on October 1. The account headings are presented below. Transactions completed during the month follow.

Assets				= Liabilities +		Owner's Equity		
Cash +	Prepaid Insurance +	Office Equipment	+ Library	Accounts Payable	Capital	, + Revenue − Expenses		

a. Strohm deposited $25,000 in a bank account in the name of the business.
b. Bought office equipment on account from Milgor Company, $11,700.
c. Strohm invested his personal law library, which cost $4,700. (Increase the account Library and increase the account S. Strohm, Capital.)
d. Paid the office rent for the month, $1,050, Ck. No. 2000 (Rent Expense).
e. Bought office supplies for cash, $475, Ck. No. 2001 (Supplies Expense).
f. Bought insurance for two years, $284, Ck. No. 2002.
g. Sold legal services for cash, $3,680 (Professional Fees).
h. Received and paid the telephone bill, $328, Ck. No. 2003 (Telephone Expense).
i. Paid the salary of the part-time receptionist, $1,060, Ck. No. 2004 (Salary Expense).
j. Received and paid the bill for utilities, $188, Ck. No. 2005 (Utilities Expense).
k. Sold legal services for cash, $3,320 (Professional Fees).
l. Paid on account to Milgor Company, a creditor, $2,500, Ck. No. 2006.
m. Strohm withdrew cash for personal use, $2,200, Ck. No. 2007 (S. Strohm, Drawing).

Check Figure

Right side of equals sign total, $40,599

Instructions

1. In the equation, write the owner's name above the term *Capital*.
2. Record the transactions and the balance after each transaction. Identify the account affected when the transaction involves revenue, expenses, or a withdrawal.
3. Write the account totals from the left side of the equals sign and add them. Write the account totals from the right side of the equals sign and add them. If the two totals are not equal, first check the addition and subtraction. If you still cannot find the error, reanalyze each transaction.

P.O. 1,2,3,4

Problem 1-4A B. G. Ellison started Ellison Plant Service on May 1 of this year. The account headings are presented below. During May, Ellison completed the transactions that follow.

Assets					= Liabilities +		Owner's Equity		
Cash +	Accounts Receivable +	Prepaid Insurance	+ Truck	+ Equipment	Accounts Payable	Capital	, + Revenue − Expenses		

a. Ellison deposited $15,000 in a bank account in the name of the business.
b. Bought a used truck from Delgado Motors for $18,250, paying $1,200 in cash, and placing the remainder on account.
c. Bought equipment on account from Fanning Company, $2,800.
d. Paid the rent for the month, $560, Ck. No. 3001 (Rent Expense).
e. Bought insurance for the truck for the year, $680, Ck. No. 3002, Policy No. 311D.
f. Sold services for cash for the first half of the month, $3,175 (Service Income).
g. Bought supplies for cash, $483, Ck. No. 3003 (Supplies Expense).
h. Sold services on account, $944 (Service Income).
i. Received and paid the bill for utilities, $186, Ck. No. 3004 (Utilities Expense).
j. Received a bill for gas and oil for the truck, $227 (Gas and Oil Expense).
k. Sold services for cash for the remainder of the month, $3,732 (Service Income).
l. Ellison withdrew cash for personal use, $1,250, Ck. No. 3005 (B. G. Ellison, Drawing).
m. Paid wages to the employees, $2,240, Ck. Nos. 3006–3008 (Wages Expense).

Check Figure

Cash, $15,308

Instructions

1. In the equation, write the owner's name above the term *Capital*.
2. Record the transactions and the balance after each transaction. Identify the account affected when the transaction involves revenue, expenses, or a withdrawal.
3. Write the account totals from the left side of the equals sign and add them. Write the account totals from the right side of the equals sign and add them. If the two totals are not equal, first check the addition and subtraction. If you still cannot find the error, reanalyze each transaction.

PROBLEM SET B

For additional help, see the demonstration problem at the beginning of each chapter in your Working Papers.

P.O. 1,2,3,4

Problem 1-1B On June 1 of this year, J. Vance, Optometrist, established the Vance Eye Clinic. The clinic's account names are presented below. Transactions completed during the month follow.

Assets		= Liabilities +	Owner's Equity		
Cash +	Office Equipment	Accounts Payable	Capital	, + Revenue −	Expenses

a. Vance deposited $20,000 in a bank account in the name of the business.
b. Paid the office rent for the month, $840, Ck. No. 1001 (Rent Expense).
c. Bought supplies for cash, $775, Ck. No. 1002 (Supplies Expense).
d. Bought office equipment on account from Espino Equipment, $9,180.
e. Bought a computer from Wesley Office Outfitters, $1,840, paying $600 in cash and placing the balance on account, Ck. No. 1003.
f. Sold professional services for cash, $2,421 (Professional Fees).

g. Paid on account to Wesley Office Outfitters, a creditor, $900, Ck. No. 1004.
h. Received and paid the bill for utilities, $243, Ck. No. 1005 (Utilities Expense).
i. Paid the salary of the assistant, $990, Ck. No. 1006 (Salary Expense).
j. Sold professional services for cash, $2,515 (Professional Fees).
k. Vance withdrew cash for personal use, $1,250, Ck. No. 1007 (J. Vance, Drawing).

Check Figure

Left side of equals sign total, $30,358

Instructions

1. In the equation, write the owner's name above the term *Capital*.
2. Record the transactions and the balance after each transaction. Identify the account affected when the transaction involves revenue, expenses, or a withdrawal.
3. Write the account totals from the left side of the equals sign and add them. Write the account totals from the right side of the equals sign and add them. If the two totals are not equal, first check the addition and subtraction. If you still cannot find the error, reanalyze each transaction.

P.O. 1,2,3,4

Problem 1-2B On July 1 of this year, R. Green established the Green Rehab Clinic. The organization's account headings are presented below. Transactions completed during the month of July follow.

Assets			= Liabilities +	Owner's Equity		
Cash +	Office Equipment	+ Professional Equipment	Accounts Payable	Capital	, + Revenue	− Expenses

a. Green deposited $15,000 in a bank account in the name of the business.
b. Paid the office rent for the month, $1,100, Ck. No. 2001 (Rent Expense).
c. Bought supplies for cash, $275, Ck. No. 2002 (Supplies Expense).
d. Bought professional equipment on account from Rehab Equipment Company, $14,200 (Professional Equipment).
e. Bought office equipment from Hi-Tech Computers, $1,870, paying $870 in cash and placing the balance on account, Ck. No. 2003.
f. Sold professional services for cash, $3,280 (Professional Fees).
g. Paid on account to Hi-Tech Computers, a creditor, $500, Ck. No. 2004.
h. Received and paid the bill for utilities, $283, Ck. No. 2005 (Utilities Expense).
i. Paid the salary of the assistant, $1,000, Ck. No. 2006 (Salary Expense).
j. Sold professional services for cash, $3,725 (Professional Fees).
k. Green withdrew cash for personal use, $1,600, Ck. No. 2007 (R. Green, Drawing).

Check Figure

Cash, $16,377

Instructions

1. In the equation, write the owner's name above the term *Capital*.
2. Record the transactions and the balance after each transaction. Identify the account affected when the transaction involves revenue, expenses, or a withdrawal.
3. Write the account totals from the left side of the equals sign and add them. Write the account totals from the right side of the equals sign and add them. If the two totals are not equal, first check the addition and subtraction. If you still cannot find the error, reanalyze each transaction.

P.O. 1,2,3,4

Problem 1-3B S. Delaney, a graphic artist, opened a studio for her professional practice on August 1. The account headings are presented below. Transactions completed during the month follow.

Assets				= Liabilities +		Owner's Equity		
Cash +	Prepaid + Insurance	Office Equipment	+ Photo Equipment	Accounts Payable	Capital	, + Revenue	− Expenses

a. Delaney deposited $15,500 in a bank account in the name of the business.
b. Bought office equipment on account from Stark Equipment Company, $4,120.
c. Delaney invested her personal photographic equipment, $6,260. (Increase the account Photo Equipment and increase the account S. Delaney, Capital.)
d. Paid the rent for the month, $500, Ck. No. 1000 (Rent Expense).
e. Bought supplies for cash, $345, Ck. No. 1001 (Supplies Expense).
f. Bought insurance for two years, $820, Ck. No. 1002.
g. Sold graphic services for cash, $2,985 (Professional Fees).
h. Paid the salary of the part-time assistant, $500, Ck. No. 1003 (Salary Expense).
i. Received and paid the bill for telephone service, $73, Ck. No. 1004 (Telephone Expense).
j. Paid cash for minor repairs to graphics equipment, $86, Ck. No. 1005 (Repair Expense).
k. Sold graphic services for cash, $2,936 (Professional Fees).
l. Paid on account to Stark Equipment Company, a creditor, $520, Ck. No. 1006.
m. Delaney withdrew cash for personal use, $1,000, Ck. No. 1007 (S. Delaney, Drawing).

Check Figure

Right side of equals sign total, $28,777

Instructions

1. In the equation, write the owner's name above the term *Capital.*
2. Record the transactions and the balance after each transaction. Identify the account affected when the transaction involves revenue, expenses, or a withdrawal.
3. Write the account totals from the left side of the equals sign and add them. Write the account totals from the right side of the equals sign and add them. If the two totals are not equal, first check the addition and subtraction. If you still cannot find the error, reanalyze each transaction.

P.O. 1,2,3,4

Problem 1-4B On March 1 of this year, B. Gelmond established Gelmond Catering Service. The account headings are presented below. Transactions completed during the month follow.

Assets					= Liabilities +		Owner's Equity		
Cash +	Accounts + Receivable	Prepaid + Insurance	Truck +	Equipment	Accounts Payable	Capital	, + Revenue	− Expenses

a. Gelmond deposited $16,500 in a bank account in the name of the business.
b. Bought a truck from Kerry Motors for $19,490, paying $2,500 in cash and placing the balance on account, Ck. No. 500.

c. Bought catering equipment on account from Fernandez Company, $2,850.
d. Paid the rent for the month, $620, Ck. No. 501 (Rent Expense).
e. Sold catering services for cash for the first half of the month, $2,420 (Catering Income).
f. Bought supplies for cash, $180, Ck. No. 502 (Supplies Expense).
g. Bought insurance for the truck for one year, $400, Ck. No. 503.
h. Received and paid the heating bill, $104, Ck. No. 504 (Utilities Expense).
i. Received a bill from Anson Gas and Lube for gas and oil for the truck, $108 (Gas and Oil Expense).
j. Sold catering services on account, $2,824 (Catering Income).
k. Sold catering services for cash for the remainder of the month, $2,520 (Catering Income).
l. Paid the salary of the assistant, $1,120, Ck. No. 505 (Salary Expense).
m. Gelmond withdrew cash for personal use, $1,550, Ck. No. 506 (B. Gelmond, Drawing).

Check Figure

Cash, $14,966

Instructions

1. In the equation, write the owner's name above the term *Capital*.
2. Record the transactions and the balance after each transaction. Identify the account affected when the transaction involves revenue, expenses, or a withdrawal.
3. Write the account totals from the left side of the equals sign and add them. Write the account totals from the right side of the equals sign and add them. If the two totals are not equal, first check the addition and subtraction. If you still cannot find the error, reanalyze each transaction.

Citigroup, Inc. is a very large, global company consisting of many different financial services. These include banking (for example, Citibank), credit cards (for example, VISA®), and investment advising or "wealth management" (for example, the Smith Barney brokerage firm). In July 2005, Citigroup completed its sale of Travelers Life & Annuity, along with substantially all of Citigroup's international insurance businesses, to MetLife, Inc. for $10.830 billion in cash and $1.0 billion in other assets. Such large sales are governed by the Federal Securities and Exchange Commission (SEC). If you go to the SEC website, you can find a report about this sale: **http://sec.gov/Archives/edgar/data/831001/000104746906002377/a2167745z10-k.htm#06NYC1891_1**. Page 2 tells about Citigroup's business. The Citigroup, Inc. financial statements for the year ended December 31, 2005, begin on page 103 of the report. After completing this chapter you will be able to find key information in this document—and in fact, you'll know how to record such sales for your own business. At the end of the chapter you will find further discussion and questions related to this sale.

Performance Objectives

After you have completed this chapter, you will be able to do the following:

1. Determine balances of T accounts having entries recorded on both sides of the accounts.

2. Present the fundamental accounting equation with the T account form, and label the plus and minus sides.

3. Present the fundamental accounting equation with the T account form, and label the debit and credit sides.

4. Record directly in T accounts a group of business transactions involving changes in asset, liability, owner's equity, revenue, and expense accounts for a service business.

5. Prepare a trial balance.

6. Prepare (a) an income statement, (b) a statement of owner's equity, and (c) a balance sheet.

7. Recognize the effect of transpositions and slides on account balances.

W e introduced the fundamental accounting equation as *Assets = Liabilities + Owner's Equity*. We also discussed the recording of transactions involving two other classifications of accounts: *Revenue* and *Expenses*. With the addition of Revenue and Expenses, the fundamental accounting equation was brought up to its full size of five account classifications. There are only five classifications; so, as far as you go in accounting—whether you are dealing with a small, one-owner business or a large corporation—there will be these five major classifications of accounts.

In this chapter, we will record the same transactions in T account form and prove the equality of both sides of the fundamental accounting equation. We will do this using a trial balance, discussed later in this chapter.

THE T ACCOUNT FORM

So far, we have recorded business transactions in a column arrangement. For example, the Cash account column in the books of Cline's Computer Clinic is shown below.

Cash Account Column

Transaction	(a)	82,000
Transaction	(b)	−64,000
Balance		18,000
Transaction	(d)	−6,000
Balance		12,000
Transaction	(f)	+3,520
Balance		15,520
Transaction	(g)	−900
Balance		14,620
Transaction	(i)	−480
Balance		14,140
Transaction	(l)	−1,800
Balance		12,340
Transaction	(m)	−320
Balance		12,020
Transaction	(n)	−340
Balance		11,680
Transaction	(o)	−2,980
Balance		8,700
Transaction	(p)	−620
Balance		8,080
Transaction	(q)	+850
Balance		8,930
Transaction	(r)	+6,020
Balance		14,950
Transaction	(s)	−3,000
		11,950

Cash

+		−	
(a)	82,000	(b)	64,000
(f)	3,520	(d)	6,000
(q)	850	(g)	900
(r)	6,020	(i)	480
	92,390	(l)	1,800
		(m)	320
		(n)	340
		(o)	2,980
		(p)	620
		(s)	3,000
			80,440

Footings

Balance → **11,950**

As an introduction to the recording of transactions, the column arrangement had the following advantages:

1. **In the process of analyzing the transaction, you**

   a. Recognized the need to determine which accounts are involved.
   b. Determined the classification of the accounts involved.
   c. Decided whether the transaction resulted in an increase or a decrease in each of these accounts.

2. **You further realized that, after each transaction had been recorded, the two sides of the fundamental accounting equation were in balance. In other words, the total of one side of the accounting equation equaled the total of the other side.**

Now, instead of recording transactions in a column for each account, we will use a **T account form** for each account. *The T account form has the advantage of providing two sides for each account; one side is used to record increases in the account, and the other side is used to record decreases.*

OBJECTIVE 1

Determine balances of T accounts having entries recorded on both sides of the accounts.

After we record a group of transactions in a T account, we add both sides and record the totals in small, pencil-written figures called **footings**. Next, we subtract one footing from the other to determine the balance of the account. For the Cash account, shown previously, the balance is $11,950 ($92,390 − $80,440).

We now record the balance on the side of the account having the larger footing, which, with a few minor exceptions, is the plus (+) side. The plus side of a T account is the side that represents the **normal balance** of that account. The normal balance may, however, fall on either the left or the right side of an account, depending on what type of account it is. To review, we presented the T account for Cash; Cash is classified as an asset, and all assets look like the following T account:

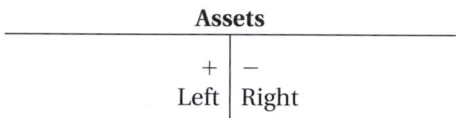

However, **not all classifications of accounts have the increase side on the left.**

Recall that we placed revenue and expenses under the umbrella of owner's equity. Revenue increases owner's equity, and expenses decrease owner's equity. The T accounts for this situation are as follows:

Expenses cause a decrease in owner's equity

Revenues cause an increase in owner's equity

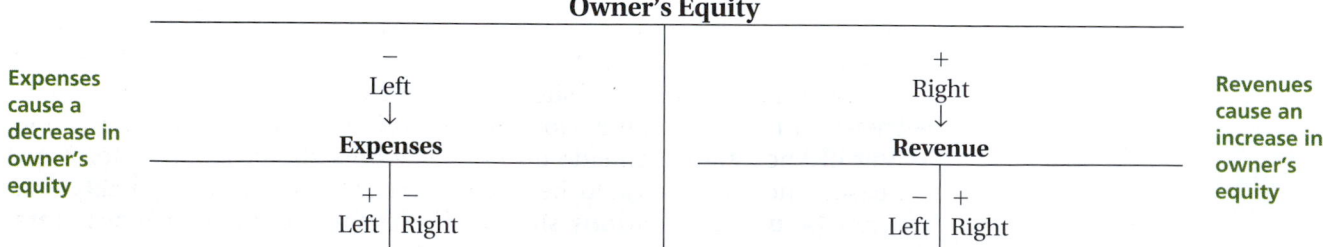

Increases in owner's equity are recorded on the right side of the account. Because revenue increases owner's equity, additions to revenue are also recorded on the right side.

Decreases in owner's equity are recorded on the left side of the account. Because expenses decrease owner's equity, additions to expenses are also recorded on the left side.

Using the five classifications of accounts, the fundamental accounting equation looks like this:

$$\text{Assets} = \text{Liabilities} + \underbrace{\overbrace{\hspace{4cm}}^{\text{Owner's Equity}}}_{\text{Capital} + \text{Revenue} - \text{Expenses}}$$

REMEMBER!

The entry for a business transaction may include any combination of pluses and minuses: pluses and pluses, pluses and minuses, or minuses and minuses.

Because revenue and expenses appear separately in the income statement, we will stretch out the equation to include them as separate headings, as shown here:

$$\text{Assets} = \text{Liabilities} + \text{Capital} + \text{Revenue} - \text{Expenses}$$

We can now restate the equation with the T account forms and plus and minus signs for each account classification:

Assets	=	Liabilities	+	Owner's Equity	+	Revenue	−	Expenses
+ | −		− | +		− | +		− | +		+ | −
Left | Right		Left | Right		Left | Right		Left | Right		Left | Right

OBJECTIVE 2

Present the fundamental accounting equation with the T account form, and label the plus and minus sides.

Before we go on, let us point out the increase, or plus, side of each account classification. You can recognize these in the accounting equation using T accounts.

Assets	The *left* side is the *increase* side.
Liabilities	The *right* side is the *increase* side.
Owner's Equity	The *right* side is the *increase* side.
Revenue	The *right* side is the *increase* side.
Expenses	The *left* side is the *increase* side.

Because revenue is an addition to owner's equity, the placement of the plus and minus signs is the same as for owner's equity. On the other hand, because expenses are treated as deductions from owner's equity, the placement of the plus and minus signs is reversed. We will use this form of the fundamental accounting equation throughout the remainder of the text.

Your accounting background up to this point has taught you to analyze business transactions to determine which accounts are involved and to recognize that each amount should be recorded as either an increase or a decrease in these accounts. Now the recording process becomes a simple matter of knowing which side of the T accounts should be used to record increases and which should be used to record decreases. **Generally, you will not be using the minus side of the revenue and expense accounts, since transactions involving revenue and expense accounts usually result in increases in these accounts.** An exception to this statement is where errors have been made and require correction. Let's now add the last element to the T account before we record the familiar Cline's Computer Clinic transactions.

THE T ACCOUNT FORM WITH DEBITS AND CREDITS

OBJECTIVE 3

Present the fundamental accounting equation with the T account form, and label the debit and credit sides.

The left side of a T account is called the **debit** side; the right side is called the **credit** side. The T accounts representing the accounting equation now contain both the signs and the words *Debit* and *Credit*. There are only five classifications of accounts. These classifications are contained in the fundamental accounting equation:

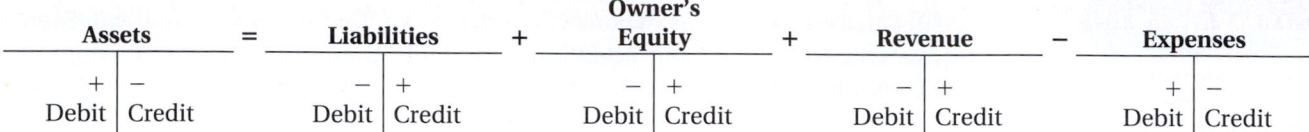

Assets	=	Liabilities	+	Owner's Equity	+	Revenue	−	Expenses
+ | −		− | +		− | +		− | +		+ | −
Debit | Credit		Debit | Credit		Debit | Credit		Debit | Credit		Debit | Credit

The following table summarizes debits and credits and how they are affected by increases and decreases. **The critical rule to remember is that the amount placed on the debit side of one or more accounts MUST equal the amount placed on the credit side of another account or accounts.**

Debits Signify		Credits Signify	
Increases in	Assets Drawing Expenses	Decreases in	Assets Drawing Expenses
Decreases in	Liabilities Capital Revenue	Increases in	Liabilities Capital Revenue

Debit is always the left side of the account, and credit is always the right side of the account. The + or −, however, changes with the type of account.

Before we begin recording, notice the new T account below the Capital account, Drawing. Recall that the Capital account is increased when amounts are invested and decreased when amounts are taken out.

Capital

−	+
Debit	Credit
	Amounts invested

Drawing

+	−
Debit	Credit
Amounts withdrawn	

We reserve the minus or debit side of the Capital account for permanent withdrawals, those made when the owner decides to reduce the size of the business permanently or when a net loss forces such a reduction. This concept is best illustrated by showing the Drawing T account under the umbrella of the Capital T account.

	Capital	
−		+
Debit		Credit

Drawing	
+	−
Debit	Credit

RECORDING BUSINESS TRANSACTIONS IN T ACCOUNTS

OBJECTIVE 4

Record directly in T accounts a group of business transactions involving changes in asset, liability, owner's equity, revenue, and expense accounts for a service business.

Our task now is to learn how to record business transactions in the T account form. First, let's review the steps in analyzing a business transaction.

1. **Decide which accounts are involved.**
2. **Classify the accounts involved** (asset, liability, capital, revenue, expense).
3. **Decide if the accounts involved are increased or decreased.**
4. **Decide which accounts are debited and which accounts are credited.**
5. **Check to see if the equation is in balance after the transaction has been recorded.**

For example, let's analyze the first transaction of the Cline's Computer Clinic transactions using this five-step process. To formulate the entry, you must be able to visualize the fundamental accounting equation in the form of T accounts. With that in mind, the first transaction is as follows:

In transaction (a), Cline deposited $82,000 in a bank account in the name of the business. This transaction results in an increase to Cash with a debit and an increase in the Capital account with a credit.

1. **Decide which accounts are involved.** The two accounts involved are Cash and R. P. Cline, Capital.
2. **Classify the accounts involved (asset, liability, capital, revenue, expense).** Cash is an asset and R. P. Cline, Capital, is an owner's equity account.
3. **Decide if the accounts involved are increased or decreased.** Cash is being deposited in the bank account, an increase to Cash. The owner has invested that cash in the business and has increased R. P. Cline, Capital.
4. **Write the transaction as a debit to one account (or accounts) and a credit to another account (or accounts).** Since Cash is an asset and Cash is increased, Cash is debited. We now need an offsetting credit. R. P. Cline, Capital, is an owner's equity account and is increased. R. P. Cline, Capital, is credited. You now have a debit equal to a credit.
5. **Check:** There is at least one account debited and at least one account credited, *and* the total amount(s) debited equal the total amount(s) credited. **You now have a debit equal to a credit, an $82,000 debit to Cash and an $82,000 credit to R. P. Cline, Capital.**

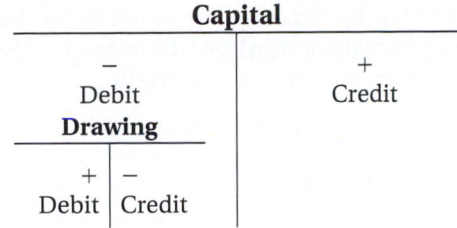

Stores such as this bike shop classify revenue accounts for each service activity—sales, repairs, and rentals. They may also classify expense accounts separately.

The resulting transaction in T account form follows:

	Cash			R. P. Cline, Capital	
	+	−		−	+
	Debit	Credit		Debit	Credit
(a)	82,000				**(a)** 82,000

In transaction (b), Cline's Computer Clinic bought equipment, paying cash, $64,000. This transaction results in an increase to Equipment with a debit and a decrease to Cash with a credit.

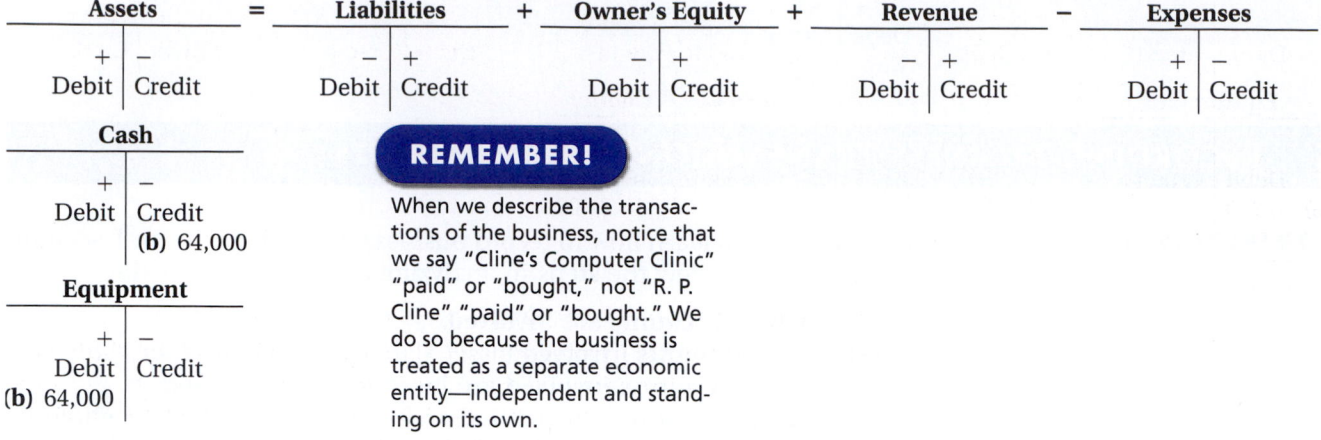

REMEMBER!

When we describe the transactions of the business, notice that we say "Cline's Computer Clinic" "paid" or "bought," not "R. P. Cline" "paid" or "bought." We do so because the business is treated as a separate economic entity—independent and standing on its own.

In transaction (c), Cline's Computer Clinic bought equipment on account from Surgo Products, $10,000. This transaction results in an increase to Equipment with a debit and an increase to Accounts Payable with a credit and is shown in T accounts as follows:

Assets	=	Liabilities	+	Owner's Equity	+	Revenue	−	Expenses
+ | −		− | +		− | +		− | +		+ | −
Debit | Credit		Debit | Credit		Debit | Credit		Debit | Credit		Debit | Credit

Equipment	Accounts Payable
+ | −	− | +
Debit | Credit	Debit | Credit
(c) 10,000	(c) 10,000

In transaction (d), Cline's Computer Clinic paid Surgo Products, a creditor, $6,000. This transaction results in a decrease to Cash with a credit and a decrease to Accounts Payable with a debit.

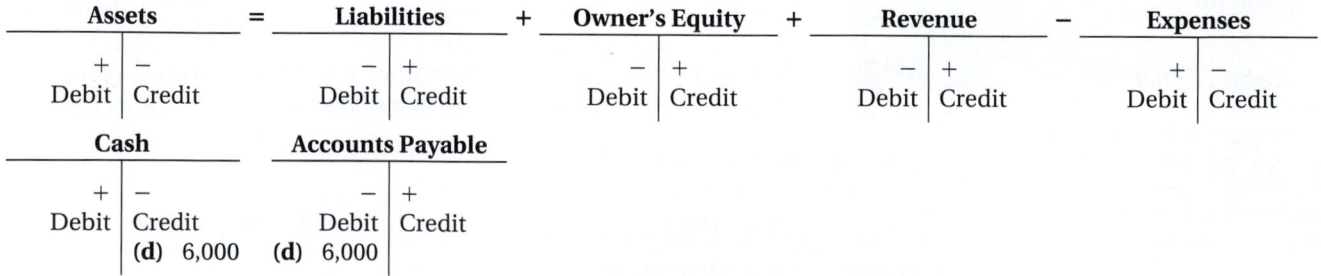

In transaction (e), R. P. Cline invests her personal computer in the business with a fair market value of $6,200.

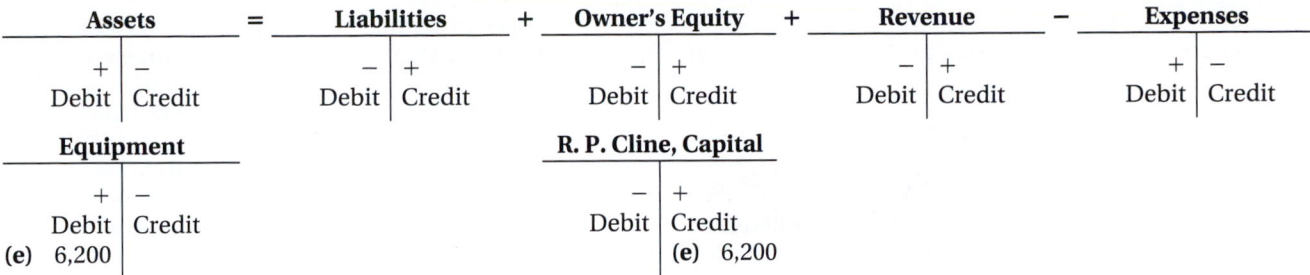

Assets	=	Liabilities	+	Owner's Equity	+	Revenue	−	Expenses
+ | −		− | +		− | +		− | +		+ | −
Debit | Credit		Debit | Credit		Debit | Credit		Debit | Credit		Debit | Credit

Equipment

+	−
Debit	Credit
(e) 6,200	

R. P. Cline, Capital

−	+
Debit	Credit
	(e) 6,200

Here is a restatement of the accounts after recording transactions (a) through (e). To test your understanding of the process, trace through the recording of each transaction and describe what happened in the transaction. Footings or subtotals (remember, always write the footings smaller than the entries and in pencil) are required to compute the balances of the accounts. The balances are written in the accounts on the side with the larger total.

Assets	=	Liabilities	+	Owner's Equity	+	Revenue	−	Expenses
+ | −		− | +		− | +		− | +		+ | −
Debit | Credit		Debit | Credit		Debit | Credit		Debit | Credit		Debit | Credit

Cash

+	−
Debit	Credit
(a) 82,000	(b) 64,000
	(d) 6,000
	70,000
Bal. 12,000	

Accounts Receivable

+	−
Debit	Credit

Prepaid Insurance

+	−
Debit	Credit

Equipment

+	−
Debit	Credit
(b) 64,000	
(c) 10,000	
(e) 6,200	
Bal. 80,200	

Accounts Payable

−	+
Debit	Credit
(d) 6,000	(c) 10,000
	Bal. 4,000

R. P. Cline, Capital

−	+
Debit	Credit
	(a) 82,000
	(e) 6,200
	Bal. 88,200

R. P. Cline, Drawing

+	−
Debit	Credit

Income from Services

−	+
Debit	Credit

Wages Expense

+	−
Debit	Credit

Rent Expense

+	−
Debit	Credit

Supplies Expense

+	−
Debit	Credit

Advertising Expense

+	−
Debit	Credit

Utilities Expense

+	−
Debit	Credit

REMEMBER!

The normal balance of an account classification is on the plus side.

FYI

The T account is not only a learning tool; it will serve you well as a problem-solving device when you need to analyze a transaction prior to recording it—manually or on a computer.

Let's pause to see if the two sides of the equation are equal by listing the balances of the accounts:

Account Name	Accounts with Normal Balances on the Left or Debit Side	Accounts with Normal Balances on the Right or Credit Side
	Assets Drawing Expenses	Liabilities Capital Revenue
Cash	$12,000	
Equipment	80,200	
Accounts Payable		$ 4,000
R. P. Cline, Capital		88,200
	$92,200	$92,200

In transaction (f), Cline's Computer Clinic sold services for cash, $3,520. This transaction results in an increase to Cash with a debit and an increase to Income from Services with a credit.

Assets	=	Liabilities	+	Owner's Equity	+	Revenue	−	Expenses
+ | −		− | +		− | +		− | +		+ | −
Debit | Credit		Debit | Credit		Debit | Credit		Debit | Credit		Debit | Credit

Cash		Income from Services
+ | −		− | +
Debit | Credit		Debit | Credit
(f) 3,520		(f) 3,520

In transaction (g), Cline's Computer Clinic paid rent for the month, $900. This transaction results in an increase to Rent Expense with a debit and a decrease to Cash with a credit.

Assets	=	Liabilities	+	Owner's Equity	+	Revenue	−	Expenses
+ | −		− | +		− | +		− | +		+ | −
Debit | Credit		Debit | Credit		Debit | Credit		Debit | Credit		Debit | Credit

Cash		Rent Expense
+ | −		+ | −
Debit | Credit		Debit | Credit
(g) 900		(g) 900

In transaction (h), Cline's Computer Clinic bought CD-R recordable compact discs and holders, manuals, and invoice forms for $870 on account from Freeman Company. This transaction results in an increase to Supplies Expense with a debit and an increase to Accounts Payable with a credit.

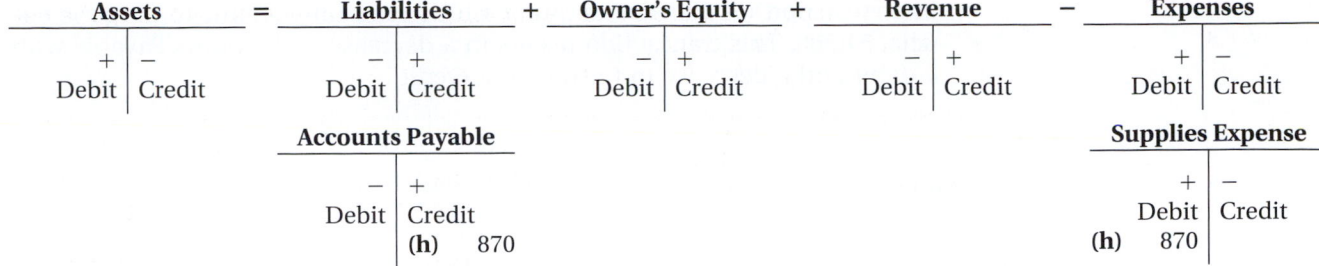

Assets	=	Liabilities	+	Owner's Equity	+	Revenue	−	Expenses
+ −		− +		− +		− +		+ −
Debit Credit		Debit Credit		Debit Credit		Debit Credit		Debit Credit

Accounts Payable

−   +
Debit   Credit
(h)   870

Supplies Expense

+   −
Debit   Credit
(h)   870

In transaction (i), Cline's Computer Clinic bought a one-year liability insurance policy, $480. This transaction results in an increase to Prepaid Insurance with a debit and a decrease to Cash with a credit.

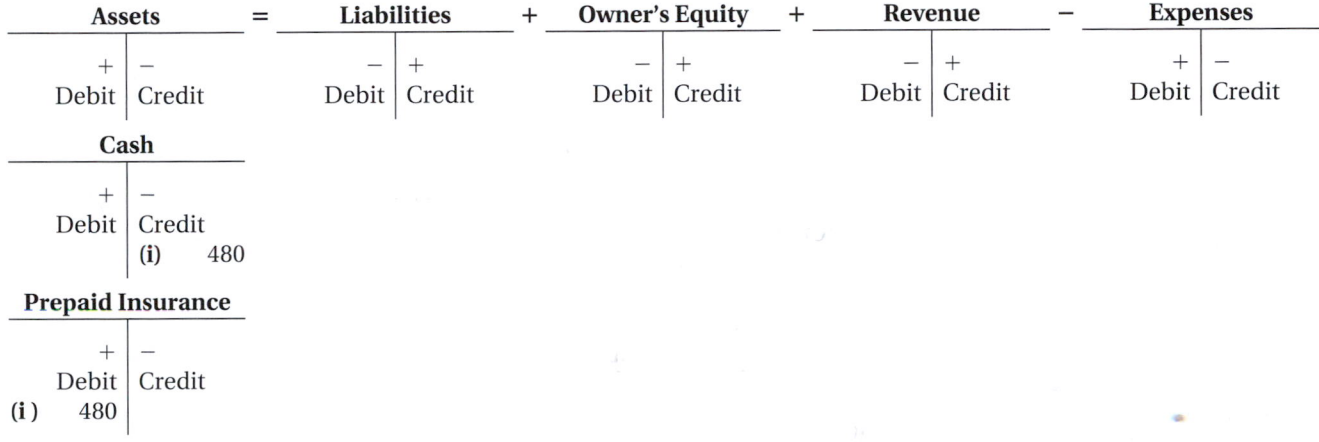

Assets	=	Liabilities	+	Owner's Equity	+	Revenue	−	Expenses
+ −		− +		− +		− +		+ −
Debit Credit		Debit Credit		Debit Credit		Debit Credit		Debit Credit

Cash

+   −
Debit   Credit
(i)   480

Prepaid Insurance

+   −
Debit   Credit
(i)   480

In transaction (j), Cline's Computer Clinic received a bill for newspaper advertising from the *Daily*, $340. This results in an increase to Advertising Expense with a debit and an increase to Accounts Payable with a credit.

Assets	=	Liabilities	+	Owner's Equity	+	Revenue	−	Expenses
+ −		− +		− +		− +		+ −
Debit Credit		Debit Credit		Debit Credit		Debit Credit		Debit Credit

Accounts Payable

−   +
Debit   Credit
(j)   340

Advertising Expense

+   −
Debit   Credit
(j)   340

In transaction (k), Cline's Computer Clinic sold services on account to Computer Makeovers, $1,470. This results in an increase to Accounts Receivable with a debit and an increase to Income from Services with a credit.

Assets	=	Liabilities	+	Owner's Equity	+	Revenue	−	Expenses
+ −		− +		− +		− +		+ −
Debit Credit		Debit Credit		Debit Credit		Debit Credit		Debit Credit

Accounts Receivable

+   −
Debit   Credit
(k)   1,470

Income from Services

−   +
Debit   Credit
(k)   1,470

In transaction (l), Cline's Computer Clinic paid on account to Surgo Products, $1,800. This transaction results in a decrease to Accounts Payable with a debit and a decrease to Cash with a credit.

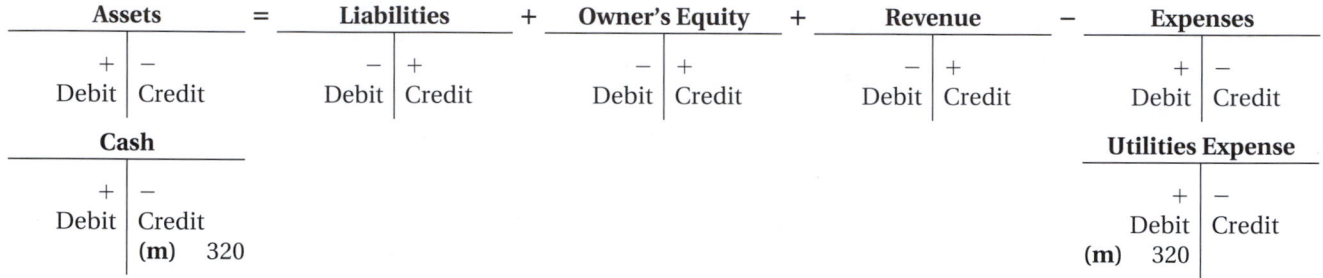

In transaction (m), Cline's Computer Clinic received and paid the electric bill, $320. The result of this transaction is an increase to Utilities Expense with a debit and a decrease to Cash with a credit.

Assets	=	Liabilities	+	Owner's Equity	+	Revenue	−	Expenses
+ | −		− | +		− | +		− | +		+ | −
Debit | Credit		Debit | Credit		Debit | Credit		Debit | Credit		Debit | Credit

Cash		Utilities Expense
+ | −		+ | −
Debit | Credit		Debit | Credit
| (m) 320		(m) 320 |

In transaction (n), Cline's Computer Clinic paid on account to the *Daily*, $340. This transaction results in a decrease to Accounts Payable with a debit and a decrease to Cash with a credit.

Assets	=	Liabilities	+	Owner's Equity	+	Revenue	−	Expenses
+ | −		− | +		− | +		− | +		+ | −
Debit | Credit		Debit | Credit		Debit | Credit		Debit | Credit		Debit | Credit

Cash	Accounts Payable
+ | −	− | +
Debit | Credit	Debit | Credit
| (n) 340	(n) 340 |

In transaction (o), Cline's Computer Clinic paid the wages of the part-time employee, $2,980. This transaction results in an increase to Wages Expense with a debit and a decrease to Cash with a credit.

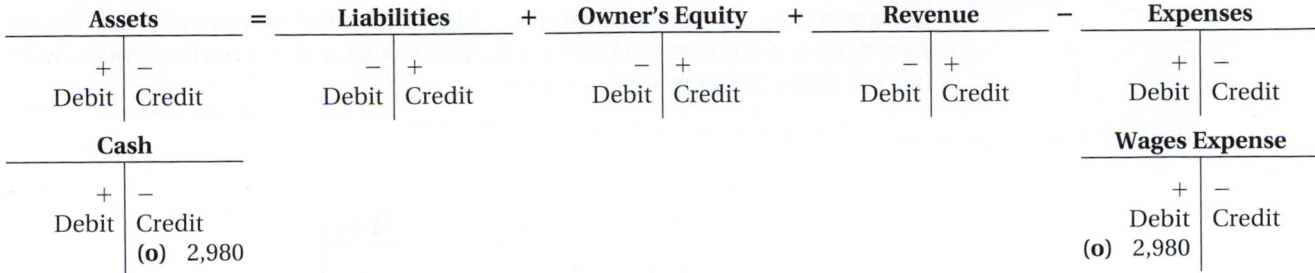

In transaction (p), Cline's Computer Clinic bought additional equipment from Surgo Products, $3,520, paying $620 in cash and placing the balance on account. This transaction results in an increase to Equipment with a debit, an increase to Accounts Payable with a credit, and a decrease to Cash with a credit. This is called a **compound entry**; that is, more than one debit or more than one credit is recorded.

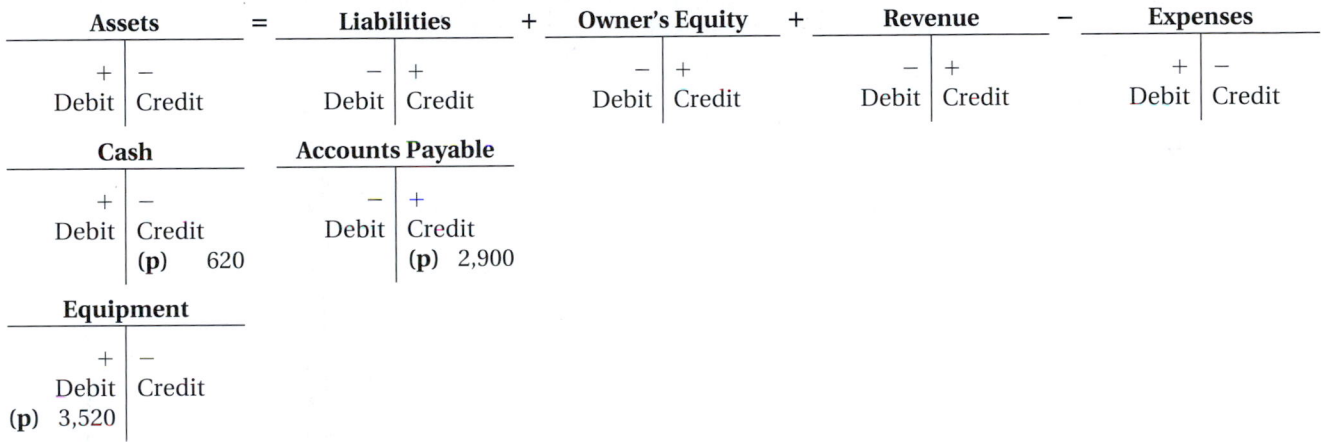

In transaction (q), Cline's Computer Clinic received cash from Computer Makeovers on account, $850. This transaction results in an increase to Cash with a debit and a decrease to Accounts Receivable with a credit.

Assets	=	Liabilities	+	Owner's Equity	+	Revenue	−	Expenses
+ | −		− | +		− | +		− | +		+ | −
Debit | Credit		Debit | Credit		Debit | Credit		Debit | Credit		Debit | Credit

Cash

+	−
Debit	Credit
(q) 850	

Accounts Receivable

+	−
Debit	Credit
	(q) 850

In transaction (r), Cline's Computer Clinic sold services for cash, $6,020. This transaction results in an increase to Cash with a debit and an increase to Income from Services with a credit.

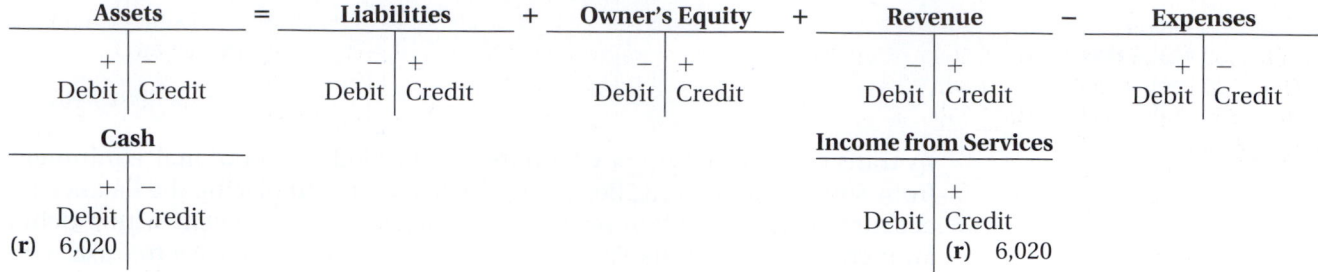

In transaction (s), R. P. Cline withdrew cash for her personal use, $3,000. This transaction increases R. P. Cline, Drawing with a debit and decreases Cash with a credit.

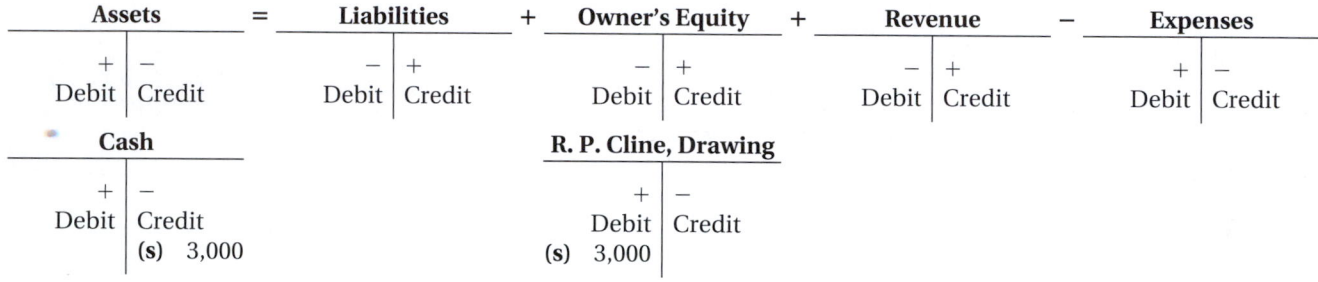

The Drawing account is used to record temporary decreases in Owner's Equity. The owner takes money out of the business for his or her living expenses hoping that the withdrawals will be offset by net income. If, instead, the owner permanently reduces his or her investment in the business, the Capital account is debited.

Summary of Transactions

The following T accounts show the transactions as they are ordinarily recorded. Footings are shown in color. You will notice that the balance of each account is normally on the plus side. Note that, in recording expenses, you place the entries only on the plus, or debit, side. Also, in recording revenue, you place the entries only on the plus, or credit, side.

Assets	=	Liabilities	+	Owner's Equity	+	Revenue	−	Expenses
+ −		− +		− +		− +		+ −
Debit Credit		Debit Credit		Debit Credit		Debit Credit		Debit Credit

Cash

+	−
(a) 82,000	(b) 64,000
(f) 3,520	(d) 6,000
(q) 850	(g) 900
(r) 6,020	(i) 480
92,390	(l) 1,800
	(m) 320
	(n) 340
	(o) 2,980
	(p) 620
	(s) 3,000
	80,440
Bal. 11,950	

Accounts Receivable

+	−
(k) 1,470	(q) 850
Bal. 620	

Prepaid Insurance

+	−
(i) 480	

Equipment

+	−
(b) 64,000	
(c) 10,000	
(e) 6,200	
(p) 3,520	
Bal. 83,720	

Accounts Payable

−	+
(d) 6,000	(c) 10,000
(l) 1,800	(h) 870
(n) 340	(j) 340
8,140	(p) 2,900
	14,110
	Bal. 5,970

R. P. Cline, Capital

−	+
	(a) 82,000
	(e) 6,200
	Bal. 88,200

R. P. Cline, Drawing

+	−
(s) 3,000	

Income from Services

−	+
	(f) 3,520
	(k) 1,470
	(r) 6,020
	Bal. 11,010

Wages Expense

+	−
(o) 2,980	

Rent Expense

+	−
(g) 900	

Supplies Expense

+	−
(h) 870	

Advertising Expense

+	−
(j) 340	

Utilities Expense

+	−
(m) 320	

FYI

A memory tool that helps some students to memorize debits and credits in T accounts is the trial balance equation A + D + E = L + C + R.

THE TRIAL BALANCE

OBJECTIVE 5

Prepare a trial balance.

You can now prepare a trial balance by simply recording the balances of the T accounts in two columns. The **trial balance** is a listing of account balances in two columns—one labeled Debit and one labeled Credit—to prove that the total of all the debit balances equals the total of all the credit balances. A trial balance is not considered a financial statement; it is, as the name implies, a trial run by the accountant to prove that the total of the debit balances equals the total of the credit balances. This is evidence of the equality of the two sides of the fundamental accounting equation. The accountant must prove that the accounts are in balance before preparing the company's financial statements.

Column headings identify information in each column

Cline's Computer Clinic
Trial Balance
June 30, 20—

ACCOUNT NAME		DEBIT		CREDIT	
Cash ——————— *Accounts listed*		11 9 5 0 00			*Dollar signs not used on a trial balance*
Accounts Receivable *in order of the*		6 2 0 00			
Prepaid Insurance *chart of accounts*		4 8 0 00			
Equipment		83 7 2 0 00			
Accounts Payable				5 9 7 0 00	
R. P. Cline, Capital				88 2 0 0 00	
R. P. Cline, Drawing		3 0 0 0 00			
Income from Services				11 0 1 0 00	
Wages Expense		2 9 8 0 00			
Rent Expense		9 0 0 00			
Supplies Expense		8 7 0 00			
Advertising Expense		3 4 0 00			
Utilities Expense *Single underline beneath*		3 2 0 00			
figures to be added		105 1 8 0 00		105 1 8 0 00	

Double underline beneath column totals

FIGURE 1

In preparing a trial balance, shown in Figure 1, record the accounts with balances in the same order as they are listed in the chart of accounts.

- Assets
- Liabilities
- Owner's Equity
- Revenue
- Expenses

The normal balance of each account is on its plus side. Remember that when there is more than one entry in an account, we record the totals in footings and subtract one footing from the other to determine the balance. **Record this balance on the side of the account with the larger footing.** (Here we record the Drawing account balance in the debit column because it has a debit balance. We do not deduct Drawing from the Capital account when we prepare the trial balance.) The following table indicates where each of the account balances would normally be shown in a trial balance.

	Trial Balance	
Account Titles	**Left or Debit Balances**	**Right or Credit Balances**
Assets	Assets	
Liabilities		Liabilities
Capital		Capital
Drawing	Drawing	
Revenue		Revenue
Expenses	Expenses	
Totals	XXXX XX	XXXX XX

MAJOR FINANCIAL STATEMENTS

OBJECTIVE 6a

Prepare an income statement.

Earlier we listed summarizing as one of the five basic tasks of the accounting process. To accomplish this task, accountants use financial statements. A **financial statement** is a report prepared by accountants to summarize the financial affairs of a business for managers and others, both inside and outside the business.

Note that the headings of all financial statements require three lines:

1. Name of the company (or owner, if there is no company name)
2. Title of the financial statement
3. Period of time covered by the financial statement, or its date

Also, note that dollar signs are placed at the head of each column and with each total. Single lines (drawn with a ruler) are used to show that the figures above are being added or subtracted. Lines should be drawn across the entire column. A double line is drawn under the final total in a column.

The financial statements are all interconnected. The income statement must be prepared first, followed by the statement of owner's equity, and then the balance sheet.

The Income Statement

The **income statement** shows total revenue minus total expenses, which yields the net income or net loss. The income statement shows the results of business transactions involving revenue and expense accounts—in other words, how the business has performed—over a period of time, usually a month or a year. When total revenue exceeds total expenses over the period, the result is **net income**, or profit. If the total revenue is less than the total expenses, the result is a **net loss**.

The income statement in Figure 2 shows the results of the first month of operations for Cline's Computer Clinic.

For convenience, the individual expense amounts are recorded in the first amount column. Thus, the total expenses ($5,410) may be subtracted directly from the total revenue ($11,010).

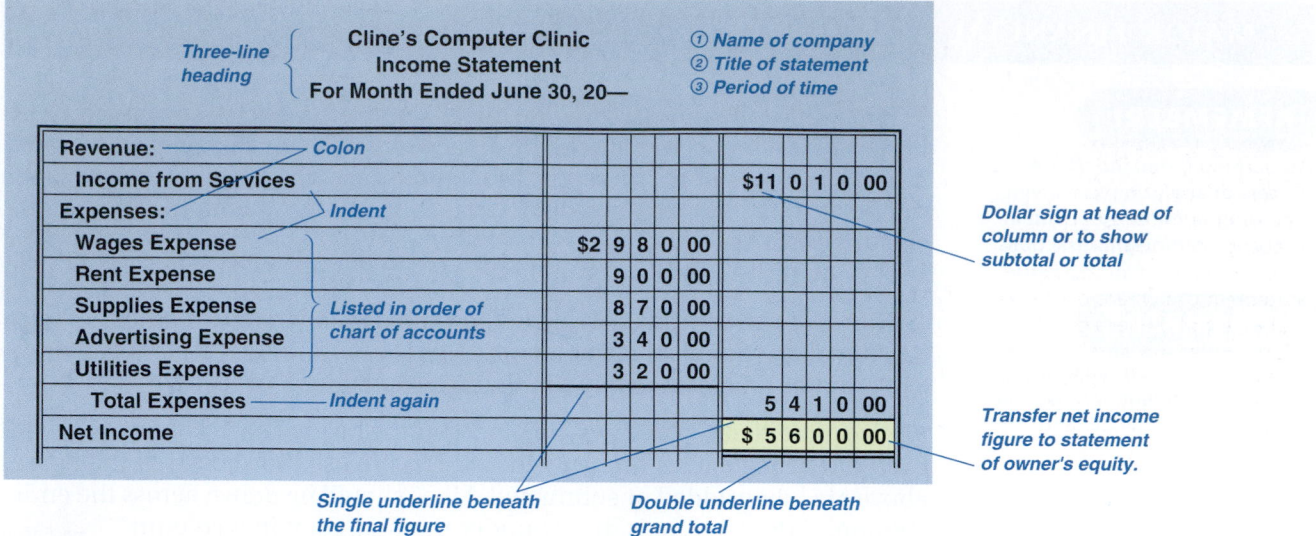

FIGURE 2

FYI

Compare the third line of the income statement heading with the third line of the balance sheet heading shown in Figure 4.

The income statement covers a period of time, whereas the balance sheet has only one date: the end of the financial period. On the income statement, the revenue for June, less the expenses for June, shows the results of operations—a net income of $5,600. To the accountant, the term *net income* means "clear" income, or profit after all expenses have been deducted. Expenses are usually listed in the same order as in the chart of accounts. Revenue and expense amounts are taken directly from the trial balance. If total expenses were greater than the revenue, then a net loss would be recorded.

The Statement of Owner's Equity

OBJECTIVE 6b

Prepare a statement of owner's equity.

We said that revenue and expenses are connected with owner's equity through the financial statements. Now let's demonstrate this by a statement of owner's equity, shown in Figure 3, which the accountant prepares after he or she has determined the net income or net loss on the income statement.

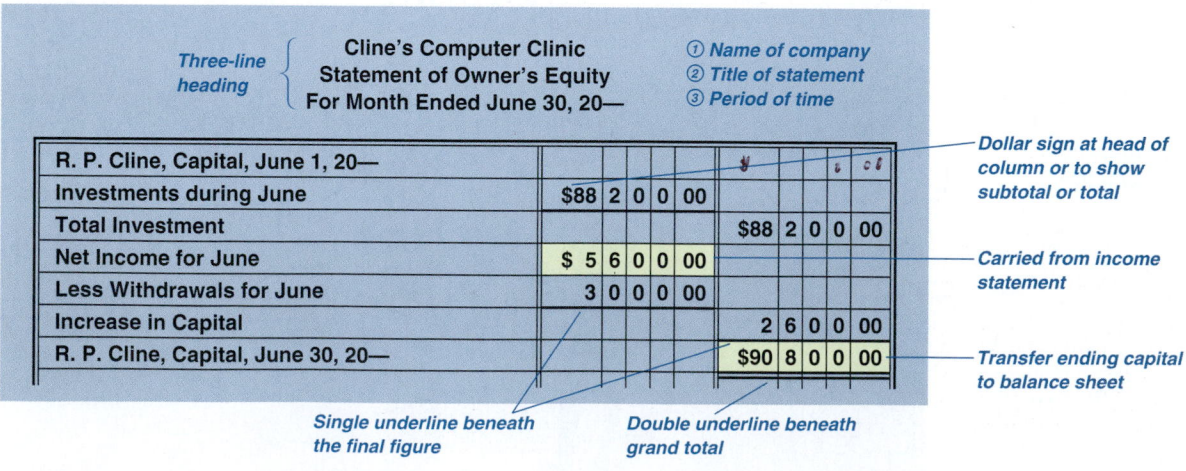

FIGURE 3

The **statement of owner's equity** shows how—and why—the owner's equity, or Capital account, has changed over a stated period of time (in this case, the month of June). Notice the third line in the heading of Figure 3. It shows that the statement of owner's equity covers the same period of time as the income statement.

Now look at the body of the statement. The first line shows the zero balance in the Capital account at the beginning of the month. An investment of $88,200 was made by R. P. Cline: total investment $88,200. Two items have affected owner's equity during the month: A net income of $5,600 was earned, and the owner withdrew $3,000. To perform the calculations smoothly, move to the left-hand column and list these two items, subtracting withdrawals from net income ($5,600 − $3,000 = $2,600). The difference ($2,600) represents an increase in capital. This difference is placed in the right-hand column to be added directly to the total capital. The final figure is the ending amount in the owner's Capital account.

REMEMBER!

The income statement is prepared first, so that the net income can be recorded in the statement of owner's equity. The statement of owner's equity is prepared second, so that the ending amount of capital can be recorded in the balance sheet, which is prepared last.

OBJECTIVE 6c

Prepare a balance sheet.

The Balance Sheet

After preparing the statement of owner's equity, we prepare a balance sheet. The **balance sheet** shows the **financial position**, or the condition of a business's assets offset by claims against them as of one particular date. It summarizes the balances of the asset, liability, and owner's equity accounts on a given date (usually the end of a month or year). The balance sheet is, thus, like a snapshot—a picture of the financial condition of the business at that particular date.

The ending capital balance in the balance sheet is taken from the statement of owner's equity. Note that the accounts appear in the same order as in the chart of accounts.

In the **report form** of the balance sheet, the elements in the accounting equation are presented one on top of the other. A balance sheet prepared on June 30 for Cline's Computer Clinic in report form would look like Figure 4.

Cline's Computer Clinic
Balance Sheet
June 30, 20—

Assets														
Cash	$11	9	5	0	00									
Accounts Receivable		6	2	0	00									
Prepaid Insurance		4	8	0	00									
Equipment	83	7	2	0	00									
Total Assets						$96	7	7	0	00					
Liabilities														
Accounts Payable						$ 5	9	7	0	00					
Owner's Equity														
R. P. Cline, Capital						90	8	0	0	00					Carried from statement of owner's equity
Total Liabilities and Owner's Equity						$96	7	7	0	00					

FIGURE 4

ERRORS EXPOSED BY THE TRIAL BALANCE

If the debit and credit columns in a trial balance are not equal, then it is evident that we have made an error. Possible mistakes include the following:

- Making errors in arithmetic, such as errors in adding the trial balance columns or in finding the balances of the accounts.
- Recording only half an entry, such as a debit without a corresponding credit, or vice versa.
- Recording both halves of the entry on the same side, such as two debits rather than a debit and a credit.
- Recording one or more amounts incorrectly.

Procedure for Locating Errors

Suppose that you are in a business situation where you have recorded transactions for a month in the account books, and the accounts do not balance. To save yourself time, you need to have a definite procedure for tracking down the errors. The best method is to do everything in reverse, as follows:

- Look at the pattern of balances to see if a normal balance was placed in the wrong column on the trial balance.
- Re-add the trial balance columns.
- Check the transferring of the figures from the accounts to the trial balance.
- Verify the footings and balances of the accounts.

As an added precaution, form the habit of verifying all addition and subtraction as you go along. You can thus correct many mistakes *before* the time comes to prepare a trial balance.

FYI

Even if debits equal credits, this does not necessarily mean that there were no errors in the recording of the transactions. For example, a transaction may have been forgotten, it may have been included twice, or it may have been written for an incorrect amount.

Although using a computer greatly reduces the occurrence of addition and subtraction errors, it does not prevent the occurrence of other kinds of errors, such as recording transactions incorrectly.

When the trial balance totals do not balance, the difference might indicate that you forgot to record half of an entry in the accounts. For example, if the difference in the trial balance totals is $20, you may have recorded $20 on the debit side of one account without recording $20 on the credit side of another account.

Another possibility is to divide the difference by 2; this may provide a clue that you accidentally recorded half an entry twice. For example, if the difference in the trial balance is $600, you may have recorded $300 on the debit side of one account and an additional $300 on the debit side of another account. Look for a transaction that involved $300 and then see if you have recorded both a debit and a credit. By knowing which transactions to check, you can save a lot of time.

Transpositions and Slides

OBJECTIVE 7

Recognize the effect of transpositions and slides on account balances.

If the difference is evenly divisible by 9, the discrepancy may be either a transposition or a slide. A **transposition** means that the digits have been transposed, or switched around, when the numbers were copied from one place to another. For example, one transposition of digits in 916 can be written as 619:

Correct Number	Number Copied	Difference	Difference Divided by 9
916	619	297	297 ÷ 9 = 33

A **slide** is an error in placing the decimal point; in other words, a slide in the decimal point. For example, $27,000 could be inadvertently written as $2,700:

Correct Number	Number Copied	Difference	Difference Divided by 9
27,000	2,700	24,300	24,300 ÷ 9 = 2,700
64,000	6,400	57,600	57,600 ÷ 9 = 6,400

Or the error may be a combination of a transposition and a slide, as when $450 is written as $54:

Correct Number	Number Copied	Difference	Difference Divided by 9
450	54	396	396 ÷ 9 = 44

Again, the difference is evenly divisible by 9 (with no remainder).

CHAPTER REVIEW

Online Study Center
ACE the test!

Review of Performance Objectives

1. Determine balances of T accounts having entries recorded on both sides of the accounts.

   Add the amounts listed on each side of the T account. The totals are called footings. To get the account balance, subtract the total of the smaller side from the total of the larger side. Record the account balance on the larger side.

2. Present the fundamental accounting equation with the T account form, and label the plus and minus sides.

Assets			=	Liabilities			+	Owner's Equity			+	Revenue			−	Expenses		
+	−			−	+			−	+			−	+			+	−	
Left	Right			Left	Right			Left	Right			Left	Right			Left	Right	

3. Present the fundamental accounting equation with the T account form, and label the debit and credit sides.

Assets			=	Liabilities			+	Owner's Equity			+	Revenue			−	Expenses		
+	−			−	+			−	+			−	+			+	−	
Left	Right			Left	Right			Left	Right			Left	Right			Left	Right	
Debit	Credit			Debit	Credit			Debit	Credit			Debit	Credit			Debit	Credit	

4. Record directly in T accounts a group of business transactions involving changes in asset, liability, owner's equity, revenue, and expense accounts for a service business.

The transactions are recorded by first recognizing and classifying the accounts involved. Next, decide whether the accounts involved are increased or decreased, and record the amounts as additions or subtractions in the accounts. The equation must always remain in balance.

5. Prepare a trial balance.

A trial balance is a list of all account balances in two columns—one labeled Debit and one labeled Credit. The trial balance shows that both sides of the accounting equation are equal. The heading consists of the company name, Trial Balance, and the date.

6. Prepare (a) an income statement, (b) a statement of owner's equity, and (c) a balance sheet.

(a) An income statement shows the results of operations of a business for a period of time. It includes revenue and expense accounts and reports either a net income or a net loss. (b) A statement of owner's equity shows the activity in the owner's equity, or Capital account, for a period of time. It includes the balance in the Capital account at the beginning of the period plus any additional investments and any increase or decrease in capital as the result of a net income (or a net loss) minus any withdrawals. (c) A balance sheet shows the financial condition of a business at a particular date in time. It summarizes the balances of the asset, liability, and owner's equity accounts on a given date.

7. Recognize the effect of transpositions and slides on account balances.

An error in a trial balance may be a transposition or a slide. The clue is whether the difference in account balances or trial balance totals is evenly divisible by 9. With a transposition, some digits have been switched around. With a slide, the decimal point has been recorded in the wrong place.

Glossary

Balance sheet A financial statement showing the financial position of an organization on a given date, such as June 30 or December 31. The balance sheet lists the balances in the asset, liability, and owner's equity accounts. (51)

Compound entry A transaction that requires more than one debit or more than one credit to be recorded. (45)

Credit The right side of a T account; to credit is to record an amount on the right side of a T account. Credits represent increases in liability, capital, or revenue accounts and decreases in asset, drawing, or expense accounts. (38)

Debit The left side of a T account; to debit is to record an amount on the left side of a T account. Debits represent increases in asset, drawing, or expense accounts and decreases in liability, capital, or revenue accounts. (38)

Financial position The resources or assets owned by an organization at a point in time, offset by the claims against those resources and owner's equity; shown on a balance sheet. (51)

Financial statement A report prepared by accountants that summarizes the financial affairs of a business. (49)

Footings The totals of each side of a T account, recorded in small, pencil-written figures. (36)

Income statement A financial statement showing the results of business transactions involving revenue and expense accounts over a period of time. (49)

Net income The result when total revenue exceeds total expenses over a period of time. (49)

Net loss The result when total expenses exceed total revenue over a period of time. (49)

Normal balance The plus side of a T account. (36)

Report form The form of the balance sheet in which assets are placed at the top and liabilities and owner's equity are placed below. (51)

Slide An error in placing the decimal point in a number. (53)

Statement of owner's equity A financial statement showing the activity in the owner's equity, or Capital account, over the financial period. (51)

T account form A form of account shaped like the letter T in which increases and decreases in the account may be recorded. One side of the T is for entries on the debit or left side. The other side of the T is for entries on the credit or right side. (36)

Transposition An error that involves interchanging, or switching around, digits during the recording of a number. (53)

Trial balance A list of all account balances to prove that the total of all the debit balances equals the total of all the credit balances. (47)

QUESTIONS, EXERCISES, AND CASES

Discussion Questions

1. Explain how a trial balance and a balance sheet differ.
2. Explain why the term *debit* doesn't always mean "increase" and why the term *credit* doesn't always mean "decrease."
3. What are footings in accounting?
4. How are the three financial statements shown in this chapter connected?
5. What is a compound entry?
6. List two reasons why the debits and credits in the trial balance might not balance.
7. Give an example of a slide and an example of a transposition. Explain how you might decide whether an error is a slide or a transposition.
8. What do we mean when we say that revenue and expense accounts are under the "umbrella" of owner's equity?

Exercises

P.O. 4

Describe transactions.

Exercise 2-1 During the first month of operation, Garza's Craft Supply recorded the following transactions. Describe what has happened in each of the transactions (a) through (k).

Cash			
(a) 3,200	**(b)**	435	
(k) 1,025	**(c)**	98	
	(e)	75	
	(g)	900	
	(i)	92	
	(j)	325	

Accounts Receivable	
(h) 615	

Equipment	
(f) 3,720	
(g) 1,835	

Accounts Payable	
(d) 280	
(g) 935	

C. S. Garza, Capital	
	(a) 3,200
	(f) 3,720

C. S. Garza, Drawing	
(j) 325	

Income from Services	
	(h) 615
	(k) 1,025

Rent Expense	
(b) 435	

Utilities Expense	
(i) 92	

Advertising Expense	
(c) 98	

Supplies Expense	
(d) 280	

Miscellaneous Expense	
(e) 75	

P.O. 2,3

Draw T accounts and record the plus and minus signs and debit and credit.

Exercise 2-2 On a sheet of paper, set up the fundamental accounting equation with T accounts under each of the five account classifications, noting plus and minus signs and debit and credit on the appropriate sides of each account. Under each of the five classifications, set up T accounts, again with the correct plus and minus signs and debit and credit, for each of the following accounts of Bevin Engine Repair.

Cash	Income from Services
Accounts Receivable	Rent Expense
Equipment	Wages Expense
Accounts Payable	Utilities Expense
A. Bevin, Capital	Supplies Expense
A. Bevin, Drawing	Miscellaneous Expense

P.O. 2,3,4

Record transactions in T accounts.

Exercise 2-3 R. Casey operates Casey's Cards. The company has the following chart of accounts:

Assets

Cash
Accounts Receivable
Prepaid Insurance
Display Equipment
Van
Office Equipment

Liabilities

Accounts Payable

Owner's Equity

R. Casey, Capital
R. Casey, Drawing

Revenue

Income from Services

Expenses

Wages Expense
Gas Expense
Utilities Expense
Supplies Expense
Advertising Expense

Using the chart of accounts above, record the following transactions in pairs of T accounts. Give the T account to be debited first and the account to be credited to the right. Show debit and credit and plus and minus signs. (Example: Received and paid the bill for the month's rent, $480.)

Rent Expense		Cash	
+	−	+	−
Dr.	Cr.	Dr.	Cr.
480			480

a. Received and paid the electric bill, $85.
b. Bought supplies on account, $245.
c. Paid for insurance for one year, $400.
d. Made a payment on account to a creditor, $555.
e. Received and paid the telephone bill, $96.
f. Sold services on account, $975.
g. Received and paid the gasoline bill for the van, $108.
h. Received cash on account from customers, $1,138.
i. Casey withdrew cash for personal use, $500.

P.O. 4

Classify accounts.

Exercise 2-4 List the classification of each of the following accounts as A (asset), L (liability), OE (owner's equity), R (revenue), or E (expense). Write Debit or Credit to indicate the increase side, the decrease side, and the normal balance side.

Account	Classification	Increase Side	Decrease Side	Normal Balance Side
0. Cash	A	Debit	Credit	Debit
1. Wages Expense				
2. Equipment				
3. J. Roth, Capital				
4. Service Revenue				
5. J. Roth, Drawing				
6. Accounts Receivable				
7. Rent Expense				
8. Fees Earned				
9. Accounts Payable				

P.O. 5

Prepare a corrected trial balance.

Exercise 2-5 At Your Service, owned by L. Mays, hired a new bookkeeper who is not entirely familiar with the process of preparing a trial balance. All the accounts have normal balances. Find the errors, and prepare a corrected trial balance for December 31 of this year.

At Your Service
Trial Balance
December 31, 20—

ACCOUNT NAME	DEBIT	CREDIT
Accounts Receivable		9 5 0 0 00
Cash	3 3 0 0 00	
Accounts Payable		8 6 0 0 00
Equipment	26 0 0 0 00	
L. Mays, Capital		26 6 0 0 00
L. Mays, Drawing		1 8 0 0 00
Prepaid Insurance		1 4 0 0 00
Income from Services		33 0 0 0 00
Rent Expense		3 6 0 0 00
Supplies Expense	1 7 0 0 00	
Utilities Expense	3 5 0 0 00	
Wages Expense	17 4 0 0 00	
	51 9 0 0 00	84 5 0 0 00

P.O. 5,6

Prepare a trial balance and financial statements.

Exercise 2-6 During the first month of operations, Hahn Modeling Agency recorded transactions in T account form. Prepare a trial balance dated March 31 of this year. Prepare an income statement, statement of owner's equity, and balance sheet.

Cash					Accounts Payable			Salary Expense	
Bal.	8,100	(b)	350			(a)	2,800	(g)	3,400
(c)	8,500	(d)	1,600			(j)	82		
(i)	7,580	(f)	175					Rent Expense	
		(g)	3,400		R. Hahn, Capital			(d)	1,600
		(h)	2,200			Bal.	8,100		

Accounts Receivable			R. Hahn, Drawing			Utilities Expense	
(e)	2,600		(h)	2,200		(f)	175

Office Furniture   **Modeling Fees**   **Supplies Expense**

(b)	350				(j)	82

Office Equipment

		Modeling Fees	
(a)	2,800	(c)	8,500
		(e)	2,600
		(i)	7,580

P.O. 7

Determine the effects of errors.

Exercise 2-7 The following errors were made in journalizing transactions. In each case, calculate the amount of the error and indicate whether the debit or the credit column of the trial balance will be understated or overstated.

	Amount of Difference	Debit or Credit Column of Trial Balance Understated or Overstated
0. Example: A $149 debit to Accounts Receivable was not recorded.	$149	Debit column understated
a. A $42 debit to Supplies Expense was recorded as $420.		
b. A $155 debit to Accounts Payable was recorded twice.		
c. A $179 debit to Prepaid Insurance was not recorded.		
d. A $65 credit to Cash was not recorded.		
e. A $190 debit to Equipment was recorded twice.		
f. A $57 debit to Utilities Expense was recorded as $75.		

P.O. 7

Determine the effects of errors.

Exercise 2-8 Which of the following errors would cause a trial balance to have unequal totals? As a result of the errors, which accounts are overstated (by how much) or understated (by how much)?

a. A purchase of office equipment for $480 was recorded as a debit to Office Equipment for $48 and a credit to Cash for $48.

b. A payment of $260 to a creditor was debited to Accounts Receivable and credited to Cash for $260 each.

c. A purchase of supplies for $145 was recorded as a debit to Equipment for $145 and a credit to Cash for $145.

d. A payment of $86 to a creditor was recorded as a debit to Accounts Payable for $86 and a credit to Cash for $68.

internet
LINKS TO ACCOUNTING

Let's review what you've learned in this chapter and apply it to Citigroup, Inc. as you look at the SEC report. Recall the steps in analyzing a business transaction in Performance Objective 4. Citigroup's sale of its insurance companies affected asset accounts, which included an $8.444 billion credit (decrease) to Ownership Interest in the insurance companies, a $10.830 billion debit (increase) to Cash, and a $1 billion debit (increase) to Investments (the other assets received were shares of MetLife stock). Notice that those debits and credits are not equal ($10.830 + $1 does not equal $8.444). The difference is a $3.386 billion gain on the sale. That gain is similar to an increase (credit) to revenue. Now the total amount of debits and the total amount of credits in this transaction are equal. Recall the fundamental accounting equation: Assets = Liabilities + Capital + Revenue − Expenses. The accounting equation has remained in balance after the transaction above. Because total debits and total credits are equal, the equation remained in balance.

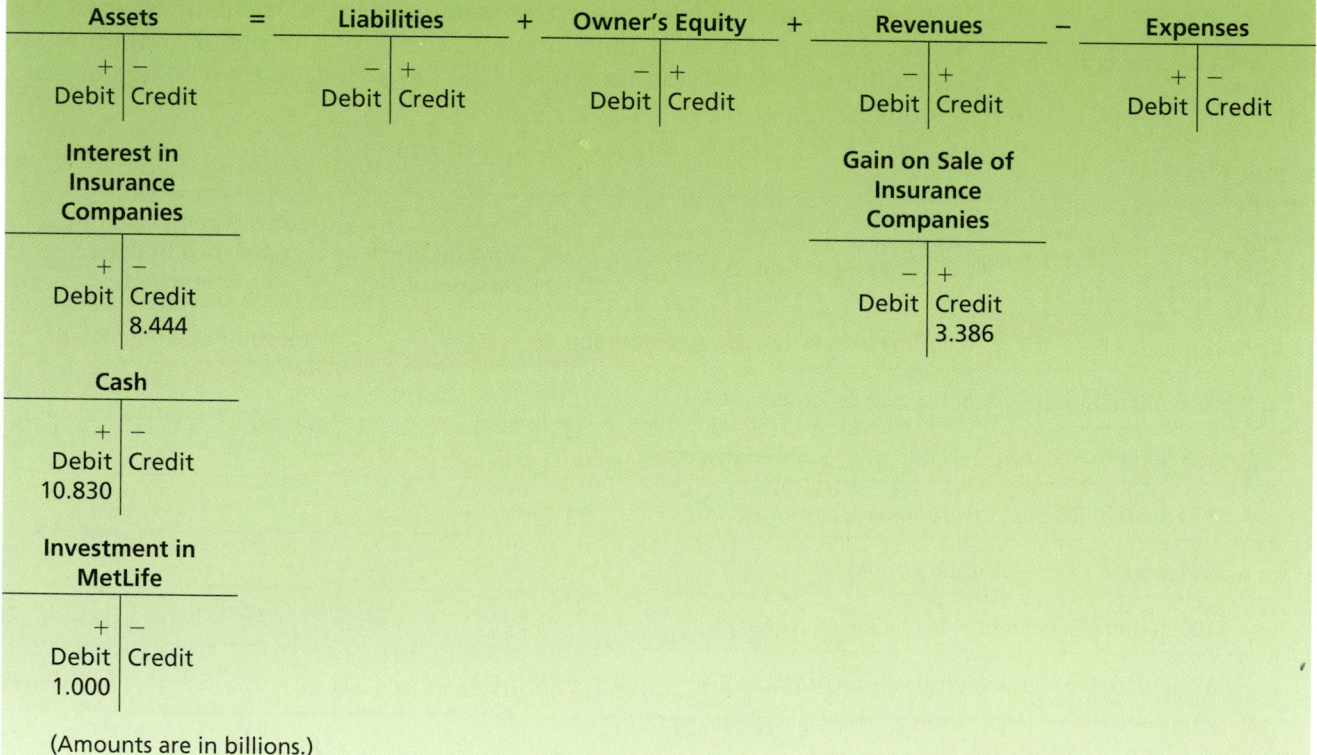

(Amounts are in billions.)

1. Is a trial balance included in the SEC 10-K report? Why or why not?
2. What was Citigroup, Inc.'s Cash and Due From Banks balance for the years ended December 31, 2004, and December 31, 2005? Place these amounts as the beginning and ending balances in a T account for Cash, and then record the sale of the insurance companies in this account. If only one other cash transaction took place during the year, what was the amount, and was it a debit or a credit to Cash?

CONSIDER AND COMMUNICATE

A fellow accounting student has difficulty understanding how the fundamental accounting equation stays in balance when a compound entry with one debit and two credits is recorded. Consider, for example, that a business bought equipment for $7,000, paid $3,000 in cash, and placed the remainder on account.

This means that there are two credits and one debit—one debit and one credit on the left side of the equation and the other credit on the right side of the equation. How does the equation stay in balance?

WHAT'S WRONG WITH THIS PICTURE?

An accounting tutor has drawn the following T accounts for two of her students who are having trouble understanding where the plus and minus signs are placed as well as where the debit and credit go. What would you do to assist these students and their tutor?

Assets	=	Liabilities	+	Owner's Equity	+	Expenses	−	Revenue
+ | −		− | +		− | +		− | +		+ | −
Debit | Credit		Credit | Debit		Credit | Debit		Credit | Debit		Credit | Debit

A QUESTION OF ETHICS

A new bookkeeper can't find the errors that are causing the month-end trial balance for her company to be out of balance. The bookkeeper is too shy to ask for help at the office, so she takes the financial records home and asks her uncle, a retired bookkeeper, to help her locate the errors. Discuss the ethics of the situation in which she has placed herself.

PROBLEM SET A

For additional help, see the demonstration problem at the beginning of each chapter in your Working Papers.

P.O. 1,2,3,4

Problem 2-1A During February of this year, R. Billand established Billand Shoe Repair. The following asset, liability, and owner's equity accounts are included in the chart of accounts:

Cash   Accounts Payable
Shop Equipment   R. Billand, Capital
Store Equipment   Supplies Expense
Office Equipment

The following transactions occurred during the month of February:

a. Billand deposited $20,000 cash in a bank account in the name of the business.
b. Bought shop equipment for cash, $1,735, Ck. No. 1000.

c. Bought supplies on account from Melland Company, $225.

d. Bought store shelving on account from Isem Hardware, $650.

e. Bought office equipment from Shreeve's Office Supply, $325, paying $125 in cash and placing the balance on account, Ck. No. 1001.

f. Paid on account to Isem Hardware, a creditor, $250, Ck. No. 1002.

g. Billand invested his personal leather working tools with a fair market value of $700 in the business.

Check Figure

Cash balance, $17,890

Instructions

1. Write the account classifications (Assets, Liabilities, Owner's Equity, Revenue, Expense) in the fundamental accounting equation, as well as the plus and minus signs and Debit and Credit.

2. Write the account names on the T accounts under the classifications, place the plus and minus signs for each T account, and label the debit and credit sides of the T accounts.

3. Record the amounts in the proper positions in the T accounts. Write the letter next to each entry to identify the transaction.

4. Foot and balance accounts.

P.O. 1,2,3,4,5

Problem 2-2A J. Cory established Cory Photo Service during June of this year. The accountant prepared the following chart of accounts:

Assets	**Revenue**
Cash	Income from Services
Computer Software	
Office Equipment	**Expenses**
Neon Sign	
	Advertising Expense
Liabilities	Supplies Expense
	Rent Expense
Accounts Payable	Utilities Expense
	Wages Expense
Owner's Equity	Miscellaneous Expense
J. Cory, Capital	
J. Cory, Drawing	

The following transactions occurred during the month of June:

a. Cory deposited $20,000 cash in a bank account in the name of the business.

b. Bought office equipment for cash, $850, Ck. No. 1001.

c. Bought computer software from Morrison Computer Center, $640, paying $340 in cash and placing the balance on account, Ck. No. 1002.

d. Paid current month's rent, $850, Ck. No. 1003 (Rent Expense).

e. Sold services for cash, $1,476 (Income from Services).

f. Bought a neon sign from The Sign Company, $1,435, paying $435 in cash and placing the balance on account, Ck. No. 1004.

g. Received bill from *The Daily* for advertising, $745 (Advertising Expense).

h. Bought supplies on account from Central Supply, $660.

i. Received and paid the electric bill, $320, Ck. No. 1005.

j. Paid on account to *The Daily*, a creditor, $745, Ck. No. 1006.

k. Sold services for cash, $3,384.

l. Paid wages to an employee, $830, Ck. No. 1007.

m. Cory invested his personal computer (Office Equipment) with a fair market value of $1,100 in the business.

n. Cory withdrew cash for personal use, $900, Ck. No. 1008.
o. Received and paid the bill for city business license, $55, Ck. No. 1009 (Miscellaneous Expense).

Check Figure

Trial balance total, $27,920

Instructions

1. Record the owner's name in the Capital and Drawing T accounts.
2. Correctly place the plus and minus signs for each T account, and label the debit and credit sides of the accounts.
3. Record the transactions in the T accounts. Write the letter of each entry to identify the transaction.
4. Foot the T accounts and show the balances.
5. Prepare a trial balance, with a three-line heading, dated June 30, 20—.

P.O. 1,2,3,4,5,6

Problem 2-3A Dr. D. Juarez, a physical therapist, opened Juarez Physical Therapy Clinic. His accountant provided the following chart of accounts:

Assets

Cash
Accounts Receivable
Office Equipment
Office Furniture

Liabilities

Accounts Payable

Owner's Equity

D. Juarez, Capital
D. Juarez, Drawing

Revenue

Professional Fees

Expenses

Rent Expense
Salary Expense
Utilities Expense
Miscellaneous Expense

The following transactions occurred during July of this year:

a. Juarez deposited $20,000 in a bank account in the name of the business.
b. Bought filing cabinets on account from Miller Office Supply (Office Equipment), $480.
c. Paid cash for chairs and carpets (Office Furniture) for the waiting room, $955, Ck. No. 1000.
d. Bought a photocopier from Rory's Office Equipment, $560, paying $200 in cash and placing the balance on account, Ck. No. 1001.
e. Received and paid the telephone bill, which included installation charges, $195, Ck. No. 1002.
f. Sold professional services on account, $2,245.
g. Received and paid the bill for the state physical therapy convention, $440, Ck. No. 1003 (Miscellaneous Expense).
h. Received and paid the electric bill, $205, Ck. No. 1004.
i. Received cash on account from credit customers, $930.
j. Paid on account to Miller Office Supply, a creditor, $220, Ck. No. 1005.
k. Paid the office rent for the current month, $845, Ck. No. 1006.
l. Sold consulting services for cash, $1,950.
m. Paid the salary of the receptionist, $850, Ck. No. 1007.
n. Juarez withdrew cash for personal use, $1,500, Ck. No. 1008.

Check Figure

Net Income, $1,660

Instructions

1. Record the owner's name in the Capital and Drawing T accounts.
2. Correctly place the plus and minus signs for each T account, and label the debit and credit sides of the accounts.

3. Record the transactions in the T accounts. Write the letter of each entry to identify the transaction.
4. Foot the T accounts and show the balances.
5. Prepare a trial balance as of July 31, 20—.
6. Prepare an income statement for July 31, 20—.
7. Prepare a statement of owner's equity for July 31, 20—.
8. Prepare a balance sheet as of July 31, 20—.

P.O. 1,2,4,5,6

Problem 2-4A On July 1, K. Rossy opened Rossy's Quick Clean. Rossy's accountant listed the following chart of accounts:

Cash
Prepaid Insurance
Equipment
Furniture and Fixtures
Accounts Payable
K. Rossy, Capital
K. Rossy, Drawing
Laundry Revenue
Wages Expense
Supplies Expense
Rent Expense
Utilities Expense
Miscellaneous Expense

During July, the following transactions were completed:

a. Rossy deposited $18,000 in a bank account in the name of the business.
b. Bought tables and chairs for cash, $625, Ck. No. 1200.
c. Paid the rent for the current month, $750, Ck. No. 1201.
d. Bought washers and dryers from Forbes Equipment, $16,500, paying $4,000 in cash and placing the balance on account, Ck. No. 1202.
e. Bought laundry supplies on account from Wicks Distributors, $515.
f. Sold services for cash, $872.
g. Bought insurance for one year, $475, Ck. No. 1203.
h. Paid on account to Forbes Equipment, a creditor, $500, Ck. No. 1204.
i. Received and paid the electric bill, $238, Ck. No. 1205.
j. Paid on account to Wicks Distributors, a creditor, $225, Ck. No. 1206.
k. Sold services to customers for cash for the second half of the month, $1,015.
l. Received and paid the bill for the business license, $65, Ck. No. 1207 (Miscellaneous Expense).
m. Paid wages to an employee, $900, Ck. No. 1208.
n. Rossy withdrew cash for personal use, $700, Ck. No. 1209.

Check Figure

Net Loss, ($581)

Instructions

1. Record the owner's name in the Capital and Drawing T accounts.
2. Correctly place the plus and minus signs for each T account, and label the debit and credit sides of the accounts.
3. Record the transactions in the T accounts. Write the letter of each entry to identify the transaction.
4. Foot the T accounts and show the balances.
5. Prepare a trial balance as of July 31, 20—.
6. Prepare an income statement for July 31, 20—.
7. Prepare a statement of owner's equity for July 31, 20—.
8. Prepare a balance sheet as of July 31, 20—.

PROBLEM SET B

For additional help, see the demonstration problem at the beginning of each chapter in your Working Papers.

P.O. 1,2,3,4

Problem 2-1B During December of this year, G. Eldridge established Gloria's Gym. The following asset, liability, and owner's equity accounts are included in the chart of accounts:

Cash
Exercise Equipment
Office Equipment
Video Equipment
Accounts Payable
G. Eldridge, Capital
Supplies Expense

During December, the following transactions occurred:

a. Eldridge deposited $25,000 in a bank account in the name of the business.
b. Bought exercise equipment for cash, $8,058, Ck. No. 1001.
c. Bought a printer on account from Horizon Company, $105.
d. Bought a computer (Office Equipment) on account from Cyber Center, $690.
e. Bought supplies on account from Office Needs, $175.
f. Eldridge invested her video equipment with a fair market value of $1,500 in the business.
g. Made a payment to Cyber Center, a creditor, $195, Ck. No. 1002.

Check Figure

Balance of Cash, $16,747

Instructions

1. Write the account classifications (Assets, Liabilities, Owner's Equity, Revenue, Expense) in the fundamental accounting equation, as well as the plus and minus signs and Debit and Credit.
2. Write the account names on the T accounts under the classifications, place the plus and minus signs for each T account, and label the debit and credit sides of the T accounts.
3. Record the amounts in the proper positions in the T accounts. Write the letter next to each entry to identify the transaction.
4. Foot and balance accounts.

P.O. 1,2,3,4,5

Problem 2-2B B. Kim established Computing Needs during November of this year. The accountant prepared the following chart of accounts:

Assets

Cash
Computer Software
Office Equipment
Neon Sign

Liabilities

Accounts Payable

Owner's Equity

B. Kim, Capital
B. Kim, Drawing

Revenue

Income from Services

Expenses

Advertising Expense
Supplies Expense
Rent Expense
Utilities Expense
Wages Expense
Miscellaneous Expense

The following transactions occurred during the month:

a. Kim deposited $25,000 in a bank account in the name of the business.
b. Paid the rent for the current month, $800, Ck. No. 2001.
c. Bought office desks and filing cabinets for cash, $785, Ck. No. 2002.
d. Bought a computer and printer (Office Equipment) from Cyber Computer Center for use in the business, $2,500, paying $1,500 in cash and placing the balance on account, Ck. No. 2003.
e. Bought a neon sign on account from Sign Co., $1,200.
f. Kim invested her personal computer software with a fair market value of $800 in the business.
g. Received a bill from *County News* for newspaper advertising, $275.
h. Sold services for cash, $1,045.
i. Received and paid the electric bill, $245, Ck. No. 2004.
j. Paid on account to *County News*, a creditor, $185, Ck. No. 2005.
k. Sold services for cash, $1,355.
l. Paid the wages to the employee, $725, Ck. No. 2006.
m. Received and paid the bill for the city business license, $55, Ck. No. 2007 (Miscellaneous Expense).
n. Kim withdrew cash for personal use, $750, Ck. No. 2008.
o. Bought printer paper and letterhead stationery on account from Office Suppliers, $108.

Check Figure

Trial balance total, $30,598

Instructions

1. Record the owner's name in the Capital and Drawing T accounts.
2. Correctly place the plus and minus signs for each T account, and label the debit and credit sides of the accounts.
3. Record the transactions in T accounts. Write the letter of each entry to identify the transaction.
4. Foot the T accounts and show the balances.
5. Prepare a trial balance, with a three-line heading, dated November 30, 20—.

P.O. 1,2,3,4,5,6

Problem 2-3B R. Morton, a dentist, opened a clinic in the name of Morton Clinic. Her accountant prepared the following chart of accounts:

Assets

Cash
Accounts Receivable
Office Equipment
Office Furniture

Liabilities

Accounts Payable

Owner's Equity

R. Morton, Capital
R. Morton, Drawing

Revenue

Professional Fees

Expenses

Rent Expense
Salary Expense
Utilities Expense
Miscellaneous Expense

The following transactions occurred during June of this year:

a. Morton deposited $28,000 in a bank account in the name of the business.
b. Bought a facsimile/copier/telephone combination from Maxie's Equipment for $495, paying $100 in cash and placing the balance on account, Ck. No. 1001.

c. Bought waiting room chairs and tables (Office Furniture), paying cash, $1,230, Ck. No. 1002.
d. Bought an intercom system on account from Regal Office Supply (Office Equipment), $275.
e. Received and paid the telephone bill, $108, Ck. No. 1003.
f. Sold professional services on account, $1,294.
g. Received and paid the electric bill, $185, Ck. No. 1004.
h. Received and paid the bill for the Regional Dental Convention, $350, Ck. No. 1005 (Miscellaneous Expense).
i. Sold professional services for cash, $1,765.
j. Paid on account to Regal Office Supply, a creditor, $100, Ck. No. 1006.
k. Paid the rent for the current month, $840, Ck. No. 1007.
l. Paid salary of the receptionist, $700, Ck. No. 1008.
m. R. Morton withdrew cash for personal use, $850, Ck. No. 1009.
n. Received $550 on account from patients who were previously billed.

Check Figure

Net Income, $876

Instructions

1. Record the owner's name in the Capital and Drawing T accounts.
2. Correctly place the plus and minus signs for each T account, and label the debit and credit sides of the accounts.
3. Record the transactions in the T accounts. Write the letter of each entry to identify the transaction.
4. Foot the T accounts and show the balances.
5. Prepare a trial balance as of June 30, 20—.
6. Prepare an income statement for June 30, 20—.
7. Prepare a statement of owner's equity for June 30, 20—.
8. Prepare a balance sheet as of June 30, 20—.

P.O. 1,2,4,5,6

Problem 2-4B On May 1, B. Brego opened Self-Service Laundry. His accountant listed the following chart of accounts:

Cash
Prepaid Insurance
Equipment
Furniture and Fixtures
Accounts Payable
B. Brego, Capital
B. Brego, Drawing
Laundry Revenue
Wages Expense
Supplies Expense
Rent Expense
Utilities Expense
Miscellaneous Expense

During May the following transactions were completed:

a. Brego deposited $25,000 in a bank account in the name of the business.
b. Bought chairs and tables (Furniture and Fixtures) paying cash, $670, Ck. No. 1000.
c. Bought laundry supplies on account from Barnes Supply Company, $325.
d. Paid the rent for the current month, $575, Ck. No. 1001.
e. Bought washing machines and dryers from Lahr Equipment Company, $11,500, paying $3,500 in cash and placing the balance on account, Ck. No. 1002.
f. Sold services for cash for the first half of the month, $925.

g. Bought insurance for one year, $560, Ck. No. 1003.

h. Paid on account to Lahr Equipment Company, a creditor, $700, Ck. No. 1004.

i. Received and paid electric bill, $208, Ck. No. 1005.

j. Sold services for cash for the second half of the month, $835.

k. Paid the wages to the employee, $740, Ck. No. 1006.

l. Brego withdrew cash for his personal use, $500, Ck. No. 1007.

m. Paid on account to Barnes Supply Company, a creditor, $275, Ck. No. 1008.

n. Received and paid bill from the county for sidewalk repair assessment, $280, Ck. No. 1009 (Miscellaneous Expense).

Check Figure

Net Loss, ($368)

Instructions

1. Record the owner's name in the Capital and Drawing T accounts.
2. Correctly place the plus and minus signs for each T account, and label the debit and credit sides of the accounts.
3. Record the transactions in the T accounts. Write the letter of each entry to identify the transaction.
4. Foot the T accounts and show the balances.
5. Prepare a trial balance as of May 31, 20—.
6. Prepare an income statement for May 31, 20—.
7. Prepare a statement of owner's equity for May 31, 20—.
8. Prepare a balance sheet as of May 31, 20—.

3

The General Journal and the General Ledger

LINKS TO ACCOUNTING

How do you keep track of the money you earn and spend? It's an important thing to know. If you were keeping the books of Peyton Manning, quarterback for the Indianapolis Colts in 2004, how would you keep track of what he earns? Or, if you were paying his salary, how would you keep track of what you pay him?

You can check out Manning's salary for 2004 at **http://asp.usatoday.com/sports/football/nfl/salaries/default.aspx.** As you read along in this chapter and learn how to record transactions such as receiving income and paying salaries, think about how you would record Manning's salary. You will learn, as well, about how these data are used in the process of creating financial statements by posting from the journal to the proper accounts and then preparing a trial balance.

Most professional athletes are not NFL superstars. How much are you likely to earn if you are a professional athlete in your state, but you aren't an NFL superstar? You can find out by going to **http://www.collegegrad.com/salaries/salaries.shtml.** Check out this website to see how much the average professional athlete in your area earns. Keep in mind, no matter how much you earn, you can be financially successful as long as you know how to track and manage your money.

Performance Objectives

After you have completed this chapter, you will be able to do the following:

1. Record a group of transactions pertaining to a service enterprise in a two-column general journal.

2. Post entries from a two-column general journal to general ledger accounts.

3. Prepare a trial balance from the ledger accounts.

4. Correct entries using the manual ruling method.

5. Correct entries using the manual or computerized correcting entry method.

Recall that *recording* is a step in the definition of accounting. Here we introduce the *journal* as the official record of business transactions. We have recorded business transactions as debits and credits to T accounts because, in the process of formulating debits and credits for business transactions, it's easier to visualize these debits and credits as the plus and minus sides of the T accounts involved. **Formulating the appropriate**

transaction debits and credits is the most important element in the accounting process. It represents the very basic foundation of accounting, and all the structure represented by financial statements and other reports is entirely dependent upon it. After determining the debits and credits, the accountant records the transaction in a journal and a ledger.

The initial steps in the accounting process are

1. Record business transactions in a journal.
2. Post entries to accounts in the ledger.
3. Prepare a trial balance.

In this chapter, we present the general journal and the posting procedure.

THE GENERAL JOURNAL

We have seen that an accountant must keep a written record of each transaction. You could record the transactions directly in T accounts; however, only part of the transaction would be listed in each T account. A **journal** is a book in which business transactions are recorded as they happen. In the journal, both the debits and the credits of the entire transaction are recorded in one place. Actually, the journal is a diary for the business, in which you record in day-by-day order all the events involving financial affairs. A journal is called a *book of original entry*. In other words, a transaction is always recorded first in the journal. The process of recording a business transaction in the journal is called **journalizing**. The information about transactions comes from business papers, such as checks, invoices, receipts, letters, and memos. These **source documents** furnish proof (objective evidence) that a transaction has taken place, and they should be identified in the journal entry whenever possible. The basic form of journal is the **two-column general journal**. The term *two-column* refers to the two columns used for debit and credit amounts.

As an example of journalizing business transactions, let's use the transactions for Cline's Computer Clinic. The pages of the journal are numbered in consecutive order. This is the first page, and so we write a 1 in the space for the page number. Also, we must write the date of each transaction. Let's begin with the first entry.

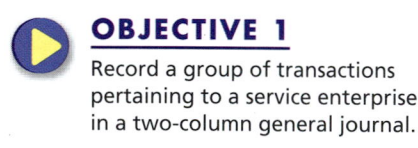

OBJECTIVE 1

Record a group of transactions pertaining to a service enterprise in a two-column general journal.

Transaction (a) June 1: R. P. Cline deposited $82,000 in a bank account in the name of Cline's Computer Clinic. First, we will show the complete journal entry.

GENERAL JOURNAL PAGE ___1___

	DATE		DESCRIPTION	POST. REF.	DEBIT	CREDIT	
1	20–						1
2	June	1	Cash		82 0 0 0 00		2
3			R. P. Cline, Capital			82 0 0 0 00	3
4			Original investment by Cline				4
5			in Cline's Computer Clinic.				5

To explain the entry, we break it down line by line. On the first line at the top of the page, we record the page number where indicated. On line one, we record the year in the left part of the Date column. On the second line, we record the month in the left part of the Date column and the day of the month in the right part of the Date column. We don't have to repeat the year and month until we start a new page, or until the year or month changes. (Because our illustrations are separated, however, the month may be repeated to eliminate confusion.)

	DATE		DESCRIPTION	POST. REF.	DEBIT	CREDIT	
1	20–		⎫				1
2	June	1	⎬ Date				2
3			⎭				3

GENERAL JOURNAL   Page number → PAGE __1__

Decide which accounts should be debited and credited. We do this by first deciding which accounts are involved and whether they are increased or decreased. We then visualize the accounts and their plus and minus sides.

Cash is involved in our example. Cash is an asset because it falls within the definition of "things owned." Cash is increased, and the increase side of Cash is the left or debit side. So we debit Cash $82,000.

R. P. Cline, Capital, is involved. R. P. Cline, Capital, is an owner's equity account because it represents the owner's investment. R. P. Cline, Capital, is increased, and the increase side of Capital is the right or credit side. So we credit R. P. Cline, Capital, $82,000. Let's show these entries by referring to our reliable fundamental accounting equation with the accompanying T accounts:

Assets	=	Liabilities	+	Owner's Equity	+	Revenue	–	Expenses
+ | –		– | +		– | +		– | +		+ | –
Debit | Credit		Debit | Credit		Debit | Credit		Debit | Credit		Debit | Credit

Cash	R. P. Cline, Capital
+ | –	– | +
82,000 |	| 82,000

You perform this process mentally. If the transaction is more complicated, draw the T accounts on scratch paper. Using T accounts is the accountant's way of drawing a picture of the transaction. You must get into the T account habit; it will be a great help to you in the future.

Always record the debit part of the entry first. Enter the account title—in this case, Cash—in the Description column. Record the amount—$82,000—in the Debit amount column.

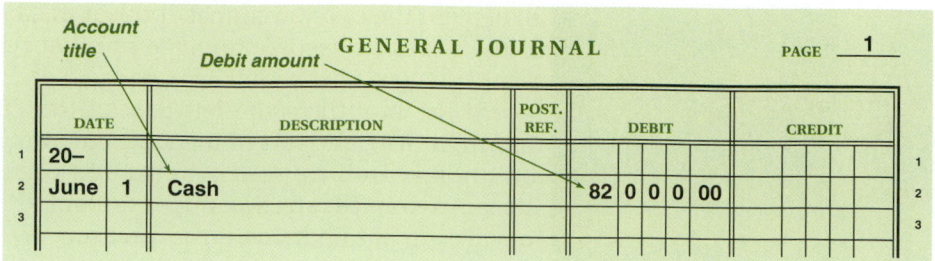

		Account title ↘ Debit amount ↘	GENERAL JOURNAL				PAGE ___1___	
	DATE	DESCRIPTION	POST. REF.	DEBIT		CREDIT	
1	20–							1
2	June 1	Cash		82 0 0 0 00				2
3								3

Customarily, accountants don't abbreviate account titles.

Next, record the credit part of the entry. Enter the account title—in this case, R. P. Cline, Capital—on the line below the debit in the Description column, indented about one-half inch. On the same line, write the amount in the Credit column.

		GENERAL JOURNAL			PAGE ___1___		
	DATE	DESCRIPTION	POST. REF.	DEBIT	CREDIT	
1	20–					1
2	June 1	Cash		82 0 0 0 00		2
3		R. P. Cline, Capital			82 0 0 0 00	3
4						4
5						5
6						6

Indent the account title that is credited

The explanation refers to the source document.

You should now write a brief explanation, in which you should refer to business papers, giving such information as check numbers, receipt numbers, or invoice numbers. You may also list names of charge customers or creditors, or terms of payment. Enter the explanation below the credit entry, indented an additional one-half inch.

		GENERAL JOURNAL			PAGE ___1___		
	DATE	DESCRIPTION	POST. REF.	DEBIT	CREDIT	
1	20–					1
2	June 1	Cash		82 0 0 0 00		2
3		R. P. Cline, Capital			82 0 0 0 00	3
4		Original investment by Cline				4
5		in Cline's Computer Clinic.				5
6						6

Indent again for the explanation

In the transaction, R. P. Cline deposited $82,000 in a bank account in the name of Cline's Computer Clinic.

For an entry in the general journal to be complete, it must contain (1) the date, (2) a debit entry, (3) a credit entry, and (4) an explanation. To anyone thoroughly familiar with the accounts, the explanation may seem quite obvious. Nevertheless, record the explanation as a required, integral part of the entry. To make the journal entries easier to read, leave one blank line between each transaction in your homework.

Transaction (b) June 2: Cline's Computer Clinic bought equipment costing $64,000, paying cash. Decide which accounts are involved. Next, determine which of the five possible classifications each part of the transaction applies to. Visualize the plus and minus signs for each classification. Decide whether the accounts are increased or decreased. When you use T accounts to analyze the transaction, the results are as follows:

Equipment		Cash	
+	−	+	−
Debit	Credit	Debit	Credit
64,000			64,000

Now journalize this analysis below the first transaction. Record the day of the month in the Date column. Remember, you do not have to record the month and year again until the month or year changes or you use a new journal page.

GENERAL JOURNAL   PAGE ___1___

	DATE		DESCRIPTION	POST. REF.	DEBIT	CREDIT	
1	20–						1
2	June	1	Cash		82 0 0 0 00		2
3			R. P. Cline, Capital			82 0 0 0 00	3
4			Original investment by Cline				4
5			in Cline's Computer Clinic.				5
6							6
7		2	Equipment		64 0 0 0 00		7
8			Cash			64 0 0 0 00	8
9			Bought equipment for cash.				9

— *Skip a line between entries in homework*

Transaction (c) June 3: Cline's Computer Clinic bought equipment costing $10,000 on credit (on account) from Surgo Products. Again start with the T accounts.

Equipment		Accounts Payable	
+	−	−	+
Debit	Credit	Debit	Credit
10,000			10,000

After skipping a line in the journal, record the day of the month and then the entry. In journalizing a transaction involving Accounts Payable, always state the name of the creditor in the explanation. Similarly, in journalizing a transaction involving Accounts Receivable, always state the name of the customer who charged the amount in the explanation.

GENERAL JOURNAL   PAGE ___1___

DATE	DESCRIPTION	POST. REF.	DEBIT	CREDIT
10					10
11	3	Equipment		10 0 0 0 00		11
12		Accounts Payable			10 0 0 0 00	12
13		Bought equipment on				13
14		account from Surgo				14
15		Products.				15

When a business buys an asset, the asset should be recorded at the actual cost (the agreed amount of a transaction). This is called the **cost principle**. For example, suppose that the $10,000 that Cline's Computer Clinic paid for the equipment from Surgo Products was a bargain price, as Surgo Products had been asking $12,500 for the equipment. The day after Cline's Computer Clinic took possession of the equipment, it received an offer of $9,500 from another party, but the offer was declined. Cline's Computer Clinic *should record the cost of the equipment as the actual amount paid in the transaction that occurred,* which is $10,000. This is true even though the fair market value may indeed be $9,500.

Transaction (d) **June 4: Cline's Computer Clinic pays $6,000 to Surgo Products as partial payment to be applied against the firm's liability of $10,000.** Picture the T accounts like this:

Cash	Accounts Payable
+ | −	− | +
Debit | Credit	Debit | Credit
| 6,000	6,000 |

In this case, we see that cash is going out, so we record it on the minus side. We now have a credit to Cash and have completed half of the entry. Next, we recognize that Accounts Payable is involved. We ask ourselves, "Do we owe more or less as a result of this transaction?" The answer is "less," so we record it on the minus, or debit, side of the account.

GENERAL JOURNAL   PAGE ___1___

DATE	DESCRIPTION	POST. REF.	DEBIT	CREDIT
16					16
17	4	Accounts Payable		6 0 0 0 00		17
18		Cash			6 0 0 0 00	18
19		Paid Surgo Products				19
20		on account.				20
21						21
22						22
23						23

CAREERS IN YOUR FUTURE

ERICA KENNEDY

Export Development Supervisor for a Global Logistics Company

Without her solid theoretical foundation in accounting fundamentals, Erica Kennedy would not be where she is today. She considers accounting an essential success factor in the business world, one that has provided endless combinations and possibilities for her career.

Erica works for an international global logistics company that has hundreds of offices in over fifty countries—each using the same accounting software, unique to the industry, that is programmed in-house and tailored for the different fiscal and legal requirements of each country. Within the company, Erica has moved from accounting, where she performed internal audits and wrote internal control procedures, to analyzing software issues and finding solutions. She focuses on the company's export software. Branches all over the world report software issues to her; she then supervises a team that tackles the software questions and finds solutions to them.

Erica has carried her accounting and software skills into this new endeavor. She will tell you that accounting trained her for her current position because she has to be very methodical, detail oriented, accurate, and thorough as she moves up in the high-tech world.

Erica also has taught accounting students at a community college. She urged her students to complete all homework, develop productive habits, and learn to write well—writing is essential in business. She also stressed to her students the importance of understanding and making journal entries. She finds that knowing about financial statement preparation and financial statement analysis are two other extremely valuable skills. What other accounting skills might be helpful in Erica's current job?

"I loved geology, but only liked accounting. On the other hand, I felt accounting would provide a better opportunity . . . to start working professionally. And because of accounting, I get to do what I love to do—teach people how to use accounting systems around the world."

Now let's list the transactions for June for Cline's Computer Clinic with the date of each transaction. The journal entries are illustrated in Figures 1, 2, and 3.

June 1 Cline invests $82,000 cash in her new business.
2 Buys equipment costing $64,000, paying cash.
3 Buys equipment costing $10,000 on credit from Surgo Products.
4 Pays $6,000 to Surgo Products to be applied against the firm's liability of $10,000.
4 Cline invests her personal equipment valued at $6,200 in her new business.
7 Receives cash revenue, $3,520.
8 Pays rent for the month, $900.
10 Buys compact discs and holders for storing troubleshooting programs and customer files during installations and repairs, as well as manuals and invoice forms, on account from Freeman Company, $870.
10 Pays for one-year liability insurance policy, $480.

FIGURE 1

GENERAL JOURNAL

PAGE __1__

	DATE		DESCRIPTION	POST. REF.	DEBIT	CREDIT	
1	20–						1
2	June	1	Cash		82 0 0 0 00		2
3			R. P. Cline, Capital			82 0 0 0 00	3
4			Original investment by Cline				4
5			in Cline's Computer Clinic.				5
6							6
7		2	Equipment		64 0 0 0 00		7
8			Cash			64 0 0 0 00	8
9			Bought equipment for cash.				9
10							10
11		3	Equipment		10 0 0 0 00		11
12			Accounts Payable			10 0 0 0 00	12
13			Bought equipment on				13
14			account from Surgo				14
15			Products.				15
16							16
17		4	Accounts Payable		6 0 0 0 00		17
18			Cash			6 0 0 0 00	18
19			Paid Surgo Products on				19
20			account.				20
21							21
22		4	Equipment		6 2 0 0 00		22
23			R. P. Cline, Capital			6 2 0 0 00	23
24			Investment by Cline in				24
25			Cline's Computer Clinic.				25
26							26
27		7	Cash		3 5 2 0 00		27
28			Income from Services			3 5 2 0 00	28
29			Cash revenue.				29
30							30
31		8	Rent Expense		9 0 0 00		31
32			Cash			9 0 0 00	32
33			For month ended June 30.				33
34							34
35		10	Supplies Expense		8 7 0 00		35
36			Accounts Payable			8 7 0 00	36
37			Bought computer supplies				37
38			on account from Freeman				38
39			Company.				39

Heavy-duty ladders, spray painting machines, and a truck to carry it all in are part of the equipment used by these house painters.

June 14 Receives bill for newspaper advertising from the *Daily*, $340.

15 Cline's Computer Clinic signs a contract with Computer Makeovers to refurbish some of the computers it receives and then bills Computer Makeovers $1,470 for services performed.

15 Pays $1,800 to Surgo Products as a partial payment on account.

GENERAL JOURNAL   PAGE ___2___

	DATE		DESCRIPTION	POST. REF.	DEBIT	CREDIT	
1	20–						1
2	June	10	Prepaid Insurance		4 8 0 00		2
3			Cash			4 8 0 00	3
4			Premium for one-year liability				4
5			insurance policy.				5
6							6
7		14	Advertising Expense		3 4 0 00		7
8			Accounts Payable			3 4 0 00	8
9			Received bill for advertising				9
10			from the *Daily.*				10
11							11
12		15	Accounts Receivable		1 4 7 0 00		12
13			Income from Services			1 4 7 0 00	13
14			Billed Computer Makeovers				14
15			for services performed.				15
16							16
17		15	Accounts Payable		1 8 0 0 00		17
18			Cash			1 8 0 0 00	18
19			Paid Surgo Products on				19
20			account.				20
21							21
22		18	Utilities Expense		3 2 0 00		22
23			Cash			3 2 0 00	23
24			Paid bill for utilities, Regional				24
25			Power, Inc.				25
26							26
27		20	Accounts Payable		3 4 0 00		27
28			Cash			3 4 0 00	28
29			Paid the *Daily* in full.				29
30							30
31		24	Wages Expense		2 9 8 0 00		31
32			Cash			2 9 8 0 00	32
33			Paid wages of part-time				33
34			employee.				34

FIGURE 2

June 18 Receives and pays bill for utilities from Regional Power, Inc., $320.

20 Pays the *Daily* for advertising, $340 in full. (This bill has been previously recorded.)

24 Pays wages of part-time employee, $2,980.

26 Buys additional equipment costing $3,520 from Surgo Products, paying $620 down with the remaining $2,900 on account.

	DATE		DESCRIPTION	POST. REF.	DEBIT		CREDIT	
1	20–							1
2	June	26	Equipment		3 5 2 0 00			2
3			Cash				6 2 0 00	3
4			Accounts Payable				2 9 0 0 00	4
5			Bought equipment on					5
6			account from Surgo					6
7			Products.					7
8								8
9		30	Cash		8 5 0 00			9
10			Accounts Receivable				8 5 0 00	10
11			Received from Computer					11
12			Makeovers to apply on					12
13			account.					13
14								14
15		30	Cash		6 0 2 0 00			15
16			Income from Services				6 0 2 0 00	16
17			Cash revenue.					17
18								18
19		30	R. P. Cline, Drawing		3 0 0 0 00			19
20			Cash				3 0 0 0 00	20
21			Withdrawal for personal use.					21

GENERAL JOURNAL   PAGE ___3___

FIGURE 3

June	30	Receives $850 from Computer Makeovers to apply on amount previously billed.
	30	Receives cash revenue, $6,020.
	30	Cline withdraws cash for personal use, $3,000.

POSTING TO THE GENERAL LEDGER

You can see that the journal is the *book of original entry.* Each transaction must first be recorded in the journal in full. However, it is difficult to determine the balance of any one account, such as Cash, from the general journal entries. So the **ledger account** has been devised to give us a complete record of the transactions recorded in each individual account. The **general ledger** contains all the accounts. It may be a loose-leaf binder so that you can add or remove pages. The process of transferring information from the journal to the ledger accounts is called **posting**.

The Chart of Accounts

The accounts in the ledger are arranged according to the chart of accounts, which **is the official list of the ledger accounts in which transactions of a business are recorded.** Assets are listed first, liabilities second, owner's equity

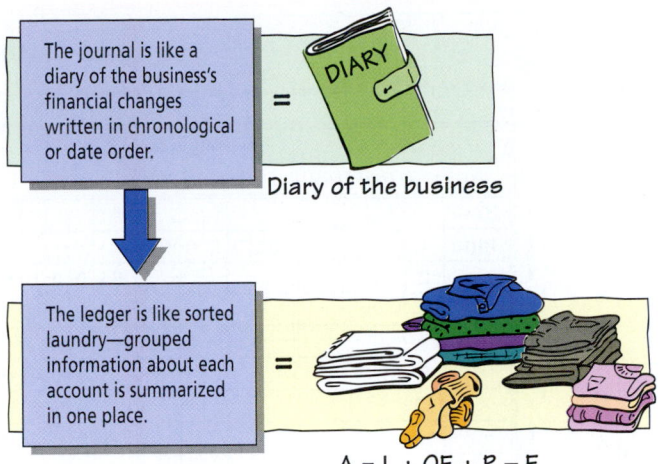

The journal is like a diary of the business's financial changes written in chronological or date order.

= **Diary of the business**

The ledger is like sorted laundry—grouped information about each account is summarized in one place.

= A = L + OE + R − E

third, revenue fourth, and expenses fifth. The chart of accounts for Cline's Computer Clinic is as follows:

Chart of Accounts

Assets (100–199)

111 Cash
113 Accounts Receivable
117 Prepaid Insurance
124 Equipment

Liabilities (200–299)

221 Accounts Payable

Owner's Equity (300–399)

311 R. P. Cline, Capital
312 R. P. Cline, Drawing

Revenue (400–499)

411 Income from Services

Expenses (500–599)

511 Wages Expense
512 Rent Expense
513 Supplies Expense
514 Advertising Expense
515 Utilities Expense

Notice that the arrangement of the chart of accounts consists of the balance sheet accounts followed by the income statement accounts. The numbers preceding the account titles are the **account numbers**. Accounts in the ledger are kept by numbers rather than by pages because it is hard to tell in advance how many pages to reserve for a particular account. When you use the number system, you can add sheets easily. The digits in the account numbers also indicate account *classifications*. For most companies, assets start with 1, liabilities with 2, owner's equity with 3, revenue with 4, and expenses with 5. The second and third digits indicate the positions of the individual accounts within their respective classifications.

The Ledger Account Form (Running Balance Format)

We have been looking at accounts in the simple T account form primarily because T accounts illustrate situations so well. The debit and credit sides are specifically labeled, making the T account form a good way to picture account activity. However, determining the balance of an account using the T account form is difficult. You must add both columns and subtract the smaller total from the larger. To overcome this disadvantage, accountants generally use the four-column account form with Balance columns in the general ledger. Let's look at the Cash account of Cline's Computer Clinic in four-column form (Figure 4) compared with the T account form. *Leave the Post. Ref. column blank for now.*

Cash

+		–	
(a)	82,000	(b)	64,000
(f)	3,520	(d)	6,000
(q)	850	(g)	900
(r)	6,020	(i)	480
	92,390	(l)	1,800
		(m)	320
		(n)	340
		(o)	2,980
		(p)	620
		(s)	3,000
			80,440

Bal. 11,950

GENERAL LEDGER

ACCOUNT **Cash**   ACCOUNT NO. __111__

	DATE	ITEM	POST. REF.	DEBIT	CREDIT	BALANCE DEBIT	BALANCE CREDIT	
1	20–							1
2	June 1			82 0 0 0 00		82 0 0 0 00		2
3	2				64 0 0 0 00	18 0 0 0 00		3
4	4				6 0 0 0 00	12 0 0 0 00		4
5	7			3 5 2 0 00		15 5 2 0 00		5
6	8				9 0 0 00	14 6 2 0 00		6
7	10				4 8 0 00	14 1 4 0 00		7
8	15				1 8 0 0 00	12 3 4 0 00		8
9	18				3 2 0 00	12 0 2 0 00		9
10	20				3 4 0 00	11 6 8 0 00		10
11	24				2 9 8 0 00	8 7 0 0 00		11
12	26				6 2 0 00	8 0 8 0 00		12
13	30			8 5 0 00		8 9 3 0 00		13
14	30			6 0 2 0 00		14 9 5 0 00		14
15	30				3 0 0 0 00	11 9 5 0 00		15

Transaction Amount (DEBIT/CREDIT columns)   *Running Balance* (BALANCE columns)

FIGURE 4

Note the calculation of the running balance. In the abbreviated form, it looks like this:

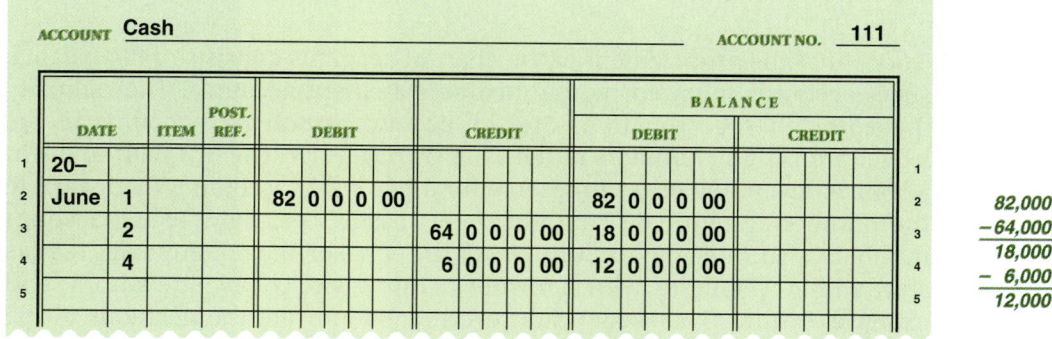

ACCOUNT **Cash**   ACCOUNT NO. __111__

	DATE	ITEM	POST. REF.	DEBIT	CREDIT	BALANCE DEBIT	BALANCE CREDIT		
1	20–							1	
2	June 1			82 0 0 0 00		82 0 0 0 00		2	82,000
3	2				64 0 0 0 00	18 0 0 0 00		3	−64,000
4	4				6 0 0 0 00	12 0 0 0 00		4	18,000
5								5	− 6,000
									12,000

The Posting Process

In the posting process, you must transfer the following information from the journal to the ledger accounts: the *date of the transaction, the debit and credit amounts,* and the *page number* of the journal. Post each account separately, using the following steps. Post the debit part of the entry first. After locating the account in the ledger, you need to do the following steps.

1. Write the date of the transaction in the account's Date column.
2. Write the amount of the transaction in the Debit or Credit column and enter the new balance in the Balance columns under Debit or Credit.

3. Write the page number of the journal in the Post. Ref. column of the ledger account. (This is a **cross-reference**; it tells where the amount came from.)

4. Record the ledger account number in the Post. Ref. column of the journal. (This is also a cross-reference; it tells where the amount was posted.)

Entering the account number in the Post. Ref. column of the journal should be the last step. It acts as a verification of the three preceding steps.

The first transaction for Cline's Computer Clinic is illustrated in Figure 5. Let's look first at the debit part of the entry.

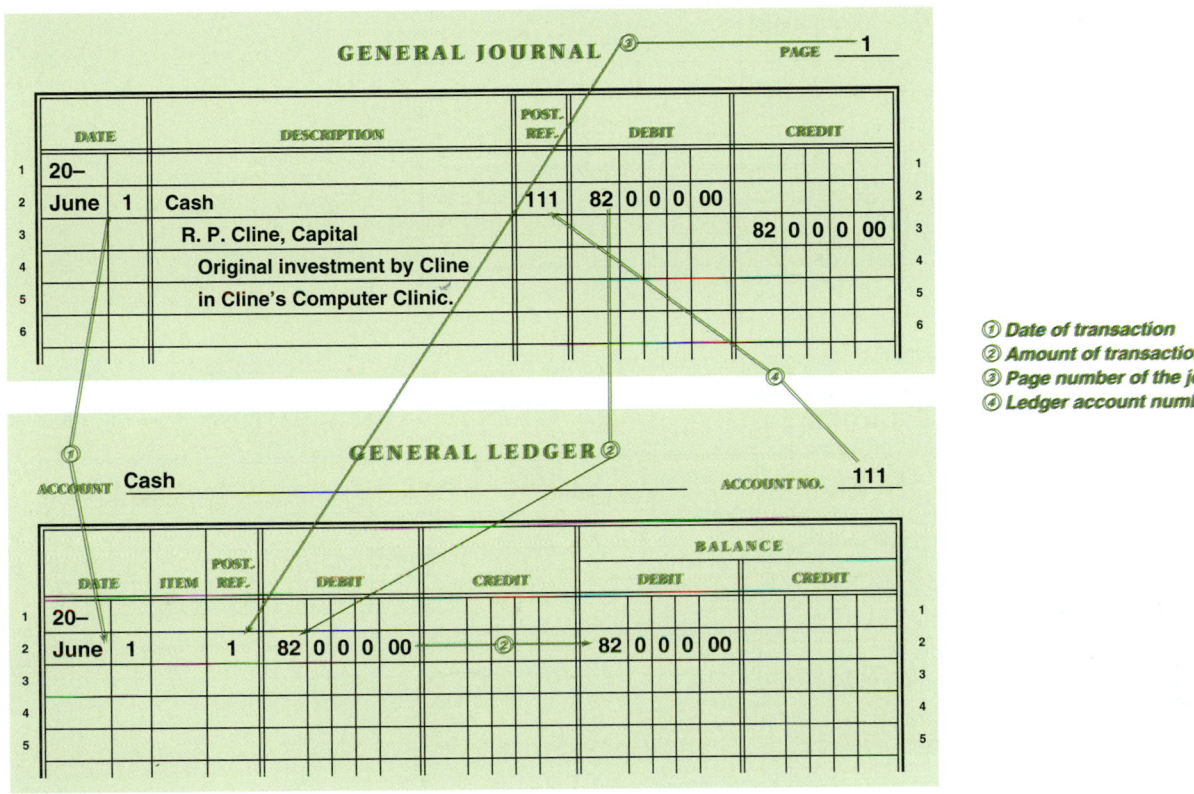

FIGURE 5

Next we post the credit part of the entry, as shown in Figure 6.

The accountant usually uses the Item column only at the end of a financial period. The words that may appear in this column are *balance, closing, adjusting,* and *reversing.* We will explain the use of these terms later.

Incidentally, some accountants use running balance–type ledger account forms that have only one balance column. However, we have used the two-balance-column arrangement to show clearly the appropriate balance of an account. For example, in Figure 5, Cash has an $82,000 balance recorded in the Debit column (normal balance). In Figure 6, R. P. Cline, Capital, has a $82,000 balance recorded in the Credit column (normal balance).

In the recording of the second transaction, shown in Figure 7, see if you can identify in order the four steps in the posting process.

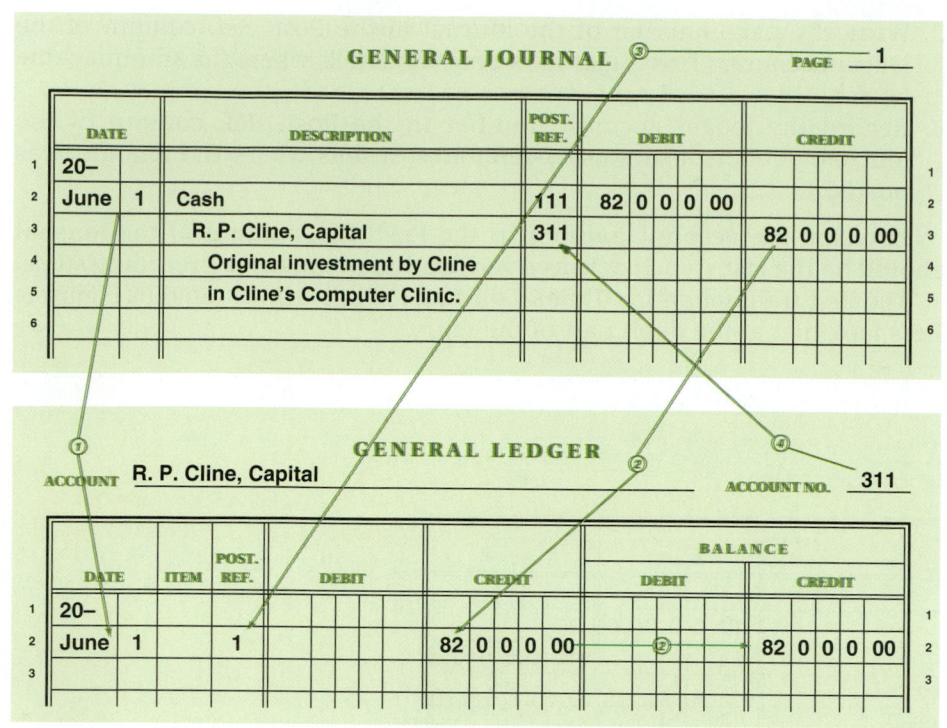

GENERAL JOURNAL   PAGE ___1___

	DATE	DESCRIPTION	POST. REF.	DEBIT	CREDIT	
1	20–					1
2	June 1	Cash	111	82 0 0 0 00		2
3		R. P. Cline, Capital	311		82 0 0 0 00	3
4		Original investment by Cline				4
5		in Cline's Computer Clinic.				5
6						6

① Date of transaction
② Amount of transaction
③ Page number of the journal
④ Ledger account number

GENERAL LEDGER

ACCOUNT   R. P. Cline, Capital   ACCOUNT NO. ___311___

	DATE	ITEM	POST. REF.	DEBIT	CREDIT	BALANCE DEBIT	BALANCE CREDIT	
1	20–							1
2	June 1		1		82 0 0 0 00		82 0 0 0 00	2
3								3

FIGURE 6

FIGURE 7

GENERAL JOURNAL   PAGE ___1___

	DATE	DESCRIPTION	POST. REF.	DEBIT	CREDIT	
7	2	Equipment	124	64 0 0 0 00		7
8		Cash	111		64 0 0 0 00	8
9		Bought equipment for cash.				9
10						10

GENERAL LEDGER

ACCOUNT   Cash   ACCOUNT NO. ___111___

	DATE	ITEM	POST. REF.	DEBIT	CREDIT	BALANCE DEBIT	BALANCE CREDIT	
1	20–							1
2	June 1		1	82 0 0 0 00		82 0 0 0 00		2
3	2		1		64 0 0 0 00	18 0 0 0 00		3

ACCOUNT   Equipment   ACCOUNT NO. ___124___

	DATE	ITEM	POST. REF.	DEBIT	CREDIT	BALANCE DEBIT	BALANCE CREDIT	
1	20–							1
2	June 2		1	64 0 0 0 00		64 0 0 0 00		2

REMEMBER!

Do not record account numbers in the Post. Ref. column of the journal until the amounts have been posted to the ledger accounts as either debits or credits.

REMEMBER!

Posting is simply transferring or copying exactly the same date and the debits and credits listed in the journal entry from the journal to the ledger.

Now let's look at the journal entries for the first month of operation for Cline's Computer Clinic. As you can see in Figure 8, the Post. Ref. column has been filled in, because the posting has been completed.

FIGURE 8

GENERAL JOURNAL   PAGE ___1___

	DATE		DESCRIPTION	POST. REF.	DEBIT	CREDIT	
1	20–						1
2	June	1	Cash	111	82 0 0 0 00		2
3			R. P. Cline, Capital	311		82 0 0 0 00	3
4			Original investment by Cline				4
5			in Cline's Computer Clinic.				5
6							6
7		2	Equipment	124	64 0 0 0 00		7
8			Cash	111		64 0 0 0 00	8
9			Bought equipment for cash.				9
10							10
11		3	Equipment	124	10 0 0 0 00		11
12			Accounts Payable	221		10 0 0 0 00	12
13			Bought equipment on				13
14			account from Surgo				14
15			Products.				15
16							16
17		4	Accounts Payable	221	6 0 0 0 00		17
18			Cash	111		6 0 0 0 00	18
19			Paid Surgo Products on				19
20			account.				20
21							21
22		4	Equipment	124	6 2 0 0 00		22
23			R. P. Cline, Capital	311		6 2 0 0 00	23
24			Investment by Cline in				24
25			Cline's Computer Clinic.				25
26							26
27		7	Cash	111	3 5 2 0 00		27
28			Income from Services	411		3 5 2 0 00	28
29			Cash revenue.				29
30							30
31		8	Rent Expense	512	9 0 0 00		31
32			Cash	111		9 0 0 00	32
33			For month ended June 30.				33
34							34
35		10	Supplies Expense	513	8 7 0 00		35
36			Accounts Payable	221		8 7 0 00	36
37			Bought computer supplies				37
38			on account from Freeman				38
39			Company.				39
40							40

(continued)

FIGURE 8 (continued)

GENERAL JOURNAL   PAGE __2__

	DATE		DESCRIPTION	POST. REF.	DEBIT	CREDIT	
1	20–						1
2	June	10	Prepaid Insurance	117	4 8 0 00		2
3			Cash	111		4 8 0 00	3
4			Premium for one-year liability				4
5			insurance policy.				5
6							6
7		14	Advertising Expense	514	3 4 0 00		7
8			Accounts Payable	221		3 4 0 00	8
9			Received bill for advertising				9
10			from the *Daily*.				10
11							11
12		15	Accounts Receivable	113	1 4 7 0 00		12
13			Income from Services	411		1 4 7 0 00	13
14			Billed Computer Makeovers				14
15			for services performed.				15
16							16
17		15	Accounts Payable	221	1 8 0 0 00		17
18			Cash	111		1 8 0 0 00	18
19			Paid Surgo Products on				19
20			account.				20
21							21
22		18	Utilities Expense	515	3 2 0 00		22
23			Cash	111		3 2 0 00	23
24			Paid bill for utilities, Regional				24
25			Power, Inc.				25
26							26
27		20	Accounts Payable	221	3 4 0 00		27
28			Cash	111		3 4 0 00	28
29			Paid the *Daily* in full.				29
30							30
31		24	Wages Expense	511	2 9 8 0 00		31
32			Cash	111		2 9 8 0 00	32
33			Paid wages of part-time				33
34			employee.				34
35							35

GENERAL JOURNAL   PAGE __3__

	DATE		DESCRIPTION	POST. REF.	DEBIT	CREDIT	
1	20–						1
2	June	26	Equipment	124	3 5 2 0 00		2
3			Cash	111		6 2 0 00	3
4			Accounts Payable	221		2 9 0 0 00	4
5			Bought equipment on				5
6			account from Surgo				6
7			Products.				7

FIGURE 8 (continued)

	DATE		POST. REF.	DEBIT	CREDIT	
9	30	Cash	111	8 5 0 00		9
10		Accounts Receivable	113		8 5 0 00	10
11		Received from Computer				11
12		Makeovers to apply on				12
13		account.				13
14						14
15	30	Cash	111	6 0 2 0 00		15
16		Income from Services	411		6 0 2 0 00	16
17		Cash revenue.				17
18						18
19	30	R. P. Cline, Drawing	312	3 0 0 0 00		19
20		Cash	111		3 0 0 0 00	20
21		Withdrawal for personal use.				21

FYI

Computerized accounting programs also require journal explanations and will generate posting references.

In making journal entries, you will sometimes find that there are not enough lines at the bottom of a page to record the entire entry. In this case, do not split up the entry; instead, record the entire entry on the next journal page. The ledger accounts and entries for Cline's Computer Clinic are shown in Figure 9.

FIGURE 9

GENERAL LEDGER

ACCOUNT **Cash**   ACCOUNT NO. **111**

	DATE	ITEM	POST. REF.	DEBIT	CREDIT	BALANCE DEBIT	BALANCE CREDIT	
1	20–							1
2	June 1		1	82 0 0 0 00		82 0 0 0 00		2
3	2		1		64 0 0 0 00	18 0 0 0 00		3
4	4		1		6 0 0 0 00	12 0 0 0 00		4
5	7		1	3 5 2 0 00		15 5 2 0 00		5
6	8		1		9 0 0 00	14 6 2 0 00		6
7	10		2		4 8 0 00	14 1 4 0 00		7
8	15		2		1 8 0 0 00	12 3 4 0 00		8
9	18		2		3 2 0 00	12 0 2 0 00		9
10	20		2		3 4 0 00	11 6 8 0 00		10
11	24		2		2 9 8 0 00	8 7 0 0 00		11
12	26		3		6 2 0 00	8 0 8 0 00		12
13	30		3	8 5 0 00		8 9 3 0 00		13
14	30		3	6 0 2 0 00		14 9 5 0 00		14
15	30		3		3 0 0 0 00	11 9 5 0 00		15

ACCOUNT **Accounts Receivable**   ACCOUNT NO. **113**

	DATE	ITEM	POST. REF.	DEBIT	CREDIT	BALANCE DEBIT	BALANCE CREDIT	
1	20–							1
2	June 15		2	1 4 7 0 00		1 4 7 0 00		2
3	30		3		8 5 0 00	6 2 0 00		3

(continued)

**FIGURE 9
(continued)**

ACCOUNT **Prepaid Insurance**   ACCOUNT NO. __117__

	DATE	ITEM	POST. REF.	DEBIT	CREDIT	BALANCE DEBIT	BALANCE CREDIT	
1	20–							1
2	June 10		2	4 8 0 00		4 8 0 00		2

ACCOUNT **Equipment**   ACCOUNT NO. __124__

	DATE	ITEM	POST. REF.	DEBIT	CREDIT	BALANCE DEBIT	BALANCE CREDIT	
1	20–							1
2	June 2		1	64 0 0 0 00		64 0 0 0 00		2
3	3		1	10 0 0 0 00		74 0 0 0 00		3
4	4		1	6 2 0 0 00		80 2 0 0 00		4
5	26		3	3 5 2 0 00		83 7 2 0 00		5

ACCOUNT **Accounts Payable**   ACCOUNT NO. __221__

	DATE	ITEM	POST. REF.	DEBIT	CREDIT	BALANCE DEBIT	BALANCE CREDIT	
1	20–							1
2	June 3		1		10 0 0 0 00		10 0 0 0 00	2
3	4		1	6 0 0 0 00			4 0 0 0 00	3
4	10		1		8 7 0 00		4 8 7 0 00	4
5	14		2		3 4 0 00		5 2 1 0 00	5
6	15		2	1 8 0 0 00			3 4 1 0 00	6
7	20		2	3 4 0 00			3 0 7 0 00	7
8	26		3		2 9 0 0 00		5 9 7 0 00	8
9								9
10								10
11								11

ACCOUNT **R. P. Cline, Capital**   ACCOUNT NO. __311__

	DATE	ITEM	POST. REF.	DEBIT	CREDIT	BALANCE DEBIT	BALANCE CREDIT	
1	20–							1
2	June 1		1		82 0 0 0 00		82 0 0 0 00	2
3	4		1		6 2 0 0 00		88 2 0 0 00	3

ACCOUNT **R. P. Cline, Drawing**   ACCOUNT NO. __312__

	DATE	ITEM	POST. REF.	DEBIT	CREDIT	BALANCE DEBIT	BALANCE CREDIT	
1	20–							1
2	June 30		3	3 0 0 0 00		3 0 0 0 00		2

FIGURE 9
(continued)

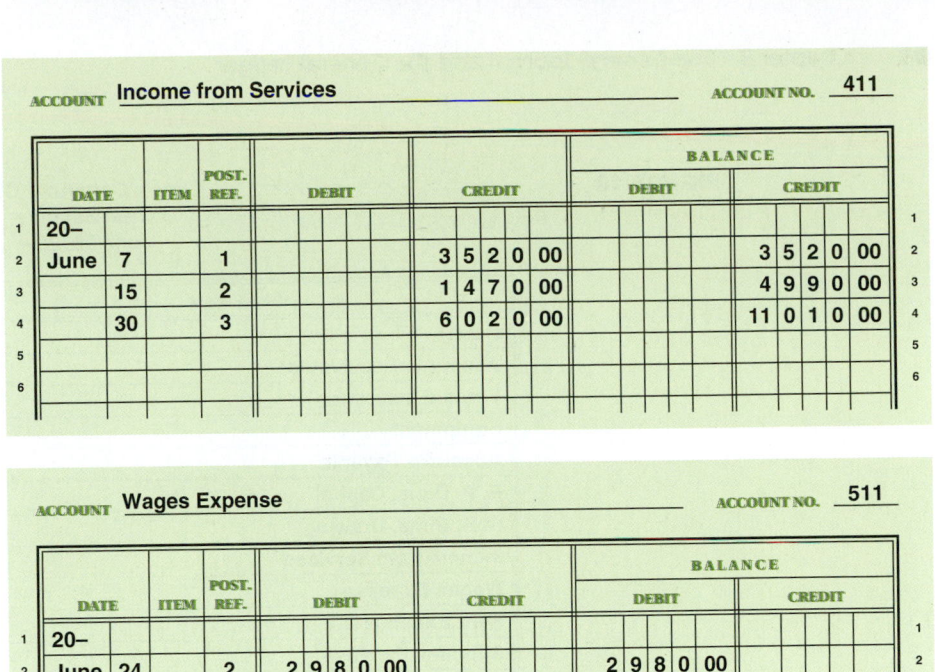

ACCOUNT Income from Services   **ACCOUNT NO.** 411

DATE	ITEM	POST. REF.	DEBIT	CREDIT	BALANCE DEBIT	BALANCE CREDIT
20–						
June 7		1		3 5 2 0 00		3 5 2 0 00
15		2		1 4 7 0 00		4 9 9 0 00
30		3		6 0 2 0 00		11 0 1 0 00

ACCOUNT Wages Expense   **ACCOUNT NO.** 511

DATE	ITEM	POST. REF.	DEBIT	CREDIT	BALANCE DEBIT	BALANCE CREDIT
20–						
June 24		2	2 9 8 0 00		2 9 8 0 00	

ACCOUNT Rent Expense   **ACCOUNT NO.** 512

DATE	ITEM	POST. REF.	DEBIT	CREDIT	BALANCE DEBIT	BALANCE CREDIT
20–						
June 8		1	9 0 0 00		9 0 0 00	

ACCOUNT Supplies Expense   **ACCOUNT NO.** 513

DATE	ITEM	POST. REF.	DEBIT	CREDIT	BALANCE DEBIT	BALANCE CREDIT
20–						
June 10		1	8 7 0 00		8 7 0 00	

ACCOUNT Advertising Expense   **ACCOUNT NO.** 514

DATE	ITEM	POST. REF.	DEBIT	CREDIT	BALANCE DEBIT	BALANCE CREDIT
20–						
June 14		2	3 4 0 00		3 4 0 00	

ACCOUNT Utilities Expense   **ACCOUNT NO.** 515

DATE	ITEM	POST. REF.	DEBIT	CREDIT	BALANCE DEBIT	BALANCE CREDIT
20–						
June 18		2	3 2 0 00		3 2 0 00	

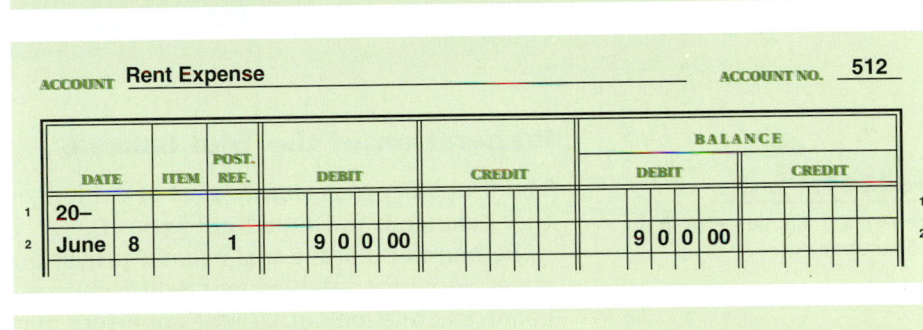

FIGURE 10

Cline's Computer Clinic
Trial Balance
June 30, 20—

ACCOUNT NAME	DEBIT	CREDIT
Cash	11 9 5 0 00	
Accounts Receivable	6 2 0 00	
Prepaid Insurance	4 8 0 00	
Equipment	83 7 2 0 00	
Accounts Payable		5 9 7 0 00
R. P. Cline, Capital		88 2 0 0 00
R. P. Cline, Drawing	3 0 0 0 00	
Income from Services		11 0 1 0 00
Wages Expense	2 9 8 0 00	
Rent Expense	9 0 0 00	
Supplies Expense	8 7 0 00	
Advertising Expense	3 4 0 00	
Utilities Expense	3 2 0 00	
	105 1 8 0 00	105 1 8 0 00

Preparation of the Trial Balance

OBJECTIVE 3

Prepare a trial balance from the ledger accounts.

The trial balance is simply a list of the ledger accounts that have balances. A trial balance is presented in Figure 10.

Remember that the trial balance proves only that the total ledger debit balances equal the total ledger credit balances. Even when the debit and credit balances are equal, other types of errors may slip through—for example,

1. Posting the correct debit or credit amounts to the incorrect account.
2. Neglecting to journalize or post an entire transaction.

If the temporary balance of an account happens to be zero, insert long dashes through both the Debit Balance and the Credit Balance columns. We'll use another business, the Becker Company, in this example. Its Accounts Receivable ledger account appears below.

ACCOUNT **Accounts Receivable** ACCOUNT NO. **113**

	DATE	ITEM	POST. REF.	DEBIT	CREDIT	BALANCE DEBIT	BALANCE CREDIT	
1	20—							1
2	Oct. 7		96	1 4 0 00		1 4 0 00		2
3	19		97	2 3 8 00		3 7 8 00		3
4	21		97		1 4 0 00	2 3 8 00		4
5	29		98		2 3 8 00	—	—	5
6	31		98	1 6 2 00		1 6 2 00		6
7								7
8								8
9								9
10								10
11								11
12								12

Steps in the Accounting Process

1. **Record the transactions of a business in a journal (book of original entry or the day-by-day record of the transactions of a firm).** An entry should be based on some source document or evidence that a transaction has occurred, such as an invoice, a receipt, or a check.
2. **Post entries to the accounts in the ledger.** Transfer the amounts from the journal to the Debit or Credit columns of the specified accounts in the ledger. Use a cross-reference system. Accounts are organized in the ledger according to the account numbers assigned to them in the chart of accounts.
3. **Prepare a trial balance.** Record the balances of the ledger accounts in the appropriate column, Debit or Credit, of the trial balance form. Prove that the total of the debit balances equals the total of the credit balances.

Source Document

A source document can be an invoice, a receipt, a check, etc. We now add an important detail in the recording of a journal entry. This detail consists of listing the related source document number, which is used as a reference for the proof of a transaction. Figure 11 is an example of a source document followed by the journal entry (Figure 12) and ledger accounts (Figure 13). Note how the explanation differs from the one we showed earlier.

FIGURE 11

FREEMAN COMPANY				No. 4-962	
220 East Ames Street					
Detroit, Michigan 48222					

Sold By: 203   Date: 6/10/20—

Name: Cline's Computer Clinic

Address: 1701 East Delaware Street

Detroit, Michigan 48228

Terms: Net 30 days

QUANTITY	DESCRIPTION	UNIT PRICE		AMOUNT	
20 bx	Compact discs	16	00	320	00
20 bx	Compact disc holders	8	00	160	00
20 ea	Manuals	10	00	200	00
10 bx	Invoice forms	12	00	120	00
	SUBTOTAL			800	00
	SALES TAX			48	00
	SHIPPING			22	00
	TOTAL			870	00

Record in the journal (Figure 12). Note how the explanation includes important information from the source document presented earlier.

GENERAL JOURNAL

PAGE __1__

DATE		DESCRIPTION	POST. REF.	DEBIT	CREDIT	
35	10	Supplies Expense	513	8 7 0 00		35
36		Accounts Payable	221		8 7 0 00	36
37		Bought computer supplies				37
38		on account from Freeman				38
39		Company, Inv. No. 4-962.				39
40						40
41						41
42						42
43						43

FIGURE 12

Post to the ledger (Figure 13).

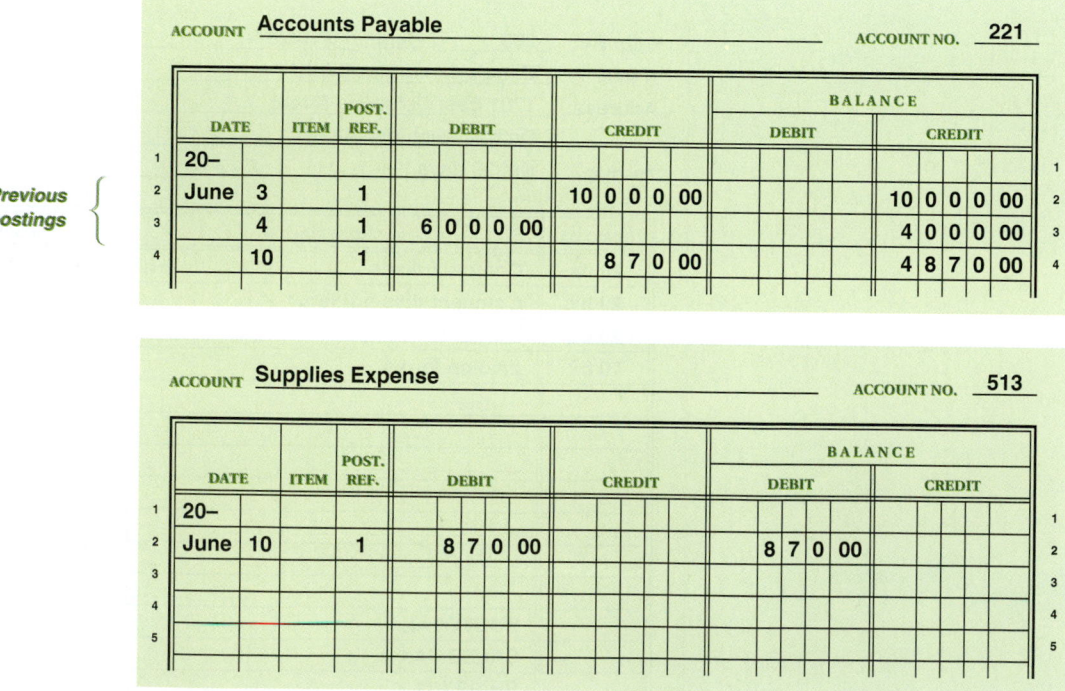

ACCOUNT **Accounts Payable** ACCOUNT NO. __221__

	DATE	ITEM	POST. REF.	DEBIT	CREDIT	BALANCE DEBIT	BALANCE CREDIT	
1	20–							1
2	June 3		1		10 0 0 0 00		10 0 0 0 00	2
3	4		1	6 0 0 0 00			4 0 0 0 00	3
4	10		1		8 7 0 00		4 8 7 0 00	4

Previous postings

ACCOUNT **Supplies Expense** ACCOUNT NO. __513__

	DATE	ITEM	POST. REF.	DEBIT	CREDIT	BALANCE DEBIT	BALANCE CREDIT	
1	20–							1
2	June 10		1	8 7 0 00		8 7 0 00		2
3								3
4								4
5								5

FIGURE 13

CORRECTION OF ERRORS—MANUAL AND COMPUTERIZED

Errors are occasionally made in recording journal entries and posting to the ledger accounts whether recording them manually or on a computer. Never erase them, because it might look as if you were trying to hide something. The method for correcting errors depends on how and when the errors were made. There are two manual methods for correcting errors; they are

1. The ruling method.
2. The correcting entry method.

Manual Ruling Method

OBJECTIVE 4

Correct entries using the manual ruling method.

You can use the ruling method to correct an error in the journal before posting or to correct an error in the ledger after an entry has been posted.

Manually Correcting Errors Before Posting Has Taken Place When an error has been made in recording an account title in a journal entry, draw a line through the incorrect account title in the journal entry, and write the correct account title immediately above. Include your initials with the correction. For example, an entry to record payment of $1,700 rent was incorrectly debited to Salary Expense.

DATE		DESCRIPTION	POST. REF.	DEBIT	CREDIT	
1	20–					1
2	Mar. 1	~~Rent Expense~~ ~~Salary Expense~~ *DJM*		1 7 0 0 00		2
3		Cash			1 7 0 0 00	3
4		Paid rent for the month.				4

When an error has been made in recording an amount, draw a line through the incorrect amount in the journal entry, and write the correct amount immediately above. For example, an entry for a $230 payment for office supplies was recorded as $320. Include your initials with the correction.

DATE		DESCRIPTION	POST. REF.	DEBIT	CREDIT	
1	20–			*DJM* 2 3 0 00 ~~3 2 0 00~~		1
2	Apr. 6	Supplies Expense			*DJM* 2 3 0 00 ~~3 2 0 00~~	2
3		Cash				3
4		Bought office stationery.				4
5						5

Manually Correcting Errors After Posting Has Taken Place When an entry was journalized correctly but one of the amounts was posted incorrectly,

Whether you are preparing accounting records manually or on computer, accuracy is of primary importance. Rapid and accurate ten-key and computer keyboard skills are a must for the accountant or bookkeeper.

correct the error by drawing a single line through the amount and recording the correct amount above. For example, an entry to record cash received for professional fees was correctly journalized as $400. However, it was posted as a debit to Cash for $400 and a credit to Professional Fees for $4,000. In the Professional Fees account, draw a line through $4,000 and insert $400 above. Change the running balance of the account and initial the corrections.

FYI

Use a ruler to draw a line through an error.

	DATE	ITEM	POST. REF.	DEBIT	CREDIT	BALANCE DEBIT	BALANCE CREDIT	
1	20–							1
2	Feb. 6		94		*DJM* 4 0 0 0 00 / 4 0 0 0 00	*DJM*	25 6 0 0 00 / 29 2 0 0 00	2

ACCOUNT **Professional Fees** ACCOUNT NO. **411**

Correcting Entry Method—Manual or Computerized

OBJECTIVE 5

Correct entries using the manual or computerized correcting entry method.

You should use the correcting entry method when incorrectly journalized amounts have been posted. There are two manual correcting entry methods; they are

1. One-step method. Simply make one entry that undoes the error and provides the correct account.
2. Two-step method. The first step reverses the error made by the original entry. The second step includes the correct entry.

The correcting entry should *always* include an explanation. For example, on January 9, a $620 payment for advertising was incorrectly journalized and posted as a debit to Miscellaneous Expense for $620 and a credit to Cash for $620. Following the one-step method, the entry would be:

	DATE		DESCRIPTION	POST. REF.	DEBIT	CREDIT	
1	20–						1
2	Jan.	27	Advertising Expense		6 2 0 00		2
3			Miscellaneous Expense			6 2 0 00	3
4			To correct error of January 9				4
5			in which a payment for				5
6			Advertising Expense was				6
7			debited to Miscellaneous				7
8			Expense.				8

Following the two-step method, if the original entry was recorded as a debit to Miscellaneous Expense and a credit to Cash, then reverse this entry by debiting Cash and crediting Miscellaneous Expense, and then record the correct entry.

	DATE		DESCRIPTION	POST. REF.	DEBIT	CREDIT	
1	20–						1
2	Jan.	27	Cash		6 2 0 00		2
3			Miscellaneous Expense			6 2 0 00	3
4			To reverse out an incorrect				4
5			entry recorded January 9.				5
6							6

	DATE		DESCRIPTION	POST. REF.	DEBIT	CREDIT	
1	20–						1
2	Jan.	27	Advertising Expense		6 2 0 00		2
3			Cash			6 2 0 00	3
4			To correct error of January 9				4
5			in which a payment for				5
6			Advertising Expense was				6
7			debited to Miscellaneous				7
8			Expense.				8

Correcting Errors on the Computer Again, never delete an error; most commercial programs will not allow deletion because if you could delete an entry, it would destroy the audit trail that tracks the life of each transaction. The procedure is to make a correcting entry with a brief and appropriate explanation followed by posting.

After the correcting entry has been journalized, the accounts are posted as for any other entry. After posting, the account balances should be correct.

CHAPTER REVIEW

Online Study Center
ACE the test!

Review of Performance Objectives

1. Record a group of transactions pertaining to a service enterprise in a two-column general journal.

Based on source documents, the transactions are analyzed to determine the accounts involved and whether the accounts are debited or credited. For each transaction, total debits must equal total credits. The journal is a book of original entry in which a day-by-day record of business transactions is maintained. The parts of a journal entry consist of the transaction date, the title of the account(s) debited, the title of the account(s) credited, the amounts recorded in the Debit and Credit columns, and an explanation.

2. Post entries from a two-column general journal to general ledger accounts.

The ledger is a book that contains all the accounts, arranged according to the chart of accounts. Posting is the process of transferring information from the journal to the ledger accounts. The posting process consists of four steps:

1. Write the date of the transaction in the account's Date column.
2. Write the amount of the transaction in the Debit or Credit column, and enter the new balance in the Balance columns under Debit or Credit.
3. Write the page number of the journal in the Post. Ref. column of the ledger account.
4. Record the ledger account number in the Post. Ref. column of the journal.

3. Prepare a trial balance from the ledger accounts.

The trial balance consists of a listing of account balances in two columns, one labeled Debit and one labeled Credit. The balances come from the ledger accounts.

4. Correct entries using the manual ruling method.

The ruling method can be used if an error is discovered before or after an entry has been posted. Draw a line through the incorrect account title or amount, and write the correct account title or amount immediately above. Include your initials with the correction.

5. Correct entries using the manual or computerized correcting entry method.

This method is used if an error is discovered after an incorrectly journalized entry has been posted. If the error consists of the wrong account(s), an entry is made to cancel out or reverse the incorrect account(s) and insert the correct account(s). Initial the correction.

Glossary

Account numbers The numbers assigned to accounts according to the chart of accounts. (79)

Cost principle The principle that a purchased asset should be recorded at its actual cost. (74)

Cross-reference The ledger account number in the Post. Ref. column of the journal and the journal page number in the Post. Ref. column of the ledger account. (81)

General ledger A loose-leaf book containing the activity (by accounts) of a business. (78)

Journal The book in which a person makes the original record of a business transaction; commonly referred to as a *book of original entry*. (70)

Journalizing The process of recording a business transaction in a journal. (70)

Ledger account A complete record of the transactions recorded in an individual account. (78)

Posting The process of transferring figures from the journal to the ledger accounts. (78)

Source documents Business papers, such as checks, invoices, receipts, letters, and memos, that furnish proof that a transaction has taken place. (70)

Two-column general journal A general journal in which there are two amount columns, one used for debit amounts and one used for credit amounts. (70)

QUESTIONS, EXERCISES, AND CASES

Discussion Questions

1. Why is the journal called a book of original entry?
2. How does the journal differ from the ledger?
3. What is the purpose of providing a ledger account for each account?
4. List by account classification the order of the accounts in the general ledger.
5. Arrange the following steps in the posting process in correct order:
   a. Write the ledger account number in the Post. Ref. column of the journal.
   b. Write the amount of the transaction.
   c. Write the date of the transaction.
   d. Write the page number of the journal in the Post. Ref. column of the ledger account.
6. What does cross-referencing mean in the posting process?
7. Why is a source document important?
8. What is the first number for each of the following accounts in a chart of accounts listed by account number?
   a. Professional Fees
   b. Utilities Expense
   c. J. R. Watson, Capital
   d. Accounts Receivable
   e. Accounts Payable

Exercises

P.O. 1

Label parts of a journal entry.

Exercise 3-1 In the two-column journal below, the capital letters represent where parts of a journal entry appear. Write the numbers 1 through 8 on a piece of paper. After each number, match the capital letter where these items appear with the number of the item.

	DATE	DESCRIPTION	POST. REF.	DEBIT	CREDIT	
1	G					1
2	H I	J	O	M		2
3		K	P		N	3
4		L				4
5						5

GENERAL JOURNAL   PAGE __1__

1. Year
2. Month
3. Explanation
4. Title of account debited
5. Ledger account number of account credited
6. Amount of debit
7. Day of the month
8. Title of account credited

Exercise 3-2 Decor Services completed the following transactions. Journalize the transactions in general journal form, including brief explanations.

Oct.   7   Received cash on account from Greg Hinton, a customer, Inv. No. 312, $830.
        15   Paid on account to Madera Brothers, a creditor, $260, Ck. No. 2242.
        20   M. Kledzik, the owner, withdrew cash for personal use, $800, Ck. No. 2243.
        23   Bought store supplies for $88 and office supplies for $74 on account from Wegner Office Supply, Inv. No. 1040.
        29   M. Kledzik, the owner, invested $2,500 cash and $3,500 of her personal equipment.

Exercise 3-3 Montoya Tutoring Service completed the following transactions. Journalize the transactions in general journal form, including brief explanations.

Mar.   1   Bought equipment for $6,075 from Teaching Partners, paying $3,000 in cash and placing the balance on account, Ck. No. 3230.
        10   Paid the wages for the first week of March, $1,435, Ck. No. 3231.
        15   Sold services for cash to Chandler District, $1,330, Sales Inv. 121.
        26   Sold services on account to Clark School, $1,700, Sales Inv. 122.
        31   Paid on account to Teaching Partners, $650, Ck. No. 3232.

Exercise 3-4 The following May journal entries all involved cash.

Increases to Cash—Debits		Decreases to Cash—Credits	
5/1	9,000	5/3	800
5/9	1,800	5/8	900
5/16	4,400	5/12	2,200
5/23	900	5/25	3,600
5/30	5,200		

Post the amounts to the ledger account for Cash, Account No. 111. Assume that all transactions appeared on page 6 of the general journal.

Exercise 3-5 Arrange the following steps in the posting process in correct order:

a. The amount of the balance of the ledger account is recorded in the Debit Balance or Credit Balance column.
b. The amount of the transaction is recorded in the Debit or Credit column of the ledger account.
c. The ledger account number is recorded in the Post. Ref. column of the journal.
d. The date of the transaction is recorded in the Date column of the ledger account.
e. The page number of the journal is recorded in the Post. Ref. column of the ledger account.

Exercise 3-6 The bookkeeper for Navarro Company has prepared the following trial balance.

Navarro Company
Trial Balance
June 30, 20—

ACCOUNT NAME	DEBIT	CREDIT
Cash		2 5 0 0 00
Accounts Receivable	8 3 0 0 00	
Prepaid Insurance	6 5 0 00	
Equipment	15 3 0 0 00	
Accounts Payable		2 7 0 0 00
M. Navarro, Capital		12 5 0 0 00
M. Navarro, Drawing	4 8 9 0 00	
Professional Fees		17 5 4 0 00
Supplies Expense	6 0 0 00	
Rent Expense	5 0 0 00	
Miscellaneous Expense	1 8 0 0 00	
	32 0 4 0 00	35 2 4 0 00

The bookkeeper has asked for your help. In examining the company's journal and ledger, you discover the following errors. Use this information to construct a corrected trial balance.

a. The debits to the Cash account total $8,000, and the credits total $3,300.
b. A $500 payment to a creditor was entered in the journal correctly but was not posted to the Accounts Payable account.
c. The first two numbers in the balance of the Accounts Receivable account were transposed in copying the balance from the ledger to the trial balance.
d. The $1,500 amount withdrawn by the owner for personal use was debited to Miscellaneous Expense by mistake—it was correctly credited to Cash.

P.O. 4,5

Determine the effect of errors.

Exercise 3-7 Determine the effect of the following errors on a company's total revenue, total expenses, and net income. Indicate the effect by writing O for "Overstated (too much)"; U for "Understated (too little)"; or NA for "Not Affected."

Transactions	Total Revenue	Total Expenses	Net Income
Example: A check for $325 was written to pay on account. The accountant debited Rent Expense for $325 and credited Cash for $325.	NA	O	U
a. $420 was received on account from customers. The accountant debited Cash for $420 and credited Professional Fees for $420.			
b. The owner withdrew $1,200 for personal use. The accountant debited Wages Expense for $1,200 and credited Cash for $1,200.			
c. A check was written for $1,250 to pay the rent. The accountant debited Rent Expense for $1,520 and credited Cash for $1,520.			
d. $1,800 was received on account from customers. The accountant debited Cash for $1,800 and credited the Capital account for $1,800.			
e. A check was written for $225 to pay the phone bill received and recorded earlier in the month. The accountant debited Phone Expense for $225 and credited Cash for $225.			

P.O. 4,5

Journalize correcting entries.

Exercise 3-8 Journalize correcting entries for each of the following errors and include a brief explanation.

a. A cash purchase of office equipment for $710 was journalized as a cash purchase of store equipment for $710. (Use the ruling method; assume the entry has not been posted.)

b. An entry for a $150 payment for office supplies was journalized as $510. (Use the ruling method; assume the entry has not been posted.)

c. A $520 payment for repairs was journalized and posted as a debit to Equipment instead of a debit to Repair Expense. (Use the correcting entry method to journalize the correction.)

d. A $650 bill for vehicle insurance was received and immediately paid. It was journalized and posted as $560. (Use the correcting entry method to journalize the correction.)

You have just learned how transactions are recorded in a general journal and then posted to the general ledger. Now, let's go back and apply this to Peyton Manning and his salary. He earned $35,037,700 in 2004!

Questions

1. If you were Manning's bookkeeper, how would you record the salary he earned for the year 2004 (assuming he gets it all in one paycheck)?

2. Now, let's look at this transaction from the giving end instead of the receiving end. If you were a bookkeeper for the Indianapolis Colts, show how you would record the payment made to Manning for his 2004 salary.

3. You probably need a reality check about now. How much *does* a professional athlete (this means the average person, not Peyton Manning) earn? To find out, go to **http://www.collegegrad.com/salaries/salaries.shtml** (or **http://www.collegegrad.com** and select Salaries and then Salary Calculator). In the Salary Wizard, select Sports and Recreation from the Job Category drop-down menu. Then, from the State/Metro Area drop-down menu, choose a listed location that is near you and click the Search button. When the search results appear, scroll through the list to find the professional athlete listing and click on Base Pay for salary information. What is the median pay indicated?

CONSIDER AND COMMUNICATE

You are the new bookkeeper in a small business. The bookkeeper whose job you are taking is training you on the business's manual system. As he journalizes, he writes the account number into the Post. Ref. column because he thinks it's easier. Then, when he posts, he won't have to be bothered writing the account numbers. How would you explain why he should *not* write the account number in the Post. Ref. column immediately and should instead enter the account number after he has posted the amount to the ledger?

CRITICAL THINKING

You work as an accounting clerk. You have received the following information supplied by a client, S. Williamson, from the client's bank statement, the client's tax returns, and a variety of other July documents. The client wants you to prepare an income statement, a statement of owner's equity, and a balance sheet for the month of July for Williamson Company.

Income from Services	8,570	Wages Expense	3,230
Beginning Capital	48,000	Utilities Expense	525
Cash	22,340	Drawing	1,200
Truck	?	Supplies Expense	612
Accounts Payable	?	Equipment	16,148
Rent Expense	1,100	Total Liabilities and Owner's Equity	54,238

PROBLEM SET A

For additional help, see the demonstration problem at the beginning of each chapter in your Working Papers.

P.O. 1

Problem 3-1A The chart of accounts of the Barkley School is shown here, followed by the transactions that took place during October of this year:

Assets

111 Cash
113 Accounts Receivable
115 Prepaid Insurance
124 Equipment
127 Furniture

Liabilities

221 Accounts Payable

Owner's Equity

311 R. Barkley, Capital
312 R. Barkley, Drawing

Revenue

411 Tuition Income

Expenses

511 Salary Expense
512 Rent Expense
513 Gas and Oil Expense
514 Advertising Expense
515 Repair Expense
516 Telephone Expense
517 Utilities Expense
529 Miscellaneous Expense

Oct.		
	1	Bought liability insurance for one year, $1,450, Ck. No. 1527.
	3	Received a bill for advertising from *Business Highlights*, $320.
	4	Paid the rent for the current month, $890, Ck. No. 1528.
	7	Received a bill for equipment repair from Speedy Service, $288, Inv. 436.
	10	Received and deposited tuition from students, $6,250.
	11	Received and paid the telephone bill, $230, Ck. No. 1529.
	15	Bought desks and chairs from Oakley Furniture Company, $1,880, paying $880 in cash and placing the balance on account, Ck. No. 1530.
	18	Paid on account to *Business Highlights*, a creditor, $320, Ck. No. 1531.
	21	R. Barkley withdrew $800 for personal use, Ck. No. 1532.
	24	Received a bill for gas and oil from West's Oil Company, $180, Inv. 682.
	25	Received and deposited tuition from students, $6,140.

Oct. 27 Paid the salary of the office assistant, $1,200, Ck. No. 1533.
28 Bought a photocopier on account from Crest Office Machines, $750, Inv. 417.
29 Received $700 tuition from a student who had charged the tuition on account last month.
30 Received and paid the bill for utilities, $360, Ck. No. 1534.
31 Paid for flower arrangements for front office, $62, Ck. No. 1535.
31 R. Barkley invested his personal computer and printer, with a fair market value of $1,230, in the business.

Instructions

Record these transactions in the general journal, including a brief explanation for each entry. Number the journal pages 31 and 32.

P.O. 2,3

Problem 3-2A The journal entries for August, Casey's Car Care's second month of business, have been journalized in the general journal in your Working Papers. The balances of the accounts as of July 31 have been recorded in the general ledger in your Working Papers. Notice the word *Balance* in the Item column, the check mark in the Post. Ref. column, and that the amount is in the Balance column only.

Check Figure

Net Income, $9,333

Instructions

1. Write the owner's name, M. Casey, in the Capital and Drawing accounts.
2. Post the general journal entries to the general ledger accounts.
3. Prepare a trial balance as of August 31, 20—.
4. Prepare an income statement for the two months ended August 31, 20—.
5. Prepare a statement of owner's equity for the two months ended August 31, 20—.
6. Prepare a balance sheet as of August 31, 20—.

P.O. 1,2,3

Problem 3-3A Following is the chart of accounts of the C. Elson Clinic.

Assets

111 Cash
113 Accounts Receivable
117 Prepaid Insurance
124 Equipment

Liabilities

221 Accounts Payable

Owner's Equity

311 C. Elson, Capital
312 C. Elson, Drawing

Revenue

411 Professional Fees

Expenses

511 Salary Expense
512 Rent Expense
513 Laboratory Expense
514 Utilities Expense
515 Supplies Expense

Dr. Elson completed the following transactions during July:

July 1 Bought laboratory equipment on account from BLM Surgical Supply Company, $3,580, paying $1,500 in cash and placing the remainder on account, Ck. No. 1730.
3 Paid the office rent for the current month, $1,100, Ck. No. 1731.
5 Received cash on account from patients, $850 (temporary abnormal balance).
6 Bought supplies on account from McReady Supply Company, $218, Inv. 3455.
7 Received and paid the bill for laboratory services, $1,110, Ck. No. 1732.

July   8   Bought insurance for one year, $1,400, Ck. No. 1733.
12   Performed medical services for patients on account, $4,990.
15   Performed medical services for patients for cash, $3,320.
16   The equipment purchased on July 1 was found to be broken. Dr. Elson returned the damaged part and received a reduction in his bill, $415, Inv. 3162, Credit Memo No. 141. (Credit Equipment.)
18   Paid the salary of the part-time nurse, $1,200, Ck. No. 1734.
24   Received and paid the telephone bill for the month, $252, Ck. No. 1735.
28   Performed medical services for patients on account, $6,250.
29   Dr. Elson withdrew cash for his personal use, $1,600, Ck. No. 1736.

Check Figure

Trial balance total, $59,265

Instructions

1. Journalize the transactions for July in the general journal, beginning on page 21.
2. Write the name of the owner next to the Capital and Drawing accounts in the general ledger. The balances of the accounts as of June 30 have been recorded in the general ledger in your Working Papers. Notice the word *Balance* in the Item column, the check mark in the Post. Ref. column, and that the amount is in the Balance column only. This indicates a balance brought forward from a prior page or month.
3. Post the entries to the general ledger accounts.
4. Prepare a trial balance.

Instructions for General Ledger Software

1. Journalize the transactions in the general journal.
2. Post the entries to the general ledger.
3. Print a trial balance as of July 31.

P.O. 1,2,3

Problem 3-4A Robbin's Landscaping Service has the following chart of accounts:

Assets

111 Cash
113 Accounts Receivable
117 Prepaid Insurance
124 Equipment

Liabilities

221 Accounts Payable

Owner's Equity

311 J. Robbin, Capital
312 J. Robbin, Drawing

Revenue

411 Landscaping Income

Expenses

511 Salary Expense
512 Rent Expense
513 Gas and Oil Expense
514 Utilities Expense
515 Supplies Expense

The following transactions were completed by Robbin's Landscaping Service:

Mar.   1   Robbin deposited $20,000 in a bank account in the name of the business.
4   Robbin invested her personal gardening equipment, with a fair market value of $1,000, in the business.
6   Bought a used trailer on account from Roth Sales, $850, Inv. 314.
7   Paid the rent for the current month, $600, Ck. No. 1000.
9   Bought a used backhoe from Mobile Equipment, $6,200, paying $3,000 in cash and placing the balance on account, Inv. 4166, Ck. No. 1001.

Mar.   10   Bought liability insurance for one year, $900, Ck. No. 1002.

13   Sold landscaping services on account to Franklin's, $3,420, Inv. 100.

14   Bought supplies on account from Office Decor, $240, Inv. 5172.

15   Sold landscaping services on account to C. Clayton, $2,560, Inv. 101.

17   Received and paid the bill from Engine Services for gas and oil for the equipment, $140, Ck. No. 1003.

19   Sold landscaping services for cash to Cass Company, $1,880, Inv. 102.

22   Paid on account to Roth Sales, a creditor, $400, Inv. 314, Ck. No. 1004.

24   Received on account from Franklin's, a customer, $700, Inv. 100.

28   Sold landscaping services on account to Simpson, Inc., $1,625, Inv. 103.

29   Received and paid the telephone bill, $186, Ck. No. 1005.

30   Paid the salary of the employee, $1,340, Ck. No. 1006.

31   Robbin withdrew cash for her personal use, $1,400, Ck. No. 1007.

Check Figure

Trial balance total, $34,375

Instructions

1. Journalize the transactions in the general journal, beginning on page 1. Write a brief explanation for each entry.
2. Write the name of the owner on the Capital and Drawing accounts.
3. Post the journal entries to the general ledger accounts.
4. Prepare a trial balance dated March 31, 20—.

PROBLEM SET B

For additional help, see the demonstration problem at the beginning of each chapter in your Working Papers.

P.O. 1

Problem 3-1B The chart of accounts of Edgar Academy is shown here, followed by the transactions that took place during December of this year:

Assets

111 Cash
113 Accounts Receivable
115 Prepaid Insurance
124 Equipment
127 Furniture

Liabilities

221 Accounts Payable

Owner's Equity

311 R. Edgar, Capital
312 R. Edgar, Drawing

Revenue

411 Tuition Income

Expenses

511 Salary Expense
512 Rent Expense
513 Gas and Oil Expense
514 Advertising Expense
515 Repair Expense
516 Telephone Expense
517 Utilities Expense
518 Supplies Expense
529 Miscellaneous Expense

Dec.   1   Bought liability insurance for one year, $1,260, Ck. No. 1627.

11   Received a bill for advertising from the *District News*, $370, Statement No. 4267.

12   Paid the rent for the current month, $950, Ck. No. 1628.

13   Received a bill for equipment repair from Electrician's Services, $360, Inv. 547.

Dec.	16	Received and deposited tuition from students, $4,860.
	17	Received and paid the telephone bill, $292, Ck. No. 1629.
	18	Bought desks and chairs from Classroom Furniture, $1,520, paying $700 in cash and placing the balance on account, Ck. No. 1630.
	20	Paid on account to the *District News*, a creditor, $370, Statement No. 4267, Ck. No. 1631.
	21	R. Edgar withdrew $900 for personal use, Ck. No. 1632.
	26	Received a bill for gas and oil from Cheapest Oil Company, $194, Inv. 591.
	27	Received and deposited tuition from students, $5,672.
	31	Paid the salary of the office assistant, $975, Ck. No. 1633.
	31	Bought a fax machine on account from OfficeCo, $192, Inv. 529.
	31	Received $910 tuition from a student who had put the tuition on account last month.
	31	Received and paid the bill for utilities, $448, Ck. No. 1634.
	31	R. Edgar invested her personal computer and printer, with a fair market value of $1,275, in the business.
	31	Bought supplies, $284, Ck. No. 1635.

Instructions

Record these transactions in the general journal, including a brief explanation for each entry. Number the journal pages 31 and 32.

P.O. 2,3

Problem 3-2B The journal entries for May, Petite Day Care's second month of business, have been journalized in the general journal in your Working Papers. The balances of the accounts as of April 30 have been recorded in the general ledger in your Working Papers. Notice the word *Balance* in the Item column, the check mark in the Post. Ref. column, and that the amount is in the Balance column only. This indicates a balance brought forward from a prior page or month.

Check Figure

Net Income, $4,994

Instructions

1. Write the owner's name, R. Ochoa, in the Capital and Drawing accounts.
2. Post the general journal entries to the general ledger accounts.
3. Prepare a trial balance as of May 31, 20—.
4. Prepare an income statement for the two months ended May 31, 20—.
5. Prepare a statement of owner's equity for the two months ended May 31, 20—.
6. Prepare a balance sheet as of May 31, 20—.

P.O. 1,2,3

Problem 3-3B Following is the chart of accounts of D. Roe, M.D.

Assets

111 Cash
113 Accounts Receivable
117 Prepaid Insurance
124 Equipment

Liabilities

221 Accounts Payable

Owner's Equity

311 D. Roe, Capital
312 D. Roe, Drawing

Revenue

411 Professional Fees

Expenses

511 Salary Expense
512 Rent Expense
513 Laboratory Expense
514 Utilities Expense
515 Supplies Expense

Dr. Roe completed the following transactions during July:

July 1 Bought laboratory equipment on account from Seger Surgical Supply Company, $6,430, paying $1,530 in cash and placing the remainder on account, Inv. 2071, Ck. No. 1930.
3 Paid the office rent for the current month, $1,250, Ck. No. 1931.
5 Received cash on account from patients, $2,753.
6 Bought supplies on account from Regan Supply, $290, Inv. 3455.
9 Received and paid the bill for laboratory services, $995, Ck. No. 1932.
10 Bought insurance for one year, $1,600, Ck. No. 1933.
12 Performed medical services for patients on account, $4,875.
14 Performed medical services for patients for cash, $3,723.
18 Part of the equipment purchased on July 1 was found to be broken. Dr. Roe returned the damaged part and received a reduction in her bill, $368, Inv. 2071, Credit Memo No. 218. (Credit Equipment.)
20 Paid the salary of the part-time nurse, $1,075, Ck. No. 1934.
22 Received and paid the telephone bill for the month, $235, Ck. No. 1935.
24 Performed medical services for patients on account, $3,857.
30 Dr. Roe withdrew cash for her personal use, $1,400, Ck. No. 1936.

Check Figure

Trial balance total, $43,925

Instructions

1. Journalize the transactions for July in the general journal, beginning on page 21.
2. Write the name of the owner next to the Capital and Drawing accounts in the general ledger. The balances of the accounts as of June 30 have been recorded in the general ledger in your Working Papers. Notice the word *Balance* in the Item column, the check mark in the Post. Ref. column, and that the amount is in the Balance column only. This indicates a balance brought forward from a prior page or month.
3. Post the entries to the general ledger accounts.
4. Prepare a trial balance.

Instructions for General Ledger Software

1. Journalize the transactions in the general journal.
2. Post the entries to the general ledger.
3. Print a trial balance as of July 31.

P.O. 1,2,3

Problem 3-4B Lara's Landscaping Service maintains the following chart of accounts.

Assets

111 Cash
113 Accounts Receivable
117 Prepaid Insurance
124 Equipment

Liabilities

221 Accounts Payable

Owner's Equity

311 J. Lara, Capital
312 J. Lara, Drawing

Revenue

411 Landscaping Income

Expenses

511 Salary Expense
512 Rent Expense
513 Gas and Oil Expense
514 Utilities Expense
515 Supplies Expense

The following transactions were completed by Lara:

Apr.   1   Lara deposited $20,000 in a bank account in the name of the business.

4   Lara invested his personal gardening equipment, with a fair market value of $1,600, in the business.

6   Bought a used trailer on account from Trailer Sales, $1,800, Inv. 415.

7   Paid the rent for the current month, $510, Ck. No. 100.

9   Bought a used bulldozer from Digger's Equipment, $11,000, paying $3,000 in cash and placing the balance on account, Inv. 3255, Ck. No. 101.

10   Bought liability insurance for one year, $800, Ck. No. 102.

13   Sold landscaping services on account to Felton Homes, $4,253, Inv. 100.

14   Bought supplies on account from Padilla Supply, $318, Inv. 4281.

15   Sold landscaping services on account to Britton Inc., $3,878, Inv. 101.

17   Received and paid the bill from The Tanks for gas and oil for the equipment, $105, Ck. No. 103.

19   Sold landscaping services for cash to Scheck Company, $1,214, Inv. 102.

22   Paid on account to Trailer Sales, a creditor, $600, Inv. 415, Ck. No. 104.

24   Received on account from Felton Homes, a customer, $700, Inv. 100.

28   Sold landscaping services on account to Lester Inc., $1,820, Inv. 103.

29   Received and paid the telephone bill, $238, Ck. No. 105.

30   Paid the salary of the employee, $1,650, Ck. No. 106.

30   Lara withdrew cash for his personal use, $1,800, Ck. No. 107.

Check Figure

Trial balance total, $42,283

Instructions

1. Journalize the transactions in the general journal, beginning on page 1. Write a brief explanation for each entry.
2. Write the name of the owner on the Capital and Drawing accounts.
3. Post the journal entries to the general ledger accounts.
4. Prepare a trial balance dated April 30, 20—.

The Computer Clinic

Meet the owner.

Determine owner's needs.

Gather information and make assessment.

Journalizing, Posting, and Preparing a Trial Balance

A friend of yours, Anika Valli, has decided to open a spa to serve her small resort town of about 7,000 people and 4 million tourists annually. She has named the business All About You Spa to convey the idea that the business intends to pamper those who enter its doors. She will operate the spa five days a week, Tuesday through Saturday, but a phone line will always be available to answer questions and take appointments. Hours will be from 8 A.M. to 8 P.M. She has asked you to be the bookkeeper for this new business. At the end of the month of June, the owner, Anika Valli, would like you to provide the following:

1. General journal
2. General ledger
3. Trial balance
4. Income statement
5. Statement of owner's equity
6. Balance sheet

She has kept a checkbook and a file folder with summary evidence of June's spa activity: a check register, a summary report of charges by customers for services provided, all receipts that were issued, and a summary of charges made by All About You Spa. Most of the income from services is received in cash and as charges to credit cards. No checks are accepted, except from approved clients (primarily conference planners and other organizations that book packages as prizes for attendees or gifts for employees, speakers, or other people they want to thank with a spa service or package of services). Anika deposits cash receipts on the 7th, 14th, 21st, and last day of each month.

The first page in the file folder contains the following chart of accounts.

Chart of Accounts for All About You Spa

111 Cash	411 Income from Services
113 Accounts Receivable	
117 Prepaid Insurance	511 Wages Expense
124 Spa Equipment	512 Rent Expense
128 Office Equipment	513 Office Supplies Expense
	514 Spa Supplies Expense
211 Accounts Payable	515 Laundry Expense
	516 Advertising Expense
311 A. Valli, Capital	517 Utilities Expense
312 A. Valli, Drawing	530 Miscellaneous Expense

Clipped to the front of the file folder is a brochure listing the services of All About You Spa. Part of the brochure is shown on the next page.

All About You Spa Services

Massages

Type	Time	Description	Price
Deep-Tissue Destresser	90 min.	Vigorous, prescriptive	$90.00
Herbal Body Sea Wrap	90 min.	Gentle, cleansing	$90.00
Aromatherapy Healing Experience	90 min.	Gentle, relaxing	$90.00
Healing Stones Experience	90 min.	Healing, relaxing	$90.00
Post-Workout Massage	90 min.	Invigorating, prescriptive	$90.00
Exfoliating Ginger and Sea Salt Scrub	90 min.	Cleansing, invigorating	$90.00
Custom Massage	60 min.	Highlights problem areas	$60.00

Other Spa Experiences

Type	Time	Description	Price
Reflexology Points Experience	60 min.	Problem areas, relaxing	$60.00
Reiki Healing Experience	60 min.	Full body, relaxing	$60.00
All About You Women's Facial	60 min.	Relaxing, individualized	$60.00
All About You Men's Facial	60 min.	Relaxing, individualized	$60.00
All About You Pedicure	60 min.	Beautifying, relaxing	$60.00
Day of Beauty	Full day or Half day	Let us help you select a memorable combination of services.	
Body Analysis and Consultation	60 min.	Informative, prescriptive	$60.00
All About You Makeup Consultation	60 min.	Beautifying, individualized	$60.00

Packages and Gift Certificates

Type	Time	Description	Price
Package of three 90-minute services	270 min.	Mix and match to your needs.	$250.00
Package of two 90-minute services	180 min.	Select your favorite duo.	$160.00
Package of three 60-minute services	180 min.	Mix and match to your needs.	$160.00
Package of two 60-minute services	120 min.	Select your favorite duo.	$110.00
Gift certificates available at any price		Reward employees, friends, or relatives.	

WHERE TO START
Enter chart of accounts.

WHAT TO DO FIRST
Enter June's transactions from documents and/or input form.

1. Load and log into your general ledger software.
2. Enter the chart of accounts. In future chapters, other accounts will have to be added as you need them.
3. There are no beginning balances since this is a new business.
4. Journalize and post the transactions prompted by the following documents (save often):

   a. Checkbook entries (deposits made and checks written)

Check No.	Date	Explanation	√	Deposits	Check Amount
	6/1	Invested cash in business.		15,000.00	
1011	6/3	Bought 6-month liability insurance policy.			960.00
1012	6/3	Bought spa equipment for $4,235.00, putting $2,000.00 cash down.			2,000.00
1013	6/3	Paid June rent.			1,650.00
1014	6/5	Bought office supplies.			248.00
1015	6/5	Purchased flowers and balloons for grand opening (Misc. Exp.).			112.00
1016	6/7	Paid first week's wages.			1,847.50
	6/7	Deposited first week's cash revenue.		2,630.00	
1017	6/11	Paid on account payable for spa equipment (June 3).			873.00
	6/14	Deposited second week's cash revenue.		3,703.00	
1018	6/14	Paid second week's wages.			1,847.50
1019	6/18	Paid on account payable for spa equipment (June 3).			1,200.00
	6/21	Deposited third week's cash revenue.		4,758.00	
1020	6/21	Paid third week's wages.			1,847.50
1021	6/25	Paid on account payable for spa equipment (June 3).			73.00
1022	6/28	Paid fourth week's wages.			1,847.50
1023	6/28	Paid month's laundry bill.			84.00
	6/30	Deposited end of month's cash revenue.		5,992.00	
1024	6/30	A. Valli withdrew $1,850 for personal use.			1,850.00
1025	6/30	Paid June telephone bill.			225.00
1026	6/30	Paid June power and water bill.			248.00

b. Other documents that also require journal entries:

Receipt: 6/1

A. Valli, owner of All
About You Spa, invested
her personal spa equipment
valued at $3,158.00.

June Accounts Payable Charges Summary Report:

6/3 Bought spa supplies on account from Spa Supplies, Inv. 804	$492.00
6/5 Bought office equipment on account from Office Equipment, Inv. 3415	$318.00
6/5 Bought advertising pamphlets on account from Adco, Inv. 512	$397.00
6/5 Bought office equipment on account from Office Equipment, Inv. 3445	$832.00
6/5 Bought office supplies on account from Office Staples, Inv. 522	$120.00

June Sales to Customers on
Account Summary Report:

6/7	Jill Anson	$325.00
6/14	Jack Morgan	$486.00
6/21	Tory Ligman	$344.00
6/28	Judy Wilcox	$109.00

WHAT TO DO AT THE END OF THE MONTH
Month-end wrap-up.

Check Figures

5. Trial balance total, $38,753
6. Net Income, $7,381
7. Ending balance of A. Valli, Capital, $23,689
8. Total Assets, $25,937

5. Print a trial balance dated June 30, 20—.
6. Print the income statement for the month ended June 30, 20—.
7. Print the statement of owner's equity for the month ended June 30, 20—.
8. Print the balance sheet dated June 30, 20—.

Note: The trial balance and financial statements are unadjusted. In the next chapter, you will learn that certain accounts need to be adjusted. These adjustments will change some of the figures in these reports.

PART I: Multiple-Choice Questions

_____ 1. Which of the following is not considered an account?

    a. Cash
    b. Prepaid Insurance
    c. Equipment
    d. Assets
    e. Accounts Receivable

_____ 2. In which of the following transactions would an expense be recorded?

    a. Received a bill for advertising.
    b. Paid on an account payable for the utility bill.
    c. Received and paid a bill for repairs.
    d. All of these should be recorded as an expense.
    e. Only a and c should be recorded as an expense.

_____ 3. The ending capital balance appears on which of the following statements?

    a. Statement of owner's equity
    b. Balance sheet
    c. Income statement
    d. Statement of owner's equity and balance sheet
    e. Statement of owner's equity and income statement

_____ 4. On a statement of owner's equity, if beginning capital is $42,000 and there are an additional investment of $5,000, a net loss of $9,000, and owner withdrawals of $15,000, the ending capital amount would be

    a. $70,000.
    b. $23,000.
    c. $40,000.
    d. $54,000.
    e. none of these.

_____ 5. If a $26 cash purchase of supplies is recorded as a $62 debit to Supplies Expense and a $62 credit to Cash, the result will be that

    a. the trial balance will be in balance.
    b. the Supplies Expense account will be overstated.
    c. the Cash account will be understated.
    d. Supplies Expense will be overstated and Cash will be understated.
    e. all of these will be true.

Note: Answers to Before a Test Check begin on page A-1.

_____ 6. A person who wanted to know the balance of an account would look in

    a. the ledger.
    b. the chart of accounts.
    c. the journal.
    d. the source documents.
    e. none of these.

PART II: The Accounting Cycle

Journalizing, Posting, Trial Balance, and Financial Statements

The accounts and their balances, as of December 1 of this year, for Antec Services are listed below:

111	Cash	$18,900	311 J. Dunn, Capital	$49,590
113	Accounts Receivable	6,300	312 J. Dunn, Drawing	11,200
116	Prepaid Insurance	1,230	411 Service Income	39,600
124	Equipment	31,200	511 Wages Expense	10,450
221	Accounts Payable	6,340	512 Utilities Expense	2,760
			513 Rent Expense	12,620
			514 Supplies Expense	870

Check Figure

Net Income, $21,153

Instructions

1. Journalize the following December transactions in general journal form on journal page 31.

    Dec. 1 Sold services for cash, $9,500.
          4 Received and paid the bill for the rent for December, $1,000, Ck. No. 2331.
        11 Received $1,750 on account from customers, Cash Receipt Nos. 1430–1438.
        19 Sold services on account, $2,075, Sales Inv. No. 2591.
        22 Received and paid the bill for utilities, $255, Ck. No. 2332.
        23 Bought supplies on account from Office Works, $292, Inv. No. 2606.
        31 Paid the wages for the month, $1,775, Ck. No. 2333.
        31 Dunn withdrew $1,500 for personal use, Ck. No. 2334.

2. Label T accounts with the above account names.

3. Correctly place the plus and minus signs under all T accounts, and label the debit and credit sides of each T account.

4. Post the entries to the T accounts by date, and foot and balance the accounts.

5. Prepare a trial balance as of December 31.

6. Prepare an income statement for the year ended December 31.

7. Prepare a statement of owner's equity for the year ended December 31.

8. Prepare a balance sheet as of December 31.

internet
LINKS TO ACCOUNTING

Whether a small company is doing all its accounting work manually or a large corporation is using a general ledger software package, the process of transforming the information in a company's accounting records into financial statements is the same. Take for instance Activision, a leading producer of video games for systems such as Sony's PlayStation®2, Microsoft's Xbox™, and Nintendo's GameCube™ and Game Boy® Advance. Activision's annual report for 2005 can be viewed at **http://investor.activision.com/reports.cfm**. Find Activision's balance sheet on page 54 of the annual report. The company reports its property and equipment value as Property and Equipment, net. What does this mean? Review Note 7, Property and Equipment, in the Notes to Consolidated Financial Statements, which begin on page 59. What was the total cost of Activision's property and equipment as of March 31, 2005? How much depreciation had accumulated? As you learn about adjustments for depreciation of equipment, think about the steps that Activision took to determine the amounts reported on the balance sheet in its 2005 annual report. The company used the same process you will learn about here.

In this chapter you will also learn about fiscal periods. After you read about fiscal periods, find out when Activision's fiscal year begins and ends. Where do you find this information in the annual report?

Performance Objectives

After you have completed this chapter, you will be able to do the following:

1. Define *fiscal period* and *fiscal year*.

2. List the classifications of the accounts that occupy each column of a ten-column work sheet.

3. Complete a work sheet for a service enterprise, involving adjustments for expired insurance, depreciation, and accrued wages.

4. Prepare an income statement, a statement of owner's equity, and a balance sheet for a service business directly from the work sheet.

5. Journalize and post the adjusting entries.

6. Prepare (a) an income statement involving more than one revenue account and a net loss, (b) a statement of owner's equity with an additional investment and either a net income or a net loss, (c) a balance sheet for a business having more than one accumulated depreciation account, and (d) a balance sheet containing the statement of owner's equity information.

REMEMBER!

Accounting steps:

Analyzing: Which accounts are involved?

Classifying: assets, liabilities, capital, revenue, and expenses

Recording: journalizing

Summarizing: financial statements

Interpreting: drawing conclusions

As part of the *summarizing* step in the definition of accounting, here we introduce the work sheet and the financial statements. Now that you are familiar with the classifying and recording phases of accounting for a service business, let's look at the remaining steps in the accounting process.

FISCAL PERIOD

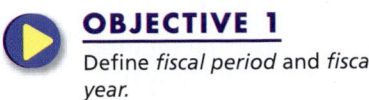

OBJECTIVE 1
Define *fiscal period* and *fiscal year.*

A **fiscal period** is any period of time covering a complete accounting cycle. A **fiscal year** is a fiscal period consisting of twelve consecutive months. It does not have to coincide with the calendar year. If a business has seasonal peaks, it is a good idea to complete the accounting operations at the end of the most active season. At that time, management wants to know the results of the year and where the business stands financially. The fiscal year of a resort that operates during the summer may be from October 1 of one year to September 30 of the next. The government has a fiscal year from October 1 of one year to September 30 of the following year. Department stores often use a fiscal period from February 1 of one year to January 31 of the next. For income tax purposes, any period of twelve consecutive months may be selected. However, you have to be consistent and use the same fiscal period each year.

THE ACCOUNTING CYCLE

The **accounting cycle** represents the sequence of steps in the accounting process completed during the fiscal period. Figure 1 shows how we introduce these steps on a chapter-by-chapter basis. This outline brings you up to date on what we have accomplished so far and how each chapter fits into the steps in the accounting cycle.

FIGURE 1

REMEMBER!

The yellow color represents source documents, which are evidence of transactions.

Chapter 1
> Analysis of Business Transactions
> Assets = Liabilities + Owner's Equity
> Analysis of Business Transactions
> Assets = Liabilities + Owner's Equity + Revenue − Expenses

Chapter 2
> Analysis of Business Transactions
> Assets = Liabilities + Owner's Equity + Revenue − Expenses
> $\overline{+|-}$ $\overline{-|+}$ $\overline{-|+}$ $\overline{-|+}$ $\overline{+|-}$

Chapter 3
> Journalize and Post Business Transactions.
> Prepare a Trial Balance.

Chapter 4
> Gather the Adjustment Data.
> Complete a Work Sheet.
> Prepare Financial Statements.
> Journalize and Post Adjusting Entries.

Chapter 5
> Journalize and Post Closing Entries.
> Prepare a Post-Closing Trial Balance.

THE WORK SHEET

FYI

The use of computerized accounting software can eliminate the preparation of the work sheet, which can be prepared manually or electronically. It does not, however, eliminate the journalizing and posting of the adjusting entries.

The **work sheet** is a working paper used by accountants to record necessary adjustments and provide up-to-date account balances needed to prepare the financial statements. **The work sheet is a tool that accountants use to help in preparing the financial statements.** As a tool, the work sheet serves as a central place for bringing together the information needed to record the adjustments. With up-to-date account balances, the accountant can prepare the financial statements.

First, we present the work sheet form so that you can see the big picture. Next, we describe and show examples of adjustments. Finally, we show how the adjustments are entered on the work sheet and how the work sheet is completed.

We will use a ten-column work sheet—so called because two amount columns are provided for each of the work sheet's five major sections. We will explain the function of each of these sections, again basing our discussion on the accounting activities of Cline's Computer Clinic. But first we need to fill in the heading, which consists of three lines: (1) the name of the company, (2) the title of the working paper, and (3) the period of time covered.

Cline's Computer Clinic
Work Sheet
For Month Ended June 30, 20—

ACCOUNT NAME	TRIAL BALANCE		ADJUSTMENTS		ADJUSTED TRIAL BALANCE		INCOME STATEMENT		BALANCE SHEET	
	DEBIT	CREDIT	DEBIT	CREDIT	DEBIT	CREDIT	DEBIT	CREDIT	DEBIT	CREDIT

Next, we want to point out the account classifications that are placed in each column. We start with the Trial Balance columns and then move across the work sheet, discussing each pair of columns separately.

The Columns of the Work Sheet

OBJECTIVE 2

List the classifications of the accounts that occupy each column of a ten-column work sheet.

Trial Balance Columns   When you use a work sheet, you do not have to prepare a trial balance on a separate sheet of paper. Instead, you enter the account balances from the general ledger in the first two amount columns of the work sheet. List the accounts that have balances in the Account Name column in the same order in which they appear in the chart of accounts. Assuming **normal balances,** the account classifications are listed in the Trial Balance Debit and Credit columns of the work sheet as shown at the top of the next page.

As we move along in this chapter, we will discuss the adjustments. The Adjusted Trial Balance columns contain the same account classifications as the Trial Balance columns. **The Adjusted Trial Balance columns are merely extensions of the Trial Balance columns, plus or minus any adjustment amounts.** If an adjustment is required, the amounts are carried from the Trial Balance columns through the Adjustments columns and into the Adjusted Trial Balance columns.

REMEMBER!

You have already prepared a trial balance. Record the normal balances in the Trial Balance Debit or Credit column. The normal balance is the + side of any account.

Account Name	Trial Balance		Adjustments		Adjusted Trial Balance		Income Statement		Balance Sheet	
	Debit	Credit	Debit	Credit	Debit	Credit	Debit	Credit	Debit	Credit
	Assets				→Assets					
		Liabilities				→Liabilities				
		Capital				→Capital				
	Drawing				→Drawing					
		Revenue				→Revenue				
	Expenses				→Expenses					

Income Statement Columns An income statement contains the revenues minus the expenses. Revenue accounts have credit balances, so they are recorded in the Income Statement Credit column. Expense accounts have debit balances, so they are recorded in the Income Statement Debit column.

Account Name	Trial Balance		Adjustments		Adjusted Trial Balance		Income Statement		Balance Sheet	
	Debit	Credit	Debit	Credit	Debit	Credit	Debit	Credit	Debit	Credit
	Assets				→Assets					
		Liabilities				→Liabilities				
		Capital				→Capital				
	Drawing				→Drawing					
		Revenue				→Revenue	→Revenue			
	Expenses				→Expenses		→Expenses			

Balance Sheet Columns As you recall, the balance sheet is a statement showing assets, liabilities, and owner's equity. Asset accounts have debit balances, so they are recorded in the Balance Sheet Debit column. Liability accounts have credit balances, so they are recorded in the Balance Sheet Credit column. The Capital account has a credit balance, so it is recorded in the Balance Sheet Credit column. Because the Drawing account is a deduction from Capital, it has a debit balance and is recorded in the Balance Sheet Debit column (the opposite column from that in which Capital is recorded).

Account Name	Trial Balance		Adjustments		Adjusted Trial Balance		Income Statement		Balance Sheet	
	Debit	Credit	Debit	Credit	Debit	Credit	Debit	Credit	Debit	Credit
	Assets				→Assets				→Assets	
		Liabilities				→Liabilities				→Liabilities
		Capital				→Capital				→Capital
	Drawing				→Drawing				→Drawing	
		Revenue				→Revenue	→Revenue			
	Expenses				→Expenses		→Expenses			

ADJUSTMENTS

OBJECTIVE 3

Complete a work sheet for a service enterprise, involving adjustments for expired insurance, depreciation, and accrued wages.

The Financial Picture Before Adjustments

The Financial Picture After Adjustments

Without adjustments, the financial statements would be out of focus.

Adjustments are a way of updating the ledger accounts. They may be considered *internal transactions*. They have not been recorded in the accounts up to this time because no outside party has been involved. Adjustments are determined after the trial balance has been prepared. Adjustments fine-tune the accounts to present a more accurate concept of the accounts.

Only a few accounts are adjusted. To describe the reasons for making adjustments, let's return to Cline's Computer Clinic. First, we select the accounts that require adjustments. Next, we show the adjustments recorded in T accounts so you can see the effect on the accounts. **However, bear in mind that the adjustments are first recorded on the work sheet when using a manual accounting system.** When using general ledger software, adjustments are recorded in the general journal.

Prepaid Insurance

The $480 balance in Prepaid Insurance represents the premium paid in advance for a one-year liability insurance policy. One month of the twelve months of premium has now expired, which amounts to $40.

$$12 \text{ months } \overline{)\begin{array}{l} \$\ 40 \text{ per month} \\ \$480 \end{array}}$$

In the adjustment, Cline's Computer Clinic deducts the expired or used portion from Prepaid Insurance and adds it to Insurance Expense.

(a)	Prepaid Insurance				Insurance Expense		
		+	−			+	−
(Old)	Balance	480	**Adjusting** 40	**Adjusting**	40		
(New)	Balance	440					

The new balance of Prepaid Insurance, $440 ($480 − $40), represents the cost of insurance that remains paid in advance and should therefore appear in the Balance Sheet Debit column. The $40 amount in Insurance Expense represents the cost of insurance that has expired and should therefore appear in the Income Statement Debit column.

Depreciation of Equipment

We have recorded durable items, such as appliances and fixtures, under Equipment because they will last longer than one year. The benefits of these assets will eventually be used up (the assets will either wear out or become obsolete). Therefore, we should systematically spread out the cost of these assets over their useful lives. That is, we allocate the cost of the equipment as an expense *over its estimated useful life* and call this **depreciation** because such equipment loses its usefulness. A part of this depreciation expense is allotted to each fiscal period. In the case of Cline's Computer Clinic, the

REMEMBER!

When using a manual accounting system, adjustments are recorded in the work sheet first. They will be journalized and posted later in the accounting cycle.

REMEMBER!

For the adjustment of insurance, you are given the amount used (expired). So, in the adjusting entry, take the amount used directly out of Prepaid Insurance and put it into Insurance Expense.

FYI

There are several methods of depreciation for assets. Straight-line depreciation is shown here—equal amounts are taken each year. There are also accelerated methods that assign larger amounts to expense in the early years of the life of an asset.

Equipment account has a balance of $83,720. Suppose we estimate that the equipment will have a useful life of seven years, with a trade-in (salvage) value of $13,160 at the end of that time. Using **straight-line depreciation**, we can allocate the cost of an asset, less any trade-in value, evenly over the useful life of the asset. Depreciation for one month is figured like this:

1. Subtract the trade-in (salvage) value from the cost to get the full depreciation.

   $83,720 − $13,160 = $70,560

2. Divide the full depreciation by the number of years in the asset's useful life to get the depreciation for one year.

   $$\frac{\$10{,}080 \text{ per year}}{7 \text{ years })\overline{\$70{,}560 \text{ full depreciation}}}$$

3. Divide the depreciation for one year by 12 to get the depreciation for one month.

   $$\frac{\$\quad 840 \text{ per month}}{12 \text{ months })\overline{\$10{,}080}}$$

When depreciation is recorded, we do not subtract it directly from the asset account. In asset accounts, such as Equipment or Building, we must keep the original cost recorded in the account. Consequently, the amount of depreciation has to be recorded in another account; that account is Accumulated Depreciation.

Always record the adjusting entry for depreciation as a debit to Depreciation Expense (an income statement item) and a credit to Accumulated Depreciation (a balance sheet item), which increases both accounts. The adjustment in T account form would appear as follows:

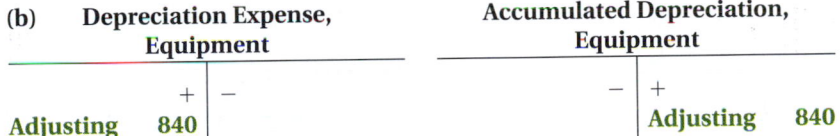

Accumulated Depreciation, Equipment, is contrary to, or a deduction from, Equipment, so we call it a **contra account**. To show the accounts under their proper headings, let's look at the fundamental accounting equation. Brackets indicate that Accumulated Depreciation, Equipment, is a deduction from the Equipment account. Note that the plus and minus signs are opposite.

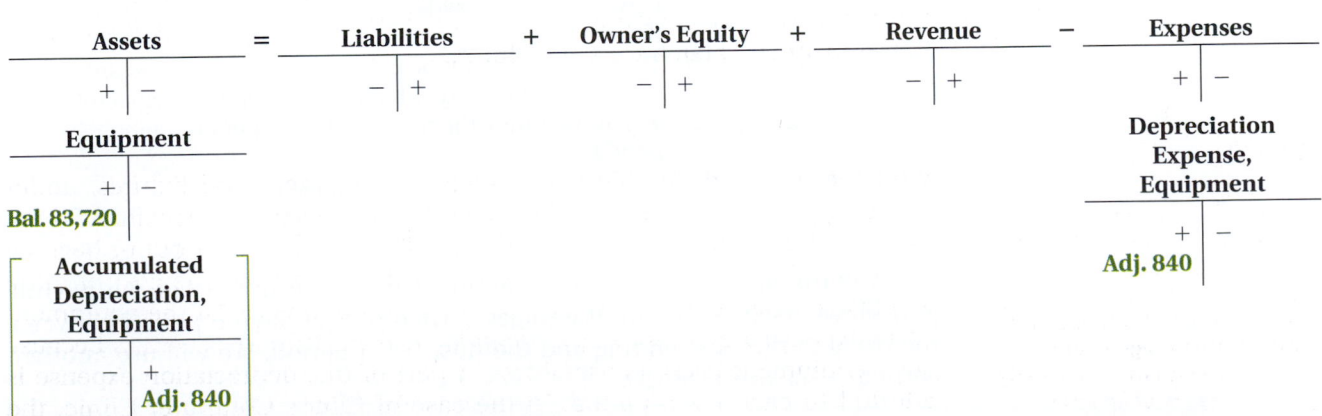

On the work sheet, Equipment (an asset) appears in the Balance Sheet Debit column. Accumulated Depreciation (a deduction from an asset) appears in the opposite column, which is the Balance Sheet Credit column.

Accumulated Depreciation, Equipment, as the title implies, is the total depreciation that the company has taken since the original purchase of the asset. Rather than crediting the Equipment account, Cline's Computer Clinic keeps track of the total depreciation taken since it first acquired the asset in a separate account. The maximum depreciation it could take would be the cost of the equipment, $83,720, less the trade-in value of $13,160. So, for the first year, Accumulated Depreciation, Equipment, will increase at the rate of $840 per month, assuming that no additional equipment has been purchased. For example, at the end of the second month, Accumulated Depreciation, Equipment, will amount to $1,680 ($840 + $840).

On the balance sheet, the balance of Accumulated Depreciation is deducted from the balance of the related asset account as illustrated on the following partial balance sheet for Cline's Computer Clinic. The net amount shown, $82,880, is referred to as the book value of the asset. Thus, **book value** (or **carrying value**) is the cost of an asset minus accumulated depreciation.

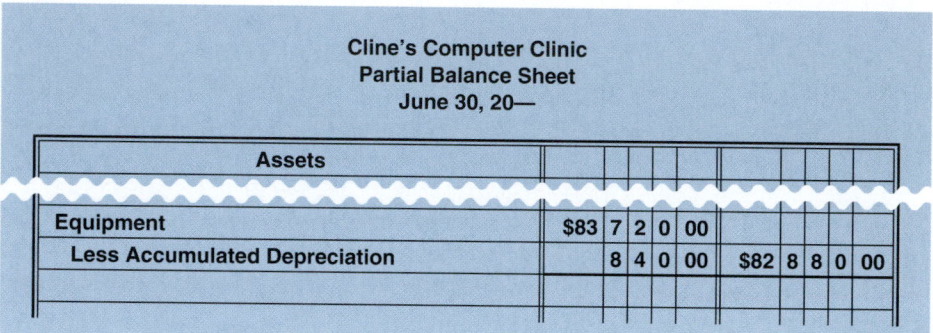

Wages Expense

The end of the fiscal period and the end of the employees' payroll period rarely fall on the same day. A diagram of the situation looks like this:

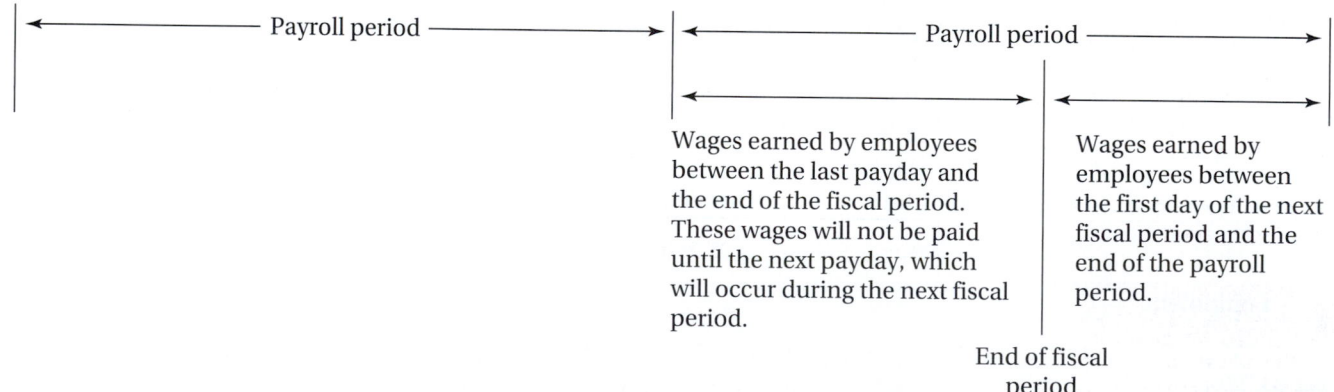

Since the last day of the fiscal period falls in the middle of the payroll period, we have to split up the wages earned in that payroll period between the fiscal period just ending and the next fiscal period. We will use another company for this example.

Assume that Brown Company pays its employees a total of $400 per day and that payday falls on Friday throughout the year. The employees work a five-day week. When the employees pick up their paychecks on Friday, the amount of the checks includes their wages for that day and for the preceding four days. Suppose that the last day of the fiscal period falls on Wednesday, December 31. The diagram below illustrates this situation.

					End of Fiscal Period				
				Dec. 26	Dec. 29	Dec. 30	Dec. 31	Jan. 1	Jan. 2
Mon	Tue	Wed	Thur	Fri	Mon	Tue	Wed	Thur	Fri
$400	$400	$400	$400	$400	$400	$400	$400	$400	$400
← Payroll period →					← Payroll period →				
				Payday $2,000					Payday $2,000
						$1,200		$800	

December						
S	M	T	W	T	F	S
	1	2	3	4	⑤	6
7	8	9	10	11	⑫	13
14	15	16	17	18	⑲	20
21	22	23	24	25	㉖	27
28	29	30	31			

— Paydays

To have the Wages Expense account show an accurate balance for the fiscal period, you need to add $1,200 for the cost of labor between the last payday, December 26, and the end of the year, December 31 ($400 for December 29; $400 for December 30; $400 for December 31). Because the $1,200 will not be paid at this time but is owed to the employees as of December 31, you also need to add $1,200 to Wages Payable, a liability account, because the company owes this amount to employees.

REMEMBER!

If the end of the fiscal period (or end of the fiscal year) occurs during the middle of a payroll period, Wages Expense must be adjusted to bring it up to date. In the adjusting entry, add the amount employees have earned between the end of the last payroll period and the end of the fiscal period.

REMEMBER!

In the adjusting entry for accrued wages, increase both the Wages Expense and the Wages Payable accounts.

Wages Expense			**Wages Payable**	
	+	−	−	+
(Old) Balance 104,000				**Adjusting 1,200**
Adjusting	**1,200**			
(New) Balance 105,200				

Returning to our illustration of Cline's Computer Clinic, the last payday was June 24. Between June 24 and the end of the month, Cline's Computer Clinic owes an additional $240 in wages to its employee. Accountants refer to this extra amount that has not been recorded at the end of the month as **accrued wages**. In accounting terms, **accrual** means recognition of an expense or a revenue that has been incurred (expense) or earned (revenue) but has not yet been recorded.

(c)	Wages Expense			Wages Payable	
	+	−		−	+
(Old) Balance	2,980				**Adjusting** 240
Adjusting	**240**				
(New) Balance	3,220				

Placement of Accounts on the Work Sheet

We have to enter the adjustments on the work sheet, but before doing so, let's briefly discuss the Drawing and Accumulated Depreciation accounts, as well as net income, and their effect on the work sheet.

Capital and Drawing Account Balances The Drawing account is a contra account (contrary to Capital). In the statement of owner's equity, Drawing is deducted from Capital. To show one account as a deduction from another, the plus and minus signs are switched around. The T accounts look like this:

R. P. Cline, Capital		R. P. Cline, Drawing	
−	+	+	−
Debit	Credit	Debit	Credit
	Balance	Balance	

The normal balance for the Capital account is recorded in the Credit columns of the Trial Balance, the Adjusted Trial Balance, and the Balance Sheet sections. The normal balance for the Drawing account is recorded in the Debit columns of the Trial Balance, the Adjusted Trial Balance, and the Balance Sheet sections.

Equipment and Accumulated Depreciation, Equipment, Account Balances
The Accumulated Depreciation, Equipment, account is a contra account (contrary to Equipment). In the balance sheet, Accumulated Depreciation, Equipment, is deducted from Equipment. The T accounts look like this:

Equipment		Accumulated Depreciation, Equipment	
+	−	−	+
Debit	Credit	Debit	Credit
Balance			Balance

The normal balance for the Equipment account is recorded in the Debit columns of the Trial Balance, the Adjusted Trial Balance, and the Balance Sheet sections. The normal balance for the Accumulated Depreciation, Equipment, account is recorded in the Credit columns of the Trial Balance, the Adjusted Trial Balance, and the Balance Sheet sections.

Net Income

Net income (or net loss) is the difference between revenue and expenses. It is used to balance the Income Statement columns; since revenue is normally larger than expenses, the balancing amount must be added to the expense side. Net income (or net loss) is also used to balance the Balance Sheet columns. On the statement of owner's equity, you add net income to the owner's beginning Capital balance. Since the Capital balance is located in the Balance Sheet Credit column, net income must also be added to that side. The following diagram shows these relationships:

Account Name	Trial Balance		Adjustments		Adjusted Trial Balance		Income Statement		Balance Sheet	
	Debit	Credit	Debit	Credit	Debit	Credit	Debit	Credit	Debit	Credit
	A + Draw. + E	Accum. Depr. + L + Cap. + R			A + Draw. + E	Accum. Depr. + L + Cap. + R	E	R	A + Draw.	Accum. Depr. + L + Cap.
Net Income							NI			NI

On the other hand, if expenses are larger than revenue, the result is a net loss. You must add net loss to the revenue side to balance the Income Statement columns. Also, because a net loss is deducted from the owner's beginning Capital balance, you must include net loss in the debit side of the Balance Sheet columns, thereby balancing these columns. To show this, let's look at the Income Statement and Balance Sheet columns diagramed here.

	Income Statement		Balance Sheet	
	Debit	Credit	Debit	Credit
	E	R	A + Draw.	Accum. Depr. + L + Cap.
Net Loss		NL	NL	

Summary of Adjustments by T Accounts

To test your understanding, describe why the following adjustments are necessary. The answers are shown below the accounts.

(a) Prepaid Insurance

	+	−
Balance	480	Adjusting 40

Insurance Expense

	+	−
Adjusting	40	

(b) Depreciation Expense, Equipment

	+	−
Adjusting	840	

Accumulated Depreciation, Equipment

	−	+
		Adjusting 840

(c) Wages Expense

	+	−
Balance	2,980	
Adjusting	240	

Wages Payable

	−	+
		Adjusting 240

a. To record the insurance expired during June, $40.
b. To record the depreciation for the month of June, $840.
c. To record accrued wages owed at the end of June, $240.

Cline's Computer Clinic
Work Sheet
For Month Ended June 30, 20—

	ACCOUNT NAME	TRIAL BALANCE DEBIT A + Draw. + E	TRIAL BALANCE CREDIT Accum. Depr. + L + Cap. + R	ADJUSTMENTS DEBIT	ADJUSTMENTS CREDIT
1	Cash	11 9 5 0 00			
2	Accounts Receivable	6 2 0 00			
3	Prepaid Insurance	4 8 0 00			(a) 4 0 00
4	Equipment	83 7 2 0 00			
5	Accounts Payable		5 9 7 0 00		
6	R. P. Cline, Capital		88 2 0 0 00		
7	R. P. Cline, Drawing	3 0 0 0 00			
8	Income from Services		11 0 1 0 00		
9	Wages Expense	2 9 8 0 00		(c) 2 4 0 00	
10	Rent Expense	9 0 0 00			
11	Supplies Expense	8 7 0 00			
12	Advertising Expense	3 4 0 00			
13	Utilities Expense	3 2 0 00			
14		105 1 8 0 00	105 1 8 0 00		
15	Insurance Expense			(a) 4 0 00	
16	Depreciation Expense, Equipment			(b) 8 4 0 00	
17	Accumulated Depreciation, Equipment				(b) 8 4 0 00
18	Wages Payable				(c) 2 4 0 00
				1 1 2 0 00	1 1 2 0 00

FIGURE 2

Mixed Accounts At this point, take special notice of the fact that each **adjusting entry contains an income statement account (revenue or expense) and a balance sheet account (asset, contra asset, or liability).** Accountants refer to these accounts as **mixed accounts**—accounts with balances that are partly income statement amounts and partly balance sheet amounts. The income statement and balance sheet accounts involved are separate accounts having a part of their name in common, like Prepaid Insurance and Insurance Expense. Prepaid Insurance is recorded as $480 in the Trial Balance columns but is apportioned as $40 in Insurance Expense in the Income Statement columns and $440 in Prepaid Insurance in the Balance Sheet columns. In other words, portions of these trial balance amounts are recorded in each section.

In the previous examples, we used T accounts to explain how to handle adjustments. T accounts help organize any type of accounting entry into debits and credits. But now it is time to record the adjustments on the work sheet. To help you remember which classifications of accounts appear in each column of the work sheet, we will label the columns with letters specifying each classification of accounts; for example, A for assets, L for liabilities, etc., as shown in Figure 2.

Steps in the Completion of the Work Sheet

A completed work sheet is shown in Figure 3. Before we complete the work sheet, let's list the recommended steps to follow.

REMEMBER!

The Trial Balance columns are exactly the same as they are listed in the Trial Balance presented in Chapter 2.

1. Complete the Trial Balance columns, total, and rule.
2. Complete the Adjustments columns, total, and rule.
3. Complete the Adjusted Trial Balance columns, total, and rule.
4. Record balances in the Income Statement and Balance Sheet columns and total each column.
5. Record net income or net loss in the Income Statement columns by subtracting the smaller side from the larger side and adding the difference to the smaller side, total, and rule.
6. Record net income or net loss in the Balance Sheet columns by subtracting the smaller side from the larger side and adding the difference to the smaller side (the amount should be the same as the difference between the Income Statement column totals—if not, there is an error), total, and rule.

The steps assume the work sheet is prepared manually. The work sheet can also be prepared using a computer spreadsheet program, such as Microsoft Excel®. Whether the work sheet is prepared manually or on a computer, the columns must be completed, totaled, and ruled. An Excel version of the work sheet is shown in Figure 5 on page 128.

Step 1: Trial Balance Columns   Note that the trial balance in Figure 2 is the same trial balance presented earlier for Cline's Computer Clinic. You will be able to follow the completion of the entire work sheet for Cline's Computer Clinic in Figure 3.

Step 2: Adjustments Columns   When we enter the adjustments, we identify them as **(a)**, **(b)**, **(c)**, to indicate the relationships between the debit and credit sides and the sequence of the individual adjusting entries (see Figure 3).

Note that Insurance Expense; Depreciation Expense, Equipment; Accumulated Depreciation, Equipment; and Wages Payable did not appear in the trial balance because there were no balances in the accounts at that time. We wrote them below the Trial Balance totals to complete the work sheet.

Here is a brief review of the adjustments:

REMEMBER!

After the first fiscal period, Accumulated Depreciation will have a balance, so it will be listed immediately below the asset being depreciated (which in this example is Equipment). Consequently, Accumulated Depreciation will not appear at the bottom of next month's work sheet.

a. To record the $40 cost of insurance expired during June.
b. To record $840 depreciation for the month of June.
c. To record $240 of accrued wages owed at the end of June.

Now let's look at the work sheet shown in Figure 4. To reinforce the idea of adjusting entries, see the brief explanation of each adjustment at the right of the work sheet. Again, the completed work sheet is shown in Figure 3.

After the first fiscal period, Accumulated Depreciation will always have a balance until the related asset is sold or disposed of. Consequently, it will be listed in the Trial Balance columns immediately below the appropriate asset (Equipment, in this case).

Again, we emphasize that the work sheet is strictly a tool used to gather all the up-to-date information needed to prepare the financial statements. **The adjustments are always recorded in the work sheet first.**

REMEMBER!

Insurance is adjusted by adding the amount expired to Insurance Expense while deducting the same amount from Prepaid Insurance.

Depreciation is added to both Depreciation Expense and Accumulated Depreciation.

Accrued wages are added to both Wages Expense and Wages Payable.

Step 3: Adjusted Trial Balance Columns   Once the Adjustments columns are totaled and ruled, extend each Trial Balance amount, plus or minus any adjustment from the Adjustments columns, to the Adjusted Trial Balance columns as shown in Figure 3.

Step 4: Income Statement and Balance Sheet Columns   Extend the balances in the Adjusted Trial Balance columns to either the Income Statement or the Balance Sheet columns (see Figure 3).

FIGURE 3

Cline's Computer Clinic
Work Sheet
For Month Ended June 30, 20—

	ACCOUNT NAME	TRIAL BALANCE						ADJUSTMENTS						
		DEBIT			CREDIT			DEBIT			CREDIT			
		A + Draw. + E			Accum. Depr. + L + Cap. + R									
1	Cash	11 9 5 0	00											
2	Accounts Receivable	6 2 0	00											
3	Prepaid Insurance	4 8 0	00								(a)	4 0	00	
4	Equipment	83 7 2 0	00											
5	Accounts Payable				5 9 7 0	00								
6	R. P. Cline, Capital				88 2 0 0	00								
7	R. P. Cline, Drawing	3 0 0 0	00											
8	Income from Services				11 0 1 0	00								
9	Wages Expense	2 9 8 0	00					(c)	2 4 0	00				
10	Rent Expense	9 0 0	00											
11	Supplies Expense	8 7 0	00											
12	Advertising Expense	3 4 0	00											
13	Utilities Expense	3 2 0	00											
14		105 1 8 0	00		105 1 8 0	00								
15	Insurance Expense							(a)	4 0	00				
16	Depr. Exp., Equip.			Step 1				(b)	8 4 0	00				
17	Accum. Depr., Equip.										(b)	8 4 0	00	
18	Wages Payable										(c)	2 4 0	00	
19									1 1 2 0	00		1 1 2 0	00	
20	Net Income													
21										Step 2				
22														
23														
24														
25														
26	(a) Insurance expired, $40			Step 1						Step 2				
27	(b) Depr. of equip., $840	In the Account Name column,						Enter the adjustments,						
28	(c) Accrued wages, $240	list the accounts that have						labeling each adjustment						
29		balances. Enter the account						as (a), (b), (c), and so on.						
30		balances in the Trial Balance						Total and rule the columns.						
31		columns. Total and rule the												
32		columns.												
33														
34														
35														
36														

	ADJUSTED TRIAL BALANCE		INCOME STATEMENT		BALANCE SHEET		
	DEBIT A + Draw. + E	**CREDIT** Accum. Depr. + L + Cap. + R	**DEBIT** E	**CREDIT** R	**DEBIT** A + Draw.	**CREDIT** Accum. Depr. + L + Cap.	
	11 9 5 0 00				11 9 5 0 00		1
	6 2 0 00				6 2 0 00		2
	4 4 0 00				4 4 0 00		3
	83 7 2 0 00				83 7 2 0 00		4
		5 9 7 0 00				5 9 7 0 00	5
		88 2 0 0 00				88 2 0 0 00	6
	3 0 0 0 00				3 0 0 0 00		7
		11 0 1 0 00		11 0 1 0 00			8
	3 2 2 0 00		3 2 2 0 00				9
	9 0 0 00		9 0 0 00				10
	8 7 0 00		8 7 0 00				11
	3 4 0 00		3 4 0 00				12
	3 2 0 00		3 2 0 00				13
							14
	4 0 00		4 0 00				15
	8 4 0 00		8 4 0 00				16
		8 4 0 00				8 4 0 00	17
		2 4 0 00				2 4 0 00	18
	106 2 6 0 00	106 2 6 0 00	6 5 3 0 00	11 0 1 0 00	99 7 3 0 00	95 2 5 0 00	19
			4 4 8 0 00			4 4 8 0 00	20
	Step 3		11 0 1 0 00	11 0 1 0 00	99 7 3 0 00	99 7 3 0 00	21
							22
			Steps 4, 5, 6				23
							24
							25

Step 3

Carry amounts across from the Trial Balance columns plus or minus any amounts appearing in the *Adjustments* columns. Total and rule the columns.

Step 4

From the top of the Adjusted Trial Balance columns, go down line by line carrying each amount over to the Income Statement or Balance Sheet columns. Total the columns.

Step 5

Write Net Income or Net Loss in the Account Name column and the amount in the appropriate Income Statement column. Total and rule the columns.

Step 6

Enter the net income or loss amount in the appropriate Balance Sheet column. Total, balance, and rule the columns.

FIGURE 4

	ACCOUNT NAME	TRIAL BALANCE					
		DEBIT			CREDIT		
					Accum. Depr.		
		A + Draw. + E			*+ L + Cap. + R*		
1	Cash	11 9 5 0 00					
2	Accounts Receivable	6 2 0 00					
3	Prepaid Insurance	4 8 0 00					
4	Equipment	83 7 2 0 00					
5	Accounts Payable				5 9 7 0 00		
6	R. P. Cline, Capital				88 2 0 0 00		
7	R. P. Cline, Drawing	3 0 0 0 00					
8	Income from Services				11 0 1 0 00		
9	Wages Expense	2 9 8 0 00					
10	Rent Expense	9 0 0 00					
11	Supplies Expense	8 7 0 00					
12	Advertising Expense	3 4 0 00					
13	Utilities Expense	3 2 0 00					
14		105 1 8 0 00			105 1 8 0 00		
15	Insurance Expense						
16	Depreciation Expense, Equipment			*Step 1*			
17	Accumulated Depreciation, Equipment						
18	Wages Payable						
19							
20	(a) Insurance expired, $40						
21	(b) Depreciation of equipment, $840						
22	(c) Accrued wages, $240						

Depreciation can occur from everyday wear and tear, or assets can simply become obsolete.

Step 5: Net Income or Net Loss—Income Statement Columns   Total each of the two Income Statement columns. Subtract the smaller side from the larger side, write the difference under the smaller Income Statement column total, and total and rule as shown in Figure 3.

Step 6: Net Income or Net Loss—Balance Sheet Columns   Total the two Balance Sheet columns. Subtract the smaller side from the larger side, write the difference under the smaller Balance Sheet column total (the amount should equal the difference between the Income Statement column totals—if not, there is an error), and total and rule as shown in Figure 3.

If there is a net income, the credit side of the Income Statement columns will be larger than the debit side—more revenue than expenses. In this case, write Net Income in the Account Name column on the same line as the difference you calculated. If there is a net loss, the debit side of the Income Statement columns will be larger than the credit side—more expenses than revenue. In this case, write Net Loss in the Account Name column on the same line as the difference you calculated.

Cline's Computer Clinic
Work Sheet
For Month Ended June 30, 20—

ADJUSTMENTS DEBIT		ADJUSTMENTS CREDIT		ADJUSTED TRIAL BALANCE DEBIT (A + Draw. + E)	ADJUSTED TRIAL BALANCE CREDIT Accum. Depr. + L + Cap. + R	INCOME STATEMENT DEBIT (E)	INCOME STATEMENT CREDIT (R)	BALANCE SHEET DEBIT (A + Draw.)	BALANCE SHEET CREDIT Accum. Depr. + L + Cap.	
				11 9 5 0 00		No adjustment, so carry over amount directly				1
				6 2 0 00						2
		(a)	4 0 00	4 4 0 00		Adjustment involved, subtract $40 (expired) from $480				3
				83 7 2 0 00		No adjustment, so carry over amount directly				4
					5 9 7 0 00					5
					88 2 0 0 00					6
				3 0 0 0 00						7
					11 0 1 0 00					8
(c)	2 4 0 00			3 2 2 0 00		Adjustment involved, add $240 (accrued) to $2,980				9
				9 0 0 00		No adjustment, so carry over amount directly				10
				8 7 0 00						11
				3 4 0 00						12
				3 2 0 00						13
						This line is blank because of the trial balance total				14
(a)	4 0 00			4 0 00		Adjustment involved, carry $40 over to the same column				15
(b)	8 4 0 00			8 4 0 00		Adjustment involved, carry $840 over to the same column				16
		(b)	8 4 0 00		8 4 0 00	Adjustment involved, carry $840 over to the same column				17
		(c)	2 4 0 00		2 4 0 00	Adjustment involved, carry $240 over to the same column				18
1 1 2 0 00		1 1 2 0 00		106 2 6 0 00	106 2 6 0 00					19
										20
Step 2				Step 3						21
										22

Work Sheet Requiring Two Pages

If a large number of accounts is involved, it may be necessary to continue the work sheet to a second page.

REMEMBER!

When a work sheet requires two pages, the totals at the bottom of the first sheet do not have to be equal. Debits must equal credits by the end of the last page.

(First Page)

Account Name	Trial Balance		Adjustments	
Wages Expense	3,240 00		(c) 220 50	
Totals carried forward	98,312 00	91,146 10	962 50	126 50

Note that the totals at the bottom of the first page are labeled "Totals carried forward" in the Account Name column. At the top of the second page, the totals are repeated and labeled "Totals brought forward" in the Account Name column. Continue listing account names and balances below the totals brought forward.

FIGURE 5

Cline's Computer Clinic
Work Sheet
For Month Ended June 30, 20—

ACCOUNT NAME	TRIAL BALANCE DEBIT	TRIAL BALANCE CREDIT	ADJUSTMENTS DEBIT	ADJUSTMENTS CREDIT	ADJUSTED TRIAL BALANCE DEBIT	ADJUSTED TRIAL BALANCE CREDIT	INCOME STATEMENT DEBIT	INCOME STATEMENT CREDIT	BALANCE SHEET DEBIT	BALANCE SHEET CREDIT
	A+Draw.+E	Accum. Depr. +L+Cap.+R			A+Draw.+E	Accum. Depr. +L+Cap.+R	E	R	A+Draw.	Accum. Depr. +L+Cap.
Cash	11,950.00				11,950.00				11,950.00	
Accounts Receivable	620.00				620.00				620.00	
Prepaid Insurance	480.00			(a) 40.00	440.00				440.00	
Equipment	83,720.00				83,720.00				83,720.00	
Accounts Payable		5,970.00				5,970.00				5,970.00
R. P. Cline, Capital		88,200.00				88,200.00				88,200.00
R. P. Cline, Drawing	3,000.00				3,000.00				3,000.00	
Income from Services		11,010.00				11,010.00		11,010.00		
Wages Expense	2,980.00		(c) 240.00		3,220.00		3,220.00			
Rent Expense	900.00				900.00		900.00			
Supplies Expense	870.00				870.00		870.00			
Advertising Expense	340.00				340.00		340.00			
Utilities Expense	320.00				320.00		320.00			
	105,180.00	105,180.00								
Insurance Expense			(a) 40.00		40.00		40.00			
Depr. Exp., Equip.			(b) 840.00		840.00		840.00			
Accum. Depr., Equip.				(b) 840.00		840.00				840.00
Wages Payable				(c) 240.00		240.00				240.00
			1,120.00	1,120.00	106,260.00	106,260.00	6,530.00	11,010.00	99,730.00	95,250.00
Net Income							4,480.00			4,480.00
							11,010.00	11,010.00	99,730.00	99,730.00

Sheet1 Sheet2 Sheet3

What you want to do	Button Name	Button*	Where to find it - or how to do it
Center a column heading over two or more cells	Merge and Center		Format toolbar—Highlight cells, then click button
Add numbers in a range of cells	Auto Sum	Σ	Function toolbar—Highlight cell in which you want total to appear, click button, highlight cells to add, then press the enter key
Rule a cell	Borders		Format toolbar—Highlight cell(s), then click arrow on right side of button, make your selection
Add commas to numbers	Comma Style	,	Format toolbar—Highlight cell(s), then click button
Center labels in a cell	Center		Format toolbar—Highlight cell(s), then click button
Adjust column width		Format	Select Format from Menu bar, then Column from drop-down menu, then Width
Format cell contents		Format	Select Format from Menu bar, then click Cells on drop-down menu

Menu Bar

File Edit View Insert Format Tools Data Window Help

Function Bar

Format Bar

Arial   12   B I U

* These tools may have additional uses or be accessed in different ways in more sophisticated applications.

	(Second Page)			
	Trial Balance		**Adjustments**	
Account Name	Debit	Credit	Debit	Credit
Totals brought forward	98,312 00	91,146 10	962 50	126 50
Wages Payable				(c) 220 50

Finding Errors in the Income Statement and Balance Sheet Columns

As you have seen, the amount of the net income or net loss must be recorded in both an Income Statement column and a Balance Sheet column. Suppose that, after the net income is added to the Balance Sheet Credit column, the Balance Sheet columns are not equal. To find the error, follow this procedure:

1. Check to see that the amount of the net income or loss is recorded in the correct columns. For example, net income is placed in the Income Statement Debit column and the Balance Sheet Credit column.
2. Verify the addition of all the columns.
3. Look to see if the appropriate amounts have been recorded in the Income Statement and Balance Sheet columns. For example, asset amounts should be listed in the Balance Sheet Debit column, expense amounts should be listed in the Income Statement Debit column, and so forth.
4. Verify, by adding or subtracting across each line, that the amounts carried over from the Trial Balance columns through the Adjustments columns into the Adjusted Trial Balance columns are correct.
5. The correct amounts of the revenue and expense accounts are transferred to the Income Statement columns.
6. The correct amounts of assets, liabilities, and owner's equity accounts are transferred to the Balance Sheet columns.

Generally, one of these steps will expose the error.

Completion of the Financial Statements

OBJECTIVE 4

Prepare an income statement, a statement of owner's equity, and a balance sheet for a service business directly from the work sheet.

As we stated, the purpose of the work sheet is to help the accountant prepare the financial statements. Since we have completed the work sheet for Cline's Computer Clinic, we can now prepare the income statement, the statement of owner's equity, and the balance sheet by taking the figures directly from the work sheet. These statements are shown in Figure 6.

Note that you record Accumulated Depreciation, Equipment, in the asset section of the balance sheet as a direct deduction from Equipment. As we have said, accountants refer to this as a **contra asset account** because it is contrary to its companion account. The difference, $82,880, is called the book value or carrying value because it represents the cost of the asset after Accumulated Depreciation has been deducted.

When preparing the statement of owner's equity, always remember to check the beginning balance of Capital against the balance shown in the Capital account in the general ledger. An additional investment may have been made during the fiscal period, and you need to record any such additional investment in the statement of owner's equity.

Cline's Computer Clinic
Income Statement
For Month Ended June 30, 20—

Revenue:										
Income from Services						$11	0	1	0	00
Expenses:										
Wages Expense	$3	2	2	0	00					
Rent Expense		9	0	0	00					
Supplies Expense		8	7	0	00					
Advertising Expense		3	4	0	00					
Utilities Expense		3	2	0	00					
Insurance Expense			4	0	00					
Depreciation Expense, Equipment		8	4	0	00					
Total Expenses						6	5	3	0	00
Net Income						$ 4	4	8	0	00

Cline's Computer Clinic
Statement of Owner's Equity
For Month Ended June 30, 20—

R. P. Cline, Capital, June 1, 20—						$88	2	0	0	00
Net Income for June	$4	4	8	0	00					
Less Withdrawals for June	3	0	0	0	00					
Increase in Capital						1	4	8	0	00
R. P. Cline, Capital, June 30, 20—						$89	6	8	0	00

Cline's Computer Clinic
Balance Sheet
June 30, 20—

Assets										
Cash						$11	9	5	0	00
Accounts Receivable							6	2	0	00
Prepaid Insurance							4	4	0	00
Equipment	$83	7	2	0	00					
Less Accumulated Depreciation		8	4	0	00	82	8	8	0	00
Total Assets						$95	8	9	0	00
Liabilities										
Accounts Payable	$ 5	9	7	0	00					
Wages Payable		2	4	0	00					
Total Liabilities						$ 6	2	1	0	00
Owner's Equity										
R. P. Cline, Capital						89	6	8	0	00
Total Liabilities and Owner's Equity						$95	8	9	0	00

FIGURE 6

JOURNALIZING ADJUSTING ENTRIES

OBJECTIVE 5

Journalize and post the adjusting entries.

To change the balance of a ledger account, you need a journal entry as evidence of the change. So far, we have been listing adjustments only in the Adjustments columns of the work sheet. The work sheet is not a journal, so we must journalize **adjusting entries** to update the ledger accounts. **Take the information for these entries directly from the Adjustments columns of the work sheet, debiting and crediting exactly the same accounts and amounts in the journal entries.**

In the Description column of the general journal, write "Adjusting Entries" before you begin making these entries. This can eliminate the need to write an explanation for each entry. The adjusting entries for Cline's Computer Clinic are shown in Figure 7.

REMEMBER!

Each adjusting entry consists of an income statement account and a balance sheet account.

GENERAL JOURNAL   PAGE __4__

	DATE		DESCRIPTION	POST. REF.	DEBIT	CREDIT	
1	20–		**Adjusting Entries**				1
2	June	30	Insurance Expense	516	4 0 00		2
3			Prepaid Insurance	117		4 0 00	3
4							4
5		30	Depr. Expense, Equipment	517	8 4 0 00		5
6			Accum. Depr., Equipment	125		8 4 0 00	6
7							7
8		30	Wages Expense	511	2 4 0 00		8
9			Wages Payable	222		2 4 0 00	9

FIGURE 7

When you post the adjusting entries to the ledger accounts, write the word "Adjusting" in the Item column of the ledger account. The adjusting entry for Prepaid Insurance is posted as follows:

GENERAL LEDGER

ACCOUNT **Prepaid Insurance**   ACCOUNT NO. __117__

	DATE	ITEM	POST. REF.	DEBIT	CREDIT	BALANCE DEBIT	BALANCE CREDIT	
1	20–							1
2	June 10		2	4 8 0 00		4 8 0 00		2
3	30	Adj.	4		4 0 00	4 4 0 00		3
4								4

| ACCOUNT | Insurance Expense | | | | | | ACCOUNT NO. | 516 |

| | | | POST. | | | | BALANCE | |
DATE		ITEM	REF.	DEBIT	CREDIT	DEBIT		CREDIT
1	20–							1
2	June 30	Adj.	4	4 0 00		4 0 00		2
3								3

Accounting Treatment for the Cost of Supplies

In Chapter 1, when Cline's Computer Clinic bought supplies, the amount paid was recorded as an expense. Generally, most service businesses expense supplies when they buy them. An alternative to expensing supplies is to record the cost as an asset (debit to Supplies, credit to Cash). At the end of the accounting period, an inventory is taken to determine the amount of supplies used in operations. The debit would be to Supplies Expense for the amount of supplies used during the accounting period, and the credit would be to Supplies (an asset account). The ending balance in Supplies (asset account) would be the supplies on hand at the end of the accounting period.

If supplies are a major cost to a business and expensing the supplies when they are purchased would distort the income statement, then recording the cost as an asset and adjusting accordingly would be the preferable method of accounting for supplies. **We will continue expensing supplies in this text.**

Income Statement Involving More than One Revenue Account and a Net Loss

OBJECTIVE 6a

Prepare an income statement involving more than one revenue account and a net loss.

When an organization has more than one distinct source of revenue, a separate revenue account is set up for each source. See, for example, the income statement of Haro Miniature Golf presented in Figure 8. Also note that expenses are greater than revenues, resulting in a net loss.

FIGURE 8

Haro Miniature Golf
Income Statement
For Month Ended September 30, 20—

Revenue:			
Admissions Income	$9 6 2 4 00		
Concessions Income	2 7 1 2 00		
Total Revenue		$12 3 3 6 00	
Expenses:			
Wages Expense	$4 1 2 3 00		
Advertising Expense	3 1 7 00		
Total Expenses		13 4 7 5 00	
Net Loss		($ 1 1 3 9 00)	

L. A. Grady Company Statement of Owner's Equity For Month Ended April 30, 20—								
L. A. Grady, Capital, April 1, 20—						$ 96	0 0 0	00
Additional Investment, April 12, 20—						10	0 0 0	00
Total Investment						$106	0 0 0	00
Net Income for April	$5	2 0 0	00					
Less Withdrawals for April	4	0 0 0	00					
Increase in Capital						1	2 0 0	00
L. A. Grady, Capital, April 30, 20—						$107	2 0 0	00

FIGURE 9

Statement of Owner's Equity with an Additional Investment and a Net Income

OBJECTIVE 6b

Prepare a statement of owner's equity with an additional investment and either a net income or a net loss.

Any additional investment by the owner during the period covered by the financial statements should be shown on the statement of owner's equity, since such a statement should show everything that has affected the Capital account from the *beginning* until the *end* of the period covered by the financial statements. For example, in Figure 9, assume that the following information is true for L. A. Grady Company, which has a net income:

Balance of L. A. Grady, Capital, on April 1	$96,000
Additional investment by L. A. Grady on April 12	10,000
Net income for the month (from income statement)	5,200
Total withdrawals for the month	4,000

The additional investment may be in the form of cash. Or the investment may be in the form of other assets, such as tools, equipment, and similar items. In the case of investments of assets other than cash, the assets should be recorded at their fair market value. Fair market value is the present worth of an asset, or the amount that would be received if the asset were sold to an outsider on the open market. Fair market value may differ greatly from the amount the owner originally paid for the asset.

Statement of Owner's Equity with an Additional Investment and a Net Loss

Assume the following for J. D. Roe Company, which has a net loss:

J. D. Roe, Capital, on Oct. 1	$70,000
Additional investment by J. D. Roe on Oct. 25	6,000
Net loss for the month (from income statement)	2,500
Total withdrawals for the month	5,100

The statement of owner's equity in Figure 10 shows this information.

FIGURE 10

J. D. Roe Company
Statement of Owner's Equity
For Month Ended October 31, 20—

J. D. Roe, Capital, October 1, 20—				$70 0 0 0	00
Additional Investment, October 25, 20—				6 0 0 0	00
Total Investment				$76 0 0 0	00
Less: Net Loss for October	$2 5 0 0	00			
Withdrawals for October	5 1 0 0	00			
Decrease in Capital				7 6 0 0	00
J. D. Roe, Capital, October 31, 20—				$68 4 0 0	00

OBJECTIVE 6c

Prepare a balance sheet for a business having more than one accumulated depreciation account.

Businesses with More than One Depreciation Expense Account and More than One Accumulated Depreciation Account

Figures 11 and 12 show the income statement and the balance sheet for Moen Veterinary Clinic. In Figure 12, note that the company has two assets subject to depreciation: Building and Equipment. In the financial statements, Depreciation Expense and Accumulated Depreciation must be listed for each asset.

In the adjusted accounts, notice that the intent is to make sure that the expenses recorded match up or compare with the revenues for the same period of time. In other words, for the month of June, we record all the revenues for June and all the expenses for June. Thus the revenues and expenses for the same time period are matched. This is called the **matching principle**.

Land supposedly lasts forever, so land is not depreciated. Adjustments would have been made in the work sheet for depreciation of the equipment and the building. The balance sheet for Moen Veterinary Clinic is shown in Figure 12.

FIGURE 11

Moen Veterinary Clinic
Income Statement
For Year Ended December 31, 20—

Revenue:				
Professional Fees	$335 1 6 0	00		
Boarding Fees	66 1 8 0	00		
Total Revenue			$401 3 4 0	00
Expenses:				
Salary Expense	$252 0 0 0	00		
Depreciation Expense, Building	19 4 4 0	00		
Depreciation Expense, Equipment	11 5 2 0	00		
Supplies Expense	11 1 6 0	00		
Insurance Expense	2 1 6 0	00		
Miscellaneous Expense	6 4 8 0	00		
Total Expenses			302 7 6 0	00
Net Income			$ 98 5 8 0	00

FIGURE 12

Moen Veterinary Clinic
Balance Sheet
December 31, 20—

Assets				
Cash			$ 18 7 2 0 00	
Supplies			6 0 0 00	
Land			13 2 0 0 00	
Building	$353 1 0 0 00			
Less Accumulated Depreciation	109 2 0 0 00	243 9 0 0 00		
Equipment	$127 8 0 0 00			
Less Accumulated Depreciation	87 6 0 0 00	40 2 0 0 00		
Total Assets		$316 6 2 0 00		
Liabilities				
Accounts Payable		$ 8 4 0 0 00		
Owner's Equity				
R. N. Moen, Capital		308 2 2 0 00		
Total Liabilities and Owner's Equity		$316 6 2 0 00		

Balance Sheet with Statement of Owner's Equity Included

OBJECTIVE 6d

Prepare a balance sheet containing the statement of owner's equity information.

The information normally shown in the statement of owner's equity is sometimes included as part of the owner's equity section of the balance sheet, as shown in Figure 13.

FIGURE 13

Cline's Computer Clinic
Balance Sheet
June 30, 20—

Assets				
Cash			$11 9 5 0 00	
Accounts Receivable			6 2 0 00	
Prepaid Insurance			4 4 0 00	
Equipment	$83 7 2 0 00			
Less Accumulated Depreciation	8 4 0 00	82 8 8 0 00		
Total Assets		$95 8 9 0 00		
Liabilities				
Accounts Payable	$ 5 9 7 0 00			
Wages Payable	2 4 0 00			
Total Liabilities		$ 6 2 1 0 00		
Owner's Equity				
R. P. Cline, Capital, June 1, 20—		$88 2 0 0 00		
Net Income	$ 4 4 8 0 00			
Less Withdrawals for June	3 0 0 0 00			
Increase in Capital		1 4 8 0 00		
R. P. Cline, Capital, June 30, 20—		$89 6 8 0 00		
Total Liabilities and Owner's Equity		$95 8 9 0 00		

FYI

Computerized accounting programs frequently do not produce a separate statement of owner's equity.

CHAPTER REVIEW

Review of Performance Objectives

1. Define *fiscal period* and *fiscal year*.

   A fiscal period is any period of time covering a complete accounting cycle. A fiscal year consists of twelve consecutive months.

2. List the classifications of the accounts that occupy each column of a ten-column work sheet.

Trial Balance Debit	Assets + Drawing + Expenses
Trial Balance Credit	Accum. Depr. + Liabilities + Capital + Revenue
Adjustments Debit	Expenses
Adjustments Credit	Assets + Liabilities + Contra Assets
Adj. Trial Balance Debit	Assets + Drawing + Expenses
Adj. Trial Balance Credit	Accum. Depr. + Liabilities + Capital + Revenue
Income Statement Debit	Expenses
Income Statement Credit	Revenue
Balance Sheet Debit	Assets + Drawing
Balance Sheet Credit	Accumulated Depreciation + Liabilities + Capital

3. Complete a work sheet for a service enterprise, involving adjustments for expired insurance, depreciation, and accrued wages.

   Adjustment for expired insurance: debit Insurance Expense and credit Prepaid Insurance.
   Adjustment for depreciation: debit Depreciation Expense and credit Accumulated Depreciation.
   Adjustment for accrued wages: debit Wages Expense and credit Wages Payable.

4. Prepare an income statement, a statement of owner's equity, and a balance sheet for a service business directly from the work sheet.

   Prepare the income statement directly from the amounts listed in the Income Statement Debit and Credit columns. The net income should equal the net income previously determined on the work sheet. For the statement of owner's equity, use the amount of the beginning capital listed in the Balance Sheet Credit column after checking the general ledger for any additional investment(s), the amount of the net income from the Balance Sheet Credit column, and the amount of Drawing from the Balance Sheet Debit column. Prepare the balance sheet directly from the amounts listed in the Balance Sheet Debit and Credit columns (except Drawing and Capital).

5. Journalize and post the adjusting entries.

6. Prepare (a) an income statement involving more than one revenue account and a net loss, (b) a statement of owner's equity with an additional investment and either a net income or a net loss, (c) a balance sheet for a business having more than one accumulated depreciation account, and (d) a balance sheet containing the statement of owner's equity information.

   (a) An income statement containing more than one revenue account requires an additional line for each type of revenue, followed by a total amount of revenue.

   (b) A statement of owner's equity involving an additional investment requires a line for each additional investment beneath the beginning capital amount, followed by a total amount of investment.

   (c) Businesses that have more than one source of revenue or more than one type of asset that is subject to depreciation must show a separate account for each on the income statement and the balance sheet.

(d) A balance sheet sometimes contains in the owner's equity section the information normally placed in a separate statement of owner's equity. The section would contain the beginning capital, plus the amount of net income (or minus the net loss), minus total withdrawals. The result is the same amount that would be calculated in a separate statement of owner's equity—the ending capital.

Glossary

Accounting cycle The sequence of steps in the accounting process completed during the fiscal period. (113)

Accrual Recognition of an expense or a revenue that has been incurred or earned but has not yet been recorded. (119)

Accrued wages Unpaid wages owed to employees for the time between the end of the last pay period and the end of the fiscal period. (119)

Adjusting entries Entries that bring the books up to date at the end of the fiscal period. (131)

Adjustments Internal transactions that bring ledger accounts up to date, as a planned part of the accounting procedure. They are first recorded in the Adjustments columns of the work sheet when using a manual accounting system. (116)

Book value or carrying value The cost of an asset minus the accumulated depreciation. (118)

Contra account An account that is contrary to, or a deduction from, another account; for example, Accumulated Depreciation is listed as a deduction from Equipment. (117)

Contra asset account An account that is contrary to or a deduction from its companion asset account. (129)

Depreciation An expense based on the expectation that an asset will gradually decline in usefulness due to time, wear and tear, or obsolescence; the cost of the asset is therefore spread out over its estimated useful life. A part of depreciation expense is apportioned to each fiscal period. (116)

Fiscal period Any period of time covering a complete accounting cycle, generally consisting of twelve consecutive months. (113)

Fiscal year A fiscal period consisting of twelve consecutive months. (113)

Matching principle The principle that the revenue for one time period is matched up with the related expenses for the same time period. (134)

Mixed accounts Certain accounts that appear on the trial balance with balances that are partly income statement amounts and partly balance sheet amounts—for example, Prepaid Insurance and Insurance Expense. (122)

Straight-line depreciation A means of calculating depreciation in which the cost of an asset, less any trade-in value, is allocated evenly over the useful life of the asset. (117)

Work sheet A working paper used by accountants to record necessary adjustments and provide up-to-date account balances needed to prepare the financial statements. (114)

QUESTIONS, EXERCISES, AND CASES

Discussion Questions

1. What is the purpose of a work sheet in a manual system?
2. What is the purpose of adjusting entries?

3. What is a mixed account? A contra account? Give an example of each.

4. In which column of the work sheet—Income Statement (IS) or Balance Sheet (BS)—would the adjusted balances of the following accounts appear?

Account	IS or BS?	Account	IS or BS?
a. Prepaid Insurance		e. Accumulated Depreciation, Equipment	
b. Wages Expense		f. T. Klein, Drawing	
c. Wages Payable		g. Insurance Expense	
d. Income from Services		h. Depreciation Expense, Equipment	

5. Why is it necessary to make an adjustment if wages for work performed for the pay period Monday through Friday are paid on Friday and the accounting period ends on a Wednesday?

6. Define depreciation as it relates to a van you bought for your business.

7. Define an internal transaction and provide an example.

8. Why is it necessary to journalize and post adjusting entries?

Exercises

P.O. 2

List account classifications in work sheet columns.

Exercise 4-1 List the following classifications of accounts in all the columns in which they appear on the work sheet, with the exception of the Adjustments columns. (Example: Assets.)

Assets
Accumulated Depreciation (with
    previous balance)
Liabilities

Capital
Drawing
Revenue
Expenses

Write Net Income in the appropriate columns.

Account Name	Trial Balance Debit	Trial Balance Credit	Adjustments Debit	Adjustments Credit	Adjusted Trial Balance Debit	Adjusted Trial Balance Credit	Income Statement Debit	Income Statement Credit	Balance Sheet Debit	Balance Sheet Credit
	Assets				Assets				Assets	
Net Income										

P.O. 2

Classify accounts and indicate normal balances and statement columns.

Exercise 4-2 Classify each of the accounts listed below as assets (A), liabilities (L), owner's equity (OE), revenue (R), or expenses (E). Indicate the normal debit or credit balance of each account. Indicate whether each account will appear in the Income Statement columns (IS) or the Balance Sheet columns (BS) of the work sheet. Item 0 is given as an example.

Account	Classification	Normal Balance	IS or BS Columns
0. Example: Wages Expense	E	Debit	IS
a. Prepaid Insurance			
b. Accounts Payable			
c. T. Robley, Capital			
d. Accounts Receivable			
e. Accumulated Depreciation, Building			
f. T. Robley, Drawing			
g. Rental Income			
h. Equipment			
i. Depreciation Expense, Equipment			
j. Supplies Expense			

P.O. 3

Choose accounts that require adjustment.

Exercise 4-3 Place a check mark next to any account(s) requiring adjustment. Explain why those accounts must be adjusted.

✓	Account Name (in trial balance order)	Reason for Adjusting This Account
	a. Cash	
	b. Prepaid Insurance	
	c. Equipment	
	d. Accumulated Depreciation, Equipment	
	e. Accounts Payable	
	f. L. Lawson, Capital	
	g. L. Lawson, Drawing	
	h. Wages Expense	

P.O. 3

Prepare adjustments on the work sheet.

Exercise 4-4 Below is a partial work sheet for Peg's Place. Prepare the following adjustments on this work sheet for the month ended June 30, 20—.

a. Expired or used-up insurance, $350.

b. Depreciation expense on equipment, $750—remember to credit the Accumulated Depreciation account for equipment, not Equipment.

c. Wages accrued or earned since the last payday, $136 (owed and to be paid on the next payday).

	ACCOUNT NAME	TRIAL BALANCE DEBIT	TRIAL BALANCE CREDIT	ADJUSTMENTS DEBIT	ADJUSTMENTS CREDIT
1	Cash	5 6 2 1 00			
2	Prepaid Insurance	9 0 0 00			
3	Equipment	4 6 8 0 00			
4	Accumulated Depreciation, Equipment		1 2 5 0 00		
5	Accounts Payable		2 6 4 9 00		
6	P. Ryan, Capital		4 6 2 4 00		
7	P. Ryan, Drawing	2 2 0 0 00			
8	Service Income		6 8 4 7 00		
9	Rent Expense	9 5 6 00			
10	Supplies Expense	3 8 5 00			
11	Wages Expense	5 6 0 00			
12	Miscellaneous Expense	6 8 00			
13		15 3 7 0 00	15 3 7 0 00		
14					

P.O. 3

Prepare adjustments and adjusted trial balance.

Exercise 4-5 Complete the work sheet through the adjusted trial balance using the following adjustment information:

a. Expired or used-up insurance, $350.

b. Depreciation expense on equipment, $870—remember to credit the Accumulated Depreciation account for equipment, not Equipment.

c. Wages accrued or earned since the last payday, $288 (owed and to be paid on the next payday).

	ACCOUNT NAME	TRIAL BALANCE DEBIT	TRIAL BALANCE CREDIT	ADJUSTMENTS DEBIT	ADJUSTMENTS CREDIT	ADJUSTED TRIAL BALANCE DEBIT	ADJUSTED TRIAL BALANCE CREDIT
1	Cash	4 6 2 0 00					
2	Prepaid Insurance	1 1 0 0 00					
3	Equipment	5 6 7 8 00					
4	Accumulated Depreciation,						
5	Equipment		1 4 5 6 00				
6	Accounts Payable		1 9 7 5 00				
7	D. Lee, Capital		6 1 2 6 00				
8	D. Lee, Drawing	1 8 0 0 00					
9	Service Fees		5 7 3 6 00				
10	Rent Expense	8 6 5 00					
11	Supplies Expense	3 6 7 00					
12	Wages Expense	7 8 5 00					
13	Miscellaneous Expense	7 8 00					
14		15 2 9 3 00	15 2 9 3 00				
15							

P.O. 3

Calculate the missing adjustments.

Exercise 4-6 Journalize the three adjusting entries from the partial work sheet below for the month ended May 31. (*Hint:* Use what you know about opening new accounts for adjusting entries.)

	ACCOUNT NAME	INCOME STATEMENT DEBIT	INCOME STATEMENT CREDIT	BALANCE SHEET DEBIT	BALANCE SHEET CREDIT	
1	Cash			4 7 3 1 00		1
2	Prepaid Insurance			8 4 1 00		2
3	Equipment			5 8 3 2 00		3
4	Accumulated Depreciation, Equipment				1 8 2 0 00	4
5	Accounts Payable				9 8 5 00	5
6	B. Ray, Capital				6 8 1 0 00	6
7	B. Ray, Drawing			2 1 5 0 00		7
8	Professional Fees		8 6 7 3 00			8
9	Salary Expense	2 7 8 7 00				9
10	Rent Expense	1 2 0 0 00				10
11	Supplies Expense	3 8 4 00				11
12	Miscellaneous Expense	1 3 4 00				12
13						13
14	Insurance Expense	1 8 5 00				14
15	Depreciation Expense, Equipment	3 6 4 00				15
16	Salaries Payable				3 2 0 00	16
17		5 0 5 4 00	8 6 7 3 00	13 5 5 4 00	9 9 3 5 00	17
18	Net Income	3 6 1 9 00			3 6 1 9 00	18
19		8 6 7 3 00	8 6 7 3 00	13 5 5 4 00	13 5 5 4 00	19
20						20

P.O. 5

Journalize adjusting entries from the work sheet.

Exercise 4-7 Journalize the adjustments for James Company as of August 31.

	ACCOUNT NAME	TRIAL BALANCE DEBIT	TRIAL BALANCE CREDIT	ADJUSTMENTS DEBIT	ADJUSTMENTS CREDIT	
1	Cash	3 9 7 1 00				1
2	Prepaid Insurance	4 8 7 3 00			(a) 2 6 5 00	2
3	Equipment	5 6 7 8 00				3
4	Accumulated Depreciation, Equipment		6 4 5 00		(b) 2 0 6 00	4
5	Accounts Payable		8 4 3 00			5
6	L. James, Capital		12 7 5 2 00			6
7	L. James, Drawing	2 0 0 0 00				7
8	Service Fees		4 6 8 3 00			8
9	Rent Expense	7 9 5 00				9
10	Supplies Expense	6 6 3 00				10
11	Wages Expense	8 6 5 00		(c) 1 6 8 00		11
12	Miscellaneous Expense	7 8 00				12
13		18 9 2 3 00	18 9 2 3 00			13
14	Insurance Expense			(a) 2 6 5 00		14
15	Depreciation Expense, Equipment			(b) 2 0 6 00		15
16	Wages Payable				(c) 1 6 8 00	16
17				6 3 9 00	6 3 9 00	17
18						18

P.O. 5

Journalize adjusting entries.

Exercise 4-8 Journalize the following adjusting entries that were included on the work sheet for the month ended December 31. Assume the financial statements have been prepared.

Dec.   31   Salaries for two days are unpaid at December 31, $1,800 (verify). Salaries are $4,500 for a five-day week.

31   Insurance was bought on September 1 for $2,400 for 12 months' coverage. Four months' coverage has expired, $800 (verify).

31   Depreciation for the month on equipment, $20, based on an asset costing $3,200 with a trade-in value of $2,000 and an estimated life of 5 years (verify).

LINKS TO ACCOUNTING

As you have learned, companies report the financial results of the year at the end of a twelve-month period called the fiscal year. Businesses with seasonal peaks usually end their accounting cycles at the end of the most active season.

1. Is Activision a company that might have seasonal peaks and that would want a fiscal year that is different from the calendar year? What is its fiscal year and where do you find this information in the annual report? (Access Activision's annual report for 2005 at **http://investor.activision.com/reports.cfm**.)

2. In this chapter, financial information entered into the general journal is transformed into the financial statements. Let's go back to Activision and analyze the Property and Equipment account on its balance sheet. This account is listed as Property and Equipment, *net* on the balance sheet on page 54. What does this mean?

3. If Property and Equipment, net was $30,490,000 as of March 31, 2005, what was the total cost of Activision's property and equipment? (*Hint:* What was Accumulated Depreciation, Property and Equipment as of March 31, 2005? Review Note 7, Property and Equipment, in the Notes to Consolidated Financial Statements, which begin on page 59 of the annual report.)

CONSIDER AND COMMUNICATE

You are the bookkeeper for a small but thriving business. You have asked the owner for the information you need in order to make adjusting entries for depreciation, insurance, and wages. He says he's really busy, and what you've done so far is "close enough." Explain the need for adjusting entries and how they can affect his balance sheet and the "bottom line" on the income statement.

A QUESTION OF ETHICS

Your client is preparing financial statements to show the bank. You know that he has incurred a refrigeration repair expense during the month, but you see no such expense on the books. When you question the client, he tells you that he has not paid the $1,250 bill yet. Your client is on the accrual basis of accounting. He does not want the refrigeration repair expense on the books as of the end of the month because he wants his profits to look good for the bank. Is your client behaving ethically by suggesting that the refrigeration repair expense should not be booked until the $1,250 is paid? Are you behaving ethically if you go along with the client's request? What principle is involved here?

CRITICAL THINKING

Your supervisor just finished a work sheet, but all the columns except the following were destroyed by a spilled latte. You have been asked to journalize the adjusting entries using the surviving partial work sheet.

	ACCOUNT NAME	INCOME STATEMENT		BALANCE SHEET	
		DEBIT	CREDIT	DEBIT	CREDIT
1	Cash			8 4 7 6 00	
2	Accounts Receivable			1 4 8 6 00	
5	Equipment			12 3 6 7 00	
6	Accumulated Depreciation, Equipment				3 6 1 0 00
7	Accounts Payable				2 8 1 3 00
8	G. Kramer, Capital				11 7 0 7 00
9	G. Kramer, Drawing			1 1 0 0 00	
10	Income from Services		11 2 1 6 00		
11	Rent Expense	1 4 0 0 00			
12	Supplies Expense	1 1 1 0 00			
13	Wages Expense	2 4 6 7 00			
14					
15	Insurance Expense	2 1 0 00			
16	Depreciation Expense, Equipment	7 5 0 00			
17	Wages Payable				6 2 0 00
18		5 9 3 7 00	11 2 1 6 00	24 0 2 9 00	18 7 5 0 00

PROBLEM SET A

For additional help, see the demonstration problem at the beginning of each chapter in your Working Papers.

P.O. 3

Problem 4-1A The trial balance for Maxie's Insurance Agency as of August 31, after the firm has completed its first month of operations, follows:

ACCOUNT NAME	DEBIT					CREDIT				
Cash	3	4	2	7	00					
Accounts Receivable	1	3	1	9	00					
Prepaid Insurance		3	6	2	00					
Office Equipment	4	9	3	9	00					
Accounts Payable						1	0	7	1	00
C. Maxie, Capital						9	0	2	0	00
C. Maxie, Drawing		9	0	0	00					
Commissions Earned						2	5	2	0	00
Rent Expense		6	9	5	00					
Travel Expense		2	2	5	00					
Supplies Expense		4	9	2	00					
Utilities Expense		1	9	8	00					
Miscellaneous Expense			5	4	00					
	12	6	1	1	00	12	6	1	1	00

Maxie's Insurance Agency
Trial Balance
August 31, 20—

Check Figure

Net Loss, $50

Instructions

1. Record the amounts in the Trial Balance columns of the work sheet.
2. Complete the work sheet by making the following adjustments and lettering each adjustment:
   a. Expired or used-up insurance, $106.
   b. Depreciation expense on office equipment, $800—remember to credit the Accumulated Depreciation account for office equipment, not Office Equipment.

P.O. 4,5

Problem 4-2A The completed work sheet for J. Marquez Design for the month of March is in your Working Papers.

Check Figure

Total Assets, $15,164

Instructions

1. Prepare an income statement.
2. Prepare a statement of owner's equity. Assume that no additional investments were made in March.
3. Prepare a balance sheet.
4. Journalize the adjusting entries.

P.O. 3,5

Problem 4-3A The trial balance of The New Directions Center for the month ended September 30 is presented on the following page.

The New Directions Center
Trial Balance
September 30, 20—

ACCOUNT NAME	DEBIT	CREDIT
Cash	2 3 7 8 00	
Prepaid Insurance	1 3 4 5 00	
Equipment	32 9 7 8 00	
Accumulated Depreciation, Equipment		16 2 3 5 00
Accounts Payable		2 7 5 1 00
C. Bock, Capital		45 2 0 8 00
C. Bock, Drawing	22 4 4 5 00	
Income from Services		43 7 9 1 00
Wages Expense	29 7 6 1 00	
Rent Expense	14 9 3 2 00	
Supplies Expense	8 6 4 00	
Utilities Expense	1 5 7 3 00	
Telephone Expense	1 2 7 1 00	
Miscellaneous Expense	4 3 8 00	
	107 9 8 5 00	107 9 8 5 00

Data for the adjustments are as follows:

a. Expired or used-up insurance, $325.
b. Depreciation expense on equipment, $2,700—remember to credit the Accumulated Depreciation account for equipment, not Equipment.
c. Wages accrued or earned since the last payday, $455 (owed and to be paid on the next payday).

Instructions

1. Complete the work sheet.   2. Journalize the adjusting entries.

Problem 4-4A See the trial balance for Wes's Pitch and Putt on June 30 below.

Wes's Pitch and Putt
Trial Balance
June 30, 20—

ACCOUNT NAME	DEBIT	CREDIT
Cash	4 5 3 2 00	
Prepaid Insurance	1 2 8 4 00	
Equipment	23 6 8 7 00	
Accumulated Depreciation, Equipment		1 2 7 8 00
Repair Equipment	6 2 8 9 00	
Accumulated Depreciation, Repair Equipment		1 4 8 5 00
Accounts Payable		9 6 0 00
W. Wygle, Capital		23 0 1 0 00
W. Wygle, Drawing	1 5 6 5 00	
Golf Fees Income		12 3 8 7 00
Concessions Income		2 8 6 3 00
Wages Expense	2 1 6 3 00	
Rent Expense	1 3 5 0 00	
Utilities Expense	3 5 7 00	
Repair Expense	2 7 1 00	
Supplies Expense	3 4 6 00	
Miscellaneous Expense	1 3 9 00	
	41 9 8 3 00	41 9 8 3 00

Data for month-end adjustments are as follows:

a. Expired or used-up insurance, $370.
b. Depreciation expense on equipment, $950 (remember to credit the Accumulated Depreciation account for equipment, not Equipment).
c. Depreciation expense on repair equipment, $1,350 (remember to credit the Accumulated Depreciation account for repair equipment, not Repair Equipment).
d. Wages accrued or earned since the last payday, $485 (owed and to be paid on the next payday).

Check Figure

Net Income, $7,469

Instructions

1. Complete the work sheet for the month.
2. Prepare an income statement, a statement of owner's equity, and a balance sheet. Assume that no additional investments were made during June.
3. Journalize the adjusting entries.

Instructions for General Ledger Software

1. Journalize the adjusting entries in the general journal. (No work sheet is required.)
2. Post the adjusting entries.
3. Print an income statement, a statement of owner's equity, and a balance sheet. Assume that no additional investments were made during the month.

PROBLEM SET B

For additional help, see the demonstration problem at the beginning of each chapter in your Working Papers.

P.O. 3

Problem 4-1B The trial balance of Marty's Insurance Agency as of September 30, after the firm has completed its first month of operations, follows:

Marty's Insurance Agency
Trial Balance
September 30, 20—

ACCOUNT NAME	DEBIT	CREDIT
Cash	3 5 3 7 00	
Accounts Receivable	1 2 2 8 00	
Prepaid Insurance	6 7 5 00	
Office Equipment	5 2 4 6 00	
Accounts Payable		1 2 6 7 00
S. Marty, Capital		9 6 2 8 00
S. Marty, Drawing	1 1 0 0 00	
Commissions Earned		2 8 4 3 00
Rent Expense	7 8 5 00	
Supplies Expense	3 8 7 00	
Travel Expense	4 8 8 00	
Utilities Expense	2 2 7 00	
Miscellaneous Expense	6 5 00	
	13 7 3 8 00	13 7 3 8 00

Check Figure

Net Income, $41

Instructions

1. Record the amounts in the Trial Balance columns of the work sheet.
2. Complete the work sheet by making the following adjustments and lettering each adjustment:
   a. Expired or used-up insurance, $200.
   b. Depreciation expense on office equipment, $650—remember to credit the Accumulated Depreciation account for office equipment, not Office Equipment.

P.O. 4,5

Problem 4-2B The completed work sheet for Delta Decorators for the month of March is in your Working Papers.

Check Figure

Total Assets, $20,134

Instructions

1. Prepare an income statement.
2. Prepare a statement of owner's equity. Assume no additional investments were made in March.
3. Prepare a balance sheet.
4. Journalize the adjusting entries.

P.O. 3,5

Problem 4-3B The trial balance of Gentle Cleaners for the month ended September 30 is presented below.

Gentle Cleaners
Trial Balance
September 30, 20—

ACCOUNT NAME	DEBIT	CREDIT
Cash	2 4 8 9 00	
Prepaid Insurance	1 2 3 6 00	
Equipment	22 7 5 2 00	
Accumulated Depreciation, Equipment		14 3 5 7 00
Accounts Payable		2 6 4 7 00
D. Nguyen, Capital		28 1 6 9 00
D. Nguyen, Drawing	20 3 5 9 00	
Income from Services		40 8 5 0 00
Wages Expense	24 9 8 3 00	
Rent Expense	10 6 7 3 00	
Utilities Expense	1 1 5 4 00	
Supplies Expense	7 5 2 00	
Telephone Expense	1 2 4 4 00	
Miscellaneous Expense	3 8 1 00	
	86 0 2 3 00	86 0 2 3 00

Data for the adjustments are as follows:

a. Expired or used-up insurance, $685.
b. Depreciation expense on equipment, $2,800 (remember to credit the Accumulated Depreciation account for equipment, not Equipment).
c. Wages accrued or earned since the last payday, $485 (owed and to be paid on the next payday).

Check Figure

Net Loss, $2,307

P.O. 3,4,5,6

Instructions

1. Complete the work sheet.
2. Journalize the adjusting entries.

Problem 4-4B The trial balance for Game Town on July 31 is shown below.

Game Town
Trial Balance
July 31, 20—

ACCOUNT NAME	DEBIT	CREDIT
Cash	3 6 2 1 00	
Prepaid Insurance	1 2 9 5 00	
Equipment	28 6 4 2 00	
Accumulated Depreciation, Equipment		2 3 8 7 00
Repair Equipment	1 8 6 5 00	
Accumulated Depreciation, Repair Equipment		7 8 0 00
Accounts Payable		8 4 2 00
A. Wata, Capital		23 9 7 1 00
A. Wata, Drawing	1 0 0 0 00	
Game Fees Income		8 9 5 4 00
Concessions Income		2 7 5 2 00
Wages Expense	1 2 6 8 00	
Rent Expense	9 8 0 00	
Utilities Expense	2 4 6 00	
Repair Expense	3 8 0 00	
Supplies Expense	2 5 7 00	
Miscellaneous Expense	1 3 2 00	
	39 6 8 6 00	39 6 8 6 00

Data for month-end adjustments are as follows:

a. Expired or used-up insurance, $280.
b. Depreciation expense on equipment, $750 (remember to credit the Accumulated Depreciation account for equipment, not Equipment).
c. Depreciation expense on repair equipment, $350 (remember to credit the Accumulated Depreciation account for repair equipment, not Repair Equipment).
d. Wages accrued or earned since the last payday, $425 (owed and to be paid on the next payday).

Check Figure

Net Income, $6,638

Instructions

1. Complete the work sheet for the month.
2. Prepare an income statement, a statement of owner's equity, and a balance sheet. Assume that no additional investments were made during July.
3. Journalize the adjusting entries.

Instructions for General Ledger Software

1. Journalize the adjusting entries in the general journal. (No work sheet is required.)
2. Post the adjusting entries.
3. Print an income statement, a statement of owner's equity, and a balance sheet. Assume no additional investments were made during the month.

The Computer Clinic

Adjustments

Although you printed the trial balance and financial statements to get an idea of how All About You Spa is doing, some accounts are not accurate. You need to make adjusting entries to provide a clearer picture of how the spa is doing.

How to Compute the Adjustments

Month-end adjusting entries

1. Compute the adjustment amounts for the month of June, using the following information:

Adjustment (a): Liability insurance for six months was purchased during the first days of the month. That protection for one month has been used or expended (Insurance Expense), and the asset (Prepaid Insurance) is not worth what the balance sheet says. Therefore, since All About You Spa paid $960 for a six-month policy and one month of the coverage has been used, $160 of that policy is no longer an asset and represents an expense to the company. How was the figure $160 computed?

Adjustments (b) and (c): Spa equipment and office equipment have depreciated. That means that they have been in use for a month and have, for accounting purposes, lost some usefulness. This is an estimate, of course, which allows us to expense the depreciation and, in effect, lowers the book value (value on the books) of both types of equipment.

(b) The owner, Anika Valli, invested spa equipment totaling $7,393 in the business ($3,158 of her own spa equipment, plus $4,235 of new spa equipment purchased). The spa equipment will be depreciated using the straight-line method. The spa equipment is estimated to have a trade-in or salvage value of $3,500 and is expected to last five years. Therefore, the spa equipment is estimated to have depreciated $64.88 for the month of June. How was the figure $64.88 computed? Remember, you want to compute the depreciation for one month, not one year.

(c) Anika Valli purchased office equipment totaling $1,150. The office equipment will be depreciated using the straight-line method. The office equipment is estimated to have a trade-in or salvage value of $550 and is expected to last five years. Therefore, the office equipment is estimated to have depreciated $10 for the month of June. How was the figure $10 computed? Remember, you want to compute the depreciation for one month, not one year.

Adjustment (d): All About You Spa owes one day of wages to its employees. The month's total wages paid in June amounted to $7,390. The employees worked twenty-one days, but were paid for only twenty days because payday for the last day worked is in the next pay period. Therefore, the spa owes them one day's pay ($369.50), which also needs to be expensed. How was the figure $369.50 computed?

What to Do with the Adjustment Amounts

Note: You will need to add six new accounts to the chart of accounts:

125 Accumulated Depreciation, Spa Equipment
129 Accumulated Depreciation, Office Equipment
212 Wages Payable
518 Insurance Expense
519 Depreciation Expense, Spa Equipment
520 Depreciation Expense, Office Equipment

2. a. If you are completing a work sheet, enter the adjusting entries and complete the work sheet by extending totals to the Adjusted Trial Balance columns and those totals to either the Income Statement or Balance Sheet columns. Total and compute the adjusted net income or net loss.

   b. Using general ledger software, journalize and post the four adjusting entries.

3. Print an adjusted trial balance.

4. Print an after-adjustment income statement for the month ended June 30, 20—.

5. Print an after-adjustment statement of owner's equity for the month ended June 30, 20—.

6. Print an after-adjustment balance sheet as of June 30, 20—.

7. Compare the statements before adjustments with the statements after adjustments. What do you find?

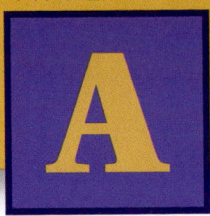

Methods of Depreciation

Performance Objectives

After you have completed this appendix, you will be able to do the following:

1. Prepare a schedule of depreciation using the straight-line method.

2. Prepare a schedule of depreciation using the double-declining-balance method.

3. Prepare a schedule of depreciation for five-year property under the Modified Accelerated Cost Recovery System.

Two methods of depreciation will be illustrated using the example of a delivery truck. Assume that the truck was bought at the beginning of Year 1 and at a cost of $24,000. The truck is estimated to have a useful life of five years and a trade-in value of $6,000 at the end of the five-year period. The two methods to be described are straight-line and double-declining-balance.

STRAIGHT-LINE METHOD

OBJECTIVE 1

Prepare a schedule of depreciation using the straight-line method.

We showed this method in Chapter 4, providing for an equal amount of depreciation each year.

$$\text{Yearly depreciation} = \frac{\text{Cost of asset} - \text{Trade-in value}}{\text{Years of life}} = \frac{\$24,000 - \$6,000}{5 \text{ years}}$$

$$= \frac{\$18,000}{5 \text{ years}} = \$3,600 \text{ per year}$$

Year	Depreciation for the Year	Accumulated Depreciation	Book Value (Cost Less Accumulated Depreciation)
1	$18,000 ÷ 5 years = $ 3,600	$ 3,600	$24,000 − $ 3,600 = $20,400
2	18,000 ÷ 5 years = 3,600	$ 3,600 + $3,600 = 7,200	24,000 − 7,200 = 16,800
3	18,000 ÷ 5 years = 3,600	7,200 + 3,600 = 10,800	24,000 − 10,800 = 13,200
4	18,000 ÷ 5 years = 3,600	10,800 + 3,600 = 14,400	24,000 − 14,400 = 9,600
5	18,000 ÷ 5 years = 3,600	14,400 + 3,600 = 18,000	24,000 − 18,000 = 6,000
	$18,000		

Double-Declining-Balance Method

OBJECTIVE 2

Prepare a schedule of depreciation using the double-declining-balance method.

The term *double* refers to double the straight-line rate. With an estimated useful life of five years, the straight-line rate is ⅕, or 0.2. Twice, or double, the straight-line rate is ⅖ (⅕ × 2) or 0.4. The trade-in value is not taken into account until the end of the schedule. Multiply *book value* at beginning of year by twice the straight-line rate.

Year	Depreciation for the Year	Accumulated Depreciation	Book Value (Cost Less Accumulated Depreciation)
1	$24,000 × 0.4 = $ 9,600	$ 9,600	$24,000 − $ 9,600 = $14,400
2	$14,400 × 0.4 = 5,760	$ 9,600 + $5,760 = 15,360	24,000 − 15,360 = 8,640
3	$8,640 − $6,000 = 2,640	15,360 + 2,640 = 18,000	24,000 − 18,000 = 6,000
4	0	18,000	24,000 − 18,000 = 6,000
5	0	18,000	24,000 − 18,000 = 6,000
	$18,000		

If the schedule is continued for Year 3, depreciation expense would be $3,456 ($8,640 × 0.4). Accumulated depreciation would be $18,816 ($15,360 + $3,456). And book value would be $5,184 ($24,000 − $18,816). However, the book value cannot drop below the established trade-in value of $6,000. So for Year 3 an adjustment must be made limiting the depreciation for the year to $2,640, which will bring the accumulated depreciation up to $18,000. Consequently, the book value at the end of the year will be $6,000 ($24,000 cost − $18,000 accumulated depreciation).

TAX REQUIREMENT—MACRS

OBJECTIVE 3

Prepare a schedule of depreciation for five-year property under the Modified Accelerated Cost Recovery System.

Modified Accelerated Cost Recovery System (MACRS) is the title given by the Internal Revenue Service for a variety of tax rate schedules. The term *recovery* is used because MACRS is a means of recovering or deducting the cost of an asset. Most small businesses use MACRS for financial statement reporting and tax reporting. MACRS is a combination of the declining-balance and straight-line depreciation methods. For more information, see IRS Publication 946, available at **http://www.irs.gov.**

According to MACRS, property is divided into eight classes, as follows:

3-year property—certain horses and tractor units for use over the road
5-year property—autos, light trucks, computers, office machines, and copiers
7-year property—office furniture and fixtures and any property that does not have a class life and that is not, by law, in any other class
10-year property—vessels, barges, tugs, and similar water transportation equipment
15-year property—land improvements including parking lots and roads
20-year property—certain farm buildings
27.5-year residential rental property—rental houses and apartments
39-year property—office buildings and warehouses (nonresidential real property) placed in service after May 13, 1993

Under MACRS, trade-in value is ignored. The following table lists the depreciation rates that a business typically may use for tax purposes.

	Depreciation for Recovery Period			
Year	3-Year	5-Year	7-Year	10-Year
1	33.33%	20.00%	14.29%	10.00%
2	44.45	32.00	24.49	18.00
3	14.81	19.20	17.49	14.40
4	7.41	11.52	12.49	11.52
5		11.52	8.93	9.22
6		5.76	8.92	7.37
7			8.93	6.55
8			4.46	6.55
9				6.56
10				6.55
11				3.28

Our light truck qualifies as five-year property.

Year	Depreciation for the Year		Accumulated Depreciation	Book Value (Cost Less Accumulated Depreciation)
1	$24,000 × 0.20 =	$ 4,800.00	$ 4,800.00	$24,000.00 − $ 4,800.00 = $19,200.00
2	24,000 × 0.32 =	7,680.00	$ 4,800.00 + $7,680.00 = 12,480.00	24,000.00 − 12,480.00 = 11,520.00
3	24,000 × 0.192 =	4,608.00	12,480.00 + 4,608.00 = 17,088.00	24,000.00 − 17,088.00 = 6,912.00
4	24,000 × 0.1152 =	2,764.80	17,088.00 + 2,764.80 = 19,852.80	24,000.00 − 19,852.80 = 4,147.20
5	24,000 × 0.1152 =	2,764.80	19,852.80 + 2,764.80 = 22,617.60	24,000.00 − 22,617.60 = 1,382.40
6	24,000 × 0.0576 =	1,382.40	22,617.60 + 1,382.40 = 24,000.00	24,000.00 − 24,000.00 = 0
		$24,000.00		

PROBLEMS

P.O. 1

Check Figure

Year 1 depreciation, $4,000

Problem A-1 A delivery van was bought for $18,000. The estimated life of the van is four years. The trade-in value at the end of four years is estimated to be $2,000. Prepare a depreciation schedule for the four-year period using the straight-line method.

P.O. 3

Check Figure

Year 3 depreciation, $3,456

Problem A-2 Assume the van is 5-year property. Using the information in Problem A-1, prepare a schedule of depreciation under MACRS. Round figures to the nearest whole dollar.

internet
LINKS TO ACCOUNTING

If you had your own shop and sold something to a customer on credit, when would you record the revenue from that sale? Would you record it when the sale was made, even though you haven't received any cash for the item yet? Or would you wait and record the revenue when you actually received the payment? Your answer to this question depends on what method of accounting you use to record your transactions. As you learn about the different methods in this chapter, think about which method you might use and why. What about Dell, Inc., the computer manufacturer? Look up financial highlights by going to **htpp://www .dell.com** and searching for SEC Reports. Select 2005 and then Form 10-K. Think about the method that Dell uses. Can you tell from looking at its financial statements?

Performance Objectives

After you have completed this chapter, you will be able to do the following:

1. List the steps in the accounting cycle.

2. Journalize and post closing entries for a service enterprise.

3. Prepare a post-closing trial balance.

4. Define the following methods of accounting: cash basis and accrual basis.

5. Prepare interim statements.

L et's review the steps in the accounting cycle for an entire fiscal period. Remember that a fiscal period is generally twelve consecutive months, but it can also consist of other time frames like three months or six months.

OBJECTIVE 1

List the steps in the accounting cycle.

1. **Analyze source documents and record business transactions in a journal.**
2. **Post journal entries to the accounts in the ledger.**
3. **Prepare a trial balance.**
4. **Gather adjustment data and record the adjusting entries on a work sheet.**
5. **Complete the work sheet.**
6. **Prepare financial statements from the data on the work sheet.**
7. **Journalize and post the adjusting entries from the data on the work sheet.**

8. **Journalize and post the closing entries.**
9. **Prepare a post-closing trial balance.**

This chapter explains the procedure for completing the final steps: closing entries and the post-closing trial balance.

Adjusting entries, closing entries, and a post-closing trial balance are prepared at the end of a fiscal period. The number of months in a fiscal period varies. To introduce you to these final steps in the accounting cycle, we assume here that the fiscal period for Cline's Computer Clinic is one month. We make this assumption so that we can thoroughly cover the material and give you a chance to practice its application. The entire accounting cycle is outlined in Figure 1.

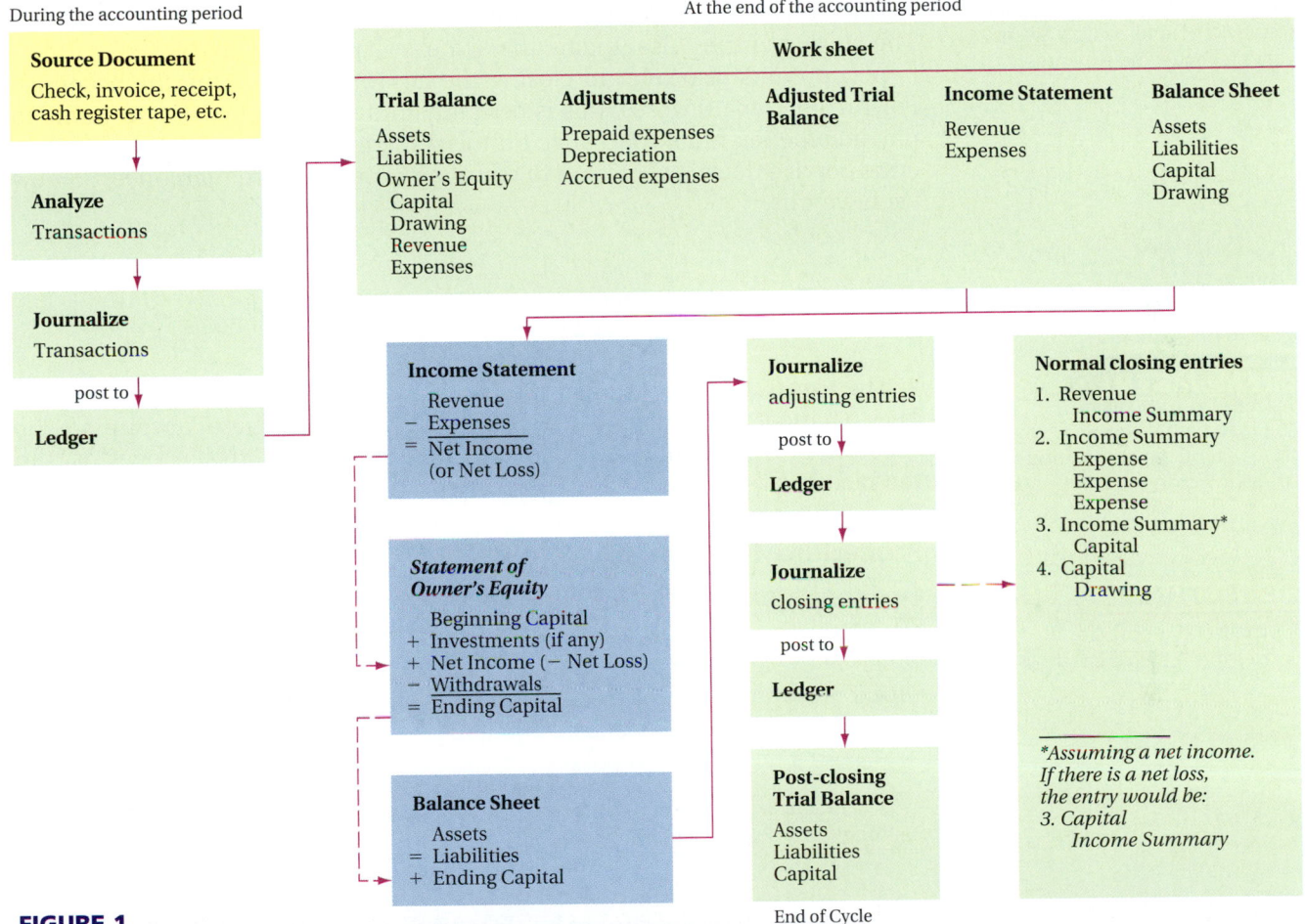

FIGURE 1

CLOSING ENTRIES

To help you understand the reason for the closing entries, let's repeat the fundamental accounting equation:

Assets = Liabilities + Owner's Equity + Revenue − Expenses

Closing entries empty or zero out temporary owner's equity accounts and prepare the accounts for the new accounting period—emptying out folders for one year so they can be filled with the new year's revenue and expenses.

We know that the income statement, as stated in the third line of its heading, covers a period of time. The income statement consists of revenue minus expenses for this period of time only. So, when the next fiscal period begins, we should start with zero balances. We start all over again each period.

Purpose of Closing Entries

This brings us to the *purpose* of the **closing entries**, which is to close (or zero) the temporary-equity or nominal accounts (revenue, expense, and Drawing accounts). We do this because their balances apply to only one fiscal period. Closing entries are made after the last adjusting entry. With the coming of the next fiscal period, we want to start from zero, recording revenue and expenses for the new fiscal period. The closing entries also update the owner's Capital account.

Accountants also refer to closing the accounts as clearing the accounts. For income tax purposes, this is certainly understandable. No one wants to pay income tax more than once on the same income, and the Internal Revenue Service doesn't allow you to count an expense more than once. So now we have this:

$$\text{Assets} = \text{Liabilities} + \underset{\text{(Capital)}}{\text{Owner's Equity}} + \overset{\text{(closed)}}{\cancel{\text{Revenue}}} - \overset{\text{(closed)}}{\cancel{\text{Expenses}}}$$

The matching principle is why we close revenue, expense, and Drawing accounts.

The assets, the liabilities, and the owner's Capital account remain open. The balance sheet gives the present balances of these accounts. The accountant carries the asset, liability, and Capital account balances over to the next fiscal period.

Procedure for Closing

OBJECTIVE 2
Journalize and post closing entries for a service enterprise.

The procedure for closing is simply to balance off the account; in other words, to make the balance *equal to zero*. This meets our objective, which is to start from zero in the next fiscal period. Let's illustrate this first with T accounts. Suppose an account to be closed has a debit balance of $960; then, to make the balance equal to zero, we *credit* the account for $960.

Debit		Credit	
Balance	960	Closing	960

Now suppose an account to be closed has a credit balance of $1,200; then, to make the balance equal to zero, we *debit* the account for $1,200.

Debit		Credit	
Closing	1,200	Balance	1,200

Remember, every entry must have at least one debit and one credit. So, to record the other half of the closing entry, we bring into existence the **Income Summary account**. The Income Summary account does not have plus and minus signs, just debit and credit.

At the end of a fiscal period, closing entries allow a business to start a new income statement period with a clean slate. Revenue and expense accounts are closed.

There are four steps in the closing procedure:

1. **Close the revenue accounts into Income Summary.**
2. **Close the expense accounts into Income Summary.**
3. **Close the Income Summary account into the Capital account, transferring the net income or loss to the Capital account.**
4. **Close the Drawing account into the Capital account.**

To illustrate, we return to Cline's Computer Clinic. For the purpose of the illustration, assume that Cline's Computer Clinic's fiscal period consists of one month. We have the following T account balances in the revenue and expense accounts after the adjustments have been posted.

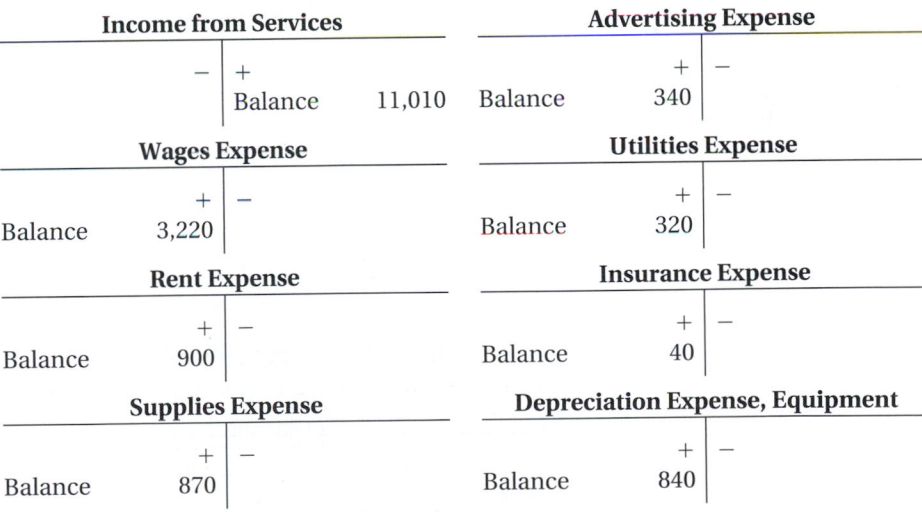

Step 1 **Close the revenue account or accounts into Income Summary.** In order to make the balance of Income from Services equal to zero, we *balance it off*, or debit it, in the amount of $11,010. Because we need an offsetting credit, we credit Income Summary for the same amount. Notice that there

are no signs in Income Summary, only Debit and Credit like the other accounts.

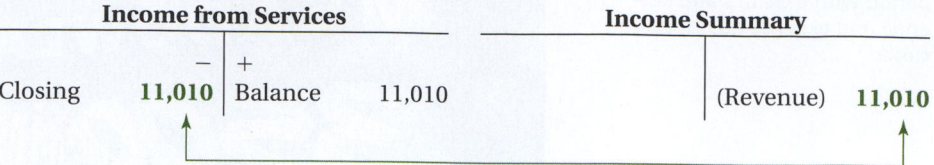

Income from Services				Income Summary		
	–	+				
Closing	**11,010**	Balance	11,010		(Revenue)	**11,010**

The balance of Income from Services is transferred to Income Summary.

Step 2 **Close the expense accounts into Income Summary.** To make the balances of the expense accounts equal to zero, we need to balance them off, or credit them. Again the T accounts are useful for formulating this journal entry.

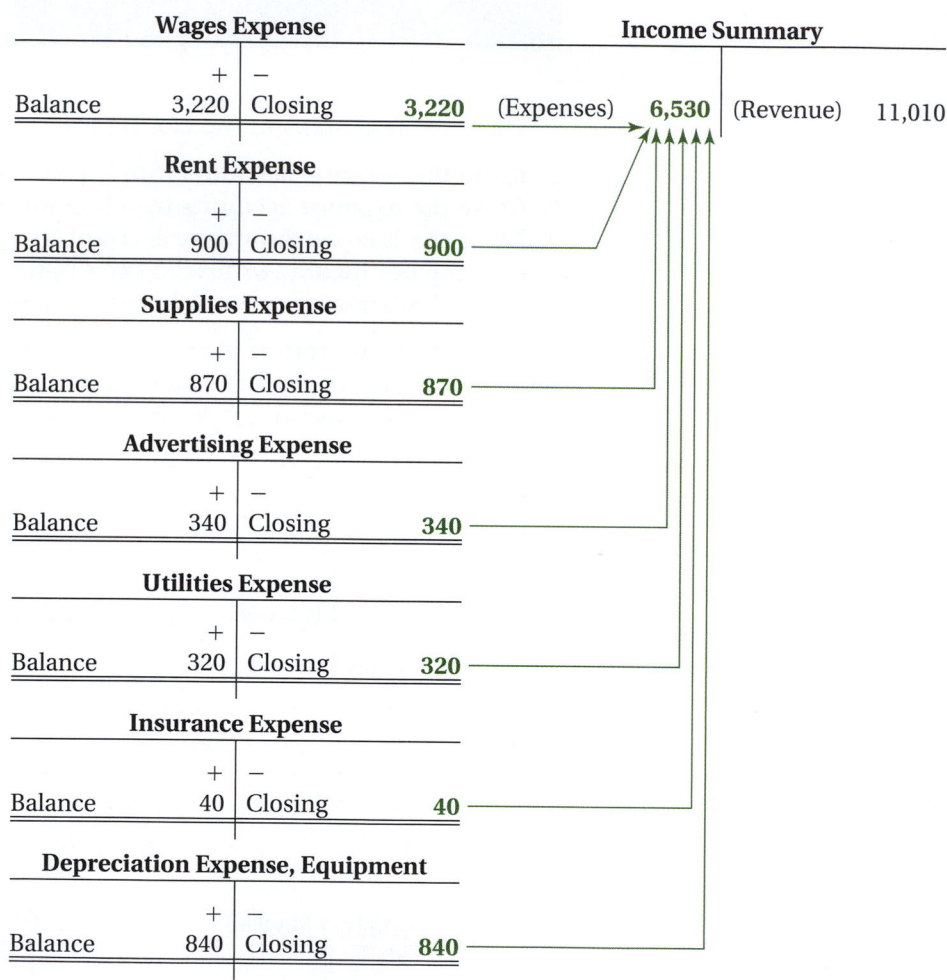

Wages Expense

	+	–		**Income Summary**			
Balance	3,220	Closing	**3,220**	(Expenses)	**6,530**	(Revenue)	11,010

Rent Expense

	+	–	
Balance	900	Closing	**900**

Supplies Expense

	+	–	
Balance	870	Closing	**870**

Advertising Expense

	+	–	
Balance	340	Closing	**340**

Utilities Expense

	+	–	
Balance	320	Closing	**320**

Insurance Expense

	+	–	
Balance	40	Closing	**40**

Depreciation Expense, Equipment

	+	–	
Balance	840	Closing	**840**

Step 3 Recall that we created Income Summary so that we could have a debit and a credit in each closing entry. Now that it has done its job, we close it out. We use the same procedure as before, in that we make the balance equal to zero, or balance off the account. We transfer, or close, the balance of the Income Summary account into the Capital account, as shown in the T accounts and in Figure 2.

Income Summary		R. P. Cline, Capital	
		− | +	
(Expenses) 6,530 | (Revenue) 11,010		Balance 88,200	
Closing **4,480**		(Net Inc.) **4,480**	

Income Summary is always closed into the Capital account by the amount of the net income (Revenue minus Expenses) or the net loss. Comparing net income or net loss on the work sheet with the closing entry for Income Summary can serve as a check point or verification for you.

FIGURE 2

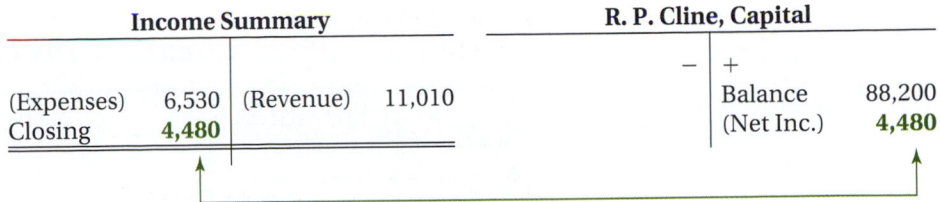

	DATE	DESCRIPTION	POST. REF.	DEBIT	CREDIT	
14	Step	Closing Entries				14
15	1 · 30	Income from Services		11 0 1 0 00		15
16		Income Summary			11 0 1 0 00	16
17						17
18	30	Income Summary		6 5 3 0 00		18
19		Wages Expense			3 2 2 0 00	19
20		Rent Expense			9 0 0 00	20
21	Step	Supplies Expense			8 7 0 00	21
22	2	Advertising Expense			3 4 0 00	22
23		Utilities Expense			3 2 0 00	23
24		Insurance Expense			4 0 00	24
25		Depreciation Expense,				25
26		Equipment			8 4 0 00	26
27						27
28	30	Income Summary		4 4 8 0 00		28
29		R. P. Cline, Capital			4 4 8 0 00	29

GENERAL JOURNAL — PAGE 4

Net income is added (credited) to the Capital account because, as shown in the statement of owner's equity, net income is treated as an addition. Net loss, on the other hand, is subtracted from (debited to) the Capital account, because net loss is treated as a deduction in the statement of owner's equity. Here's how to close Income Summary for J. Doe Company (net loss of $200):

Income Summary		J. Doe, Capital	
		− | +	
(Expenses) 2,600 | (Revenue) **2,400**	(Net Loss) **200** | Balance	30,000
| Closing **200**			

The entry to close Income Summary into J. Doe's Capital account would look like the following.

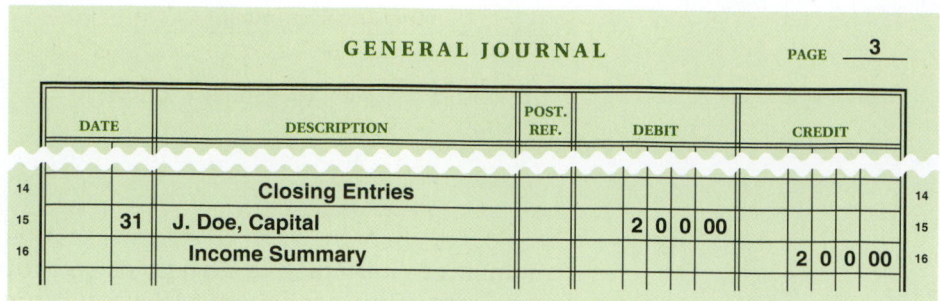

Step 4   Let's return to the example of Cline's Computer Clinic. The Drawing account applies to only one fiscal period, and so it too must be closed. Drawing is not an expense because it did not help the business generate revenue. And because Drawing is not an expense, it cannot affect net income or net loss. It appears in the statement of owner's equity as a deduction from the Capital account, so it is closed directly into the Capital account. We balance off the Drawing account, or make the balance of it equal to zero. The balance of Drawing is transferred to the Capital account.

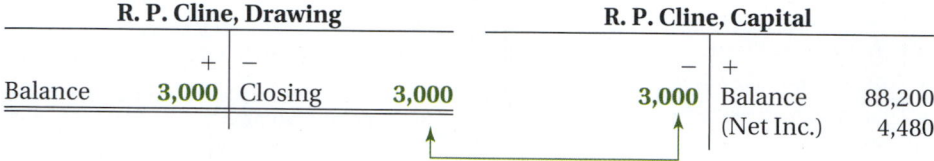

The journal entries in the closing procedure are shown in Figure 3.

FIGURE 3

GENERAL JOURNAL   PAGE ___4___

	DATE	DESCRIPTION	POST. REF.	DEBIT	CREDIT	
14	Step	**Closing Entries**				14
15	1 30	Income from Services	411	11 0 1 0 00		15
16		Income Summary	313		11 0 1 0 00	16
17						17
18	30	Income Summary	313	6 5 3 0 00		18
19		Wages Expense	511		3 2 2 0 00	19
20		Rent Expense	512		9 0 0 00	20
21	Step	Supplies Expense	513		8 7 0 00	21
22	2	Advertising Expense	514		3 4 0 00	22
23		Utilities Expense	515		3 2 0 00	23
24		Insurance Expense	516		4 0 00	24
25		Depreciation Expense,				25
26		Equipment	517		8 4 0 00	26
27						27
28	Step 30	Income Summary	313	4 4 8 0 00		28
29	3	R. P. Cline, Capital	311		4 4 8 0 00	29
30						30
31	Step 30	R. P. Cline, Capital	311	3 0 0 0 00		31
32	4	R. P. Cline, Drawing	312		3 0 0 0 00	32

FYI

As a memory tool for the sequence of steps in the closing procedure, use the letters of the closing elements, **REID**: Revenue, Expenses, Income Summary, Drawing.

These closing entries show that Cline's Computer Clinic has net income of $4,480, the owner has withdrawn $3,000 for personal expenses, and $1,480 has been retained in the business, thereby increasing capital.

Closing Entries Taken Directly from the Work Sheet

You can gather the information for the closing entries either directly from the ledger accounts or from the work sheet. Since the Income Statement columns of the work sheet consist entirely of revenues and expenses, you can pick up the figures for three of the four closing entries from these columns. Figure 4 shows a partial work sheet for Cline's Computer Clinic.

	ACCOUNT NAME	TRIAL BALANCE DEBIT	TRIAL BALANCE CREDIT	ADJUSTMENTS DEBIT	ADJUSTMENTS CREDIT	INCOME STATEMENT DEBIT	INCOME STATEMENT CREDIT
1	Cash	11 950 00					
2	Accounts Receivable	620 00					
3	Prepaid Insurance	480 00			(a) 40 00		
4	Equipment	83 720 00					
5	Accounts Payable		5 970 00				
6	R. P. Cline, Capital		88 200 00				
7	R. P. Cline, Drawing	3 000 00					
8	Income from Services		11 010 00				11 010 00
9	Wages Expense	2 980 00		(c) 240 00		3 220 00	
10	Rent Expense	900 00				900 00	
11	Supplies Expense	870 00				870 00	
12	Advertising Expense	340 00				340 00	
13	Utilities Expense	320 00				320 00	
14		105 180 00	105 180 00				
15	Insurance Expense			(a) 40 00		40 00	
16	Depreciation Expense,						
17	Equipment			(b) 840 00		840 00	
18							
19	Accumulated Dep.,						
20	Equipment				(b) 840 00		
21	Wages Payable				(c) 240 00		
22				1 120 00	1 120 00	6 530 00	11 010 00
23	Net Income					4 480 00	
24						11 010 00	11 010 00
25							
26							

FIGURE 4

You may plan the closing entries by balancing off all the figures that appear in the Income Statement columns. For example, in the Income Statement Credit column, there is a credit for $11,010 (Income from Services), so we debit that account for $11,010 and credit Income Summary for $11,010.

There are debits for $3,220, $900, $870, $340, $320, $40, and $840 (expense accounts). So now we *credit* these accounts for the same amounts, and we debit Income Summary for their total ($6,530).

Next, we close Income Summary into Capital, using the net income figure already shown on the work sheet in Figure 4.

We do, of course, have to get the last closing entry from the Balance Sheet columns to close Drawing.

Incidentally, accountants call the accounts that are to be closed (such as revenue, expenses, Income Summary, and Drawing) **nominal** or **temporary-equity accounts**. These accounts are *temporary* in that their balances apply to only one fiscal period. The *equity* aspect pertains because these accounts all come under the umbrella of owner's equity.

On the other hand, accountants call the accounts that remain open (such as assets, liabilities, and Capital) **real** or **permanent accounts**. These accounts have balances that will be carried over to the next fiscal period. They are *permanent* because as long as the company exists, there will be balances in these accounts.

Posting the Closing Entries

In the Item column of the ledger account, we write the word *Closing*. To show that the balance of an account is zero, we draw a line through both the Debit Balance and the Credit Balance columns.

After we have posted the closing entries, the Capital, Drawing, Income Summary, revenue, and expense accounts of Cline's Computer Clinic appear as follows:

GENERAL LEDGER

ACCOUNT   R. P. Cline, Capital   ACCOUNT NO. 311

	DATE		ITEM	POST. REF.	DEBIT	CREDIT	BALANCE DEBIT	BALANCE CREDIT	
1	20–								1
2	June	1		1		82 0 0 0 00		82 0 0 0 00	2
3		4		1		6 2 0 0 00		88 2 0 0 00	3
4		30	Closing	4		4 4 8 0 00		92 6 8 0 00	4
5		30	Closing	4	3 0 0 0 00			89 6 8 0 00	5

ACCOUNT   R. P. Cline, Drawing   ACCOUNT NO. 312

	DATE		ITEM	POST. REF.	DEBIT	CREDIT	BALANCE DEBIT	BALANCE CREDIT	
1	20–								1
2	June	30		3	3 0 0 0 00		3 0 0 0 00		2
3		30	Closing	4		3 0 0 0 00	—	—	3

ACCOUNT   Income Summary   ACCOUNT NO. 313

	DATE		ITEM	POST. REF.	DEBIT	CREDIT	BALANCE DEBIT	BALANCE CREDIT	
1	20–								1
2	June	30	Closing	4		11 0 1 0 00		11 0 1 0 00	2
3		30	Closing	4	6 5 3 0 00			4 4 8 0 00	3
4		30	Closing	4	4 4 8 0 00		—	—	4

ACCOUNT __Income from Services__   ACCOUNT NO. __411__

	DATE		ITEM	POST. REF.	DEBIT	CREDIT	BALANCE DEBIT	BALANCE CREDIT	
1	20–								1
2	June	7		1		3 5 2 0 00		3 5 2 0 00	2
3		15		2		1 4 7 0 00		4 9 9 0 00	3
4		30		3		6 0 2 0 00		11 0 1 0 00	4
5		30	Closing	4	11 0 1 0 00		—	—	5
6									6

ACCOUNT __Wages Expense__   ACCOUNT NO. __511__

	DATE		ITEM	POST. REF.	DEBIT	CREDIT	BALANCE DEBIT	BALANCE CREDIT	
1	20–								1
2	June	24		2	2 9 8 0 00		2 9 8 0 00		2
3		30	Adj.	4	2 4 0 00		3 2 2 0 00		3
4		30	Closing	4		3 2 2 0 00	—	—	4

ACCOUNT __Rent Expense__   ACCOUNT NO. __512__

	DATE		ITEM	POST. REF.	DEBIT	CREDIT	BALANCE DEBIT	BALANCE CREDIT	
1	20–								1
2	June	8		1	9 0 0 00		9 0 0 00		2
3		30	Closing	4		9 0 0 00	—	—	3

ACCOUNT __Supplies Expense__   ACCOUNT NO. __513__

	DATE		ITEM	POST. REF.	DEBIT	CREDIT	BALANCE DEBIT	BALANCE CREDIT	
1	20–								1
2	June	10		1	8 7 0 00		8 7 0 00		2
3		30	Closing	4		8 7 0 00	—	—	3

ACCOUNT __Advertising Expense__   ACCOUNT NO. __514__

	DATE		ITEM	POST. REF.	DEBIT	CREDIT	BALANCE DEBIT	BALANCE CREDIT	
1	20–								1
2	June	14		2	3 4 0 00		3 4 0 00		2
3		30	Closing	4		3 4 0 00	—	—	3

ACCOUNT **Utilities Expense**   ACCOUNT NO. __515__

									BALANCE			
	DATE		ITEM	POST. REF.		DEBIT		CREDIT		DEBIT		CREDIT
1	20–											
2	June	18		2	3 2 0	00				3 2 0	00	
3		30	Closing	4				3 2 0	00	—		—

ACCOUNT **Insurance Expense**   ACCOUNT NO. __516__

									BALANCE			
	DATE		ITEM	POST. REF.		DEBIT		CREDIT		DEBIT		CREDIT
1	20–											
2	June	30	Adj.	4	4 0	00				4 0	00	
3		30	Closing	4				4 0	00	—		—

ACCOUNT **Depreciation Expense, Equipment**   ACCOUNT NO. __517__

									BALANCE			
	DATE		ITEM	POST. REF.		DEBIT		CREDIT		DEBIT		CREDIT
1	20–											
2	June	30	Adj.	4	8 4 0	00				8 4 0	00	
3		30	Closing	4				8 4 0	00	—		—

Office supplies—such as those supplied by major chains like Office Depot and Staples—consist of a wide variety of items that are used up and reordered frequently in the course of doing business.

THE POST-CLOSING TRIAL BALANCE

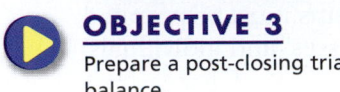

OBJECTIVE 3

Prepare a post-closing trial balance.

After posting the closing entries and before going on to the next fiscal period, verify the balances of the accounts that remain open. To do so, prepare a **post-closing trial balance**, using the final balance figures from the ledger accounts. The purpose of the post-closing trial balance is to make sure that the debit balances equal the credit balances.

Note that the accounts listed in the post-closing trial balance (assets, liabilities, and Capital) are the *real* or *permanent accounts* (see Figure 5). The accountant carries forward the balances of the permanent accounts from one fiscal period to another.

FIGURE 5

Cline's Computer Clinic
Post-Closing Trial Balance
June 30, 20—

ACCOUNT NAME	DEBIT	CREDIT
Cash	11 9 5 0 00	
Accounts Receivable	6 2 0 00	
Prepaid Insurance	4 4 0 00	
Equipment	83 7 2 0 00	
Accumulated Depreciation, Equipment		8 4 0 00
Accounts Payable		5 9 7 0 00
Wages Payable		2 4 0 00
R. P. Cline, Capital		89 6 8 0 00
	96 7 3 0 00	96 7 3 0 00

Contrast this to the handling of *nominal* or *temporary-equity accounts* (revenue, expenses, Income Summary, and Drawing), which are closed at the end of each fiscal period.

If the total debits and total credits of the post-closing trial balance are not equal, here's a recommended procedure for tracking down the error.

1. Re-add the trial balance columns.
2. Check to see that the figures were correctly transferred from the ledger accounts to the post-closing trial balance.
3. Verify the posting of the adjusting entries and the recording of the new balances.
4. Make sure that the closing entries have been posted and that all revenue, expense, Income Summary, and Drawing accounts have zero balances.

THE BASES OF ACCOUNTING: CASH AND ACCRUAL

OBJECTIVE 4

Define the following methods of accounting: cash basis and accrual basis.

The basis of accounting that a company chooses has a direct effect on the company's net income and the company's income tax. The business must use the same basis of accounting from year to year, and the basis of accounting must clearly reflect the net income of the business.

FYI

For income tax purposes, the availability of the cash method is explained by the IRS in Publication 538. Most service businesses with average annual gross receipts of $5 million or less will be allowed to use the cash method rather than the accrual method, which is more complicated and time consuming. Most businesses use the same method of accounting for their financial statements and income tax reporting. IRS Publication 538 is available on the IRS website at **http://www.irs.gov.**

Under the **cash basis of accounting**, revenue is counted when it is received in cash, and generally expenses are counted when they are paid in cash. If the expenditures have an economic life of more than one year, for example equipment purchases and insurance, then the cost of these items must be prorated or spread out over their useful lives. Many small businesses' and individuals' personal income taxes are recorded on the cash basis.

Under the **accrual basis of accounting**, revenue is recorded when it is earned, and expenses are recorded when they are incurred (when they occur or the bill is received). For example, in the sale of goods, revenue is counted by the seller when the buyer accepts delivery of the goods. Expenses are recorded by the seller of the goods when the costs are incurred. This is called the *matching* principle, since revenue in one fiscal period is matched up with expenses incurred in the same period. If your business produces, purchases, or sells merchandise, the business must keep an inventory and use the accrual method for sales and purchases of merchandise. A business may also use a combination of cash and accrual bases of accounting, called the *hybrid method.*

INTERIM STATEMENTS

OBJECTIVE 5

Prepare interim statements.

The owner of a business understandably does not want to wait until the end of the twelve-month fiscal period to determine whether the company made a profit or a loss. Instead, most owners want financial statements at the end of each month. Financial statements prepared during the fiscal year, for periods of less than twelve months, are called **interim statements**. (They are given this name because they are prepared within the fiscal period.) For example, a business may prepare the income statement, the statement of owner's equity, and the balance sheet *monthly.* These statements provide up-to-date information about the results and status of operations. For example, a company might have the following interim statements:

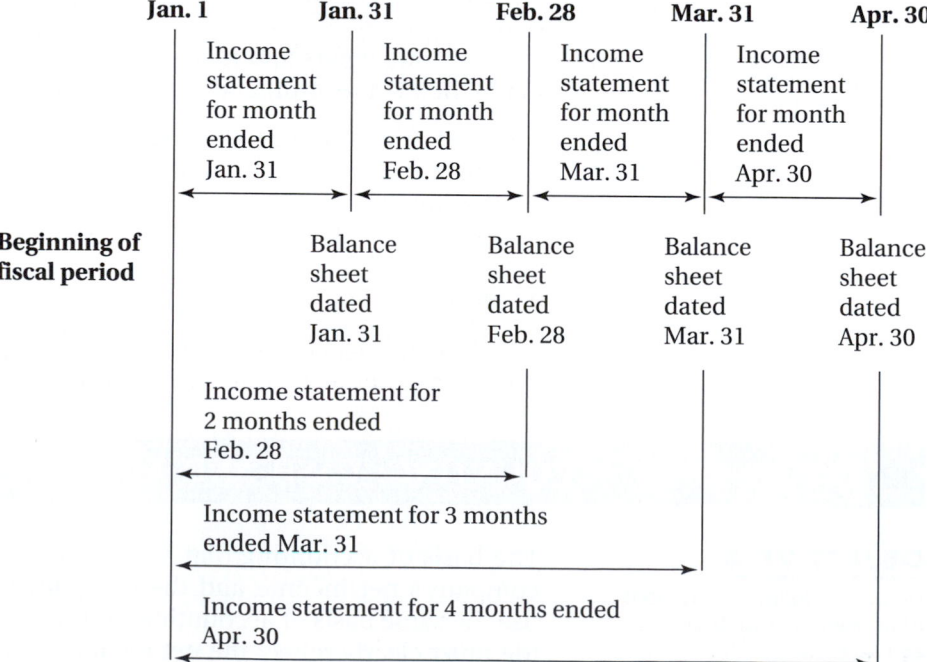

In this case, the accountant would prepare a work sheet at the end of each month. Next, based on these work sheets, he or she would prepare the financial statements. *However, the remaining steps—journalizing the adjusting and closing entries and preparing the post-closing trial balance—would be performed only at the end of the year.*

CHAPTER REVIEW

Online Study Center
ACE the test!

Review of Performance Objectives

1. List the steps in the accounting cycle.

   1. Analyze source documents and record business transactions in a journal.
   2. Post journal entries to the accounts in the ledger.
   3. Prepare a trial balance.
   4. Gather adjustment data and record the adjusting entries on a work sheet.
   5. Complete the work sheet.
   6. Prepare financial statements from the data on the work sheet.
   7. Journalize and post the adjusting entries from the data on the work sheet.
   8. Journalize and post the closing entries.
   9. Prepare a post-closing trial balance.

2. Journalize and post closing entries for a service enterprise.

   The four steps in the closing procedure are as follows:

   1. Close the revenue accounts into Income Summary.
   2. Close the expense accounts into Income Summary.
   3. Close the Income Summary account into the Capital account, transferring the net income or loss to the Capital account.
   4. Close the Drawing account into the Capital account.

3. Prepare a post-closing trial balance.

   A post-closing trial balance consists of the final balances of the accounts remaining open. It is the final proof that the debit balances equal the credit balances before the posting for the new fiscal period begins.

4. Define the following methods of accounting: cash basis and accrual basis.

   Under the *cash basis* of accounting, revenue is recorded when it is received and expenses are generally counted when they are paid in cash. Under the *accrual basis* of accounting, revenue is recorded when earned, even if cash is received at a later date, and expenses are recorded when incurred, even if cash is to be paid at a later date.

5. Prepare interim statements.

   Interim statements consist of year-to-date income statements, statements of owner's equity, and balance sheets as of various dates during the fiscal period.

Glossary

Accrual basis of accounting An accounting method under which revenue is recorded when it is earned, regardless of when it is received, and expenses are recorded when they are incurred, regardless of when they are paid. (166)

Cash basis of accounting An accounting method under which revenue is recorded only when it is received in cash. Most expenses are recorded only when they are paid in cash. However, exceptions are made for expenditures on items having a useful life of more than one year and for certain prepaid items. Expenditures for insurance premiums can be *prorated,* or spread out, over the fiscal periods covered. Expenditures for long-lived items are recorded as assets and later depreciated as an expense over their useful lives. (166)

Closing entries Entries made at the end of a fiscal period to close off the revenue, expense, and Drawing accounts—that is, to make the balances of the temporary-equity accounts equal to zero. Closing is also called *clearing the accounts.* (156)

Income Summary account An account brought into existence in order to have a debit and credit in each closing entry. The revenue and expense account balances are transferred to this account to allow calculations of net income or net loss. (156)

Interim statements Financial statements prepared during the fiscal year, covering a period of time less than twelve months. (166)

Nominal or **temporary-equity accounts** Accounts that apply to only one fiscal period and that are to be closed at the end of that fiscal period, such as revenue, expense, Income Summary, and Drawing accounts. This category may also be described as all accounts except assets, liabilities, and the Capital account. (162)

Post-closing trial balance The listing of the final balances of the real accounts at the end of the fiscal period. (165)

Real or **permanent accounts** The accounts that remain open (assets, liabilities, and the Capital account in owner's equity) and that have balances that will be carried over to the next fiscal period. (162)

QUESTIONS, EXERCISES, AND CASES

Discussion Questions

1. Number in order the following steps in the accounting cycle.
   a. Prepare a trial balance on the first two columns of the work sheet.
   b. Post journal entries to accounts in the ledger.
   c. Journalize and post adjusting entries.
   d. Analyze source documents and record transactions in the journal.
   e. Prepare financial statements.
   f. Gather adjusting data and write adjusting entries on the work sheet.

g. Journalize and post closing entries.

h. Prepare a post-closing trial balance.

i. Complete the work sheet (this assumes a manual system).

2. List the steps in the closing procedure in the correct order.

3. What is the purpose of closing entries? Consider the consequence of forgetting to make closing entries.

4. What happens if you do not print, save, and back up your financial statements before the closing entries occur?

5. What are real accounts? What are nominal accounts? Give examples of each.

6. What is the purpose of the Income Summary account, and how does it relate to the revenue and expense accounts?

7. What is the purpose of the post-closing trial balance? What is the difference between a trial balance and a post-closing trial balance?

8. Write the third closing entry to transfer the profit or loss to the B. Corson, Capital account, assuming the following:

   a. A profit of $3,765 during the first quarter (Jan.–Mar.)

   b. A loss of $1,689 during the second quarter (Apr.–Jun.)

Exercises

P.O. 2

Classify accounts and show where they are listed on the work sheet.

Exercise 5-1 Classify the accounts listed below as real (permanent) or nominal (temporary), and indicate with an X whether the account is closed. Also, indicate the financial statement in which each account will appear. The Building account is given as an example.

Account Title	Real	Nominal	Closed Yes	Closed No	Income Statement	Balance Sheet
0. Example: Building	X			X		X
a. Prepaid Insurance						
b. Accounts Payable						
c. Wages Payable						
d. Services Income						
e. Rent Expense						
f. Supplies Expense						
g. Accum. Depr.,						

P.O. 2

Journalize closing entries from T account balances.

Exercise 5-2 Number the closing entries as steps 1 through 4. Journalize the closing entries shown on the next page.

Assets	=	Liabilities	+	Owner's Equity	+	Revenue	−	Expenses
Dr. | Cr.		Dr. | Cr.		Dr. | Cr.		Dr. | Cr.		Dr. | Cr.
+ | −		− | +		− | +		− | +		+ | −

Prepaid Insurance

Bal. 990	(c) 360
Bal. 630	

Accum. Depr., Equipment

	Bal. 3,200
	(b) 700
	Bal. 3,900

Wages Payable

	(a) 210

J. Ramsey, Capital

560	Bal. 24,000
500	
	Bal. 22,940

J. Ramsey, Drawing

Bal. 500	500

Income Summary

4,210	3,650
	560

Professional Fees

3,650	Bal. 3,650

Wages Expense

Bal. 2,800	
(a) 210	
Bal. 3,010	3,010

Insurance Expense

(c) 360	360

Depr. Expense, Equipment

(b) 700	700

Misc. Expense

Bal. 140	140

P.O. 2

Journalize closing entries from account balances.

Exercise 5-3 As of December 31, the end of the current year, the ledger of Harris Company contained the following account balances after adjustment. All accounts have normal balances. Journalize the closing entries.

Cash	$ 8,540	H. Harris, Drawing	$1,698
Equipment	11,486	Professional Fees	6,875
Accumulated Depreciation,		Wages Expense	1,468
Equipment	2,687	Rent Expense	990
Accounts Payable	1,574	Depreciation Expense,	
Wages Payable	658	Equipment	1,243
H. Harris, Capital	13,876	Miscellaneous Expense	245

P.O. 2

Journalize closing entries from work sheet columns—a profit.

Exercise 5-4 The Income Statement columns of the work sheet of Dwyer Company for the fiscal year ended June 30 appear below. During the year, N. Dwyer withdrew $4,200. Journalize the closing entries.

	ACCOUNT NAME	INCOME STATEMENT DEBIT	INCOME STATEMENT CREDIT
1	Service Income		6 8 9 7 00
2	Rental Income		3 6 7 6 00
3	Rent Expense	2 7 0 0 00	
4	Wages Expense	1 9 5 4 00	
5	Utilities Expense	3 6 5 00	
6	Miscellaneous Expense	1 5 9 00	
7		5 1 7 8 00	10 5 7 3 00
8	Net Income	5 3 9 5 00	
9		10 5 7 3 00	10 5 7 3 00

P.O. 2

Journalize closing entries from work sheet columns—a loss.

Exercise 5-5 The Income Statement columns of the work sheet of Salas Company for the fiscal year ended December 31 appear on the following page. During the year, S. Salas withdrew $18,000. Journalize the closing entries.

	ACCOUNT NAME	INCOME STATEMENT	
		DEBIT	CREDIT
1	Service Income		32 7 4 0 00
2	Rental Income		12 0 0 0 00
3	Wages Expense	43 5 2 0 00	
4	Utilities Expense	4 6 3 0 00	
5	Miscellaneous Expense	9 2 0 0 00	
6		57 3 5 0 00	44 7 4 0 00
7	Net Loss		12 6 1 0 00
8		57 3 5 0 00	57 3 5 0 00

P.O. 2

Journalize closing entries three and four from account balances.

Exercise 5-6 After all revenue and expenses have been closed at the end of the fiscal period ended December 31, Income Summary has a debit of $46,550 and a credit of $37,520. On the same date, E. Masters, Drawing, has a debit balance of $13,500, and E. Masters, Capital, had a beginning credit balance of $64,410.

a. Journalize the entries to close the remaining temporary accounts.
b. What is the new balance of E. Masters, Capital, after closing the remaining temporary accounts? Show your calculations.

P.O. 5

Place accounts on financial statements.

Exercise 5-7 Indicate with an X whether each of the following would appear on the income statement, statement of owner's equity, or balance sheet. An item may appear on more than one statement. The first item is provided as an example.

Item	Income Statement	Statement of Owner's Equity	Balance Sheet
0. Example: The total liabilities of the business at the end of the year.			X
a. The amount of the owner's Capital balance at the end of the year.			
b. The amount of depreciation expense on equipment during the year.			
c. The amount of the company's net income for the year.			
d. The book value of the equipment.			
e. Total insurance expired during the year.			
f. Total accounts receivable at the end of the year.			
g. Total withdrawals by the owner.			
h. The cost of utilities used during the year.			
i. The amount of the owner's Capital balance at the beginning of the year.			

P.O. 5

Prepare a statement of owner's equity from T accounts.

Exercise 5-8 Prepare a statement of owner's equity for The Dunn Clinic for the year ended December 31. P. Dunn's capital amount on January 1 was $125,000, and there was an additional investment of $8,000 on May 12 and withdrawals of $32,500 for the year. Net income for the year was $21,418.

You just learned about the methods of accounting a company can use when recording transactions, such as sales. This would be a good time to review the methods discussed in Performance Objective 4. Then, see if you can answer some questions about Dell. Go to **http://www.dell.com** and then search for SEC Reports. Select 2005 and then Form 10-K. Use the financial statements that begin on page 33 of the 10-K report.

1. For 2005, how much is net revenue on Dell's income statement? How much are accounts receivable, net, and accounts payable on the balance sheet?
2. What method of accounting does Dell use? How can you tell by looking at its financial statements?

CONSIDER AND COMMUNICATE

Your uncle owns a small sole proprietorship. He does his own bookkeeping, although he didn't finish the chapter on closing entries before he opened his business. He mentions to you that closing entries look like they take a long time. He wonders why he should bother to do them, because all he really looks at is the checkbook anyway. What would you say to convince him that closing entries are necessary?

CRITICAL THINKING

Following is the post-closing trial balance submitted to you by the book-keeper. Assume that the debit total ($41,048) is correct.

a. Analyze the work and prepare a response to what you have reviewed.
b. Journalize the closing entries.
c. What is the net income or net loss?
d. Is there an increase or a decrease in Capital?
e. What would be the ending amount of Capital?
f. What is the new balance of the post-closing trial balance?

Tafoya Consulting Company
Post-Closing Trial Balance
December 31, 20—

ACCOUNT NAME	DEBIT	CREDIT
Cash	3 4 1 2 00	
Accounts Receivable	1 6 9 3 00	
Prepaid Insurance	2 1 4 7 00	
Accounts Payable		
C. Tafoya, Capital		13 8 1 8 00
C. Tafoya, Drawing	6 3 6 0 00	
Consulting Income		25 6 0 3 00
Wages Expense	11 9 9 4 00	
Rent Expense	9 6 0 0 00	
Advertising Expense	2 5 8 2 00	
Supplies Expense	9 1 4 00	
Insurance Expense	1 6 1 0 00	
Miscellaneous Expense	7 3 6 00	
	41 0 4 8 00	41 0 4 8 00

A QUESTION OF ETHICS

You are preparing a post-closing trial balance for the company where you work, but it doesn't balance. You are tired, and besides, you don't think they pay you for this kind of hassle and extra time. You decide to increase the balance of an asset account to make the totals balance. Discuss this action and whether it is ethical or illegal.

WHAT'S WRONG WITH THIS PICTURE?

The bookkeeper has completed a work sheet and has journalized and posted the closing entries, but he forgot to journalize and post the adjusting entries from the work sheet. What are the effects of these actions and omissions? How would these actions and omissions affect the accounting records and the resulting financial statements?

PROBLEM SET A

For additional help, see the demonstration problem at the beginning of each chapter in your Working Papers.

P.O. 2

Problem 5-1A After the accountant posted the adjusting entries for M. Waldon, Designer, the general ledger contained the following account balances on May 31:

	ACCOUNT NAME	ADJUSTED TRIAL BALANCE	
		DEBIT	CREDIT Accum. Deprec.
		A + Draw. + E	+ L + C + R
1	Cash	2 3 1 8 00	
2	Accounts Receivable	1 4 0 8 00	
3	Prepaid Insurance	9 8 7 00	
4	Office Equipment	5 7 9 0 00	
5	Accumulated Depreciation, Office Equipment		1 3 6 4 00
6	Accounts Payable		8 8 0 00
7	M. Waldon, Capital		8 2 4 7 00
8	M. Waldon, Drawing	1 8 0 0 00	
9	Commissions Earned		3 8 9 7 00
10	Rent Expense	7 9 0 00	
11	Supplies Expense	3 8 1 00	
12	Depreciation Expense, Office Equipment	5 2 0 00	
13	Utilities Expense	2 7 6 00	
14	Miscellaneous Expense	1 1 8 00	
15		14 3 8 8 00	14 3 8 8 00

Check Figure

Net Income, $1,812

Instructions

a. Write the owner's name on the Capital and Drawing T accounts.
b. Record the account balances in the T accounts for owner's equity, revenue, and expenses.
c. Journalize the closing entries with the four steps in correct order. Number the closing entries 1 through 4.
d. Post the closing entries to the T accounts right after you journalize each one to see the effect of the closing entries. Number the closing entries 1 through 4.

P.O. 2

Problem 5-2A The partial work sheet for Kessley Consulting for the month of May is shown on the next page.

ACCOUNT NAME	INCOME STATEMENT		BALANCE SHEET		
	DEBIT	CREDIT	DEBIT	CREDIT Accum. Depr.	
	E	R	A + Draw.	+ L + C	
1 Cash			2 2 4 8 00		1
2 Prepaid Insurance			8 5 9 00		2
3 Equipment			5 7 3 1 00		3
4 Accumulated Depreciation, Equipment				2 3 7 9 00	4
5 Accounts Payable				8 4 1 00	5
6 K. Kessley, Capital				2 4 1 5 00	6
7 K. Kessley, Drawing			1 8 0 0 00		7
8 Consulting Income		8 5 4 6 00			8
9 Rent Expense	8 0 0 00				9
10 Wages Expense	1 6 3 3 00				10
11 Supplies Expense	3 6 5 00				11
12 Miscellaneous Expense	1 6 8 00				12
13					13
14 Insurance Expense	2 6 4 00				14
15 Depreciation Expense, Equipment	7 0 0 00				15
16 Wages Payable				3 8 7 00	16
17	3 9 3 0 00	8 5 4 6 00	10 6 3 8 00	6 0 2 2 00	17
18 Net Income	4 6 1 6 00			4 6 1 6 00	18
19	8 5 4 6 00	8 5 4 6 00	10 6 3 8 00	10 6 3 8 00	19
20					20

Check Figure

Debit to Income Summary, second entry, $3,930

Check Figure

Post-closing trial balance total, $7,408

Instructions

a. Write the owner's name on the Capital and Drawing T accounts.
b. Record the account balances in the T accounts for owner's equity, revenue, and expenses.
c. Journalize the closing entries with the four steps in correct order. Number the closing entries 1 through 4.
d. Post the closing entries to the T accounts right after you journalize each one to see the effect of the closing entries. Number the closing entries 1 through 4.

P.O. 1,2,3

Problem 5-3A The completed work sheet for Ulmer Tour Company as of December 31 is presented in your Working Papers, along with the general ledger as of December 31 before adjustments.

Instructions

1. Write the name of the owner, K. Ulmer, in the Capital and Drawing accounts.
2. Write the balances from the unadjusted trial balance in the general ledger.
3. Journalize and post the adjusting entries.
4. Journalize and post the closing entries in the correct order.
5. Prepare a post-closing trial balance.

P.O. 1,2,3

Problem 5-4A The account balances of Morrow's Tutoring Service as of June 30, the end of the current fiscal year, are as follows:

	ACCOUNT NAME	TRIAL BALANCE DEBIT	TRIAL BALANCE CREDIT
1	Cash	5 4 9 1 00	
2	Accounts Receivable	6 2 4 00	
3	Prepaid Insurance	1 2 8 0 00	
4	Equipment	6 4 9 7 00	
5	Accumulated Depreciation, Equipment		2 6 7 2 00
6	Van	18 6 7 4 00	
7	Accumulated Depreciation, Van		4 3 6 8 00
8	Accounts Payable		1 0 3 6 00
9	B. Morrow, Capital		4 8 4 8 00
10	B. Morrow, Drawing	12 0 0 0 00	
11	Fees Earned		53 2 8 0 00
12	Salary Expense	18 0 0 0 00	
13	Advertising Expense	1 2 0 0 00	
14	Van Operating Expense	6 0 5 00	
15	Utilities Expense	1 2 4 8 00	
16	Supplies Expense	3 2 7 00	
17	Miscellaneous Expense	2 5 8 00	
18		66 2 0 4 00	66 2 0 4 00

Check Figure

Net Income, $28,248

Instructions

1. Complete the work sheet:

   Data for the adjustments:
   a. Expired or used up insurance, $350.
   b. Depreciation expense on equipment, $980 (remember to credit the Accumulated Depreciation, Equipment account, not Equipment).
   c. Depreciation expense on the van, $1,690 (remember to credit the Accumulated Depreciation, Van account, not Van).
   d. Salary accrued (earned) since the last payday, $374 (owed and to be paid on the next payday).

2. Prepare an income statement.
3. Prepare a statement of owner's equity; assume there was an additional investment of $2,000 on July 10.
4. Prepare a balance sheet.
5. Journalize the adjusting entries.
6. Journalize the closing entries with the four steps in the correct sequence.

Instructions for General Ledger Software

1. Print a trial balance.
2. Journalize the adjusting entries in the general journal and post to the general ledger. (No work sheet is required on the computer.)

3. Print an income statement, a statement of owner's equity, and a balance sheet.
4. Journalize the closing entries in the general journal.
5. Post the closing entries.
6. Print a post-closing trial balance.

PROBLEM SET B

For additional help, see the demonstration problem at the beginning of each chapter in your Working Papers.

P.O. 2

Problem 5-1B After the accountant posted the adjusting entries for C. Lynn, Designer, the general ledger contained the following account balances on May 31:

	ACCOUNT NAME	ADJUSTED TRIAL BALANCE	
		DEBIT	CREDIT Accum. Deprec.
		A + Draw. + E	+ L + C + R
1	Cash	2 4 2 9 00	
2	Accounts Receivable	8 8 6 00	
3	Prepaid Insurance	1 4 6 0 00	
4	Office Equipment	4 6 7 2 00	
5	Accumulated Depreciation, Office Equipment		1 2 5 3 00
6	Accounts Payable		9 4 3 00
7	C. Lynn, Capital		6 5 2 0 00
8	C. Lynn, Drawing	1 6 5 0 00	
9	Commissions Earned		4 6 7 9 00
10	Rent Expense	8 9 5 00	
11	Supplies Expense	5 7 0 00	
12	Depreciation Expense, Office Equipment	4 6 7 00	
13	Utilities Expense	2 6 4 00	
14	Miscellaneous Expense	1 0 2 00	
15		13 3 9 5 00	13 3 9 5 00

Check Figure

Net Income, $2,381

Instructions

a. Write the owner's name on the Capital and Drawing T accounts.
b. Record the account balances in the T accounts for owner's equity, revenue, and expenses.
c. Journalize the closing entries with the four steps in correct order. Number the closing entries 1 through 4.
d. Post the closing entries to the T accounts right after you journalize each one to see the effect of the closing entries. Number the closing entries 1 through 4.

P.O. 2

Problem 5-2B The partial work sheet for Kwan Consulting for the month of June is as follows.

	ACCOUNT NAME	INCOME STATEMENT DEBIT E	INCOME STATEMENT CREDIT R	BALANCE SHEET DEBIT A + Draw.	BALANCE SHEET CREDIT Accum. Depr. + L + C	
1	Cash			6 1 0 4 00		1
2	Prepaid Insurance			1 3 4 4 00		2
3	Equipment			6 7 5 1 00		3
4	Accumulated Depreciation, Equipment				3 3 9 3 00	4
5	Accounts Payable				1 3 5 6 00	5
6	L. Kwan, Capital				1 3 6 7 00	6
7	L. Kwan, Drawing			2 4 0 0 00		7
8	Consulting Income		15 0 6 0 00			8
9	Rent Expense	1 1 0 0 00				9
10	Wages Expense	1 9 0 8 00				10
11	Miscellaneous Expense	2 4 0 00				11
12						12
13	Supplies Expense	4 3 2 00				13
14	Insurance Expense	3 4 5 00				14
15	Depreciation Expense, Equipment	9 0 0 00				15
16	Wages Payable				3 4 8 00	16
17		4 9 2 5 00	15 0 6 0 00	16 5 9 9 00	6 4 6 4 00	17
18	Net Income	10 1 3 5 00			10 1 3 5 00	18
19		15 0 6 0 00	15 0 6 0 00	16 5 9 9 00	16 5 9 9 00	19
20						20

Check Figure

Debit to Income Summary, second entry, $4,925

Instructions

a. Write the owner's name on the Capital and Drawing T accounts.
b. Record the account balances in the T accounts for owner's equity, revenue, and expenses.
c. Journalize the closing entries with the four steps in correct order. Number the closing entries 1 through 4.
d. Post the closing entries to the T accounts right after you journalize each one to see the effect of the closing entries. Number closing entries 1 through 4.

P.O. 1,2,3

Problem 5-3B The completed work sheet for Valenti Insurance Agency as of December 31 is presented in your Working Papers, along with the general ledger as of December 31 before adjustments.

Check Figure

Post-closing trial balance total, $8,889.60

Instructions

1. Write the name of the owner, M. Valenti, in the Capital and Drawing accounts.
2. Write the balances from the unadjusted trial balance in the general ledger.
3. Journalize and post the adjusting entries.
4. Journalize and post the closing entries in the correct order.
5. Prepare a post-closing trial balance.

P.O. 1,2,3

Problem 5-4B The account balances of Braden Company as of June 30, the end of the current fiscal year, are as follows.

	ACCOUNT NAME	TRIAL BALANCE DEBIT	TRIAL BALANCE CREDIT
1	Cash	4 3 8 1 00	
2	Accounts Receivable	5 7 8 00	
3	Prepaid Insurance	1 1 3 8 00	
4	Equipment	5 7 1 3 00	
5	Accumulated Depreciation, Equipment		2 4 8 7 00
6	Van	12 6 7 8 00	
7	Accumulated Depreciation, Van		3 3 1 8 00
8	Accounts Payable		9 9 7 00
9	B. Braden, Capital		5 9 6 4 00
10	B. Braden, Drawing	18 0 0 0 00	
11	Fees Earned		48 3 1 7 00
12	Salary Expense	16 0 0 0 00	
13	Advertising Expense	8 8 7 00	
14	Supplies Expense	3 9 7 00	
15	Van Operating Expense	4 6 2 00	
16	Utilities Expense	6 8 5 00	
17	Miscellaneous Expense	1 6 4 00	
18		61 0 8 3 00	61 0 8 3 00

Check Figure

Net income, $26,822

Instructions

1. Complete the work sheet.

   Data for the adjustments:

   a. Expired or used up insurance, $490.
   b. Depreciation expense on equipment, $680 (remember to credit the Accumulated Depreciation, Equipment account, not Equipment).
   c. Depreciation expense on the van, $1,090 (remember to credit the Accumulated Depreciation, Van account, not Van).
   d. Salary accrued (earned) since the last payday, $640 (owed and to be paid on the next payday).

2. Prepare an income statement.
3. Prepare a statement of owner's equity; assume there was an additional investment of $3,000 on October 10.
4. Prepare a balance sheet.
5. Journalize the adjusting entries.
6. Journalize the closing entries with the four steps in the proper sequence.

Instructions for General Ledger Software

1. Print a trial balance.
2. Journalize the adjusting entries in the general journal and post to the general ledger. (No work sheet is required on the computer.)
3. Print an income statement, a statement of owner's equity, and a balance sheet.
4. Journalize the closing entries in the general journal.
5. Post the closing entries.
6. Print a post-closing trial balance.

The Computer Clinic

Closing Entries

Before the Month-End Closing Entries

What to do *before* you perform the closing entries:

1. a. Print out all financial statements.
   b. Make a copy of your pre-closing file.
   c. Add the Income Summary account (399) to the chart of accounts.

Month-End Closing Entries

What to do to *close* (or zero out) the temporary owner's equity accounts (revenue(s), expenses, Income Summary, and Drawing), a process that transfers the net income into or deducts the net loss and the withdrawals from the Capital account. In addition, the closing process prepares the records for the new fiscal period:

2. a. Debit each revenue account and credit the Income Summary account. Now, all revenue accounts have a zero balance and the Income Summary account has a credit representing all revenue earned this fiscal period.
   b. Debit the Income Summary account for the total of all expenses and credit each expense account. Now, all expenses have a zero balance and the Income Summary account has a debit representing all expenses incurred this fiscal period.
   c. The Income Summary account has a larger credit (revenue) than debit (expenses), which indicates that there is a net income. This is consistent with the income statement you printed in Chapter 4. The balance in the Income Summary account is $6,776.62. Therefore, to close the Income Summary account with a credit balance, debit Income Summary for the balance and credit A. Valli, Capital. The balance of the Income Summary account is now zero and the net income of $6,776.62 has been transferred to the Capital account.
   d. Finally, debit A. Valli, Capital for the amount of the A. Valli, Drawing account and credit A. Valli, Drawing. The balance of A. Valli, Drawing is now zero, and you have reduced A. Valli, Capital by the amount of the owner withdrawal.

After the Month-End Closing Entries

What to do *after* the closing entries:

3. a. Print a post-closing trial balance from the general ledger. *Post* means "after," so you are printing a trial balance *after* closing.
   b. Look at the post-closing trial balance. What do you see? How does it differ from the other trial balances you have seen? It should be shorter than the trial balances you are used to seeing. What classifications of accounts are present or open (that is, they have balances over zero)? You should see only assets, liabilities, and the owner's Capital account. Why? Because the purpose of the post-closing trial balance is to be assured that all temporary owner's equity accounts (revenues, expenses, Income Summary, and Drawing) are closed or have zero balances, readying the records to receive revenues, expenses, and drawing entries in the new fiscal period. You have experienced not only accrual-basis accounting, but the matching principle as well.

Before a Test Check: Chapters 4–5

PART I: Multiple-Choice Questions

____ 1. The net income appears on all of the following statements except

    a. the statement of owner's equity.
    b. the balance sheet.
    c. the income statement.
    d. all of these.
    e. none of these.

____ 2. Which of the following entries records the withdrawal of cash for personal use by Dolan, the owner of a business firm?

    a. Debit Cash and credit Drawing.
    b. Debit Salary Expense and credit Cash.
    c. Debit Cash and credit Salary Expense.
    d. Debit Drawing and credit Cash.
    e. None of these.

____ 3. Which of the following errors, considered individually, would cause the trial balance totals to be unequal?

    a. A payment of $52 for supplies was posted as a debit of $52 to Supplies and a credit of $25 to Cash.
    b. A payment of $625 to a creditor was posted as a debit of $625 to Accounts Payable and a debit of $625 to Cash.
    c. Cash received from customers on account was posted as a debit of $380 to Cash and a credit of $38 to Accounts Receivable.
    d. All of these.
    e. None of these.

____ 4. The balance in the Prepaid Insurance account before adjustment at the end of the year is $600. This represents six months' insurance paid on November 1. The monthly adjusting entry required on December 31 is

    a. debit Insurance Expense, $200; credit Prepaid Insurance, $200.
    b. debit Prepaid Insurance, $100; credit Insurance Expense, $100.
    c. debit Prepaid Insurance, $600; credit Insurance Expense, $600.
    d. debit Insurance Expense, $600; credit Prepaid Insurance, $600.
    e. none of these.

____ 5. If an accountant fails to make an adjusting entry to record expired insurance at the end of a fiscal period, the omission will cause

    a. total expenses to be understated.
    b. total revenue to be understated.
    c. total assets to be understated.
    d. all of these.
    e. none of these.

Note: Answers to Before a Test Check begin on page A-1.

___ 6. Farmer Company bought equipment on January 2 of this year for $9,000. At the time of purchase, the equipment was estimated to have a useful life of eight years and a trade-in value of $1,000 at the end of eight years. Using the straight-line method, the amount of depreciation for the first year is

   a. $900.
   b. $1,000.
   c. $800.
   d. $950.
   e. none of these.

___ 7. If expenses are greater than revenue, the Income Summary account will be closed by a debit to

   a. Cash and a credit to Income Summary.
   b. Income Summary and a credit to Cash.
   c. Capital and a credit to Income Summary.
   d. Income Summary and a credit to Capital.
   e. none of these.

___ 8. In preparing closing entries, it is helpful to refer to which of the following columns of the work sheet first?

   a. The Balance Sheet columns
   b. The Adjusted Trial Balance columns
   c. The Income Statement columns
   d. Both the Adjusted Trial Balance and the Income Statement columns
   e. None of these

PART II: Practical Application

On December 31, the ledger accounts of Kristopher's Upholstery Shop have the following balances after all adjusting entries have been posted.

Cash	$ 1,200
Equipment	15,400
Accumulated Depreciation,	
Equipment	1,100
Accounts Payable	300
K. Payton, Capital	16,500
K. Payton, Drawing	16,400
Income Summary	
Income from Services	35,900
Wages Expense	11,500
Rent Expense	2,400
Utilities Expense	1,000
Depreciation Expense,	
Equipment	500
Supplies Expense	4,100
Miscellaneous Expense	900

Instructions

Journalize the four closing entries in the proper order.

PART III: Matching Questions

____ 1. Creditor

____ 2. Business entity

____ 3. Fundamental accounting equation

____ 4. Income statement

____ 5. Owner's equity

____ 6. Accounts Receivable

____ 7. Net loss

____ 8. Ledger

____ 9. Credit

____ 10. Compound entry

____ 11. Trial balance

____ 12. Journalizing

____ 13. Posting

____ 14. Cross-reference

____ 15. Journal

____ 16. Work sheet

____ 17. Book value

____ 18. Depreciation

____ 19. Accounting cycle

____ 20. Fiscal year

____ 21. Contra account

____ 22. Mixed accounts

____ 23. Temporary-equity accounts

____ 24. Real accounts

____ 25. Debit

a. The book of original entry

b. One to whom money is owed

c. Accounts that are partly income statement and partly balance sheet accounts

d. Assets − Liabilities

e. A listing of the ending balances of all ledger accounts that proves the equality of total debits and total credits

f. The process of recording transactions in a journal

g. The left side of a T account

h. A business enterprise, separate and distinct from the person who owns its assets

i. The process of transferring accounts and amounts from the journal to the ledger

j. An account that is deducted from another account

k. Amounts owed by charge customers

l. Balance sheet accounts

m. Assets = Liabilities + Owner's Equity

n. A bookkeeping device for referring from journal to ledger or ledger to journal

o. The right side of a T account

p. Allocation of the cost of a plant asset over its estimated life

q. Financial statement that shows the net results of operations

r. Accounts that belong to only one fiscal period and are closed out at the end of each fiscal period

s. A transaction that has two or more debits and/or credits

t. Paper used to record adjustments and provide balances to prepare financial statements

u. Excess of total expenses over total revenues

v. A period of twelve consecutive months

w. A book containing all the accounts of a business

x. The cost of an asset minus its accumulated depreciation

y. Steps in the accounting process, completed during the fiscal period

Accounting Cycle Review Problem A

This problem is designed to enable you to apply the knowledge you have acquired in the preceding chapters. In accounting, the ultimate test is being able to handle data in real-life situations. This problem will give you valuable experience.

Chart of Accounts

Assets

111 Cash
112 Accounts Receivable
114 Prepaid Insurance
121 Land
122 Building
123 Accumulated Depreciation, Building
124 Pool/Slide Facility
125 Accumulated Depreciation, Pool/Slide Facility
126 Pool Furniture
127 Accumulated Depreciation, Pool Furniture

Liabilities

221 Accounts Payable
222 Wages Payable
223 Mortgage Payable

Owner's Equity

311 W. Wong, Capital
312 W. Wong, Drawing
313 Income Summary

Revenue

411 Income from Services
412 Concessions Income

Expenses

511 Pool Maintenance Expense
512 Wages Expense
513 Advertising Expense
514 Utilities Expense
515 Interest Expense
517 Insurance Expense
518 Depreciation Expense, Building
519 Depreciation Expense, Pool/Slide Facility
520 Depreciation Expense, Pool Furniture
522 Miscellaneous Expense

You are to record transactions in a two-column general journal. Assume that the fiscal period is one month. You will then be able to complete all the steps in the accounting cycle.

When you are analyzing the transactions, think them through by visualizing the T accounts or by writing them down on scratch paper. For unfamiliar types of transactions, specific instructions for recording them are included. However, reason them out for yourself as well. Check off each transaction as it is recorded.

July 1 Wong deposited $150,000 in a bank account for the purpose of buying Splashdown. The business is a recreation area offering three large waterslides (called "tubes"), one children's slide, an inner tube run, and a looping extreme slide.

2 Bought Splashdown in its entirety for a total price of $540,800. The assets include pool furniture, $3,800; the pool/slide facility (includes filter system, pools, pump, and slides), $148,800; building, $96,200; and land, $292,000. Paid $120,000 down and signed a mortgage note for the remainder. (Debit the assets, and credit Cash and Mortgage Payable.)

July 2 Received and paid the bill for a one-year premium for insurance, $12,240.

2 Bought 125 inner tubes from Worn Tires for $1,225, paying $500 down, with the remainder due in twenty days. (Debit Pool/Slide Facility.)

3 Signed a contract with a video game company to lease space for video games and to provide a food concession. The rental income agreed upon is 10 percent of the revenues generated from the machines and food, with the estimated monthly rental income paid in advance. Received cash payment for July, $250. (Debit Cash and credit Concessions Income.)

5 Received bills totaling $1,320 for the grand opening/Fourth of July party. The bill from Party Rentals for the promotional hand-outs, balloons, decorations, and prizes was $620, and the newspaper advertising bills from the *City Star* were $700. (These expenses should all be considered advertising expense.)

6 Signed a one-year contract for the pool maintenance with All-Around Maintenance and paid the maintenance fee for July of $800.

6 Paid cash for employee picnic food and beverages, $128. (Debit Miscellaneous Expense.)

7 Received $12,086 in cash as income for the use of the facilities.

9 Bought parts for the filter system on account from Arlen's Pool Supply, $646. (Debit Pool Maintenance Expense.)

14 Received $10,445 in cash as income for the use of the facilities.

15 Paid wages to employees for the period ending July 14, $8,460.

16 Paid $1,150 on account for promotional expenses recorded on July 5.

16 Wong withdrew cash for personal use, $2,500.

17 Bought additional pool furniture from Pool Suppliers for $2,100; payment due in thirty days.

18 Paid cash to seamstress for alterations and repairs to the character costumes, $248. (Debit Miscellaneous Expense.)

21 Received $10,330 in cash as income for the use of the facilities.

21 Paid cash to Worn Tires as partial payment on account, $600.

23 Received a $225 reduction of our account from Pool Suppliers for lawn chairs received in damaged condition.

25 Received and paid telephone bill, $292.

29 Paid wages for the period July 15 through 28 of $8,227.

31 Received $11,870 in cash as income for the use of the facilities.

31 Paid cash to Arlen's Pool Supply to apply on account, $360.

31 Received and paid water bill, $684.

31 Paid cash as an installment payment on the mortgage, $3,890. Of this amount, $1,910 represents a reduction in the principal, and the remainder is interest. (Debit Mortgage Payable, debit Interest Expense, and credit Cash.)

31 Received and paid electric bill, $824.

31 Bought additional inner tubes from Worn Tires for $480, paying $100 down, with the remainder due in thirty days.

31 Wong withdrew cash for personal use, $2,200.

31 Sales for the video and food concessions amounted to $4,840, and 10 percent of $4,840 equals $484. Since you have already recorded $250 as concessions income, record the additional $234 revenue due from the concessionaire (cash was not received).

Instructions

1. Journalize the transactions, starting on page 1 of the general journal.
2. Post the transactions to the ledger accounts.
3. Prepare a trial balance in the first two columns of the work sheet.
4. Complete the work sheet. Data for the adjustments are as follows:
   a. Insurance expired during the month, $1,020.
   b. Depreciation of building for the month, $480.
   c. Depreciation of pool/slide facility for the month, $675.
   d. Depreciation of pool furniture for the month, $120.
   e. Wages accrued at July 31, $920.
5. Prepare the income statement.
6. Prepare the statement of owner's equity.
7. Prepare the balance sheet.
8. Journalize adjusting entries.
9. Post adjusting entries to the ledger accounts.
10. Journalize closing entries.
11. Post closing entries to the ledger accounts.
12. Prepare a post-closing trial balance.

Accounting Cycle Review Problem B

This problem is designed to enable you to apply the knowledge you have acquired in the preceding chapters. In accounting, the ultimate test is being able to handle data in real-life situations. This problem will give you valuable experience.

Chart of Accounts

Assets

111 Cash
112 Accounts Receivable
114 Prepaid Insurance
121 Land
125 Pool Structure
126 Accumulated Depreciation, Pool Structure
127 Fan System
128 Accumulated Depreciation, Fan System
129 Sailboats
130 Accumulated Depreciation, Sailboats

Liabilities

221 Accounts Payable
222 Wages Payable
223 Mortgage Payable

Owner's Equity

311 R. Erdmon, Capital
312 R. Erdmon, Drawing
313 Income Summary

Revenue

411 Income from Services
412 Concessions Income

Expenses

511 Sailboat Rental Expense
512 Wages Expense
513 Advertising Expense
514 Utilities Expense
515 Interest Expense
516 Insurance Expense
517 Depreciation Expense, Pool Structure
518 Depreciation Expense, Fan System
519 Depreciation Expense, Sailboats
522 Miscellaneous Expense

You are to record transactions in a two-column general journal. Assume that the fiscal period is one month. You will then be able to complete all the steps in the accounting cycle.

When you are analyzing the transactions, think them through by visualizing the T accounts or by writing them down on scratch paper. For unfamiliar types of transactions, specific instructions for recording them are included. However, reason them out for yourself as well. Check off each transaction as it is recorded.

June   1   Erdmon deposited $85,000 in a bank account for the purpose of buying Wind Riders, a business offering the use of small sailboats to the public at a large indoor pool with a fan system that provides wind.

        2   Bought Wind Riders in its entirety for a total price of $216,100. The assets include sailboats, $25,800; fan system, $13,300; pool structure, $140,000; land, $37,000. Paid $60,000 down, and signed a mortgage note for the remainder. (Debit each asset and credit Cash and Mortgage Payable.)

June 3 Received and paid bill for newspaper advertising, $350.
  3 Received and paid bill for a one-year premium for insurance, $12,000.
  3 Bought additional boats from Larkin Manufacturing Co. for $7,200, paying $3,200 down, with the remainder due in thirty days.
  3 Signed a contract with a vending machine service to lease space for vending machines. The rental income agreed upon is 10 percent of the sales generated from the machines, with the estimated total rental income payable in advance. Received estimated cash payment for June, $150. (Debit Cash and credit Concessions Income.)
  3 Received bill from Quick Printing for promotional handouts, $460 (Advertising Expense).
  3 Signed a contract for leasing sailboats from K. Erdmon Boat Co. and paid rental fee for June, $700.
  5 Paid cash for miscellaneous expenses, $96.
  8 Received $2,855 in cash as income for the use of the boats.
  9 Bought an addition for the fan system on account from Stark Pool Supply, $745.
  15 Paid wages to employees for the period ending June 14, $3,900.
  16 Paid on account for promotional handouts already recorded on June 3, $460.
  16 Erdmon withdrew cash for personal use, $1,200.
  16 Bought additional sails from Canvas Products, Inc., $850; payment due in thirty days. (Debit Sailboats.)
  16 Received $4,850 in cash as income for the use of the boats.
  19 Paid cash for miscellaneous expenses, $40.45.
  20 Paid cash to Larkin Manufacturing Co. as part payment on account, $1,300.
  22 Received $8,260 in cash for the use of the boats (Income from Services).
  23 Received a reduction in the outstanding bill from Larkin Manufacturing Co. for a boat received in a damaged condition, $380. (Debit Accounts Payable, credit Sailboats.)
  24 Received and paid telephone bill, $284.
  29 Paid wages for period June 15 through 28, $4,973.
  30 Paid cash to Stark Pool Supply to apply on account, $475.
  30 Received and paid electric bill, $345.
  30 Paid cash as an installment payment on the mortgage, $1,848. Of this amount, $497 represents a reduction in the principal, and the remainder is interest. (Debit Mortgage Payable, debit Interest Expense, and credit Cash.)
  30 Received and paid water bill, $590.
  30 Bought additional boats from Ranger and Son for $5,320, paying $1,550 down, with the remainder due in thirty days.
  30 Erdmon withdrew cash for personal use, $1,500.
  30 Received $5,902 in cash as income for the use of the boats.
  30 Sales from vending machines for the month amounted to $1,780. Ten percent of $1,780 equals $178. Since you have already recorded $150 as concessions income, list the additional $28 revenue earned from the vending machine operator. (Cash was not received.)

Check Figures

Net income, $5,290.55; total of post-closing trial balance, $253,068.55

Instructions

1. Journalize the transactions, starting on page 1 of the general journal.
2. Post the transactions to the ledger accounts.
3. Prepare a trial balance in the first two columns of the work sheet.
4. Complete the work sheet. Data for the adjustments are as follows:
   a. Insurance expired during the month, $1,000.
   b. Depreciation of pool structure for the month, $715.
   c. Depreciation of fan system for the month, $260.
   d. Depreciation of sailboats for the month, $900.
   e. Wages accrued at June 30, $790.
5. Prepare the income statement.
6. Prepare the statement of owner's equity.
7. Prepare the balance sheet.
8. Journalize adjusting entries.
9. Post adjusting entries to the ledger accounts.
10. Journalize closing entries.
11. Post closing entries to the ledger accounts.
12. Prepare a post-closing trial balance.

Accounting systems for professional companies such as architecture firms, law firms, and physician's offices require users to document such items as fees for services rendered, utility bills, travel expenses, supplies, and insurance. But each type of profession uses an individualized set of accounts to record business transactions. These professionals would probably find that a combined journal, which has special columns to record frequently used accounts, is more efficient than a general journal. As you learn about combined journals in this chapter, think about how the accounts you would commonly use in your accounting records might differ if you were an architect or a doctor.

A little later in this chapter, you will also learn how the entries in the combined journal (or general journal) are transformed into financial statements, which are prepared for professional enterprises as well as major corporations. How does Dr. Hanna's balance sheet in this chapter differ from Best Buy's balance sheet? How is it the same? You can find Best Buy's 2005 balance sheet by going to **http://www.sec.gov/edgar/searchedgar/companysearch.html**. Search by company name (Best Buy Co Inc) and either scroll through the listing or search for Form 10-K. Select the 2005 filing. You will find the 2005 balance sheet on page 58 of Form 10-K.

Performance Objectives

After you have completed this chapter, you will be able to do the following:

1. Describe the accounting records for a professional enterprise.

2. Record transactions for both a professional enterprise and a service enterprise in a combined journal.

3. Post from the combined journal and determine the cash balance.

4. Prepare a work sheet for a professional enterprise.

5. Prepare financial statements for a professional enterprise.

6. Record adjusting and closing entries in a combined journal.

A professional enterprise offers a specialized service for a fee. The fee may be charged on a per hour basis, a per visit basis, or a per job or task basis. **Professional enterprises** include practices of medicine, dentistry, law, architecture, engineering, accounting, and so forth. Your knowledge of accounting procedures can be readily applied to professional enterprises. Professional enterprises generally use the cash basis of accounting.

EXAMPLE: RECORDS OF A DENTIST

 OBJECTIVE 1

Describe the accounting records for a professional enterprise.

To understand the cash basis of accounting used by a professional enterprise, let's look at the records of Dr. S. A. Hanna, a dentist. The basic records used in his office are the appointment record and the patient's ledger record. We will assume the patient records are kept manually. Specialized computer software is available for professional businesses, such as dentists, that combines the accounting for patient records and the accounting records of the business. Following is the chart of accounts for the office:

Chart of Accounts

Assets

111 Cash
115 Prepaid Insurance
121 Dental Equipment
122 Accumulated Depreciation, Dental Equipment
123 Office Furniture and Equipment
124 Accumulated Depreciation, Office Furniture and Equipment

Liabilities

211 Notes Payable

Owner's Equity

311 S. A. Hanna, Capital
312 S. A. Hanna, Drawing
313 Income Summary

Revenue

411 Professional Fees

Expenses

511 Dental Instruments Expense
512 Laundry and Cleaning Expense
513 Salary Expense
514 Laboratory Expense
515 Dental Supplies Expense
516 Rent Expense
517 Depreciation Expense, Dental Equipment
518 Depreciation Expense, Office Furniture and Equipment
519 X-ray Supplies Expense
521 Office Supplies Expense
522 Insurance Expense
523 Telephone Expense
524 Utilities Expense
525 Repairs and Maintenance Expense
526 Miscellaneous Expense

Appointment Record

The dentist's receptionist keeps a daily appointment record, showing the time of each appointment and the name of the patient, and gives a copy of the appointment record to the dentist the day before the scheduled appointments. Dr. Hanna's appointment record is shown in Figure 1.

FIGURE 1

APPOINTMENT RECORD

DATE 12/1/20—

HOUR	PATIENT	SERVICE RENDERED	FEES	RECEIPTS
8:00	Edna Dixon			
15	John Freed			
30				
45	Carlos Flores			
9:00				
15				
30				
45	Rita Irvine			
10:00	M. L. Lilly			
15				
30				
45	R. D. Petrie			
11:00	Carl Ryan			
15				
30				
45				
1:00	Glen C. Smith			
15				
30	C. K. Wyse			
45				
2:00	Alice Cheney			
15				
30	Ralph Farr			
45	Paul Hayes			
3:00				
15	Nancy Kirby			
30				
45	C. L. McKoy			
4:00				
15	Juan Tyra			

Patient's Ledger Record

The receptionist also maintains a **patient's ledger record** card for each patient. One side of this card shows a daily record of the services performed, amount of any cost estimate given, plan of payment, and information regarding collections. This side of the card is shown in Figure 2.

The other side of the card contains a diagram of the patient's teeth and a space for personal information about the patient.

After Dr. Hanna completes the work, he (or an assistant) describes the services performed and writes the amount of the fees in the Debit column. The card is returned to the receptionist, who records the services rendered and the fees charged on the appointment record.

The patient's ledger record for M. L. Lilly is shown in Figure 2. **As with Accounts Receivable, debits mean increases in the amounts owed by patients, and credits mean decreases in the amounts owed by patients.** The

FIGURE 2

M. L. Lilly
2416 Bryan Ave., E
Chicago, IL 60644

360-365-2619
Account No. 46-4128

DATE		SERVICE RENDERED	TIME	DEBIT	CREDIT	BALANCE
June	15	#31—M.O.D. (4)	10:00	1 5 7 00		1 5 7 00
July	4	Ck.			1 5 7 00	
	16	#27—D.O. (Amal.)	9:15	1 4 1 00		1 4 1 00
Aug.	5	Ck.			1 4 1 00	
Sept.	24	#25—P.J.C.	10:00	1 1 1 0 00		1 1 1 0 00
Oct.	6	Ck.			1 8 0 00	9 3 0 00
	18	#24—D. (Porc.)	9:00	1 2 0 00		1 0 5 0 00
Nov.	3	Ck.			1 8 0 00	8 7 0 00
	9	#18—full gold crown	10:00	8 2 5 00		1 6 9 5 00
Dec.	1	B. W. X-rays (6)	10:00	1 4 4 00		1 8 3 9 00
		Full upper denture		1 3 5 0 00		3 1 8 9 00
	1	Ck.			3 0 0 00	2 8 8 9 00

PLAN OF SERVICE		PLAN OF PAYMENT	COLLECTION EFFORTS
1–2 surf.	amalgam	30-day basis	
2–3 surf.	1 full gold crown	or $150 per month	
1–1 surf.	1 ceramic crown		
2 anterior porcelain			

ESTIMATE IF ANY	
$900 upper denture (6 appt.)	$225 per month

Balance column shows the amount owed by the patient at the time of the latest entry.

The services to be performed may require a number of appointments. Some patients may make partial payments each time they have an appointment. Others may pay the entire amount at—or after—the last appointment. Patients' bills are compiled directly from the patient's ledger record. The dentist or receptionist regularly reviews the patients' ledger records to determine which accounts are past due. Figure 3 on page 194 shows the statement that was mailed to M. L. Lilly at the end of December.

Receipt of Payments from Patients

Depending on the size of the office, the person who receives payments may be the receptionist or the cashier in the accounting office. Whoever receives the payments issues a written receipt for all incoming cash, filled out in duplicate, giving the first copy to the patient and filing the second copy as evidence of the transaction. Receipts should be prenumbered so that they can be accounted for. The payment is recorded in the Receipts column of the appointment record.

When a patient sends in a payment, the receptionist records the amount on the appointment record and on the patient's ledger record in the Credit column on the day the payment was received.

REMEMBER!

The fees charged are not recorded in the Professional Fees account until they are received in cash when using the cash basis.

FIGURE 3

S. A. HANNA, D.D.S.
1710 CARTER AVE., E
CHICAGO, IL 60642

STATEMENT

M. L. Lilly
2416 Bryan Ave., E
Chicago, IL 60644

December 31, 20—
Account No. 46-4128

DATE	PROFESSIONAL SERVICE	CHARGES		PAYMENTS		BALANCE	
6/15	#31—MOD (4)	157	00			157	00
7/4	Ck.			157	00	—	
7/16	#27—DO (Amal.)	141	00			141	00
8/5	Ck.			141	00	—	
9/24	#25—PJC	1,110	00			1,110	00
10/6	Ck.			180	00	930	00
10/18	#24—D (Porc.)	120	00			1,050	00
11/3	Ck.			180	00	870	00
11/9	#18—full gold crown	825	00			1,695	00
12/1	B.W. X-rays (6)	144	00			1,839	00
	Full upper denture	1,350	00			3,189	00
12/1	Ck.			300	00	2,889	00

PAY LAST AMOUNT IN BALANCE COLUMN.

The form in Figure 4 is a typical appointment record for a day, showing services rendered, fees (recorded by the dentist on the patients' ledger records), and payments received (recorded by the receptionist). The receptionist deposits $2,048 in the bank. A journal entry would now be made debiting Cash and crediting Professional Fees for $2,048.

Summary of Procedures

1. Patients request appointments.
2. Receptionist records appointments on appointment record: date, time, and name of patient.
3. Receptionist furnishes dentist with appointment record for the day, plus the patients' ledger records.
4. Dentist performs services and records descriptions of the services performed on each patient's ledger card, listing the fees to be charged in the Debit column.
5. Receptionist accepts payments from patients both in the office and through the mail and records receipt of payments in the Receipts column of the appointment record. Any difference between the fee charged amount and the insurance company approved amount for the services rendered can be shown in the Debit column and a note made in the Service Rendered column. (For purposes of this text, cash receipts are recorded weekly.)
6. At the end of the day, receptionist deposits cash received in the bank.

FIGURE 4

APPOINTMENT RECORD

DATE <u>12/1/20—</u>

HOUR	PATIENT	SERVICE RENDERED	FEES		RECEIPTS	
8:00	Edna Dixon	Extraction	90	00		
15	John Freed	Three amalgam fillings				
30		D.O. (3)	460	00	130	00
45	Carlos Flores	Gold inlay filling	632	00		
9:00						
15						
30						
45	Rita Irvine	Amalgam filling D.O.	138	00		
10:00	M. L. Lilly	B.W. X-rays (6)	144	00	300	00
15		Full upper denture				
30		(6 appointments)	1,350	00		
45	R. D. Petrie	Prophylaxis	108	00	108	00
11:00	Carl Ryan	Endodontia treatment	338	00	75	00
15						
30						
45						
1:00	Glen C. Smith	Amalgam filling M.O.D.	156	00	78	00
15						
30	C. K. Wyse	Ceramco crown	870	00		
45						
2:00	Alice Cheney	Extraction	75	00		
15						
30	Ralph Farr	Amalgam filling 1 surf.	112	00		
45	Paul Hayes	Prophylaxis and full-				
3:00		mouth X-ray (14)	196	00		
15	Nancy Kirby	Fixed bridge 3 units				
30		(Gold) (5 appointments)	2,460	00	187	00
45	C. L. McKoy	Prophylaxis & bitewing				
4:00		X-rays	138	00		
15	Juan Tyra	Periodontal treatment	426	00		
	Robert L. Moyer				180	00
	Rita Davis				165	00
	Gene Roxang				204	00
	Sidney Woods				81	00
	N. T. Wyatt				279	00
	S. T. Mendoza				111	00
	Gilbert Lamont				150	00
			7,693	00	2,048	00

7. Receptionist lists the description of services and the amount charged on the appointment record.
8. Receptionist records payments received on the patients' ledger cards in the Credit column. The source is the appointment record.

9. Receptionist compiles monthly statements directly from patient's ledger records.

This procedure may vary, depending on the size of the office staff. Also, the monthly statement may consist of a duplicate copy of the patient's ledger card. If the size of the office staff is sufficiently large, the function of accepting and depositing money should be separated from the function of recording payments.

Here is a list of Dr. Hanna's transactions for December, the last month of the fiscal period. **To save time and space, cash receipts are recorded on a weekly basis.**

Dec.	1	Issued Ck. No. 416 for rent for December, $3,000.
	1	Issued Ck. No. 417 for telephone bill for November, $107.
	1	Issued Ck. No. 418 for electric bill for November, $168.
	3	Issued Ck. No. 419 to First-Rate Printing for patient statement forms, $198.
	5	Issued Ck. No. 420 to Milner Dental Supply for drills, $381.
	5	Total cash received from patients during the week, $10,716.
	8	Issued Ck. No. 421 to Monroe Office Supply for repair of copier, $138.
	9	Issued Ck. No. 422 to S. A. Hanna for personal use, $1,125.
	11	Issued Ck. No. 423 to Ready Cleaning Service for janitorial service, $210.

We will first record these transactions in general journal form (Figure 5). However, since our objective is to introduce the combined journal, we will also record the same transactions in a combined journal.

FIGURE 5

GENERAL JOURNAL

DATE		DESCRIPTION	POST. REF.	DEBIT	CREDIT
20—					
Dec.	1	Rent Expense		3 0 0 0 00	
		Cash			3 0 0 0 00
		Rent for December,			
		Ck. No. 416.			
	1	Telephone Expense		1 0 7 00	
		Cash			1 0 7 00
		Telephone bill for November,			
		Ck. No. 417.			
	1	Utilities Expense		1 6 8 00	
		Cash			1 6 8 00
		Electric bill for November,			
		Ck. No. 418.			
	3	Office Supplies Expense		1 9 8 00	
		Cash			1 9 8 00
		First-Rate Printing for			
		statement forms, Ck. No. 419.			

**FIGURE 5
(continued)**

5	Dental Instruments Expense		3 8 1 00			
	Cash				3 8 1 00	
	Milner Dental Supply for					
	drills, Ck. No. 420.					
5	Cash		10 7 1 6 00			
	Professional Fees				10 7 1 6 00	
	For period Dec. 1 through 5.					
8	Repairs and Maint. Expense		1 3 8 00			
	Cash				1 3 8 00	
	Monroe Office Supply, for					
	repair of copier, Ck. No. 421.					
9	S. A. Hanna, Drawing		1 1 2 5 00			
	Cash				1 1 2 5 00	
	For personal use, Ck. No. 422.					
11	Laundry and Cleaning Expense		2 1 0 00			
	Cash				2 1 0 00	
	Ready Cleaning Service,					
	Ck. No. 423.					

THE COMBINED JOURNAL

OBJECTIVE 2

Record transactions for both a professional enterprise and a service enterprise in a combined journal.

The **combined journal** is designed to make the recording and posting of transactions more efficient. It is used widely by professional and service enterprises, where **it replaces the general journal.** No explanations are given in the combined journal. **Special columns** are set up to record accounts that are used frequently by a particular business. Most transactions can be recorded on one line.

Compare the first nine transactions in the combined journal in Figure 6 (pages 198–199) with the same transactions recorded in the general journal in Figure 5. In the first transaction (paid rent for the month, $3,000), the entry is a debit to Rent Expense and a credit to Cash. There is a Cash Credit column in the combined journal, so $3,000 is listed in this column; that $3,000 will be posted as part of the column total. The Other Accounts columns are used to record any accounts for which there are no special columns. Since there is no Rent Expense Debit column, the $3,000 debit to Rent Expense must be recorded in the Other Accounts Debit column. Notice that the Other Accounts column does not tell you where to post the $3,000. Therefore, you need to write the title of the account to be posted in the Account Name column. This amount is posted separately.

In the December 5 entry to record professional fees received in cash, special columns are available to handle both the debit to Cash and the credit to Professional Fees. In cases where the special columns can handle both the entire debit and credit amounts, it is not necessary to use the Account Name

COMBINED JOURNAL

	CASH		CK. NO.	DATE	ACCOUNT NAME	POST. REF.	OTHER ACCOUNTS	
	DEBIT	CREDIT					DEBIT	CREDIT
1				20—				
2		3 0 0 0 00	416	Dec. 1	Rent Expense	516	3 0 0 0 00	
3		1 0 7 00	417	1	Telephone Expense	523	1 0 7 00	
4		1 6 8 00	418	1	Utilities Expense	524	1 6 8 00	
5		1 9 8 00	419	3	Office Supplies Expense	521	1 9 8 00	
6		3 8 1 00	420	5	Dental Instruments Expense	511	3 8 1 00	
7	10 7 1 6 00			5	————————	—		
8		1 3 8 00	421	8	Repairs and Maintenance Expense	525	1 3 8 00	
9		1 1 2 5 00	422	9	S. A. Hanna	—		
10		2 1 0 00	423	11	Ready Cleaning Service	—		
11	3 6 1 6 00			12	————————	—		
12		6 4 8 00	424	16	Davies Dental Supply	—		
13		1 4 5 5 00	425	16	C. R. Jarvis	—		
14		1 4 5 5 00	426	16	D. C. Yang	—		
15				19	Dental Equipment	121	8 6 6 8 00	
16		2 6 6 8 00	427	19	Notes Payable	211		6 0 0 0 00
17	1 8 3 0 00			19	————————	—		
18		1 2 1 5 00	428	22	S. A. Hanna	—		
19		4 4 4 00	429	23	Nollen Dental Laboratory	—		
20		6 0 0 00	430	23	Notes Payable	211	6 0 0 00	
21	2 0 9 4 00			27	————————	—		
22		3 3 9 00	431	29	Briggs Automotive	—		
23		3 2 8 00	432	31	Milner Dental Supply	—		
24		1 4 5 5 00	433	31	C. R. Jarvis	—		
25		1 4 5 5 00	434	31	D. C. Yang	—		
26		1 7 8 5 00	435	31	S. A. Hanna	—		
27		8 1 00	436	31	Jersey Publishers Service	—		
28		1 2 6 00	437	31	Clement Linen Supply	—		
29	2 9 6 4 00			31	————————	—		
30	21 2 2 0 00	19 3 8 1 00		31			13 2 6 0 00	6 0 0 0 00
31	(1 1 1)	(1 1 1)					(X)	(X)

END OF MONTH
Post the column totals to the Cash account in the general ledger at the end of the month. The account number in parentheses at the foot of each column indicates that posting has been completed.

DAILY
Post each amount in the Other Accounts columns to an account in the general ledger. The account number recorded in the Post. Ref. column indicates that posting has been completed. The (X) indicates that the column total is not to be posted.

FIGURE 6

		S. A. HANNA, DRAWING	PROFESSIONAL FEES	LAUNDRY AND CLEANING EXPENSE	SALARY EXPENSE	LABORATORY EXPENSE	DENTAL SUPPLIES EXPENSE	MISC. EXPENSE	
		DEBIT	CREDIT	DEBIT	DEBIT	DEBIT	DEBIT	DEBIT	
									1
									2
									3
									4
									5
									6
			10 7 1 6 00						7
									8
		1 1 2 5 00							9
				2 1 0 00					10
			3 6 1 6 00						11
							6 4 8 00		12
					1 4 5 5 00				13
					1 4 5 5 00				14
									15
									16
			1 8 3 0 00						17
		1 2 1 5 00							18
						4 4 4 00			19
									20
			2 0 9 4 00						21
		3 3 9 00							22
							3 2 8 00		23
					1 4 5 5 00				24
					1 4 5 5 00				25
		1 7 8 5 00							26
								8 1 00	27
				1 2 6 00					28
			2 9 6 4 00						29
		4 4 6 4 00	21 2 2 0 00	3 3 6 00	5 8 2 0 00	4 4 4 00	9 7 6 00	8 1 00	30
		(3 1 2)	(4 1 1)	(5 1 2)	(5 1 3)	(5 1 4)	(5 1 5)	(5 2 6)	31
		↑	↑	↑	↑	↑	↑	↑	32
									33
									34

END OF MONTH
Post the column totals to their general ledger accounts. Account numbers in parentheses indicate that posting has been completed.

Owners of dry cleaners and service stations as well as doctors and lawyers can buy premade combined journals targeted directly for their own professions. These combined journals are set up to help channel routine transactions into the journal.

column except to write the name of the check payee. To show that the Account Name column has not been overlooked, we draw a long line through it and put a dash in the Post. Ref. column. The individual amounts are posted as parts of the totals of the special columns. The rest of the month's transactions follow:

Dec.	12	Total cash received from patients during the week, $3,616.
	16	Issued Ck. No. 424 to Davies Dental Supply for miscellaneous dental supplies, $648.
	16	In payment of salaries, issued Ck. No. 425 to C. R. Jarvis, $1,455 and Ck. No. 426 to D. C. Yang, $1,455. (Use two lines.)
	19	Bought new dental chair from Milner Dental Supply, $8,668. Issued Ck. No. 427 as a down payment, $2,668. The balance is to be paid in ten monthly payments of $600 each (Notes Payable). (Use two lines.)
	19	Total cash received from patients during the week, $1,830.
	22	Issued Ck. No. 428 to S. A. Hanna for personal use, $1,215.
	23	Issued Ck. No. 429 to Nollen Dental Laboratory for laboratory expense, $444.
	23	Issued Ck. No. 430 to Milner Dental Supply as the first contract payment (Notes Payable) on dental equipment purchased on December 19, $600.
	27	Total cash received from patients during the week, $2,094.
	29	Hanna wrote Ck. No. 431 payable to Briggs Automotive for repairing his car, $339 (to be recorded as Drawing).
	31	Issued Ck. No. 432 to Milner Dental Supply for miscellaneous dental supplies, $328.
	31	In payment of salaries, issued Ck. No. 433 to C. R. Jarvis, $1,455 and Ck. No. 434 to D. C. Yang, $1,455. (Use two lines.)
	31	Issued Ck. No. 435 to S. A. Hanna for personal use, $1,785.
	31	Issued Ck. No. 436 to Jersey Publishers Service for magazines for the office, $81.
	31	Issued Ck. No. 437 to Clement Linen Supply for laundry services, $126.
	31	Total cash received from patients this week up until last day of year, $2,964.

After you have added all columns at the end of the month, prove on scratch paper that the sum of the debit totals equals the sum of the credit totals.

Column	Debit totals	Credit totals
Cash	$21,220.00	$19,381.00
Other Accounts	13,260.00	6,000.00
S. A. Hanna, Drawing	4,464.00	
Professional Fees		21,220.00
Laundry and Cleaning Expense	336.00	
Salary Expense	5,820.00	
Laboratory Expense	444.00	
Dental Supplies Expense	976.00	
Miscellaneous Expense	81.00	
	$46,601.00	$46,601.00

Posting from the Combined Journal

OBJECTIVE 3

Post from the combined journal and determine the cash balance.

REMEMBER!

Special columns are posted as one total. Amounts in Other Accounts columns are posted individually.

The person who keeps records posts items in the Other Accounts columns individually, usually daily, using the specific transaction date. **After posting the ledger account, the person records the ledger account number in the Post. Ref. column of the combined journal.** This procedure is similar to posting from a general journal.

Special columns, used only for debits or credits to specific accounts, are posted as totals at the end of the month. **After posting the ledger account, the ledger account number is recorded in the special column immediately below the total.** The account number is placed in parentheses. The total of the Cash Debit column in Figure 6 on pages 198–199 is an example. After the Cash account in the general ledger has been debited for $21,220.00, the account number of Cash (111) is placed in parentheses below the total of the Cash Debit column in the combined journal. Notice the X's in parentheses below the totals of the Other Accounts columns. These totals were not posted because the individual amounts recorded in the columns were posted separately. The separate amounts listed in the Other Accounts columns should not be posted twice.

The Cash, Dental Supplies Expense, and Rent Expense accounts from Dr. Hanna's completed general ledger are shown in Figure 7 to illustrate the posting process.

FIGURE 7

GENERAL LEDGER

ACCOUNT **Cash**   ACCOUNT NO. __111__

DATE		ITEM	POST. REF.	DEBIT	CREDIT	BALANCE DEBIT	BALANCE CREDIT	
20—								1
Dec.	1	Balance	✓			9 9 3 0 00		2
	31		12	21 2 2 0 00		31 1 5 0 00		3
	31		12		19 3 8 1 00	11 7 6 9 00		4

ACCOUNT **Dental Supplies Expense**   ACCOUNT NO. __515__

DATE		ITEM	POST. REF.	DEBIT	CREDIT	BALANCE DEBIT	BALANCE CREDIT	
20—								1
Dec.	1	Balance	✓			7 2 4 4 00		2
	31		12	9 7 6 00		8 2 2 0 00		3

ACCOUNT **Rent Expense**   ACCOUNT NO. __516__

DATE		ITEM	POST. REF.	DEBIT	CREDIT	BALANCE DEBIT	BALANCE CREDIT	
20—								1
Dec.	1	Balance	✓			24 0 0 0 00		2
	1		12	3 0 0 0 00		27 0 0 0 00		3

FIGURE 8

	ACCOUNT NAME	TRIAL BALANCE	
		DEBIT	CREDIT
1	Cash	11 7 6 9 00	
2	Prepaid Insurance	3 6 7 2 00	
3	Dental Equipment	172 8 5 1 00	
4	Accumulated Depreciation, Dental Equipment		25 8 0 0 00
5	Office Furniture and Equipment	11 7 0 0 00	
6	Accum. Depr., Office Furniture and Equipment		6 3 0 0 00
7	Notes Payable		11 4 0 0 00
8	S. A. Hanna, Capital		107 2 4 7 00
9	S. A. Hanna, Drawing	69 4 2 0 00	
10	Professional Fees		241 5 3 6 00
11	Dental Instruments Expense	2 9 7 3 00	
12	Laundry and Cleaning Expense	4 5 3 6 00	
13	Salary Expense	61 2 0 0 00	
14	Laboratory Expense	8 7 8 4 00	
15	Dental Supplies Expense	8 2 2 0 00	
16	Rent Expense	27 0 0 0 00	
17	X-ray Supplies Expense	1 9 6 2 00	
18	Office Supplies Expense	4 1 4 3 00	
19	Telephone Expense	6 1 8 00	
20	Utilities Expense	1 1 6 7 00	
21	Repairs and Maintenance Expense	1 3 3 2 00	
22	Miscellaneous Expense	9 3 6 00	
23		392 2 8 3 00	392 2 8 3 00
24	Depreciation Expense, Dental Equipment		
25	Depreciation Expense, Office Furn. and Equipment		
26	Insurance Expense		
27			
28	Net Income		
29			
30			

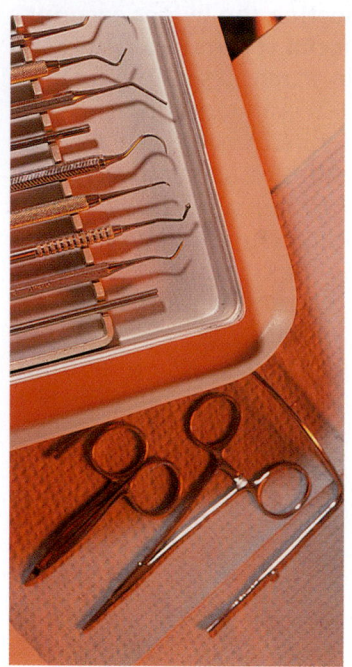

A combined journal allows businesses to set up special columns for frequently used accounts, such as Dental Supplies Expense, for this professional firm.

Determining Cash Balance

The cash balance may be determined at any time during the month by taking the beginning balance of cash, adding the total cash debits so far during the month, and subtracting the total cash credits so far during the month. For example, to determine the balance of cash on December 5:

Beginning balance (Dec. 1)	$ 9,930
Add cash debits	10,716
Total	$20,646
Less cash credits	3,854
Ending balance (Dec. 5)	$16,792

COMBINED JOURNAL   PAGE __12__

	CASH		CK.	DATE		ACCOUNT NAME
	DEBIT	CREDIT	NO.			
1				20—		
2		3 0 0 0 00	416	Dec.	1	Rent Expense
3		1 0 7 00	417		1	Telephone Expense
4		1 6 8 00	418		1	Utilities Expense
5		1 9 8 00	419		3	Office Supplies Expense
6		3 8 1 00	420		5	Dental Instruments Expense
7	10 7 1 6 00				5	——————————
8	10 7 1 6 00	3 8 5 4 00				

S. A. Hanna, D.D.S.
Work Sheet
For Year Ended December 31, 20—

ADJUSTMENTS DEBIT	ADJUSTMENTS CREDIT	ADJUSTED TRIAL BALANCE DEBIT	ADJUSTED TRIAL BALANCE CREDIT	INCOME STATEMENT DEBIT	INCOME STATEMENT CREDIT	BALANCE SHEET DEBIT	BALANCE SHEET CREDIT	
		11 7 6 9 00				11 7 6 9 00		1
	(c) 2 7 5 4 00	9 1 8 00				9 1 8 00		2
		172 8 5 1 00				172 8 5 1 00		3
	(a)12 6 0 0 00		38 4 0 0 00				38 4 0 0 00	4
		11 7 0 0 00				11 7 0 0 00		5
	(b) 2 2 8 0 00		8 5 8 0 00				8 5 8 0 00	6
			11 4 0 0 00				11 4 0 0 00	7
			107 2 4 7 00				107 2 4 7 00	8
		69 4 2 0 00				69 4 2 0 00		9
			241 5 3 6 00		241 5 3 6 00			10
		2 9 7 3 00		2 9 7 3 00				11
		4 5 3 6 00		4 5 3 6 00				12
		61 2 0 0 00		61 2 0 0 00				13
		8 7 8 4 00		8 7 8 4 00				14
		8 2 2 0 00		8 2 2 0 00				15
		27 0 0 0 00		27 0 0 0 00				16
		1 9 6 2 00		1 9 6 2 00				17
		4 1 4 3 00		4 1 4 3 00				18
		6 1 8 00		6 1 8 00				19
		1 1 6 7 00		1 1 6 7 00				20
		1 3 3 2 00		1 3 3 2 00				21
		9 3 6 00		9 3 6 00				22
								23
(a) 12 6 0 0 00		12 6 0 0 00		12 6 0 0 00				24
(b) 2 2 8 0 00		2 2 8 0 00		2 2 8 0 00				25
(c) 2 7 5 4 00		2 7 5 4 00		2 7 5 4 00				26
17 6 3 4 00	17 6 3 4 00	407 1 6 3 00	407 1 6 3 00	140 5 0 5 00	241 5 3 6 00	266 6 5 8 00	165 6 2 7 00	27
				101 0 3 1 00			101 0 3 1 00	28
				241 5 3 6 00	241 5 3 6 00	266 6 5 8 00	266 6 5 8 00	29

Work Sheet for a Professional Enterprise

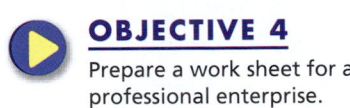

OBJECTIVE 4

Prepare a work sheet for a professional enterprise.

Assume that Dr. Hanna's receptionist posted the journal entries to the ledger accounts and recorded the trial balance in the first two columns of the work sheet. Dr. Hanna uses the cash basis of accounting, recording revenue only when he has received it in cash and recording expenses only when he has paid for them in cash. However, when Dr. Hanna buys an item that is going to last a number of years, he records this item as an asset and writes it off or depreciates it by making an adjusting entry each year of its useful life. He also makes adjusting entries for expired insurance. Data for the adjustments are given below.

a. Additional depreciation on dental equipment, $12,600.
b. Additional depreciation on office furniture and equipment, $2,280.
c. Insurance expired, $2,754.

With these adjusting entries, the rest of the work sheet can be completed as shown in Figure 8. First the balances of the accounts that were adjusted are brought up to date in the Adjusted Trial Balance columns. Then these amounts are carried forward to the remaining columns.

Medical professionals have their uniforms or lab coats cleaned by outside services. Their work sheets are likely to include an account for Laundry and Cleaning Expense.

Financial Statements

From the work sheet, Dr. Hanna's accountant prepares the financial statements shown in Figure 9. In this case, there was no additional investment made by S. A. Hanna during the year.

FIGURE 9

S. A. Hanna, D.D.S.
Income Statement
For Year Ended December 31, 20—

Revenue:		
Professional Fees		$241 5 3 6 00
Expenses:		
Dental Instruments Expense	$ 2 9 7 3 00	
Laundry and Cleaning Expense	4 5 3 6 00	
Salary Expense	61 2 0 0 00	
Laboratory Expense	8 7 8 4 00	
Dental Supplies Expense	8 2 2 0 00	
Rent Expense	27 0 0 0 00	
Depreciation Expense, Dental		
Equipment	12 6 0 0 00	
Depreciation Expense, Office		
Furniture and Equipment	2 2 8 0 00	
X-ray Supplies Expense	1 9 6 2 00	
Office Supplies Expense	4 1 4 3 00	
Insurance Expense	2 7 5 4 00	
Telephone Expense	6 1 8 00	
Utilities Expense	1 1 6 7 00	
Repairs and Maintenance Expense	1 3 3 2 00	
Miscellaneous Expense	9 3 6 00	
Total Expenses		140 5 0 5 00
Net Income		$101 0 3 1 00

FIGURE 9
(continued)

REMEMBER!

Whenever you are preparing a statement of owner's equity, always check the Capital account in the general ledger to see if any additional investment was recorded.

S. A. Hanna, D.D.S.
Statement of Owner's Equity
For Year Ended December 31, 20—

S. A. Hanna, Capital, January 1, 20—			$107 2 4 7 00
Net Income for Year	$101 0 3 1 00		
Less Withdrawals for Year	69 4 2 0 00		
Increase in Capital			31 6 1 1 00
S. A. Hanna, Capital, December 31, 20—			$138 8 5 8 00

S. A. Hanna, D.D.S.
Balance Sheet
December 31, 20—

Assets			
Cash			$ 11 7 6 9 00
Prepaid Insurance			9 1 8 00
Dental Equipment	$172 8 5 1 00		
Less Accumulated Depreciation	38 4 0 0 00		134 4 5 1 00
Office Furniture and Equipment	$ 11 7 0 0 00		
Less Accumulated Depreciation	8 5 8 0 00		3 1 2 0 00
Total Assets			$150 2 5 8 00
Liabilities			
Notes Payable			$ 11 4 0 0 00
Owner's Equity			
S. A. Hanna, Capital			138 8 5 8 00
Total Liabilities and Owner's Equity			$150 2 5 8 00

Adjusting and Closing Entries

OBJECTIVE 6

Record adjusting and closing entries in a combined journal.

Dr. Hanna (or his receptionist) records the adjusting and closing entries entirely in the Other Accounts columns of the combined journal. These entries must be posted individually, so the special columns are never used for them.

The adjusting and closing entries are shown in Figure 10 on page 206, two pages of a shortened combined journal. These adjusting and closing entries are shown here on two pages to make the concept clear. In practice, the closing entries would be written right below the adjusting entries. Be careful not to split up any individual entry between two pages. The totals are included because it is customary to show totals of all columns of a combined journal. In the Account Name column, accounts to be credited do not have to be indented.

COMBINED JOURNAL

| | CASH | | CK. | DATE | | ACCOUNT NAME | POST. REF. | OTHER ACCOUNTS | |
	DEBIT	CREDIT	NO.					DEBIT	CREDIT
1				20—		**Adjusting Entries**			
2				Dec.	31	Depr. Expense, Dental Equipment	517	12 6 0 0 00	
3						Accum. Depr., Dental Equipment	122		12 6 0 0 00
4					31	Depreciation Expense, Office			
5						Furniture and Equipment	518	2 2 8 0 00	
6						Accumulated Depreciation, Office			
7						Furniture and Equipment	124		2 2 8 0 00
8					31	Insurance Expense	522	2 7 5 4 00	
9						Prepaid Insurance	115		2 7 5 4 00
10					31			17 6 3 4 00	17 6 3 4 00
11								(X)	(X)
12									
13									
14									
15									
16									
17									

COMBINED JOURNAL

| | CASH | | CK. | DATE | | ACCOUNT NAME | POST. REF. | OTHER ACCOUNTS | |
	DEBIT	CREDIT	NO.					DEBIT	CREDIT
1				20—		**Closing Entries**			
2				Dec.	31	Professional Fees	411	241 5 3 6 00	
3						Income Summary	313		241 5 3 6 00
4					31	Income Summary	313	140 5 0 5 00	
5						Dental Instruments Expense	511		2 9 7 3 00
6						Laundry and Cleaning Expense	512		4 5 3 6 00
7						Salary Expense	513		61 2 0 0 00
8						Laboratory Expense	514		8 7 8 4 00
9						Dental Supplies Expense	515		8 2 2 0 00
10						Rent Expense	516		27 0 0 0 00
11						Depr. Expense, Dental Equipment	517		12 6 0 0 00
12						Depr. Expense, Office Furniture			
13						and Equipment	518		2 2 8 0 00
14						X-ray Supplies Expense	519		1 9 6 2 00
15						Office Supplies Expense	521		4 1 4 3 00
16						Insurance Expense	522		2 7 5 4 00
17						Telephone Expense	523		6 1 8 00
18						Utilities Expense	524		1 1 6 7 00
19						Repairs and Maintenance Expense	525		1 3 3 2 00
20						Miscellaneous Expense	526		9 3 6 00
21					31	Income Summary	313	101 0 3 1 00	
22						S. A. Hanna, Capital	311		101 0 3 1 00
23					31	S. A. Hanna, Capital	311	69 4 2 0 00	
24						S. A. Hanna, Drawing	312		69 4 2 0 00
25					31			552 4 9 2 00	552 4 9 2 00
26								(X)	(X)

FIGURE 10

DESIGNING A COMBINED JOURNAL

REMEMBER!

A combined journal can be used for either the accrual or the cash basis of accounting.

Since the combined journal is widely used in professional offices and service business firms, it is interesting to look over the varieties of combined journals available at stores selling office supplies. Some are bound journals; others are loose-leaf books. The number of columns varies from six to twenty, and they are available with or without column headings. Those that have printed column headings represent a "canned" type of combined journal. These journals are available for service stations, dry cleaners, doctors' offices, and many other types of businesses.

Combined journals with blank columns can be customized to meet the specific requirements of a given business. Prior to labeling the columns, first study the operations of the business and make up a chart of accounts. Next, identify those accounts that are likely to be used frequently to record typical transactions of the business. Naturally, if these accounts are used over and over, you need to set up special columns for them.

CHAPTER REVIEW

Online Study Center
ACE the test!

Review of Learning Objectives

1. Describe the accounting records for a professional enterprise.

   The records for a professional enterprise generally consist of an appointment record, a recording of charges levied for services rendered, and patients' or clients' (customers') ledger cards. A combined journal is generally used to record transactions that are posted to a general ledger.

2. Record transactions for both a professional enterprise and a service enterprise in a combined journal.

   Special columns are set up to record transactions involving frequently used accounts. Transactions involving other accounts are recorded in the Other Accounts columns. A long line in the Account Name column and a dash in the Post. Ref. column indicate that all debits and credits for a transaction have been entered in special columns.

3. Post from the combined journal and determine the cash balance.

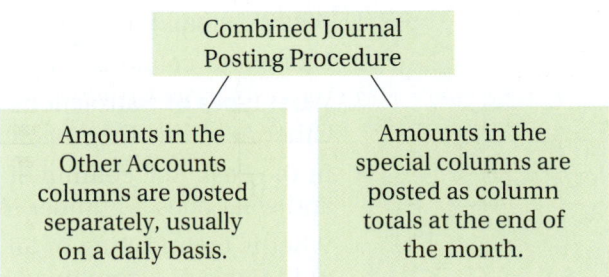

An account number in the Post. Ref. column indicates that the amount in the Other Accounts column has been posted; a dash in that column indicates that the amount is being posted as part of a column total. Below the totals of the Other Accounts columns, an X in parentheses indicates that the column total was not posted; accounts were posted individually. Below the totals of the special columns, the account numbers in parentheses indicate that each column has been posted.

4. Prepare a work sheet for a professional enterprise.

The work sheet for a professional enterprise is the same as the work sheet presented in Chapter 4 for a service enterprise.

5. Prepare financial statements for a professional enterprise.

The financial statements for professional enterprises are the same as the financial statements presented previously for service enterprises, except for some new account titles.

6. Record adjusting and closing entries in a combined journal.

Adjusting and closing entries are recorded in the Account Name column and the Other Accounts Debit and Credit columns. The closing entries may be recorded immediately below the adjusting entries. However, if it is necessary to carry over any one entry to a second page, you should not split up the entry.

Glossary

Combined journal A journal format widely used by professional and service enterprises in place of a general journal; designed to make the recording and posting of transactions more efficient. (197)

Patient's ledger record A record of amounts charged to patients, amounts received from patients, estimates given, and the remaining amounts owed by patients, which are called debit balances. In the event that a patient overpaid, the remainder is called a credit balance, which indicates a liability exists to the patient. (192)

Professional enterprise A business that provides a highly specialized service for a fee. (191)

Special columns Columns in a journal that are used to record amounts that occur frequently. (197)

QUESTIONS, EXERCISES, AND CASES

Discussion Questions

1. Why do small businesses find the combined journal convenient to use?
2. Name four columns that should always appear in a combined journal.
3. What types of transactions are recorded in the Other Accounts Debit and Other Accounts Credit columns?
4. In the Post. Ref. column of a combined journal, what does a dash signify and what does a number indicate?
5. What is the meaning of an X or a number in parentheses under the column totals of a combined journal?
6. When an amount is placed in the Other Accounts Debit or Other Accounts Credit column, what would be written in the Account Name column?
7. You have been asked to design a combined journal for Jody's Hair Salon. Customers pay in cash only. The business buys supplies on account from

creditors. Rent and utilities are paid monthly. Employees are paid wages weekly. The owner, Jody Wallace, makes withdrawals weekly. The firm advertises frequently. List the special columns needed plus the four columns that always appear in a combined journal.

8. Describe the process of proving the combined journal at the end of the month.

Exercises

P.O. 1

Record receipt of cash under the cash basis.

Exercise 6-1 On June 4, the appointment record for a psychiatrist shows that the total of the Fees column is $926 and the total of the Receipts column is $287. At the end of the day, $287 is deposited in the bank. Record the journal entry for the deposit in the general journal. Assume that the cash basis is used.

P.O. 2

List the columns to record transactions.

Exercise 6-2 Zambrano Advertising Agency uses a combined journal with the following columns. Assume that the accrual basis of accounting is used.

Cash Debit	Accounts Receivable Debit
Cash Credit	Accounts Receivable Credit
Ck. No.	Accounts Payable Debit
Date	Accounts Payable Credit
Account Name	Commissions Earned Credit
Post. Ref.	Salary Expense Debit
Other Accounts Debit	Utilities Expense Debit
Other Accounts Credit	

For each of the following, (a) list all of the columns that would be used to record the transaction and (b) describe what would be shown in each of the columns. (You do not have to indicate the Date column, since it would be used in the same way for each of the transactions.)

a. Payment of rent for the month.
b. Charge of commission to a client.
c. Payment of an electric bill.
d. Investment of equipment by the owner.

P.O. 2

Designate columns to record transactions.

Exercise 6-3 J. L. Larson, an attorney, uses a combined journal with the columns listed below.

a. Cash Debit
b. Cash Credit
c. Other Accounts Debit
d. Other Accounts Credit
e. Accounts Receivable Debit
f. Accounts Receivable Credit
g. Fees Earned Credit
h. Office Supplies Expense Debit
i. Salary Expense Debit
j. Travel Expense Debit

For each of the following, (a) list all of the columns that would be used to record the transaction and (b) describe what would be shown in each of the columns.

1. Issued a check for $235 for the purchase of a filing cabinet.
2. Sold services on account, $4,680.

 3. Received and paid the electric bill, $168.
 4. Received and paid the bill for airline ticket, $485.
 5. Sold services for cash, $600.
 6. Received and paid the bill for rent for the month, $1,600.
 7. Received $3,300 on account from customers.
 8. J. L. Larson withdrew $2,000 for personal use.
 9. Issued a check for $250 payment of court fees on behalf of a client (client owes J. L. Larson).

P.O. 2

Designate columns to record transactions.

Exercise 6-4 The books of Baylor and Associates, Certified Public Accountants, are kept on a cash basis. The client record of Alice Benson is presented below.

BAYLOR AND ASSOCIATES
CERTIFIED PUBLIC ACCOUNTANTS
242 SELVA AVENUE
MIAMI, FLORIDA 32906

CLIENT RECORD

Alice Benson
1429 Garfield Avenue
Miami, Florida 32909

DATE		SERVICE	CHG		REC		BAL	
20—								
May	6	Tax prep.	164	00			164	00
June	2				90	00	74	00

Record the June 2 transaction in a combined journal.

P.O. 2

Journalize a withdrawal.

Exercise 6-5 Assume that on June 14, Baylor and Associates issues business check number 311 for $1,950 to Miami National Bank for payment on N. Baylor's home mortgage. Explain how the transaction would be recorded in a combined journal.

P.O. 2

List the special columns to accommodate a situation.

Exercise 6-6 Ahmad Dental Laboratory maintains charge accounts for eight dentists. The owner is R. A. Ahmad. Frequent payments include supplies, salaries, delivery, and owner's withdrawals. List the most important special columns for the company's combined journal.

P.O. 3

Describe the posting procedure.

Exercise 6-7 Clayton Landscaping Services uses a combined journal that includes the following columns:

Cash Debit
Cash Credit
Other Accounts Debit
Other Accounts Credit
Fees Earned Credit

Truck Expense Debit
Supplies Expense Debit
Wages Expense Debit
Miscellaneous Expense Debit

Indicate the columns that are posted individually and those that are posted as a column total. Indicate the columns that are posted daily and those that are posted at the end of the month.

P.O. 3

Determine up-to-date cash balance.

Exercise 6-8 Determine the cash balance after November 11.

Cash

Beginning
Nov. 1 Bal.
642.50

	CASH					CK. NO.	DATE	
	DEBIT			CREDIT				
1							20—	
2	9 2 1 64						Nov.	1
3				7 5 42		121		3
4	3 8 9 00							5
5				4 1 6 20		122		8
6	8 4 0 00			2 1 9 00		123		9
7				8 4 59		124		11

internet
LINKS TO ACCOUNTING

Now that you have learned about recording transactions in a combined journal and preparing financial statements, let's go back to the questions we asked at the beginning of the chapter.

1. How would the accounts you would commonly use in a combined journal for a doctor differ from the accounts for an architect?
2. Give some examples of how Dr. Hanna's balance sheet in this chapter differs from Best Buy's balance sheet (found on page 58 of the 2005 Form 10-K report) by going to **http://www.sec.gov/edgar/searchedgar/companysearch.html** and searching for Best Buy Co Inc. Then, either scroll through the listing or do a search for Form 10-K. Select the 2005 filing.
3. The information found on the Internet seems endless. Choose any professional/service enterprise you know about and see if you can find its financial statements online.

CONSIDER AND COMMUNICATE

You do the bookkeeping for a small animal veterinarian. She has no formal accounting system yet, but she does save all source documents.

1. Convince her of the benefits of a combined journal.
2. Design the format for a combined journal with Debit and Credit columns and headings to accommodate the entries for a small animal veterinarian using the cash basis.

WHAT'S WRONG WITH THIS PICTURE?

Your friend, a psychotherapist, has been using a general journal for his sole proprietorship practice. He needs a better journal solution because he does the accounting himself. Discuss how you think a combined journal could save him time.

A QUESTION OF ETHICS

It is Friday at 6 P.M. It is your responsibility to count the money in the cash register, prepare the deposit slip for the bank, and lock up. You have counted the money, prepared the bank deposit, and cleared the cash register, when a customer comes in to buy something. You finish the sale for $19.50. The customer has the exact change. You are in a hurry and do not want to redo the deposit, so you put the $19.50 in your bag (the safe is locked and you don't have the combination). You intend to add it to Monday's deposit. Over the weekend you have a flat tire and need the $19.50 for repairs and lunch. Discuss the possible problems that arise from this action.

PROBLEM SET A

For additional help, see the demonstration problem at the beginning of each chapter in your Working Papers.

P.O. 2

Problem 6-1A M. L. Green, M.D., uses the following chart of accounts:

Assets

111 Cash
121 Medical Equipment
122 Accumulated Depreciation, Medical Equipment
123 Office Furniture and Equipment
124 Accumulated Depreciation, Office Furniture and Equipment
125 Vehicle
126 Accumulated Depreciation, Vehicle

Liabilities

211 Notes Payable

Owner's Equity

311 M. L. Green, Capital
312 M. L. Green, Drawing
313 Income Summary

Revenue

411 Professional Fees

Expenses

511 Nurse Salary Expense
512 Office Salary Expense
513 Equipment Rental Expense
514 Rent Expense
515 Medical Supplies Expense
516 X-ray Supplies Expense
517 Laboratory Expense
518 Cleaning Expense
519 Office Supplies Expense
521 Depreciation Expense, Medical Equipment
522 Depreciation Expense, Office Furniture and Equipment
523 Depreciation Expense, Vehicle
524 Vehicle Expense
525 Insurance Expense
526 Telephone Expense
527 Utilities Expense
528 Miscellaneous Expense

Dr. Green's records consist of an appointment record book, examination and charge reports, patients' ledger records, a combined journal, and a general ledger. The doctor fills out an examination and charge report each time a patient visits. The report contains a listing of the treatments and tests administered, coded for insurance purposes, as well as the amounts of the charges. The charges are then recorded in the patient's ledger record. Monthly statements based on the patient's ledger record are mailed to the patient. Dr. Green's books are kept on the cash basis. These transactions took place during April:

Apr.		
	1	Paid April's rent, $1,790 (Ck. No. 636).
	2	Paid salary for the part-time office person, $775 (Ck. No. 637).
	4	Bought medical supplies for cash from Park Medical Supply, $670 (Ck. No. 638).
	6	Received cash from patients during week, $7,680.
	9	Paid telephone bill, $170 (Ck. No. 639).
	12	Paid Technical Labs for laboratory expense, $855 (Ck. No. 640).
	13	Received cash from patients during week, $6,593.
	15	Dr. M. L. Green withdrew $1,050 for personal use (Ck. No. 641).
	17	Bought x-ray supplies for cash, $214 (Ck. No. 642).
	18	Paid for gas and oil for vehicle used in business, $135 (Vehicle Expense) (Ck. No. 643).
	20	Received cash from patients during week, $3,742.
	23	Bought postage stamps for cash, $30 (Miscellaneous Expense) (Ck. No. 644).
	24	Paid $110 to Carson Laundry for laundry service (Cleaning Expense) (Ck. No. 645).
	27	Paid Kramer News for waiting room magazines, $86.50 (Miscellaneous Expense) (Ck. No. 646).
	30	Paid nurse's salary for the month, $2,010 (Ck. No. 647).
	30	Paid A-One Cleaning for janitorial services, $132 (Cleaning Expense) (Ck. No. 648).
	30	Received cash from patients (April 21 through 30), $3,246.
	30	Dr. M. L. Green withdrew $1,750 for personal use (Ck. No. 649).

Check Figure

Total debits, $31,038.50

Instructions

1. Record these transactions on page 9 of the combined journal. Insert the name of the Drawing account.
2. Prove the equality of the debit and credit totals in the Account Name column below the totals.

P.O. 6

Problem 6-2A The completed work sheet for S. R. Lindell, Psychologist, is shown in Figure 11 on pages 214 and 215.

Check Figure

Total Other Accounts Debit column, $172,626.20

Instructions

Record the adjusting and closing entries on page 5 of the combined journal. Remember to total the columns and insert an X in parentheses below each total.

P.O. 2,3

Problem 6-3A Dr. Terrence T. Cascone operates the Cascone Allergy Clinic. The transactions were completed during September of this year. Following is his chart of accounts.

FIGURE 11

	ACCOUNT NAME	TRIAL BALANCE DEBIT	TRIAL BALANCE CREDIT
1	Cash	6 2 7 0 00	
2	Office Equipment	56 4 1 0 25	
3	Accumulated Depreciation, Office Equipment		16 9 8 4 16
4	S. R. Lindell, Capital		38 8 7 2 94
5	S. R. Lindell, Drawing	24 7 8 5 00	
6	Professional Fees		70 9 2 9 20
7	Salary Expense	16 3 2 4 60	
8	Advertising Expense	4 5 7 5 10	
9	Rent Expense	7 6 7 0 00	
10	Vehicle Expense	2 0 6 2 75	
11	Travel Expense	2 2 4 1 32	
12	Entertainment Expense	7 9 6 12	
13	Supplies Expense	5 2 6 0 00	
14	Miscellaneous Expense	3 9 1 16	
15		126 7 8 6 30	126 7 8 6 30
16	Depreciation Expense, Office Equipment		
17			
18	Net Income		
19			
20			

Assets

111 Cash
112 Accounts Receivable
114 Prepaid Insurance
121 Equipment
122 Accumulated Depreciation, Equipment

Liabilities

221 Accounts Payable

Owner's Equity

311 T. T. Cascone, Capital
312 T. T. Cascone, Drawing
313 Income Summary

Revenue

411 Professional Fees

Expenses

511 Salary Expense
512 Rent Expense
513 Laboratory Expense
514 Utilities Expense
515 Depreciation Expense, Equipment
516 Supplies Expense
517 Miscellaneous Expense

Sept. 2 Bought medical equipment on account from Wing Medical Supplies, $1,560. (Use two lines.)

2 Paid office rent for month, $1,200 (Ck. No. 516).

2 Received cash on account from patients, $5,129: D. R. Crain, $1,152.50; Deanne Skeller, $1,372; Jason Neeles, $1,317; Terense Garner, $1,287.50. These patients were billed last month for services performed in August. (Dr. Cascone uses the

S. R. Lindell, Psychologist
Work Sheet
For Year Ended December 31, 20—

ADJUSTMENTS		ADJUSTED TRIAL BALANCE		INCOME STATEMENT		BALANCE SHEET		
DEBIT	CREDIT	DEBIT	CREDIT	DEBIT	CREDIT	DEBIT	CREDIT	
		6 2 7 0 00				6 2 7 0 00		1
		56 4 1 0 25				56 4 1 0 25		2
	(a)5 9 8 2 80		22 9 6 6 96				22 9 6 6 96	3
			38 8 7 2 94				38 8 7 2 94	4
		24 7 8 5 00				24 7 8 5 00		5
			70 9 2 9 20		70 9 2 9 20			6
		16 3 2 4 60		16 3 2 4 60				7
		4 5 7 5 10		4 5 7 5 10				8
		7 6 7 0 00		7 6 7 0 00				9
		2 0 6 2 75		2 0 6 2 75				10
		2 2 4 1 32		2 2 4 1 32				11
		7 9 6 12		7 9 6 12				12
		5 2 6 0 00		5 2 6 0 00				13
		3 9 1 16		3 9 1 16				14
								15
(a)5 9 8 2 80		5 9 8 2 80		5 9 8 2 80				16
5 9 8 2 80	5 9 8 2 80	132 7 6 9 10	132 7 6 9 10	45 3 0 3 85	70 9 2 9 20	87 4 6 5 25	61 8 3 9 90	17
				25 6 2 5 35			25 6 2 5 35	18
				70 9 2 9 20	70 9 2 9 20	87 4 6 5 25	87 4 6 5 25	19
								20

accrual basis. Use four lines, recording individual amounts in both the Cash Debit column and the Accounts Receivable Credit column. List each patient's name in the Account Name column.)

Sept.

3 Received cash for professional services rendered, $3,229.

5 Received and paid electric bill to Mid-State Power, $258.40 (Ck. No. 517).

8 Received and paid telephone bill to Western Telephone Company for month, $183 (Ck. No. 518).

9 Recorded fees charged to patients on account for professional services rendered, $830.50: F. Radewan, $484.50; M. Parkhill, $346. (Use two lines.)

15 Paid salary of L. Mance (assistant), $847.50 (Ck. No. 519).

19 Received cash for professional services, $1,608.

23 Returned part of the equipment purchased on September 2 and received a reduction on the bill, $184.

28 Billed patients on account for professional services rendered, $2,045: C. R. Roberts, $1,486; Marnie Lendal, $516.50; Dave Hensen, $42.50.

30 Paid salary of C. Barnes (part-time assistant), $720.75 (Ck. No. 520).

30 Paid salary of R. Carson (receptionist), $942 (Ck. No. 521).

30 Dr. Cascone withdrew $1,700 cash for personal use (Ck. No. 522).

Check Figure

Total debits (combined journal), $20,437.15

Instructions

1. Record these transactions in the combined journal, page 37.
2. Prove the equality of the debit and credit totals in the Account Name column below the totals.
3. Fill in owner's equity accounts and post to the accounts in the general ledger.
4. Prepare a trial balance.

P.O. 2

Problem 6-4A On September 1 of this year, T. W. Baptiste started a limousine service serving the local area. The following transactions related to Luscious Limousine Service were completed during September.

Sept.	1	Baptiste opened an account at the Golden State Bank in the name of the business and deposited $34,000.
	2	Bought two used limousines from Laughlin Motors for $80,900, paying $20,900 down, with the balance payable in 30 days (Ck. No. 1).
	3	Bought heavy-duty vacuum and car-cleaning equipment for $380, paying cash (Ck. No. 2).
	4	Paid Valley Service for gas and oil for limousines, $243 (Ck. No. 3).
	5	Paid rent for subletting office space, $725 (Ck. No. 4).
	7	Paid wages to G. Baugh, $540 (Ck. No. 5).
	7	Received revenue for the week, $2,315.
	9	Paid for city business license, $175 (Ck. No. 6).
	11	Bought desk and filing cabinet on account from Murray Office Supply, $480.
	14	Paid for telephone answering service for the month, $225 (Ck. No. 7).
	14	Paid wages to G. Baugh, $540 (Ck. No. 8).
	14	Baptiste withdrew $1,800 for personal use (Ck. No. 9).
	14	Received revenue for the week, $2,784.
	17	Paid Laughlin Motors $2,800 as part payment on account (Ck. No. 10).
	18	Paid $342 for advertising in the telephone directory (Ck. No. 11).
	18	Paid Valley Service for gas and oil for limousines, $295 (Ck. No. 12).
	20	Paid utilities for the month, $208 (Ck. No. 13).
	21	Received revenue for the week, $2,405.
	23	Paid wages to G. Baugh, $540 (Ck. No. 14).
	30	Received revenue for the period September 22–30, $2,010.
	30	Paid Security Insurance Agency for vehicle insurance for six months, $857 (Ck. No. 15).
	30	Paid wages to G. Baugh, $540 (Ck. No. 16).
	30	Baptiste withdrew $1,500 for personal use (Ck. No. 17).

Check Figure

Total debits (combined journal), $136,604

Instructions

1. Review the transactions for Luscious Limousine Service and then develop an appropriate chart of accounts. The company uses the cash basis. All revenue is in the form of cash.
2. Label the appropriate columns in the combined journal. Next to the Date column, list a Ck. No. column and record checks beginning with number 1.
3. Record the transactions in the combined journal beginning with page 1.
4. Show proof of the equality of debit and credit totals in the Account Name column below the totals.

PROBLEM SET B

For additional help, see the demonstration problem at the beginning of each chapter in your Working Papers.

P.O. 2

Problem 6-1B L. Swanson, M.D., uses the following chart of accounts:

Assets

111 Cash
121 Medical Equipment
122 Accumulated Depreciation, Medical Equipment
123 Office Furniture and Equipment
124 Accumulated Depreciation, Office Furniture and Equipment
125 Vehicle
126 Accumulated Depreciation, Vehicle

Liabilities

211 Notes Payable

Owner's Equity

311 L. Swanson, Capital
312 L. Swanson, Drawing
313 Income Summary

Revenue

411 Professional Fees

Expenses

511 Salary Expense
512 Rent Expense
513 Equipment Rental Expense
514 Medical Supplies Expense
515 X-ray Supplies Expense
516 Laboratory Expense
517 Cleaning Expense
518 Office Supplies Expense
519 Depreciation Expense, Medical Equipment
521 Depreciation Expense, Office Furniture and Equipment
522 Depreciation Expense, Vehicle
523 Vehicle Expense
524 Insurance Expense
525 Telephone Expense
526 Utilities Expense
527 Miscellaneous Expense

Dr. Swanson's records consist of an appointment record book, examination and charge reports, patients' ledger records, a combined journal, and a general ledger. The doctor fills out an examination and charge report each time a patient visits. The reports contain a listing of the treatments and tests administered, coded for insurance purposes, as well as the amounts of the charges. The charges are then recorded in the patient's ledger record. Monthly statements based on the patients' ledger records are mailed to patients. Dr. Swanson's books are kept on the cash basis. These transactions took place during November:

Nov. 1 Bought medical supplies for cash from Martin Surgical Supply, $679.50 (Ck. No. 214).
  1 Paid November's rent, $1,450 (Ck. No. 215).
  4 Paid salary for the part-time office person, $820 (Ck. No. 216).
  6 Received cash from patients during the week, $7,325.
  7 Bought an examination table from Martin Surgical Supply, costing $1,560, paying $560 in cash and agreeing by contract to pay the balance in four monthly installments of $250 each (credit Notes Payable) (Ck. No. 217).
  8 Paid Runyan Laboratories for laboratory expense, $854 (Ck. No. 218).
  9 Paid telephone bill, $184 (Ck. No. 219).

FIGURE 12

	ACCOUNT NAME	TRIAL BALANCE	
		DEBIT	CREDIT
1	Cash	8 1 0 5 00	
2	Equipment	35 2 1 9 00	
3	Accumulated Depreciation, Equipment		7 4 9 0 00
4	T. R. Berman, Capital		27 9 4 5 40
5	T. R. Berman, Drawing	14 8 8 0 00	
6	Professional Fees		65 9 5 2 00
7	Salary Expense	31 3 1 5 00	
8	Advertising Expense	1 0 6 0 80	
9	Rent Expense	1 8 3 0 00	
10	Vehicle Expense	1 9 7 5 00	
11	Travel Expense	3 1 2 4 60	
12	Entertainment Expense	9 3 5 00	
13	Supplies Expense	2 2 4 2 40	
14	Miscellaneous Expense	7 0 0 60	
15		101 3 8 7 40	101 3 8 7 40
16	Depreciation Expense, Equipment		
17			
18	Net Income		
19			
20			

Nov. 13 Received cash from patients during the week, $5,230.
  16 Dr. L. Swanson withdrew $1,500 for personal use (Ck. No. 220).
  16 Bought x-ray supplies for cash, $398 (Ck. No. 221).
  20 Received cash from patients during the week, $3,622.
  23 Bought postage stamps for cash, $30 (Miscellaneous Expense) (Ck. No. 222).
  26 Paid for gas and oil for vehicle used in business, $100.25 (Vehicle Expense) (Ck. No. 223).
  28 Paid Selton and Company for janitorial services, $195 (Cleaning Expense) (Ck. No. 224).
  30 Paid nurse's salary for the month, $2,100 (Ck. No. 225).
  30 Dr. L. Swanson withdrew $1,500 for personal use (Ck. No. 226).
  30 Received cash from patients (November 21 through 30), $3,450.
  30 Paid $112 to Pro Laundry for laundry service through November 30 (Cleaning Expense) (Ck. No. 227).

Check Figure

Total debits, $31,109.75

Instructions

1. Record these transactions in the combined journal, page 26. Insert the name in the Drawing account.
2. Prove the equality of the debits and credits in the Account Name column below the totals.

P.O. 6

Problem 6-2B The completed work sheet for Berman Development Company is shown in Figure 12 above.

Berman Development Company
Work Sheet
For Month Ended December 31, 20—

ADJUSTMENTS DEBIT	ADJUSTMENTS CREDIT	ADJUSTED TRIAL BALANCE DEBIT	ADJUSTED TRIAL BALANCE CREDIT	INCOME STATEMENT DEBIT	INCOME STATEMENT CREDIT	BALANCE SHEET DEBIT	BALANCE SHEET CREDIT	
		8 1 0 5 00				8 1 0 5 00		1
		35 2 1 9 00				35 2 1 9 00		2
	(a) 1 2 2 1 00		8 7 1 1 00				8 7 1 1 00	3
			27 9 4 5 40				27 9 4 5 40	4
		14 8 8 0 00				14 8 8 0 00		5
			65 9 5 2 00		65 9 5 2 00			6
		31 3 1 5 00		31 3 1 5 00				7
		1 0 6 0 80		1 0 6 0 80				8
		1 8 3 0 00		1 8 3 0 00				9
		1 9 7 5 00		1 9 7 5 00				10
		3 1 2 4 60		3 1 2 4 60				11
		9 3 5 00		9 3 5 00				12
		2 2 4 2 40		2 2 4 2 40				13
		7 0 0 60		7 0 0 60				14
								15
(a) 1 2 2 1 00		1 2 2 1 00		1 2 2 1 00				16
1 2 2 1 00	1 2 2 1 00	102 6 0 8 40	102 6 0 8 40	44 4 0 4 40	65 9 5 2 00	58 2 0 4 00	36 6 5 6 40	17
				21 5 4 7 60			21 5 4 7 60	18
				65 9 5 2 00	65 9 5 2 00	58 2 0 4 00	58 2 0 4 00	19
								20

Check Figure

Total Other Accounts Debit column, $148,005

P.O. 2,3

Instructions

Record the adjusting and closing entries on page 6 of the combined journal. Remember to total the columns and insert an X in parentheses below each total.

Problem 6-3B Tara Eng, D.C., operates the Eng Chiropractic Clinic. The transactions described on page 220 were completed during September of this year. Her chart of accounts is as follows:

Assets

111 Cash
112 Accounts Receivable
114 Prepaid Insurance
121 Equipment
122 Accumulated Depreciation, Equipment

Liabilities

221 Accounts Payable

Owner's Equity

311 T. Eng, Capital
312 T. Eng, Drawing
313 Income Summary

Revenue

411 Professional Fees

Expenses

511 Salary Expense
512 Rent Expense
513 Laboratory Expense
514 Utilities Expense
515 Depreciation Expense, Equipment
516 Supplies Expense
517 Miscellaneous Expense

Sept.	1	Bought x-ray equipment on account from Radiological Associates, $1,640. (Use two lines.)
	2	Paid office rent for the month, $1,725 (Ck. No. 423).
	2	Received cash on account from patients, $926: R. Whitten, $375; Ellen Briggs, $412; Andy Corde, $139. These patients were billed last month for services performed in August. (Dr. Eng uses the accrual basis. Use three lines, recording individual amounts in both the Cash Debit column and the Accounts Receivable Credit column. List each patient's name in the Account Name column.)
	4	Received cash for professional services rendered, $2,790.75.
	6	Received and paid electric bill to Universal Electric, $145.50 (Ck. No. 424).
	7	Received and paid telephone bill for month to Southern Telephone Company, $151 (Ck. No. 425).
	9	Recorded fees charged to patients on account for professional services rendered, $945.50: T. Wang, $335; H. Carver, $610.50. (Use two lines.)
	15	Paid salary of K. Olsen (assistant), $1,230 (Ck. No. 426).
	19	Received cash for professional services, $1,581.
	22	Returned part of equipment purchased on September 1 and received a reduction on the bill, $265.
	27	Billed patients on account for professional services rendered, $1,532: N. Carol, $280; J. Ortiz, $390; S. Archer, $862.
	30	Paid salary of D. Canton (part-time assistant), $625 (Ck. No. 427).
	30	Paid salary of J. Grand (receptionist), $1,155 (Ck. No. 428).
	30	Dr. Eng withdrew $1,500 cash for personal use (Ck. No. 429).

Check Figure

Total debits (combined journal), $16,211.75

Instructions

1. Record these transactions in the combined journal, page 43.
2. Prove the equality of the debit and credit totals in the Account Name column below the totals.
3. Fill in owner's equity accounts and post to the accounts in the general ledger.
4. Prepare a trial balance.

P.O. 2

Problem 6-4B On July 1 of this year, K. A. Bremer started a landscaping business. The following transactions related to Bremer's Landscaping were completed during July.

July	1	Bremer opened an account at the Carter National Bank in the name of the business and deposited $18,000.
	1	Paid rent for office and warehouse space for the month, $1,425 (Ck. No. 1).
	2	Bought a used truck from Nelson Motors for $15,200, paying $5,000 as a down payment, with the balance on account due in 30 days (Ck. No. 2).
	3	Bought landscaping equipment from Glade Equipment for $3,750, paying $1,750 as a down payment, with the balance due in 30 days (Ck. No. 3).
	3	Paid Zelda's Fast Serve for gas and oil for the truck, $136 (Ck. No. 4).
	4	Received and paid bill for advertising from the *City Review,* $248 (Ck. No. 5).

July 4 Bought fertilizers on account from Drager's Lawn and Garden Store, $1,145 (Supplies Expense).

4 Bought beauty bark from R&L Distributing Company on account, $430 (Supplies Expense).

6 Received revenue for the week, $2,392.

7 Paid wages to part-time employee, $492 (Ck. No. 6).

7 Paid for telephone answering service for the month, $244 (Ck. No. 7).

10 Paid Zelda's Fast Serve for gas and oil for the truck, $185 (Ck. No. 8).

13 Received revenue for the week, $2,515.

17 Bremer withdrew $1,020 for personal use (Ck. No. 9).

20 Received revenue for the week, $2,368.

21 Paid wages to part-time employee, $412 (Ck. No. 10).

27 Paid for city business license, $157 (Ck. No. 11).

27 Paid utilities for the month, $228 (Ck. No. 12).

30 Paid Nelson Motors $2,500 to apply on account (Ck. No. 13).

30 Paid Zelda's Fast Serve for gas and oil for the truck, $145, plus $115 for a tune-up (Ck. No. 14).

31 Received revenue for the period July 21–31, $2,525.

31 Paid wages to part-time employee, $415 (Ck. No. 15).

31 Bremer withdrew $1,850 for personal use (Ck. No. 16).

Check Figure

Total debits (combined journal), $57,897

Instructions

1. Review the transactions for Bremer's Landscaping and then develop an appropriate chart of accounts. Bremer uses the cash basis of accounting. All revenue is in the form of cash.
2. Label the appropriate columns in the combined journal. Next to the Date column, list a Ck. No. column and record checks beginning with number 1.
3. Record the transactions in the combined journal beginning with page 1.
4. Show proof of the equality of debit and credit totals in the Account Name column below the totals.

Bank Accounts and Cash Funds

Performance Objectives

After you have completed this chapter, you will be able to do the following:

1. Describe the procedure for depositing checks.

2. Reconcile a bank statement.

3. Record the required journal entries from the bank reconciliation.

4. Record journal entries to establish and reimburse a Petty Cash Fund.

5. Complete petty cash vouchers and petty cash payments records.

6. Record the journal entries to establish a Change Fund.

7. Record journal entries for transactions involving Cash Short and Over.

A very important aspect of any system of financial accounting, either for an individual or for a business enterprise, is the accurate and efficient management of cash. For a business of any size, all cash received during a work day should be deposited at the end of the day, and all disbursements—with the exception of payments from Petty Cash—should be made by check or paid electronically. The handling of cash in this manner is an example of **internal control**. Internal control is the system of policies and procedures to (1) protect assets against fraud and waste, (2) provide for accurate accounting data, (3) promote an efficient operation, and (4) encourage adherence to management policies.

When we talk about cash, we mean currency, coins, checks, money orders, traveler's checks, and bank drafts or bank cashier's checks. Personal checks are accepted conditionally—that is, based on the condition that they are valid. In other words, we consider checks to be good until they are otherwise proven not to be good.

Internal control of cash is a critical activity in a business. Divide the cash activities among several people to deter mishandling.

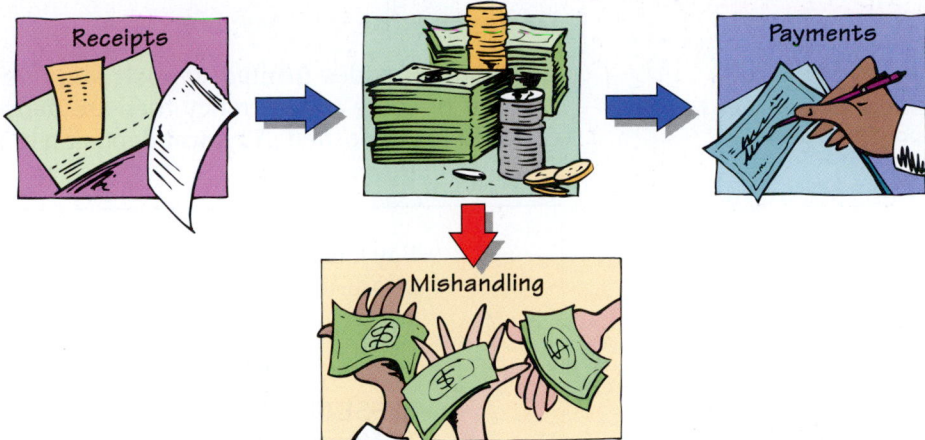

In this chapter, besides discussing bank accounts, we are going to talk about **cash funds**—petty cash funds and change funds—which are separately held reserves of cash set aside for specific purposes.

USING A CHECKING ACCOUNT

Although you may be familiar with the process of opening a checking account, making deposits, and writing checks, let's review these and other procedures associated with opening and maintaining a business checking account. We will discuss signature cards, deposit slips, automated teller machines, electronic funds transfer, night deposits, and endorsements.

Signature Card

FYI

As a means of preventing employee theft, many companies require more than one signature on checks over a certain dollar amount.

When Paula C. Boyd founded Bay Cleaners, she opened a checking account in the name of the business. When she opened the account, she filled out a **signature card** for the bank's files. Because Boyd gave her assistant Maria R. Ruiz the right to sign checks too, the assistant also signed the card. The signature card gives the bank a copy of the official signatures of any persons authorized to sign checks. The bank can use it to verify the signatures on any checks of Bay Cleaners presented for payment. This card helps the bank detect forgeries. Figure 1 shows a typical signature card.

FIGURE 1

Title **Bay Cleaners**	Account Number **5008-3007**

In consideration of the acceptance by   BESSETT NATIONAL BANK   of my/our account of the type indicated below, I/we agree to be bound by such rules and regulations and/or such schedules of interest, fees and charges applicable to such account as may now or hereafter be adopted by and in effect at said Bank, and also by the provisions printed hereon. It is understood that the acceptance by said Bank of my/our account is subject to the receipt by said Bank of satisfactory credit information.

(1) Sign Here *Paula C. Boyd*

(2) Sign Here *Maria R. Ruiz*

Address **625 Montes Avenue**

City **San Diego**   State **California**   Zip **92109**

☑ CHECKING   ☐ MULTIPLE MATURITY   ☐ CASH MANAGER

☐ SAVINGS   ☐ GUARANTEED INTEREST (Multiple Maturity)   ☐ SAFE DEPOSIT   ☐ OTHER _____

IF THIS IS A JOINT ACCOUNT, BOTH OWNERS MUST SIGN ABOVE

Each of the signers guarantees the genuineness of the signature of the other. Each signer also agrees with the other and the Bank that deposits now or hereafter made to this account may be withdrawn in whole or part by either or survivor, and that each may endorse for deposit to this account any instrument payable to the order of either or both. Provisions respecting this agreement shall be modified only upon receipt by the Bank of written notice, signed by both.

Deposit Slips

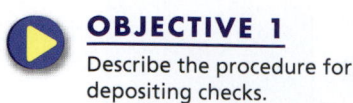

OBJECTIVE 1

Describe the procedure for depositing checks.

The bank provides printed **deposit slips** on which customers record the amount of coins and currency they are depositing and list each individual check being deposited. A typical deposit slip is shown in Figure 2.

FIGURE 2

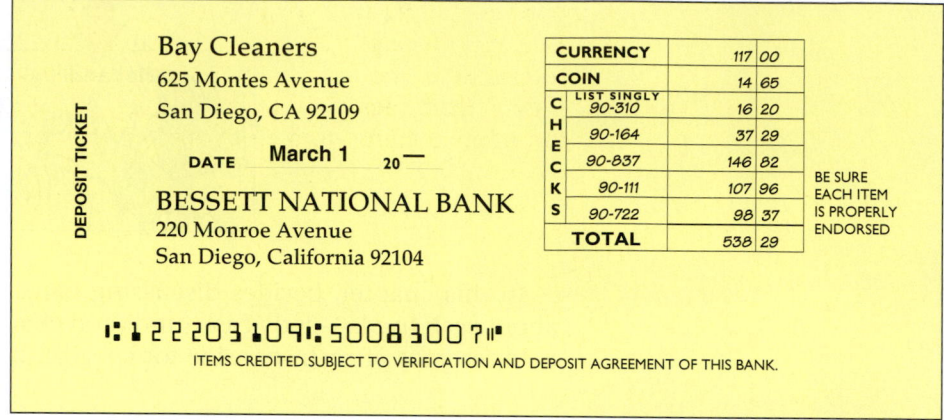

Each check should be listed according to its American Bankers Association (ABA) transit number. The **ABA number** is the small fraction located in the upper right corner of a check. The numerator (top of the fraction) indicates the city or state in which the bank is located and the specific bank on which the check is drawn. The denominator (bottom of the fraction) indicates the Federal Reserve District in which the check is cleared and the routing number used by the Federal Reserve Bank. For example,

$$\frac{90\text{-}310}{1222}$$

FYI

The 12 in the denominator represents the Twelfth Federal Reserve District, and the 22 represents the routing number used by the Federal Reserve Bank.

The 90 identifies the city or state, and the 310 indicates the specific bank within that area (see Figures 3 and 5).

For a business account, the depositor fills out the deposit slip in duplicate, giving the original to the bank teller and keeping the copy. (This procedure may vary from bank to bank.)

The bank prints the amount of each deposited check on the lower right side of the check in a distinctive script called **MICR**, which stands for *magnetic ink character recognition*. The routing number (as well as the depositor's number) used by the Federal Reserve Bank was printed on the lower left side of the blank check before it was sent to the account holder. The electronic equipment used to process the checks is able to rapidly read the script identifying the bank on which the check is drawn and the amount of the check.

Automated Teller Machines

Deposits, withdrawals, and transfers can be made at all hours at banks with **ATMs (automated teller machines)**. Each depositor uses a plastic card that contains a code number and has a personal identification number (PIN). The amount to be deposited, withdrawn, or transferred is keyed in by the depositor. To make a deposit, the customer inserts an envelope containing cash and/or checks and, if required, a copy of the deposit slip into the ATM. To make a withdrawal, the customer requests an amount, the ATM dispenses it, and the customer removes the cash. In addition to deposits and withdrawals, a customer may transfer amounts from one account to another (for example, from savings to checking).

Electronic Funds Transfer

A transfer of funds initiated through an electronic terminal, such as a telephone, computer, or magnetic tape, is an **Electronic Funds Transfer (EFT)**. There is no paper document, such as a check or deposit slip, starting the transaction. The monthly bank statement will list the EFT deposits and payments. Examples of EFTs include an ATM transaction, a wire transfer in or out of an account, and electronic bill paying.

Night Deposits

Most banks provide night depositories so that businesses and individuals can make deposits after regular hours. These are secured chutes into which a business's representative can drop a bag of cash and checks, knowing that the day's receipts will be safe until the bank opens in the morning.

Endorsements

The bank may not accept for deposit a check made out to a business until someone from the business has endorsed the check by signature or by stamp. The endorsement should appear on the back of the left end of a check, as it does in Figure 3. The **endorsement** (1) transfers title to the money and (2) authorizes the payment of the check. In other words, if the check is not good, NSF (not sufficient funds), then the bank, in order to protect itself, will deduct the amount of the check from the depositor's account.

FIGURE 3

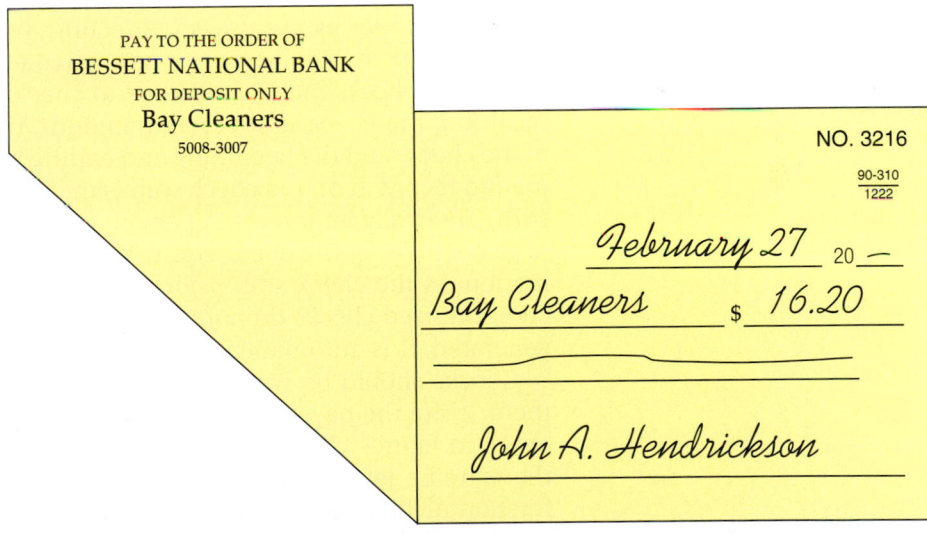

Restrictive Endorsement All checks made payable to Bay Cleaners are endorsed by stamping on the back of the checks "Pay to the Order of Bessett National Bank, For Deposit Only, Bay Cleaners." This is called a **restrictive endorsement** because it restricts or limits any further transfer of the check. This endorsement also forces the deposit of the check, because the endorsement is not valid for any other purpose.

Blank Endorsement When the party to whom a check is made payable (the payee) endorses the check by signing only her or his name on the back

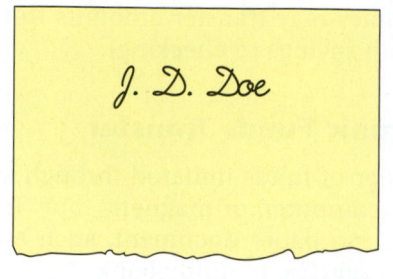

Restrictive Endorsement
(with rubber stamp)
           Blank Endorsement
           Qualified Endorsement

FIGURE 4

of the check, this is known as a **blank endorsement** (Figure 4). With a blank endorsement, there are no restrictions attached.

Qualified Endorsement A third type of endorsement is a **qualified endorsement** (see Figure 4), which generally includes the phrase "Pay to the order of," followed by the name of the person to whom the check is being transferred, and then followed by the phrase "without recourse." Such an endorsement frees the endorser from future liability in case the drawer of the check does not have sufficient funds to cover the check.

WRITING CHECKS

People generally use a check to withdraw money from a bank checking account. The party who writes the check is called the **drawer**. A check represents an order by the drawer, directing the bank to pay a designated person or company. The party to whom payment is to be made is the **payee**.

Manual checks may be attached to check stubs. Each stub has spaces for recording the check number and amount, the date and payee, the purpose of the check, and the beginning and ending balances of cash. *Note:* The information recorded on the check stub is the basis for the journal entry, so check stubs are vitally important. A person in a hurry or under pressure sometimes neglects to fill in the check stubs. Therefore, it is best to record all the information on the check stub *before making out the check*. Businesses that use computerized checks do not need check stubs. When the check is computer generated, it is automatically entered into the accounting system.

Checks should be written carefully so that no one can successfully alter them. Write the payee's name on the first long line. Write the amount of the check in figures close to the dollar sign, then write the amount in words at the extreme left of the line provided for this information. Write cents as a fraction of 100. For example, write $727.50 as "seven hundred twenty-seven and 50/100," or $89.00 as "eighty-nine and NO/100." Legally, if there is a discrepancy between the amount in figures and the written amount, the written amount prevails. However, generally, the bank gets in touch with the drawer and asks what the correct amount should be.

Finally, the drawer's signature on the face of the check should match that on the signature card on file at the drawer's bank.

Figure 5 is a manual check, with the accompanying stub, drawn on the account of Bay Cleaners. A description of the script appears in Figure 6.

FIGURE 5

FIGURE 6

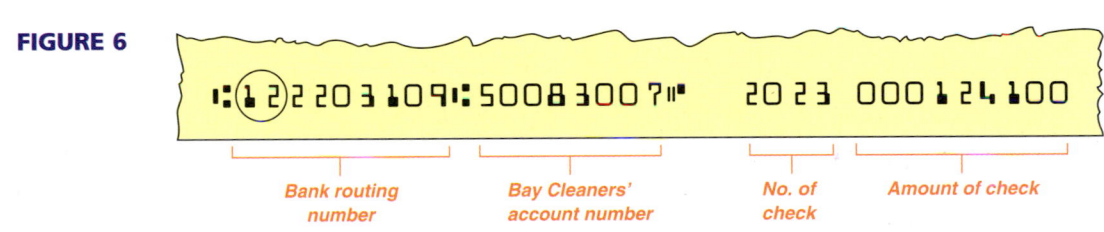

Bank routing number | Bay Cleaners' account number | No. of check | Amount of check

BANK STATEMENTS

The bank prepares the **bank statement**, which is created from the bank's viewpoint. Keep in mind that, to the bank, a customer's account is a liability and, therefore, has a credit balance. Once a month, the bank sends each of its customers the following information with the bank statement:

- The balance at the beginning of the month
- Additions in the form of deposits and credit memos
- Deductions in the form of checks and debit memos
- Electronic transactions
- The final balance at the end of the month

A bank statement for Bay Cleaners is shown in Figure 7 on page 228. The following legend of symbols is listed on the bottom of the statement:

- **CM (credit memo)** Increases in or credits to the account, such as notes or accounts left with the bank for collection and interest income earned.
- **DM (debit memo)** Decreases in or debits to the account, such as NSF checks and service charges. Service charges are based on the number of items processed and the average account balance. Special charges may also be levied against the account for collections and other services performed, including check printing.

BESSETT NATIONAL BANK
220 Monroe Avenue
San Diego, California 92104

| STATEMENT OF ACCOUNT | **Bay Cleaners**
 625 Montes Avenue
 San Diego, CA 92109 | ACCOUNT NUMBER
 5008-3007
 STATEMENT DATE
 September 30, 20 — – October 31, 20 —
 TAX ID NUMBER
 83-424 9732 |

SUMMARY

Balance Last Statement	$10,633.69
Amount of Checks and Debits	$37,732.36
Number of Checks	66
Amount of Deposits and Credits	$40,547.67
Number of Deposits	23
Balance This Statement	$13,449.00

CHECKS/OTHER DEBITS

CHECKS

CHECK NUMBER	DATE POSTED	AMOUNT	CHECK NUMBER	DATE POSTED	AMOUNT
1952	10-01	50.00	1988	10-17	61.22
1953	10-01	200.00	1989	10-17	463.29
1954	10-01	400.00	1990	10-18	520.00
1955	10-02	46.00	1991	10-19	14.57
1956	10-02	174.23	1992	10-19	23.98
1957	10-02	671.74	1993	10-19	115.16
1958	10-03	846.20	1994	10-20	117.37
1984	10-14	664.56	2018	10-30	126.70
1985	10-15	719.00	2019	10-30	943.64
1986	10-16	61.68	2020	10-31	843.17
1987	10-16	591.84	2021	10-31	21.92

OTHER DEBITS

DESCRIPTION	DATE POSTED	AMOUNT
DM NSF check from A. L. Sanders	10-15	193.00
DM Automated Teller Trans. 062142 customer N3162241 at terminal 30962—cash	10-16	20.00
DM Service charge	10-31	9.50

DEPOSITS/OTHER CREDITS

DEPOSITS

DATE POSTED	AMOUNT	DATE POSTED	AMOUNT
10-01	921.00	10-17	873.19
10-02	1,476.22	10-18	946.78
10-03	463.62	10-21	329.49
10-04	789.44	10-22	1,116.27
10-07	1,063.14	10-23	734.13
10-08	1,211.96	10-26	227.69
10-14	992.27	10-28	439.45
10-15	759.41	10-29	611.12
10-16	641.33	10-30	764.35

OTHER CREDITS

DESCRIPTION	DATE POSTED	AMOUNT
CM Note collected, principal $900, interest $9	10-29	909.00

PLEASE EXAMINE THIS STATEMENT CAREFULLY. REPORT ANY POSSIBLE ERRORS IN 10 DAYS.

CODE SYMBOLS

CM Credit Memo   OD Overdraft

DM Debit Memo   EC Error Correction

FIGURE 7

- **OD (overdraft)** The withdrawal of more than the cash balance in the account, resulting in a negative balance.
- **EC (error correction)** Corrections of errors made by the bank, such as encoding mistakes.

The bank statement is a valuable aid to efficiency and accuracy because it provides a double record of the Cash account. If a business entity deposits all cash receipts in the bank and makes all payments by check, then the bank is keeping an independent record of the business's cash. You might think that the two balances—the business's and the bank's—should be equal, but this is unlikely. Some transactions may have been recorded in the business's account before being entered in the bank's records. In addition, there are unavoidable delays (by either the business or the bank) in recording transactions. Ordinarily, there is a delay of one or more days between the date on which a check is written and the date when it is presented to the bank for payment. Also, banks may not record deposits until the following business day. During this time lag, deposits made or checks written are recorded in the business's check register, but they are not yet listed on the bank statement.

The bank mails statements to its depositors each month. The **canceled checks** (checks that have been paid or cleared by the bank) are listed on the bank statement. They are called *canceled checks* because they are canceled by a stamp on the back, indicating that they have been paid. Debit or credit memos are generally described on the bank statement.

Recording Deposits or Withdrawals

Each business entity keeps its accounts from its *own* point of view. As far as the bank is concerned, each customer's deposits are liabilities, in that the bank owes the customer the amount of the deposits. Using T accounts, it looks like this:

Liabilities

−	+
Debits	Credits

Deposits Payable

−	+
Debits	Credits

Debit memos {
Checks written	Deposits
Service charges	Notes
NSF checks	collected
ATM withdrawals	Interest income
Electronic	Wire transfers
payments made	received
} **Credit memos**

When the bank receives a cash deposit from a customer, the bank credits Deposits Payable, because it owes more to its customer. When the bank cashes a check (pays out) for a customer, the bank debits Deposits Payable, because it owes less to its customer.

The customer, on the other hand, uses the account titled Cash, or Cash in Bank, or simply the name of the bank. Deposits are recorded as debits and withdrawals are recorded as credits in the account. On a bank reconciliation, the balance of the account is listed as the **ledger balance of cash** before reconciliation with the bank statement.

REMEMBER!

Debit memos represent deductions from and credit memos represent additions to a bank account.

CAREERS IN YOUR FUTURE

JERRY DUNN
*Co-founder, Co-owner, and President of
Aviation Finance Group*

How do you go from reconciling bank statements to owning a company that finances private jets for high-net-worth individuals on a nationwide basis? Jerry Dunn says you apply common sense and problem-solving skills as you learn accounting rather than relying on rote memorization. He believes that the successful accounting student and businessperson must understand the "big picture" of the business transaction before applying accounting procedures and principles. In other words, you mustn't get buried in the procedures and lose sight of what the numbers mean, where they are going, and what impact they have on the business as a whole.

"The statement of cash flows is king in business along with the fundamental foundation of successful business—INTEGRITY."

Jerry believes that *cash flow is king* in business and that *integrity is essential*—beliefs shared by many successful businesses and individuals. Integrity is a fundamental foundation of a successful business. And building on these beliefs,

Jerry's career has taken an exciting path. After working on Wall Street in the finance industry, he later became an entrepreneur. Although he has never prepared financial statements, he certainly uses them almost every day. There's that solid accounting foundation and big-picture combination again; they are inseparable.

Besides selling jets to high-net-worth people, as president of the Aviation Finance Group, Jerry is responsible for the day-to-day internal operations of the company—human resources, operations, and systems. Part of that responsibility includes managing the financial health of the company. It is very hard to stay in any business without a healthy cash flow. And without his accounting and finance background, he wouldn't be able to balance the responsibilities involved with financing jets and keeping up his own company's cash flow and monetary return.

OBJECTIVE 2

Reconcile a bank statement.

Need for Reconciling Bank Balance and Ledger Balance

Since the bank statement balance and the ledger balance of cash are not equal, a business prepares a **bank reconciliation** to uncover the reasons for the difference between the two balances and to correct any errors that may have been made by either the bank or the business. This makes it possible to arrive at the same balance in each account, which is called the *adjusted balance,* or *true balance,* of the Cash account.

Because identity theft and white-collar crimes are potential problems for a business, another purpose of the bank reconciliation is to make sure all of the amounts paid out from the account are proper disbursements for the business. It is a mark of good internal control to have the bank reconciliation prepared by someone other than the check signer (if someone other than the business owner is signing checks). The person performing the bank reconciliation will be making sure (a) the dollar amount of each check has not been altered, (b) all of the charges, checks, and electronic transfers belong to the company, and (c) deposits are made in a timely way.

FYI

When a bank agrees to accept payments on behalf of a customer, the fee the bank charges does not necessarily mean that the bank will follow up on collection of a payment or notify the customer that the payment is late.

There are a variety of reasons for differences between the bank statement balance and the customer's cash balance. Here are some of the more common ones:

- **Deposit in transit** A deposit made after the bank statement was issued. The depositor has already added the amount to the Cash account in his or her books, but the deposit has not been recorded by the bank (this is also called a *late deposit*).
- **Outstanding checks** Checks that have been written by the company but not yet received for payment by the time the bank sends out its statement. The company employee, when preparing the checks, deducted the amounts from the Cash account in the company's books, which explains the difference.
- **Collections** Money collected by the bank for the customer. When the bank acts as a collection point for its customers by accepting payments on their behalf, it adds the proceeds to the customer's bank account and sends a credit memorandum to notify the customer of the transaction or includes it on the next bank statement.
- **Interest income** Interest earned for keeping cash in the bank account. Some checking accounts are interest bearing or earning. The depositor will not learn how much interest the bank has credited to the bank account until the bank statement is received.
- **NSF (not sufficient funds) check** A deposited check that the bank cannot process because the check writer's account does not contain enough money. When a bank customer deposits a check, it is recorded as cash on the customer's books. Occasionally, however, a check is not paid (bounces). When the bank notifies the customer of this, the customer must make a deduction from the Cash account. Simultaneously, the depositor records an increase in accounts receivable because the client's debt to the depositor remains unpaid. An NSF check may also be called a *dishonored check*.
- **Service charge** A bank charge for services rendered: for handling checks, for collecting money, for receiving payment of notes turned over to it by the customer for collection, for check printing, and for other such services. The bank immediately deducts the fee from the balance of the bank account and identifies the charges on the bank statement.
- **Errors** Mistakes made by the customer or the bank. In spite of internal controls and systems designed to double-check to prevent errors, sometimes either the customer or the bank makes a mistake. Often these errors do not become evident until the bank reconciliation is performed.

Steps in Reconciling the Bank Statement

Follow these steps to reconcile a bank statement:

1. **Canceled checks**
   a. Compare the amount of each canceled check with the bank statement and note any differences. The amount of the machine-readable characters should appear at the lower right-hand corner of the check, which should match the amount written on the check and the bank statements.
   b. In the checkbook beside the check number, list the date of the bank statement. In some cases, a bank may not pay a check until one or two months after it was written. If a question arises as to whether or not you have paid a particular bill, you can look at the checkbook. Then you can refer directly to the bank statement to pick up the accompanying canceled check as proof of payment.

Besides their core activities of providing financial transactions, many banks are actively committed to community service by supporting various causes, such as the JPMorgan Chase. The bank sponsors the JPMorgan Chase Corporate Challenge, which is run in various locations all over the world. Learn more about the race at **http://www .jpmorganchaseco.com.**

2. **Deposits**

a. Compare the deposits in transit (not recorded by the bank at the time of the statement) listed on last month's bank reconciliation with the deposits shown on the bank statement. All of last month's deposits in transit should be listed on this month's bank statement. If they are not, notify the bank immediately.

b. Compare the remaining deposits listed on this month's bank statement with deposits written in the company's accounting records. Consider any deposits not shown on the bank statement as deposits in transit.

3. **Outstanding checks**

a. Arrange the canceled checks in order by check number.

b. Look over the list of outstanding checks left over from last month's bank reconciliation, and note the checks that have now been returned or cleared.

c. For each canceled check, compare the amount recorded in MICR numbers at the lower right-hand corner of the check with the amount recorded in the checkbook. Next, compare the canceled check with the numerical listing in the statement. Use a check mark (✓) to indicate that the check has been paid and that the amount is correct. Any payments that have not been marked off, including the outstanding checks from last month's bank reconciliation, are the present outstanding checks.

d. Review the endorsements on the backs of the checks to verify that money has been sent to the correct payee.

4. **Bank memoranda** Trace the credit memos and debit memos to the journal. If the memos have not been recorded, make separate entries for them.

For businesses that have computerized check registers, the bank reconciliation can also be done on the computer. The procedures are similar as there is still the need to compare canceled checks, compare deposits, identify outstanding checks and deposits, and record adjustments.

The Check Clearing for the 21st Century Act (Check 21), a federal law that became effective in 2004, enables banks to create a new negotiable instrument called a *substitute check*. Substitute checks, which are special paper copies of the front and back of the original checks, are easily converted into an electronic form that can be processed quickly and inexpensively. The banks are also allowed to return copies of substitute checks rather than original checks with the bank statement. The Federal Reserve's website (**http://www .federalreserve.gov/pubs/check21/consumer_guide.htm**) provides more information about Check 21.

Examples of Bank Reconciliations

Let's go through the reconciliation process for two businesses, M. K. Young Company and Bay Cleaners.

M. K. Young Company   The bank statement of M. K. Young Company indicates a balance of $6,357 as of March 31. The balance of the Cash account in Young's ledger as of that date is $4,656. Young's accountant has taken the following steps:

1. Verified that canceled checks were recorded correctly on the bank statement.
2. Noted that the deposit made on March 31 was not recorded on the bank statement, $2,286.
3. Noted outstanding checks: no. 921, $1,878; no. 985, $207; no. 986, $1,314.
4. Noted credit memo: note collected by the bank from T. Chang, $600, not recorded in the journal.
5. Noted debit memo: collection charge and service charge not recorded in the journal, $12.

The note received from T. Chang is called a promissory note. A **promissory note** is a written promise to pay a definite amount at a definite future time. Let's assume that M. K. Young Company received the sixty-day non-interest-bearing note from T. Chang for services performed. In recording the transaction, Young's accountant debited Notes Receivable and credited Income from Services. (The account Notes Receivable is similar to Accounts Receivable. However, Accounts Receivable is reserved for customer charge accounts, with payments usually due in thirty days.) Next, M. K. Young Company turned the note over to its bank for collection.

The bank will use a credit memo form to notify M. K. Young Company that the note has been collected and that the company's bank account has been increased by the amount of the note. Based on the credit memo, Young's accountant will make a journal entry debiting Cash and crediting Notes Receivable.

Think of the bank reconciliation in terms of the following:

1. Bring the bank statement balance up to date by recording the events that we knew about but the bank did not know about when it prepared the statement (deposits in transit and outstanding checks as shown in our checkbook, for example).
2. Bring the balance of the Cash account up to date by recording the events that the bank knew about but we did not know about until we received the statement (debit memos and credit memos as shown on the bank statement, for example).

Figure 8 shows M. K. Young Company's bank reconciliation. The items in the reconciliation that require journal entries are shown in color, and the entries are shown below.

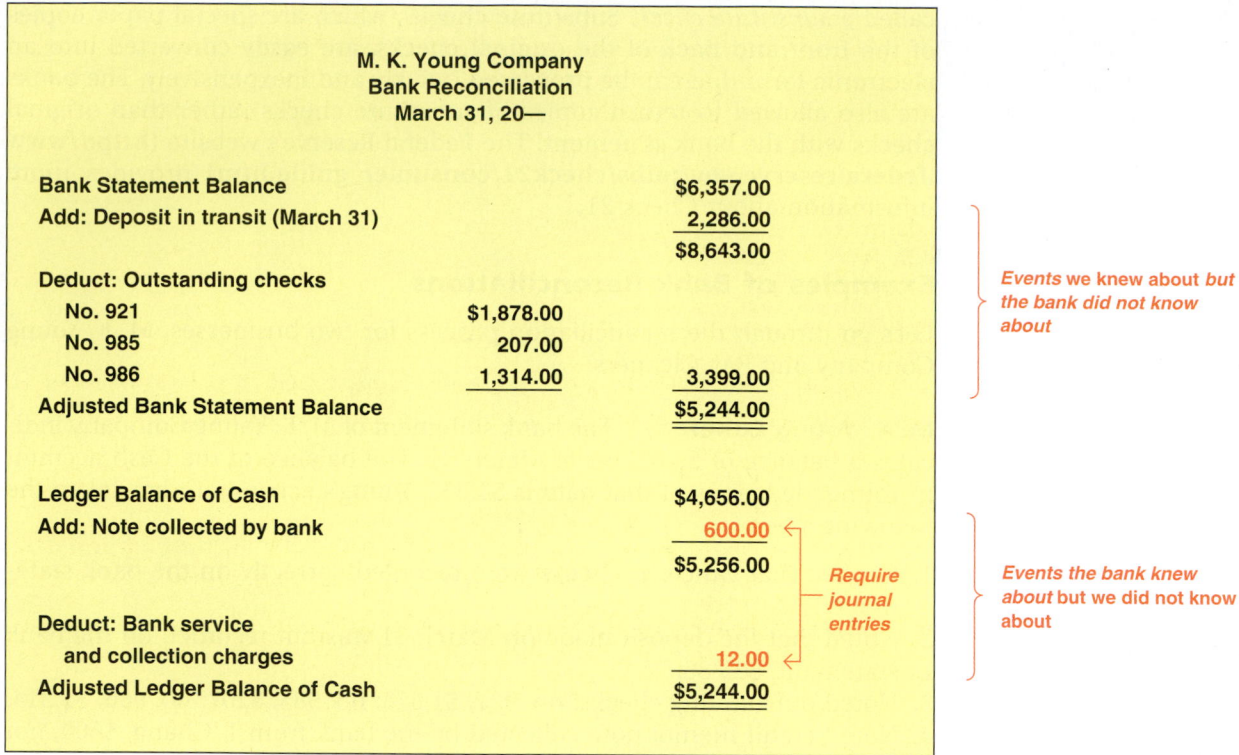

M. K. Young Company
Bank Reconciliation
March 31, 20—

Bank Statement Balance		$6,357.00
Add: Deposit in transit (March 31)		2,286.00
		$8,643.00
Deduct: Outstanding checks		
No. 921	$1,878.00	
No. 985	207.00	
No. 986	1,314.00	3,399.00
Adjusted Bank Statement Balance		$5,244.00
Ledger Balance of Cash		$4,656.00
Add: Note collected by bank		600.00
		$5,256.00
Deduct: Bank service		
and collection charges		12.00
Adjusted Ledger Balance of Cash		$5,244.00

Events we knew about but the bank did not know about

Require journal entries

Events the bank knew about but we did not know about

FIGURE 8

OBJECTIVE 3

Record the required journal entries from the bank reconciliation.

Note that the journal entries are based on the items used to adjust the ledger balance of Cash. These items represent the transactions that the bank has knowledge of but the business does not. According to the bank reconciliation, the true balance of Cash is $5,244, which is the balance we wish to show on the business's books. We can't change the balance of an account unless we first make a journal entry and then post the entry to the accounts involved. **Consequently, we have to make journal entries for items in the Ledger Balance of Cash section of the bank reconciliation.** The additions are debited to the Cash account, and the deductions are credited to the Cash account. M. K. Young Company records the entries in its general journal:

GENERAL JOURNAL   PAGE _____

DATE		DESCRIPTION	POST. REF.	DEBIT	CREDIT
20—					
Mar.	31	Cash		6 0 0 00	
		Notes Receivable			6 0 0 00
		Non-interest-bearing note			
		signed by T. Chang was			
		collected by the bank.			
	31	Miscellaneous Expense		1 2 00	
		Cash			1 2 00
		Service charge and collection			
		charge levied by bank.			

Here bank service and collection charges are recorded in Miscellaneous Expense because the amounts are relatively small. Some accountants may use a separate expense account, such as Bank Charge Expense. After the entries have been posted, the T account for Cash looks like this:

Cash			
Balance	4,656	Mar. 31	12
Mar. 31	600		
Bal.	**5,244**		

Note that the balance in the T account is now equal to both the adjusted bank statement balance and the adjusted ledger balance of cash.

Form of Bank Reconciliation

Now that you have seen an example of a bank reconciliation, let's look at the standard form of a bank reconciliation for an imaginary company.

Bank Statement Balance (last figure on the statement)		$4,000
Add		
Deposits in transit (deposits made after the bank statement was issued and already added to the ledger balance of Cash)	$300	
Bank errors (that understate balance)	20	320
		$4,320
Deduct		
Outstanding checks and transfers (they have already been deducted from the Cash account)	$960	
Bank errors (that overstate balance)	40	1,000
Adjusted Bank Statement Balance (the true balance of Cash)		$3,320
Ledger Balance of Cash (the latest balance of the Cash account if it has been posted up to date; otherwise take the beginning balance of Cash, plus cash receipts, minus cash payments)		$2,850
Add		
Credit memos (additions by the bank not recorded in the Cash account, such as collections of notes)	$500	
Book errors (that understate balance)	40	540
		$3,390
Deduct		
Debit memos (deductions by the bank not recorded in the Cash account, such as service charges or collection charges and NSF checks)	$ 20	
Book errors (that overstate balance)	50	70
Adjusted Ledger Balance of Cash (the true balance of Cash)		$3,320

REMEMBER!

When placing each item on the bank reconciliation, ask yourself if it has been recorded only by the bank or only by the depositor. If an item has been recorded by both the bank and the depositor, there is nothing to do. If an item has been recorded only by the bank, then record it in a similar manner in the Ledger Balance of Cash section. If an item has been recorded only by the depositor, then record it in a similar manner in the Bank Statement Balance section.

Bay Cleaners The bank statement of Bay Cleaners shows a final balance of $13,449 as of October 31 (see Figure 7). The present balance of the Cash account in the ledger, after Bay Cleaners' accountant has posted from the journal, is $12,495.50. The accountant took the following steps:

1. Verified that canceled checks were recorded correctly on the bank statement.
2. Discovered that a deposit of $1,955 made on October 31 was not recorded on the bank statement.
3. Noted outstanding checks: no. 1916, $692; no. 2022, $179; no. 2023, $1,241; no. 2024, $101.
4. Noted that a credit memo for a note collected by the bank from Lee and Camara, $900 principal plus $9 interest, was not recorded in the journal.
5. Found that check no. 2001 for $845, payable to Dennis, Inc., on account, was recorded in the journal as $854. (The correct amount is $845.)
6. Noted that a debit memo for a collection charge and service charge of $9.50 was not recorded in the journal.
7. Noted that a debit memo for an NSF check for $193 from A. L. Sanders was not recorded.
8. Noted that a $20 personal withdrawal by Paula C. Boyd, the owner, using an ATM, was not recorded.

Look at Figure 9 to see how each step relates to the bank reconciliation.

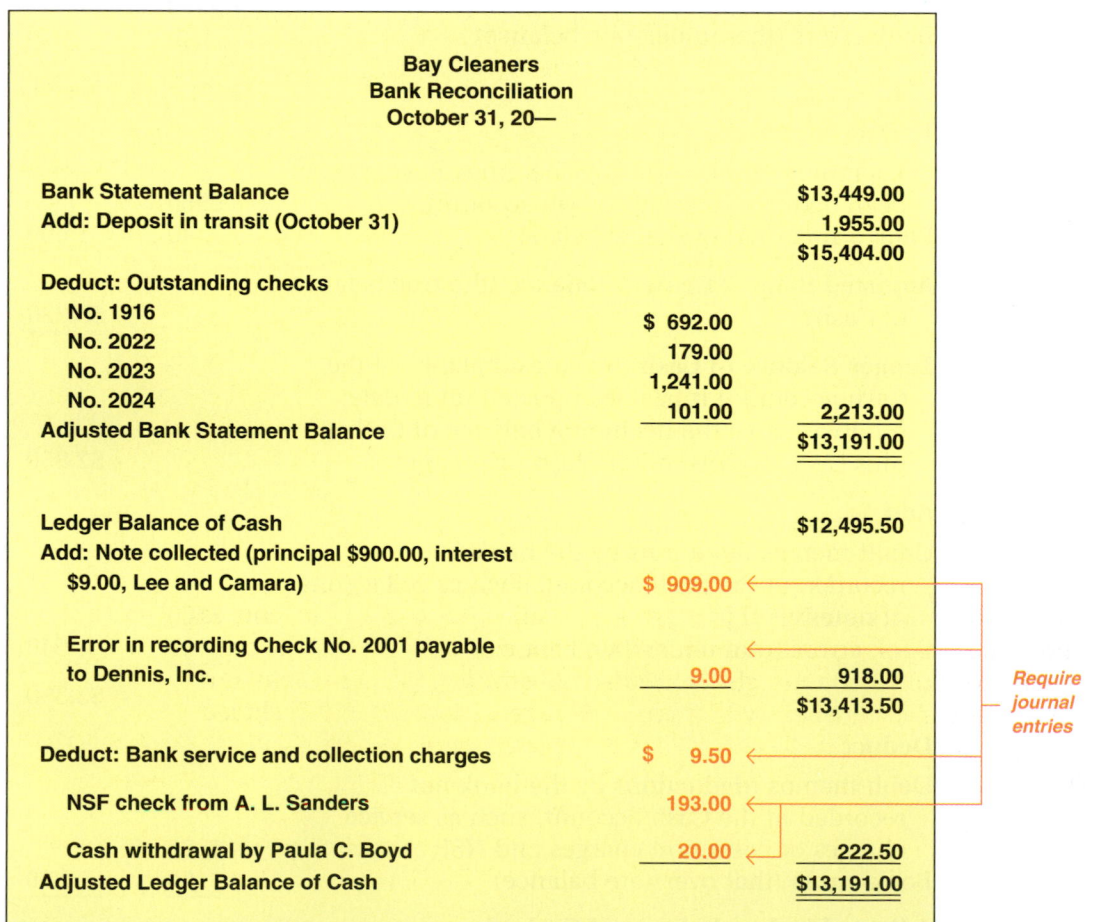

FIGURE 9

FIGURE 10

GENERAL JOURNAL   PAGE _____

DATE		DESCRIPTION	POST. REF.	DEBIT	CREDIT
20—					
Oct.	31	Cash		9 0 9 00	
		Notes Receivable			9 0 0 00
		Interest Income			9 00
		Bank collected note signed			
		by Lee and Camara.			
	31	Cash		9 00	
		Accounts Payable			9 00
		Error in recording Ck. No.			
		2001 payable to Dennis, Inc.			
	31	Miscellaneous Expense		9 50	
		Cash			9 50
		Bank service charge and			
		collection charge.			
	31	Accounts Receivable		1 9 3 00	
		Cash			1 9 3 00
		NSF check received from			
		A. L. Sanders.			
	31	P. C. Boyd, Drawing		2 0 00	
		Cash			2 0 00
		Withdrawal for personal use.			

The accountant makes journal entries for the items indicated in Figure 9 to change the balance of the Cash account from its present balance of $12,495.50 to the true balance of $13,191.00. Again, those items that require journal entries are highlighted in Figure 9 and shown in Figure 10.

The account Interest Income is classified as a revenue account. It represents the amount received on the promissory note that is over and above the face value of the note.

As for the NSF check, upon being notified by the bank, Bay Cleaners calls its customer (A. L. Sanders). Sanders can now take steps to cover the check. Review Bay Cleaners' transaction with A. L. Sanders. In return for service provided, Bay Cleaners received Sanders's check for $193. At that time, Bay Cleaners' accountant recorded the transaction as a debit to Cash for $193 and a credit to Income from Services for $193. Then the bank, through its debit memorandum, notified Bay Cleaners about Sanders's NSF check. To avoid overdrawing its own bank account, Bay Cleaners makes an entry crediting Cash (to correct its earlier debit to Cash) and debiting Accounts Receivable (to put the amount into Accounts Receivable). Since A. L. Sanders owes the money, it is logical to add the amount to Accounts Receivable.

A bank reconciliation form is ordinarily printed on the back of the bank statement. The adjusted balance of the ledger balance of cash has already been determined. Consequently, the bank form is provided only for calculating the adjusted bank statement balance of the bank reconciliation. The bank form for Bay Cleaners is shown in Figure 11 on page 238.

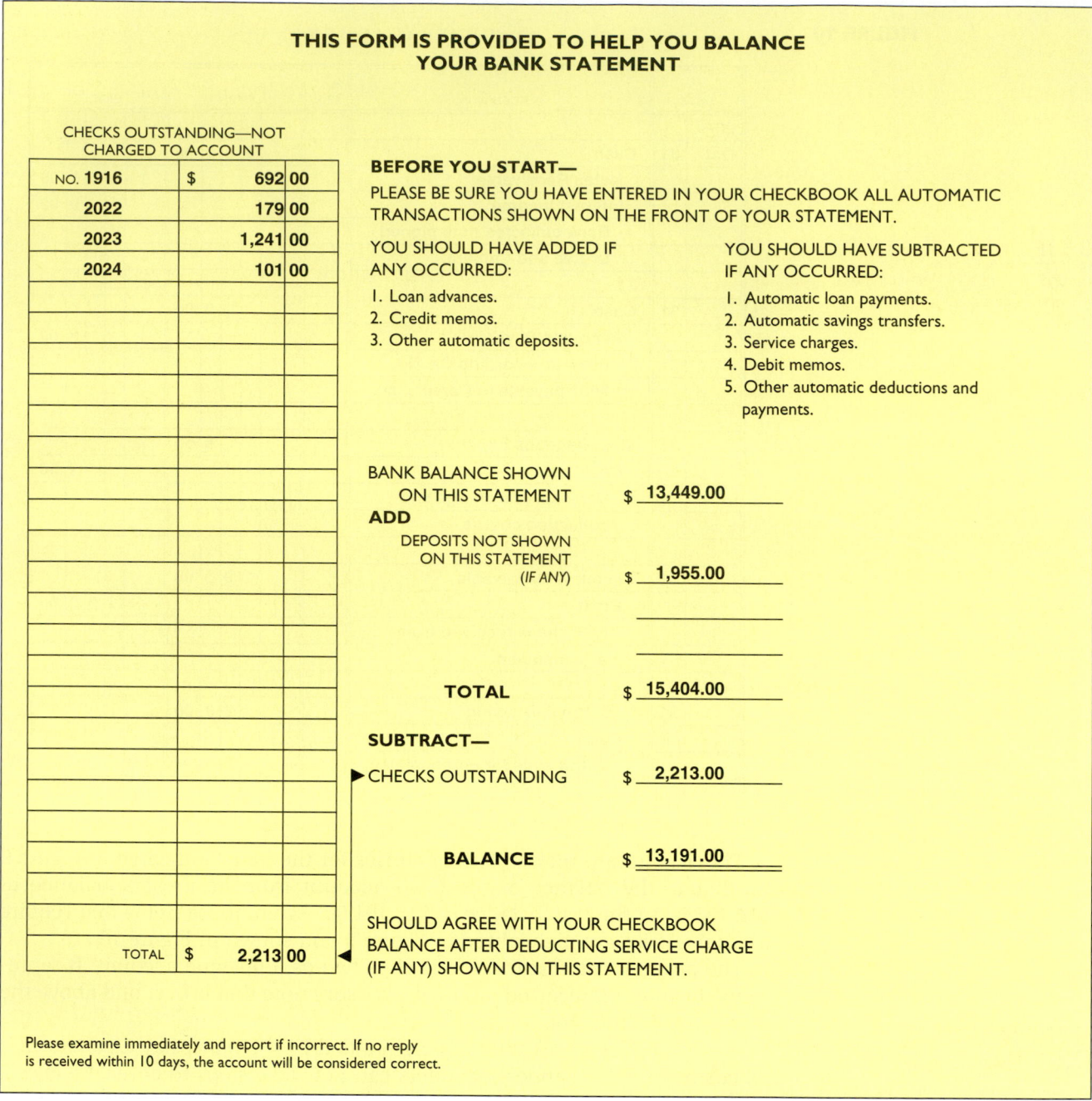

THIS FORM IS PROVIDED TO HELP YOU BALANCE YOUR BANK STATEMENT

CHECKS OUTSTANDING—NOT CHARGED TO ACCOUNT

NO.			
1916	$	692	00
2022		179	00
2023		1,241	00
2024		101	00
TOTAL	$	2,213	00

BEFORE YOU START—

PLEASE BE SURE YOU HAVE ENTERED IN YOUR CHECKBOOK ALL AUTOMATIC TRANSACTIONS SHOWN ON THE FRONT OF YOUR STATEMENT.

YOU SHOULD HAVE ADDED IF ANY OCCURRED:

1. Loan advances.
2. Credit memos.
3. Other automatic deposits.

YOU SHOULD HAVE SUBTRACTED IF ANY OCCURRED:

1. Automatic loan payments.
2. Automatic savings transfers.
3. Service charges.
4. Debit memos.
5. Other automatic deductions and payments.

BANK BALANCE SHOWN ON THIS STATEMENT $ 13,449.00

ADD

DEPOSITS NOT SHOWN ON THIS STATEMENT (IF ANY) $ 1,955.00

_____

_____

TOTAL $ 15,404.00

SUBTRACT—

▶CHECKS OUTSTANDING $ 2,213.00

BALANCE $ 13,191.00

SHOULD AGREE WITH YOUR CHECKBOOK BALANCE AFTER DEDUCTING SERVICE CHARGE (IF ANY) SHOWN ON THIS STATEMENT.

Please examine immediately and report if incorrect. If no reply is received within 10 days, the account will be considered correct.

FIGURE 11

THE PETTY CASH FUND

Day after day, businesses are confronted with transactions requiring small immediate payments, such as paying for delivery charges, birthday cards, or pizza for after-hours workers. If the business had to make all payments by check, the time consumed would be frustrating and the whole process would be unduly expensive. For many businesses, the cost of writing each check is more than $10; this includes the cost of an employee's time for writing and reconciling the check. Suppose you buy five stamps from an employee for $1.95, and you want to reimburse her. To write a check would not be practical. It only makes sense to pay in cash, using the **Petty Cash Fund**. *Petty* means "small," so the business sets a maximum amount that can be paid immediately out of petty cash. Payments that exceed this maximum must be processed by regular check through the journal.

Establishing the Petty Cash Fund

OBJECTIVE 4

Record journal entries to establish and reimburse a Petty Cash Fund.

After the business has set the maximum amount of a payment from petty cash, the next step is to estimate how much cash will be needed during a given period of time, such as a month. It is also important to consider the element of security when keeping cash in the office. If the risk is great, the amount kept in the fund should be small. Bay Cleaners decides to establish a Petty Cash Fund of $100 and put it under the control of the assistant. Accordingly, Bay Cleaners' accountant writes a check, cashes it at the bank, and records this transaction in the journal as follows:

	DATE		DESCRIPTION	POST. REF.	DEBIT	CREDIT	
1	20—						1
2	Sept.	1	Petty Cash Fund		1 0 0 00		2
3			Cash			1 0 0 00	3
4			Established a Petty Cash				4
5			Fund, Ck. No. 1880.				5

GENERAL JOURNAL   PAGE _____

T accounts for the entry look like this:

Petty Cash Fund			Cash	
+	−		+	−
100				100

Because the Petty Cash Fund is an asset account, it is listed on the balance sheet immediately below Cash.

Once the fund has been created, it is not debited again unless the original amount is not large enough to handle the necessary transactions. In that case, the accountant has to increase the Petty Cash Fund—perhaps from $100 to $200. **But, if no change is made in the size of the fund, Petty Cash Fund is debited only once.**

The check is written to the assistant, "Maria Ruiz, Petty Cash Fund." She converts it into convenient **denominations**, which are varieties of coins and currency, such as quarters and dimes and $1 and $5 bills. Then the assistant puts the money in a locked drawer and will not pay anything larger than $20 (or whatever is the agreed-upon amount) out of petty cash.

REMEMBER!

The Petty Cash Fund account is debited only once, and this happens when the fund is first established.

Payments from the Petty Cash Fund

OBJECTIVE 5

Complete petty cash vouchers and petty cash payments records.

The assistant is designated as the only person who can make payments from the Petty Cash Fund. In case of her illness, another employee should be named as stand-in. A **petty cash voucher** must be used to account for every payment from the fund. The voucher constitutes a receipt signed by the person who authorized the payment and by the person who received payment as well as the purpose of the payment. Thus, even for small payments of $20 or less, there would have to be collusion between the payee and the assistant for any theft to occur. Figure 12 is a petty cash voucher.

FIGURE 12

PETTY CASH VOUCHER

No. __1__   Date __September 2, 20—__

Paid to __Mark Delivery Service__ $ __10.00__

For ____Delivery____

Account __Delivery Expense__

Approved by   *Payment received by*

_____M. Ruiz_____   _____D. Stanton_____

Petty Cash Payments Record

Some businesses prefer to have a written record on one sheet of paper, so they keep a **petty cash payments record**. In a petty cash payments record,

FIGURE 13

Petty Cash Payments Record
Month of September 20—

	DATE	VOU. NO.	EXPLANATION	PAYMENTS	OFFICE SUPPLIES EXPENSE	
1	Sept. 1		Establish fund, Ck. No. 1880, $100			
2	2	1	Mark Delivery Service	10 00		
3	3	2	Pencils and pens	4 59	4 59	
4	5	3	Local newspapers	2 00		
5	7	4	Postage on incoming packages	3 70		
6	10	5	Paula C. Boyd	20 00		
7	14	6	Reimburse employee for stamps	1 95		
8	21	7	Stick-on tabs	4 10	4 10	
9	22	8	Mark Delivery Service	14 00		
10	26	9	Postage for mailings	3 60		
11	27	10	Fast Way Delivery	9 00		
12	29	11	Memo pads	4 40	4 40	
13	29	12	Making duplicate keys	3 19		
14	30	13	Mark Delivery Service	8 20		
15	30	14	Trash removal	5 00		
16	30		Totals	93 73	13 09	
17			Balance in Fund $ 6.27			
18			Reimburse fund, Ck. No. 1926 93.73			
19			Total $100.00			
20						
21						

petty cash vouchers and the accounts that are to be charged are listed as well as the purpose of the expenditure. Special columns for frequent types of expenditures are included in the Distribution of Payments section. The petty cash payments record is not a journal.

Bay Cleaners made the following payments from its Petty Cash Fund during September:

Sept.   2   Paid $10 to Mark Delivery Service, voucher no. 1.
        3   Bought pencils and pens, $4.59, voucher no. 2.
        5   Bought local newspapers for article related to Bay Cleaners, $2, voucher no. 3.
        7   Paid postage on incoming packages, $3.70, voucher no. 4.
     10   Paula C. Boyd, the owner, withdrew $20 for personal use, voucher no. 5.
     14   Reimbursed employee for stamps, $1.95, voucher no. 6.
     21   Bought stick-on tabs, $4.10, voucher no. 7.
     22   Paid $14 to Mark Delivery Service, voucher no. 8.
     26   Paid for mailing packages, $3.60, voucher no. 9.
     27   Paid $9 to Fast Way Delivery, voucher no. 10.
     29   Bought memo pads, $4.40, voucher no. 11.
     29   Paid for making duplicate keys, $3.19, voucher no. 12.
     30   Paid $8.20 to Mark Delivery Service, voucher no. 13.
     30   Paid for trash removal, $5, voucher no. 14.

Figure 13 below shows how these payments are recorded.

PAGE ___1___

	DELIVERY EXPENSE	MISCELLANEOUS EXPENSE	OTHER ACCOUNTS – ACCOUNT	OTHER ACCOUNTS – AMOUNT	
					1
	10 00				2
					3
		2 00			4
	3 70				5
			P. C. Boyd, Drawing	20 00	6
		1 95			7
					8
	14 00				9
	3 60				10
	9 00				11
					12
		3 19			13
	8 20				14
		5 00			15
	48 50	12 14		20 00	16
					17
					18
					19
					20
					21

A petty cash fund is an effective and efficient way to deal with small cash payments that need to be made immediately. These caterers, delivering food for an office party, can be paid on the spot, saving their own company the expense of billing and the recipient the expense of writing a check.

Reimbursement of the Petty Cash Fund

To bring the fund back up to the original amount when it is nearly exhausted (for instance, at the end of the month), the accountant reimburses the fund for expenditures made. Consequently, the Petty Cash Fund may be considered a revolving fund. If the amount initially put in the Petty Cash Fund is $100 and at the end of the month only $6.27 is left, the accountant puts $93.73 in the fund as a reimbursement, thereby bringing the fund back up to $100 to start the new month.

Bear in mind that the petty cash payments record is only a supplementary record for gathering information. A less formal way of compiling the information concerning petty cash payments might consist of collecting one month's petty cash vouchers, then sorting them by accounts, such as Office Supplies Expense, Delivery Expense, and the like. Then run a calculator tape for each account. At the end of the month, the accountant makes a summarizing entry to officially journalize the transactions that have taken place. The journal and T accounts of Bay Cleaners are shown below.

Note that, in the summarizing entry, the accountant debits the accounts for which the payments were made and credits the Cash account. No entry is made to the Petty Cash Fund account alone. Then the assistant cashes a check for $93.73 and puts the cash in a locked place, thereby restoring the amount in the Petty Cash Fund to the original $100.

> **REMEMBER!**
>
> The petty cash payments record is not a journal; it is simply used as a basis for compiling information for the journal entry. Remember, to change an account, we have to make a journal entry.

	DATE		DESCRIPTION	POST. REF.	DEBIT	CREDIT	
1	20—						1
2	Sept.	30	Office Supplies Expense		1 3 09		2
3			Delivery Expense		4 8 50		3
4			Miscellaneous Expense		1 2 14		4
5			P. C. Boyd, Drawing		2 0 00		5
6			Cash			9 3 73	6
7			Reimbursed the Petty Cash				7
8			Fund, Ck. No. 1926.				8
9							9
10							10

GENERAL JOURNAL   PAGE _____

Cash		P. C. Boyd, Drawing		Miscellaneous Expense	
+	−	+	−	+	−
	93.73	20.00		12.14	

Office Supplies Expense		Delivery Expense	
+	−	+	−
13.09		48.50	

THE CHANGE FUND

OBJECTIVE 6

Record the journal entries to establish a Change Fund.

Anyone who has tried to pay for a small item with a $20 bill knows that any business that carries out numerous cash transactions needs a **Change Fund**.

Establishing the Change Fund

Before setting up a Change Fund, you have to decide two things: (1) how much money needs to be in the fund, and (2) what denominations of bills and coins are needed. Like the Petty Cash Fund, **the Change Fund is debited only once: when it is established.** It is left at the initial figure unless the person in charge decides to make it larger. The Change Fund account, like the Petty Cash Fund account, is an asset. It is recorded in the balance sheet immediately below Cash. If the Petty Cash Fund account is larger than the Change Fund account, it precedes the Change Fund.

The owner of Bay Cleaners, Paula C. Boyd, decides to establish a Change Fund; she decides this at the same time she sets up the company's Petty Cash Fund. The entries for the two transactions look like this:

			DESCRIPTION	POST. REF.	DEBIT	CREDIT	
	GENERAL JOURNAL					PAGE ____	
1	20—						1
2	Sept.	1	Petty Cash Fund		1 0 0 00		2
3			Cash			1 0 0 00	3
4			Established a Petty Cash Fund.				4
5							5
6		1	Change Fund		1 5 0 00		6
7			Cash			1 5 0 00	7
8			Established a Change Fund.				8
9							9

The T accounts for establishing the Change Fund are as follows:

Change Fund		Cash	
+	−	+	−
150			150

Boyd cashes a check for $150 and gets the money in several denominations. She is now prepared to make change for any normal business transactions.

Depositing Cash

At the end of each business day, Bay Cleaners' accountant deposits the cash taken in during the day but holds back the amount of the Change Fund, being sure that it is in convenient denominations. Let's say that on September 1, Bay Cleaners had $1,475 on hand at the end of the day.

$1,475 Total cash count
− 150 Change Fund

$1,325 New cash deposit

The T accounts look like this:

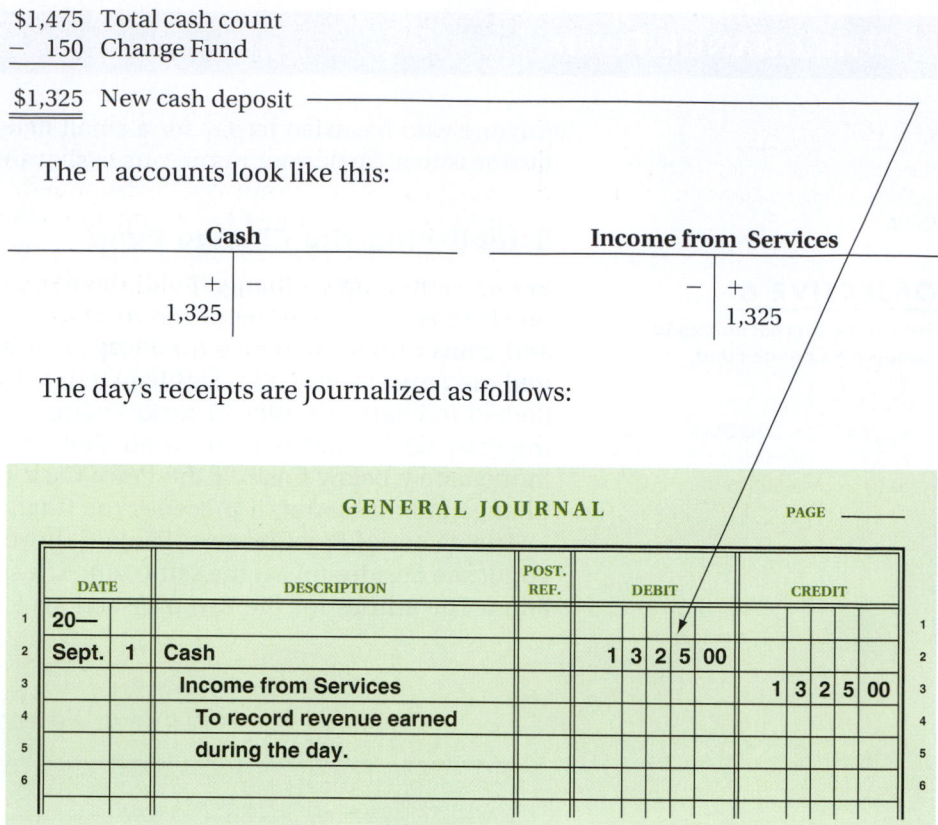

Cash			Income from Services	
+	−		−	+
1,325				1,325

The day's receipts are journalized as follows:

GENERAL JOURNAL   PAGE _____

	DATE		DESCRIPTION	POST. REF.	DEBIT	CREDIT	
1	20—						1
2	Sept.	1	Cash		1 3 2 5 00		2
3			Income from Services			1 3 2 5 00	3
4			To record revenue earned				4
5			during the day.				5
6							6

The amount of the cash deposit is the total cash count less the amount of the Change Fund. This should be equal to the income earned.
On September 9, the cash count is $1,583. So the accountant deposits $1,433 ($1,583 − $150). Bay Cleaners' accountant makes the following entry to record the day's receipts:

GENERAL JOURNAL   PAGE _____

	DATE		DESCRIPTION	POST. REF.	DEBIT	CREDIT	
1	20—						1
2	Sept.	9	Cash		1 4 3 3 00		2
3			Income from Services			1 4 3 3 00	3
4			To record revenue earned				4
5			during the day.				5
6							6

Some businesses label the Cash account *Cash in Bank* and label the Change Fund *Cash on Hand*.

CASH SHORT AND OVER

OBJECTIVE 7
Record journal entries for transactions involving Cash Short and Over.

FYI
The Cash Short and Over account may also be used to handle shortages and overages in the Petty Cash Fund.

FYI
Like the Income Summary account, which has no normal balance, the Cash Short and Over account has no signs.

There is an inherent danger in making change: Human beings make mistakes, especially when there are many customers to be waited on or when the business is temporarily short-handed. Because mistakes do happen, accounting records must be set up to cope with the situation. One reason that a business uses a cash register is to detect mistakes in handling cash. **If, after removing the Change Fund, the day's receipts are less than the register reading, then a cash shortage exists. Conversely, when the day's receipts are greater than the register reading, a cash overage exists.** Both shortages and overages are recorded in the same account, which is called Cash Short and Over. Shortages are considered an expense of operating a business, and therefore shortages are recorded on the debit side of the account. Overages are treated as another form of revenue, and therefore overages are recorded on the credit side of the account.

Let's say that on September 14, Bay Cleaners is faced with the following situation:

Cash Register Tape	Cash Count	Amount of the Change Fund
$1,515	$1,661	$150

After deducting the $150 in the Change Fund, Boyd will deposit $1,511 ($1,661 − $150). Note that this amount is $4 less than the amount indicated by the cash register ($1,515 − $1,511); therefore, a $4 cash shortage exists. The following T accounts show how the accountant entered this transaction into the books:

Cash	Income from Services	Cash Short and Over
+ | −	− | +	
1,511 |	| 1,515	4 |

The next day, September 15, the pendulum happens to swing in the other direction:

Cash Register Tape	Cash Count	Amount of the Change Fund
$1,574	$1,726	$150

The amount to be deposited is $1,576 ($1,726 − $150). This figure is $2 greater than the $1,574 in income from services indicated by the cash register tape. Thus, there is a $2 cash overage ($1,576 − $1,574). The analysis of this transaction is shown in the following T accounts:

Cash	Income from Services	Cash Short and Over
+ | −	− | +	
1,576 |	| 1,574	| 2

Bay Cleaners' revenue for September 14 and 15 is recorded in the general journal as follows:

GENERAL JOURNAL — PAGE ___

	DATE	DESCRIPTION	POST. REF.	DEBIT	CREDIT	
1	20—					1
2	Sept. 14	Cash		1 5 1 1 00		2
3		Cash Short and Over		4 00		3
4		Income from Services			1 5 1 5 00	4
5		To record revenue earned				5
6		for the day involving a				6
7		cash shortage of $4.				7
8						8
9	15	Cash		1 5 7 6 00		9
10		Income from Services			1 5 7 4 00	10
11		Cash Short and Over			2 00	11
12		To record revenue earned				12
13		during the day involving a				13
14		cash overage of $2.				14

A scanner can speed customer checkout or taking inventory of goods still on the shelves. The scanner, however, is only as accurate as the amount for each item entered in the computer.

As far as errors are concerned, one would think that shortages would be offset by overages. However, customers receiving change are more likely to report shortages than overages. **Consequently, the business usually experiences a greater number of shortages.** A business may set a tolerance level for the cashiers. If the shortages consistently exceed the level of tolerance, either fraud is being committed or somebody is making entirely too many careless mistakes.

Now let's summarize our discussion of the Cash Short and Over account by drawing the following conclusions from the illustration:

1. At the close of the business day, the business deposits the difference between the amount in the cash drawer and the amount in the Change Fund.
2. The business records the amount shown on the cash register tape as its income from services.
3. If the amount of the cash deposit disagrees with the record of receipts, Cash Short and Over makes up the difference. In the first situation just described, there was a shortage of $4, and so there was a debit to Cash Short and Over. In the second situation, there was an overage of $2, and so there was a credit to Cash Short and Over. It is apparent that, as a result of these transactions, the account looks like this:

Cash Short and Over		
Shortage 4	2	Overage

Throughout any fiscal period, the accountant must continually record shortages and overages in the Cash Short and Over account. Let's say that

Chapter Review   **247**

Bay Cleaners' final balance is $21 on the debit side. Bay Cleaners winds up with a net shortage of $21.

At the end of the fiscal period, **if the account has a debit balance or net shortage, the accountant classifies it as an expense and credits Cash Short and Over and debits Miscellaneous Expense, so that the amount is put in the income statement under Miscellaneous Expense.** The T-account would look like this:

Cash Short and Over

Shortage				Overage
	4	2		
	4	1		
	3	2		
	7	2		
	5	1		
	2	2		
	3	1		
	4			
Bal.	**21**			

Conversely, **if the account has a credit balance or net overage, the accountant classifies it as a revenue account and debits Cash Short and Over and credits Miscellaneous Income, so that the amount is put in the income statement under Miscellaneous Income.** This is an exception to the policy of recording accounts under their exact account title in financial statements. Rather than attaching plus and minus signs to the Cash Short and Over account immediately, we wait until we find out its final balance, then make a journal entry to send the balance to the correct account classification.

CHAPTER REVIEW

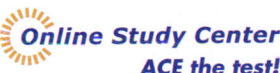
Online Study Center
ACE the test!

Review of Performance Objectives

1. Describe the procedure for depositing checks.

   The procedure for depositing checks consists of first endorsing each check and then completing a deposit slip. On the deposit slip, record the date, the amount of currency to be deposited, the amount and ABA number of each check, and the total amount to be deposited. The checks to be deposited should accompany the deposit slip.

2. Reconcile a bank statement.

   The standard form for a bank reconciliation is as follows:

   Bank Statement Balance

   Add
   Deposits in transit
   Bank errors that understate bank statement balance

   Deduct
   Outstanding checks or electronic transfers
   Bank errors that overstate bank statement balance

   Adjusted Bank Statement Balance

Ledger Balance of Cash

Add

Notes collected
Interest income earned
Checkbook errors that understate the ledger balance of cash
Bank credit memos

Deduct

Bank service charges
Checkbook errors that overstate the ledger balance of cash
NSF checks
Bank debit memos

Adjusted Ledger Balance of Cash

3. Record the required journal entries from the bank reconciliation.

   Journal entries for the Ledger Balance of Cash section are required. The entry for notes and interest collected is a debit to Cash and credits to Notes Receivable and Interest Income. The entry for a bank service charge is a debit to Miscellaneous Expense and a credit to Cash. The entry for an NSF check is a debit to Accounts Receivable and a credit to Cash.

4. Record journal entries to establish and reimburse a Petty Cash Fund.

   The entry to establish a Petty Cash Fund is a debit to Petty Cash Fund and a credit to Cash. The entry to reimburse the Petty Cash Fund consists of debits to the items for which payments from the Petty Cash Fund were made and one credit to Cash for the total payments.

5. Complete petty cash vouchers and petty cash payments records.

   A petty cash voucher is made out for each payment from the Petty Cash Fund. In the petty cash payments record, each voucher is listed and a notation is made concerning the accounts involved; also, an explanation of why the money was paid out is recorded. The petty cash payments record is used as a source of information for making the journal entry to reimburse the Petty Cash Fund.

6. Record the journal entries to establish a Change Fund.

   The entry to establish the Change Fund is a debit to Change Fund and a credit to Cash.

7. Record journal entries for transactions involving Cash Short and Over.

   The Cash Short and Over account provides a way to keep a record of errors in making change. A debit balance in Cash Short and Over denotes a shortage, which is listed as Miscellaneous Expense; the entry is a debit to Miscellaneous Expense and a credit to Cash Short and Over. A credit balance in Cash Short and Over denotes an overage, which becomes Miscellaneous Income; the entry is a debit to Cash Short and Over and a credit to Miscellaneous Income.

Glossary

ABA number The number assigned by the American Bankers Association to a given bank. The first part of the numerator denotes the city or state in which the bank is located; the second part denotes the bank on which the check is drawn. The denominator indicates the Federal Reserve District in which the check is cleared and the routing number used by the Federal Reserve Bank. (224)

ATM (automated teller machine) A machine that enables depositors to make deposits, withdrawals, and transfers using a coded plastic card. (224)

Bank reconciliation A process by which an accountant determines whether and why there is a difference between the balance shown on the bank statement and the balance of the Cash account in the business's general ledger. The object is to determine the adjusted (or true) balance of the Cash account. (230)

Bank statement A periodic statement that a bank sends to the drawer/ depositor of a checking account listing deposits received and checks paid by the bank, debit and credit memos, electronic transactions, and beginning and ending balances. (227)

Blank endorsement An endorsement in which the holder (payee) of a check simply signs her or his name on the back of the check. There are no restrictions attached. (226)

Canceled checks Checks issued by the depositor that have been paid (cleared) by the bank and listed on the bank statement. They are called canceled checks because they are canceled by a stamp or perforation, indicating that they have been paid. (229)

Cash funds Separately held reserves of cash set aside for specific purposes. (223)

Change Fund A cash fund used by a business to make change for customers who pay cash for goods or services. (243)

Collections Payments collected by the bank and added to the customer's bank account in the form of a credit memorandum. (231)

Denominations Varieties of coins and currency, such as quarters, dimes, and nickels and $1 and $5 bills and so on. (239)

Deposit in transit A deposit not recorded on the bank statement because the deposit was made between the time of the bank's closing date for compiling items for its statement and the time the statement is received by the depositor; also known as a *late deposit.* (231)

Deposit slips Printed forms provided by a bank on which customers can list all items being deposited; also known as *deposit tickets.* (224)

Drawer The party who writes the check. (226)

Electronic Funds Transfer (EFT) A transfer of funds initiated through an electronic terminal, such as a telephone, computer, or magnetic tape. (225)

Endorsement The process by which the payee transfers ownership of the check to a bank or another party. A check must be endorsed when deposited in a bank, because the bank must have legal title to it in order to collect payment from the drawer of the check (the person or firm who wrote the check). In case the check cannot be collected, the endorser guarantees all subsequent holders (*exception:* an endorsement "without recourse"). (225)

Interest income The amount earned from lending money to another person or business. (231)

Internal control Plans and procedures built into the accounting system with the following objectives: (1) to protect assets against fraud and waste; (2) to provide accurate accounting data; (3) to promote an efficient operation; and (4) to encourage adherence to management policies. (222)

Ledger balance of cash The balance of the Cash account in the general ledger before it is reconciled with the bank statement. (229)

MICR Magnetic ink character recognition; the characters the bank uses to print the number of the depositor's account and the bank's number at the bottom of checks and deposit slips. The bank also prints the amount of the check in MICR when the check is deposited. A number written in these characters can be read by electronic equipment used by banks in clearing checks. (224)

NSF (not sufficient funds) checks Checks drawn against an account in which there are *not sufficient funds* and returned by the payee's bank to the drawer's bank because of nonpayment; also known as *dishonored checks*. (231)

Outstanding checks Checks that have been written by the drawer and deducted on his or her records but have not reached the bank for payment and are not deducted from the bank balance by the time the bank issues its statement. (231)

Payee The person to whom a check is payable. (226)

Petty Cash Fund A cash fund used to make small, immediate cash payments. (239)

Petty cash payments record A record indicating the amount of each petty cash voucher, the accounts to which it should be charged, and the purpose of the expenditure. (240)

Petty cash voucher A form stating who requested cash from the Petty Cash Fund, signed by (1) the person in charge of the fund and (2) the person who received the cash, and indicating the purpose of the petty cash payment. (240)

Promissory note A written promise to pay a definite sum at a definite future time. (233)

Qualified endorsement An endorsement in which the holder (payee) of a check avoids future liability, in case the drawer of the check does not have sufficient funds to cover the check, by adding the words "Pay to the order of" and "without recourse" to the endorsement on the back of the check. (226)

Restrictive endorsement An endorsement, such as "Pay to the order of (name of bank), for deposit only," that restricts or limits any further negotiation of a check. It forces the check's deposit, because the endorsement is not valid for any other purpose. (225)

Service charge The fee the bank charges for handling checks, collections, and other items. It is in the form of a debit memorandum. (231)

Signature card The form a depositor signs to give the bank a copy of the official signatures of any persons authorized to sign checks. The bank can use it to verify the depositors' signatures on checks. (223)

QUESTIONS, EXERCISES, AND CASES

Discussion Questions

1. Why does a bank keep a signature card on file for your account(s)?
2. What is the purpose of endorsing a check?

3. Why is there generally a difference between the balance in the Cash account on the company's books and the balance on the bank statement?

4. Indicate whether the following items in a bank reconciliation should be (1) added to the Cash account balance, (2) deducted from the Cash account balance, (3) added to the bank statement balance, or (4) deducted from the bank statement balance.
   a. NSF check
   b. Deposit in transit
   c. Outstanding check
   d. Bank error charging the business's account with another company's check
   e. Bank service charge

5. Why is it necessary to make general journal entries for the ledger balance side of the bank reconciliation?

6. a. Why would a business use a Petty Cash Fund?
   b. Describe the entry needed to establish a $50 Petty Cash Fund and an entry to reimburse the fund.

7. a. What does a debit balance in Cash Short and Over mean?
   b. Where does a debit balance in Cash Short and Over appear in the financial statements?
   c. What does a credit balance in Cash Short and Over mean?
   d. Where does a credit balance in Cash Short and Over appear in the financial statements?

Exercises

P.O. 2

Determine missing amounts on a bank reconciliation.

Exercise 7-1 Fill in the missing amounts for the following bank reconciliation:

Bank Reconciliation March 31, 20—		
Bank Statement Balance		$3,754.00
Add: Deposit in transit		(a)
		$4,021.00
Deduct: Outstanding checks		
No. 210	$210.00	
No. 224	(b)	
No. 227	320.00	851.00
Adjusted Bank Statement Balance		(c)
Ledger Balance of Cash		$2,840.00
Add: Note collected by bank		427.00
		(d)
Deduct: Bank service and collection charge	(e)	
NSF check from customer	85.00	97.00
Adjusted Ledger Balance of Cash		(f)

P.O. 3

Journalize entries from a bank reconciliation.

Exercise 7-2 The Ledger Balance of Cash section of the bank reconciliation for Jeon Company for July 31 is shown on the following page.

Ledger Balance of Cash	$6,357.00
Add: Note collected (principal, $700, interest $41, signed by L. Diaz) $741.00	
Error in recording Ck. No. 2225 payable to Fenton Company (recorded check for $18 too much) 18.00	759.00
	$7,116.00
Deduct: NSF check from J. Kelton $ 85.00	
Bank service and collection charges 21.00	106.00
Adjust Ledger Balance of Cash	$7,010.00

Journalize the entries required to bring the general ledger up to date as of July 31 of this year.

P.O. 2

Determine amount of outstanding checks.

Exercise 7-3 When the bank statement is received on December 3, it shows a balance, before reconciliation, of $3,000 as of November 30. After reconciliation, the adjusted balance is $2,500. If there was one deposit in transit amounting to $500, what was the total of the outstanding checks, assuming that there were no other adjustments to be made to the bank statement?

P.O. 2

Place items on a bank reconciliation.

Exercise 7-4 Write a check mark in the column that indicates the location of each item that would be found on a bank reconciliation. The checks are written correctly.

Item	Add to Bank Statement Balance	Subtract from Bank Statement Balance	Add to Ledger Balance of Cash	Subtract from Ledger Balance of Cash
a. A check-printing charge				
b. An outstanding check				
c. A deposit for $187 listed incorrectly on the bank statement as $178				
d. A collection charge the bank made for a note it collected for its depositor				
e. A check written for $40.73 and recorded incorrectly in the checkbook as $40.37				
f. A deposit in transit				
g. An NSF check received from a customer				
h. A check written for $72.39 and recorded incorrectly in the checkbook as $720.39				

P.O. 2

Determine the adjusted ledger balance of cash.

Exercise 7-5 Mysung Company's Cash account shows a balance of $752 as of August 31 of this year. The balance on the bank statement on that date is $1,250.50. Checks for $263.70, $437.05, and $327 are outstanding. The bank statement shows a check issued by another depositor for $237.25 (in other words, the bank made an error and charged Mysung Company for a check written by another company). The bank statement also shows an NSF check for $280 received from one of Mysung's customers. Service charges for the month were $12. What is the adjusted ledger balance of cash as of August 31?

P.O. 4

Journalize entries pertaining to a Petty Cash Fund.

Exercise 7-6 Record entries in general journal form to record the following:

a. Established a Petty Cash Fund, $150. Issued Ck. No. 857.
b. Reimbursed the Petty Cash Fund for expenditures of $102: Store Supplies Expense, $28; Office Supplies Expense, $36; Miscellaneous Expense, $38. Issued Ck. No. 889.
c. Increased the amount of the fund by an additional $25. Issued Ck. No. 891.
d. Reimbursed the Petty Cash Fund for expenditures of $91.84: Store Supplies Expense, $45.92; Delivery Expense, $36; Miscellaneous Expense, $9.92. Issued Ck. No. 936.

P.O. 7

Journalize entry for the receipt of cash.

Exercise 7-7 At the end of the day, the cash register tape lists $827.27 as total income from services. Cash on hand consists of $15.27 in coins, $694 in currency, $80 in traveler's checks, and $236 in customers' checks. The amount of the Change Fund is $200. In general journal form, record the entry to record the day's cash revenue.

P.O. 6,7

Describe entries related to the Change Fund and Cash Short and Over.

Exercise 7-8

a. Describe the entries that have been posted to the following accounts after the Change Fund was established.

Change Fund		Sales		Cash	
200		1,521	Jan. 3	Jan. 3 1,523	
		1,420	4	4 1,419	
		1,663	6	6 1,660	

Cash Short and Over			
Jan. 4	1	2	Jan. 3
	6	3	

b. How will the balance of Cash Short and Over be reported on the income statement?

internet
LINKS TO ACCOUNTING

You have just learned about checking accounts, reconciling bank statements, and managing Petty Cash Funds. Using an online banking service can provide many advantages to managing your cash.

1. What advantages are there to having access to your bank statement online?
2. What are the disadvantages, if any?

CONSIDER AND COMMUNICATE

As the new bookkeeper at a small business, you find the Petty Cash Fund is accessed by several people, usually without anyone leaving any written explanation of what the money was used for. The amount of cash does not match the recorded amount of the fund. Explain how the Petty Cash Fund operation can be made more efficient in order to maintain an accurate accounting of how the money is used.

CRITICAL THINKING

Jamal Page, a college student, plans to provide keyboarding services to graduate students at the university near his home. He must determine how much money to deposit initially in his business account to cover the start-up of the new business. The deposit must cover the start-up costs and leave him with a balance of $5,000 in his business account. He plans to buy a computer/printer and a copier for $4,500 cash. The fax machine and the telephone system he needs are available for $2,500, and he will put down $300. He will buy paper for the copier for $275 on account.

1. Determine the required amount of the beginning investment Jamal needs to make if he is to meet his goal of having $5,000 in his business account after his anticipated transactions.
2. Use the practice grid to complete each transaction. Balance the fundamental accounting equation after each transaction.

	Quality Keyboarding Service				
	Cash	+ Equipment =	Accounts Payable	+ J. Page, Capital	− Supplies Expense
(a) Make needed beginning investment.					
Balance					
(b) Buy equipment for cash, $4,500.					
Balance					
(c) Buy equipment, $2,500, paying $300 down.					
Balance					
(d) Buy supplies on account, $275.					
Balance					

3. Prepare a balance sheet for Jamal's business as of June 10, 20—.

WHAT'S WRONG WITH THIS PICTURE?

You work as a cashier in a service business. Some days you are short of cash at the end of the day, and some days you have more cash than the cash register tape says was earned. You are embarrassed when your cash is short and don't want the owner to know, so you use your own money to make up the difference. On days when you are over, you keep the difference to help pay back what you paid to cover your shortages. What do you think of this practice and why?

PROBLEM SET A

P.O. 2,3

Problem 7-1A Amelio's Men's Shop deposits all receipts in the bank each evening and makes all payments by check. On November 30 its ledger balance of cash is $2,370.65. The bank statement balance of cash as of November 30 is $2,235.25. Use the following information to reconcile the bank statement:

a. The reconciliation for October, the previous month, showed three checks outstanding on October 31: no. 1416 for $85, no. 1419 for $75.75, and no. 1420 for $126. Checks no. 1416 and 1420 were returned with the November bank statement; however, check no. 1419 was not returned.
b. Checks no. 1499 for $40, no. 1516 for $22, no. 1517 for $115, and no. 1518 for $24.85 were written during November and have not been returned by the bank.
c. A deposit of $810 was placed in the night depository on November 30 and did not appear on the bank statement.
d. The canceled checks were compared with the entries in the checkbook, and it was observed that check no. 1487, for $78, was written correctly, payable to M. A. Garson, the owner, for personal use, but was recorded in the checkbook as $87.
e. A bank debit memo for service charges, $24.
f. A bank credit memo for collection of a note signed by T. R. Ritz, $412, including $400 principal and $12 interest.

Check Figure

Adjusted ledger balance of cash, $2,767.65

Instructions

1. Prepare a bank reconciliation as of November 30, assuming that the debit and credit memos have not been recorded.
2. Record the necessary entries in general journal form.

P.O. 4,5

Problem 7-2A On May 1 of this year, Estes and Company established a Petty Cash Fund. The following petty cash transactions took place during the month:

May	1	Cashed check no. 956 for $80 to establish a Petty Cash Fund, and put the $80 in a locked drawer in the office.
	3	Bought postage stamps, $7.80, voucher no. 1 (Miscellaneous Expense).
	4	Issued voucher no. 2 for taxi fare, $8 (Miscellaneous Expense).
	6	Issued voucher no. 3 for delivery charges on outgoing parts, $5.
	9	N. Estes, the owner, withdrew $10 for personal use, voucher no. 4.
	13	Paid $8.15 for postage, voucher no. 5 (Miscellaneous Expense).
	19	Bought pens for office, $6.58, voucher no. 6.

May   23   Paid $1.98 for a box of staples, voucher no. 7.
            28   Paid $12 for window cleaning service, voucher no. 8 (Miscellaneous Expense).
            29   Paid $1.85 for pencils for office, voucher no. 9.
            31   Issued for cash check no. 1098 for $61.36 to reimburse Petty Cash Fund.

Check Figure

Office Supplies Expense, $10.41

Instructions

1. Journalize the entry establishing the Petty Cash Fund in the general journal.
2. Record the disbursements of petty cash in the petty cash payments record.
3. Journalize the summarizing entry to reimburse the Petty Cash Fund.

P.O. 7

Problem 7-3A Emie Harold, owner of Harold's Dry Cleaners, makes bank deposits in the night depository at the close of each business day. The following information for the last four days of July is available.

	July			
	28	**29**	**30**	**31**
Cash register tape	$785.20	$ 965.70	$894.50	$1,021.60
Cash count	883.50	1,068.40	992.60	1,124.40

Check Figure

Cash Short and Over, July 31, $2.80 cash overage

Instructions

In general journal form, record the cash deposit for each day, assuming that there is a $100 Change Fund.

P.O. 2,3

Problem 7-4A On August 31, Bronski and Company receives its bank statement (on the following page). The company deposits its receipts in the bank and makes all payments by check. The debit memo for $49 is for an NSF check written by N. Corday. Check no. 924 for $37, payable to Jackson Company (a creditor), was recorded in the checkbook and journal as $73.

The ledger balance of cash as of August 31 is $1,321. Outstanding checks as of August 31 are: no. 928, $140; no. 929, $245. The accountant notes that the deposit of August 31 for $368 did not appear on the bank statement.

Check Figure

Adjusted ledger balance of cash, $1,306

Instructions

1. Prepare a bank reconciliation as of August 31, assuming that the debit memos have not been recorded.
2. Record the necessary journal entries.
3. Complete the bank form to determine the adjusted balance of cash.

Instructions for General Ledger Software

1. Prepare a bank reconciliation as of August 31. Errors made by the company or the bank, as well as service charges, must be entered as debit or credit memos.
2. Print the bank reconciliation.
3. Record the necessary journal entries.
4. Print the journal entries.

PROBLEM SET B

P.O. 2,3

Problem 7-1B Madox Company deposits all receipts in the bank each evening and makes all payments by check. On November 30 its ledger balance of cash is $3,219.72. The bank statement balance of cash as of November 30 is $3,185.90. You are given the following information with which to reconcile the bank statement:

a. A deposit of $518.32 was placed in the night depository on November 30 and did not appear on the bank statement.

b. The reconciliation for October, the previous month, showed three checks outstanding on October 31: no. 727 for $81.30, no. 730 for $127.40, and no. 732 for $46.84. Checks no. 727 and 730 were returned with the November bank statement; however, check no. 732 was not returned.

c. Checks no. 742 for $27, no. 743 for $20.20, no. 744 for $101, and no. 745 for $15.46 were written during November but were not returned by the bank.

d. A $36 personal withdrawal by C. R. Madox, the owner, using an ATM, was not recorded in the checkbook.

e. Included in the bank statement was a bank debit memo for service charges, $18.

f. A bank credit memo was also enclosed for the collection of a note signed by L. B. Leonard, $256, including $250 principal and $6 interest.

Check Figure

Adjusted ledger balance of cash, $3,493.72

Instructions

1. Prepare a bank reconciliation as of November 30, assuming that the debit and credit memos have not been recorded.
2. Record the necessary entries in general journal form.

P.O. 4,5

Problem 7-2B On March 1 of this year, Stein Company established a Petty Cash Fund, and the following petty cash transactions took place during the month:

Mar.	1	Cashed check no. 314 for $70 to establish a Petty Cash Fund, and put the $70 in a locked drawer in the office.
	4	Issued voucher no. 1 for taxi fare, $7 (Miscellaneous Expense).
	7	Issued voucher no. 2 for memo pads, $8.20 (Office Supplies Expense).
	9	Paid $11.50 for an advertisement in a college basketball program, voucher no. 3.
	16	Bought postage stamps, $7.80, voucher no. 4 (Miscellaneous Expense).
	20	Paid $10 to have snow removed from office front sidewalk, voucher no. 5 (Miscellaneous Expense).
	25	Issued voucher no. 6 for delivery charge, $5.55.
	28	R. C. Stein, the owner, withdrew $10 for personal use, voucher no. 7.
	29	Paid $3.82 for postage, voucher no. 8 (Miscellaneous Expense).
	30	Paid $5.60 for delivery charge, voucher no. 9.
	31	Issued for cash check no. 372 for $69.47 to reimburse Petty Cash Fund.

Check Figure

Office Supplies Expense, $8.20

Instructions

1. Journalize the entry establishing the Petty Cash Fund in the general journal.
2. Record the disbursements of petty cash in the petty cash payments record.
3. Journalize the summarizing entry to reimburse the Petty Cash Fund.

P.O. 7

Problem 7-3B Betty Ferrari, owner of Betty's Beauty Salon, makes bank deposits in the night depository at the close of each business day. The following information for the first four days of April is available.

	April			
	1	**2**	**3**	**4**
Cash register tape	$374.75	$580.25	$586.65	$633.25
Cash count	473.50	681.25	685.75	732.15

Check Figure

Cash Short and Over, April 3, $0.90 cash shortage

Instructions

In general journal form, record the cash deposit for each day, assuming that there is a $100 Change Fund.

P.O. 2,3

Problem 7-4B On August 2, Northway Hotel receives its bank statement (below). The company deposits its receipts in the bank and makes all payments by check. The debit memo for $37 is for an NSF check written by T. N. Ross. Check no. 1617 for $72.50, payable to Michaels Company (a creditor), was incorrectly recorded in the checkbook and journal as $27.50.

The balance of the Cash account as of July 31 is $1,877.46. Outstanding checks as of July 31 are: no. 1631, $115.35; no. 1632, $75.10; no. 1633, $173.25. The accountant notes that the July 31 deposit of $580 did not appear on the bank statement.

Check Figure

Adjusted ledger balance of cash, $1,792.36

Instructions

1. Prepare a bank reconciliation as of July 31, assuming that the debit memos have not been recorded.
2. Record the necessary journal entries.
3. Complete the bank form to determine the adjusted balance of cash.

STANTON NATIONAL BANK

Northway Hotel
410 W. Lang Street
Rockford, Illinois 61104

ACCOUNT NO.
761-145-792

STATEMENT DATE
July 1–31, 20—

SUMMARY		
Balance Last Statement	$1,153.80
Amount of Checks and Debits	$2,105.91
Number of Checks	14
Amount of Deposits and Credits	$2,528.17
Number of Deposits	7
Balance This Statement	$1,576.06

CHECKS/OTHER DEBITS — CHECKS

CHECK NUMBER	DATE POSTED	AMOUNT	CHECK NUMBER	DATE POSTED	AMOUNT
1617	7-03	72.50	1624	7-08	120.00
1618	7-03	167.00	1625	7-09	429.60
1619	7-03	124.20	1626	7-12	37.40
1620	7-05	137.20	1627	7-14	38.49
1621	7-06	236.25	1628	7-22	182.71
1622	7-06	159.89	1629	7-25	96.87
1623	7-08	244.50	1630	7-26	19.20

OTHER DEBITS

DESCRIPTION	DATE POSTED	AMOUNT
DM NSF check	7-22	37.00
DM Service charge	7-31	3.10

DEPOSITS/OTHER CREDITS — DEPOSITS

DATE POSTED	AMOUNT	DATE POSTED	AMOUNT
7-03	491.50	7-15	291.76
7-06	415.72	7-18	142.90
7-09	439.16	7-28	368.93
7-11	378.20		

PLEASE EXAMINE THIS STATEMENT CAREFULLY. REPORT ANY POSSIBLE ERRORS IN 10 DAYS.

CODE SYMBOLS

CM Credit Memo   DM Debit Memo   OD Overdraft   EC Error Correction

Instructions for General Ledger Software

1. Prepare a bank reconciliation as of July 31. Errors made by the company or the bank, as well as service charges, must be entered as debit or credit memos.
2. Print the bank reconciliation.
3. Record the necessary journal entries.
4. Print the journal entries.

B Bad Debts

Performance Objectives

After you have completed this appendix, you will be able to do the following:

1. Prepare the adjusting entry for bad debts using the allowance method, based on a percentage of credit sales.

2. Prepare the entry to write off an account as uncollectible when the allowance method is used.

3. Prepare the entry to write off an account as uncollectible when the specific charge-off method is used.

As you know, not all credit customers pay their bills. In this appendix, we turn our attention to the accounts receivable that will not be collected. There are two basic methods of providing for writing or charging off credit customers' accounts that are considered uncollectible. They are the allowance method and the specific charge-off method.

ALLOWANCE METHOD

The allowance method provides for bad debt losses in advance, by estimating them. Though there are a number of ways to estimate the amount of future losses from open accounts, we will base our estimate on a percentage of credit sales.

For example, based on its experience with bad debt losses, Miami Printing estimates that 1 percent of its revenue from services on account for the year will be uncollectible. Obviously, Miami Printing does not know which credit customers will not pay their bills. If the company were certain that a particular customer would not pay his or her bill, then it wouldn't perform services without requiring cash in advance.

Adjusting Entry and Writing Off an Account

 **OBJECTIVE 1**

Prepare the adjusting entry for bad debts using the allowance method, based on a percentage of credit sales.

Miami Printing's total income from services on account for last year was $500,000. One percent of $500,000 is $5,000. On its work sheet, Miami Printing makes an adjusting entry. We show this in T account form.

Bad Debts Expense				Allowance for Doubtful Accounts		
	+	−		−	+	
Dec. 31 Adjusting	5,000				5,000	Dec. 31 Adjusting

Allowance for Doubtful Accounts is treated as a deduction from Accounts Receivable. Consequently, Allowance for Doubtful Accounts is a contra account. The adjusting entry is similar to the entry for depreciation in that there is a debit to an expense account and a credit to a contra-asset account. In T account form, the adjustment for depreciation looks like this:

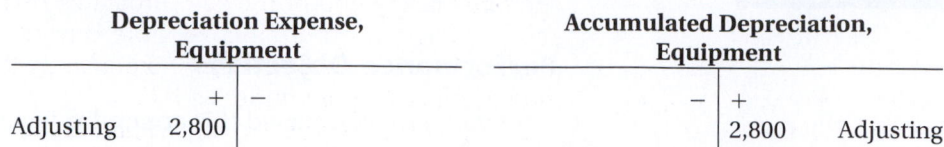

	Depreciation Expense, Equipment			Accumulated Depreciation, Equipment	
	+	−	−	+	
Adjusting	2,800			2,800	Adjusting

Assume that Miami Printing's Accounts Receivable balance is $90,000 and its Equipment balance is $75,000. Let's show the accounts and the adjusting entries in T account form.

Assets	=	Liabilities	+	Owner's Equity	+	Revenue	−	Expenses
+ | −		− | +		− | +		− | +		+ | −

Accounts Receivable

+	−
Bal. 90,000	

Allowance for Doubtful Accounts

−	+
	Bal. 170
	Adj. 5,000
	Bal. 5,170

Equipment

+	−
Bal. 75,000	

Accumulated Depreciation, Equipment

−	+
	Bal. 7,000
	Adj. 2,800
	Bal. 9,800

Income from Services

−	+
	Bal. 500,000

Bad Debts Expense

+	−
Adj. 5,000	

Depreciation Expense, Equipment

+	−
Adj. 2,800	

The Depreciation Expense, Equipment, account comes into existence as an adjusting entry at the end of the year. It is closed immediately after being brought into existence. The same thing happens to Bad Debts Expense; it comes into existence as an adjusting entry, and then it is immediately closed during the closing process.

FYI

Companies generally have a credit balance left in the Allowance account.

 OBJECTIVE 2

Prepare the entry to write off an account as uncollectible when the allowance method is used.

As certain charge customers' accounts are determined to be uncollectible and are written off, the losses are taken out of Allowance for Doubtful Accounts. Think of the Allowance for Doubtful Accounts as a reservoir. By means of the adjusting entry, the account is filled up at the end of the year and then is gradually drained off (reduced) during the next year by write-offs of charge customer accounts. The $170 balance in Allowance for Doubtful Accounts at the end of the year indicates that less accounts receivable were actually written off as uncollectible during the year than previously estimated. As a result, Bad Debts Expense in the period was overstated and therefore net income understated.

Let's go on to the next year. On January 2, Miami Printing finally gives up on its attempts to collect $720 from its credit customer Ace Computer, which is included in Accounts Receivable. Miami Printing now writes off the account in the amount of $720, shown below in T account form.

Accounts Receivable				Allowance for Doubtful Accounts			
	+	−			−	+	
Bal.	90,000		Jan. 2	Jan. 2		5,170	Bal.
		720	(write-off)	(write-off)	720		
Bal.	**89,280**					**4,450**	**Bal.**

As you can see, the write-off has reduced both the balance of Accounts Receivable and the balance of Allowance for Doubtful Accounts but has not changed the net realizable value of accounts receivable. The general journal entry is shown below.

						PAGE _____	
	DATE		DESCRIPTION	POST. REF.	DEBIT	CREDIT	
1	20—						1
2	Jan.	2	Allowance for Doubtful Accounts		7 2 0 00		2
3			Accounts Receivable			7 2 0 00	3
4			Wrote off the account of				4
5			Ace Computer as uncollectible.				5
6							6

An Advantage and a Disadvantage of the Allowance Method

The allowance method is consistent with the accrual basis of accounting in that it matches revenues of one year with expenses of the same year. The bad-debt loss potential is provided in the same year in which the revenue is earned. The conformity with the matching principle places the allowance method in compliance with generally accepted accounting principles as recognized by the FASB. However, the allowance method cannot be used for federal income tax purposes. This means that if a business uses the allowance method, the net income shown on the company's income statement will differ from the net income shown on its federal income tax return. The tax return shows a reconciliation between income reported for book purposes and income reported for tax purposes.

SPECIFIC CHARGE-OFF METHOD

OBJECTIVE 3

Prepare the entry to write off an account as uncollectible when the specific charge-off method is used.

Under the specific charge-off method, when a credit customer's account is determined to be uncollectible, the account is simply written off. The terms *write-off* and *charge-off* mean the same thing. No allowance account is used with the specific charge-off method because no estimate of uncollectible accounts receivable is calculated. As an illustration, Walter Company uses the specific charge-off method. On May 5, Walter Company writes off the account of Garber Construction, $1,220. For the purpose of this example, we will use a separate Accounts Receivable account for Garber Construction. T accounts pertaining to Garber's account look like this:

Accounts Receivable				Bad Debts Expense		
+	−				+	−
Balance 1,220				May 5		
	1,220	May 5	May 5	(write-off)	1,220	
		(write-off)	(write-off)			

The general journal entry is shown below.

PAGE _____

	DATE		DESCRIPTION	POST. REF.	DEBIT	CREDIT	
1	20—						1
2	May	5	Bad Debts Expense		1 2 2 0 00		2
3			Accounts Receivable			1 2 2 0 00	3
4			Wrote off the account of Garber				4
5			Construction as uncollectible.				5
6							6

Under this method, entries will be made directly into the Bad Debts Expense account during the year. No adjusting entry is needed, and Allowance for Doubtful Accounts is not used.

Advantages of the Specific Charge-off Method

The main advantage is that the method may be used for federal income tax purposes. It is not necessary to make an adjusting entry. Also, one less account (Allowance for Doubtful Accounts) is required.

Disadvantage of the Specific Charge-off Method

This method is not consistent with the accrual basis of accounting (recognizing revenue when it is earned and expenses when they are incurred). The method does not match up the revenue of one year with the expense of the same year. This lack of conformity with the matching principle places the specific charge-off method in violation of generally accepted accounting principles. For example, the sale of services on account to Garber Construction could have been made two years ago. Since the account receivable will never be collected, the revenue for that year was too high (overstated). Consequently, net income is also overstated during that year. Now, two years later, $1,220 is written off as an expense. So net income for this year is too low (understated) because of the added expense.

PROBLEMS

P.O. 1,2

Check Figure

Adjusting entry amount, $3,270

Problem B-1 Regis Company's total sales on account for the year amounted to $327,000. The company, which uses the allowance method, estimated bad debts at 1 percent of its charge sales. Journalize the following selected entries:

20X8
Dec. 31 The adjusting entry.

20X9
Mar. 2 Write-off of the account of B. L. Giroux as uncollectible, $584.

June 6 Write-off of the account of A. P. Bollard as uncollectible, $492.

P.O. 1,2

Check Figure

Adjusting entry amount, $1,366.03

Problem B-2 Harron's Landscape Service's total revenue on account for 2008 amounted to $273,205. The company, which uses the allowance method, estimates bad debts at ½ percent of total revenue on account. Journalize the following selected entries:

20X8
Dec. 12 Performed services on account for D. A. Wallace, $245.
          31 The adjusting entry for Bad Debts Expense.
          31 The closing entry for Bad Debts Expense.

20X9
Feb. 18 Wrote off the account of D. A. Wallace as uncollectible, $245.

P.O. 3

Check Figure

Total amount debited to Bad Debts Expense in 20X8, $677

Problem B-3 Spin City uses the specific charge-off method for recording bad debts. Journalize the following selected entries:

20X8
Apr. 10 Write-off of the account of J. C. Sargent as uncollectible, $286.

July 27 Write-off of the account of B. R. Warner as uncollectible, $391.

When you graduate from college, where will you work? If you move to another state, will that affect the amount of taxes deducted from your paycheck? As you learn about recording payroll deductions, think about how these deductions affect you. You can learn more about payroll tax information for each state at Payroll-Taxes.com **(http://www. payroll-taxes.com).** How does your state compare to one you might want to move to, as far as payroll deductions for income taxes are concerned? You can find out by using the paycheck calculator provided at this site. Also, visit the IRS website at **www.irs.gov** to view the wage-bracket tax tables in Publication 15 (Circular E) as you cover the material under Objective 3.

Performance Objectives

After you have completed this chapter, you will be able to do the following:

1. Understand the role of laws that affect payroll deductions and contributions.

2. Calculate total earnings based on an hourly, piece-rate, or commission basis.

3. Determine deductions using tables of employees' income tax withholding.

4. Complete a payroll register.

5. Journalize the payroll entry from a payroll register.

6. Maintain employees' individual earnings records.

Up to now, we've been recording employees' earnings as a debit to Salary or Wages Expense and a credit to Cash, but we've really been talking only about **gross pay**: the total amount of an employee's pay before deductions. We haven't mentioned the various deductions that we all know are taken out of our gross pay before we get to the **net pay**, or take-home pay. In this chapter, we will talk about types of deductions and how to enter them in the payroll records, and about journal entries to record the payroll and pay the employees.

OBJECTIVES OF PAYROLL RECORDS AND ACCOUNTING

There are two primary reasons to maintain accurate payroll records. First, we must collect the data necessary to compute the compensation for each employee for each payroll period.

Second, we must provide the information needed to complete the various government reports—federal and state—required of all employers. All business enterprises, both large and small, are required by law to withhold certain amounts from employees' pay for taxes, to make payments to government agencies by specific deadlines, and to submit reports on official forms. Because governments impose penalties if the requirements are not met, employers are vitally concerned with payroll accounting.

The employer is required to keep records of the following information:

1. **Personal data on employee** Name, address, Social Security number, date of birth
2. **Data on wage payments** Dates and amounts of payments, and payroll periods
3. **Amount of taxable wages paid** Dates and amount earned year to date for the calendar year involved
4. **Amount of tax withheld from each employee's earnings by pay period**

Many companies use software, such as Excel or Quickbooks, or outside payroll services, such as ADP or Paychex, to assist with their payroll acounting.

EMPLOYER/EMPLOYEE RELATIONSHIPS

FYI

Examples of independent contractors include a self-employed appliance repair person, plumber, or CPA.

Payroll accounting is concerned with employees and their compensation, withholdings, records, reports, and taxes. There is a distinction between an employee and an independent contractor. An **employee** is one who is under the direction and control of the employer, such as a bookkeeper, salesclerk, assistant, vice president, controller, and so on. An **independent contractor** is engaged for a definite job or service and may choose his or her own means of doing the work. Payments made to independent contractors are in the form of fees or charges. Independent contractors submit bills or invoices for the work they do. The payment is not subject to any withholding or payroll taxes by the person or firm paying that invoice. Such taxes are the responsibility of the independent contractor.

LAWS AFFECTING EMPLOYEES' PAY DEDUCTIONS

Both federal and state laws require the employer to act as a collecting agent and deduct specified amounts from employees' gross earnings. The employer sends the withholdings to the appropriate government agencies, along with reports substantiating the figures. Let's look at some of the more important laws that pertain to employees' pay.

OBJECTIVE 1

Understand the role of laws that affect payroll deductions and contributions.

Fair Labor Standards Act

The **Fair Labor Standards Act** of 1938 is referred to as "the Act" or "FLSA." The Act provides for minimum standards for both wages and overtime. Included in the Act are also provisions related to child labor and equal pay for equal work. In addition, the Act exempts specified employees or groups of employees from the application of certain of its provisions. Details of the Act may be read at **http://www.opm.gov.**

Federal Income Tax Withholding

The **Current Tax Payment Act**, passed in 1943, requires employers not only to withhold the tax and then pay it to the U.S. Treasury but also to keep records of the names and addresses of persons employed, their earnings and withholdings, and the amounts and dates of payment. The employer has to submit reports to the Internal Revenue Service on a quarterly basis (Form 941) and to the employee on an annual basis (W-2 form). With few exceptions, this requirement applies to employers of one or more persons. We will discuss these reports and the related deposits in Chapter 9.

FICA Tax (Employees' Share)

The **Social Security Act of 1935** began as an attempt to provide retired workers with benefits based upon their work history. Several amendments have added benefits for spouses and minor children of retired workers, disability insurance, lowering the age when benefits may be collected, Medicare, and supplemental security income.

Currently, FICA consists of Social Security and Medicare. At the writing of this text, employees contribute 6.2 percent (.062) on the first $94,200 earned in a calendar year for Social Security. Employees contribute 1.45 percent (.0145) on all earnings in a calendar year with no limit for Medicare. Throughout this chapter, we will use these percentages and earnings limitations for our calculations.

LAWS AFFECTING EMPLOYER'S PAYROLL TAX CONTRIBUTIONS (PAYROLL TAX EXPENSE)

Certain payroll taxes, based on the total wages paid to employees, are levied on the employer. Let's look at some of the more important laws that pertain to the pay of employees.

FICA Tax (Employer's Share)

The employer has to match the amount of FICA tax withheld from the employees' wages, and the employer's share is recorded under Payroll Tax Expense. Every three months the employer has to submit reports to the U.S. Treasury, recording the information on Form 941, the same form that is used to report the income tax withheld. The employer's payment to the Internal Revenue Service consists of (1) the employee's share of the FICA tax, (2) the employer's matching portion of the FICA tax, and (3) the employee's income tax withheld. We will talk about this in detail in Chapter 9.

State Unemployment Taxes (SUTA)

Each state is responsible for paying its own unemployment compensation benefits. The revenue provided by **state unemployment taxes** is used exclusively for this purpose. However, there is considerable variation among the states concerning the tax rates and the amount of taxable income. **This tax is paid by employers only.** Most states, under a State Unemployment Tax Act, charge their employers a percentage of the first $7,000 based on the taxable income stipulated in the Federal Unemployment Tax Act. In this text, we will use 5.4 percent (.054) of the first $7,000. States require employers to file reports on a quarterly, or three-month, basis. Included in these reports are a listing of employees' names, Social Security numbers, amounts of wages paid to each employee, and computations of unemployment taxes.

Federal Unemployment Tax Act (FUTA)

The purpose of the Federal Unemployment Tax Act is to provide financial support for the maintenance of government-run employment offices throughout the country. **FUTA taxes are paid by employers only.** Generally this includes all employers except nonprofit schools and charities.

The federal unemployment tax is based on the total earnings of each employee during the calendar year. Congress has frequently changed the rates and the taxable income base.

For the examples and problems in this text, we will assume that employers pay an effective federal unemployment tax rate of 0.8 percent (.008) of the first $7,000 of earnings of each employee during the calendar year.

Reports to the federal government (Form 940) must be submitted annually. We will discuss these reports in Chapter 9.

Workers' Compensation Laws

Workers' compensation laws protect employees and their dependents against losses due to death or injury incurred on the job. Most states require employers either to contribute to a state compensation insurance fund or to buy similar insurance from a private insurance company. The employer ordinarily pays the cost of the insurance premiums. The premium rates vary according to the degree of danger inherent in each job category and the employer's number of accidents. The employer has to keep records of job descriptions and classifications as well as claims of insured persons.

HOW EMPLOYEES GET PAID

Employees may be paid salaries or wages, depending on the type of work and the period of time covered. Money paid to a person for managerial or administrative services is usually called a salary, and the time period covered is generally a month or a year. Money paid for either skilled or unskilled labor is usually called wages, and the time period covered is hours or weeks. Wages may also be paid on a piecework basis. A company may supplement an employee's salary or wage by commissions, bonuses, cost-of-living adjustments, and profit-sharing plans. As a rule, employees are paid by check, in cash, or by a direct deposit to their bank account. However, their compensation may take the form of merchandise, lodging, meals, or other property as well. When the compensation is in these forms, you have to determine the fair value of the property or service given in payment for an employee's labor.

Calculating Total Earnings

OBJECTIVE 2

Calculate total earnings based on an hourly, piece-rate, or commission basis.

When compensation is based on the amount of time worked, the accountant has to have a record of the number of hours worked by each employee. When there are only a few employees, this can be accomplished by means of a time book. When there are many employees, time clocks or other electronic time-keeping systems are used.

Employees may be paid weekly, biweekly, semimonthly, or monthly. Biweekly is every two weeks. Semimonthly is twice a month.

Wages

Although wages are more often paid by check or direct deposit, some industries or companies still pay employees in cash. From an internal control point of view, however, it is better to have a permanent record, which a check or direct deposit slip provides.

Consider Mark E. Amano, who works for Goren Company. His regular rate of pay is $22.95 per hour. The company pays time-and-a-half for hours worked in excess of 40 per week. In addition, it pays him double time for any work he does on Sundays and holidays. Amano has a ½-hour lunch break during an 8½-hour day. He is not paid for the lunch break nor is he paid for minutes before 8 AM or after 4:30 PM unless hours of overtime are authorized in advance. His time card for the week is shown in Figure 1.

TIME CARD

Name   Amano, Mark E.

Week ending   Oct. 7, 20—

Day	In	Out	In	Out	Hours Worked Regular	Overtime
M	7:57	12:00	12:20	4:32	8	
T	7:56	12:06	12:36	4:37	8	
W	7:57	12:02	12:31	4:31	8	
T	8:00	12:11	12:40	6:32	8	2
F	8:00	12:03	12:33	5:33	8	1
S	7:59	11:02				3
S						

FIGURE 1

Amano's gross wages can be computed by one of two methods. The first method works like this:

40 hours at straight time	40 × $22.95 per hour =	$ 918.00
2 hours overtime on Thursday ($22.95 × 1.5 = $34.43)	2 × $34.43 per hour =	68.86
1 hour overtime on Friday	1 × $34.43 per hour =	34.43
3 hours overtime on Saturday	3 × $34.43 per hour =	103.29
Total gross wages	46	$1,124.58

The second method of calculating gross wages is often used when it is necessary to identify or track overtime premium.

FYI

Minimum wages are set by Congress or state legislature—whichever is higher. Originally, in 1938, the minimum wage was $.25 per hour.

46 hours at straight time: 46 × $22.95 per hour = $1,055.70
Overtime premium:
6 hours × $11.48 per hour premium =   68.88

Total gross wages $1,124.58

Salaries

Employees who are paid a regular salary may also be entitled to extra pay for overtime. It is necessary to figure out their regular hourly rate of pay before you can determine their overtime rate. Consider R. Henry, who gets a salary of $2,350 per month. She is entitled to overtime pay for all hours worked in excess of 40 during a week at the rate of 1½ times her regular hourly rate. This past week she worked 44 hours, so we calculate her gross pay as follows:

$2,350 per month × 12 months = $28,200 per year
$28,200 per year ÷ 52 weeks = $542.31 per week
$542.31 per week ÷ 40 hours = $13.56 per regular hour
$13.56 × 1.5 = $20.34 per overtime hour

Earnings for 44 hours:
40 hours at straight time, as calculated above   = $542.31
4 hours overtime   4 × $20.34 =   81.36

Total gross earnings $623.67

Piece Rate

Workers under the piece-rate system are paid at the rate of so much per unit of production. For example, Ben Frost, a pear picker, gets paid $8 for picking a bin of pears. If he picks 6 bins during the day, his total earnings are 6 × $8 = $48.

Workers paid by the piece-rate system are paid according to how much they produce. The number of heads of lettuce picked or flags sewn determines the worker's total compensation.

Commissions

Some salespersons are paid on a purely commission basis. However, a more common arrangement is a salary plus a commission or bonus. Assume that Lori Borsca receives an annual salary of $22,000. Her employer agrees to pay her a 5 percent commission on all sales during the year in excess of $100,000. Her sales for the year total $245,000. Her commission is $7,250 ($145,000 × 0.05). Therefore, her total earnings are $29,250 ($22,000 + $7,250).

DEDUCTIONS FROM TOTAL EARNINGS

Anyone who has ever earned a paycheck has encountered some of the many types of deductions. Total earnings minus deductions equal net pay. The most common deductions are for

1. Federal income tax withholding
2. State income tax withholding
3. FICA tax (Social Security and Medicare), employee's share
4. Union dues
5. Medical and life insurance premiums
6. Contributions to a charitable organization
7. Repayment of personal loans from the company credit union or retirement savings
8. Savings through the company credit union or retirement savings
9. Purchase of U.S. savings bonds

> **FYI**
>
> For purposes of this text, medical insurance premiums are treated as an after-tax deduction, similar to union dues and charitable contributions. However, in the real world, medical insurance premiums as usually deducted *pre-tax*. If a pre-tax deduction, the employee does not have to pay income tax, nor does the employee or employer have to pay payroll taxes, on the amount of the premium.

Employees' Federal Income Tax Withholding

Employers are required not only to withhold employees' taxes and then pay them to the U.S. Treasury but also to keep records of the names and addresses of persons employed, their **taxable earnings** (the earnings subject to tax) and withholdings, and the amounts and dates of payment.

The amount of federal income tax withheld from an employee's earnings depends on the amount of her or his total earnings, marital status, and number of withholding allowances claimed. A **withholding allowance** is an amount of an individual's earnings that is exempt from income taxes (nontaxable). An employee is entitled to one personal allowance for the taxpayer, one for his or her spouse, and one for each dependent. An **exemption** is an amount of an employee's annual earnings not subject to income tax. Each employee has to fill out an **Employee's Withholding Allowance Certificate (Form W-4)**, shown in Figure 2.

The employer retains this form as authorization to withhold money for the employee's federal income tax.

> **FYI**
>
> Federal tax rates change frequently, but the procedure stays the same. We will use the tax table given in this chapter for all computations.

Publication 15 (Circular E), Employer's Tax Guide

OBJECTIVE 3

Determine deductions using tables of employees' income tax withholding.

Publication 15 (Circular E) contains withholding tables for federal income, Social Security, and Medicare taxes, along with the rules for depositing these taxes. It is regularly updated to reflect changes in tax laws and withholding rates. It also describes filing requirements for official employer reports. Publication 15 (Circular E) is provided free of charge by the Internal Revenue Service. Accountants responsible for preparation of payroll registers and forms should be familiar with the contents of Publication 15 (Circular E).

Form **W-4** Department of the Treasury Internal Revenue Service	**Employee's Withholding Allowance Certificate** ▶ Whether you are entitled to claim a certain number of allowances or exemption from withholding is subject to review by the IRS. Your employer may be required to send a copy of this form to the IRS.	OMB No. 1545-0074 20**XX**

1 Type or print your first name and middle initial. Mark E.	Last name Amano	**2** Your social security number 543 : 24 : 1680

Home address (number and street or rural route) 6357 Boston Lane	**3** ☐ Single ☑ Married ☐ Married, but withhold at higher Single rate. **Note.** If married, but legally separated, or spouse is a nonresident alien, check the "Single" box.
City or town, state, and ZIP code Bangor, Maine 04401	**4** If your last name differs from that shown on your social security card, check here. You must call 1-800-772-1213 for a new card. ▶ ☐

5 Total number of allowances you are claiming (from line **H** above **or** from the applicable worksheet on page 2) **5** | 0

6 Additional amount, if any, you want withheld from each paycheck . . . . **6** $

7 I claim exemption from withholding for 2006, and I certify that I meet **both** of the following conditions for exemption.
● Last year I had a right to a refund of **all** federal income tax withheld because I had **no** tax liability **and**
● This year I expect a refund of **all** federal income tax withheld because I expect to have **no** tax liability.
If you meet both conditions, write "Exempt" here . . . . ▶ | **7**

Under penalties of perjury, I declare that I have examined this certificate and to the best of my knowledge and belief, it is true, correct, and complete.

Employee's signature
(Form is not valid
unless you sign it.) ▶ *Mark E. Amano*   Date ▶ *January 2, 20--*

8 Employer's name and address (Employer: Complete lines 8 and 10 only if sending to the IRS.)	**9** Office code (optional)	**10** Employer identification number (EIN)

For Privacy Act and Paperwork Reduction Act Notice, see page 2.   Cat. No. 10220Q   Form **W-4** (20XX)

FIGURE 2

> **FYI**
>
> Publication 15 (Circular E) is available in paper form or can be downloaded from the Internet at **www.irs.gov**.

The **wage-bracket tax tables** cover monthly, semimonthly, biweekly, weekly, and daily payroll periods. The tables are also subdivided on the basis of marital status. First locate the wage bracket in the first two columns of the table. Next, find the column for the number of allowances claimed and read down this column until you get to the appropriate wage-bracket line. A portion of the weekly federal income tax withholding table for married persons is reproduced in Figure 3 on page 274.

Assume that Mark E. Amano, who claims zero allowances as of the October 7 payroll, has gross wages of $1,124.58 for the week. As $1,124.58 falls in the $1,120–$1,130 bracket, you can see from the table that $131 should be withheld.

Note the headings of the bracket columns: "At least" and "But less than." A strict interpretation of the $1,120–$1,130 bracket really means $1,120–$1,129.99. Therefore, if Amano's salary were $1,130, it would fall into the $1,130–$1,140 bracket.

Employees' State Income Tax Withholding

Many states that levy state income taxes also furnish employers with withholding tables. Other states use a fixed percentage of the federal income tax withholding as the amount to be withheld for state taxes. In our illustration, we assume that the amount of each employee's state income tax deduction is 20 percent (.20) of that employee's federal income tax deduction.

Employees' FICA Tax Withholding (Social Security and Medicare)

The Federal Insurance Contributions Act provides for retirement pensions after a worker reaches age 62, disability benefits for any worker who becomes disabled (and for her or his dependents), and a health insurance program

MARRIED Persons—WEEKLY Payroll Period
(For Wages Paid in 2006)

If the wages are—		And the number of withholding allowances claimed is—										
At least	But less than	0	1	2	3	4	5	6	7	8	9	10
		The amount of income tax to be withheld is—										
$740	$750	$74	$65	$55	$46	$36	$27	$21	$15	$8	$2	$0
750	760	76	66	57	47	38	28	22	16	9	3	0
760	770	77	68	58	49	39	30	23	17	10	4	0
770	780	79	69	60	50	41	31	24	18	11	5	0
780	790	80	71	61	52	42	33	25	19	12	6	0
790	800	82	72	63	53	44	34	26	20	13	7	1
800	810	83	74	64	55	45	36	27	21	14	8	2
810	820	85	75	66	56	47	37	28	22	15	9	3
820	830	86	77	67	58	48	39	29	23	16	10	4
830	840	88	78	69	59	50	40	31	24	17	11	5
840	850	89	80	70	61	51	42	32	25	18	12	6
850	860	91	81	72	62	53	43	34	26	19	13	7
860	870	92	83	73	64	54	45	35	27	20	14	8
870	880	94	84	75	65	56	46	37	28	21	15	9
880	890	95	86	76	67	57	48	38	29	22	16	10
890	900	97	87	78	68	59	49	40	30	23	17	11
900	910	98	89	79	70	60	51	41	32	24	18	12
910	920	100	90	81	71	62	52	43	33	25	19	13
920	930	101	92	82	73	63	54	44	35	26	20	14
930	940	103	93	84	74	65	55	46	36	27	21	15
940	950	104	95	85	76	66	57	47	38	28	22	16
950	960	106	96	87	77	68	58	49	39	30	23	17
960	970	107	98	88	79	69	60	50	41	31	24	18
970	980	109	99	90	80	71	61	52	42	33	25	19
980	990	110	101	91	82	72	63	53	44	34	26	20
990	1,000	112	102	93	83	74	64	55	45	36	27	21
1,000	1,010	113	104	94	85	75	66	56	47	37	28	22
1,010	1,020	115	105	96	86	77	67	58	48	39	29	23
1,020	1,030	116	107	97	88	78	69	59	50	40	31	24
1,030	1,040	118	108	99	89	80	70	61	51	42	32	25
1,040	1,050	119	110	100	91	81	72	62	53	43	34	26
1,050	1,060	121	111	102	92	83	73	64	54	45	35	27
1,060	1,070	122	113	103	94	84	75	65	56	46	37	28
1,070	1,080	124	114	105	95	86	76	67	57	48	38	29
1,080	1,090	125	116	106	97	87	78	68	59	49	40	30
1,090	1,100	127	117	108	98	89	79	70	60	51	41	32
1,100	1,110	128	119	109	100	90	81	71	62	52	43	33
1,110	1,120	130	120	111	101	92	82	73	63	54	44	35
1,120	1,130	131	122	112	103	93	84	74	65	55	46	36
1,130	1,140	133	123	114	104	95	85	76	66	57	47	38
1,140	1,150	134	125	115	106	96	87	77	68	58	49	39
1,150	1,160	136	126	117	107	98	88	79	69	60	50	41
1,160	1,170	137	128	118	109	99	90	80	71	61	52	42
1,170	1,180	139	129	120	110	101	91	82	72	63	53	44
1,180	1,190	140	131	121	112	102	93	83	74	64	55	45
1,190	1,200	142	132	123	113	104	94	85	75	66	56	47
1,200	1,210	143	134	124	115	105	96	86	77	67	58	48
1,210	1,220	145	135	126	116	107	97	88	78	69	59	50
1,220	1,230	146	137	127	118	108	99	89	80	70	61	51
1,230	1,240	148	138	129	119	110	100	91	81	72	62	53
1,240	1,250	149	140	130	121	111	102	92	83	73	64	54
1,250	1,260	151	141	132	122	113	103	94	84	75	65	56
1,260	1,270	152	143	133	124	114	105	95	86	76	67	57
1,270	1,280	154	144	135	125	116	106	97	87	78	68	59
1,280	1,290	155	146	136	127	117	108	98	89	79	70	60
1,290	1,300	157	147	138	128	119	109	100	90	81	71	62
1,300	1,310	158	149	139	130	120	111	101	92	82	73	63
1,310	1,320	161	150	141	131	122	112	103	93	84	74	65
1,320	1,330	163	152	142	133	123	114	104	95	85	76	66
1,330	1,340	166	153	144	134	125	115	106	96	87	77	68
1,340	1,350	168	155	145	136	126	117	107	98	88	79	69
1,350	1,360	171	156	147	137	128	118	109	99	90	80	71
1,360	1,370	173	158	148	139	129	120	110	101	91	82	72
1,370	1,380	176	160	150	140	131	121	112	102	93	83	74
1,380	1,390	178	162	151	142	132	123	113	104	94	85	75
1,390	1,400	181	165	153	143	134	124	115	105	96	86	77

$1,400 and over   Use Table 1(b) for a **MARRIED person** on page 36. Also see the instructions on page 34.

FIGURE 3

after age 65 (Medicare). Both the employee and the employer have to pay **FICA taxes**, which are commonly referred to as **Social Security taxes** and **Medicare taxes**. The employer withholds FICA taxes from employees' wages and pays them to the U.S. Treasury.

FICA tax rates apply to the gross earnings of an employee during the **calendar year** (January 1 through December 31). After an employee has paid Social Security tax on the maximum taxable earnings, the employer stops deducting Social Security tax until the next calendar year begins. Congress has frequently changed the schedule of rates and taxable incomes.

In this text, we assume a Social Security rate of 6.2 percent (.062) of the first \$94,200 for each employee and a Medicare rate of 1.45 percent (.0145) of all earnings for each employee. Both tax rates apply to earnings during the calendar year. (Tables for Social Security and Medicare tax withholdings are available in the Internal Revenue Service Publication 15 (Circular E), Employer's Tax Guide.)

Let's return to Mark E. Amano, who had gross wages of \$1,124.58 for the week ending October 7. Suppose that his total accumulated gross wages earned this year *prior to this payroll period* are \$44,960. Amano's total gross wages including this payroll period were \$46,084.58 (\$44,960 + \$1,124.58). Since the Social Security tax applies to the first \$94,200 and the Medicare tax applies to all earnings, Amano's earnings are subject to both taxes. For Amano's Social Security tax, multiply \$1,124.58 by 6.2 percent (\$1,124.58 $\times$ 0.062 = \$69.72). For Amano's Medicare tax, multiply \$1,124.58 by 0.0145 = \$16.31.

Here's another example. At the beginning of the pay period, Susan Walker had cumulative earnings of \$91,300, which is \$2,900 less than \$94,200. During this pay period, she earned \$3,010.35, which is greater than \$2,900. Thus, she must pay Social Security tax of \$179.80 (\$2,900 $\times$ 0.062) on \$2,900. However, because the Medicare tax applies to all earnings, she is not exempt from any Medicare tax. Her Medicare tax is \$43.65 (\$3,010.35 $\times$ 0.0145).

PAYROLL REGISTER

OBJECTIVE 4

Complete a payroll register.

The **payroll register** is a multicolumn form prepared for each payroll period listing the earnings, deductions, and net pay for each employee. In Figure 4 (shown on the next page) we see a payroll register that shows the data for each employee on a separate line. This would be suitable for a firm, like Goren Company, that has a small number of employees.

First, we'll show the entire payroll register; then, we'll break it down and explain it column by column. The number at the foot of each column refers to the related text description.

The payroll period shown in Figure 4 covers October 1 through October 7. The first part consists of employees' names, hours worked, beginning cumulative earnings, and taxable earnings.

(1) Total Hours—Taken from employees' time cards.

(2) Beginning Cumulative Earnings—The amount each employee has earned between January 1 and September 30 (the last day of the previous payroll period). It is taken from each employee's individual earnings record. (See Figure 7, pages 282–283.)

(3) Regular Earnings—Earnings for hours worked up to and including 40. In other words, the first 40 hours multiplied by each employee's regular hourly rate.

			EARNINGS				
NAME	TOTAL HOURS	BEGINNING CUMULATIVE EARNINGS	REGULAR	OVERTIME	TOTAL	ENDING CUMULATIVE EARNINGS	UNEMPLOYMENT
1 Amano, Mark E.	46	44,960.00	918.00	206.58	1,124.58	46,084.58	
2 Barkov, Anna E.	45	5,987.00	626.20	118.00	744.20	6,731.20	744.20
3 Dorn, David L.	49	6,786.00	686.00	230.00	916.00	7,702.00	214.00
4 Felding, Sarah H.	40	38,462.00	1,084.50	0.00	1,084.50	39,546.50	
5 Graham, Jason W.	40	68,600.00	1,798.45	0.00	1,798.45	70,398.45	
6 Kilmer, Richard B.	40	68,500.00	1,895.58	0.00	1,895.58	70,395.58	
7 Mankowitz, Jim L.	55	37,850.00	1,264.30	580.00	1,844.30	39,694.30	
8 Orlene, Barbara A.	40	45,820.00	1,487.20	0.00	1,487.20	47,307.20	
9 Parker, William R.	44	46,430.00	1,581.58	194.70	1,776.28	48,206.28	
10 Rumberg, Shelly L.	45	54,867.00	1,674.16	275.00	1,949.16	56,816.16	
11 Tabor, Annette G.	40	42,740.00	1,168.83	0.00	1,168.83	43,908.83	
12 Walker, Susan	52	91,300.00	2,215.15	795.20	3,010.35	94,310.35	
13		552,302.00	16,399.95	2,399.48	18,799.43	571,101.43	958.20
14	(1)	(2)	(3)	(4)	(5)	(6)	(7A)
15							

16,399.95 + 2,399.48 = 18,799.43

552,302.00 + 18,799.43 = 571,101.43

FIGURE 4

(4) **Overtime Earnings**—Hours in excess of 40 (relative to a 40-hour week) worked by each employee, multiplied by that employee's overtime rate.

(5) **Total Earnings**—Regular earnings plus overtime earnings.

(6) **Ending Cumulative Earnings**—Beginning Cumulative Earnings plus Total Earnings.

(7) **Taxable Earnings**—The amount of earnings subject to taxation, **not the tax itself.** We'll use these columns later to figure the amount of each tax. In other words, **Taxable Earnings is the base on which to figure the tax. Taxable Earnings multiplied by the tax rate equals the amount of the tax.**

(7A) **Unemployment Taxable Earnings**—In our illustration, we are using a maximum of $7,000 for unemployment tax liability on the employer for each employee. This column represents the previously untaxed portion remaining of the $7,000 for the individual employees. **Unemployment tax is paid only by the employer in most states. An unemployment tax may be paid both to the state and to the federal government.** Actually, states may use different maximum earnings and different rates than does the federal government. However, many states use $7,000, which at the time of this writing is the amount used by the federal government. There are three possibilities for Unemployment Taxable Earnings, as follows:

a. **Employee's cumulative earnings including this pay period have not reached $7,000.** When an employee's cumulative earnings so far during the calendar year (since January 1) are less than $7,000, we record the total earnings for the payroll period in the Unemployment Taxable Earnings column. For example, Anna E. Barkov's cumulative earnings before this

PAYROLL REGISTER FOR WEEK ENDED October 7, 20—

(7) TAXABLE EARNINGS		(8) DEDUCTIONS					
SOCIAL SECURITY	MEDICARE	FEDERAL INCOME TAX	STATE INCOME TAX	SOCIAL SECURITY TAX	MEDICARE TAX	MEDICAL INSURANCE	OTHER
1 1 2 4 58	1 1 2 4 58	1 3 1 00	2 6 20	6 9 72	1 6 31	1 8 50	0 00
7 4 4 20	7 4 4 20	7 4 00	1 4 80	4 6 14	1 0 79	1 1 50	UW 3 5 00
9 1 6 00	9 1 6 00	1 0 0 00	2 0 00	5 6 79	1 3 28	1 5 50	UW 2 5 00
1 0 8 4 50	1 0 8 4 50	1 1 6 00	2 3 20	6 7 24	1 5 73	1 7 20	0 00
1 7 9 8 45	1 7 9 8 45	2 8 1 00	5 6 20	1 1 1 50	2 6 08	3 0 50	0 00
1 8 9 5 58	1 8 9 5 58	3 0 6 00	6 1 20	1 1 7 53	2 7 49	3 2 00	UW 1 5 00
1 8 4 4 30	1 8 4 4 30	2 9 3 00	5 8 60	1 1 4 35	2 6 74	3 0 00	UW 1 5 00
1 4 8 7 20	1 4 8 7 20	2 0 4 00	4 0 80	9 2 21	2 1 56	2 5 00	UW 2 0 00
1 7 7 6 28	1 7 7 6 28	2 7 6 00	5 5 20	1 1 0 13	2 5 76	3 0 50	0 00
1 9 4 9 16	1 9 4 9 16	3 1 9 00	6 3 80	1 2 0 85	2 8 26	3 5 00	AR 3 0 00
1 1 6 8 83	1 1 6 8 83	1 3 7 00	2 7 40	7 2 47	1 6 95	2 0 00	UW 2 5 00
2 9 0 0 00	3 0 1 0 35	6 0 1 00	1 2 0 20	1 7 9 80	4 3 65	5 5 00	UW 5 0 00
18 6 8 9 08	18 7 9 9 43	2 8 3 8 00	5 6 7 60	1 1 5 8 73	2 7 2 60	3 2 0 70	2 1 5 00
(7 B)	(7 C)	(8 A)	(8 B)	(8 C)	(8 D)	(8 E)	(8 F)

2,838.00 + 567.60 + 1,158.73 + 272.60 + 320.70 + 215.00 = 5,372.63

PAGE 56

(9) PAYMENTS			(10) EXPENSE ACCOUNT DEBITED		
TOTAL	NET AMOUNT	CK. NO.	SALES WAGES EXPENSE	OFFICE WAGES EXPENSE	
2 6 1 73	8 6 2 85	931	1 1 2 4 58		1
1 9 2 23	5 5 1 97	932	7 4 4 20		2
2 3 0 57	6 8 5 43	933	9 1 6 00		3
2 3 9 37	8 4 5 13	934		1 0 8 4 50	4
5 0 5 28	1 2 9 3 17	935	1 7 9 8 45		5
5 5 9 22	1 3 3 6 36	936		1 8 9 5 58	6
5 3 7 69	1 3 0 6 61	937	1 8 4 4 30		7
4 0 3 57	1 0 8 3 63	938		1 4 8 7 20	8
4 9 7 59	1 2 7 8 69	939	1 7 7 6 28		9
5 9 6 91	1 3 5 2 25	940	1 9 4 9 16		10
2 9 8 82	8 7 0 01	941	1 1 6 8 83		11
1 0 4 9 65	1 9 6 0 70	942	3 0 1 0 35		12
5 3 7 2 63	13 4 2 6 80		14 3 3 2 15	4 4 6 7 28	13
(8 G)	(9 A)	(9B)	(1 0 A)	(1 0 B)	14
					15

5,372.63 + 13,426.80 = 18,799.43   14,332.15 + 4,467.28 = 18,799.43

FYI

Social Security and Medicare taxes are recorded separately in the payroll register because there is no limit on Medicare as there is on Social Security.

week were $5,987. Barkov's cumulative earnings after this week are $6,731.20 ($5,987 + $744.20). Because Barkov's cumulative earnings are still less than $7,000 (after the current check of $744.20), her entire $744.20 in wages earned during this pay period is listed in the Unemployment Taxable Earnings column.

b. **Employee's cumulative earnings were less than $7,000 before this week and are more than $7,000 after this week.** Look at the line for David L. Dorn and notice that his cumulative earnings before this week were $6,786. Dorn's new cumulative earnings (ending) are $7,702 ($6,786 + $916), putting him over the $7,000 maximum. Therefore, to bring Dorn up to the $7,000 limit, $214 ($7,000 − $6,786) of his earnings for the week are taxable. After this week, none of Dorn's earnings for the remainder of this calendar year will be taxable for unemployment.

c. **Employee's cumulative earnings before this week were more than $7,000.** After an employee's earnings top $7,000 during the calendar year, record a dash in the Unemployment Taxable Earnings column to indicate that the column has not been forgotten or overlooked. For example, Mark Amano's total earnings before the payroll period ended October 7 (beginning) were $44,960 (as shown in his individual earnings record in Figure 7). Since he had previously earned more than $7,000 this year, we record a dash in the Unemployment Taxable Earnings column.

(7B) **Social Security Taxable Earnings**—The first $94,200 for each employee. We assume a Social Security tax rate of 6.2 percent of the first $94,200 paid to each employee during the calendar year.

a. **Employee's cumulative earnings including this pay period have not reached $94,200.** When an employee's cumulative earnings so far during the year are less than $94,200, we record the total earnings for the payroll period in the Social Security Taxable Earnings column. For example, Anna Barkov's cumulative earnings so far this year amount to $6,731.20. Because Barkov's total earnings are less than $94,200, the entire $744.20 of wages earned during this pay period is listed in the Social Security Taxable Earnings column. Note that this is true of all the employees except Susan Walker.

The United Way is a large charitable organization that collects and compiles contributions from companies and individuals and allocates funds to various agencies under its umbrella. United Way agencies reach out to all ages as well as providing funding for research on many health issues.

b. **Employee's cumulative earnings were less than $94,200 before this week and are more than $94,200 after this week.** The line for Susan Walker shows her cumulative earnings before the payroll period ended October 7 were $91,300. However, the cumulative earnings including those of this payroll period total $94,310.35, which is greater than the $94,200 limit. That means only $2,900 ($94,200 − $91,300) of her current pay period earnings is recorded in the Social Security Taxable Earnings column. After an employee's earnings top $94,200 during the calendar year, record a dash to indicate that the column has not been forgotten or overlooked. (Use the same procedure as for the Unemployment Taxable Earnings column.)

(7C) **Medicare Taxable Earnings**—All earnings for this period. We have assumed a Medicare tax rate of 1.45 percent (.0145) on all earnings that are paid to each employee during the calendar year. Therefore, all earnings for this period are taxable and are recorded in the Medicare Taxable Earnings column.

(8) **Deductions**—Amounts taken away (withheld) from total earnings.

(8A) **Federal Income Tax Deductions**—The amount of the federal income tax deduction for each employee can be located directly on the wage bracket tables or calculated on a percentage basis.

(8B) **State Income Tax Deductions**—States that impose income taxes also provide wage-bracket tables. The state tax deduction for each employee can be located directly in the appropriate table. As stated previously, we are assuming a rate of 20 percent of the federal income tax.

(8C) **Social Security Tax Deductions**—For each employee's Social Security tax deduction, we first go to the Social Security Taxable Earnings column and note the amount subject to tax. Next, we multiply the Social Security taxable earnings by 6.2 percent (.062). For example, Barkov's taxable earnings are $744.20, and her Social Security tax deduction is $46.14 ($744.20 × .062).

(8D) **Medicare Tax Deductions**—For each employee's Medicare tax deduction, we go to the Medicare Taxable Earnings column and note the amount subject to tax. Next, we multiply the Medicare taxable earnings by 1.45 percent. For example, Barkov's taxable earnings are $744.20, and her Medicare tax deduction is $10.79 ($744.20 × .0145).

(8E) **Medical Insurance Deductions**—Premiums paid by the employee through payroll withholding. The amount of the premium for each employee depends on the number of dependents claimed, among other things. For example, Barkov's premium is $11.50 per week.

(8F) **Other Deductions**—Employees' voluntary withholdings. In our illustration, UW represents the United Way, and AR stands for Accounts Receivable (employee pays off charge account to the company). For example, Shelly Rumberg paid $30 on her charge account.

(8G) **Total Deductions**—The combined total of each employee's deductions for taxes, insurance, and other. For example, Barkov's total deduction is $192.23 ($74.00 + $14.80 + $46.14 + $10.79 + $11.50 + $35.00).

(9) **Payments**—The amount of each employee's payroll check (take-home pay).

(9A) **Net Amount**—Each employee's Total Earnings minus Total Deductions. For example, Barkov's net amount is $551.97 ($744.20 − $192.23).

(9B) **Ck. No.**—The number of each employee's payroll check.

(10) **Expense Account Debited**—Columns used for distributing each amount into the appropriate wages expense account. Goren Company uses Sales Wages Expense and Office Wages Expense. The sum of these two columns equals the total earnings.

(10A) **Sales Wages Expense**—Amounts earned by employees involved in sales activities.

(10B) **Office Wages Expense**—Amounts earned by employees involved in office activities.

REMEMBER!

Taxable earnings multiplied by the tax rate equals the tax.

THE PAYROLL ENTRY

OBJECTIVE 5

Journalize the payroll entry from a payroll register.

Because the payroll register summarizes the payroll data for the period, it is used as the basis for recording the payroll in the ledger accounts. Since the payroll register does not have the status of a journal, a journal entry is necessary. Figure 5 on page 280 shows the entry in general journal form.

GENERAL JOURNAL   PAGE ___31___

DATE		DESCRIPTION	POST. REF.	DEBIT		CREDIT	
1	20—						1
2	Oct. 7	Sales Wages Expense *gross*		14 3 3 2 15			2
3		Office Wages Expense		4 4 6 7 28			3
4		Employees' Federal Income					4
5		Tax Payable			2 8 3 8 00		5
6		FICA Tax Payable			1 4 3 1 33		6
7		Employees' State Income Tax					7
8		Payable			5 6 7 60		8
9		Employees' Medical Insurance					9
10		Payable			3 2 0 70		10
11		Employees' United Way					11
12		Payable			1 8 5 00		12
13		Accounts Receivable			3 0 00		13
14		Wages Payable *Net Amt.*			13 4 2 6 80		14
15		Payroll register, page 56,					15
16		for week ended October 7.					16

FIGURE 5

Note that the accountant records the total cost to the company for services of employees as debits to the Wages Expense accounts.

Also note that the total Social Security tax deductions ($1,158.73) and the total Medicare tax deductions ($272.60) are combined to become FICA Tax Payable of $1,431.33 ($1,158.73 + $272.60). The two tax deductions are combined into the one liability account because they are paid together at the same time. Social Security and Medicare taxes are recorded separately in the payroll register because they must be listed separately on each employee's W-2 form (Wage and Tax Statement).

To pay the employees from the company's regular checking account, the accountant now makes the following journal entry:

		DESCRIPTION		DEBIT		CREDIT	
17	8	Wages Payable		13 4 2 6 80			17
18		Cash—M. Amano			8 6 2 85		18
19		Cash—A. Barkov			5 5 1 97		19
20		Cash—D. Dorn			6 8 5 43		20
21		Cash—S. Felding			8 4 5 13		21
22		Cash—J. Graham			1 2 9 3 17		22
23		Cash—R. Kilmer			1 3 3 6 36		23
24		Cash—J. Mankowitz			1 3 0 6 61		24
25		Cash—B. Orlene			1 0 8 3 63		25
26		Cash—W. Parker			1 2 7 8 69		26
27		Cash—S. Rumberg			1 3 5 2 25		27
28		Cash—A. Tabor			8 7 0 01		28
29		Cash—S. Walker			1 9 6 0 70		29

Special Payroll Bank Account—An Alternative

A firm with a large number of employees would probably open a special **payroll bank account** with its bank. One check drawn on the regular bank account is made payable to the special payroll account for the amount of the total net pay for a payroll period. All payroll checks for the period are then written on the special payroll account. To record this, the accountant makes the following journal entry. In this book, assume the entry to debit Cash—Payroll Bank Account and to credit Cash has already been made.

GENERAL JOURNAL   PAGE ___1___

	DATE	DESCRIPTION	POST. REF.	DEBIT	CREDIT	
17	8	Wages Payable		13 4 2 6 80		17
18		Cash—Payroll Bank Account			13 4 2 6 80	18
19		Paid wages for week				19
20		ended October 7.				20
21						21
22						22
23						23
24						24
25						25
26						26

Paycheck

All the data needed to make out a payroll check are available in the payroll register. Mark E. Amano's paycheck is shown in Figure 6.

FIGURE 6

EMPLOYEE	TOTAL HOURS	O.T. HOURS	REG. PAY	O.T. PREM. PAY	GROSS PAY	FED INC. TAX	STATE INC. TAX	SOCIAL SECURITY TAX	MEDICARE TAX	MEDICAL INSURANCE	OTHER	TOTAL DED.	NET PAY
Mark E. Amano	46	6	918.00	206.58	1,124.58	131.00	26.20	69.72	16.31	18.50	—	261.73	862.85

CENTRAL NATIONAL BANK   98-461 / 252

Payroll Account

Goren Company
610 First Avenue
Bangor, Maine 04401

October 8 20 _—_ No. _931_

PAY TO THE ORDER OF _Mark E. Amano_ $ _862.85_

Eight hundred sixty-two and 85/100 _____ DOLLARS

Eileen Goren

⑆252⑈046⑈

EMPLOYEE'S INDIVIDUAL EARNINGS RECORD

NAME **Mark E. Amano**

ADDRESS **6357 Boston Lane**

Bangor, Maine 04401

MALE **X** FEMALE _____

MARRIED **X** SINGLE _____

PHONE NO. **663-2556** DATE OF BIRTH **9/19/72**

EMPLOYEE NO. **5**

SOC. SEC. NO. **543-24-1680**

PAY RATE **$22.95**

EQUIVALENT HOURLY RATE **$22.95**

DATE TERMINATED _____

CLASSIFICATION FOR WORKERS' COMPENSATION INSURANCE **Sales floor**

PERIOD ENDED	DATE PAID	HOURS WORKED REG	HOURS WORKED O.T.	EARNINGS REGULAR	EARNINGS OVERTIME	EARNINGS TOTAL	ENDING CUMULATIVE EARNINGS	FEDERAL INCOME TAX	STATE INCOME TAX
9/2	9/3	40	8	918 00	275 44	1193 44	40 771 55	142 00	28 40
9/9	9/10	40	2	918 00	68 86	986 86	41 758 41	110 00	22 00
9/16	9/17	40	2	918 00	68 86	986 86	42 745 27	110 00	22 00
9/23	9/24	40	5	918 00	172 15	1090 15	43 835 42	127 00	25 40
9/30	10/1	40	6	918 00	206 58	1124 58	44 960 00	131 00	26 20
10/7	10/8	40	6	918 00	206 58	1124 58	46 084 58	131 00	26 20

FIGURE 7

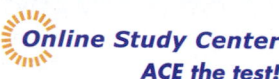

OBJECTIVE 6

Maintain employees' individual earnings records.

Employees' Individual Earnings Records

To comply with government regulations, a firm has to keep current data on each employee's accumulated earnings, deductions, and net pay. The information contained in the payroll register is recorded each payday in each **employee's individual earnings record**. Figure 7 shows a portion of the earnings record for Mark E. Amano.

CHAPTER REVIEW

Online Study Center
ACE the test!

Review of Performance Objectives

1. Understand the role of laws that affect payroll deductions and contributions.

   Those employees and employers involved in the computation and paying of employees for their work must understand the laws, know the percentages and limits involved, and when and to whom to submit the funds deducted from employees and contributed by employees.

2. Calculate total earnings based on an hourly, piece-rate, or commission basis.

   Earnings calculated on an *hourly basis* equal the hourly rate multiplied by the number of hours worked. Earnings calculated on a *piece-rate basis* equal the total number of products produced multiplied by the rate per unit of product. Earnings calculated on a *commission basis* equal the total number of units sold or the price of units sold multiplied by the commission rate.

3. Determine deductions using tables of employees' income tax withholding.

   Using the appropriate income tax withholding table in IRS Publication 15 (Circular E), first determine marital status and payroll period and then locate the wage bracket containing the amount of earnings. Next, on the same horizontal line, select the vertical column containing the number of allowances claimed.

4. Complete a payroll register.

   List the employees' names, hours worked, and beginning cumulative earnings. Add the total earnings to the beginning cumulative earnings to get ending cumulative earnings. The Unemployment Taxable Earnings column is used for the first

DATE EMPLOYED __2/1/—__

NO. OF EXEMPTIONS __0__

PER HOUR __X__   PER DAY _____

PER WEEK _____   PER MONTH _____

	DEDUCTIONS							PAID	
	SOCIAL SECURITY TAX	MEDICARE TAX	MEDICAL INSURANCE	OTHER		TOTAL		NET AMOUNT	CK. NO.
				CODE	AMOUNT				
	73 99	17 30	18 50	UW	5 00	285 19		908 25	871
	61 19	14 31	18 50	UW	—	226 00		760 86	883
	61 19	14 31	18 50	UW	5 00	231 00		755 86	895
	67 59	15 81	18 50	UW	—	254 30		835 85	907
	69 72	16 31	18 50	UW	5 00	266 73		857 85	919
	69 72	16 31	18 50	UW	—	261 73		862 85	931

$7,000 of each employee's earnings for FUTA and SUTA. The Social Security Taxable Earnings column is used for an assumed first $94,200. The Medicare Taxable Earnings column is used for all earnings. Under the Deductions columns, list the income taxes withheld, the Social Security taxes withheld, the Medicare taxes withheld, and other deductions. The Social Security tax deduction equals the Social Security taxable earnings multiplied by an assumed rate of 6.2 percent. The Medicare tax deduction equals the Medicare taxable earnings multiplied by an assumed rate of 1.45 percent. Net amount equals total (gross) earnings minus total deductions. The Expense Account Debited columns are used to distribute salaries and wages expense to the appropriate accounts.

5. Journalize the payroll entry from a payroll register.

Totals are taken directly from the payroll register. Refer to the general journal illustrations on pages 280 and 281 for an example of the first payroll entry and examples of two ways to journalize the payment of the payroll—one from the company's regular checking account, and one from a special payroll bank account.

6. Maintain employees' individual earnings records.

In the employees' individual earnings records, list the personal data for each employee. Based on the information contained in the payroll register, record the earnings and deductions for each payroll period.

Glossary

Calendar year A twelve-month period beginning on January 1 and ending on December 31 of the same year. (275)

Current Tax Payment Act (Income Tax Withholding) An act to require employers to withhold and pay to the U.S. Treasury employee funds. (268)

Employee One who works for compensation under the direction and control of the employer. (267)

Employee's individual earnings record A supplementary record for each employee showing personal payroll data and yearly cumulative earnings, deductions, and net pay. (282)

Employee's Withholding Allowance Certificate (Form W-4) A form that specifies the number of allowances claimed by each employee and gives the employer the authority to withhold money for an employee's federal income taxes and FICA taxes. (272)

Exemption An amount of an employee's annual earnings not subject to income tax for the taxpayer, taxpayer's spouse, and dependents (usually children). (272)

Fair Labor Standards Act (FLSA) The act of 1938 that provides for minimum standards for wages and overtime, including provisions related to child labor and equal pay for equal work. (268)

FICA taxes Social Security taxes plus Medicare taxes, paid by both employee and employer under the provisions of the Federal Insurance Contributions Act. The proceeds are used to pay old-age and disability pensions and to fund the Medicare program. (275)

Gross pay The total amount of an employee's pay before any deductions. (266)

Independent contractor Someone who is engaged for a definite job or service, and who may choose his or her own means of doing the work. This person is not an employee of the firm for which the service is provided. (267)

Medicare taxes Federal government taxes levied on employees and employers; proceeds are used for medical insurance for eligible people age 65 or over. (275)

Net pay Gross pay minus deductions. Also called *take-home pay*. (266)

Payroll bank account A special checking account used to pay a company's employees. (281)

Payroll register A multicolumn form prepared for each payroll period listing the earnings, deductions, and net pay for each employee. (275)

Social Security Act of 1935 An act to provide for worker retirement funding through deductions from their wages and matching amounts from the employers. (268)

Social Security taxes Federal government taxes levied on employees and employers; proceeds are used for old-age pensions and disability benefits. (275)

Taxable earnings The amount of an employee's earnings subject to a tax. (272)

Wage-bracket tax tables A chart providing the amounts to be deducted for income taxes based on amount of earnings, marital status, and number of allowances claimed. (273)

Withholding allowance An amount of an employee's annual earnings not subject to income tax. (272)

Workers' compensation laws Laws that protect employees and dependents against losses due to death or injury incurred on the job. (269)

QUESTIONS, EXERCISES, AND CASES

Discussion Questions

1. Why must employers maintain employees' individual earnings records?
2. What information is included in an employee's individual earnings record?

3. What is the purpose of the payroll register?

4. Explain the difference between gross earnings and net earnings for a payroll period.

5. Describe how a special payroll bank account is useful in paying the wages and salaries of employees.

6. List three required deductions and four voluntary deductions from an employee's total earnings.

7. What is the difference between an employee and an independent contractor? List two examples of an independent contractor.

8. What information is included in a wage-bracket withholding table? Are there overlapping amounts of gross earnings in the table?

Exercises

P.O. 1,2

Calculate gross pay.

Exercise 8-1 Determine the gross pay for each employee listed below.

a. Gary Dale is paid time-and-a-half for all hours over forty. He worked forty-four hours during the week. His regular pay rate is $10.80 per hour.

b. Moira Nole worked fifty hours during the week. She is entitled to time-and-a-half for all hours in excess of forty per week. Her regular pay rate is $12.50 per hour.

c. Lora Mikel is paid a commission of 8 percent of her sales, which amounted to $10,885.

d. Margo Best's yearly salary is $40,800. During the week, Best worked forty-three hours, and she is entitled to time-and-a-half for all hours over forty.

P.O. 1,2,3

Determine gross pay and withholding.

Exercise 8-2 Lisa Meilo works for Palo Company, which pays its employees time-and-a-half for all hours worked in excess of forty per week. Meilo's pay rate is $18.50 per hour. Her wages are subject to federal income tax, a Social Security tax deduction at the rate of 6.2 percent, and a Medicare tax deduction at the rate of 1.45 percent. She is married and claims three allowances. Meilo has an unpaid half-hour lunch break during an eight-and-one-half-hour day. In the most recent pay period, she worked fifty hours. Meilo's beginning cumulative earnings are $36,827.

Complete the following using Meilo's most recent time card shown at the top of page 286.

a. _____ hours at straight time × $_____
per hour $_____

b. _____ hours overtime × $_____
per hour   _____

c. Total gross pay $_____

d. Federal income tax withholding (from tax
tables in Figure 3, page 274) $_____

e. Social Security tax withholding at 6.2 percent   _____

f. Medicare tax withholding at 1.45 percent   _____

g. Total withholding   _____

h. Net pay $_____

TIME CARD

Name   Meilo, Lisa

Week ending   March 11, 20—

Day	In	Out	In	Out	Hours Worked Regular	Hours Worked Overtime
M	7⁵⁶	12⁰⁹	12³⁹	4³²	8	
T	7⁵²	12⁰⁵	12³⁵	5⁰⁴	8	½
W	7⁵⁹	12²⁰	12⁴⁰	5⁰³	8	½
T	8⁰⁰	12⁰⁸	12³⁸	4³⁴	8	
F	7⁵⁶	12⁰⁹	12³⁹	6³³	8	2
S	8⁰⁰	12⁰¹	12⁴⁰	3⁴⁰		7
S						

P.O. 1,2,3,4

Determine net pay.

Exercise 8-3 Using the income tax withholding table in Figure 3, page 274, for each employee of Miles Company, determine the net pay for the week ended January 21. Assume a Social Security tax of 6.2 percent and a Medicare tax of 1.45 percent. All employees have cumulative earnings, including this pay period, of less than $94,200. Assume all employees are married.

Employee	Allowances	Total Earnings	Social Security Tax Withheld	Medicare Tax Withheld	Federal Income Tax Withheld	Union Dues Withheld	Medical Insurance Withheld	Net Pay
a. Aston, F. B.	1	$ 900	$	$	$	$ 25	$ 35	$
b. Dwyer, S. J.	2	920				25	35	
c. Flynn, K. A.	3	1,110				25	40	
d. Harden, J. L.	0	1,025				25	40	
e. Nguyen, H.	2	925				25	35	
Totals		$4,880	$	$	$	$125	$185	$

FIGURE 8

NAME	BEGINNING CUMULATIVE EARNINGS	EARNINGS REGULAR	EARNINGS OVERTIME	EARNINGS TOTAL	ENDING CUMULATIVE EARNINGS	TAXABLE EARNINGS UNEMPLOYMENT	TAXABLE EARNINGS SOCIAL SECURITY	TAXABLE EARNINGS MEDICARE
	245 7 5 4 00	6 7 2 4 00	1 2 2 0 00	7 4 9 4 00	253 2 4 8 00	2 4 5 6 00	7 9 4 4 00	7 9 4 4 00

P.O. 1,4

Locate errors in a payroll register.

Exercise 8-4 For the week ended September 7, the totals of the payroll register for Benton, Inc., are presented in Figure 8. The regular and overtime earnings are correct. List six errors that exist. All earnings are subject to Social Security and Medicare taxes.

P.O. 1,4

Determine taxable earnings.

Exercise 8-5 For tax purposes, assume that the maximum taxable earnings are $94,200 for Social Security and $7,000 for the unemployment tax, and that all earnings are taxable for Medicare. For the payroll register for the month of November in Figure 9, determine the taxable earnings for each employee.

EMPLOYEE	BEGINNING CUMULATIVE EARNINGS	TOTAL EARNINGS	ENDING CUMULATIVE EARNINGS	TAXABLE EARNINGS		
				UNEMPLOYMENT	SOCIAL SECURITY	MEDICARE
Axton, C.	94 0 0 0 00	7 6 9 1 00	101 6 9 1 00			
Edgar, E.	45 4 6 5 00	3 6 8 0 00	49 1 4 5 00			
Gorman, L.	36 8 7 9 00	3 0 6 4 00	39 9 4 3 00			
Jolson, R.	24 6 3 4 00	2 3 2 5 00	26 9 5 9 00			
Nixel, P.	6 8 5 0 00	2 4 6 3 00	9 3 1 3 00			

FIGURE 9

P.O. 1,4,5

Determine FICA withholdings and journalize the payroll entry.

Exercise 8-6 On January 21, the column totals of the payroll register for Cory Company showed that its sales employees had earned $14,960, its trucking employees had earned $10,692, and its office employees had earned $8,670. Social Security taxes were withheld at an assumed rate of 6.2 percent, and Medicare taxes were withheld at an assumed rate of 1.45 percent. Other deductions consisted of federal income tax, $3,975; medical insurance, $1,480; union dues, $560. Determine the amount of Social Security and Medicare taxes withheld, and record the general journal entry for the payroll, crediting Salaries Payable for the net pay. All earnings were taxable.

	DEDUCTIONS					PAYMENTS		WAGES EXPENSE
FEDERAL INCOME TAX	SOCIAL SECURITY TAX	MEDICARE TAX	UNION DUES	MEDICAL INSURANCE	TOTAL	NET AMOUNT	CK. NO.	DEBIT
9 4 9 00	4 2 9 53	1 1 5 19	1 9 3 00	2 9 2 00	2 0 8 3 00	5 4 5 6 00		7 4 9 4 00

P.O. 1,2,3

Determine missing amounts.

Exercise 8-7 Lehn Labs has two employees. The information shown below was taken from its individual earnings records for the month of September. Determine the missing amounts, assuming that the Social Security tax is 6.2 percent and the Medicare tax is 1.45 percent. All earnings are subject to Social Security and Medicare taxes. Round amounts to nearest penny.

	Barton	Ringness	Total
Regular earnings	$1,750.00	$?	$?
Overtime earnings	?	120.00	?
Total earnings	$1,860.00	$?	$?
Federal income tax withheld	$ 335.00	$?	$?
State income tax withheld	?	92.00	?
Social Security tax withheld	115.32	111.60	?
Medicare tax withheld	25.38	26.10	?
Medical insurance withheld	26.97	97.00	?
Total deductions	$ 688.88	$ 554.70	$?
Net pay	$?	$1,245.30	$?

P.O. 5

Journalize the payroll entry.

Exercise 8-8 Assume that the employees in Exercise 8-7 are paid from the company's regular bank account (check numbers 981 and 982). Prepare the entry to record and pay the payroll in general journal form, dated September 30.

As you've learned about recording payroll taxes in this chapter, have you thought about how they affect you?

Find out whether you would have more or less deducted from your paycheck if you moved from Massachusetts to Oklahoma. Then, consider moving to Wyoming. Use the paycheck calculator provided at Payroll-Taxes.com (http://www.paycheckcity.com/copayroll-taxes/netpaycalculator.asp). For each state, assume it is the 2006 tax year, you are single, you would make $2,000 per week, and you claim no federal or state exemptions or other deductions. If the amounts differ, explain how they differ.

CONSIDER AND COMMUNICATE

Norton Company pays its employees weekly by issuing checks on its regular bank account. The owner thinks it would be too much trouble to have a second checking account. Explain to the owner why this might be worth the additional effort.

WHAT'S WRONG WITH THIS PICTURE?

You have just completed the payroll register for this week's payroll. You have crossfooted the register—that is, you have added the columns vertically and horizontally to see if you come up with the same totals both ways. There is just one problem: The total of the Net Amount column does not equal the total of the Gross Amount column minus the total of the Total Deductions column. How could this happen? What would you do to obtain correctly crossfooted totals?

A QUESTION OF ETHICS

An employee who is married and has three children submits a W-4 form to his employer and checks the box that says "Single," and writes zero in the "Deductions Claimed" box. Is this action ethical, unethical, or illegal? Explain your reasoning.

PROBLEM SET A

For additional help, see the demonstration problem at the beginning of each chapter in your Working Papers.

P.O. 1,2,3

Problem 8-1A Violet Ross, an employee of Hofman Company, worked forty-eight hours during the week of February 9 through 15. Her rate of pay is $16.50 per hour, and she gets time-and-a-half for work in excess of forty hours per week. She is married and claims two allowances on her W-4 form. Her wages are subject to the following deductions:

a. Federal income tax (use the table in Figure 3, page 274).
b. Social Security tax at 6.2 percent.
c. Medicare tax at 1.45 percent.
d. Union dues, $30.00.
e. Medical insurance, $32.00.

Check Figure

Net pay, $658.36

Instructions

Compute her regular pay, overtime pay, gross pay, and net pay.

P.O. 1,2,4,5

Problem 8-2A Payroll information for Ridge Homes for the week ended February 21 is shown at the top of page 290.

Taxable earnings for Social Security are based on the first $94,200. Taxable earnings for Medicare are based on all earnings. Taxable earnings for federal and state unemployment are based on the first $7,000. Employees are paid time-and-a-half for work in excess of forty hours per week.

Name	Earnings at End of Previous Week	Daily Time							Pay Rate	Federal Income Tax
		S	M	T	W	T	F	S		
Arms, P.	1,950.00	8	8	8	8	8			12.00	125.00
Bill, D.	2,060.00			8	8	8	8	8	12.50	138.00
Carn, W.	2,085.00	8	8	8			8	8	12.95	155.00
Dorf, J.	748.00				8	8			22.00	130.00
Edgar, L.	2,687.00	8	8	8			8	8	12.90	178.00
Fitz, G. W.	2,075.00	8	8		8	8	8	8	12.45	140.00

Check Figure

Net amount, $1,916.88

Instructions

1. Complete the payroll register, page 37. The Social Security tax rate is 6.2 percent, and the Medicare tax rate is 1.45 percent. Begin payroll checks with No. 208.
2. Prepare a general journal entry to record the payroll. The firm's general ledger contains a Wages Expense account and a Wages Payable account.
3. Assuming that the firm has transferred funds from its regular bank account to its special payroll bank account, and that this entry has been made, prepare a general journal entry to record the payment of wages.

P.O. 1,2,3,4,5

Problem 8-3A Austin Company pays its employees time-and-a-half for hours worked in excess of forty per week. The information available from time cards and employees' individual earnings records for the pay period ended October 14 is shown in the chart below.

Name	Earnings at End of Previous Week	Daily Time						Pay Rate	Income Tax Allowances
		M	T	W	T	F	S		
Bardin, J.	43,627.00	8	8	8	8	8	2	21.30	2
Caris, A.	44,340.00	8	8	8	8	8	8	21.60	1
Drew, W.	43,845.00	8	10	10	8	8	0	21.50	1
Garen, S.	93,030.00	8	8	8	8	8	0	49.00	3
North, M.	43,875.00	8	8	8	8	8	5	21.40	3
Ovid, N.	40,150.00	8	8	8	8	8	0	21.50	1
Ross, J.	6,430.00	8	8	8	8	8	4	20.50	1
Springer, O.	44,175.00	8	8	8	8	8	3	21.25	2

Taxable earnings for Social Security are based on the first $94,200. Taxable earnings for Medicare are based on all earnings. Taxable earnings for federal and state unemployment are based on the first $7,000.

Check Figure

Net amount, $7,167.58

Instructions

1. Complete the payroll register, page 72, using the wage-bracket income tax withholding table in Figure 3 (page 274). The Social Security tax rate is 6.2 percent, and the Medicare tax rate is 1.45 percent. Assume that all employees are married. Garen's federal income tax is $312. In the payroll register, begin payroll checks with No. 945.
2. Prepare a general journal entry to record the payroll. The firm's general ledger contains a Wages Expense account and a Wages Payable account.
3. Assuming that the firm has transferred funds from its regular bank account to its special payroll bank account, and that this entry has been made, prepare a general journal entry to record the payment of wages.

P.O. 1,4,5

Problem 8-4A The information for Tanger Company, shown in the chart below, is available from Tanger's time cards and the employees' individual earnings records for the pay period ended December 22.

Name	Hours Worked	Earnings at End of Previous Week	Total Earnings	Class.	Federal Income Tax	Other Deduct.	
Cgo, C.	44	31,670	1,650	Sales	199.00	UW	25.00
Don, V.	42	36,410	1,940	Sales	218.00	AR	95.00
Fine, J.	40	36,860	1,868	Sales	222.00	UW	25.00
Ginny, N.	46	33,590	1,785	Office	190.00	UW	35.00
John, M.	47	36,980	1,835	Office	210.00	UW	25.00
Lund, D.	43	93,240	2,100	Office	325.00	UW	20.00
Maya, R.	42	36,860	1,846	Sales	238.00	AR	70.00
Nord, P.	41	36,750	1,850	Sales	224.00	UW	20.00
Oscar, T.	43	33,480	1,750	Sales	208.00	UW	25.00
Troy, B.	40	47,250	1,170	Sales	116.00	UW	20.00

Taxable earnings for Social Security are based on the first $94,200. Taxable earnings for Medicare are based on all earnings. Taxable earnings for federal and state unemployment are based on the first $7,000.

Check Figure

Net amount, $13,993.41

Instructions

1. Complete the payroll register, page 56, using a Social Security tax rate of 6.2 percent and a Medicare tax rate of 1.45 percent. Concerning Other Deductions, AR refers to Accounts Receivable and UW refers to United Way. Begin payroll checks in the payroll register with No. 914.

2. Prepare the general journal entry to record the payroll. The firm's general ledger contains a Salary Expense account and a Salaries Payable account.
3. Prepare the general journal entry to pay the payroll. Assume that funds for this payroll have been transferred to Cash—Payroll Bank Account and that this entry has been made.

PROBLEM SET B

For additional help, see the demonstration problem at the beginning of each chapter in your Working Papers.

P.O. 1,2,3

Problem 8-1B Ina Provo, an employee of Gellen Company, worked forty-four hours during the week of October 11 through 17. Her rate of pay is $17.50 per hour, and she receives time-and-a-half for all work in excess of forty hours per week. Provo is married and claims two allowances on her W-4 form. Her wages are subject to the following deductions:

a. Federal income tax (use the table in Figure 3, page 274).
b. Social Security tax at 6.2 percent.
c. Medicare tax at 1.45 percent.
d. Union dues, $32.00.
e. Medical insurance, $44.75.

Check Figure

Net pay, $602.67

Instructions

Compute her regular pay, overtime pay, gross pay, and net pay.

P.O. 1,2,4,5

Problem 8-2B Harris Company has the following payroll information for the pay period ended May 14:

| Name | Earnings at End of Previous Week | Daily Time | | | | | | Pay Rate | Federal Income Tax |
		M	T	W	T	F	S		
Grant, L.	7,536.00	8	8	8	8	8	0	18.00	132.00
Hamn, R.	6,496.00	8	8	8	8	8	0	18.10	124.00
Lisk, J.	6,798.00	0	8	8	8	8	8	17.80	126.00
Myre, G.	9,589.00	8	8	8	0	8	8	19.25	155.00
Segel, T.	6,585.00	8	8	8	8	8	6	17.95	135.00
Torgel, I.	7,501.00	0	8	8	8	8	8	18.70	133.00

Taxable earnings for Social Security are based on the first $94,200. Taxable earnings for Medicare are based on all earnings. Taxable earnings for federal and state unemployment are based on the first $7,000. Employees are paid time-and-a-half for work in excess of forty hours per week.

Instructions

1. Complete the payroll register, page 34. The Social Security tax rate is 6.2 percent, and the Medicare tax rate is 1.45 percent. Begin payroll checks with No. 744.
2. Prepare a general journal entry to record the payroll. The firm's general ledger contains a Wages Expense account and a Wages Payable account.
3. Assuming that the firm has transferred funds from its regular bank account to its special payroll bank account, and that this entry has been made, prepare a journal entry to record the payment of wages.

P.O. 1,2,3,4,5

Problem 8-3B Wilke Company pays its employees time-and-a-half for hours worked in excess of forty per week. The information available from time cards and employees' individual earnings records for the pay period ended September 21 is shown in the chart below.

Name	Earnings at End of Previous Week	Daily Time						Pay Rate	Income Tax Allowances
		M	T	W	T	F	S		
Bolt, D.	6,745.00	8	8	8	10	8	0	19.50	1
Dore, C.	36,240.00	8	8	8	8	8	0	25.00	2
Gayle, A.	32,730.00	8	10	8	8	8	0	24.50	2
Hale, R.	92,250.00	8	8	8	8	8	4	53.00	3
Jilly, B.	35,154.00	8	8	8	8	8	0	49.50	0
Karn, S.	29,938.00	8	8	9	8	8	0	20.50	2
Ober, N.	6,795.00	8	8	8	9	9	4	21.00	1
Wong, J.	27,252.00	8	8	10	8	8	0	20.00	2

Taxable earnings for Social Security are based on the first $94,200. Taxable earnings for Medicare are based on all earnings. Taxable earnings for federal and state unemployment are based on the first $7,000.

Instructions

1. Complete the payroll register, page 72, using the wage-bracket income tax withholding table in Figure 3 (page 274). The Social Security tax rate is 6.2 percent, and the Medicare tax rate is 1.45 percent. Assume that all employees are married. Note: Hale's federal income tax deduction is $393. Jilly's federal income tax deduction is $295. In the payroll register, begin payroll checks with No. 863.
2. Prepare a general journal entry to record the payroll. The firm's general ledger contains a Wages Expense account and a Wages Payable account.
3. Assuming that the firm has transferred funds from its regular bank account to its special payroll bank account, and that this entry has been made, prepare a general journal entry to record the payment of wages.

P.O. 1,4,5

Problem 8-4B For Morley Company, the information available from the time books and employees' individual earnings records for the pay period ended December 29 is shown in the chart below.

Name	Hours Worked	Earnings at End of Previous Week	Total Earnings	Class.	Federal Income Tax	Other Deduct.	
Chang, C.	44	33,900.00	1,740.00	Sales	180.00	AR	80.00
Dugan, T.	42	38,270.00	1,935.00	Sales	212.00	UW	20.00
Fancher, K.	40	37,680.00	1,848.00	Sales	200.00	UW	25.00
Gannon, T.	44	33,245.00	1,740.00	Office	187.00		———
Jones, L.	48	37,789.00	1,845.00	Office	289.00	UW	25.00
Lange, M.	40	93,700.00	2,005.00	Office	302.00	UW	35.00
Milton, D.	43	37,684.00	1,938.00	Sales	206.00	UW	20.00
Naylor, B.	40	37,499.00	1,856.00	Sales	209.00		———
Orton, A.	44	34,338.00	1,780.00	Sales	201.00	AR	70.00
Tiosha, J.	42	48,120.00	1,065.00	Sales	190.00	UW	25.00

Taxable earnings for Social Security are based on the first $94,200. Taxable earnings for Medicare are based on all earnings. Taxable earnings for federal and state unemployment are based on the first $7,000.

Check Figure

Net amount, $14,011.28

Instructions

1. Complete the payroll register, page 56, using a Social Security tax rate of 6.2 percent and a Medicare tax rate of 1.45 percent. Concerning Other Deductions, AR refers to Accounts Receivable and UW refers to United Way. Begin payroll checks in the payroll register with No. 914.
2. Prepare the general journal entry to record the payroll. The firm's general ledger contains a Salary Expense account and a Salaries Payable account.
3. Prepare the general journal entry to pay the payroll. Assume that funds for this payroll have been transferred to Cash—Payroll Bank Account and that this entry has been made.

Not only do you pay payroll taxes, but your employers pay their share, also! They deposit the federal taxes they withhold from your paycheck, as well as the FICA taxes they are required to pay, in an authorized commercial bank or in the Federal Reserve Bank using federal tax deposit coupons (Form 8109-B). Electronic deposits are required for companies with larger payrolls. The whole process of withholding and paying taxes can often seem complicated and confusing. As a service to taxpayers, the Internal Revenue Service (IRS) website provides convenient access to tax information, forms, and publications. Employers' requirements for making deposits begin on page 19 of Publication 15 (Circular E), which can be found at **http://www.irs.gov/pub/irs-pdf/p15.pdf.** You might be surprised at the extent of the requirements for something as simple as making a deposit!

Performance Objectives

After you have completed this chapter, you will be able to do the following:

1. Calculate the amount of payroll tax expense and journalize the entry.

2. Journalize the entry for the deposit of employees' federal income taxes withheld and FICA taxes (both employees' withheld and employer's matching share) and prepare the deposit coupon.

3. Journalize the entries for the payment of employer's state and federal unemployment taxes.

4. Journalize the entry for the deposit of employees' state income taxes withheld.

5. Complete Employer's Quarterly Federal Tax Return, Form 941.

6. Prepare W-2 and W-3 forms and Form 940.

7. Calculate the premium for workers' compensation insurance, and prepare the entry for payment in advance.

8. Determine the amount of the end-of-the-year adjustments for (a) workers' compensation insurance and (b) accrued salaries and wages, and record the adjustments.

We have talked about computing and recording such payroll data as gross pay, employees' income tax withheld, employees' FICA tax withheld, and various deductions requested by employees. Now we will pay these withholding liabilities and the taxes levied on the employer.

EMPLOYER IDENTIFICATION NUMBER

Everyone who works must have a Social Security number, a vital part of federal income tax returns. An employer's counterpart to the Social Security number is the **employer identification number** assigned by the Internal Revenue Service. Employers of one or more persons are required to have such a number, and it must be listed on all reports and payments of employees' federal income tax withholding and FICA taxes.

EMPLOYER'S PAYROLL TAXES

An employer's payroll taxes are based on the gross wages paid to employees. Payroll taxes—like property taxes—are an expense of doing business. Goren Company records these taxes in the **Payroll Tax Expense** account and debits the account for the company's portion of FICA taxes and for state and federal unemployment taxes. In T account form, Payroll Tax Expense for Goren Company would look like the following example.

<table>
<tr><th colspan="2" align="center">Payroll Tax Expense</th></tr>
<tr><td align="center">+</td><td align="center">−</td></tr>
<tr><td>FICA tax (employer's
  matching portion)
State unemployment tax
Federal unemployment tax</td><td>Closed at the end of the
  year along with all other
  expense accounts</td></tr>
</table>

The skyrocketing costs of Medicare have caused Congress and the president to try to make sweeping reforms. The issues are far-reaching. Medicare affects a large percentage of the population—who fear their benefits may be reduced.

As you can see, **FICA tax (employer's share), state unemployment tax, and federal unemployment tax are included under the Payroll Tax Expense heading.** In most states, the unemployment taxes are levied on the employer only.

Employer's Matching Portion of FICA Tax (Social Security Plus Medicare)

FICA tax is imposed equally on both employer and employee. After the firm's accountant deducts the employee's share from gross wages and records it in the payroll entry under FICA Tax Payable, he or she then determines the employer's share by multiplying the employer's tax rates (assumed to be 6.2 percent (.062) for Social Security and 1.45 percent (.0145) for Medicare) by the taxable earnings (assumed to be a maximum of $94,200 for Social Security and all earnings for Medicare). The same tax rates apply to both the employer and the employees.

The accountant gets the Social Security and Medicare taxable earnings amounts from the payroll register. In Figure 1, on the following page, we present the Taxable Earnings columns taken from the payroll register for the week ended October 7.

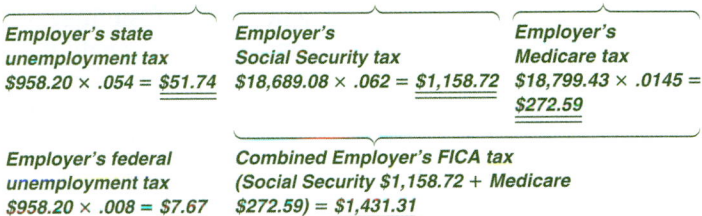

| | | | (7) TAXABLE EARNINGS | | |
| | | | Amount of employees' earnings for the period that has not, as yet, been taxed as part of the $7,000 maximum liability | Amount of employees' earnings that are less than $94,200 per employee for the year | Amount of all employees' earnings |

	NAME	TOTAL HOURS	TOTAL	ENDING CUMULATIVE EARNINGS	UNEMPLOYMENT	SOCIAL SECURITY	MEDICARE
1	Amano, Mark E.	46	1 1 2 4 58	46 0 8 4 58		1 1 2 4 58	1 1 2 4 58
2	Barkov, Anna E.	45	7 4 4 20	6 7 3 1 20	7 4 4 20	7 4 4 20	7 4 4 20
3	Dorn, David L.	49	9 1 6 00	7 7 0 2 00	2 1 4 00	9 1 6 00	9 1 6 00
4	Felding, Sarah H.	40	1 0 8 4 50	39 5 4 6 50		1 0 8 4 50	1 0 8 4 50
5	Graham, Jason W.	40	1 7 9 8 45	70 3 9 8 45		1 7 9 8 45	1 7 9 8 45
6	Kilmer, Richard B.	40	1 8 9 5 58	70 3 9 5 58		1 8 9 5 58	1 8 9 5 58
7	Mankowitz, Jim J.	55	1 8 4 4 30	39 6 9 4 30		1 8 4 4 30	1 8 4 4 30
8	Orlene, Barbara A.	40	1 4 8 7 20	47 3 0 7 20		1 4 8 7 20	1 4 8 7 20
9	Parker, William R.	44	1 7 7 6 28	48 2 0 6 28		1 7 7 6 28	1 7 7 6 28
10	Rumberg, Shelly L.	45	1 9 4 9 16	56 8 1 6 16		1 9 4 9 16	1 9 4 9 16
11	Tabor, Annette G.	40	1 1 6 8 83	43 9 0 8 83		1 1 6 8 83	1 1 6 8 83
12	Walker, Susan	52	3 0 1 0 35	94 3 1 0 35		2 9 0 0 00	3 0 1 0 35
13			18 7 9 9 43	571 1 0 1 43	9 5 8 20	18 6 8 9 08	18 7 9 9 43

FIGURE 1

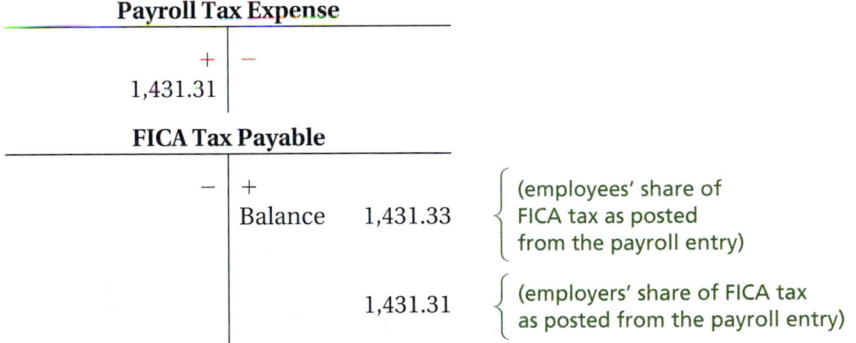

Employer's state unemployment tax
$958.20 × .054 = $51.74

Employer's Social Security tax
$18,689.08 × .062 = $1,158.72

Employer's Medicare tax
$18,799.43 × .0145 = $272.59

Employer's federal unemployment tax
$958.20 × .008 = $7.67

Combined Employer's FICA tax
(Social Security $1,158.72 + Medicare $272.59) = $1,431.31

Before we look at the journal entry to record the employer's share of FICA tax, let's look at the entry in T account form.

Payroll Tax Expense

+	−
1,431.31	

FICA Tax Payable

−	+
	Balance 1,431.33 { (employees' share of FICA tax as posted from the payroll entry)
	1,431.31 { (employers' share of FICA tax as posted from the payroll entry)

Note particularly that the FICA Tax Payable account is often used for both the tax liability of the employer and the amounts withheld from the employees. This is logical because both FICA taxes are paid at the same time and to the same place. There may be a slight difference between the employer's and the employees' share of FICA taxes because of the rounding process. For the employees' share, the accountant uses the total of the employees' Social Security and Medicare tax deductions. For the employer's share, the accountant multiplies the total taxable earnings (Social Security and Medicare) by the tax rates.

Employer's State Unemployment Tax

The proceeds of the state unemployment tax (SUTA), which is levied only on the employer in most states, are used to pay subsistence benefits to unemployed workers. The rate of the state unemployment tax varies considerably among the states. Assume that Goren Company is subject to a rate of 5.4 percent (.054) of the first $7,000 of each employee's earnings (the same base amount as for the federal unemployment tax). As shown in the portion of the payroll register illustrated in Figure 1, $958.20 of earnings are subject to the state unemployment tax. Accordingly, by T accounts, the state unemployment tax based on taxable earnings is as follows:

Payroll Tax Expense		State Unemployment Tax Payable	
+	−	−	+
(958.20 × .054)			(958.20 × .054)
51.74			51.74

Employer's Federal Unemployment Tax

The federal unemployment tax (FUTA) is paid only by the employer. Congress may from time to time change the rate. Let's assume a rate of 0.8 percent (.008) of the first $7,000 earned by each employee during the calendar year. For the weekly payroll period for Goren Company, the tax liability is $7.67 ($958.20 of unemployment taxable earnings, taken from the payroll register, multiplied by .008, the tax rate). The T account is as follows:

Payroll Tax Expense		Federal Unemployment Tax Payable	
+	−	−	+
(958.20 × .008)			(958.20 × .008)
7.67			7.67

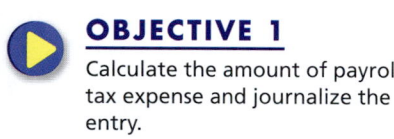

OBJECTIVE 1

Calculate the amount of payroll tax expense and journalize the entry.

To make things clearer, figures for the employer's three payroll taxes have been presented separately. Now let's combine all of this information into one entry, which follows the regular payroll entry. Goren Company pays its employees weekly, so it also makes its Payroll Tax Expense entry weekly.

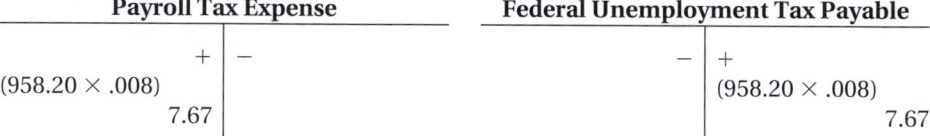

	DATE		DESCRIPTION	POST. REF.	DEBIT	CREDIT	
17	Oct.	7	Payroll Tax Expense		1 4 9 0 72		17
18			FICA Tax Payable			1 4 3 1 31	18
19			State Unemployment Tax				19
20			Payable			5 1 74	20
21			Federal Unemployment Tax				21
22			Payable			7 67	22
23			To record employer's share				23
24			of FICA tax and employer's				24
25			state and federal				25
26			unemployment taxes.				26
27							27
28							28

JOURNAL ENTRIES FOR RECORDING PAYROLL

At this point, let's restate in general journal form the entries that have already been recorded. We'll do this so that you can see the sequence of the payroll entries. First, the entry to record the payroll is journalized.

	DATE		DESCRIPTION	POST. REF.	DEBIT	CREDIT	
1	20–						1
2	Oct.	7	Sales Wages Expense		14 3 3 2 15		2
3			Office Wages Expense		4 4 6 7 28		3
4			Employees' Federal Income				4
5			Tax Payable			2 8 3 8 00	5
6			FICA Tax Payable			1 4 3 1 33	6
7			Employees' State Income Tax				7
8			Payable			5 6 7 60	8
9			Employees' Medical Insurance				9
10			Payable			3 2 0 70	10
11			Employees' United Way				11
12			Payable			1 8 5 00	12
13			Accounts Receivable			3 0 00	13
14			Wages Payable			13 4 2 6 80	14
15			Payroll register, page 56,				15
16			for week ended October 7.				16
17							17

Next, the entry to record the employer's payroll taxes is journalized.

REMEMBER!

The sequence of steps for recording the payroll entries is: (1) record the payroll for the present period in the payroll register; (2) based on the payroll register, record the payroll entry in the journal; (3) based on the Taxable Earnings columns of the payroll register, record Payroll Tax Expense in the journal; (4) make a journal entry to pay the employees.

	DATE		DESCRIPTION	POST. REF.	DEBIT	CREDIT	
18		7	Payroll Tax Expense		1 4 9 0 72		18
19			FICA Tax Payable			1 4 3 1 31	19
20			State Unemployment Tax				20
21			Payable			5 1 74	21
22			Federal Unemployment Tax				22
23			Payable			7 67	23
24			To record employer's share				24
25			of FICA tax and employer's				25
26			state and federal				26
27			unemployment taxes.				27
28							28

Finally, the entry to pay the employees is journalized. Goren Company issues one check payable to a payroll bank account. To pay its employees, it will draw separate payroll checks on this payroll account. (The entry to transfer cash to the payroll bank account is not shown here.)

DATE		DESCRIPTION	POST. REF.	DEBIT	CREDIT	
29	8	Wages Payable		13 4 2 6 80		29
30		Cash—Payroll Bank Account			13 4 2 6 80	30
31		Paid salaries for week				31
32		ended October 7.				32
33						33

As stated previously, in the first payroll entry, small employers will credit Cash directly instead of Wages Payable. These employers issue separate checks out of their regular bank accounts for each employee.

Next, we describe the entries for paying withholdings for employees' federal income tax and FICA tax and the employer's matching share of FICA tax. We also show the entries for paying the federal and state unemployment taxes and the withholdings for employees' state income tax.

PAYMENTS OF FICA TAX AND EMPLOYEES' FEDERAL INCOME TAX WITHHOLDING

OBJECTIVE 2

Journalize the entry for the deposit of employees' federal income taxes withheld and FICA taxes (both employees' withheld and employer's matching share) and prepare the deposit coupon.

FYI

There are penalties applied for late deposits of federal taxes.

After paying employees, the employer must make payments in the form of federal tax deposits. A deposit includes the combined total of three items: (1) employees' federal income taxes withheld, (2) employees' FICA taxes withheld, and (3) employer's share of FICA taxes. Employers make these deposits on a pay-as-you-go basis.

Deposits are made to authorized commercial banks or Federal Reserve banks and handled through automated clearing-houses. Electronic deposits are required for companies with larger payrolls. The timing of these deposits depends on the amounts owed. The calendar year is broken into days, semi-weekly periods, months, and **quarters** (3 consecutive months).

Employers submit a return, Form 941, every quarter. The due dates for filing this return are as follows:

Quarter	Ending Date of Quarter	Due Date for Form 941
January–February–March	March 31	April 30
April–May–June	June 30	July 31
July–August–September	September 30	October 31
October–November–December	December 31	January 31

Federal Tax Deposit Coupon

FYI

We will show a Form 941 later in this chapter.

Let's go back to Goren Company, where tax payments were up to date. From the payroll of October 7, the following federal taxes are owed:

Employees' federal income taxes withheld	$2,838.00
Employees' FICA taxes withheld	1,431.33
Employer's share of FICA taxes	1,431.31
Total federal undeposited taxes	$5,700.64

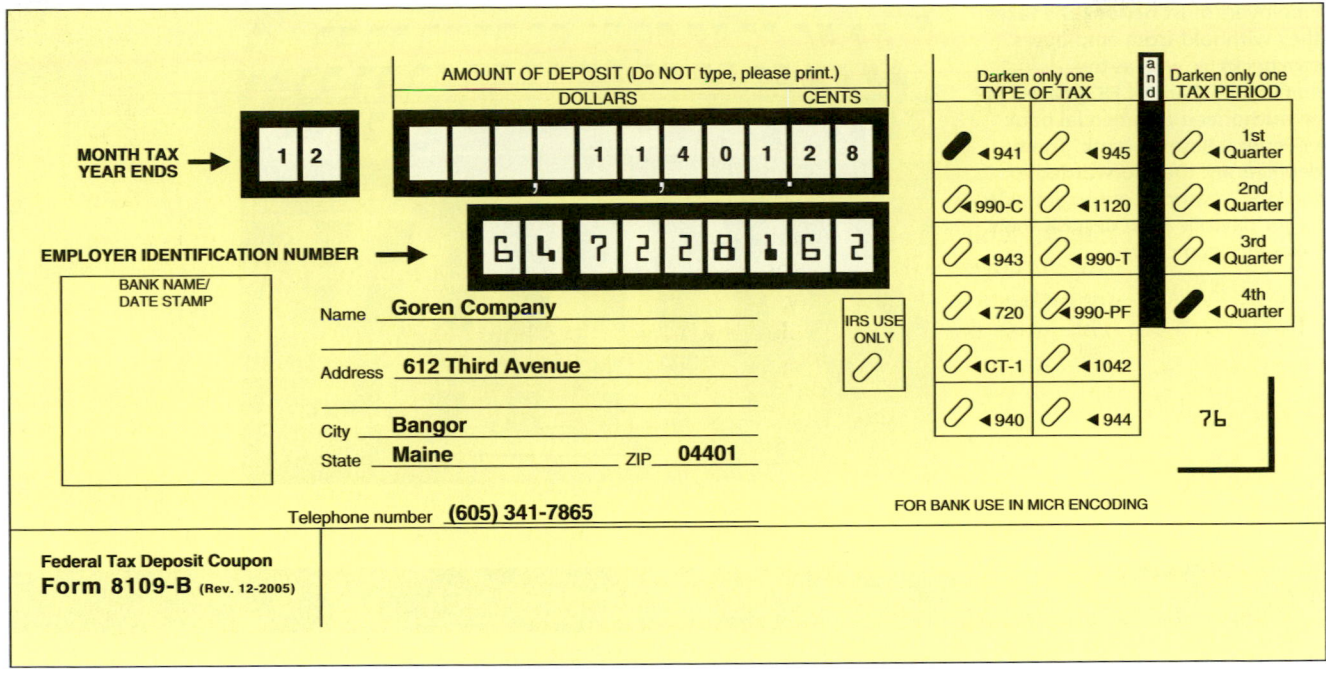

FIGURE 2

We continue on for the next payroll period, ended October 14. Assuming the payroll information for the week is the same as it was for the week ended October 7, the two periods would be:

	Oct. 7	Oct. 14	Total
Employees' federal income taxes withheld	$2,838.00	$2,838.00	$ 5,676.00
Employees' FICA taxes withheld	1,431.33	1,431.33	2,862.66
Employer's share of FICA taxes	1,431.31	1,431.31	2,862.62
Total federal undeposited taxes	$5,700.64	$5,700.64	$11,401.28

Goren Company, which deposits taxes semiweekly, receives a federal tax deposit card (printed with the company's name and employer identification number) from the Internal Revenue Service (Figure 2).

The accountant records the amount of the deposit, the employer identification number (unless preprinted), the type of tax, the tax period, and the name and address of the company. The entry in general journal form to record the deposit of two weeks' taxes looks like the following.

FYI

Because of rounding differences, the employee and employer amounts of FICA taxes may differ slightly. Line 7a of the 941 Form accommodates this difference.

	DATE		DESCRIPTION	POST. REF.	DEBIT	CREDIT	
1	20–						1
2	Oct.	15	Employees' Federal Income Tax				2
3			Payable		5 6 7 6 00		3
4			FICA Tax Payable		5 7 2 5 28		4
5			Cash			11 4 0 1 28	5
6			Issued check for federal tax				6
7			deposit, Bangor Bank.				7

Employers must deposit the taxes they withhold from employees' paychecks, as well as the employer's share of FICA taxes, in an authorized commercial bank or Federal Reserve bank. These deposits are then forwarded to the U.S. Treasury. Companies with larger payrolls must deposit their taxes electronically.

PAYMENTS OF STATE UNEMPLOYMENT INSURANCE

OBJECTIVE 3

Journalize the entries for the payment of employer's state and federal unemployment taxes.

As we stated before, states differ with regard to both the rate and the taxable base for unemployment insurance. In our example, we assume that the state tax is 5.4 percent (.054) of the first $7,000 paid to each employee during the calendar year. **The state tax is usually paid quarterly and is due by the end of the month following the end of the quarter (the same as the due dates for Form 941).** Here's the entry in general journal form made by Goren Company for the first quarter (covering the months of January, February, and March). We assume that $60,325 was taxable for the quarter. The amount of the tax is $3,257.55 ($60,325 × 0.054).

	DATE		DESCRIPTION	POST. REF.	DEBIT	CREDIT	
1	20–						1
2	Apr.	30	State Unemployment Tax				2
3			Payable		3 2 5 7 55		3
4			Cash			3 2 5 7 55	4
5			Issued check for payment of				5
6			state unemployment tax.				6

The T accounts are as follows:

Cash		State Unemployment Tax Payable	
+	−	−	+
	Apr. 30 3,257.55		Mar. 31
		Apr. 30 3,257.55	Balance 3,257.55

The March 31 balance in State Unemployment Tax Payable is the result of weekly entries recording the state unemployment portion of payroll tax expense. After the payment is made on April 30, the balance is shown as zero for illustrative purposes. However, throughout the month of April, the company would be making weekly entries to record the tax liability and tax expense.

PAYMENTS OF FEDERAL UNEMPLOYMENT TAX

The FUTA tax is calculated quarterly, during the month following the end of each calendar quarter. **If the accumulated tax liability is greater than $100, the tax is deposited in a commercial bank or Federal Reserve bank, accompanied by a preprinted federal tax deposit card** like that used to deposit employees' federal income tax withholding and FICA taxes. The deposit may also be made electronically. The due date for this deposit is the last day of the month following the end of the quarter, the same as the due dates for the Employer's Quarterly Federal Tax Return and for state unemployment taxes.

Here is the entry in general journal form made by Goren Company for the first quarter. In our example, since the FUTA and state unemployment taxable earnings are the same (the first $7,000 for each employee), we assume that $60,325 was taxable for the quarter. The amount of the tax is $482.60 ($60,325 × 0.008).

	DATE		DESCRIPTION	POST. REF.	DEBIT	CREDIT	
1	20–						1
2	Apr.	30	Federal Unemployment Tax				2
3			Payable		4 8 2 60		3
4			Cash			4 8 2 60	4
5			Issued check for deposit of				5
6			federal unemployment tax.				6
7							7

The T accounts are as follows:

Cash			Federal Unemployment Tax Payable		
+	–		–	+	
	Apr. 30 482.60			Mar. 31	
			Apr. 30 482.60	Balance 482.60	

The balance in Federal Unemployment Tax Payable is the result of weekly entries recording the federal unemployment portion of payroll tax expense.

DEPOSITS OF EMPLOYEES' STATE INCOME TAX WITHHOLDING

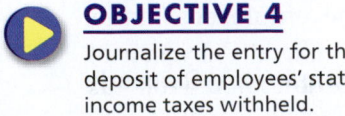

OBJECTIVE 4

Journalize the entry for the deposit of employees' state income taxes withheld.

Assume that the withholdings for employees' state income taxes are deposited on a quarterly basis, payable at the same time as state unemployment tax. Also, as of March 31, the credit balance of Employees' State Income Tax Payable is $1,674.10. The entry in general journal form to record the payment for the first quarter takes the following form.

	DATE		DESCRIPTION	POST. REF.	DEBIT	CREDIT	
1	20–						1
2	Apr.	30	Employees' State Income Tax				2
3			Payable		1 6 7 4 10		3
4			Cash			1 6 7 4 10	4
5			Issued check for state				5
6			income tax deposit.				6
7							7

The T accounts are as follows:

Cash			
+	−		
	Apr. 30	1,674.10	

Employees' State Income Tax Payable			
−		+	
		Mar. 31	
Apr. 30	1,674.10	Balance	1,674.10

EMPLOYER'S QUARTERLY FEDERAL TAX RETURN (FORM 941)

OBJECTIVE 5

Complete Employer's Quarterly Federal Tax Return, Form 941.

If you are an employer, you must file a quarterly **Form 941**, Employer's Quarterly Federal Tax Return. The purpose of Form 941 is to report the tax liability for withholdings of employees' federal income tax and FICA taxes, and also the employer's share of FICA taxes. Total tax deposits are also listed. As the title implies, the time period is three months. Remember that the due dates for the calendar year are: first quarter, April 30; second quarter, July 31; third quarter, October 31; fourth quarter, January 31.

A completed Form 941 for Goren Company is shown in Figure 3. There are six parts to this form. Figure 3 shows the information for Goren Company for Parts 1 and 2. Part 3 is used when you close your business and stop paying wages—this will also stop the IRS from automatically sending 941 forms. Part 4 is for you to give the IRS permission—or not—to speak with your third-party designee (employee, paid tax preparer for example). Part 5 is the signature, title, and date block for the employer. Part 6 is the signature, firm information, employer identification number (EIN), and date block for any paid preparer of the 941 form. You can go online at **http://www.irs.gov** and enter Form 941 into the search window. For the instructions, type 941 instructions into the search window.

The top of the form contains basic information about the employer. Once an employer has secured an identification number and has filed the first return, the Internal Revenue Service automatically sends forms directly to the employer. These subsequent forms will have the employer's name, address, and identification number filled in.

Now let's look at completed Parts 1 and 2 of an Employer's Quarterly Federal Tax Return (Form 941) starting with its heading.

Form 941 for 2006: Employer's QUARTERLY Federal Tax Return

(Rev. January 2006)   Department of the Treasury — Internal Revenue Service

990106

OMB No. 1545-0029

(EIN)
Employer identification number   6 4 – 7 2 2 8 1 6 2

Name (not your trade name)

Trade name (if any)   **Goren Company**

Address   **612 Third Avenue**
Number   Street   Suite or room number

Bangor   **ME**   **04401**
City   State   ZIP code

Report for this Quarter ...
(Check one.)

☐ 1: January, February, March
☐ 2: April, May, June
☐ 3: July, August, September
☒ 4: October, November, December

Read the separate instructions before you fill out this form. Please type or print within the boxes.

Part 1: Answer these questions for this quarter.

1 Number of employees who received wages, tips, or other compensation for the pay period including: *Mar. 12* (Quarter 1), *June 12* (Quarter 2), *Sept. 12* (Quarter 3), *Dec. 12* (Quarter 4)   1   **12**

2 Wages, tips, and other compensation   2   **216,252.00**

3 Total income tax withheld from wages, tips, and other compensation   3   **39,768.00**

4 If no wages, tips, and other compensation are subject to social security or Medicare tax .   ☐ Check and go to line 6.

5 Taxable social security and Medicare wages and tips:

	Column 1		Column 2
5a Taxable social security wages	130,080.00	× .124 =	16,129.92
5b Taxable social security tips	.	× .124 =	.
5c Taxable Medicare wages & tips	216,252.00	× .029 =	6,271.31

5d Total social security and Medicare taxes (*Column 2*, lines 5a + 5b + 5c = line 5d) .   5d   **22,401.23**

6 Total taxes before adjustments (lines 3 + 5d = line 6)   6   **62,169.23**

7 **TAX ADJUSTMENTS** (Read the instructions for line 7 before completing lines 7a through 7h.):

7a Current quarter's fractions of cents . . . .   — .

7b Current quarter's sick pay . . . .   — .

7c Current quarter's adjustments for tips and group-term life insurance   — .

7d Current year's income tax withholding (attach Form 941c) . .   — .

7e Prior quarters' social security and Medicare taxes (attach Form 941c)   — .

7f Special additions to federal income tax (attach Form 941c) . . .   — .

7g Special additions to social security and Medicare (attach Form 941c)   — .

7h **TOTAL ADJUSTMENTS** (Combine all amounts: lines 7a through 7g.) . . . .   7h   — .

8 Total taxes after adjustments (Combine lines 6 and 7h.)   8   **62,169.23**

9 Advance earned income credit (EIC) payments made to employees   9   — .

10 Total taxes after adjustment for advance EIC (line 8 – line 9 = line 10)   10   **62,169.23**

11 Total deposits for this quarter, including overpayment applied from a prior quarter . . .   11   **62,169.23**

12 Balance due (If line 10 is more than line 11, write the difference here.)   12   **-0-.**
Make checks payable to *United States Treasury*.

13 Overpayment (If line 11 is more than line 10, write the difference here.)   — .   Check one ☐ Apply to next return
☐ Send a refund.

▶ You **MUST** fill out both pages of this form and **SIGN** it.   Next ➡

Part 2: Tell us about your deposit schedule and tax liability for this quarter.

If you are unsure about whether you are a monthly schedule depositor or a semiweekly schedule depositor, see *Pub. 15 (Circular E)*, section 11.

14   **M E**   Write the state abbreviation for the state where you made your deposits OR write "MU" if you made your deposits in *multiple* states.

15 Check one: ☐ Line 10 is less than $2,500. Go to Part 3.

☐ You were a monthly schedule depositor for the entire quarter. Fill out your tax liability for each month. Then go to Part 3.

Tax liability: Month 1   .

Month 2   .

Month 3   .

Total liability for quarter   .   Total must equal line 10.

☒ You were a semiweekly schedule depositor for any part of this quarter. Fill out *Schedule B (Form 941): Report of Tax Liability for Semiweekly Schedule Depositors*, and attach it to this form.

FIGURE 3

Questions Listed on Form 941 (Figure 3)

Tax forms can be somewhat intimidating. The best approach to completing a tax form is to have accurate and complete records, read and complete the form line by line, and don't look ahead. Goren Company's fourth quarter form, shown in Figure 3, has been completed as follows. Note that the employees at Goren earn wages. Had they also earned tips or other compensation, such as bonuses, those would have been included in the form.

Part 1:

1. Line 1 indicates the number of employees (12) who received wages.
2. Line 2 shows the total of those wages for the quarter ($216,252.00).
3. Line 3 shows the total income tax withheld from wages for the quarter ($39,768.00).
4. Line 4 is not checked because all wages during the quarter are subject to Medicare tax.
5. Lines 5a–d provide information that indicates how the total of the Social Security and Medicare taxes ($16,129.92 + $6,271.31 = $22,401.23) is calculated. Note that the multipliers represent the combined employee and employer contributions (for Social Security, $.062 \times 2 = .124$; for Medicare, $.0145 \times 2 = .029$).
6. Line 6 ($62,169.23) is the total of the income taxes withheld (line 3) and the Social Security and Medicare taxes (line 5d), before adjustments.
7. Lines 7a–h indicate any tax adjustments that may be needed. Goren Company did not have any of those for the quarter. Note that these adjustments may be for fractions of cents due to rounding (line 7a), corrections of errors in earlier filings of Form 941 (lines 7b–e), or as a result of a notice from the IRS (lines 7f and 7g).
8. Line 8 shows the total taxes after adjustments (line 6 plus line 7h = $62,169.23).
9. Line 9 discloses any payments of advanced earned income credit (EIC), a refundable federal income tax credit for low-income working individuals and families, that may have been made to employees. Goren Company did not have any this quarter.
10. Line 10 is the total of lines 8 and 9 ($62,169.23).
11. Line 11 shows the total deposits ($62,169.23) made by Goren Company for this quarter and includes any overpayments from prior quarters. As indicated, the company has made deposits equaling the total due for this quarter.
12. Lines 12 (underpayment) and 13 (overpayment), which indicate the difference between lines 10 and 11, show that the company's balance for the quarter is zero.

Part 2:

13. Line 14 shows ME, the abbreviation for Maine, the state in which the deposits were made.
14. Line 15 shows a checkmark in the third box because Goren Company was a semiweekly scheduled depositor for part of this quarter.

As stated earlier, the remaining parts of the 941 form require stating whether your business is closing, permission to allow third-party inquiries, signatures and titles of the preparer, and the date Form 941 is submitted. For thorough instructions to assist you in filling out any IRS form, go to **http://www.irs.gov** and enter the form or descriptive words into the search box.

a Control number		Safe, accurate, FAST! Use 	Visit the IRS website at www.irs.gov/efile.
22222 OMB No. 1545-0008			

b Employer identification number (EIN)	1 Wages, tips, other compensation	2 Federal income tax withheld
64-7228162	58,404.58	10,920.00

c Employer's name, address, and ZIP code	3 Social security wages	4 Social security tax withheld
	58,404.58	3,621.08
Goren Company	5 Medicare wages and tips	6 Medicare tax withheld
612 Third Avenue	58,404.58	846.87
Bangor, Maine 04401	7 Social security tips	8 Allocated tips
	0	

d Employee's social security number	9 Advance EIC payment	10 Dependent care benefits
543-24-1680	0	0

e Employee's first name and initial Last name Suff.	11 Nonqualified plans	12a See instructions for box 12
	0	
Mark E. Amano	13 Statutory employee ☐ Retirement plan ☐ Third-party sick pay ☐	12b
6357 Boston Lane		
Bangor, Maine 04401	14 Other	12c
		12d

f Employee's address and ZIP code

15 State	Employer's state ID number	16 State wages, tips, etc.	17 State income tax	18 Local wages, tips, etc.	19 Local income tax	20 Locality name
ME	464-729	58,404.58	2,184.00	0	0	0

Form **W-2** Wage and Tax Statement   **20____**   Department of the Treasury—Internal Revenue Service

Copy B—To Be Filed With Employee's FEDERAL Tax Return.
This information is being furnished to the Internal Revenue Service.

FIGURE 4

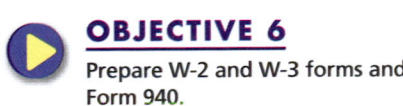

Wage Withholding Statements for Employees (Form W-2)

OBJECTIVE 6

Prepare W-2 and W-3 forms and Form 940.

After the end of a year (December 31) and by the following January 31, the employer must furnish for each employee a Wage and Tax Statement, known as **Form W-2**. This form contains information about the employee's earnings and tax deductions for the year. The source of the information used to complete Form W-2 is the employee's individual earnings record. The amounts used to complete Mark E. Amano's W-2 form (in Figure 4) represent the amounts taken from his earnings record at the end of the calendar year, December 31.

Box 9 shows the total paid to the employee as advance earned income credit (EIC) payments. Box 13 is used for miscellaneous items, such as sick pay that is not included in income because the employee contributed to the sick pay plan. This box is also used for employer-provided group term life insurance in excess of $50,000. Statutory employees are life insurance and traveling salespersons. Box 14 may include the value of noncash fringe benefits, such as providing a vehicle for the employee.

The accountant will prepare at least four copies of the W-2 form for each employee.

Copy A—Employer sends to the Social Security Administration.

Copy B—Employer gives to employee to be attached to the employee's individual federal income tax return.

Copy C—Employer gives to employee to be kept for his or her personal records.

Copy D—Employer keeps this copy as a record of payments made.

If state and local income taxes are withheld, the employer prepares additional copies to be sent to the appropriate tax agency.

Employer's Annual Federal Income Tax Reports (Form W-3)

Accompanying copy A of the employees' W-2 forms, Goren Company sends **Form W-3**, Transmittal of Wage and Tax Statements, to the Social Security Administration. This form is due on February 28, following the end of the calendar year.

For all employees, Form W-3 shows the total wages and tips, total federal income tax withheld, total Social Security and Medicare taxable wages, total Social Security and Medicare tax withheld, and other information. These amounts must be the same as the grand totals of the W-2 forms and the four quarterly 941 forms for the year. Goren Company's completed Form W-3 is presented in Figure 5.

Some boxes deserve an explanation. Box d, establishment number, may be used for a company that has separate establishments, with each establishment filing W-2 and W-3 forms separately. Box 9 is used for recording the amount of advance earned income credits shown on W-2 forms for qualified employees. Box h is used by a company that had more than one employer identification number (EIN) during the year.

To sum up thus far: The employer must submit the following at the end of the calendar year: Employer's Quarterly Federal Tax Return, Form 941, for the fourth quarter by January 31; Wage and Tax Statements, Form W-2, for all employees by January 31; Transmittal of Wage and Tax Statements, Form W-3, by February 28.

REPORTS AND PAYMENTS OF FEDERAL UNEMPLOYMENT TAX

As we stated previously, generally all employers are subject to the Federal Unemployment Tax Act. These employers must submit an Employer's Annual Federal Unemployment Tax Return, Form 940, not later than January 31 following the close of the calendar year. This deadline may be extended until February 10 if the employer has made deposits paying the FUTA tax liability in full. **Form 940** shows total wages paid to employees, total wages subject to federal unemployment tax, and other information.

DO NOT STAPLE

a Control number	33333	For Official Use Only ▶ OMB No. 1545-0008		

b Kind of Payer ▶	941 [X] Military [ ] 943 [ ] 944 [ ] CT-1 [ ] Hshld. emp. [ ] Medicare govt. emp. [ ] Third-party sick pay [ ]	1 Wages, tips, other compensation **861,530.00**	2 Federal income tax withheld **103,383.60**
		3 Social security wages **775,358.00**	4 Social security tax withheld **48,072.20**
c Total number of Forms W-2 **12**	d Establishment number – – – – – –	5 Medicare wages and tips **861,530.00**	6 Medicare tax withheld **12,492.19**
e Employer identification number (EIN) **64-7228162**		7 Social security tips **0**	8 Allocated tips **0**
f Employer's name **Goren Company** **612 Third Avenue** **Bangor, Maine 04401**		9 Advance EIC payments **0**	10 Dependent care benefits **0**
		11 Nonqualified plans **0**	12 Deferred compensation **0**
		13 For third-party sick pay use only	
		14 Income tax withheld by payer of third-party sick pay **0**	
g Employer's address and ZIP code			
h Other EIN used this year **0**			
15 State Employer's state ID number **464-729**		16 State wages, tips, etc.	17 State income tax
		18 Local wages, tips, etc.	19 Local income tax
Contact person **Eileen Goren**	Telephone number **(605) 341-1465**	For Official Use Only
Email address **egoren@fastlink.net**	Fax number **(605) 341-1477**	

Under penalties of perjury, I declare that I have examined this return and accompanying documents, and, to the best of my knowledge and belief, they are true, correct, and complete.

Signature ▶ *Eileen Goren*   Title ▶ *Owner*   Date ▶ 2/27/20--

Form **W-3** **Transmittal of Wage and Tax Statements**   **20__**   Department of the Treasury Internal Revenue Service

FIGURE 5

Using Goren Company as our example, federal unemployment taxable earnings by quarter are as follows:

Federal Unemployment Tax	1st Quarter	2nd Quarter	3rd Quarter	4th Quarter	Cumulative Total
Taxable earnings	$60,325	$9,485	$10,316	$3,520	$83,646
Tax rate	× .008	× .008	× .008	× .008	× .008
Tax liability	$482.60	$75.88	$ 82.53	$28.16	$669.17

We now repeat the journal entry for the first quarter, in which $482.60 was deposited on April 30.

	DATE		DESCRIPTION	POST. REF.	DEBIT	CREDIT	
1	20–						1
2	Apr.	30	Federal Unemployment Tax				2
3			Payable		4 8 2 60		3
4			Cash			4 8 2 60	4
5			Issued check for deposit of				5
6			federal unemployment tax.				6
7							7

During the second quarter, many employees' total earnings passed the $7,000 limit of taxable earnings, and the firm's tax liability was reduced accordingly. Because Goren's total accumulated liability ($75.88) was less than $100, a deposit covering that quarter was not made. However, because of an expansion of the company, three new employees were hired during the middle of the quarter.

For the third quarter, the tax liability amounted to $82.53. The total cumulative tax liability was now $158.41 ($75.88 second quarter plus $82.53 third quarter). Consequently, $158.41 was deposited on October 31.

By the end of the fourth quarter, each of the twelve employees' earnings passed the $7,000 mark. The total liability for the quarter is $28.16. This amount will be paid by January 31, accompanied by the completed Employer's Annual Federal Unemployment Tax Return, Form 940.

The T account for Federal Unemployment Tax Payable follows. The credits to the account were part of the entries to record the federal unemployment tax portion of Payroll Tax Expense for each payroll period.

Federal Unemployment Tax Payable

	−	+	
Apr. 30 deposit	482.60	1st quarter (liability)	482.60
Oct. 31 deposit	158.41	2nd quarter (liability)	75.88
		3rd quarter (liability)	82.53
Jan. 31 deposit	28.16	4th quarter (liability)	28.16

Employer's Annual Federal Unemployment (FUTA) Tax Return (Form 940)

Figure 6 shows a completed Form 940-EZ for Goren Company. This form has three sections. (Bear in mind that all forms change from time to time. Go to **http://www.irs.gov** for updates.)

Form 940-EZ

Employer's Annual Federal Unemployment (FUTA) Tax Return

Department of the Treasury
Internal Revenue Service

▶ See the separate Instructions for Form 940-EZ for information on completing this form.

OMB No. 1545-1110

20__

T	
FF	
FD	
FP	
I	
T	

You must complete this section. ▶

Name (as distinguished from trade name)

Trade name, if any
Goren Company

Address (number and street)
612 Third Avenue

Calendar year
20--

Employer identification number (EIN)
64-7228162

City, state, and ZIP code
Bangor, ME 04401

Answer the questions under **Who May Use Form 940-EZ** on page 2. If you cannot use Form 940-EZ, you must use Form 940.

A Enter the amount of contributions paid to your state unemployment fund (see the separate instructions) . . ▶ $ ....

B (1) Enter the name of the state where you have to pay contributions . . . . ▶ ....

(2) Enter your state reporting number as shown on your state unemployment tax return. ▶

If you will not have to file returns in the future, check here (see **Who Must File** in separate instructions) **and complete and sign the return.** ▶ ☐

If this is an Amended Return, check here (see **Amended Returns** in the separate instructions) . . . . ▶ ☐

Part I Taxable Wages and FUTA Tax

1	Total payments (including payments shown on lines 2 and 3) during the calendar year for services of employees	**1**	861,530	00	
2	Exempt payments. (Explain all exempt payments, attaching additional sheets if necessary.) ▶	**2**	—		
3	Payments of more than $7,000 for services. Enter only amounts over the first $7,000 paid to each employee (**see the separate instructions**)	**3**	777,884	00	
4	Add lines 2 and 3	**4**	777,884	00	
5	**Total taxable wages** (subtract line 4 from line 1) . . . . ▶	**5**	83,646	00	
6	**FUTA tax.** Multiply the wages on line 5 by .008 and enter here. (**If the result is over $500, also complete Part II.**)	**6**	669	17	
7	Total FUTA tax deposited for the year, including any overpayment applied from a prior year	**7**	669	17	
8	**Balance due** (subtract line 7 from line 6). Pay to the "United States Treasury." . . . . ▶	**8**	—		
	If you owe more than $500, see **Depositing FUTA tax** in the separate instructions.				
9	**Overpayment** (subtract line 6 from line 7). Check if it is to be: ☐ **Applied to next return** or ☐ **Refunded** ▶	**9**	—		

Part II Record of Quarterly Federal Unemployment Tax Liability (Do not include state liability.) **Complete only if line 6 is over $500.**

Quarter	First (Jan. 1 – Mar. 31)	Second (Apr. 1 – June 30)	Third (July 1 – Sept. 30)	Fourth (Oct. 1 – Dec. 31)	Total for year
Liability for quarter	482.60	75.88	82.53	28.16	669.17

Third-Party Designee

Do you want to allow another person to discuss this return with the IRS (see the separate instructions)? ☐ **Yes.** Complete the following. ☒ **No**

Designee's name ▶

Phone no. ▶ ( )

Personal identification number (PIN) ▶

Under penalties of perjury, I declare that I have examined this return, including accompanying schedules and statements, and, to the best of my knowledge and belief, it is true, correct, and complete, and that no part of any payment made to a state unemployment fund claimed as a credit was, or is to be, deducted from the payments to employees.

Signature ▶ *Eileen Goren* Title (Owner, etc.) ▶ *Owner* Date ▶ *1/31/20--*

For Privacy Act and Paperwork Reduction Act Notice, see the separate instructions. ▼ **DETACH HERE** ▼ Cat. No. 10983G Form **940-EZ** (2005)

FIGURE 6

Part I: Taxable Wages and FUTA Tax.

Line 1 Record total wages paid.

Line 2 Record certain exempt wages—this includes such items as agricultural labor, family employment, and the value of meals and lodging.

Line 3 Record exempt wages paid—wages paid to each employee over and above $7,000 for the calendar year.

Line 4 Total exempt payments.

Line 5 Total taxable wages.

Line 6 Computation of tax due.

Line 7   Total FUTA tax deposited.

Line 8   Balance due.

Line 9   Overpayment.

Part II: Record of Quarterly Federal Unemployment Tax Liability.

WORKERS' COMPENSATION INSURANCE

OBJECTIVE 7

Calculate the premium for workers' compensation insurance, and prepare the entry for payment in advance.

Most states require employers to provide **workers' compensation insurance** or industrial accident insurance for employees killed or injured on the job, either through plans administered by the state or through private insurance companies authorized by the state. The employer usually has to pay all the premiums. The premium rate varies with the amount of risk the job entails and the company's claims history. For example, handling molten steel ingots is much more dangerous than typing reports. Thus, it is very important that employees be identified properly in terms of the insurance premium classifications. The rates as percentages of the payroll may be 0.15 percent for office work, 0.5 percent for sales work, and 3.5 percent for industrial labor in heavy manufacturing. These same rates may be expressed as $0.15 per $100 of the salaries or wages for office work, $0.50 per $100 for sales work, and $3.50 per $100 for industrial labor.

REMEMBER!

Workers' compensation for the year is first estimated based on the anticipated year's payroll; debit Prepaid Insurance, Workers' Compensation, and credit Cash. At the end of the year, when the actual payroll is known, the exact insurance premium is calculated; debit Workers' Compensation Insurance Expense and credit Prepaid Insurance, Workers' Compensation, for the amount paid at the beginning of the year.

If the amount of the estimated payroll is less than the actual payroll, debit Workers' Compensation Insurance Expense and credit Workers' Compensation Insurance Payable for the difference between the actual premium and the estimated premium.

Generally, the employer pays a premium in advance, based on the estimated payroll for the year. After the year ends, the employer knows the exact amount of the payroll and can calculate the exact premium. At that time, depending on the difference between the estimated and exact premiums, the employer either pays an additional premium or gets a credit for having made an overpayment.

At Goren Company, there are two work classifications: office work and sales work. At the beginning of the year, the firm's accountant computed the estimated annual premium as follows:

Classification	Predicted Payroll	Rate (Percent)	Estimated Premium
Office work	$182,000	.15	$182,000 × .0015 = $ 273.00
Sales work	660,000	.50	660,000 × .0050 = 3,300.00
			Total estimated premium $3,573.00

As shown by T accounts, the accountant made the following entry.

Prepaid Insurance, Workers' Compensation		**Cash**	
+	−	+	−
Jan. 10 3,573.00			3,573.00 Jan. 10

Workers' compensation premiums are based on the level of risk involved. A decimal rating is given to the employer for each type of job.

Then, at the end of the calendar year, the accountant calculated the exact premium:

Classification	Actual Payroll	Rate (Percent)	Estimated Premium
Office work	$188,990	.15	$188,990 × .0015 = $ 283.49
Sales work	672,540	.50	672,540 × .0050 = 3,362.70
			Total estimated premium $3,646.19

Therefore, the amount of the unpaid premium is

$3,646.19	Total exact premium
3,573.00	Less total estimated premium paid
$ 73.19	Additional premium owed

OBJECTIVE 8a

Determine the amount of the end-of-the-year adjustment for workers' compensation insurance, and record the adjustment.

Now the accountant makes an adjusting entry, similar to the adjusting entry for expired insurance; this entry appears on the work sheet. The accountant then makes an additional adjusting entry for the extra premium owed. By T accounts, the entries are as follows:

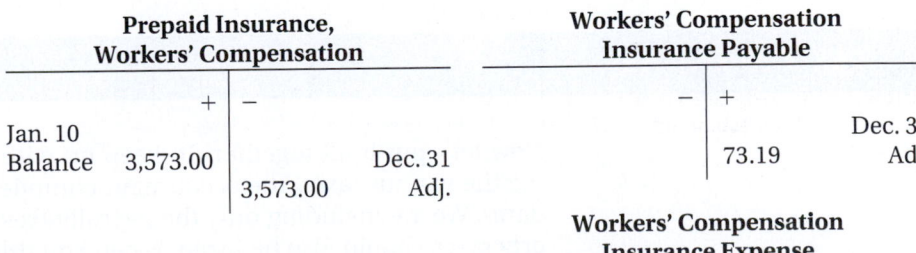

Prepaid Insurance, Workers' Compensation			Workers' Compensation Insurance Payable	
	+	−	−	+
Jan. 10				Dec. 31
Balance 3,573.00		Dec. 31		73.19 Adj.
		3,573.00 Adj.		

Workers' Compensation Insurance Expense	
+	−
Dec. 31 Adj. 3,573.00	
Dec. 31 Adj. 73.19	

Goren Company will pay $73.19, the amount of unpaid premium, in January, together with the estimated premium for the next year.

ADJUSTING FOR ACCRUED SALARIES AND WAGES

OBJECTIVE 8b

Determine the amount of the end-of-the-year adjustment for accrued salaries and wages, and record the adjustment.

Assume that $1,200 of salaries accrue for the time between the last payday and the end of the year. An adjusting entry is necessary.

	DATE		DESCRIPTION	POST. REF.	DEBIT	CREDIT	
1	20–		**Adjusting Entry**				1
2	Dec.	31	Salary Expense		1 2 0 0 00		2
3			Salaries Payable			1 2 0 0 00	3
4							4

Salaries Payable is considered a liability account, as are employees' withholding taxes and deductions payable. Federal income tax and FICA tax levied on employees do not become legal obligations until the employees are paid. Therefore, for the purpose of recording the adjusting entry, the entire liability of the gross salaries and wages is included under Salaries Payable or Wages Payable. In other words, in the adjusting entry, such accounts as Employees' Federal Income Tax Payable, FICA Tax Payable (employees' share), and Employees' Union Dues Payable are not used.

Adjusting Entry for Accrual of Payroll Taxes

As you have seen, the following taxes come under the umbrella of the Payroll Tax Expense account: the employer's share of the FICA tax, the state unemployment tax, and the federal unemployment tax. The employer becomes liable for these taxes only when the employees are actually paid, rather than at the time the liability to the employees is incurred. From the standpoint of legal liability, there should be no adjusting entry for Payroll Tax Expense.

TAX CALENDAR

Now let's put it all together. To keep up with the task of paying and reporting the various taxes, the accountant compiles a chronological list of the due dates. We are including only the payroll taxes here, but sales taxes and property taxes should also be listed. When you think about the penalties for non-payment of taxes by the due dates, this chronological list seems to be well worth the effort. The employer is a monthly depositor for the federal tax deposit.

Jan.   10   Pay estimated annual premium for workers' compensation insurance. (This is an approximate date, as it varies among the states.)

Compiling a chronological list of tax due dates helps accountants keep up with paying and reporting the various taxes.

Jan.	15	Make federal tax deposit for employees' income tax withholding, employees' FICA taxes withheld, and employer's FICA taxes for wages paid during the month of December.
	31	Complete Employer's Quarterly Federal Tax Return, Form 941, for the fourth quarter.
	31	Issue copies B and C of Wage and Tax Statement, Form W-2, to employees.
	31	Pay state unemployment tax liability for the previous quarter, and submit state return, employer's tax report.
	31	Pay any remaining federal unemployment tax liability for the previous year, and submit Form 940, Employer's Annual Federal Unemployment Tax Return.
	31	Make state deposit for employees' state income tax withholding and submit any required state payroll reports. (Timing and required reports may differ from state to state.)
Feb.	15	Make federal tax deposit for employees' income tax withholding, employees' FICA tax withholding, and employer's FICA tax for wages paid during the month of January.
	28	Complete Transmittal of Wage and Tax Statements, Form W-3, and attach copy A of W-2 forms for employees.
Mar.	15	Make federal tax deposit for employees' income tax withholding, employees' FICA tax withholding, and employer's FICA tax for wages paid during the month of February.
Apr.	15	Make federal tax deposit for employees' income tax withholding, employees' FICA tax withholding, and employer's FICA tax for wages paid during the month of March.
	30	Pay state unemployment tax liability for the previous quarter and submit state return, employer's tax report.
	30	Complete Employer's Quarterly Federal Tax Return, Form 941, for the first quarter.
	30	Make federal tax deposit for federal unemployment tax liability if it exceeds $100.
	30	Make state deposit for employees' state income tax withholding.

CHAPTER REVIEW

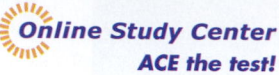
Online Study Center
ACE the test!

Review of Performance Objectives

1. **Calculate the amount of payroll tax expense and journalize the entry.**

   Payroll tax expense consists of the employer's matching portion of FICA taxes, plus the state unemployment tax, plus the federal unemployment tax. The *FICA tax* consists of Social Security and Medicare taxes. *Social Security tax* equals total Social Security taxable earnings multiplied by .062 (6.2 percent assumed rate) on the taxable earnings. For this text, the maximum taxable is assumed to be $94,200. Total *Medicare tax* equals Medicare taxable earnings multiplied by .0145 (1.45 percent assumed rate). There is no maximum limit for Medicare—all earnings are taxable. *State unemployment tax* equals unemployment taxable earnings multiplied by .054 (5.4 percent assumed rate). *Federal unemployment tax* equals unemployment taxable earnings multiplied by .008 (.8 percent assumed rate). Refer to the related journal entry on page 298.

2. **Journalize the entry for the deposit of employees' federal income taxes withheld and FICA taxes (both employees' withheld and employer's matching share) and prepare the deposit coupon.**

   Refer to this journal entry on page 301.

3. **Journalize the entries for the payment of employer's state and federal unemployment taxes.**

   State unemployment tax is paid on a quarterly basis. Payment is due by the end of the next month following the end of the calendar quarter. Refer to this journal entry on page 302.

   If the amount of the accumulated federal unemployment tax liability exceeds $100 at the end of any quarter, the tax is due by the end of the next month following the end of the quarter. If the federal unemployment tax payable is less than $100 at the end of the year, it is due by January 31 of the next year. Refer to this journal entry on page 303.

4. **Journalize the entry for the deposit of employees' state income taxes withheld.**

   Employees' state income taxes withheld are paid on a quarterly basis or as required by the state. Payment may be due by the end of the next month following the end of the calendar quarter. Refer to this journal entry on page 304.

5. **Complete Employer's Quarterly Federal Tax Return, Form 941.**

   Form 941 is illustrated on page 305.

6. **Prepare W-2 and W-3 forms and Form 940.**

   W-2 form (Wage and Tax Statement) is illustrated on page 307. W-3 form (Transmittal of Wage and Tax Statements) is illustrated on page 309. Form 940 is illustrated on page 311.

7. **Calculate the premium for workers' compensation insurance, and prepare the entry for payment in advance.**

   Rates vary depending on the degree of physical risk involved in different occupations. The amount of the premium equals the predicted annual payroll multiplied by the premium rate. The entry is a debit to Prepaid Insurance, Workers' Compensation, and a credit to Cash.

8. Determine the amount of the end-of-the-year adjustments for (a) workers' compensation insurance and (b) accrued salaries and wages, and record the adjustments.

When the total annual payroll is known, the exact cost of workers' compensation insurance can be determined by multiplying the total payroll by the premium rate. Two adjusting entries are required. The first adjusting entry records the expired insurance as a debit to Workers' Compensation Insurance Expense and a credit to Prepaid Insurance, Workers' Compensation. The second adjusting entry records the difference between the estimated and the actual premiums. If the actual premium is greater than the premium that was paid in advance, the entry is a debit to Workers' Compensation Insurance Expense and a credit to Workers' Compensation Insurance Payable. The adjustment for accrued salaries and wages accounts for the additional amount of salaries or wages paid in the next payroll that are incurred in the current fiscal period—a debit to Wages (or Salary) Expense. The credit to Wages (or Salaries) Payable accounts for the additional amount of liability incurred in the current period that will be paid with the next payroll that occurs in the following fiscal period.

Glossary

Employer identification number The number assigned each employer by the Internal Revenue Service for use in the submission of reports and payments for FICA taxes and federal income tax withheld. (296)

Federal unemployment tax (FUTA) A tax levied only on the employer, equal to 0.8 percent of the first $7,000 of total earnings paid to each employee during the calendar year. This tax is used to administer the funds. (298)

Form 940 An annual report filed by employers showing total wages paid to employees, total wages subject to federal unemployment tax, total federal unemployment tax, and other information. Also called the *Employer's Annual Federal Unemployment Tax Return.* (308)

Form 941 A quarterly report showing the tax liability for withholdings of employees' federal income tax and FICA tax and the employer's share of FICA tax. Total tax deposits made in the quarter are also listed on this *Employer's Quarterly Federal Tax Return.* (304)

Form W-2 A form containing information about employee earnings and tax deductions for the year. Also called *Wage and Tax Statement.* (307)

Form W-3 An annual report sent to the Social Security Administration listing the total wages and tips, total federal income tax withheld, total Social Security and Medicare taxable wages, total Social Security and Medicare tax withheld, and other information for all employees of a firm. Also called the *Transmittal of Wage and Tax Statements.* (308)

Payroll Tax Expense A general expense account used for recording the employer's matching portion of the FICA tax, the federal unemployment tax, and the state unemployment tax. (296)

Quarters Three consecutive months, also referred to as *calendar quarters.* (300)

State unemployment tax (SUTA) A tax levied only on the employer in most states. Rates differ among the various states; however, they are generally 5.4 percent or higher of the first $7,000 of total earnings paid to each employee during the calendar year. The proceeds are used to pay subsistence benefits to unemployed workers. (298)

Workers' compensation insurance This insurance, primarily paid for by the employer, provides benefits for employees injured or killed on the job. The rates vary according to the degree of risk inherent in the job. The plans may be sponsored by states or by private firms. The employer pays the premium in advance at the beginning of the year, based on the estimated payroll. The rates are adjusted after the exact payroll is known. (312)

QUESTIONS, EXERCISES, AND CASES

Discussion Questions

1. What taxes are employers accounting for that increase the debit to Payroll Tax Expense?
2. Describe the journal entry to
   a. record the payroll.
   b. record the employer's payroll tax contributions.
   c. pay the payroll.
3. Explain the deposit requirement for federal unemployment tax.
4. What is the purpose of Form 941? How often is it prepared, and what are the due dates?
5. How many copies are made of a Form W-2, and who uses the copies of the W-2 form?
6. What is the purpose of Form 940? How often is it prepared, and what is the due date?
7. Generally, what is the time schedule for payment of workers' compensation insurance premiums?
8. Explain the advantage of establishing a tax calendar.

Exercises

P.O. 1

Journalize the entry for payroll tax expense.

Exercise 9-1 Salerno Company's partial payroll register for the week ended January 7 is shown below.

	NAME	BEGINNING CUMULATIVE EARNINGS	TOTAL EARNINGS	ENDING CUMULATIVE EARNINGS	TAXABLE EARNINGS		
					UNEMPLOYMENT	SOCIAL SECURITY	MEDICARE
1	Bonney, R. S.		932 00	932 00	932 00	932 00	932 00
2	Fisk, M. C.		567 00	567 00	567 00	567 00	567 00
3	Hayes, W. O.		483 00	483 00	483 00	483 00	483 00
4	Lee, L. B.		679 00	679 00	679 00	679 00	679 00
5	Parks, S. J.		578 00	578 00	578 00	578 00	578 00
6	Tempy, E. B.		546 00	546 00	546 00	546 00	546 00
7			3785 00	3785 00	3785 00	3785 00	3785 00
8							
9							
10							
11							

Assume that the payroll is subject to a Social Security tax of 6.2 percent of the first $94,200 and a Medicare tax of 1.45 percent on all earnings. Also assume that the federal unemployment tax is 0.8 percent of the first $7,000, and the state unemployment tax is 5.4 percent of the first $7,000. Give the entry in general journal form to record the payroll tax expense.

P.O. 1

Journalize the entry for payroll tax expense.

Exercise 9-2 On January 14, at the end of the second week of the year, the totals of Carson Company's payroll register showed that its store employees' wages amounted to $33,482 and its warehouse wages amounted to $13,560. Withholdings consisted of federal income taxes, $5,110; Social Security taxes at the rate of 6.2 percent of the first $94,200 and no employee has reached the limit; Medicare taxes at the rate of 1.45 percent on all earnings; union dues, $845.

p 280

notes

a. Calculate the amount of Social Security and Medicare taxes to be withheld, and write the general journal entry to record the payroll.
b. Write the general journal entry to record the employer's payroll taxes, assuming that the federal unemployment tax is 0.8 percent of the first $7,000, that the state unemployment tax is 5.4 percent of the same base, and that no employee has surpassed the $7,000 limit.

P.O. 1

Journalize the payroll entries.

Exercise 9-3 Fennell Systems had the following payroll data for wages for the week ended February 5. These calculations for state income tax (20% of federal income tax) are exceptions.

| | | TAXABLE EARNINGS | | | DEDUCTIONS | | | |
TOTAL EARNINGS	ENDING CUMULATIVE EARNINGS	UNEMPLOYMENT	SOCIAL SECURITY	MEDICARE	FEDERAL INCOME TAX	STATE INCOME TAX	SOCIAL SECURITY TAX	MEDICARE TAX
6 7 7 0 00	72 8 5 0 00	6 7 7 0 00	6 7 7 0 00	6 7 7 0 00	8 2 4 00	1 5 7 00	4 1 9 74	9 8 17

a. Write the general journal entry to record the payroll.
b. Write the general journal entry to record the employer's payroll taxes. Assume rates of 0.8 percent for federal unemployment tax and 5.4 percent for state unemployment tax based on the first $7,000 for each employee and that no employee has earned more than $7,000.

P.O. 1

Journalize the entry for payroll tax expense.

Exercise 9-4 The information on earnings and deductions for the pay period ended December 14 from Larry Company's payroll records is shown on the following page.

For each employee, the Social Security tax is 6.2 percent of the first $94,200 and the Medicare tax is 1.45 percent on all earnings. The federal unemployment tax is 0.8 percent of the first $7,000 of earnings of each employee. The state unemployment tax is 5.4 percent of the same base. Determine the total taxable earnings for unemployment, Social Security, and Medicare. Prepare a general journal entry to record the employer's payroll taxes.

Name	Gross Pay	Beginning Cumulative Earnings
Biliken, J. L.	$ 410	$ 6,750
Clayton, M. E.	785	40,200
Drugden, T. F.	860	38,500
Rich, L. W.	990	39,700
Sparks, C. R.	2,094	93,650
Stevers, D. H.	850	6,810

P.O. 2

Journalize entries for payment of federal payroll taxes.

Exercise 9-5 Selected columns of Linch Company's payroll register for the month of January are as follows. The employees' FICA taxes are matched by the employer.

Payment Date	Employees' Federal Income Tax	Employees' Social Security Tax	Employees' Medicare Tax
Jan. 7	1,192.00	475.00	112.25
14	1,135.00	518.14	122.31
21	1,245.00	572.62	124.24
28	1,452.00	561.27	143.26

Linch Company deposits taxes monthly. In general journal form, record the entry for the February 15 payment of FICA and federal income taxes for employees and employer.

P.O. 2,3

Journalize entries for payment of payroll taxes.

Exercise 9-6 On September 30, Kaplin Company's selected account balances are as follows:

Employees' Federal Income Tax Payable	$ 2,369.00
FICA Tax Payable (employer and employee)	2,604.46
State Unemployment Tax Payable	1,250.00 } (Some employees have
Federal Unemployment Tax Payable	195.00 } reached the limit.)

In general journal form, prepare the entries to record the following:

Oct.   15   Payment of liabilities for FICA and federal income tax.
       31   Payment of liability for state unemployment tax.
       31   Payment of liability for federal unemployment tax.

P.O. 2,3

Journalize entries for payment of payroll taxes.

Exercise 9-7 On September 30, Mitchel Company's selected payroll accounts are as follows:

FICA Tax Payable				State Unemployment Tax Payable		
−	+			−	+	
	Sept. 30	2,314.84			Sept. 30	1,183.40
	Sept. 30	2,314.84				

Federal Unemployment Tax Payable				Employees' Federal Income Tax Payable		
−	+			−	+	
	Sept. 30	200.15			Sept. 30	3,210.85

Prepare general journal entries to record the following:

Oct. 15 Payment of federal tax deposit of FICA and federal income tax.
     31 Payment of state unemployment tax.
     31 Payment of federal unemployment tax.

P.O. 7,8

Journalize entries for workers' compensation insurance.

Exercise 9-8 Megan Company received and paid a premium notice on January 2 for workers' compensation insurance stating the rates for the new year. Estimated employees' earnings for the year are as follows:

Classification	Estimated Wages and Salaries	Rate Per Hundred	Estimated Premium
Office clerical	$ 92,000	.11	$ 101.20
Warehouse work	29,000	.92	266.80
Manufacturing	264,000	1.20	3,168.00
			$3,536.00

At the end of the year, the exact figures for the payroll are as follows:

Classification	Estimated Wages and Salaries	Rate Per Hundred	Exact Premium
Office clerical	$ 93,000	.11	$ 102.30
Warehouse work	30,000	.92	276.00
Manufacturing	267,000	1.20	3,204.00
			$3,582.30

a. Record the entry in general journal form for payment of the estimated premium.
b. Record the adjusting entries on December 31 for the insurance expired and for the additional premium.

internet
LINKS TO ACCOUNTING

The previous chapter covered payroll taxes, collected by the employer, that the employee pays. In this chapter, you learned about the taxes the employer must pay. The whole process can be very complicated and confusing for the employer!

Are any methods other than Form 8109-B available for making deposits? See if you can find out by visiting the IRS website at **www.irs.gov.** If so, what are they and how are they used?

WHAT'S WRONG WITH THIS PICTURE?

The payroll clerk is working on the payroll for May 31. Several employees' gross earnings are about to exceed the limits for unemployment and FICA taxes. For each employee whose cumulative earnings were near the limit, the payroll clerk multiplied the tax rate by the amount by which the employee's earnings exceeded the tax ceiling (not the amount between the beginning cumulative earnings and the tax limit). Comment on this procedure.

CRITICAL THINKING

It is December 15, and you are the payroll clerk for Lincoln Company. The owner has come to you for help; two employees have asked for a 3 percent pay raise, and the owner wants to know how much more such a raise will cost her next year. Present gross salaries are as follows:

Employee A
$40,000/year   Married, with 2 allowances   Paid weekly
Employee B
$42,000/year   Married, with 1 allowance   Paid weekly

Assume the following tax rates and limits:

Social Security, 6.2 percent with a limit of $94,200
Medicare, 1.45 percent with no limit (all earnings taxable)
SUTA, 5.4 percent with a limit of $7,000
FUTA, 0.8 percent with a limit of $7,000

What will be the cost to the employer of giving Employee A and Employee B the pay raise?

A QUESTION OF ETHICS

Between the end of one month and the fifteenth day of the next month, the balance in the employer's business bank account has been getting smaller and smaller. An employee prepares the next payroll and correctly computes the necessary withholding taxes. The employer is supposed to pay accumulated employment taxes on the fifteenth of the next month. Payday is the last day of the month. However, the employer has used the funds withheld from employees to pay some of the business's bills. He hopes that enough of the customers who owe him money will pay their outstanding debts. If his assumption is true, the checking account will have enough in it to pay the federal deposit on the fifteenth of the month. Is the employer acting ethically? After all, he says he intends to have enough money in the account for the deposit.

PROBLEM SET A

For additional help, see the demonstration problem at the beginning of each chapter in your Working Papers.

P.O. 1

Problem 9-1A Migiro Labs had the following payroll for the week ended February 28:

Salaries		Deductions	
Technicians' salaries	$6,955.00	Federal income tax withheld	$ 695.00
Office salaries	2,260.00	Social Security tax withheld	571.33
		Medicare tax withheld	133.62
Total	$9,215.00	Union dues withheld	165.00
		Medical insurance	450.00
		Total	$2,014.95

Assumed tax rates are as follows:

a. FICA: Social Security, 6.2 percent (.062) on the first $94,200 for each employee, and Medicare, 1.45 percent (.0145) on all earnings for each employee.
b. State unemployment tax, 5.4 percent (.054) on the first $7,000 for each employee.
c. Federal unemployment tax, 0.8 percent (.008) on the first $7,000 for each employee.

Check Figure

Payroll Tax Expense, $1,107.33

Instructions

Record the following entries in general journal form:

1. The payroll entry as of February 28.
2. The entry to record the employer's payroll taxes as of February 28, assuming that the total payroll is subject to the FICA tax (combined Social Security and Medicare) and that $6,490.00 is subject to unemployment taxes.
3. The payment to the employees on March 2. (Assume that the company has transferred cash to Cash—Payroll Bank Account for this payroll.)

P.O. 1

Problem 9-2A Timely Services has the following payroll information for the week ended December 7. State income tax is computed as 20% of federal income tax.

	NAME	BEGINNING CUMULATIVE EARNINGS	TOTAL EARNINGS	DEDUCTIONS FEDERAL INCOME TAX	STATE INCOME TAX
1	Delong, T.	6 8 2 0 00	4 8 0 00	3 9 00	7 80
2	Herrera, M.	6 8 4 0 00	4 7 0 00	3 7 00	7 40
3	Joyner, J.	36 3 2 0 00	7 4 0 00	4 6 00	9 20
4	King, L.	26 2 0 0 00	5 4 0 00	5 0 00	1 0 00
5	Wisniewski, M.	93 3 6 0 00	1 7 2 0 00	2 8 9 00	5 7 80
6	Yee, N.	28 4 2 6 00	6 0 5 00	6 4 00	1 2 80
7					
8					
9					
10					
11					
12					
13					
14					

Assumed tax rates are as follows:

a. FICA: Social Security, 6.2 percent (.062) on the first $94,200 for each employee, and Medicare, 1.45 percent (.0145) on all earnings for each employee.
b. State unemployment tax, 5.4 percent (.054) on the first $7,000 for each employee.
c. Federal unemployment tax, 0.8 percent (.008) on the first $7,000 for each employee.

Check Figure

Payroll Tax Expense, $314.98

Instructions

1. Complete the payroll register, page 72. Payroll checks begin with Ck. No. 714 in the payroll register.
2. Prepare a general journal entry to record the payroll as of December 7. The company's general ledger contains a Salary Expense account and a Salaries Payable account.
3. Prepare a general journal entry to record the payroll taxes as of December 7.
4. Journalize the entry to pay the payroll on December 9. (Assume that the company has transferred cash to the Cash—Payroll Bank Account for this payroll.)

P.O. 5

Problem 9-3A For the third quarter of the year, Jackson Company, 415 Circle Avenue, Chicago, Illinois 60652, received Form 941 from the Internal Revenue Service. The identification number of Jackson Company is 76-4213171. Its payroll for the quarter ended September 30 is as follows.

		TAXABLE EARNINGS		DEDUCTIONS		
NAME	TOTAL EARNINGS	SOCIAL SECURITY	MEDICARE	FEDERAL INCOME TAX	SOCIAL SECURITY TAX	MEDICARE TAX
1 Barker, D. D.	6 6 2 9 00	6 6 2 9 00	6 6 2 9 00	8 4 3 00	4 1 1 00	9 6 12
2 Carey, L. R.	8 5 2 8 00	8 5 2 8 00	8 5 2 8 00	8 2 5 00	5 2 8 74	1 2 3 66
3 Domzalski, T. P.	4 6 6 5 00	4 6 6 5 00	4 6 6 5 00	6 8 9 00	2 8 9 23	6 7 64
4 Grisson, R. O.	3 7 2 1 00	3 7 2 1 00	3 7 2 1 00	4 7 8 00	2 3 0 70	5 3 95
5 Tyler, J. L.	7 4 0 6 00	7 4 0 6 00	7 4 0 6 00	8 6 5 00	4 5 9 17	1 0 7 39
6 Vardic, K. R.	5 2 8 7 00	5 2 8 7 00	5 2 8 7 00	7 9 5 00	3 2 7 79	7 6 66
7	36 2 3 6 00	36 2 3 6 00	36 2 3 6 00	4 4 9 5 00	2 2 4 6 63	5 2 5 42
8						

The company has had six employees throughout the year. Assume that the Social Security tax is 6.2 percent of the first $94,200 and that the Medicare tax is 1.45 percent of all earnings. The employer matches the employees' FICA (Social Security and Medicare) taxes. There are no taxable tips, adjustments, backup withholding, or earned income credits. Jackson Company has submitted the following federal tax deposits and written the accompanying checks:

On August 15 for the July Payroll

Employees' income tax withheld	$1,380.00
Employees' Social Security and Medicare tax withheld	851.10
Employer's Social Security and Medicare tax contributed	851.10
	$3,082.20

On September 15 for the August Payroll

Employees' income tax withheld	$1,892.00
Employees' Social Security and Medicare tax withheld	875.92
Employer's Social Security and Medicare tax contributed	875.92
	$3,643.84

On October 15 for the September Payroll

Employees' income tax withheld	$1,223.00
Employees' Social Security and Medicare tax withheld	1,045.03
Employer's Social Security and Medicare tax contributed	1,045.03
	$3,313.06

Check Figure

Total taxes, $10,039.10

P.O. 1,2,3

Instructions

Complete Part 1 of Form 941 for the third quarter for the owner, Maxwell Jackson.

Problem 9-4A Leidel Company has the following balances in its general ledger as of June 1 of this year:

a. FICA Tax Payable (liability for May), $1,719.40 (employee and employer).
b. Employees' Federal Income Tax Payable (liability for May), $995.00.
c. Federal Unemployment Tax Payable (liability for April and May), $180.00.
d. State Unemployment Tax Payable (liability for April and May), $1,205.75.
e. Employees' Medical Insurance Payable (liability for April and May), $1,289.00.

The company completed the following transactions involving the payroll during June and July:

June 13 Issued check for $2,709.40 payable to Security Bank, for the monthly deposit of May FICA taxes and employees' federal income tax withheld.

      30 Recorded the payroll entry in the general journal from the payroll register for June. The payroll register has the following column totals:

Sales salaries	$11,490.00	
Office salaries	5,147.00	
Total earnings		$16,637.00
Employees' federal income tax deductions	$ 1,725.00	
Employees' Social Security tax deductions	1,031.49	
Employees' Medicare tax deductions	241.24	
Employees' medical insurance deductions	755.00	
Total deductions		3,752.73
Net pay		$12,884.27

      30 Recorded payroll taxes. Employer matches the employees' FICA taxes. State unemployment tax is 5.4 percent, and federal unemployment tax is 0.8 percent. At this time, all employees' earnings are taxable for FICA and unemployment taxes.

      30 Issued check for $12,884.27 from Cash—Payroll Bank Account to pay salaries for the month.

July 14 Issued check for $2,044, payable to Carson Insurance Company, in payment of employees' medical insurance for April, May, and June.

      14 Issued check for $4,270.46, payable to Security Bank, for the monthly deposit of June FICA taxes (employee and employer matching) and employees' federal income tax withheld.

      31 Issued check for $2,104.15, payable to the State Tax Commission, for state unemployment tax for April, May, and June. The check was accompanied by the quarterly tax return.

      31 Issued check for $313.10, payable to Security Bank, for the deposit of federal unemployment tax for the months of April, May, and June.

Check Figure

Payroll Tax Expense, $2,304.23

Instructions

Record the transactions in the general journal, pages 77–78.

Instructions for General Ledger Software

1. Record the transactions in the general journal.
2. Print the journal entries.

PROBLEM SET B

For additional help, see the demonstration problem at the beginning of each chapter in your Working Papers.

P.O. 1

Problem 9-1B Kovich Company had the following payroll for the week ended March 21:

Salaries		Deductions	
Sales salaries	$7,620.00	Federal income tax withheld	$ 894.00
Office salaries	1,790.00	Social Security tax withheld	583.42
		Medicare tax withheld	136.45
Total	$9,410.00	Union dues withheld	153.00
		Medical insurance	200.00
		Total	$1,966.87

Assumed tax rates are as follows:

a. FICA: Social Security, 6.2 percent (.062) on the first $94,200 for each employee, and Medicare, 1.45 percent (.0145) on all earnings for each employee.
b. State unemployment tax, 5.4 percent (.054) on the first $7,000 for each employee.
c. Federal unemployment tax, 0.8 percent (.008) on the first $7,000 for each employee.

Check Figure

Payroll Tax Expense, $1,027.70

Instructions

Record the following entries in general journal form:

1. The payroll entry as of March 21.
2. The entry to record the employer's payroll taxes as of March 21, assuming that the total payroll is subject to the FICA tax (combined Social Security and Medicare) and that $4,965 is subject to unemployment taxes.
3. The payment of the employees on March 23. (Assume that the company has transferred cash to Cash—Payroll Bank Account for this payroll.)

P.O. 1

Problem 9-2B Kyle Agency has the following payroll information for the week ended December 14. State income tax is computed as 20% of federal income tax.

	NAME	BEGINNING CUMULATIVE EARNINGS	TOTAL EARNINGS	DEDUCTIONS FEDERAL INCOME TAX	DEDUCTIONS STATE INCOME TAX
1	Abraham, R.	10 650 00	4 600 00	3 5 00	7 00
2	Baca, T.	38 820 00	9 700 00	1 09 00	21 80
3	Eubanks, E.	93 255 00	17 900 00	2 05 00	41 00
4	Ling, D.	6 750 00	3 850 00	2 8 00	5 60
5	Metcalf, S.	31 670 00	6 940 00	5 2 00	10 40
6	Quinn, D.	48 961 00	10 400 00	1 10 00	22 00
7					

Assumed tax rates are as follows:

a. FICA: Social Security, 6.2 percent (.062) on the first $94,200 for each employee, and Medicare, 1.45 percent (.0145) on all earnings for each employee.
b. State unemployment tax, 5.4 percent (.054) on the first $7,000 for each employee.
c. Federal unemployment tax, 0.8 percent (.008) on the first $7,000 for each employee.

Check Figure

Payroll Tax Expense, $371.55

Instructions

1. Complete the payroll register, page 72. Payroll checks begin with Ck. No. 923 in the payroll register.
2. Prepare a general journal entry to record the payroll as of December 14. The company's general ledger contains a Salary Expense account and a Salaries Payable account.
3. Prepare a general journal entry to record the payroll taxes as of December 14.
4. Journalize the entry to pay the payroll on December 16. (Assume that the company has transferred cash to the Cash—Payroll Bank Account for this payroll.)

P.O. 5

Problem 9-3B For the third quarter of the year, Farley Construction, of 715 Red Rock Boulevard, San Francisco, California 94421, received Form 941 from the District Office of the Internal Revenue Service. The identification number for Farley Construction is 78-7382476. Its payroll for the quarter ended September 30 is as follows:

	NAME	TOTAL EARNINGS	TAXABLE EARNINGS SOCIAL SECURITY	MEDICARE	FEDERAL INCOME TAX	SOCIAL SECURITY TAX	MEDICARE TAX
1	Brinnon, D. L.	3 3 8 7 00	3 3 8 7 00	3 3 8 7 00	3 1 0 00	2 0 9 99	4 9 11
2	Finn, J. A.	6 7 5 3 00	6 7 5 3 00	6 7 5 3 00	7 0 4 00	4 1 8 69	9 7 92
3	Harrell, N. E.	7 7 8 0 00	7 7 8 0 00	7 7 8 0 00	8 2 0 00	4 8 2 36	1 1 2 81
4	Kelly, T. L.	6 2 4 3 00	6 2 4 3 00	6 2 4 3 00	6 6 0 00	3 8 7 07	9 0 52
5	Morton, S. M.	4 2 1 5 00	4 2 1 5 00	4 2 1 5 00	3 8 4 00	2 6 1 33	6 1 12
6	Rieck, A. J.	10 2 6 4 00	10 2 6 4 00	10 2 6 4 00	1 2 2 4 00	6 3 6 37	1 4 8 83
7		38 6 4 2 00	38 6 4 2 00	38 6 4 2 00	4 1 0 2 00	2 3 9 5 81	5 6 0 31

The company has had six employees throughout the year. Assume that the Social Security tax is 6.2 percent of the first $94,200, and that the Medicare tax is 1.45 percent of all earnings. The employer matches the employees' FICA (Social Security and Medicare) taxes. There are no taxable tips, adjustments, backup withholding, or earned income credits. Farley Construction has submitted the following federal tax deposits and written the accompanying checks:

On August 15 for the July Payroll		**On September 15 for the August Payroll**		**On October 15 for the September Payroll**	
Employees' income tax withheld	$1,440.00	Employees' income tax withheld	$1,394.00	Employees' income tax withheld	$1,268.00
Employees' Social Security and Medicare tax withheld	984.80	Employees' Social Security and Medicare tax withheld	1,138.40	Employees' Social Security and Medicare tax withheld	832.92
Employer's Social Security and Medicare tax contributed	984.80	Employer's Social Security and Medicare tax contributed	1,138.40	Employer's Social Security and Medicare tax contributed	832.92
	$3,409.60		$3,670.80		$2,933.84

Check Figure

Total taxes, $10,014.24

P.O. 1,2,3

Instructions

Complete Part 1 of Form 941 for the third quarter for the owner, Tom Farley.

Problem 9-4B Degrande Company has the following balances in its general ledger as of March 1 of this year:

a. FICA Tax Payable (liability for February), $1,459.80 (employee and employer).
b. Employees' Federal Income Tax Payable (liability for February), $915.00.
c. State Unemployment Tax Payable (liability for January and February), $965.20.
d. Federal Unemployment Tax Payable (liability for January and February), $151.40.
e. Employees' Medical Insurance Payable (liability for January and February), $935.00.

The company completed the following transactions involving the payroll during March and April:

Mar. 12 Issued check for $2,374.80 payable to Coastal Bank, for monthly deposit of February FICA taxes and employees' federal income tax withheld.

31 Recorded the payroll entry in the general journal from the payroll register for March. The payroll register had the following column totals:

Sales salaries	$7,654.00	
Office salaries	1,982.00	
Total earnings		$9,636.00
Employees' federal income tax deductions	$ 795.00	
Employees' Social Security tax deductions	597.43	
Employees' Medicare tax deductions	139.72	
Employees' medical insurance deductions	485.00	
Total deductions		2,017.15
Net pay		$7,618.85

Mar. 31 Recorded payroll taxes. Employer matches the employees' FICA taxes. State unemployment tax is 5.4 percent. Federal unemployment tax is 0.8 percent. At this time, all employees' earnings are taxable for FICA and unemployment taxes.

31 Issued check for $7,618.85 from Cash—Payroll Bank Account to pay the salaries for the month.

Apr. 3 Issued check for $1,420, payable to Orange Insurance Company, for employees' medical insurance for January, February, and March.

14 Issued check for $2,269.30, payable to Coastal Bank, for monthly deposit of March FICA taxes and employees' federal income tax withheld.

30 Issued check for $1,485.54, payable to State Department of Revenue, for state unemployment tax for January, February, and March. The check was accompanied by the quarterly tax return.

30 Issued check for $228.49, payable to Coastal Bank, for deposit of federal unemployment tax for January, February, and March.

Check Figure

Payroll Tax Expense, $1,334.58

Instructions

Record the transactions in the general journal, pages 77 and 78.

Instructions for General Ledger Software

1. Record the transactions in the general journal.
2. Print the journal entries.

Before a Test Check: Chapters 7–9

PART I: Completion

1. Checks issued by the depositor that have been paid or have cleared the bank are called _____ checks.

2. A deposit that is not recorded on the bank statement because it was made after the bank's closing date for preparation of bank statements is called a(n) _____.

3. The process by which the payee transfers ownership of the check to a bank or other party is called a(n) _____.

4. The person to whom a check is payable is called the _____.

5. A cash fund used to make small immediate cash payments is called a(n) _____.

PART II: Application

1. Clara Thompson's salary is $1,775 per month. If she works more than 40 hours in one week, she is entitled to overtime pay at the rate of 1½ times her regular hourly rate. During the current week, she worked 45 hours. Calculate her gross pay.

2. On June 30, the column totals of Midtown Cleaning's payroll register showed that its cleaning employees had earned $9,000 and its office employees had earned $3,000. Social Security taxes were withheld at 6.2 percent, and Medicare taxes were withheld at 1.45 percent. All earnings are taxable. Other deductions consisted of federal income tax, $1,500; U.S. savings bonds, $500; and medical insurance, $962. Determine the amount of Social Security and Medicare taxes that should be withheld. Record the general journal entry to record the payroll, crediting Salaries Payable for the net pay.

3. Roxy Company's payroll for the week ended December 31 is as follows:

Gross earnings of employees	$155,000
Social Security taxable earnings	143,000
Medicare taxable earnings	155,000
Federal unemployment taxable earnings	22,000
State unemployment taxable earnings	22,000

Assume that the payroll is subject to Social Security tax of 6.2 percent (.062), Medicare tax of 1.45 percent (.0145), federal unemployment tax of 0.8 percent (.008), and state unemployment tax of 5.4 percent (.054). Write the entry in general journal form to record the employer's payroll tax expense.

Note: Answers to Before a Test Check begin on page A-1.

PART III: True/False

T F 1. There is no limit on the amount of taxable earnings for Medicare.

T F 2. When journalizing the entry to reimburse the Petty Cash Fund, include a credit to Petty Cash Fund.

T F 3. When journalizing the entry to account for a customer's NSF check, debit Accounts Payable.

T F 4. An employee's net pay is the result of subtracting his or her deductions from gross pay.

T F 5. The gross pay for an employee who works 45 hours, earns $8.50 per hour, and receives time and a half for hours worked over 40 hours is $402.75.

How many times have you purchased something from Target, only to return it later because you changed your mind? How does this affect Target's sales figures? As you learn about sales transactions in this chapter, think about what accounts might be involved to record the sale and return of merchandise. You can view Target's financial statements at **http://www.target.com.** (At the bottom of the site, click on Investors. Select Annual Reports. Once you open up one of the annual reports, you will be able to select the statement of operations from a pull-down menu.) Can you tell the amount of sales returns from looking at the financial statements?

Performance Objectives

After you have completed the chapter, you will be able to do the following:

1. Describe the specific accounts used by a merchandising firm.

2. Journalize transactions in a sales journal.

3. Post sales journal transactions to an accounts receivable ledger and a general ledger.

4. Prepare a schedule of accounts receivable.

5. Journalize sales returns and allowances, including credit memorandums and returns involving sales tax, in a general journal, and post to the accounts receivable ledger and general ledger.

6. Journalize transactions in a three-column purchases journal.

7. Post purchases journal transactions to an accounts payable ledger and a general ledger.

8. Prepare a schedule of accounts payable.

9. Journalize transactions involving purchases returns and allowances in a general journal, and post to the accounts payable ledger and general ledger.

10. Describe the procedures for handling freight charges on merchandise and other goods.

Ｗe begin this chapter by briefly introducing four special journals that are helpful when accounting for merchandising businesses. A **merchandising business** is one that buys and sells goods. It can be a wholesale or a retail business. A **wholesale business**, which is sometimes called a "middleman" or a "distributor," buys goods from manufacturers and sells them to retailers. A **retail business** sells goods directly to consumers ("the public"). An example of a wholesaler is a business that supplies Target with soaps, shampoos, and other "health and beauty" items. Target, then, is a retailer of those same products.

SPECIAL JOURNALS

Special journals are books of original entry used to simplify the recording process. One or more of these journals may be used in a manual accounting system, or they may be used in certain computerized systems designed to facilitate specialized types of repetitive transactions. The four most commonly used special journals are:

Sales journal (S) Used to record sales of merchandise sold on account *only*. For example, if a wholesale business sells televisions to Best Buy (the retailer), on account, the wholesaler could use this journal to record that sale. However, if Best Buy paid cash for the televisions, the sale would not be recorded in this journal. Also, if a company sells some of its old computer equipment, on account, this journal would not be used because the equipment was not part of the business's merchandise sales.

Purchases journal (P) Used to record purchases of merchandise purchased for resale on account *only*. For example, this journal could be used by a shoe store for its purchase, on account, of a supply of shoes to resell to customers. However, this journal would not be used by a company buying a copy machine or supplies for the office, even though purchased on account, because those goods are not intended for resale to customers.

Cash receipts journal (CR) Used to record all transactions that include a debit to Cash, such as cash sales, checks received, or interest earned on a checking account.

Cash payments journal (CP) Used to record all transactions that include a credit to Cash, such as payments by check or bank service charges.

All other transactions are recorded in the general journal (J). A business would use only those journal(s) that it needs.

SPECIFIC ACCOUNTS FOR MERCHANDISING FIRMS

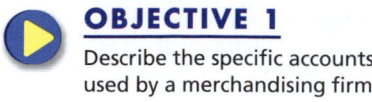

OBJECTIVE 1

Describe the specific accounts used by a merchandising firm.

Merchandise inventory consists of a stock of goods that a company buys and intends to resell at a profit. Merchandise should be differentiated from other assets, such as furniture and equipment, that are acquired for use in the business and are not for resale. Here is the fundamental accounting equation with the T accounts for merchandising businesses.

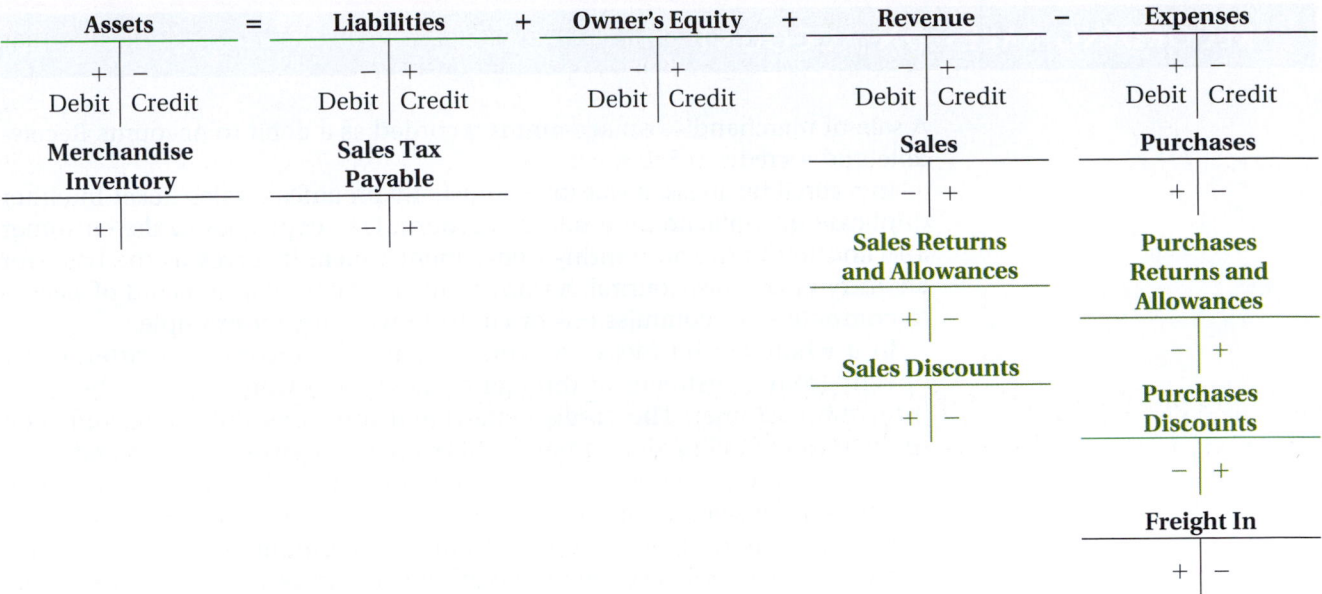

The **Sales account** is a revenue account used for recording sales of merchandise.

The **Purchases account** is used strictly to record the cost of merchandise bought for resale. The plus and minus signs are the same as the signs for Merchandise Inventory. The Purchases account is placed under the Expenses heading because the accountant closes it along with the expense accounts at the end of the fiscal period. (This is explained more in Chapter 17.)

The **Sales Returns and Allowances account** is used to record the physical return of merchandise by customers or a reduction in a bill because merchandise was damaged. It is treated as a deduction from Sales.

The **Sales Tax Payable account** is used to record a tax levied by a state or city government on the retail sale of goods and services. The tax is paid by the consumer but collected by the retailer.

The **Purchases Returns and Allowances account** is used to record the company's returns of merchandise it had purchased from suppliers or reductions in bills because of damaged merchandise. It is treated as a deduction from Purchases.

The **Sales Discounts account** and **Purchases Discounts account** are used to record cash discounts granted for prompt payments, in accordance with the credit terms.

The **Freight In account** is used to record the transportation charges on incoming merchandise intended for resale. Debits to this account increase the cost of purchases.

The T accounts for returns and allowances and for discounts are shown in green to emphasize that we are treating them as deductions from the related accounts placed above them. We list these accounts as deductions because they appear as deductions in the financial statements. Their relationship is similar to that between the Drawing account and the Capital account; remember that we deduct Drawing from Capital in the statement of owner's equity. These same types of accounts pertain to both retail and wholesale businesses.

RECORDING SALES ON ACCOUNT

A sale of merchandise on account is recorded as a debit to Accounts Receivable and a credit to Sales.

In a retail business, a salesperson usually prepares a sales ticket in either duplicate or triplicate for a sale on account. One copy goes to the customer and another to the accounting department, where it serves as the basis for an entry in the sales journal. A third copy may be used as a record of sales—to compute sales commissions or control inventory, for example.

In a wholesale business, the company usually receives a written order directly from a customer or through a salesperson who obtained the order from the customer. The credit department approves the order, and then sends it to the billing department, where the sales invoice is prepared.

Invoices are prepared in multiple copies. Figure 1 shows one possible distribution of sales invoice copies to various parties.

Just as we used Cline's Computer Clinic as a continuous example of a service business, we will use Rainier Plumbing Supply as a continuous example of a merchandising business. Rainier Plumbing Supply is a wholesaler.

FIGURE 1

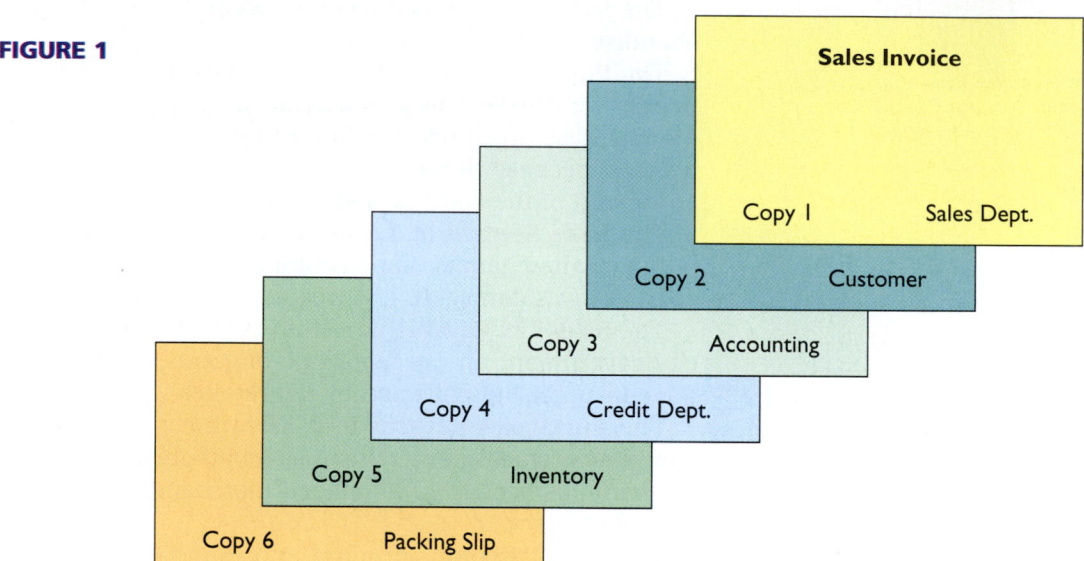

We will introduce the sales journal by looking at three transactions on the books of Rainier Plumbing Supply:

Aug. 1 Sold merchandise on account to Betterbuilt Homes Co., invoice no. 1320, $1,564.86.
3 Sold merchandise on account to Arnold, Inc., invoice no. 1321, $1,116.
6 Sold merchandise on account to Gonzales Construction, invoice no. 1322, $1,394.

Here's how the accounts appear in the fundamental accounting equation.

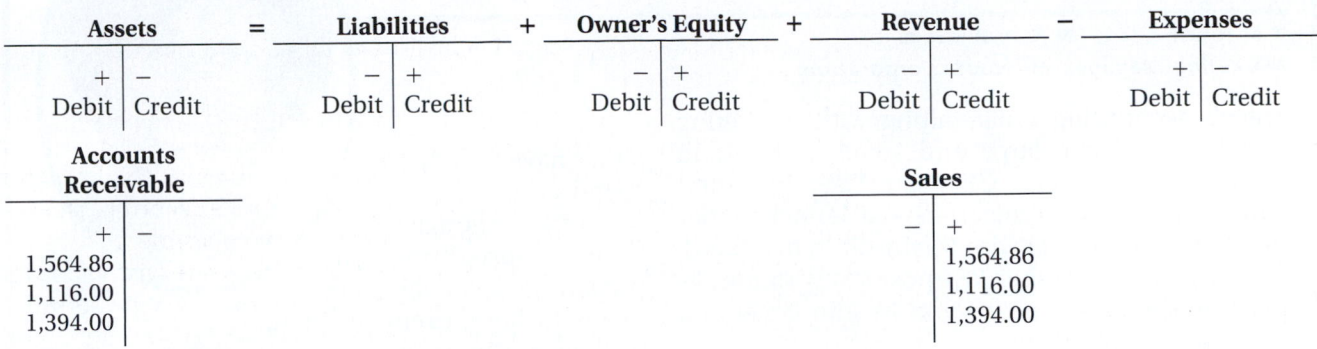

Assets	=	Liabilities	+	Owner's Equity	+	Revenue	−	Expenses
+ | −		− | +		− | +		− | +		+ | −
Debit | Credit		Debit | Credit		Debit | Credit		Debit | Credit		Debit | Credit

Accounts Receivable

+ | −
1,564.86
1,116.00
1,394.00

Sales

− | +
1,564.86
1,116.00
1,394.00

The sales invoice for the sale to Betterbuilt Homes Co. is shown in Figure 2.

FIGURE 2

> **REMEMBER!**
>
> The sales invoice is a source document and as such is evidence that serves as the basis for recording a transaction.

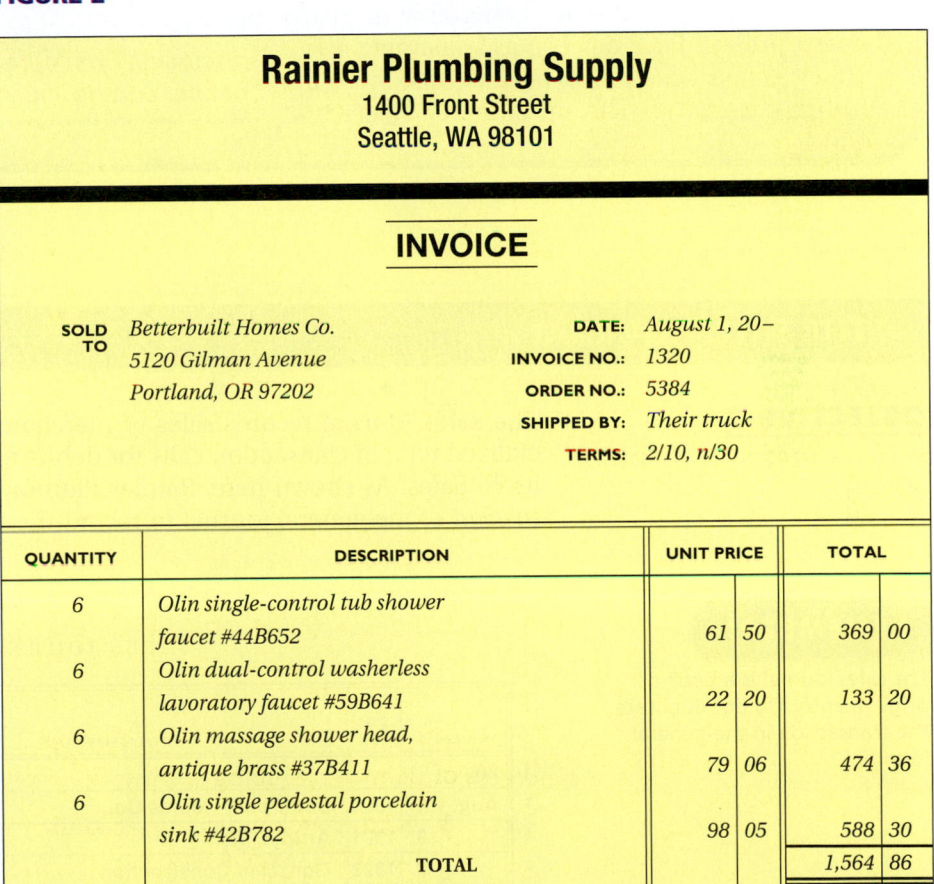

Rainier Plumbing Supply
1400 Front Street
Seattle, WA 98101

INVOICE

SOLD TO	Betterbuilt Homes Co.	DATE:	August 1, 20–
	5120 Gilman Avenue	INVOICE NO.:	1320
	Portland, OR 97202	ORDER NO.:	5384
		SHIPPED BY:	Their truck
		TERMS:	2/10, n/30

QUANTITY	DESCRIPTION	UNIT PRICE	TOTAL
6	Olin single-control tub shower faucet #44B652	61 | 50	369 | 00
6	Olin dual-control washerless lavatory faucet #59B641	22 | 20	133 | 20
6	Olin massage shower head, antique brass #37B411	79 | 06	474 | 36
6	Olin single pedestal porcelain sink #42B782	98 | 05	588 | 30
	TOTAL		1,564 | 86

CAREERS IN YOUR FUTURE

TRACY L. NEWKIRK
Marketing Manager, Microsoft Corporation

Tracy's accounting skills—along with marketing positions in three large and small, public and private corporations (GE, CareWise, Inc., and Experience Music Project)—have launched her into her dream career with Microsoft in Redmond, Washington. Unlike her last position with a non-profit museum, she now works in a far larger and more global company.

Tracy works as a marketing manager in a relatively small, product-incubation-like group within Microsoft. But her responsibilities are not all related to marketing. Along with all the marketing efforts comes greater fiscal responsibility, including showing the return on investment (ROI) for marketing campaign efforts and being able to justify the next project. Each day brings something new.

Tracy enjoys accounting because she loves the number crunching. The outcome is clear—you either have money to spend on a project or you don't. Although she is not journalizing or preparing financial statements in her current position, her accounting experience sets her apart from many in the marketing field.

"Absorb all that you can in accounting and hang onto it so that you can apply it in your everyday life. Put it on your resume. If you can sit in a room with the controller and/or director of finance and hold your own during a budget discussion, you'll be doing very well. Not many people can do that."

THE SALES JOURNAL

OBJECTIVE 2

Journalize transactions in a sales journal.

The **sales journal** records sales of merchandise **on account only.** This specialized type of transaction calls for debits to Accounts Receivable and credits to Sales. As shown here, Rainier Plumbing Supply uses the sales journal *instead of* the general journal to record the three transactions.

REMEMBER!

The sales journal is a book of original entry. Do not duplicate the transaction in the general journal.

SALES JOURNAL   PAGE __38__

	DATE	INV. NO.	CUSTOMER'S NAME	POST. REF.	ACCOUNTS RECEIVABLE DR. SALES CR.	
1	20–					1
2	Aug. 1	1320	Betterbuilt Homes Co.		1 5 6 4 86	2
3	3	1321	Arnold, Inc.		1 1 1 6 00	3
4	6	1322	Gonzales Construction		1 3 9 4 00	4
5						5
6						6
7						7
8						8
9						9

Because *one* column is headed Accounts Receivable Dr./Sales Cr., each transaction requires only a single line. Repetition is avoided, and all entries for sales of merchandise on account are found in one place. Listing the invoice number makes it easier to check the details of a particular sale at a later date.

The amount of each sale will be posted daily to the account of each charge customer in the accounts receivable ledger. The accounts receivable ledger is introduced on page 341.

Posting from the Sales Journal

OBJECTIVE 3
Post sales journal transactions to an accounts receivable ledger and a general ledger.

Using the sales journal also saves time and space in posting to the ledger accounts. The transactions involving the sales of merchandise on account for the entire month of August are shown in Figure 3 on page 340.

Because every entry is a debit to Accounts Receivable and a credit to Sales, you can make a single posting to these accounts for the amount of the total as of the last day of the month. This entry is called a **summarizing entry** because it summarizes one month's transactions. In the Post. Ref. columns of the ledger accounts, the letter S designates the sales journal.

REMEMBER!

The T accounts look like this:

Accounts Receivable

+	−
32,973.82	

Sales

−	+
	32,973.82

GENERAL LEDGER

ACCOUNT **Accounts Receivable**   ACCOUNT NO. **113**

	DATE	ITEM	POST. REF.	DEBIT	CREDIT	BALANCE DEBIT	BALANCE CREDIT	
1	20–							1
2	Aug. 31		S38	32 9 7 3 82		32 9 7 3 82		2
3								3
4								4
5								5

ACCOUNT **Sales**   ACCOUNT NO. **411**

	DATE	ITEM	POST. REF.	DEBIT	CREDIT	BALANCE DEBIT	BALANCE CREDIT	
1	20–							1
2	Aug. 31		S38		32 9 7 3 82		32 9 7 3 82	2
3								3
4								4
5								5

REMEMBER!

The purpose of posting reference numbers is to tell where in the ledger an amount was posted or the journal from which it came.

After posting the total of the sales journal to the Accounts Receivable account in the general ledger, write the account number of Accounts Receivable at the left below the total of the sales journal. Repeat the process of posting for the total of the sales journal to the Sales account in the general ledger, placing the account number of Sales at the right below the total of the sales journal. **Don't record these account numbers until you have completed the postings.**

FIGURE 3

REMEMBER!

The sales journal is used to record only the sales of merchandise (goods) on account.

SALES JOURNAL

PAGE ___38___

	DATE	INV. NO.	CUSTOMER'S NAME	POST. REF.	ACCOUNTS RECEIVABLE DR. SALES CR.	
1	20–					1
2	Aug. 1	1320	Betterbuilt Homes Co.		1 5 6 4 86	2
3	3	1321	Arnold, Inc.		1 1 1 6 00	3
4	6	1322	Gonzales Construction		1 3 9 4 00	4
5	9	1323	Harris Service Company		5 9 6 1 00	5
6	11	1324	Carmel Hardware		3 7 7 2 24	6
7	16	1325	Howard and Sons, Inc.		2 4 4 1 00	7
8	20	1326	Green Plumbing and Heating		1 7 1 0 00	8
9	23	1327	Chin Building Supplies		3 3 8 4 00	9
10	24	1328	Carmel Hardware		1 2 9 3 22	10
11	28	1329	Howard and Sons, Inc.		2 4 8 7 00	11
12	30	1330	Chin Building Supplies		3 6 1 4 00	12
13	31	1331	Betterbuilt Homes Co.		1 3 7 5 50	13
14	31	1332	Quality Builders, Inc.		2 8 6 1 00	14
15	31				32 9 7 3 82	15
16					(113)(411)	16
17						17

Sales Journal Provision for Sales Tax

Most states and some cities levy a sales tax on retail sales of goods and services. The retailer collects the sales tax from customers and later pays it to the tax authorities.

When goods or services are sold on credit, the sales tax is charged to the customer and recorded at the time of the sale. The sales journal must be designed to handle this type of transaction. For example, if a retail store sells an item for $500 and the sales tax is 8 percent, the transaction would be recorded in T accounts like this:

Accounts Receivable	Sales	Sales Tax Payable
+ –	– +	– +
540	500	40

Incidentally, when the sales tax is paid to the state, the accountant debits Sales Tax Payable and credits Cash.

Because we want to illustrate a sales journal for a retail merchandising firm operating in a state that has a sales tax, we will talk about the transactions of Dixon Office Furniture Co., another company. Its sales journal is shown in Figure 4.

Column totals would be posted as a debit to Accounts Receivable, a credit to Sales Tax Payable, and a credit to Sales. After posting, the respective account numbers are recorded in parentheses below the totals.

FIGURE 4

				ACCOUNTS RECEIVABLE DEBIT	SALES TAX PAYABLE CREDIT	SALES CREDIT
DATE	INV. NO.	CUSTOMER'S NAME	POST. REF.			
20–						
Apr. 1	9382	C. D. Barnes		1 6 7 4 00	1 2 4 00	1 5 5 0 00
1	9383	Best Child Care		1 1 0 3 76	8 1 76	1 0 2 2 00
1	9384	Land Use Planners		2 2 1 4 00	1 6 4 00	2 0 5 0 00
2	9385	R. M. Allen		3 3 6 0 96	2 4 8 96	3 1 1 2 00
30	10121	Link Accountants		1 2 0 9 60	8 9 60	1 1 2 0 00
30				49 9 1 7 60	3 6 9 7 60	46 2 2 0 00
				(1 1 3)	(2 1 4)	(4 1 1)

SALES JOURNAL   PAGE 96

REMEMBER!

With a sales journal that has more than one column, use the column totals to prove that the total debits equal the total credits. Do this before posting to the general ledger accounts.

THE ACCOUNTS RECEIVABLE LEDGER

In order to know how much each charge customer owes a business, the firm maintains an **accounts receivable ledger**. This ledger is a separate book or record containing a list of the charge customers with their respective balances listed in either alphabetical order or by account number. If the company's accounting system is not computerized, accountants prefer a loose-leaf binder, so that they can insert accounts for new customers and remove closed accounts.

The Accounts Receivable account in the general ledger should still be maintained. When all the postings are up to date, the balance of this account should equal the total of all the charge customers' individual account balances. The Accounts Receivable account in the general ledger is called a **controlling account**. The accounts receivable *ledger,* containing the accounts of all the charge customers, is really a special type of ledger, called a **subsidiary ledger**. Figure 5 diagrams the interrelationship of these ledgers.

The accountant posts the individual amounts to the accounts receivable ledger every day, so that this ledger will have up-to-date information. At the end of the month, the accountant posts the sales journal total of $12,900 (in Figure 5) to the general ledger accounts as a debit to the Accounts Receivable controlling account and a credit to the Sales account. The schedule of accounts receivable is merely a listing of charge customers' individual account balances.

In the simplified illustration in Figure 5, it just so happens that, since no payments were received from charge customers, the total of the sales journal equals the balance of Accounts Receivable. However, if $1,200 had been received from charge customers, both the balance of the Accounts Receivable controlling account and the total of the schedule of accounts receivable would be $11,700 ($12,900 − $1,200). The total of the sales journal would still be $12,900.

REMEMBER!

The balance of the Accounts Receivable controlling account at the end of the month must equal the total of the balances of the charge customer accounts in the accounts receivable ledger.

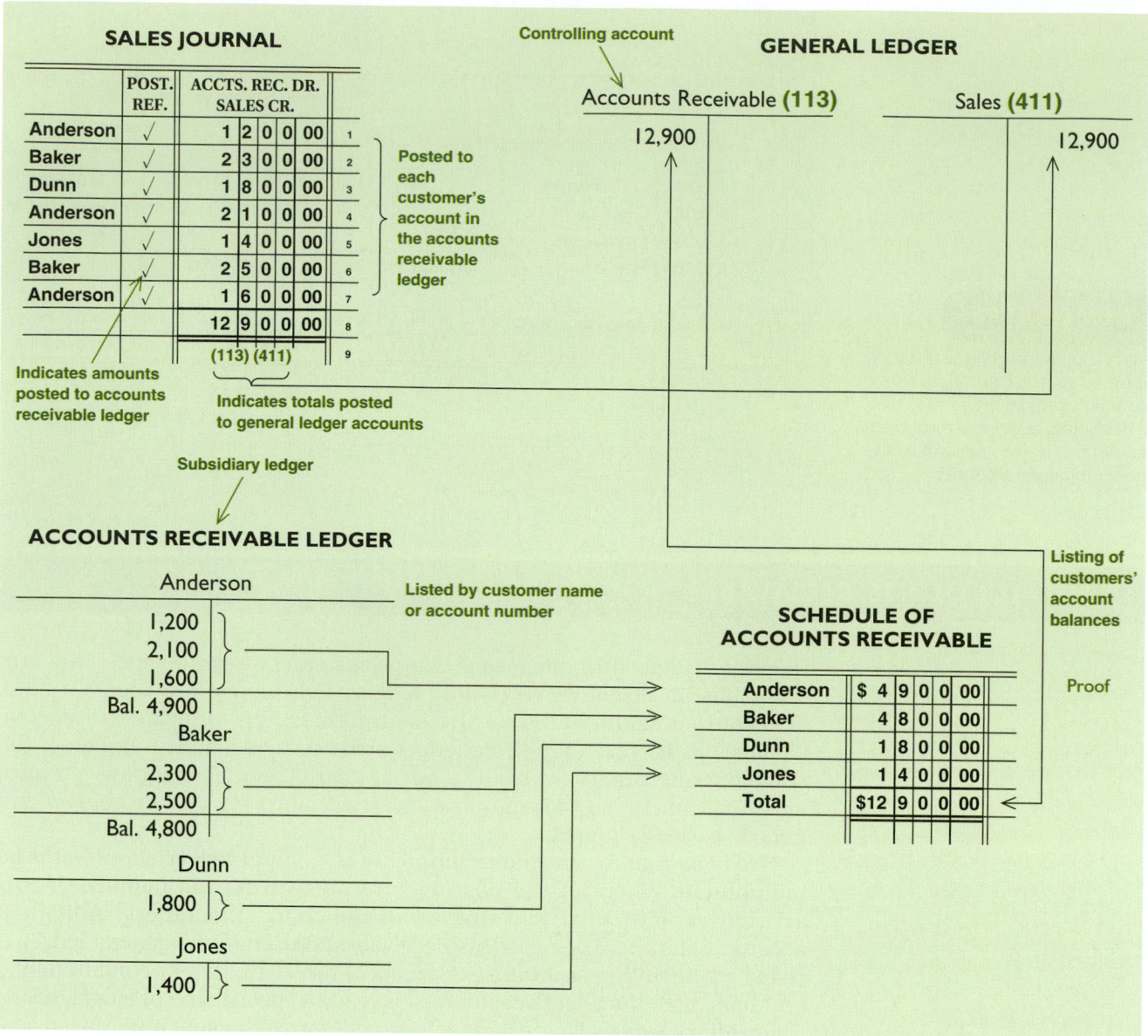

FIGURE 5

After you post an amount from the sales journal to a charge customer's account in the accounts receivable ledger, put a check mark (✓) in the Post. Ref. column of the sales journal. Figure 6 shows the posting procedure for a single-column sales journal.

Let's go back to the sales journal of Rainier Plumbing Supply for August. We will cover the daily postings that its accountant has made to the accounts receivable ledger. Then we'll see the schedule of accounts receivable. These entries are shown in Figure 6 and the ledger accounts that follow. Note that the ruling consists of a single line under the amount column and double lines extended through the Date, Post. Ref., and amount columns. The last day of the month is recorded on the same line as the total.

FIGURE 6

SALES JOURNAL   PAGE ___38___

	DATE	INV. NO.	CUSTOMER'S NAME	POST. REF.	ACCOUNTS RECEIVABLE DR. SALES CR.	
1	20–					1
2	Aug. 1	1320	Betterbuilt Homes Co.	✓	1 5 6 4 86	2
3	3	1321	Arnold, Inc.	✓	1 1 1 6 00	3
4	6	1322	Gonzales Construction	✓	1 3 9 4 00	4
5	9	1323	Harris Service Company	✓	5 9 6 1 00	5
6	11	1324	Carmel Hardware	✓	3 7 7 2 24	6
7	16	1325	Howard and Sons, Inc.	✓	2 4 4 1 00	7
8	20	1326	Green Plumbing and Heating	✓	1 7 1 0 00	8
9	23	1327	Chin Building Supplies	✓	3 3 8 4 00	9
10	24	1328	Carmel Hardware	✓	1 2 9 3 22	10
11	28	1329	Howard and Sons, Inc.	✓	2 4 8 7 00	11
12	30	1330	Chin Building Supplies	✓	3 6 1 4 00	12
13	31	1331	Betterbuilt Homes Co.	✓	1 3 7 5 50	13
14	31	1332	Quality Builders, Inc.	✓	2 8 6 1 00	14
15	31				32 9 7 3 82	15
16					(113)(411)	16
17						17

> **REMEMBER!**
>
> The check marks (✓) indicate that each amount has been posted to a charge customer's account.

ACCOUNTS RECEIVABLE LEDGER

NAME Arnold, Inc.

ADDRESS 1457 Lincoln Street
Seattle, WA 98101

DATE	ITEM	POST. REF.	DEBIT	CREDIT	BALANCE
20–					
Aug. 3		S38	1 1 1 6 00		1 1 1 6 00

NAME Betterbuilt Homes Co.

ADDRESS 5120 Gilman Avenue
Portland, OR 97202

DATE	ITEM	POST. REF.	DEBIT	CREDIT	BALANCE
20–					
Aug. 1		S38	1 5 6 4 86		1 5 6 4 86
31		S38	1 3 7 5 50		2 9 4 0 36

> **REMEMBER!**
>
> The normal balance in the accounts receivable ledger is a debit, because the customer accounts represent assets.

(continued)

**FIGURE 6
(continued)**

NAME **Carmel Hardware**
ADDRESS **2168 Tenth Street**
Seattle, WA 98101

DATE		ITEM	POST. REF.	DEBIT					CREDIT					BALANCE				
20–																		
Aug.	11		S38	3	7	7	2	24						3	7	7	2	24
	24		S38	1	2	9	3	22						5	0	6	5	46

NAME **Chin Building Supplies**
ADDRESS **2242 Lakeside Avenue**
Seattle, WA 98101

DATE		ITEM	POST. REF.	DEBIT					CREDIT					BALANCE				
20–																		
Aug.	23		S38	3	3	8	4	00						3	3	8	4	00
	30		S38	3	6	1	4	00						6	9	9	8	00

NAME **Gonzales Construction**
ADDRESS **3680 Paseo Avenue**
Seattle, WA 98115

DATE		ITEM	POST. REF.	DEBIT					CREDIT					BALANCE				
20–																		
Aug.	6		S38	1	3	9	4	00						1	3	9	4	00

NAME **Green Plumbing and Heating**
ADDRESS **1620 Salazar Road**
Tacoma, WA 98405

DATE		ITEM	POST. REF.	DEBIT					CREDIT					BALANCE				
20–																		
Aug.	20		S38	1	7	1	0	00						1	7	1	0	00

**FIGURE 6
(continued)**

NAME **Harris Service Company**

ADDRESS **5196 Eighteenth Street**
Seattle, WA 98102

DATE		ITEM	POST. REF.	DEBIT	CREDIT	BALANCE
20–						
Aug.	9		S38	5 9 6 1 00		5 9 6 1 00

NAME **Howard and Sons, Inc.**

ADDRESS **4142 Adams Avenue**
Tacoma, WA 98422

DATE		ITEM	POST. REF.	DEBIT	CREDIT	BALANCE
20–						
Aug.	16		S38	2 4 4 1 00		2 4 4 1 00
	28		S38	2 4 8 7 00		4 9 2 8 00

NAME **Quality Builders, Inc.**

ADDRESS **424 Fifteenth Street**
Seattle, WA 98115

DATE		ITEM	POST. REF.	DEBIT	CREDIT	BALANCE
20–						
Aug.	31		S38	2 8 6 1 00		2 8 6 1 00

OBJECTIVE 4

Prepare a schedule of accounts receivable.

Next, the accountant prepares a schedule of accounts receivable, like the one shown in Figure 7, on page 346, listing each charge customer's account balance.

We assume that there were no previous balances in the customers' accounts. Under this circumstance, the Accounts Receivable controlling account in the general ledger will have the same balance, $32,973.82, as the schedule of accounts receivable.

REMEMBER!

Posting to the Accounts Receivable account from the sales journal took place at the end of the month.

GENERAL LEDGER

ACCOUNT **Accounts Receivable**   ACCOUNT NO. **113**

	DATE		ITEM	POST. REF.	DEBIT	CREDIT	BALANCE DEBIT	BALANCE CREDIT	
1	20–								1
2	Aug.	31		S38	32 9 7 3 82		32 9 7 3 82		2
3									3

FIGURE 7

Rainier Plumbing Supply
Schedule of Accounts Receivable
August 31, 20—

Arnold, Inc.	$ 1 1 1 6 00
Betterbuilt Homes Co.	2 9 4 0 36
Carmel Hardware	5 0 6 5 46
Chin Building Supplies	6 9 9 8 00
Gonzales Construction	1 3 9 4 00
Green Plumbing and Heating	1 7 1 0 00
Harris Service Company	5 9 6 1 00
Howard and Sons, Inc.	4 9 2 8 00
Quality Builders, Inc.	2 8 6 1 00
Total Accounts Receivable	$ 32 9 7 3 82

SALES RETURNS AND ALLOWANCES

OBJECTIVE 5

Journalize sales returns and allowances, including credit memorandums and returns involving sales tax, in a general journal, and post to the accounts receivable ledger and general ledger.

The Sales Returns and Allowances account handles two types of transactions related to merchandise that has previously been sold. A *return* is a physical return of the goods. An *allowance* is a reduction from the original price because the goods were defective or damaged. It may not be economically worthwhile to have customers return the goods; each situation is a special case. To avoid writing a separate letter each time to inform customers of their account adjustments, businesses use a special form called a **credit memorandum**. A credit memorandum (Figure 8) is a written statement indicating a seller's willingness to reduce the amount of a buyer's debt.

FIGURE 8

Rainier Plumbing Supply
1400 Front Street
Seattle, WA 98101

CREDIT MEMORANDUM

No. 1069

CREDIT TO: *Chin Building Supplies*
2242 Lakeside Avenue
Seattle, WA 98101

DATE: *September 2, 20–*

WE CREDIT YOUR ACCOUNT AS FOLLOWS:

QUANTITY	DESCRIPTION	TOTAL	
50	*Olin pop-up tub drain antique finish*		
	1½-inch brass overflow tube #46C72	254	00

The Sales Returns and Allowances account is a deduction from Sales. Using an account separate from Sales provides a better record of the total returns and allowances. Accountants deduct Sales Returns and Allowances from Sales on the income statement.

Using T accounts, here's an example of a return. The original sale is shown first, followed by the issuance of a credit memorandum.

Transaction (a)   On August 30, Rainier Plumbing Supply sold merchandise on account to Chin Building Supplies, $3,614, and recorded the sale in the sales journal.

Transaction (b)   On September 2, Chin Building Supplies returned $254 worth of the merchandise. Rainier Plumbing Supply issued credit memorandum no. 1069 (see Figure 8).

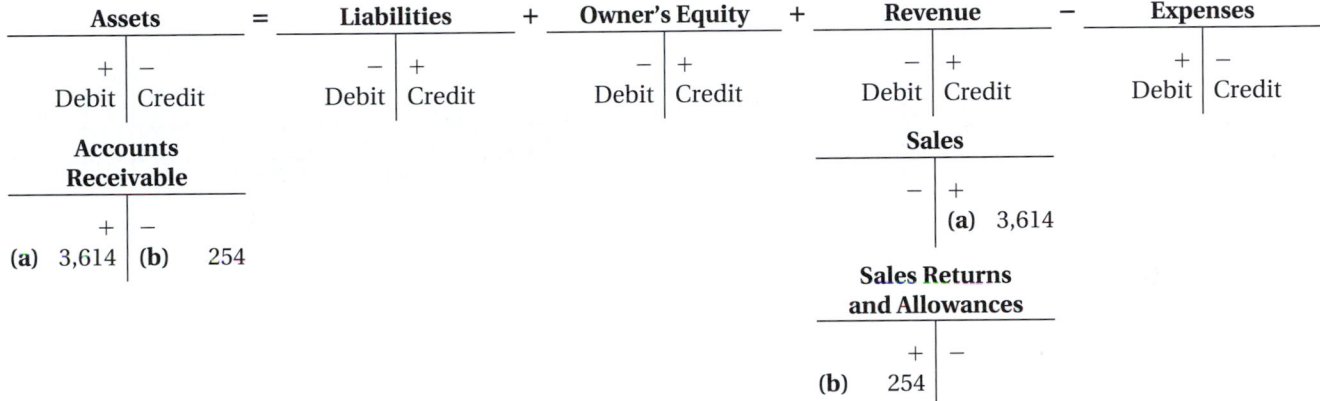

Rainier Plumbing Supply's accountant debits Sales Returns and Allowances to increase it; then, the accountant credits Accounts Receivable to decrease it because the charge customer, Chin Building Supplies, owes less than before.

The general journal entry serves as the posting source for crediting the Accounts Receivable controlling account in the general ledger. It also serves as the posting source for updating the accounts receivable ledger and therefore includes the name of the charge customer. If the balance of the Accounts Receivable controlling account is to equal the total of the individual account balances in the accounts receivable ledger, one must post to *both* the Accounts Receivable account in the general ledger *and* the account of Chin Building Supplies in the accounts receivable ledger. To take care of this double posting, the accountant draws a slanted line in the Post. Ref. column. When the amount has been posted as a credit to the general ledger account, the accountant writes the account number of Accounts Receivable in the left part of the Post. Ref. column. After the account of Chin Building Supplies has been posted as a credit, the accountant puts a check mark in the right portion of the Post. Ref. column. Sales Returns and Allowances is posted in the usual manner. The entry after posting is complete is shown on the following page.

GENERAL JOURNAL PAGE **27**

	DATE		DESCRIPTION	POST. REF.	DEBIT	CREDIT	
1	20–						1
2	Sept.	2	Sales Returns and Allowances	412	2 5 4 00		2
3			Accounts Receivable, Chin				3
4			Building Supplies	113 ✓		2 5 4 00	4
5			Issued credit memo no. 1069.				5
6							6

GENERAL LEDGER

ACCOUNT **Accounts Receivable** ACCOUNT NO. **113**

	DATE		ITEM	POST. REF.	DEBIT	CREDIT	BALANCE DEBIT	BALANCE CREDIT	
1	20–								1
2	Aug.	31		S38	32 9 7 3 82		32 9 7 3 82		2
3	Sept.	2		J27		2 5 4 00	32 7 1 9 82		3
4									4

ACCOUNT **Sales Returns and Allowances** ACCOUNT NO. **412**

	DATE		ITEM	POST. REF.	DEBIT	CREDIT	BALANCE DEBIT	BALANCE CREDIT	
1	20–								1
2	Sept.	2		J27	2 5 4 00		2 5 4 00		2
3									3

ACCOUNTS RECEIVABLE LEDGER

NAME **Chin Building Supplies**
ADDRESS **2242 Lakeside Avenue**
Seattle, WA 98101

DATE		ITEM	POST. REF.	DEBIT	CREDIT	BALANCE
20–						
Aug.	23		S38	3 3 8 4 00		3 3 8 4 00
	30		S38	3 6 1 4 00		6 9 9 8 00
Sept.	2		J27		2 5 4 00	6 7 4 4 00

Sales Return Involving a Sales Tax

If a customer who returns merchandise to a retail store was originally charged a sales tax, the sales tax must be returned to the customer. Refer back to the sales journal of Dixon Office Furniture Company on page 341, which included sales taxes. On April 3, assume that C. D. Barnes returns the furniture bought on April 1 for $1,550 plus $124 sales tax. Following is the general journal entry required for this type of return:

	GENERAL JOURNAL				PAGE 12	
DATE	DESCRIPTION	POST. REF.	DEBIT		CREDIT	
20–						
Apr. 3	Sales Returns and Allowances		1 5 5 0 00			
	Sales Tax Payable		1 2 4 00			
	Accounts Receivable, C. D. Barnes				1 6 7 4 00	
	Issued credit memo no. 1371.					

PURCHASING PROCEDURES

In a small retail store, the owner may do the buying. In large retail and wholesale businesses, department heads or division managers do the buying, after which the Purchasing Department goes into action: It places purchase orders, follows up the orders, and sees that deliveries are made to the right departments. The Purchasing Department also acts as a source of information on current prices, price trends, quality of goods, prospective suppliers, and reliability of suppliers.

The Purchasing Department normally requires that any requests to buy merchandise be in writing, in the form of a **purchase requisition**. After the purchase requisition is approved, the Purchasing Department sends a purchase order to the supplier. A **purchase order** is the company's written offer to buy certain goods. The accountant does not make any entry at this point because the supplier has not yet indicated acceptance of the order. A purchase order has at least four copies. The original goes to the supplier; copies go to the Purchasing Department (as proof of what was ordered), the department that issued the requisition (telling it that the goods it wanted have been ordered), the Accounting Department, and a blind copy (with quantities omitted) goes to Receiving.

To continue with the accounts of Rainier Plumbing Supply, the Fixtures Department submits a purchase requisition to the Purchasing Department, as shown in Figure 9 on page 350.

FIGURE 9

Rainier Plumbing Supply

No. C-726

1400 Front Street
Seattle, WA 98101

PURCHASE REQUISITION

| DEPARTMENT | *Fixtures* | DATE OF REQUEST | *July 2, 20–* |
| ADVISE ON DELIVERY | *C. Fenwick* | DATE REQUIRED | *Aug. 5, 20–* |

QUANTITY	DESCRIPTION
50	*Drominex shower heads #772R*

APPROVED BY *D. M. Bruce*   REQUESTED BY *J. C. Garcia*

FOR PURCHASING DEPT. USE ONLY

PURCHASE ORDER NO.   *7918*   ISSUED TO: *Collins, Inc.*
DATE *July 5, 20–*   *1614 Olivera Street*
                                                                  San Francisco, CA 94129

The Purchasing Department completes the rest of the purchase requisition and then sends out the purchase order shown in Figure 10.

FIGURE 10

Rainier Plumbing Supply

1400 Front Street
Seattle, WA 98101

PURCHASE ORDER

TO: *Collins, Inc.*   DATE: *July 5, 20–*
1614 Olivera Street   ORDER NO.: *7918*
San Francisco, CA 94129   SHIPPED BY:
                                                      TERMS: *2/10, n/30*

QUANTITY	DESCRIPTION	UNIT PRICE	TOTAL
50	*Drominex shower heads #772R*	34	20	1,710	00
	Total			1,710	00

D. M. Bruce

The seller then sends an invoice to the buyer as shown in Figure 11. This invoice should arrive in advance of the goods (or at least *with* the goods).

FIGURE 11

Collins, Inc.	**No. 2706**
1614 Olivera Street	
San Francisco, CA 94129	

INVOICE

SOLD TO *Rainier Plumbing Supply*
1400 Front Street
Seattle, WA 98101

DATE: *July 31, 20–*
ORDER NO.: *7918*
SHIPPED BY: *Western Freight Line*
TERMS: *2/10, n/30*

YOUR ORDER NO.	SALESPERSON	TERMS
7918	*C. L.*	2/10, n/30

DATE SHIPPED	SHIPPED BY	FOB
July 31, 20–	*Western Freight Line*	*San Francisco*

QUANTITY	DESCRIPTION	UNIT PRICE	TOTAL	
50	*Drominex shower heads #772R*	34 20	1,710	00
	Freight		85	50
	Total		1,795	50

Collins, Inc. (the seller) prepaid the freight cost and added the $85.50 to the bill, listing it separately; this is similiar to buying something by mail order or through the Internet. Freight In is discussed in more detail on **pages 358–360.** The transaction is recorded in T accounts below. Note that the transaction is recorded on August 2, the day the merchandise is received.

Purchases		Freight In		Accounts Payable	
+	−	+	−	−	+
Aug. 2 1,710.00		Aug. 2 85.50			Aug. 2 1,795.50

PURCHASES JOURNAL (THREE-COLUMN)

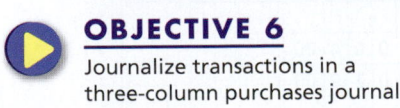

OBJECTIVE 6

Journalize transactions in a three-column purchases journal.

The **purchases journal** for Rainier Plumbing Supply for the month of August appears on page 352. By including a separate column for each account, we can record a typical purchase of merchandise on account on one line.

Terms means the terms of payment. For example, 2/10, n/30 means that if we pay the amount due within 10 days, we will receive a 2 percent discount; otherwise, the entire amount is due in 30 days.

PURCHASES JOURNAL

PAGE ___29___

	DATE		SUPPLIER'S NAME	INVOICE NO.	INVOICE DATE	TERMS	POST. REF.	ACCOUNTS PAYABLE CREDIT	FREIGHT IN DEBIT	PURCHASES DEBIT	
1	20–										1
2	Aug.	2	Collins, Inc.	2706	7/31	2/10, n/30		1 7 9 5 50	8 5 50	1 7 1 0 00	2
3		3	Langseth and Son	982	8/2	n/30		2 9 2 9 00	1 5 7 00	2 7 7 2 00	3
4		5	Dana Manufacturing Co.	10611	8/3	2/10, n/30		5 6 4 00		5 6 4 00	4
5		9	Gardner Products Co.	B643	8/6	1/10, n/30		1 2 4 5 00	9 0 00	1 1 5 5 00	5
6		18	C. A. Waters	46812	8/17	n/60		2 2 2 8 00		2 2 2 8 00	6
7		25	Delaney and Cox	1024	8/23	2/10, n/30		3 4 7 6 00	1 1 4 00	3 3 6 2 00	7
8		26	Collins, Inc.	2801	8/25	2/10, n/30		2 6 0 6 00	2 2 2 00	2 3 8 4 00	8
9		31						14 8 4 3 50	6 6 8 50	14 1 7 5 00	9
10								(2 1 2)	(5 1 4)	(5 1 1)	10
11											11
12											12

Posting from the Purchases Journal to the General Ledger

OBJECTIVE 7

Post purchases journal transactions to an accounts payable ledger and a general ledger.

Figures 12 and 13 show the journal entries for all transactions involving the purchase of merchandise on account for August and the related ledger accounts for the same time period. In the Post. Ref. column of the ledger accounts, P designates the purchases journal. After posting the column totals for the month to the ledger accounts, the accountant goes back to the purchases journal and records the account numbers in parentheses directly below the total.

FIGURE 12

REMEMBER!

Transactions involving the buying of supplies or other assets should not be journalized in the three-column purchases journal, because this purchases journal may be used only for purchases of merchandise for resale.

GENERAL LEDGER

ACCOUNT   **Accounts Payable**

ACCOUNT NO. __212__

	DATE	ITEM	POST. REF.	DEBIT	CREDIT	BALANCE DEBIT	BALANCE CREDIT	
1	20–							1
2	Aug. 1	Balance	✓				1 5 0 4 00	2
3	31		P29		14 8 4 3 50		16 3 4 7 50	3
4								4

ACCOUNT   **Purchases**

ACCOUNT NO. __511__

	DATE	ITEM	POST. REF.	DEBIT	CREDIT	BALANCE DEBIT	BALANCE CREDIT	
1	20–							1
2	Aug. 1	Balance	✓			89 9 0 4 00		2
3	31		P29	14 1 7 5 00		104 0 7 9 00		3
4								4

FIGURE 12 (continued)

ACCOUNT   **Freight In**   ACCOUNT NO.   **514**

	DATE	ITEM	POST. REF.	DEBIT	CREDIT	BALANCE DEBIT	BALANCE CREDIT	
1	20–							1
2	Aug. 1	Balance	✓			4 6 7 9 50		2
3	31		P29	6 6 8 50		5 3 4 8 00		3
4								4

PURCHASES JOURNAL   PAGE   **29**

	DATE		SUPPLIER'S NAME	INVOICE NO.	INVOICE DATE	TERMS	POST. REF.	ACCOUNTS PAYABLE CREDIT	FREIGHT IN DEBIT	PURCHASES DEBIT	
1	20–										1
2	Aug.	2	Collins, Inc.	2706	7/31	2/10, n/30	✓	1 7 9 5 50	8 5 50	1 7 1 0 00	2
3		3	Langseth and Son	982	8/2	n/30	✓	2 9 2 9 00	1 5 7 00	2 7 7 2 00	3
4		5	Dana Manufacturing Co.	10611	8/3	2/10, n/30	✓	5 6 4 00		5 6 4 00	4
5		9	Gardner Products Co.	B643	8/6	1/10, n/30	✓	1 2 4 5 00	9 0 00	1 1 5 5 00	5
6		18	C. A. Waters	46812	8/17	n/60	✓	2 2 2 8 00		2 2 2 8 00	6
7		25	Delaney and Cox	1024	8/23	2/10, n/30	✓	3 4 7 6 00	1 1 4 00	3 3 6 2 00	7
8		26	Collins, Inc.	2801	8/25	2/10, n/30	✓	2 6 0 6 00	2 2 2 00	2 3 8 4 00	8
9		31						14 8 4 3 50	6 6 8 50	14 1 7 5 00	9
10								(2 1 2)	(5 1 4)	(5 1 1)	10

FIGURE 13

THE ACCOUNTS PAYABLE LEDGER

REMEMBER!

Creditors are companies or individuals to whom we owe money.

REMEMBER!

Increases in Accounts Payable are recorded in the Credit column. Decreases in Accounts Payable are recorded in the Debit column.

Previously, we called the Accounts Receivable account in the general ledger a **controlling** account, and we saw that the accounts receivable ledger consists of an individual account for each charge customer. We also saw that the accountant posts to the accounts receivable ledger every day.

Accounts Payable is a parallel case; it, too, is a controlling account in the general ledger. **The accounts payable ledger is a subsidiary ledger, and it consists of individual accounts for all the creditors.** Again, posting to the accounts payable ledger is usually done daily. After posting to the individual creditors' accounts, the accountant puts a check mark (✓) in the Post. Ref. column of the purchases journal. After the accountant has finished the posting to the controlling account at the end of the period, the total of the schedule of accounts payable should equal the balance of the Accounts Payable (controlling) account. The three-column form is used for the accounts payable ledger.

Now let's look at the purchases journal (Figure 13) and the postings to the ledger. Note that in the accounts payable ledger—as in the accounts receivable ledger—the accounts of the individual creditors are listed in either alphabetical or numerical order. Firms that handle all of their bookkeeping and accounting on computer may assign an account number to each individual account.

REMEMBER!

Signs for Accounts Payable

Debit	Credit
−	+

Columns for Accounts Payable Ledger

DEBIT	CREDIT	BALANCE
−	+	

ACCOUNTS PAYABLE LEDGER

NAME Collins, Inc.

ADDRESS 1614 Olivera Street

San Francisco, CA 94129

DATE		ITEM	POST. REF.	DEBIT	CREDIT	BALANCE
20–						
Aug.	2		P29		1 7 9 5 50	1 7 9 5 50
	26		P29		2 6 0 6 00	4 4 0 1 50

NAME Dana Manufacturing Company

ADDRESS 254 Calle Mancha

Los Angeles, CA 90025

DATE		ITEM	POST. REF.	DEBIT	CREDIT	BALANCE
20–						
Aug.	5		P29		5 6 4 00	5 6 4 00

NAME Delaney and Cox

ADDRESS 2426 Reilly Way, N.E.

Los Angeles, CA 90101

DATE		ITEM	POST. REF.	DEBIT	CREDIT	BALANCE
20–						
Aug.	25		P29		3 4 7 6 00	3 4 7 6 00

NAME Gardner Products Company

ADDRESS 2154 Springer St.

Boston, MA 02107

DATE		ITEM	POST. REF.	DEBIT	CREDIT	BALANCE
20–						
Aug.	9		P29		1 2 4 5 00	1 2 4 5 00

NAME Langseth and Son

ADDRESS 142 Grant Road

Cleveland, OH 44102

DATE		ITEM	POST. REF.	DEBIT	CREDIT	BALANCE
20–						
July	27		P28		1 1 8 0 00	1 1 8 0 00
Aug.	3		P29		2 9 2 9 00	4 1 0 9 00

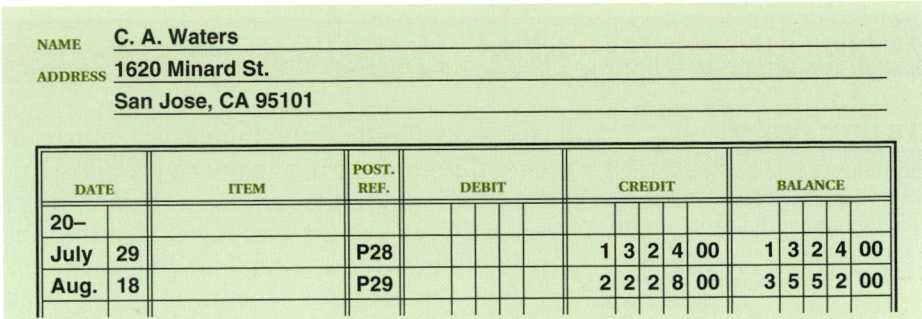

NAME   C. A. Waters

ADDRESS 1620 Minard St.
         San Jose, CA 95101

DATE		ITEM	POST. REF.	DEBIT	CREDIT	BALANCE
20–						
July	29		P28		1 3 2 4 00	1 3 2 4 00
Aug.	18		P29		2 2 2 8 00	3 5 5 2 00

Schedule of Accounts Payable

OBJECTIVE 8

Prepare a schedule of accounts payable.

Assuming that no other transactions involved Accounts Payable, the schedule of accounts payable would appear as shown in Figure 14. Note that the balance of Dana Manufacturing Company is taken from the accounts payable ledger.

The posting to the Accounts Payable controlling account in the general ledger below is now up to date.

GENERAL LEDGER

ACCOUNT Accounts Payable   ACCOUNT NO. 212

	DATE		ITEM	POST. REF.	DEBIT	CREDIT	BALANCE DEBIT	BALANCE CREDIT	
1	20–								1
2	Aug.	1	Balance	✓				2 5 0 4 00	2
3		31		P29		14 8 4 3 50		17 3 4 7 50	3
4									4

FIGURE 14

Rainier Plumbing Supply
Schedule of Accounts Payable
August 31, 20—

Collins, Inc.	$ 4 4 0 1 50
Dana Manufacturing Company	5 6 4 00
Delaney and Cox	3 4 7 6 00
Gardner Products Company	1 2 4 5 00
Langseth and Son	4 1 0 9 00
C. A. Waters	3 5 5 2 00
Total Accounts Payable	$17 3 4 7 50

PURCHASES RETURNS AND ALLOWANCES

OBJECTIVE 9

Journalize transactions involving purchases returns and allowances in a general journal, and post to the accounts payable ledger and general ledger.

As its title implies, the Purchases Returns and Allowances account handles either a return of merchandise previously purchased or an allowance made for merchandise that arrived in damaged condition. In both cases, there is a reduction in the amount owed to the supplier. The buyer sends a letter or printed form to the supplier, who acknowledges the reduction by sending a credit memorandum. The buyer should wait for notice of the agreed deduction before making an entry.

The Purchases Returns and Allowances account is considered to be a deduction from Purchases. Using a separate account provides a better record of the total returns and allowances. Purchases Returns and Allowances is deducted from the Purchases account on the income statement. (We'll talk about this point later.) For now, let's look at an example consisting of a return on the books of Rainier Plumbing Supply.

Transaction (a) On September 2, bought merchandise on account from Dana Manufacturing Company, $830. Journalized this entry as a debit to Purchases and a credit to Accounts Payable.

Transaction (b) On September 8, received credit memorandum no. 1629 from Dana Manufacturing Company for $270. Journalized this as a debit to Accounts Payable and a credit to Purchases Returns and Allowances.

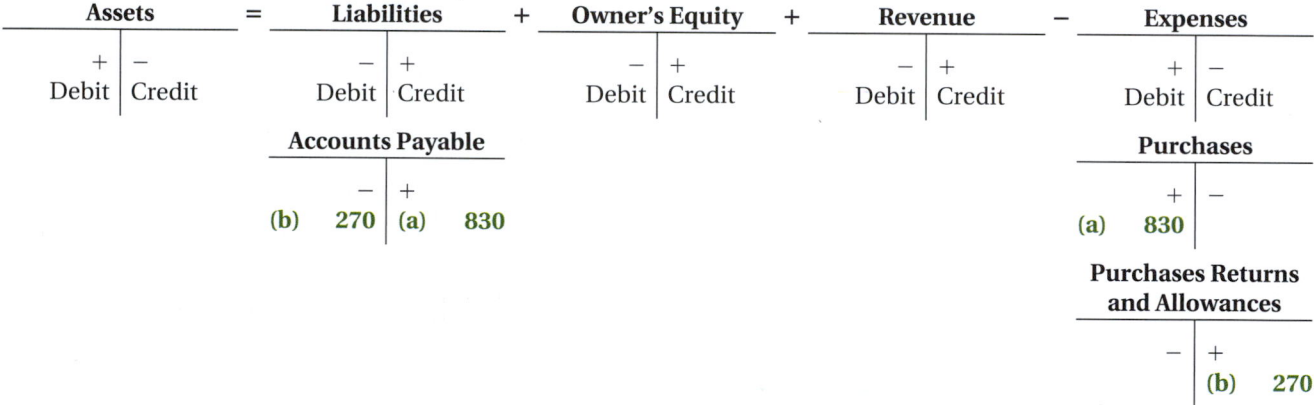

Purchases Returns and Allowances is credited because Rainier Plumbing Supply has more returns and allowances than before. Accounts Payable is debited because Rainier Plumbing Supply owes less than before. The related entry including the postings is shown on the next page. Note that Accounts Payable is followed by the name of the individual creditor's account. **The accountant must post the amount to both the Accounts Payable controlling account and the individual creditor's account in the accounts payable ledger.** The account numbers in the Post. Ref. column indicate postings to the accounts in the general ledger, and the check marks indicate postings to the accounts in the accounts payable ledger.

GENERAL JOURNAL PAGE 27

	DATE		DESCRIPTION	POST. REF.	DEBIT	CREDIT	
1	20–						1
2	Sept.	8	Accounts Payable, Dana				2
3			Manufacturing Company	212 ✓	2 7 0 00		3
4			Purchases Returns and				4
5			Allowances	512		2 7 0 00	5
6			Credit memo no. 1629 for				6
7			return of merchandise.				7
8							8

GENERAL LEDGER

ACCOUNT Accounts Payable   ACCOUNT NO. 212

	DATE		ITEM	POST. REF.	DEBIT	CREDIT	BALANCE DEBIT	BALANCE CREDIT	
1	20–								1
2	Sept.	1	Balance	✓				17 3 4 7 50	2
3		8		J27	2 7 0 00			17 0 7 7 50	3
4									4

ACCOUNT Purchases Returns and Allowances   ACCOUNT NO. 512

	DATE		ITEM	POST. REF.	DEBIT	CREDIT	BALANCE DEBIT	BALANCE CREDIT	
1	20–								1
2	Sept.	1	Balance	✓				1 6 4 0 00	2
3		8		J27		2 7 0 00		1 9 1 0 00	3
4									4

ACCOUNTS PAYABLE LEDGER

NAME Dana Manufacturing Company
ADDRESS 254 Calle Mancha
Los Angeles, CA 90025

DATE		ITEM	POST. REF.	DEBIT	CREDIT	BALANCE
20–						
Sept.	1	Balance	✓			5 6 4 00
	2		P30		8 3 0 00	1 3 9 4 00
	8		J27	2 7 0 00		1 1 2 4 00

FREIGHT CHARGES ON INCOMING MERCHANDISE

OBJECTIVE 10

Describe the procedures for handling freight charges on merchandise and other goods.

FYI

Some accountants call the Freight In account *Transportation In*.

Companies use the Freight In account to keep a record of all separately charged delivery costs on incoming merchandise.

Freight costs are expressed as FOB (free on board) destination or shipping point. **(Destination is the buyer's location; shipping point is the seller's location.)** In both cases, the supplier loads the goods free on board the carrier. Beyond that point, there must be an understanding as to who is responsible for paying the freight charges. **If the seller assumes the entire cost of transportation, without any reimbursement from the buyer, the terms are** FOB destination. In this case, title or ownership changes hands when the buyer receives the goods. **If the buyer is responsible for paying the freight cost, the shipping terms are called** FOB shipping point. In this case, title or ownership changes hands when goods are transferred to a common carrier (freight company).

Briefly, when goods are shipped FOB destination, the freight charges are not stated, and the seller simply pays the amount of the freight. Suppose Rainier Plumbing Supply, which is in Seattle, buys merchandise from a supplier in Chicago with shipping terms of FOB Seattle listed on the invoice. The total of the invoice is $1,740, and there is no separate listing of freight charges. In other words, the seller has included the transportation costs in the price.

When goods are shipped FOB shipping point, with the buyer responsible for paying the freight charges, transportation costs may be handled in two ways:

1. The buyer may pay the freight charges directly to the transportation company. For example, an automobile dealer in Houston buys cars FOB Detroit. In this case, the automobile dealer makes one check payable to the manufacturer and another check payable to the carrier for the freight charges. (FOB Detroit is the same as FOB shipping point.)
2. The transportation or shipping costs may be listed separately on the invoice. For example, suppose a person orders a computer from an Internet company. The Internet company has prepaid (paid in advance) the freight charges as a favor or convenience for the buyer. However, the

To record the transportation costs of merchandise purchased for resale, such as automobiles, accountants use an expense account called Freight In (also called Transportation In).

freight charges are listed on the bill or invoice, and the buyer is responsible for reimbursing the Internet company for the freight charges. Similarly, when a business buys merchandise, the amount of the freight charges may be prepaid by the seller and listed separately on the invoice.

Look again at the invoice from Collins, Inc., on page 351. Note that the freight cost is listed separately, and the terms are FOB shipping point (San Francisco). Collins paid the transportation cost; Rainier must reimburse Collins for this cost.

Let's proceed with three transactions for Rainier Plumbing Supply. We first record the transactions in a general journal. Then, as a means of reemphasizing the advantages of special journals as opposed to a general journal, we record the same transactions in a special journal. In practice, the transactions would be recorded *in only one journal, not both.*

During the first week in August, the following transactions took place:

Aug.   2   Bought merchandise on account from Collins, Inc., invoice no. 2706, $1,710; terms 2/10, n/30; dated July 31; FOB San Francisco, freight prepaid and added to the invoice, $85.50 (total $1,795.50).

3   Bought merchandise on account from Langseth and Son, invoice no. 982, $2,772; terms net 30 days; dated August 2; FOB Cleveland, freight prepaid and added to the invoice, $157 (total $2,929).

5   Bought merchandise on account from Dana Manufacturing Company, invoice no. 10611, $564; terms 2/10, n/30; dated August 3; FOB Los Angeles.

Notice that the transactions with Collins, Inc., and Langseth and Son are both FOB shipping point with the freight charges listed separately. Consequently, the buyer (Rainier) must reimburse the sellers for the transportation costs by paying the total of the invoices. However, in the transaction with Dana Manufacturing Company, which is FOB shipping point without freight charges listed, the buyer (Rainier) must pay the freight costs separately, perhaps when the goods are delivered.

TRANSPORTATION CHARGES ON THE BUYING OF GOODS AND SERVICES OTHER THAN MERCHANDISE

Any freight charges incurred when buying any other assets, such as supplies or equipment, should be debited to the respective asset accounts. Let's return to Rainier Plumbing Supply and assume that this company bought display cases on account from Carter Cabinet Shop, at a cost of $2,700 plus freight charges of $290. The seller of the display cases prepaid the transportation costs for Rainier Plumbing Supply and then added the $290 to the invoice price of the cases. Let's visualize this with T accounts.

Store Equipment		Accounts Payable	
+	−	−	+
2,990			2,990

If Rainier Plumbing Supply had paid the freight charges separately, the entry for the payment would be a debit to Store Equipment for $290 and a credit to Cash for $290.

INTERNAL CONTROL OF PURCHASES

Purchases is one of the areas in which internal control is essential. Efficiency and security require most companies to work out careful procedures for buying and paying for goods. This is understandable, as large sums of money are usually involved. The control aspect generally involves the following measures:

1. Purchases are made only after proper authorization is given. Purchase requisitions and purchase orders are all prenumbered, so that each form can be accounted for.
2. The receiving department carefully checks all goods upon receipt for count, damages, and description. Later, the report of the receiving department is verified against the purchase order and the purchase invoice.
3. The person who authorizes the payment is neither the person doing the ordering nor the person actually writing the check. Payment is authorized only after verifying the purchase invoice data against the receiving report and purchase order.
4. The person who actually writes the check has not been involved in any of the foregoing purchasing procedures.

CHAPTER REVIEW

Online Study Center
ACE the test!

Picture the T accounts involved in transactions. Here are examples of transactions. Sold merchandise on account to Chin Building Supplies, $3,384.

Assets	=	Liabilities	+	Owner's Equity	+	Revenue	−	Expenses
+ | −		− | +		− | +		− | +		+ | −
Debit | Credit		Debit | Credit		Debit | Credit		Debit | Credit		Debit | Credit

Accounts Receivable						Sales
+ | −						− | +
3,384						3,384

REMEMBER!

Always think of the T accounts involved in each transaction. Get and stay in the T account habit.

Sold merchandise on account to C. D. Barnes, $1,550 plus sales tax $124.

Assets	=	Liabilities	+	Owner's Equity	+	Revenue	−	Expenses
+ | −		− | +		− | +		− | +		+ | −
Debit | Credit		Debit | Credit		Debit | Credit		Debit | Credit		Debit | Credit

Accounts Receivable		Sales Tax Payable				Sales		
+ | −		− | +				− | +		
1,674 |		| 124				| 1,550		

Chin Building Supplies returned $254 of merchandise.

Assets	=	Liabilities	+	Owner's Equity	+	Revenue	−	Expenses
+ | −		− | +		− | +		− | +		+ | −
Debit | Credit		Debit | Credit		Debit | Credit		Debit | Credit		Debit | Credit

Accounts Receivable						Sales Returns and Allowances		
+ | −						+ | −		
| 254						254 |		

REMEMBER!

Sales Returns and Allowances are a deduction from Sales.

Purchased merchandise from Gardner Products Co., $1,155 plus $90 freight, total $1,245.

Assets	=	Liabilities	+	Owner's Equity	+	Revenue	−	Expenses
+ | −		− | +		− | +		− | +		+ | −
Debit | Credit		Debit | Credit		Debit | Credit		Debit | Credit		Debit | Credit

		Accounts Payable						Purchases
		− | +						+ | −
		| 1,245						1,155 |

Freight In

+ | −
90 |

Returned merchandise to Dana Manufacturing Co., $270, and received a credit memorandum.

Assets	=	Liabilities	+	Owner's Equity	+	Revenue	−	Expenses
+ | −		− | +		− | +		− | +		+ | −
Debit | Credit		Debit | Credit		Debit | Credit		Debit | Credit		Debit | Credit

		Accounts Payable						Purchases Returns and Allowances
		− | +						− | +
		270 |						| 270

Review of Performance Objectives

1. Describe the specific accounts used by a merchandising firm.

   The Merchandise Inventory account is an asset account representing the cost of goods bought for resale.

   The Sales Tax Payable account is a liability account representing amounts owed to state or city governments.

   The Sales account is a revenue account representing the total sales of merchandise.

   The Sales Returns and Allowances account is a deduction from the Sales account, representing amounts allowed for returns of merchandise and damaged goods.

   The Sales Discounts account is a deduction from the Sales account, representing amounts deducted for prompt payments.

   The Purchases account is a cost (expense) account representing the costs of goods bought for resale.

   The Purchases Returns and Allowances account is a deduction from the Purchases account, representing amounts granted by suppliers for the return of merchandise or damaged goods.

   The Purchases Discounts account is a deduction from the Purchases account, representing amounts suppliers allow for prompt payments.

   The Freight In account is a cost (expense) representing the transportation charges on incoming merchandise.

2. Journalize transactions in a sales journal.

   The sales journal is used to record only sales of merchandise on account.

   The entries are posted daily to the accounts receivable ledger. At the end of the month, the total is posted to the general ledger as a debit to the Accounts Receivable controlling account and a credit to the Sales account.

3. Post sales journal transactions to an accounts receivable ledger and a general ledger.

   During the month, as customers charge merchandise, the amounts must be posted to their individual accounts as debits and a running balance maintained.

   At the end of the month, the total of the amounts charged by customers for purchase of merchandise must be posted to the general ledger as a debit to Accounts Receivable and a credit to Sales.

4. Prepare a schedule of accounts receivable.

   The schedule of accounts receivable consists of a listing of the individual account balances of the charge customers taken from the accounts receivable ledger.

5. Journalize sales returns and allowances, including credit memorandums and returns involving sales tax, in a general journal, and post to the accounts receivable ledger and general ledger.

   When a customer returns merchandise, or when his or her bill is reduced owing to an allowance for defective or damaged merchandise, the Sales Returns and Allowances account is debited and the Accounts Receivable account is credited. The entry is recorded in the general journal and posted to both the general ledger and the accounts receivable ledger.

6. Journalize transactions in a three-column purchases journal.

   The three-column purchases journal handles the purchase of merchandise on account and freight charges that are prepaid by the seller and included in the invoice total.

7. Post purchases journal transactions to an accounts payable ledger and a general ledger.

   Amounts in the Accounts Payable Credit column are posted daily to the accounts payable ledger. At the end of the month, the totals are posted to the general ledger as a debit to Purchases, a debit to Freight In, and a credit to Accounts Payable.

8. Prepare a schedule of accounts payable.

   A schedule of accounts payable, listing the balance of each individual creditor's account, is prepared from the accounts payable ledger.

9. Journalize transactions involving purchases returns and allowances in a general journal, and post to the accounts payable ledger and general ledger.

   When a credit memo is received for the return of merchandise or as an allowance for damaged merchandise, the buyer credits Purchases Returns and Allowances. If the merchandise was bought on account, the buyer debits Accounts Payable. The transaction is journalized in the general journal.

10. Describe the procedures for handling freight charges on merchandise and other goods.

   The Freight In account is debited for the cost of transportation charges on incoming merchandise intended for resale. Freight costs that apply to nonmerchandise assets purchased are added to the asset account that applies. For example, $300 freight on a large freezer for a restaurant would be debited to that freezer account as part of the cost of that asset.

Glossary

Accounts payable ledger A subsidiary ledger that lists the individual accounts of creditors in either alphabetical or numerical order with their respective balances. (353)

Accounts receivable ledger A subsidiary ledger that lists the individual accounts of charge customers in either alphabetical or numerical order, with their respective transactions and balances. (341)

Controlling account An account in the general ledger that summarizes the balances of a subsidiary ledger. (341)

Credit memorandum A written statement indicating a seller's willingness to reduce the amount of a buyer's debt. The seller records the amount of the credit memorandum in the Sales Returns and Allowances account. (346)

FOB destination Shipping terms under which the seller pays the freight charges and includes them in the selling price. Title or ownership changes hands when the buyer receives the goods. (358)

FOB shipping point Shipping terms under which the buyer pays the freight charges between the point of shipment and the destination. Payment may be made directly to the carrier upon receiving the goods or to the supplier if the supplier prepaid the freight charges on behalf of the buyer. Title or ownership changes hands when goods are transferred to the freight company. (358)

Freight In account The account used to record transportation charges on incoming merchandise intended for resale. (335)

Invoices Business forms prepared by the seller that list the items shipped, their cost, the terms of the sale, and the mode of shipment. They may also state the freight charges. The buyer considers them purchase invoices; the seller considers them sales invoices. (336)

Merchandise inventory A stock of goods (an asset account) that a company buys and intends to resell at a profit. (334)

Merchandising business A business that buys and sells goods. (334)

Purchase order A written order from the buyer of goods to the supplier, listing the items wanted and the terms of the transaction. (349)

Purchase requisition A form used to request that the Purchasing Department buy something. This form is intended for internal use within a company. (349)

Purchases account An account for recording the cost of merchandise acquired for resale. (335)

Purchases Discounts account An account that records cash discounts granted by suppliers in return for prompt payment; it is treated as a deduction from Purchases. (335)

Purchases journal A special journal used to record only the buying of goods on account. It may be used to record the purchase of merchandise only. (351)

Purchases Returns and Allowances account An account that records a company's return of merchandise it has purchased or a reduction in the bill because of damaged merchandise; it is treated as a deduction from Purchases. (335)

Retail business A business that sells goods directly to consumers. (334)

Sales account A revenue account for recording the sale of merchandise. (335)

Sales Discounts account An account that records a deduction from the original price, granted by the seller to the buyer for the prompt payment of an invoice. (335)

Sales journal A special journal for recording only the sale of merchandise on account. (338)

Sales Returns and Allowances account The account a seller uses to record the physical return of merchandise by customers or a reduction in a bill because merchandise was damaged. Sales Returns and Allowances is treated as a deduction from Sales. This account is usually evidenced by a credit memorandum issued by the seller. (335)

Sales Tax Payable account An account used to record a tax levied by a state or city government on the retail sale of goods and services. The tax is paid by the consumer but collected by the retailer. (335)

Special journals Books of original entry in which specialized types of repetitive transactions are recorded. (334)

Subsidiary ledger A group of accounts representing individual subdivisions showing the debits and credits of a controlling account. (341)

Summarizing entry An entry made to post the column totals of a special journal to the appropriate accounts in the general ledger. (339)

Wholesale business A business that buys goods from manufacturers and sells those goods (normally in large quantities) to retailers for resale. (334)

QUESTIONS, EXERCISES, AND CASES

Discussion Questions

1. Describe the posting procedures and rules for totaling and ruling the:
   a. Sales journal   b. Purchases journal

2. What is the purpose of a:
   a. Schedule of accounts receivable?
   b. Schedule of accounts payable?

3. Describe the procedure for posting:
   a. From the sales journal to the accounts receivable ledger.
   b. From the purchases journal to the accounts payable ledger.

4. With regard to goods sold and purchased, explain how sales returns and allowances and purchases returns and allowances are different from each other.

5. Explain the meaning and importance of the shipping terms FOB destination and FOB shipping point. Who has title to the goods once they have been shipped?

6. Why is an accounts receivable ledger or an accounts payable ledger necessary for a business with large numbers of charge customers or large numbers of vendors/suppliers?

7. Why is it a good practice to post daily to the accounts receivable or accounts payable ledgers?

8. Describe the four procedures that most companies follow to maintain internal control of purchases of merchandise.

Exercises

P.O. 3,4,7,8

Post to general and subsidiary ledgers; prepare schedules of accounts receivable and accounts payable.

Exercise 10-1 Milcer Company has completed October's sales and purchases journals (see below and on the following page). Your job is to:

a. Total and post the journals to T accounts for the general ledger and the accounts receivable and accounts payable ledgers.
b. Complete a schedule of accounts receivable for October 31, 20—.
c. Complete a schedule of accounts payable for October 31, 20—.
d. Compare the balances of the schedules with their respective general ledger accounts. If they are not the same, find and correct the error(s).

SALES JOURNAL   PAGE ___18___

	DATE	INV. NO.	CUSTOMER'S NAME	POST. REF.	ACCOUNTS RECEIVABLE DR. SALES CR.	
1	20–					1
2	Oct. 3	414	Anderson Company		4 4 3 24	2
3	4	415	R. T. Holcomb		1 4 2 6 90	3
4	7	416	Gray and Malo		1 6 4 7 00	4
5	11	417	Mercer Mobil		3 1 1 2 16	5
6	16	418	J. L. Anthony		2 1 3 0 00	6
7	22	419	C. A. Goldschmidt		1 9 4 4 05	7
8	31	420	F. A. Baumann		2 7 9 1 00	8
9	31					9
10					( )( )	10

PURCHASES JOURNAL PAGE 10

	DATE	SUPPLIER'S NAME	INVOICE NO.	INVOICE DATE	TERMS	POST. REF.	ACCOUNTS PAYABLE CREDIT	FREIGHT IN DEBIT	PURCHASES DEBIT	
1	20–									1
2	Oct. 2	Colter, Inc.	2706	7/31	2/10, n/30		7 5 9 00	4 9 00	7 1 0 00	2
3	3	Thomas and Son	982	8/2	n/30		8 2 9 00	5 7 00	7 7 2 00	3
4	5	Archer Manufacturing Co.	10611	8/3	2/10, n/30		5 6 4 00		5 6 4 00	4
5	9	Spence Products Co.	B643	8/6	1/10, n/30		1 6 5 00	1 0 00	1 5 5 00	5
6	18	L. C. Walter	46812	8/17	n/60		2 2 8 00		2 2 8 00	6
7	25	Delaney and Cox	1024	8/23	2/10, n/30		3 7 6 00	1 4 00	3 6 2 00	7
8	26	Colter, Inc.	2801	8/25	2/10, n/30		4 0 6 00	2 2 00	3 8 4 00	8
9	31									9
10							( )	( )	( )	10

P.O. 3,5

Describe transactions involving a sale, a return, and a payment.

Exercise 10-2 Describe the transactions recorded in the following T accounts:

Cash		Sales Tax Payable		Sales Returns and Allowances	
(c) 358.75		(b) 3.75	(a) 67.50	(b) 49.95	

Accounts Receivable		Sales	
(a) 967.50	(b) 53.70		(a) 900.00
	(c) 358.75		

P.O. 3,5

Record entries involving a sale, a return, and a receipt of cash.

Exercise 10-3 Record the following transactions in general journal form:

a. Sold merchandise on account to C. Heald, $560 plus $48.80 sales tax (invoice no. D446).
b. Heald returned $81 of the merchandise. Issued credit memo no. 114 for $87.48 ($81 for the amount of the sale plus $6.48 for the amount of the sales tax).
c. Received $517.32 from C. Heald in full payment of account.

P.O. 5

Post to general and accounts receivable ledgers.

Exercise 10-4 Post the following entry to the general ledger and subsidiary ledger:

GENERAL JOURNAL PAGE 52

	DATE	DESCRIPTION	POST. REF.	DEBIT	CREDIT	
1	20–					1
2	June 16	Sales Returns and Allowances		2 4 1 27		2
3		Accounts Receivable, R. D. Moen			2 4 1 27	3
4		Issued credit memo no. 131.				4
5						5

GENERAL LEDGER

ACCOUNT Accounts Receivable   ACCOUNT NO. 113

DATE		ITEM	POST. REF.	DEBIT	CREDIT	BALANCE DEBIT	BALANCE CREDIT
20–							
June	1	Balance	✓			6 5 1 1 19	

ACCOUNT Sales Returns and Allowances   ACCOUNT NO. 412

DATE		ITEM	POST. REF.	DEBIT	CREDIT	BALANCE DEBIT	BALANCE CREDIT
20–							
June	1	Balance	✓			3 1 4 60	

ACCOUNTS RECEIVABLE LEDGER

NAME R. D. Moen

ADDRESS 416 Fifth Avenue

Dallas, Texas 75204

DATE		ITEM	POST. REF.	DEBIT	CREDIT	BALANCE
20–						
May	31		S26	3 1 2 60		3 1 2 60

P.O. 5,9

Record a sales return and a purchases return.

Exercise 10-5 Using the following source document (credit memo issued by Akura Electronics), record the transaction in general journal form on the books of Akura Electronics, then on the books of The Merchandise Market.

Akura Electronics
4160 Broad Street
Chicago, Illinois 60627

CREDIT MEMORANDUM   No. 121

DATE: November 6, 20—

CREDIT TO:

The Merchandise Market

2241 Sullivan Street

Chicago, Illinois   60632

Your account has been credited for:

1 CPU tower $725.50

P.O. 9

Describe entries involving a purchase and return.

Exercise 10-6 Describe the transactions recorded in the following T accounts:

Cash				Purchases		
	(c)	1,024		(a)	1,100	

Accounts Payable				Purchases Returns and Allowances		
(b)	160	(a)	1,184		(b)	160
(c)	1,024					

			Freight In		
		(a)	84		

P.O. 9

Record journal entries for a purchase and return.

Exercise 10-7 Journalize the following transactions in general journal form:

a. Bought merchandise on account from Jabari, Inc., invoice no. C3009; net 30 days; FOB destination, $1,125.
b. Received credit memo no. 117 from Jabari, Inc., for merchandise returned, $127.
c. Issued a check to Jabari, Inc., in full payment of account.

P.O. 9

Post to accounts payable ledger and general ledger.

Exercise 10-8 Post the following entry to the general ledger and the subsidiary ledger:

GENERAL JOURNAL PAGE __92__

	DATE		DESCRIPTION	POST. REF.	DEBIT	CREDIT	
1	20–						1
2	July	14	Accounts Payable, Bullock and				2
3			Hendricks		1 9 2 30		3
4			Purchases Returns and				4
5			Allowances			1 9 2 30	5
6			Credit memo no. 942 for				6
7			return of merchandise.				7
8							8

GENERAL LEDGER

ACCOUNT __Accounts Payable__ ACCOUNT NO. __212__

	DATE	ITEM	POST. REF.	DEBIT	CREDIT	BALANCE DEBIT	BALANCE CREDIT	
1	20–							1
2	July 1	Balance	✓				2 7 6 1 24	2
3								3

ACCOUNT   **Purchases Returns and Allowances**   ACCOUNT NO.   **512**

	DATE	ITEM	POST. REF.	DEBIT	CREDIT	BALANCE DEBIT	BALANCE CREDIT	
1	20–							1
2	July	1	Balance	✓				2 3 0 16	2
3								3

ACCOUNTS PAYABLE LEDGER

NAME   **Bullock and Hendricks**

ADDRESS   **542 Roselle Blvd.**

Richmond, CA 94879

DATE	ITEM	POST. REF.	DEBIT	CREDIT	BALANCE
20–					
June	13		P73		2 1 8 00	2 1 8 00

internet
LINKS TO ACCOUNTING

You have just learned about recording transactions related to a company's sales. Sales returns and allowances, as well as discounts, affect the amount of a company's net sales.

1. Can you tell from looking at Target's financial statements, how much merchandise was returned during a year? You can view Target's financial statements at **http://www.target.com/**.

2. Target is a retail merchandising company. The company purchases merchandise inventory and then resells it. In Target's chart of accounts, which accounts are related to the purchase and sale of merchandise inventory? (Hint: Look at the statement of operations and the statement of financial position.)

3. In Chapter 5, we discussed the net sales and accounts receivable amounts of Dell, Inc. Now that you have learned about recording sales on account, let's go back to the same question and take another look. Use the financial statements that begin on page 35 of the 2006 10-K report. For 2006, what is the net sales amount (assume that all revenue is from sales) on Dell's income statement (statement of income)? How much is accounts receivable on the balance sheet (statement of financial position)? What can you tell from these two amounts? What is their relation to each other?

CONSIDER AND COMMUNICATE

You are the bookkeeper at a small merchandising firm. You are comparing the income statements from the last three years. You notice that the Purchases Returns and Allowances account (as a percentage of net sales) has been increasing at an alarming rate. If you were a manager, who would you speak to in the organization to help you understand why so much merchandise is being returned?

CRITICAL THINKING

TO: Accounting Clerk   SUBJECT: Errors in trial balance
FROM: Senior Accountant   DATE: April 1, 20—

Following is a trial balance prepared just before you were hired. There are two accounts missing, and the amount for Sales is off. Here are a few facts to consider. Our business is in a state that collects sales tax. I ran some totals, and we collected $1,800 in sales tax. Customers returned $900 in goods, which would reduce the above sales tax by $70. Our books need to reflect these events. The former accounting clerk said she did record everything—somewhere. She said she may have credited the $1,800 sales tax to Sales and not to Sales Tax Payable. Plus, she looked confused when Sales Returns and Allowances was mentioned. She asked, "Why not just debit Sales?" Please determine the two missing accounts and correct the accounts that are off.

Cox Retail Outlet
Trial Balance
March 31, 20—

ACCOUNT NAME	DEBIT	CREDIT
Cash	8 9 4 0 00	
Accounts Receivable	4 8 0 00	
Supplies	1 7 5 00	
Store Equipment	9 4 6 0 00	
Accounts Payable		9 5 8 00
D. Cox, Capital		11 9 5 9 00
D. Cox, Drawing	4 4 8 0 00	
Sales		18 0 0 0 00
Rent Expense	2 4 0 0 00	
Wages Expense	4 8 6 4 00	
Miscellaneous Expense	1 1 8 00	
	30 9 1 7 00	30 9 1 7 00

1. Think about where these amounts might have been put, think about what accounts are missing, and use T accounts to solve the problems.
2. Prepare a corrected trial balance.

A QUESTION OF ETHICS

Ms. Winters, an employee, accidentally dropped a pallet of boxes containing televisions off the forklift she was driving in the warehouse. No one saw what happened. She couldn't see (or hear) any damage to the televisions, so she reloaded the boxes and did not tell her supervisor. Is Ms. Winters behaving in an ethical manner when she withholds this information? Assume that the televisions were damaged and were delivered to customers. How might this damage affect the income statement?

PROBLEM SET A

For additional help, see the demonstration problem at the beginning of each chapter in your Working Papers.

P.O. 2,3,4,5

Problem 10-1A Brandmeir Company sells electrical supplies on a wholesale basis. The following transactions took place during April of this year:

Apr. 1 Sold merchandise on account to Meyer Company, invoice no. 761, $570.40.
5 Sold merchandise on account to L. R. Feldman Company, invoice no. 762, $486.10.
6 Issued credit memo no. 50 to Meyer Company for merchandise returned, $40.70.
10 Sold merchandise on account to Danton Hardware, invoice no. 763, $293.35.
14 Sold merchandise on account to Blair and Barnes, invoice no. 764, $640.16.
17 Sold merchandise on account to Pope and Rogers, invoice no. 765, $582.12.
21 Issued credit memo no. 51 to Blair and Barnes for merchandise returned, $68.44.
24 Sold merchandise on account to Oberman Company, invoice no. 766, $652.87.
26 Sold merchandise on account to Danton Hardware, invoice no. 767, $832.19.
30 Issued credit memo no. 52 to Danton Hardware for damage to merchandise, $98.50.

Check Figure

Accounts Receivable account balance, $5,018.97 debit

Instructions

1. Record these sales of merchandise on account in the sales journal (page 39). Record the sales returns and allowances in the general journal (page 74).
2. Immediately after recording each transaction, post to the accounts receivable ledger.
3. Post the amounts from the general journal daily. Post the sales journal amounts as a total at the end of the month; Accounts Receivable 113, Sales 411, Sales Returns and Allowances 412.
4. Prepare a schedule of accounts receivable. Compare the balance of the Accounts Receivable controlling account with the total of the schedule of accounts receivable.

Instructions for General Ledger Software

1. Record these transactions in either the sales journal or the general journal and post.
2. Print the entries from the general journal.
3. Print the entries from the sales journal.
4. Print a schedule of accounts receivable and compare its total with the balance of the Accounts Receivable controlling account.

P.O. 2,3,4,5

Problem 10-2A Marconi Florists sells flowers on a retail basis. Most of the sales are for cash; however, a few steady customers have charge accounts. Marconi's sales staff fills out a sales slip for each sale. There is a state retail sales tax of 5 percent, which is collected by the retailer and submitted to the state. The following represent Marconi Florists' charge sales for March:

Mar.
4 Sold potted plant on account to C. Marlo, sales slip no. 242, $27, plus sales tax of $1.35, total $28.35.
6 Sold floral arrangement on account to R. Dresher, sales slip no. 267, $54, plus sales tax of $2.70, total $56.70.
12 Sold corsage on account to B. Carter, sales slip no. 279, $16, plus sales tax of $0.80, total $16.80.
16 Sold wreath on account to American Legion, sales slip no. 296, $104, plus sales tax of $5.20, total $109.20.
18 Sold floral arrangements on account to Turner Funeral Home, sales slip no. 314, $260, plus sales tax of $13, total $273.00.
21 Turner Funeral Home complained about a wrinkled ribbon on the floral arrangement. Marconi Florists allowed a $30 credit and the sales tax of $1.50, credit memo no. 27.
23 Sold flower arrangements on account to Ponderosa Savings and Loan Association for their fifth anniversary, sales slip no. 337, $180, plus sales tax of $9, total $189.
24 Allowed Ponderosa Savings and Loan Association credit, $25, plus sales tax of $1.25, because of a few withered blossoms in floral arrangements, credit memo no. 28.

Check Figure

Schedule of Accounts Receivable total, $726.52

Instructions

1. Record these transactions in either the sales journal (page 23) or the general journal (page 57).
2. Immediately after recording each transaction, post to the accounts receivable ledger.
3. Post the amounts from the general journal daily. Post the sales journal amounts as a total at the end of the month; Accounts Receivable 113, Sales Tax Payable 214, Sales 411, Sales Returns and Allowances 412.
4. Prepare a schedule of accounts receivable and compare its total with the balance of the Accounts Receivable controlling account.

P.O. 6,7,8

Problem 10-3A Bhanu Appliance uses a three-column purchases journal. The company is located in Fresno, California. On January 1 of this year, the balances of the ledger accounts are Accounts Payable, $559.06; Purchases, zero; Freight In, zero. In addition to a general ledger, Bhanu Appliance also uses an accounts payable ledger. Transactions for January related to the purchase of merchandise are as follows:

Jan. 2 Bought eighty 12-inch, 3-speed Brighton Oscillating Fans from Sweet and Alyn, $1,890, invoice no. 268J, dated January 2; terms net 60 days; FOB Fresno.

4 Bought ten 35-pint-capacity Crystal Humidifiers from Shasta Company, $2,300, invoice no. 39426, dated January 2; terms 2/10, n/30; FOB Durango, freight prepaid and added to the invoice, $90 (total $2,390).

7 Bought ten 16-inch Axel Window Fans from Teter, Inc., $360, invoice no. 452AD, dated January 6; terms 1/10, n/30; FOB Fresno.

10 Bought twenty-four 4-blade Tiempo Ceiling Fans, Model 2760, from Ukele Company, $3,550, invoice no. D7742, dated January 7; terms 2/10, n/30; FOB Sacramento, freight prepaid and added to the invoice, $84 (total $3,634).

14 Bought four Charger Electric Hedge Trimmers from Famous Products Company, $186, invoice no. 2542, dated January 13; terms net 30 days; FOB Fresno.

22 Bought forty Lindon Electric Bug Killers from Sweet and Alyn, $2,265, invoice no. 392J, dated January 22; terms net 60 days; FOB Fresno.

28 Bought ten Charger Electric Blowers from Famous Products Company, $830, invoice no. 2691, dated January 27; terms net 30 days; FOB Fresno.

30 Bought ten Kole Powered Attic Ventilators from Pinder Company, $446, invoice no. 664CC, dated January 27; terms 2/10, n/30; FOB Seattle, freight prepaid and added to the invoice, $48 (total $494).

Check Figure

Accounts Payable account balance, $12,608.06 credit

Instructions

1. Open the following accounts in the accounts payable ledger and record the January 1 balances, if any, as given: Famous Products Company; Pinder Company, $163.17; Shasta Company, $167.19; Sweet and Alyn; Teter, Inc., $228.70; Ukele Company. For the accounts having balances, write "Balance" in the Item column and place a check mark in the Post. Ref. column.

2. Record the balance of $559.06 in the Accounts Payable controlling account as of January 1. Write "Balance" in the Item column and place a check mark in the Post. Ref. column.

3. Record the transactions in the purchases journal beginning on page 81.

4. Post to the accounts payable ledger daily.

5. Post to the general ledger at the end of the month.

6. Prepare a schedule of accounts payable, and compare the balance of the Accounts Payable controlling account with the total of the schedule of accounts payable.

P.O. 2,3,4,5,6,7,8,9

Problem 10-4A The following transactions relate to Brady Company during April of this year. Terms of sale are 2/10, n/30. The company is located in Atlanta.

Apr. 2 Sold merchandise on account to Slover Company, invoice no. 1126, $1,746.

4 Bought merchandise on account from Pedro Company, invoice no. 16521, $800; terms 1/10, n/30; dated April 2; FOB Atlanta.

9 Sold merchandise on account to Pima and Lane, invoice no. 1127, $860.

Apr. 12 Bought merchandise on account from Varder Company, invoice no. L8552, $2,482; terms 2/10, n/30; dated April 11; FOB Rome, freight prepaid and added to the invoice, $49 (total $2,531).

15 Received credit memo no. 79 for merchandise returned to Kraig and Company, for $120.

17 Sold merchandise on account to C. N. Hague, invoice no. 1128, $1,015.

19 Issued credit memo no. 34 to Pima and Lane for merchandise returned, $86.

26 Bought merchandise on account from M. R. Parker, Inc., invoice no. 7447, $1,482; terms 2/10, n/30; dated April 23; FOB Macon, freight prepaid and added to the invoice, $45 (total $1,527).

29 Bought office supplies on account from Tillman Stationery Company, invoice no. S336, $152; terms net 30 days; dated April 29.

30 Sold merchandise on account to Schilling and Mark, invoice no. 1129, $2,601.

30 Issued credit memo no. 35 to Schilling and Mark for merchandise returned, $153.

Check Figure

Accounts Payable account balance, $5,268 credit

Instructions

1. Open the following accounts in the accounts receivable ledger and record the balances as of April 1: C. N. Hague; Pima and Lane, $426; Schilling and Mark, $974; Slover Company. For the accounts having balances, write "Balance" in the Item column and place a check mark in the Post. Ref. column.

2. Open the following accounts in the accounts payable ledger and record the balances as of April 1: Kraig and Company, $262; M. R. Parker, Inc., $116; Pedro Company; Tillman Stationery Company; Varder Company. For the accounts having balances, write "Balance" in the Item column and place a check mark in the Post. Ref. column.

3. Record the transactions in the sales, purchases, or general journal, as appropriate.

4. Post the entries to the accounts receivable ledger daily.

5. Post the entries to the accounts payable ledger daily.

6. Post the entries in the general journal immediately after you make each journal entry.

7. Post the totals from the special journals at the end of the month.

8. Prepare a schedule of accounts receivable.

9. Prepare a schedule of accounts payable.

10. Compare the totals of the schedules with the balances of the controlling accounts.

Instructions for General Ledger Software

1. Record the transactions in the sales, purchases, or general journal.
   a. For efficiency, analyze the transactions, indicate into which journal each transaction goes, and key the entries in three batches—the sales journal, the purchases journal, and the general journal.
   b. If the program uses a single-column purchases journal, add the amount of the freight to the amount of the purchases.

2. Print the journals.

3. Post the amounts from the sales, purchases, and general journals.

4. Print the general ledger.

5. Print a schedule of accounts receivable and compare the total with the balance of the Accounts Receivable controlling account.

6. Print a schedule of accounts payable and compare the total with the balance of the Accounts Payable controlling account.

PROBLEM SET B

For additional help, see the demonstration problem at the beginning of each chapter in your Working Papers.

P.O. 2,3,4,5

Problem 10-1B C. H. Barton Company sells electrical supplies on a wholesale basis. The following transactions took place during April of this year.

Apr.		
	3	Sold merchandise on account to Meyer Company, invoice no. 822, $652.80.
	7	Sold merchandise on account to L. R. Feldman Company, invoice no. 823, $462.15.
	8	Sold merchandise on account to Danton Hardware, invoice no. 824, $205.60.
	13	Issued credit memo no. 61 to L. R. Feldman Company for merchandise returned, $136.50.
	15	Sold merchandise on account to Blair and Barnes, invoice no. 825, $831.47.
	21	Sold merchandise on account to Pope and Rogers, invoice no. 826, $590.34.
	24	Issued credit memo no. 62 to Blair and Barnes for merchandise returned, $80.45.
	26	Sold merchandise on account to Oberman Company, invoice no. 827, $569.90.
	28	Issued credit memo no. 63 to Danton Hardware for damage to merchandise, $52.48.
	30	Sold merchandise on account to Danton Hardware, invoice no. 828, $735.50.

Check Figure

Accounts Receivable account balance, $4,947.75 debit

Instructions

1. Record these sales of merchandise on account in the sales journal (page 39). Record the sales returns and allowances in the general journal (page 74).
2. Immediately after recording each transaction, post to the accounts receivable ledger.
3. Post the amounts from the general journal daily. Post the sales journal amount as a total at the end of the month; Accounts Receivable 113, Sales 411, Sales Returns and Allowances 412.
4. Prepare a schedule of accounts receivable. Compare the balance of the Accounts Receivable controlling account with the total of the schedule of accounts receivable.

Instructions for General Ledger Software

1. Record these transactions in either the sales journal or the general journal and post.
2. Print the entries from the general journal.
3. Print the entries from the sales journal.
4. Print a schedule of accounts receivable and compare its total with the balance of the Accounts Receivable controlling account.

P.O. 2,3,4,5

Problem 10-2B Marconi Florists sells flowers on a retail basis. Most of the sales are for cash; however, a few steady customers have charge accounts. Marconi's sales staff fills out a sales slip for each sale. There is a state retail tax of 5 percent, which is collected by the retailer and submitted to the state. Marconi Florists' charge sales for March are as follows:

Mar.   4   Sold floral arrangement on account to R. Dresher, sales slip no. 236, $45, plus sales tax of $2.25, total $47.25.

   7   Sold potted plant on account to C. Marlo, sales slip no. 272, $61, plus sales tax of $3.05, total $64.05.

   12   Sold wreath on account to American Legion, sales slip no. 294, $63, plus sales tax of $3.15, total $66.15.

   17   Sold floral arrangements on account to Turner Funeral Home, sales slip no. 299, $170, plus sales tax of $8.50, total $178.50.

   20   Turner Funeral Home returned a flower spray, complaining that there were dead blooms. Marconi Florists allowed a credit of $36 and the sales tax of $1.80, credit memo no. 27.

   21   Sold flower arrangements on account to Ponderosa Savings and Loan Association for their anniversary, sales slip no. 310, $236, plus sales tax of $11.80, total $247.80.

   22   Allowed Ponderosa Savings and Loan Association credit, $25, plus sales tax of $1.25, because of withered blossoms in floral arrangements, credit memo no. 28.

   27   Sold corsage on account to B. Carter, sales slip no. 332, $30, plus sales tax of $1.50, total $31.50.

Check Figure

Schedule of Accounts Receivable total, $682.42

Instructions

1. Record these transactions in either the sales journal (page 23) or the general journal (page 57).
2. Immediately after recording each transaction, post to the accounts receivable ledger.
3. Post the amounts from the general journal daily. Post the sales journal amount as a total at the end of the month; Accounts Receivable 113, Sales Tax Payable 214, Sales 411, Sales Returns and Allowances 412.
4. Prepare a schedule of accounts receivable and compare its total with the balance of the Accounts Receivable controlling account.

P.O. 6,7,8

Problem 10-3B Urban Bicycle Shop uses a three-column purchases journal. The company is located in Topeka, Kansas. On January 1 of this year, the balances of the ledger accounts are Accounts Payable, $423.08; Purchases, zero; Freight In, zero. In addition to a general ledger, the company also uses an accounts payable ledger. Transactions for January related to the purchase of merchandise are as follows:

Jan.   4   Bought fifty 10-speed bicycles from Nakita Company, $4,775, invoice no. 26145, dated January 3; terms net 60 days; FOB Topeka.

   7   Bought tires from Bergen Tire Company, $792, invoice no. 9763, dated January 5; terms 2/10, n/30; FOB Topeka.

   8   Bought bicycle lights and reflectors from Goodwin Products Company, $384, invoice no. 17317, dated January 6; terms net 30 days; FOB Topeka.

   11   Bought hand brakes from Barlow, Inc., $470, invoice no. 291GE, dated January 9; terms 1/10, n/30; FOB Kansas City, freight prepaid and added to the invoice, $36 (total $506).

Jan. 19 Bought handle grips from Goodwin Products Company, $96.50, invoice no. 17520, dated January 17; terms net 30 days; FOB Topeka.

24 Bought thirty 5-speed bicycles from Nakita Company, $1,487, invoice no. 26942, dated January 23; terms net 60 days; FOB Topeka.

29 Bought knapsacks from Dunn Manufacturing Company, $304.80, invoice no. 762AC, dated January 26; terms 2/10, n/30; FOB Topeka.

31 Bought locks from Lincoln Safety Net, $415.47, invoice no. 27712, dated January 26; terms 2/10, n/30; FOB Dodge City, freight prepaid and added to the invoice, $22 (total $437.47).

Check Figure

Accounts Payable account balance, $9,205.85 credit

Instructions

1. Open the following creditor accounts in the accounts payable ledger and record the January 1 balances, if any, as given: Bergen Tire Company, $156; Barlow, Inc.; Dunn Manufacturing Company, $82.88; Goodwin Products Company; Lincoln Safety Net, $184.20; Nakita Company. For the accounts having balances, write "Balance" in the Item column and place a check mark in the Post. Ref. column.
2. Record the balance of $423.08 in the Accounts Payable controlling account as of January 1. Write "Balance" in the Item column and place a check mark in the Post. Ref. column.
3. Record the transactions in the purchases journal beginning with page 81.
4. Post to the accounts payable ledger daily.
5. Post to the general ledger at the end of the month.
6. Prepare a schedule of accounts payable, and compare the balance of the Accounts Payable controlling account with the total of the schedule of accounts payable.

P.O. 2,3,4,5,6,7,8,9

Problem 10-4B The following transactions relate to Kelly Metal Products during April of this year. Terms of sale are 2/10, n/30. The company is located in Los Angeles.

Apr. 1 Sold merchandise on account to Helpful Hardware, invoice no. 5522, $607.40.

4 Bought merchandise on account from Rama Manufacturing Company, invoice no. C1142, $556; terms 1/10, n/30; dated April 2; FOB San Diego, freight prepaid and added to the invoice, $34 (total $590).

9 Sold merchandise on account to Bocci Stores, invoice no. 5523, $1,025.30.

11 Bought merchandise on account from Bali Products Company, invoice no. 8990, $1,756.80; terms 2/10, n/30; dated April 11; FOB San Francisco, freight prepaid and added to the invoice, $75 (total $1,831.80).

16 Sold merchandise on account to C. D. Alvarez, invoice no. 5524, $921.56.

19 Issued credit memo no. 32 to Bocci Stores for merchandise returned, $86.

24 Bought merchandise on account from Ashley Manufacturing Company, invoice no. P1981, $1,432.80; terms 2/10, n/30; dated April 22; FOB Santa Rosa, freight prepaid and added to the invoice, $76 (total $1,508.80).

Apr. 27 Bought office supplies on account from China and Duncan, invoice no. E621A, $84.40; terms net 30 days; dated April 25.

28 Sold merchandise on account to Grady Specialty Company, invoice no. 5525, $3,598.70.

29 Issued credit memo no. 33 to C. D. Alvarez for allowance on damaged merchandise, $80.

30 Received credit memo no. 79 for merchandise returned to Bjorn, Inc., for $115.20.

Check Figure

Accounts Payable account balance, $4,277.80 credit

Instructions

1. Open the following accounts in the accounts receivable ledger and record the balances as of April 1: C. D. Alvarez; Bocci Stores, $352.50; Grady Specialty Company, $225.50; Helpful Hardware, $822. For the accounts having balances, write "Balance" in the Item column and place a check mark in the Post. Ref. column.

2. Open the following accounts in the accounts payable ledger and record the balances as of April 1: Ashley Manufacturing Company; Bali Products Company, $122.46; Bjorn, Inc., $255.54; China and Duncan; Rama Manufacturing Company. For the accounts having balances, write "Balance" in the Item column and place a check mark in the Post Ref. column.

3. Record the transactions in the sales, purchases, or general journal, as appropriate.

4. Post the entries to the accounts receivable ledger daily.

5. Post the entries to the accounts payable ledger daily.

6. Post the entries in the general journal immediately after you make each journal entry.

7. Post the totals from the special journals at the end of the month.

8. Prepare a schedule of accounts receivable.

9. Prepare a schedule of accounts payable.

10. Compare the totals of the schedules with the balances of the controlling accounts.

Instructions for General Ledger Software

1. Record the transactions in the sales, purchases, or general journal.

   a. For efficiency, analyze the transactions, indicate into which journal each transaction goes, and key the entries in three batches—the sales journal, the purchases journal, and the general journal.

   b. If the program uses a single-column purchases journal, add the amount of the freight to the amount of the purchases.

2. Print the journals.

3. Post the amounts from the sales, purchases, and general journals.

4. Print the general ledger.

5. Print a schedule of accounts receivable and compare the total with the balance of the Accounts Receivable controlling account.

6. Print a schedule of accounts payable and compare the total with the balance of the Accounts Payable controlling account.

The Computer Clinic

Sales and Purchases Journals

Ms. Valli of All About You Spa has decided to expand her business by adding two lines of merchandise—a selection of products used in the salon for the body, the feet, and the face, as well as logo mugs, T-shirts, and baseball caps that can provide advertising benefits. She believes she will be able to increase her profits significantly. She has provided paper copies and computer files that report her revenues, operating expenses, and other accounting activity that occurred in June.

The first thing you want to do is to look at the post-closing trial balance as of June 30, 20— shown below. As you look at the post-closing trial balance for the spa, answer the question, "Why is the trial balance so short?"

Why is the trial balance so short?

All About You Spa
Post-Closing Trial Balance
June 30, 20—

ACCOUNT NAME	DEBIT	CREDIT
Cash	15 1 7 0 00	
Accounts Receivable	1 2 6 4 00	
Prepaid Insurance	8 0 0 00	
Spa Equipment	7 3 9 3 00	
Accumulated Depreciation, Spa Equipment		6 4 88
Office Equipment	1 1 5 0 00	
Accumulated Depreciation, Office Equipment		1 0 00
Accounts Payable		2 2 4 8 00
Wages Payable		3 6 9 50
A. Valli, Capital		23 0 8 4 62
	25 7 7 7 00	25 7 7 7 00

If you answered "There are no revenue, expense, or drawing accounts," you are correct. But why are there no revenue, expense, or drawing accounts? What happened to them?*

Directions for July Journal Entries

What do I do next?

1. If you are beginning the Computer Clinic problem at Chapter 10, journalize the post-closing trial balance accounts and amounts in the general journal. Do this as one big compound entry prior to recording the July journal entries.

*Answer: There are no temporary owner's equity accounts (revenue, expense, or drawing accounts) because they were closed; their balances were made zero to prepare the books for the next fiscal period. The only accounts remaining open (having a balance) are the real accounts—assets, liabilities, and Owner's Capital.

These amounts are the June 30 balances that become the beginning balances for July.

2. Then, make the following reversing entry, dated July 1. (The purpose of this entry is to reverse or undo the adjusting entry you made in Chapter 4. Reversing entries are explained in Chapter 13.)

Wages Payable			Wages Expense	
+	−		+	−
369.50				369.50

So that you can complete the journal entries for the month of July, Ms. Valli has also left the information you will need and directions on how to proceed.

3. Add new accounts to the chart of accounts as needed (for example, Merchandise Sales). Since All About You Spa now needs a Purchases account, the chart of accounts needs to be modified as follows: All expense accounts need to be in the 600–699 range; for example, Wages Expense changes from 511 to 611. The 500–599 range is now used for the purchase-related accounts; for example, make Purchases 511 and Freight In 515. (*Hint:* Four new accounts need to be added to the chart of accounts.)

4. a. Journalize the checks written in July and shown in the checkbook register, which also shows deposits made to the account. Record these events in the *general journal*. (*Notes:* Payroll taxes related to wages will be ignored here for purposes of simplification. All About You Spa is located in a state that levies sales tax on both merchandise and services. Some states do not tax services.)

   b. Journalize in the *purchases journal* all of the July purchases of merchandise on account, which are shown in the list of invoices provided.

   c. Journalize in the *sales journal* all of the July sales of merchandise on account, which are shown in the list of merchandise sales invoices provided.

> Remember to journalize a transaction in only one journal—either the sales journal *or* the purchases journal *or* the general journal.

5. Set up an accounts receivable ledger and an accounts payable ledger. Use the following opening balances. All other accounts have a zero opening balance.

Accounts Receivable Ledger		Accounts Payable Ledger	
Jill Anson	$325.00	Adco, Inc.	$ 397.00
Troy Ligman	344.00	Golden Spa Supplies	492.00
Jack Morgan	486.00	Office Staples	120.00
Judy Wilcox	109.00	Spa Equipment, Inc.	89.00
		Superior Equipment	1,150.00

6. After journalizing and posting all transactions to the general ledger and subsidiary ledgers, print a trial balance dated July 31, 20—. Do not include those accounts that have a zero balance at the end of the month.

7. Print a schedule of accounts receivable dated July 31, 20—.

8. Print a schedule of accounts payable dated July 31, 20—.

Checkbook Register

Check No.	Date	Explanation	✔	Deposits	Check Amount
	7/1	Owner invested cash in business.		25,000.00	
1027	7/3	Bought additional spa equipment from Spa Equipment, Inc., for $8,235.00, paying $2,000.00 cash down, invoice no. 2731; terms 2/10, n/60.			2,000.00
1028	7/3	Paid July's rent.			1,650.00
1029	7/3	Paid on account to Spa Equipment, Inc., invoice no. 2013, dated June 3 (no discount). Paid in full.			89.00
1030	7/5	Paid on account to Golden Spa Supplies, invoice no. 804, dated June 3 (no discount). Paid in full.			492.00
1031	7/5	Paid on account to Office Staples, invoice no. 522, dated June 5 (no discount). Paid in full.			120.00
1032	7/5	Paid Celebrate, Inc., for flowers and balloons for lobby (Miscellaneous Expense).			98.00
1033	7/5	Paid on account to Adco, Inc., invoice no. 512, dated June 5 (no discount). Paid in full.			397.00
1034	7/5	Paid week's wages.			1,845.50
	7/7	Deposited first week's cash sales: merchandise $1,410.00; services $3,110.00; sales tax collected $361.60. (Open new accounts Merchandise Sales 412 and Sales Tax Payable 215.)		4,881.60	
	7/7	Deposited check from Jill Anson, invoice no. 10, dated June 7 (balance due in August, $175.00).		150.00	
1035	7/12	Paid week's wages.			1,845.50
	7/14	Deposited check from Jack Morgan, invoice no. 11, dated June 14 (balance due in August, $286.00).		200.00	
	7/14	Deposited second week's cash sales: merchandise $1,220.00; services $2,630.00; sales tax collected $308.00.		4,158.00	

Check No.	Date	Explanation	✔	Deposits	Check Amount
1036	7/18	Paid on account to Superior Equipment, invoice no. 3140, dated June 5 (no discount). Paid in full.			1,150.00
1037	7/19	Paid week's wages.			1,840.50
	7/21	Deposited check from Tory Ligman, invoice no. 12, dated June 21 (balance due in August, $164.00).		180.00	
	7/21	Deposited third week's cash sales: merchandise $1,940.00; services $2,920.00; sales tax collected $388.80.		5,248.80	
1038	7/25	Bought new nail cart for cash (debit Spa Equipment).			173.00
1039	7/26	Paid week's wages.			1,842.00
1040	7/28	Paid month's laundry bill.			84.00
	7/28	Deposited check from Judy Wilcox, invoice no. 13, dated June 28 (paid in full).		109.00	
	7/31	Deposited end of month's cash sales: merchandise $1,930.00; services $4,062.00; sales tax collected $479.36.		6,471.36	
1041	7/31	Owner withdrew cash for personal use.			2,500.00
1042	7/31	Paid July telephone bill.			225.00
1043	7/31	Paid July power and water bill.			248.00

Purchases Invoices for Merchandise Bought on Account During July

All About You Spa will pay all freight costs associated with purchases of merchandise to the supplier. Two new accounts are needed: Purchases 511 and Freight In 515.

Date of Purchase	Transaction Information	Amount
July 1	Bought aromatherapy products from Spa Goods; invoice no. 312, dated 7/1; terms 2/10, n/60.	$5,300.00 plus $145.00 freight
1	Bought logo merchandise from Logo Products; invoice no. 1579, dated 7/1; terms 2/10, n/60.	$3,692.00 plus $104.00 freight
2	Bought bath and beauty products from Spa Magic; invoice no. 5033, dated 7/2; 2/10, n/30.	$2,623.00 plus $98.00 freight
5	Bought logo merchandise from Giftco; invoice no. 316, dated 7/5; terms 2/10, n/60.	$1,253 plus $56.00 freight

Sales Invoices for Gift Certificates Sold on Account During July

All About You Spa is responsible for collecting and paying the sales tax on merchandise that it sells. The sales tax rate where All About You Spa does business is 8 percent of each sale; for example, $325.00 × 0.08 = $26.00.

Date of Sale	Transaction Information	Sales Amount (Before Tax)
July 2	Los Obrigados Lodge, invoice no.14.	$ 325.00
4	Chaco's, invoice no.15.	481.50
5	Pleasant Spa, invoice no.16.	1,815.95
10	Holmes Condos, invoice no.17.	340.25
10	Mini Spa, invoice no.18.	206.00
12	About Face Spa, invoice no.19.	482.95

Note: All certificates for services were redeemed and the services were provided by the end of the month.

Other July Transactions

There were five other transactions in July. None involved cash.

Date	Transaction Information	Amount
July 1	Bought spa supplies on account from Golden Spa Supplies, invoice no. 1836, terms n/45.	$490.00
5	Bought office equipment on account from Superior Equipment, invoice no. 3608, terms 2/10, n/60.	$420.00
5	Bought self-help books for the waiting room on account (Miscellaneous Expense) from Office Staples, invoice no. 1417, n/30.	$186.00
5	Bought office supplies on account from Office Staples, invoice no. 1418, terms n/30.	$118.00
31	Owner invested additional personal spa equipment (treadmill and bicycle) valued at $1,800.00.	

C

Sales and Purchases on Account: An Alternative to Special Journals

Performance Objectives

After you have completed this appendix, you will be able to do the following:

1. Record transactions pertaining to the sale and purchase of merchandise in a general journal.

2. Maintain an accounts receivable ledger and an accounts payable ledger.

3. Prepare schedules of accounts receivable and accounts payable.

Although most merchandising enterprises set up special journals, some businesses elect to record sales and purchases of merchandise on account in the general journal because of personal preference or the desire to record all transactions chronologically in one place.

JOURNALIZING SALES OF MERCHANDISE ON ACCOUNT

Refer to Figures 1 (page 336), 2 (page 337), and 8 (page 346) in Chapter 10, which illustrate the forms that drive and support the merchandising transactions to be journalized.

Here are the merchandising accounts in T account form. Refer to the glossary at the end of Chapter 10 on pages 363 and 364 for definitions of these accounts. The same accounts are used whether transactions are journalized in special journals (as in Chapter 10) or in a general journal. The outcomes will be the same.

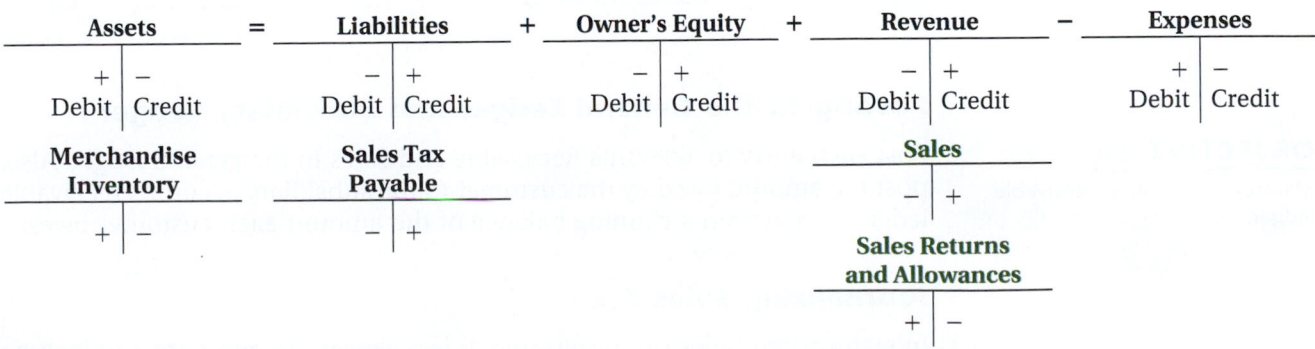

RECORDING SALES ON ACCOUNT IN A GENERAL JOURNAL

OBJECTIVE 1a

Record transactions pertaining to the sale of merchandise in a general journal.

We will introduce journalizing sales of merchandise on account in a general journal by looking at three transactions on the books of Rainier Plumbing Supply:

Aug.   1   Sold merchandise on account to Betterbuilt Homes Co., invoice no. 1320, $1,564.86.

3   Sold merchandise on account to Arnold, Inc., invoice no. 1321, $1,116.

6   Sold merchandise on account to Gonzales Construction, invoice no. 1322, $1,394.

		GENERAL JOURNAL			PAGE 26
	DATE	DESCRIPTION	POST. REF.	DEBIT	CREDIT
1	20–				1
2	Aug. 1	Accounts Receivable, Betterbuilt			2
3		Homes Co.		1 5 6 4 86	3
4		Sales			1 5 6 4 86	4
5		Sold merchandise to Betterbuilt			5
6		Homes Co., invoice no. 1320.			6
7					7
8	3	Accounts Receivable, Arnold, Inc.		1 1 1 6 00	8
9		Sales			1 1 1 6 00	9
10		Sold merchandise to Arnold,			10
11		Inc., invoice no. 1321.			11
12					12
13	6	Accounts Receivable, Gonzales			13
14		Construction		1 3 9 4 00	14
15		Sales			1 3 9 4 00	15
16		Sold merchandise to Gonzales			16
17		Construction, invoice no. 1322.			17
18					18
19					19

Posting to the General Ledger and Subsidiary Ledger

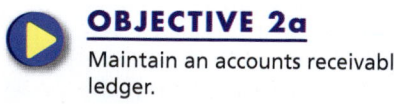

OBJECTIVE 2a

Maintain an accounts receivable ledger.

Post each entry to Accounts Receivable and Sales in the general ledger. Also, post the amount owed by the customer to the subsidiary accounts receivable ledger to maintain a running balance of the amount each customer owes.

Journalizing Sales Tax

In states where sales tax is collected, it is necessary to compute and include the amount of the sales tax for each transaction. That is, the customer owes the amount of the sale plus the applicable sales tax.

Following are three transactions that include sales tax computed on the amount of the sale of merchandise on account in a state that requires sales tax to be collected:

Apr. 1 Sold merchandise on account to C. D. Barnes, invoice no. 9382, $1,550, plus sales of tax $124, total $1,674.

1 Sold merchandise on account to Best Child Care, invoice no. 9383, $1,022, plus sales tax of $81.76, total $1,103.76.

1 Sold merchandise on account to Land Use Planners, invoice no. 9384, $2,050, plus sales tax of $164, total $2,214.

GENERAL JOURNAL   PAGE **10**

	DATE		DESCRIPTION	POST. REF.	DEBIT	CREDIT	
1	20–						1
2	Apr.	1	Accounts Receivable, C. D. Barnes		1 6 7 4 00		2
3			Sales			1 5 5 0 00	3
4			Sales Tax Payable			1 2 4 00	4
5			Sold merchandise to C. D.				5
6			Barnes, invoice no. 9382.				6
7							7
8		1	Accounts Receivable, Best Child Care		1 1 0 3 76		8
9			Sales			1 0 2 2 00	9
10			Sales Tax Payable			8 1 76	10
11			Sold merchandise to Best Child				11
12			Care, invoice no. 9383.				12
13							13
14		1	Accounts Receivable, Land Use				14
15			Planners		2 2 1 4 00		15
16			Sales			2 0 5 0 00	16
17			Sales Tax Payable			1 6 4 00	17
18			Sold merchandise to Land Use				18
19			Planners, invoice no. 9384.				19
20							20

Posting to the General Ledger and Subsidiary Ledger

Post each entry to Accounts Receivable, Sales, and Sales Tax Payable in the general ledger. Also, post the amount owed by the customer to the subsidiary accounts receivable ledger to maintain a running balance of the amount each customer owes.

Schedule of Accounts Receivable

OBJECTIVE 3a

Prepare a schedule of accounts receivable.

At the end of the month, the accountant lists the customer names and amounts owed and totals the amounts. This listing is called the schedule of accounts receivable. The total of this schedule should equal the total of the Accounts Receivable controlling account in the general ledger. If the two amounts are different, reverse the process of adding and posting to discover and correct the error.

Sales Returns and Allowances

Refer to pages 346–348 in Chapter 10 for information on journalizing and posting credit memorandums, which give customers permission to return all or part of the goods sold to them. Since we debited the customer's Accounts

Receivable account and credited Sales and Sales Tax Payable, we must undo or reverse the accounts for the amount the customer is returning in addition to the sales tax on that amount.

JOURNALIZING PURCHASES OF MERCHANDISE (FOR RESALE) ON ACCOUNT

Refer to Figures 9 (page 350), 10 (page 350), and 11 (page 351) in Chapter 10, which illustrate the forms that drive and support the merchandising transactions to be journalized.

Here are the merchandising accounts in T account form. Refer to the glossary at the end of Chapter 10 on pages 363 and 364 for definitions of these accounts. The same accounts are used whether transactions are journalized in special journals (as in Chapter 10) or in a general journal. The outcomes will be the same.

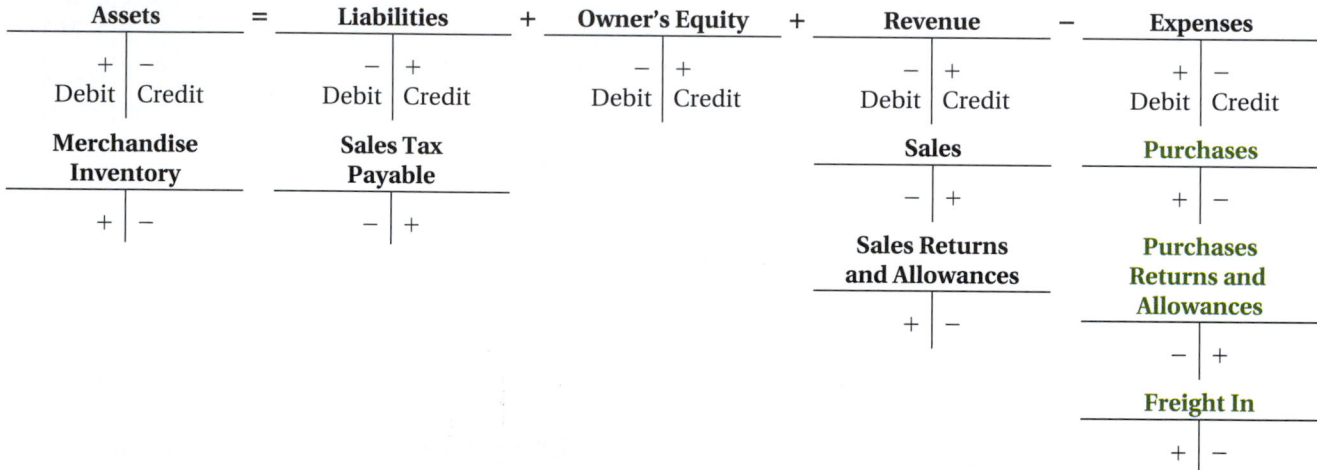

RECORDING PURCHASES ON ACCOUNT IN A GENERAL JOURNAL

OBJECTIVE 1b

Record transactions pertaining to the purchase of merchandise in a general journal.

We will introduce journalizing purchases of merchandise on account in a general journal by looking at three transactions on the books of Rainier Plumbing Supply. These transactions include the cost of delivering the merchandise, called Freight In.

Aug. 2 Bought merchandise on account from Collins, Inc., invoice no. 2706, $1,710; terms 2/10, n/30; dated July 31; FOB San Francisco, freight prepaid and added to the invoice, $85.50 (total $1,795.50).

3 Bought merchandise on account from Langseth and Son, invoice no. 982, $2,772; terms net 30 days; dated August 2; FOB Cleveland, freight prepaid and added to the invoice, $157 (total $2,929).

5 Bought merchandise on account from Dana Manufacturing Company, invoice no. 10611, $564; terms 2/10, n/30; dated August 3; FOB Los Angeles.

			GENERAL JOURNAL			PAGE _26_	
	DATE		DESCRIPTION	POST. REF.	DEBIT	CREDIT	
1	20–						1
2	Aug.	2	Purchases		1 7 1 0 00		2
3			Freight In		8 5 50		3
4			Accounts Payable, Collins, Inc.			1 7 9 5 50	4
5			Purchased merchandise from				5
6			Collins, Inc., invoice no. 2706,				6
7			invoice dated 7/31, terms 2/10, n/30.				7
8							8
9		3	Purchases		2 7 7 2 00		9
10			Freight In		1 5 7 00		10
11			Accounts Payable, Langseth and Son			2 9 2 9 00	11
12			Purchased merchandise from				12
13			Langseth and Son, invoice no. 982,				13
14			invoice dated 8/2, terms n/30.				14
15							15
16		5	Purchases		5 6 4 00		16
17			Accounts Payable, Dana Mfg. Co.			5 6 4 00	17
18			Purchased merchandise from				18
19			Dana Mfg. Co., invoice no. 10611,				19
20			invoice dated 8/3, terms 2/10, n/30.				20
21							21
22							22

Posting to the General Ledger and Subsidiary Ledger

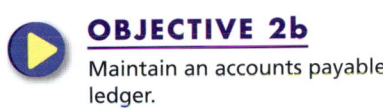

OBJECTIVE 2b

Maintain an accounts payable ledger.

Post each entry to Accounts Payable, Purchases, and Freight In in the general ledger. Also, post the amount owed to the vendor to the subsidiary accounts payable ledger to maintain a running balance of the amount owed to each vendor.

Schedule of Accounts Payable

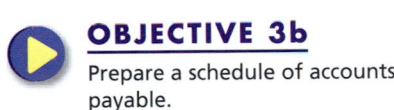

OBJECTIVE 3b

Prepare a schedule of accounts payable.

At the end of the month, the accountant lists the vendor names and amounts owed and totals the amounts. This listing is called the schedule of accounts payable. The total of this schedule should equal the total of the Accounts Payable controlling account in the general ledger. If the two amounts are different, reverse the process of adding and posting to discover and correct the error.

Purchases Returns and Allowances

Refer to pages 356–357 in Chapter 10 for information on journalizing and posting credit memorandums, which give the purchaser permission from the vendor to return all or part of the goods purchased from them. Since we debited Purchases and sometimes Freight In and credited the customer's Accounts Payable account, we must undo or reverse these accounts for the amount we are returning.

PROBLEMS

P.O. 1, 2, 3

Check Figures

Schedule of Accounts Receivable total, $7,383; Schedule of Accounts Payable total, $5,268

Problem C-1A Complete Problem 10-4A on pages 373–375 *except* journalize transactions in a general journal instead of in special journals.

P.O. 1, 2, 3

Check Figures

Schedule of Accounts Receivable total, $7,386.96; Schedule of Accounts Payable total, $4,277.80

Problem C-1B Complete Problem 10-4B on pages 377–378 *except* journalize transactions in a general journal instead of in special journals.

Most Americans have at least one credit card. Many have more than one. Are you aware of the different charges that are paid when you use a credit card? Online, you can find many websites explaining how credit card use affects you as a consumer. Check out *How Stuff Works,* **http://money .howstuffworks.com/credit-card.htm** for some very useful information.

Even though consumers don't have to pay cash up front for a purchase, using their credit card starts a series of transactions that involve cash. Go to **http://wfhummel.cnchost.com/creditcards.html** to learn all about the transactions involved in a credit card purchase. After reading this article, and as you read this chapter, think about who receives cash and who pays cash for credit card transactions, and how the different parties involved might record these transactions.

Performance Objectives

After you have completed this chapter, you will be able to do the following:

1. Journalize transactions for a merchandising business in a cash receipts journal.

2. Post from a cash receipts journal to a general ledger and an accounts receivable ledger.

3. Determine cash discounts according to credit terms, and record cash receipts from charge customers who are entitled to deduct the cash discount.

4. Journalize transactions in a cash payments journal for a service enterprise.

5. Post from a cash payments journal to a general ledger and an accounts payable ledger.

6. Journalize transactions involving cash discounts in a cash payments journal for a merchandising enterprise.

7. Journalize transactions in a check register.

8. Journalize transactions involving trade discounts.

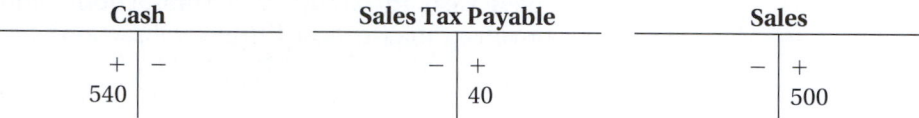

e have seen that using a sales journal and a purchases journal enables an accountant to carry out the journalizing and posting processes much more efficiently. These special journals make it possible to post column totals rather than individual figures. They also make the division of labor more efficient because the journalizing functions can be delegated to different persons. The *cash receipts journal* and the *cash payments journal* further extend these advantages.

THE CASH RECEIPTS JOURNAL

 OBJECTIVE 1

Journalize transactions for a merchandising business in a cash receipts journal.

The **cash receipts journal** contains all transactions in which cash is received, or increases. When a cash receipts journal is used, all transactions in which cash is debited *must* be recorded in it. It may be used for a service as well as a merchandising business. Let's list some typical transactions of a retail merchandising business that result in an increase in cash. To get a better picture of the transactions, let's first record them in T accounts.

May 3 Sold merchandise for cash, $500, plus $40 sales tax.

Cash	Sales Tax Payable	Sales
+ −	− +	− +
540	40	500

May 4 Sold merchandise, $500, plus $40 sales tax, and the customer used a bank charge card. The bank issuing the card bills the customer directly each month. The business, on the other hand, deposits the bank credit card receipts every day. The bank *deducts a discount* and credits the firm's account with cash. We will assume that the discount is 4 percent. The firm therefore records the amount of the discount under Credit Card Expense: $540.00 × .04 = $21.60 credit card expense; $500.00 + $40.00 − $21.60 = $518.40.

Cash	Sales Tax Payable	Sales	Credit Card Expense
+ −	− +	− +	+ −
518.40	40.00	500.00	21.60

May 5 Collected cash on account from L. R. Ray, a charge customer, $416.

Cash	Accounts Receivable
+ −	+ −
416	416

May 7 The owner, J. R. Hall, invested cash in the business, $10,000.

Cash	J. R. Hall, Capital
+ −	− +
10,000	10,000

Cash transactions can take place anywhere in the world through ATM machines, with clients never entering their banks.

May 8 Sold computer equipment for cash at cost, $500.

Cash		Computer Equipment	
+	−	+	−
500			500

The same transactions are shown in general journal form as follows:

		GENERAL JOURNAL			PAGE _____	
	DATE	DESCRIPTION	POST. REF.	DEBIT	CREDIT	
1	20–					1
2	May 3	Cash		5 4 0 00		2
3		Sales			5 0 0 00	3
4		Sales Tax Payable			4 0 00	4
5		Sold merchandise for cash.				5
6						6
7	4	Cash		5 1 8 40		7
8		Credit Card Expense		2 1 60		8
9		Sales			5 0 0 00	9
10		Sales Tax Payable			4 0 00	10
11		Sold merchandise involving				11
12		a bank charge card.				12
13						13
14	5	Cash		4 1 6 00		14
15		Accounts Receivable, L. R. Ray			4 1 6 00	15
16		Collected cash on account.				16
17						17
18	7	Cash		10 0 0 0 00		18
19		J. R. Hall, Capital			10 0 0 0 00	19
20		Owner invested cash.				20
21						21
22	8	Cash		5 0 0 00		22
23		Computer Equipment			5 0 0 00	23
24		Sold computer equipment				24
25		at cost.				25
26						26

Now let's analyze these five transactions: The first three would occur frequently; the last two would occur less frequently. When designing a cash receipts journal, it is logical to include a Cash Debit column because all the transactions involve an increase in cash. If a business regularly collects cash from charge customers, there should be an Accounts Receivable Credit column. If a firm often sells merchandise for cash and collects a sales tax, there should be a Sales Credit column and a Sales Tax Payable Credit column. If the business accepts bank charge cards and wants to record the amount of the discount at the time of each transaction, there should be a Credit Card Expense Debit column for the amount deducted by the bank.

However, the credit to J. R. Hall, Capital, and the credit to Computer Equipment do not occur very often, so it would not be practical to set up

CASH RECEIPTS JOURNAL   PAGE __41__

	DATE	ACCOUNT CREDITED	POST. REF.	CASH DEBIT	CREDIT CARD EXPENSE DEBIT	ACCOUNTS RECEIVABLE CREDIT	SALES CREDIT	SALES TAX PAYABLE CREDIT	OTHER ACCOUNTS CREDIT	
1	20–									1
2	May 3	————		5 4 0 00			5 0 0 00	4 0 00		2
3	4	————		5 1 8 40	2 1 60		5 0 0 00	4 0 00		3
4	5	L. R. Ray		4 1 6 00		4 1 6 00				4
5	7	J. R. Hall,								5
6		Capital		10 0 0 0 00					10 0 0 0 00	6
7	8	Computer								7
8		Equipment		5 0 0 00					5 0 0 00	8
9										9

FIGURE 1

special columns for these credits. They can be handled adequately by an Other Accounts Credit column, which can be used for credits to all accounts that have no special column.

Now let's record these transactions in a cash receipts journal (see Figure 1). First, we repeat the transactions:

May 3 Sold merchandise for cash, $500, plus $40 sales tax.
     4 Sold merchandise, $500, plus $40 sales tax, and the customer used a bank charge card. Discount charged by the bank is 4 percent of the total of sales plus sales tax.
     5 Collected cash on account from L. R. Ray, a charge customer, $416.
     7 The owner, J. R. Hall, invested cash in the business, $10,000.
     8 Sold computer equipment for cash at cost, $500.

> **REMEMBER!**
>
> The amount of credit card expense is based on the total of sales *plus* sales tax payable.

> **REMEMBER!**
>
> Special journals include a sales journal, a purchases journal, a cash receipts journal, and a cash payments journal. They are used to save time by posting totals of the special columns rather than individual amounts to the general ledger.

As an alternative, many businesses postpone recording the amount of bank credit card expense until they actually receive notification from their bank on their bank statement. For example, total credit card sales for a restaurant for a time period amount to $10,600 plus 8 percent sales tax. The entry is as follows:

Cash	Sales Tax Payable	Sales
+ | −	− | +	− | +
11,448 |	| 848	| 10,600

The restaurant's next bank statement includes a debit memorandum for credit card charges of $457.92, using an assumed 4 percent discount rate ($11,448 × .04). The business handles this in a similar manner to a check service charge:

Credit Card Expense	Cash
+ | −	+ | −
457.92 |	| 457.92

Posting from the Cash Receipts Journal

Here are some other transactions made during the month that involve increases in cash. (Remember that these transactions are for a retail business.)

May 11 Borrowed $9,000 from the bank, receiving cash and giving the bank a promissory note.

16 Sold merchandise for cash, $200, plus $16 sales tax.

21 Sold merchandise, $100, plus $8 sales tax; customer used a bank charge card. Credit card expense charge is 4 percent of sales plus sales tax.

26 Collected cash from B. Sanchez, a charge customer, on account, $262.40.

28 Sold merchandise for cash, $160, plus $12.80 sales tax.

31 Sold merchandise, $150, plus $12 sales tax; customer used a bank charge card. Credit card expense charge is 4 percent of sales plus sales tax.

31 Collected cash from T. Nguyen, a charge customer, on account, $140.

In the transaction of May 11, in which $9,000 was borrowed from the bank, the bank was given a **promissory note** (a written promise to pay a specified amount at a specified time) as evidence of the debt. The account **Notes Payable**, instead of Accounts Payable, is used to represent the amount owed on the promissory note. The Accounts Payable account is reserved for charge accounts with creditors, which are normally paid on a thirty-day basis.

Let's assume that all the month's transactions involving debits to Cash have now been recorded in the cash receipts journal. The cash receipts journal (see Figure 2 on the following page) and the T accounts following it illustrate the postings to the general ledger and the accounts receivable ledger.

Individual amounts in the Accounts Receivable Credit column of the cash receipts journal are usually posted daily to the accounts receivable ledger. Individual amounts in the Other Accounts Credit column are usually posted daily.

At the end of the month, we can post the special column totals in the cash receipts journal to the general ledger accounts. These columns include Cash Debit, Credit Card Expense Debit, Accounts Receivable Credit, Sales Credit, and Sales Tax Payable Credit.

In the Post. Ref. column, the check marks (✓) indicate that the amounts in the Accounts Receivable Credit column have been posted to the individual charge customers' accounts as credits. The account numbers show that the amounts in the Other Accounts Credit column have been posted separately to the accounts described in the Account Credited column. An (X) goes under the total of the Other Accounts Credit column; it means "do not post—the figures have already been posted separately." This column is totaled to make it easier to prove that the debits equal the credits.

Note the ruling. A single rule is placed above the column totals, and double rules extend through all but the Account Credited column. Also, on the last line, the last day of the month is recorded in the Date column.

Let's say it's the end of the month. Total the columns first. Then begin crossfooting the journal by proving that the sum of the debit totals equals the sum of the credit totals. This process must be completed before you post the totals to the general ledger accounts.

OBJECTIVE 2

Post from a cash receipts journal to a general ledger and an accounts receivable ledger.

FYI

The dash is a placeholder indicating that nothing has been left out or forgotten.

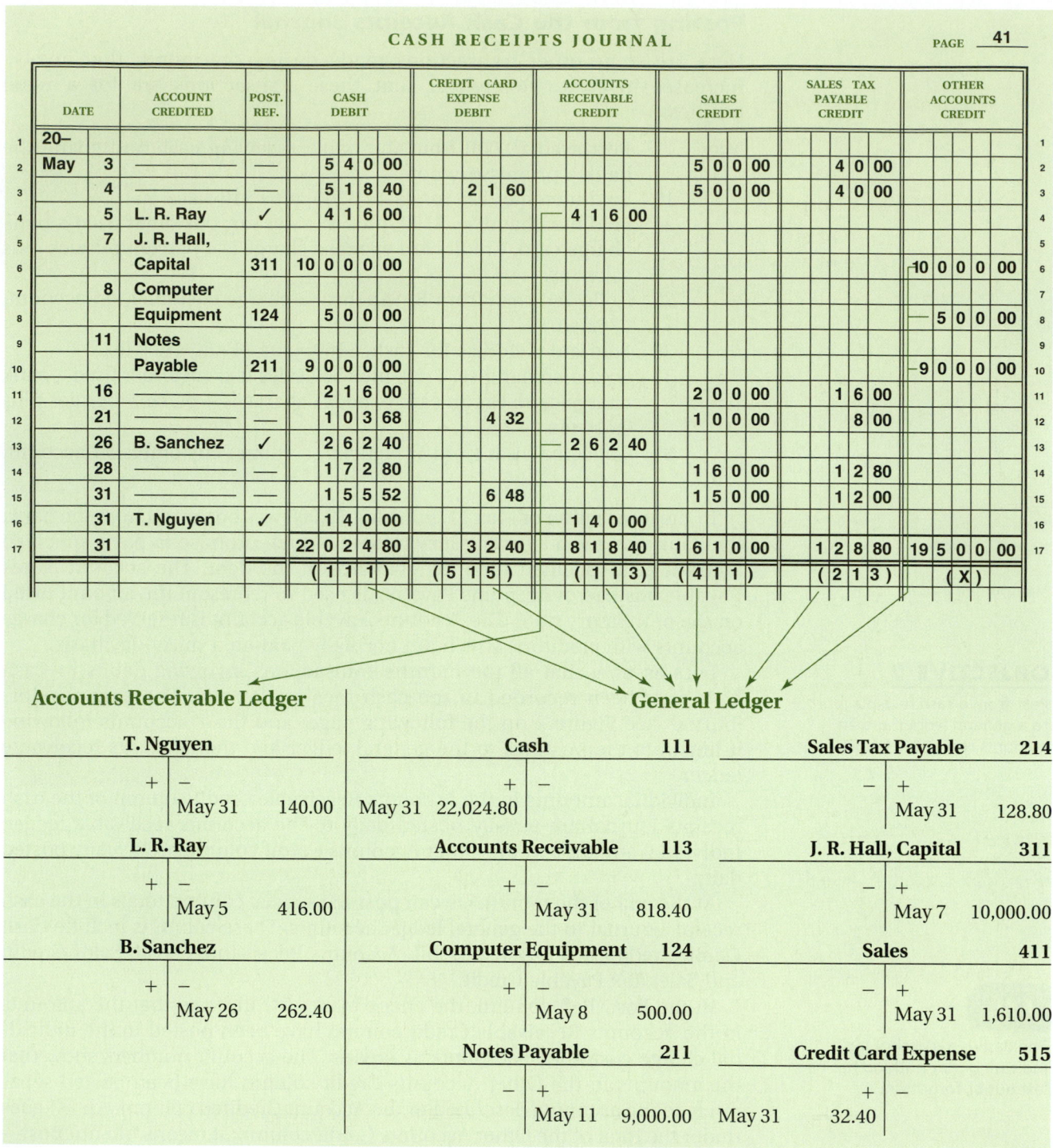

CASH RECEIPTS JOURNAL PAGE 41

	DATE	ACCOUNT CREDITED	POST. REF.	CASH DEBIT	CREDIT CARD EXPENSE DEBIT	ACCOUNTS RECEIVABLE CREDIT	SALES CREDIT	SALES TAX PAYABLE CREDIT	OTHER ACCOUNTS CREDIT	
1	20–									1
2	May 3	————	—	5 4 0 00			5 0 0 00	4 0 00		2
3	4	————	—	5 1 8 40	2 1 60		5 0 0 00	4 0 00		3
4	5	L. R. Ray	✓	4 1 6 00		4 1 6 00				4
5	7	J. R. Hall,								5
6		Capital	311	10 0 0 0 00					10 0 0 0 00	6
7	8	Computer								7
8		Equipment	124	5 0 0 00					5 0 0 00	8
9	11	Notes								9
10		Payable	211	9 0 0 0 00					9 0 0 0 00	10
11	16	————	—	2 1 6 00			2 0 0 00	1 6 00		11
12	21	————	—	1 0 3 68	4 32		1 0 0 00	8 00		12
13	26	B. Sanchez	✓	2 6 2 40		2 6 2 40				13
14	28		—	1 7 2 80			1 6 0 00	1 2 80		14
15	31	————	—	1 5 5 52	6 48		1 5 0 00	1 2 00		15
16	31	T. Nguyen	✓	1 4 0 00		1 4 0 00				16
17	31			22 0 2 4 80	3 2 40	8 1 8 40	1 6 1 0 00	1 2 8 80	19 5 0 0 00	17
				(1 1 1)	(5 1 5)	(1 1 3)	(4 1 1)	(2 1 3)	(X)	

Accounts Receivable Ledger

General Ledger

T. Nguyen	
+ | –	
May 31	140.00

L. R. Ray	
+ | –	
May 5	416.00

B. Sanchez	
+ | –	
May 26	262.40

Cash	111
+ | –	
May 31 22,024.80	

Accounts Receivable	113
+ | –	
	May 31 818.40

Computer Equipment	124
+ | –	
	May 8 500.00

Notes Payable	211
– | +	
	May 11 9,000.00

Sales Tax Payable	214
– | +	
	May 31 128.80

J. R. Hall, Capital	311
– | +	
	May 7 10,000.00

Sales	411
– | +	
	May 31 1,610.00

Credit Card Expense	515
+ | –	
May 31 32.40	

FIGURE 2

Debit Totals		Credit Totals	
Cash	$22,024.80	Accounts Receivable	$ 818.40
Credit Card Expense	32.40	Sales	1,610.00
		Sales Tax Payable	128.80
		Other Accounts	19,500.00
	$22,057.20		$22,057.20

Post the special column totals to the general ledger, using the letters CR as the posting reference. Next, write the general ledger account number in parentheses below the total in the appropriate column.

Advantages of a Cash Receipts Journal

1. Transactions generally can be recorded on one line.
2. All transactions involving debits to Cash are recorded in one place.
3. It eliminates much repetition in posting when there are numerous transactions involving Cash debits. The Cash Debit side can be posted as one total.
4. Special columns can be used for specialized transactions and posted as one total.

CREDIT TERMS

OBJECTIVE 3

Determine cash discounts according to credit terms, and record cash receipts from charge customers who are entitled to deduct the cash discount.

The seller always stipulates credit terms: How much credit can a customer be allowed? And, how much time should the customer be given to pay the full amount? The **credit period** is the time the seller allows the buyer before full payment has to be made. Retailers generally allow twenty-five to thirty days.

Wholesalers and manufacturers often specify a **cash discount** in their credit terms. A cash discount is an amount that a customer can deduct if a bill is paid within a specified time. The discount is based on the *total amount of the invoice after any returns and allowances and freight charges billed on the invoice have been deducted.* Naturally, this discount acts as an incentive for charge customers to pay their bills promptly.

Let's say that a wholesaler offers customers credit terms of 2/10, n/30. These terms mean that the customer gets a 2 percent discount if the bill is paid within ten days after the invoice date. The discount period begins the day after the invoice date. If the bill is not paid within the ten days, the entire amount is due within thirty days after the invoice date. Other types of cash discounts that may be used are the following:

The cash receipts journal and the cash payments journal are used by both service and merchandising businesses to record all transactions in which cash comes into or goes out of the business.

- **1/15, n/60** The seller offers a 1 percent discount if the bill is paid within fifteen days after the invoice date, and the whole bill must be paid within sixty days after the invoice date.
- **2/10, EOM, n/60** The seller offers a 2 percent discount if the bill is paid within ten days after the end of the month, and the whole bill must be paid within sixty days after the last day of the month.

A wholesaler or manufacturer that offers a cash discount adopts a single cash discount as a credit policy and makes this available to all its customers. The seller considers cash discounts as sales discounts; the buyer, on the other hand, considers cash discounts as purchases discounts. In this section we are concerned with the sales discount. *The Sales Discounts account, like Sales Returns and Allowances, is a deduction from Sales.*

To illustrate, we return to Rainier Plumbing Supply. We will record the following transactions in T accounts.

Transaction (a) August 1: Sold merchandise on account to Betterbuilt Homes Co., invoice no. 1320, $1,564.86; terms 2/10, n/30.

Transaction (b) August 10: Received check from Betterbuilt Homes Co. for $1,533.56 in payment of invoice no. 1320, less cash discount ($1,564.86 × .02 = $31.30; $1,564.86 − $31.30 = $1,533.56).

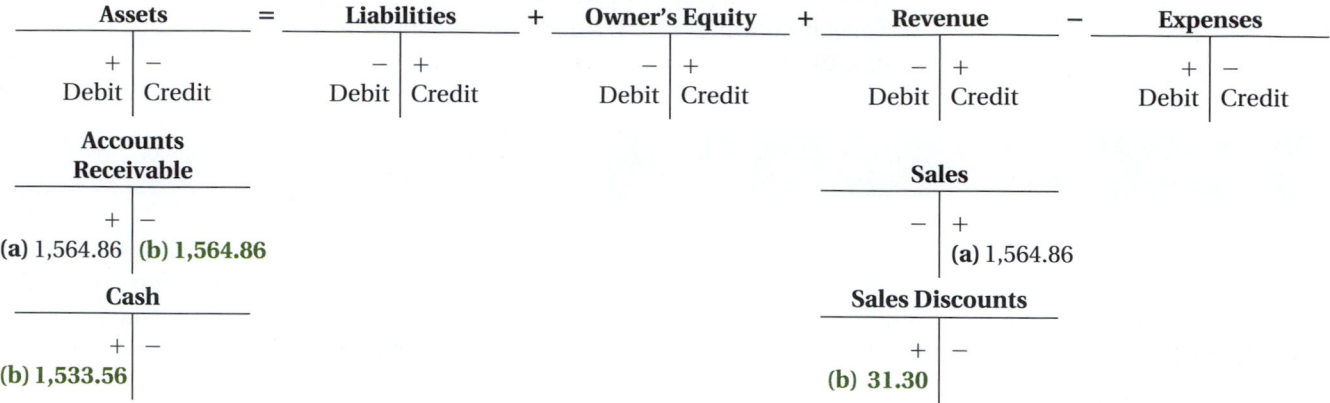

Since Rainier Plumbing Supply offers this cash discount to all its customers, and since charge customers often pay their bills within the discount period, Rainier Plumbing Supply sets up a Sales Discounts Debit column in the cash receipts journal. Note that Rainier Plumbing Supply is a wholesaler. Therefore, a column for Sales Tax Payable is not used since few states levy a tax on sales at the wholesale level.

CASH RECEIPTS JOURNAL   PAGE 18

	DATE	ACCOUNT CREDITED	POST. REF.	CASH DEBIT	SALES DISCOUNTS DEBIT	ACCOUNTS RECEIVABLE CREDIT	SALES CREDIT	OTHER ACCOUNTS CREDIT	
1	20–								1
2	Aug. 10	Betterbuilt Homes Co.		1 5 3 3 56	3 1 30	1 5 6 4 86			2
3									3

Several other transactions of Rainier Plumbing Supply involve increases in cash during August. Remember that the standard credit terms for all charge customers are 2/10, n/30.

Aug. 15 Cash sales for first half of the month, $2,460.
16 Received check from Gonzales Construction for $1,366.12 in payment of invoice no. 1322, less cash discount ($1,394.00 − $27.88 = $1,366.12).
17 Received payment on a promissory note given by John R. Bryant, $500 principal, plus $10 interest. (The amount of the interest is recorded in Interest Income.)

Aug. 21 Received check from Carmel Hardware for $3,696.80 in payment of invoice no. 1324, less cash discount ($3,772.24 − $75.44 = $3,696.80).

23 Sold equipment for cash at cost, $126.

26 C. F. Rainier, the owner, invested an additional $4,000 cash in the business.

26 Received a check from Howard and Sons, Inc., for $2,392.18 in payment of invoice no. 1325, less cash discount ($2,441.00 − $48.82 = $2,392.18).

30 Received check from Green Plumbing and Heating for $1,675.80 in payment of invoice no. 1326, less cash discount ($1,710.00 − $34.20 = $1,675.80).

31 Cash sales for second half of the month, $2,620.

31 Received check from Arnold, Inc., for $1,116 in payment of invoice no. 1321. (This is longer than the ten-day period, so the cash discount is not allowed.)

Rainier Plumbing Supply records these transactions in its cash receipts journal (Figure 3).

After that has been done, the company's accountant proves the equality of debits and credits:

> **REMEMBER!**
>
> When journalizing a cash receipt involving a sales discount, be sure to credit Accounts Receivable for the total amount of the sales transaction.

Debit Totals		Credit Totals	
Cash	$21,496.46	Accounts Receivable	$11,998.10
Sales Discounts	217.64	Sales	5,080.00
		Other Accounts	4,636.00
	$21,714.10		$21,714.10

FIGURE 3

CASH RECEIPTS JOURNAL   PAGE 18

	DATE	ACCOUNT CREDITED	POST. REF.	CASH DEBIT	SALES DISCOUNTS DEBIT	ACCOUNTS RECEIVABLE CREDIT	SALES CREDIT	OTHER ACCOUNTS CREDIT	
1	20–								1
2	Aug. 10	Betterbuilt Homes Co.	✓	1 5 3 3 56	3 1 30	1 5 6 4 86			2
3	15	——————	—	2 4 6 0 00			2 4 6 0 00		3
4	16	Gonzales Construction	✓	1 3 6 6 12	2 7 88	1 3 9 4 00			4
5	17	Notes Receivable	112					5 0 0 00	5
6		Interest Income	422	5 1 0 00				1 0 00	6
7	21	Carmel Hardware	✓	3 6 9 6 80	7 5 44	3 7 7 2 24			7
8	23	Equipment	124	1 2 6 00				1 2 6 00	8
9	26	C. F. Rainier, Capital	311	4 0 0 0 00				4 0 0 0 00	9
10	26	Howard and Sons, Inc.	✓	2 3 9 2 18	4 8 82	2 4 4 1 00			10
11	30	Green Plumbing and Heating	✓	1 6 7 5 80	3 4 20	1 7 1 0 00			11
12	31	——————	—	2 6 2 0 00			2 6 2 0 00		12
13	31	Arnold, Inc.	✓	1 1 1 6 00		1 1 1 6 00			13
14	31			21 4 9 6 46	2 1 7 64	11 9 9 8 10	5 0 8 0 00	4 6 3 6 00	14
15				(1 1 1)	(4 1 3)	(1 1 3)	(4 1 1)	(X)	15
16									16
17									17

SALES RETURNS AND ALLOWANCES AND SALES DISCOUNTS ON AN INCOME STATEMENT

In the fundamental accounting equation, to be consistent with the income statement, we placed Sales Returns and Allowances and Sales Discounts under Sales with the plus and minus signs reversed. Both accounts are contra revenue accounts, so we subtract their totals from Sales on the income statement. Here is the Revenue from Sales section of the annual income statement of Rainier Plumbing Supply.

Rainier Plumbing Supply
Income Statement
For Year Ended December 31, 20—

Revenue from Sales:			
Sales		$255 1 8 0 00	
Less: Sales Returns and Allowances	$ 8 4 0 00		
Sales Discounts	1 8 8 0 00	2 7 2 0 00	
Net Sales			$252 4 6 0 00

THE CASH PAYMENTS JOURNAL: SERVICE ENTERPRISE

The **cash payments journal**, as the name implies, is a special journal used to record all transactions in which cash goes out, or decreases. When the cash payments journal is used, all transactions in which cash is credited *must* be recorded in it. This journal may be used for either a service or a merchandising business.

To get acquainted with the cash payments journal, let's list some typical transactions of a professional service firm (such as an attorney's office) that result in a decrease in cash. To illustrate, we record the following transactions in T accounts:

May 2 Paid Brown Paper Co., a creditor, on account, Ck. No. 2063, $1,220.

Accounts Payable		Cash	
−	+	+	−
1,220			1,220

May 4 Paid cash for liability insurance, Ck. No. 2064, $4,890.

Prepaid Insurance		Cash	
+	−	+	−
4,890			4,890

May 5 Paid wages for two weeks, Ck. No. 2065, $6,220 (previously recorded in the payroll entry).

Wages Payable		Cash	
−	+	+	−
6,220			6,220

May 6 Paid rent for the month, Ck. No. 2066, $2,950.

Rent Expense		Cash	
+	−	+	−
2,950			2,950

The same transactions are now shown in general journal form.

	DATE		DESCRIPTION	POST. REF.	DEBIT	CREDIT	
			GENERAL JOURNAL			PAGE _____	
1	20–						1
2	May	2	Accounts Payable,				2
3			Brown Paper Co.		1 2 2 0 00		3
4			Cash			1 2 2 0 00	4
5			Paid on account, Ck. No. 2063.				5
6							6
7		4	Prepaid Insurance		4 8 9 0 00		7
8			Cash			4 8 9 0 00	8
9			Paid cash for liability				9
10			insurance, Ck. No. 2064.				10
11							11
12		5	Wages Payable		6 2 2 0 00		12
13			Cash			6 2 2 0 00	13
14			Paid wages for two weeks,				14
15			Ck. No. 2065.				15
16							16
17		6	Rent Expense		2 9 5 0 00		17
18			Cash			2 9 5 0 00	18
19			Paid rent for month,				19
20			Ck. No. 2066.				20

Let's analyze these four transactions. The first one would occur frequently, as payments to creditors are made several times a month. Of the last three transactions, the debit to Wages Payable might occur twice a month, the debit to Rent Expense once a month, and the debit to Prepaid Insurance only occasionally.

It is logical to include a Cash Credit column in a cash payments journal because all transactions recorded in this journal involve a decrease in cash. Since payments to creditors are made often, there should also be an

Accounts Payable Debit column. You can set up any other column that is used often enough to warrant it. Otherwise, an Other Accounts Debit column takes care of all the other transactions.

Now let's record these same transactions in a cash payments journal and include a column titled Ck. No. If you think a moment, you will see that this is consistent with good management of cash. All expenditures except Petty Cash expenditures should be paid for by check. Let's repeat the transactions.

OBJECTIVE 4

Journalize transactions in a cash payments journal for a service enterprise.

May			
	2	Paid Brown Paper Co., a creditor, on account, Ck. No. 2063, $1,220.	
	4	Paid cash for liability insurance, Ck. No. 2064, $4,890.	
	5	Paid wages for two weeks, Ck. No. 2065, $6,220 (previously recorded in the payroll entry).	
	6	Paid rent for the month, Ck. No. 2066, $2,950.	

CASH PAYMENTS JOURNAL   PAGE __62__

	DATE	CK. NO.	ACCOUNT DEBITED	POST. REF.	OTHER ACCOUNTS DEBIT	ACCOUNTS PAYABLE DEBIT	CASH CREDIT	
1	20–							1
2	May 2	2063	Brown Paper Co.			1 2 2 0 00	1 2 2 0 00	2
3	4	2064	Prepaid Insurance		4 8 9 0 00		4 8 9 0 00	3
4	5	2065	Wages Payable		6 2 2 0 00		6 2 2 0 00	4
5	6	2066	Rent Expense		2 9 5 0 00		2 9 5 0 00	5
6								6

Other transactions involving decreases in cash during May are as follows:

May		
	7	Paid a one-year premium for fire insurance, Ck. No. 2067, $360.
	9	Paid Morris, Inc., a creditor, on account, Ck. No. 2068, $418.
	11	Issued Ck. No. 2069 in payment of delivery expense, $62.
	14	Paid Russet and Son, a creditor, on account, Ck. No. 2070, $110.
	16	Issued Ck. No. 2071 to the Logan State Bank for a Note Payable, $6,396, $6,000 on the principal and $396 interest.
	19	Voided Ck. No. 2072.
	19	Bought equipment from Snyder Company, Ck. No. 2073, $200.
	20	Paid wages for two weeks, Ck. No. 2074, $3,340 (previously recorded in the payroll entry).
	22	Issued Ck. No. 2075 to Scheel Advertising Agency for advertising, $94 (not previously recorded).
	26	Paid telephone bill, Ck. No. 2076, $326.
	31	Issued Ck. No. 2077 for freight bill on equipment purchased on May 19, $58.
	31	Paid Trask & Co., a creditor, on account, Ck. No. 2078, $160.

You should list all checks in consecutive order, even those checks that must be voided. In this way, *every* check is accounted for, which is necessary for internal control.

These transactions are recorded in the cash payments journal illustrated in Figure 4. Notice that an (X) is placed under the Other Accounts column. That means "do not post—the individual figures have already been posted."

FIGURE 4

	DATE	CK. NO.	ACCOUNT DEBITED	POST. REF.	OTHER ACCOUNTS DEBIT	ACCOUNTS PAYABLE DEBIT	CASH CREDIT	
1	20–							1
2	May 2	2063	Brown Paper Co.	✓		1 2 2 0 00	1 2 2 0 00	2
3	4	2064	Prepaid Insurance	113	4 8 9 0 00		4 8 9 0 00	3
4	5	2065	Wages Payable	214	6 2 2 0 00		6 2 2 0 00	4
5	6	2066	Rent Expense	512	2 9 5 0 00		2 9 5 0 00	5
6	7	2067	Prepaid Insurance	114	3 6 0 00		3 6 0 00	6
7	9	2068	Morris, Inc.	✓		4 1 8 00	4 1 8 00	7
8	11	2069	Delivery Expense	513	6 2 00		6 2 00	8
9	14	2070	Russet and Son	✓		1 1 0 00	1 1 0 00	9
10	16	2071	Notes Payable	211	6 0 0 0 00			10
11			Interest Expense	518	3 9 6 00		6 3 9 6 00	11
12	19	2072	Void	—				12
13	19	2073	Equipment	121	2 0 0 00		2 0 0 00	13
14	20	2074	Wages Payable	214	3 3 4 0 00		3 3 4 0 00	14
15	22	2075	Advertising					15
16			Expense	515	9 4 00		9 4 00	16
17	26	2076	Telephone					17
18			Expense	516	3 2 6 00		3 2 6 00	18
19	31	2077	Equipment	121	5 8 00		5 8 00	19
20	31	2078	Trask & Co.	✓		1 6 0 00	1 6 0 00	20
21	31				24 8 9 6 00	1 9 0 8 00	26 8 0 4 00	21
22					(X)	(2 1 2)	(1 1 1)	22

CASH PAYMENTS JOURNAL   PAGE __62__

At the end of the month, after totaling the columns, check the accuracy of the footings by proving that the sum of the debit totals equals the sum of the credit totals. Since you have posted the individual amounts in the Other Accounts Debit column to the general ledger, the only posting that remains is the credit to the Cash account for $26,804 and the debit to the Accounts Payable (controlling) account for $1,908.

Debit Totals		Credit Totals	
Accounts Payable	$ 1,908.00	Cash	$26,804.00
Other Accounts	24,896.00		
	$26,804.00		$26,804.00

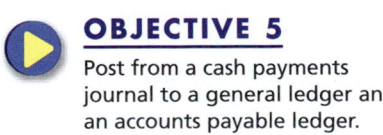

OBJECTIVE 5

Post from a cash payments journal to a general ledger and an accounts payable ledger.

The posting process for the cash payments journal is similar to the posting process for the cash receipts journal. Individual amounts in the Accounts Payable Debit column are usually posted daily to the subsidiary ledger. After posting, put a check mark (✓) in the Post. Ref. column. Individual amounts in the Other Accounts Debit column are usually posted daily to the general ledger. Post these figures individually, then place the account number in the Post. Ref. column. Totals of the Cash Credit column and the Accounts Payable Debit column are posted to the general ledger accounts at the end of the month. Write the appropriate general ledger account number in parentheses below the column totals. Print an (X) below the total of the Other Accounts Debit column to indicate that the total amount is not posted. The posting letter designation for the cash payments journal is CP.

REMEMBER!

The (X) below the total of the Other Accounts Debit column means "do not post total."

The advantages of the cash payments journal are similar to the advantages of the cash receipts journal:

1. Transactions generally can be recorded on one line.
2. All the transactions involving credits to Cash are recorded in one place.
3. For numerous transactions involving Cash credits, the Cash Credit side can be posted as one total.
4. Special columns can be used for specialized transactions and posted as one total.

THE CASH PAYMENTS JOURNAL: MERCHANDISING ENTERPRISE

OBJECTIVE 6

Journalize transactions involving cash discounts in a cash payments journal for a merchandising enterprise.

There is one slight difference between the cash payments journal for a merchandising enterprise and that for a service enterprise. This difference has to do with the cash discounts available to a merchandising business. Recall that a cash discount is the amount that the buyer may deduct from the bill; this acts as an incentive to get the buyer to pay the bill promptly. The buyer considers the cash discount to be a purchases discount, because it relates to the buyer's purchase of merchandise. The Purchases Discounts account, like Purchases Returns and Allowances, is treated as a deduction from Purchases on the buyer's income statement.

Let us return to Rainier Plumbing Supply and assume that the following transactions take place. To demonstrate the debits and credits, let's show some typical transactions in the form of T accounts.

REMEMBER!

The cash discount does not apply to freight charges billed separately on an invoice.

Transaction (a) August 2: Bought merchandise on account from Collins, Inc., $1,710, invoice no. 2706, dated July 31; terms 2/10, n/30; FOB San Francisco, freight prepaid and added to the invoice, $85.50 (total $1,795.50).

Transaction (b) August 8: Issued Ck. No. 2076 to Collins, Inc., in payment of invoice no. 2706, less cash discount of $34.20, $1,761.30 ($1,795.50 − $34.20), which is recorded in the cash payments journal. Notice that the discount applies only to the amount billed for the merchandise (2 percent of $1,710). Here are the transactions shown in T accounts:

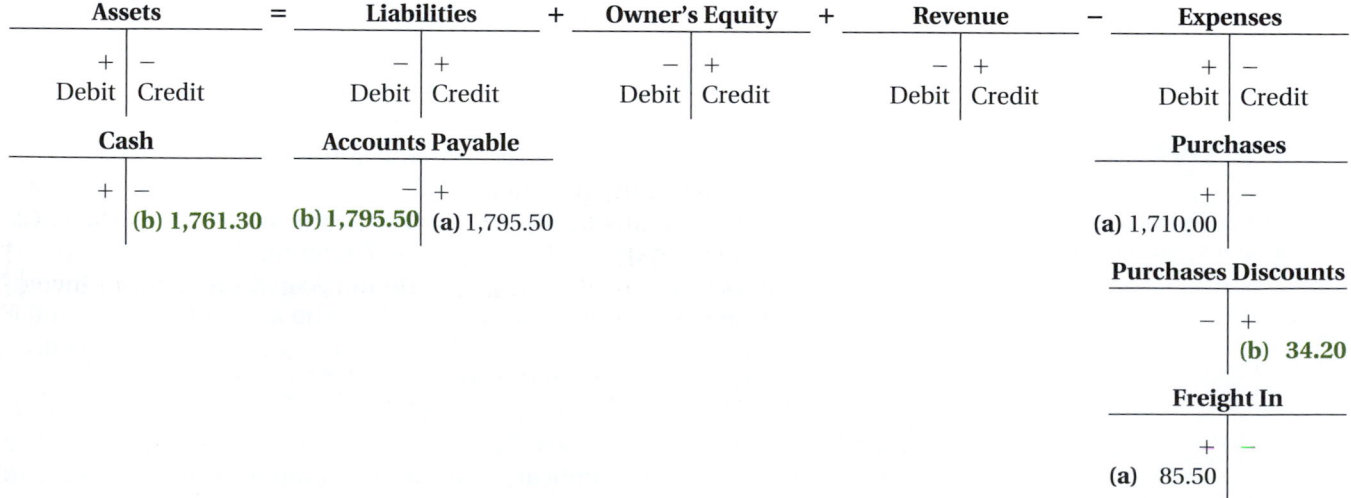

Any well-managed business takes advantage of a purchases discount whenever possible. So, if a discount is generally available to the business, it is worthwhile to set up a special Purchases Discounts Credit column in the cash payments journal. Transaction (b), August 8, looks like this in the cash payments journal:

CASH PAYMENTS JOURNAL   PAGE ___26___

	DATE	CK. NO.	ACCOUNT DEBITED	POST. REF.	OTHER ACCOUNTS DEBIT	ACCOUNTS PAYABLE DEBIT	PURCHASES DISCOUNTS CREDIT	CASH CREDIT	
1	20–								1
2	Aug. 8	2076	Collins, Inc.			1 7 9 5 50	3 4 20	1 7 6 1 30	2
3									3

Here are some other transactions of Rainier Plumbing Supply involving decreases in cash during August. Note that credit terms vary among the different creditors.

Aug. 10 Paid wages for two-week period, Ck. No. 2077, $1,680 (previously recorded in the payroll entry).

11 Issued Ck. No. 2078 to Dana Manufacturing Company, in payment of invoice no. 10611 ($564), less return ($270); less cash discount, 2/10, n/30; $288.12 ($564 − $270 = $294; $294.00 × 0.02 = $5.88; $294.00 − $5.88 = $288.12).

12 Bought supplies for cash, Ck. No. 2079, payable to Davenport Office Supplies, $70. (Debit Supplies Expense.)

15 Issued Ck. No. 2080 to Gardner Products Company, in payment of invoice no. B643 ($1,245), less return ($315); less cash discount, 1/10, n/30; $921.60 [$1,245 − $315 = $930; freight charges totaled $90 ($930 − $90 = $840); $840.00 × 0.01 = $8.40; $930.00 − $8.40 = $921.60].

16 Bought merchandise for cash, Ck. No. 2081, payable to Jones and Son, $200.

19 Received bill and issued Ck. No. 2082 to Monroe Express for freight charges on merchandise purchased earlier from Dana Manufacturing Company, $60.

23 Voided Ck. No. 2083.

23 Issued Ck. No. 2084 to American Fire Insurance Company for insurance premium for one year, $420.

25 Paid wages for two-week period, Ck. No. 2085, $1,750 (previously recorded in the payroll entry).

27 Paid F. P. Franz for merchandise he returned on a cash sale, Ck. No. 2086, $51.

27 Issued Ck. No. 2087 to Langseth and Son in payment of invoice no. 902, net 30 days, $1,180.

The transaction of August 19 paying the freight bill to Monroe Express increases the Freight In account, as the transportation charges are for merchandise purchased.

					OTHER ACCOUNTS DEBIT	ACCOUNTS PAYABLE DEBIT	PURCHASES DISCOUNTS CREDIT	CASH CREDIT	
	DATE	CK. NO.	ACCOUNT DEBITED	POST. REF.					
1	20–								1
2	Aug. 8	2076	Collins, Inc.	✓		1 7 9 5 50	3 4 20	1 7 6 1 30	2
3	10	2077	Wages Payable	213	1 6 8 0 0 00			1 6 8 0 00	3
4	11	2078	Dana Manufacturing Company	✓		2 9 4 00	5 88	2 8 8 12	4
5	12	2079	Supplies Expense	625	7 0 00			7 0 00	5
6	15	2080	Gardner Products Company	✓		9 3 0 00	8 40	9 2 1 60	6
7	16	2081	Purchases	511	2 0 0 00			2 0 0 00	7
8	19	2082	Freight In	514	6 0 00			6 0 00	8
9	23	2083	Void	—					9
10	23	2084	Prepaid Insurance	116	4 2 0 00			4 2 0 00	10
11	25	2085	Wages Payable	213	1 7 5 0 00			1 7 5 0 00	11
12	27	2086	Sales Returns and Allowances	412	5 1 00			5 1 00	12
13	27	2087	Langseth and Son	✓		1 1 8 0 00		1 1 8 0 00	13
14	31				4 2 3 1 00	4 1 9 9 50	4 8 48	8 3 8 2 02	14
15					(X)	(2 1 2)	(5 1 3)	(1 1 1)	15
16									16

CASH PAYMENTS JOURNAL PAGE __26__

NOTE: The Supplies account is explained in Chapter 12.

FIGURE 5

REMEMBER!

After posting to the accounts payable subsidiary ledger from the cash payments journal, record a check mark in the Post. Ref. column in the cash payments journal.

Now let's record these transactions in the cash payments journal (Figure 5). After that is completed, Rainier Plumbing Supply's accountant proves the equality of debits and credits:

Debit Totals		Credit Totals	
Accounts Payable	$4,199.50	Purchases Discounts	$ 48.48
Other Accounts	4,231.00	Cash	8,382.02
	$8,430.50		$8,430.50

PURCHASES RETURNS AND ALLOWANCES, PURCHASES DISCOUNTS, AND FREIGHT IN ON AN INCOME STATEMENT

In the fundamental accounting equation, to be consistent with the income statement, we placed Purchases Returns and Allowances and Purchases Discounts under Purchases with the plus and minus signs reversed. Both accounts are considered contra accounts and are subtracted from Purchases on the income statement. Since Freight In increases the cost of purchases, it must be added. A portion of the Cost of Goods Sold section of the annual income statement of Rainier Plumbing Supply, as well as the Revenue from Sales section (taken from the illustration in Chapter 13), is shown in Figure 6.

Rainier Plumbing Supply
Income Statement
For Year Ended December 31, 20—

Revenue from Sales:					
Sales			$255 1 8 0 00		
Less: Sales Returns and Allowances	$ 8 4 0 00				
Sales Discounts	1 8 8 0 00		2 7 2 0 00		
Net Sales				$252 4 6 0 00	
Cost of Goods Sold:					
Merchandise Inventory, January 1, 20—			$ 67 0 0 0 00		
Purchases	$87 1 4 0 00				
Less: Purchases Returns and					
Allowances	$ 832.00				
Purchases Discounts	1,248.00	2 0 8 0 00			
Net Purchases		$85 0 6 0 00			
Add Freight In		2 4 6 0 00			
Delivered Cost of Purchases			87 5 2 0 00		
Goods Available for Sale			$154 5 2 0 00		

FIGURE 6

CHECK REGISTER

OBJECTIVE 7
Journalize transactions in a check register.

Instead of using a cash payments journal as a book of original entry, you can use a check register. Businesses often use a large checkbook with perforations that make it easy to tear out the checks. The page opposite the checks, known as the **check register**, has columns labeled for special accounts, such as Bank Credit (in place of Cash), Accounts Payable Debit, and so on. The checks are prenumbered, and each check issued is recorded on the columnar sheet. This is common practice for a small business in which the owner writes the checks personally. Transactions are posted directly from the check register.

Suppose Rainier Plumbing Supply had used a check register instead of the cash payments journal. Its August transactions would appear as they do in Figure 7 on page 408.

You can see that the difference between the cash payments journal and the check register is minor. The Bank Credit column substitutes for the Cash Credit column. The check register lists the payee of the check.

Two additional columns, Deposits and Bank Balance, can be added to give the current balance of the City Bank or Cash account. The posting process for each book of original entry is the same.

REMEMBER!

In the Post. Ref. column, a check mark indicates that the amount has been posted to the creditor's account in the accounts payable ledger; below the total of the Other Accounts Debit column, an (X) indicates that the total is not to be posted.

In a small business, the owner or manager usually signs all the checks. However, if the owner delegates the authority to sign checks to some other person, that person should *not* have access to the accounting records. Why? This helps prevent fraud, because a dishonest employee could conceal a cash disbursement in the accounting records. In other words, for a medium- to large-size business, a manager should keep a separate book, which in this case is the cash payments journal. One person writes the checks; another person records the checks in the cash payments journal; and a third person does the bank reconciliation. In this way, each person acts as a control on the others. There would have to be cooperation among the three people for

DATE	CK. NO.	PAYEE	ACCOUNT DEBITED	POST. REF.	OTHER ACCOUNTS DEBIT	ACCOUNTS PAYABLE DEBIT	PURCHASES DISCOUNTS CREDIT	CITY BANK CREDIT	
20–									1
Aug. 8	2076	Collins, Inc.	Collins, Inc.	✓		1795 50	34 20	1761 30	2,3
10	2077	Payroll	Wages Payable	213	1680 00			1680 00	4
11	2078	Dana Manufacturing Company	Dana Manufacturing Company	✓		294 00	5 88	288 12	5,6,7
12	2079	Davenport Office Supplies	Supplies Expense	625	70 00			70 00	8,9
15	2080	Gardner Products Co.	Gardner Products Co.	✓		930 00	8 40	921 60	10,11
16	2081	Jones and Son	Purchases	511	200 00			200 00	12
19	2082	Monroe Express	Freight In	514	60 00			60 00	13
23	2083	Void	————	—					14
23	2084	American Fire Ins. Co.	Prepaid Insurance	116	420 00			420 00	15,16
25	2085	Payroll	Wages Payable	213	1750 00			1750 00	17
27	2086	F. P. Franz	Sales Ret. and Allowances	412	51 00			51 00	18,19
27	2087	Langseth and Son	Langseth and Son	✓		1180 00		1180 00	20
31					4231 00	4199 50	48 48	8382 02	21
					(X)	(212)	(513)	(111)	

FIGURE 7

embezzlement to take place. This precaution is consistent with a good system of internal control, because more than one person is involved in the process of recording cash payments. This system also provides protection against errors. One person can double-check the other person's work.

Transactions for Two Companies' Purchases and Sales

> **REMEMBER!**
>
> To the seller, a cash discount is a sales discount and is recorded in the cash receipts journal as a debit. To the purchaser, a cash discount is a purchases discount and is recorded in the cash payments journal as a credit.

Purchaser's Books—Able Company	Seller's Books—Baker Company
Bought merchandise from Baker Company, $500; terms 2/10, n/30.	Sold merchandise to Able Company, $500; terms 2/10, n/30.

Dr. Purchases, 500
    Cr. Accounts Payable, 500
	Dr. Accounts Receivable, 500
	    Cr. Sales, 500

Received credit memo from Baker Company for return of merchandise, $100.	Issued credit memo to Able Company for return of merchandise, $100.

Dr. Accounts Payable, 100
    Cr. Purchases Returns and
        Allowances, 100
	Dr. Sales Returns and Allowances, 100
	    Cr. Accounts Receivable, 100

Paid Baker Company within the discount period, $392 ($500 − $100 = $400; $400 × .02 = $8; $400 − $8 = $392).	Received cash from Able Company within the discount period, $392.

Dr. Accounts Payable, 400
    Cr. Cash, 392
    Cr. Purchases Discounts, 8
	Dr. Cash, 392
	Dr. Sales Discounts, 8
	    Cr. Accounts Receivable, 400

TRADE DISCOUNTS

OBJECTIVE 8

Journalize transactions involving trade discounts.

Manufacturers and wholesalers of many lines of products publish annual catalogs listing their products at retail prices. These organizations offer their customers substantial reductions (often as much as 40 percent) from the list or catalog prices. The reductions from the list prices are called **trade discounts**. Trade discounts are not journalized. Remember, firms grant cash discounts for prompt payment of invoices. Trade discounts are *not related* to cash payments. Manufacturers and wholesalers use trade discounts to avoid the high cost of reprinting catalogs when selling prices change. To change prices, the manufacturer or wholesaler simply issues a sheet showing a new list of trade discounts to be applied to the catalog prices. Trade discounts can also be used to differentiate between classes of customers. For example, a manufacturer may use one schedule of trade discounts for wholesalers and another schedule for retailers.

Firms may quote trade discounts as a single percentage. *Example:* A distributor of furnaces grants a single discount of 40 percent off the listed catalog price of $8,000. In this case, the selling price is calculated as follows:

List or catalog price	$8,000
Less trade discount of 40% ($8,000 × .40)	3,200
Selling price	$4,800

Neither the seller nor the buyer records trade discounts in the accounts; they enter only the selling price. Using T accounts, the furnace distributor records the sale like this:

Accounts Receivable		Sales	
+	−	−	+
4,800			4,800

The buyer records the purchase as follows:

Purchases		Accounts Payable	
+	−	−	+
4,800			4,800

Firms may also quote trade discounts as a chain, or series, of percentages. For example, a distributor of automobile parts grants discounts of 30 percent, 10 percent, and 10 percent off the listed catalog price of $900. In this case, the selling price is calculated as follows:

List or catalog price	$900.00
Less first trade discount of 30% ($900 × .30)	270.00
Remainder after first discount	$630.00
Less second trade discount of 10% ($630 × .10)	63.00
Remainder after second discount	$567.00
Less third discount of 10% ($567 × .10)	56.70
Selling price	$510.30

Using T accounts, the automobile parts distributor records the sale as follows:

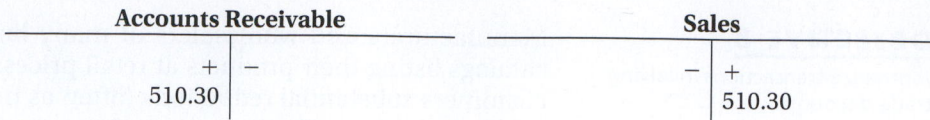

The buyer records the purchase as follows:

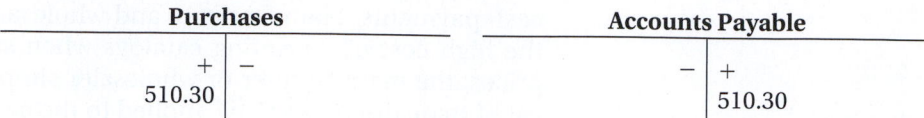

In the situation involving a chain of discounts, the additional discounts are granted for large-volume transactions, either in dollar amount or in size of shipment, such as carload lots.

Cash discounts could also apply in situations involving trade discounts. *Example:* Suppose that the credit terms of the preceding sale include a cash discount of 2/10, n/30, and that the buyer pays the invoice within ten days. The seller applies the cash discount to the selling price. The seller records the transaction as shown in the following T accounts:

Cash	Sales Discounts	Accounts Receivable
+ −	+ −	+ −
500.09	10.21	510.30

The buyer records the transaction as follows:

Cash	Purchases Discounts	Accounts Payable
+ −	− +	− +
500.09	10.21	510.30

COMPARISON OF THE FIVE TYPES OF JOURNALS

We have now looked at four special journals and the general journal. It is very important for a business to select and use the journals that provide the most efficient accounting system possible. Figure 8 summarizes the applications of the journals we have discussed and the correct procedures for using them.

Recommended Order of Posting to the Subsidiary Ledgers and the General Ledger

To avoid errors and negative balances in accounts, post from the special journals in this order:

1. Sales journal
2. Purchases journal
3. Cash receipts journal
4. Cash payments journal

Types of Transactions

Sale of merchandise on account	Purchase of merchandise on account	Receipt of cash	Payment of cash	All other

Evidenced by Source Documents

Sales invoice	Purchase invoice	Credit card receipts Cash Checks	Check stub	Miscellaneous

Types of Journals

Sales journal	Purchases journal	Cash receipts journal	Cash payments journal	General journal

Posting to Ledger Accounts

Individual amounts posted daily to the accounts receivable ledger and the total posted monthly to the general ledger.	*Individual amounts posted daily to the accounts payable ledger and the totals of the special columns posted monthly to the general ledger.*	*Individual amounts in the Accounts Receivable Credit column posted daily to the accounts receivable ledger.* *Individual amounts in the Other Accounts columns posted daily to the general ledger.* *Totals of special columns posted monthly to the general ledger.*	*Individual amounts in the Accounts Payable Debit column posted daily to the accounts payable ledger.* *Individual amounts in the Other Accounts columns posted daily to the general ledger.* *Totals of special columns posted monthly to the general ledger.*	*Entries posted daily to the subsidiary ledgers and the general ledger.*

FIGURE 8

REMEMBER!

Again, always think of the T accounts involved in each transaction.

Posting of general journal entries depends on the dates of the specific transactions.

Picture the T accounts involved in transactions. Here are examples of the transactions we have introduced.

Sold merchandise, $500, plus $40 sales tax, and the customer used a bank charge card. Bank discount rate is 4 percent.

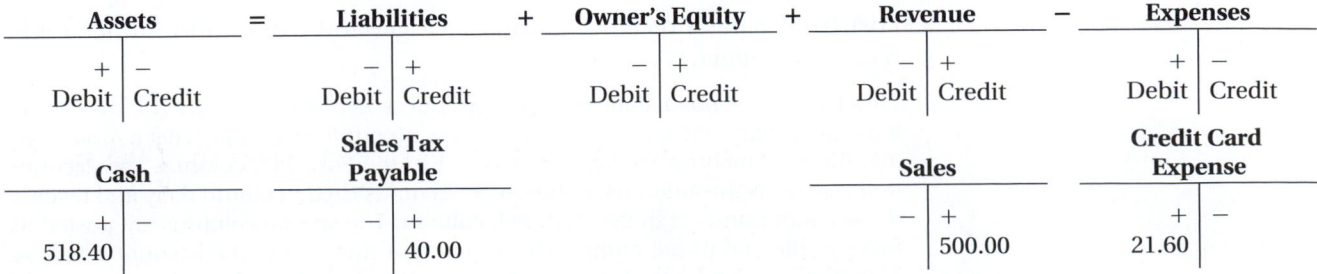

Received check from Betterbuilt Homes Co. for $1,533.56 in payment of $1,564.86 invoice less $31.30 cash discount.

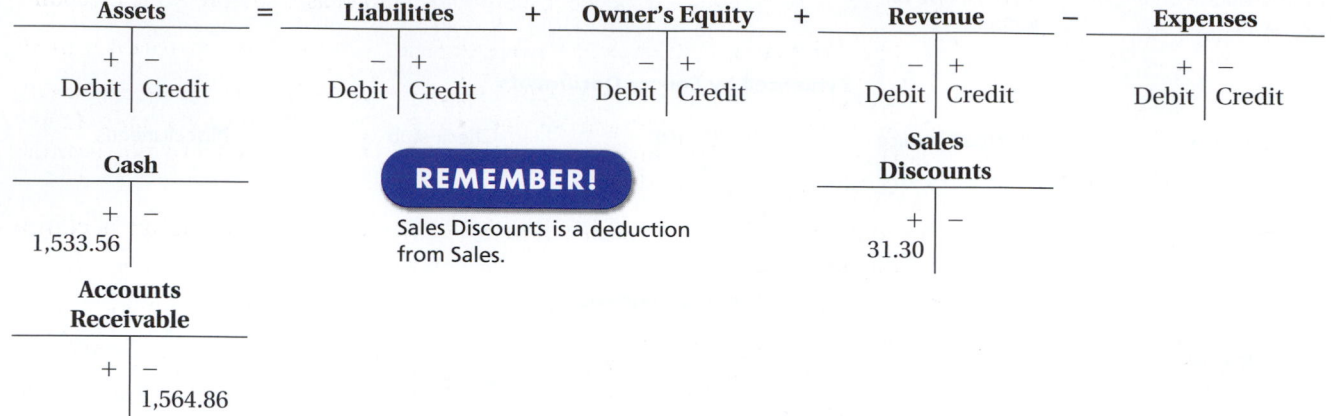

Issued check to Collins, Inc., in payment of $1,795.50 invoice less $34.20 cash discount.

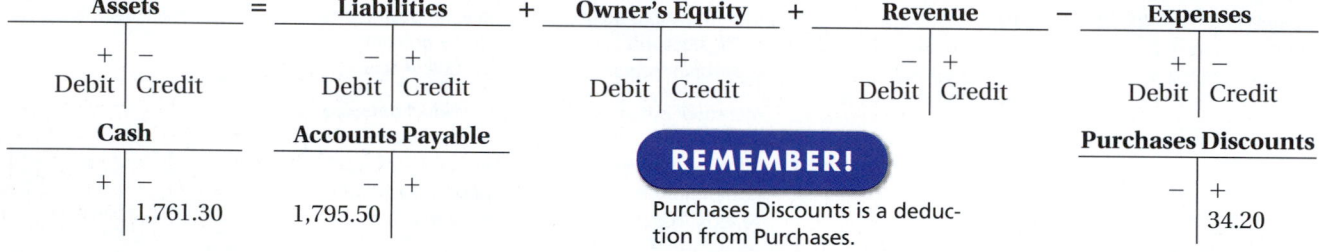

CHAPTER REVIEW

Online Study Center
ACE the test!

Review of Performance Objectives

1. Journalize transactions for a merchandising business in a cash receipts journal.

   A transaction for a retail merchandising business can be recorded on one line in a cash receipts journal. The cash receipts journal usually contains the following columns: Date, Account Credited, Post. Ref., Cash Debit, Credit Card Expense Debit, Accounts Receivable Credit, Sales Credit, Sales Tax Payable Credit, and Other Accounts Credit.

2. Post from a cash receipts journal to a general ledger and an accounts receivable ledger.

   The accountant posts daily from the Accounts Receivable Credit column to the individual charge customers' accounts in the accounts receivable ledger. After posting, the accountant puts a check mark (✓) in the Post. Ref. column. The accountant also posts the amounts in the Other Accounts Credit column daily and records the account numbers in the Post. Ref. column. The special columns are posted as totals at the end of the month. The accountant then writes the account numbers in parentheses under the totals. An (X) below the total of the Other Accounts Credit column shows that amounts are posted individually and the total is not posted.

3. Determine cash discounts according to credit terms, and record cash receipts from charge customers who are entitled to deduct the cash discount.

The same cash discount is available to all the supplier's customers. The amount of the discount is determined by multiplying the invoice total (excluding freight charges and any returns and allowances) by the cash discount rate (usually 1 or 2 percent). The amount of the discount is recorded as a debit to Sales Discounts.

4. Journalize transactions in a cash payments journal for a service enterprise.

A cash payment by a service enterprise can be handled on one line in a cash payments journal. The cash payments journal usually contains the following columns: Date, Ck. No., Account Debited, Post. Ref., Other Accounts Debit, Accounts Payable Debit, and Cash Credit.

5. Post from a cash payments journal to a general ledger and an accounts payable ledger.

The accountant posts daily from the Accounts Payable Debit column to the individual suppliers' accounts in the accounts payable ledger. After posting, the accountant puts a check mark (✓) in the Post. Ref. column. The accountant also posts the amounts in the Other Accounts Debit column daily and records the account numbers in the Post. Ref. column. The special columns are posted as totals at the end of the month. The accountant then writes the account numbers in parentheses under the totals. An (X) below the total of the Other Accounts Debit column shows that amounts are posted individually and the total is not posted.

6. Journalize transactions involving cash discounts in a cash payments journal for a merchandising enterprise.

A cash payment by a merchandising enterprise that includes a purchase discount can be recorded on one line in a cash payments journal. The cash payments journal usually contains the following columns: Date, Ck. No., Account Debited, Post. Ref., Other Accounts Debit, Accounts Payable Debit, Purchases Discounts Credit, and Cash Credit.

7. Journalize transactions in a check register.

Transactions can be recorded on one line in a check register. The check register is similar to the cash payments journal. However, the check register has an additional column entitled Payee, and instead of a Cash Credit column there is often a column with the name of the bank (City Bank Credit, for example).

8. Journalize transactions involving trade discounts.

In transactions involving trade discounts, the trade discounts are deducted from the list prices to arrive at the selling prices. Both sellers and buyers record the transactions at the selling prices.

Glossary

Bank charge card A bank credit card, like the credit cards used by millions of private citizens. The cardholder pays what she or he owes directly to the issuing bank. The business deposits the credit card receipts; the amount of the deposit equals the total of the receipts, less a discount deducted by the bank. (392)

Cash discount The amount a customer can deduct for paying a bill within a specified period of time; used to encourage prompt payment. Not all sellers offer cash discounts. (397)

Cash payments journal A special journal used to record all transactions involving cash payments or decreases. (400)

Cash receipts journal A special journal used to record all transactions involving cash receipts or increases. (392)

Check register A journal in which checks are listed as they are written. A check register replaces a cash payments journal. (407)

Credit period The time the seller allows the buyer before full payment on a charge sale has to be made. (397)

Notes Payable The account containing the balance of promissory notes. (395)

Promissory note A written promise to pay a specified amount at a specified time. (395)

Trade discount A substantial discount from the list or catalog prices of goods, granted by the seller; not recorded by the buyer or the seller. (409)

QUESTIONS, EXERCISES, AND CASES

Discussion Questions

1. What are the normal balances of (a) Purchases? (b) Sales Discounts? (c) Purchases Returns and Allowances? (d) Sales? (e) Purchases Discounts? (f) Sales Returns and Allowances?

2. What does an X under the total of a special journal's Other Accounts column signify?

3. Explain the following credit terms: (a) n/30; (b) 2/10, n/60; (c) 1/15, EOM, n/30.

4. In a cash receipts journal, both the Accounts Receivable Credit column and the Cash Debit column were mistakenly underadded by $700. How will this error be discovered?

5. If a cash payments journal is supposed to save writing, why are there so many entries in the Other Accounts Debit column?

6. Describe the posting procedure for a cash payments journal with an Other Accounts Debit column and several special columns, including an Accounts Payable Debit column.

7. An electronics business purchased speakers for resale. The total of the invoice is $2,580, and it is subject to trade discounts of 15 percent, 10 percent, and 5 percent. Compute the amount the dealer will pay for the speakers.

8. What is the difference between a cash discount and a trade discount?

Exercises

P.O. 1

Describe a recorded transaction involving sale of merchandise with sales tax, paid by credit card.

Exercise 11-1 Describe the transaction recorded.

Cash	Sales Tax Payable	Sales	Credit Card Expense
322.56	16.00	320.00	13.44

P.O. 1,3

Label column headings.

Exercise 11-2 Label the blanks in the column heads as either debit or credit.

CASH RECEIPTS JOURNAL   PAGE _____

DATE	ACCOUNT CREDITED	POST. REF.	OTHER ACCOUNTS	ACCOUNTS RECEIVABLE	SALES	SALES DISCOUNTS	CASH
1							1

P.O. 5,6

Describe posted transactions.

Exercise 11-3 Describe the transactions recorded in the following T accounts:

Cash		Accounts Payable				Purchases		
(c)	1,176	(b)	150	(a)	1,350	(a)	1,350	
		(c)	1,200					

Purchases Returns and Allowances		Purchases Discounts	
(b)	150	(c)	24

P.O. 6

Calculate amounts paid for merchandise purchases involving returns and cash discounts.

Exercise 11-4 For the following purchases of merchandise, determine the amount of cash to be paid:

Purchase	Invoice Date	Credit Terms	FOB	Amount of Purchase	Freight Charges	Total Invoice Amount	Returns and Allowances	Date Paid
a.	June 1	2/10, n/30	Destination	$550	—	$ 550	—	June 30
b.	June 12	1/10, n/30	Destination	700	—	700	$100	June 21
c.	June 14	2/10, n/30	Shipping point	940	$60	1,000	—	June 20
d.	June 21	n/30	Shipping point	830	70	900	130	July 20
e.	June 24	1/10, n/30	Shipping point	760	50	810	90	July 3

P.O. 1,6

Designate the appropriate journal.

Exercise 11-5 Indicate the journal in which each of the following transactions should be recorded. Assume a three-column purchases journal.

Transaction	Journal				
	S	P	CR	CP	J
a. Paid a creditor on account.					
b. Bought merchandise on account.					
c. Sold merchandise for cash.					
d. Adjusted for insurance expired.					
e. Received payment on account from a charge customer.					
f. Received a credit memo for merchandise returned.					
g. Bought equipment on credit.					
h. Sold merchandise on account.					
i. Recorded a customer's NSF check.					
j. Invested personal noncash assets in the business.					
k. Withdrew cash for personal use.					

P.O. 3

Journalize transactions involving sales and purchases of merchandise with returns and cash discounts.

Exercise 11-6 Record the following transactions in general journal form:

May 4   Sold merchandise on account to Seymour, Inc., $640; terms 2/10, n/30.
     10   Bought merchandise on account from Mann Company, $750; terms 1/10, n/60; FOB shipping point.
     11   Paid Gordon Freight Lines for freight charges on merchandise purchased from Mann Company, $22.
     13   Received full payment from Seymour, Inc.
     14   Received a credit memo from Mann Company for defective merchandise returned, $104.
     19   Paid Mann Company in full within the discount period.
     28   Bought merchandise on account from Bean Company, $900; terms 2/10, n/30; freight prepaid and added to the invoice, $47 (total $947).

P.O. 3

Journalize transactions involving sale and purchase of merchandise, a return, and a cash discount.

Exercise 11-7 Record the following transactions in general journal form, first on the books of the seller (Fry Company) and then on the books of the buyer (Lee Company).

Fry Company

a. Sold merchandise on account to Lee Company, $1,500; terms 2/10, n/30.
b. Issued a credit memo to Lee Company for damaged merchandise, $100.
c. Lee Company paid the account in full within the discount period.

Lee Company

a. Purchased merchandise on account from Fry Company, $1,500; terms 2/10, n/30.
b. Received a credit memo from Fry Company for damaged merchandise, $100.
c. Paid Fry Company in full within the discount period.

P.O. 8

Make correcting entries involving freight charges, returns, and trade discounts.

Exercise 11-8 Record general journal entries to correct the errors described below. Assume that the incorrect entries were posted in the same period in which the errors occurred.

a. A freight cost of $57 incurred on equipment purchased for use in the business was debited to Freight In.
b. The issuance of a credit memo to Merino Company for $126 for merchandise returned was recorded as a debit to Purchases Returns and Allowances and a credit to Accounts Receivable, Merino Company.
c. A cash purchase of $114 of store supplies for the business was recorded as office supplies.
d. A cash sale of $92 to M. A. Marx was recorded as a sale on account.
e. A purchase of merchandise from Ames Company in the amount of $1,000 with a 30 percent trade discount was recorded as a debit to Purchases and a credit to Accounts Payable of $1,000 each.

internet
LINKS TO ACCOUNTING

1. Who pays for and who receives money from a credit card transaction?
2. If Arcadia Bank pays the merchant 98 percent of the sale amount, how might the grocer record the sale in its cash receipts journal?

CONSIDER AND COMMUNICATE

You are the manager of the Accounts Receivable Department for a merchandising business. Your billing clerk sent a bill for $2 to a customer who had charged $100 in goods (including sales tax) with terms 2/10, n/30. The customer has called and indicated his displeasure; he can't understand an error like this, since he paid on time. Explain to your billing clerk why Accounts Receivable is credited for $100 and not $98. How was permission given to send less than the full amount?

WHAT'S WRONG WITH THIS PICTURE?

Suppose we collected cash from a charge customer, and our debit was to Cash and the credit to Sales. How and when would this error be discovered?

CRITICAL THINKING

You work for Garson Plumbing Supply. You are responsible for training a new accounting clerk. He has the following questions for you to answer about this invoice:

Garson Plumbing Supply				No. 320
14 Indiana Avenue				
Chicago, Illinois 60612				

INVOICE

SOLD TO	C. P. Lund Company	DATE:	August 1, 20–
	5210 Gilman Avenue	ORDER NO.:	5384
	San Diego, CA 92102	SHIPPED BY:	Faster Freight
		TERMS:	2/10, n/30
		SALESPERSON:	H. T.

QUANTITY	DESCRIPTION	UNIT PRICE	TOTAL
6	Olin single-control tub shower faucet #44B652	51 50	309 00
6	Olin dual-control washerless lavatory faucet #59B641	22 20	133 20
12	Olin massage shower head, antique brass #37B411	11 56	138 72
	Subtotal		580 92
	Freight		63 80
	Total		644 72

1. Who is the buyer?
2. Who is paying the freight?

3. What is the customer's order number?
4. What percentage of the goods bought is the cost of the freight?
5. What are the credit terms and what do they mean?
6. How much will the buyer actually have to pay if the money is received within ten days?
7. What is the dollar amount of the discount?
8. Who receives the discount?
9. What is the due date for payment to get the discount?
10. Why would a seller give a buyer a discount?

A QUESTION OF ETHICS

When the new accountant started to work, the owner took him out to lunch each Friday to discuss problems, progress, and suggestions to improve the business. One Friday, the owner couldn't go to lunch with the accountant. The accountant took the money for his lunch from petty cash and charged it to the owner's drawing account. He reasoned that the owner always took him to lunch on Friday, and he didn't have money for lunch. This happened several Fridays during the year. Was this a fair assumption for the accountant to make? Was it ethical?

PROBLEM SET A

For additional help, see the demonstration problem at the beginning of each chapter in your Working Papers.

P.O. 1,2

Problem 11-1A Winters and Company, a retail flooring store, sells on the bases of (1) cash, (2) charge accounts, and (3) bank credit cards. The following transactions involved cash receipts for the firm during May of this year. The state imposes a 7 percent sales tax on retail sales. The bank charges 4 percent on the total of the credit card sales plus sales tax. (For all sales involving credit cards, record credit card expense at the time of the sale.)

May
- 8 Total cash sales for the week, $1,248, plus $87.36 sales tax.
- 8 Total sales for the week paid for by bank credit cards, $1,560, plus $109.20 sales tax.
- 11 D. C. Winters, the owner, invested an additional $2,500.
- 11 Collected cash from N. D. Payson, a charge customer, $71.70.
- 12 Sold store equipment at cost for cash, $360.
- 15 Total cash sales for the week, $1,780, plus $124.60 sales tax.
- 15 Total sales for the week paid for by bank credit cards, $1,130, plus $79.10 sales tax.
- 19 Borrowed $2,300 from the bank, receiving the same in cash and giving the bank a promissory note.
- 21 Collected cash from R. Binder, a charge customer, $85.
- 22 Total cash sales for the week, $2,834, plus $198.38 sales tax.
- 22 Total sales for the week paid for by bank credit cards, $1,385, plus $96.95 sales tax.
- 24 Received cash as refund for the return of merchandise purchased, $127.
- 26 Collected cash from C. Fisher, a charge customer, $147.

May 31 Total sales for the week paid for by bank credit cards, $362, plus $25.34 sales tax.

31 Collected cash from R. D. Thompson, a charge customer, $120.

31 Total cash sales for the remainder of the month, $2,892, plus $202.44 sales tax.

Check Figure

Total Sales Credit, $13,191

Instructions

1. Open the following accounts in the accounts receivable ledger and record the May 1 balances as given: R. Binder, $85; C. Fisher, $147; N. D. Payson, $71.70; S. R. Potts, $114.72; R. D. Thompson, $176.47; F. N. Warren, $79.52. Place a check mark in the Post. Ref. column.
2. Record a balance of $674.41 in the Accounts Receivable controlling account as of May 1.
3. Record the transactions in the cash receipts journal beginning with page 62.
4. Post daily to the accounts receivable ledger.
5. Total and rule the cash receipts journal.
6. Prove the equality of debit and credit totals.
7. Post to the Accounts Receivable controlling account in the general ledger.

P.O. 1,3

Problem 11-2A Parker Company sells candy wholesale to vending machine operators. Terms of sales on account are 2/10, n/30, FOB shipping point. The following transactions involving cash receipts and sales of merchandise took place in May of this year:

May 1 Received $1,960 cash from L. Reagon in payment of April 22 invoice of $2,000, less cash discount.

4 Received $896 cash in payment of $800 note receivable and interest of $96.

7 Received $784 cash from K. L. Shaw in payment of April 29 invoice of $800, less cash discount.

8 Sold merchandise on account to D. Pang, invoice no. 272, $396.

16 Cash sales for first half of May, $3,367.

17 Received cash from D. Pang in payment of invoice no. 272, less cash discount.

20 Received $325 cash from L. N. Saranden in payment of April 16 invoice, no discount.

21 Sold merchandise on account to R. O. Winston, invoice no. 285, $935.

24 Received $220 cash refund for return of defective equipment that was originally bought for cash.

27 Sold merchandise on account to R. James, invoice no. 292, $450.

31 Cash sales for second half of May, $3,956.

Check Figure

Total sales on account, $1,781

Instructions

1. Journalize the transactions for May in the cash receipts journal and the sales journal.
2. Total and rule the journals.
3. Prove the equality of debit and credit totals.

P.O. 7

Problem 11-3A Martinson Bookshop uses a check register to keep track of expenditures. The following transactions occurred during February of this year.

Feb. 3 Issued Ck. No. 4312, $804.68, to Kendall Company for invoice no. 68172, recorded previously for $821.10, less 2 percent cash discount.

4 Issued Ck. No. 4313 to King Express Company for freight charges, $46, for books purchased.

6 Issued Ck. No. 4314 to Morton Land Company for monthly rent, $590.

11 Received and paid bill for advertising in the *Ballard News*, $98, Ck. No. 4315.

11 Issued Ck. No. 4316, $970.20, to Corwin Book Company for invoice no. A3322, recorded previously for $980, less 1 percent cash discount.

17 Paid wages recorded previously for first half of February, $598; Ck. No. 4317.

21 R. D. Martinson, the owner, withdrew $800 for personal use; Ck. No. 4318.

26 Issued Ck. No. 4319 to First National Bank for payment on bank loan, $560, consisting of $500 on the principal and $60 interest.

27 Issued Ck. No. 4320, $877, to Grayson Publishing Company for invoice no. 7768, recorded previously (no discount).

28 Voided Ck. No. 4321.

28 Paid wages recorded previously for second half of February, $552; Ck. No. 4322.

Check Figure

Total First Nat'l Bank Credit, $5,895.88

P.O. 1,2,3,5,6

Instructions

1. Record the transactions in the check register.
2. Total and rule the check register.
3. Prove the equality of the debit and credit totals.

Problem 11-4A The following transactions were completed by Hammel Auto Supply during January, which is the first month of this fiscal year. Terms of sale are 2/10, n/30.

Jan. 2 Issued Ck. No. 6981 for monthly rent, $775.

2 J. Hammel, the owner, invested an additional $3,500 in the business.

4 Bought merchandise on account from Vaughn and Company, $2,930, invoice no. A691, dated January 2; terms 2/10, n/30.

4 Received check from Vessey Appliance for $980 in payment of $1,000 invoice less discount.

4 Sold merchandise on account to L. Parker, invoice no. 6483, $850.

6 Received check from Peterson, Inc., $637, in payment of $650 invoice less discount.

7 Issued Ck. No. 6982, $588, to Franklin and Son, in payment of invoice no. C1272 for $600 less discount.

7 Bought supplies on account from Duncan Office Supply, $108, invoice no. 1906B; terms net 30 days. (Debit Supplies Expense—Chapter 12 explains when to use the asset account Supplies.)

7 Sold merchandise on account to English and Cole, invoice no. 6484, $787.

9 Issued credit memo no. 43 to L. Parker, $54, for merchandise returned.

11 Cash sales for January 1 through January 10, $4,863.20.

11 Issued Ck. No. 6983, $2,871.40, to Vaughn and Company, in payment of $2,930 invoice less discount.

Jan. 14 Sold merchandise on account to Vessey Appliance, invoice no. 6485, $2,050.

18 Bought merchandise on account from Crosby Products, $4,854, invoice no. 7281D, dated January 16; terms 2/10, n/60; FOB shipping point, freight prepaid and added to the invoice, $147 (total $5,001).

21 Issued Ck. No. 6984, $194, to *The Newsline* for advertising not recorded previously. (Miscellaneous Expense)

21 Cash sales for January 11 through January 20, $4,591.

23 Issued Ck. No. 6985 to Fastest Freight, $96, for freight charges on merchandise purchased on January 4.

23 Received credit memo no. 163, $376, from Crosby Products for merchandise returned.

29 Sold merchandise on account to Bryan Supply, invoice no. 6486, $1,835.

31 Cash sales for January 21 through January 31, $4,428.

31 Issued Ck. No. 6986, $53, to M. Doore for miscellaneous expenses not recorded previously.

31 Recorded payroll entry from the payroll register: total salaries, $6,200; employees' federal income tax withheld, $872; FICA tax withheld, $474.30.

31 Recorded the payroll taxes: FICA, $474.30; state unemployment tax, $334.80; federal unemployment tax, $49.60.

31 Issued Ck. No. 6987, $4,853.70, for salaries for the month.

31 J. Hammel, the owner, withdrew $1,000 for personal use, Ck. No. 6988.

Check Figure

Trial balance totals, $65,288.80

Instructions

1. Record the transactions for January, using a sales journal, page 73; a purchases journal, page 56; a cash receipts journal, page 38; a cash payments journal, page 45; a general journal, page 100. The chart of accounts is as follows:

111	Cash	311	J. Hammel, Capital
113	Accounts Receivable	312	J. Hammel, Drawing
114	Merchandise Inventory		
116	Prepaid Insurance	411	Sales
121	Equipment	412	Sales Returns and Allowances
		413	Sales Discounts
212	Accounts Payable		
215	Salaries Payable	511	Purchases
216	Employees' Federal Income Tax Payable	512	Purchases Returns and Allowances
217	FICA Tax Payable	513	Purchases Discounts
218	State Unemployment Tax Payable	514	Freight In
219	Federal Unemployment Tax Payable	621	Salary Expense
		622	Payroll Tax Expense
		625	Supplies Expense
		627	Rent Expense
		631	Miscellaneous Expense

2. Post daily all entries involving customer accounts to the accounts receivable ledger.

3. Post daily all entries involving creditor accounts to the accounts payable ledger.

4. Post daily those entries involving the Other Accounts columns and the general journal to the general ledger. Write the owner's name in the Capital and Drawing accounts.

5. Add the columns of the special journals, and prove the equality of debit and credit totals on scratch paper.
6. Post the appropriate totals of the special journals to the general ledger.
7. Prepare a trial balance.
8. Prepare a schedule of accounts receivable and a schedule of accounts payable. Do the totals equal the balances of the related controlling accounts?

Instructions for General Ledger Software

1. Record the transactions in the sales journal, purchases journal, cash receipts journal, cash payments journal, and general journal.
   a. For efficiency, analyze the transactions, indicate what journal each transaction goes into, and key the entries in five groups or batches, one for each journal.
   b. Because the program uses a single-column purchases journal, add the amount of the freight to the amount of purchases.
2. Print the journals.
3. Post the amounts from the sales, purchases, cash receipts, cash payments, and general journals.
4. Print a trial balance.
5. Print a schedule of accounts receivable and compare the total with the balance of the Accounts Receivable controlling account.
6. Print a schedule of accounts payable and compare the total with the balance of the Accounts Payable controlling account.

PROBLEM SET B

For additional help, see the demonstration problem at the beginning of each chapter in your Working Papers.

P.O. 1,2

Problem 11-1B Bilden Furniture, a home furnishings store, sells on the bases of (1) cash, (2) charge accounts, and (3) bank credit cards. The following transactions involve cash receipts for the firm for November of this year. The state imposes a 7 percent sales tax on retail sales. The bank charges 4 percent of the total credit card sales plus sales tax. (For all sales involving credit cards, record credit card expense at the time of the sale.)

Nov.
- 7 Total cash sales for the week, $1,800, plus $126 sales tax.
- 7 Total sales from bank credit cards for the week, $1,900, plus $133 sales tax.
- 11 M. R. Victor, the owner, invested an additional $4,800.
- 12 Sold office equipment for cash at cost, $358.
- 12 Collected cash from T. R. Alex, a charge customer, $55.80.
- 14 Total cash sales for the week, $3,490.05, plus $244.30 sales tax.
- 14 Total sales from bank credit cards for the week, $1,540, plus $107.80 sales tax.
- 18 Collected cash from N. P. Tempe, a charge customer, $87.54.
- 19 Borrowed $5,700 from the bank, receiving the same in cash and giving the bank a promissory note.
- 21 Total cash sales for the week, $3,500, plus $245 sales tax.
- 21 Total sales from bank credit cards for the week, $1,535, plus $107.45 sales tax.

Nov. 22 Collected cash from C. E. Baker, a charge customer, $235.
24 Received cash as refund for the return of merchandise purchased, $234.
27 Collected cash from O. Hauge, a charge customer, $150.15.
30 Total cash sales for the week, $3,855, plus $269.85 sales tax.
30 Total sales from bank credit cards for the week, $430.25, plus $30.12 sales tax.

Check Figure

Total Sales Credit, $18,050.30

Instructions

1. Open the following accounts in the accounts receivable ledger and record the November 1 balances as given: T. R. Alex, $193.84; C. E. Baker, $235; L. R. Case, $110; L. P. Dane, $180; O. Hauge, $150.15; N. P. Tempe, $87.54. Place a check mark in the Post. Ref. column.
2. Record a balance of $956.53 in the Accounts Receivable controlling account as of November 1.
3. Record the transactions in the cash receipts journal beginning with page 16.
4. Post daily to the accounts receivable ledger.
5. Total and rule the cash receipts journal.
6. Prove the equality of debit and credit totals.
7. Post to the Accounts Receivable controlling account in the general ledger.

P.O. 1,3

Problem 11-2B C. R. McCain Company sells candy wholesale, primarily to vending machine operators. Terms of sales on account are 2/10, n/30, FOB shipping point. The following transactions involving cash receipts and sales of merchandise took place in May of this year:

May 2 Received $784 cash from N. Rockey in payment of April 23 invoice of $800, less cash discount.
5 Received $1,120 cash in payment of $1,000 note receivable and interest of $120.
8 Sold merchandise on account to G. Solter, invoice no. 862, $830.
9 Received $960.40 cash from D. Maxton in payment of April 30 invoice of $980, less cash discount.
15 Received cash from G. Solter in payment of invoice no. 862, less cash discount.
16 Cash sales for first half of May, $4,326.
19 Received $296 cash from R. O. Hintz in payment of April 14 invoice, no discount.
22 Sold merchandise on account to N. T. Johns, invoice no. 887, $753.
25 Received $239 cash refund for return of defective equipment bought in April for cash.
28 Sold merchandise on account to M. E. Mulder, invoice no. 910, $964.
31 Cash sales for second half of May, $3,617.

Check Figure

Total sales on account, $2,547

Instructions

1. Journalize the transactions for May in the cash receipts journal and the sales journal.
2. Total and rule the journals.
3. Prove the equality of debit and credit totals.

P.O. 7

Problem 11-3B Jason Company uses a check register to keep track of expenditures. The following transactions occurred during February of this year.

Feb.	1	Issued Ck. No. 4311, $637, to Barnet Company for invoice no. 3113E, recorded previously for $650, less cash discount of $13.
	2	Issued Ck. No. 4312 to Boxer Express Company for freight charges, $48, for merchandise purchased.
	4	Issued Ck. No. 4313 to Dixie Realty for monthly rent, $560.
	9	Received and paid bill for advertising in *The Nickel News*, $84, Ck. No. 4314.
	10	Issued Ck. No. 4315, $990, to Dieter Company for invoice no. D642, recorded previously for $1,000, less 1 percent cash discount.
	15	Paid wages recorded previously for first half of month, $1,678; Ck. No. 4316.
	19	R. Jason, the owner, withdrew $900 for personal use; Ck. No. 4317.
	25	Issued Ck. No. 4318 to First National Bank for payment on bank loan, $896, consisting of $800 on principal and $96 interest.
	27	Issued Ck. No. 4319, $430, to Lopez Company for invoice no. 6317, recorded previously (no discount).
	28	Voided Ck. No. 4320.
	28	Paid wages recorded previously for second half of month, $1,648; Ck. No. 4321.
	28	Received and paid telephone bill, $86; Ck. No. 4322, payable to Western Telephone Company.

Check Figure

Total First Nat'l Bank Credit, $7,957

Instructions

1. Record the transactions in the check register.
2. Total and rule the check register.
3. Prove the equality of the debit and credit totals.

P.O. 1,2,3,5,6

Problem 11-4B The following transactions were completed by Ye Restaurant Equipment during January, the first month of this fiscal year. Terms of sale are 2/10, n/30.

Jan.	2	Issued Ck. No. 6981 for monthly rent, $850.
	2	L. Ye, the owner, invested an additional $4,500 in the business.
	4	Bought merchandise on account from Vaughn and Company, $2,830, invoice no. A694, dated January 2; terms 2/10, n/30.
	4	Received check from Vessey Appliance for $980 in payment of invoice for $1,000 less discount.
	4	Sold merchandise on account to L. Parker, invoice no. 6483, $755.
	6	Received check from Peterson, Inc., for $637 in payment of $650 invoice less discount.
	7	Issued Ck. No. 6982, $588, to Franklin and Son, in payment of invoice no. C127 for $600 less discount.
	7	Bought supplies on account from Duncan Office Supply, $93.54, invoice no. 190B; terms net 30 days. (Debit Supplies Expense— Chapter 12 explains when to use the asset account Supplies.)
	7	Sold merchandise on account to English and Cole, invoice no. 6484, $1,115.
	9	Issued credit memo no. 43 to L. Parker, $47, for merchandise returned.
	11	Cash sales for January 1 through January 10, $4,454.87.
	11	Issued Ck. No. 6983, $2,773.40, to Vaughn and Company, in payment of $2,830 invoice less discount.

Jan. 14 Sold merchandise on account to Vessey Appliance, invoice no. 6485, $2,100.

14 Received check from L. Parker, $693.84, in payment of $755 invoice, less return of $47 and less discount.

19 Bought merchandise on account from Crosby Products, $3,700, invoice no. 7281, dated January 16; terms 2/10, n/60; FOB shipping point, freight prepaid and added to invoice, $142 (total $3,842).

21 Issued Ck. No. 6984, $245, to Barclay Agency for advertising not recorded previously. (Miscellaneous Expense)

21 Cash sales for January 11 through January 20, $3,689.

23 Received credit memo no. 163, $87, from Crosby Products for merchandise returned.

29 Sold merchandise on account to Bryan Supply, invoice no. 6486, $1,697.20.

29 Issued Ck. No. 6985 to Pacific Freight, $64, for freight charges on merchandise purchased January 4.

31 Cash sales for January 21 through January 31, $3,862.

31 Issued Ck. No. 6986, $65, to M. Pierce for miscellaneous expenses not recorded previously.

31 Recorded payroll entry from the payroll register: total salaries, $5,900; employees' federal income tax withheld, $795; FICA tax withheld, $451.35.

31 Recorded the payroll taxes: FICA, $451.35; state unemployment tax, $265.50; federal unemployment tax, $47.20.

31 Issued Ck. No. 6987, $4,653.65, for salaries for the month.

31 L. Ye, the owner, withdrew $1,000 for personal use, Ck. No. 6988.

Check Figure

Trial balance totals, $63,187.61

Instructions

1. Record the transactions for January, using a sales journal, page 91; a purchases journal, page 74; a cash receipts journal, page 56; a cash payments journal, page 63; a general journal, page 119. The chart of accounts is as follows:

111	Cash	311	L. Ye, Capital
113	Accounts Receivable	312	L. Ye, Drawing
114	Merchandise Inventory		
116	Prepaid Insurance	411	Sales
121	Equipment	412	Sales Returns and Allowances
		413	Sales Discounts
212	Accounts Payable		
215	Salaries Payable	511	Purchases
216	Employees' Federal Income Tax Payable	512	Purchases Returns and Allowances
		513	Purchases Discounts
217	FICA Tax Payable	514	Freight In
218	State Unemployment Tax Payable		
		621	Salary Expense
219	Federal Unemployment Tax Payable	622	Payroll Tax Expense
		625	Supplies Expense
		627	Rent Expense
		631	Miscellaneous Expense

2. Post daily all entries involving customer accounts to the accounts receivable ledger.

3. Post daily all entries involving creditor accounts to the accounts payable ledger.

4. Post daily those entries involving the Other Accounts columns and the general journal to the general ledger. Write the owner's name in the Capital and Drawing accounts.
5. Add the columns of the special journals, and prove the equality of debit and credit totals on scratch paper.
6. Post the appropriate totals of the special journals to the general ledger.
7. Prepare a trial balance.
8. Prepare a schedule of accounts receivable and a schedule of accounts payable. Do the totals equal the balances of the related controlling accounts?

Instructions for General Ledger Software

1. Record the transactions in the sales journal, purchases journal, cash receipts journal, cash payments journal, and general journal.

   a. For efficiency, analyze the transactions, indicate what journal each transaction goes into, and key the entries in five groups or batches, one for each journal.

   b. Because the program uses a single-column purchases journal, add the amount of the freight to the amount of purchases.

2. Print the journals.
3. Post the amounts from the sales, purchases, cash receipts, cash payments, and general journals.
4. Print a trial balance.
5. Print a schedule of accounts receivable and compare the total with the balance of the Accounts Receivable controlling account.
6. Print a schedule of accounts payable and compare the total with the balance of the Accounts Payable controlling account.

The Computer Clinic

Cash Receipts and Cash Payments Journals

Since All About You Spa decided to streamline accounting operations by adding purchases and sales journals, Ms. Valli believes it would be logical and efficient to add two more special journals: a cash receipts journal for all increases to cash and a cash payments journal for all decreases to cash. That will leave only a few entries that will go into the general journal—for instance, returns and allowances, payroll entries (except the payment of the net payroll, which goes in the cash payments journal), adjusting and closing entries, and any other entry that does not fit the definition of what goes in a particular special journal.

As of July 31, the chart of accounts contained the following:

Chart of Accounts

All About You Spa

111	Cash	511	Purchases
113	Accounts Receivable	515	Freight In
117	Prepaid Insurance		
124	Spa Equipment	611	Wages Expense
125	Accumulated Depreciation, Spa Equipment	612	Rent Expense
		613	Office Supplies Expense
128	Office Equipment	614	Spa Supplies Expense
129	Accumulated Depreciation, Office Equipment	615	Laundry Expense
		616	Advertising Expense
		617	Utilities Expense
211	Accounts Payable	618	Insurance Expense
212	Wages Payable	619	Depreciation Expense, Spa Equipment
215	Sales Tax Payable		
		620	Depreciation Expense, Office Equipment
311	A. Valli, Capital	630	Miscellaneous Expense
312	A. Valli, Drawing		
399	Income Summary		
411	Income from Services		
412	Merchandise Sales		

Ms. Valli has provided the trial balance as of July 31, schedules of accounts receivable and payable, as well as transactions for the month of August to be recorded in one of the four special journals or the general journal.

All About You Spa
Trial Balance
July 31, 20—

ACCOUNT NAME	DEBIT	CREDIT
Cash	44 9 6 9 26	
Accounts Receivable	4 5 6 8 79	
Prepaid Insurance	8 0 0 00	
Spa Equipment	17 6 0 1 00	
Accumulated Depreciation, Spa Equipment		6 4 88
Office Equipment	1 5 7 0 00	
Accumulated Depreciation, Office Equipment		1 0 00
Accounts Payable		20 7 2 0 00
Sales Tax Payable		1 8 2 9 90
A. Valli, Capital		49 8 8 4 62
A. Valli, Drawing	2 5 0 0 00	
Income from Services		12 7 2 2 00
Merchandise Sales		10 1 5 1 65
Purchases	12 8 6 8 00	
Freight In	4 0 3 00	
Wages Expense	7 0 0 4 00	
Rent Expense	1 6 5 0 00	
Office Supplies Expense	1 1 8 00	
Spa Supplies Expense	4 9 0 00	
Laundry Expense	8 4 00	
Utilities Expense	4 7 3 00	
Miscellaneous Expense	2 8 4 00	
	95 3 8 3 05	95 3 8 3 05

All About You Spa
Schedule of Accounts Receivable
July 31, 20—

About Face Spa	$ 5 2 1 59
Jill Anson	1 7 5 00
Chaco's	5 2 0 02
Holmes Condos	3 6 7 47
Tory Ligman	1 6 4 00
Los Obrigados Lodge	3 5 1 00
Mini Spa	2 2 2 48
Jack Morgan	2 8 6 00
Pleasant Spa	1 9 6 1 23
Total Accounts Receivable	$4 5 6 8 79

All About You Spa
Schedule of Accounts Payable
July 31, 20—

Giftco	$ 1 3 0 9 00
Golden Spa Supplies	4 9 0 00
Logo Products	3 7 9 6 00
Office Staples	3 0 4 00
Spa Equipment, Inc.	6 2 3 5 00
Spa Goods	5 4 4 5 00
Spa Magic	2 7 2 1 00
Superior Equipment	4 2 0 00
Total Accounts Payable	$20 7 2 0 00

Directions for August Journal Entries

1. If you are beginning the Computer Clinic problem at Chapter 11, journalize the trial balance accounts and amounts in the general journal as one big compound entry prior to recording the August journal entries. These are the July 31 balances that become the beginning balances for August.

   So that you can complete the journal entries for the month of August, Ms. Valli has also left the information you will need and directions on how to proceed.

2. Add new accounts to the chart of accounts as needed. One account that should be added is Purchases Discounts 512. Although no discounts have been taken by All About You Spa, they may be in the future. Add Sales Discounts 413 as well, since such discounts may be given to customers in the future.

3. a. Journalize in the *purchases journal* all of the August purchases of merchandise on account, which are shown in the list of invoices provided.

   b. Journalize in the *sales journal* all of the August sales of merchandise on account, which are shown in the list of merchandise sales invoices provided.

   c. Journalize the list of transactions that are to be entered in the cash receipts journal OR cash payments journal OR general journal. (*Notes:* Payroll taxes related to wages will be ignored here for purposes of simplification. All About You Spa is located in a state that levies sales tax on both merchandise and services. Some states do not tax services.)

4. After journalizing and posting all transactions to the general ledger and the subsidiary ledgers, print a trial balance dated August 31, 20—. Do not include those accounts that have a zero balance at the end of the month.

5. Print a schedule of accounts receivable dated August 31, 20—.

6. Print a schedule of accounts payable dated August 31, 20—.

Checkbook Register

Check No.	Date	Explanation	✓	Deposits	Check Amount
1044	8/1	Paid August's rent.			1,650.00
	8/1	Deposited Chaco's payment received on account, invoice no. 15.		400.00	
	8/1	Deposited Mini Spa's payment received on account, invoice no. 18 paid in full.		222.48	
1045	8/1	Paid accumulated sales tax payable to State Revenue Dept.			1,829.90
1046	8/2	Paid advertising expense for August photo ad.			455.00
1047	8/2	Paid week's wages.			1,845.50
1048	8/2	Paid Spa Magic for invoice no. 5033, dated June 2. Paid in full.			2,721.00
1049	8/3	Bought silk flower arrangement for the salon (Miscellaneous Expense).			87.90
	8/3	Deposited Tory Ligman's payment received on account, paid in full.		164.00	
1050	8/4	Bought spa supplies—5 cases of bottled water for clients (debit Spa Supplies).			45.00
	8/4	Deposited Jill Anson's payment received on account.		87.50	
1051	8/5	Bought a digital camera for confidential before-and-after pictures (debit Spa Equipment).			482.00
1052	8/5	Paid Office Staples for invoice 1417, dated July 5. Paid in full.			186.00
1053	8/5	Paid on account to Giftco, invoice no. 316, dated July 5.			709.00
	8/6	Deposited Pleasant Spa's payment received on account, invoice no. 16.		997.42	
1054	8/6	Paid Golden Spa Supplies for invoice no. 1836, dated July 1. Paid in full.			490.00
	8/7	Deposited first week's cash sales: merchandise $1,630.00; services $3,350.00; sales tax collected $398.40.		5,378.40	
	8/8	Deposited Los Obrigados Lodge's payment received on account, invoice no. 14.		200.00	
	8/9	Deposited Holmes Condo's payment received on account, invoice no. 17.		200.00	
1055	8/9	Paid week's wages.			1,850.00
	8/14	Deposited second week's cash sales: merchandise $1,330.00; services $2,340.00; sales tax collected $293.60.		3,963.60	
	8/15	Deposited About Face Spa's payment received on account, invoice no. 19.		265.00	
1056	8/16	Paid week's wages.			1,853.00

Check No.	Date	Explanation	✓	Deposits	Check Amount
1057	8/18	Paid Superior Equipment for invoice no. 3608, dated July 5. Paid in full.			420.00
	8/19	Deposited Jack Morgan's payment received on account, paid in full.		286.00	
	8/21	Deposited third week's cash sales: merchandise $2,220.00; services $2,810.00; sales tax collected $402.40.		5,432.40	
1058	8/22	Paid on account to Logo Products, invoice no. 1579, dated July 1.			2,500.00
1059	8/23	Paid on account to Spa Goods, invoice no. 312, dated July 1.			2,000.00
1060	8/23	Paid week's wages.			1,847.50
1061	8/28	Paid month's laundry bill.			95.00
1062	8/28	Owner withdrew cash for personal use.			2,500.00
1063	8/30	Paid week's wages.			1,850.00
	8/31	Deposited end of month's cash revenue: merchandise sales $2,030.00; services $4,176.00; $496.48 sales tax.		6,702.48	
1064	8/31	Paid August telephone bill.			235.00
1065	8/31	Paid on account to Spa Equipment, Inc., invoice no. 2731, dated July 3.			3,000.00
1066	8/31	Paid August power and water bill.			255.00

Purchases Invoices for Merchandise Bought on Account During August

All About You Spa will pay all freight costs associated with purchases of merchandise to the supplier.

Date of Purchase	Transaction Information	Amount
Aug. 1	Bought logo merchandise from Giftco; invoice no. 416, dated 8/1; terms 2/10, n/30.	$4,100.00 plus $180.00 freight
1	Bought bath and beauty products from Spa Magic; invoice no. 5235, dated 8/1; 2/10, n/30.	$3,562.00 plus $155.00 freight
2	Bought logo merchandise from Logo Products; invoice no. 1680, dated 8/2; terms 2/10, n/30.	$2,451.00 plus $144.00 freight
5	Bought spa accessories from Spa Goods; invoice no. 387, dated 8/5; terms 2/10, n/30.	$1,120 plus $110.00 freight

Sales Invoices for Gift Certificates Sold on Account During August

All About You Spa is responsible for collecting and paying the sales tax on merchandise that it sells. The sales tax rate where All About You Spa does business is 8 percent of each sale; for example, $650.00 \times 0.08 = \$52.00$.

Date of Sale	Transaction Information	Sales Amount (Before Tax)
Aug. 1	About Face Spa, invoice no. 20.	$ 650.00
5	Chaco's, invoice no. 21.	395.00
8	Holmes Condos, invoice no. 22.	1,294.00
9	Pleasant Spa, invoice no. 23.	1,560.00
11	Los Obrigados Lodge, invoice no. 24.	356.00
14	Mini Spa, invoice no. 25.	873.00

Note: All certificates for services were redeemed and the services were provided by the end of the month.

Other August Transactions

There were two other transactions in August. Neither involved cash.

Date	Transaction Information	Amount
Aug. 9	Issued credit memorandum no. 1 to About Face Spa, allowance for damaged goods. (New account Sales Returns and Allowances 414.)	$ 88.00
29	Received a credit memo for damaged spa accessories from Spa Magic. (New account Purchases Returns and Allowances 513.)	$123.00

Before a Test Check: Chapters 10–11

PART I: Completion

Complete each of the following statements by writing the appropriate word(s) in the spaces provided.

1. The normal balance of the Purchases Discounts account is on the _____ side.

2. Entries in the Accounts Payable Debit column of a cash payments journal are posted daily to the _____.

3. A _____ is the amount a customer may deduct for paying a bill within a specified period of time.

4. The form sent to the supplier of merchandise is called a(n) _____.

5. The _____ account is used to record the buying of merchandise only.

6. If the freight charges are FOB shipping point, the _____ pays the transportation charges.

7. The time the seller allows the buyer before full payment has to be made is the _____.

8. Increases in Sales Returns and Allowances are recorded on the _____ side.

9. The sales journal is used to record all _____.

10. The schedule of accounts receivable lists the balances of all the _____ accounts at the end of the month.

PART II: Matching

For each numbered item, choose the appropriate journal, and write the identifying letter.

____ 1. Paid freight bill on merchandise purchased.

____ 2. Bought office equipment on account.

____ 3. Received a credit memo for merchandise returned.

____ 4. Bought office equipment for cash.

____ 5. Sold merchandise on account.

S   Sales journal
P   Purchases journal (3 columns)
CR   Cash receipts journal
CP   Cash payments journal
J   General journal

Note: Answers to Before a Test Check begin on page A-1.

____ 6. Journalized the closing entries.

____ 7. Paid state sales tax to the state revenue department.

____ 8. Bought merchandise on account.

____ 9. Sold merchandise for cash.

____ 10. Bought merchandise for cash.

PART III: True/False

For each question circle T if it is True or circle F if it is False.

T   F   1. The Purchases Discounts account is classified as a revenue account.

T   F   2. The normal balance of the Sales Discounts account is on the debit side.

T   F   3. Check marks in the Posting Reference column of the sales journal indicate that the amounts are not to be posted.

T   F   4. When you post directly from the purchases invoice, you eliminate the accounts payable ledger.

T   F   5. The purchases journal is used for the buying of merchandise for cash and on account.

Cash Receipts and Cash Payments: An Alternative to Special Journals

Performance Objectives

After you have completed this appendix, you will be able to do the following:

1. Record transactions pertaining to cash receipts and cash payments in a general journal.

2. Maintain an accounts receivable ledger and an accounts payable ledger.

3. Prepare schedules of accounts receivable and accounts payable.

Although most merchandising enterprises set up special journals, some businesses elect to record cash receipts and cash payments in the general journal because of personal preference or the desire to record all transactions chronologically in one place.

JOURNALIZING INCREASES TO CASH

Here are the merchandising accounts in T account form. Refer to the glossary at the end of Chapter 10 on pages 363–364 for definitions of these accounts. The same accounts are used whether transactions are journalized in special journals (as in Chapters 10 and 11) or in a general journal. The outcomes will be the same.

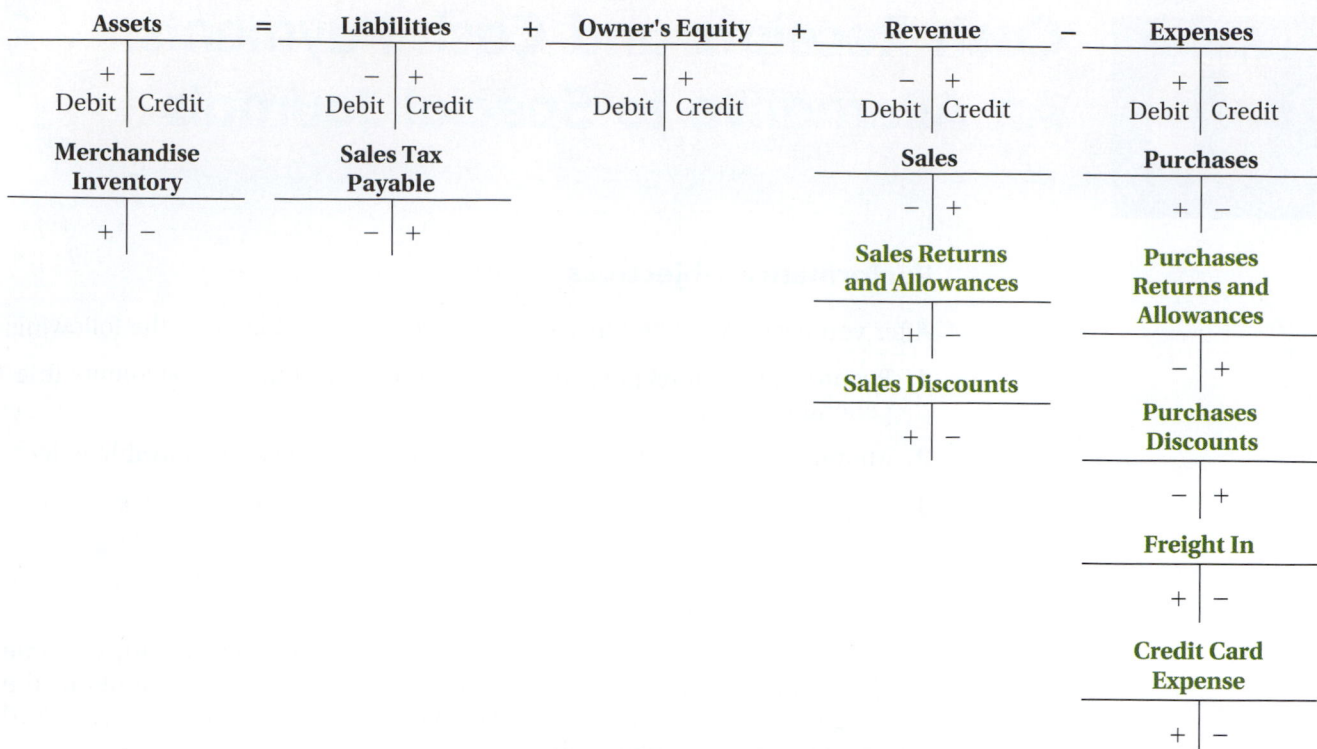

RECORDING CASH RECEIPTS (INCREASES TO CASH) IN A GENERAL JOURNAL

OBJECTIVE 1a

Record transactions pertaining to cash receipts in a general journal.

We will introduce journalizing increases (debits) to cash from a variety of sources in a general journal by looking at the following five transactions:

May   3   Sold merchandise for cash, $500, plus $40 sales tax.
4   Sold merchandise for cash. The customer charged the $500 sale on a credit card, and the cost of using the credit card was $21.60. Sales tax amounted to $40.
5   Collected cash on account from L. R. Ray, a charge customer, $416.
7   The owner, J. R. Hall, invested cash in the business, $10,000.
8   Sold computer equipment for cash at cost, $500.

	DATE		DESCRIPTION	POST. REF.	DEBIT	CREDIT	
1	20–						1
2	May	3	Cash		5 4 0 00		2
3			Sales			5 0 0 00	3
4			Sales Tax Payable			4 0 00	4
5			Sold merchandise for cash.				5
6							6
7		4	Cash		5 1 8 40		7
8			Credit Card Expense		2 1 60		8
9			Sales			5 0 0 00	9
10			Sales Tax Payable			4 0 00	10
11			Sold merchandise involving				11
12			a bank charge card and				12
13			sales tax.				13
14							14
15		5	Cash		4 1 6 00		15
16			Accounts Receivable, L. R. Ray			4 1 6 00	16
17			Collected cash on account.				17
18							18
19		7	Cash		10 0 0 0 00		19
20			J. R. Hall, Capital			10 0 0 0 00	20
21			Owner invested cash.				21
22							22
23		8	Cash		5 0 0 00		23
24			Computer Equipment			5 0 0 00	24
25			Sold computer equipment				25
26			at cost.				26

GENERAL JOURNAL   PAGE **15**

Posting to the General Ledger and Subsidiary Ledger

OBJECTIVE 2a

Maintain an accounts receivable ledger.

Post each entry to Cash and any other accounts involved in the general ledger. Also, post the amounts paid by customers to the subsidiary accounts receivable ledger to maintain a running balance of the amount each customer owes.

Schedule of Accounts Receivable

OBJECTIVE 3a

Prepare a schedule of accounts receivable.

At the end of the month, the accountant lists the customer names and amounts owed and totals the amounts. This listing is called the schedule of accounts receivable. The total of this schedule should equal the total of the Accounts Receivable controlling account in the general ledger. If the two amounts are different, reverse the process of adding and posting to discover and correct the error.

JOURNALIZING PURCHASES OF MERCHANDISE (FOR RESALE) ON ACCOUNT

Refer to Figures 9 (page 350), 10 (page 350), and 11 (page 351) in Chapter 10; they illustrate the forms that drive and support the merchandising transactions to be journalized.

Here are the merchandising accounts in T account form. Refer to the glossary at the end of Chapter 10 on pages 363–364 for definitions of these accounts. The same accounts are used whether transactions are journalized in special journals (as in Chapters 10 and 11) or in a general journal. The outcomes will be the same.

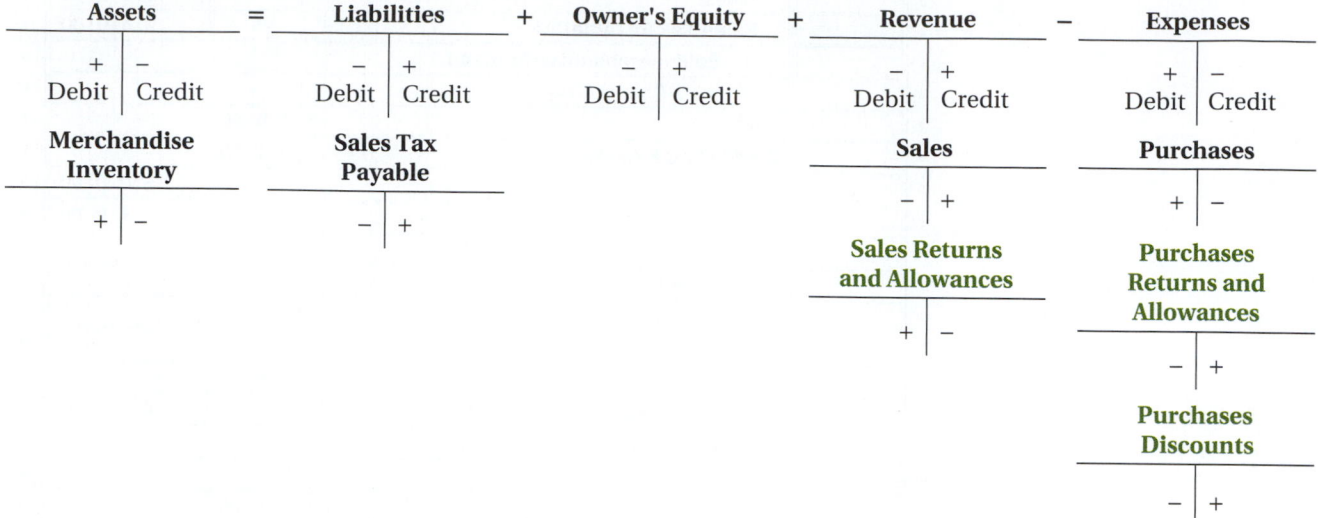

RECORDING CASH PAYMENTS (DECREASES TO CASH) IN A GENERAL JOURNAL

OBJECTIVE 1b

Record transactions pertaining to cash payments in a general journal.

We will introduce journalizing decreases (credits) to cash from a variety of sources in a general journal by looking at the following six transactions:

Aug. 8 Issued Ck. No. 2076 to Collins, Inc., in payment of invoice no. 2706, less cash discount of $34.20, $1,761.30 ($1,795.50 − $34.20). Notice that the discount applies only to the amount billed for the merchandise (2 percent of $1,710).

10 Paid wages for two-week period, Ck. No. 2077, $1,680 (previously recorded in the payroll entry).

11 Issued Ck. No. 2078 to Dana Manufacturing Company, in payment of invoice no. 10611 ($564), less return ($270); less cash discount, 2/10, n/30; $288.12 ($564 − $270 = $294; $294.00 × 0.02 = $5.88; $294.00 − $5.88 = $288.12).

12 Bought supplies for cash, Ck. No. 2079, payable to Davenport Office Supplies, $70. (Debit Supplies Expense.)

15 Issued Ck. No. 2080 to Gardner Products Company, in payment of invoice no. B643 ($1,245), less return ($315); less cash discount, 1/10, n/30; $921.60 [$1,245 − $315 = $930; freight charges totaled $90 ($930 − $90 = $840); $840.00 × 0.01 = $8.40; $930.00 − $8.40 = $921.60].

16 Bought merchandise for cash, Ck. No. 2081, payable to Jones and Son, $200.

GENERAL JOURNAL   PAGE ___27___

	DATE	DESCRIPTION	POST. REF.	DEBIT	CREDIT	
1	20–					1
2	Aug. 8	Accounts Payable, Collins, Inc.		1 7 9 5 50		2
3		Cash			1 7 6 1 30	3
4		Purchases Discounts			3 4 20	4
5		Paid Collins, Inc., for invoice				5
6		no. 2706, Ck. No. 2076.				6
7						7
8	10	Wages Payable		1 6 8 0 00		8
9		Cash			1 6 8 0 00	9
10		Paid wages for two-week				10
11		period, Ck. No. 2077.				11
12						12
13	11	Accounts Payable, Dana Mfg. Co.		2 9 4 00		13
14		Cash			2 8 8 12	14
15		Purchases Discounts			5 88	15
16		Paid Dana Mfg. Co. for				16
17		invoice no. 10611,				17
18		Ck. No. 2078.				18
19						19
20	12	Supplies Expense		7 0 00		20
21		Cash			7 0 00	21
22		Bought supplies from				22
23		Davenport Office Supplies,				23
24		Ck. No. 2079.				24
25						25
26	15	Accounts Payable, Gardner		9 3 0 00		26
27		Products Co.				27
28		Cash			9 2 1 60	28
29		Purchases Discounts			8 40	29
30		Paid Gardner Products Co.				30
31		for invoice no. B643,				31
32		Ck. No. 2080.				32
33						33
34	16	Purchases		2 0 0 00		34
35		Cash			2 0 0 00	35
36		Bought merchandise from				36
37		Jones and Son, Ck. No. 2081.				37

Posting to the General Ledger and Subsidiary Ledger

OBJECTIVE 2b

Maintain an accounts payable ledger.

Post each entry to Cash, Accounts Payable, and any other accounts involved in the general ledger. Also, post the amount owed to the vendor to the subsidiary accounts payable ledger to maintain a running balance of the amount owed to each vendor.

OBJECTIVE 3b

Prepare a schedule of accounts payable.

Schedule of Accounts Payable

At the end of the month, the accountant lists the vendor names and amounts owed and totals the amounts. This listing is called the schedule of accounts payable. The total of this schedule should equal the total of the Accounts Payable controlling account in the general ledger. If the two amounts are different, reverse the process of adding and posting to discover and correct the error.

PROBLEMS

P.O. 1, 2, 3

Check Figures

Trial Balance totals, $65,288.80; Schedule of Accounts Receivable total, $5,468; Schedule of Accounts Payable total, $4,733

Problem D-1A Complete Problem 11-4A on pages 420–422 *except* journalize transactions in a general journal instead of in special journals.

P.O. 1, 2, 3

Check Figures

Trial Balance totals, $63,187.61; Schedule of Accounts Receivable total, $4,912.20; Schedule of Accounts Payable total, $3,848.54

Problem D-1B Complete Problem 11-4B on pages 424–426 *except* journalize transactions in a general journal instead of in special journals.

12 Work Sheet and Adjusting Entries

internet LINKS TO ACCOUNTING

Anyone who subscribes to a magazine has probably received subscription renewal notices enticing them to renew now and save! And the savings can seem substantial, such as save 65 percent off the newsstand price or buy one year and get one year free. Many subscribers take advantage of these offers, extending their subscriptions into future years. When subscription fees are collected more than a year in advance, they represent unearned revenue. This unearned revenue is a liability to the company because it is money received for a product or service that has not yet been provided to the customer. *TV Guide* is a weekly magazine that focuses on the scheduled television programs for the week. How do you think GEMSTAR-TV Guide International, Inc., the publisher of the magazine, records these advance sales? When does the company consider the revenue to be earned and how does it record it? Look at the company's 2005 annual report, found by going to **http://www.gemstartvguide.com,** clicking on Investors at the top of the screen, then Financial Reports in the list on the left side, and then on 2005 Annual Report. Think about the answer to this as you learn about adjusting entries for unearned revenue in this chapter.

Performance Objectives

After you have completed this chapter, you will be able to do the following:

1. Prepare an adjustment for supplies.

2. Prepare an adjustment for merchandise inventory under the periodic inventory system.

3. Prepare an adjustment for unearned revenue.

4. Record the adjustment data in a work sheet (including merchandise inventory, unearned revenue, supplies remaining, expired insurance, depreciation, and accrued wages or salaries).

5. Complete the work sheet.

6. Journalize the adjusting entries for a merchandising business under the periodic inventory system.

7. Journalize the adjusting entry for merchandise inventory under the perpetual inventory system.

We have talked about the special journals and accounts kept by a merchandising business. Now we take another step toward completing the accounting cycle by presenting the related adjustments and the work sheet. Many of the adjustments made by a service business are also made by a merchandising firm. First, let's briefly review the adjusting entries described so far. To begin, look over the following accounts. Here are the data for the adjustments, along with the related adjusting entries:

Insurance expired, $2,600. (The amount expired is the amount used.)

Prepaid Insurance						Insurance Expense		
	+	−				+	−	
Bal.	3,000	Adj.	2,600		Adj.	2,600		
Bal.	400							

Additional depreciation, $2,800. (Add to both accounts.)

Depreciation Expense				Accumulated Depreciation		
	+	−		−	+	
Adj.	2,800				Bal.	10,000
					Adj.	2,800
					Bal.	12,800

Accrued wages (owed but not yet paid), $3,900. (Add to both accounts.)

Wages Expense				Wages Payable		
	+	−		−	+	
Bal.	26,000				Adj.	3,900
Adj.	3,900					
Bal.	29,900					

In this chapter, we introduce three more adjusting entries. One adjustment is for supplies. This adjustment can be used for merchandising and manufacturing businesses. One adjustment is for merchandise inventory, which is used exclusively for a merchandising business. Another adjustment is for unearned revenue, which could apply to either a merchandising or a service business. We also discuss how to handle the specialized accounts of a merchandising business in the work sheet. Finally, we briefly describe the perpetual inventory system and the accompanying adjustment.

ADJUSTMENT FOR SUPPLIES

OBJECTIVE 1

Prepare an adjustment for supplies.

Previously, when we were talking about the buying of supplies for a service business, we debited Supplies Expense and credited Cash or Accounts Payable.

When a merchandising business buys supplies for cash or on credit, the accounting would generally be the same as for a service business. However, if the amount of supplies held at the end of the accounting period is substantial, then an adjustment should be made to capitalize the supplies that were not consumed during the accounting period. The adjustment would be to debit Supplies (an asset account) and credit Supplies Expense. The amount is determined by a physical count of the supplies left over. For a retail business, supplies would consist of everything from paper or plastic bags to paper forms.

As an illustration, let's say that Mullene & Co. has a balance of $62,000 in the Supplies Expense account as a result of buying supplies all during the fiscal period. Now, by taking a count of the supplies on hand, it is determined that $12,000 of supplies are left.

To record the amount of the supplies used, Mullene & Co. has to make an adjusting entry. The purpose of an adjusting entry is to bring the books up to date at the end of the accounting period.

Let's look at this in T account form. We need to add to the balance sheet the supplies still on hand at the end of the accounting period (debit Supplies, an asset account) and reduce the amount of supplies expensed during the accounting period (credit Supplies Expense).

> **REMEMBER!**
>
> For the adjustment of supplies, first find the amount by determining the amount of the supplies that remain. In the adjusting entry, deduct the amount of the remaining supplies from Supplies Expense and add it to the asset account Supplies.

	Supplies				**Supplies Expense**			
	+	−			+	−		
Adj.	12,000			Bal.	62,000	Adj.	12,000	
				Bal.	50,000			

ADJUSTMENT FOR MERCHANDISE INVENTORY USING THE PERIODIC INVENTORY SYSTEM

OBJECTIVE 2

Prepare an adjustment for merchandise inventory under the periodic inventory system.

Under the **periodic inventory system**, we do not make an entry in the Merchandise Inventory account until an actual **physical inventory** or count of the stock of goods on hand has been taken. Instead, we record the purchase of merchandise as a debit to Purchases for the amount of the cost and the sale of the merchandise as a credit to Sales for the amount of the selling price. Finally, after a physical count of merchandise has been taken, one method of adjusting inventory is to make two adjusting entries to record the dollar amount of the inventory. The first adjusting entry is to remove the beginning inventory. The second entry is to enter the ending inventory.

Consider this example. A firm has a Merchandise Inventory balance of $174,000, which represents the cost of the inventory at the beginning of the fiscal period. At the end of the fiscal period, the firm takes an actual count of the stock on hand and determines the cost of the ending inventory to be $180,000. Naturally, in any business, goods are constantly being bought, sold, and replaced. The cost of the ending inventory is larger than the cost of the beginning inventory because the firm bought more than it sold. When we adjust the Merchandise Inventory account, we place the new figure of $180,000 in the account. This method can require two steps.

Step 1 Eliminate the amount of the beginning inventory from the Merchandise Inventory account by transferring the amount into Income Summary. (Remove the beginning inventory.)

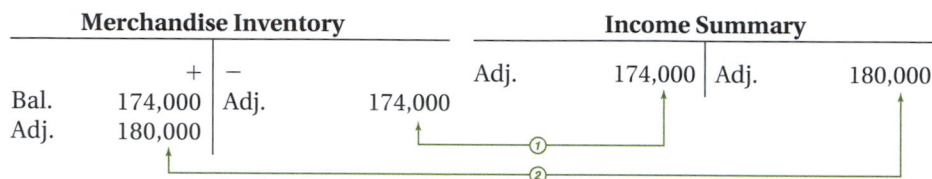

We credit Merchandise Inventory and then debit Income Summary.

Step 2 Enter the ending Merchandise Inventory, because you must record on the books the cost of the asset remaining on hand. (Enter the ending inventory.)

Let's repeat the T accounts, showing step 1 and adding step 2.

Merchandise Inventory		Income Summary	
+	−	Adj. 174,000	Adj. 180,000
Bal. 174,000	Adj. 174,000		
Adj. 180,000			

In step 2, we debit Merchandise Inventory (recording the asset on the plus side of the account) and do the opposite to Income Summary.

The reason for adjusting the Merchandise Inventory account in these two steps is that both the beginning and the ending amounts appear as distinct figures in the Income Statement columns of a work sheet, and these columns are used as the basis for preparing the income statement.

ADJUSTMENT FOR UNEARNED REVENUE

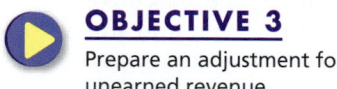

OBJECTIVE 3

Prepare an adjustment for unearned revenue.

Now let's introduce another adjusting entry, **unearned revenue,** which is cash received in advance for goods or services to be delivered or performed later. This entry could pertain to a service business as well as to a merchandising or manufacturing business. Frequently, cash is received in advance for services to be performed in the future. For example, a professional sports team sells tickets in advance, a concert association sells season tickets in advance, a magazine publisher sells subscriptions in advance, and an insurance company receives premiums in advance. If the cash amounts received by each of these organizations will be earned during the present fiscal period, the amounts should be credited to revenue accounts. On the other hand, if the amounts received will *not* be earned during the present fiscal period, the amounts should be credited to unearned revenue accounts. **An unearned revenue account is classified as a liability,** because an organization is liable for (owes) the amount received in advance until it is earned.

College students pay in advance to participate in a meal plan. Until all those meals are consumed, this money represents unearned revenue for the college or university dining hall services.

To illustrate, assume that on April 1, Bell Publishing Company receives $82,000 in cash for subscriptions covering two years and records them originally as debits to Cash and credits to Unearned Subscriptions. At the end of the year, Bell finds that $30,750 of the subscriptions have been earned. Accordingly, Bell's accountant makes an adjusting entry, debiting Unearned Subscriptions and crediting Subscriptions Income. In other words, the accountant takes the earned portion out of Unearned Subscriptions and adds it to Subscriptions Income. T accounts show the situation as follows:

Cash				**Unearned Subscriptions**		
	+	−		−	+	
April 1	82,000		Dec. 31 Adj. 30,750	April 1	82,000
			(9 months)	(24 months)	
				Bal.	**51,250**

Subscriptions Income	
−	+
	Dec. 31 Adj. 30,750
	(9 months)

To take another example, suppose that Rainier Plumbing Supply offers a course in plumbing repairs for home owners and apartment managers. On November 1, Rainier Plumbing Supply receives $1,200 in fees for a three-month course. Because Rainier Plumbing Supply's present fiscal period ends on December 31, the three months' worth of fees received in advance will not all be earned during this fiscal period. Therefore, Rainier Plumbing Supply's accountant records the transaction as a debit to Cash of $1,200 and a credit to Unearned Course Fees of $1,200. Unearned Course Fees is a liability account, because Rainier Plumbing Supply must complete the how-to course or refund a portion of the money it collected. **Any account beginning with the word *Unearned* is always a liability.**

On December 31, because two months' worth of course fees have now been earned, Rainier Plumbing Supply's accountant makes an adjusting entry to transfer $800 (⅔ of $1,200) from Unearned Course Fees to Course Fees Income. By T accounts, the situation looks like this:

Cash				**Unearned Course Fees**		
	+	−		−	+	
Nov. 1	1,200		Dec. 31 Adj.	800	Nov. 1	1,200
			(2 months)		(3 months)	
					Bal.	**400**

Course Fees Income	
−	+
	Dec. 31 Adj. 800
	(2 months)

Rainier Plumbing Supply's chart of accounts is presented on the next page. The account number arrangement will be discussed in Chapter 13.

Assets (100–199)

111	Cash
112	Notes Receivable
113	Accounts Receivable
114	Merchandise Inventory
115	Supplies
116	Prepaid Insurance
121	Land
122	Building
123	Accumulated Depreciation, Building
124	Equipment
125	Accumulated Depreciation, Equipment

Liabilities (200–299)

211	Notes Payable
212	Accounts Payable
213	Wages Payable
217	Unearned Course Fees
221	Mortgage Payable

Owner's Equity (300–399)

311	C. F. Rainier, Capital
312	C. F. Rainier, Drawing
313	Income Summary

Revenue (400–499)

411	Sales
412	Sales Returns and Allowances
413	Sales Discounts
421	Course Fees Income
422	Interest Income

Cost of Goods Sold (500–599)

511	Purchases
512	Purchases Returns and Allowances
513	Purchases Discounts
514	Freight In

Expenses (600–699)

611	Wages Expense
622	Supplies Expense
623	Insurance Expense
624	Depreciation Expense, Building
625	Depreciation Expense, Equipment
626	Taxes Expense
634	Interest Expense

Before we demonstrate how to record adjustments, let's first look at the trial balance section of Rainier Plumbing Supply's work sheet (Figure 1).

DATA FOR THE ADJUSTMENTS

OBJECTIVE 4

Record the adjustment data in a work sheet (including merchandise inventory, unearned revenue, supplies remaining, expired insurance, depreciation, and accrued wages or salaries).

Listing the adjustment data appears to be a relatively minor task. In a business situation, however, one must take actual physical counts of the inventories and match them up with costs. One must check insurance policies to determine the amount of insurance that has expired. Finally, one must systematically write off, or depreciate, the cost of buildings and equipment.

For income tax and accounting purposes, land cannot be depreciated. Even if the building and lot were bought as one package for one price, the buyer must separate the cost of the building from the cost of the land. For real estate taxes, the county assessor appraises the building and the land separately. If there is no other qualified appraisal available, one can use the assessor's ratio or percentage as a basis for separating building cost and land cost.

Here are the adjustment data for Rainier Plumbing Supply. We will show the adjustments recorded in T accounts.

a–b. Ending merchandise inventory, $65,800. The adjustments for inventory are generally placed first.

	Merchandise Inventory				Income Summary		
	+	−					
Bal.	67,000	**(a)** Adj.	67,000	**(a)** Adj.	67,000	**(b)** Adj.	65,800
(b) Adj.	65,800						

Rainier Plumbing Supply
Work Sheet
For Year Ended December 31, 20—

	ACCOUNT NAME	TRIAL BALANCE DEBIT	TRIAL BALANCE CREDIT	ADJUSTMENTS DEBIT	ADJUSTMENTS CREDIT
1	Cash	24 1 5 4 00			
2	Notes Receivable	4 0 0 0 00			
3	Accounts Receivable	29 4 4 6 00			
4	Merchandise Inventory	67 0 0 0 00			
5	Prepaid Insurance	9 6 0 00			
6	Land	120 1 0 0 00			
7	Building	130 0 0 0 00			
8	Accumulated Depreciation, Building		52 0 0 0 00		
9	Equipment	33 6 0 0 00			
10	Accumulated Depreciation, Equipment		16 4 0 0 00		
11	Notes Payable		36 4 0 0 00		
12	Accounts Payable		3 0 0 0 00		
13	Unearned Course Fees		1 2 0 0 00		
14	Mortgage Payable		8 0 0 0 00		
15	C. F. Rainier, Capital		253 6 7 4 00		
16	C. F. Rainier, Drawing	76 9 0 0 00			
17	Sales		255 1 8 0 00		
18	Sales Returns and Allowances	8 4 0 00			
19	Sales Discounts	1 8 8 0 00			
20	Interest Income		1 2 0 00		
21	Purchases	87 1 4 0 00			
22	Purchases Returns and Allowances		8 3 2 00		
23	Purchases Discounts		1 2 4 8 00		
24	Freight In	2 4 6 0 00			
25	Wages Expense	45 8 0 0 00			
26	Supplies Expense	1 4 4 0 00			
27	Taxes Expense	1 9 6 0 00			
28	Interest Expense	3 7 4 00			
29		628 0 5 4 00	628 0 5 4 00		

FIGURE 1

c. Course fees earned, $800

Unearned Course Fees				Course Fees Income		
	−	+			−	+
(c) Adj.	800	Bal.	1,200			(c) Adj. 800

d. Ending supplies inventory, $412

Supplies				Supplies Expense		
	+	−			+	−
(d) Adj.	412			Bal. 1,440	(d) Adj.	412

Rainier Plumbing Supply
Work Sheet
For Year Ended December 31, 20—

	ACCOUNT NAME	TRIAL BALANCE DEBIT	TRIAL BALANCE CREDIT	ADJUSTMENTS DEBIT	ADJUSTMENTS CREDIT
1	Cash	24 1 5 4 00			
2	Notes Receivable	4 0 0 0 00			
3	Accounts Receivable	29 4 4 6 00			
4	Merchandise Inventory	67 0 0 0 00		(b)65 8 0 0 00	(a)67 0 0 0 00
5	Prepaid Insurance	9 6 0 00			(e) 3 2 0 00
6	Land	120 1 0 0 00			
7	Building	130 0 0 0 00			
8	Accumulated Depreciation, Building		52 0 0 0 00		(f) 4 0 0 0 00
9	Equipment	33 6 0 0 00			
10	Accumulated Depreciation, Equipment		16 4 0 0 00		(g) 4 8 0 0 00
11	Notes Payable		36 4 0 0 00		
12	Accounts Payable		3 0 0 0 00		
13	Unearned Course Fees		1 2 0 0 00	(c) 8 0 0 00	
14	Mortgage Payable		8 0 0 0 00		
15	C. F. Rainier, Capital		253 6 7 4 00		
16	C. F. Rainier, Drawing	76 9 0 0 00			
17	Sales		255 1 8 0 00		
18	Sales Returns and Allowances	8 4 0 00			
19	Sales Discounts	1 8 8 0 00			
20	Interest Income		1 2 0 00		
21	Purchases	87 1 4 0 00			
22	Purchases Returns and Allowances		8 3 2 00		
23	Purchases Discounts		1 2 4 8 00		
24	Freight In	2 4 6 0 00			
25	Wages Expense	45 8 0 0 00		(h) 1 1 2 0 00	
26	Supplies Expense	1 4 4 0 00			(d) 4 1 2 00
27	Taxes Expense	1 9 6 0 00			
28	Interest Expense	3 7 4 00			
29		628 0 5 4 00	628 0 5 4 00		
30	Income Summary			(a)67 0 0 0 00	(b)65 8 0 0 00
31	Course Fees Income				(c) 8 0 0 00
32	Supplies			(d) 4 1 2 00	
33	Insurance Expense			(e) 3 2 0 00	
34	Depreciation Expense, Equipment			(g) 4 8 0 0 00	
35	Depreciation Expense, Building			(f) 4 0 0 0 00	
36	Wages Payable				(h) 1 1 2 0 00
37				144 2 5 2 00	144 2 5 2 00

FIGURE 2

e. Insurance expired, $320

Prepaid Insurance				Insurance Expense	
+	−			+	−
Bal. 960	(e) Adj. 320	(e) Adj. 320			

f. Additional year's depreciation of building, $4,000

Accumulated Depreciation, Building			Depreciation Expense, Building	
−	+	(f) Adj. 4,000	+	−
	Bal. 52,000		4,000	
	(f) Adj. 4,000			

g. Additional year's depreciation of equipment, $4,800

Accumulated Depreciation, Equipment			Depreciation Expense, Equipment	
−	+	(g) Adj.	+	−
	Bal. 16,400	4,800	4,800	
	(g) Adj. 4,800			

h. Wages owed but not paid to employees at end of year, $1,120

Wages Payable			Wages Expense	
−	+	Bal. 45,800	+	−
	(h) Adj. 1,120	(h) Adj. 1,120		

We now record these in the Adjustments columns of the work sheet, using the same letters to identify the adjustments (see Figure 2).

COMPLETION OF THE WORK SHEET

OBJECTIVE 5

Complete the work sheet.

Previously, in introducing work sheets, we included the Adjusted Trial Balance columns as a means of verifying that the accounts were in balance after recording the adjusting entries. At this time, to reduce the number of columns in the work sheet, we will eliminate the Adjusted Trial Balance columns. The account balances after the adjusting entries will be carried directly into the Income Statement and Balance Sheet columns.

The completed work sheet looks like Figure 3 on pages 450 and 451.

Observe in particular the way we carry forward the figures for Merchandise Inventory and Income Summary. **Income Summary is the only account in which we don't combine the debit and credit figures. Instead, we carry them into the Income Statement columns in Figure 3 as two distinct figures.** The reason is that both figures appear in the income statement itself. The amount listed as Income Summary in the Income Statement Debit column is the beginning merchandise inventory. The amount listed as Income Summary in the Income Statement Credit column is the

Rainier Plumbing Supply
Work Sheet
For Year Ended December 31, 20—

	ACCOUNT NAME	TRIAL BALANCE DEBIT	TRIAL BALANCE CREDIT	
1	Cash	24 1 5 4 00		
2	Notes Receivable	4 0 0 0 00		
3	Accounts Receivable	29 4 4 6 00		
4	Merchandise Inventory	67 0 0 0 00		
5	Prepaid Insurance	9 6 0 00		
6	Land	120 1 0 0 00		
7	Building	130 0 0 0 00		
8	Accumulated Depreciation, Building		52 0 0 0 00	
9	Equipment	33 6 0 0 00		
10	Accumulated Depreciation, Equipment		16 4 0 0 00	
11	Notes Payable		36 4 0 0 00	
12	Accounts Payable		3 0 0 0 00	
13	Unearned Course Fees		1 2 0 0 00	
14	Mortgage Payable		8 0 0 0 00	
15	C. F. Rainier, Capital		253 6 7 4 00	
16	C. F. Rainier, Drawing	76 9 0 0 00		
17	Sales		255 1 8 0 00	
18	Sales Returns and Allowances	8 4 0 00		
19	Sales Discounts	1 8 8 0 00		
20	Interest Income		1 2 0 00	
21	Purchases	87 1 4 0 00		
22	Purchases Returns and Allowances		8 3 2 00	
23	Purchases Discounts		1 2 4 8 00	
24	Freight In	2 4 6 0 00		
25	Wages Expense	45 8 0 0 00		
26	Supplies Expense	1 4 4 0 00		
27	Taxes Expense	1 9 6 0 00		
28	Interest Expense	3 7 4 00		
29		628 0 5 4 00	628 0 5 4 00	
30	Income Summary			
31	Course Fees Income			
32	Supplies			
33	Insurance Expense			
34	Depreciation Expense, Equipment			
35	Depreciation Expense, Building			
36	Wages Payable			
37				
38	Net Income			
39				
40				
41				
42				

FIGURE 3

ADJUSTMENTS DEBIT	ADJUSTMENTS CREDIT	INCOME STATEMENT DEBIT	INCOME STATEMENT CREDIT	BALANCE SHEET DEBIT	BALANCE SHEET CREDIT	
				24 1 5 4 00		1
				4 0 0 0 00		2
				29 4 4 6 00		3
(b)65 8 0 0 00	(a)67 0 0 0 00			65 8 0 0 00		4
	(e) 3 2 0 00			6 4 0 00		5
				120 1 0 0 00		6
				130 0 0 0 00		7
	(g) 4 0 0 0 00				56 0 0 0 00	8
				33 6 0 0 00		9
	(f) 4 8 0 0 00				21 2 0 0 00	10
					36 4 0 0 00	11
					3 0 0 0 00	12
(c) 8 0 0 00					4 0 0 00	13
					8 0 0 00	14
					253 6 7 4 00	15
				76 9 0 0 00		16
			255 1 8 0 00			17
		8 4 0 00				18
		1 8 8 0 00				19
			1 2 0 00			20
		87 1 4 0 00				21
			8 3 2 00			22
			1 2 4 8 00			23
		2 4 6 0 00				24
(h) 1 1 2 0 00		46 9 2 0 00				25
	(d) 4 1 2 00	1 0 2 8 00				26
		1 9 6 0 00				27
		3 7 4 00				28
						29
(a)67 0 0 0 00	(b)65 8 0 0 00	67 0 0 0 00	65 8 0 0 00			30
	(c) 8 0 0 00		8 0 0 00			31
(d) 4 1 2 00				4 1 2 00		32
(e) 3 2 0 00		3 2 0 00				33
(f) 4 8 0 0 00		4 8 0 0 00				34
(g) 4 0 0 0 00		4 0 0 0 00				35
	(h) 1 1 2 0 00				1 1 2 0 00	36
144 2 5 2 00	144 2 5 2 00	218 7 2 2 00	323 9 8 0 00	485 0 5 2 00	379 7 9 4 00	37
		105 2 5 8 00			105 2 5 8 00	38
		323 9 8 0 00	323 9 8 0 00	485 0 5 2 00	485 0 5 2 00	39
						40
						41
						42

ending merchandise inventory. We will talk about this topic in greater detail in Chapter 13.

Using an electronic spreadsheet, such as Excel, can be a more efficient way of preparing a work sheet. When developing the work sheet, complete one stage at a time:

1. Record the trial balance, and make sure that the total of the Debit column equals the total of the Credit column.
2. Record the adjustments in the Adjustments columns, and make sure that the totals are equal.
3. Complete the Income Statement and Balance Sheet columns by recording the adjusted balance of each account. The accounts and classifications pertaining to a merchandising business appear in these columns:

Income Statement		Balance Sheet	
Debit	Credit	Debit	Credit
Expenses + Sales Returns and Allowances + Sales Discounts + Purchases + Freight In + Income Summary	Revenues + Purchases Returns and Allowances + Purchases Discounts + Income Summary	Assets + Drawing	Accumulated Depreciation + Liabilities + Capital

Study the following example, noting especially the way we treat these accounts for a merchandising business:

	Location in Work Sheet			
	Income Statement		Balance Sheet	
Account Name	Debit	Credit	Debit	Credit
Merchandise Inventory			65,800.00	
Sales		255,180.00		
Sales Returns and Allowances	840.00			
Sales Discounts	1,880.00			
Purchases	87,140.00			
Purchases Returns and Allowances		832.00		
Purchases Discounts		1,248.00		
Freight In	2,460.00			
Income Summary	67,000.00	65,800.00		
Supplies Expense	1,028.00			

ADJUSTING ENTRIES UNDER THE PERIODIC INVENTORY SYSTEM

Figure 4 shows the adjusting entries as taken from the Adjustments columns of the work sheet and recorded in the general journal.

FIGURE 4

OBJECTIVE 6

Journalize the adjusting entries for a merchandising business under the periodic inventory system.

	DATE		DESCRIPTION	POST. REF.	DEBIT	CREDIT	
1	20–		**Adjusting Entries**				1
2	Dec.	31	Income Summary		67 0 0 0 00		2
3	(a)		Merchandise Inventory			67 0 0 0 00	3
4							4
5	(b)	31	Merchandise Inventory		65 8 0 0 00		5
6			Income Summary			65 8 0 0 00	6
7							7
8	(c)	31	Unearned Course Fees		8 0 0 00		8
9			Course Fees Income			8 0 0 00	9
10							10
11	(d)	31	Supplies		4 1 2 00		11
12			Supplies Expense			4 1 2 00	12
13							13
14	(e)	31	Insurance Expense		3 2 0 00		14
15			Prepaid Insurance			3 2 0 00	15
16							16
17	(f)	31	Depreciation Expense, Equipment		4 8 0 0 00		17
18			Accumulated Depreciation,				18
19			Equipment			4 8 0 0 00	19
20							20
21	(g)	31	Depreciation Expense,				21
22			Building		4 0 0 0 00		22
23			Accumulated Depreciation,				23
24			Building			4 0 0 0 00	24
25							25
26	(h)	31	Wages Expense		1 1 2 0 00		26
27			Wages Payable			1 1 2 0 00	27
28							28

GENERAL JOURNAL   PAGE **96**

ADJUSTMENT FOR MERCHANDISE INVENTORY UNDER THE PERPETUAL INVENTORY SYSTEM

OBJECTIVE 7

Journalize the adjusting entry for merchandise inventory under the perpetual inventory system.

Under the **perpetual inventory system,** a business continually maintains a record of each item in stock. **Under the perpetual inventory system, when merchandise is purchased, the Merchandise Inventory account (not the Purchases account) is debited for the cost of the merchandise and Accounts Payable or Cash is credited. When merchandise is sold, the Merchandise Inventory account is credited for the cost of the merchandise and the Cost of Goods Sold account is debited for the cost of the merchandise.**

Many firms use electronic devices to keep track of stock items. For example, when a sale is made at a supermarket checkout counter, as the bar code on each item is scanned, the price and stock number are recorded. The cash register is connected to a computer that updates the inventory record and records the cost of the item. So the business perpetually (always) knows how much inventory it should have on hand.

However, to verify the inventory record, a physical count should be taken from time to time. The amount shown by the physical count may be less than the recorded amount as a result of errors, shrinkage, or shoplifting. If this is the case, an adjusting entry must be made to record the amount of the loss. This entry is a debit to the Cost of Goods Sold account (an expense account) and a credit to the Merchandise Inventory account.

ADJUSTING ENTRY UNDER THE PERPETUAL INVENTORY SYSTEM

Here is a comparison of entries in T-account form under both the periodic and the perpetual inventory systems. Assume a beginning inventory of $80,000.

1. Bought merchandise on account, $50,000.

Periodic Inventory		Perpetual Inventory	

Purchases	Accounts Payable	Merchandise Inventory	Accounts Payable
+ | −	− | +	+ | −	− | +
(1) 50,000	(1) 50,000	Bal. 80,000	(1) 50,000
		(1) 50,000	

2. Sold merchandise for $82,000 having a cost of $61,200.

Periodic Inventory		Perpetual Inventory	

Accounts Receivable	Sales	Accounts Receivable	Sales
+ | −	− | +	+ | −	− | +
(2) 82,000	(2) 82,000	(2) 82,000	(2) 82,000

		Cost of Goods Sold	Merchandise Inventory
		+ | −	+ | −
		(2) 61,200	Bal. 80,000 | (2) 61,200
			(1) 50,000

REMEMBER!

The ending inventory of one period becomes the beginning inventory of the next period.

3. Adjusting entry for ending inventory by physical count, $68,400. The recorded balance of the perpetual inventory is $68,800 ($80,000 + $50,000 − $61,200).

Periodic Inventory		Perpetual Inventory	

Income Summary	Merchandise Inventory	Cost of Goods Sold	Merchandise Inventory
+ | −	+ | −	+ | −	+ | −
(3a) Adj. | (3b) Adj.	Bal. 80,000 | (3a) Adj.	(2) 61,200	Bal. 80,000 | (2) 61,200
80,000 | 68,400	(3b) Adj. | 80,000	(3) Adj. 400	(1) 50,000 | (3) Adj. 400
	68,400 |		

FYI

This entry would have been previously listed in the Adjustments columns of the work sheet.

The difference of $400 ($68,800 − $68,400) is the adjustment amount under the perpetual inventory system (actual physical count versus the accounting records). The adjusting entry required to record the $400 loss is shown in Figure 5.

FIGURE 5

			POST. REF.	DEBIT	CREDIT	
DATE		**DESCRIPTION**				
1	20–		**Adjusting Entries**				1
2	Dec.	31	Cost of Goods Sold		4 0 0 00		2
3			Merchandise Inventory			4 0 0 00	3
4			or				4
5		31	Merchandise Inventory		5 0 0 00		5
6			Cost of Goods Sold			5 0 0 00	6

GENERAL JOURNAL   PAGE __96__

Suppose, on the other hand, that the physical count of the stock of merchandise ($68,900) were more than the recorded amount ($68,400). The adjusting entry is to debit Merchandise Inventory and credit Cost of Goods Sold (account) for the difference ($68,900 − $68,400 = $500). (See Figure 5.)

Additional adjusting entries would follow, such as those for supplies remaining, insurance expired, accrued wages, and other such expenses.

In the income statement, under the perpetual inventory system, the Cost of Goods Sold account is listed under one line, rather than there being a Cost of Goods Sold section.

Here is a comparison of income statements under each of the two systems.

Periodic			**Perpetual**	
Sales		$82,000	Sales	$82,000
Cost of Goods Sold:			Cost of Goods Sold	61,600
Merchandise Inventory (beginning)	$ 80,000		Gross Profit	$20,400
Purchases (net)	50,000			
Cost of Goods Available for Sale	$130,000			
Less Merchandise Inventory (ending)	68,400			
Cost of Goods Sold		61,600		
Gross Profit		$20,400		

CHAPTER REVIEW

Online Study Center
ACE the test!

Review of Performance Objectives

1. Prepare an adjustment for supplies.

   When supplies are bought during the year, they are recorded by debiting (increasing) Supplies Expense. At the end of the year, an inventory is taken to determine the amount of supplies on hand. If the ending inventory of supplies is significant, then an adjusting entry is made for the amount remaining, debiting Supplies (an asset account) and crediting Supplies Expense.

2. Prepare an adjustment for merchandise inventory under the periodic inventory system.

The adjustment for merchandise inventory under the periodic inventory system requires two adjusting entries. In the first adjusting entry (to remove the beginning inventory), debit Income Summary and credit Merchandise Inventory. In the second adjusting entry (to enter the ending inventory), debit Merchandise Inventory and credit Income Summary.

3. Prepare an adjustment for unearned revenue.

For revenue received in advance, an adjustment is required to separate the portion that has been earned from the portion that is unearned. We assume that the amount of cash received in advance was originally recorded as unearned revenue, which is a liability. In the adjusting entry for the amount actually earned, debit the unearned revenue account (Unearned Course Fees) and credit the revenue account (Course Fees Income).

4. Record the adjustment data in a work sheet (including merchandise inventory, unearned revenue, supplies remaining, expired insurance, depreciation, and accrued wages or salaries).

In the Adjustments columns of the work sheet, record the following adjusting entries:

For merchandise inventory: first, debit Income Summary and credit Merchandise Inventory (to remove the beginning inventory); next, debit Merchandise Inventory and credit Income Summary (to enter the ending inventory).
For unearned revenue: debit the unearned revenue account and credit the revenue account (to record revenue earned).
For supplies remaining: debit Supplies and credit Supplies Expense.
For expired insurance: debit Insurance Expense and credit Prepaid Insurance.
For depreciation: debit Depreciation Expense and credit Accumulated Depreciation.
For accrued wages or salaries: debit Wages Expense or Salaries Expense and credit Wages Payable or Salaries Payable.

5. Complete the work sheet.

Carry the Income Summary account from the Adjustments columns into the Income Statement columns as two separate figures. For merchandise inventory, record the amount of the ending inventory in the Balance Sheet Debit column. For unearned revenue, record the unearned revenue account in the Balance Sheet Credit column and the revenue account in the Income Statement Credit column.

6. Journalize the adjusting entries for a merchandising business under the periodic inventory system.

Take the adjusting entries recorded in the journal directly from the Adjustments columns of the work sheet.

7. Journalize the adjusting entry for merchandise inventory under the perpetual inventory system.

Assuming that the amount of the physical count of the stock of merchandise is less than the recorded amount, the adjusting entry is a debit to Cost of Goods Sold and a credit to Merchandise Inventory for the amount of the difference. On the other hand, if the physical count of the stock of merchandise is more than the recorded amount, the adjusting entry is to debit Merchandise Inventory and credit Cost of Goods Sold for the amount of the difference.

Glossary

Periodic inventory system The system under which the buying of merchandise during the year is recorded as a debit to Purchases and a credit to Accounts Payable or Cash. At the end of the year, a physical count of the stock of goods is taken and adjusting entries are made to record the amount of the physical count. (443)

Perpetual inventory system The system under which the buying of merchandise during the year is recorded as a debit to Merchandise Inventory and a credit to Accounts Payable or Cash. When merchandise is sold, the cost of the merchandise is recorded as a debit to Cost of Goods Sold and a credit to Merchandise Inventory. At the end of the year, a physical count of the stock of goods is taken and an adjusting entry is made to record the difference between the amount of the count and the amount previously recorded. (453)

Physical inventory An actual count of the stock of goods on hand. (443)

Unearned revenue Revenue received in advance for goods or services to be delivered later; considered to be a liability until the revenue is earned. (444)

QUESTIONS, EXERCISES, AND CASES

Discussion Questions

1. What is a physical inventory? What does the word *periodic* mean in the term *periodic inventory*?

2. On the Income Summary line of a work sheet, $126,200 appears in the Income Statement Debit column, and $124,100 appears in the Income Statement Credit column. Which figure represents the beginning inventory?

3. Using the perpetual inventory system, what account is debited when a business buys more merchandise?

4. On a work sheet, where will the amount of the ending merchandise inventory be recorded?

5. Explain what is meant by unearned revenue and why it is treated as a liability.

6. Why is it necessary to adjust the Merchandise Inventory account under a periodic inventory system?

7. A merchandising company shows $952 in the Supplies Expense account on the preadjusted trial balance. After taking inventory of the actual supplies, they still own $627.

    a. Write the adjusting entry.
    b. How much was used or expired?

8. When a college receives one semester's dormitory rent in advance, an entry is made debiting Cash and crediting Unearned Rent. At the end of the year, a large portion of the rent has been earned. What adjusting entry would you suggest?

Exercises

P.O. 2

Journalize adjustments for merchandise inventory.

Exercise 12-1 After adjusting entries are posted, the Merchandise Inventory account appears as follows. Journalize the complete entries that support these postings. The Income Summary account is numbered 313.

ACCOUNT __Merchandise Inventory__ ACCOUNT NO. __114__

	DATE		ITEM	POST. REF.	DEBIT	CREDIT	BALANCE DEBIT	BALANCE CREDIT	
1	2006								1
2	Dec.	31	Balance	✓			96 4 0 0 00		2
3	2007								3
4	Dec.	31	Adjusting	J112		96 4 0 0 00	—	—	4
5		31	Adjusting	J112	97 1 0 0 00		97 1 0 0 00		5
6									6
7									7
8									8

P.O. 3

Journalize the adjustment for unearned revenue.

Exercise 12-2 On October 31, the Vermillion Igloos Hockey Club received $800,000 in cash in advance for season tickets for eight home games. The transaction was recorded as a debit to Cash and a credit to Unearned Admissions. By December 31, the end of the fiscal year, the team had played three home games and received an additional $450,000 cash admissions income at the gate.

a. Journalize the adjusting entry as of December 31.
b. List the title of the account and the related balance that will appear on the income statement.
c. List the title of the account and the related balance that will appear on the balance sheet.

P.O. 3

Determine the entries in an unearned revenue account.

Exercise 12-3 For the basketball federation's Unearned Season Tickets account, list the debits and credits for each amount posted to the account and briefly describe the transaction.

ACCOUNT __Unearned Season Tickets__ ACCOUNT NO. __214__

	DATE		ITEM	POST. REF.	DEBIT	CREDIT	BALANCE DEBIT	BALANCE CREDIT	
1	20—								1
2	Jan.	1	Balance	✓				10 4 0 0 00	2
3	Oct.	15		CR42		12 6 0 0 00		23 0 0 0 00	3
4	Nov.	1		CR43		22 1 0 0 00		45 1 0 0 00	4
5	Dec.	31	Adjusting	J99	22 6 0 0 00			22 5 0 0 00	5
6									6
7									7

P.O. 1

Determine entries in the Supplies Expense account.

Exercise 12-4 For the following Supplies Expense ledger account, determine the debits and credits for each amount posted to the account and briefly describe each transaction. The entry of December 9 involved the return of defective goods. The purchases of December 17 involved the Odom Company.

ACCOUNT **Supplies Expense**   ACCOUNT NO. **615**

	DATE		ITEM	POST. REF.	DEBIT	CREDIT	BALANCE DEBIT	BALANCE CREDIT	
1	20—								1
2	Jan.	1	Balance	✓			4 2 0 00		2
3	Apr.	6		CP42	1 6 0 00		5 8 0 00		3
4	May	31		CP44	9 0 00		6 7 0 00		4
5	Nov.	21		CP53	2 2 5 00		8 9 5 00		5
6	Dec.	9		CR41		4 2 00	8 5 3 00		6
7		17		J77	1 4 1 00		9 9 4 00		7
8		31	Adjusting	J78		2 2 0 00	7 7 4 00		8
9									9

P.O. 5

Place account balances in work sheet columns.

Exercise 12-5 Indicate the work sheet columns (Income Statement Debit, Income Statement Credit, Balance Sheet Debit, Balance Sheet Credit) in which the balances of the following accounts should appear:

a. F. Dexter, Drawing
b. Advertising Expense
c. Merchandise Inventory (ending)
d. Purchases Discounts
e. Unearned Fees
f. Sales Returns and Allowances
g. Accumulated Depreciation, Building
h. Income Summary
i. Fees Income
j. Prepaid Rent

P.O. 6

Journalize adjustments for expired insurance, unearned revenue, and depreciation.

Exercise 12-6 Journalize the required adjusting entries for the year ended December 31 for Mallory Dance Studio. Begin on journal page 42.

a. On June 1 of this year, $600 was paid for a one-year insurance policy.
b. On October 1 of this year, $160 was paid for four months of advertising.
c. As of December 31, the balance of the Unearned Membership Fees account is $12,400. Of this amount, $8,200 has now been earned.
d. Equipment purchased on April 1 of this year for $3,400 is expected to have a useful life of five years, with a trade-in value of $400. All other equipment has been fully depreciated. The straight-line method is used.
e. As of December 31, two days' wages at $240 per day had accrued.

P.O. 6

Journalize adjusting entries.

Exercise 12-7 On December 31, the end of the year, the accountant for *Fidelity Magazine* was called away suddenly because of an emergency. However, before leaving, the accountant jotted down a few notes pertaining to the adjustments. Record the necessary adjusting entries.

a. Subscriptions received in advance amounting to $136,400 were recorded as Unearned Subscriptions. At year-end, $90,200 has been earned.
b. Depreciation of equipment for the year is $18,600.
c. The amount of expired insurance for the year is $916.

d. The balance of Prepaid Rent is $2,800, representing four months' rent. Three months' rent has now expired.

e. Three days' salaries will be unpaid at the end of the year; total weekly (five days') salaries are $3,600.

P.O. 7

Journalize adjustment for merchandise inventory using the perpetual inventory system.

Exercise 12-8 On December 31, Bold Company took a physical count of its merchandise inventory. It operates under the perpetual inventory system. The physical count amounted to $178,400. The Merchandise Inventory account shows a balance of $180,200. Journalize the adjusting entry.

internet
LINKS TO ACCOUNTING

Let's go back to the publisher of *TV Guide* again and take a look at the unearned revenues from advance magazine subscriptions and publications sales. Look at page 70 (labeled F-12) of GEMSTAR-TV Guide International, Inc.'s 2005 annual report, found by going to **http://www.gemstartvguide.com.**

1. When does GEMSTAR-TV Guide International, Inc., recognize revenue from its magazine sales?
2. Where would you find GEMSTAR-TV Guide International, Inc.'s unearned (or deferred) revenue in the financial statements, and what was the account balance as of December 31, 2005?
3. How would GEMSTAR-TV Guide International, Inc., record the receipt of cash for these advance subscription sales?
4. How would GEMSTAR-TV Guide International, Inc., record the current portion of unearned subscription revenues when it becomes earned?

CONSIDER AND COMMUNICATE

You have a friend who is a seamstress specializing in western ensembles. She receives cash well in advance of the required date, often in the fiscal period prior to the date of delivery of the ensemble, not only to enable her to purchase material, but to cover her labor. She always debits Cash and credits Ensemble Income. First, explain to her why this entry violates the matching principle. Second, identify the classification of Unearned Revenue. Third, explain when the Unearned Revenue account is used.

WHAT'S WRONG WITH THIS PICTURE?

What would happen if a business spent the cash it had received in advance for services it promised to perform at a later date?

CRITICAL THINKING

On November 1, an exterior painting company received $3,420 for a paint job that will not be finished for a few months. As of December 31, which is the end of the fiscal period, $1,200 worth of painting will have been completed. The bookkeeper completed the following entries prior to leaving on vacation:

Cash		Painting Income		Unearned Painting Income	
11/1 3,420		12/31 2,220	11/1 3,420		12/31 2,220

The owner wants to get a bank loan by December 1. The bank requires interim financial statements to be submitted as of December 1. How will the bookkeeper's entries affect the accuracy of the interim balance sheet and income statements? What difference will the bookkeeper's methods make in the December 31 balance sheet and income statement?

A QUESTION OF ETHICS

The owner of a motorcycle shop allows his two sons to take motorcycles home to try them out on different types of ground because he believes that they need to be familiar with the products they sell. Sometimes the motorcycles are not returned to the store by the time the physical count of inventory takes place. Respond to this practice.

PROBLEM SET A

P.O. 4, 5

Problem 12-1A The trial balance of Swenson Company as of December 31, the end of its current fiscal year, is as follows:

Swenson Company
Trial Balance
December 31, 20—

	ACCOUNT NAME	TRIAL BALANCE DEBIT	TRIAL BALANCE CREDIT
1	Cash	9 5 6 3 92	
2	Merchandise Inventory	63 5 2 2 84	
3	Prepaid Insurance	9 6 0 00	
4	Store Equipment	37 4 8 0 00	
5	Accumulated Depreciation, Store Equipment		24 3 2 0 00
6	Accounts Payable		14 5 7 8 80
7	Sales Tax Payable		2 4 3 36
8	D. N. Swenson, Capital		55 6 3 0 00
9	D. N. Swenson, Drawing	29 4 4 0 00	
10	Sales		179 0 3 6 74
11	Sales Returns and Allowances	1 4 4 3 04	
12	Purchases	76 3 6 8 46	
13	Purchases Returns and Allowances		1 8 7 8 94
14	Purchases Discounts		1 4 9 7 90
15	Freight In	4 8 7 5 00	
16	Salary Expense	36 6 5 8 80	
17	Rent Expense	14 4 0 0 00	
18	Store Supplies Expense	1 4 4 1 12	
19	Miscellaneous Expense	1 0 3 2 56	
20		277 1 8 5 74	277 1 8 5 74
21			

Here are the data for the adjustments.

a–b. Merchandise Inventory at December 31, $65,945.36.
c. Store supplies inventory, $401.50.
d. Insurance expired, $570.
e. Salaries accrued, $652.
f. Depreciation of store equipment, $3,990.

Check Figure

Net income, $43,806.62

Instructions

Complete the work sheet after entering the account names and balances onto the work sheet.

P.O. 4,5,6

Problem 12-2A The balances of the ledger accounts of Pedigo Furniture as of December 31, the end of its fiscal year, are as follows:

Cash	$ 10,592
Accounts Receivable	43,962
Merchandise Inventory	120,838
Prepaid Insurance	2,628
Store Equipment	35,924
Accumulated Depreciation, Store Equipment	29,420
Office Equipment	10,436
Accumulated Depreciation, Office Equipment	1,720
Notes Payable	5,000
Accounts Payable	29,822
Unearned Rent	3,200
P. Pedigo, Capital	120,532
P. Pedigo, Drawing	29,000
Sales	653,000
Sales Returns and Allowances	9,748
Purchases	519,374
Purchases Returns and Allowances	12,440
Purchases Discounts	8,634
Freight In	24,724
Wages Expense	54,200
Supplies Expense	1,570
Interest Expense	772

Data for the adjustments are as follows:

a–b. Merchandise Inventory at December 31, $102,765.
c. Wages accrued at December 31, $1,834.
d. Supplies inventory at December 31, $645.
e. Depreciation of store equipment, $5,782.
f. Depreciation of office equipment, $1,791.
g. Insurance expired during the year, $845.
h. Rent earned, $2,500.

Check Figure

Net income, $38,506

Instructions

1. Complete the work sheet after entering the account names and balances onto the work sheet.
2. Journalize the adjusting entries.

P.O. 4,5,6

Problem 12-3A The accounts in the ledger of Mickey's Mountain Shop, with the balances as of December 31, the end of its fiscal year, are as follows:

Cash	$ 11,600
Accounts Receivable	3,040
Merchandise Inventory	119,600
Prepaid Insurance	3,940
Land	20,000
Building	88,000
Accumulated Depreciation, Building	37,600
Store Equipment	57,100
Accumulated Depreciation, Store Equipment	12,600
Notes Payable	11,800
Accounts Payable	18,260
Sales Tax Payable	4,940
B. Mickey, Capital	171,000
B. Mickey, Drawing	54,000
Sales	469,000
Sales Returns and Allowances	7,700
Purchases	285,850
Purchases Returns and Allowances	5,900
Purchases Discounts	5,800
Freight In	17,180
Salary Expense	53,500
Advertising Expense	5,150
Utilities Expense	6,610
Store Supplies Expense	1,620
Taxes Expense	300
Miscellaneous Expense	900
Interest Expense	810

Data for the adjustments are as follows:

a–b. Merchandise Inventory at December 31, $125,700.
c. Store supplies inventory at December 31, $440.
d. Depreciation of building, $3,200.
e. Depreciation of store equipment, $3,400.
f. Salaries accrued at December 31, $1,450.
g. Insurance expired during the year, $2,480.

Check Figure

Net income, $97,090

Instructions

1. Complete the work sheet after entering the account names and balances onto the work sheet.
2. Journalize the adjusting entries.

Instructions for General Ledger Software

1. Record the adjusting entries in the general journal.
2. Print the journal.
3. Post the general journal amounts to the general ledger.
4. Print a trial balance.
5. Print the income statement, statement of owner's equity, and balance sheet.

P.O. 4,5,6

Problem 12-4A A portion of the work sheet of Hurst Company for the year ended December 31 is as follows:

	ACCOUNT NAME	INCOME STATEMENT DEBIT	INCOME STATEMENT CREDIT	BALANCE SHEET DEBIT	BALANCE SHEET CREDIT	
1	Cash			9 3 4 0 00		1
2	Merchandise Inventory			76 9 4 0 00		2
3	Prepaid Insurance			2 4 0 00		3
4	Store Equipment			39 2 8 0 00		4
5	Accumulated Depreciation, Store Equipment				26 2 2 0 00	5
6	Accounts Payable				14 6 0 0 00	6
7	P. R. Hurst, Capital				68 9 4 0 00	7
8	P. R. Hurst, Drawing			27 6 0 0 00		8
9	Sales		173 4 2 0 00			9
10	Sales Returns and Allowances	1 5 2 0 00				10
11	Purchases	82 3 1 2 00				11
12	Purchases Returns and Allowances		9 4 0 00			12
13	Purchases Discounts		1 6 0 0 00			13
14	Freight In	1 9 4 8 00				14
15	Salary Expense	37 5 6 0 00				15
16	Rent Expense	14 8 0 0 00				16
17	Supplies Expense	9 4 4 00				17
18						18
19	Income Summary	65 6 8 0 00	76 9 4 0 00			19
20	Depreciation Expense, Store Equipment	4 0 4 0 00				20
21	Insurance Expense	7 6 0 00				21
22	Supplies			2 5 6 00		22
23	Salaries Payable				5 6 0 00	23
24		209 5 6 4 00	252 9 0 0 00	153 6 5 6 00	110 3 2 0 00	24

Check Figure

Salaries accrued, $560

Instructions

1. Determine the entries that appeared in the Adjustments columns and present them in general journal form.
2. Determine the net income for the year.
3. What is the amount of the ending capital?

PROBLEM SET B

P.O. 4,5

Problem 12-1B The trial balance of Hakala Company as of December 31, the end of its current fiscal year, is on the next page.

Here are the data for the adjustments:

a–b. Merchandise Inventory at December 31, $65,982.90.
c. Store supplies inventory, $510.30.
d. Insurance expired, $853.
e. Salaries accrued, $675.60.
f. Depreciation of store equipment, $3,810.

Hakala Company
Trial Balance
December 31, 20—

	ACCOUNT NAME	TRIAL BALANCE DEBIT	TRIAL BALANCE CREDIT
1	Cash	9 1 3 6 54	
2	Merchandise Inventory	62 8 5 4 82	
3	Prepaid Insurance	1 0 2 0 00	
4	Store Equipment	37 3 4 0 00	
5	Accumulated Depreciation, Store Equipment		24 8 3 6 00
6	Accounts Payable		14 2 8 6 96
7	Sales Tax Payable		2 4 6 98
8	R. P. Hakala, Capital		55 0 5 9 84
9	R. P. Hakala, Drawing	29 0 0 0 00	
10	Sales		177 9 6 6 34
11	Sales Returns and Allowances	1 4 9 3 84	
12	Purchases	78 8 0 0 84	
13	Purchases Returns and Allowances		1 8 5 7 82
14	Purchases Discounts		1 5 0 3 64
15	Freight In	2 6 3 7 00	
16	Salary Expense	36 5 6 8 86	
17	Rent Expense	14 4 0 0 00	
18	Store Supplies Expense	1 4 6 6 84	
19	Miscellaneous Expense	1 0 3 8 84	
20		275 7 5 7 58	275 7 5 7 58

Check Figure

Net income, $43,221.36

P.O. 4,5,6

Instructions

Complete the work sheet after entering the account names and balances onto the work sheet.

Problem 12-2B The balances of the ledger accounts of Bolston Home Center as of June 30, the end of its fiscal year, are as follows:

Cash	$ 13,775
Accounts Receivable	52,300
Merchandise Inventory	71,900
Prepaid Insurance	2,080
Store Equipment	25,790
Accumulated Depreciation, Store Equipment	15,200
Office Equipment	10,600
Accumulated Depreciation, Office Equipment	5,815
Notes Payable	4,600
Accounts Payable	41,900
Unearned Rent	2,700
F. C. Bolston, Capital	95,340
F. C. Bolston, Drawing	24,000
Sales	465,500
Sales Returns and Allowances	2,210
Purchases	367,010
Purchases Returns and Allowances	6,170
Purchases Discounts	3,280

Freight In	$22,490
Salary Expense	45,250
Supplies Expense	1,470
Interest Expense	1,630

Here are the data for the adjustments:

a–b. Merchandise Inventory at June 30, $115,800.
 c. Salaries accrued at June 30, $1,560.
 d. Insurance expired during the year, $800.
 e. Supplies inventory at June 30, $385.
 f. Depreciation of store equipment, $3,240.
 g. Depreciation of office equipment, $1,870.
 h. Rent earned, $2,490.

Check Figure

Net income, $74,195

Instructions

1. Complete the work sheet after entering the account names and balances onto the work sheet.
2. Journalize the adjusting entries.

P.O. 4,5,6

Problem 12-3B Here are the accounts in the ledger of VonBehren's Jewel Box, with the balances as of December 31, the end of its fiscal year.

Cash	$ 12,280
Accounts Receivable	2,554
Merchandise Inventory	114,100
Prepaid Insurance	1,785
Land	16,000
Building	77,000
Accumulated Depreciation, Building	28,340
Store Equipment	76,490
Accumulated Depreciation, Store Equipment	18,160
Accounts Payable	13,070
Sales Tax Payable	2,784
Mortgage Payable	44,860
L. VonBehren, Capital	150,830
L. VonBehren, Drawing	46,500
Sales	380,254
Sales Returns and Allowances	3,388
Purchases	251,768
Purchases Returns and Allowances	2,760
Purchases Discounts	4,410
Freight In	11,200
Salary Expense	24,400
Advertising Expense	1,426
Store Supplies Expense	1,784
Utilities Expense	1,658
Taxes Expense	162
Miscellaneous Expense	613
Interest Expense	2,360

Here are the data for the adjustments.

a–b. Merchandise Inventory at December 31, $110,130.
c. Insurance expired during the year, $1,354.
d. Depreciation of building, $4,300.
e. Depreciation of store equipment, $7,580.
f. Salaries accrued at December 31, $560.
g. Store supplies inventory at December 31, $439.

Check Figure

Net income, $71,340

Instructions

1. Complete the work sheet after entering the account names and balances onto the work sheet.
2. Journalize the adjusting entries.

Instructions for General Ledger Software

1. Record the adjusting entries in the general journal.
2. Print the journal.
3. Post the general journal amounts to the general ledger.
4. Print a trial balance.
5. Print the income statement, statement of owner's equity, and balance sheet.

P.O. 4,5,6

Problem 12-4B A portion of the work sheet of Susan's Flowers for the year ended December 31 appears below.

	ACCOUNT NAME	INCOME STATEMENT DEBIT	INCOME STATEMENT CREDIT	BALANCE SHEET DEBIT	BALANCE SHEET CREDIT	
1	Cash			7 7 3 6 00		1
2	Merchandise Inventory			74 2 9 8 00		2
3	Prepaid Insurance			2 5 0 00		3
4	Store Equipment			37 9 6 0 00		4
5	Accumulated Depreciation, Store Equipment				29 4 4 0 00	5
6	Accounts Payable				13 7 6 0 00	6
7	S. R. Ramirez, Capital				75 1 4 2 00	7
8	S. R. Ramirez, Drawing			30 8 0 0 00		8
9	Sales		171 8 1 6 00			9
10	Sales Returns and Allowances	1 4 3 4 00				10
11	Purchases	85 9 3 4 00				11
12	Purchases Returns and Allowances		9 6 4 00			12
13	Purchases Discounts		1 6 3 6 00			13
14	Freight In	2 6 5 8 00				14
15	Salary Expense	37 8 5 2 00				15
16	Rent Expense	14 4 0 0 00				16
17	Supplies Expense	8 8 4 00				17
18						18
19	Income Summary	68 2 2 8 00	74 2 9 8 00			19
20	Depreciation Expense, Store Equipment	4 3 6 0 00				20
21	Insurance Expense	5 5 2 00				21
22	Supplies			2 9 8 00		22
23	Salaries Payable				5 8 8 00	23
24		216 3 0 2 00	248 7 1 4 00	151 3 4 2 00	118 9 3 0 00	24

Check Figure

Salaries accrued, $588

Instructions

1. Determine the entries that appeared in the Adjustments columns and present them in general journal form.
2. Determine the net income for the year.
3. What is the amount of the ending capital?

The Computer Clinic

What additional accounts need to be adjusted?

Work Sheet and Adjusting Entries

Two months (July and August) have passed since Ms. Valli has seen the financial statements for All About You Spa. It is time to begin their preparation. Several accounts need adjusting. These include the accounts you adjusted in Chapter 4 as well as any accounts involved with merchandising.

Following is the information you will need to make adjustments that need to be journalized whether you are constructing a work sheet on paper or in Excel or you are journalizing the adjustments directly into your general ledger program.

Work Sheet and Adjusting Entry Information

Complete the work sheet using the following information. If you are using a general ledger software package, enter the adjustments directly into the general journal and post. The preadjusted trial balance for August 31 is as follows:

Check Figures

Adjustments total	$13,961.43
Income Statement Debit total	47,364.33
Income Statement Credit total	61,120.65
Balance Sheet Debit total	86,259.70
Balance Sheet Credit total	72,503.38
Net Income	13,756.32

All About You Spa
Trial Balance
August 31, 20 —

ACCOUNT NAME	DEBIT	CREDIT
Cash	4 0 3 6 1 74	
Accounts Receivable	7 1 9 6 63	
Prepaid Insurance	8 0 0 00	
Spa Equipment	1 8 0 8 3 00	
Accumulated Depreciation, Spa Equipment		6 4 88
Office Equipment	1 5 7 0 00	
Accumulated Depreciation, Office Equipment		1 0 00
Accounts Payable		2 0 3 9 3 00
Sales Tax Payable		2 0 0 1 12
A. Valli, Capital		4 9 8 8 4 62
A. Valli, Drawing	5 0 0 0 00	
Income from Services		3 0 5 2 6 00
Merchandise Sales		1 7 3 6 1 65
Sales Returns and Allowances	8 8 00	
Purchases	2 4 1 0 1 00	
Purchases Returns and Allowances		1 2 3 00
Freight In	9 9 2 00	
Wages Expense	1 6 2 5 0 00	
Rent Expense	3 3 0 0 00	
Office Supplies Expense	1 1 8 00	
Spa Supplies Expense	5 3 5 00	
Laundry Expense	1 7 9 00	
Advertising Expense	4 5 5 00	
Utilities Expense	9 6 3 00	
Miscellaneous Expense	3 7 1 90	
	12 0 3 6 4 27	12 0 3 6 4 27

469

Merchandise Inventory Adjustment (a) and (b)

Add a new account, Merchandise Inventory 115, to the chart of accounts. The August 31 pre-adjustment balance in that account is zero. But you know that merchandise has been purchased for resale and that you have sold merchandise. In addition, there is possible inventory shrinkage for several reasons: breakage, theft, misplacement, use as samples, etc. A physical count was taken, and the inventory was valued at $13,110.

> The inventory adjustment takes two entries.

Recall that the merchandise inventory adjustment under the periodic inventory system is a two-step adjustment.

First step (a): Get rid of the old inventory amount on the pre-adjusted trial balance (zero) by crediting Merchandise Inventory and debiting Income Summary. This may look strange on the work sheet, but it is probably the only time Merchandise Inventory would be zero. It is appropriate, but not required, to journalize and post this memo entry as a kind of placeholder so that anyone looking at the books can see exactly how it was handled.

Second step (b): Enter the latest inventory count by debiting Merchandise Inventory and crediting Income Summary.

Supplies Adjustments (c) and (d)

> Remember, you must determine the amount of supplies left and then make the adjustment.

A physical count has been taken of the two supplies accounts. The values of the remaining inventories of supplies are:

Office Supplies	$ 75.00
Spa Supplies	345.00

You will need to make two adjusting entries on the work sheet and then journalize and post them. Add two new accounts to the chart of accounts: Spa Supplies 113 and Office Supplies 114.

Prepaid Insurance Adjustment (e)

> Remember, do *not* do any calculations; the amount given *is* the amount of the adjustment.

A review of the insurance records determined that $281.67 in liability insurance coverage had been used during the last two months.

Depreciation Adjustments (f) and (g)

> There are several types of depreciation methods—all of them are an estimate of the loss of usefulness—that GAAP and the IRS allow a business to write off against its revenue.

Estimated depreciation amounts for the two equipment accounts are:

Spa Equipment	$129.76
Office Equipment	20.00

Remember to credit the accumulated depreciation account (a contra asset), *not* the equipment accounts.

Wages Expense/Wages Payable Adjustment

There is no need for a Wages Expense/Wages Payable adjustment because the end of the fiscal period did not come in the middle of a pay period. (The spa was closed on August 31.)

Completing the Adjustment Process

1. Journalize and post the adjusting entries in the general journal, page 11.
2. Print a copy of the general journal, page 11.
3. Print a copy of the general ledger.

You will prepare financial statements in Chapter 13 *before* making the closing entries. Do not close the accounts now.

13

Financial Statements, Closing Entries, and Reversing Entries

Barnes & Noble, acclaimed to be the world's largest bookseller and a *Fortune 500* company, operates 799 bookstores in fifty states. For the fourth year in a row, the company is the nation's top retail brand for quality, according to the EquiTrend® Brand Study. Barnes & Noble is also the Internet's largest bookstore. Through expanded Internet sales, the company ranks among the top five Web properties in the world at Barnes & Noble.com. In this chapter you will learn about two measures, working capital and current ratio, used to help determine whether a company has sufficient capital to operate and to pay its debts. You can find the figures you need to compute Barnes & Noble's working capital and current ratio in its 2005 annual report on the Web at **http://www .barnesandnoble.com.** Click on Investor Relations at the bottom of the screen and then select the link for the annual reports.

Performance Objectives

After you have completed this chapter, you will be able to do the following:

1. Prepare a classified income statement for a merchandising firm.

2. Prepare a classified balance sheet for any type of business.

3. Compute working capital and current ratio.

4. Journalize the closing entries for a merchandising firm.

5. Determine which adjusting entries can be reversed, and journalize the reversing entries.

This chapter again demonstrates how to prepare financial statements directly from a work sheet. We also explain the functions of closing entries and reversing entries as means of completing the accounting cycle. Finally, we look at the financial statements in their entirety, and explain their various subdivisions.

First, here is the chart of accounts for Rainier Plumbing Supply.

FYI

Accountants sometimes number contra accounts as subaccounts. For example, Accumulated Depreciation, Building, is 122.1, Sales Returns and Allowances is 411.1, Sales Discounts is 411.2, Purchases Returns and Allowances is 511.1, and so on.

Assets (100–199)

111 Cash
112 Notes Receivable
113 Accounts Receivable
114 Merchandise Inventory
115 Supplies
116 Prepaid Insurance
121 Land
122 Building
123 Accumulated Depreciation, Building
124 Equipment
125 Accumulated Depreciation, Equipment

Liabilities (200–299)

211 Notes Payable
212 Accounts Payable
213 Wages Payable
217 Unearned Course Fees
221 Mortgage Payable

Owner's Equity (300–399)

311 C. F. Rainier, Capital
312 C. F. Rainier, Drawing
313 Income Summary

Revenue (400–499)

411 Sales
412 Sales Returns and Allowances
413 Sales Discounts
421 Course Fees Income
422 Interest Income

Cost of Goods Sold (500–599)

511 Purchases
512 Purchases Returns and Allowances
513 Purchases Discounts
514 Freight In

Expenses (600–699)

611 Wages Expense
622 Supplies Expense
623 Insurance Expense
624 Depreciation Expense, Building
625 Depreciation Expense, Equipment
626 Taxes Expense
634 Interest Expense

THE INCOME STATEMENT

OBJECTIVE 1

Prepare a classified income statement for a merchandising firm.

As you know, the work sheet is merely a tool used by accountants to prepare the financial statements. In Figure 1, shown on page 474, we present the part of the work sheet for Rainier Plumbing Supply that includes the Income Statement columns. Of course, **each of the amounts that appear in the Income Statement columns of the work sheet will also be used in the income statement.** Notice that the amounts for the beginning and ending merchandise inventory appear separately on the Income Summary line. Figure 2 on page 475 shows the entire income statement. Pause for a while and look it over carefully; then we will break it down into its components.

The income statement follows a logical pattern that is much the same for any type of merchandising business. The ability to interpret the income statement and extract parts from it is very useful when gathering information for decisions. To realize the full value of an income statement, however, you need to know the basic format of an income statement. Let's look at the statement section by section.

Net Sales	$252,460
− Cost of Goods Sold	88,720
Gross Profit	$163,740
− Operating Expenses	59,028
Income from Operations	$104,712

Rainier Plumbing Supply
Work Sheet
For Year Ended December 31, 20—

#	ACCOUNT NAME	TRIAL BALANCE DEBIT	TRIAL BALANCE CREDIT	ADJUSTMENTS DEBIT	ADJUSTMENTS CREDIT	INCOME STATEMENT DEBIT	INCOME STATEMENT CREDIT
1	Cash	24 1 5 4 00					
2	Notes Receivable	4 0 0 0 00					
3	Accounts Receivable	29 4 4 6 00					
4	Merchandise Inventory	67 0 0 0 00		(b) 65 8 0 0 00	(a) 67 0 0 0 00		
5	Prepaid Insurance	9 6 0 00			(e) 3 2 0 00		
6	Land	120 1 0 0 00					
7	Building	130 0 0 0 00					
8	Accumulated Depr.,						
9	Building		52 0 0 0 00		(g) 4 0 0 0 00		
10	Equipment	33 6 0 0 00					
11	Accumulated Depr.,						
12	Equipment		16 4 0 0 00		(f) 4 8 0 0 00		
13	Notes Payable		36 4 0 0 00				
14	Accounts Payable		3 0 0 0 00				
15	Unearned Course Fees		1 2 0 0 00	(c) 8 0 0 00			
16	Mortgage Payable		8 0 0 0 00				
17	C. F. Rainier, Capital		253 6 7 4 00				
18	C. F. Rainier, Drawing	76 9 0 0 00					
19	Sales		255 1 8 0 00				255 1 8 0 00
20	Sales Returns and						
21	Allowances	8 4 0 00				8 4 0 00	
22	Sales Discounts	1 8 8 0 00				1 8 8 0 00	
23	Interest Income		1 2 0 00				1 2 0 00
24	Purchases	87 1 4 0 00				87 1 4 0 00	
25	Purchases Returns						
26	and Allowances		8 3 2 00				8 3 2 00
27	Purchases Discounts		1 2 4 8 00				1 2 4 8 00
28	Freight In	2 4 6 0 00				2 4 6 0 00	
29	Wages Expense	45 8 0 0 00		(h) 1 1 2 0 00		46 9 2 0 00	
30	Supplies Expense	1 4 4 0 00			(d) 4 1 2 00	1 0 2 8 00	
31	Taxes Expense	1 9 6 0 00				1 9 6 0 00	
32	Interest Expense	3 7 4 00				3 7 4 00	
33		628 0 5 4 00	628 0 5 4 00				
34	Income Summary			(a) 67 0 0 0 00	(b) 65 8 0 0 00	67 0 0 0 00	65 8 0 0 00
35	Course Fees Income				(c) 8 0 0 00		8 0 0 00
36	Supplies			(d) 4 1 2 00			
37	Insurance Expense			(e) 3 2 0 00		3 2 0 00	
38	Depreciation Expense,						
39	Equipment			(f) 4 8 0 0 00		4 8 0 0 00	
40	Depreciation Expense,						
41	Building			(g) 4 0 0 0 00		4 0 0 0 00	
42	Wages Payable				(h) 1 1 2 0 00		
43				144 2 5 2 00	144 2 5 2 00	218 7 2 2 00	323 9 8 0 00
44	Net Income					105 2 5 8 00	
45						323 9 8 0 00	323 9 8 0 00
46							

FIGURE 1

Rainier Plumbing Supply
Income Statement
For Year Ended December 31, 20—

Revenue from Sales:			
Sales		$255 180 00	
Less: Sales Returns and Allowances	$ 840 00		
Sales Discounts	1 880 00	2 720 00	
Net Sales			$252 460 00
Cost of Goods Sold:			
Merchandise Inventory, January 1, 20—		$ 67 000 00	
Purchases	$87 140 00		
Less: Purchases Returns and			
Allowances $ 832.00			
Purchases Discounts 1,248.00	2 080 00		
Net Purchases	$85 060 00		
Add Freight In	2 460 00		
Delivered Cost of Purchases		87 520 00	
Cost of Goods Available for Sale		$154 520 00	
Less Merchandise Inventory, December 31, 20—		65 800 00	
Cost of Goods Sold			88 720 00
Gross Profit			$163 740 00
Operating Expenses:			
Wages Expense		$ 46 920 00	
Supplies Expense		1 028 00	
Insurance Expense		320 00	
Depreciation Expense, Equipment		4 800 00	
Depreciation Expense, Building		4 000 00	
Taxes Expense		1 960 00	
Total Operating Expenses			59 028 00
Income from Operations			$104 712 00
Other Income:			
Course Fees Income		$ 800 00	
Interest Income		120 00	
Total Other Income		$ 920 00	
Other Expenses:			
Interest Expense		374 00	546 00
Net Income			$105 258 00

FIGURE 2

To illustrate the concepts of **gross** and **net,** here is an example of a simple single-sale transaction.

Several years ago, Della Reyes bought an antique table at a second-hand store for $900. She sold the table for $1,700. She advertised it in the daily newspaper at a cost of $50. How much did she make as clear profit?

Sale of Table	$1,700
Less Cost of Table	900
Gross Profit	$ 800
Less Advertising Expense	50
Net Income or Net Profit (gain on the sale)	$ 750

Gross Profit is the profit on the sale of the table before any expenses have been deducted; in this case, it is $800. **Net Income**, or **Net Profit**, is the final or clear profit after all expenses have been deducted. In a single-sale situation such as this, we refer to the final outcome as the net profit. But for a business that has many sales and expenses, most accountants prefer the term *net income*. Regardless of which word you use, *net* refers to clear profit—after all expenses have been deducted.

Revenue from Sales

Now let's look at the Revenue from Sales section of the income statement for Rainier Plumbing Supply:

Revenue from Sales:			
Sales		$255 1 8 0 00	
Less: Sales Returns and Allowances	$ 8 4 0 00		
Sales Discounts	1 8 8 0 00	2 7 2 0 00	
Net Sales			$252 4 6 0 00

When we introduced Sales Returns and Allowances and Sales Discounts, we treated them as deductions from Sales. You can see that on the income statement, they are deducted from Sales to give us **Net Sales**. Note that we record these items in the same order in which they appear in the ledger.

REMEMBER!

Returns and Allowances (Sales or Purchases) is listed on one line, and Discounts (Sales or Purchases) is listed below.

Cost of Goods Sold

The section of the income statement that requires the greatest amount of concentration is the **Cost of Goods Sold** section, where the cost of the goods we sold is computed. Let's repeat it in its entirety:

Cost of Goods Sold:				
Merchandise Inventory, January 1, 20—			$ 67 0 0 0 00	
Purchases		$87 1 4 0 00		
Less: Purchases Returns and				
Allowances	$ 832.00			
Purchases Discounts	1,248.00	2 0 8 0 00		
Net Purchases		$85 0 6 0 00		
Add Freight In		2 4 6 0 00		
Delivered Cost of Purchases			87 5 2 0 00	
Cost of Goods Available for Sale			$154 5 2 0 00	
Less Merchandise Inventory, December 31, 20—			65 8 0 0 00	
Cost of Goods Sold				$88 7 2 0 00

First, let's look closely at the Purchases section.

Purchases		$87	1	4	0	00							
Less: Purchases Returns													
and Allowances	$ 832.00												
Purchases Discounts	1,248.00	2	0	8	0	00							
Net Purchases		$85	0	6	0	00							
Add Freight In		2	4	6	0	00							
Delivered Cost of Purchases							$87	5	2	0	00		

Note the parallel to the Revenue from Sales section. To arrive at **Net Purchases**, we deduct the sum of Purchases Returns and Allowances and Purchases Discounts from Purchases. To complete the Purchases section we add Freight In to Net Purchases to get **Delivered Cost of Purchases**.

Now let's look at the full Cost of Goods Sold section. You might think of Cost of Goods Sold like this:

Amount we started with (beginning inventory)	$ 67,000
+ Net amount we purchased, including freight charges	87,520
Total amount that could have been sold (available)	$154,520
− Amount left over (ending inventory)	65,800
Cost of the goods that were actually sold	$ 88,720

Here's the Cost of Goods Sold expressed in proper wording.

Merchandise Inventory, January 1, 20—	$ 67,000
+ Delivered Cost of Purchases	87,520
Cost of Goods Available for Sale	$154,520
− Merchandise Inventory, December 31, 20—	65,800
Cost of Goods Sold	$ 88,720

Operating Expenses

Operating expenses, as the name implies, are the regular expenses of doing business. We list the accounts and their respective balances in the order in which they appear in the ledger.

Many firms use subclassifications of operating expenses, such as the following:

1. **Selling Expenses** Any expenses directly connected with the selling activity, such as

   - Sales Salary Expense
   - Sales Commissions Expense
   - Advertising Expense
   - Store Supplies Expense
   - Delivery Expense
   - Depreciation Expense, Store Equipment

2. **General Expenses** Any expenses related to the office or administration, or any expense that cannot be directly connected with a selling activity:

   - Office Salary Expense
   - Taxes Expense

FYI

In preparing the income statement, classifying expense accounts as selling expenses or general expenses is a matter of judgment. The only reason we're not using this breakdown here is that we're trying to keep the number of accounts to a basic few.

- Depreciation Expense, Office Equipment
- Rent Expense
- Insurance Expense
- Office Supplies Expense

If the Cash Short and Over account has a debit balance (net shortage), the balance is added to and reported as Miscellaneous General Expense. Conversely, if the Cash Short and Over account has a credit balance (net overage), the balance is added to and reported as Miscellaneous Income, which is classified as Other Income.

Income from Operations

Now let's repeat the skeleton outline:

Net Sales
− Cost of Goods Sold

Gross Profit
− Operating Expenses

Income from Operations

If Operating Expenses are the regular, recurring expenses of doing business, then Income from Operations should be the regular or recurring income from normal business operations. When you compare the results of operations over a number of years, Income from Operations is the figure to use as a basis for comparison.

Other Income and Other Expenses

The Other Income classification, as the name implies, includes any revenue account other than Revenue from Sales. What we are trying to do is to isolate Sales at the top of the income statement as the major revenue account, so that the Gross Profit figure represents the profit made on the sale of merchandise *only*. Additional accounts that may appear under the heading of Other Income are Rent Income (the firm is subletting part of its premises), Interest Income (the firm holds an interest-bearing note or contract), Gain on Disposal of Property and Equipment (the firm makes a profit on the sale of property and equipment), and Miscellaneous Income (the firm has an overage recorded in the Cash Short and Over account).

The classification Other Expenses records various nonoperating expenses, such as Interest Expense or Loss on Disposal of Property and Equipment.

THE STATEMENT OF OWNER'S EQUITY AND THE BALANCE SHEET

REMEMBER!

Net income appears on both the income statement and the statement of owner's equity.

Figure 3 is a partial work sheet for Rainier Plumbing Supply. Here again we find that **every figure in the Balance Sheet columns of the work sheet is used in either the statement of owner's equity or the balance sheet.**

Preparation of the financial statements follows the same order we presented before: first, the income statement; second, the statement of owner's equity; third, the balance sheet. The statement of owner's equity shows why the balance of the Capital account has changed from the beginning of the

Rainier Plumbing Supply
Work Sheet
For Year Ended December 31, 20—

	ACCOUNT NAME	TRIAL BALANCE DEBIT	TRIAL BALANCE CREDIT	ADJUSTMENTS DEBIT	ADJUSTMENTS CREDIT	BALANCE SHEET DEBIT	BALANCE SHEET CREDIT	
1	Cash	24 1 5 4 00				24 1 5 4 00		1
2	Notes Receivable	4 0 0 0 00				4 0 0 0 00		2
3	Accounts Receiv.	29 4 4 6 00				29 4 4 6 00		3
4	Merchandise Inven.	67 0 0 0 00		(b) 65 8 0 0 00	(a) 67 0 0 0 00	65 8 0 0 00		4
5	Prepaid Insurance	9 6 0 00			(e) 3 2 0 00	6 4 0 00		5
6	Land	120 1 0 0 00				120 1 0 0 00		6
7	Building	130 0 0 0 00				130 0 0 0 00		7
8	Accum. Depr., Build.		52 0 0 0 00		(g) 4 0 0 0 00		56 0 0 0 00	8
9	Equipment	33 6 0 0 00				33 6 0 0 00		9
10	Accum. Depr., Equip.		16 4 0 0 00		(f) 4 8 0 0 00		21 2 0 0 00	10
11	Notes Payable		36 4 0 0 00				36 4 0 0 00	11
12	Accounts Payable		3 0 0 0 00				3 0 0 0 00	12
13	Unearn. Course Fees		1 2 0 0 00	(c) 8 0 0 00			4 0 0 00	13
14	Mortgage Payable		8 0 0 0 00				8 0 0 0 00	14
15	C. F. Rainier,							15
16	Capital		253 6 7 4 00				253 6 7 4 00	16
17	C. F. Rainier, Draw.	76 9 0 0 00				76 9 0 0 00		17
18	Sales		255 1 8 0 00					18
19	Sales Returns and							19
20	Allowances	8 4 0 00						20
21	Sales Discounts	1 8 8 0 00						21
22	Interest Income		1 2 0 00					22
23	Purchases	87 1 4 0 00						23
24	Purchases Returns							24
25	and Allowances		8 3 2 00					25
26	Purchases Discounts		1 2 4 8 00					26
27	Freight In	2 4 6 0 00						27
28	Wages Expense	45 8 0 0 00		(h) 1 1 2 0 00				28
29	Supplies Expense	1 4 4 0 00			(d) 4 1 2 00			29
30	Taxes Expense	1 9 6 0 00						30
31	Interest Expense	3 7 4 00						31
32		628 0 5 4 00	628 0 5 4 00					32
33	Income Summary			(a) 67 0 0 0 00	(b) 65 8 0 0 00			33
34	Course Fees Income				(c) 8 0 0 00			34
35	Supplies			(d) 4 1 2 00		4 1 2 00		35
36	Insurance Expense			(e) 3 2 0 00				36
37	Depr. Expense,							37
38	Equipment			(f) 4 8 0 0 00				38
39	Depr. Expense,							39
40	Building			(g) 4 0 0 0 00				40
41	Wages Payable				(h) 1 1 2 0 00		1 1 2 0 00	41
42				144 2 5 2 00	144 2 5 2 00	485 0 5 2 00	379 7 9 4 00	42
43	Net Income						105 2 5 8 00	43
44						485 0 5 2 00	485 0 5 2 00	44
45								45

FIGURE 3

fiscal period to the end of it. In preparing the statement of owner's equity, always look into the ledger for the owner's Capital account to find any changes, such as additional investments, made during the year.

In Figure 4 we observe the balance of C. F. Rainier, Capital, listed on the work sheet as $253,674. We note from the ledger account a credit of $8,000 representing an additional investment. Therefore, the beginning balance of C. F. Rainier, Capital, was $245,674 ($253,674 − $8,000).

REMEMBER!

The columns *do not* represent debit or credit columns. The columns are for making computations and listing totals.

FIGURE 4

Rainier Plumbing Supply Statement of Owner's Equity For Year Ended December 31, 20—			
C. F. Rainier, Capital, January 1, 20—			$ 245 6 7 4 00
Additional Investment, August 26, 20—			8 0 0 0 00
Total Investment			$ 253 6 7 4 00
Net Income for the Year		$ 105 2 5 8 00	
Less Withdrawals for the Year		76 9 0 0 00	
Increase in Capital			28 3 5 8 00
C. F. Rainier, Capital, December 31, 20—			$ 282 0 3 2 00

BALANCE SHEET CLASSIFICATIONS

OBJECTIVE 2

Prepare a classified balance sheet for any type of business.

Balance sheet classifications are generally uniform for all types of business enterprises. You are strongly urged to take the time to learn the following definitions of the classifications and the order of accounts within them. As you read, refer to Figure 5.

Current Assets

FYI

Some companies are so successful that they accumulate cash from earnings that is not needed to pay current obligations. Rather than leaving the cash in a bank account, companies may prefer to invest it in short-term government or corporate notes or bonds. These are called marketable securities. On the balance sheet, Marketable Securities is a separate account listed just below Cash.

Current Assets consist of cash and any other assets or resources that are expected to be realized in cash or to be sold or consumed during the normal operating cycle of the business (or one year, if the normal operating cycle is less than twelve months).

Accountants list current assets in the order of their convertibility into cash—in other words, their **liquidity**. (If you've got an asset such as a car or a stereo and you sell it quickly and turn it into cash, you are said to be turning it into a *liquid* state.) If the first four accounts shown under Current Assets in Figure 5 are present, they are always recorded in the same order: (1) Cash, (2) Notes Receivable, (3) Accounts Receivable, and (4) Merchandise Inventory.

Notes Receivable (current) are short-term (one year or less) promissory notes (promise-to-pay notes) held by the firm. A note is generally received from a customer as a substitute for a charge account.

Prepaid Insurance and Supplies are considered prepaid items that will be used up or will expire within the following operating cycle or year. Generally, these prepaid items are not converted into cash and that's why they appear

Rainier Plumbing Supply
Balance Sheet
December 31, 20—

Assets														
Current Assets:														
Cash						$ 24	1	5	4	00				
Notes Receivable						4	0	0	0	00				
Accounts Receivable						29	4	4	6	00				
Merchandise Inventory						65	8	0	0	00				
Prepaid Insurance							6	4	0	00				
Supplies							4	1	2	00				
Total Current Assets											$124	4	5	2	00
Property and Equipment:														
Land						$120	1	0	0	00				
Building	$130	0	0	0	00									
Less Accumulated Depreciation	56	0	0	0	00	74	0	0	0	00				
Equipment	$ 33	6	0	0	00									
Less Accumulated Depreciation	21	2	0	0	00	12	4	0	0	00				
Total Property and Equipment											206	5	0	0	00
Total Assets											$330	9	5	2	00
Liabilities														
Current Liabilities:														
Notes Payable						$ 36	4	0	0	00				
Mortgage Payable (current portion)						2	0	0	0	00				
Accounts Payable						3	0	0	0	00				
Wages Payable						1	1	2	0	00				
Unearned Course Fees							4	0	0	00				
Total Current Liabilities											$ 42	9	2	0	00
Long-Term Liabilities:														
Mortgage Payable											6	0	0	0	00
Total Liabilities											$ 48	9	2	0	00
Owner's Equity														
C. F. Rainier, Capital											282	0	3	2	00
Total Liabilities and Owner's Equity											$330	9	5	2	00

FIGURE 5

at the bottom of the Current Assets section. There is no particular reason to list Prepaid Insurance before Supplies. Supplies could just as easily have preceded Prepaid Insurance.

Property and Equipment

Property and Equipment are relatively long-lived assets that are held for use in the production or sale of other assets or services; some accountants refer to them as *fixed assets*. The three types of accounts that usually appear in this category are Land, Building, and Equipment (refer to Figure 5). Note that

The barn, the tractor, and the land this man is working are all classified as fixed assets in the Property and Equipment section. Only the barn and tractor, however, are subject to depreciation.

OBJECTIVE 3

Compute working capital and current ratio.

the Building and Equipment accounts are followed by their respective Accumulated Depreciation accounts. We list these assets in order of their length of life, with the longest-lived asset placed first.

Current Liabilities

Current Liabilities are debts that will become due within the normal operating cycle of the business, usually within one year; they normally will be paid, when due, from current assets. List current liabilities in the order of their expected payment. Notes Payable represents the amount owed on promissory notes. Mortgage Payable is the payment one makes to reduce the principal of the mortgage in a given year. Accounts Payable are debts owed to creditors. Wages Payable and any other accrued liabilities, such as Commissions Payable and the current portion of unearned revenue accounts, usually fall at the bottom of the list of current liabilities.

Long-Term Liabilities

Long-Term Liabilities are debts that are payable over a comparatively long period, usually longer than one year. The current portion of notes, contracts, and loans (the amount of principal due within the next year) is shown as a current liability. The remaining amount is shown as a long-term liability.

Working Capital and Current Ratio

Both the management and the short-term creditors of a firm are vitally interested in two questions:

1. Does the firm have a sufficient amount of capital to operate?
2. Does the firm have the ability to pay its debts?

Two measures used to answer these questions are a firm's working capital and its current ratio; the necessary data are taken from a classified balance sheet.

Working capital is determined by subtracting current liabilities from current assets; thus,

Working Capital = Current Assets − Current Liabilities

The normal operating cycle for most firms is less than one year. Because current assets equal cash—or items that can be converted into cash or used up within one year—and current liabilities equal the total amount that the company must pay out within one year, working capital is appropriately named. It is the amount of capital the company has available to use or to work with. The working capital for Rainier Plumbing Supply is as follows:

Working Capital = $124,452 − $42,920 = $81,532

The **current ratio** is useful in revealing a firm's ability to pay its bills. It is determined by dividing current assets by current liabilities:

$$\text{Current Ratio} = \frac{\text{Current Assets (amount coming in within one year)}}{\text{Current Liabilities (amount going out within one year)}}$$

The current ratio for Rainier Plumbing Supply is calculated like this:

$$\text{Current Ratio} = \frac{\$124,452}{\$\ 42,920} \qquad 42,920\overline{)\ 124,452} = 2.8996$$

In the case of Rainier Plumbing Supply, \$2.90 in current assets is available to pay every dollar currently due on December 31.

Chart of Accounts

When we introduced the chart of accounts and the account number arrangement, we said that the first digit represents the classification of an account. Since you are now acquainted with classified income statements and balance sheets, we can introduce the second digit. The second digit stands for the subclassification.

Assets	1– –	Revenue	4– –
Current Assets	11–	Revenue from Sales	41–
Property and Equipment	12–	Other Income	42–
Liabilities	2– –	Cost of Goods Sold	5– –
Current Liabilities	21–	Purchases	51–
Long-Term Liabilities	22–	Expenses	6– –
Owner's Equity	3– –	Selling Expenses	61–
Capital	31–	General Expenses	62–
		Other Expenses	63–

The third digit indicates the placement of the account within the subclassification. For example, account number 411 represents Sales, which is the first account listed under Revenue. Account number 512 represents Purchases Returns and Allowances, which is the second account listed under Cost of Goods Sold. Account number 312 represents Drawing, which is the second account listed under Owner's Equity.

CLOSING ENTRIES

OBJECTIVE 4

Journalize the closing entries for a merchandising firm.

Now let's look at closing entries for a merchandising business. You follow the same four steps to close or zero out the revenue, expense, and Drawing accounts as you do for a service business.

At the end of a fiscal period, you close the revenue and expense accounts so that you can start the next fiscal period with zero balances. You close the Drawing account because it, too, applies to one fiscal period. Recall that these accounts are called **temporary-equity accounts**, or *nominal accounts*.

Figure 6, shown on page 484, shows the isolated Income Statement columns. After you have looked them over, let us look at the four steps of the closing procedure.

Four Steps in the Closing Procedure

These four steps should be followed when closing:

1. Close the revenue accounts and the other accounts that appear on the income statement and have credit balances (all temporary or nominal

	ACCOUNT NAME	TRIAL BALANCE DEBIT	TRIAL BALANCE CREDIT	INCOME STATEMENT DEBIT	INCOME STATEMENT CREDIT
1	Cash	24 1 5 4 00			
2	Notes Receivable	4 0 0 0 00			
3	Accounts Receivable	29 4 4 6 00			
4	Merchandise Inventory	67 0 0 0 00			
5	Prepaid Insurance	9 6 0 00			
6	Land	120 1 0 0 00			
7	Building	130 0 0 0 00			
8	Accumulated Depreciation, Building		52 0 0 0 00		
9	Equipment	33 6 0 0 00			
10	Accumulated Depreciation, Equipment		16 4 0 0 00		
11	Notes Payable		36 4 0 0 00		
12	Accounts Payable		3 0 0 0 00		
13	Unearned Course Fees		1 2 0 0 00		
14	Mortgage Payable		8 0 0 0 00		
15	C. F. Rainier, Capital		253 6 7 4 00		
16	C. F. Rainier, Drawing	76 9 0 0 00			
17	Sales		255 1 8 0 00		255 1 8 0 00
18	Sales Returns and Allowances	8 4 0 00		8 4 0 00	
19	Sales Discounts	1 8 8 0 00		1 8 8 0 00	
20	Interest Income		1 2 0 00		1 2 0 00
21	Purchases	87 1 4 0 00		87 1 4 0 00	
22	Purchases Returns and Allowances		8 3 2 00		8 3 2 00
23	Purchases Discounts		1 2 4 8 00		1 2 4 8 00
24	Freight In	2 4 6 0 00		2 4 6 0 00	
25	Wages Expense	45 8 0 0 00		46 9 2 0 00	
26	Supplies Expense	1 4 4 0 00		1 0 2 8 00	
27	Taxes Expense	1 9 6 0 00		1 9 6 0 00	
28	Interest Expense	3 7 4 00		3 7 4 00	
29		628 0 5 4 00	628 0 5 4 00		
30	Income Summary			67 0 0 0 00	65 8 0 0 00
31	Course Fees Income				8 0 0 00
32	Supplies				
33	Insurance Expense			3 2 0 00	
34	Depreciation Expense, Equipment			4 8 0 0 00	
35	Depreciation Expense, Building			4 0 0 0 00	
36	Wages Payable				
37				218 7 2 2 00	323 9 8 0 00
38	Net Income			105 2 5 8 00	
39				323 9 8 0 00	323 9 8 0 00
40					

FIGURE 6

accounts with credit balances). **(Debit the figures that are credited in the Income Statement columns of the work sheet, except the figure on the Income Summary line.)** This entry is illustrated as follows:

	GENERAL JOURNAL			PAGE 97	
DATE	**DESCRIPTION**	**POST. REF.**	**DEBIT**	**CREDIT**	
20–	**Closing Entries**				1
Dec. 31	Sales		255 1 8 0 00		2
	Interest Income		1 2 0 00		3
	Purchases Returns and				4
	Allowances		8 3 2 00		5
	Purchases Discounts		1 2 4 8 00		6
	Course Fees Income		8 0 0 00		7
	Income Summary			258 1 8 0 00	8

2. Close the expense accounts and the other accounts appearing on the income statement that have debit balances (all temporary or nominal accounts with debit balances). **(Credit the figures that are debited in the Income Statement columns of the work sheet, except the figure on the Income Summary line.)**

    Note that you close Purchases Discounts and Purchases Returns and Allowances in step 1 along with the revenue accounts. Note also that in step 2 you close Sales Discounts and Sales Returns and Allowances along with the expense accounts.

	GENERAL JOURNAL			PAGE 97	
DATE	**DESCRIPTION**	**POST. REF.**	**DEBIT**	**CREDIT**	
Dec. 31	Income Summary		151 7 2 2 00		9
	Sales Returns and Allowances			8 4 0 00	10
	Sales Discounts			1 8 8 0 00	11
	Purchases			87 1 4 0 00	12
	Freight In			2 4 6 0 00	13
	Wages Expense			46 9 2 0 00	14
	Supplies Expense			1 0 2 8 00	15
	Taxes Expense			1 9 6 0 00	16
	Interest Expense			3 7 4 00	17
	Insurance Expense			3 2 0 00	18
	Depreciation Expense, Equip.			4 8 0 0 00	19
	Depreciation Expense, Build.			4 0 0 0 00	20
					21

3. Close the Income Summary account into C. F. Rainier, Capital. **(Debit Income Summary by the amount of the net income; credit it by the amount of a net loss.)**

	GENERAL JOURNAL					PAGE 97	
DATE	DESCRIPTION	POST. REF.	DEBIT		CREDIT		
Dec. 31	Income Summary		105 2 5 8 00				22
	C. F. Rainier, Capital				105 2 5 8 00		23
							24

Here is what the T accounts look like. Note that the Income Summary account already contains adjusting entries for merchandise inventory.

Income Summary

Adjusting (Beginning Merchandise Inventory)	67,000	Adjusting (Ending Merchandise Inventory)	65,800
(Expenses and other debit balance accounts)	151,722	(Revenue and other credit balance accounts)	258,180
(Net Income)	105,258		
		Balance	————

C. F. Rainier, Capital

−	+	
	Balance	253,674
	(Net Income)	105,258

Like service businesses, merchandisers such as this CD store need to prepare closing entries to track net income.

4. Close the Drawing account into the Capital account.

	DATE		DESCRIPTION	POST. REF.	DEBIT	CREDIT	
			GENERAL JOURNAL			PAGE __97__	
25	Dec.	31	C. F. Rainier, Capital		76 9 0 0 00		25
26			C. F. Rainier, Drawing			76 9 0 0 00	26
27							27
28							28

Here is what the T accounts would look like:

C. F. Rainier, Drawing				C. F. Rainier, Capital		
	+	−			−	+
Balance	76,900	Closing	76,900	(Drawing)	76,900	Balance 253,674
						(Net Income) 105,258
Bal.	———					Bal. 282,032

REVERSING ENTRIES

FYI

The use of reversing entries is optional.

Reversing entries are general journal entries that are the exact reverse of certain adjusting entries. A reversing entry enables the accountant to record routine transactions in the usual manner, *even though* an adjusting entry affecting one of the accounts involved in the transaction has intervened. We can understand this concept best by looking at an example.

Suppose there is an adjusting entry for accrued wages owed to employees at the end of the fiscal year. Assume that all the employees of Michaelson Company earn, altogether, $400 per day for a five-day week and that payday occurs every Friday throughout the year. When the employees get their checks at 5:00 P.M. on Friday, the checks include their wages for that day and for the preceding four days. And assume that, one year, the last day of the fiscal year happens to fall on Wednesday, December 31. A diagram of this situation would look like this:

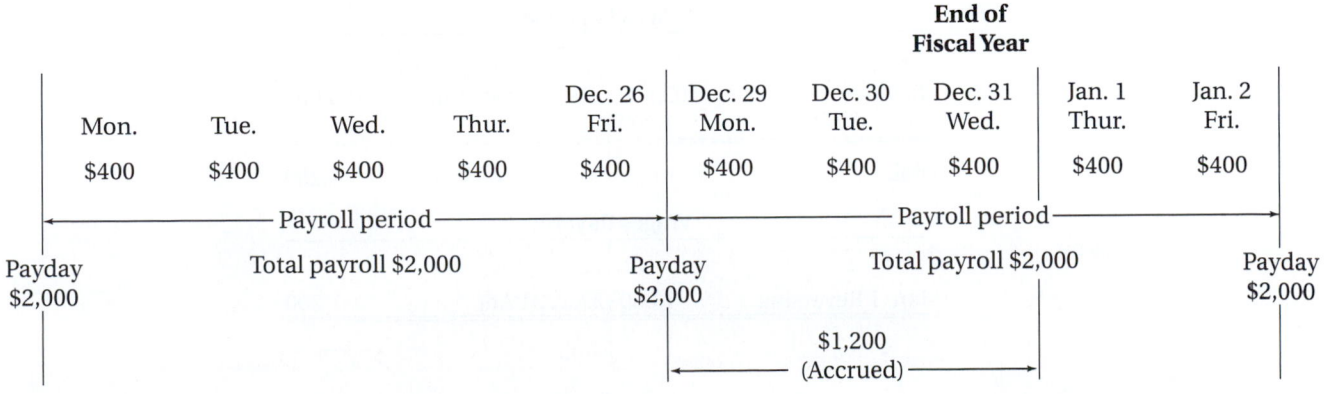

Each Friday during the year, the payroll has been debited to the Wages Expense account and credited to the Cash account. As a result, Wages Expense has a debit balance of $102,800. Here is the adjusting entry in T account form:

Wages Expense

	+	−
Bal.	102,800	
Dec. 31 Adj.	1,200	

Wages Payable

−	+
	Dec. 31
	Adj. 1,200

Next, when all the expense accounts are closed, Wages Expense is closed by crediting it for $104,000. However, Wages Payable continues to have a credit balance of $1,200. The $2,000 payroll on January 2 must be split up by debiting Wages Payable $1,200, debiting Wages Expense $800, and crediting Cash $2,000.

The employee who records the payroll not only has to record this particular payroll differently from all other weekly payrolls for the year but also has to refer back to the adjusting entry to determine what portion of the $2,000 is debited to Wages Payable and what portion is debited to Wages Expense. In many companies, however, the employee who records the payroll does not have access to the adjusting entries.

There is a solution to this problem. The need to refer to the earlier entry and divide the debit total between the two accounts is eliminated *if a reversing entry is made on the first day of the following fiscal period.* You make an entry that is the exact reverse of the adjusting entry, as follows:

GENERAL JOURNAL   PAGE **118**

	DATE		DESCRIPTION	POST. REF.	DEBIT	CREDIT	
27							27
28	20–		Reversing Entries				28
29	Jan.	1	Wages Payable		1 2 0 0 00		29
30			Wages Expense			1 2 0 0 00	30
31							31

Now let's bring the T accounts up to date.

Wages Expense

	+	−		
Balance	102,800	Dec. 31 Closing	104,000
Dec. 31 Adj.	1,200		
Bal.	———	Jan. 1 Reversing	1,200

Wages Payable

	−	+	
Jan. 1 Reversing	1,200	Dec. 31 Adj.	1,200
		Bal.	———

The reversing entry has the effect of transferring the $1,200 liability from Wages Payable to the credit side of Wages Expense. Wages Expense will temporarily have a credit balance until the next payroll is recorded in the routine manner. In our example, this occurs on January 2 as shown below.

Wages Expense

	+	−	
Balance	102,800	Dec. 31 Closing	104,000
Dec. 31 Adj.	1,200		
Bal.	———		
Jan. 2	2,000	Jan. 1 Reversing	1,200
Bal.	800		

Wages Payable

	−	+	
Jan. 1 Reversing	1,200	Dec. 31 Adj.	1,200
		Bal.	———

Cash

	+	−	
		Jan. 2	2,000

There is now a *net debit balance* of $800 in Wages Expense, which is the correct amount ($400 for January 1 and $400 for January 2). To see this, look at the following ledger accounts. December 26 was the last payday of one year, and January 2 is the first payday of the next year.

GENERAL LEDGER

ACCOUNT **Wages Expense**   ACCOUNT NO. **611**

	DATE	ITEM	POST. REF.	DEBIT	CREDIT	BALANCE DEBIT	BALANCE CREDIT	
11	20—							11
12	Dec. 26		CP16	2 0 0 0 00		102 8 0 0 00		12
13	31	Adjusting	J116	1 2 0 0 00		104 0 0 0 00		13
14	31	Closing	J117		104 0 0 0 00	—	—	14
15	20—							15
16	Jan. 1	Reversing	J118		1 2 0 0 00		1 2 0 0 00	16
17	2		CP17	2 0 0 0 00		8 0 0 00		17

ACCOUNT **Wages Payable**   ACCOUNT NO. **213**

	DATE	ITEM	POST. REF.	DEBIT	CREDIT	BALANCE DEBIT	BALANCE CREDIT	
1	20—							1
2	Dec. 31	Adjusting	J116		1 2 0 0 00		1 2 0 0 00	2
3	20—							3
4	Jan. 1	Reversing	J118	1 2 0 0 00		—	—	4

OBJECTIVE 5

Determine which adjusting entries can be reversed, and journalize the reversing entries.

The reversing entry for accrued salaries or wages applies to service as well as merchandising companies. You can see that a reversing entry simply switches around an adjusting entry. The question is: Which adjusting entries should be reversed? Here are two handy rules for reversing. **If an adjusting entry is to be reversed, it must meet both of the following qualifications:**

1. **The adjusting entry increases an asset or liability account.**
2. **The asset or liability account did not have a previous balance.**

With the exception of the first year of operations, Merchandise Inventory and contra accounts—such as Accumulated Depreciation—always have previous balances. Consequently, adjusting entries involving these accounts should never be reversed.

Let's apply these rules to the adjusting entries for Rainier Plumbing Supply.

(Do not reverse; Merchandise Inventory is an asset, but it was decreased. Also, it has a previous balance.)

Merchandise Inventory						Income Summary	
	+	−					
Balance	67,000	Adj.	67,000	Adj.	67,000		

(Do not reverse; Merchandise Inventory is an asset, but it has a previous balance.)

Merchandise Inventory						Income Summary	
	+	−					
Balance	67,000	Adj.	67,000	Adj.	67,000	Adj.	65,800
Adj.	65,800						

(Do not reverse; Unearned Course Fees is a liability, but it was decreased. Also, it has a previous balance.)

Course Fees Income						Unearned Course Fees	
	−	+			−	+	
		Adj.	800	Adj.	800	Balance	1,200

(Reverse; Supplies is an asset account. It was increased, and it had no previous balance.

Supplies						Supplies Expense	
	+	−			+	−	
Adj.	412			Balance	1,440	Adj.	412

(Do not reverse; Prepaid Insurance is an asset account, but it was decreased. Also, it has a previous balance.)

Insurance Expense						Prepaid Insurance	
	+	−			+	−	
Adj.	320			Balance	960	Adj.	320

(Do not reverse; Accumulated Depreciation is a contra-asset, and it always has a previous balance after the first year.)

Depreciation Expense, Equipment						Accumulated Depreciation, Equipment	
	+	−			−	+	
Adj.	4,800					Balance	16,400
						Adj.	4,800

(Do not reverse; Accumulated Depreciation is a contra-asset, and it always has a previous balance after the first year.)

Depreciation Expense, Building						Accumulated Depreciation, Building	
	+	−			−	+	
Adj.	4,000					Balance	52,000
						Adj.	4,000

(Reverse; Wages Payable is a liability account. It was increased, and it had no previous balance.)

Wages Expense						Wages Payable	
	+	−			−	+	
Balance	45,800					Adj.	1,120
Adj.	1,120						

REMEMBER!

Reversing entries are optional.

Whenever we introduce additional adjusting entries, we will make it a point to state whether they can be reversed.

CHAPTER REVIEW

Review of Performance Objectives

1. Prepare a classified income statement for a merchandising firm.

   The outline of the income statement looks like this:

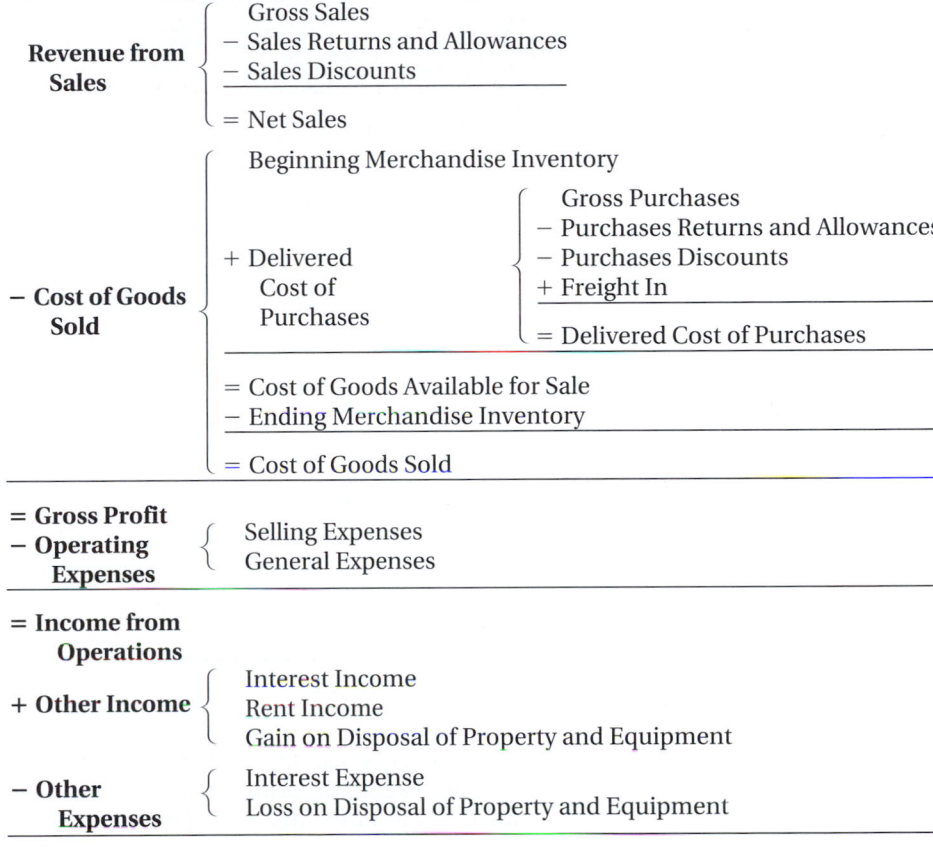

   Revenue from Sales
   - Gross Sales
   - − Sales Returns and Allowances
   - − Sales Discounts
   - = Net Sales

   − Cost of Goods Sold
   - Beginning Merchandise Inventory
   - + Delivered Cost of Purchases
     - Gross Purchases
     - − Purchases Returns and Allowances
     - − Purchases Discounts
     - + Freight In
     - = Delivered Cost of Purchases
   - = Cost of Goods Available for Sale
   - − Ending Merchandise Inventory
   - = Cost of Goods Sold

   = Gross Profit
   − Operating Expenses
   - Selling Expenses
   - General Expenses

   = Income from Operations
   + Other Income
   - Interest Income
   - Rent Income
   - Gain on Disposal of Property and Equipment

   − Other Expenses
   - Interest Expense
   - Loss on Disposal of Property and Equipment

   = Net Income

2. Prepare a classified balance sheet for any type of business.

   The outline of the balance sheet looks like this:

   Assets **Current Assets** (listed in the order of their convertibility into cash)

   1. Cash
   2. Notes Receivable
   3. Accounts Receivable
   4. Merchandise Inventory
   5. Prepaid items (Supplies; Prepaid Insurance)

   Property and Equipment (listed in the order of their length of life; the asset with the longest life is placed first)

   1. Land
   2. Buildings
   3. Equipment

   Liabilities **Current Liabilities** (listed in the order of their urgency of payment; the most pressing obligation is placed first)

1. Notes Payable
2. Mortgage Payable or Contracts Payable (current portion)
3. Accounts Payable
4. Accrued liabilities (Wages Payable; Commissions Payable)
5. Unearned Revenue

Long-Term Liabilities (Contracts Payable; Mortgage Payable)

Owner's Equity Capital balance at end of the fiscal year

3. Compute working capital and current ratio.

These two measures help analysts determine whether a firm has enough capital to operate and whether it can pay its debts.

Working capital = Current assets − Current liabilities

$$\text{Current ratio} = \frac{\text{Current assets}}{\text{Current liabilities}}$$

4. Journalize the closing entries for a merchandising firm.

There are four steps in making closing entries for a merchandising business:

Step 1. Close all revenue accounts, Purchases Returns and Allowances, and Purchases Discounts into Income Summary (any accounts listed as credits in the work sheet Income Statement columns except Income Summary).

Step 2. Close all expense accounts, Sales Returns and Allowances, and Sales Discounts into Income Summary (any accounts listed as debits in the work sheet Income Statement columns except Income Summary).

Step 3. Close Income Summary into Capital (transfer net income or net loss into the owner's Capital account). The Income Summary balance should now be zero.

Step 4. Close Drawing into Capital.

5. Determine which adjusting entries can be reversed, and journalize the reversing entries.

The use of reversing entries is optional. Reverse the adjusting entries that increase either asset or liability accounts that do not have previous balances. A contra-account like Accumulated Depreciation should not be reversed. Reversing entries are dated as of the first day of the next fiscal period.

Glossary

Cost of Goods Sold A section of the income statement in which the amount of the cost of the goods the business sold is calculated. Terms often used to describe the same thing are *cost of merchandise sold* and *cost of sales*.

Merchandise Inventory (beginning)
+ Delivered Cost of Purchases
_____

Cost of Goods Available for Sale
− Merchandise Inventory (ending)
_____

Cost of Goods Sold (476)

Current Assets Cash and any other assets or resources that are expected to be realized in cash or to be sold or consumed during the normal operating cycle of the business (or one year, if the normal operating cycle is less than twelve months). (480)

Current Liabilities Debts that will become due within the normal operating cycle of a business, usually within one year, and that are normally paid from current assets. (482)

Current ratio A firm's current assets divided by its current liabilities. Portrays a firm's short-term debt-paying ability. (482)

Delivered Cost of Purchases Net Purchases plus Freight In:

Net Purchases
+ Freight In
_____

Delivered Cost of Purchases   (477)

General Expenses Expenses incurred in the administration of a business, including office expenses and any expenses that are not completely classified as Selling Expenses or Other Expenses. (477)

Gross Profit Net Sales minus Cost of Goods Sold, or profit before deducting expenses:

Net Sales
− Cost of Goods Sold
_____

Gross Profit   (476)

Liquidity The ability of an asset to be quickly turned into cash, either by selling it or by putting it up as security for a loan. (480)

Long-Term Liabilities Debts payable over a comparatively long period, usually more than one year. (482)

Net Income or **Net Profit** The final figure on an income statement after all expenses have been deducted from revenues. (476)

Net Purchases Purchases minus Purchases Returns and Allowances and minus Purchases Discounts:

Purchases
− Purchases Returns and Allowances
− Purchases Discounts
_____

Net Purchases   (477)

Net Sales Sales minus Sales Returns and Allowances and minus Sales Discounts:

Sales
− Sales Returns and Allowances
− Sales Discounts
_____

Net Sales   (476)

Notes Receivable (current) Written promises to pay the seller/lender the amount due in a period of less than one year. (480)

Property and Equipment Long-lived assets that are held for use in the production or sale of other assets or services; also called *fixed assets.* (481)

Reversing entries The reverse of certain adjusting entries, recorded as of the first day of the following fiscal period. The use of reversing entries is optional. (487)

Selling Expenses Expenses directly connected with the selling activity, such as salaries of sales staff, advertising expenses, and delivery expenses. (477)

Temporary-equity accounts Accounts whose balances apply to one fiscal period only, such as revenues, expenses, and the Drawing account. Temporary-equity accounts are also called *nominal accounts.* (483)

Working capital A firm's current assets less its current liabilities. The amount of capital a firm has available to use or to work with during a normal operating cycle. (482)

QUESTIONS, EXERCISES, AND CASES

Discussion Questions

1. What is the order for listing accounts in the Current Assets section of the balance sheet?
2. What is the difference between the cost of goods available for sale and the cost of goods sold?
3. What are the basic classifications found on an income statement for a merchandising business as compared to a service business?
4. On a balance sheet, what is the difference between Current Liabilities and Long-Term Liabilities? Give an example of an account in each classification.
5. On an income statement, what is the difference between income from operations and net income? Which is more useful in comparing the results of operations over a number of years?
6. Explain the calculation of net sales and net purchases.
7. In the closing procedure, what happens to (a) Purchases Discounts, (b) Sales Returns and Allowances, (c) Freight In, (d) Gain on Disposal of Property and Equipment?
8. What are the rules for recognizing whether or not an adjusting entry should be reversed?

P.O. 1

Provide missing amounts on an income statement.

Exercises

Exercise 13-1 Calculate the missing items in the following:

Sales	Sales Returns and Allowances	Net Sales	Beginning Merchandise Inventory	Net Purchases	Cost of Goods Available for Sale	Ending Merchandise Inventory	Cost of Goods Sold	Gross Profit
a. $248,000	$ 6,000	—	$148,000	$170,000	—	$136,000	$182,000	—
b. 304,000	—	$296,000	144,000	—	$404,000	196,000	208,000	—
c. —	12,000	628,000	—	412,000	496,000	92,000	—	—

P.O. 1

Prepare the Cost of Goods Sold section.

Exercise 13-2 Using the following information, prepare the Cost of Goods Sold section of an income statement.

Purchases Discounts	$ 9,000
Merchandise Inventory, December 31	192,000
Purchases	480,000
Merchandise Inventory, January 1	188,000
Purchases Returns and Allowances	16,000
Freight In	27,000

P.O. 1

Classify income statement accounts.

Exercise 13-3 Identify each of the following items relating to sections of an income statement as Revenue from Sales (S), Cost of Goods Sold (CGS), Selling Expenses (SE), General Expenses (GE), Other Income (OI), or Other Expenses (OE).

a. Advertising Expense
b. Rent Expense
c. Purchases Discounts
d. Sales Returns and Allowances
e. Interest Income
f. Freight In
g. Depreciation Expense, Building
h. Interest Expense
i. Insurance Expense
j. Delivery Expense

P.O. 1

Prepare an income statement.

Exercise 13-4 The Income Statement columns of the June 30 (year-end) work sheet for Barker Company are shown here. From the information given, prepare an income statement for the company. To save time and space, the expenses have been grouped together into two categories.

		INCOME STATEMENT	
ACCOUNT NAME		DEBIT	CREDIT
21	Income Summary	27 0 0 0 00	23 0 0 0 00
22	Sales		291 0 0 0 00
23	Sales Returns and Allowances	11 1 0 0 00	
24	Sales Discounts	4 1 0 0 00	
25	Purchases	116 0 0 0 00	
26	Purchases Returns and Allowances		1 2 0 0 00
27	Purchases Discounts		1 0 0 0 00
28	Freight In	7 5 0 0 00	
29	Selling Expenses	56 0 0 0 00	
30	General Expenses	49 0 0 0 00	
31		270 7 0 0 00	316 2 0 0 00
32	Net Income	45 5 0 0 00	
		316 2 0 0 00	316 2 0 0 00

P.O. 2

Classify balance sheet items.

Exercise 13-5 Identify each of the following items relating to sections of a balance sheet as Current Assets (CA), Property and Equipment (PE), Current Liabilities (CL), Long-Term Liabilities (LTL), or Owner's Equity (OE).

a. Accounts Receivable
b. Building
c. Wages Payable
d. Prepaid Taxes
e. Mortgage Payable (current)
f. Mortgage Payable (due in 3 years)
g. Unearned Fees
h. D. Marlor, Capital
i. Notes Payable (due in 3 months)

P.O. 3

Determine working capital and current ratio.

Exercise 13-6 On December 31, 20—, the following selected accounts and amounts appeared on the balance sheet. Determine the amount of the working capital and the current ratio.

Building	$160,000
Prepaid Insurance	600
Merchandise Inventory	72,000
Store Equipment	14,000
Unearned Fees	700
Notes Payable	7,000
Accumulated Depreciation, Building	72,000
Accounts Payable	22,000
Land	40,000
Cash	9,000
Accumulated Depreciation, Store Equipment	6,000
Notes Receivable	4,000
Mortgage Payable (current portion)	4,400
Salaries Payable	2,000
C. Rorson, Capital	101,500
Mortgage Payable (due in 4 years)	85,000

P.O. 4

Journalize closing entries.

Exercise 13-7 From the following T accounts, journalize the closing entries dated December 31:

Salary Expense				H. Beal, Drawing				Purchases Returns and Allowances	
+	–			+	–			–	+
68,000				54,000					7,600

Purchases				Miscellaneous Expense				Rent Expense	
+	–			+	–			+	–
236,800				13,200				24,000	

Sales Returns and Allowances				Freight In				Sales	
+	–			+	–			–	+
8,000				15,200					504,000

Income Summary				H. Beal, Capital				Purchases Discounts	
88,000	104,000			–	+			–	+
					336,000				5,600

P.O. 4

From T accounts, prepare a statement of owner's equity.

Exercise 13-8 From the following information, journalize the last two closing entries, and present a statement of owner's equity for Nakamura Company:

T. H. Nakamura, Capital		
–	+	
	Jan. 1 Balance	440,000
	Apr. 7	16,000

Income Summary			
Dec. 31 Adj.	192,000	Dec. 31 Adj.	204,000
Dec. 31 Closing	410,000	Dec. 31 Closing	490,000

T. H. Nakamura, Drawing		
	+	–
Mar. 1	32,000	
Dec. 9	37,000	

Let's analyze Barnes & Noble's working capital and current ratio for 2005. The 2005 annual report can be found at **http://www.barnesandnoble.com.** Click on Investor Relations at the bottom of the screen and then select the link for the annual reports.

1. What was Barnes & Noble's working capital for 2005, and what does it say about the business?
2. What was Barnes & Noble's current ratio for 2005, and what does it say about the business?

CONSIDER AND COMMUNICATE

A music store sells new instruments. The store also sells used instruments for people who are willing to give the store part of the sales price. The sales of used instruments, called commissions, amount to about one-fourth of total sales. On the firm's classified income statement under the Revenue heading are both New Instrument Sales and Sales Commissions. Comment on this practice.

WHAT'S WRONG WITH THIS PICTURE?

What if the freight charges on a new desk for the owner were journalized and posted to the Freight In account? Would this affect the Cost of Goods Sold section? If so, how?

CRITICAL THINKING

You are an owner/bookkeeper in a country whose economy has been nearly destroyed. Goods are scarce; in fact, you have no goods to sell at the start of each day. You go out early each morning to purchase goods and haul them back to sell. At the end of the day, you have sold everything. Prepare a Cost of Goods Sold section for a day when you purchased $400 in goods. What conclusion can you draw?

A QUESTION OF ETHICS

Marty is an accountant. Sometimes printouts of financial statements have errors and are not usable. Marty doesn't like to waste anything, so he takes the unusable financial statements to his son's day care center to use for drawing paper. Explain why you think this is or is not unethical behavior.

PROBLEM SET A

P.O. 1,4

For additional help, see the demonstration problem at the beginning of each chapter in your Working Papers.

Problem 13-1A A partial work sheet for Preslie Music Store is presented here. The merchandise inventory at the beginning of the fiscal period was $49,584. F. L. Preslie, the owner, withdrew $35,000 during the year.

Preslie Music Store
Work Sheet
For Year Ended December 31, 20—

	ACCOUNT NAME	INCOME STATEMENT DEBIT	INCOME STATEMENT CREDIT
21	Sales		326 5 9 2 80
22	Sales Returns and Allowances	5 2 2 9 20	
23	Sales Discounts	1 9 0 8 00	
24	Interest Income		3 2 4 98
25	Purchases	195 1 9 1 00	
26	Purchases Returns and Allowances		1 6 5 6 00
27	Freight In	14 2 6 5 00	
28	Wages Expense	39 5 2 4 00	
29	Rent Expense	9 3 6 0 00	
30	Commissions Expense	9 4 4 0 00	
31	Supplies Expense	6 3 7 20	
32	Interest Expense	6 5 6 32	
33	Income Summary	49 5 8 4 00	43 9 7 2 00
34	Insurance Expense	9 3 6 00	
35	Depreciation Expense, Equipment	3 3 4 0 00	
36	Depreciation Expense, Building	4 8 0 0 00	
38		334 8 7 0 72	372 5 4 5 78
39	Net Income	37 6 7 5 06	
40		372 5 4 5 78	372 5 4 5 78
41			
42			
43			
44			
45			
46			
47			
48			
49			

Check Figure

Cost of Goods Sold, $213,412

Instructions

1. Prepare an income statement.
2. Journalize the closing entries.

P.O. 2,3

Problem 13-2A Here is the partial work sheet for Olsen Mountain Shop.

Olsen Mountain Shop
Work Sheet
For Year Ended December 31, 20—

	ACCOUNT NAME	BALANCE SHEET DEBIT	BALANCE SHEET CREDIT	
1	Cash	9 7 2 3 00		1
2	Notes Receivable	3 6 0 0 00		2
3	Accounts Receivable	42 8 7 9 60		3
4	Merchandise Inventory	56 6 9 7 00		4
5	Prepaid Taxes	6 1 3 50		5
6	Prepaid Insurance	6 3 0 00		6
7	Land	8 4 0 0 00		7
8	Building	63 0 0 0 00		8
9	Accumulated Depreciation, Building		21 6 0 0 00	9
10	Computer Equipment	5 4 2 4 00		10
11	Accumulated Depreciation, Computer Equipment		4 1 7 0 00	11
12	Store Equipment	6 5 7 0 00		12
13	Accumulated Depreciation, Store Equipment		4 9 9 5 00	13
14	Delivery Equipment	5 5 6 5 00		14
15	Accumulated Depreciation, Delivery Equipment		4 3 0 5 00	15
16	Notes Payable		5 4 3 0 00	16
17	Accounts Payable		29 5 9 1 70	17
18	Mortgage Payable (current portion)		2 7 0 0 00	18
19	Mortgage Payable		55 7 1 3 00	19
20	N. Olsen, Capital		65 0 5 8 90	20
21	N. Olsen, Drawing	25 1 9 4 00		21
23	Wages Payable		1 2 7 8 00	23
24		228 2 9 6 10	194 8 4 1 60	24
25	Net Income		33 4 5 4 50	25
26		228 2 9 6 10	228 2 9 6 10	26
27				27
28				28
29				29
30				30
31				31
32				32

Check Figure

Working capital, $75,617.40

Instructions

1. Prepare a statement of owner's equity (no additional investment).
2. Prepare a balance sheet.
3. Determine the amount of the working capital.
4. Determine the current ratio (carry to two decimal places).

P.O. 4,5   **Problem 13-3A** The following partial work sheet covers the affairs of Komo and Company for the year ending June 30:

Komo and Company
Work Sheet
For Year Ended June 30, 20—

	ACCOUNT NAME	INCOME STATEMENT DEBIT	INCOME STATEMENT CREDIT	BALANCE SHEET DEBIT	BALANCE SHEET CREDIT	
1	Cash			33 4 1 6 34		1
2	Accounts Receivable			104 6 3 4 54		2
3	Merchandise Inventory			119 4 5 6 00		3
4	Prepaid Insurance			1 3 2 0 00		4
5	Delivery Equipment			12 9 2 0 00		5
6	Accumulated Depreciation, Delivery Equipment				6 4 8 0 00	6
7	Store Equipment			36 5 0 0 00		7
8	Accumulated Depreciation, Store Equipment				10 3 6 0 00	8
9	Accounts Payable				67 4 3 7 34	9
10	C. P. Komo, Capital				195 9 2 1 14	10
11	C. P. Komo, Drawing			37 4 4 0 00		11
12	Sales		536 3 5 2 40			12
13	Purchases	393 9 3 0 00				13
14	Purchases Returns and Allowances		7 8 2 8 00			14
15	Purchases Discounts		5 7 4 6 00			15
16	Freight In	23 3 5 0 00				16
17	Salary Expense	51 4 0 0 00				17
18	Truck Expense	9 3 4 2 00				18
19	Supplies Expense	2 5 6 4 00				19
20	Miscellaneous Expense	1 4 1 8 00				20
21						21
22	Income Summary	115 2 2 6 00	119 4 5 6 00			22
23	Salaries Payable				8 5 2 00	23
24	Insurance Expense	1 9 2 0 00				24
25	Depreciation Expense, Delivery Equipment	2 7 0 0 00				25
26	Depreciation Expense, Store Equipment	2 8 9 6 00				26
27		604 7 4 6 00	669 3 8 2 40	345 6 8 6 88	281 0 5 0 48	27
28	Net Income	64 6 3 6 40			64 6 3 6 40	28
29		669 3 8 2 40	669 3 8 2 40	345 6 8 6 88	345 6 8 6 88	29
30						30
31						31
32						32

Check Figure

Reversing entry amount, $852

Instructions

1. Journalize the seven adjusting entries.
2. Journalize the closing entries.
3. Journalize the reversing entry.

P.O. 1,2,4,5

Problem 13-4A The following accounts appear in the ledger of Shirley Company on January 31, the end of this fiscal year:

Cash	$ 6,400
Accounts Receivable	13,100
Merchandise Inventory	54,500
Prepaid Insurance	2,080
Store Equipment	26,900
Accumulated Depreciation, Store Equipment	3,700
Accounts Payable	12,800
M. R. Shirley, Capital	112,620
M. R. Shirley, Drawing	37,000
Sales	223,000
Sales Returns and Allowances	2,000
Purchases	172,000
Purchases Returns and Allowances	2,450
Purchases Discounts	3,400
Freight In	6,000
Wages Expense	23,000
Advertising Expense	4,900
Rent Expense	8,400
Store Supplies Expense	1,690

The data needed for adjustments on January 31 are as follows:

a–b. Merchandise inventory, January 31, $54,600
c. Insurance expired for the year, $1,015
d. Depreciation for the year, $5,395
e. Accrued wages on January 31, $996

Check Figure

Net income, $4,134

Instructions

1. Prepare a work sheet for the fiscal year ended January 31.
2. Prepare an income statement.
3. Prepare a statement of owner's equity. No additional investments were made during the year.
4. Prepare a balance sheet.
5. Journalize the adjusting entries.
6. Journalize the closing entries.
7. Journalize the reversing entry.

Instructions for General Ledger Software

1. Record the adjusting entries in the general journal and print a copy of the entries.
2. Post the general journal amounts to the general ledger.
3. Print an adjusted trial balance and the general ledger after adjustments.
4. Print the income statement, statement of owner's equity, and balance sheet.
5. Record the closing entries in the general journal and print a copy of the entries.
6. Post the general journal amounts to the general ledger.
7. Print a post-closing trial balance.
8. Record the reversing entry in the general journal at the beginning of the next month.

PROBLEM SET B

P.O. 1,4

For additional help, see the demonstration problem at the beginning of each chapter in your Working Papers.

Problem 13-1B A partial work sheet for The Town Shop is presented here. The merchandise inventory at the beginning of the year was $53,200. C. A. Ochs, the owner, withdrew $26,500 during the year.

The Town Shop
Work Sheet
For Year Ended December 31, 20—

	ACCOUNT NAME	INCOME STATEMENT DEBIT	INCOME STATEMENT CREDIT
21	Sales		328 0 0 0 00
22	Sales Returns and Allowances	4 4 8 0 00	
23	Sales Discounts	3 7 0 7 32	
24	Interest Income		1 8 4 0 00
25	Purchases	199 4 9 0 00	
26	Purchases Returns and Allowances		2 9 8 0 00
27	Freight In	12 7 5 0 00	
28	Wages Expense	43 2 0 0 00	
29	Rent Expense	9 6 0 0 00	
30	Commissions Expense	10 3 2 0 00	
31	Supplies Expense	8 3 2 46	
32	Interest Expense	9 6 4 22	
33	Income Summary	53 2 0 0 00	44 3 6 0 00
34	Insurance Expense	1 0 4 0 00	
35	Depreciation Expense, Equipment	3 6 0 0 00	
36	Depreciation Expense, Building	4 8 0 0 00	
38		347 9 8 4 00	377 1 8 0 00
39	Net Income	29 1 9 6 00	
40		377 1 8 0 00	377 1 8 0 00
41			
42			
43			
44			
45			
46			

Check Figure

Cost of Goods Sold, $218,100

Instructions

1. Prepare an income statement.
2. Journalize the closing entries.

P.O. 2,3

Problem 13-2B Here is the partial work sheet for Westhaven Stereo.

Westhaven Stereo
Work Sheet
For Year Ended December 31, 20—

	ACCOUNT NAME	BALANCE SHEET	
		DEBIT	CREDIT
1	Cash	12 9 1 5 00	
2	Notes Receivable	6 3 0 0 00	
3	Accounts Receivable	33 2 7 0 00	
4	Merchandise Inventory	55 3 4 4 00	
5	Prepaid Taxes	1 0 1 5 00	
6	Prepaid Insurance	5 4 0 00	
7	Land	7 8 0 0 00	
8	Building	60 0 0 0 00	
9	Accumulated Depreciation, Building		18 9 0 0 00
10	Computer Equipment	4 3 9 2 00	
11	Accumulated Depreciation, Computer Equipment		1 6 7 4 00
12	Testing Equipment	7 2 3 0 00	
13	Accumulated Depreciation, Testing Equipment		5 4 2 4 00
14	Delivery Equipment	5 4 0 0 00	
15	Accumulated Depreciation, Delivery Equipment		4 4 7 0 00
16	Notes Payable		4 2 1 5 00
17	Accounts Payable		28 1 4 0 00
18	Mortgage Payable (current portion)		1 8 0 0 00
19	Mortgage Payable		55 2 0 0 00
20	C. R. Gonzales, Capital		67 3 1 4 00
21	C. R. Gonzales, Drawing	22 4 4 0 00	
23	Wages Payable		9 8 4 00
24		216 6 8 1 00	188 1 2 1 00
25	Net Income		28 5 6 0 00
26		216 6 8 1 00	216 6 8 1 00

Check Figure

Working capital, $74,280

Instructions

1. Prepare a statement of owner's equity (no additional investment).
2. Prepare a balance sheet.
3. Determine the amount of the working capital.
4. Determine the current ratio (carry to two decimal places).

P.O. 4,5

Problem 13-3B The following partial work sheet covers the affairs of Breski and Company for the year ended June 30:

Breski and Company
Work Sheet
For Year Ended June 30, 20—

	ACCOUNT NAME	INCOME STATEMENT DEBIT	INCOME STATEMENT CREDIT	BALANCE SHEET DEBIT	BALANCE SHEET CREDIT	
1	Cash			29 0 3 4 61		1
2	Accounts Receivable			92 0 0 6 00		2
3	Merchandise Inventory			112 4 0 0 00		3
4	Prepaid Insurance			1 2 2 0 00		4
5	Delivery Equipment			12 4 0 0 00		5
6	Accumulated Depreciation, Delivery Equipment				5 8 0 0 00	6
7	Store Equipment			33 4 0 0 00		7
8	Accumulated Depreciation, Store Equipment				9 6 0 0 00	8
9	Accounts Payable				60 2 0 0 00	9
10	L. Breski, Capital				167 8 2 0 00	10
11	L. Breski, Drawing			28 0 0 0 00		11
12	Sales		520 0 0 0 00			12
13	Purchases	380 0 0 0 00				13
14	Purchases Returns and Allowances		7 6 0 0 00			14
15	Purchases Discounts		4 8 0 0 00			15
16	Freight In	24 0 0 0 00				16
17	Salary Expense	48 0 0 0 00				17
18	Truck Expense	8 6 0 0 00				18
19	Supplies Expense	2 2 0 0 48				19
20	Miscellaneous Expense	1 9 5 9 52				20
21						21
22	Income Summary	109 2 0 0 00	112 4 0 0 00			22
23	Salaries Payable				1 2 4 0 00	23
24	Insurance Expense	1 8 4 0 00				24
25	Depreciation Expense, Delivery Equipment	2 4 0 0 00				25
26	Depreciation Expense, Store Equipment	2 8 0 0 00				26
27		581 0 0 0 00	644 8 0 0 00	308 4 6 0 00	244 6 6 0 00	27
28	Net Income	63 8 0 0 00			63 8 0 0 00	28
29		644 8 0 0 00	644 8 0 0 00	308 4 6 0 00	308 4 6 0 00	29
30						30
31						31
32						32

Check Figure

Reversing entry amount, $1,240

Instructions

1. Journalize the seven adjusting entries.
2. Journalize the closing entries.
3. Journalize the reversing entry.

P.O. 1,2,4,5

Problem 13-4B The following accounts appear in the ledger of Clark and Company as of June 30, the end of this fiscal year:

Cash	$ 5,349.00
Accounts Receivable	13,910.00
Merchandise Inventory	50,480.00
Prepaid Insurance	1,085.00
Store Equipment	28,640.00
Accumulated Depreciation, Store Equipment	6,880.00
Accounts Payable	10,085.00
D. E. Clark, Capital	96,404.52
D. E. Clark, Drawing	27,260.00
Sales	201,630.00
Sales Returns and Allowances	1,640.00
Purchases	136,050.00
Purchases Returns and Allowances	3,395.00
Purchases Discounts	3,565.00
Freight In	8,260.00
Wages Expense	32,100.00
Advertising Expense	7,150.00
Rent Expense	9,200.00
Store Supplies Expense	835.52

The data needed for the adjustments on June 30 are as follows:

a–b. Merchandise inventory, June 30, $47,296
c. Insurance expired for the year, $380.80
d. Depreciation for the year, $5,290
e. Accrued wages on June 30, $572

Check Figure

Net income, $3,927.68

Instructions

1. Prepare a work sheet for the fiscal year ended June 30.
2. Prepare an income statement.
3. Prepare a statement of owner's equity. No additional investments were made during the year.
4. Prepare a balance sheet.
5. Journalize the adjusting entries.
6. Journalize the closing entries.
7. Journalize the reversing entry.

Instructions for General Ledger Software

1. Record the adjusting entries in the general journal and print a copy of the entries.
2. Post the general journal amounts to the general ledger.
3. Print an adjusted trial balance and the general ledger after adjustments.
4. Print the income statement, statement of owner's equity, and balance sheet.
5. Record the closing entries in the general journal and print a copy of the entries.
6. Post the general journal amounts to the general ledger.
7. Print a post-closing trial balance.
8. Record the reversing entry in the general journal at the beginning of the next month.

The Computer Clinic

Financial Statements, Closing Entries, and Reversing Entry

It is now August 31. You have journalized and posted the adjustments in the All About You Spa accounting records, and Ms. Valli wants to see financial statements in order to compare the results of the last two months (July and August) to those of June.

A partial copy of the August 31 work sheet after adjustments is shown on the following page.

Using the Income Statement and Balance Sheet columns of the partial work sheet, you are to do the following:

Print all statements before entering the closing entries.

Check Figures

Net Income	$13,756.32
Aug. 31 Capital	58,640.94
Total assets	81,035.06

1. Prepare and print the following financial statements:

   a. Income statement for the two months ended August 31, 20— using the Income Statement columns of the partial work sheet.

   The following expenses have been split between selling expenses and general expenses:

Wages Expense	Selling	$12,070	General	$4,180
Utilities Expense	Selling	632	General	331

   The following are also considered general expenses: rent, office supplies, depreciation on office equipment, medical insurance, and miscellaneous. All other expenses are considered selling expenses.

   b. Statement of owner's equity for the two months ended August 31, 20— using the Income Statement and Balance Sheet (for the Capital and Drawing accounts) columns of the partial work sheet. Don't forget the two additional investments of $25,000 and $1,800.

   c. Balance sheet dated August 31, 20— using the Balance Sheet columns of the partial work sheet.

2. Journalize the four closing entries in the following order:

   a. Close the revenue accounts (every amount on the credit side of the Income Statement columns *except the Income Summary account amount*) to the Income Summary account.

   b. Close the expense accounts (every amount on the debit side of the Income Statement columns *except the Income Summary account amount*) to the Income Summary account.

   c. Close the Income Summary account to the Capital account.

      i. If the balance is a debit, it means expenses were greater than revenue and therefore you had a loss. To close the Income Summary account if there is a debit balance, credit Income Summary and debit the Capital account.

      ii. If the balance is a credit, it means revenue was greater than expenses and therefore you had a profit or net income. To close the Income Summary account if there is a credit balance, debit Income Summary and credit the Capital account.

   d. Close the Drawing account to the Capital account. Since the Drawing account will have a debit balance, credit it to achieve a zero balance and debit the Capital account.

Why is it essential that you save and print your financial statements before zeroing out or closing the temporary owner's equity accounts?

All About You Spa
Work Sheet
August 31, 20—

#	ACCOUNT NAME	INCOME STATEMENT DEBIT	INCOME STATEMENT CREDIT	BALANCE SHEET DEBIT	BALANCE SHEET CREDIT	#
1	Cash			40 3 6 1 74		1
2	Accounts Receivable			7 1 9 6 63		2
3	Prepaid Insurance			5 1 8 33		3
4	Spa Equipment			18 0 8 3 00		4
5	Accumulated Depreciation, Spa Equipment				1 9 4 64	5
6	Office Equipment			1 5 7 0 00		6
7	Accumulated Depreciation, Office Equipment				3 0 00	7
8	Accounts Payable				20 3 9 3 00	8
9	Sales Tax Payable				2 0 0 1 12	9
10	A. Valli, Capital				49 8 8 4 62	10
11	A. Valli, Drawing			5 0 0 0 00		11
12	Income from Services		30 5 2 6 00			12
13	Merchandise Sales		17 3 6 1 65			13
14	Sales Returns and Allowances	8 8 00				14
15	Purchases	24 1 0 1 00				15
16	Purchases Returns and Allowances		1 2 3 00			16
17	Freight In	9 9 2 00				17
18	Wages Expense	16 2 5 0 00				18
19	Rent Expense	3 3 0 0 00				19
20	Office Supplies Expense	4 3 00				20
21	Spa Supplies Expense	1 9 0 00				21
22	Laundry Expense	1 7 9 00				22
23	Advertising Expense	4 5 5 00				23
24	Utilities Expense	9 6 3 00				24
25	Miscellaneous Expense	3 7 1 90				25
26						26
27	Income Summary	0 00	13 1 1 0 00			27
28	Merchandise Inventory			13 1 1 0 00		28
29	Office Supplies			7 5 00		29
30	Spa Supplies			3 4 5 00		30
31	Insurance Expense	2 8 1 67				31
32	Depreciation Expense, Spa Equipment	1 2 9 76				32
33	Depreciation Expense, Office Equipment	2 0 00				33
34		47 3 6 4 33	61 1 2 0 65	86 2 5 9 70	72 5 0 3 38	34
35	Net Income	13 7 5 6 32			13 7 5 6 32	35
36		61 1 2 0 65	61 1 2 0 65	86 2 5 9 70	86 2 5 9 70	36
37						37
38						38
39						39
40						40
41						41

3. Print the closing entries from the general journal, page 12.

4. Post the closing entries to the general ledger and print the general ledger.

5. Print a post-closing trial balance from the general ledger. You should only show assets, liabilities, and the owner's equity account—therefore, a relatively short trial balance. If you find any account open beyond the Capital account, you either failed to include it in the closing entries or you forgot to post it before taking this final trial balance to see if the temporary accounts are closed and only the real or permanent accounts remain open for the start of the new fiscal period.

Congratulations! You have completed your work with All About You Spa.

PART I: Completion

Complete each of the following statements by writing the appropriate word(s) in the spaces provided.

1. An actual count of a stock of goods is called a(n) _____.

2. Under the _____ system, entries to record the purchase of merchandise are recorded in the Merchandise Inventory account.

3. Unearned revenue is classified as a(n) _____.

4. Under the periodic inventory system, the first adjustment is to debit _____ for the amount of the beginning inventory.

5. Under the perpetual inventory system, after recording the sale of the goods, the accountant debits _____ and credits _____.

6. An increase in Rent Expense results in a(n) _____ to net income.

7. Gross Profit is calculated by subtracting _____ from Net Sales.

8. Current Assets minus Current Liabilities equals _____.

9. Gross Profit minus Total Operating Expenses equals _____.

10. Net Purchases plus _____ equals Delivered Cost of Purchases.

PART II: True/False

T	F	1. The second adjustment for Merchandise Inventory under the periodic inventory system is to debit Cost of Goods Sold and credit Merchandise Inventory.
T	F	2. Unearned Rent Income is classified as a revenue.
T	F	3. The perpetual inventory system requires that each sale of goods has two entries: one to reduce inventory and affix the cost of the goods sold and one to record the sale.
T	F	4. The periodic inventory system requires two adjusting entries: one to remove the old inventory amount and one to enter the latest inventory amount.
T	F	5. The adjustment to unearned revenue allows the correct amount of liability and revenue to be applied to each fiscal period involved.
T	F	6. Freight In is classified in the Operating Expenses section of an income statement.
T	F	7. Under the perpetual inventory system, the cost of goods sold is calculated by subtracting ending inventory from the cost of goods available for sale.
T	F	8. Reversing entries are optional, and only some adjusting entries are reversed.

Note: Answers to Before a Test Check begin on page A-1.

T   F   9. Delivery Expense is added to net purchases to arrive at delivered cost of purchases.

T   F   10. Purchases Returns and Allowances increases Income from Operations.

PART III: Application

1. Alphonse Company uses the periodic inventory system. Employees have just taken a physical count of its inventory. This ending inventory has been valued at $136,000. The company's accounting records show the Merchandise Inventory account with a debit balance of $132,000. Journalize the entries on December 31 to adjust the records for this situation.

2. Regletto Company uses the perpetual inventory system. Employees have just taken a physical count of its inventory. This ending inventory has been valued at $146,000. The company's accounting records show the Merchandise Inventory account with a debit balance of $148,000. Journalize the entry on December 31 to adjust the records for this situation.

3. On December 1, Wesley Company collected $20,000 for a remodeling job that will be completed on March 31 of the following year. The revenue will be earned evenly over four months. Wesley Company's fiscal period ends December 31. Make the entries to record the collection of the cash and the year-end adjustment to reflect the amount of revenue earned in December.

4. Yorkland Company has total assets of $250,000, of which noncurrent assets amount to $140,000. The company also has total liabilities of $130,000, of which $80,000 are long-term liabilities. Calculate (a) working capital and (b) current ratio.

Comprehensive Review Problem

You are to record transactions completed by Fine Fabrics during the month of February of this year. This company is located in Dallas. To gain practice in completing the steps in the accounting cycle, assume that the fiscal period consists of one month.

CHART OF ACCOUNTS

Assets

111	Cash
112	Petty Cash Fund
113	Accounts Receivable
114	Merchandise Inventory
117	Supplies
118	Prepaid Insurance
122	Equipment
123	Accumulated Depreciation, Equipment

Liabilities

221	Accounts Payable
226	Employees' Income Tax Payable
227	FICA Tax Payable
228	State Unemployment Tax Payable
229	Federal Unemployment Tax Payable
230	Salaries Payable

Owner's Equity

311	J. L. Fisher, Capital
312	J. L. Fisher, Drawing
313	Income Summary

Revenue

411	Sales
412	Sales Returns and Allowances

Cost of Goods Sold

511	Purchases
512	Purchases Returns and Allowances
513	Purchases Discounts
514	Freight In

Operating Expenses

611	Salary Expense
612	Payroll Tax Expense
613	Rent Expense
614	Utilities Expense
616	Supplies Expense
617	Insurance Expense
618	Depreciation Expense, Equipment
619	Miscellaneous Expense

JOURNALS

Sales Journal, page 56
Purchases Journal, page 62
Cash Receipts Journal, page 69
Cash Payments Journal, page 75
General Journal, pages 89–92

ACCOUNTS RECEIVABLE

Hotel Bentnor
Jerome and Woods
Wilkes Decorators

ACCOUNTS PAYABLE

Byran, Inc.
Keller Textiles
Meldon Fabrics
Taylor Manufacturing Company

TRANSACTIONS

The following transactions were completed during February of this year.

Feb. 1 Reversed the adjusting entry for accrued salaries, $710.

1 Sold merchandise on account to Hotel Bentnor, $13,052.97, invoice no. 5221.

2 Issued Ck. No. 7216, $17,271.62, to Keller Textiles, in payment of its invoice no. D1739 for $17,624.10 less 2 percent discount.

5 Bought merchandise on account from Meldon Fabrics, $4,551.90; invoice no. RE275, dated February 2; terms 1/10, n/30; FOB Orlando; freight prepaid and added to the invoice, $147 (total, $4,698.90).

5 Received an electric bill and paid Regional Power, Ck. No. 7217, $121.

6 Received check from Jerome and Woods for $11,619.50 in payment of account.

7 Issued Ck. No. 7218, $9,519.84, to Meldon Fabrics, in payment of its invoice no. RE64 for $9,616 less 1 percent discount.

9 Cash sales for February 1 through February 9, $7,951.60.

12 Recorded the payroll in the payroll register for regular semi-monthly salaries for period ended February 12. Salaries: M. B. Corson, $2,730; K. L. Vickers, $2,240. Income tax withholdings are $382.20 for Corson and $313.60 for Vickers. Assume the following tax rates and taxable earnings limits (see the payroll register in your Working Papers for beginning cumulative earnings):

- Social Security taxable earnings, $94,200, with a rate of 6.2 percent.
- Medicare taxable earnings, all earnings, with a rate of 1.45 percent.

12 Recorded the payroll entry in the general journal, crediting Salaries Payable.

Feb.   12   Issued Ck. No. 7219, $2,138.95, to M. B. Corson. Issued Ck. No. 7220, $1,755.04, to K. L. Vickers. Use two lines and debit Salaries Payable. (Verify these amounts.)

12   Recorded payroll taxes. Assume the following tax rates and taxable earnings:

- Federal unemployment taxable earnings, $7,000, with a rate of 0.8 percent.
- State unemployment taxable earnings, $7,000, with a rate of 5.4 percent. *Note:* Corson's taxable earnings for unemployment amount to $1,540 and Vickers's amount to $2,240.

12   Received a credit memo from Meldon Fabrics for defective merchandise, $542, credit memo no. 916.

14   Issued Ck. No. 7221, $2,912.44, to State Bank for monthly deposit of January employees' federal income tax withheld, $1,391.60, and FICA taxes, $1,520.84.

14   Sold merchandise on account to Jerome and Woods, $15,692.50, invoice no. 5222.

14   Issued Ck. No. 7222, $4,116.80, to Meldon Fabrics, in payment of its invoice no. RE275 less the credit memo for defective merchandise and less the discount ($40.10). *Note:* Debit Accounts Payable, $4,156.90, and credit Purchases Discounts, $40.10. Verify these amounts: $4,698.90, less $147 freight, less $542 return, less 1 percent cash discount (cash discounts can't be taken on freight). Remember to add $147 freight back to compute the cash credit.

18   Bought merchandise on account from Byran, Inc., $20,488.20; invoice no. 164M, dated February 14; terms 2/10, n/30; FOB Miami; freight prepaid and added to the invoice, $1,152 (total, $21,640.20).

18   Cash sales for February 10 through February 18, $7,994.14.

19   Issued Ck. No. 7223 payable to Faster Printing for invoice forms, $327 (not previously recorded). (Debit Supplies Expense.)

19   Received check from Wilkes Decorators for $4,920.14 in payment of account.

22   Issued Ck. No. 7224, $12,710, to Taylor Manufacturing Company, in payment of its invoice no. 9264D.

22   Sold merchandise on account to Wilkes Decorators, $16,721.42, invoice no. 5223.

24   Issued credit memo no. 214 to Wilkes Decorators, $156, for merchandise returned.

24   Bought merchandise on account from Keller Textiles, $16,448.01; invoice no. D1797, dated February 22; terms 2/10, n/30; FOB Dallas.

26   Recorded the payroll in the payroll register for regular semimonthly salaries for period ended February 26. Salaries: M. B. Corson, $2,730; K. L. Vickers, $2,240. Income tax withholdings are $382.20 for Corson and $313.60 for Vickers. *Note:* See the entry of February 12 for taxable earnings limits and tax rates. See the payroll register in your Working Papers for beginning cumulative earnings.

26   Recorded the payroll entry in the general journal, crediting Salaries Payable.

26   Issued Ck. No. 7225, $2,138.95, to M. B. Corson. Issued Ck. No. 7226, $1,755.04, to K. L. Vickers. Use two lines and debit Salaries Payable.

Feb. 26 Ck. No. 7227 voided.

26 Recorded payroll taxes. *Note:* Vickers's taxable earnings for unemployment amount to $280.

27 Issued Ck. No. 7228, $994, to Greater Freight Line for transportation charge on merchandise purchased from Keller Textiles.

28 Issued Ck. No. 7229, $48.63, payable to Cash to reimburse the petty cash fund. Petty cash payments consist of Supplies Expense, $27.16, and Miscellaneous Expense, $21.47.

28 Cash sales for February 19 through February 28, $7,685.20.

28 Issued Ck. No. 7230, $650, to Grandy Realty for monthly rent.

28 J. L. Fisher (owner) withdrew $3,000 for personal use, Ck. No. 7231.

INSTRUCTIONS

1. Journalize and post the transactions completed during February.

   a. Post the amounts in the Other Accounts columns of the special journals daily.
   b. Post the general journal daily.
   c. Post the totals of the special columns of the special journals at the end of the month.

2. Prepare a schedule of accounts receivable and a schedule of accounts payable.

3. Complete the work sheet for February.
   Data for the month-end adjustments are as follows:

   a–b. Merchandise inventory at February 28, $44,262
   c. Salaries accrued at February 28, $710
   d. Insurance expired during February, $40
   e. Depreciation of equipment during February, $105

4. Journalize and post the adjusting entries.
5. Prepare an income statement.
6. Prepare a statement of owner's equity. (No additional investment was made during the month.)
7. Prepare a balance sheet.
8. Journalize and post the closing entries.
9. Prepare a post-closing trial balance.

INSTRUCTIONS FOR GENERAL LEDGER SOFTWARE

1. Journalize and post the transactions completed during February.
2. Print the journals and the general ledger.
3. Print a trial balance.
4. Print a schedule of accounts receivable and a schedule of accounts payable.

5. Journalize and post the month-end adjustments:

   a–b. Merchandise inventory at February 28, $44,262
   c. Salaries accrued at February 28, $710
   d. Insurance expired during February, $40
   e. Depreciation of equipment during February, $105

6. Print the adjusting entries, an adjusted trial balance, and the general ledger after adjustments.
7. Print the income statement, the statement of owner's equity, and the balance sheet.
8. Journalize and post the closing entries.
9. Print the closing entries.
10. Print a post-closing trial balance.

Inventory Methods

Performance Objectives

After you have completed this appendix, you will be able to do the following:

1. Determine the amount of the ending merchandise inventory by the weighted-average-cost method.

2. Determine the amount of the ending merchandise inventory by the first-in, first-out method (FIFO).

3. Determine the amount of the ending merchandise inventory by the last-in, first-out method (LIFO).

To determine the dollar amount of the ending merchandise inventory, it is necessary to take a physical count of the various items in stock and match them up with their costs. In other words, the ending inventory consists of the number of units of each type of item on hand multiplied by the cost of each unit.

If each unit were purchased at exactly the same price, the job of determining the total cost of the inventory would be simple. For example, if there are 100 units of Product A on hand, and all 100 units were bought at $15, the total cost of the ending inventory is $1,500 (100 × $15). However, over a period of time, costs of individual purchases of units may differ. Changes in costs of individual units make the different methods of inventory valuation necessary.

We will use Carlson Appliances, a distributor of dishwashers, to illustrate the three methods of inventory valuation. Carlson's ending inventory consists of 176 Model M43 dishwashers acquired through various purchases, as follows:

Specific Purchase	Number of Units	Cost per Unit	Total Cost
Beginning inventory	34	$270	$ 9,180
First purchase	60	282	16,920
Second purchase	256	298	76,288
Third purchase	164	312	51,168
Total units available	514		$153,556

Of the 514 units available for sale, 176 units are still on hand and 338 have been sold (514 − 176).

Carlson Appliances may choose any one of the following three methods of recording the total cost of the 176 units in the ending inventory of dishwashers.

WEIGHTED-AVERAGE-COST METHOD

OBJECTIVE 1

Determine the amount of the ending merchandise inventory by the weighted-average-cost method.

$$\text{Average Cost per Unit} = \frac{\text{Total Cost}}{\text{Total Units Available}} = \frac{\$153,556}{514} = \$298.75 \text{ (rounded)}$$

$$\text{Cost of 176 units} = \$298.75 \times 176 \text{ units} = \$52,580$$

FIRST-IN, FIRST-OUT METHOD

OBJECTIVE 2

Determine the amount of the ending merchandise inventory by the first-in, first-out method (FIFO).

This method is based on the **assumption** that the first units of dishwashers purchased will be sold first. The costs of the units left will be those of the most recently purchased units. You may think of this as the way a grocery store sells milk. Because milk will sour, the oldest milk is moved to the front of the display shelf and is sold first. Consequently, the cartons of milk remaining on the shelf are the freshest milk.

Relating to our illustration of dishwashers:

Specific Purchase	Number of Units	Cost per Unit	Total Cost
Beginning inventory	34	$270	$ 9,180
First purchase	60	282	16,920
Second purchase	256	298	76,288
Third purchase	164	312	51,168
Total units available	514		$153,556

The cost of the 176 dishwashers on hand (most recently purchased) is as follows:

164 units (third purchase)   @ $312 each = $51,168
 12 units (second purchase) @ $298 each =   3,576
176 units $54,744

LAST-IN, FIRST-OUT METHOD

OBJECTIVE 3

Determine the amount of the ending merchandise inventory by the last-in, first-out method (LIFO).

This method is based on the **assumption** that the last units of dishwashers purchased will be sold first. The costs of the units left over will be those of the earliest purchased units. You may think of this as the way a coal yard sells coal. When the coal yard sells coal to its customers, it takes coal off the top of the pile. Consequently, the tons of coal in the ending inventory consist of those first few tons at the bottom of the pile.

Relating to our illustration of dishwashers shown above, the cost of the 176 dishwashers on hand (earliest purchased) is as follows:

34 units (beginning inventory) @ $270 each = $ 9,180
60 units (first purchase)   @ $282 each = 16,920
82 units (second purchase)   @ $298 each = 24,436
176 units $50,536

Comparison of Three Methods		
Method	**Ending Inventory (176 units)**	**Cost of Goods Sold (Goods Available for Sale − Ending Inventory) (338 units = 514 − 176)**
Weighted-average-cost	$52,580	$100,976 ($153,556 − $52,580)
First-in, first-out	54,744	98,812 ($153,556 − $54,744)
Last-in, first-out	50,536	103,020 ($153,556 − $50,536)

Assume that the dishwashers were sold for $450 each.

	Weighted-Average-Cost	**First-in, First-out**	**Last-in, First-out**
Sales (338 units × $450 each)	$152,100	$152,100	$152,100
Cost of Goods Sold	100,976	98,812	103,020
Gross Profit	$ 51,124	$ 53,288	$ 49,080

As you can see, the inventory method used can have a dramatic effect on the gross profit of a business. Once an inventory method is adopted by a business, the method must be consistently used. If a company wants to change its inventory method for tax purposes, the company must request permission from the Internal Revenue Service.

PROBLEMS

P.O. 1

Check Figure

Cost of ending inventory, $399.24

Problem E-1 Bexley Nursery sells bark to its customers at retail. Bexley buys bark from a plywood mill in bulk and transports the bark in its own trucks. Information relating to the beginning inventory and purchases of bark is as follows:

Beginning inventory	1,500 cubic yards @ $0.30 per cubic yard
First purchase	2,100 cubic yards @ $0.32 per cubic yard
Second purchase	1,400 cubic yards @ $0.36 per cubic yard
Third purchase	1,000 cubic yards @ $0.37 per cubic yard

Find the cost of 1,200 cubic yards in the ending inventory by the weighted-average-cost method. Carry average cost per cubic yard to four decimals.

P.O. 2

Check Figure

Cost of ending inventory, $442

Problem E-2 Using the information presented in Problem E-1, find the cost of the ending inventory by the first-in, first-out method.

P.O. 3

Check Figure

Cost of ending inventory, $360

Problem E-3 Using the information presented in Problem E-1, find the cost of the ending inventory by the last-in, first-out method.

APPENDIX

F

Financial Statement Analysis

Performance Objectives

After you have completed this appendix, you will be able to do the following:

1. Determine gross profit percentage.

2. Determine merchandise inventory turnover.

3. Determine accounts receivable turnover.

4. Determine return on investment.

An important function of accounting is to provide tools for interpreting the financial statements or the results of operations. This appendix presents a number of percentages and ratios that are frequently used to analyze financial statements.

GROSS PROFIT PERCENTAGE

OBJECTIVE 1
Determine gross profit percentage.

Southern Office Furniture will serve as our example (see the comparative income statement on the next page).

For each year, net sales is the base (100 percent). All other items on the income statement can be expressed as a percentage of net sales for the particular year involved. For example, let's look at the following percentages:

$$\text{Gross Profit \% (2008)} = \frac{\text{Gross Profit for 2008}}{\text{Net Sales for 2008}} = \frac{\$250,000}{\$528,000} = 0.473 = 47\%$$

$$\text{Gross Profit \% (2007)} = \frac{\text{Gross Profit for 2007}}{\text{Net Sales for 2007}} = \frac{\$252,000}{\$500,000} = 0.504 = 50\%$$

$$\text{Sales Salary Expense \% (2008)} = \frac{\text{Sales Salary Expense for 2008}}{\text{Net Sales for 2008}}$$

$$= \frac{\$63,600}{\$528,000} = 0.120 = 12\%$$

$$\text{Sales Salary Expense \% (2007)} = \frac{\text{Sales Salary Expense for 2007}}{\text{Net Sales for 2007}}$$

$$= \frac{\$58,000}{\$500,000} = 0.116 = 11.6\%$$

Here's how you might interpret a few of the percentages:

2008

- For every $100 in net sales, gross profit amounted to $47.
- For every $100 in net sales, sales salary expense amounted to $12.
- For every $100 in net sales, net income amounted to $22.

519

Southern Office Furniture
Comparative Income Statement
For Years Ended January 31, 2008, and January 31, 2007

	2008		2007	
	AMOUNT	PERCENT	AMOUNT	PERCENT
Revenue from Sales:				
Sales	$533 6 0 0 00	101	$510 0 0 0 00	102
Less Sales Returns and Allowances	5 6 0 0 00	1	10 0 0 0 00	2
Net Sales	$528 0 0 0 00	100	$500 0 0 0 00	100
Cost of Goods Sold:				
Merchandise Inventory, February 1	$ 46 0 0 0 00	9	$ 64 0 0 0 00	13
Delivered Cost of Purchases	290 0 0 0 00	55	230 0 0 0 00	46
Cost of Goods Available for Sale	$336 0 0 0 00	64	$294 0 0 0 00	59
Less Merchandise Inventory, January 31	58 0 0 0 00	11	46 0 0 0 00	9
Cost of Goods Sold	$278 0 0 0 00	53	$248 0 0 0 00	50
Gross Profit	$250 0 0 0 00	47	$252 0 0 0 00	50
Operating Expenses:				
Sales Salary Expense	$ 63 6 0 0 00	12	$ 58 0 0 0 00	12
Rent Expense	24 0 0 0 00	5	24 0 0 0 00	5
Advertising Expense	21 4 0 0 00	4	16 0 0 0 00	3
Depreciation Expense, Equipment	20 0 0 0 00	4	18 0 0 0 00	4
Insurance Expense	2 0 0 0 00	—	2 0 0 0 00	—
Store Supplies Expense	1 0 0 0 00	—	1 0 0 0 00	—
Miscellaneous Expense	1 0 0 0 00	—	1 0 0 0 00	—
Total Operating Expenses	$133 0 0 0 00	25	$120 0 0 0 00	24
Net Income	$117 0 0 0 00	22	$132 0 0 0 00	26

2007

- For every $100 in net sales, gross profit amounted to $50.
- For every $100 in net sales, sales salary expense amounted to $12.
- For every $100 in net sales, net income amounted to $26.

The gross profit percentage declined from 50% in 2007 to 47% in 2008 because the Cost of Goods Sold percentage increased from 50% in 2007 to 53% in 2008.

MERCHANDISE INVENTORY TURNOVER

OBJECTIVE 2
Determine merchandise inventory turnover.

Merchandise inventory turnover is the number of times a firm's average inventory is sold during a given year.

$$\text{Merchandise Inventory Turnover} = \frac{\text{Cost of Goods Sold}}{\text{Average Merchandise Inventory}}$$

$$\text{Average Merchandise Inventory} = \frac{\text{Beginning Merchandise Inventory} + \text{Ending Merchandise Inventory}}{2}$$

	2008	**2007**
Beginning Merchandise Inventory (from the Cost of Goods Sold section of the income statement)	$46,000	$ 64,000
Ending Merchandise Inventory (from the Cost of Goods Sold section of the income statement or the balance sheet)	58,000	46,000

2008

$$\text{Average Merchandise Inventory} = \frac{\$46,000 + \$58,000}{2} = \frac{\$104,000}{2} = \underline{\$52,000}$$

$$\text{Merchandise Inventory Turnover} = \frac{\$278,000}{\$52,000} = \underline{5.35} \text{ times per year}$$

2007

$$\text{Average Merchandise Inventory} = \frac{\$64,000 + \$46,000}{2} = \frac{\$110,000}{2} = \underline{\$55,000}$$

$$\text{Merchandise Inventory Turnover} = \frac{\$248,000}{\$55,000} = \underline{4.51} \text{ times per year}$$

With each turnover of merchandise, the company makes a gross profit, so the higher the turnover, the better.

The inventory turnover improved from 4.51 in 2007 to 5.35 in 2008 because the inventory was lower on average in 2008 as compared to 2007. Over the same period, net sales increased 5.6% from $500,000 in 2007 to $528,000 in 2008.

ACCOUNTS RECEIVABLE TURNOVER

OBJECTIVE 3
Determine accounts receivable turnover.

Accounts receivable turnover is the number of times charge accounts are turned over (paid off) during a given year. A turnover implies a sale on account followed by the cash collection of the amount owed.

$$\text{Accounts Receivable Turnover} = \frac{\text{Net Sales on Account}}{\text{Average Accounts Receivable}}$$

$$\text{Average Accounts Receivable} = \frac{\text{Beginning Accounts Receivable} + \text{Ending Accounts Receivable}}{2}$$

Going back to Southern Office Furniture, let's assume the following information for 2008 and 2007.

	2008	**2007**
Net sales on account (from the sales journal)	$330,000	$302,000
Beginning accounts receivable (from Accounts Receivable account)	39,680	37,500
Ending accounts receivable (from Accounts Receivable account)	45,840	39,680

2008

$$\text{Average Accounts Receivable} = \frac{\$39,680 + \$45,840}{2} = \frac{\$85,520}{2} = \$42,760$$

$$\text{Accounts Receivable Turnover} = \frac{\$330,000}{\$42,760} = 7.72 \text{ times per year}$$

2007

$$\text{Average Accounts Receivable} = \frac{\$37,500 + \$39,680}{2} = \frac{\$77,180}{2} = \$38,590$$

$$\text{Accounts Receivable Turnover} = \frac{\$302,000}{\$38,590} = 7.83 \text{ times per year}$$

A lower turnover rate indicates that a firm is experiencing greater difficulty in collecting charge accounts. In addition, more investment capital is tied up in accounts receivable.

The receivable turnover deteriorated slightly from 7.83 in 2007 to 7.72 in 2008, possibly because the seller granted easier credit terms or the buyers incurred cash flow problems because of a declining economy. From the end of 2007 to the end of 2008, the receivables balance increased almost 16% from $39,680 to $45,840. However, over the same period, net sales increased only 5.6%. This trend would be of concern to management and owners.

RETURN ON INVESTMENT (YIELD)

OBJECTIVE 4
Determine return on investment.

Return on investment represents the earning power of the owner's investment in the business.

$$\text{Return on Investment} = \frac{\text{Net Income for the Year}}{\text{Average Capital}}$$

$$\text{Average Capital} = \frac{\text{Beginning Capital} + \text{Ending Capital}}{2}$$

Getting back to Southern Office Furniture, let's assume the following information for 2008 and 2007:

	2008	2007
Beginning balance of owner's Capital account	$515,000	$530,000
Ending balance of owner's Capital account	530,000	510,000

2008

$$\text{Average Capital} = \frac{\$515,000 + \$530,000}{2} = \frac{\$1,045,000}{2} = \$522,500$$

$$\text{Return on Investment} = \frac{\$117,000}{\$522,500} = 0.224 = 22.4\%$$

2007

$$\text{Average Capital} = \frac{\$530,000 + \$510,000}{2} = \frac{\$1,040,000}{2} = \underline{\$520,000}$$

$$\text{Return on Investment} = \frac{\$132,000}{\$520,000} = 0.254 = \underline{\underline{25.4\%}}$$

As a result, we can state the following:

- In 2008, for an average investment of $100, the business earned $22.40.
- In 2007, for an average investment of $100, the business earned $25.40.

The return on investment deteriorated from 25.4% in 2007 to 22.4% in 2008 because net income declined 11% from $132,000 in 2007 to $117,000 in 2008.

PROBLEMS

P.O. 1

Problem F-1 Pena Company's abbreviated comparative income statement for years 2008 and 2007 is as follows:

Pena Company
Comparative Income Statement
For Years Ended December 31, 2008 and December 31, 2007

	2008	2007
Net Sales	$587 2 0 0 00	$562 0 0 0 00
Cost of Goods Sold	287 4 0 0 00	277 2 0 0 00
Gross Profit	$299 8 0 0 00	$284 8 0 0 00
Total Operating Expenses	152 2 4 0 00	146 1 6 0 00
Net Income	$147 5 6 0 00	$138 6 4 0 00

Check Figure

Net income % (2007), 24.7%

Instructions

1. For the years 2008 and 2007, determine gross profit as a percentage of net sales.
2. For the years 2008 and 2007, determine net income as a percentage of net sales.

P.O. 2

Problem F-2 Pena Company's merchandise inventory figures are:

	2008	2007
Beginning merchandise inventory (January 1)	$188,420	$206,110
Purchases	402,190	359,510
Ending merchandise inventory (December 31)	203,210	188,420

Check Figure

Merchandise inventory turnover (2008), 2 times

Instructions

Determine the merchandise inventory turnover for the years 2008 and 2007.

P.O. 4

Problem F-3 A. L. Pena, Capital, account balances are as follows:

January 1, 2007	$475,670
January 1, 2008	593,970
December 31, 2008	626,820

Check Figure

Return on investment (2007), 25.9%

Instructions

Determine the return on investment for the years 2008 and 2007 if net income is $147,560 for 2008 and $138,640 for 2007.

G The Statement of Cash Flows

Performance Objectives

After you have completed this appendix, you will be able to do the following:

1. Classify cash flows as Operating Activities, Investing Activities, and Financing Activities.

2. Prepare a statement of cash flows.

The fourth major financial statement is the statement of cash flows. This statement explains in detail how the balance of Cash has changed between the beginning and the end of the fiscal period. Some accountants refer to the statement as the "where got, where gone" statement of cash.

SECTIONS OF THE STATEMENT OF CASH FLOWS

OBJECTIVE 1

Classify cash flows as Operating Activities, Investing Activities, and Financing Activities.

The statement has three main sections: Operating Activities, Investing Activities, and Financing Activities. Cash flows are subdivided as cash inflows and cash outflows.

Operating Activities

This section covers cash received and used in carrying out the company's operations.

Cash Inflows

- Cash from selling of services or merchandise
- Cash from collection of miscellaneous income

Cash Outflows

- Payments for purchases of merchandise and supplies from suppliers
- Payments of salaries or wages
- Payments of rent, utilities, insurance
- Payment of interest to creditors

Investing Activities

This section covers cash used in or received from buying or selling of property and equipment assets and all other noncurrent assets, such as long-term investments.

Cash Inflows

- Cash received from the sale of noncurrent assets

Cash Outflows

- Cash payments to buy noncurrent assets

Financing Activities

This section covers cash related to changes in the owner's equity accounts and long-term liabilities accounts.

Cash Inflows

- Investment of cash by the owner
- Borrowing from creditors

Cash Outflows

- Withdrawals of cash by the owner
- Repayment of loans to creditors

Cash, for purposes of the cash flow statement, includes checking and savings accounts and also cash equivalents. A company that has idle cash temporarily during the year may prefer to invest in short-term interest-bearing notes or money market funds. These short-term funds are considered to be cash equivalents.

FINANCIAL STATEMENTS NEEDED FOR PREPARING THE STATEMENT OF CASH FLOWS

The financial statements required for preparing the statement of cash flows consist of the income statement and the statement of owner's equity for the fiscal period, the balance sheet at the end of the fiscal period, and the balance sheet at the end of the previous fiscal period. Using the two balance sheets, we can prepare a comparative balance sheet for the two fiscal periods, showing the increases and decreases in the various accounts.

ILLUSTRATION OF THE STATEMENT OF CASH FLOWS

OBJECTIVE 2

Prepare a statement of cash flows.

The financial statements for Kelley Company are shown here. Based on the comparative balance sheet, the first step is to record the increases and decreases in the accounts.

Kelley Company
Income Statement
For Year Ended December 31, 2007

Revenue from Sales:												
Net Sales	$847	0	0	0	00							
Less Cost of Goods Sold	500	0	0	0	00							
Gross Profit						$347	0	0	0	00		
Operating Expenses:												
Salary Expense	$ 70	0	0	0	00							
Rent Expense	10	0	0	0	00							
Depreciation Expense, Equipment	6	0	0	0	00							
Supplies Expense	1	0	0	0	00							
Total Operating Expenses						87	0	0	0	00		
Net Income						$260	0	0	0	00		

Kelley Company
Statement of Owner's Equity
For Year Ended December 31, 2007

B. Kelley, Capital, January 1, 2007		$120 0 0 0 00
Additional Investment, March 2, 2007		10 0 0 0 00
Total Investment		$130 0 0 0 00
Net Income for the Year	$260 0 0 0 00	
Less Withdrawals for the Year	150 0 0 0 00	
Increase in Capital		110 0 0 0 00
B. Kelley, Capital, Dec. 31, 2007		$240 0 0 0 00

Kelley Company
Comparative Balance Sheet
December 31, 2007, and December 31, 2006

	2007		2006		INCREASE (DECREASE)
Assets					
Cash		$ 12 0 0 0 00		$ 7 0 0 0 00	$ 5 0 0 0 00
Accounts Receivable		70 0 0 0 00		66 0 0 0 00	4 0 0 0 00
Merchandise Inventory		220 0 0 0 00		113 0 0 0 00	107 0 0 0 00
Supplies		3 0 0 0 00		4 0 0 0 00	(1 0 0 0 00)
Equipment	$72 0 0 0 00		$60 0 0 0 00		12 0 0 0 00
Less Accumulated Deprec.	(62 0 0 0 00)	10 0 0 0 00	(56 0 0 0 00)	4 0 0 0 00	(6 0 0 0 00)
Total Assets		$315 0 0 0 00		$194 0 0 0 00	$121 0 0 0 00
Liabilities					
Accounts Payable	$71 0 0 0 00		$69 0 0 0 00		$ 2 0 0 0 00
Salaries Payable	4 0 0 0 00		5 0 0 0 00		(1 0 0 0 00)
Total Liabilities		$ 75 0 0 0 00		$ 74 0 0 0 00	$ 1 0 0 0 00
Owner's Equity					
B. Kelley, Capital		240 0 0 0 00		120 0 0 0 00	120 0 0 0 00
Total Liabilities and					
Owner's Equity		$315 0 0 0 00		$194 0 0 0 00	$121 0 0 0 00

Note the $5,000 increase in Cash. First let's see how this increase comes about.

- Cash flows related to operating activities involve changes in current asset and current liability accounts.
- Cash flows related to investing activities involve changes in property and equipment (long-term asset) accounts (with the exception of Accumulated Depreciation).
- Cash flows related to financing activities involve changes in owner's equity accounts and long-term liabilities accounts.

Now let's present the statement of cash flows.

Kelley Company
Statement of Cash Flows
For Year Ended December 31, 2007

Cash Flows from (Used by) Operating Activities													
Net Income	$260	0	0	0	00								
Add (Deduct) Items to Convert Net Income from Accrual Basis to Cash Basis													
Depreciation Expense	6	0	0	0	00								
Increase in Accounts Receivable	(4	0	0	0	00)								
Increase in Merchandise Inventory	(107	0	0	0	00)								
Decrease in Supplies	1	0	0	0	00								
Increase in Accounts Payable	2	0	0	0	00								
Decrease in Salaries Payable	(1	0	0	0	00)								
Net Cash Flows from Operating Activities						$157	0	0	0	00			
Cash Flows from (Used by) Investing Activities													
Purchase of Equipment	$ (12	0	0	0	00)								
Net Cash Flows Used by Investing Activities						(12	0	0	0	00)			
Cash Flows from (Used by) Financing Activities													
Cash Investment by Owner	$ 10	0	0	0	00								
Cash Withdrawals by Owner	(150	0	0	0	00)								
Net Cash Flows Used by Financing Activities						(140	0	0	0	00)			
Net Increase (Decrease) in Cash						$ 5	0	0	0	00			

EXPLANATION OF ITEMS IN THE STATEMENT OF CASH FLOWS

Cash Flows from Operating Activities

- Net income of $260,000, from the income statement, included such items as sale of services or merchandise, miscellaneous income, and payment of expenses such as salaries or wages, utilities, and interest.
- Depreciation of $6,000 was included as an expense on the income statement, but it did not result in the payment of cash to anyone. Since depreciation expense was deducted on the income statement, we now add $6,000 back in. Depreciation expense is always an addition under Cash Flows from Operating Activities.
- Accounts Receivable increased by $4,000. Of the amount shown as Sales on the income statement, $4,000 was in the form of additional charge account balances and therefore were not cash inflows. So we deduct $4,000 from Cash Flows from Operating Activities.
- Merchandise Inventory increased by $107,000. Because the inventory increased by $107,000 during the year (more merchandise was bought than was sold), we can assume that the change resulted in a $107,000 decrease in Cash Flows from Operating Activities.
- Decrease in Supplies of $1,000 means that the company used up supplies bought in a previous fiscal period and included the entire amount of supplies used as Supplies Expense on the income statement. In other words, the $1,000 of Supplies Expense shown on the income statement did not result in a payment of cash in the current period. For this appendix, Supplies is considered a significant asset of the business, so the ending inventory is recorded as an asset.

- Increase in Accounts Payable of $2,000 in this case means that $2,000 of the amount listed as Purchases on the income statement (not shown because we included Purchases in Cost of Goods Sold) did not result in the payment of cash. So we add $2,000 to Cash Flows from Operating Activities.
- Decrease in Salaries Payable of $1,000 means that the amount listed as Salary Expense on the income statement is $1,000 less than the amount of cash spent by the company. So we deduct $1,000 from Cash Flows from Operating Activities.

Cash Flows from Investing Activities

Equipment increased by $12,000. We would have to look at the journal entry to determine how much cash was involved. In this case, we assume that the purchase of equipment resulted in a payment of $12,000 cash. So we deduct $12,000 from Cash Flows from Investing Activities.

Cash Flows from Financing Activities

- The owner's Capital account increased by $10,000 as a result of an additional investment. We would have to look at the journal entry to determine how much cash was involved. In this case, we assume that the investment was in the form of cash. So we add $10,000 to Cash Flows from Financing Activities.
- The owner's Drawing account increased by $150,000. We would have to look at the journal entries to determine how much cash was involved. In this case, we assume that the withdrawals were in the form of cash. So we deduct $150,000 from Cash Flows from Financing Activities.

Here are some handy guidelines for preparing a statement of cash flows.

Add to Net Income	Why?
If Current Assets decrease	If an account like Accounts Receivable decreases, this means that we received more cash than the amount listed as Net Sales.
If Current Liabilities increase	If an account like Accounts Payable increases, this means that we bought more merchandise or supplies than we paid for in cash.
Deduct from Net Income	**Why?**
If Current Assets increase	If an account like Prepaid Insurance increases, this means that we paid more cash for insurance than the amount listed as Insurance Expense on the income statement.
If Current Liabilities decrease	If an account like Notes Payable decreases, this means that we paid out cash to pay off the note.

The statement of cash flows can be used as a source in the preparation of a cash budget. The cash budget is an important management tool that focuses on understanding and managing the cash flow of a business.

PROBLEMS

P.O. 1,2

Problem G-1 Monroe Company has the following financial statements for 2006 and 2007. Assume that the withdrawals were in the form of cash.

Check Figure

Net cash flows from operating activities, $44,500

Instructions

Prepare a statement of cash flows for the year ended December 31, 2007.

Monroe Company
Income Statement
For Year Ended December 31, 2007

Revenue:			
Income from Services			$134 0 0 0 00
Expenses:			
Wages Expense	$77 0 0 0 00		
Rent Expense	8 0 0 0 00		
Depreciation Expense, Equipment	5 0 0 0 00		
Supplies Expense	2 0 0 0 00		
Total Expenses		92 0 0 0 00	
Net Income		$ 42 0 0 0 00	

Monroe Company
Statement of Owner's Equity
For Year Ended December 31, 2007

B. N. Monroe, Capital, January 1, 2007		$94 0 0 0 00
Net Income for the Year	$42 0 0 0 00	
Less Withdrawals for the Year	40 0 0 0 00	
Increase in Capital		2 0 0 0 00
B. N. Monroe, Capital, December 31, 2007		$96 0 0 0 00

Monroe Company
Comparative Balance Sheet
December 31, 2007, and December 31, 2006

	2007		2006		INCREASE (DECREASE)
Assets					
Cash		$ 9 0 0 0 00		$ 6 5 0 0 00	$2 5 0 0 00
Supplies		5 0 0 0 00		2 5 0 0 00	2 5 0 0 00
Equipment	$100 0 0 0 00		$98 0 0 0 00		2 0 0 0 00
Less Accumulated Depreciation	(18 0 0 0 00)	82 0 0 0 00	(13 0 0 0 00)	85 0 0 0 00	(5 0 0 0 00)
Total Assets		$96 0 0 0 00		$94 0 0 0 00	$2 0 0 0 00
Owner's Equity					
B. N. Monroe, Capital		$96 0 0 0 00		$94 0 0 0 00	$2 0 0 0 00
Total Liabilities and					
Owner's Equity		$96 0 0 0 00		$94 0 0 0 00	$2 0 0 0 00

P.O. 1,2

Problem G-2 The financial statements for Rhyne and Company follow. Assume that the additional investment and the withdrawals were in the form of cash.

Check Figure

Net cash flows from operating activities, $77,000

Instructions

Prepare a statement of cash flows for the year ended December 31, 2007.

Rhyne and Company
Income Statement
For Year Ended December 31, 2007

Revenue:		
Income from Services		$270 0 0 0 00
Expenses:		
Wages Expense	$161 0 0 0 00	
Rent Expense	18 0 0 0 00	
Depreciation Expense, Equipment	12 0 0 0 00	
Supplies Expense	4 0 0 0 00	
Insurance Expense	1 0 0 0 00	
Total Expenses		196 0 0 0 00
Net Income		$ 74 0 0 0 00

Rhyne and Company
Statement of Owner's Equity
For Year Ended December 31, 2007

S. T. Rhyne, Capital, January 1, 2007		$150 0 0 0 00
Additional Investment, April 1, 2007		2 0 0 0 00
Total Investment		$152 0 0 0 00
Net Income for the Year	$74 0 0 0 00	
Less Withdrawals for the Year	70 0 0 0 00	
Increase in Capital		4 0 0 0 00
S. T. Rhyne, Capital, December 31, 2007		$156 0 0 0 00

Rhyne and Company
Comparative Balance Sheet
December 31, 2007 and December 31, 2006

	2007	2006	INCREASE (DECREASE)
Assets			
Cash	$ 11 8 0 0 00	$ 2 8 0 0 00	$ 9 0 0 0 00
Accounts Receivable	32 0 0 0 00	26 0 0 0 00	6 0 0 0 00
Supplies	10 0 0 0 00	9 4 0 0 00	6 0 0 00
Prepaid Insurance	3 2 0 0 00	6 0 0 00	2 6 0 0 00
Equipment	$145 4 0 0 00	$145 4 0 0 00	
Less Accumulated Depreciation	(36 0 0 0 00) 109 4 0 0 00	(24 0 0 0 00) 121 4 0 0 00	(12 0 0 0 00)
Total Assets	$166 4 0 0 00	$160 2 0 0 00	$ 6 2 0 0 00
Liabilities			
Accounts Payable	$ 10 4 0 0 00	$ 10 2 0 0 00	$ 2 0 0 00
Owner's Equity			
S. T. Rhyne, Capital	156 0 0 0 00	150 0 0 0 00	6 0 0 0 00
Total Liabilities and			
Owner's Equity	$166 4 0 0 00	$160 2 0 0 00	$ 6 2 0 0 00

P.O. 1,2

Problem G-3 The financial statements for Salinas Company follow. Assume that the withdrawals were in the form of cash.

Check Figure

Net cash flows used by financing activities, ($70,000)

Instructions

Prepare a statement of cash flows for the year ended December 31, 2007.

Salinas Company
Income Statement
For Year Ended December 31, 2007

Net Sales	$942 0 0 0 00		
Less Cost of Goods Sold	753 6 0 0 00		
Gross Profit		$188 4 0 0 00	
Operating Expenses:			
Salary Expense	$ 86 9 0 0 00		
Rent Expense	18 0 0 0 00		
Depreciation Expense, Equipment	10 0 0 0 00		
Supplies Expense	4 7 0 0 00		
Insurance Expense	2 8 0 0 00		
Total Operating Expenses		122 4 0 0 00	
Net Income		$ 66 0 0 0 00	

Salinas Company
Statement of Owner's Equity
For Year Ended December 31, 2007

C. L. Salinas, Capital, January 1, 2007		$196 0 0 0 00
Net Income for the Year	$66 0 0 0 00	
Less Withdrawals for the Year	70 0 0 0 00	
Decrease in Capital		(4 0 0 0 00)
C. L. Salinas, Capital, December 31, 2007		$192 0 0 0 00

Salinas Company
Comparative Balance Sheet
December 31, 2007 and December 31, 2006

	2007	2006	INCREASE (DECREASE)
Assets			
Cash	$ 9 4 0 0 00	$ 10 9 0 0 00	$ (1 5 0 0 00)
Accounts Receivable	56 0 0 0 00	48 6 0 0 00	7 4 0 0 00
Merchandise Inventory	104 6 0 0 00	104 4 0 0 00	2 0 0 00
Supplies	8 2 0 0 00	6 0 0 0 00	2 2 0 0 00
Prepaid Insurance	1 6 0 0 00	1 8 0 0 00	(2 0 0 00)
Equipment	$156 0 0 0 00	$156 0 0 0 00	————
Less Accumulated Depreciation	(76 4 0 0 00) 79 6 0 0 00	(66 4 0 0 00) 89 6 0 0 00	(10 0 0 0 00)
Total Assets	$259 4 0 0 00	$261 3 0 0 00	$ (1 9 0 0 00)
Liabilities			
Accounts Payable	$ 62 7 0 0 00	$ 60 4 0 0 00	$ 2 3 0 0 00
Salaries Payable	4 7 0 0 00	4 9 0 0 00	(2 0 0 00)
Total Liabilities	$ 67 4 0 0 00	$ 65 3 0 0 00	$ 2 1 0 0 00
Owner's Equity			
C. L. Salinas, Capital	192 0 0 0 00	196 0 0 0 00	(4 0 0 0 00)
Total Liabilities and			
Owner's Equity	$259 4 0 0 00	$261 3 0 0 00	$ (1 9 0 0 00)

14

Notes Payable

LINKS TO ACCOUNTING

Defense spending represents big bucks. It also represents big borrowing. According to the notes in its financial statements, Raytheon, a large manufacturer of special-mission aircraft, business aviation, and defense electronics, had promised to pay its lenders over $4 billion as of December 31, 2005. And that doesn't even include the interest!

When Raytheon managers sign a promissory note, they are promising to pay the original amount plus interest in the future. Notes payable are promissory notes due in as little as a few days or, perhaps, as many as fifty years. To find more information about Raytheon's notes payable, go to **http://www.raytheon.com/investor/2005/index.html** and click on 10-K in the Downloads list at the top of the screen. Go to Note H, on page 69, and find the actual amount of Raytheon's notes payable on December 31, 2005 and the weighted-average interest rate on its notes. Think about how much interest Raytheon pays as you learn how to calculate interest on notes payable in this chapter, and consider how Raytheon might record that interest when it becomes due.

Performance Objectives

After you have completed this chapter, you will be able to do the following:

1. Define *promissory note*.

2. Calculate the interest on promissory notes.

3. Determine the due dates of promissory notes.

4. Make journal entries for (a) notes given to secure an extension of time on an open account; (b) payment of an interest-bearing note at maturity; (c) notes given in exchange for merchandise or other property purchased; (d) notes given to secure a cash loan, when the borrower receives the full face value of the note; (e) notes given to secure a cash loan, when the bank discounts the note; (f) payment of a non-interest-bearing note at maturity; and (g) renewal of a note at maturity.

5. Complete a notes payable register.

6. Make journal entries for (a) adjustment for accrued interest on notes payable, (b) adjustment for Discount on Notes Payable, and (c) conversion of Discount on Notes Payable to Interest Expense.

Credit plays an extremely important role in the operation of most business enterprises. Credit may be extended on a charge-account basis, with payment generally due in twenty-five to thirty days. This type of credit involves the Accounts Payable and Accounts Receivable accounts. Credit may also be granted by giving or receiving notes for specific transactions. This sort of credit involves the Notes Payable and Notes Receivable accounts. The notes, which represent formal instruments of credit, are known as *promissory notes*. They are customarily used as evidence of credit transactions for periods longer than thirty days. For example, promissory notes may be used in sales of equipment on the installment plan and for transactions involving large amounts of money.

Promissory notes are also used to grant extensions of credit beyond the original credit terms. For example, suppose that Mills Company buys merchandise from Benson Company with terms of 2/10, n/30. Mills Company finds that it can't pay its bill within the thirty-day period. To preserve its credit standing, Mills Company offers a note. The advantages to Benson Company are as follows: (1) Benson now has specific evidence of the transaction, (2) the note may carry interest, and (3) Benson can borrow from the bank by pledging the note as security for a loan. Business concerns may also borrow from banks by issuing their own promissory notes.

Most companies become involved with notes at one time or another, either by issuing notes to creditors, by receiving notes from customers, or by issuing notes to banks in order to borrow money. Consequently, an accountant must be acquainted with the procedures for handling promissory notes.

PROMISSORY NOTES

OBJECTIVE 1

Define *promissory note*.

A **promissory note**—usually referred to simply as a *note*—is a written promise to pay a certain sum at a fixed or determinable future time. Like a check, it must be payable to the order of a particular person or firm, known as the **payee**. It must also be signed by the person or firm making the promise, known as the **maker**. In Figure 1, Dana Manufacturing Company is the payee, and Rainier Plumbing Supply is the maker.

FIGURE 1

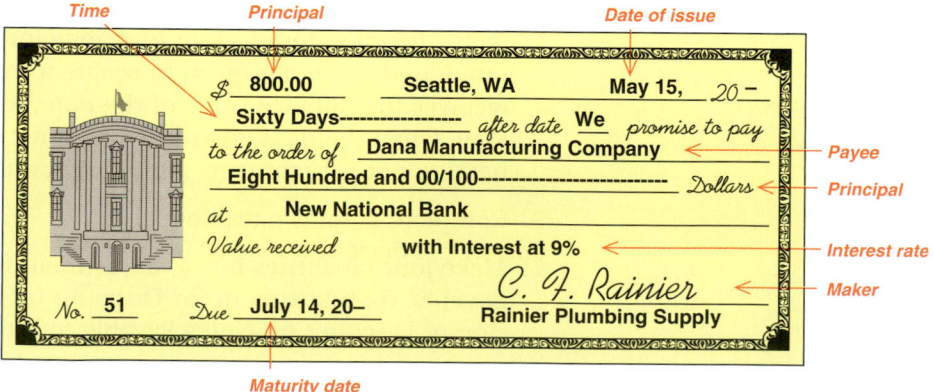

CALCULATING INTEREST

OBJECTIVE 2

Calculate the interest on promissory notes.

The liability incurred when borrowing money can be short-term or long-term in nature. Some debts last only a few days, whereas others—such as those for major construction projects—can last thirty, or even fifty, years.

Interest is a charge made for the use of money. To the maker of the note, interest is an expense. The amount of interest a maker pays is expressed as a certain percentage of the principal of the note for a period of one year (or less). The following formula is used to calculate interest:

Interest = **Principal** of note × **Rate** of interest × **Time** of note
(in dollars) (in dollars) (as a percentage (expressed as a
                of the principal) year or fraction
                                    of a year)

The **principal** is the face amount of the note. The *rate of interest* is a percentage of the principal, such as 10 percent or 11 percent. Since 1 percent equals $\frac{1}{100}$ or 0.01, then 10 percent equals $\frac{10}{100}$ or 0.10.

Time, or the length of life of the note, is usually expressed in days or months. It is the period between the note's date of issue (starting date) and its **maturity date** (the due date or interest payment date). It is stated in terms of a year or fraction of a year. Examples are

$$1 \text{ year} = 1 \qquad 6 \text{ months} = \frac{6}{12} \qquad 3 \text{ months} = \frac{3}{12}$$

$$90 \text{ days} = \frac{90}{360} \qquad 24 \text{ days} = \frac{24}{360}$$

The usual commercial practice is to use a 360-day year, making the denominator of the fraction 360. However, agencies of the federal government use the actual number of days in the year.

Example 1 $6,000, 8 percent, 1 year.

Interest = Principal × Rate × Time

Interest = $6,000 × 0.08 × 1 = $480

Example 2 $4,000, 9 percent, 3 months.

Interest = Principal × Rate × Time

$$\textbf{Interest} = \textbf{\$4,000} \times \textbf{0.09} \times \frac{\textbf{3}}{\textbf{12}}$$

$$= \textbf{\$4,000} \times \textbf{0.09} \times \textbf{3} \div \textbf{12} = \textbf{\$90}$$

Example 3 $9,000, 7 percent, 60 days.

Interest = Principal × Rate × Time

$$\textbf{Interest} = \textbf{\$9,000} \times \textbf{0.07} \times \frac{\textbf{60}}{\textbf{360}}$$

$$= \textbf{\$9,000} \times \textbf{0.07} \times \textbf{60} \div \textbf{360} = \textbf{\$105}$$

REMEMBER!

A note is a formal written promise to pay an amount of money at a definite time, as opposed to the "open account" relationship in Accounts Receivable or Accounts Payable.

DETERMINING DUE DATES

OBJECTIVE 3

Determine the due dates of promissory notes.

The period of time between a promissory note's issue date and its maturity date is called the **duration** of the note. The duration of a note, as we have said, may be expressed in either days or months. If the time of the note is expressed in months, the maturity date is the corresponding day in the month after the specified number of months have elapsed. For example, a note dated March 15 with a time period of three months has a due date of June 15. In those cases in which there is no date in the month of maturity that corresponds to the issuance date, the due date becomes the last day of the month. For example, a three-month note dated March 31 would be due on June 30.

But suppose that the period of time a note has to run is expressed in days. When counting the number of days, begin with the day after the date the note was issued, since the note states "after date." The last day, however, is counted. Let's say that the due date of a promissory note is specified as 60 days after April 8. The due date is June 7.

April						
S	M	T	W	T	F	S
		1	2	3	4	5
6	7	8	9	10	11	12
13	14	15	16	17	18	19
20	21	22	23	24	25	26
27	28	29	30			

22 days
8th through the 30th
30 − 8 = 22 days left

May						
S	M	T	W	T	F	S
				1	2	3
4	5	6	7	8	9	10
11	12	13	14	15	16	17
18	19	20	21	22	23	24
25	26	27	28	29	30	31

+ 31 days

June						
S	M	T	W	T	F	S
1	2	3	4	5	6	7
8	9	10	11	12	13	14
15	16	17	18	19	20	21
22	23	24	25	26	27	28
29	30					

= 53 days have passed
60 − 53 = 7 days remaining after May 31
June 7 due date

The due date is determined by the following steps:

1. Determine the number of days remaining in the month of issue by subtracting the date of the note from the number of days in the month in which it is dated.
2. Add as many full months as possible without exceeding the number of days in the note, counting the full number of days in these months.
3. Determine the number of days remaining in the month in which the note matures by subtracting the total days counted so far from the number of days in the note, as shown here.

April (30 − 8)	= 22 days left in April
May	= 31 days
Total days so far	= 53 days
June (60 − 53)	= 7th day of June (due date)

Now, suppose you have a 120-day note dated May 20:

May (31 – 20)	= 11 days left in May
June	= 30 days
July	= 31 days
August	= 31 days
Total days so far	= 103 days
September (120 – 103)	= 17th day of September (due date)

TRANSACTIONS INVOLVING NOTES PAYABLE

The following types of transactions involve the issuance and payment of notes payable:

1. Note given to a supplier in return for an extension of time for payment of an open account (charge account)
2. Note given in exchange for merchandise or other property purchased
3. Note given as evidence of a loan
4. Note renewed at maturity

In our examples, we assume that all the notes are due within one year; thus they are classified on the balance sheet as Current Liabilities. However, if notes are not due within one year, that portion of the note that is due within one year is a Current Liability, and the remainder is classified as a Long-Term Liability. Interest expense is classified on the income statement as Interest Expense (if significant) or Other Expense.

Note Given to Secure an Extension of Time on an Open Account

OBJECTIVE 4a

Make journal entries for notes given to secure an extension of time on an open account.

When a firm wishes to obtain an extension of time for the payment of an account, the firm may ask a supplier to accept a note for all or part of the amount due. For example, let's say that Rainier Plumbing Supply prefers not to pay its open account with Dana Manufacturing Company when it becomes due. Dana Manufacturing Company agrees to accept a 60-day, 9 percent, $800 note from Rainier Plumbing Supply in settlement of the account. The entry that caused the account to be put on Dana Manufacturing Company's books came about when Rainier Plumbing Supply bought merchandise on account on April 15, with terms 2/10, n/30.

Original Purchase   In general journal form, the entry looks like this:

		GENERAL JOURNAL			PAGE _____	
DATE		**DESCRIPTION**	**POST. REF.**	**DEBIT**	**CREDIT**	
20–						1
Apr.	15	Purchases		8 0 0 00		2
		Accounts Payable, Dana			8 0 0 00	3
		Manufacturing Company				4
		Terms 2/10, n/30.				5

Payment by Note On May 15, Rainier Plumbing Supply records the issuance of the note in its general journal.

	DATE		DESCRIPTION	POST. REF.	DEBIT	CREDIT	
1	20–						1
2	May	15	Accounts Payable, Dana				2
3			Manufacturing Company		8 0 0 00		3
4			Notes Payable			8 0 0 00	4
5			Gave a 60-day, 9 percent				5
6			note, in settlement of our				6
7			open account.				7
8							8

GENERAL JOURNAL   PAGE _____

By T accounts, the transactions look like this:

Purchases		Accounts Payable		Notes Payable	
+	–	–	+	–	+
Apr. 15 800		May 15 800	Apr. 15 800		May 15 800

Observe that the above entry cancels out the Accounts Payable, Dana Manufacturing Company, account and substitutes Notes Payable. The note does not *pay* the debt, it merely changes the liability status from an account payable to a note payable. Dana Manufacturing Company prefers the note to the open account because, in the case of default and a subsequent lawsuit to collect, the possession of the note improves Dana Manufacturing Company's legal position. The note is written evidence of the debt and the amount owed. In addition, Dana Manufacturing Company is, in this case, entitled to 9 percent interest.

Payment of an Interest-Bearing Note at Maturity

OBJECTIVE 4b

Make journal entries for payment of an interest-bearing note at maturity.

When a note payable falls due, payment may be made directly to the holder, or it may be made to a bank with which the note was left for collection. The maker knows the identity of the original payee, of course, but he or she may not know who the holder of the note is at maturity. The payee may have transferred the note by endorsement to another party or may have left it with a bank for collection. When a note is left with a bank for collection, the bank usually mails the maker a **notice of maturity** specifying the terms, the due date of the note, and the **maturity value** (the principal of the note plus the interest). For example, Dana Manufacturing Company turned the note over to its bank, the New National Bank, for collection. Accordingly, the bank sent Rainier Plumbing Supply a notice of maturity of the note.

Rainier Plumbing Supply pays the note on July 14. In general journal form, the entry is as follows:

		GENERAL JOURNAL			PAGE ___
DATE		DESCRIPTION	POST. REF.	DEBIT	CREDIT
20–					
July	14	Notes Payable		8 0 0 00	
		Interest Expense		1 2 00	
		Cash			8 1 2 00
		Paid note to Dana			
		Manufacturing Company			

Because Interest = Principal × Rate × Time, we perform this calculation:

Interest = $800 × 0.09 × 60 ÷ 360 = $12

Cash			Notes Payable			Interest Expense	
+	**−**		**−**	**+**		**+**	**−**
Bal. 10,000	July 14 812	July 14 800	May 15 800		July 14 12		

OBJECTIVE 4c

Make journal entries for notes given in exchange for merchandise or other property purchased.

In practice, if special journals are used, transactions like this one are recorded directly in the cash payments journal rather than in the general journal. However, to simplify the discussion of the entries, all transactions are presented here in general journal form.

Note Given in Exchange for Assets Purchased

Occasionally, when the price of an item is high or the credit period is long, a buyer gives a note instead of buying the item on account. For example, Rainier Plumbing Supply issues a 90-day, 7 percent interest-bearing note for $5,000 to Wagner Display Company in exchange for equipment purchased June 3 and records the transaction in the general journal as follows:

DATE		DESCRIPTION	POST. REF.	DEBIT	CREDIT
20–					
June	3	Store Equipment		5 0 0 0 00	
		Notes Payable			5 0 0 0 00
		Acquired shelves and			
		counters from Wagner			
		Display Company, 90 days,			
		7 percent.			

When Rainier Plumbing Supply pays the note at maturity, the entry in its books is the same as the entry it makes for the payment of any interest-bearing note. The entry, in general journal form, is shown on the next page.

	DATE		DESCRIPTION	POST. REF.	DEBIT	CREDIT	
1	20–						1
2	Sept.	1	Notes Payable		5 0 0 0 00		2
3			Interest Expense		8 7 50		3
4			Cash			5 0 8 7 50	4
5			Paid note to Wagner				5
6			Display Company.				6
7							7

Determining the Due Date

June (30 – 3)   = 27 days left in June

July   = 31 days

August   = 31 days

Total days so far   = 89 days

September (90 – 89) = 1st day of September (due date)

And because Interest = Principal × Rate × Time,

Interest = $5,000 × 0.07 × 90 ÷ 360 = $87.50

Note Given to Secure a Cash Loan

Businesses frequently need to stock up on merchandise in large amounts in order to meet seasonal demands. Sometimes their usual receipts from customers are not enough to cover the sudden volume of purchases. During such periods, firms customarily borrow money from banks, through the medium of short-term notes, to finance their operations.

Borrowing from a Bank When Borrower Receives Full Face Value of Note

OBJECTIVE 4d

Make journal entries for notes given to secure a cash loan, when the borrower receives the full face value of the note.

In one type of bank loan, a business firm signs an interest-bearing note and receives the full face value of the note. The borrower repays the principal plus interest. For example, on June 11, Rainier Plumbing Supply borrows $4,700 from Finley National Bank for 120 days with interest of 9 percent payable at maturity. The entry to record the transaction is as follows:

	DATE		DESCRIPTION	POST. REF.	DEBIT	CREDIT	
1	20–						1
2	June	11	Cash		4 7 0 0 00		2
3			Notes Payable			4 7 0 0 00	3
4			Gave Finley National Bank a				4
5			120-day, 9 percent note.				5
6							6

Transactions Involving Notes Payable 543

Note Paid to the Bank at Maturity

After Rainier Plumbing Supply has paid the note and interest, its accountant makes the following entry on the books:

	DATE		DESCRIPTION	POST. REF.	DEBIT	CREDIT	
1	20–						1
2	Oct.	9	Notes Payable		4 7 0 0 00		2
3			Interest Expense		1 4 1 00		3
4			Cash			4 8 4 1 00	4
5			Paid note to Finley National				5
6			Bank.				6
7							7

> **REMEMBER!**
>
> The debit to Notes Payable represents the face value of the note.

Interest = Principal × Rate × Time

Interest = \$4,700 × 0.09 × 120 ÷ 360 = \$141

Borrowing from a Bank When Bank Discounts Note (Deducts Interest in Advance)

In another type of bank loan, the bank deducts the interest in advance, which is called **discounting a note payable**. For example, on June 19, Rainier Plumbing Supply borrows \$8,800 for 90 days from Western National Bank, and the bank requires Rainier Plumbing Supply to sign a note. From the face value of the note, the bank deducts 9.5 percent interest for 90 days, so Rainier Plumbing Supply actually gets only \$8,591. This interest deducted in advance by a bank is called the **discount**. The principal of the loan left after the discount has been subtracted is called the **proceeds**, which is the amount the borrower has available to use. Since all the interest is deducted at the time the loan is made, the note must state that only the face amount is to be paid at maturity. The calculation is as follows:

Interest = Principal × Rate × Time

Interest = \$8,800 × 0.095 × 90 ÷ 360 = \$209

The bank deducts the discount from the face amount of the note before making the money available to the borrower.

Principal	\$8,800
− Discount	209
Proceeds	\$8,591

Banks assist businesses by providing loans to finance their operations. In exchange for a note payable, the bank makes the loan either with the interest payable at maturity or with the interest already deducted in advance.

Entry When Note Discounted at Bank Matures Before End of Fiscal Period

OBJECTIVE 4e

Make journal entries for notes given to secure a cash loan, when the bank discounts the note.

As long as a note begins and matures during the same fiscal period, the borrower may debit all the interest (or discount) to Interest Expense. The 90-day note that Rainier Plumbing Supply submits to the bank is dated June 19 and therefore matures September 17. Since Rainier Plumbing Supply's fiscal period is from January 1 to December 31, the company can include the entire amount of interest in Interest Expense. Accordingly, Rainier Plumbing Supply records the transaction as follows:

	DATE		DESCRIPTION	POST. REF.	DEBIT	CREDIT	
1	20–						1
2	June	19	Cash		8 5 9 1 00		2
3			Interest Expense		2 0 9 00		3
4			Notes Payable			8 8 0 0 00	4
5			Discounted our 90-day				5
6			non-interest-bearing note				6
7			at Western National Bank,				7
8			discount rate 9.5 percent.				8
9							9

REMEMBER!

When a note is discounted, the proceeds received are reduced by the amount of the interest expense.

Note Paid to the Bank at Maturity

OBJECTIVE 4f

Make journal entries for payment of a non-interest-bearing note at maturity.

When the note becomes due, Rainier Plumbing Supply pays the bank only the *face value of the note* and records the transaction as follows:

	DATE		DESCRIPTION	POST. REF.	DEBIT	CREDIT	
1	20–						1
2	Sept.	17	Notes Payable		8 8 0 0 00		2
3			Cash			8 8 0 0 00	3
4			Paid Western National Bank				4
5			on our note payable				5
6			discounted June 19.				6
7							7

Entry When Note Discounted at Bank Matures After End of Fiscal Period

Instead of the entire duration of the note (such as 90 or 60 days) being included in one 12-month fiscal period, assume that the duration extends into the next fiscal period. In this case, the journal entry must include a debit to Discount on Notes Payable instead of a debit to Interest Expense. In other words, Discount on Notes Payable is substituted for Interest Expense, using the same dollar amount.

Discount on Notes Payable is a contra-liability account; it is a deduction from Notes Payable. Recall that we defined the Accumulated Depreciation account as a contra-asset account—for example, a deduction from Equipment with the plus and minus signs reversed. Similarly, Discount on Notes Payable is a contra account—a deduction from Notes Payable with the plus and minus signs reversed. In T account form, these accounts look like this:

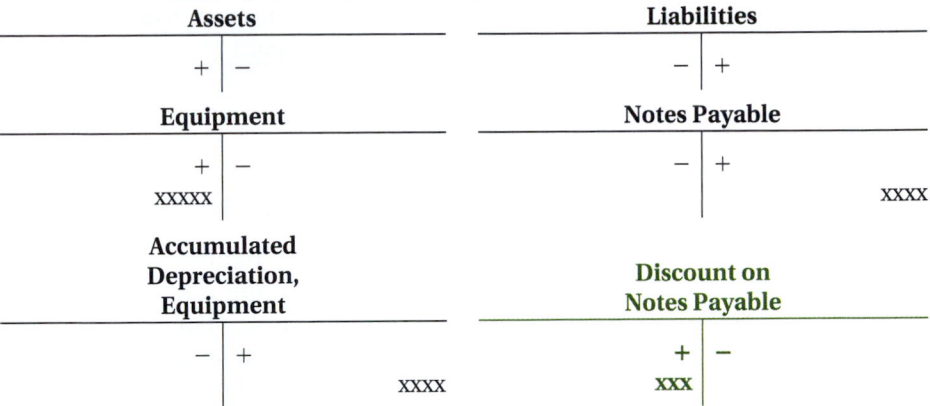

On a balance sheet, the contra account is deducted as follows:

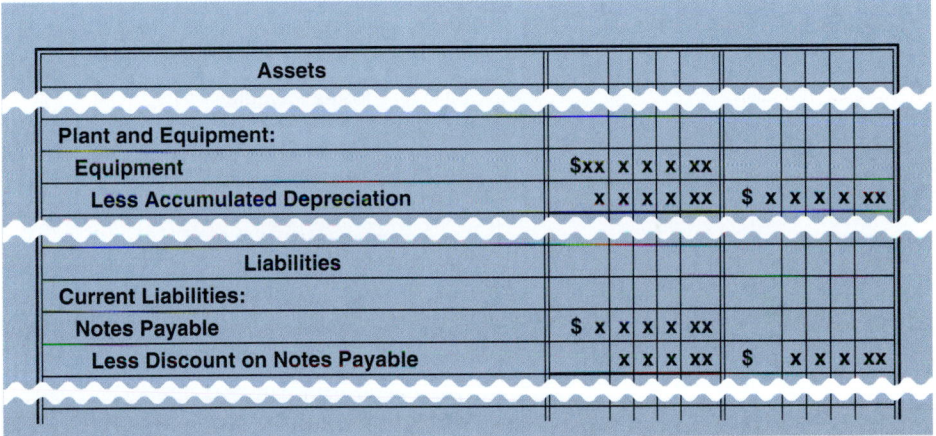

At the end of the fiscal period, an adjusting entry must be made to record the accrued interest expense and the discount on notes payable for the time between the date the note is issued and the end of the fiscal period. The note is outstanding during the period. We will describe this type of adjusting entry in the section "End-of-Fiscal-Period Adjustments" later in the chapter.

Let's say that on December 1, Rainier Plumbing Supply borrows $9,000 from Mid State Bank for 120 days. The bank deducts 9 percent interest (in advance) for 120 days, $270, and gives Rainier Plumbing Supply $8,730. Rainier Plumbing Supply's fiscal period is from January 1 through December 31, so the entry in the general journal is as shown on the following page.

REMEMBER!

If a note payable discounted at a bank comes due *before* the end of the fiscal period, debit Interest Expense for the amount of the discount. If the note comes due *after* the end of the fiscal period, debit Discount on Notes Payable for the amount of the discount.

DATE		DESCRIPTION	POST. REF.	DEBIT	CREDIT	
20–						1
Dec.	1	Cash		8 7 3 0 00		2
		Discount on Notes Payable		2 7 0 00		3
		Notes Payable			9 0 0 0 00	4
		Discounted our 120-day,				5
		non-interest-bearing note at				6
		Mid State Bank; discount rate				7
		9 percent.				8
						9

OBJECTIVE 4g

Make journal entries for renewal of a note at maturity.

Renewal of Note at Maturity

A maker (or borrower) unable to pay a note in full at maturity may arrange to renew all or part of the note. At this time, the company usually pays the interest on the old note. For example, assume that on June 27, Rainier Plumbing Supply issues a 45-day note to Bailey, Inc., for $9,800, with interest at 8 percent. The original entry in general journal form is as follows:

DATE		DESCRIPTION	POST. REF.	DEBIT	CREDIT	
20–						1
June	27	Accounts Payable, Bailey, Inc.		9 8 0 0 00		2
		Notes Payable			9 8 0 0 00	3
		Issued a 45-day, 8 percent				4
		note.				5
						6

Renewal of Note with Payment of Interest

When a firm renews an interest-bearing note, while paying interest owed, the accountant first makes an entry for payment of the interest on the existing note up to the present date. This entry occurs on August 11, the maturity date of the note:

DATE		DESCRIPTION	POST. REF.	DEBIT	CREDIT	
20–						1
Aug.	11	Interest Expense		9 8 00		2
		Cash			9 8 00	3
		Interest payment on note to				4
		Bailey, Inc.				5
						6

Interest = Principal × Rate × Time

Interest = $9,800 × 0.08 × 45 ÷ 360 = $98

The accountant then makes a separate entry for the issuance of the new note, to run for 30 days at 9 percent (the interest rate has been increased and the number of days decreased), as follows:

	DATE		DESCRIPTION	POST. REF.	DEBIT	CREDIT	
11	Aug.	11	Notes Payable		9 8 0 0 00		11
12			Notes Payable			9 8 0 0 00	12
13			Canceled note to Bailey, Inc.,				13
14			by issuing a 30-day,				14
15			9 percent note.				15

Renewal of Note with Payment of Interest and Part Payment of Principal

REMEMBER!

For a renewal of a note payable, debit the old note to take it off the books, and credit the new note to put it on the books.

What if the maker decides to pay only *part* of a note at maturity? Let's assume that, instead of taking the course of action we have just described, Rainier Plumbing Supply pays $1,600 on the principal of the note that is due (the old note), and also pays the entire interest on it. In other words, the maker pays the interest up to the present date for the old note, plus $1,600 to reduce the principal from $9,800 to $8,200, and issues a *new* note for $8,200.

	DATE		DESCRIPTION	POST. REF.	DEBIT	CREDIT	
11	Aug.	11	Notes Payable		1 6 0 0 00		11
12			Interest Expense		9 8 00		12
13			Cash			1 6 9 8 00	13
14			Interest payment on 45-day,				14
15			8 percent note to Bailey, Inc.,				15
16			and partial payment on the				16
17			principal.				17
18							18
19		11	Notes Payable		8 2 0 0 00		19
20			Notes Payable			8 2 0 0 00	20
21			Canceled note to Bailey, Inc.,				21
22			by issuing a 30-day,				22
23			9 percent note.				23
24							24

Ordinarily, small businesses issue notes to relatively few creditors. These firms can record the details of the notes on stubs similar to check stubs, or they can just keep duplicate copies of the notes. However, if a firm issues many notes, it may be more convenient to keep a separate record listing the details of each note. This type of record is called a **notes payable register**.

In an abbreviated form, here's an illustration of a notes payable register for Rainier Plumbing Supply through August 11:

NOTES PAYABLE REGISTER

DATE		PAYEE	AMOUNT	TIME	RATE	INTEREST	DUE DATE	DATE PAID	REMARKS
20–									
May	15	Dana Manufacturing Company	8 0 0 00	60 days	9%	1 2 00	7/14	7/14	Open account.
June	3	Wagner Display Company	5 0 0 0 00	90 days	7%	8 7 50	9/1	9/1	Bought equipment.
	11	Finley National Bank	4 7 0 0 00	120 days	9%	1 4 1 00	10/9	10/9	Loan, received full principal.
	19	Western National Bank	8 8 0 0 00	90 days	9.5%	2 0 9 00	9/17	9/17	Loan, discount $209.
	27	Bailey, Inc.	9 8 0 0 00	45 days	8%	9 8 00	8/11	Renewed	Open account.
Aug.	11	Bailey, Inc.	9 8 0 0 00	30 days	9%	7 3 50	9/10		Renewed June 27 note.
		OR IF PARTIAL PAYMENT							
		Bailey, Inc.	8 2 0 0 00	30 days	9%	6 1 50	9/10		Renewed June 27 note with partial payment of $1,600.

More elaborate notes payable registers may include columns listing note numbers, addresses of payees, and similar information.

At the end of the fiscal period, the firm may prepare a schedule of notes payable by listing the unpaid notes that appear in the notes payable register. This schedule is similar to a schedule of accounts payable. The total of the schedule is compared with the balance of Notes Payable.

END-OF-FISCAL-PERIOD ADJUSTMENTS

REMEMBER!

Accrual-basis accounting requires adjustment for notes spanning two or more fiscal periods so that interest expense and discount on notes payable are allocated properly to the periods benefited.

When notes start in one fiscal period and mature in the next, adjusting entries must be made both for accrued interest and for discounts on notes payable. Otherwise, neither the expenses incurred by the business firm during a fiscal period nor its liabilities at the end of the fiscal period would be correctly stated.

Accrued Interest on Notes Payable

On all interest-bearing notes, interest expense *accrues*, or *accumulates*, daily. Consequently, if any notes payable are outstanding at the end of a fiscal period, the **accrued interest on notes payable** (that is, the interest due but not yet paid) should be calculated and recorded. For example, assume that a firm has two notes payable outstanding as of December 31, the end of the current fiscal period.

$12,000, 60 days, 8%, dated December 10
$7,200, 90 days, 7%, dated December 2

We can diagram the period of each note like this:

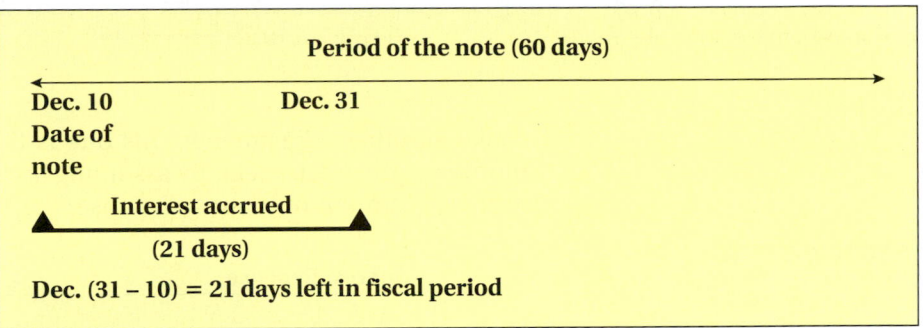

Interest = Principal × Rate × Time

Interest = $12,000 × 0.08 × 21 ÷ 360 = $56

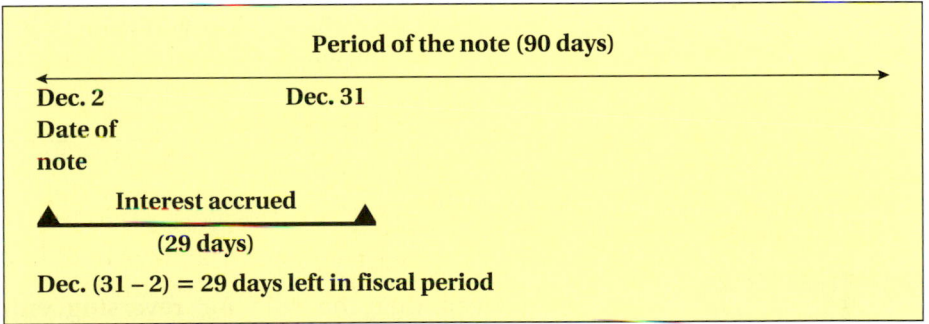

Interest = Principal × Rate × Time

Interest = $7,200 × 0.07 × 29 ÷ 360 = $40.60

OBJECTIVE 6a

Make journal entries for adjustment for accrued interest on notes payable.

Obviously, both notes extend into the next fiscal period; if they didn't, there would be no need for an adjustment. When paying interest on notes—except for notes discounted at a bank—you usually pay the principal and interest together on the day the note matures, or becomes due. But since *these* notes have not matured, the interest expense has been neither paid nor recorded. Therefore, the firm has to make an adjustment, because the accountant tries to portray the firm's expenses and liabilities for the current fiscal period as accurately as possible. In general journal form, the adjusting entry for the interest expense accrued on the two notes is as shown on the following page.

DATE		DESCRIPTION	POST. REF.	DEBIT	CREDIT	
1	20–	**Adjusting Entry**				1
2	Dec.	31	Interest Expense		9 6 60		2
3			Interest Payable			9 6 60	3
4			($56.00 + $40.60)				4
5							5
6							6
7							7

REMEMBER!

Calculations are included to show how the amounts were determined. They would not normally appear in journal entries.

Like all other adjustments, this one is first recorded in the Adjustments columns of the work sheet. By assuming an Interest Expense balance of $825 before adjustment of Interest Expense, the T accounts are as follows:

Interest Expense		Interest Payable	
+	–	–	+
Dec. 31 Bal. 825.00			Dec. 31 Adj. 96.60
Dec. 31 Adj. 96.60			

REMEMBER!

Any account name ending in Payable is always a liability account.

This situation parallels the adjustment for accrued salaries, in which the objective is to record the additional amount of salaries incurred and owed at the end of the year. In each adjusting entry, debit an expense account and credit a payable account.

Salary Expense		Salaries Payable	
+	–	–	+
Dec. 31 Adj. xxx			Dec. 31 Adj. xxx

Recall that **the rule for reversing entries is: If an adjusting entry increases an asset or liability account that does not have a previous balance, then you may reverse the adjusting entry.** Entries involving contra accounts are never reversed.

REMEMBER!

Reversing entries are not required.

Discount on Notes Payable

When a note payable is discounted at a bank, the bank deducts the interest (based on the principal of the note) in advance. **If the note begins and ends during one fiscal period, the interest is recorded as Interest Expense, and no adjustment is needed. But if the note extends into the next fiscal period, the interest is recorded as Discount on Notes Payable.** An adjusting entry is needed to record the interest for the number of days the note was outstanding during the fiscal period.

Recall our original entry made on December 1, in which the firm discounted its $9,000, 120-day, non-interest-bearing note at the bank; discount rate 9 percent.

REMEMBER!

Discount on Notes Payable is a contra-liability account and a deduction from Notes Payable.

DATE		DESCRIPTION	POST. REF.	DEBIT	CREDIT
20–					
Dec.	1	Cash		8 7 3 0 00	
		Discount on Notes Payable		2 7 0 00	
		Notes Payable			9 0 0 0 00
		Discounted our 120-day,			
		non-interest-bearing note at			
		Mid State Bank; discount rate			
		9 percent.			

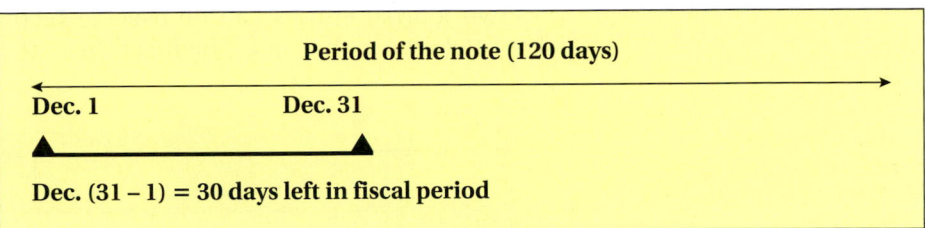

Period of the note (120 days)

Dec. 1   Dec. 31

Dec. (31 – 1) = 30 days left in fiscal period

Interest = Principal × Rate × Time

Interest = $9,000 × 0.09 × 30 ÷ 360 = <u>$67.50</u>

OBJECTIVE 6b

Make journal entries for adjustment for Discount on Notes Payable.

Since there are 30 days between December 1 and December 31, Rainier Plumbing Supply's accountant has to make an adjusting entry to record the Interest Expense:

DATE		DESCRIPTION	POST. REF.	DEBIT	CREDIT
20–		Adjusting Entry			
Dec.	31	Interest Expense		6 7 50	
		Discount on Notes Payable			6 7 50

In T accounts, it looks this way:

Interest Expense		Discount on Notes Payable	
+	–	+	–
Dec. 31 Adj. 67.50		Dec. 1 270.00	Dec. 31 Adj. 67.50

In addition to recording Interest Expense, the adjusting entry also reduces the balance of Discount on Notes Payable to its correct amount. This adjustment and the adjusting entry for accrued interest payable are

FIGURE 2

ACCOUNT NAME	TRIAL BALANCE	
	DEBIT	CREDIT
Discount on Notes Payable	2 7 0 00	
Interest Expense	8 2 5 00	
Interest Payable		

shown on the partial work sheet in Figure 2. At the end of the year, the Interest Expense account is closed along with all the other expense accounts.

Two journal entries can be used to record the final payment of the discounted note to the bank. The first is like the payment of any discounted note.

DATE	DESCRIPTION	POST. REF.	DEBIT	CREDIT
20–				
Mar. 31	Notes Payable		9 0 0 0 00	
	Cash			9 0 0 0 00
	Paid the bank the 120-day,			
	non-interest-bearing note,			
	dated December 1 and			
	discounted at 9 percent.			

OBJECTIVE 6c

Make journal entries for conversion of Discount on Notes Payable to Interest Expense.

The Discount on Notes Payable that was on the books has now become entirely an expense, and so it is converted into Interest Expense.

	DATE	DESCRIPTION		DEBIT	CREDIT
9	31	Interest Expense		2 0 2 50	
10		Discount on Notes Payable			2 0 2 50
11		To expense the discount for			
12		the current year for the 120-			
13		day note, dated December 1			
14		and discounted at 9 percent.			
15		($9,000 × 0.09 × 90/360)			

In T accounts, the entries for the discounted note payable look like this:

Interest Expense				Discount on Notes Payable			
	+	–			+	–	
Bal.	825.00						
Dec. 31 Adj.	96.60						
Dec. 31 Adj.	67.50	Dec. 31 Clos.	989.10	Dec. 1	270.00	Dec. 31 Adj.	67.50
Mar. 31	202.50			Bal.	202.50	Mar. 31	202.50

		ADJUSTMENTS		INCOME STATEMENT		BALANCE SHEET	
		DEBIT	CREDIT	DEBIT	CREDIT	DEBIT	CREDIT
	(b)		6 7 50			2 0 2 50	
	(a)	9 6 60		9 8 9 10			
	(b)	6 7 50					
	(a)		9 6 60				9 6 60

CHAPTER REVIEW

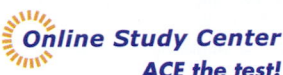
Online Study Center
ACE the test!

Review of Performance Objectives

1. Define *promissory note*.

   A promissory note is a written promise to pay a certain sum at a fixed or determinable future time.

2. Calculate the interest on promissory notes.

   The formula used to calculate interest is as follows:

   Interest = **Principal** of note × **Rate** of interest × **Time** of note
   (in dollars) (in dollars)   (as a percentage   (expressed as a year
                                    of the principal)   or fraction of a year)

3. Determine the due dates of promissory notes.

   Use the following steps to determine the due date:

   1. Determine the number of days remaining in the month of issue by subtracting the date of the note from the number of days in the month in which it is dated.
   2. Add as many full months as possible without exceeding the number of days in the note, counting the full number of days in these months.
   3. Determine the number of days remaining in the month in which the note matures by subtracting the total days counted so far from the number of days in the note.

4. Make journal entries for (a) notes given to secure an extension of time on an open account; (b) payment of an interest-bearing note at maturity; (c) notes given in exchange for merchandise or other property purchased; (d) notes given to secure a cash loan, when the borrower receives the full face value of the note; (e) notes given to secure a cash loan, when the bank discounts the note; (f) payment of a non-interest-bearing note at maturity; and (g) renewal of a note at maturity.

   (a) Notes given to secure an extension of time on an open account.

   May 15 Issued a 60-day, 9 percent note for $800 payable to Dana Manufacturing Company, in place of the open account.

GENERAL JOURNAL PAGE _____

	DATE		DESCRIPTION	POST. REF.	DEBIT	CREDIT	
1	20–						1
2	May	15	Accounts Payable, Dana				2
3			Manufacturing Company		8 0 0 00		3
4			Notes Payable			8 0 0 00	4

(b) Payment of an interest-bearing note at maturity.

July   14   Paid at maturity the note given to Dana Manufacturing Company.

CASH PAYMENTS JOURNAL PAGE _____

	DATE	CK. NO.	ACCOUNT NAME	POST. REF.	OTHER ACCOUNTS DEBIT	ACCOUNTS PAYABLE DEBIT	PURCHASES DISCOUNT CREDIT	CASH CREDIT	
1	20–								1
2	July	14	Notes Payable		8 0 0 00				2
3			Interest Expense		1 2 00			8 1 2 00	3

(c) Notes given in exchange for merchandise or other property purchased.

June   3   Issued a 90-day, 7 percent note for $5,000 payable to Wagner Display Company, for equipment.

GENERAL JOURNAL PAGE _____

	DATE		DESCRIPTION	POST. REF.	DEBIT	CREDIT	
1	20–						1
2	June	3	Store Equipment		5 0 0 0 00		2
3			Notes Payable			5 0 0 0 00	3

(d) Notes given to secure a cash loan, when the borrower receives the full face value of the note.

June   11   Borrowed $4,700 from Finley National Bank, giving in exchange a 120-day, 9 percent note (received full face amount).

CASH RECEIPTS JOURNAL PAGE _____

	DATE		ACCOUNT NAME	POST. REF.	OTHER ACCOUNTS DEBIT	OTHER ACCOUNTS CREDIT	CASH DEBIT	
1	20–							1
2	June	11	Notes Payable			4 7 0 0 00	4 7 0 0 00	2
3								3

(e) Notes given to secure a cash loan, when the bank discounts the note.

June 19 Borrowed $8,800 from Western National Bank for 90 days; discount rate is 9.5 percent; issued a note for $8,800.

CASH RECEIPTS JOURNAL   PAGE _____

DATE	ACCOUNT NAME	POST. REF.	OTHER ACCOUNTS DEBIT	OTHER ACCOUNTS CREDIT	CASH DEBIT	
20–						1
June 19	Interest Expense		2 0 9 00			2
	Notes Payable			8 8 0 0 00	8 5 9 1 00	3
						4

(f) Payment of a non-interest-bearing note at maturity.

Sept. 17 Paid $8,800 to Western National Bank for 90-day note payable.

CASH PAYMENTS JOURNAL   PAGE _____

DATE	CK. NO.	ACCOUNT NAME	POST. REF.	OTHER ACCOUNTS DEBIT	ACCOUNTS PAYABLE DEBIT	PURCHASES DISCOUNTS CREDIT	CASH CREDIT	
20–								1
Sept. 17		Notes Payable		8 8 0 0 00			8 8 0 0 00	2
								3

(g) Renewal of a note at maturity.

Aug. 11 Canceled a 45-day note payable to Bailey, Inc., for $9,800, with interest at 8 percent, by issuing a new note to run for 30 days at 9 percent.

GENERAL JOURNAL   PAGE _____

DATE	DESCRIPTION	POST. REF.	DEBIT	CREDIT	
20–					1
Aug. 11	Notes Payable		9 8 0 0 00		2
	Notes Payable			9 8 0 0 00	3
					4

5. Complete a notes payable register.

For each note, list the date, payer, amount, time, rate, interest, due date, date paid, and relevant remarks.

NOTES PAYABLE REGISTER

DATE		PAYEE	AMOUNT					TIME	RATE	INTEREST				DUE DATE	DATE PAID	REMARKS
20–																
May	15	Dana Manufacturing Company	8	0	0	00		60 days	9%		1	2	00	7/14	7/14	Open account.
June	3	Wagner Display Company	5	0	0	0	00	90 days	7%		8	7	50	9/1	9/1	Bought equipment.
	11	Finley National Bank	4	7	0	0	00	120 days	9%	1	4	1	00	10/9	10/9	Loan, received full principal.

6. Make journal entries for (a) adjustment for accrued interest on notes payable, (b) adjustment for Discount on Notes Payable, and (c) conversion of Discount on Notes Payable to Interest Expense.

(a) Adjustment for accrued interest on notes payable (see pages 549–550).

When the time period of the note spans two fiscal periods, record interest expense incurred for the number of days the note is outstanding during the fiscal period.

(b) Adjustment for Discount on Notes Payable (see page 551).

If a discounted note extends into the next fiscal period, the Discount on Notes Payable is adjusted to reflect the portion of the discount that has become interest expense for the current fiscal period.

(c) Conversion of Discount on Notes Payable to Interest Expense (see page 552).

Upon payment of a discounted note spanning two fiscal periods, the remainder of the Discount on Notes Payable has become an expense and must be converted to Interest Expense.

Glossary

Accrued interest on notes payable The interest that is due (not yet paid) on notes payable that are outstanding at the end of the fiscal period. (549)

Contra-liability account A deduction from a liability, such as Discount on Notes Payable, which is a deduction from the balance of Notes Payable. (545)

Discount Interest deducted in advance by a bank that makes a loan. (543)

Discounting a note payable The procedure by which a bank deducts interest in advance when it loans money with a note. (543)

Duration The period of time a note is outstanding; the length of time in days or months from a note's issue date to its maturity date. (538)

Interest A charge made for the use of money. (537)

Maker An individual or firm that signs a promissory note. (536)

Maturity date The due date of a promissory note. (537)

Maturity value The principal of the note plus interest. (540)

Notes payable register An auxiliary record used for listing the details of notes issued. (548)

Notice of maturity A notice specifying the terms and due date of a promissory note that has been left with a bank for collection; mailed by the bank to the maker. (540)

Payee The party receiving payment, such as on a note receivable or an account receivable. (536)

Principal The face amount of a note. (537)

Proceeds The principal of a loan less the discount. (543)

Promissory note A written promise to pay a certain sum at a fixed or determinable future time. (536)

QUESTIONS, EXERCISES, AND CASES

Discussion Questions

1. Why is it necessary to make an adjusting entry for accrued interest on an interest-bearing note payable? Should the entry be reversed?
2. Define *promissory note* and identify the two major parties involved.
3. Explain how to determine the maturity date of a note.
4. Describe the basic formula for the calculation of interest on a note. Explain each element.
5. Distinguish between a regular note and a discounted note.
6. Differentiate between the principal value of a note and the maturity value of a note.
7. Explain the difference when making an entry for a note discounted at a bank in which the note matures before the end of the fiscal period and one in which the note matures after the end of the fiscal period. Does either situation require an adjusting entry?
8. Briefly explain the Discount on Notes Payable account. What is its classification?

Exercises

P.O. 2,3

Determine interest amounts.

Exercise 14-1 Part A: Calculate the interest on the following notes:

Principal	Interest Rate (percent)	Number of Days
1. $14,400	9.5	33 days
2. 1,200	7.5	45 days
3. 6,000	8	90 days
4. 9,800	10.5	60 days
5. 2,500	9	120 days

Determine maturity dates.

Part B: Determine the maturity dates on the following notes:

Date of Issue	Life of Note
1. January 18	90 days
2. February 12	6 months
3. June 21	60 days
4. September 10	4 months
5. November 17	30 days

P.O. 2,3,4a,b

Determine interest and due date, and journalize entries to issue and pay the note.

Exercise 14-2 On April 3, B. M. Sibon gives a 60-day, 10 percent note, dated April 3, to Como Company, a creditor, in the amount of $7,640.

a. What is the due date of the note?
b. How much interest is to be paid on the note at maturity?
c. Write the entries in general journal form to record both issuance of the note by the maker and payment of the note at maturity as they would appear on Sibon's books.

P.O. 4e,f

Journalize issuance and payment of a discounted note.

Exercise 14-3 As a result of a loan from Plains State Bank, Tony Company signed a 120-day note, dated March 12, for $12,000 that the bank discounted at 8 percent. Write the entries for the maker in general journal form to record the following, assuming that the note is paid in the same fiscal period:

a. Issuance of the note on March 12.
b. Payment of the note at maturity.

P.O. 2,4d,e

Calculate interest and proceeds of a note.

Exercise 14-4 In arranging for a 90-day loan from a bank, Marley Company has the option of either (1) giving a $52,000, 10 percent interest-bearing note, dated November 3, that will be accepted at face value; or (2) giving a $52,000 note that will be discounted at 10 percent.

a. What is the amount of interest in each case?
b. What is the amount of cash Marley Company actually receives in each case?

P.O. 2,3,5

Complete a notes payable register.

Exercise 14-5 Make entries in a notes payable register to document the following events. Show the computation of the interest and due dates.

Mar. 15   Gave a 45-day, 9 percent note, dated March 15, for $3,600, to Donlet Company to apply on account.
Apr. 10   Borrowed $5,800 from Drew State Bank, giving a 90-day, 10.5 percent note, dated April 10 (received full face value).
         20   Bought merchandise from Morris, Inc., with a $3,330, 45-day, 11 percent note, dated April 20.
         29   Paid Donlet Company the amount owed on the note of March 15.

P.O. 4b,c,g,6a

Journalize note renewal, partial payment, and adjusting entry.

Exercise 14-6 Gruner Supply Company completed the following transactions. Record them in general journal form.

a. Purchased merchandise for $18,300 on November 17, giving a 30-day, 8.5 percent note dated November 17 to Lester Company in exchange for the merchandise.
b. On December 17, Gruner is unable to pay the principal of the note due but pays the interest due.
c. On December 17, Gruner renews the $18,300 note for 60 days at 9 percent, dated December 17.
d. On December 31, Gruner makes the adjusting entry for accrued interest.

P.O. 4a,b,6a

Journalize note issuance, adjusting entry, reversing entry, and payment.

Exercise 14-7 On September 10, H. H. Hanson issued a 120-day, 10 percent note, dated September 10, to Swazey Construction, a creditor, for $9,800. Write the entries in general journal form to record the following transactions. Assume that closing entries were made at the appropriate time.

a. Issuance of the note on September 10.
b. Adjusting entry for accrued interest on December 31, the end of the fiscal year.
c. Reversing entry on January 1.
d. Payment of the note plus interest on January 8.

P.O. 4e,f,6b,c

Journalize note issuance, adjustment, payment, and conversion of Discount on Notes Payable to Interest Expense.

Exercise 14-8 On December 5, B. M. Valentine borrowed $7,500 from Cosley State Bank for 45 days, with a discount rate of 9 percent. Accordingly, B. M. Valentine signed a note for $7,500, dated December 5. The end of B. M. Valentine's fiscal year is December 31. Write entries in general journal form to record the following transactions. Assume the closing entries were made at the appropriate time.

a. Issuance of the note on December 5.
b. Adjusting entry on December 31.
c. Payment of the note at maturity on January 19.
d. Conversion of the Discount on Notes Payable to Interest Expense for the current year.

internet
LINKS TO ACCOUNTING

Now that you have a better understanding of notes payable and the related interest payments, let's go back to Raytheon's notes payable as of December 31, 2005. Go to **http://www.raytheon.com/investor/2005/index.html** and click on 10-K in the Downloads list at the top of the screen. Look at Note H, on page 69.

1. As of December 31, 2005, what was the total of Raytheon's current notes payable and the weighted-average interest rate on these notes?
2. Assume these notes have a duration of six months. What would be the total interest Raytheon would pay on them?
3. Assume that these notes were issued on September 1, 2005. What would Raytheon's December 31, 2005, adjusting entry have been for accrued interest on these notes?

CONSIDER AND COMMUNICATE

Your friend needs to buy an $800 component to replace some essential sound equipment. He has neither that much cash nor credit available. He has heard of promissory notes and asks for your help. Explain the concept of a promissory note, what it will mean when your friend signs it, and why the total of the payments on the note at maturity will be greater than the original $800.

WHAT'S WRONG WITH THIS PICTURE?

The owner of a business told her accountant that she "paid" her personal revolving charge account with a 30-day, 9 percent note for $10,000, signed by her business. At the end of the 30 days, the owner told her accountant that she paid off the interest due and signed another 30-day, 9 percent note. What problems, if any, do you see with this scenario?

CRITICAL THINKING

Your supervisor has asked you to audit some journal entries recorded by her client's bookkeeper. Review the following transactions. If there is an error, rejournalize the entry. If the bookkeeper's entry is correct, write OK next to the date on your paper. The fiscal period begins January 1 and ends on December 31.

Apr. 5 Borrowed $3,000 from Star Bank for 90 days, discount rate 9 percent. Signed a discounted note for $3,000 dated April 5.

June 30 Bought a new air conditioning system (Building), giving a 90-day, 9.5 percent note, dated June 30, to Yocum Company, $65,300.

July 4 Paid the $3,000 note to Star Bank dated April 5.

Sept. 28 Paid the entire interest due to Yocum Company as well as $30,000 toward the principal. Issued a new $35,300, 120-day, 9.5 percent note, dated September 28.

Nov. 20 Borrowed $4,000 from Larson Bank for 45 days, discount rate 9.5 percent. Signed a discounted note for $4,000 dated November 20.

Dec. 31 Journalized the adjusting entries for the outstanding notes owed to Yocum Company and Larson Bank.

GENERAL JOURNAL — PAGE _____

DATE		DESCRIPTION	POST. REF.	DEBIT	CREDIT
20–					
Apr.	5	Cash		3 0 0 0 00	
		Interest Expense			6 7 50
		Notes Payable			2 9 3 2 50
June	30	Building		65 3 0 0 00	
		Notes Payable			65 3 0 0 00
July	4	Notes Payable		3 0 0 0 00	
		Discount on Notes Payable		6 7 50	
		Cash			3 0 6 7 50
Sept.	28	Notes Payable		30 0 0 0 00	
		Cash			30 0 0 0 00
	28	Notes Payable		35 3 0 0 00	
		Notes Payable			35 3 0 0 00
Nov.	20	Cash		3 9 5 2 50	
		Interest Expense		4 7 50	
		Notes Payable			4 0 0 0 00
		Adjusting Entries			
Dec.	31	Interest Expense		9 1 8 92	
		Interest Payable			9 1 8 92
	31	Discount on Notes Payable		4 4 33	
		Interest Payable			4 4 33

PROBLEM SET A

For additional help, see the demonstration problem at the beginning of each chapter in your Working Papers.

P.O. 2,4a,b,d

Problem 14-1A The following were among this year's transactions of Moore Appliances, which uses a periodic inventory system:

Jan.	15	Bought merchandise on account from Jang Wholesalers, $4,550; terms 3/10, n/30.
	21	Paid Jang Wholesalers for the invoice of January 15.
Feb.	25	Bought merchandise on account from Marvin Company, $3,850; terms net 30 days.
Mar.	27	Gave a 60-day, 9 percent note, dated March 27, for $3,850 to Marvin Company to apply on account.
May	26	Paid Marvin Company the amount owed on the note of March 27.
June	18	Borrowed $9,000 from Tower Bank, giving a 90-day, 8 percent note, dated June 18, for that amount (received full face value).
Sept.	16	Paid Tower Bank the amount due on the note of June 18.

Check Figure

May 26 Interest Expense, $57.75

Instructions

Record these transactions in a general journal (page 36).

P.O. 4a,b,e,g

Problem 14-2A The following were among this year's transactions of U.S. Yarn Shop, which uses a periodic inventory system:

Jan.	25	Bought merchandise on account from Geneva Mills, $4,000; terms net 30 days.
Feb.	23	Gave a 45-day, 10 percent note, dated February 23, for $4,000 to Geneva Mills to apply on account.
Apr.	9	Paid Geneva Mills the amount owed on the note of February 23.
May	24	Bought merchandise on account from Tildon Company, $8,200; terms net 30 days.
June	23	Gave a 30-day, 9.5 percent note, dated June 23, for $8,200 to Tildon Company to apply on account.
July	23	Paid Tildon Company the interest due on the note of June 23 and renewed the obligation by issuing a new 60-day, 9.5 percent note, dated July 23, for $8,200 (two entries).
Sept.	21	Paid Tildon Company the amount owed on the note of July 23.
	25	Borrowed $12,500 from Valley Bank for 90 days; discount rate is 11 percent. Accordingly, signed a discounted note for $12,500, dated September 25. (Use Interest Expense because the note will mature in the present fiscal period.)
Dec.	24	Paid Valley Bank at maturity of note.

Check Figure

April 9 Interest Expense, $50

Instructions

Record these transactions in a general journal (pages 27 and 28).

Instructions for General Ledger Software

1. Journalize the entries in the general journal.
2. Print the journal entries.

P.O. 3,4a,b,c,e,f,g,5,6a

Problem 14-3A The following were among the transactions of Cliff Shop during this year. The firm, whose fiscal year ends on December 31, uses a periodic inventory system.

Jan.	11	Bought merchandise on account from Harris Company, $4,600; terms net 30 days.
Feb.	10	Gave a 30-day, 10 percent note, dated February 10, for $4,600 to Harris Company to apply on account.
Mar.	12	Paid $2,600 as partial payment on principal as well as the full interest on the note given to Harris Company (Ck. No. 819). Issued a new 60-day, 10.5 percent note, dated March 12, for $2,000.
May	10	Borrowed $10,500 from Washington Bank for 120 days; discount rate is 10.25 percent. Accordingly, signed a discounted note for $10,500, dated May 10.
	11	Paid Harris Company the amount owed on the note of March 12 (Ck. No. 911).
Sept.	7	Paid Washington Bank the amount owed on the note of May 10 (Ck. No. 1051).
Nov.	17	Bought a laptop computer for $2,290 from Data Equipment. Issued a 90-day, 10 percent note, dated November 17.
Dec.	31	Recorded the adjusting entry for accrued interest on the note given to Data Equipment.
Jan.	1	Recorded the reversing entry. (Assume the closing entries were journalized and posted.)

Check Figure

Adjusting entry, Interest Expense, $27.99

Instructions

1. Record these transactions in one of the following journals: cash receipts journal (page 13), cash payments journal (page 18), or general journal (page 10).
2. Immediately after each journal entry, record each note in the notes payable register (page 5). Fill in the date paid after journalizing the entry to pay the note, or fill in "renewed" if not paid.

P.O. 4a,b,c,d,e,g,5,6a,b,c

Problem 14-4A The following were among the transactions of Klisky Company during this year. The firm, whose fiscal year ends on December 31, uses a periodic inventory system.

May	24	Gave a 60-day, 9.5 percent note, dated May 24, for $63,000 to Dean Builders for additional office space.
June	20	Borrowed $16,300 from First Bank, signing a 3-month, 10 percent note, dated June 20, for that amount (received full face value).
July	15	Gave a 120-day, 10 percent note, dated July 15, for $12,800 to Castle Carpentry for shelving units. The invoice was not previously recorded.
	23	Paid Dean Builders the amount owed on the note of May 24.
Sept.	20	Paid interest on the note issued to First Bank; renewed the loan by issuing a new 60-day, 10.75 percent note, dated September 20.
Oct.	27	Gave two notes to Chapman Company in settlement of its October 27 invoice for merchandise, as follows: $12,300 note for 45 days at 9.5 percent, dated October 27; $12,300 note for 60 days at 9.75 percent, dated October 27. The invoice was not previously recorded.

Nov. 12 Paid Castle Carpentry the amount owed on the note of July 15.
     19 Paid the note given to First Bank.
Dec. 11 Paid the amount owed on the 45-day note given to Chapman Company.
     15 Issued a 60-day, 10 percent note, dated December 15, to McNeil Company in settlement of November 15 invoice for merchandise, $11,460. The invoice was previously recorded.
     18 Borrowed $20,500 from Horner Bank for 60 days; discount rate is 10.75 percent. Accordingly, signed a discounted note for $20,500, dated December 18. (Debit Discount on Notes Payable, since the note extends into next fiscal period.)
Dec. 26 Paid the amount owed on the 60-day note given to Chapman Company.

Check Figure

December 18 Discount on Notes Payable, $367.29

Instructions

1. Record these transactions in a general journal (pages 26–29).
2. Immediately after each journal entry, record each note in the notes payable register (page 7). Fill in the date paid after journalizing the entry to pay the note, or fill in "renewed" if not paid.
3. On December 31, record the adjusting entries to adjust for accrued interest expense for the McNeil Company note and Discount on Notes Payable for the Horner Bank note.
4. On January 1, record the reversing entry. (Assume that closing entries have been made.)
5. On February 13, record the payment of the note to McNeil Company.
6. On February 16, record the payment of the note to Horner Bank.
7. On February 16, record the entry to expense the discount on the Horner Bank note.

PROBLEM SET B

For additional help, see the demonstration problem at the beginning of each chapter in your Working Papers.

P.O. 2,4a,b,d

Problem 14-1B The following were among this year's transactions of Borumbi Company, which uses a periodic inventory system:

Jan. 8 Bought merchandise on account from Laris Company, $4,450; terms 3/10, n/30.
     18 Paid Laris Company for the invoice of January 8.
Feb. 14 Bought merchandise on account from Rory Company, $3,800; terms net 30 days.
Mar. 16 Gave a 45-day, 10 percent note, dated March 16, for $3,800 to Rory Company to apply on account.
Apr. 30 Paid Rory Company the amount owed on the note of March 16.
May 24 Borrowed $10,800 from Kingston Bank, giving a 90-day, 9.75 percent note, dated May 24, for that amount (received full face value).
Aug. 22 Paid Kingston Bank the amount due on the note of May 24.

Check Figure

April 30 Interest Expense, $47.50

Instructions

Record these transactions in the general journal (page 47).

P.O. 4a,b,e,g

Problem 14-2B The following were among this year's transactions of Zamora Company, which uses a periodic inventory system:

Jan. 31 Bought merchandise on account from Markle Company, $3,345; terms net 30 days.

Mar. 2 Gave a 60-day, 9 percent note, dated March 2, for $3,345 to Markle Company to apply on account.

May 1 Paid Markle Company the amount owed on the note of March 2.
5 Bought merchandise on account from Best Company, $8,400; terms 3/10, n/30.

June 4 Gave a 45-day, 10.5 percent note, dated June 4, for $8,400 to Best Company to apply on account.

July 19 Paid Best Company the interest due on the note of June 4 and renewed the obligation by issuing a new 60-day, 10.5 percent note, dated July 19, for $8,400 (two entries).

Sept. 17 Paid Best Company the amount owed on the note of July 19.

Oct. 18 Borrowed $15,700 from River Bank for 60 days; discount rate is 10 percent. Accordingly, signed a discounted note for $15,700, dated October 18. (Use Interest Expense because the note will mature in the present fiscal period.)

Dec. 17 Paid River Bank at maturity of note.

Check Figure

May 1 Interest Expense, $50.18

Instructions

Record these transactions in the general journal (pages 36 and 37).

Instructions for General Ledger Software

1. Journalize the entries in the general journal.
2. Print the journal entries.

P.O. 3,4a,b,c,e,f,g,5,6a

Problem 14-3B The following were among the transactions of Ken's Crafts during this year. The firm, whose fiscal year ends on December 31, uses a periodic inventory system.

Jan. 25 Bought merchandise on account from Rose Company, $3,360; terms 2/10, n/30.

Feb. 24 Gave a 30-day, 8 percent note, dated February 24, for $3,360 to Rose Company to apply on account.

Mar. 26 Paid $1,500 as partial payment on principal as well as the full interest on the note given to Rose Company (Ck. No. 4120). Issued a new 45-day, 8.5 percent note, dated March 26, for $1,860 (two entries).

May 10 Paid Rose Company the amount owed on the note of March 26 (Ck. No. 4215).

June 26 Borrowed $6,960 from Old Bank for 90 days; discount rate is 9.5 percent. Accordingly, signed a discounted note for $6,960, dated June 26.

Sept. 24 Paid Old Bank the amount owed on the note of June 26 (Ck. No. 4310).

Oct. 28 Bought display racks for $1,980 from Cain's Fixtures. Issued a 90-day, 8.25 percent note, dated October 28.

Dec. 31 Recorded the adjusting entry for accrued interest on the note given to Cain's Fixtures.

Jan. 1 Recorded the reversing entry. (Assume closing entries were journalized and posted.)

Check Figure

Adjusting Entry, Interest Expense, $29.04

Instructions

1. Record these transactions in one of the following journals: cash receipts journal (page 16), cash payments journal (page 21), or general journal (page 12).
2. Immediately after each journal entry, record each note in the notes payable register (page 5). Fill in the date paid after journalizing the entry to pay the note, or fill in "renewed" if not paid.

P.O. 4a,b,c,d,e,g,5,6a,b,c

Problem 14-4B The following were among the transactions of Cort Company during this year. The firm, whose fiscal year ends on December 31, uses a periodic inventory system.

June 12 Gave a 30-day, 9.5 percent note, dated June 12, for $62,000 to Parker, Inc., for an addition to the building.

15 Borrowed $27,400 from Mesa Bank, signing a 3-month, 8.5 percent note, dated June 15, for that amount (received full face value).

July 12 Paid Parker, Inc., the amount owed on the note of June 12.

12 Gave a 120-day, 8.5 percent note, dated July 12, for $9,342 to C. J., Inc., for office equipment. The invoice was not previously recorded.

Sept. 15 Paid interest on the note issued to Mesa Bank; renewed the loan by issuing a new 60-day, 9 percent note, dated September 15.

Nov. 9 Paid C. J., Inc., the amount owed on the note of July 12.

14 Gave two notes to NesCo in settlement of its November 14 invoice for merchandise, as follows: $12,300 note for 30 days at 8 percent, dated November 14; $12,300 note for 60 days at 8 percent, dated November 14. The invoice was not previously recorded.

14 Paid the note given to Mesa Bank.

Dec. 14 Paid the amount owed on the 30-day note given to NesCo.

15 Issued a 90-day, 8.5 percent note, dated December 15, to Hall Company in settlement of November 15 invoice for merchandise, $18,950. The invoice was previously recorded.

18 Borrowed $36,000 from Trent Bank for 30 days; discount rate is 8.25 percent. Accordingly, signed a discounted note for $36,000, dated December 18. (Debit Discount on Notes Payable, since the note extends into the next fiscal period.)

Check Figure

Adjusting Entry, Interest Payable, $200.06

Instructions

1. Record these transactions in a general journal (pages 18–21).
2. Immediately after each journal entry, record each note in the notes payable register (page 7). Fill in the date paid after journalizing the entry to pay the note, or fill in "renewed" if not paid.
3. On December 31, record the adjusting entries to adjust for accrued interest expense for the NesCo and Hall notes, as well as the adjustment of Discount on Notes Payable on the Trent Bank note.
4. On January 1, record the reversing entry. (Assume that closing entries have been made.)
5. On January 13, record the payment of the note to NesCo.
6. On January 17, record the payment of the note to Trent Bank.
7. On January 17, record the entry to expense the discount on the Trent note.
8. On March 15, record the payment of the note to Hall Company.

15

Notes Receivable

Do you have some extra cash? Are you looking for a good investment? Using promissory notes, investors lend money to a firm in exchange for a fixed amount of income. A promissory note with a duration of as little as a few days or, perhaps, as much as 50 years is called a note receivable. This might be a good way for you to invest that extra cash, but you need to do a little homework first! The Securities and Exchange Commission (SEC) found that, in fraudulent cases, promoters promise very high returns (can you believe 200%!?) and make assurances that the investment's safety is guaranteed by insurance companies or that bonds or other collateral back up the notes. In most cases, however, the issuers have little or no insurance, collateral, or other means to guarantee payment. What happens when you invest in notes receivable and the borrower doesn't repay the debt when it is due? Go to **http://www.sec.gov/litigation/litreleases.shtml** to learn about cases in which the SEC has brought charges against fraudulent companies and individuals. The SEC has also issued a warning about fraudulent "prime bank" schemes, which can be found by going to **http://www.sec.gov/divisions/enforce/primebank/howtheywork.shtml.** It's shocking how bold and widespread this type of scam is. Be cautious of promises of high returns that sound too good to be true!

Performance Objectives

After you have completed this chapter, you will be able to do the following:

1. Write the journal entries to record (a) receipt of a note from a charge customer; (b) receipt of payment of an interest-bearing note at maturity; (c) receipt of a note as a result of granting a personal loan; (d) receipt of a note in exchange for merchandise or other property; (e) renewal of a note at maturity and payment of interest; (f) renewal of a note with payment of interest and partial payment of principal; (g) a dishonored note receivable; (h) collection of a note receivable formerly dishonored; (i) discounting an interest-bearing note receivable.

2. Complete a notes receivable register.

3. Write the journal entry to record the adjustment for accrued interest on notes receivable.

FYI

Notes receivable may be written for short periods of time, even days or weeks. They can also be written for very long periods of time, as when a bank receives a 30-year mortgage note. The life of a note is whatever is agreed upon by all parties.

Business firms receive promissory notes either regularly or occasionally for a variety of reasons. Sometimes a business firm accepts a promissory note from a customer at the time of sale. Companies frequently accept promissory notes from charge account customers who request an extension of time to settle past-due accounts. In effect, they substitute notes

FYI

Banks may grant loans for 100 percent of the face value of notes but a lesser percentage of the face value of open accounts.

receivable for accounts receivable. The net result is that the charge customer gets an extension of time for the payment of a debt.

Obviously, getting a note receivable is not as good as having cash in hand. However, it offers several advantages to the company: (1) the note represents proof of the original transaction, (2) the note may bear interest, and (3) the note may be pledged as security for a loan from a bank. Banks, in fact, loan a higher proportion of the face value on notes (Notes Receivable) than of open accounts (Accounts Receivable).

REMEMBER!

A note receivable on the books of the payee company is a note payable on the books of the company signing the note.

Notes receivable also come into being when a company grants loans to employees or preferred customers or suppliers. In some industries, the credit period is often longer than thirty days; here, the transactions are frequently evidenced by notes rather than by open accounts. Examples are sales of farm machinery, construction equipment, and trucks.

Now let's see how to journalize transactions involving notes receivable. The accounts involved are Notes Receivable (classified as a current asset on the balance sheet in our examples, although it could be classified as a long-term asset if the repayment period is longer than a year) and Interest Income (classified as other income on the income statement).

TRANSACTIONS FOR NOTES RECEIVABLE

First, let's say that all notes received are recorded in a single current asset account: Notes Receivable. Second, throughout this chapter, we are going to use Rainier Plumbing Supply to illustrate such transactions. All notes are payable at New National Bank. Now let's begin with a simple exchange.

Notes from Charge Customers to Extend Time on Their Accounts

 OBJECTIVE 1a

Write the journal entry to record receipt of a note from a charge customer.

On March 7, Rainier Plumbing Supply sold $840 worth of merchandise to Green Plumbing and Heating, with the customary terms of 2/10, n/30, and made the original entry in its sales journal. On April 6, Green Plumbing and Heating sent Rainier Plumbing Supply a note for $840, payable within 30 days, at 8 percent interest. The note, dated April 6, was in settlement of the transaction of March 7. Rainier Plumbing Supply recorded this new development in its general journal as follows:

REMEMBER!

A note receivable and an account receivable differ in the strength of legal claim they represent and in the way interest is earned—a note is more formal.

	DATE		DESCRIPTION	POST. REF.	DEBIT	CREDIT	
1	20–						1
2	Apr.	6	Notes Receivable		8 4 0 00		2
3			Accounts Receivable, Green				3
4			Plumbing and Heating			8 4 0 00	4
5			Received a 30-day, 8 percent				5
6			note, dated April 6, in				6
7			settlement of open account.				7
8							8

GENERAL JOURNAL   PAGE _____

T accounts for the transactions look like this:

Accounts Receivable				Sales			Notes Receivable		
+	−			−	+		+	−	
Mar. 7	840	Apr. 6	840		Mar. 7	840	Apr. 6	840	

Receipt of Payment of an Interest-Bearing Note at Maturity

OBJECTIVE 1b

Write the journal entry to record receipt of payment of an interest-bearing note at maturity.

On May 6, Green Plumbing and Heating paid Rainier Plumbing Supply in full: principal plus interest. Rainier Plumbing Supply recorded the transaction in the general journal as follows:

	DATE		DESCRIPTION	POST. REF.	DEBIT	CREDIT	
1	20–						1
2	May	6	Cash		8 4 5 60		2
3			Notes Receivable			8 4 0 00	3
4			Interest Income			5 60	4
5			Received full payment of				5
6			Green Plumbing and				6
7			Heating's note.				7
8			($840 × 0.08 × 30/360)				8
9							9
10							10
11							11

REMEMBER!

Calculations are included to show how the amounts were determined. They would not normally appear in journal entries.

Let's look at the T accounts for this entry:

Cash				Notes Receivable			
+	−			+	−		
May 6	845.60			Apr. 6	840.00	May 6	840.00

Interest Income		
−	+	
	May 6	5.60

Businesses may accept a promissory note from a customer for several reasons. Customers may be making a large purchase or need an extension on a past-due account. A note receivable is a promise to pay the amount due, with interest, at a future date.

In practice, this transaction would be recorded directly in the cash receipts journal rather than in the general journal. But, for the sake of simplicity and clarity, we will use the general journal format to illustrate entries throughout this chapter.

Notes Received as a Result of Granting Personal Loans

OBJECTIVE 1c

Write the journal entry to record receipt of a note as a result of granting a personal loan.

Sometimes employees, preferred customers, or suppliers may want to borrow cash from the business. When that is the case, the business often accepts a note receivable. Let's say that Glenda Moore, an employee of Rainier Plumbing Supply, borrows $600 from her employer, for 3 months at 6 percent. Her note is dated April 8. In general journal form, the entry is as shown below:

	DATE		DESCRIPTION	POST. REF.	DEBIT	CREDIT	
1	20–						1
2	Apr.	8	Notes Receivable		6 0 0 00		2
3			Cash			6 0 0 00	3
4			Granted a loan to Glenda				4
5			Moore, 3 months, 6 percent,				5
6			dated April 8.				6
7							7

When the loan reaches maturity, Moore pays the principal plus interest.

	DATE		DESCRIPTION	POST. REF.	DEBIT	CREDIT	
1	20–						1
2	July	8	Cash		6 0 9 00		2
3			Notes Receivable			6 0 0 00	3
4			Interest Income			9 00	4
5			Received full payment of				5
6			Glenda Moore's note, dated				6
7			April 8.				7
8			($600 × 0.06 × 3/12)				8
9							9
10							10

Note Received in Exchange for Merchandise or Other Property

OBJECTIVE 1d

Write the journal entry to record receipt of a note in exchange for merchandise or other property.

Business firms that sell high-priced durable goods for which the credit period is longer than the normal thirty days may regularly accept notes from their customers.

On April 9, Rainier Plumbing Supply sold merchandise to M. L. Klaus and Company for $920. M. L. Klaus and Company gave Rainier Plumbing Supply a promissory note, promising to pay the full amount within 60 days; the note specified 7 percent interest. When this type of transaction occurs occasionally, the transaction is recorded in the general journal as follows:

	DATE		DESCRIPTION	POST. REF.	DEBIT	CREDIT	
1	20—						1
2	Apr.	9	Notes Receivable		9 2 0 00		2
3			Sales			9 2 0 00	3
4			M. L. Klaus and Company,				4
5			60-day, 7 percent				5
6			note, dated April 9.				6
7							7
8							8

Renewal of Note at Maturity and Payment of Interest

OBJECTIVE 1e

Write the journal entries to record renewal of a note at maturity and payment of interest.

If the maker of a note is unable to pay the entire principal at maturity, the company may be allowed to renew all or part of the note.

Now suppose that M. L. Klaus and Company is not able to pay the note at maturity and offers to pay the interest on the current note and to issue a new note, for 30 days at 8 percent. Rainier Plumbing Supply makes the entries in the general journal as shown below. Note that two entries are required. One entry records the interest on the old note. The second entry cancels the old note and records the new note.

	DATE		DESCRIPTION	POST. REF.	DEBIT	CREDIT	
1	20—						1
2	June	8	Cash		1 0 73		2
3			Interest Income			1 0 73	3
4			Received payment of interest				4
5			on M. L. Klaus and Company				5
6			note, dated April 9.				6
7			($920 × 0.07 × 60/360)				7
8							8
9		8	Notes Receivable		9 2 0 00		9
10			Notes Receivable			9 2 0 00	10
11			M. L. Klaus and Company,				11
12			renewal of note, dated April 9;				12
13			new note is dated June 8,				13
14			30 days, 8 percent.				14
15							15

REMEMBER!

For a renewal of a note receivable, credit the old note to take it off the books, and debit the new note to put it on the books.

Actually, there is only one Notes Receivable ledger account. However, when a note is renewed, it is customary for the debtor or maker to pay up the interest on the old note and then issue a new note.

Renewal of Note with Payment of Interest and Partial Payment of Principal

OBJECTIVE 1f

Write the journal entries to record renewal of a note with payment of interest and partial payment of principal.

Sometimes the maker of a note cancels the original note by paying the interest, plus part of the principal, and issuing a new note. Suppose that, as a substitute for the $920 note described earlier, M. L. Klaus and Company gives Rainier Plumbing Supply $300 toward the principal and a new note for $620 in addition to the interest on the old note.

Rainier Plumbing Supply records the transactions in the general journal as follows:

	DATE		DESCRIPTION	POST. REF.	DEBIT	CREDIT	
1	20–						1
2	June	8	Cash		3 1 0 73		2
3			Notes Receivable			3 0 0 00	3
4			Interest Income			1 0 73	4
5			M. L. Klaus and Company				5
6			note, dated April 9, partial				6
7			payment of the principal and				7
8			interest payment.				8
9							9
10		8	Notes Receivable		6 2 0 00		10
11			Notes Receivable			6 2 0 00	11
12			M. L. Klaus and Company,				12
13			renewal of note dated April 9;				13
14			the new note is dated June 8,				14
15			30 days, 8 percent.				15
16							16

DISHONORED NOTES RECEIVABLE

OBJECTIVE 1g

Write the journal entry to record a dishonored note receivable.

When the maker of a note fails to pay the principal amount or to renew the note at maturity, the note is said to be a dishonored note receivable. The maker of the note is still obligated to pay the principal plus interest, and the creditor should take legal steps to collect the debt. However, the balance of the Notes Receivable account shows only the principal of notes that have not yet matured. A note that is past due, or dishonored, should be removed from the Notes Receivable account and added to the Accounts Receivable account; the amount listed should be the principal plus interest. In other words, once a note receivable comes due and is not collected, it is "dead." But the maker still owes the payee, so the amount owed (principal plus interest) is put back into Accounts Receivable.

For example, Rainier Plumbing Supply holds a 60-day, 8 percent note for $850 dated April 20, from Chin Building Supplies, which fails to pay by the due date. Thus the note is dishonored at maturity. Rainier Plumbing Supply then makes an entry in its general journal to remove the dishonored note from the Notes Receivable account as shown on the next page.

	DATE		DESCRIPTION	POST. REF.	DEBIT	CREDIT	
1	20–						1
2	June	19	Accounts Receivable, Chin				2
3			Building Supplies		8 6 1 33		3
4			Notes Receivable			8 5 0 00	4
5			Interest Income			1 1 33	5
6			Chin Building Supplies				6
7			dishonored its 60-day,				7
8			8 percent note for $850,				8
9			dated April 20.				9
10			($850 × 0.08 × 60/360)				10
11							11

REMEMBER!

Rainier Plumbing Supply records Interest Income, which is consistent with the accrual basis of accounting (record income when earned and expenses when incurred).

Chin Building Supplies owes both the principal and the interest, and the account should reflect the full amount owed. Note particularly that Rainier Plumbing Supply credits the Interest Income account, even though Chin Building Supplies did not pay the interest. This is consistent with the accrual basis of accounting: revenue is recorded when it is *earned*, rather than when it is received. If Chin Building Supplies should ever ask Rainier Plumbing Supply to act as a credit reference, or if Chin Building Supplies ever asks for credit in the future, subsidiary records will show all past dealings, including the dishonored note.

Collection of a Note Formerly Dishonored

OBJECTIVE 1h

Write the journal entry to record collection of a note receivable formerly dishonored.

Now suppose that, 30 days after its note has been dishonored, Chin Building Supplies pays up the balance of its account, plus an additional 30 days' interest at 8 percent on the amount owed. The entry in Rainier Plumbing Supply's general journal is shown below:

GENERAL JOURNAL   PAGE _____

	DATE		DESCRIPTION	POST. REF.	DEBIT	CREDIT	
1	20–						1
2	July	19	Cash		8 6 7 07		2
3			Accounts Receivable, Chin				3
4			Building Supplies			8 6 1 33	4
5			Interest Income			5 74	5
6			Chin Building Supplies				6
7			paid the dishonored note,				7
8			plus interest for 30 days at				8
9			8 percent.				9
10			($861.33 × 0.08 × 30/360)				10
11							11

Rainier Plumbing Supply gets its money in the long run anyway, and it can now consider the matter closed.

DISCOUNTING NOTES RECEIVABLE

OBJECTIVE 1i

Write the journal entry to record discounting an interest-bearing note receivable.

Instead of keeping notes receivable until they come due, a firm can raise cash by selling its notes receivable to a bank or finance company. This type of financing is called **discounting notes receivable** because the bank deducts the interest or discount from the maturity value of the note to determine the proceeds (that is, the amount of money received by the payee). The **maturity value** is the principal (face value) of the note plus interest from the date of the note until the due date.

In the process of discounting a note receivable, the payee endorses the note (as it would a check) and delivers it to the financial institution. The

financial institution gives out cash now in exchange for the right to collect the principal and interest when the note comes due. The discount rate is the annual rate (percentage of maturity value) charged by the financial institution for buying the note. The financial institution generally discounts at a higher interest rate than stated in the note because the financial institution assumes increased risk of the maker's possible default.

A Discounted Note: Example 1 Rainier Plumbing Supply granted an extension on an open account by accepting a 60-day, 8 percent note for $1,080, dated April 20, from Carmel Hardware. To raise cash to buy additional merchandise, Rainier Plumbing Supply sold the note to New National Bank on May 5. The bank charged a discount rate of 9 percent. A diagram of the situation looks like this:

Sometimes notes receivable are discounted; that is, the lender sells the note to someone else to collect. The reason for doing this is the need for money before the borrower would pay his or her debt.

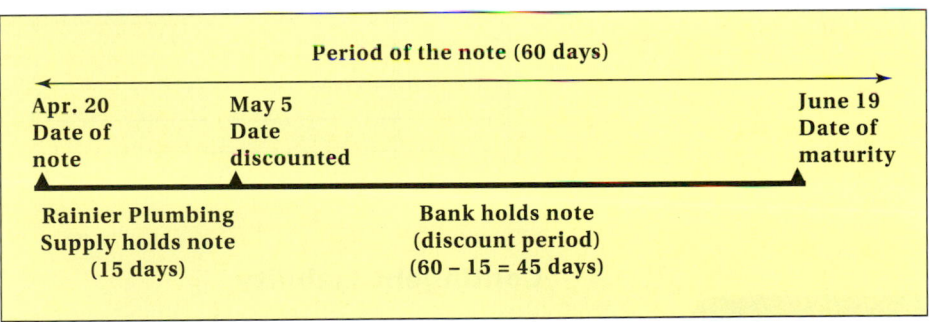

The **discount period** of the note consists of the interval between the date the note is given to the bank and the maturity date of the note. (In other words, the discount period is the time the note has left to run.)

Next we determine the value of the note at maturity and deduct the amount of the bank's discount from it, using the following formula:

Principal ($1,080)
+ Interest to maturity date (8%, 60 days)
_____
  Value at maturity
− Discount (9%, 45 days)
_____
  Proceeds

After we set up the problem, we can complete the calculation:

Principal	$1,080.00	Interest = Principal × Rate × Time
+ Interest (8%, 60 days)	14.40	
Value at maturity	$1,094.40	Interest = $1,080 × 0.08 × $\frac{60}{360}$ = $14.40
− Discount (9%, 45 days)	12.31	Discount = $1,094.40 × 0.09 × $\frac{45}{360}$ = $12.31
Proceeds	$1,082.09	

Note that, in our calculations, we figure the discount on the value of the note at maturity ($1,094.40, 9 percent, 45 days). The proceeds are the amount that Rainier Plumbing Supply receives from the bank; this amount is therefore debited to Cash. *If the amount of the proceeds is greater than the amount of the principal, the difference represents Interest Income,* because Rainier Plumbing Supply made money on the deal. *If the amount of the proceeds is less than the principal, on the other hand, the deficiency represents Interest Expense because Rainier Plumbing Supply lost money in the deal.* Look at the entry in Rainier Plumbing Supply's general journal:

	DATE		DESCRIPTION	POST. REF.	DEBIT	CREDIT	
1	20–						1
2	May	5	Cash		1 0 8 2 09		2
3			Notes Receivable			1 0 8 0 00	3
4			Interest Income			2 09	4
5			Discounted at the bank				5
6			Carmel Hardware's note,				6
7			dated April 20. The bank				7
8			discount rate is 9 percent.				8
9							9
10							10
11							11
12							12

Contingent Liability

> **REMEMBER!**
>
> If the maker dishonors the note, the endorser is liable to the bank to pay the note; thus, it is necessary to show such potential liability on the endorser's balance sheet.

At the time Rainier Plumbing Supply discounted Carmel's note at the bank, Rainier Plumbing Supply had to endorse the note. By this endorsement, Rainier Plumbing Supply agreed to pay the note when it became due if the maker did not pay it. Therefore the endorser has a **contingent liability** for payment of the note. If the maker dishonors the note, the endorser is liable. In other words, the liability of the endorser is contingent upon the possible dishonoring of the note by the maker. It follows that, if the credit rating of the endorser of the note is good, a bank is usually willing to accept and discount a note. The endorser, by virtue of his or her endorsement, or guarantee, agrees to pay the note at maturity *if* it is not paid by the maker. The fact that the note receivable is pledged as security, along with the amount of the contingent liability, should be shown as a note to the endorser's balance sheet.

Payment of a Discounted Note by the Maker

The bank collects the principal plus the interest on a discounted note directly from the maker. When the maker pays the bank, the endorser no longer has any contingent liability; the note to the endorser's balance sheet can be eliminated when the note is paid. A journal entry is not required.

A Discounted Note: Example 2   On April 25, Rainier Plumbing Supply received a 90-day, 6 percent, $2,300 note, dated April 24, from Harris Service Company. On May 4, Rainier Plumbing Supply discounted the note at New National Bank. The discount rate charged by the bank is 7 percent. In handling discounted notes receivable, you should follow a definite step-by-step procedure.

REMEMBER!

The discount period is the time the note is held by the bank.

1. Diagram the situation.

	Period of the note (90 days)	
Apr. 24 **Date of** **note**	**May 4** **Date** **discounted**	**July 23** **Date of** **maturity**
Rainier Plumbing Supply holds note (10 days)	Bank holds note (discount period) (90 − 10 = 80 days)	

2. Determine the discount period.

April 30 − 24 = 6 days left in April
May _____ = 4 days in May

Days held by = 10 days
endorser

Discount period (bank holds note),
(Total days − days held by endorser)
90 days − 10 days = 80 days

3. Record the formula.

Principal ($2,300)
+ Interest (6%, 90 days)

Value at maturity
− Discount (7%, 80 days)

Proceeds

4. Complete the formula.

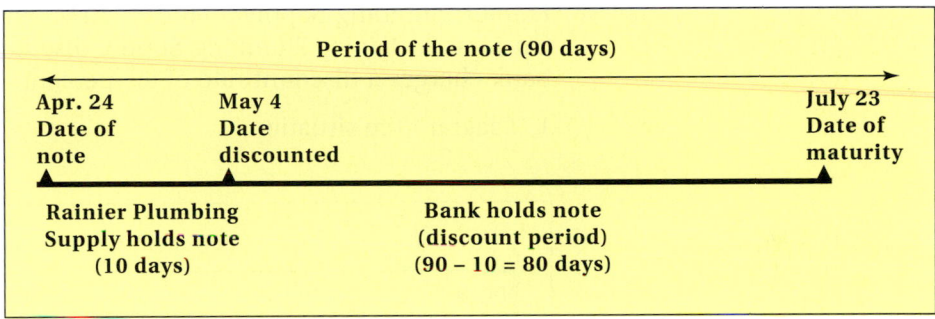

Principal	$2,300.00	Interest = Principal × Rate × Time
+ Interest (6%, 90 days)	34.50	$Interest = \$2{,}300 \times 0.06 \times \dfrac{90}{360} = \underline{\$34.50}$
Value at maturity	$2,334.50	
− Discount (7%, 80 days)	36.31	$Discount = \$2{,}334.50 \times 0.07 \times \dfrac{80}{360}$
Proceeds	$2,298.19	$= \underline{\$36.31}$

5. Make the entry, recognizing that the amount of the proceeds is a debit to Cash. If the amount of the proceeds is less than the principal, debit Interest Expense for the difference.

	DATE		DESCRIPTION	POST. REF.	DEBIT	CREDIT	
1	20–						1
2	May	4	Cash		2 2 9 8 19		2
3			Interest Expense		1 81		3
4			Notes Receivable			2 3 0 0 00	4
5			Discounted at the bank Harris				5
6			Service Company's note,				6
7			dated April 24. The bank				7
8			discount rate is 7 percent.				8

A Discounted Note: Example 3 On May 10, Martinez and Son gave Rainier Plumbing Supply a 60-day, 8 percent note for $3,960, dated May 9. On June 2, Rainier Plumbing Supply discounted the note at the bank. The bank charges a discount rate of 8.5 percent.

1. Diagram the situation.

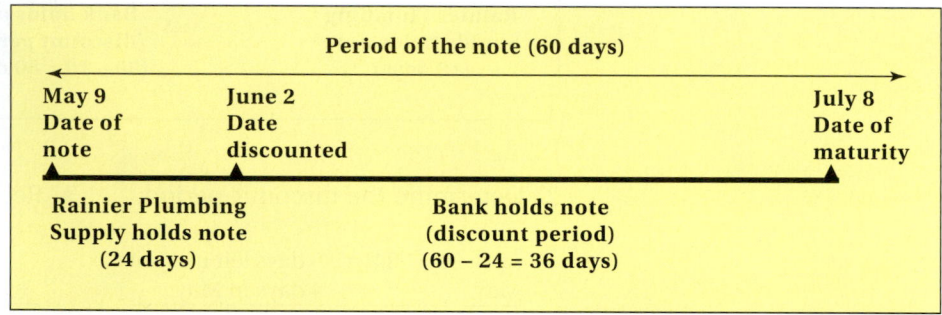

Companies with seasonal peaks and lows may need to sign a promissory note for a certain period of time to increase their inventory prior to the time it will actually be sold.

2. Determine the discount period.

May (31 − 9)	=	22 days left in May
June	=	2 days in June
Days held by endorser	=	24 days

Discount period (bank holds note),
(Total days − days held by endorser)
60 days – 24 days = 36 days

3. Record the formula.

Principal ($3,960)
+ Interest (8%, 60 days)

Value at maturity
− Discount (8.5%, 36 days)

Proceeds

4. Complete the formula.

Principal	$3,960.00
+ Interest (8%, 60 days)	52.80
Value at maturity	$4,012.80
− Discount (8.5%, 36 days)	34.11
Proceeds	$3,978.69

$\text{Interest} = \text{Principal} \times \text{Rate} \times \text{Time}$

$\text{Interest} = \$3,960 \times 0.08 \times \dfrac{60}{360} = \underline{\$52.80}$

$\text{Discount} = \$4,012.80 \times 0.085 \times \dfrac{36}{360}$

$= \underline{\$34.11}$

5. Record the entry as shown. If the amount of the proceeds is greater than the principal, credit Interest Income for the difference.

	DATE		DESCRIPTION	POST. REF.	DEBIT	CREDIT	
1	20–						1
2	June	2	Cash		3 9 7 8 69		2
3			Notes Receivable			3 9 6 0 00	3
4			Interest Income			1 8 69	4
5			Discounted at bank the note				5
6			received from Martinez and				6
7			Son dated May 9; discount				7
8			rate, 8.5 percent.				8
9							9

Notes Receivable Register

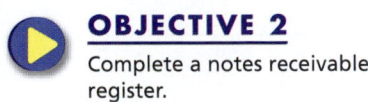

OBJECTIVE 2

Complete a notes receivable register.

Companies that have a significant number of notes receivable may find it worthwhile to set up a separate list to keep track of them. This list is called a **notes receivable register** (see Figure 1 on page 578). Information is taken from the face of each note. Columns are included to record the specifics of each note. At the end of the fiscal period, the accountant makes a schedule of notes receivable by listing the unpaid notes that appear in the notes receivable register. Also, the total of the schedule is compared with the balance of the Notes Receivable account. The two should match.

NOTES RECEIVABLE REGISTER

DATE		MAKER	WHERE PAYABLE	AMOUNT		TIME	RATE	INTEREST		DUE DATE	DISCOUNTED BANK	DATE	DATE PAID	REMARKS
20–														
Apr.	6	Green Plumbing and Heating	New Nat.	8 4 0	00	30 d	8%		5 60	5/6			5/6	Open account.
	8	Glenda Moore	New Nat.	6 0 0	00	3 m	6%		9 00	7/8			7/8	Employee loan.
	9	M. L. Klaus and Company	New Nat.	9 2 0	00	60 d	7%	1 0 73		6/8			Ren.	Open account.
	20	Chin Bldg. Supp.	New Nat.	8 5 0	00	60 d	8%	1 1 33		6/19			7/19	Dishonored
	20	Carmel Hardware	New Nat.	1 0 8 0	00	60 d	8%	1 4 40		6/19	New Nat.	5/5	—	Discount. @ 9%, $1,082.09 proceeds.
	24	Harris Service Company	New Nat.	2 3 0 0	00	90 d	6%	3 4 50		7/23	New Nat.	5/4	—	Discount. @ 7%, $2,298.19 proceeds.
May	9	Martinez and Son	New Nat.	3 9 6 0	00	60 d	8%	5 2 80		7/8	New Nat.	6/2		Discount. @ 8.5%, $3,978.69 proceeds.
June	8	M. L. Klaus and Company	New Nat.	9 2 0	00	30 d	8%		6 13	7/8				Renewed 4/9 note.
		Or if partial payment:												
June	8	M. L. Klaus and Company	New Nat.	6 2 0	00	30 d	8%		4 13	7/8				Renewed 4/9 note with part. payment of $300 plus interest.

FIGURE 1

END-OF-FISCAL-PERIOD ADJUSTMENT: ACCRUED INTEREST ON NOTES RECEIVABLE

OBJECTIVE 3

Write the journal entry to record the adjustment for accrued interest on notes receivable.

Accrued interest income on notes receivable is the interest that is due (not yet received) on notes receivable that are outstanding at the end of the fiscal period. Whenever a firm receives *or* issues an interest-bearing note, the interest accrues daily. As a result, any interest-bearing note that overlaps fiscal periods requires an adjusting entry in order for the financial statements to present a true picture of the firm's net income and financial condition.

For example, let's say that a firm has two notes receivable on December 31, the end of the fiscal period:

$9,000, 90 days, 8%, dated November 28
$5,200, 60 days, 7%, dated December 20

We can diagram the situation as follows:

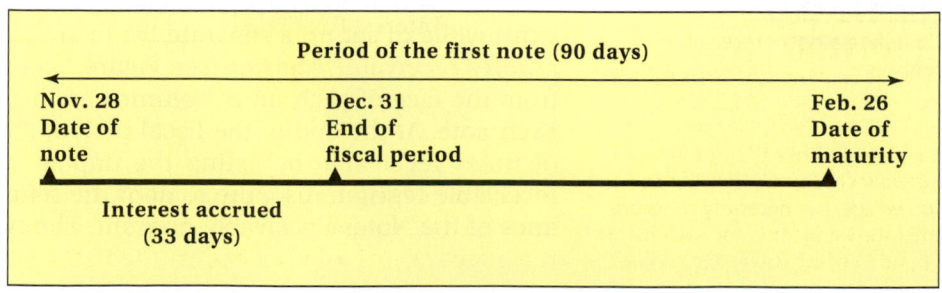

Nov. $(30 - 28) =$ 2 days left in November
Dec. $= 31$ days in December
_____

Total   33 days left in the fiscal period

Interest $=$ Principal $\times$ Rate $\times$ Time

Interest $= \$9,000 \times 0.08 \times \dfrac{33}{360} = \underline{\underline{\$66.00}}$

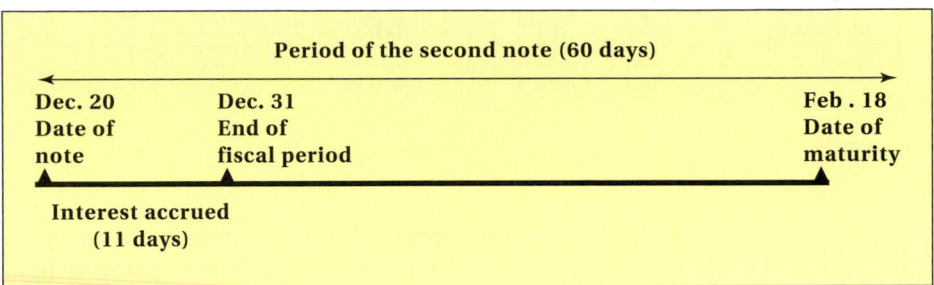

Period of the second note (60 days)

Dec. 20	Dec. 31	Feb . 18
Date of	End of	Date of
note	fiscal period	maturity

Interest accrued
(11 days)

Dec. $(31 - 20) = 11$ days left in the fiscal period

Interest $=$ Principal $\times$ Rate $\times$ Time

Interest $= \$5,200 \times 0.07 \times \dfrac{11}{360} = \underline{\underline{\$11.12}}$

The maker doesn't ordinarily pay the interest until the note comes due. Since these notes have not matured, the interest income has been neither paid nor recorded ($\$66.00 + \$11.12 = \$77.12$).

In the firm's general journal, the adjusting entry for the interest income accrued on the two notes looks like this:

GENERAL JOURNAL   PAGE _____

	DATE		DESCRIPTION	POST. REF.	DEBIT	CREDIT	
1	20–		**Adjusting Entry**				1
2	Dec	31	Interest Receivable		7 7 12		2
3			Interest Income			7 7 12	3

Like all other adjustments, this entry was first recorded in the Adjustments columns of the work sheet. Here is a T account picture of the situation, assuming a balance in Interest Income of $674.10 before adjustment:

Interest Receivable		Interest Income	
+	–	–	+
			Dec. 31 Bal. 674.10
Dec. 31 Adj. 77.12			Dec. 31 Adj. 77.12

The adjusting entry is this: debit Interest Receivable and credit Interest Income. On the partial work sheet shown in Figure 2 (page 580), you can see the effect of this adjustment on the financial statements.

REMEMBER!

When a firm has notes that extend from one fiscal period into the next, an adjusting entry is required. Since the interest is not collected until the note becomes due, it is necessary to record the interest income for each fiscal period in which interest is earned.

ACCOUNT NAME	TRIAL BALANCE		ADJUSTMENTS		INCOME STATEMENT		BALANCE SHEET
	DEBIT	CREDIT	DEBIT	CREDIT	DEBIT	CREDIT	DEBIT
Notes Receiv.	14 2 0 0 00						14 2 0 0 00
Int. Income		6 7 4 10		(a) 7 7 12		7 5 1 22	
Int. Receiv.			(a) 7 7 12				7 7 12

FIGURE 2

Remember that the interest accompanying notes receivable is Interest Income. On the balance sheet, Interest Receivable is classified as a current asset if it is to be received during the coming year.

The accountant may reverse this adjusting entry as of the first day of the next fiscal period because it increases a balance sheet account. When the note matures, the reversing entry makes it possible for the accountant to make the routine entry for the receipt of payment of an interest-bearing note: a debit to Cash, a credit to Notes Receivable, and a credit to Interest Income. This procedure is most convenient, especially when a significant number of notes is involved.

CHAPTER REVIEW

Online Study Center
ACE the test!

FYI

Selected transactions are now repeated and shown in the appropriate journal.

Review of Performance Objectives

The performance objectives require you to write general journal entries, because those entries allow for the clearest analysis of the debits and credits in each transaction. We will repeat these entries, but to conserve space, we omit explanations. Ordinarily, any firm using a cash receipts journal and a cash payments journal would record any transactions involving cash in one of these journals.

1a. Write the journal entry to record receipt of a note from a charge customer.

April 6 Received a note for $840 from Green Plumbing and Heating in settlement of the sale of March 7, 30 days, 8 percent.

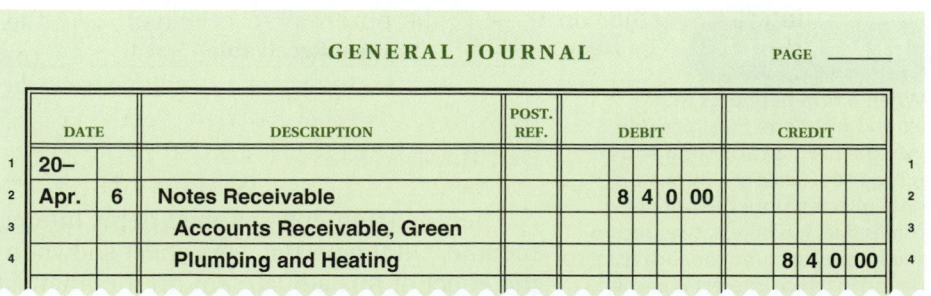

	DATE		DESCRIPTION	POST. REF.	DEBIT	CREDIT	
1	20–						1
2	Apr.	6	Notes Receivable		8 4 0 00		2
3			Accounts Receivable, Green				3
4			Plumbing and Heating			8 4 0 00	4

GENERAL JOURNAL   PAGE _____

1b. Write the journal entry to record receipt of payment of an interest-bearing note at maturity.

> **May**   6   Received payment at maturity of principal plus interest on Green Plumbing and Heating's note.

CASH RECEIPTS JOURNAL   PAGE _____

	DATE		ACCOUNT CREDITED	POST. REF.	OTHER ACCOUNTS CREDIT	ACCOUNTS RECEIVABLE CREDIT	SALES CREDIT	SALES DISCOUNTS DEBIT	CASH DEBIT	
1	20–									1
2	May	6	Notes Receivable		8 4 0 00					2
3			Interest Income		5 60				8 4 5 60	3
4										4

1c. Write the journal entry to record receipt of a note as a result of granting a personal loan.

> **April**   8   Granted a loan to Glenda Moore, an employee, for $600 for 3 months, 6 percent, dated April 8.

CASH PAYMENTS JOURNAL   PAGE _____

	DATE	CK. NO.	ACCOUNT NAME	POST. REF.	OTHER ACCOUNTS DEBIT	ACCOUNTS PAYABLE DEBIT	PURCHASES DISCOUNTS CREDIT	CASH CREDIT	
1	20–								1
2	Apr.	8	Notes Receivable		6 0 0 00			6 0 0 00	2
3									3

1d. Write the journal entry to record receipt of a note in exchange for merchandise or other property.

> **April**   9   Received a note for $920 from M. L. Klaus and Company for merchandise sold, 60 days, 7 percent, dated April 9.

GENERAL JOURNAL   PAGE _____

	DATE		DESCRIPTION	POST. REF.	DEBIT	CREDIT	
1	20–						1
2	Apr.	9	Notes Receivable		9 2 0 00		2
3			Sales			9 2 0 00	3

1e. Write the journal entries to record renewal of a note at maturity and payment of interest.

> **June**   8   Received interest from M. L. Klaus and Company on its note of April 9.

CASH RECEIPTS JOURNAL
PAGE _____

	DATE	ACCOUNT CREDITED	POST. REF.	OTHER ACCOUNTS CREDIT	ACCOUNTS RECEIVABLE CREDIT	SALES CREDIT	SALES DISCOUNTS DEBIT	CASH DEBIT	
1	20–								1
2	June 8	Interest Income		1 0 73				1 0 73	2

Then it was agreed to renew the note by issuing a new note, 30 days, 8 percent, dated June 8.

GENERAL JOURNAL
PAGE _____

	DATE	DESCRIPTION	POST. REF.	DEBIT	CREDIT	
1	20–					1
2	June 8	Notes Receivable		9 2 0 00		2
3		Notes Receivable			9 2 0 00	3
4						4

1f. Write the journal entries to record renewal of a note with payment of interest and partial payment of principal.

Two examples are shown, one for a business with only a general journal and the other for a business with a cash receipts journal.

GENERAL JOURNAL
PAGE _____

	DATE	DESCRIPTION	POST. REF.	DEBIT	CREDIT	
1	20–					1
2	June 8	Cash		3 1 0 73		2
3		Notes Receivable			3 0 0 00	3
4		Interest Income			1 0 73	4
5						5
6	8	Notes Receivable		6 2 0 00		6
7		Notes Receivable			6 2 0 00	7
8						8

CASH RECEIPTS JOURNAL
PAGE _____

	DATE	ACCOUNT CREDITED	POST. REF.	OTHER ACCOUNTS CREDIT	ACCOUNTS RECEIVABLE CREDIT	SALES CREDIT	SALES DISCOUNTS DEBIT	CASH DEBIT	
1	20–								1
2	June 8	Notes Receivable		3 0 0 00					2
3		Interest Income		1 0 73				3 1 0 73	3
4									4

1g. Write the journal entry to record a dishonored note receivable.

June   19   Chin Building Supplies dishonored its note of April 20 for $850 at 8 percent, for 60 days.

GENERAL JOURNAL   PAGE _____

	DATE		DESCRIPTION	POST. REF.	DEBIT	CREDIT	
1	20–						1
2	June	19	Accounts Receivable, Chin				2
3			Building Supplies		8 6 1 33		3
4			Notes Receivable			8 5 0 00	4
5			Interest Income			1 1 33	5

1h. Write the journal entry to record collection of a note receivable formerly dishonored.

July   19   Chin Building Supplies paid its dishonored note, plus additional interest for 30 days at 8 percent.

CASH RECEIPTS JOURNAL   PAGE _____

	DATE		ACCOUNT CREDITED	POST. REF.	OTHER ACCOUNTS CREDIT	ACCOUNTS RECEIVABLE CREDIT	SALES CREDIT	SALES DISCOUNTS DEBIT	CASH DEBIT	
1	20–									1
2	July	19	Chin Bldg. Supplies			8 6 1 33				2
3			Interest Income		5 74				8 6 7 07	3
4										4

1i. Write the journal entry to record discounting an interest-bearing note receivable.

May   5   Discounted at New National Bank the note received from Carmel Hardware, dated April 20, $1,080, 8 percent, 60 days. The discount rate is 9 percent.

CASH RECEIPTS JOURNAL   PAGE _____

	DATE		ACCOUNT CREDITED	POST. REF.	OTHER ACCOUNTS CREDIT	ACCOUNTS RECEIVABLE CREDIT	SALES CREDIT	SALES DISCOUNTS DEBIT	CASH DEBIT	
1	20–									1
2	May	5	Notes Receivable		1 0 8 0 00					2
3			Interest Income		2 09				1 0 8 2 09	3
4										4

2. Complete a notes receivable register.

For each note, list the date, the maker, where the note is payable, the amount, the time period, the interest rate, the amount of interest, the due date, the date paid, and relevant remarks.

NOTES RECEIVABLE REGISTER

DATE		MAKER	WHERE PAYABLE	AMOUNT	TIME	RATE	INTEREST	DUE DATE	DISCOUNTED BANK	DATE	DATE PAID	REMARKS
20–												
Apr.	6	Green Plumbing	New Nat.	8 4 0 00	30 d	8%	5 60	5/6			5/6	Open account.
		and Heating										
	8	Glenda Moore	New Nat.	6 0 0 00	3 m	6%	9 00	7/8			7/8	Employee loan.
	9	M. L. Klaus and	New Nat.	9 2 0 00	60 d	7%	1 0 73	6/8			Ren.	Open account.
		Company										
June	8	M. L. Klaus and	New Nat.	9 2 0 00	30 d	8%	6 13	7/8				Renewed 4/9 note.
		Company										

3. Write the journal entry to record the adjustment for accrued interest on notes receivable.

    Here is the adjusting entry for two notes: a $9,000, 90-day, 8 percent note dated November 28, and a $5,200, 60-day, 7 percent note dated December 20.

GENERAL JOURNAL   PAGE _____

	DATE		DESCRIPTION	POST. REF.	DEBIT	CREDIT	
1	20–		**Adjusting Entry**				1
2	Dec.	31	Interest Receivable		7 7 12		2
3			Interest Income			7 7 12	3
4							4

Glossary

Accrued interest income on notes receivable The interest that is due (not yet received) on notes receivable, which are outstanding at the end of the fiscal period. (578)

Contingent liability A liability that is dependent upon certain conditions or events taking place—for example, if a note receivable is discounted at a bank and then the maker does not pay. The payee or endorser of the dishonored note is then liable to pay the bank. (574)

Discounting notes receivable The process by which a firm may raise cash by selling a note receivable to a bank or finance company. The bank deducts the discount from the maturity value of the note to determine the proceeds (amount of money) that the firm receives. (573)

Discount period The time between the date a note receivable is discounted and the date it matures. (573)

Dishonored note receivable A note whose maker fails to pay the principal amount or to renew the note at maturity. (571)

Maturity value The principal (face value) of a note plus interest from the date of the note until the due date. (573)

Notes receivable register A supplementary record in which a firm lists details of notes received. (577)

QUESTIONS, EXERCISES, AND CASES

Discussion Questions

1. When is it necessary to make an adjusting entry for accrued interest on an interest-bearing note receivable, and why? What is the adjusting entry? Can the adjusting entry be reversed?

2. From the point of view of a creditor, what are the advantages of having a note receivable over having an account receivable?

3. Describe the formula for calculating the proceeds of an interest-bearing note receivable discounted at a bank. Define the terms.

4. Explain why a business would sell its notes receivable to a bank or finance company.

5. In discounting an interest-bearing note receivable, why is the discount figured on the maturity value of the note?

6. Explain how to record a discounted note receivable.

7. Explain what *contingent liability* means in relation to the endorser of a note.

8. What is the purpose of maintaining a notes receivable register?

Exercises

P.O. 1a,b

Calculate due date and interest, and journalize issuance and payment of note on the books of payee and maker.

Exercise 15-1 On March 11, T. L. Reid Company received a 90-day, 9 percent note for $1,600, dated March 11, from D. Alaniz, a charge customer, to satisfy his open account receivable.

a. What is the due date of the note?
b. How much interest is due at maturity?

Given the preceding data, write entries in general journal form on the books of T. L. Reid Company to record the following:

c. Receipt of the note from Alaniz in settlement of his account.
d. Receipt of the principal and interest at maturity.

Given the same data, write entries in general journal form on Alaniz's books to record the following:

e. Issuance of the note by Alaniz in settlement of his account.
f. Payment of the note at maturity.

P.O. 1b,c

Journalize entries to loan money with a note and collect the principal and interest.

Exercise 15-2 Prepare entries in general journal form to record the following:

May   5 Received a 2-month, 8 percent note from Pat Davis for a $450 personal loan.
July   5 Received the total amount due from Davis.

P.O. 1e,f

Record renewal of note with payment of interest and full or partial payment of principal.

Exercise 15-3 Prepare entries in general journal form to record the following:

June   4 Received payment from Parker Company of interest on a 45-day, 7 percent note for $8,000, dated April 20, and renewal of the note for 60 days at 7.5 percent.
July   8 Received payment of interest from Newell Company on a 60-day, 7.5 percent note for $7,500, dated May 9, and partial payment of $2,000 on the principal. Received an 8 percent, 30-day note for $5,500 dated July 8.

P.O. 1d,i

Discount a note at the bank.

Exercise 15-4 On May 10, Von Behren Company received a 90-day, 9.5 percent note for $8,500, dated May 10, for merchandise sold to Burr Company. Von Behren Company endorsed the note in favor of its bank on May 28. The bank discounted the note at 11 percent, paying the proceeds to Von Behren Company. Determine the following facts:

a. Number of days Von Behren Company held the note
b. Number of days in the discount period
c. Face value
d. Maturity value
e. Discount
f. Proceeds
g. Interest income or expense recorded by the payee (Von Behren Company)

P.O. 1a,i

Journalize a sale on account, settlement of the account with a note, and discount of the note at the bank.

Exercise 15-5 Prepare entries in general journal form to record the following:

June	12	Sold merchandise on account to K. M. Prine; terms 3/10, n/30; $1,800.
July	12	Received $400 in cash from K. M. Prine and a 60-day, 9 percent note for $1,400 dated July 12.
Aug.	17	Discounted the note at the bank at 11 percent.

P.O. 1a,b

Describe transactions concerning sales on account and payments of those accounts.

Exercise 15-6 The T accounts below show a series of four transactions concerning a sale of merchandise on account and subsequent payment of the amount owed. Describe what happened in each transaction.

Cash		Accounts Receivable		Sales		Interest Income	
+	−	+	−	−	+	−	+
(d) 1,090.02		(a) 1,200.00	(b) 120.00		(a) 1,200.00		(d) 10.02
			(c) 1,080.00				

Notes Receivable		Sales Returns and Allowances	
+	−	+	−
(c) 1,080.00	(d) 1,080.00	(b) 120.00	

P.O. 1g,h

Record dishonored note and collection of dishonored note.

Exercise 15-7 Prepare entries in general journal form to record the following:

| Aug. | 6 | Wilson Company failed to pay its 30-day, 8 percent note for $700, dated July 7. The note is thus dishonored at maturity. |
| Sept. | 5 | Wilson Company pays the balance of its account, plus an additional 30 days' interest at 8 percent on the amount owed. |

P.O. 1a,b,3

Journalize entries to receive a note, adjust for interest accrued, close, reverse, and record receipt of payment.

Exercise 15-8 Write entries in general journal form to record the following transactions for Badillo Company, whose fiscal year ends on December 31:

Year 1

Dec.	3	Badillo Company received from BRB Services a $9,500, 120-day, 10.5 percent note, dated December 3, as an extension of a charge account.
	31	The adjusting entry for accrued interest.
	31	The closing entry (for practice), assuming all other closing entries were made.

Year 2
Jan. 1 The reversing entry.
Apr. 2 Receipt of the principal and interest at maturity.

LINKS TO ACCOUNTING

Now that you've learned about recording different types of transactions involving notes receivable, let's assume you decide to invest in 90-day notes that pay 25 percent interest! You feel confident about this investment because you've done your research regarding the maker of the notes. On May 1, you give the maker a check for $1,000. But, on July 30, the maturity date of the note, you try to contact the maker and find that the phone has been disconnected and the doors to the building are locked. This note has been dishonored.

1. How would you record the dishonored note receivable?
2. The maker of your note contacts you 30 days after the note's maturity date and agrees to pay you the full amount owed. How would you record the collection of this formerly dishonored note?

CONSIDER AND COMMUNICATE

The term *discount* or *discounting* is used repeatedly in accounting. For example, it is common to see references to "a sales discount of 2 percent," "discounting our note at the bank," "discounting a customer's note at the bank," and "trade discount." Explain how discounting is similar in these cases and how these situations differ.

WHAT'S WRONG WITH THIS PICTURE?

You loaned $20,000 to a close friend to buy an off-road vehicle. You planned to have him sign a note receivable, with the off-road vehicle becoming collateral or security for the note in case your friend failed to pay you. However, in the excitement and rush to get the vehicle, you forgot to have your friend sign the note, and you also forgot to make the arrangements for collateral. Nothing was signed prior to your giving your friend the cash. How should this transaction have been handled? What are the possible consequences of this transaction between you and your friend?

CRITICAL THINKING

A client would like you to explain some options he has regarding discounting of a 10 percent, 60-day, $2,000 note receivable. He wants to know what he will receive in proceeds and what will be his interest income (or expense) if he discounts the note (a) after 10 days with a discount rate of 10 percent, (b) after 50 days with a 10 percent discount rate, or (c) after 5 days with a discount rate of 12 percent. Make the calculations for the client and explain the different outcomes to him.

PROBLEM SET A

For additional help, see the demonstration problem at the beginning of each chapter in your Working Papers.

P.O. 1a,b,d

Problem 15-1A Hines Company carried out the following transactions this year:

Jan.	19	Sold merchandise on account to Cross Company; 2/10, n/30; $2,890.
	29	Received a check from Cross Company for the sale on January 19.
Feb.	23	Sold merchandise on account to Ryan Company; 3/10, n/30; $1,683.
Mar.	25	Received a 60-day, 9.5 percent note, dated this day, for $1,683 from Ryan Company for the amount owed on account.
May	24	Received a check from Ryan Company for the amount owed on the note of March 25.
June	8	Sold merchandise to Jan's Interiors for $4,520, receiving a 120-day, 10 percent note, dated June 8 (not previously recorded).
Oct.	6	Received payment from Jan's Interiors for the amount owed on its note of June 8.

Check Figure

Interest on Ryan Company note, $26.65

Instructions

Record these transactions in the general journal (page 23).

P.O. 1a,b,d,e,i,2

Problem 15-2A Hayashikawa, Inc. carried out the following transactions this year:

Jan.	11	Sold merchandise on account to L. Hans; 1/10, n/30; $4,620.
Feb.	10	Received a 30-day, 9 percent note, dated this day, for $4,620 from L. Hans on account. Assume 28 days in February.
Mar.	12	Received payment from L. Hans for the amount owed on its note of February 10.
Apr.	28	Sold merchandise on account to EMP Gallery; 1/10, n/30; $5,900.
May	28	Received a 60-day, 9.5 percent note, dated this day, for $5,900 from EMP Gallery on account.
July	27	EMP Gallery paid the interest on its note of May 28 and renewed the obligation by issuing a new 60-day, 10 percent note for $5,900, dated July 27.
Sept.	25	Received a check from EMP Gallery for the amount owed on its note of July 27.
Oct.	11	Sold merchandise to Newton, Inc., for $6,300, receiving a 30-day, 10 percent note, dated this day (not previously recorded).
	21	Discounted the note received from Newton, Inc., at Calkins Bank; discount rate, 11 percent.

Check Figure

Interest Income on the L. Hans note, $34.65

Instructions

1. Record these transactions in the general journal (pages 11 and 12).
2. Immediately after each journal entry, record each note receivable in the notes receivable register (page 7).

   a. All notes are payable at Calkins Bank.
   b. Fill in the date paid after journalizing the receipt of payment of the note, or fill in "renewed" or "discounted" when appropriate.

P.O. 1a,b,d,e,f,i

Problem 15-3A Here are some selected transactions carried out by Calabrese Nursery this year.

Jan.	7	Sold merchandise on account to Alpine Gardens; 2/10, n/30; $4,800.
Feb.	6	Received a 30-day, 10 percent note, dated February 6, for $4,800 from Alpine Gardens to apply on account. Assume 28 days in February.
Mar.	8	Received $1,890 from Alpine Gardens as payment on its note dated February 6: $1,850 as partial payment on the principal, and $40 as interest on $4,800 for 30 days at 10 percent. Received a new 30-day, 10 percent note for $2,950, dated March 8.
Apr.	7	Received a check from Alpine Gardens for the amount owed on its note of March 8.
	13	Sold merchandise to K. T. Frank for $2,800, receiving a 60-day, 10 percent note, dated April 13 (not previously recorded).
	21	Discounted the note received from K. T. Frank at Kundert Bank; discount rate, 10 percent.
May	23	Sold merchandise on account to Hogan Company; 3/10, n/30; $1,366.
June	22	Received a 60-day, 11 percent note, dated June 22, for $1,366 from Hogan Company for the amount owed on account.

Check Figure

Proceeds of the K. T. Frank note dated April 13, $2,805.55

Instructions

Record these transactions in one of the following journals: sales journal (page 37), cash receipts journal (page 32), or general journal (page 17).

Instructions for General Ledger Software

1. Journalize transactions in either the sales journal, the cash receipts journal, or the general journal.
2. Print the journal entries from each journal.

P.O. 1a,b,c,d,e,i,3

Problem 15-4A Epler's Printing Company completed the following transactions during the year ended December 31:

June	16	Received a 60-day, 9 percent note, dated June 16, for $1,830 from City Office Supply for the sale of services. (The sale was not previously recorded.)
	26	Received a 30-day, 10 percent note, dated June 26, for $3,524 from Dawson, Inc., a charge customer, for a sale previously recorded.
July	7	Received a 90-day, 11 percent note, dated July 7, for $4,980 from Colin Office Supply, a charge customer, for a sale previously recorded.
	26	Received a check from Dawson, Inc., in payment of principal and interest on its note.
Aug.	15	Received payment of interest from City Office Supply for its note of June 16 and also a new 30-day, 10 percent note, dated August 15, for $1,830. (two entries)
	22	Received a 90-day, 9.5 percent note, dated August 22, for $2,600 from E. Morris and Company, a charge customer, for a sale previously recorded.

Sept.   14   City Office Supply paid its note dated August 15, principal plus interest.

14   Discounted the note received from E. Morris and Company at Harris Bank; discount rate, 10 percent.

Oct.   5   Received a check from Colin Office Supply in payment of principal and interest on its note.

Dec.   16   Received a 60-day, 10.5 percent note, dated December 16, for $6,258 from Largent and Ryan Company, a charge customer, for a sale previously recorded.

19   Received a 45-day, 10 percent note, dated December 19, for $450 from B. Jorn, an employee, for a personal loan.

Check Figure

Adjustment for interest receivable, $28.88

Instructions

1. Record these transactions in the general journal (pages 47–49).
2. Show the calculation of each due date.
3. On December 31, record the adjusting entry to account for accrued interest receivable for the Largent and Ryan Company and B. Jorn notes, which are not due to be paid until the next fiscal period.
4. On January 1, record the reversing entry. (Assume closing entries have been made.)
5. On February 2, record the receipt of payment from B. Jorn on February 2 of the new fiscal period.

PROBLEM SET B

For additional help, see the demonstration problem at the beginning of each chapter in your Working Papers.

P.O. 1a,b,d

Problem 15-1B Following are selected transactions carried out by Bloomfield Company this year:

Jan.   12   Sold merchandise on account to H. Lee; 3/10, n/30; $2,530.
22   Received check from H. Lee for the sale of January 12.
Feb.   17   Sold merchandise on account to L. Bliss; 2/10, n/30; $3,460.
Mar.   19   Received a 30-day, 9.5 percent note, dated this day, for $3,460 from L. Bliss on account.
Apr.   18   Received a check from L. Bliss for the amount owed on the note of March 19.
June   1   Sold merchandise to Maloney Company for $4,272, receiving a 60-day, 9.5 percent note, dated this day. (This sale was not previously recorded.)
July   31   Received payment from Maloney Company for the amount owed on the note of June 1.

Check Figure

Interest on Bliss note, $27.39

Instructions

Record these transactions in the general journal (page 23).

P.O. 1a,b,d,e,i,2

Problem 15-2B Here are some of the transactions carried out by Gary Company this year:

Jan.   7   Sold merchandise on account to Eagle Imports; 2/10, n/30; $2,960.

Feb.	6	Received a 30-day, 9 percent note, dated this day, for $2,960 from Eagle Imports on account. Assume 28 days in February.
Mar.	8	Received payment from Eagle Imports for the amount owed on its note of February 6.
Apr.	25	Sold merchandise on account to Klein's Gift Shop; 2/10, n/30; $3,152.
May	25	Received a 45-day, 10 percent note, dated May 25, for $3,152 from Klein's Gift Shop on account.
July	9	Klein's Gift Shop paid the interest on its note of May 25 and renewed the obligation by issuing a new 60-day, 12 percent note for $3,152, dated July 9.
Sept.	7	Received a check from Klein's Gift Shop for the amount owed on its note of July 9.
	15	Sold merchandise to Rikki Boe, Inc., for $4,286, receiving a 30-day, 10.25 percent note, dated this day (not previously recorded).
	25	Discounted the note received from Rikki Boe, Inc., at Salem State Bank; discount rate, 11 percent.

Check Figure

Interest Income on Eagle Imports note, $22.20

Instructions

1. Record these transactions in the general journal (pages 11 and 12).
2. Immediately after each journal entry, record each note receivable in the notes receivable register (page 7).

   a. All notes are payable at Salem State Bank.
   b. Fill in the date paid after journalizing the receipt of payment of the note, or fill in "renewed" or "discounted" when appropriate.

P.O. 1a,b,d,e,f,i

Problem 15-3B Selected transactions of Lou's Center carried out this year are as follows:

Jan.	10	Sold merchandise on account to Osborn Stores; 3/10, n/30; $5,820.
Feb.	9	Received a 30-day, 9 percent note, dated February 9, for $5,820 from Osborn Stores to apply on account. Assume 28 days in February.
Mar.	11	Received $2,493.65 from Osborn Stores as partial payment on its note dated February 9: $2,450 as partial payment on the principal, and $43.65 interest on $5,820 for 30 days at 9 percent. Received a new 30-day, 11 percent note for $3,370, dated March 11.
Apr.	4	Sold merchandise to Fisher Sports for $2,790, receiving a 60-day, 9 percent note, dated April 4 (not previously recorded).
	10	Received a check from Osborn Stores for the amount owed on its note of March 11.
	12	Discounted the note received from Fisher Sports at Lundgren Bank; discount rate, 10 percent.
May	10	Sold merchandise on account to Laxtrom, Inc.; 2/10, n/30; $2,848.
June	9	Received a 45-day, 9 percent note, dated June 9, for $2,848 from Laxtrom, Inc., to apply on account.

Check Figure

Proceeds of the Fisher Sports note dated April 4, $2,790.95

Instructions

Record these transactions in one of the following journals: sales journal (page 37), cash receipts journal (page 32), or general journal (page 17).

P.O. 1a,b,c,d,e,i,3

Instructions for General Ledger Software

1. Journalize transactions in either the sales journal, the cash receipts journal, or the general journal.
2. Print the journal entries from each journal.

Problem 15-4B Here are selected transactions of Wally's Grocery Supply carried out during the year ended December 31:

June	9	Received a 60-day, 9.5 percent note, dated June 9, for $3,680 from Mark's Foods for merchandise. (The sale was not previously recorded.)
	21	Received a 30-day, 10 percent note, dated June 21, for $2,973 from Lindsey Restaurants, a charge customer, for a sale previously recorded.
July	11	Received a 90-day, 10 percent note, dated July 11, for $1,980 from Armstrong, Inc., a charge customer, for a sale previously recorded.
	21	Received a check from Lindsey Restaurants in payment of principal and interest on its note.
Aug.	8	Received payment of interest from Mark's Foods for its note of June 9 and also a new 30-day, 9 percent note, dated August 8, for $3,680 (two entries).
	20	Received a 60-day, 10 percent note, dated August 20, for $3,010 from C. T. Tamparo, a charge customer, for a sale previously recorded.
Sept.	7	Mark's Foods paid its note, dated August 8, principal plus interest.
	9	Discounted the note received from C. T. Tamparo at Hammond Bank; discount rate, 10 percent.
Oct.	9	Received a check from Armstrong, Inc., in payment of principal and interest on its note.
Dec.	6	Received a 60-day, 8.5 percent note, dated December 6, for $2,642 from C. L. Chan, a charge customer, for a sale previously recorded.
	8	Received a 30-day, 9.5 percent note, dated December 8, for $780 from J. Brannon, an employee, for a personal loan.

Check Figure

Adjustment for interest receivable, $20.33

Instructions

1. Record these transactions in the general journal (pages 47–49).
2. Show the calculation of each due date.
3. On December 31, record the adjusting entry to account for accrued interest receivable for the C. L. Chan and J. Brannon notes, which are not due to be paid until the next fiscal period.
4. On January 1, record the reversing entry. (Assume closing entries have been made.)
5. On January 7, record the receipt of payment on the J. Brannon note on January 7 of the new fiscal year.

Before a Test Check: Chapters 14–15

PART I: Notes Payable

A. On September 20 of this year, B. Mann issued a 120-day, 9 percent note, dated September 20, to L. Roo, a creditor, for $12,000. Answer the following questions about the note:

1. What is the due date?
2. What is the face value?
3. How much is the total interest?
4. What is the maturity value?
5. What is the amount of the adjusting entry for interest expense on December 31?

B. On October 20 of this year, D. Dagostino borrowed $8,000 from the bank, signing a 90-day, discounted 8 percent note dated October 20. Answer the following questions about the note:

1. What is the due date?
2. What is the face value?
3. How much is the total interest?
4. On October 20, the entry to record the note includes a debit to Cash. Is the other debit to Interest Expense or to Discount on Notes Payable? How much is that debit?
5. What is the maturity value?
6. What is the amount of the adjusting entry on December 31?
7. What are the debit and credit accounts in the December 31 adjusting entry?
8. On the date of payment of the note, besides debiting Notes Payable and crediting Cash for the face value of the note, what are the debit and credit accounts and amounts needed to report the entire amount of interest on the note?

PART II: Notes Receivable

A. The Glen Company received a $9,000, 60-day, 8.5 percent note, dated December 3 of this year, as an extension of a charge account for Fryer Company. Determine the following:

1. The debit and credit accounts involved in recording the $9,000 note
2. The debit and credit accounts and amounts involved in the December 31 adjusting entry
3. The due date
4. The maturity value
5. The debit and credit accounts and amounts involved in the receipt of payment from Fryer Company, assuming a reversing entry was made on January 1

Note: Answers to Before a Test Check begin on page A-1.

B. On April 8 of this year, Tickner Company received a 90-day, 8 percent note for $6,500, dated April 8, for merchandise sold to Ward Company. Tickner endorsed the note in favor of its bank on April 28. The bank discounted the note at 8.5 percent, paying the proceeds to Tickner Company. Determine the following:

1. Number of days Tickner Company held the note
2. Number of days in the discount period
3. Face value
4. Maturity value
5. Discount
6. Proceeds
7. Will interest income or interest expense be recorded by the payee (Tickner Company)?
8. What is the amount of interest income or interest expense recorded by the payee (Tickner Company)?

16

Uncollectible Accounts

Most Americans will take out a loan at one point or another during their lives, either when they purchase a car or a home, or by carrying a balance on their credit card. Citigroup Inc. provides loans, mortgages, and credit card services to individuals and businesses around the world. Citigroup (and every other organization involved in the lending business) realizes that the loan business carries with it a certain amount of credit risk. This means there is a likelihood that a certain percentage of loans will not be paid back. If a loan is not paid when it is due, it goes into default. If it is not eventually paid, it must be written off. How many people and businesses do you think actually default on their credit card loans?

At the end of 2005, U.S. Cards, a part of Citigroup Inc. and the largest provider of credit cards in North America, had more than 130 million customer accounts in the United States, Canada, and Puerto Rico! What is the risk that Citigroup's customers won't make their credit card payments? You can view Citigroup's 2005 financial information by going to **http://www.citi.com/citigroup/fin/index.htm,** selecting SEC Filings, and clicking on Citigroup Inc.'s Form 10-K for 2005. Go to page 42 of this report to find out about U.S. Card's net revenue and provision for loan losses (bad debt expense) for 2005.

Performance Objectives

After you have completed this chapter, you will be able to do the following:

1. Make the adjusting entry to record estimated bad debt losses by using the allowance method of recording bad debts. (a) Determine the amount of the adjusting entry by aging Accounts Receivable. (b) Determine the amount of the adjusting entry by using a percentage of Accounts Receivable. (c) Calculate the amount of the adjusting entry by using a percentage of net sales or net credit sales.

2. Journalize the entries to write off accounts receivable as being uncollectible, using the allowance method of accounting for bad debt losses.

3. Journalize entries to reinstate accounts receivable previously written off, using the allowance method.

4. Journalize the entries to write off accounts receivable as being uncollectible, using the specific charge-off method.

5. Journalize entries to reinstate accounts receivable previously written off, using the specific charge-off method.

The use of credit for both buying and selling goods and services has become standard practice for businesses of all types and levels: retailers, wholesalers, and manufacturers. You have learned to record sales of goods on account as a debit to Accounts Receivable and a credit to Sales. You have also learned to record collections on account as a debit to Cash and a credit to Accounts Receivable.

Business firms selling goods or services on credit will find that not all the accounts receivable (charge accounts) are collected in full. As a result, the unpaid accounts must eventually be written off as uncollectible or as bad debts. In other words, a firm that grants credit will not collect from everyone, and therefore the firm needs to plan for these anticipated losses. In this chapter, we discuss ways to provide for losses as well as to write off customer accounts that are no longer collectible.

TWO METHODS OF ACCOUNTING FOR UNCOLLECTIBLE ACCOUNTS

There are two methods of accounting for uncollectible accounts: the allowance method and the specific charge-off method.

The Allowance Method

The allowance method is consistent with the matching principle, in that it enables firms to match sales of one period with bad debt losses of the same period; and it is consistent with the accrual method of accounting required by generally accepted accounting principles (GAAP).

The Specific Charge-off Method

FYI

Write-off and *charge-off* mean the same thing.

The specific charge-off method traditionally has been used by small businesses. The specific charge-off method is the only method approved for federal income tax purposes. Many companies, especially larger firms, use the allowance method for their own accounting system for external reporting—that is, for their own financial statements. They use the specific charge-off method for federal income tax reporting. The adjustments required on their tax returns are not entered in the companies' books.

THE CREDIT DEPARTMENT

The Credit Department has to keep a watchful eye on customers. It evaluates the debt-paying ability of prospective customers and determines the maximum amount of credit to extend to each customer. Retail stores selling to individuals rely on reports from local retail credit bureaus. When wholesalers and manufacturers grant credit to customers, they use reports from national credit-rating institutions, wholesale credit bureaus, and the financial statements of prospective customers. Firms that make many sales on credit find it worthwhile to subscribe to these credit bureaus or credit-rating agencies. These credit-reporting organizations maintain files of current

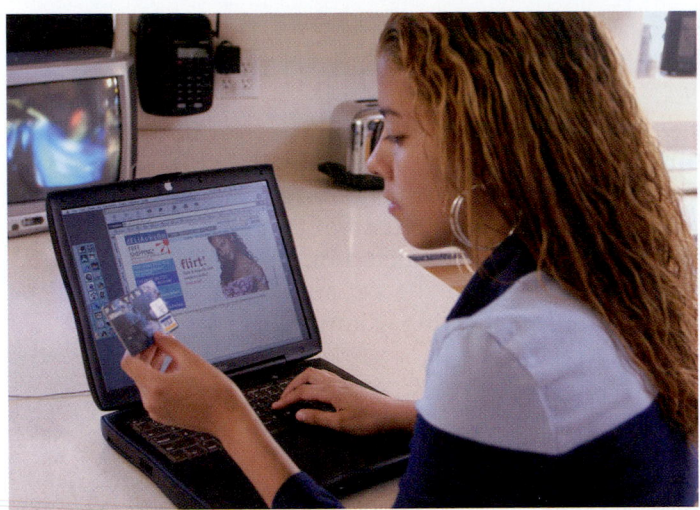

Most companies—including those selling goods on the Internet—lend money to customers by extending credit. This is a convenience to consumers, but some customers don't repay the debt. Businesses write off those accounts and record the amount in the Bad Debts Expense account.

financial information on charge customers, establish credit ratings for each charge customer, and conduct special investigations on request from their clients.

Incurring excessive credit losses is always unfavorable for a seller because any firm needs to be paid for its sales on account. Surprisingly, it may also be bad if a firm has no credit losses. Such a record may indicate that the firm is turning down applications for credit, even though most applicants would indeed pay their bills. If credit requirements are too rigid, the firm not only loses many immediate sales but may create considerable ill will. A sound credit policy should provide for a limited amount of credit losses. It is the responsibility of the Credit Department to keep these losses within acceptable limits.

MATCHING BAD DEBT LOSSES WITH SALES

REMEMBER!

The matching principle attempts to match the amount of expenses incurred with the revenue earned for the same fiscal period.

A basic principle of the accrual basis of accounting is that revenue for a fiscal period be matched with the expenses incurred to earn that revenue. This matching principle is consistent with our earlier presentation of adjusting entries. For example, depreciation represents the allocation of the cost of equipment to the particular periods or years benefited. In making the adjustment, we allocate this expense to that year. Thus, we debit Depreciation Expense, Equipment, and credit Accumulated Depreciation, Equipment. Similarly, when a firm sells merchandise on account to a customer who may eventually refuse to pay the bill for the merchandise, the firm has a bad debt loss potential. The firm must try to match the loss with the revenue earned for the year in which the sale is made.

At the time of the sale, the company does not *know* that it has incurred a loss; it believes that the customer will pay the debt. If it did not, the company would not have extended credit to that customer in the first place. In other words, the firm making the credit sale has increased its revenue account, but it does not know at the time of the sale whether the money earned will be collected. As a matter of fact, the firm will not be certain of the loss until it has repeatedly failed in its attempts to collect the bill. The final recognition of the loss will probably occur many months after the sale. *In order to match the bad debt losses for the year with the sales for the same year, the firm must make an estimate of the losses as a means of providing for them in advance.* The allowance method of accounting for bad debt losses provides the means for matching bad debt losses with the applicable sales in the company's financial statements.

THE ALLOWANCE METHOD OF ACCOUNTING FOR BAD DEBTS

REMEMBER!

With the accrual method of accounting, revenue is recorded when it is earned rather than when it is received.

Most big firms use the **allowance method of accounting for bad debt losses** for financial reporting, which is consistent with the accrual method of accounting required by generally accepted accounting principles (GAAP). An adjusting entry is recorded first in the Adjustments columns of the work sheet—much like the adjustment for depreciation. In general journal and T account form, the adjusting entry for the estimated bad debt losses for Hobson Company is shown in the following examples.

	DATE	DESCRIPTION	POST. REF.	DEBIT	CREDIT	
1	20–	Adjusting Entry				1
2	Dec. 31	Bad Debts Expense		1 6 0 0 00		2
3		Allowance for Doubtful				3
4		Accounts			1 6 0 0 00	4

Bad Debts Expense

+	–
Adj. 1,600	

Allowance for Doubtful Accounts

–	+
	Bal. 2,200
	Adj. 1,600
	3,800

OBJECTIVE 1

Make the adjusting entry to record estimated bad debt losses by using the allowance method of recording bad debts.

The purpose of the adjusting entry is to increase Bad Debts Expense by the amount of the estimated loss and to produce a collectible figure for the book value of Accounts Receivable. **Allowance for Doubtful Accounts is classified as a deduction from Accounts Receivable. As such, it is a contra account, similar to Accumulated Depreciation.** Just as the book value of Equipment equals the cost of Equipment minus Accumulated Depreciation, Equipment, the **book value of Accounts Receivable** equals Accounts Receivable minus Allowance for Doubtful Accounts. Accountants also refer to the

FIGURE 1

		TRIAL BALANCE	
ACCOUNT NAME		DEBIT	CREDIT
Accounts Receivable		60 0 0 0 00	
Allowance for Doubtful Accounts			2 2 0 0 00
Equipment		74 0 0 0 00	
Accumulated Depreciation, Equipment			22 0 0 0 00
Bad Debts Expense			
Depreciation Expense, Equipment			

book value of Accounts Receivable as the **net expected realizable value of Accounts Receivable**.

Because a firm cannot know with certainty which accounts won't be fully collected, it's not possible to credit Accounts Receivable directly. However, on the basis of its experience, a firm is able to estimate what this year's bad debt losses will be. The firm bases its estimate on a year's sales, but it can't say with certainty *which* specific credit sales, by customer name, will not be paid.

Prior to adjustments, the **Bad Debts Expense account has no previous balance, as the account is not used during the fiscal period.** The firm's accountant makes an adjusting entry to increase Bad Debts Expense and immediately closes the account along with all other expense accounts. Allowance for Doubtful Accounts, on the other hand, has a balance that is carried over from previous years and is not closed. Notice where these accounts appear in the partial work sheet shown in Figure 1.

Note that Accounts Receivable is recorded in the debit column, and Allowance for Doubtful Accounts is recorded in the credit column. The $1,600 adjustment is added to the previous credit balance of $2,200, resulting in $3,800 being recorded in the Balance Sheet Credit column. As you can see, Allowance for Doubtful Accounts is handled much like Accumulated Depreciation. Both are recorded as credits in the Adjustments and Balance Sheet columns of the work sheet; also, the adjustments are never reversed because both accounts have previous balances after the first year of operation.

Bad Debts Expense and Allowance for Doubtful Accounts on Financial Statements

The Bad Debts Expense account appears on the income statement as an operating expense. Some firms subdivide operating expenses into selling expenses and general expenses, in which case they list Bad Debts Expense as a general expense. (*Reason:* The decision to grant credit is usually a function of the administrative rather than the sales staff.)

Allowance for Doubtful Accounts is listed immediately below Accounts Receivable in the Current Assets section of the balance sheet, as shown in Figure 2 on the following page.

The $56,200 ($60,000 − $3,800) represents the anticipated net realizable value of Accounts Receivable; this is also known as the *book value of Accounts Receivable*. The net realizable value is the amount of cash the seller

REMEMBER!

Allowance for Doubtful Accounts is a contra account. It is used to record an estimate of the accounts receivable that will not be collected in the future. Its signs are opposite to those of Accounts Receivable.

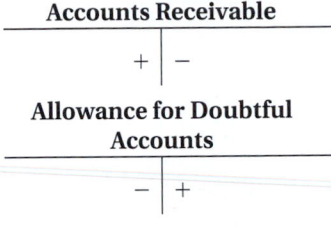

Accounts Receivable

| + | − |

Allowance for Doubtful Accounts

| − | + |

FYI

Sometimes accountants use other names for this account, such as Allowance for Bad Debts, Allowance for Uncollectible Accounts, and Estimated Uncollectible Accounts.

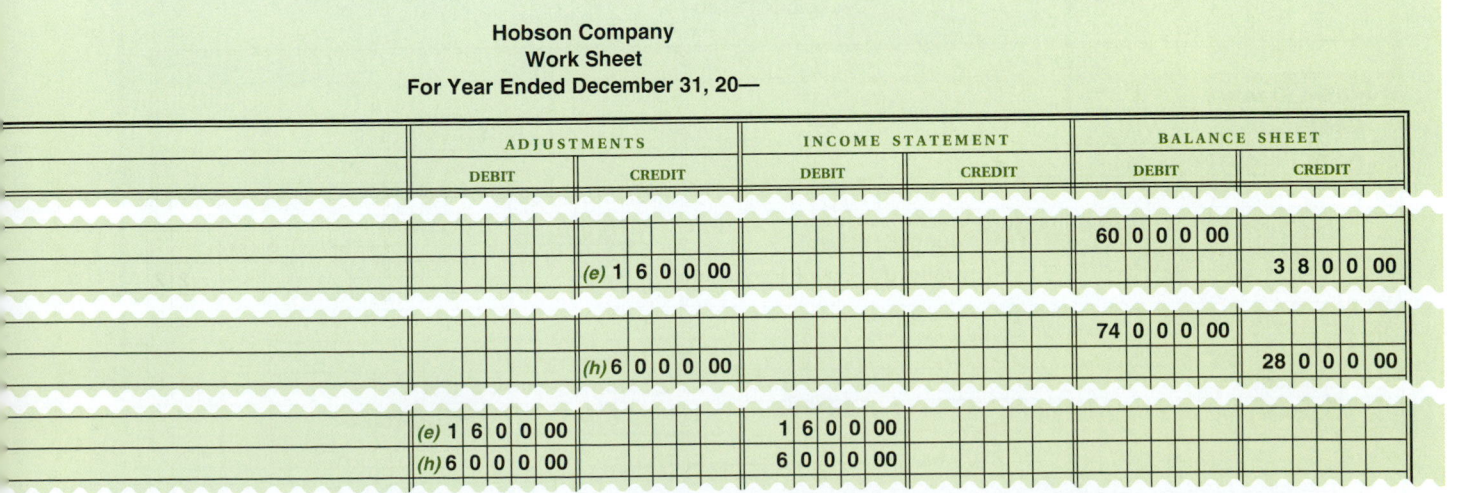

Hobson Company
Work Sheet
For Year Ended December 31, 20—

	ADJUSTMENTS		INCOME STATEMENT		BALANCE SHEET	
	DEBIT	CREDIT	DEBIT	CREDIT	DEBIT	CREDIT
					60 000 00	
		(e) 1 600 00				3 800 00
					74 000 00	
		(h) 6 000 00				28 000 00
	(e) 1 600 00		1 600 00			
	(h) 6 000 00		6 000 00			

CAREERS IN YOUR FUTURE

STACIE O. KELLEY

Student and Teaching and Research Assistant with the Goal of Becoming an Accounting Professor

Stacie believes that accounting is not just sitting in a cubicle making entries into an electronic system. Accounting is truly the "language of business." There are accounting opportunities in every type of business, from movie studios to ski resorts to multinational telecommunications companies. Accounting is critical to their success. Besides these somewhat glamorous industries, equally satisfying and lucrative opportunities abound in public companies, private companies, the U.S. government, and overseas companies.

While it may seem difficult to compete successfully for these positions, Stacie stresses that it is well worth the effort. The great news is that it is not just the 4.0 students who get great jobs. Companies look for people with exceptional communication and critical thinking skills, as well as those with exceptional grade-point averages. Yes, strong technical skills are necessary, but they are not the only ingredients for success.

"The accounting cycle and accompanying details play a critical role in students' understanding of financial statements and eventually in their ability to use them to make decisions."

In addition to strong communication and technical skills, Stacie has found that flexibility in respect to the work environment is essential. You need to be flexible in terms of work space, hours of work required, personalities, and geography. Rather than sitting at your desk each day, you might instead be out of the office (and maybe the city) to do audits or handle other duties. The ability to cope with change is also required by the computer hardware and software you may encounter. In other words, spreadsheets, word processing, data base manipulation, and graphics programs for presentations won't always be the version or brand that you used in school. The basics will be similar; but you must adjust to the situations that will come your way each day.

So, whether you start at a big accounting firm, work in a corporate setting, or decide to go into academia and teach, you will find a myriad of exciting opportunities when you are armed with polished accounting skills, the ability to communicate, and a sense of adventure for what lies ahead in the accounting field.

FIGURE 2

Hobson Company
Balance Sheet
December 31, 20—

Assets																			
Current Assets:																			
Cash							$12	0	0	0	00								
Notes Receivable							8	0	0	0	00								
Accounts Receivable	$60	0	0	0	00														
Less Allowance for Doubtful Accounts	3	8	0	0	00		56	2	0	0	00								
Merchandise Inventory							96	0	0	0	00								
Supplies								4	0	0	00								
Total Current Assets													$172	6	0	0	00		
Property and Equipment:																			
Equipment	$74	0	0	0	00														
Less Accumulated Depreciation	28	0	0	0	00		$46	0	0	0	00								

eventually expects to collect from gross accounts receivable. Allowance for Doubtful Accounts is classified as a *contra account,* because it is a deduction from an asset.

Using the Allowance Method—Three Ways of Estimating the Amount of Bad Debts Expense

Based on the aging of Accounts Receivable
Based on a percentage of Accounts Receivable
Based on a percentage of net sales or net credit sales

Management—on the basis of its judgment and past experience—has to make a reasonable estimate of the amount of its uncollectible accounts. It stands to reason that any such estimate is modified by business trends. In a period of prosperity and high employment, you can usually expect fewer losses from uncollectible accounts than in a period of recession.

The next question is: "For the adjusting entry, how does management estimate the dollar amount of bad debts expense?" The estimate can be made in several ways. Figure 3 illustrates the adjustment approaches to estimate the amount of bad debts expense.

FIGURE 3

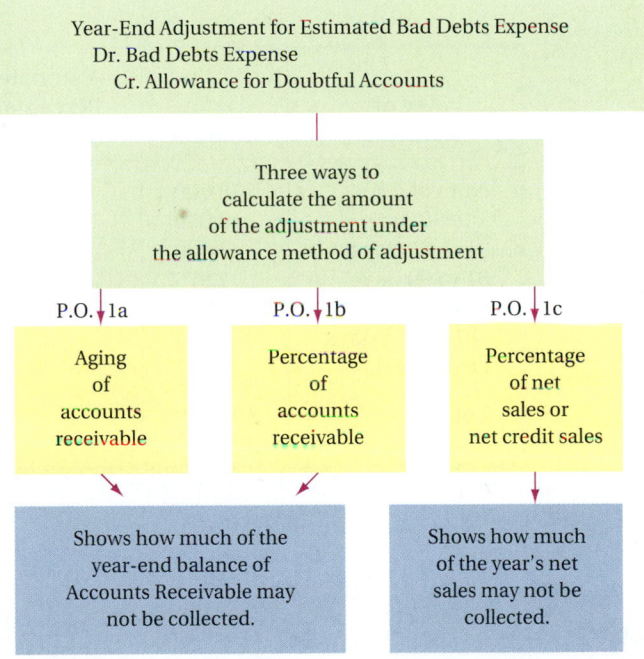

Adjusting Entry Based on Aging Accounts Receivable

OBJECTIVE 1a

Determine the amount of the adjusting entry by aging Accounts Receivable.

The most common technique for estimating the total uncollectible amount of Accounts Receivable is to **age** each charge customer's account by (1) determining the age, in number of days, of each account and (2) determining the number of days the account is past due. On a working paper, the accounts in a company's accounts receivable ledger are listed by name and amount. Columns are set up for various age groups. As an example, we use the accounts receivable of Walker Company. Here is the partial aging schedule.

ANALYSIS OF ACCOUNTS RECEIVABLE BY AGE

CUSTOMER NAME	BALANCE	NOT YET DUE	1–30	31–60	61–90	91–180	181–365	OVER 365
					DAYS PAST DUE			
A. R. Ayres	792.00	792.00						
B. N. Burns	464.00				464.00			
C. L. Casey	136.90			136.90				
D. R. Dewey	914.00	914.00						
E. V. Eaton	593.10			593.10				
Total	94,000.00	78,200.00	8,030.00	3,280.00	1,975.00	1,260.00	834.00	421.00

REMEMBER!

The older the account, the greater the possibility that it is uncollectible.

Based on its past experience, a company can estimate that a given percentage of accounts in each age group will be uncollectible. Next, the accountant multiplies the total amount for each age group by the percentage for that group. This results in the amount estimated to be uncollectible for that group. Let's continue with the Accounts Receivable of Walker Company.

Age of Accounts	Amount	Estimated Percentage Uncollectible	Allowance for Doubtful Accounts
Not yet due	$78,200	2	$78,200 × .02 = $1,564.00
1 to 30 days	8,030	4	8,030 × .04 = 321.20
31 to 60 days	3,280	10	3,280 × .10 = 328.00
61 to 90 days	1,975	20	1,975 × .20 = 395.00
91 to 180 days	1,260	30	1,260 × .30 = 378.00
181 to 365 days	834	50	834 × .50 = 417.00
Over 365 days	421	80	421 × .80 = 336.80
Total	$94,000		$3,740.00

FIGURE 4

ACCOUNT NAME	TRIAL BALANCE DEBIT	TRIAL BALANCE CREDIT
Accounts Receivable	94 0 0 0 00	
Allowance for Doubtful Accounts		3 2 0 00
Bad Debts Expense		

Many companies offer credit opportunities to increase business, but they should screen their customers carefully. The longer an account is past due, the greater the possibility that it will be uncollectible.

In the ledger of Walker Company, the new balance in Allowance for Doubtful Accounts should be $3,740 (the amount estimated by the aging to be uncollectible). **The accountant now makes an adjusting entry large enough to make the balance of Allowance for Doubtful Accounts the same as the estimated uncollectible amount.** Walker Company had a credit balance of $320 in Allowance for Doubtful Accounts. We now make an adjusting entry to bring the balance of the account up to $3,740. The amount of the adjusting entry is $3,420 ($3,740 − $320). This situation is illustrated by T accounts:

Bad Debts Expense		Allowance for Doubtful Accounts	
+ −		− +	
Adj. 3,420		Bal.	320
		Adj.	3,420
			3,740

To sum up: The firm estimates that $3,740 of Accounts Receivable are uncollectible. *It now has to bring the balance of Allowance for Doubtful Accounts up to the desired amount of $3,740.* Allowance for Doubtful Accounts has a present credit balance of $320, so the firm adjusts for the difference, $3,420. After the accountant posts the adjusting entry, the footing of Allowance for Doubtful Accounts indicates the desired balance, as determined by the aging analysis. The adjusting data and their effects on the accounts are illustrated in Figure 4.

Walker Company
Work Sheet
For Year Ended December 31, 20—

	ADJUSTMENTS		INCOME STATEMENT		BALANCE SHEET	
	DEBIT	CREDIT	DEBIT	CREDIT	DEBIT	CREDIT
					94 0 0 0 00	
		(a) 3 4 2 0 00				3 7 4 0 00
	(a) 3 4 2 0 00		3 4 2 0 00			

Bad Debts Expense ($3,420) appears on the income statement in the general expense portion of Operating Expenses. Like all expenses, it is closed into Income Summary at the end of the fiscal period. For emphasis, let's repeat the placement of the accounts on the balance sheet.

FYI

Aging of Accounts Receivable is easily accomplished by computer accounting programs.

Walker Company Balance Sheet December 31, 20—			
Assets			
Current Assets:			
Cash			$ 9 2 0 0 00
Notes Receivable			4 0 0 0 00
Accounts Receivable	$94 0 0 0 00		
Less Allowance for Doubtful Accounts	3 7 4 0 00		90 2 6 0 00

Adjusting Entry Based on Estimating Bad Debts as a Percentage of Accounts Receivable

OBJECTIVE 1b

Determine the amount of the adjusting entry by using a percentage of Accounts Receivable.

Some firms feel that the aging procedure is too time consuming; they prefer a quicker but less exact method for estimating the amount of uncollectible Accounts Receivable. These firms take an average of the actual bad debt losses of previous years as a percentage of Accounts Receivable. For example, we'll use a different company, Reyes Company. The firm calculated the amount of the adjustment for uncollectible accounts as follows:

End of Year	Balance of Accounts Receivable	Total Actual Losses from Accounts Receivable (Accounts Receivable Written Off)
20x4	$ 44,000	$1,540
20x5	56,000	1,528
20x6	48,000	1,372
	$148,000	$4,440

FIGURE 5

ACCOUNT NAME	TRIAL BALANCE	
	DEBIT	CREDIT
Cash	16 8 9 1 00	
Notes Receivable	1 6 0 0 00	
Accounts Receivable	59 2 0 0 00	
Allowance for Doubtful Accounts		2 9 4 00
Bad Debts Expense		

The firm's average loss over three consecutive years is:

$$\frac{\$4,440}{\$148,000} = .03 = \underline{\underline{3\%}}$$

Assume that, at the end of 20x7, the balance of Accounts Receivable is $59,200 and the credit balance of Allowance for Doubtful Accounts is $294. The amount of Accounts Receivable the company estimates to be uncollectible is $1,776 ($59,200 × .03 = $1,776). Since $1,776 is the desired balance, the amount of the adjustment is $1,482 ($1,776 − $294 = $1,482). As in the case of aging Accounts Receivable, when you figure the adjustment for bad debts as a percentage of Accounts Receivable, **you make an adjusting entry to bring the balance of Allowance for Doubtful Accounts up to the desired amount.** Notice how the adjusting entry looks:

Bad Debts Expense		Allowance for Doubtful Accounts	
+	−	−	+
Adj. 1,482			Bal. 294
			Adj. 1,482
			1,776

You would then record the adjustment in the work sheet as shown in Figure 5 below.

Let's examine a portion of the balance sheet derived from the work sheet.

Reyes Company
Balance Sheet
December 31, 20—

Assets			
Current Assets:			
Cash			$16 8 9 1 00
Notes Receivable			1 6 0 0 00
Accounts Receivable		$59 2 0 0 00	
Less Allowance for Doubtful Accounts		1 7 7 6 00	57 4 2 4 00

In this statement, the book value of Accounts Receivable is shown as $57,424 ($59,200 − $1,776).

Reyes Company
Work Sheet
For Year Ended December 31, 20—

	ADJUSTMENTS		INCOME STATEMENT		BALANCE SHEET	
	DEBIT	CREDIT	DEBIT	CREDIT	DEBIT	CREDIT
					16 8 9 1 00	
					1 6 0 0 00	
					59 2 0 0 00	
		(e) 1 4 8 2 00				1 7 7 6 00
	(e) 1 4 8 2 00		1 4 8 2 00			

REMEMBER!

No matter what method is used to determine the amount of the adjustment for bad debts, the resulting amount is an estimate only.

FIGURE 6

ACCOUNT NAME	TRIAL BALANCE	
	DEBIT	CREDIT
Accounts Receivable	63 2 0 0 00	
Allowance for Doubtful Accounts		3 1 0 00
Sales		711 0 0 0 00
Sales Returns and Allowances	31 0 0 0 00	
Sales Discounts	1 6 0 0 00	
Bad Debts Expense		

Adjusting Entry Based on Estimating Bad Debts as a Percentage of Net Sales or Net Credit Sales

OBJECTIVE 1c

Calculate the amount of the adjusting entry by using a percentage of net sales or net credit sales.

Some businesses prefer a simplified method for determining the amount of the adjustment for Bad Debts Expense. They multiply the current year's sales by a set percentage rate and then record the adjusting entry for that amount. We'll use a different company as an illustration, Packer Company.

Estimate Based on Net Sales   For example, the actual losses from sales on account for the Packer Company have averaged approximately 1 percent of net sales (Sales less Sales Returns and Allowances and less Sales Discounts). The firm makes virtually all sales on credit. Based on this information, the company computes the amount of the adjustment for bad debts expense as 1 percent of net sales.

The figure for net sales is shown in the partial income statement below:

Packer Company
Income Statement
For Year Ended June 30, 20—

Revenue from Sales:				
Sales			$711 0 0 0 00	
Less: Sales Returns and Allowances	$31 0 0 0 00			
Sales Discounts	1 6 0 0 00	32 6 0 0 00		
Net Sales				$678 4 0 0 00

One percent of net sales is $6,784 ($678,400 × .01), **so the firm uses this amount directly for the adjusting entry, adding it to both accounts,** as shown in the T accounts on the next page. In contrast to the previously illustrated aging and percentage of accounts receivable methods, the sales methods ignore any existing balance in the allowance account to calculate Bad Debts Expense.

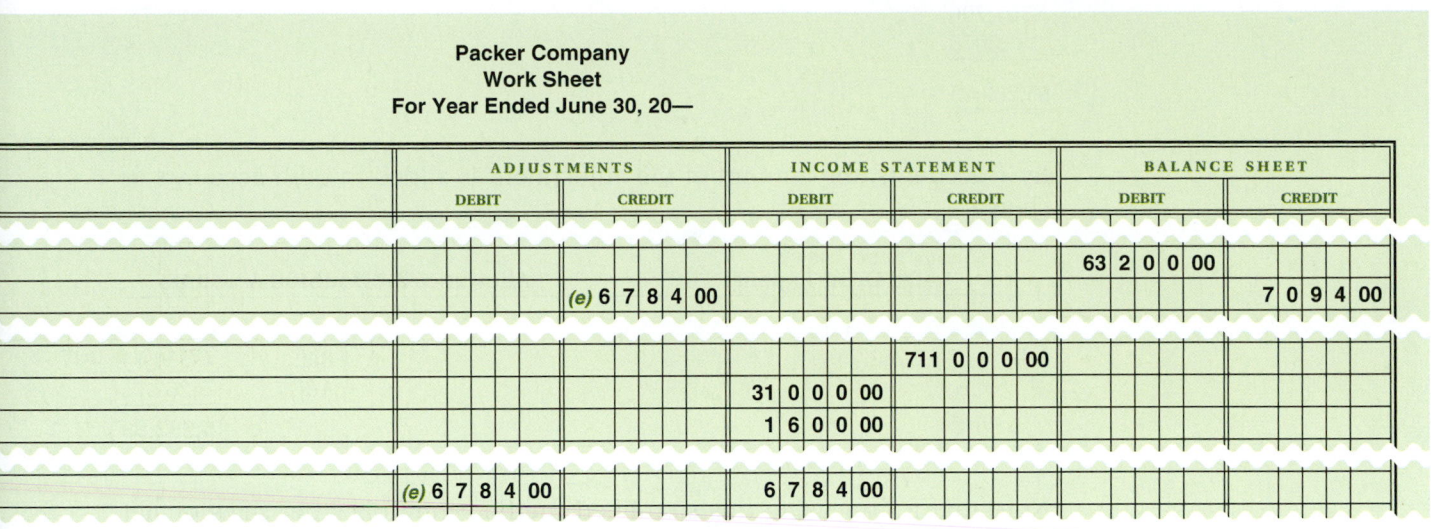

Packer Company
Work Sheet
For Year Ended June 30, 20—

	ADJUSTMENTS		INCOME STATEMENT		BALANCE SHEET	
	DEBIT	CREDIT	DEBIT	CREDIT	DEBIT	CREDIT
		(e) 6 7 8 4 00			63 2 0 0 00	
						7 0 9 4 00
				711 0 0 0 00		
			31 0 0 0 00			
			1 6 0 0 00			
	(e) 6 7 8 4 00		6 7 8 4 00			

Bad Debts Expense			Allowance for Doubtful Accounts		
	+	−		−	+
Adj.	6,784			Bal.	310
				Adj.	6,784
					7,094

Figure 6 above shows how to record the adjustment in the work sheet. A portion of the balance sheet is as follows:

Packer Company
Balance Sheet
June 30, 20—

Assets					
Current Assets:					
Accounts Receivable		$63 2 0 0 00			
Less Allowance for Doubtful Accounts		7 0 9 4 00		56 1 0 6 00	

Estimate Based on Net Credit Sales   Many companies that sell on both a cash and a credit basis compute the amount of their adjustment for bad debts on net credit sales only. As an example, we'll use a different business firm, Rea Company. The business's credit sales, recorded in a sales journal, total $735,000. Sales Returns and Allowances and Sales Discounts relating to credit sales are $27,000 and $6,300, respectively. Rea Company records the adjustment for bad debts at ¾ percent of net credit sales. Look at the calculation and adjustment that follow:

Credit (charge) sales		$735,000
Less: Sales Returns and Allowances	$27,000	
Sales Discounts	6,300	33,300
Net credit sales		$701,700

$701,700
× .0075
_____
$5,262.75

By T accounts, the amount of the adjustment is added to both accounts as shown:

Bad Debts Expense				Allowance for Doubtful Accounts		
	+	−			−	+
Adj.	5,262.75				Bal.	330.14
					Adj.	5,262.75
						5,592.89

Note that a firm using this simplified method multiplies net sales or net credit sales by the given percentage in order to determine the amount of the adjustment. **The present balance of Allowance for Doubtful Accounts is not involved in determining the amount of the adjustment.** If the given percentage does not adequately provide for the firm's losses (that is, if it yields either too little or too much), the firm merely changes the percentage.

CLOSING THE BAD DEBTS EXPENSE ACCOUNT

Up to now, we have seen that the firm's accountant first records the adjusting entry for bad debts in the appropriate columns of the work sheet. The T accounts for Rea Company are repeated here.

Bad Debts Expense				Allowance for Doubtful Accounts		
	+	−			−	+
Adj.	5,262.75				Bal.	330.14
					Adj.	5,262.75
						5,592.89

Next, the accountant closes Bad Debts Expense, along with all other expenses, into the Income Summary account. **The Bad Debts Expense account is not used during the year, so the only entries in it are the adjusting entry and the closing entry.** This represents the beginning and the end of Bad Debts Expense for the fiscal period. In other words, the only entry in Bad Debts Expense is the adjusting entry, and, as we said, this account is immediately closed out. After the adjusting entry and closing entry have been posted, the accounts look like this:

Bad Debts Expense				Allowance for Doubtful Accounts		
	+	−			−	+
Adj.	5,262.75	Clos.	5,262.75		Bal.	330.14
					Adj.	5,262.75
						5,592.89

Allowance for Doubtful Accounts

It is apparent that Allowance for Doubtful Accounts remains open. Rather than have the balance continually increase because of the successive adjustments on the credit side of the account, the accountant uses the debit side of the account to write off charge accounts that are considered uncollectible.

Consider Allowance for Doubtful Accounts as a reservoir: We fill it up at the end of the year through the medium of the adjusting entry by crediting the account. During the following year, we drain off the reservoir through the medium of write-offs by debiting the account. To avoid the possibility of the reservoir's "running dry," *the accountant should make the adjusting entry large enough to provide for all possible write-offs.*

REMEMBER!

Allowance for Doubtful Accounts increases when the adjustment is made at the end of the year (credit) and decreases as write-offs occur during the year (debits).

WRITING OFF ACCOUNTS AS UNCOLLECTIBLE

Entry to Write Off a Charge Account in Full

OBJECTIVE 2

Journalize the entries to write off accounts receivable as being uncollectible, using the allowance method of accounting for bad debt losses.

Suppose that, after all attempts to collect a customer's debt have failed, a firm decides that the account is definitely uncollectible. In such a case, the firm should write off the amount due. To pick out one company to use as an illustration, let's use Packer Company. Assume that in July the firm decides that the $971.40 account of a customer, L. N. Lee, is uncollectible. The accountant records the write-off by making the following entry:

GENERAL JOURNAL   PAGE **116**

	DATE		DESCRIPTION	POST. REF.	DEBIT	CREDIT	
1	20–						1
2	July	15	Allowance for Doubtful Accounts		9 7 1 40		2
3			Accounts Receivable, L. N. Lee			9 7 1 40	3
4			Wrote off the account as				4
5			uncollectible.				5
6							6

By T accounts, the entry looks like this:

Accounts Receivable					Allowance for Doubtful Accounts			
	+	–				–	+	
Bal.	63,200.00	July 15	971.40		July 15	971.40	Bal.	7,094.00
					(Lee's write-off)			
Bal.	62,228.60						Bal.	6,122.60

The accountant also posts the entry to the account of L. N. Lee in the accounts receivable subsidiary ledger.

NAME	L. N. Lee
ADDRESS	217 Barclay Road
	Boston, MA 02101

DATE		ITEM	POST. REF.	DEBIT	CREDIT	BALANCE
20–						
June	30	Balance	✓			9 7 1 40
July	15	Written off	J116		9 7 1 40	—

Note that the entry just shown does not change the net realizable value or book value of Accounts Receivable.

REMEMBER!

An entry to write off an account receivable does not change the book value of Accounts Receivable because Accounts Receivable and Allowance for Doubtful Accounts are reduced by the same amount.

Account Name	Balances Before Write-off	Balances After Write-off
Accounts Receivable	$63,200.00	$62,228.60
Less Allowance for Doubtful Accounts	7,094.00	6,122.60
Book value (net realizable value)	$56,106.00	$56,106.00

Also note that **the entry to write off an account does not involve an expense account.** The adjusting entry, which was made on June 30, provides for the expense. The estimated expense was recorded *during the year in which the sale was made,* even though this account is written off in a later year.

Entry to Write Off a Charge Account Paid in Part

Sometimes a partial payment is involved in a write-off of an account. When this happens, it may be due to a bankruptcy settlement. The federal laws governing **bankruptcy** legally excuse a debtor from paying off certain obligations. For example, on April 21, Packer Company received 10 cents on the dollar (10 percent) in settlement of a $442 account owed by its customer R. E. Linn, a bankrupt customer. In general journal form, the entry is as follows:

	DATE		DESCRIPTION	POST. REF.	DEBIT	CREDIT	
1	20–						1
2	Apr.	21	Cash		4 4 20		2
3			Allowance for Doubtful Accounts		3 9 7 80		3
4			Accounts Receivable, R. E. Linn			4 4 2 00	4
5			Settlement in bankruptcy,				5
6			wrote off account balance				6
7			as uncollectible.				7
8							8

When a company does not have adequate cash to pay its bills, it may file for bankruptcy protection to reorganize or simply sell off its inventory and other assets and go out of business. If the company files for bankruptcy protection to reorganize, it may pay off only part of its debt to its creditors.

Compound Entry to Write Off a Number of Accounts as Uncollectible

Rather than writing off each uncollectible account separately during the year, a firm may write off a number of accounts at the end of the year by using a compound entry. For example, assume that on December 31, a different business, Ortiz Company, writes off the following accounts of charge customers as being uncollectible: C. D. Lem, $111.00; D. T. Rios, $94.00; O. C. Rose, $47.10; and M. A. See, $193.27. The accountant records the write-offs by making the following entry:

REMEMBER!

With the allowance method, the Bad Debts Expense account is used only as part of the adjusting entry at the end of the fiscal period. Bad Debts Expense is not used during the period.

	DATE	DESCRIPTION	POST. REF.	DEBIT	CREDIT	
1	20–					1
2	Dec. 31	Allowance for Doubtful Accounts		4 4 5 37		2
3		Accounts Receivable, C. D. Lem			1 1 1 00	3
4		Accounts Receivable, D. T. Rios			9 4 00	4
5		Accounts Receivable, O. C. Rose			4 7 10	5
6		Accounts Receivable, M. A. See			1 9 3 27	6
7		Wrote off the accounts				7
8		as uncollectible.				8
9						9

Write-offs Seldom Agree with Previous Estimates

The total amount of Accounts Receivable written off during a given year does not ordinarily agree with the estimate of uncollectible accounts previously debited to Bad Debts Expense and credited to Allowance for Doubtful Accounts. In the usual situation, the amounts written off as uncollectible turn out to be less than the estimated amount. At the end of a given year, there is normally a credit balance in Allowance for Doubtful Accounts.

However, if the amounts written off are greater than the estimated amounts, Allowance for Doubtful Accounts temporarily has a debit balance. The debit balance is eliminated by the adjusting entry at the end of the year, which results in a credit to, or increase in, Allowance for Doubtful Accounts.

COLLECTION OF ACCOUNTS PREVIOUSLY WRITTEN OFF

OBJECTIVE 3

Journalize entries to reinstate accounts receivable previously written off, using the allowance method.

Occasionally an account that was previously written off as uncollectible may later be recovered, either in part or in full. In such cases, the firm's accountant restores the account to the books, or reinstates it, by an entry that is the exact opposite of the write-off entry.

As an example, Packer Company sells merchandise on account to P. E. Norris for $495 on May 5, 20—. Here is the entry in general journal form:

	DATE		DESCRIPTION	POST. REF.	DEBIT	CREDIT	
1	20—						1
2	May	5	Accounts Receivable, P. E. Norris		4 9 5 00		2
3			Sales			4 9 5 00	3
4			Sold merchandise on account,				4
5			2/10, n/30.				5
6							6

REMEMBER!

A write-off requires two credits—one to the controlling account, Accounts Receivable, and one to the accounts receivable subsidiary ledger account for the customer.

Packer Company makes many unsuccessful attempts to collect the Norris debt, and the **statute of limitations** finally expires. Since the statute of limitations is set at three years in many states, let's say that Packer Company has not been able to collect any money at all from Norris during a three-year period and that Norris has remained within the jurisdiction of the court. This means that the debt is outlawed by the statute of limitations. In other words, the firm cannot use the courts to force the debtor to pay up. Accordingly, three years later, on June 10, the accountant for Packer Company writes off the account of P. E. Norris as uncollectible.

FYI

As a result of some people's failure to pay their accounts, everyone else pays higher prices for goods they buy.

	DATE		DESCRIPTION	POST. REF.	DEBIT	CREDIT	
1	20—						1
2	June	10	Allowance for Doubtful Accounts		4 9 5 00		2
3			Accounts Receivable, P. E.				3
4			Norris			4 9 5 00	4
5			Wrote off the account as				5
6			uncollectible.				6

But on September 15, 20—, P. E. Norris suddenly pays her account in full! The entry to reinstate the account is the reverse of the entry used to write off the account.

	DATE		DESCRIPTION	POST. REF.	DEBIT	CREDIT	
1	20—						1
2	Sept.	15	Accounts Receivable, P. E. Norris		4 9 5 00		2
3			Allowance for Doubtful				3
4			Accounts			4 9 5 00	4
5			Reinstated the account.				5
6							6

The way is now clear to record the collection of the account.

	DATE		DESCRIPTION	POST. REF.	DEBIT	CREDIT	
1	20—						1
2	Sept.	15	Cash		4 9 5 00		2
3			Accounts Receivable, P. E.				3
4			Norris			4 9 5 00	4
5			Collected account in full.				5
6							6

Now suppose that P. E. Norris had gone into bankruptcy and settled her account with Packer Company by paying it 5 cents on the dollar. Packer Company would realize that there was no hope of collecting any more, so the accountant would reinstate the account only for the amount collected, like this:

	DATE		DESCRIPTION	POST. REF.	DEBIT	CREDIT	
1	20—						1
2	Sept.	15	Accounts Receivable, P. E. Norris		2 4 75		2
3			Allowance for Doubtful				3
4			Accounts			2 4 75	4
5			Settlement in bankruptcy,				5
6			5 percent of $495, so reinstated				6
7			the account to the extent of the				7
8			settlement.				8

The subsequent entry to record the cash receipt would be as follows:

	DATE		DESCRIPTION	POST. REF.	DEBIT	CREDIT	
8	Sept.	15	Cash		2 4 75		8
9			Accounts Receivable, P. E.				9
10			Norris			2 4 75	10
11			Settlement in bankruptcy,				11
12			5 percent of $495.				12

SPECIFIC CHARGE-OFF OF BAD DEBTS

OBJECTIVE 4

Journalize the entries to write off accounts receivable as being uncollectible, using the specific charge-off method.

The **specific charge-off method of accounting for bad debt losses** is a simpler system for writing off charge accounts determined to be uncollectible. No adjusting entry is made because there is no attempt to provide for bad debt losses in advance or to match revenue with related expenses. Instead, when a firm decides that a specific customer account is never going to be collected, the accountant makes an entry in the general journal debiting Bad Debts Expense and crediting Accounts Receivable. Thus Allowance for Doubtful Accounts does not exist in the firm's chart of accounts. Traditionally, this method has been used primarily by small companies and professional enterprises. As we stated previously, the specific charge-off method is required for federal income tax reporting, but is not allowed under GAAP. We'll use a different business as an illustration, Roy Company.

For example, on April 16, 20—, Roy Company sold merchandise on account to H. N. Morgan for $179.10, making the following entry in the general journal:

DATE	DESCRIPTION	POST. REF.	DEBIT	CREDIT	
20—					1
Apr. 16	Accounts Receivable, H. N.				2
	Morgan		1 7 9 10		3
	Sales			1 7 9 10	4
	Sold merchandise on				5
	account, n/30.				6

Morgan never paid his bill. Finally, three years later, on September 1, the account is written off as follows:

REMEMBER!

The specific charge-off method is simple to use but can cause inaccurate matching of revenue and expenses; for example, a sale on account made in one fiscal period is found to be uncollectible in the next fiscal period. Nevertheless, this method is used for tax purposes by most businesses, even though they may use the allowance method for financial reporting.

DATE	DESCRIPTION	POST. REF.	DEBIT	CREDIT	
20—					1
Sept. 1	Bad Debts Expense		1 7 9 10		2
	Accounts Receivable, H. N.				3
	Morgan			1 7 9 10	4
	Wrote off an uncollectible				5
	account.				6

By T accounts, the entries look like this:

Accounts Receivable			Sales			Bad Debts Expense	
+	−		−	+		+	−
20—	20—			20—		20—	
Apr. 16 179.10	Sept. 1 179.10			Apr. 16 179.10		Sept. 1 179.10	

You can see that revenue does not match expenses for a particular year. Roy Company counted the original sale of $179.10 in 20—, thereby overstating true revenue for that year. It counted Bad Debts Expense three years later, thereby overstating expenses for that year. Note that Roy Company did not use the account titled Allowance for Doubtful Accounts. In other words, if you wait until you consider an account to be a bad debt and then write it off, with no provision for realistically estimating the losses in advance, you are making unrealistic assumptions. On the balance sheet, Accounts Receivable is stated at the gross amount only; there is no book value or net realizable value. As a result, both assets and owners' equity are overstated.

To reinstate an account previously written or charged off, let's say that on May 2, 20—, H. N. Morgan returns and pays his $179.10 bill. We show the entries in general journal form.

OBJECTIVE 5

Journalize entries to reinstate accounts receivable previously written off, using the specific charge-off method.

GENERAL JOURNAL

	DATE		DESCRIPTION	POST. REF.	DEBIT	CREDIT	
1	20—						1
2	May	2	Accounts Receivable, H. N.				2
3			Morgan		1 7 9 10		3
4			Bad Debts Recovered			1 7 9 10	4
5			Reinstated the account.				5
6							6
7		2	Cash		1 7 9 10		7
8			Accounts Receivable, H. N.				8
9			Morgan			1 7 9 10	9
10			Collected account in full.				10
11							11
12							12
13							13
14							14
15							15
16							16
17							17

With T accounts, the entries look like this:

Accounts Receivable			Bad Debts Recovered		Cash	
+	−		−	+	+	−
20—	20—			20—	20—	
May 2 179.10	May 2 179.10			May 2 179.10	May 2 179.10	

For a small company that uses the specific charge-off method alone, the account entitled Bad Debts Recovered is classified as a revenue account and would be listed in the Other Income section of the income statement. The Accounts Receivable account was placed back on the books, so that the firm would have a record of H. N. Morgan's account. Note that this method of accounting is not consistent with the accrual method. The following chart illustrates a comparison of journal entries involved in the allowance method and the specific charge-off method.

Comparison of Two Methods of Write-off, Reinstatement, and Collection		
	Allowance Method	**Specific Charge-off Method**

Original sale	Accounts Receivable, J. Smith
	    Sales
		Accounts Receivable, J. Smith
		    Sales

Write-off	Allowance for Doubtful Accounts
	    Accounts Receivable, J. Smith
		Bad Debts Expense
		    Accounts Receivable, J. Smith

Reinstatement	Accounts Receivable, J. Smith
	    Allowance for Doubtful Accounts
		Accounts Receivable, J. Smith
		    Bad Debts Recovered (Other Income)

Collection	Cash
	    Accounts Receivable, J. Smith
		Cash
		    Accounts Receivable, J. Smith

FEDERAL INCOME TAX REQUIREMENT

All firms except financial institutions are required to use the specific charge-off method for reporting on their federal income tax returns. A separate record should be maintained for reporting bad debt losses. For each account charged off, this record must contain the following:

1. A description of the debt, including the amount, and the date it became due
2. The name of the debtor
3. The efforts that have been made to collect the debt
4. Why it has been decided that the debt is worthless

CHAPTER REVIEW

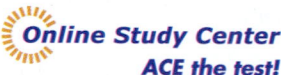
Online Study Center
ACE the test!

Review of Performance Objectives

1. Make the adjusting entry to record estimated bad debt losses by using the allowance method of recording bad debts.

   The adjusting entry is a debit to Bad Debts Expense and a credit to Allowance for Doubtful Accounts.

   (a) **Determine the amount of the adjusting entry by aging Accounts Receivable.**
   Classify each charge customer's account according to the number of days past due (thirty days, sixty days, and so on).
   Multiply the total for each time period by a given percentage deemed to be uncollectible, and sum the totals.

Assuming that Allowance for Doubtful Accounts has a credit balance, subtract the amount of the credit balance from the amount estimated to be uncollectible to get the amount of the adjusting entry.

(b) **Determine the amount of the adjusting entry by using a percentage of Accounts Receivable.**

Multiply the balance of Accounts Receivable by the given percentage. Next, assuming that Allowance for Doubtful Accounts has a credit balance, subtract the amount of the credit balance from the percentage amount to get the amount of the adjusting entry.

(c) **Calculate the amount of the adjusting entry by using a percentage of net sales or net credit sales.**

Multiply the amount of net sales or net credit sales by the given percentage and make the adjusting entry for the amount determined.

2. Journalize the entries to write off accounts receivable as being uncollectible, using the allowance method of accounting for bad debt losses.

Debit Allowance for Doubtful Accounts and credit Accounts Receivable.

3. Journalize entries to reinstate accounts receivable previously written off, using the allowance method.

Debit Accounts Receivable and credit Allowance for Doubtful Accounts (the opposite of a write-off).

4. Journalize the entries to write off accounts receivable as being uncollectible, using the specific charge-off method.

Debit Bad Debts Expense and credit Accounts Receivable.

5. Journalize entries to reinstate accounts receivable previously written off, using the specific charge-off method.

Debit Accounts Receivable and credit Bad Debts Recovered.

Glossary

Age (accounts receivable) To analyze the accounts receivable by classifying the outstanding balance of each charge customer's account according to the amount of time it has been outstanding. Multiply the total for each time period by a percentage deemed to be uncollectible and sum the totals to determine the balance of Allowance for Doubtful Accounts. (601)

Allowance method of accounting for bad debt losses A method that requires an adjusting entry to debit Bad Debts Expense and to credit Allowance for Doubtful Accounts to match losses from uncollectible accounts with sales of the same period. Write-offs of uncollectible accounts are debited to Allowance for Doubtful Accounts and credited to Accounts Receivable. (598)

Bankruptcy A condition governed by federal law in which a debtor is excused from certain obligations incurred. (610)

Book value of Accounts Receivable The balance of Accounts Receivable after deducting the balance of Allowance for Doubtful Accounts; also called the *net expected realizable value of Accounts Receivable*. The amount of cash expected to be collected eventually from gross receivables. (598)

Net expected realizable value of Accounts Receivable The balance of Accounts Receivable after deducting the balance of Allowance for Doubtful Accounts; also called the *book value of Accounts Receivable*. The amount of cash expected to be collected eventually from gross receivables. (599)

Specific charge-off method of accounting for bad debt losses A method of recognizing bad debts that requires no adjusting entry. The accountant debits Bad Debts Expense and credits Accounts Receivable. This method is required for federal income tax reporting but is not allowed under GAAP. (614)

Statute of limitations Laws that limit the period of time in which legal action may be taken; with regard to bad debts, laws limiting the period of time during which the courts may force a debtor to pay a debt, usually three years for charge accounts. (612)

QUESTIONS, EXERCISES, AND CASES

Discussion Questions

1. What is meant by aging of Accounts Receivable?
2. When an account is written off under the allowance method of accounting for bad debts, why doesn't the book value of Accounts Receivable decrease?
3. Explain how the book value of Accounts Receivable is calculated.
4. Describe the concept of Allowance for Doubtful Accounts, how it comes into existence, and what happens to it during the accounting period.
5. Suppose that the estimate of bad debts is based on the aging method and that Allowance for Doubtful Accounts has a debit balance. Explain how this situation is handled in terms of accounting procedure.
6. If the allowance method of accounting for bad debts is used to determine the amount of the adjusting entry, explain the difference between using a percentage of Accounts Receivable and a percentage of net sales.
7. Discuss why the allowance method of handling bad debts is considered more in accordance with GAAP than the specific charge-off method. Is it ever acceptable to use the specific charge-off method?
8. Assume that a customer's account was written off as uncollectible and is paid at a later date. What journal entries are made on the seller's books using the allowance method? What entry is made on the buyer's books?

Exercises

P.O. 1a

Estimate uncollectible accounts based on aging and make the adjusting entry.

Exercise 16-1 Nigel Company uses the allowance method of estimating losses from bad debts. Management analyzed its accounts receivable balances on December 31 and determined the following aged balances:

Age of Accounts	Balance	Estimated Percentage Uncollectible	Allowance for Doubtful Accounts
Not yet due	$120,000	1	_____
31 to 60 days	16,000	2	_____
61 to 120 days	9,000	5	_____
121 to 365 days	1,400	30	_____
Over 365 days	4,800	60	_____
	$151,200		_____

Compute the estimate of the amount of uncollectible accounts. Write the adjusting entry for estimated credit losses on December 31. The credit balance of Allowance for Doubtful Accounts is $3,040.

P.O. 1b

Journalize the adjusting entry based on a percentage of Accounts Receivable.

Exercise 16-2 Gable Company uses the allowance method of estimating losses from bad debts. Gable Company considers estimated losses to be 3 percent of Accounts Receivable. On December 31, the Accounts Receivable balance was $63,000, and Allowance for Doubtful Accounts had a credit balance of $320. Journalize the adjusting entry to record the estimated bad debt losses.

P.O. 1c

Journalize the adjusting entry based on a percentage of net sales.

Exercise 16-3 Espinoza Company uses the allowance method of estimating losses due to bad debts. On December 31, before any adjustments have been recorded, the ledger contains the following balances:

Sales	$180,000
Sales Returns and Allowances	27,000

The company estimates that bad debt losses will be ¾ percent of net sales. Journalize the adjusting entry to record the estimated bad debt losses. The Allowance for Doubtful Accounts account has a credit balance of $320.

P.O. 1a,c

Journalize the adjusting entry based on (a) aging and (b) a percentage of net sales.

Exercise 16-4 Gore Company uses the allowance method of handling losses due to bad debts. Gore Company's Accounts Receivable account has a balance of $82,000. Net sales for the year total $104,000. Write the adjusting entry to record the estimated bad debt losses under each of the following conditions. Assume that Allowance for Doubtful Accounts has a credit balance of $650.

a. Aging of the charge accounts in the accounts receivable ledger indicates doubtful accounts of $1,570.
b. Bad debt losses are estimated at ¾ percent of net sales.

P.O. 2

Journalize the write-off of an account using the allowance method, compute net realizable value of Accounts Receivable, and prepare a partial balance sheet.

Exercise 16-5 On June 1, Roy Supply's Accounts Receivable balance was $26,436. The balance of the contra account Allowance for Doubtful Accounts was $1,630 credit. On June 20, the account balance of Mel's Bakery of $570 was written off.

a. Journalize the write-off of the Mel's Bakery account using the allowance method.
b. Using T accounts, determine what is now the net realizable value of Accounts Receivable. How would this be shown in the financial statements? (The period ends December 31, 20—.)

P.O. 1c,2,3

Allowance method: write off, reinstate, and collect on an account; journalize adjusting entry based on percentage of net sales.

Exercise 16-6 Manor Shop had the following selected transactions this year. Assuming that Manor Shop uses the allowance method of accounting for bad debt losses, record the three transactions in general journal form. Allowance for Doubtful Accounts has a credit balance of $346.

a. Wrote off the account of D. Yarro as uncollectible, $280.
b. Reinstated the account of R. Flanigan, which had been written off during the preceding year, $65; received $65 cash in full payment.
c. Estimated bad debt losses to be 1 percent of net sales of $82,350.

P.O. 4,5

Specific charge-off method: write off, reinstate, and collect on an account.

Exercise 16-7 Using the same data as in Exercise 16-6, assume that Manor Shop uses the specific charge-off method of accounting for bad debt losses. Record transactions *a* and *b* in general journal form.

P.O. 4,5

Journalize the write-off, the reinstatement, and the collection of an account using the specific charge-off method.

Exercise 16-8 With reference to Exercise 16-5:

a. Use the specific charge-off method of accounting for bad debt losses to write off the Mel's Bakery account.
b. Reinstate the Mel's Bakery account and collect the amount due.

Let's take another look at Citigroup Inc.'s 2005 financial information. Go to **http://www.citi.com/citigroup/fin/index.htm**, select SEC Filings, and click on Citigroup Inc.'s Form 10-K for 2005. Find the U.S. Cards section of the report, which begins on page 42.

1. What was the net revenue from credit cards for 2005, and what was the amount of the bad debts expense from those credit cards that Citigroup recognized that year? (Remember, Citigroup uses the term *provision for loan losses*.)
2. Now, look at page 143 of the Citigroup report. Can you tell from the information given which method Citigroup uses to account for uncollectible accounts?
3. Based on the information provided for 2005, how would Citigroup have written the adjusting entry to record its bad debts expense related to its credit card services?

CONSIDER AND COMMUNICATE

The owner of the business where you work is puzzled. He asks you how he can write off bad accounts. You know about the allowance method and the specific charge-off method.

Explain why the allowance method of accounting for bad debts is preferable to the specific charge-off method for financial reporting.

CRITICAL THINKING

Your supervisor has asked you to do some work for her on Martin Company's accounts receivables.

Below is selected information from Martin Company:

	12/31/06	12/31/07
Net Credit Sales	$250,000	$300,000
Accounts Receivable	48,000	65,000
Allowance for Doubtful Accounts (credit balance)	800	800

For each situation, your supervisor suggests you do the following:

1. Write the correct entry for Martin Company to record either estimated Bad Debts Expense or actual Bad Debts Expense, depending upon the method used to value Accounts Receivable.
2. Determine the balance of Allowance for Doubtful Accounts at the end of December 2007.

Situation A—Martin Company ages Accounts Receivable to determine the amount of the adjustment for estimated Bad Debts Expense.
The following facts are available:

Age of Accounts	12/31/07 Balance	Estimated Percentage Uncollectible
Not yet due	$45,000	1
1 to 30 days	12,000	3
31 to 60 days	4,000	6
61 to 90 days	3,000	12
Over 90 days	1,000	30

Situation B—Martin Company uses a percentage of Accounts Receivable to determine the amount of the adjustment for estimated Bad Debts Expense. The firm's average actual bad debt losses over the prior three consecutive years were 3 percent. The firm feels that this is a reasonable estimate of Bad Debts Expense.

A QUESTION OF ETHICS

As the company bookkeeper reviewing delinquent accounts receivable, you find that a relative of yours has not paid his account amounting to $550. You know that he has been experiencing financial difficulties, and so you set his account aside and do not include it with the other past due accounts sent to a credit collection agency. Comment on this action.

PROBLEM SET A

For additional help, see the demonstration problem at the beginning of each chapter in your Working Papers.

P.O. 1a,2

Problem 16-1A On December 31 of last year, the accountant for Bolt Co. prepared a balance sheet that included $197,900 in Accounts Receivable and $12,618 (credit) in Allowance for Doubtful Accounts. Selected transactions occurred during January of this year, as follows:

a. Sales of merchandise on account, $181,900.
b. Sales returns and allowances related to sales of merchandise on account, $4,922.

c. Cash payments by charge customers (no cash discounts), $168,461.24.
d. Account of Cooke Company written off as uncollectible, $1,217.27.
e. By the process of aging Accounts Receivable, on January 31 it was decided that Allowance for Doubtful Accounts should be adjusted to a balance of $22,354.20.
f. Closed the Bad Debts Expense account.

Check Figure

Bad Debts Expense Debit, $10,953.47

Instructions

1. Record the entries in general journal form, page 36. Record the letter in the Date column.
2. Record the balance in Allowance for Doubtful Accounts.
3. Post the appropriate entries to the accounts for Allowance for Doubtful Accounts and Bad Debts Expense.

Instructions for General Ledger Software

1. Account balances already appear in the general ledger.
2. Record the entries in the general journal. Record the letter in the Explanation.
3. Post the amounts in the general journal to the general ledger. Print the general ledger.

P.O. 1a

Problem 16-2A Malcore Company uses the aging method of estimating bad debts as of December 31, the end of the fiscal year. Terms of sales are net 30 days. While preparing the aging schedule, the accountant became very ill and was unable to finish the job. The accountant's report, as he left it, appears below:

Customer Name	Balance	Not Yet Due	Days Past Due			
			1–30	31–60	61–90	Over 90
Balance Forward	$352,292	$192,800	$94,400	$37,452	$14,960	$12,680

The accountant still had to analyze the following accounts:

Account	Amount	Due Date
P. Gallegos	$3,780	January 12 (next year)
R. Novak	2,910	December 22
L. Pomeroy	7,830	November 2
C. Quinnly	8,540	August 18
T. Renn	1,620	December 3
P. Roma	1,290	January 22 (next year)

From past experience, the company has found that the following percentages for estimated uncollectible accounts produce an adequate balance for Allowance for Doubtful Accounts:

Time Past Due	Estimated Percentage Uncollectible
Not yet due	2
1 to 30 days	4
31 to 60 days	20
61 to 90 days	30
Over 90 days	50

Prior to aging the accounts receivable, Allowance for Doubtful Accounts had a credit balance of $7,248.

Check Figure

Total of Allowance for Doubtful Accounts, $32,069

Instructions

1. Enter the Balance Forward balances and complete the aging schedule.
2. Complete the table for estimating an allowance for doubtful accounts.
3. Record the adjusting entry in general journal form.

P.O. 1c,2,3

Problem 16-3A On January 1 of this year, Roland's Wholesale Meats had a credit balance of $4,234 in Allowance for Doubtful Accounts. During the year, the company completed the following selected transactions:

Feb.	8	Wrote off as uncollectible a $462 account of Sealish Market, which had gone out of business, leaving no assets.
May	3	Wrote off the account of Marci's Catering as uncollectible, $220.80.
	17	Collected 5 percent of the $1,777 owed by Lee Company, a bankrupt customer. Wrote off the remainder as worthless.
Aug.	2	Received $228.40 unexpectedly from Day Company, whose account had been written off two years earlier in the amount of $228.40. Reinstated the account and recorded the collection of $228.40.
Sept.	11	Received $173 from Marci's Catering as partial payment of the account written off on May 3. She wrote a letter saying that she expects to pay the balance soon. Accordingly, reinstated the account for the amount of the original obligation, $220.80.
Dec.	30	Journalized a compound entry to write off the following accounts as uncollectible: C. D. Finch, $326.32; Southway Inn, $282.52; Hall's Drive-In, $566.30.
	31	Recorded the adjusting entry for estimated bad debt losses at ½ percent of net sales of $584,290.
	31	Closed the Bad Debts Expense account.

Check Figure

December 31 balance of Allowance for Doubtful Accounts, $4,058.56

Instructions

1. Record the opening balance in the ledger account for Allowance for Doubtful Accounts.
2. Record the entries in general journal form, pages 73 and 74.
3. Post the entries to the ledger accounts for Allowance for Doubtful Accounts and Bad Debts Expense.

P.O. 1a,2,3

Problem 16-4A The following transactions were among those completed by Calder Wholesale Jewelers this year:

Feb.	15	Wrote off as uncollectible the account of Malin, Inc., $1,762.50. The company had gone out of business, leaving no assets.

Mar. 14 Reinstated the account of Golding, Inc., which had been written off in the preceding year; received $323.12 in full payment of account.

July 27 Received $214.26 unexpectedly from Craig and Son, whose account had been written off last year in the amount of $214.26. Reinstated the account and recorded the collection of $214.26.

Oct. 14 Reinstated the account of C. P. Stewart, which had been written off two years earlier, and received $674 in full payment.

Dec. 28 Journalized a compound entry to write off the following accounts as uncollectible: L. Browning, $365.00; C. Godfrey, $327.16; Engle and Burns, $716.42; Gable Jewelry, $2,379.60.

31 On the basis of an aged analysis of Accounts Receivable of $184,164.22, estimated that $5,597 will be uncollectible. Recorded the adjusting entry.

31 Recorded the entry to close the appropriate account to Income Summary.

Check Figure

Total Current Assets, $519,642.03

Instructions

1. Open the following accounts, recording the credit balance of Allowance for Doubtful Accounts as of January 1 of this fiscal year:

114 Allowance for Doubtful Accounts $5,112.16
313 Income Summary   —
642 Bad Debts Expense   —

2. Record in general journal form, pages 24 and 25, the transactions and the adjusting and closing entries described above. After each entry, post to the three selected ledger accounts.

3. Prepare the Current Assets section of the balance sheet. Other pertinent accounts are: Cash, $14,421.40; Notes Receivable, $2,720.00; Merchandise Inventory, $323,213.41; Prepaid Insurance, $720.00.

PROBLEM SET B

For additional help, see the demonstration problem at the beginning of each chapter in your Working Papers.

P.O. 1a,2

Problem 16-1B The balance sheet prepared by D. H. Ellen Co. for December 31 of last year includes $206,400 in Accounts Receivable and $12,192 (credit) in Allowance for Doubtful Accounts. The following transactions occurred during January of this year:

a. Sales of merchandise on account, $197,300.
b. Sales returns and allowances related to sales of merchandise on account, $5,627.
c. Cash payments by charge customers (no cash discounts), $181,946.
d. Account of Sims and Towne written off as uncollectible, $1,219.
e. By the process of aging Accounts Receivable, on January 31 it was decided that Allowance for Doubtful Accounts should be adjusted to a balance of $19,369.
f. Closed the Bad Debts Expense account.

Check Figure

Bad Debts Expense Debit, $8,396

Instructions

1. Record the entries in general journal form, page 36. Record the letter in the Date column.
2. Record the balance in Allowance for Doubtful Accounts.
3. Post the appropriate entries to the accounts for Allowance for Doubtful Accounts and Bad Debts Expense.

Instructions for General Ledger Software

1. Account balances already appear in the general ledger.
2. Record the entries in the general journal. Record the letter in the Explanation.
3. Post the amounts in the general journal to the general ledger. Print the general ledger.

P.O. 1a

Problem 16-2B Johnson Company uses the aging method of estimating bad debts as of December 31, the end of the fiscal year. Terms of sales are net 30 days. While in the process of completing the aging schedule, the accountant became very ill and was unable to finish the job. The accountant's report, as she left it, appears as follows:

Customer Name	Balance	Not Yet Due	Days Past Due			
			1–30	31–60	61–90	Over 90
Balance Forward	$389,900	$249,200	$76,280	$38,848	$15,032	$10,540

The accountant still had to analyze the following accounts:

Account	Amount	Due Date
B. Finchly	$3,650	November 28
L. Flanagan	935	January 16 (next year)
C. Gillerman	6,830	November 17
L. Hernandez	9,420	January 27 (next year)
P. Lamb	3,700	September 10
C. Newly	1,268	October 16

From past experience, the company has found that the following percentages for estimated uncollectible accounts produce an adequate balance for Allowance for Doubtful Accounts:

Time Past Due	Estimated Percentage Uncollectible
Not yet due	2
1–30 days	4
31–60 days	20
61–90 days	30
Over 90 days	50

Prior to aging the accounts receivable, Allowance for Doubtful Accounts had a credit balance of $4,346.

Instructions

1. Enter the Balance Forward balances and complete the aging schedule.
2. Complete the table for estimating an allowance for doubtful accounts.
3. Record the adjusting entry in general journal form.

P.O. 1c,2,3

Problem 16-3B On January 1 of this year, Ness Company had a credit balance of $1,926 in Allowance for Doubtful Accounts. During the year, Ness Company completed the following selected transactions:

Feb.	11	Wrote off as uncollectible a $694 account of Newly Company, which had gone out of business, leaving no assets.
May	5	Wrote off the account of C. Tidwell as uncollectible, $348.32.
	19	Received $189 unexpectedly from C. Weiss, whose account had been written off two years earlier in the amount of $189. Reinstated the account and recorded the collection of $189.
Aug.	3	Collected 10 percent of the $269 owed by C. C. Mack, a bankrupt customer. Wrote off the remainder as worthless.
Sept.	24	Received $195 from C. Tidwell as partial payment of the account written off on May 5. He wrote a letter stating that he expects to pay the balance soon. Accordingly, reinstated the account for the amount of the original obligation, $348.32.
Dec.	29	Journalized a compound entry to write off the following accounts as uncollectible: N. C. Allen, $372.40; R. L. Barnes, $248.72; C. Ellis, $288.00.
	31	Recorded the adjusting entry for estimated bad debt losses at ½ percent of net sales of $302,526.
	31	Closed the Bad Debts Expense account.

Instructions

1. Record the opening balance in the ledger account for Allowance for Doubtful Accounts.
2. Record the entries in general journal form, pages 73 and 74.
3. Post the entries to the ledger accounts for Allowance for Doubtful Accounts and Bad Debts Expense.

P.O. 1a,2,3

Problem 16-4B The following are among the transactions completed by Wheaton Building Supplies this year:

Feb.	6	Wrote off as uncollectible the account of Malo, Inc., $1,251.17. The company had gone out of business, leaving no assets.
Mar.	15	Reinstated the account of L. Ward, which had been written off in the preceding year; received $217.16 in full payment of account.
Aug.	17	Received $154 unexpectedly from C. P. Beech, whose account had been written off last year in the amount of $154. Reinstated the account and recorded the collection of $154.
Oct.	15	Reinstated the account of Dahl and Son, which had been written off two years earlier, and received $839.70 in full payment.
Dec.	29	Journalized a compound entry to write off the following accounts as uncollectible: D. C. Lang, $368.00; R. R. Mann, $752.28; N. Shearer, $1,374.91; D. Terry, $1,962.15.

Dec. 31 On the basis of an aged analysis of Accounts Receivable of $87,811.14, estimated that $5,772.55 will be uncollectible. Recorded the adjusting entry.

31 Recorded the entry to close the appropriate account to Income Summary.

Check Figure

Total Current Assets, $243,529.21

Instructions

1. Open the following accounts, recording the credit balance of Allowance for Doubtful Accounts as of January 1 of this fiscal year:

    114 Allowance for Doubtful Accounts $5,272.36
    313 Income Summary   —
    642 Bad Debts Expense   —

2. Record in general journal form, pages 24 and 25, the transactions and the adjusting and closing entries described above. After each entry, post to the three selected ledger accounts.

3. Prepare the Current Assets section of the balance sheet. Other pertinent accounts are: Cash, $14,227.12; Merchandise Inventory, $146,507.50; Prepaid Insurance, $756.00.

During the early 2000s, Target ran a series of TV ads focusing on merchandise of a specific color. All products displayed were made or packaged in the color selected for that ad. Scenes might show fully stocked shelves lined with a parade of orange boxes of Tide® laundry detergent or green bottles of Sprite™ soft drink. All these items represent inventory the store has on hand. An effective inventory system will likely increase the company's chances of a stronger bottom line. Buyers will be able to purchase what is needed based on past sales, and the stores will not find themselves overstocked, which is costly. How much inventory do you think Target carries? And, how does the company account for that inventory? When items are sold, how does it figure the cost of goods sold? You will be able to answer these questions and others as you learn about ending merchandise inventory in this chapter. Look for the answers to these questions in Target's annual report for 2005, which can be found at **http://www.target.com.** Click on Investors at the bottom of the screen and then on Annual Reports.

Performance Objectives

After you have completed this chapter, you will be able to do the following:

1. Determine the overstatement or understatement of cost of goods sold, gross profit, and net income resulting from a change in the ending merchandise inventory amount.

2. Determine unit cost, the value of the ending inventory, and the cost of goods sold by the following methods: (a) specific identification; (b) weighted-average-cost; (c) first-in, first-out; and (d) last-in, first-out.

3. Journalize transactions relating to perpetual inventories.

4. Complete a perpetual inventory record card.

One of the most important aspects of the operation of any merchandising business is the accounting for and valuation of the merchandise in stock. We define *merchandise inventory* as goods purchased by the company and held for resale to customers in the ordinary course of business. Merchandise Inventory and the related T accounts are as follows:

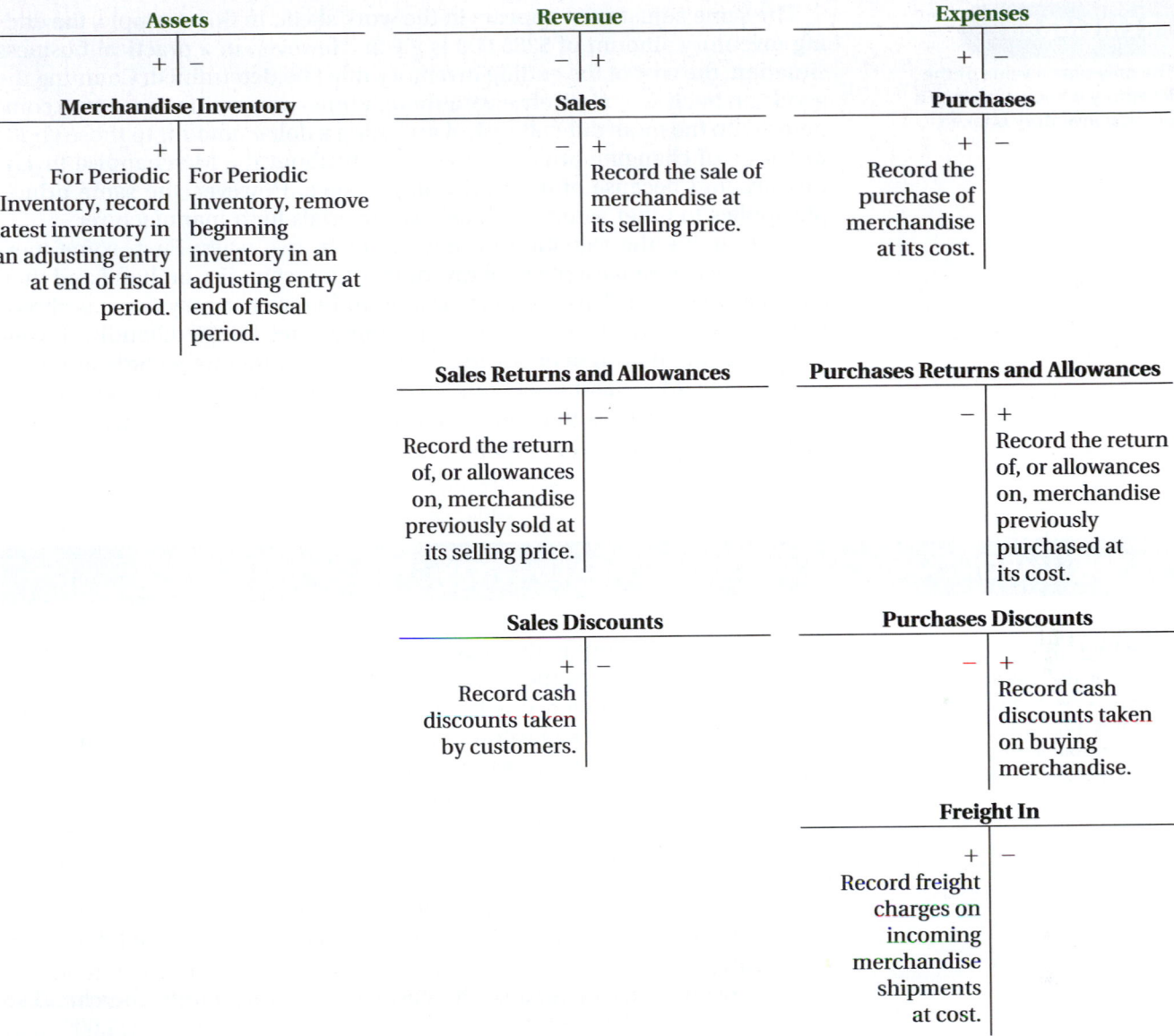

Firms take a physical inventory at the end of their fiscal periods. At this time, the most up-to-date figure is included in the Adjustments columns of the work sheet. Remember, under the periodic inventory system, Merchandise Inventory requires two adjusting entries:

a. The first entry removes or "reverses out" the value of the beginning merchandise inventory.
b. The second adds in the value of the ending merchandise inventory.

Assume that a firm has a beginning merchandise inventory amounting to $277,000. The cost of the ending merchandise inventory is $285,000. The adjustment is described by T accounts as follows:

	Merchandise Inventory				Income Summary		
	+	−					
Bal.	277,000	(a)	277,000	(a)	277,000	(b)	285,000
(b)	285,000						

The same adjustment appears in the work sheet. In this example, the ending inventory amount of $285,000 is given. However, in a practical business situation, the cost of the ending inventory must be determined. Counting the goods on hand is a relatively easy although time-consuming procedure compared with the more difficult task of assigning a dollar amount to those goods in a time of changing prices. We talk mainly about the Merchandise Inventory account because of its relative importance. However, the same principle applies to other assets, such as raw materials for a manufacturer.

We examine the valuation of inventories in two ways: First, some merchandising firms take a physical inventory of merchandise on hand and then attach a value to it. This is known as a **periodic inventory system**, as shown in the example involving the two adjusting entries for Merchandise Inventory. Second, other merchandising firms keep continuous records of inventories by recording all transactions, so that at any given time they know what they should have on hand and the current cost of each item. This is known as a **perpetual inventory system**.

THE IMPORTANCE OF INVENTORY VALUATION

OBJECTIVE 1

Determine the overstatement or understatement of cost of goods sold, gross profit, and net income resulting from a change in the ending merchandise inventory amount.

Merchandise Inventory is the only account that can appear on both major financial statements. On the balance sheet, it appears under Current Assets. On the income statement, it is listed under Cost of Goods Sold. Why is the valuation of merchandise inventory so important? In many firms, merchandise inventory is the current asset with the largest dollar amount. Likewise, as a part of Cost of Goods Sold, it materially affects the net income because the cost of goods sold is the largest deduction from sales. As a result, inventory determination plays an important role in matching costs with revenue for a given period.

Differing costs of ending merchandise inventory have a dramatic effect on net income. We can see this in the partial income statements that follow (Figures 1 through 5).

Now assume that instead of the correct value for ending merchandise inventory of $285,000 (Figure 1), you in error set its value at $235,000, that

FIGURE 1

YEAR 1—CORRECT ENDING INVENTORY STATED				
Net Sales			$905 0 0 0 00	
Cost of Goods Sold:				
Merchandise Inventory (beginning)	$277 0 0 0 00			
Purchases (net)	420 0 0 0 00			
Cost of Goods Available for Sale	$697 0 0 0 00			
Less Merchandise Inventory (ending)	285 0 0 0 00			
Cost of Goods Sold			412 0 0 0 00	
Gross Profit			$493 0 0 0 00	
Operating Expenses			227 0 0 0 00	
Net Income			$266 0 0 0 00	

FIGURE 2

YEAR 1—ENDING INVENTORY UNDERSTATED BY $50,000

Net Sales										$905	0	0	0	00
Cost of Goods Sold:														
Merchandise Inventory (beginning)	$277	0	0	0	00									
Purchases (net)	420	0	0	0	00									
Cost of Goods Available for Sale	$697	0	0	0	00									
Less Merchandise Inventory (ending)	235	0	0	0	00									
Cost of Goods Sold						462	0	0	0	00				
Gross Profit						$443	0	0	0	00				
Operating Expenses						227	0	0	0	00				
Net Income						$216	0	0	0	00				

REMEMBER!

The ending inventory of one year becomes the beginning inventory of the next year.

is, it was understated (too low) by $50,000. The result would be a net income of only $216,000 (Figure 2).

From Figures 1 and 2, you can see that if the ending merchandise inventory is understated (too low) by $50,000, the net income will be understated (too low) by $50,000 because the two are directly related to each other. Similarly, **if the ending merchandise inventory is overstated (too high), net income will be overstated (too high; Figure 3).**

From Figures 1 and 3 you can see that if the *ending* inventory is overstated (too high) by $50,000, net income is overstated (too high) by $50,000.

But there is something else you have to take into account. Because the *ending* inventory of one year becomes the beginning inventory of the following year, the net income of the following year is also affected, but in an opposite direction. Let's continue our examples into year 2. The understated $235,000 *ending* inventory of year 1 (Figure 2) becomes the *beginning* inventory of year 2 (Figure 4 on the following page). Similarly, if the *beginning* inventory (the *ending* inventory of the prior year) is understated by $50,000, the net income will be overstated because the two are inversely related to each other. Similarly, **if the beginning inventory is overstated, the net income will be understated.**

FIGURE 3

YEAR 1—ENDING INVENTORY OVERSTATED BY $50,000

Net Sales										$905	0	0	0	00
Cost of Goods Sold:														
Merchandise Inventory (beginning)	$277	0	0	0	00									
Purchases (net)	420	0	0	0	00									
Cost of Goods Available for Sale	$697	0	0	0	00									
Less Merchandise Inventory (ending)	335	0	0	0	00									
Cost of Goods Sold						362	0	0	0	00				
Gross Profit						$543	0	0	0	00				
Operating Expenses						227	0	0	0	00				
Net Income						$316	0	0	0	00				

FIGURE 4

YEAR 2—UNDERSTATED ENDING INVENTORY ($235,000) OF YEAR 1 BECOMES BEGINNING INVENTORY OF YEAR 2

Net Sales									$973	0	0	0	00
Cost of Goods Sold:													
Merchandise Inventory (beginning)	$235	0	0	0	00								
Purchases (net)	468	0	0	0	00								
Cost of Goods Available for Sale	$703	0	0	0	00								
Less Merchandise Inventory (ending)	200	0	0	0	00								
Cost of Goods Sold						503	0	0	0	00			
Gross Profit						$470	0	0	0	00			
Operating Expenses						225	0	0	0	00			
Net Income						$245	0	0	0	00			

FIGURE 5

YEAR 2—OVERSTATED ENDING INVENTORY ($335,000) OF YEAR 1 BECOMES BEGINNING INVENTORY OF YEAR 2

Net Sales									$973	0	0	0	00
Cost of Goods Sold:													
Merchandise Inventory (beginning)	$335	0	0	0	00								
Purchases (net)	468	0	0	0	00								
Cost of Goods Available for Sale	$803	0	0	0	00								
Less Merchandise Inventory (ending)	200	0	0	0	00								
Cost of Goods Sold						603	0	0	0	00			
Gross Profit						$370	0	0	0	00			
Operating Expenses						225	0	0	0	00			
Net Income						$145	0	0	0	00			

REMEMBER!

An error made in the ending inventory in one period will be carried to the next period in the beginning inventory. This is important because of the direct relationship between ending inventory and net income.

Now look at Figure 5 to see what happens when the overstated $335,000 ending inventory of year 1 becomes the beginning inventory of year 2.

If the *beginning* inventory is overstated by $50,000, the net income will be understated by $50,000, because the two are inversely related to each other. And similarly, **if the *beginning* inventory is understated, the net income will be overstated.**

In other words, over a two-year period, the total net income will be correct, because the overstatement of one year cancels out the understatement of the following year, and vice versa. At the end of a two-year period, the balance sheet is correct because *ending* inventory and *ending* capital are both correctly stated. We can summarize this in the following table:

Year	Ending Inventory of $235,000 ($50,000 understatement)	Ending Inventory of $335,000 ($50,000 overstatement)
	Net Income	Net Income
1	$216,000	$316,000
2	245,000	145,000
Total	$461,000	$461,000

If *ending* inventory is *understated,* net income for the period will be *understated.*

If *ending* inventory is *overstated,* net income for the period will be *overstated.*

If *beginning* inventory is *understated,* net income for the period will be *overstated.*

If *beginning* inventory is *overstated,* net income for the period will be *understated.*

THE NEED FOR AND THE TAKING OF INVENTORIES

Firms that want to satisfy their customers have to maintain large and varied inventories of goods. Efficient purchasing also requires that the company take advantage of quantity discounts and of special buys of seasonal or distressed merchandise.

Care should be taken to count all goods belonging to the firm. Sometimes the goods may not be physically present; this occurs while the goods are being transported. **From the seller's position, merchandise sold FOB destination should be included in the seller's inventory** because the seller is paying the freight charges. **From the buyer's position, merchandise purchased FOB shipping point should be included in the buyer's inventory** because the buyer is paying the freight charges. Title transfer or ownership of the goods depends on who has paid the freight.

Inventory Control

A small business such as a bicycle shop or an antique store may keep track of its inventories manually. However, to have up-to-date counts of inventory items on hand, most firms use computers. Software programs that record transactions and produce inventory reports are readily available. These reports include a description of each item in stock, the number of units on hand, the cost of each unit, and the number of units sold, as well as the number of units to be reordered. Also, management can use inventory reports to determine and analyze buying and selling trends.

Maintaining accurate and up-to-the-minute inventory counts is critical to the success of any business, and hand-held scanners make that a reality.

METHODS OF ASSIGNING COSTS TO ENDING INVENTORY

OBJECTIVE 2

Determine unit cost, the value of the ending inventory, and the cost of goods sold by the following methods:
(a) specific identification;
(b) weighted-average-cost;
(c) first-in, first-out; and
(d) last-in, first-out.

After the items have been described and counted, the unit costs are inserted on the inventory sheet and the total costs are extended. How do you determine unit cost? You might think that this is rather elementary. Indeed, it would be *if* all the purchases of a given article had been made at the same price per unit. In that case, to determine the total unit cost, you would need only to look up one invoice, check the unit price, then multiply it by the number of items present. But nothing is ever that simple. A firm usually buys a number of batches of a given item during the year, and the unit costs can vary. A bottle of shampoo that cost $2.62 in January might cost $2.76 in October. Which unit cost should you assign to the goods on hand?

There are four main methods of assigning costs to goods in the ending inventory: (1) specific identification; (2) weighted-average-cost; (3) first-in, first-out; and (4) last-in, first-out.

Example of Inventory Evaluation Rainier Plumbing Supply keeps an inventory of Deco single-handle kitchen faucets (#810) purchased from Dana Manufacturing Company. This year, Rainier Plumbing sells eighty of these faucets and has twenty-six remaining in stock. The company started the year with twenty-two in stock and bought more as the year went on, as follows:

Jan. 1	Beginning inventory	22 units @ $57 each = $1,254
Mar. 16	Purchase	30 units @ $62 each = 1,860
July 29	Purchase	36 units @ $65 each = 2,340
Nov. 18	Purchase	18 units @ $68 each = 1,224
	Total available	106 units $6,678

Now let's compute the cost of goods sold (eighty faucets) and the value of the ending inventory (twenty-six faucets) using the four different methods.

Specific Identification Method

When a firm sells big-ticket items (cars, appliances, furniture, jewelry), the cost is low to keep track of the purchase price of each individual article and determine the exact cost of the goods sold. Such a firm uses the **specific identification method** of inventory control. Because faucets have imprinted manufactured date codes, Rainier Plumbing Supply can identify each faucet with a specific purchase invoice listing the unit cost. When Rainier Plumbing Supply takes inventory at the end of the year, it finds that there are twenty-six faucets left in stock; four of these were bought in March, ten were bought in July, and twelve were bought in November. Costs are assigned to the ending inventory as follows:

Mar. 16	Purchase	4 units @ $62 each = $ 248
July 29	Purchase	10 units @ $65 each = 650
Nov. 18	Purchase	12 units @ $68 each = 816
	Total	26 units $1,714

Rainier Plumbing Supply determines the cost of goods sold by subtracting the value of the ending inventory from the total cost of goods available for sale:

Total kitchen faucets available (106 units)	$6,678
Less ending inventory (26 units)	1,714
Cost of goods sold (80 units)	$4,964

Weighted-Average-Cost Method

An alternative to keeping track of the cost of each item purchased is to use the **weighted-average-cost method** to find the cost per unit of all like articles available for sale during the period. First, Rainier Plumbing Supply finds the total cost of the faucets it had on hand during the year by multiplying the number of units by their respective purchase costs.

Jan. 1	Beginning inventory	22 units @ $57 each = $1,254
Mar. 16	Purchase	30 units @ $62 each = 1,860
July 29	Purchase	36 units @ $65 each = 2,340
Nov. 18	Purchase	18 units @ $68 each = 1,224
	Total available	106 units $6,678

Accountants calculate the value of the ending inventory. These amounts are needed not only to keep track of changing inventory but also to compute the cost of goods sold on the income statement.

Next Rainier Plumbing Supply finds the average cost per faucet.

Average Cost per Unit = Total Cost ÷ Total Units

Average Cost per Unit = $6,678 ÷ 106 units = $63 per unit

Value of Ending Inventory = Number of Units × Average Cost per Unit

Value of Ending Inventory = 26 × $63 = $1,638

According to this method, the beginning inventory is *weighted* (that is, multiplied by the number of units it comprises). Each purchase thereafter is weighted by the number of units involved in that purchase. In other words, the more you buy at a time, the more that purchase influences the average cost.

Total kitchen faucets available (106 units)	$6,678
Less ending inventory (26 units)	1,638
Cost of goods sold (80 units)	$5,040

First-In, First-Out (FIFO) Method

REMEMBER!

First-in, first-out refers to the assumed flow of costs. The ending inventory is assumed to consist of those items purchased most recently.

The **first-in, first-out (FIFO) method** is based on the flow-of-cost assumption that costs of merchandise sold should be charged against revenue in the order in which the costs were incurred. To determine the cost of goods sold, the accountant records the oldest (first) cost first, then the next-oldest cost, and so on. First-in, first-out is a logical way for a firm to rotate its stock of merchandise. Think of a grocery store selling milk. Because milk will sour, the oldest milk is moved up to the front of the shelf. As a result, the ending inventory consists of the freshest milk.

Again, let's return to Rainier Plumbing Supply's kitchen faucets. To repeat, 106 faucets were available for sale during the year:

Jan. 1	Beginning inventory	22 units @ $57 each = $1,254
Mar. 16	Purchase	30 units @ $62 each = 1,860
July 29	Purchase	36 units @ $65 each = 2,340
Nov. 18	Purchase	18 units @ $68 each = 1,224
	Total available	106 units $6,678

Rainier Plumbing Supply sold eighty units. The accountant calculates the total cost of the faucets sold on a first-in, first-out (FIFO) basis, as follows:

Jan. 1	Beginning inventory	22 units @ $57 each = $1,254
Mar. 16	Purchase	30 units @ $62 each = 1,860
July 29	Purchase	28 units @ $65 each = 1,820
	Total	80 units $4,934

Rainier Plumbing Supply has the twenty-six newest or most recently purchased units on hand in the ending inventory. The accountant records the ending inventory at the most recent costs, like this:

Nov. 18	Purchase	18 units @ $68 each = $1,224
July 29	Purchase	8 units @ $65 each = 520
	Total	26 units $1,744

The accountant now verifies the total cost of the eighty units sold:

Cost of Goods Sold = Total Available − Ending Inventory

$4,934 = $6,678 − $1,744

Last-In, First-Out (LIFO) Method

The **last-in, first-out (LIFO) method** is based on the flow-of-cost assumption that the most recently purchased articles are sold first and the articles remaining in the ending inventory are the oldest items. As an example, think of a coal yard selling coal. When the coal yard buys coal from its supplier, the new coal is added to the top of the pile. When the coal yard sells coal to its customer, coal is taken off the top of the pile. Consequently, the ending inventory consists of those first few tons at the bottom of the pile. And, unless the pile is exhausted, they will never be sold.

Meanwhile, back at Rainier Plumbing Supply, the firm sold eighty units. The accountant calculates the cost of the faucets sold on a last-in, first-out (LIFO) basis:

Nov. 18	Purchase	18 units @ $68 each = $1,224
July 29	Purchase	36 units @ $65 each = 2,340
Mar. 16	Purchase	26 units @ $62 each = 1,612
	Total	80 units $5,176

Rainier Plumbing Supply has the twenty-six oldest units (or the units at the bottom of the pile) on hand in the ending inventory. The accountant records the ending inventory at the earliest costs, like this:

Jan. 1	Beginning inventory	22 units @ $57 each = $1,254
Mar. 16	Purchase	4 units @ $62 each = 248
	Total	26 units $1,502

The accountant now verifies the total cost of the eighty units sold:

Cost of Goods Sold = Total Available − Ending Inventory

　　　$5,176　　=　　$6,678　　−　　$1,502

Comparison of Methods

If prices don't change very much, all inventory methods give just about the same results. However, in a dynamic market where prices are constantly rising and falling, each method may yield different amounts. Here is a comparison of the results of the sale of the faucets, using the four methods we described.

Method	Cost of Goods Sold (80 Units)	Ending Inventory (26 Units)
Specific identification	$4,964	$1,714
Weighted-average-cost	5,040	1,638
First-in, first-out	4,934	1,744
Last-in, first-out	5,176	1,502

Assume that Rainier Plumbing Supply sells the eighty kitchen faucets for $110 apiece, for a total of $8,800. The four methods yield the following gross profits:

	Specific Identification	Weighted-Average-Cost	First-In, First-Out	Last-In, First-Out
Sales	$8,800	$8,800	$8,800	$8,800
Cost of goods sold	4,964	5,040	4,934	5,176
Gross profit	$3,836	$3,760	$3,866	$3,624

The effects of the methods are as follows:

1. Specific identification matches costs exactly with revenues.
2. Weighted-average-cost is a compromise between LIFO and FIFO, both for the amount of the ending inventory and for the cost of goods sold.
3. FIFO provides the most realistic amount for ending merchandise inventory in the Current Assets section of the balance sheet. The ending inventory is valued at the most recent costs, referred to as replacement cost.
4. LIFO provides the most realistic amount for the Cost of Goods Sold section of the income statement, because the items that have been sold will have to be replaced at the most recent costs.

Tax Effect of LIFO

In a period of rising prices, LIFO yields the lowest gross profit and hence the lowest income taxes because the most recent (higher) costs are assigned to the cost of goods sold (expense). For the past forty years, prices in most industries have just kept going up, providing a built-in income tax advantage for users of LIFO. In effect, a business using LIFO is postponing paying income taxes. Since the money is not paid to the government, the business has the use of the money. Consequently, the money saved can be used to finance more inventory or to pay off interest-bearing debts. When prices fall, companies using LIFO are at a disadvantage from the standpoint of income taxes.

Bear in mind that the cost figure determined by the different methods may have nothing to do with the physical flow of the goods. By physical flow, we mean the order in which specific items are taken out of inventory and sold.

The **consistency principle** is a fundamental principle of accounting. We have seen that a firm can increase or decrease its gross profit, and likewise its net income and income taxes, by changing the flow-of-cost assumption from one method to another—from FIFO to LIFO, for example. Although a firm may change its method of assigning inventory costs, it may not change back and forth repeatedly. Consistency in the method of determining cost of goods sold and the related cost of the ending inventory is necessary to conform with generally accepted accounting principles. A business must disclose any change it makes in its method of accounting for inventories for book purposes. For income tax purposes, a business must consistently use the same method of accounting for inventories. Only with IRS approval can a company change its accounting method for inventories.

> **REMEMBER!**
>
> The cost figure determined by the different methods may have nothing to do with the physical flow of goods.

LOWER-OF-COST-OR-MARKET RULE

All the methods for determining the cost of ending inventory are based on cost per unit. In our examples, prices were generally rising. However, sometimes the replacement cost of items in stock is *less* than the original market cost. The word *market* refers to the current price charged in the market. It is the price at which, *at the time of taking the inventory*, the items could be bought through the usual channels and in the usual quantities. The current prices may be quoted in catalogs or reflect contract quotations.

The **lower-of-cost-or-market (LCM) rule** says that, under certain conditions, when the replacement or market cost is lower than the original cost, the inventory should be valued at the lower cost to comply with the accounting concept of conservatism. For example, the inventory of a store includes twenty leather vests originally purchased for $22 each (total, $440). At the time the inventory is being taken, the same type of leather vest may be purchased (replaced) for $18 each (total, $360). Under the lower-of-cost-or-market rule, the inventory is valued at $360. In this example, the original cost of $22 may have been determined by the specific identification method, the weighted-average-cost method, or the FIFO method. Under the tax law, the lower-of-cost-or-market rule may *not* be used when the original cost is determined by the LIFO method because this method already offers tax advantages.

PERPETUAL INVENTORIES

OBJECTIVE 3

Journalize transactions relating to perpetual inventories.

Firms that sell a limited variety of products of relatively high value, such as equipment or appliance dealers, maintain records in real time of their inventories on hand. They *record additions to or deductions from their inventories directly in Merchandise Inventory accounts.* This is known as the perpetual inventory system because the firms perpetually (or continually) *know the amount* of goods on hand. With computers, many firms have adopted the perpetual inventory system. This system involves the following accounts:

Merchandise Inventory		Cost of Goods Sold		Sales	
+	−	+	−	−	+
Record the purchase of merchandise at cost.	Record the sale of merchandise at cost.	Record the sale of merchandise at cost.			Record the sale of merchandise at selling price.

FYI

Companies also have the option of eliminating the Purchases Discounts account and making the credit to the Merchandise Inventory account.

The adjusting entries at the end of the year are the only entries firms using the periodic inventory system make in Merchandise Inventory. But firms using the perpetual inventory system make entries directly in the Merchandise Inventory account throughout the year. The perpetual inventory system enables the firm to do away with the Purchases, Purchases Discounts, and Purchases Returns and Allowances accounts.

To illustrate the perpetual inventory system, let's look at a series of entries in general journal form, with transactions recorded at the gross amount.

Feb. 14 Bought merchandise on account from Hong, Inc.; 2/10, n/30; $4,800.

REMEMBER!

Under the perpetual inventory system, when goods are bought for resale, Merchandise Inventory is debited instead of Purchases. Similarly, when the goods are sold, Merchandise Inventory is credited for the amount of their cost.

	DATE		DESCRIPTION	POST. REF.	DEBIT	CREDIT	
1	20–						1
2	Feb.	14	Merchandise Inventory		4 8 0 0 00		2
3			Accounts Payable, Hong, Inc.			4 8 0 0 00	3
4			Terms 2/10, n/30.				4
5							5

	Merchandise Inventory			Accounts Payable	
	+	−		−	+
Feb. 14	4,800				Feb. 14	4,800

Feb.   24   Paid the invoice within the discount period.

	DATE		DESCRIPTION	POST. REF.	DEBIT	CREDIT	
1	20–						1
2	Feb.	24	Accounts Payable, Hong, Inc.		4 8 0 0 00		2
3			Cash			4 7 0 4 00	3
4			Merchandise Inventory			9 6 00	4
5			Paid invoice within discount				5
6			period.				6

Accounts Payable				Cash				Merchandise Inventory			
−		+		+		−		+		−	
Feb. 24	4,800	Feb. 14	4,800			Feb. 24	4,704	Feb. 14	4,800	Feb. 24	96

Mar.   5   Sold the merchandise on account to S. P. Hahn for $9,600. (The cost of the merchandise is $4,704. Two entries are required to record a sale under the perpetual inventory system.)

	DATE		DESCRIPTION	POST. REF.	DEBIT	CREDIT	
1	20–						1
2	Mar.	5	Accts. Receivable, S. P. Hahn		9 6 0 0 00		2
3			Sales			9 6 0 0 00	3
4			Sold merchandise on acct.				4
5							5
6		5	Cost of Goods Sold		4 7 0 4 00		6
7			Merchandise Inventory			4 7 0 4 00	7
8			Relating to $9,600 sale to				8
9			S. P. Hahn.				9

Accounts Receivable				Sales		
+		−		−	+	
Mar. 5	9,600				Mar. 5	9,600

Cost of Goods Sold				Merchandise Inventory		
+		−		+		−
Mar. 5	4,704			Bal.	4,704	Mar. 5	4,704

For a firm using the perpetual inventory system, you can compare the Cost of Goods Sold account to an expense account: Both are increased by debits, and both are closed at the end of the year.

Apr. 2 S. P. Hahn returned merchandise for credit having a sale price of $3,200 and a cost of $1,568.

Under the perpetual inventory system, two entries are required for each sale—one for the sale and one for the cost.

	DATE		DESCRIPTION	POST. REF.	DEBIT	CREDIT	
1	20–						1
2	Apr.	2	Sales Returns and Allowances		3 2 0 0 00		2
3			Accts. Receivable, S. P. Hahn			3 2 0 0 00	3
4			Issued credit memo for				4
5			the return of merchandise.				5
6							6
7		2	Merchandise Inventory		1 5 6 8 00		7
8			Cost of Goods Sold			1 5 6 8 00	8
9			Merchandise returned				9
10			by S. P. Hahn.				10
11							11
12							12
13							13

	Accounts Receivable				**Sales Returns and Allowances**		
	+	–			+	–	
Bal.	9,600	Apr. 2	3,200	Apr. 2	3,200		

	Cost of Goods Sold				**Merchandise Inventory**		
	+	–			+	–	
Bal.	4,704	Apr. 2	1,568	Bal.	4,704	Mar. 5	4,704
				Apr. 2	1,568		

Using a scanner to check out merchandise allows a store to eliminate the tedious (and often error-ridden) process of a clerk's entering code numbers. Scanners also allow inventory tracking by maintaining a perpetual or up-to-the-moment count of goods sold and goods remaining.

Firms may take physical inventories both during and at the end of the year to verify the book value of the perpetual inventory. If there is a difference between the book value and the physical count, an adjustment is made to the Merchandise Inventory account. In this adjustment, Cost of Goods Sold is used as the offsetting account. Suppose the book value amount for Merchandise Inventory is $52,756 and the physical count shows $51,980 of merchandise on hand on June 30. The ending inventory is short by $776 ($52,756 − $51,980). The adjusting entry looks like this:

	DATE		DESCRIPTION	POST. REF.	DEBIT	CREDIT	
1	20–		Adjusting Entry				1
2	June	30	Cost of Goods Sold		7 7 6 00		2
3			Merchandise Inventory			7 7 6 00	3
4							4

Here is a comparison of the periodic and perpetual inventory systems.

Comparison: Periodic Versus Perpetual Inventory Systems		
Transaction	**Periodic Inventory System**	**Perpetual Inventory System**

Purchased merchandise from supplier on account, $4,800.	Purchases 4,800
	    Accounts Payable,
	    Hong, Inc. 4,800
		Merchandise Inventory 4,800
		    Accounts Payable,
		    Hong, Inc. 4,800

Paid the invoice within the discount period.	Accounts Payable,
	 Hong, Inc. 4,800
	    Cash 4,704
	    Purchases Discounts 96
		Accounts Payable,
		 Hong, Inc. 4,800
		    Cash 4,704
		    Merchandise Inventory 96

Returned merchandise to supplier, $1,200.	Accounts Payable,
	 Hong, Inc. 1,200
	    Purchases Returns and
	    Allowances 1,200
		Accounts Payable,
		 Hong, Inc. 1,200
		    Merchandise Inventory 1,200

Sold merchandise to customer on account, $9,600, having a cost of $4,704.	Accounts Receivable,
	 S. P. Hahn 9,600
	    Sales 9,600
		Accounts Receivable,
		 S. P. Hahn 9,600
		    Sales 9,600
		
		 Cost of Goods Sold 4,704
		    Merchandise Inventory 4,704

Customer returned merchandise, $3,200, having a cost of $1,568.	Sales Returns and
	 Allowances 3,200
	    Accounts Receivable,
	    S. P. Hahn 3,200
		Sales Returns and
		 Allowances 3,200
		    Accounts Receivable,
		    S. P. Hahn 3,200
		
		 Merchandise Inventory 1,568
		    Cost of Goods Sold 1,568

Adjusting entries at end of fiscal period:
 Beginning merchandise inventory, $84,380.
 Ending merchandise inventory, $51,980.
 Book record of merchandise inventory (perpetual), $52,756.
	Income Summary 84,380
	    Merchandise
	    Inventory 84,380
	
	 Merchandise Inventory 51,980
	    Income Summary 51,980
		Cost of Goods Sold 776
		    Merchandise Inventory 776
		      Book inventory $52,756
		      Physical count 51,980
		
		     Decrease in
		     Merchandise
		     Inventory $ 776

Recognize that the actual cost of the merchandise on hand is $51,980, whereas, according to the perpetual inventory records, there should be merchandise costing $52,756 on hand. What has happened to the $776 difference? Could it be due to inaccuracies in the inventory records, errors in the counting of goods, shoplifting, or employee theft? At any rate, the $776 loss will be noted or absorbed by increasing the Cost of Goods Sold account, and Merchandise Inventory will wind up with the correct inventory amount, $51,980.

Perpetual Inventory Record

When a firm uses the perpetual inventory system, Merchandise Inventory is a controlling account. The firm maintains an individual record (either manually or on the computer) for each kind of product in the subsidiary ledger,

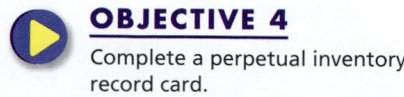

OBJECTIVE 4

Complete a perpetual inventory record card.

INVENTORY RECORD CARD

ITEM __Kitchen Sinks, Brigg No. 614__   LOCATION __Warehouse, Sink Section__

MAXIMUM __40__   MINIMUM __8__   METHOD __LIFO__

DATE	PURCHASED AT COST			SALES			COST OF GOODS SOLD			INVENTORY AT COST		
	UNITS	COST	TOTAL	UNITS	PRICE	TOTAL	UNITS	COST	TOTAL	UNITS	COST	TOTAL
1/2	Bal.									14	$72	$1,008
2/6				4	$120	$480	4	$72	$288	10	72	720
2/22	30	$75	$2,250							10	72	720
										30	75	2,250
3/14				6	120	720	6	75	450	10	72	720
										24	75	1,800
3/29				8	120	960	8	75	600	10	72	720
										16	75	1,200
Total	30		$2,250	18		$2,160	18		$1,338			

FIGURE 6

recording the number of units received as "units received" and the number of units sold as "units sold." The firm records the remaining balance after each receipt or sale. Companies may keep perpetual inventories by any of the four methods. Assume that Rainier Plumbing Supply maintains a perpetual inventory on kitchen sinks on a LIFO basis, as shown in Figure 6.

The ending balance of twenty-six units amounts to $1,920 ($720 + $1,200). Eighteen sinks were sold at $120 each, for total sales of $2,160, and gross profit is $822.

Sales	$2,160
Less Cost of Goods Sold	1,338
Gross Profit	$ 822

FYI

Further discussion of moving averages is reserved for more advanced accounting texts.

The weighted-average-cost flow can be used with a perpetual inventory system. Rather than computing the average price for each inventory item at the end of a period, the firm calculates a new average each time a purchase is made. This average method is called a **moving average**. When goods are sold, their cost is determined by multiplying the number of units sold by the moving-average cost existing at that time.

Perpetual Inventory Records in Electronic Accounting Systems

Computers—which can retrieve an item of stored information in a fraction of a second—have enabled business firms to maintain perpetual inventories even when a wide variety of products and a large volume of transactions are involved. Think of the benefits a computer terminal would provide for a car parts store connected to its regional distribution center.

Each item of stock in the inventory is assigned a code number. Whenever the amount of an item changes, information concerning the change is fed into the computer by an online data entry terminal. The computer performs the arithmetic operations and determines the new balance in accordance with the inventory method in use: LIFO, FIFO, or moving-average. Thus the firm can determine the current status of any given item instantaneously. Whenever desired, the computer can list the balances of all the items in the inventory, in terms of both units and dollars.

As another illustration, in many department stores the cash registers (terminals) are linked directly to a computer center. When a sale is made, the salesperson punches in the item number, the quantity, and the price of the item. In other stores, clerks use a wand or gun to scan bar codes on individual tickets. And in supermarkets across the country, cashiers pass purchased items over scanners at the checkout register. With the information about the sale stored in the computer, management may obtain inventory quantities, costs, and total sales at any time as well as the program's prompting reordering of items that have reached a critical level.

Our discussion of perpetual inventories has been geared to merchandising firms. However, manufacturing concerns use perpetual inventories almost exclusively. A lumber mill, for example, uses the balances of daily inventories as a basis for deciding which sizes of lumber to cut: $2'' \times 4'' \times 8'$, $1'' \times 3'' \times 6'$, and so on.

CHAPTER REVIEW

Online Study Center
ACE the test!

Review of Performance Objectives

1. Determine the overstatement or understatement of cost of goods sold, gross profit, and net income resulting from a change in the ending merchandise inventory amount.

   The amounts of the beginning and ending merchandise inventories appear in the Cost of Goods Sold section of the income statement.

If the Ending Inventory Is	Net Income Will Be
Understated	Understated
Overstated	Overstated

If the Beginning Inventory Is	Net Income Will Be
Understated	Overstated
Overstated	Understated

2. Determine unit cost, the value of the ending inventory, and the cost of goods sold by the following methods: (a) specific identification; (b) weighted-average-cost; (c) first-in, first-out; and (d) last-in, first-out.

   (a) Specific identification: Used for high-value items when a firm can identify each item on hand with its respective price.
   (b) Weighted-average-cost: Number of Units of Each Purchase × Unit Price = Cost of Each Purchase. Cost of Beginning Inventory + Costs of All Purchases = Total Cost. Total Cost ÷ Total Units = Weighted-Average Cost per Unit.

(c) First-in, first-out (FIFO): Costs are charged against revenue in the order in which they were incurred. This method produces the most realistic amount for the Current Assets section of the balance sheet.

(d) Last-in, first-out (LIFO): Costs that are charged against revenue are the most recent costs. This method produces the most realistic amount for the Cost of Goods Sold section of the income statement.

In an era of rising prices, the LIFO method yields the lowest net income. Firms must be consistent in their use of inventory methods.

3. Journalize transactions relating to perpetual inventories.

Perpetual inventories are book records of what a firm has in stock. The Merchandise Inventory account is a controlling account. Merchandise Inventory is debited when goods are bought and credited when goods are sold. Cost of Goods Sold is an expense account.

4. Complete a perpetual inventory record card.

The perpetual inventory record card contains columns for the following information: date of purchase, number of units purchased, cost per unit purchased, total cost of purchase, number of units sold, selling price per unit of goods sold, total selling price of units sold, number of units sold, cost per unit sold, total cost of goods sold, number of units in ending inventory, cost per unit of goods in ending inventory, and total cost of goods in ending inventory.

Glossary

Consistency principle An accounting principle that requires that a particular accounting procedure, once adopted, not be changed from one fiscal period to another. (638)

First-in, first-out (FIFO) method A procedure for assigning costs to merchandise sold based on the flow-of-cost assumption that units are sold in the order in which they were acquired. Unsold units on hand at date of inventory are assumed to be valued at the most recent costs. (635)

Last-in, first-out (LIFO) method A procedure for assigning costs to merchandise sold based on the flow-of-cost assumption that units sold are recorded at the costs of the most recently acquired units. Unsold units on hand at date of inventory are assumed to be valued at the earliest costs. (636)

Lower-of-cost-or-market (LCM) rule In cases where there is a difference between the original price and the market price of goods, using the lower price for determining the value of the ending inventory. The term *market price* means current replacement price. (638)

Moving average A modification of the weighted-average-cost method, used for computing the average cost of a perpetual inventory. The firm determines the moving-average unit price each time it buys more units. (643)

Periodic inventory system Determining the amount of goods on hand by periodically taking a physical count and then attaching a value to it. (630)

Perpetual inventory system A book record of the ending inventory showing the unit costs of the items received and the items sold. This gives the firm a running balance of the actual units on hand and the historical cost of each item. (630)

Specific identification method Counting the actual cost of each individual item in the ending inventory. (634)

Weighted-average-cost method A procedure for determining the cost of the ending inventory by multiplying the weighted-average cost per unit by the number of remaining units. (635)

QUESTIONS, EXERCISES, AND CASES

Discussion Questions

1. Explain the consistency principle. How can the consistency principle relate to inventory costing?

2. In periods of steadily rising prices, which inventory method (weighted-average-cost, FIFO, or LIFO) will give (a) the highest net income? (b) the lowest net income?

3. If the ending merchandise inventory of Year 1 is mistakenly understated by $3,000, what is the effect on the following:
   a. Year 1's net income?
   b. Year 1's balance sheet?
   c. Year 2's net income?

4. State an advantage and a disadvantage of LIFO.

5. What is meant by the specific identification method of pricing inventory? Give an example of a situation in which this method would be suitable.

6. Because of an error, goods costing $2,700 were omitted from the ending inventory. What effect does this omission have on the company's gross profit?

7. When a perpetual inventory system is in use, what are the necessary journal entries for buying merchandise on account and selling merchandise on account?

8. If the physical inventory count is less than the balance in the perpetual inventory record, what should be done?

Exercises

P.O. 1

Determine the effect of an error in ending inventory.

Exercise 17-1 An abbreviated income statement for Morgan Company for this fiscal year is as follows:

Net Sales			$155 0 0 0 00
Cost of Goods Sold:			
Merchandise Inventory, January 1	$132 0 0 0 00		
Purchases, net	25 0 0 0 00		
Cost of Goods Available for Sale	$157 0 0 0 00		
Less Merchandise Inventory, Dec. 31	37 0 0 0 00		
Cost of Goods Sold			120 0 0 0 00
Gross Profit			$ 35 0 0 0 00
Operating Expenses			18 0 0 0 00
Net Income			$ 17 0 0 0 00

An accountant discovers that the ending inventory is overstated by $5,700. What effect does this have on cost of goods sold, gross profit, and net income in this fiscal year?

P.O. 1

Correct errors on comparative income statements.

Exercise 17-2 Condensed income statements for Sadler Company for two years are presented here.

		2007		2006	
Net Sales			$91 0 0 0 00		$98 0 0 0 00
Cost of Goods Sold:					
Merchandise Inventory (beginning)	$12 0 0 0 00			$15 0 0 0 00	
Purchases (net)	47 0 0 0 00			49 0 0 0 00	
Cost of Goods Available for Sale	$59 0 0 0 00			$64 0 0 0 00	
Less Merchandise Inventory (ending)	14 0 0 0 00			12 0 0 0 00	
Cost of Goods Sold		45 0 0 0 00			52 0 0 0 00
Gross Profit		$46 0 0 0 00			$46 0 0 0 00
Operating Expenses		23 0 0 0 00			21 0 0 0 00
Net Income		$23 0 0 0 00			$25 0 0 0 00

After the end of 2007, it was discovered that an error had been made in 2006. Ending inventory in 2006 should have been $11,000 instead of $12,000. Determine the corrected net income for 2006 and 2007.

a. Did the error understate or overstate cost of goods sold for 2006?
b. Did the error understate or overstate net income for 2006?
c. What is the amount of total net income for the two-year period with the error ($12,000) and corrected ($11,000)?

P.O. 1

Calculate the value of ending inventory.

Exercise 17-3 The records of Krug Company show the following data as of January 31, the end of the fiscal year. Determine the value of the ending merchandise inventory.

a. Cost of goods on hand, based on physical count, $203,250.
b. Cost of defective goods (to be thrown away) included in **a**, $430.
c. Cost of goods shipped out FOB destination on January 30, with an expected delivery date of approximately four days, $2,983; not included in **a**.
d. Goods purchased January 28, FOB shipping point, delivered to the transportation company on January 31, $1,259; not included in **a**.
e. Cost of goods sold to a customer on January 30, paid for in full and awaiting shipping instructions, $1,761; not included in **a**.

P.O. 2b,c,d

Compute the value of ending inventory and cost of goods sold using three methods.

Exercise 17-4 McGower's Garden Shop maintains an inventory of mower blades. Purchases of the blades during the year are as shown.

Jan.   1   Inventory of 30 units @ $215 each.
Mar.   8   Purchased 20 units @ $220 each.
May   15   Purchased 15 units @ $225 each.
      30   Purchased 20 units @ $228 each.

The ending inventory, by physical count, is 52 units. Determine the value of the ending inventory and the cost of goods sold by the following methods: weighted-average-cost; first-in, first-out; last-in, first-out. (Round all computations to two decimal places.)

P.O. 2b,c,d

Calculate the cost of ending inventory using three methods.

Exercise 17-5 Labonte Office Supplies has a July beginning inventory of model 77 desk lamps consisting of 188 units at $84.50 each. Purchases and sales during July are as follows:

July   5   Sold 15 units.
      12   Purchased 12 units @ $86 each.

July   14   Sold 18 units.
25   Purchased 25 units @ $88 each.
30   Sold 19 units.

Calculate the cost of the ending inventory under each of the following methods: weighted-average-cost; first-in, first-out; last-in, first-out. (Round all computations to two decimal places.)

P.O. 2b,c,d

Calculate the gross profit using three methods.

Exercise 17-6 If the mower blades in Exercise 17-4 were sold during the year for $265 each, determine the gross profit using the weighted-average-cost; first-in, first-out; and last-in, first-out methods.

P.O. 3

Journalize adjusting entries under periodic and perpetual inventory methods.

Exercise 17-7 Rodgers Company's fiscal year is from January 1 through December 31. The following amounts are available:

Jan.   1   Inventory, $182,500 (by physical count).
Dec.   31   Inventory, $200,300 (by physical count).

a. Record the adjusting entries, assuming that the company uses the periodic inventory system.
b. Record the adjusting entry, assuming that the company uses the perpetual inventory system and that the book balance of the ending inventory is $201,220.

P.O. 4

Calculate the cost of goods sold and the inventory value, using FIFO.

Exercise 17-8 Envico Systems keeps perpetual inventories on energy-efficient stoves, using the first-in, first-out method. Determine the cost of goods sold in each sale and the inventory balance after each sale for the following purchases and sales of energy-efficient stoves:

Jan.   1   Inventory of 40 units @ $415 each.
25   Sold 14 units.
Mar.   4   Purchased 20 units @ $420 each.
15   Sold 12 units.
June   5   Sold 12 units.
22   Purchased 20 units @ $422 each.

internet
LINKS TO ACCOUNTING

Let's go back now and answer the questions we asked at the beginning of this chapter about Target Corporation's merchandise inventory. Its 2005 annual report can be found at **http://www.target.com.** Click on Investors at the bottom of the screen and then on Annual Reports. Note that Target's 2005 fiscal year-end was January 28, 2006.

1. What was Target Corporation's 2005 ending merchandise inventory valuation on its consolidated statements of financial position?
2. What method does Target use to account for inventory? (Hint: Look in the Notes to Consolidated Financial Statements beginning on page 28.) Why do you think it uses this method?
3. How much was Target Corporation's cost of sales for the 2005 fiscal year?

CONSIDER AND COMMUNICATE

A person you work for in the accounting department is confused about FIFO and LIFO as methods of charging cost of goods sold against revenue. Explain, for each method, which units are used to calculate the cost of the ending inventory and which financial statement is emphasized. Also indicate which method results in a lower net income (assuming rising cost per unit).

CRITICAL THINKING

Your supervisor has asked you to evaluate the following situation and conditions: Lara's Music Store has taken inventory of the flutes, saxophones, and other reed instruments, as well as miscellaneous musical items that it sells retail. As the store's accountant, you gave your assistant instructions about taking the inventory and asked that unusual items be flagged for your review. Your assistant flagged the following items that need your review to determine if the item was correctly handled on the year-end inventory:

a. Last year's Model CX-2, classical flute, is included in inventory at a cost of $357. (You happen to know that this outdated model can be purchased for $150, now that the new model is out.)
b. A purchase of 2 Native American flutes at $350 each was sent by the supplier on 12/29, FOB destination. The shipment had not arrived and was not included in inventory.
c. A purchase of 2 oboes at $450 each was sent by the supplier on 12/30, FOB shipping point. The shipment had not arrived and was not included in inventory.
d. You have received a credit memo for a damaged piccolo, cost $248, from a supplier. The supplier issued the notice based on your promise to ship the damaged unit back after the end of the year. The item is still in the warehouse, and the cost of $248 is included in the inventory.
e. A customer has paid $740 in full for a custom-made Native American flute that cost $540. The customer requested that you deliver it at the end of the first week of the new year. The value of the special flute is included in the inventory, as no one remembered to put a "sold" tag on it.
f. For the holidays, the shop owner has taken home a one-of-a-kind tenor saxophone. Retail value is $2,650; cost, $2,250. This item was not counted in inventory.
g. According to the company's layaway policy, a sale is not recorded until the merchandise is paid for in full, and then delivery is made. A customer has paid 25 percent of the $960 price of a French horn. The horn is set aside because the customer has put money down on it, and the $810 cost is not included in the inventory.

Instructions

1. What is the correct treatment for each item? Should you include it in inventory or exclude it? Why?
2. Was the item handled correctly by your assistant? If it was not correctly handled, what must be done to correct the inventory? Should you increase inventory (if so, by what amount) or decrease inventory (if so, by what amount)?

A QUESTION OF ETHICS

A large computer retailer has taken year-end inventory and has valued 80 Dellgate X computers at $1,100 each, or $88,000—the original cost of the Dellgate Xs. Current technologies have allowed the supplier to reduce the cost of the Dellgate X to $900 each, although the computer store has not purchased any Dellgate Xs at this price. Is the owner doing anything unethical by valuing the 80 Dellgate Xs at the original cost of $88,000?

PROBLEM SET A

For additional help, see the demonstration problem at the beginning of each chapter in your Working Papers.

P.O. 2b,c,d

Problem 17-1A Pardel Chemical's inventory of ND301 on January 1 was 7,500 gallons, costing $0.54 per gallon (periodic inventory). In addition to this beginning inventory, purchases during the next six months were as follows:

Date	Quantity (Gallons)	Cost per Gallon	Total Cost
Jan. 1 Inventory	7,500	$0.54	$4,050
26	9,000	0.545	4,905
Feb. 4	11,000	0.55	6,050
21	8,000	0.55	4,400
Mar. 7	10,000	0.555	5,550
24	9,000	0.55	4,950
Apr. 19	8,000	0.55	4,400
May 31	7,000	0.55	3,850
June 15	5,000	0.57	2,850

Pardel Chemical's inventory on June 30 was 12,000 gallons. During this six-month period, the firm sold ND301 at $0.70 per gallon. Assume that no liquid was lost through evaporation or leakage.

Check Figure

Ending inventory under FIFO, $6,700

Instructions

1. Find the cost of the ending inventory by the following methods:

   a. Weighted-average-cost (Round to three decimal places.)
   b. First-in, first-out
   c. Last-in, first-out

2. Determine the cost of goods sold according to the three methods of costing inventory.
3. Determine the amount of the gross profit according to the three methods of costing inventory.

P.O. 2b,c,d

Problem 17-2A Manzo Stereo uses the periodic inventory system. Data for its inventories on January 1, the beginning of the fiscal year, purchases during the year, and the inventory count at December 31 are as follows:

	Model		
	JG491	**CP925**	**8M21**
Inventory, Jan. 1	5 @ $527	5 @ $589	18 @ $327
First purchase	8 @ $456	8 @ $780	22 @ $363
Second purchase	10 @ $465	7 @ $831	34 @ $380
Third purchase	9 @ $425	6 @ $633	15 @ $358
Fourth purchase	8 @ $488		
Inventory, Dec. 31	9	8	21

Check Figure

Weighted-average-cost ending inventory, $17,572.36

Instructions

1. Determine the cost of the inventory on December 31 by the weighted-average-cost method. (Round to two decimal places.)
2. Determine the cost of the inventory on December 31 by the first-in, first-out method.
3. Determine the cost of the inventory on December 31 by the last-in, first-out method.

P.O. 3

Problem 17-3A McAfee Company carried out the following transactions during the year:

Jan.	3	Bought merchandise on account from Sanger, Inc.; terms 2/10, n/30; FOB destination; $12,700.
	5	Received credit memo no. 1642 from Sanger, Inc., for the return of merchandise bought on January 3, $810.
	12	Issued check no. 2141 to Sanger, Inc., in payment of the invoice dated January 3.
	20	Sold merchandise on account to Sorken and Son, $4,310; the cost of the merchandise was $3,122.
	30	Sold merchandise on account to Odlin and Company, $5,578; the cost of the merchandise was $3,491.
Dec.	31	Made the following adjusting entries: The ending inventory determined by physical count is $223,648. The balance in the Inventory account under the perpetual inventory system is $223,884. The beginning inventory was $194,625. Accrued interest on notes payable is $90. Accrued interest on notes receivable is $115. Allowance for Doubtful Accounts is to be increased by $1,430.

Check Figure

First adjusting entry amount, perpetual inventory system, $236

Instructions

1. Record the transactions in general journal form, assuming that McAfee Company uses the perpetual inventory system and records purchases at the gross amount.
2. Record the transactions in general journal form, assuming that McAfee Company uses the periodic inventory system and records purchases at the gross amount.

Instructions for General Ledger Software

The Problem Menu lists two versions of this problem, one for each part.

1. Assuming that McAfee Company uses the perpetual inventory system, record the transactions in the general journal, with purchases recorded at the gross amount. Print the journal entries.
2. Assuming that McAfee Company uses the periodic inventory system, record the transactions in the general journal, with purchases recorded at the gross amount. Print the journal entries.

P.O. 4

Problem 17-4A Baldwin Company's beginning inventory of D520 is 150 units at a cost of $89 each. Dates of purchases and sales for a three-month period are as follows:

Date	Purchases Units	Cost per Unit	Sales Units	Price per Unit
Jan. 16	225	$90.50		
18			70	$105.00
29			130	105.00
Feb. 2	170	92.00		
11			120	107.00
17	200	95.00		
27			160	112.00
Mar. 9			90	112.00
14	120	97.50		
22			70	112.00
29			65	112.80

Baldwin Company maintains a perpetual inventory record using the first-in, first-out method. The minimum number of units allowed in inventory is 130; the maximum is 450. Data for the month of January are recorded in the Working Papers.

Check Figure

Cost of goods sold, $64,552.50

Instructions

1. Record the data for purchases and sales of item D520 and for cost of goods sold in a perpetual inventory record using the first-in, first-out method for the months of February and March.
2. Determine the total cost of goods sold during the three-month period.
3. Determine the total sales for the three-month period.
4. Determine the gross profit from sales of item D520 for this period.

PROBLEM SET B

For additional help, see the demonstration problem at the beginning of each chapter in your Working Papers.

P.O. 2b,c,d

Problem 17-1B Boit and Company's inventory of LB163 on January 1 was 10,000 gallons, costing $0.42 per gallon (periodic inventory). In addition to this beginning inventory, purchases during the next six months were as follows:

Date	Quantity (Gallons)	Cost per Gallon	Total Cost
Jan. 1 Inventory	10,000	$0.42	$4,200
14	11,000	0.43	4,730
Feb. 21	9,000	0.44	3,960
Mar. 7	7,000	0.445	3,115
Apr. 19	10,000	0.45	4,500
May 5	9,000	0.46	4,140
June 2	10,000	0.47	4,700
29	6,000	0.48	2,880

The inventory on June 30 was 15,000 gallons. During this six-month period, Boit and Company sold LB163 for $0.60 per gallon. Assume that no liquid was lost through evaporation or leakage.

Check Figure

Ending inventory under FIFO, $7,110

Instructions

1. Find the cost of the ending inventory by the following methods:

    a. Weighted-average-cost (Round to three decimal places.)
    b. First-in, first-out
    c. Last-in, first-out

2. Determine the cost of goods sold according to the three methods of costing inventory.
3. Determine the amount of the gross profit according to the three methods of costing inventory.

P.O. 2b,c,d

Problem 17-2B Castle Jewelers uses the periodic inventory system. Data pertaining to the inventory on January 1, the beginning of the fiscal year, purchases during the year, and the inventory count on December 31 are as follows:

	Model		
	JG491	CP925	8M21
Inventory, Jan. 1	12 @ $433	4 @ $785	20 @ $319
First purchase	18 @ $445	8 @ $786	27 @ $321
Second purchase	24 @ $451	10 @ $787	29 @ $322
Third purchase	18 @ $451	7 @ $788	31 @ $324
Fourth purchase	14 @ $457		25 @ $327
Inventory, Dec. 31	16	8	30

Check Figure

Weighted-average-cost ending inventory, $23,147.68

Instructions

1. Determine the cost of the inventory on December 31 by the weighted-average-cost method. (Round to two decimal places.)
2. Determine the cost of the inventory on December 31 by the first-in, first-out method.
3. Determine the cost of the inventory on December 31 by the last-in, first-out method.

P.O. 1,3

Problem 17-3B Gloster Company carried out the following transactions during the year:

Jan.	2	Bought merchandise on account from Upson Products; terms 2/10, n/30; FOB destination; $7,860.
	4	Received credit memo no. 1421 from Upson Products for the return of merchandise bought on January 2, $530.
	11	Issued check no. 2912 to Upson Products in payment of the invoice dated January 2.
	14	Sold merchandise on account to C. N. Lester, $3,670; the cost of the merchandise was $2,495.
	30	Sold merchandise on account to S. T. Clarkson, $4,945; the cost of the merchandise was $3,327.
Dec.	31	Made adjusting entries: The ending merchandise inventory determined by physical count is $141,306. The beginning inventory was $138,182. The balance in the Inventory account under the perpetual inventory system is $142,765. Accrued interest on notes payable is $227. Accrued interest on notes receivable is $121. Allowance for Doubtful Accounts is to be increased by $1,312.

Check Figure

First adjusting entry amount, periodic inventory system, $138,182

Instructions

1. Record the transactions in general journal form, assuming that Gloster Company uses the perpetual inventory system and records purchases at the gross amount.
2. Record the transactions in general journal form, assuming that Gloster Company uses the periodic inventory system and records purchases at the gross amount.

Instructions for General Ledger Software

The Problem Menu lists two versions of this problem, one for each part.

1. Assuming that Gloster Company uses the perpetual inventory system, record the transactions in the general journal, with purchases recorded at the gross amount. Print the journal entries.
2. Assuming that Gloster Company uses the periodic inventory system, record the transactions in the general journal, with purchases recorded at the gross amount. Print the journal entries.

P.O. 4

Problem 17-4B Boroson Company's beginning inventory of R317 is 160 units at a cost of $45 each. Dates of purchases and sales for a three-month period are as follows:

	Purchases		Sales	
Date	**Units**	**Cost per Unit**	**Units**	**Price per Unit**
Jan. 16	225	$46.00		
18			70	$54.00
29			140	55.00
Feb. 5	235	47.60		
14			135	56.00
22			195	57.00
26	225	48.20		
Mar. 4			75	58.00
11	155	48.50		
17			85	59.00
30			135	59.00

Boroson Company maintains a perpetual inventory record using the first-in, first-out method. The minimum number of units allowed in inventory is 80; the maximum is 420. Data for the month of January are recorded in the Working Papers.

Instructions

1. Record the data for purchases and sales of item R317 and for cost of goods sold in a perpetual inventory record using the first-in, first-out method for the months of February and March.
2. Determine the total cost of goods sold during the three-month period.
3. Determine the total sales for the three-month period.
4. Determine the gross profit from sales of item R317 for the period.

Estimating the Value of Inventories

Performance Objectives

After you have completed this appendix, you will be able to do the following:

1. Estimate the value of inventory by the retail method.

2. Estimate the value of inventory by the gross-profit method.

To function efficiently, management must have interim income statements and balance sheets prepared monthly. Management needs a physical inventory at the end of the year, because inventory balance figures are an integral element of financial statements. However, because it is both time-consuming and expensive to take a physical inventory, management finds it more expedient to estimate the value of the ending inventory each month and to use these estimates on the monthly financial statements. Let's take a look at the two most frequently used methods of estimating the value of inventories: the retail method and the gross-profit method.

RETAIL METHOD OF ESTIMATING THE VALUE OF INVENTORIES

OBJECTIVE 1

Estimate the value of inventory by the retail method.

This **retail method**, widely used by retail concerns, is based on both the cost and retail value of the goods. The retailer buys merchandise at cost, then adds the normal markup and prices the goods at the retail level. The **normal markup**—which is the normal amount, or percentage, that you add to the cost of an item to arrive at its selling price—covers operating expenses and profit. If a firm uses the retail method of estimating inventories, it must record the purchases-related accounts at both cost and retail values. The firm's accountant records retail values in supplementary records; he or she also records the physical inventory taken at the end of the previous year at both cost and retail values.

Example 1 Hall & Company takes a physical inventory at the end of each year and estimates the value of the inventory at the end of each month for its monthly financial statements.

The accountant for Hall & Company needs the following information to estimate the value of the ending merchandise inventory at cost:

• Cost value and retail value of merchandise on hand at the beginning of the month. (The inventory at the beginning of a given month is the same as the inventory at the end of the preceding month.)

		AT COST	AT RETAIL
Merchandise Inventory (beginning)		82 4 0 0 00	137 2 0 0 00

- Delivered cost of purchases during the month, both cost value and retail value. The retail amounts include the cost plus the company's standard markup.

	AT COST		AT RETAIL	
Purchases		165 4 9 0 00		275 8 1 6 00
Less: Purchases Returns and Allowances	4 6 0 0 00		7 6 0 0 00	
Purchases Discounts	3 8 0 0 00	8 4 0 0 00	6 4 0 0 00	14 0 0 0 00
Net Purchases		157 0 9 0 00		261 8 1 6 00
Add Freight In		8 7 1 0 00		14 5 1 8 00
Delivered Cost of Purchases		165 8 0 0 00		276 3 3 4 00

- Net sales for the month. All sales are recorded at retail price levels, as listed on sales slips and cash register tapes.

		AT RETAIL
Sales		303 3 0 0 00
Less: Sales Returns and Allowances	14 0 0 0 00	
Sales Discounts	5 3 0 0 00	19 3 0 0 00
Net Sales		284 0 0 0 00

The accountant can determine the cost value of the ending inventory by following these four steps:

1. Determine the dollar value of goods available for sale, at cost and at retail. The cost amounts are the same as the Cost of Goods Available for Sale, which is part of the Cost of Goods Sold section of the income statement.

	At Cost	At Retail
Beginning inventory	$ 82,400	$137,200
Plus delivered cost of purchases	165,800	276,334
Goods available for sale	$248,200	$413,534

2. Find the ratio of the cost value of goods available for sale to the retail value of goods available for sale.

$$\frac{\text{Cost Value of Goods Available for Sale}}{\text{Retail Value of Goods Available for Sale}} = \frac{\$248,200}{\$413,534} = 60\% \text{ (rounded)}$$

3. Determine the retail value (selling price) of ending inventory.

Retail value of goods available	$413,534
Less net sales	284,000
Retail value of ending inventory	$129,534

Think of the retail value of the ending inventory this way: If the firm had $413,534 of goods available for sale, and $284,000 was actually sold, then the amount left over should be $129,534.

4. Convert the retail value of the ending inventory into the cost value of the ending inventory by using this formula and rounding to the nearest dollar:

$$\$129,534 \times 60\% = \$129,534 \times 0.60 = \underline{\$77,720} \text{ (rounded)}$$

Therefore, on its income statement for the month, Hall & Company records the value of the ending inventory as $77,720. If the retail value is $129,534 and 40 percent of this amount represents markup, the remaining 60 percent must be the cost.

Example 2   Halpin Company has the following account balances, as shown by T accounts:

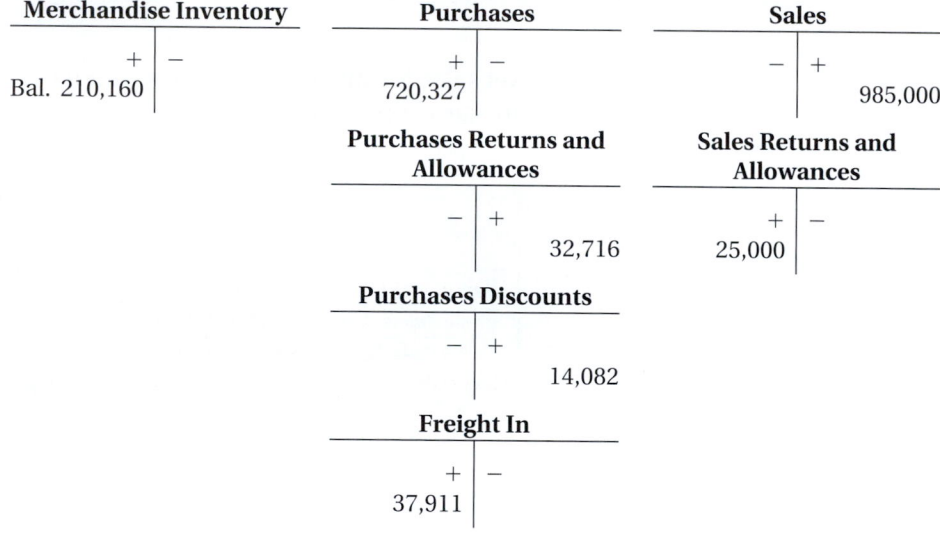

Retail value of beginning inventory is $296,000 (the accountant picks up this amount from a report dated the end of the preceding month).

Delivered Cost of Purchases = Purchases − Purchases Returns and
Allowances − Purchases Discounts + Freight In

$$= \$720,327 - \$32,716 - \$14,082 + \$37,911$$

$$= \underline{\$711,440} \text{ Delivered Cost of Purchases}$$

Retail value of delivered cost of purchases is $1,001,708 (the normal markup is added to the cost amount).

Net Sales = Sales − Sales Returns and Allowances

= **\$985,000 − \$25,000**

= **\$960,000**

Again, the information is obtained by following the four steps:

1. Determine the dollar value of goods available for sale, at cost and at retail.

	At Cost	At Retail
Beginning inventory	\$210,160	\$ 296,000
Plus delivered cost of purchases	711,440	1,001,708
Goods available for sale	\$921,600	\$1,297,708

2. Find the ratio of the cost value of goods available for sale to the retail value of goods available for sale.

$$\frac{\text{Cost Value of Goods Available for Sale}}{\text{Retail Value of Goods Available for Sale}} = \frac{\$921,600}{\$1,297,708} = 71\% \text{ (rounded)}$$

3. Find the retail value of ending inventory, as follows:

Retail value of goods available	\$1,297,708
Less net sales	960,000
Retail value of ending inventory	\$ 337,708

4. Convert retail value of ending inventory into cost value of ending inventory by using this formula:

\$337,708 × 71% = \$337,708 × 0.71 = **\$239,773** (rounded)

These examples assume that the retailer maintains the normal markup. In other words, we are assuming that the composition or mix of the items in the ending inventory, in terms of the ratio of cost price to retail price, remains the same for the entire stock of goods available for sale.

Markups and Markdowns

In our examples, the retailers used normal markups, but some stores use additional markups and markdowns. Retailers impose additional markups on top of normal markups when the merchandise involved is in great demand. Because of the highly desirable nature of certain goods (such as up-to-the-minute fashion), a store may feel that it can get higher-than-normal prices for these goods. Conversely, a store uses markdowns to sell slow-moving merchandise during a clearance sale.

When a store using the retail inventory method imposes additional markups and markdowns, it must keep track of them, so that it can calculate the ratio of the cost value of goods available to the retail value of goods available. Look at the following example of how a store keeps track of markups and markdowns:

Step 1 Goods available for sale, at cost and at retail.

	At Cost	At Retail
Beginning inventory	$ 60,000	$ 90,000
Plus delivered cost of purchases	110,000	165,000
Plus additional markups		4,000
Goods available for sale	$170,000	$259,000

Step 2   Ratio of cost value of goods available for sale to retail value of goods available for sale is as follows:

$$\frac{\text{Cost Value of Goods Available for Sale}}{\text{Retail Value of Goods Available for Sale}} = \frac{\$170,000}{\$259,000} = 66\% \text{ (rounded)}$$

Step 3   Retail value of ending inventory.

Retail value of goods available for sale	$259,000
Less net sales	200,000
Less markdowns	3,000
Retail value of ending inventory	$ 56,000

Step 4   Convert retail value of ending inventory into cost value of ending inventory:

$$\$56,000 \times 0.66 = \$36,960$$

The accountant adds any additional markups in the retail column of his or her working paper because such markups result in an increase in the retail value of the goods available for sale. For example, let's say that the price of a popular item is $40, and a store seizes the opportunity and marks it up to $49; this is a $9 increase in the retail value of the goods available for sale. On the other hand, when a store marks down the price of an item, the accountant deducts the amount of the markdown from the retail value of the goods available for sale (step 3) to obtain the retail value of the merchandise inventory at the end of a given month. For example, say that the price tag of an item is $389, but nobody is buying, so the store marks it down to $359. This means that there has been a $30 decrease in the retail value of these goods available for sale.

END-OF-YEAR PROCEDURE

It is very important to take a physical inventory at the end of the year. Physical inventories may also be taken periodically during the year to spot-check the estimated inventories. Most retail stores record items in stock on the inventory sheets at retail prices (they take the total of all the price tags). It is then necessary to convert the total of the retail values into the total of the cost values, as in step 4. For example, suppose that the total retail value of the merchandise on all the inventory sheets is $96,000, and the ratio of cost value to retail value is

$$\frac{\text{Cost Value of Goods Available}}{\text{Retail Value of Goods Available}} = 70\%$$

The cost value of the goods is $96,000 \times 0.70 = \$67,200$. The only difference between the steps taken to prepare the end-of-the-year statement and the steps taken to prepare the interim or monthly statements is that at the end of the year there is a physical count of the merchandise, and consequently you begin with step 4.

However, to find out the magnitude of shoplifting, or to verify the accuracy of the evaluation of the physical inventory, some firms go through the full procedure of estimating the value of the inventory at the end of the year. Then they take a physical count of the goods on hand and compare this value with the value of the estimated inventory.

GROSS-PROFIT METHOD OF ESTIMATING THE VALUE OF INVENTORIES

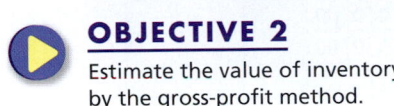

OBJECTIVE 2

Estimate the value of inventory by the gross-profit method.

Sometimes a firm may find that the total of the retail prices of the beginning inventory and purchases is not readily available; in such cases, the firm naturally cannot use the retail method of estimating the value of the ending inventory. The **gross-profit method** is an alternative procedure that achieves the same objective. The key element in this method is that the percentage of gross profit earned in the prior year will remain the same for the present year.

The term *gross profit*, as used on income statements, represents net sales less cost of goods sold:

Net sales	$60,000
Less cost of goods sold	45,000
Gross profit	$15,000

You arrive at the amount for the percentage of gross profit by dividing the gross profit by the net sales:

$$\text{Percentage of Gross Profit} = \frac{\text{Gross Profit}}{\text{Net Sales}} = \frac{\$15,000}{\$60,000} = \underline{\underline{25\%}}$$

A 25 percent gross-profit rate means that there is 25¢ of gross profit for every $1 of net sales. *Gross profit* is the profit earned on the sale of merchandise *before* other expenses are deducted. You can compute the gross-profit rate or percentage by using amounts from a recent income statement, or you may compute the percentage of gross profit from income statements from past years, using averages of amounts. The variation from year to year is usually relatively minor, unless marked changes in the firm's buying and selling policies have taken place.

You need the following information for the current year:

- Sales (balance of account to date)
- Sales Returns and Allowances (balance of account to date)
- Sales Discounts (balance of account to date)
- Beginning Merchandise Inventory (ending inventory of the previous period)
- Purchases (balance of account to date)
- Purchases Returns and Allowances (balance of account to date)
- Purchases Discounts (balance of account to date)
- Freight In (balance of account to date)

Northeast Mountain Bikes Company
Partial Income Statement
For Period January 1 through April 29, 20—

Revenue from Sales:				
Sales				$217 0 0 0 00
Less Sales Returns and Allowances				17 0 0 0 00
Net Sales				$200 0 0 0 00
Cost of Goods Sold:				
Merchandise Inventory, January 1, 20—			$ 72 0 0 0 00	
Purchases		$136 0 0 0 00		
Less: Purchases Returns and Allowances	$14 0 0 0 00			
Purchases Discounts	2 4 0 0 00	16 4 0 0 00		
Net Purchases		$119 6 0 0 00		
Add Freight In		7 4 0 0 00		
Delivered Cost of Purchases			127 0 0 0 00	
Cost of Goods Available for Sale			$199 0 0 0 00	
Less Merchandise Inventory, April 29, 20—				
Cost of Goods Sold				
Gross Profit				$

FIGURE 1

Example 1 On the night of April 29, Northeast Mountain Bikes Company was destroyed by fire. However, the company's books and records of transactions were saved. For insurance purposes, the owner must estimate the value of the inventory by the gross-profit method. The owner knows that the average gross-profit percentage for the past five years is 32 percent. By journalizing and posting the transactions of the current month, the company's accounts can be brought up to date from these sources:

- Sales (from sales journal, cash receipts journal, and invoices through April 29)
- Sales Returns and Allowances (from cash receipts journal and general journal)
- Merchandise Inventory, December 31 (ending inventory of last fiscal period)
- Purchases (from purchases journal and invoices through April 29)
- Purchases Returns and Allowances (from general journal)
- Purchases Discounts (from cash payments journal)
- Freight In (from purchases journal, cash payments journal, and invoices through April 29)

The owner of Northeast Mountain Bikes Company arranges these figures in the customary income statement format, extending from Sales to Gross Profit (see Figure 1).

$$\text{Percentage of Gross Profit} = \frac{\text{Gross Profit}}{\text{Net Sales}} = \frac{\text{Gross Profit}}{\$200,000} = \underline{\underline{32\%}}$$

$$\text{Gross Profit} = 0.32 \times \$200,000 = \underline{\$64,000}$$

Next fill in the Gross Profit blank in the income statement (see Figure 2 on the following page).

Northeast Mountain Bikes Company
Partial Income Statement
For Period January 1 through April 29, 20—

Revenue from Sales:							
Sales							$217 0 0 0 00
Less Sales Returns and Allowances							17 0 0 0 00
Net Sales							$200 0 0 0 00
Cost of Goods Sold:							
Merchandise Inventory, January 1, 20—					$ 72 0 0 0 00		
Purchases			$136 0 0 0 00				
Less: Purchases Returns and Allowances	$14 0 0 0 00						
Purchases Discounts	2 4 0 0 00		16 4 0 0 00				
Net Purchases			$119 6 0 0 00				
Add Freight In			7 4 0 0 00				
Delivered Cost of Purchases					127 0 0 0 00		
Cost of Goods Available for Sale					$199 0 0 0 00		
Less Merchandise Inventory, April 29, 20—							
Cost of Goods Sold							136 0 0 0 00
Gross Profit							$ 64 0 0 0 00

FIGURE 2

To find the cost of the merchandise at the end (April 29), we work backward. The cost of goods sold is the difference between net sales and gross profit, or $136,000 ($200,000 − $64,000). The equation follows below.

Cost of Goods Sold = Net Sales − Gross Profit

$$= \$200,000 - \$64,000$$

$$= \$136,000$$

Now that we have filled in the amounts for Gross Profit and Cost of Goods Sold, the partial income statement (from Cost of Goods Available for Sale through Gross Profit) looks like this:

Cost of Goods Available for Sale	$199,000.00
Less Merchandise Inventory, April 29, 20—	_____
Cost of Goods Sold	136,000.00
Gross Profit	$ 64,000.00

The cost of the merchandise inventory on April 29 is the difference between the cost of the goods available for sale and the cost of goods sold, or $63,000 ($199,000 − $136,000). The equation is as follows:

Cost of Ending Inventory = Cost of Goods Available for Sale − Cost of Goods Sold

$$= \mathbf{\$199,000 - \$136,000}$$

$$= \mathbf{\$63,000}$$

Cost of Goods Available for Sale	$199,000.00
Less Merchandise Inventory, April 29, 20—	63,000.00
Cost of Goods Sold	136,000.00
Gross Profit	$ 64,000.00

The income statement is a very useful device in the box of tools that you have been accumulating. That is why we suggested earlier that you memorize the form to implant it firmly in your mind; then it will always be at your fingertips when you need it to do a specific job.

Example 2 Bellows Beauty Supply has an average gross-profit rate of 34 percent. Its account balances on May 31 of this year are shown by the following T accounts and by the partial income statement in Figure 3.

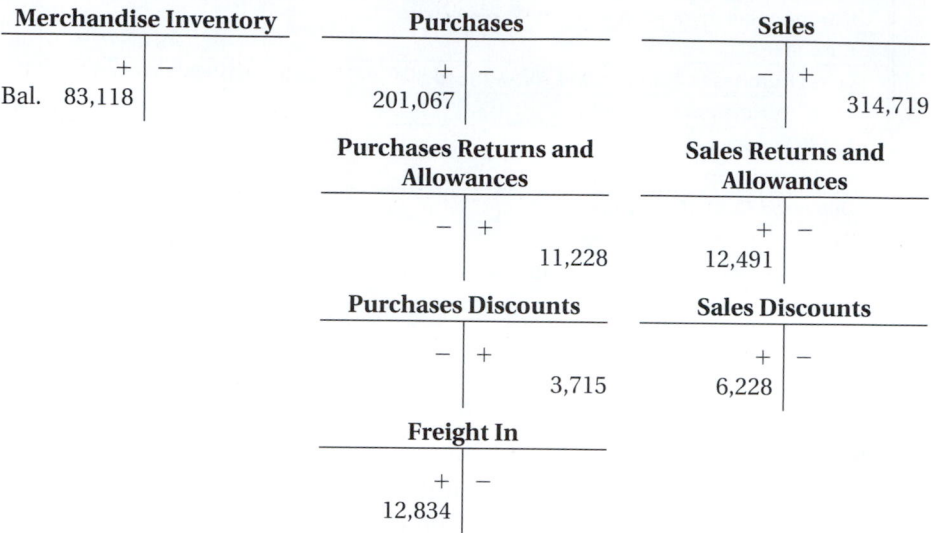

Bellows Beauty Supply Partial Income Statement For Period January 1 through May 31, 20—					
Revenue from Sales:					
Sales					$314 7 1 9 00
Less: Sales Returns and Allowances				$ 12 4 9 1 00	
Sales Discounts				6 2 2 8 00	18 7 1 9 00
Net Sales					$296 0 0 0 00
Cost of Goods Sold:					
Merchandise Inventory, January 1, 20—				$ 83 1 1 8 00	
Purchases			$201 0 6 7 00		
Less: Purchases Returns and Allowances	$11 2 2 8 00				
Purchases Discounts	3 7 1 5 00		14 9 4 3 00		
Net Purchases			$186 1 2 4 00		
Add Freight In			12 8 3 4 00		
Delivered Cost of Purchases				198 9 5 8 00	
Cost of Goods Available for Sale				$282 0 7 6 00	
Less Merchandise Inventory, May 31, 20—				86 7 1 6 00	
Cost of Goods Sold					195 3 6 0 00
Gross Profit					$100 6 4 0 00

FIGURE 3

$$\text{Percentage of Gross Profit} = \frac{\text{Gross Profit}}{\text{Net Sales}} = \frac{\text{Gross Profit}}{\$296,000} = 34\%$$

$$\text{Gross Profit} = \text{Net Sales} \times 0.34 = \$296,000 \times 0.34 = \$100,640$$
$$\text{Cost of Goods Sold} = \text{Net Sales} - \text{Gross Profit}$$
$$= \$296,000 - \$100,640 = \$195,360$$

The cost of goods sold is equal to net sales minus gross profit, or $195,360 ($296,000 − $100,640). The ending merchandise inventory is the cost of goods available for sale minus the cost of goods sold, or $86,716 ($282,076 − $195,360).

$$\text{Ending Inventory} = \text{Cost of Goods Available for Sale} - \text{Cost of Goods Sold}$$
$$= \$282,076 - \$195,360 = \$86,716$$

Glossary

Gross-profit method An alternative procedure (vs. the retail method) to estimating the value of inventories. The key element in this method is that the percentage of gross profit earned in the prior year will remain the same for the present year. (661)

Normal markup The amount or percentage that is normally added to the cost of an item to arrive at its selling price. (656)

Retail method A widely used procedure for estimating the value of inventories. The key elements in this method are the cost of the goods and the retail value of the goods both being recorded. (656)

PROBLEMS

P.O. 1

Problem H-1 You are given the following information for Walden Toys at the end of its fiscal year, October 31:

	At Cost	At Retail
Sales		$264,789
Sales Returns and Allowances		10,659
Purchases	$152,806	254,600
Purchases Returns and Allowances	7,026	11,712
Merchandise Inventory (beginning)	59,172	98,640
Freight In	8,042	13,534

Check Figure

Amount of the loss, $1,225.80

Instructions

1. Determine the cost of the ending merchandise inventory as of October 31, presenting details of your computations.
2. At the end of the year, Walden Toys takes a physical inventory at marked selling prices and finds that the retail stock totals $98,889. There is a possibility that the difference between the estimated ending inventory and the actual physical inventory is due to shoplifting. Convert the value of the physical inventory at retail into its value at cost, and determine the amount of the loss.

P.O. 2

Problem H-2   On May 10 of this year, a fire in the night destroyed the entire stock of merchandise of Kay's Crafts. Most of the accounting records were destroyed also. However, from assorted statements and documents, the firm's accountant was able to piece together the balances of several accounts. Over the past three years, the percentage of gross profit averaged 40 percent.

Merchandise Inventory, January 1	
(beginning of fiscal year)	$128,859
Account balances, as of May 10:	
Purchases	163,970
Purchases Returns and Allowances	984
Freight In	7,906
Sales	219,540
Sales Returns and Allowances	660

Check Figure

Cost of ending inventory, $168,423

Instructions

Determine the cost of the ending merchandise inventory as of May 10, giving details of your computations.

P.O. 2

Problem H-3   On the morning of July 27, the owner of Simone's opened her store and discovered that a robbery had taken place over the weekend. A large part of the stock had been stolen. However, the following information for the period January 1 through July 27 was available. Each year during the past four years, the store had earned an average 34 percent gross profit on sales.

Merchandise Inventory, January 1	
(beginning of fiscal year)	$190,389
Account balances, as of July 27:	
Purchases	408,692
Purchases Returns and Allowances	10,986
Purchases Discounts	8,244
Freight In	24,703
Sales	596,134
Sales Returns and Allowances	6,134

Check Figure

Cost of ending inventory, $215,154

Instructions

1. Determine the cost of the ending merchandise inventory as of July 27, giving details of your computations.
2. By physical count, the cost of the remaining inventory on hand is $80,940. What is the amount of the loss to be claimed for insurance purposes?

18 Property and Equipment

During the late 1990s and early 2000s, the SUV (sport utility vehicle) soared in popularity. What seems to be the latest craze on the roads? It appears that consumer appeal is now focused on the sport truck. Although pickup trucks have always enjoyed a certain amount of popularity, truck makes such as Ford F-Series, Dodge, and Nissan can now be readily found cruising the streets in 4 × 4, full-size, crew cab models. (Full-size pickups were the most popular vehicles with the American buyer in 2005.)

Have you ever thought about the equipment required to manufacture one of these trucks? With today's automated, high-tech assembly operations, manufacturers must have quite an investment in property and equipment. Find out how much General Motors Corporation invests in property and equipment by looking at its 2005 annual report, which can be found at **http://www.gm.com/company/investor_information.** Click on Stockholder Information, go to page 136, and notice Expenditures for Property under Note 26 Segment Reporting. The numbers are reported in millions.

Performance Objectives

After you have completed this chapter, you will be able to do the following:

1. Allocate costs to Land, Land Improvements, Buildings, and Leasehold Improvements accounts.

2. Calculate depreciation by the straight-line method, double-declining-balance method, and units-of-production method.

3. Differentiate among capital expenditures, revenue expenditures, and extraordinary-repairs expenditures.

4. Prepare journal entries for discarding of assets fully depreciated, discarding of assets not fully depreciated, sale of assets involving a loss, sale of assets involving a gain, exchange of assets involving a loss on the trade, and exchange of assets involving a gain on the trade.

5. Maintain a property and equipment subsidiary ledger.

6. Calculate the allowable depreciation for federal income tax returns using the Modified Accelerated Cost Recovery System.

ssets in the Property and Equipment category have a useful life longer than one year, and so they are often referred to as long-lived or fixed assets. Assets such as these are originally purchased for use in the business, unlike merchandise, which is bought for resale. Items most frequently classified as property and equipment are equipment, furniture, machinery, tools, buildings, land improvements, and land.

INITIAL COSTS OF PROPERTY AND EQUIPMENT

The original cost of property and equipment includes all normal expenditures necessary to acquire, install, and prepare the property and equipment for its intended use. For example, the cost of a delivery van includes not only its invoice price (less any discount for paying cash) but also sales tax, freight charges, insurance costs while it is being transported, and costs of dealer preparation. If the buyer of the van pays these additional charges in cash, the accountant for the buyer debits Delivery Van and credits Cash. Suppose the firm buys a second-hand delivery van that needs repair before it can be used; the cost of the repairs are debited to the appropriate asset account, in this case Delivery Van.

The accountant should debit only normal and necessary costs to the asset accounts; this rules out expenditures that result from carelessness, vandalism, and other abnormal causes. For example, suppose that an employee dented the van while parking it. The cost of the repair is not part of the cost of the van; that cost is debited to an expense account, such as Repair Expense. The cost is charged as an expense and not as an asset because the repair does not *add* to the value or usefulness of the asset—it simply restores its usefulness.

> **REMEMBER!**
>
> Normal costs of acquiring the asset, such as its transportation and installation, are debited to the asset account. Other expenditures, from abnormal causes, are debited to an expense account.

DIFFERENTIATING COSTS OF LAND, LAND IMPROVEMENTS, BUILDINGS, AND LEASEHOLD IMPROVEMENTS

OBJECTIVE 1

Allocate costs to Land, Land Improvements, Buildings, and Leasehold Improvements accounts.

A buyer usually buys a property including land, land improvements, a building, and leasehold improvements. In other words, the buyer pays one price for the property. So the question is: How should the price be allocated among the four elements?

When there is no qualified appraisal available, you accept the ratio established by the county or municipal tax assessor. For example, suppose that someone buys some real property, including land and a building, for $1,600,000. The assessor valued this property for tax purposes at $1,300,000: $700,000 for the land and $600,000 for the building. The percentage the assessor allocated to the land is $700,000/$1,300,000 = 53.8 percent. The percentage allocated to the building is $600,000/$1,300,000 = 46.2 percent. Therefore, the value that the buyer should allocate to the land is $1,600,000 × 0.538 = $860,800, and that to the building is $1,600,000 × 0.462 = $739,200. For bookkeeping purposes, you separate land improvements from buildings because of the different useful lives involved. There is no accounting recognition of depreciation of land because the useful life of land is infinite.

Land

Suppose that someone buys a piece of land—just land, no building. The cost of the land includes the amount paid for the land plus incidental charges connected with the purchase: real estate agents' commissions paid by the buyer, escrow and legal fees, delinquent taxes paid by the buyer, plus any costs of surveying, clearing, draining, or grading the land. In addition, the municipality or county—either at the time of purchase or later—may assess the buyer for such improvements as the installation of paved streets, curbs, sidewalks, and sewers. The buyer debits these items to the Land account, since the items are considered as permanent as the land. If a business entity buys land for a building site and the land happens to have old buildings standing on it, the firm debits the cost of the structures (as well as the costs of demolishing them) to the Land account.

Land Improvements

An accountant uses the asset account **Land Improvements** to record expenditures for improvements that have (1) a determinable or finite useful life or (2) are not directly associated with a building. Examples are driveways, parking lots, landscaping, fences, and outdoor lighting systems.

Buildings

REMEMBER!

If land and building are bought as one property, the assets on the land (the building) must be separated for accounting purposes.

The cost of a building includes not only labor and materials, but also architectural and engineering fees, insurance premiums during construction, interest on construction loans during the period of construction, and all other necessary and normal expenditures incurred to prepare the asset for its intended use. The cost of the building can be further broken down into components. The costs that are unrelated to the operation and maintenance of the building can be depreciated over a shorter life. Examples include carpet, cabinets, and decorative elements.

Leasehold Improvements

Leasehold Improvements is an asset account used to record improvements to rented property that are made or paid by the lessee (renter or tenant) but become the property of the lessor (owner or landlord) at the end of the lease term. An example would include remodeling an office suite to fit the business needs of the lessee.

THE NATURE AND RECORDING OF DEPRECIATION

REMEMBER!

The purpose of depreciation is to spread the cost of property and equipment over the years in which it is used to produce revenue—again, in keeping with the matching principle.

When accountants use the term *depreciation,* they mean loss in usefulness of long-lived assets (assets that will last longer than one year). Examples of long-lived assets are buildings, office furniture, store fixtures, machines, computers, trucks, and vehicles. Assets lose their usefulness for two reasons: (1) **physical depreciation**—simply wearing out or being used up, such as a vehicle's being beyond repair, and (2) **functional depreciation**—becoming obsolete or inadequate, such as a computer being outdated because more efficient and faster computers have been developed. Remember that depreciation represents a systematic procedure for spreading the cost of property

Machinery and equipment aren't the only assets that are depreciated. Professional sports teams and sponsors depreciate players as they age and become less useful to the organization in terms of their ability to produce revenue.

and equipment over the fiscal periods in which the company receives services from the assets.

An item of supplies is bought and used up in one fiscal period; its cost is charged to that fiscal period. In contrast, equipment is used over several fiscal periods. Thus, the cost of the equipment must be spread out over several periods, in accordance with the matching principle.

The firm records depreciation by debiting Depreciation Expense and crediting Accumulated Depreciation. It treats Accumulated Depreciation as a deduction from the related asset account. Accumulated Depreciation is thus a contra account. You can record depreciation as an adjusting entry at the end of each month or postpone recording it until the end of the fiscal year, except when there is a change in the assets, such as a sale or a trade-in. In that case, first record depreciation of the asset from the beginning of the fiscal year until the date of the change, and *then* make any other accounting entries to record the sale or trade-in.

Determining the Amount of Depreciation

To determine the depreciation of a long-lived asset, you must take into account three elements.

1. The **depreciation base** is the full depreciation of an asset. Full depreciation is the total cost of an asset less its trade-in or salvage value.
2. The length of the useful life of the asset.
3. The method of depreciation chosen to allocate the depreciation base over the useful life of the asset.

Depreciation Base

When a business entity first puts an asset into service, it is hard to predict the amount of the trade-in or salvage (scrap) value, especially when such a trade-in will not take place for many years. Many firms make estimates based on their own experience or on data supplied by trade associations or government agencies. If the firm expects the salvage value to be insignificant in comparison with the cost of the asset, the accountant often assumes the salvage value to be zero.

Useful Life

The length of an asset's useful life is affected not only by the amount of physical wear and tear to which it is subjected, but also by technological change and innovation. For accounting purposes, the useful life of an asset is based on the expected use of the asset, in keeping with the company's replacement policy. An average car, for example, may have a useful life of five years. However, a car rental company may replace its cars every year in order to offer customers the latest models. A company operating a fleet of cars for its sales force may replace the cars every three years.

CALCULATING DEPRECIATION

OBJECTIVE 2

Calculate depreciation by the straight-line method, double-declining-balance method, and units-of-production method.

The objective of recording depreciation is to systematically allocate the cost of a long-lived asset over the asset's useful life. However, a firm need not use the same method of depreciation for all its assets.

The most common methods of computing depreciation are the (1) straight-line method, (2) double-declining-balance method, and (3) units-of-production method. Method 2 represents **accelerated depreciation**. In accelerated depreciation, depreciation is sped up: Larger amounts of depreciation are taken during the early life of an asset, and smaller amounts are taken during the later years of an asset's life.

Straight-Line Method

A firm that uses the **straight-line method** to calculate depreciation charges an equal amount of depreciation for each year of service anticipated. The accountant computes the annual depreciation by dividing the depreciation base (cost minus trade-in value, if any) by the number of years of useful life predicted for the asset.

$$\text{Depreciation per Year} = \frac{\text{Cost} - \text{Trade-in Value}}{\text{Useful Life (in years)}}$$

The percentage rate of depreciation per year is determined by dividing the number of years of useful life into 1. For instance, take an asset with an estimated life of eight years:

$$\frac{1}{8 \text{ years}} = 0.125 \qquad 0.125 \times 100 = \underline{\underline{12.5\%}}$$

You always apply the depreciation rate against the depreciation base (cost less trade-in value).

Now let's look at two examples.

Example 1 A truck costs $60,000 and has a useful life of five years. The estimated trade-in value at the end of five years is $9,600.

$$\text{Depreciation per Year} = \frac{\$60,000 - \$9,600}{5} = \frac{\$50,400}{5} = \underline{\underline{\$10,080}}$$

$$\text{Depreciation Rate per Year} = \frac{1}{5 \text{ years}} = 0.20 \quad 0.20 \times 100 = \underline{\underline{20\%}}$$

Example 2 A neon sign costs $6,400 and has a useful life of seven years. The estimated trade-in value at the end of seven years is zero.

$$\text{Depreciation per Year} = \frac{\$6,400 - \$0}{7} = \frac{\$6,400}{7} = \underline{\underline{\$914}} \text{ (rounded)}$$

$$\text{Depreciation Rate per Year} = \frac{1}{7 \text{ years}} = 0.1429 \quad 0.1429 \times 100 = \underline{\underline{14.29\%}}$$

Double-Declining-Balance Method

The **double-declining-balance method** is an accelerated method of depreciation that allows larger amounts of depreciation to be taken in the early years of an asset's life. Some accountants reason that the amount charged to depreciation should be higher during an asset's early years, when it is more productive and efficient, to offset the higher repair and maintenance expenses of the asset's later years. The total annual expense then tends to be equalized over the entire life of the asset.

For an asset that has a life of three years or more, this method allows a firm to calculate depreciation by *multiplying the book value (cost less accumulated depreciation) at the beginning of the year by* twice *the straight-line rate.*

Trade-in or salvage value is not counted in determining depreciation by the double-declining-balance method until the end of the depreciation schedule. As with other methods, an asset may not be depreciated below its trade-in value.

To compute depreciation by the double-declining-balance method, follow these steps:

1. Calculate the straight-line depreciation rate.
2. Multiply the straight-line rate by 2.
3. Multiply the book value of the asset at the beginning of the year by double the straight-line rate.
4. When the straight-line rate is equal to or exceeds the double-declining balance, switch to the straight-line method. Do not depreciate below trade-in value.

During the first year, the book value of an asset is the same as its cost, because no depreciation has been taken. So for the first year only, multiply the cost by twice the straight-line rate.

FYI

Under the double-declining-balance method, the book value will reach zero after switching to straight-line if the asset has a zero salvage value.

Example 1 A firm's copy equipment costs $40,000 and has a useful life of five years. The estimated trade-in value at the end of five years is zero.

1. Compute the straight-line depreciation rate:

$$\text{Straight-Line Depreciation Rate} = \frac{1}{5 \text{ years}} = 0.20 \quad 0.20 \times 100 = \underline{\underline{20\%}}$$

2. Twice the straight-line rate = $0.20 \times 2 = 0.40$

3. Depreciation per Year = Book Value at Beginning of Year $\times$ 0.40.

Year	Beginning Book Value	Double-Declining-Balance Rate	Straight-Line Rate	Computation of Depreciation Expense	Ending Book Value
1	$40,000	0.40	$\frac{1}{5} = 0.20$	$40,000 \times 0.40 = $16,000	$40,000 - $16,000 = $24,000
2	24,000	0.40	$\frac{1}{4} = 0.25$	24,000 \times 0.40 = 9,600	24,000 - 9,600 = 14,400
3	14,400	0.40	$\frac{1}{3} = 0.33$	14,400 \times 0.40 = 5,760	14,400 - 5,760 = 8,640
4	8,640	0.40	$\frac{1}{2} = 0.50$	8,640 \times 0.50 = 4,320	8,640 - 4,320 = 4,320
5	4,320	0.40	$\frac{1}{1} = 1.00$	4,320 \times 1.00 = 4,320	4,320 - 4,320 = 0
Total				$40,000	

Computation of straight-line rate = 1 divided by the remaining number of years.

Notice that in the fourth year the straight-line depreciation rate is greater than the double-declining-balance rate. A company typically switches over to the straight-line method when the straight-line depreciation rate equals or exceeds the double-declining-balance rate.

Example 2 A delivery van costs $24,000 and has a useful life of six years. The estimated trade-in value at the end of six years is $4,600.

1. Compute the straight-line depreciation rate:

$$\text{Straight-Line Depreciation Rate} = \frac{1}{6 \text{ years}} = 0.1667$$

$$0.1667 \times 100 = 16.67\% = \tfrac{1}{6}$$

Since the decimal equivalent of $\tfrac{1}{6}$ has a remainder (0.1667), it is more accurate to use the fraction.

2. Twice the straight-line rate = $\tfrac{1}{6} \times 2 = \tfrac{2}{6} = \tfrac{1}{3}$.

3. Depreciation per Year = Book Value at Beginning of Year $\times \tfrac{1}{3}$.

Year	Beginning Book Value	Double-Declining-Balance Rate	Straight-Line Rate	Computation of Depreciation Expense	Ending Book Value
1	$24,000.00	$\tfrac{1}{3}$	$\tfrac{1}{6}$	$24,000.00 $\times \tfrac{1}{3}$ = $ 8,000.00	$24,000.00 − $8,000.00 = $16,000.00
2	16,000.00	$\tfrac{1}{3}$	$\tfrac{1}{5}$	16,000.00 $\times \tfrac{1}{3}$ = 5,333.33	16,000.00 − 5,333.33 = 10,666.67
3	10,666.67	$\tfrac{1}{3}$	$\tfrac{1}{4}$	10,666.67 $\times \tfrac{1}{3}$ = 3,555.56	10,666.67 − 3,555.56 = 7,111.11
4	7,111.11	$\tfrac{1}{3}$	$\tfrac{1}{3}$	7,111.11 $\times \tfrac{1}{3}$ = 2,370.37	7,111.11 − 2,370.37 = 4,740.74
5	4,740.74	$\tfrac{1}{3}$	$\tfrac{1}{2}$	4,740.74 − 4,600.00 = 140.74 $\times \tfrac{1}{2}$ = 70.37	4,740.74 − 70.37 = 4,670.37
6	4,670.37	$\tfrac{1}{3}$	$\tfrac{1}{1}$	4,670.37 − 4,600.00 = 70.37 $\times \tfrac{1}{1}$ = 70.37	4,670.37 − 70.37 = 4,600.00
Total				$19,400.00	

Observe carefully that the trade-in or salvage value is not counted until the fourth year. When you use the double-declining-balance method and there is a trade-in value involved, the book value gradually declines until it reaches the amount of the trade-in value. *An asset must not be depreciated beyond its trade-in value.* For example, take the delivery van. During the fifth year, the normal depreciation would be one-third of the book value at the beginning of the year. Normally, depreciation for the year and the ending book value would be calculated:

Depreciation Expense = $4,740.74 $\times \tfrac{1}{3}$ = $1,580.25

Book Value at End of Year = $4,740.74 − $1,580.25 = $3,160.49

Obviously, if you calculate depreciation in this manner, the book value of the van ($3,160.49) dips below the established trade-in value ($4,600). The maximum amount of depreciation that can be taken is $19,400 ($24,000 cost − $4,600 trade-in value). It should be mentioned that some accountants call book value, carrying value and trade-in value, residual value.

For each separate asset, a company should use the same method of depreciation for each year, to follow the principle of consistency. Since depreciation is an expense, its amount will be subtracted from total revenue to arrive at net income. If the depreciation method is changed from year to year, it becomes impossible to compare the firm's performance from one year to the next.

Units-of-Production Method

The **units-of-production method** allocates an asset's cost based on its usage or productivity within the period. You can obtain the depreciation charge per unit of production by dividing the depreciation base by the total estimated units of production.

$$\text{Depreciation per Unit of Production} = \frac{\text{Cost} - \text{Trade-in Value}}{\text{Estimated Units of Production}}$$

Example 1   A salesperson's car costs $24,000 and has a useful life of 60,000 miles. The estimated trade-in value at the end of 60,000 miles is $7,200. The car is driven 18,500 miles this year.

$$\text{Depreciation per Mile} = \frac{\$24,000 - \$7,200}{60,000 \text{ miles}} - \frac{\$16,800}{60,000 \text{ miles}} = \underline{\$0.28} \text{ per mile}$$

$$\text{Depreciation for 18,500 miles} = 18,500 \text{ miles} \times \$0.28 \text{ per mile} = \underline{\$5,180}$$

Example 2   A backhoe costs $82,000 and has a useful life of 4,000 hours. The estimated salvage value after 4,000 hours is $7,600. The firm uses the backhoe for 380 hours this year.

$$\text{Depreciation per Hour} = \frac{\$82,000 - \$7,600}{4,000 \text{ hours}} = \frac{\$74,400}{4,000 \text{ hours}} = \underline{\$18.60} \text{ per hour}$$

$$\text{Depreciation for 380 hours} = 380 \text{ hours} \times \$18.60 \text{ per hour} = \underline{\$7,068}$$

> **REMEMBER!**
>
> Once you have computed the depreciation per unit (mile, hour, etc.), you must then multiply the unit amount by the number of units produced.

DEPRECIATION FOR PERIODS OF LESS THAN A YEAR

Businesses do not buy nor sell nor discard all their depreciable assets on the first and last days of their fiscal period. They buy and sell assets throughout the year. How, then, do they calculate depreciation? As you look at the examples in the following table, remember that when a business entity acquires a depreciable asset during the year, the accountant usually figures depreciation to the nearest whole month. If the firm held the asset for *less* than half a given month, the accountant doesn't count that month. But if the firm held it for half of a given month or more, the accountant counts it as a whole month. All of the examples in the table assume that the firm's fiscal year ends on December 31.

Date Acquired	Cost	Trade-in Value	Method	Useful Life	Depreciation for First Year
May 12	$8,000	$1,000	Straight-line	5 years	$\dfrac{\$8,000 - \$1,000}{5\ \text{years}} = \$1,400$ per year $\$1,400 \times \frac{8}{12} = \$933.33$ for 8 months
October 19	6,000	200	Double-declining-balance	8 years	$\$6,000 \times \frac{1}{4} = \$1,500$ for first year $\$1,500 \times \frac{2}{12} = \$250$ for 2 months

Suppose a firm buys an asset on June 14. Depreciation is computed from June 1, counting the entire month. But if the firm buys that asset any time after June 15, no depreciation will be computed for the month of June. Software programs are readily available to calculate and keep track of depreciation by the various methods.

CAPITAL AND REVENUE EXPENDITURES

OBJECTIVE 3

Differentiate among capital expenditures, revenue expenditures, and extraordinary-repairs expenditures.

The term *expenditure* refers to spending, either by paying cash now or by promising to pay in the future for services received or assets purchased. After paying the initial price for an asset, you often have to pay out more, either to maintain the asset's operating efficiency or to increase its capacity. So there are two classifications of expenditures: revenue and capital.

Capital expenditures include the initial costs debited to property and equipment; they also include any costs of enlarging or increasing the capacity of assets. Capital expenditures benefit more than one accounting period. Examples are expenditures for buying a building, enlarging it, putting in air conditioning, and replacing a stairway with an elevator. All these expenditures result in debits to an asset account.

Revenue expenditures include the costs of maintaining the operation of an asset, such as the expense of making normal repairs. Examples are expenditures for painting, plumbing repairs, property taxes, and so on. These expenditures provide benefit only during the current accounting period and are recorded as debits to expense accounts.

EXTRAORDINARY-REPAIRS EXPENDITURES

Extraordinary-repairs expenditures refer to a major overhaul or reconditioning that either extends the useful life of an asset beyond its original estimated life or increases its estimated trade-in value. An accountant usually records expenditures for extraordinary repairs as a debit to the asset account and a credit to Cash or Accounts Payable.

For example, on January 3, Year 1, a firm bought a used truck for $18,000. The truck's estimated useful life is four years and its trade-in value is $5,600; straight-line annual depreciation expense is $3,100. On January 5, Year 4, the firm puts in a new engine and has other major repairs done, for which it spends $3,480 in cash. The entry in general journal form is as follows:

	DATE		DESCRIPTION	POST. REF.	DEBIT	CREDIT	
1	Year 4						1
2	Jan.	5	Truck		3 4 8 0 00		2
3			Cash			3 4 8 0 00	3
4			New engine installed in				4
5			company truck.				5
6							6

This extraordinary repair extends the life of the truck from the present one additional year to three additional years. Here are the balances, together with the $3,480 payment, as shown by T accounts:

Truck				Accumulated Depreciation, Truck		
	+	−			−	+
Jan. 3, Year 1	18,000				Dec. 31, Year 1	3,100
Jan. 5, Year 4	3,480				Dec. 31, Year 2	3,100
					Dec. 31, Year 3	3,100

REMEMBER!

When recording an extraordinary repair, debit the asset and calculate the new book value.

The truck's book value before the extraordinary repair was $8,700 ($18,000 − $9,300). The book value of the truck after the extraordinary repair is $12,180 ($18,000 + $3,480 − $9,300). We can see the increase in the Truck account in the balance sheet as follows:

Property and Equipment:			
Truck	$21 4 8 0 00		
Less Accumulated Depreciation	9 3 0 0 00	$12 1 8 0 00	

When it comes to recording the remaining depreciation on the truck, the accountant now has a new cost base, which he or she uses to determine the new depreciation base. Assume that the trade-in value is still $5,600.

New book value ($21,480 − $9,300)	$12,180
Less trade-in value	5,600
New depreciation base	$ 6,580

$6,580 ÷ 3 years = $2,193 (rounded)

The adjusting entry for depreciation of the truck at the end of Year 4 is as follows:

DATE		DESCRIPTION	POST. REF.	DEBIT	CREDIT	
1	Year 4		Adjusting Entry				1
2	Dec.	31	Depreciation Expense, Truck		2 1 9 3 00		2
3			Accumulated Depreciation, Truck			2 1 9 3 00	3
4							4

Assuming that no additional expenditures are made for extraordinary repairs, the adjusting entries for the remaining two years (Years 5 and 6) will be $2,193 for Year 5 and $2,194 for Year 6.

DISPOSITION OF PROPERTY AND EQUIPMENT

OBJECTIVE 4

Prepare journal entries for discarding of assets fully depreciated, discarding of assets not fully depreciated, sale of assets involving a loss, sale of assets involving a gain, exchange of assets involving a loss on the trade, and exchange of assets involving a gain on the trade.

Sooner or later a business entity disposes of its long-lived assets by (1) discarding or retiring them, (2) selling them, or (3) trading them in for other assets. **If the assets are not fully depreciated, the accountant must first make an entry to bring the depreciation up to date.** Let's look at some examples. (Ordinarily entries involving Cash would be recorded in the cash journals; however, for simplification and clarity, we present all the following entries in general journal form.)

Discarding or Retiring Property and Equipment

When long-lived assets are no longer useful to the business and have no market value, a firm discards them.

Discarding of Fully Depreciated Assets   A display case that originally cost $1,760, with a zero salvage value, and has been fully depreciated is given away as junk. The present status of the accounts is as follows:

Store Equipment		Accumulated Depreciation, Store Equipment	
+	−	−	+
Bal. 1,760			Bal. 1,760

The journal entry to record the disposal of the display case looks like this:

DATE		DESCRIPTION	POST. REF.	DEBIT	CREDIT	
6	July	10	Accumulated Depreciation,				6
7			Store Equipment		1 7 6 0 00		7
8			Store Equipment			1 7 6 0 00	8
9			Discarded a fully depreciated				9
10			display case.				10
11							11

Although fully depreciated assets are retained on the books as long as they remain in use, the firm may not take any additional depreciation on them. Once an asset is fully depreciated, the asset's book value remains at its estimated salvage value unless an extraordinary repair is made or the company disposes of the asset.

Discarding an Asset Not Fully Depreciated   On August 12, a firm discards a printer that originally cost $1,720. No salvage value is recognized. Accumulated Depreciation up to the end of the previous year is $1,032. Depreciation for the current year is $352. The present balances of the accounts are as follows:

Office Equipment		Accumulated Depreciation, Office Equipment	
+	−	−	+
Bal. 1,720			Bal. 1,032

Record the entry to depreciate the printer up to date:

	DATE		DESCRIPTION	POST. REF.	DEBIT	CREDIT	
12	20–						12
13	Aug.	12	Depreciation Expense, Office				13
14			Equipment		3 5 2 00		14
15			Accumulated Depreciation,				15
16			Office Equipment			3 5 2 00	16
17			Depreciation on printer				17
18			for the partial year.				18

The T accounts look like this:

Depreciation Expense, Office Equipment		Accumulated Depreciation, Office Equipment	
+	−	−	+
352			Bal. 1,032
			352
			1,384

REMEMBER!

A gain occurs when the amount received for an asset is greater than the book value. A loss occurs when the amount received is less than the book value. To calculate the book value, the depreciation must be brought up to date before a sale, disposal, or trade-in.

The journal entry to record the disposal of the printer is as follows:

	DATE		DESCRIPTION	POST. REF.	DEBIT	CREDIT	
19	Aug.	12	Accumulated Depreciation,				19
20			Office Equipment		1 3 8 4 00		20
21			Loss on Disposal of Property				21
22			and Equipment		3 3 6 00		22
23			Office Equipment			1 7 2 0 00	23
24			Discarded a printer.				24

The T accounts look like this:

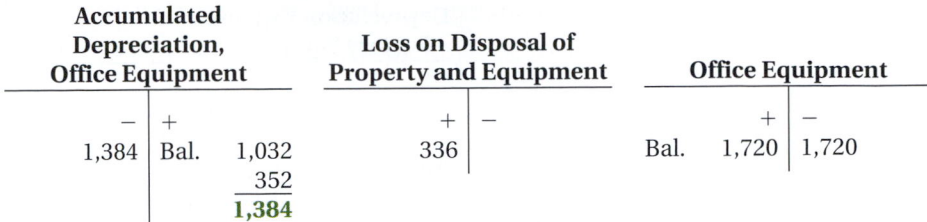

Accumulated Depreciation, Office Equipment			Loss on Disposal of Property and Equipment			Office Equipment		
−	+		+	−			+	−
1,384	Bal.	1,032	336			Bal.	1,720	1,720
		352						
		1,384						

REMEMBER!

Gains or losses from disposal of assets go in either the Other Revenue or the Other Expenses section of the income statement, unless they are significant.

The book value of the asset is $336 ($1,720 − $1,384). Because the firm realized nothing from the disposal of the asset, the loss is for the same amount as the book value.

Loss on Disposal of Property and Equipment is an expense account that appears under Other Expenses on the income statement and is used when a firm sells or trades in an asset and receives an amount less than the book value of the asset.

REMEMBER!

Market value (the amount we could sell an asset for) often differs from book value (cost less accumulated depreciation).

Selling of Property and Equipment

Naturally, it is very hard to estimate the exact trade-in or salvage value of a long-lived asset. It is quite likely that when a firm sells or trades in such an asset, the amount realized will differ from the estimated amount.

Sale of an Asset at a Loss   Suppose that a firm sells a lathe for $250. This lathe originally cost $2,100; accumulated depreciation up to the end of the previous year (December 31) was $1,680. Yearly depreciation is $210. The lathe is sold on August 21.

The present balances of the accounts are as follows:

Factory Equipment			Accumulated Depreciation, Factory Equipment		
	+	−		−	+
Bal.	2,100				Bal. 1,680

We record the depreciation of the lathe to the present date:

REMEMBER!

When disposing of property and equipment that is not fully depreciated, an entry must first be made to bring the depreciation up to date. Then the entry to discard, sell, or trade the asset may be made.

	DATE		DESCRIPTION	POST. REF.	DEBIT	CREDIT	
1	20–						1
2	Aug.	21	Depreciation Expense, Factory				2
3			Equipment		1 4 0 00		3
4			Accumulated Depreciation,				4
5			Factory Equipment			1 4 0 00	5
6			Depreciation on lathe for				6
7			8 months, $140.				7
8			($210 × 8/12)				8

By T accounts, the situation looks like this:

Depreciation Expense, Factory Equipment		Accumulated Depreciation, Factory Equipment	
+	−	−	+
140			Bal. 1,680
			140
			1,820

The entry, in general journal form, to record the sale of the lathe is as follows:

	DATE	DESCRIPTION	POST. REF.	DEBIT	CREDIT	
9	21	Cash		2 5 0 00		9
10		Accumulated Depreciation,				10
11		Factory Equipment		1 8 2 0 00		11
12		Loss on Disposal of Property				12
13		and Equipment		3 0 00		13
14		Factory Equipment			2 1 0 0 00	14
15		Sold a lathe for $250				15
16		having an orginal cost of				16
17		$2,100 and accumulated				17
18		depreciation of $1,820.				18
19						19

For purposes of illustration, let's record the above entry in the T accounts as follows:

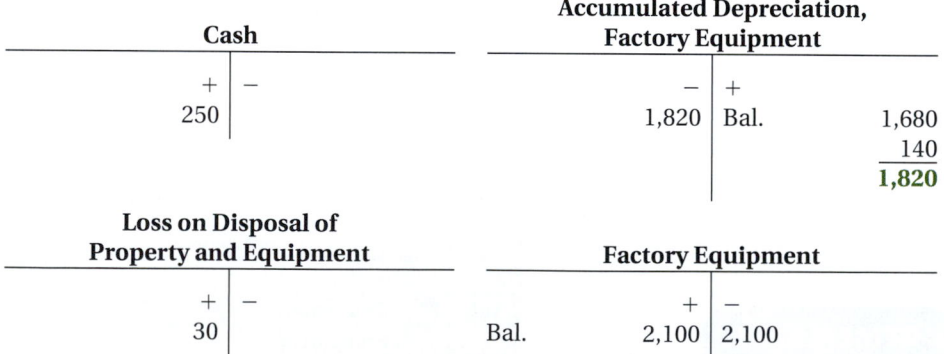

Note that the book value of the lathe is $280 ($2,100 − $1,820). When the firm sells it for $250, the loss is $30 because the amount received for the lathe is $30 less than its book value.

Sale of an Asset at a Gain   Suppose that a firm sells an electronic analyzer for $400. The firm had originally paid $4,400; accumulated depreciation to the end of the previous year, December 31, was $3,960. Yearly depreciation is $360. The electronic analyzer is sold on October 18. The present balances of the accounts are as follows:

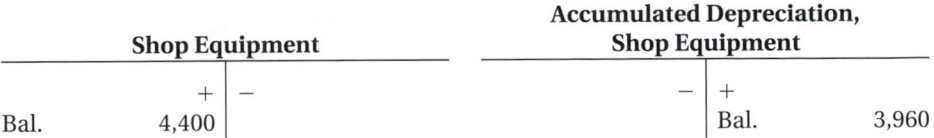

Shop Equipment		Accumulated Depreciation, Shop Equipment	
+	−	−	+
Bal. 4,400			Bal. 3,960

We record the depreciation of the electronic analyzer to the present date:

	DATE		DESCRIPTION	POST. REF.	DEBIT	CREDIT	
1	20–						1
2	Oct.	18	Depreciation Expense, Shop				2
3			Equipment		3 0 0 00		3
4			Accumulated Depreciation,				4
5			Shop Equipment			3 0 0 00	5
6			Depreciation on electronic				6
7			analyzer for 10 months, $300.				7
8			($360 × 10/12)				8
9							9

REMEMBER!

The calculations shown in the explanation are for illustration and would not normally appear in practice.

By T accounts, the situation looks like this:

Depreciation Expense, Shop Equipment		Accumulated Depreciation, Shop Equipment	
+	−	−	+
300			Bal. 3,960
			300
			4,260

The general journal entry to record the sale of the electronic analyzer is as follows:

	DATE		DESCRIPTION	POST. REF.	DEBIT	CREDIT	
10	Oct.	18	Cash		4 0 0 00		10
11			Accumulated Depreciation,				11
12			Shop Equipment		4 2 6 0 00		12
13			Shop Equipment			4 4 0 0 00	13
14			Gain on Disposal of Property				14
15			and Equipment			2 6 0 00	15
16			Sold an electronic analyzer				16
17			for $400 having an orginal				17
18			cost of $4,400 and				18
19			accumulated depreciation of				19
20			$4,260.				20

The T accounts look like this:

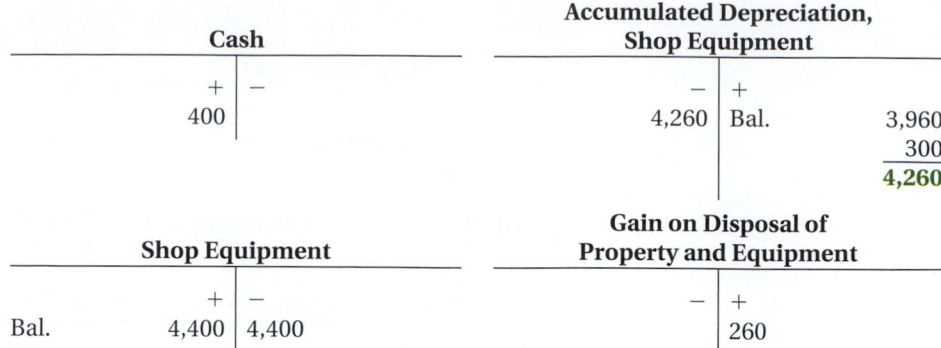

Cash			
+	−		
400			

Accumulated Depreciation, Shop Equipment		
−	+	
4,260	Bal.	3,960
		300
		4,260

Shop Equipment		
	+	−
Bal.	4,400	4,400

Gain on Disposal of Property and Equipment	
−	+
	260

The revenue account **Gain on Disposal of Property and Equipment** appears under Other Income on the income statement and is used when a firm sells or trades in an asset and receives an amount greater than the book value for that asset.

The book value of the electronic analyzer is $140 ($4,400 − $4,260). When the firm sells the electronic analyzer for $400, the firm's gain is $260 ($400 − $140). The amount received for the item is $260 more than its book value.

Exchange of Long-Lived Assets for Other Similar Assets Without Recognition of Gain or Loss

Often a business trades in one asset for another, using the old item as partial payment for the new one. The trade-in allowance may differ from the book value of the asset. If the trade-in allowance is greater than the book value, the firm has a gain; if the trade-in allowance is less than the book value, it has a loss. However, federal income tax laws state that when assets held for productive use are exchanged for similar assets (called a like-kind or Section 1031 exchange), *no gain or loss is recognized*. In effect, the gain or loss is absorbed into the recorded cost of the new asset.

Exchange When Trade-in Value Is Less Than Book Value Suppose that a firm bought a delivery truck for $30,400. Four years later, the truck has accumulated depreciation of $26,200 (book value = $30,400 − $26,200 = $4,200). The firm buys a new truck, with a list price of $35,400, trading in the old one, for which the firm is allowed only $2,800, and paying the difference in cash. Assume that the depreciation for the year is already up to date. The present status of the accounts is as follows:

Delivery Equipment		
	+	−
Bal.	30,400	

Accumulated Depreciation, Delivery Equipment		
−	+	
	Bal.	26,200

When you use the income tax method of accounting, the loss is absorbed in the cost of the new truck. In this case, the accountant adds the loss of $1,400 ($4,200 book value − $2,800 trade-in value) to the price of the new truck, as shown on the following page.

Cost of old truck	$30,400
Less accumulated depreciation	26,200
Book value	$ 4,200
Less trade-in allowance	2,800
Loss	$ 1,400
Quoted price of new truck	$35,400
Plus loss absorbed in recorded cost of new truck	1,400
Recorded cost of new truck	$36,800

The firm's accountant records the transaction by the following steps:

1. Credit Cash, $32,600 (quoted price of the new truck, $35,400, minus the $2,800 trade-in allowance on the old truck).
2. Close or clear the account of the old truck: credit Delivery Equipment, $30,400.
3. Close or clear the Accumulated Depreciation account of the old truck: debit Accumulated Depreciation, Delivery Equipment, $26,200.
4. Calculate the loss and add it to the quoted price of the new truck. Then debit the new truck for this amount.

The entry in general journal form (with the steps labeled) is as follows:

	DATE		DESCRIPTION	POST. REF.	DEBIT	CREDIT	
11		(4)	Delivery Equipment		36 8 0 0 00		11
12		(3)	Accumulated Depreciation,				12
13			Delivery Equipment		26 2 0 0 00		13
14		(1)	Cash			32 6 0 0 00	14
15		(2)	Delivery Equipment			30 4 0 0 00	15
16			Bought a new delivery truck				16
17			having a list price of $35,400.				17
18			Received a trade-in				18
19			allowance of $2,800 on old				19
20			delivery truck, having an				20
21			original cost of $30,400 and				21
22			accumulated depreciation of				22
23			$26,200.				23

REMEMBER!

For income tax purposes, gain or loss is not recognized when assets held for productive use are exchanged for similar assets—the gain or loss is absorbed into the recorded cost of the new asset.

FYI

Obviously the firm would prefer to deduct the loss when it is incurred rather than taking it as depreciation in the future. The firm does not have that option for income tax purposes.

You can also use this technique to verify the cost recorded for the new truck. For income tax purposes, the firm cannot count the $1,400 loss at this time; however, the firm does have an additional $1,400 that it can take in depreciation in the future.

Exchange When Trade-in Value Is Greater Than Book Value   A business bought a copier for $2,600. After some years, the business decides to trade it in on a new model. The old copier has accumulated depreciation of $2,480 *on the date of the trade-in*, leaving a book value of $120. The new copier has a list price of $3,350; however, the salesperson gives the firm a generous trade-in allowance of $310 on the old equipment, and the firm pays the difference in cash. The present status of the accounts is as follows:

Office Equipment			Accumulated Depreciation, Office Equipment		
	+	−		−	+
Bal.	2,600			Bal.	2,480

The accountant records the cost of the new copier at less than the list price, which indicates that a gain is involved. For income tax purposes, this gain has been absorbed in the price of the new copier.

Cost of old copier	$2,600
Less accumulated depreciation	2,480
Book value	$ 120
Trade-in allowance	$ 310
Less book value	120
Gain	$ 190
Quoted price of new copier	$3,350
Less gain absorbed in recorded cost of new copier	190
Recorded cost of new copier	$3,160

The firm's accountant records the transaction by the following steps:

1. Credit Cash, $3,040 (quoted price of new copier, $3,350, minus the $310 trade-in allowance on the old model).
2. Close or clear the account of the old copier: credit Office Equipment, $2,600.
3. Close or clear the Accumulated Depreciation account of the old copier: debit Accumulated Depreciation, Office Equipment, $2,480.
4. Calculate the gain and subtract it from the quoted price of the new copier.

Here are the entries in general journal form with the steps labeled:

	DATE		DESCRIPTION	POST. REF.	DEBIT	CREDIT	
10		(4)	Office Equipment		3 1 6 0 00		10
11		(3)	Accumulated Depreciation,				11
12			Office Equipment		2 4 8 0 00		12
13		(1)	Cash			3 0 4 0 00	13
14		(2)	Office Equipment			2 6 0 0 00	14
15			Bought a new copier having				15
16			a list price of $3,350.				16
17			Received a trade-in				17
18			allowance of $310 on old				18
19			copier, which had an original				19
20			cost of $2,600 and				20
21			accumulated depreciation of				21
22			$2,480.				22
23							23

For income tax purposes, the firm does not count the gain. However, the amount that the firm can take in depreciation in the future has been reduced by $190.

PROPERTY AND EQUIPMENT RECORDS

OBJECTIVE 5

Maintain a property and equipment subsidiary ledger.

Depreciation, which is regarded as an expense, vitally affects the net income of any business. Because net income is affected, the amount of income taxes owed is likewise affected; not only Depreciation Expense, but also Loss (or Gain) on Disposal, affects net income. For income tax purposes, the business must be able to justify the amount of depreciation taken, as well as the gain or loss on disposal of assets.

We have discussed Property and Equipment as a category on a classified balance sheet. Accountants use the term *property* to include land, land improvements, buildings, and leasehold improvements.

Following is an illustration of the Property and Equipment section of a balance sheet:

Property and Equipment:			
Land			$95 0 0 0 00	
Land Improvements	$ 3 0 0 0 00		
Less Accumulated Depreciation	2 3 0 0 00	7 0 0 00	
Building	$60 0 0 0 00		
Less Accumulated Depreciation	28 0 0 0 00	32 0 0 0 00	
Office Equipment	$ 6 0 0 0 00		
Less Accumulated Depreciation	4 5 0 0 00	1 5 0 0 00	
Store Equipment	$18 0 0 0 00		
Less Accumulated Depreciation	14 0 0 0 00	4 0 0 0 00	
Delivery Equipment	$20 0 0 0 00		
Less Accumulated Depreciation	12 0 0 0 00	8 0 0 0 00	
Total Property and Equipment			$141 2 0 0 00

The Store Equipment account represents a functional group; it includes all types of equipment used in the operation of a store. Examples of store equipment are display cases, cash registers, counters, and storage shelves. Accountants maintain a separate depreciation record for each item in the property and equipment ledger. The record may be in the form of a computer file or a card file. We will illustrate a card.

Store Equipment is a controlling account; the property and equipment ledger is a subsidiary ledger. This relationship is like that of Accounts Receivable, which is a controlling account, and the accounts receivable ledger, which is a subsidiary ledger with an account for each individual charge customer. Figure 1, on the following page, shows a record card in a firm's property and equipment ledger. Posting to the subsidiary ledger will also be noted by a check mark in the journal's Post. Ref. column when the asset accounts and the related accumulated depreciation accounts are debited or credited.

PROPERTY AND EQUIPMENT RECORD

ITEM **Cash Register**   ACCOUNT NO.   **128-1**

SERIAL NO.   **ND37-4163**   MAKER   **Security, Inc.**

FROM WHOM PURCHASED   **Tran Equipment Company**   ESTIMATED

ESTIMATED LIFE   **5**   SALVAGE VALUE   **$300**

DEPRECIATION   DEPRECIATION   DEPRECIATION   RATE OF

METHOD **Straight line**   PER YEAR **$900**   PER MONTH **$75**   DEPRECIATION   **20%**

DATE	EXPLANATION	ASSET			ACCUMULATED DEPRECIATION			BOOK VALUE
		DEBIT	CREDIT	BALANCE	DEBIT	CREDIT	BALANCE	
7/3/Yr. 1		4,800		4,800				4,800
12/31/Yr. 1						450	450	4,350
12/31/Yr. 2						900	1,350	3,450
12/31/Yr. 3						900	2,250	2,550

FIGURE 1

Account 128 is the number of the general ledger account for Store Equipment. Account 128-1 is the first piece of equipment listed under Store Equipment in the property and equipment ledger.

The property and equipment record enables the accountant to calculate the total amount of the adjusting entry to be recorded on the company's work sheet. This total amount is found by adding the fiscal period's depreciation for each separate asset contained in the property and equipment ledger. The amount of depreciation for each asset is determined by the schedule of depreciation for that asset. Also, property and equipment records are valuable when a business has to submit insurance claims in the event of insured losses.

DEPRECIATION FOR FEDERAL INCOME TAX

Business firms are entitled to deduct depreciation on their income tax returns. However, the amount recorded on a company's income statement (involving the use of the straight-line method, double-declining-balance method, or units-of-production method) may differ from the amount recorded on the company's income tax return.

Modified Accelerated Cost Recovery System

For property acquired after 1986, a schedule of depreciation called the **Modified Accelerated Cost Recovery System (MACRS)** has been established. Under MACRS, assets are divided into classes. Here are the property classes as defined:

OBJECTIVE 6

Calculate the allowable depreciation for federal income tax returns using the Modified Accelerated Cost Recovery System.

Property Class	Description
3-year property	Certain horses and tractor units for use over the road
5-year property	Autos, light and heavy duty general purpose trucks, computers, and office equipment (copiers, etc.); also, furniture, appliances, window treatments, and carpeting used in residential rental buildings
7-year property	Office furniture and fixtures and any property that does not have a class life and that is not, by law, in any other class
10-year property	Vessels, barges, tugs, and similar water transportation equipment
15-year property	Wharves, roads, fences, and any municipal wastewater treatment plant
20-year property	Certain farm buildings and municipal sewers
27.5-year residential rental property	Rental houses and apartments
39-year real property	Office buildings, store buildings, and warehouses

Following are the approved schedules of percentage of cost allocated (written off or depreciated) each year for three-year, five-year, and seven-year property. These schedules are based on the half-year convention (where only half the depreciation is taken in the first and final years of service).

Year	Three-Year	Five-Year	Seven-Year
1	33.33	20.00	14.29
2	44.45	32.00	24.49
3	14.81	19.20	17.49
4	7.41	11.52	12.49
5		11.52	8.93
6	100.00	5.76	8.92
7			8.93
8		100.00	4.46
			100.00

FYI

Depreciation for five-year property is recorded over six fiscal years because under IRS guidelines, only a half-year's depreciation is taken during the first year.

To determine the depreciation for the year, multiply the cost of the asset by the percentage figure. For example, the first year's depreciation on a desk (classified as 7-year property) having a cost of $300 is $42.87 ($300 × 0.1429). Trade-in value is not counted. Note: If more than 40 percent of the new property is placed in service during the fourth quarter of the year (October, November, and December), then a quarterly schedule must be used, known as the mid-quarter convention. The mid-quarter convention rate schedules, similar to the rate schedule shown above, are published by the IRS.

For residential and nonresidential real property, the property is considered placed in service during the middle of the month (called the mid-month convention).

From time to time Congress changes the allowable depreciation in order to stimulate business investment in equipment. The IRS makes it possible for small businesses to deduct the full cost of machines, computers, furniture, and the like, in the year placed in service (called the 179 deduction). Presently, the limit is $100,000 (indexed for inflation), but it may be changed.

The IRS has issued various publications on depreciation, including Publication 946, How to Depreciate Property. These publications are updated frequently and are available at **http://www.irs.gov.**

CHAPTER REVIEW

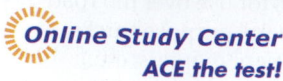

Online Study Center
ACE the test!

Review of Performance Objectives

1. **Allocate costs to Land, Land Improvements, Buildings, and Leasehold Improvements accounts.**

   Land includes amounts paid for the land plus incidental charges connected with the purchase—for example, real estate agents' commissions when the agent was retained by the buyer; legal fees; delinquent taxes paid by the buyer; and surveying, clearing, and grading the land. *Land improvements* include costs of driveways, parking lots, landscaping, and outdoor lighting systems. *Buildings* include amounts paid for labor and materials, architectural and engineering fees, premiums for insurance during construction, and interest on construction loans during the period of construction. *Leasehold improvements* include improvements to rented property that are made or paid by the lessee but become the property of the lessor at the end of the lease term.

2. **Calculate depreciation by the straight-line method, double-declining-balance method, and units-of-production method.**

   The depreciation base is the cost of the asset less its trade-in or salvage value.

$$\text{Straight-Line Method} = \frac{\text{Cost} - \text{Trade-in Value}}{\text{Useful Life (in years)}}$$

$$\text{Double-Declining-Balance Method} = \text{Book Value at Beginning of Year} \times \text{Twice Straight-Line Rate}$$

$$\text{Units-of-Production Method} = \frac{\text{Cost} - \text{Trade-in Value}}{\text{Estimated Units of Production}} \times \text{Number of Units Produced}$$

   Under the double-declining-balance method, book value never reaches zero unless the asset has no trade-in value. Also under the double-declining-balance method, the trade-in value is counted at the end of the schedule of depreciation.

3. **Differentiate among capital expenditures, revenue expenditures, and extraordinary-repairs expenditures.**

   Capital expenditures include costs incurred to buy or increase the value or capacity of assets. Costs are debited to the asset accounts. *Revenue expenditures* include the costs of maintaining the operation of an asset, such as costs for cleaning, painting, and normal repairs. Costs are debited to expense accounts. *Extraordinary-repairs expenditures* include the costs of prolonging the life of an asset or increasing its estimated salvage value, such as the cost of a new engine for a truck or a new roof for a building. The costs are debited to the asset account.

4. **Prepare journal entries for discarding of assets fully depreciated, discarding of assets not fully depreciated, sale of assets involving a loss, sale of assets involving a gain, exchange of assets involving a loss on the trade, and exchange of assets involving a gain on the trade.**

   When a firm changes its Property and Equipment accounts as a result of selling, exchanging, or discarding its assets, the accountant must close or clear the asset accounts along with their respective Accumulated Depreciation accounts. When a firm discards, sells, or trades in an asset that has not yet been fully depreciated, the accountant must first depreciate the asset up to the present date. When the amount received for the old asset is less than the asset's book value, the accountant debits Loss on Disposal of Property and Equipment. On the other hand, when a firm receives more for an asset than its book value, Gain on Disposal of Property and Equipment is credited.

   When a firm trades in one asset for a similar asset, the entry must include the following four steps:

a. Credit Cash for the difference between the quoted price of the new asset and the trade-in allowance.

b. Credit the account of the old asset.

c. Debit the Accumulated Depreciation account of the old asset.

d. Debit the account of the new asset for the cash paid plus the book value of the old asset; or the recorded (adjusted) cost of the new equipment equals the price of the equipment plus the loss or minus the gain not recognized.

5. Maintain a property and equipment subsidiary ledger.

Property and equipment records should consist of a controlling account and a subsidiary ledger. The manual subsidiary ledger should contain a card for each piece of equipment, listing the date acquired, cost, and depreciation taken to date. For income tax purposes, a subsidiary ledger is a must.

6. Calculate the allowable depreciation for federal income tax returns using the Modified Accelerated Cost Recovery System.

First, determine the class of the property. Next, multiply the cost of the asset by the percentage listed in the schedule of depreciation for the Modified Accelerated Cost Recovery System.

Glossary

Accelerated depreciation Depreciation methods in which relatively larger amounts of depreciation are recorded during the early years of an asset's use and decreasing amounts in later years. (671)

Capital expenditures Costs incurred for the purchase of property and equipment, as well as the cost of increasing the capacity or quality of assets; the firm receives services or benefits from this property and equipment for more than one accounting period. (675)

Depreciation base Total cost of an asset less its trade-in or salvage value. (670)

Double-declining-balance method An accelerated method of depreciation; book value at the beginning of the year multiplied by twice the straight-line rate. (672)

Extraordinary-repairs expenditures Costs incurred for major overhauls or reconditioning of assets; repairs that either significantly prolong the life of the asset or increase its estimated salvage value. (675)

Gain on Disposal of Property and Equipment The account in which a gain is recorded when a firm sells or trades in an asset and receives an amount in excess of the book value for that asset; it appears under Other Income on the income statement. (682)

Land Improvements An asset account covering expenditures for improvements that are (1) not as permanent as the land or (2) not directly associated with a building. These include driveways, parking lots, landscaping, fences, and outdoor lighting systems. (669)

Leasehold Improvements An asset account used to record improvements to rented property that are made or paid by the lessee (renter or tenant) but become the property of the lessor (owner or landlord) at the end of the lease term. An example would include remodeling an office suite to fit the business needs of the lessee. (669)

Loss on Disposal of Property and Equipment The account in which a loss is recorded when a firm sells or trades in an asset and receives an amount less than the book value for that asset; it appears under Other Expenses on the income statement. (679)

Modified Accelerated Cost Recovery System (MACRS) An accelerated method of depreciation that is used to determine allowable depreciation for federal income tax returns based on property acquired after 1986; assets are divided into eight classes. (686)

Revenue expenditures Costs incurred to maintain the operation of assets, such as normal repair expenses and fuel expenses. (675)

Straight-line method A method of depreciation that assigns equal amounts of depreciation to each year of the asset's depreciable life. (Cost minus trade-in value divided by useful life [in years].) (671)

Units-of-production method A method of depreciation that allocates an asset's costs based on its usage or productivity within the period. (Cost minus trade-in value divided by estimated units of production multiplied by the number of units produced.) (674)

QUESTIONS, EXERCISES, AND CASES

Discussion Questions

1. Define depreciation and discuss two ways in which assets lose their usefulness.

2. What is meant by disposition of an asset? List the situations involving disposition of assets.

3. Explain how an asset's estimated trade-in or salvage value is treated in computing depreciation under the double-declining-balance method and the straight-line method.

4. Give examples of possible expenditures that should be included in determining the total cost of an asset, such as a machine.

5. Explain the two entries usually involved in the disposition of an asset.

6. Distinguish between expenditures for ordinary repairs and expenditures for extraordinary repairs.

7. Explain how MACRS differs from other methods of depreciation.

8. Differentiate between capital expenditures and revenue expenditures. Give two examples of each type of expenditure for a truck.

Exercises

P.O. 1

Record amounts debited to Land.

Exercise 18-1 Karver Manufacturing Company purchased land adjacent to its factory for the installation of a holding area for equipment. Expenditures by the company were as follows: purchase price, $143,000; paving, $4,300; title search and other fees, $660; grading, $4,000; demolition of a shack on the property, $3,600; lighting, $10,200; signs, $1,850; broker's fees, $8,240; landscaping, $8,600. Determine the amount that should be debited to the Land account.

P.O. 2,6

Determine depreciation using four methods.

Exercise 18-2 At the beginning of the fiscal year, Info Services bought a new computer for $16,500, with an estimated trade-in value of $2,500 and an estimated useful life of five years. Determine the amount of the depreciation for the first and second years by the following methods:

a. Straight-line
b. Double-declining-balance

c. Units-of-production (Useful life is 10,400 hours. Year 1 use is 2,050 hours; Year 2 use, 1,800 hours. Compute depreciation per hour, then depreciation for Year 1 and Year 2.)

d. MACRS (Assume the asset was purchased after 1986. Calculate the depreciation for income tax reporting.)

P.O. 3

Record an extraordinary-repairs expenditure.

Exercise 18-3 Barkson Company just bought a piece of machinery for $8,000, with an estimated life of five years and an estimated trade-in value of $2,200; straight-line depreciation expense is $1,160. Record journal entries for the following transactions:

Jan.   12   Issued Ck. No. 5221 for $250 for inspection and lubrication of the machinery.

Oct.   15   Issued Ck. No. 5562 for $1,970 to replace the motor and rollers. Barkson Company estimates that this repair will extend the life of the machinery about two years.

P.O. 4

Record the disposal of a fully depreciated asset.

Exercise 18-4 On April 28, Muscle-up Mart discarded exercise equipment that cost $7,300. The Accumulated Depreciation account shows depreciation of $7,300 as of the previous December 31. Make the entry in general journal form to record the disposal of the asset.

P.O. 4

Record the update of depreciation and the discarding of office equipment at a loss.

Exercise 18-5 On June 25, Pound Company discarded office equipment with no salvage value. The following details are taken from the subsidiary ledger: cost, $800; accumulated depreciation as of the previous December 31, $620; monthly depreciation, $14. Journalize entries to record the depreciation of the office equipment to date and to record the disposal of the office equipment.

P.O. 4

Record the update of depreciation and sale of an asset at a gain.

Exercise 18-6 On June 20, BRB Communications sold editing equipment that cost $1,800 for $450. Accumulated depreciation up to the end of the previous year was $1,350. Monthly depreciation is $22. Make the necessary general journal entries.

P.O. 4

Record the update of depreciation and trade-in on a similar asset without recognizing a gain or loss.

Exercise 18-7 On June 25, Purkey Assemblers trades in a machine for a new one priced at $8,460, receiving a trade-in allowance of $1,500 on the old machine. Purkey makes a down payment of $1,200 in cash and issues a 60-day, 9 percent note for the remainder. The subsidiary account shows the following: cost (of old machine), $6,000; accumulated depreciation as of last December 31, $4,800; monthly depreciation, $100. Without recognizing gain or loss, make entries in general journal form to record the depreciation of the old machine to date and to record the trade-in and purchase of the new machine.

P.O. 4

Record the update of depreciation and trade-in on a similar asset without recognizing a gain or loss.

Exercise 18-8 On September 27, Valenzuela Florists traded in its old delivery van for a new one, which cost $15,000. Valenzuela got a trade-in allowance of $3,000 on the old van and paid the difference in cash. The subsidiary account shows the following: cost (of old van), $12,000; accumulated depreciation as of last December 31, $9,500; monthly depreciation, $200. Without recognizing gain or loss, make entries in general journal form to record the depreciation of the old van to date and to record the trade-in and purchase of the new van.

Now that you understand how a company accounts for property and equipment, let's see how much Toyota Motor Corporation had invested in those long-term assets. Go to **http://www.toyota.co.jp/en/ir/library/index.html** and click on SEC Filings to access the Form 20-F for the year ended March 31, 2005. The index of the financial statements is on page F-1, which follows page 104. Note that Form 20-F is very similar to Form 10-K but is for foreign companies. When reviewing Toyota's financial information, be careful to look at the amounts shown in U.S. dollars ($), not those shown in Japanese yen (¥).

1. What are the property, plant and equipment (PP&E) categories that Toyota Motor Corporation reported on its 2005 balance sheet?
2. As of March 31, 2005, what was the total amount that the company had invested in property, plant and equipment before accumulated depreciation was deducted? Which of Toyota's PP&E asset categories are not depreciated? (*Hint:* Two of the listed categories are not depreciated.)
3. What depreciation method(s) does Toyota use? What are the estimated useful lives used for the buildings and for the machinery and equipment? (See the note on page F-13.)
4. What percentage of the depreciable assets investment had been depreciated as of March 31, 2005?

CONSIDER AND COMMUNICATE

Tabatha Dawn owns a small catering service. The company owns a delivery van as well as ovens and large cooking containers. She is confused about the different traditional depreciation methods she may use for financial reporting. Explain briefly to her the features and consequences of using each method.

WHAT'S WRONG WITH THIS PICTURE?

Your employer, who is ordering equipment for a new office, has signed the purchase orders for new equipment without looking at them carefully. As you complete an invoice for items for the employee lunchroom, you are tempted to change the order from one microwave to two microwaves and quietly take the second one home to compensate yourself for all the hard work you have done on your own time to get the new office ready. You are a trusted employee; and you are sure that if your employer found out what you had done, there would be no real repercussions. What if you go ahead with this idea? How could it be discovered? Assume that you are the one who would accept shipment when the microwaves are delivered.

CRITICAL THINKING

Rick's Cycle Shop owns various depreciable assets, which were purchased beginning in 2001. The only record you can find on December 31, 2006 (prior to any depreciation adjustments for 2006) is the general ledger account for Equipment, which has a balance of $50,500, and the general ledger account for Accumulated Depreciation, Equipment, which has a balance of $29,690, plus the information listed on the following page. You will need to prepare supporting schedules by asset classification and expense for each prior year before you can calculate the 2006 depreciation.

Depreciable Assets					
Asset	**Bought**	**Method**	**Life**	**Cost**	**Salvage Value**
Van #1	1/1/2001	DDB	5 yrs.	$13,000	$1,000
Office Desks	7/1/2001	SL	5 yrs.	2,500	500
Van #2	7/1/2003	DDB	5 yrs.	20,000	2,000
Trailer	9/1/2005	DDB	5 yrs.	12,000	1,500
Computer	12/1/2005	SL	5 yrs.	3,000	—0—

Total Depreciation

2001	$5,400
2002	3,520
2003	6,272
2004	7,923
2005	6,575

Instructions

1. Classify assets by type: Delivery Equipment or Office Equipment.
2. Recompute depreciation for 2001, 2002, 2003, 2004, and 2005. Round each year's depreciation expense to whole dollars.
3. Compute depreciation for 2006.

PROBLEM SET A

For additional help, see the demonstration problem at the beginning of each chapter in your Working Papers.

P.O. 2

Check Figure

Double-declining-balance method, book value at end of year 5, $3,000

Problem 18-1A At the beginning of a fiscal year, Peters Company buys a truck for $21,000. The truck's estimated life is five years, and its estimated trade-in value is $3,000.

Instructions

Using the following two methods, determine the annual depreciation of the truck for each of the estimated five years of life, the accumulated depreciation at the end of each year, and the book value of the truck at the end of each year.

a. Straight-line method
b. Double-declining-balance method

P.O. 2,3,4

Problem 18-2A During a three-year period, Braxton Electric completed the following transactions related to its service truck:

Year 1

Jan.	4	Bought a used service truck for cash, $18,600.
Nov.	21	Paid garage for maintenance repairs to the truck, $146.
Dec.	31	Recorded the adjusting entry for depreciation for the fiscal year. The estimated life of the truck is four years, and it has an estimated

trade-in value of $3,800. Braxton uses the straight-line method of depreciation.

31 Closed the expense accounts to the Income Summary account.

Year 2

Apr. 2 Paid garage for tune-up of truck, $86.
May 24 Bought tires for the truck, $335.
Dec. 31 Recorded the adjusting entry for depreciation for the fiscal year.
31 Closed the expense accounts to the Income Summary account.

Year 3

June 6 Paid garage for maintenance repairs to truck, $362.
27 Traded in the used truck for a new truck that cost $22,800, receiving a trade-in allowance of $7,500 and paying the difference in cash. Recorded the entry to depreciate the truck up to the present date. Made the entry to record the exchange, assuming the gain or loss is not recognized.
Dec. 31 Recorded the adjusting entry for depreciation of the new truck for the fiscal year. The estimated life of the truck is six years, and it has an estimated trade-in value of $2,600. Braxton Electric uses the straight-line method of depreciation.
31 Closed the expense accounts to the Income Summary account.

Check Figure

Year 2, adjustment amount, $3,700

Instructions

1. Record the transactions in general journal form, pages 97 and 98.
2. After journalizing each entry, post to the following ledger accounts: Truck, No. 131; Accumulated Depreciation, Truck, No. 132; Truck Repair Expense, No. 519; and Depreciation Expense, Truck, No. 523.

P.O. 2,3,4

Problem 18-3A During a three-year period, Farnsworth Excavation completed the following transactions pertaining to its front-end loader:

Year 1

June 30 Bought a front-end loader, $43,500, paying $11,500 in cash and issuing a series of four notes for $8,000 each, to come due at six-month intervals. Payments are to include principal plus 9 percent interest to maturity of each $8,000 note.
July 1 Paid transportation charges for the loader, $750.
Dec. 31 Paid the principal, $8,000, on the first note, plus interest of $1,440 on $32,000, on all the notes.
31 Made the adjusting entry to record depreciation on the loader for the fiscal year. The estimated life of the loader is four years; it has a salvage value of $4,000. Farnsworth's accountant uses the double-declining-balance method.
31 Closed the expense accounts to the Income Summary account.

Year 2

Mar. 14 Paid for normal mechanical repairs to the front-end loader, $535.
June 30 Paid the principal, $8,000, on the second note, plus interest of $1,080 on $24,000, on the remaining notes.
Dec. 31 Paid the principal, $8,000, on the third note, plus interest of $720 on $16,000, on the remaining notes.
31 Recorded the adjusting entry for depreciation for the fiscal year.
31 Closed the expense accounts to the Income Summary account.

Year 3

Apr.	21	Paid for normal mechanical repairs to the front-end loader, $925.
June	30	Paid the principal, $8,000, plus interest of $360 on $8,000, on the fourth note.
Sept.	27	Farnsworth Excavation decided to get rid of its loader and use the services of an equipment rental firm in the future. Sold the loader for $8,200 cash. Made the entry to depreciate the loader to date ($6,222.66). Made the entry to account for the sale of the loader.
Dec.	31	Closed the expense accounts to the Income Summary account.

Check Figure

Year 3, Income Summary debit, $9,678.75

Instructions

1. Record the transactions in general journal form, pages 192–194.
2. After making each journal entry, post to the following ledger accounts: Equipment, No. 141; Accumulated Depreciation, Equipment, No. 142; Equipment Maintenance Expense, No. 529; Depreciation Expense, Equipment, No. 533; Interest Expense, No. 541; and Loss on Disposal of Property and Equipment, No. 542.

P.O. 2,4,5

Problem 18-4A The general ledger of Conger Personnel Service includes controlling accounts for Office Equipment, No. 123, and Accumulated Depreciation, Office Equipment, No. 124. Conger's accountant also records the details of each item of office equipment in a subsidiary ledger. During a three-year period, the following transactions affecting office equipment took place:

Year 1

Jan.	5	Bought the following from Abby, Inc., for cash: Filing cabinet, $240, account no. 123-1, expected life fifteen years, trade-in value zero. Executive desk, $960, account no. 123-2, expected life twelve years, trade-in value zero. Executive chair, $360, account no. 123-3, expected life twelve years, trade-in value zero. (The above assets will be depreciated using the straight-line method.)
	7	Paid Biggs and Roberts $1,280 for a custom-made counter, account no. 123-4, expected life ten years, trade-in value zero; depreciation by straight-line method.
Dec.	31	Made the adjusting entry to record depreciation of office equipment for the fiscal year (total depreciation, $254; verify this figure).
	31	Closed the Depreciation Expense, Office Equipment account into the Income Summary account.

Year 2

June	29	Bought a carpet from Bard Floor Coverings on account, $1,280, account no. 123-5, estimated life eight years, trade-in value zero; depreciation by double-declining-balance method.
Dec.	31	Recorded the adjusting entry for depreciation of office equipment for the fiscal year (depreciation for six months on the carpet; total depreciation, $414; verify this figure).
	31	Closed the Depreciation Expense, Office Equipment account into the Income Summary account.

Year 3

June 30   Traded in the executive chair for a new one from Gorzen and Weltz, account no. 123-6. The new chair cost $520, has an estimated life of eight years, and has a zero trade-in value; depreciation using the straight-line method. Conger Personnel Service received a trade-in allowance of $230 on the old chair and paid the balance in cash. Recorded the entry to depreciate the old chair to date. Made the entry to record the exchange of assets, without recognizing any gain or loss.

Dec. 31   Made the adjusting entry to record depreciation of office equipment for the fiscal year (depreciation for six months on the chair; total depreciation, $539.94; verify this figure).

       31   Closed the Depreciation Expense, Office Equipment account into the Income Summary account.

Check Figure

Year 3, Income Summary debit, $539.94

Instructions

1. Record the transactions in general journal form, pages 136 and 137.
2. With the purchase of each new asset, open an account in the subsidiary ledger.
3. After each entry, post to the two controlling accounts and to the subsidiary ledger.
4. Make a list of the balances in the subsidiary ledger accounts at the end of Year 3 and compare the totals with the balances of the two controlling accounts.

PROBLEM SET B

For additional help, see the demonstration problem at the beginning of each chapter in your Working Papers.

P.O. 2

Problem 18-1B At the beginning of a fiscal year, Yoo Company buys a machine for $42,000. The machine has an estimated life of five years and an estimated trade-in value of $4,000.

Instructions

Check Figure

Double-declining-balance method, book value at end of year 5, $4,000

Using the following two methods, determine the annual depreciation of the machine for each of the estimated five years of its life, the accumulated depreciation at the end of each year, and the book value of the machine at the end of each year.

a. Straight-line method
b. Double-declining-balance method

P.O. 2,3,4

Problem 18-2B During a three-year period, Morgan Motel completed the following transactions pertaining to its pickup truck:

Year 1

Jan. 11   Bought a used pickup truck for cash, $6,700.
Nov. 16   Paid garage for maintenance repairs to pickup truck, $152.

Dec. 31 Recorded the adjusting entry for depreciation for the fiscal year, using the straight-line method of depreciation. The estimated life of the pickup truck is four years, and it has an estimated trade-in value of $1,200.

31 Closed the expense accounts to the Income Summary account.

Year 2

Mar. 4 Paid garage for tune-up and minor repairs, $68.
May 27 Bought a tire for the truck, $72.
Dec. 31 Recorded the adjusting entry for depreciation for the fiscal year.
31 Closed the expense accounts to the Income Summary account.

Year 3

Feb. 13 Paid garage for maintenance repairs to pickup truck, $316.
June 22 Traded in the pickup truck for another pickup truck priced at $9,460, receiving a trade-in allowance of $1,040 and paying the difference in cash. Recorded the entry to depreciate the old truck to date. Made the entry to record the exchange, assuming the gain or loss is not recognized.
Dec. 31 Recorded the adjusting entry for depreciation of the new pickup truck for the fiscal year, using the straight-line method of depreciation. The estimated life of the new truck is six years, and it has an estimated trade-in value of $1,500.
31 Closed the expense accounts to the Income Summary account.

Check Figure

Year 2, adjustment amount, $1,375

Instructions

1. Record the transactions in general journal form, pages 97 and 98.
2. After journalizing each entry, post to the following ledger accounts: Truck, No. 131; Accumulated Depreciation, Truck, No. 132; Truck Repair Expense, No. 519; and Depreciation Expense, Truck, No. 523.

P.O. 2,3,4

Problem 18-3B During a three-year period, Dolan Construction Company completed the following transactions connected with its bulldozer:

Year 1

June 30 Bought a bulldozer, $120,400, paying $40,400 in cash and issuing a series of four notes for $20,000 each, to come due at six-month intervals. Payments are to include principal plus 9 percent interest to maturity of each $20,000 note.
July 2 Paid transportation charges for the bulldozer, $3,600.
Dec. 31 Paid the principal, $20,000, on the first note, plus interest of $3,600 on $80,000, on all the notes.
31 Made the adjusting entry to record depreciation on the bulldozer for the fiscal year, using the double-declining-balance method ($24,800; verify this figure). The estimated life of the bulldozer is five years, and it has an estimated salvage value of $11,600.
31 Closed the expense accounts to the Income Summary account.

Year 2

Apr. 24 Paid for maintenance repairs to the bulldozer, $5,936.
June 30 Paid the principal, $20,000, on the second note, plus interest of $2,700 on $60,000, on the remaining notes.
Dec. 31 Paid the principal, $20,000, on the third note, plus interest of $1,800 on $40,000, on the remaining notes.

Dec. 31 Recorded the adjusting entry for depreciation for the fiscal year.

31 Closed the expense accounts to the Income Summary account.

Year 3

May 19 Paid for maintenance repairs to the bulldozer, $2,185.

June 30 Paid the principal, $20,000, plus interest of $900 on $20,000, on the fourth note.

Sept. 29 Dolan Construction decided to get rid of its bulldozer and use the services of an equipment rental firm in the future. Sold the bulldozer for $24,000 cash. Made the entry to depreciate the bulldozer to date. Made the entry to account for the sale of the bulldozer.

Dec. 31 Closed the expense accounts to the Income Summary account.

Check Figure

Year 3, Income Summary debit, $38,605

Instructions

1. Record the transactions in general journal form, pages 192–194.
2. After making each journal entry, post to the following ledger accounts: Equipment, No. 141; Accumulated Depreciation, Equipment, No. 142; Equipment Maintenance Expense, No. 529; Depreciation Expense, Equipment, No. 533; Interest Expense, No. 541; and Loss on Disposal of Property and Equipment, No. 542.

P.O. 2,4,5

Problem 18-4B The general ledger of Lang Insurance Agency includes controlling accounts for Office Equipment, No. 123, and Accumulated Depreciation, Office Equipment, No. 124. Lang's accountant also records the details of each item of office equipment in a subsidiary ledger. The following transactions affecting office equipment occurred during a three-year period:

Year 1

Jan. 4 Bought the following from Gregoir Office Supplies for cash:
Executive desk, $810, account no. 123-1, estimated life ten years, trade-in value zero.
Executive chair, $285, account no. 123-2, estimated life ten years, trade-in value zero.
Filing cabinet, metal, $180, account no. 123-3, estimated life fifteen years, trade-in value zero.
(The above assets will be depreciated using the straight-line method.)

9 Paid Sabin Cabinet Shop $1,080 for a custom-made counter, account no. 123-4, estimated life ten years, trade-in value zero; depreciation by straight-line method.

Dec. 31 Made the adjusting entry to record depreciation of office equipment for the fiscal year (total depreciation, $229.50; verify this figure).

31 Closed the Depreciation Expense, Office Equipment account into the Income Summary account.

Year 2

June 27 Bought a rug from Foster Furniture on account, $720, account no. 123-5, estimated life eight years, trade-in value zero; depreciation by double-declining-balance method.

Dec.   31   Recorded the adjusting entry for depreciation of office equipment for the fiscal year (depreciation for six months on the rug; total depreciation, $319.50; verify this figure).

31   Closed the Depreciation Expense, Office Equipment account into the Income Summary account.

Year 3

June   23   Traded in the executive desk for a new one, which cost $1,020, from Silkwood, Inc., account no. 123-6, receiving a trade-in allowance of $480 on the old desk and paying the balance in cash. Expected life of the new desk is eight years, with a zero trade-in value; depreciated using straight-line method. Made the entry to depreciate the old desk to date. Made the entry to record the exchange of assets, without recognizing any gain or loss.

Dec.   31   Made the adjusting entry to record depreciation of office equipment for the fiscal year (depreciation for six months on the desk; total depreciation, $377.72; verify this figure).

31   Closed the Depreciation Expense, Office Equipment account into the Income Summary account.

Check Figure

Year 3, Income Summary debit, $418.22

Instructions

1. Record the transactions in general journal form, pages 136 and 137.
2. With the purchase of each new asset, open an account in the subsidiary ledger.
3. After each entry, post to the two controlling accounts and to the subsidiary ledger.
4. Make a list of the balances in the subsidiary ledger accounts at the end of Year 3 and compare the totals with the balances of the two controlling accounts.

Before a Test Check: Chapters 16–18

PART I: True/False Questions

For each of the following statements, circle T if the statement is true and F if the statement is false.

T   F   1. The Allowance for Doubtful Accounts account is a current liability.

T   F   2. Under the allowance method of handling bad debt losses, accounts considered uncollectible are written off by debiting Allowance for Doubtful Accounts.

T   F   3. There is an adjusting entry required when the specific charge-off method is used to handle bad debt losses.

T   F   4. FIFO will result in the lowest net income during periods of rising prices.

T   F   5. An account called Cost of Goods Sold is included in the general ledger when the perpetual inventory system is used.

T   F   6. The income statement and the balance sheet both include the balance of the ending merchandise inventory for the same fiscal period (using the periodic inventory system).

T   F   7. When an extraordinary repair on an asset is made, the cost should be credited to the asset account.

T   F   8. When a business sells equipment for an amount greater than its book value, a loss is recorded.

T   F   9. Depreciation amounts are estimates of the loss of usefulness of an asset over a period of time.

T   F   10. The FIFO inventory valuation method assumes that the items on hand are the most recent ones purchased.

PART II: Completion

Complete each of the following statements by writing the appropriate word(s) in the space provided.

1. The balance of Accounts Receivable after one has deducted the balance of Allowance for Doubtful Accounts is called the _____.

2. A method of accounting for bad debt losses that requires a debit to Bad Debts Expense and a credit to Accounts Receivable is called the _____ method.

3. A federal law excusing a debtor from certain obligations incurred is called _____.

4. A process of assigning costs to goods sold based on the flow-of-cost assumption that units sold are recorded at the costs of the most recently acquired goods is called _____.

Note: Answers to Before a Test Check begin on page A-1.

5. A method of inventory valuation requiring that the actual cost of each individual item in the ending inventory be used is called the _____ method.

6. The inventory system in which a running balance is kept of the inventory on hand and the current cost of each item is called the _____ system.

7. Expenditures for improvements that are not as permanent as the land or not directly associated with a building are debited to the _____ account.

8. The type of depreciation method that allows recording of larger amounts of depreciation in the early years of an asset's use is called a(n) _____ method.

9. The costs of normal day-to-day expenses associated with an asset are called _____.

10. The inventory system that requires a physical count and then attaches a value to that count is called the _____ inventory system.

PART III: Matching

For each numbered item, choose the matching term and write the identifying letter in the answer column.

____ 1. The systematic expensing of the cost of equipment over its useful life.

____ 2. Cost of major overhaul of an asset.

____ 3. Cost less trade-in or salvage value.

____ 4. Federal law excusing a debtor from certain obligations incurred.

____ 5. Analysis of the composition of outstanding accounts receivable.

____ 6. Cost less accumulated depreciation.

____ 7. Balance of Accounts Receivable minus Allowance for Doubtful Accounts.

____ 8. Method of inventory valuation ideal for high-priced units.

____ 9. Method of inventory valuation that yields the most realistic value of the asset.

____ 10. Method of inventory valuation that yields the lowest net income during a period of rising prices.

A. Perpetual system
B. Book value
C. Net realizable value
D. Periodic system
E. Depreciation
F. Aging
G. Capital expenditure
H. Revenue expenditure
I. Depreciation base
J. Specific identification
K. FIFO
L. LIFO
M. Weighted average
N. Bankruptcy
O. Extraordinary-repairs expenditure

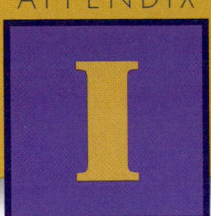
The Voucher System of Accounting

Performance Objectives

After you have completed this appendix, you will be able to do the following:

1. Prepare vouchers.

2. Record vouchers in a voucher register.

3. Record payment of vouchers in a check register.

4. Record transactions involving canceling or altering an original voucher.

T he voucher system is a means of achieving internal control and enabling the owner or manager to maintain contact with day-to-day transactions. This system promotes the delegation of duties and responsibilities.

OBJECTIVE OF THE VOUCHER SYSTEM

The objective of the voucher system is to control the incurrence of all liabilities and the payment of all expenditures—in other words, to control the purchase of (1) merchandise or materials, (2) other assets, and (3) services. The voucher system is suitable for companies of varying sizes that require a clear separation of duties. The voucher system has the following components: vouchers, voucher register, check register, unpaid voucher file, paid voucher file, and general journal.

VOUCHERS

The dictionary defines a voucher as a document that serves as proof of a transaction and, from a business point of view, also serves as a full description of the transaction. **When a business is using the voucher system, a voucher must be filled out for every invoice or bill received, whether it is to be paid immediately or in the future. The invoice or bill is usually stapled to the voucher.**

Characteristics of Vouchers

Just as the form of invoices varies from one company to another, so too the form of vouchers varies from one company to another. However, the characteristics listed on the following page are usually present.

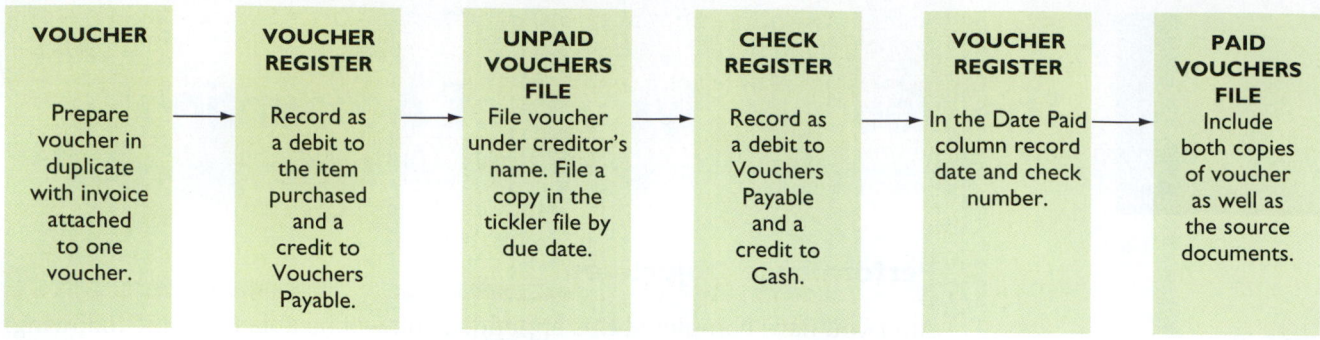

FIGURE 1

- Vouchers are numbered consecutively.
- The name and address of the payee or creditor appear on the voucher.
- The amount and credit terms of the invoice appear on the voucher.
- Vouchers state due dates so that firms can take advantage of possible cash discounts.
- For internal control, vouchers require signatures approving payment.
- Vouchers record payment: date paid and check number.

A completed voucher, with the invoice or bill stapled to it, describes an entire transaction as well as the procedure for processing the voucher. First, so that you can see the big picture, Figure 1 presents the steps involved in processing a voucher for a purchase of merchandise.

Preparation and Approval of Vouchers

OBJECTIVE 1

Prepare vouchers.

To cite a familiar example, let's assume that Rainier Plumbing Supply has now achieved such a volume of business that it is using a voucher system. Let's also assume that Rainier Plumbing Supply has received from its supplier, Collins, Inc., the invoice shown here.

Collins, Inc.
1614 Olivera Street
San Francisco, CA 94129

INVOICE

SOLD TO	*Rainier Plumbing Supply*		DATE:	*October 1, 20—*
	1400 Front Street		INVOICE NO.:	*3394*
	Seattle, WA 98101		ORDER NO.:	*9764*
			SHIPPED BY:	*Western Freight Line*
			TERMS:	*2/10, n/30*

QUANTITY	DESCRIPTION	UNIT PRICE	TOTAL
26	*Baxter oak-trimmed medicine cabinets*	26 70	694 20
	Freight		20 80
			715 00

Rainier Plumbing Supply's accountant, using the invoice as the source of information, fills out the following voucher. The face of the voucher lists the details of the transaction.

RAINIER PLUMBING SUPPLY
1400 Front Street
Seattle, WA 98101

No. 118

VOUCHER

PAY TO: Collins, Inc.
1614 Olivera St.
San Francisco, CA 94129

DATE _____ 10/1/20—_____

DATE OF INVOICE	TERMS	DESCRIPTION	AMOUNT	
10/1	2/10, n/30	Invoice No. 3394	694	20
		Less discount	13	88
		Freight	20	80
		Net amount payable	701	12

APPROVAL	DATES	APPROVED BY
Extensions and footings verified	10/2	M. C. L.
Prices in agreement with purchase order	10/2	S. T.
Credit terms in agreement with purchase order	10/2	S. T.
Quantities in agreement with receiving report	10/2	J. D. S.
Approved for payment	10/7	R. L. R.

ACCOUNT DISTRIBUTION

VOUCHER NO. _118_

ACCOUNT DEBITED	AMOUNT
Purchases	694.20
Freight In	20.80
Wages Payable	
Supplies Expense	
Miscellaneous Expense	
Total Vouchers Payable Cr.	715.00

Due Date 10/8

Pay To Collins, Inc.
1614 Olivera Street
San Francisco, CA 94129

SUMMARY OF CHARGES

Amount of invoice	$715.00
Less cash discount	13.88
Net amount	$701.12

RECORD OF PAYMENT

Paid by check no.	390
Date of check	10/8
Amount of check	701.12

ACCOUNT DISTRIBUTION by _____ R. R. H. _____

ENTERED IN VOUCHER REG. by _____ M. C. L. _____

	DATE	VOU. NO.	CREDITOR	PAYMENT DATE	CK. NO.	VOUCHERS PAYABLE CREDIT	PURCHASES DEBIT	
1	20–							
2	Oct. 1	117	Fast-Way Freight	10 1	383	6 3 00		
3	1	118	Collins, Inc.	10 8	390	7 1 5 00	6 9 4 20	
4	3	119	Dell Office Supply	10 3	384	4 8 72		
5	5	120	Stable Ins. Company	10 5	387	1 7 4 00		
6	9	121	Langseth and Son	10 18	404	3 2 8 00	3 0 6 00	
7	10	122	Payroll Bank Account	10 10	393	1 6 9 0 00		
8	12	123	Southland Journal			1 7 6 00		
9	12	124	Bradley Construction	10 12	395	1 1 6 00		
10	15	125	C. F. Rainier	10 15	399	5 0 0 00		
11	15	126	C. A. Waters, Inc.	10 18	By note	4 2 1 00	4 2 1 00	
28	29	149	Dana Mfg. Company			7 1 4 00	7 1 4 00	
29	30	150	Safety National Bank	10 30	412	1 5 0 7 50		
30								
31	31					10 9 1 9 68	4 3 6 1 90	
32						(2 1 2)	(5 1 1)	
33								
34								

REMEMBER!

Since the check register replaces the cash payments journal and the voucher register replaces the purchases journal, the special-column totals from the voucher register must be posted before those from the check register.

	Debits
Purchases	$ 4,361.90
Freight In	212.30
Wages Payable	3,314.00
Supplies Expense	121.79
Miscellaneous Expense	83.69
Other Accounts	2,826.00
	$10,919.68

The *due date* represents the last day on which one can take advantage of the cash discount. For example, the invoice of Collins, Inc., was dated October 1, with terms of 2/10, n/30. The discount period ends on October 11. Therefore, at the latest, send the check on October 8 to receive the discount.

The Account Distribution section is used to record the account titles and amounts to be debited, the total amount to be credited to Vouchers Payable, and the initials of the person authorized to determine the distribution.

THE VOUCHERS PAYABLE ACCOUNT

When you use a voucher system, you substitute the Vouchers Payable account for Accounts Payable. For example, when a firm buys merchandise on account, the accountant enters it as a debit to Purchases and a credit to Vouchers Payable. Similarly, when a firm buys store equipment on account, the accountant records it as a debit to Store Equipment and a credit to Vouchers Payable. Also, if a company incurs an expense on account, such as Advertising, the entry is a debit to Advertising Expense and a credit to Vouchers Payable.

FREIGHT-IN DEBIT	WAGES PAYABLE DEBIT	SUPPLIES EXPENSE DEBIT	MISCELLANEOUS EXPENSE DEBIT	OTHER ACCOUNTS DEBIT — ACCOUNT	POST. REF.	AMOUNT	
							1
	6 3 00						2
	2 0 80						3
		4 8 72					4
				Prepaid Insurance	116	1 7 4 00	5
	2 2 00						6
		1 6 9 0 00					7
				Advertising Expense	518	1 7 6 00	8
				Sales Returns and Allowances	412	1 1 6 00	9
				C. F. Rainier, Drawing	312	5 0 0 00	10
							11
							28
				Notes Payable	211	1 5 0 0 00	29
				Interest Expense	534	7 50	30
2 1 2 30	3 3 1 4 00	1 2 1 79	8 3 69			2 8 2 6 00	31
(5 1 4)	(2 1 3)	(1 1 5)	(5 1 9)			(X)	32
							33
							34

Credit

Vouchers Payable $10,919.68

When a check is issued in payment of a voucher, record the entry in the check register as a debit to Vouchers Payable and a credit to Cash. Again, we emphasize that *all* liabilities are recorded in the Vouchers Payable account.

THE VOUCHER REGISTER

OBJECTIVE 2

Record vouchers in a voucher register.

The **voucher register** has the status of a journal; it is a book of original entry. All vouchers must be recorded in it, in numerical order. Think of it as a multicolumn purchases journal. The voucher register has only one credit column, Vouchers Payable Credit, but a number of debit columns. Headings for the debit columns are selected on the basis of their frequency of use. In addition to the special columns, the voucher register also has space for recording the voucher number, the name of the creditor, the date of payment, and the check number. The voucher register for Rainier Plumbing Supply is shown above.

When you first record the voucher, leave the Payment Date and Ck. No. columns blank. After you have recorded the payment in the check register, go back to the voucher register and enter the date of payment and the number of the check.

Posting from the Voucher Register

The entries in the Other Accounts columns are posted *daily* to the general ledger, just as the Other Accounts columns of the other special journals are posted daily. The (X) under the column total means "do not post." At the end of the month, total all the columns, and prove the equality of the debit and credit entries by comparing the combined total of the debit columns with the total of the Vouchers Payable Credit column.

THE CHECK REGISTER

OBJECTIVE 3

Record payment of vouchers in a check register.

Any company or organization using a voucher system uses both the voucher register and the check register as books of original entry. Now let's look at the procedure for the check register. Since checks are issued only in payment of approved and recorded vouchers, the entry in the check register is always a debit to Vouchers Payable and a credit to Cash. A Vouchers Payable Debit column in the check register offsets the Vouchers Payable Credit column in the voucher register. Recall that after you record the entry in the check register, you enter the date and check number on the appropriate line in the voucher register and on the outside of the voucher in the Record of Payment section.

CHECK REGISTER   CH 10 & 11   PAGE __11__

	DATE	CK. NO.	PAYEE	VOU. NO.	VOUCHERS PAYABLE DEBIT	PURCHASES DISCOUNTS CREDIT	CASH CREDIT	
1	20–							1
2	Oct. 1	383	Fast-Way Freight	117	6 3 00		6 3 00	2
3	3	384	Dell Office Supply	119	4 8 72		4 8 72	3
4	3	385	Gardner Products Company	114	2 0 6 00	2 06	2 0 3 94	4
5	4	386	Dana Manufacturing Company	115	5 4 0 00	1 0 80	5 2 9 20	5
6	5	387	Stable Insurance Company	120	1 7 4 00		1 7 4 00	6
7	6	388	Void					7
8	6	389	Langseth and Son	116	4 6 4 00	9 28	4 5 4 72	8
9	8	390	Collins, Inc.	118	7 1 5 00	1 3 88	7 0 1 12	9
24	30	412	Safety National Bank	150	1 5 0 7 50		1 5 0 7 50	24
25	31				6 5 2 5 98	7 5 42	6 4 5 0 56	25
26					(2 1 2)	(5 1 3)	(1 1 1)	26
27								27

Debit

$6,525.98

Credits

$ 75.42
6,450.56
$6,525.98

HANDLING OF UNPAID VOUCHERS

Firms usually prepare vouchers in duplicate. In the system used by Rainier Plumbing Supply, the invoice is attached to the original copy of the voucher. Then the voucher is circulated within the company for the necessary signatures. After a voucher is recorded in the voucher register, it is filed under the name of the creditor. (Other companies may prepare only one copy of the voucher and file it only under the date on which it is supposed to be paid.)

At Rainier Plumbing Supply, the Unpaid Vouchers file contains all outstanding vouchers or credit memos. This file, organized by names of creditors, now acts as a subsidiary ledger. In fact, at Rainier Plumbing Supply, this file substitutes for the accounts payable ledger.

The *second* copy of the voucher goes to the treasurer, who files it chronologically by due date. This tickler file (a file of unpaid vouchers filed by due date) helps the treasurer forecast the amount of cash that will be needed to pay outstanding bills and take advantage of cash discounts.

At the end of the month, the accountant lists all the vouchers payable, taking the information directly from the Unpaid Vouchers file.

Rainier Plumbing Supply
Schedule of Vouchers Payable
October 31, 20—

VOU. NO.	NAME OF CREDITOR	AMOUNT
123	Southland Journal	$1 7 6 00
149	Dana Manufacturing Company	7 1 4 00
	Total Vouchers Payable	$8 9 0 00

FILING PAID VOUCHERS

Now let's assume that the firm has paid its bill. The payment is recorded in the check register and in the Payment columns of the voucher register. Then the voucher is stapled to the copy in the tickler file, marked paid, and filed in numerical order in a Paid Vouchers file.

SITUATIONS REQUIRING SPECIAL TREATMENT

OBJECTIVE 4

Record transactions involving canceling or altering an original voucher.

When a firm is using the voucher system, it inevitably runs into an occasional nonroutine transaction that does not fit into the fixed channels of the voucher system and therefore may require an entry in the general journal. You can consider such treatment as an adjustment to the voucher system.

Return of a Purchase Before Original Voucher Has Been Recorded

Normally, if a business with an efficient purchasing department is going to return any merchandise, it returns the merchandise before the vouchers are recorded in the voucher register. The accountant records the deduction right on the invoice and records the invoice in the voucher register for the net amount.

Return of a Purchase After Original Voucher Has Been Recorded

Assume that a business purchased merchandise for $566. The transaction was recorded in the voucher register as a debit to Purchases and a credit to Vouchers Payable. Later, the company returns $26 worth of defective merchandise. The return is recorded in the general journal as a debit to Vouchers Payable and a credit to Purchases Returns and Allowances. A notation "Return" is entered in the Payment column of the voucher register.

Installment Payments Planned at Time of Original Purchase

In a voucher system, invoices not subject to cash discounts are generally paid in full. Sometimes, however, management prefers to pay for an item in installments. When this happens, the company's accountant prepares a separate voucher for each installment and records each of these vouchers in the voucher register. Each voucher's due date corresponds to the date on which that installment is to be paid.

Installment Payments After Original Voucher Has Been Recorded

However, suppose that the buyer records the entire amount of the invoice on one voucher and *later* decides to pay the invoice in installments. The accountant must now cancel the original voucher by means of a general journal entry and issue a new voucher for each installment. A notation listing the new voucher numbers is made in the Payment column of the voucher register.

Correcting an Amount After Original Voucher Has Been Recorded

If an error in the purchase of merchandise is discovered after the voucher has been recorded in the voucher register, the original voucher must be canceled by means of a general journal entry debiting Vouchers Payable and crediting Purchases. Next, a new entry is made in the voucher register for the correct amount, debiting Purchases and crediting Vouchers Payable. A notation listing the new voucher number is made in the Payment column of the voucher register.

Issuing a Note Payable After Original Voucher Has Been Recorded

If a note is issued for the amount of an unpaid invoice after the voucher has been recorded, an entry must be made in the general journal to cancel the original voucher. The entry is a debit to Vouchers Payable and a credit to Notes Payable. A notation, "by Note," is made in the Date Paid column of the voucher register. When the note is to be paid, a new voucher is issued for the amount of the principal and interest, debiting Notes Payable and Interest Expense and crediting Vouchers Payable.

PROBLEMS

P.O. 2,3

Problem I-1 Alfonso Company uses a voucher system in which it records invoices at the **gross amount.** The following vouchers were issued during February and were unpaid on March 1:

Voucher Number	Company	For	Date of Voucher	Amount
1729	Kepper Company	Merchandise, FOB destination	Feb. 26	$3,436
1732	F. N. Karl	Merchandise, FOB destination	Feb. 28	$4,710

The following transactions were completed during March:

Mar.
3   Issued voucher no. 1734 in favor of Lindon Company for March rent, $1,220.

3   Issued Ck. No. 1829 in payment of voucher no. 1734, $1,220.

5   Bought merchandise on account from Loren, Inc., $3,890; terms 2/10, n/30; FOB shipping point; freight prepaid and added to the invoice, $72 (total, $3,962). Issued voucher no. 1735.

5   Issued Ck. No. 1830 in payment of voucher no. 1729, $3,401.64 ($3,436 less 1 percent cash discount).

9   Issued voucher no. 1736 in favor of Marner Electric Company for electric bill, $216.

9   Issued Ck. No. 1831 in payment of voucher no. 1736, $216.

9   Issued Ck. No. 1832 in payment of voucher no. 1732, $4,615.80 ($4,710 less 2 percent cash discount).

13 Issued Ck. No. 1833 in payment of voucher no. 1735, less the cash discount, $3,884.20. Recall that the freight portion is not eligible for discount.

16 Bought merchandise on account from Markle Manufacturing Company, $6,260; terms 2/10 EOM; FOB destination. Issued voucher no. 1737.

25 Issued voucher no. 1738 for note payable previously recorded in the general journal: principal, $4,000, plus $30 interest. The note is payable to the Southsound State Bank.

Mar. 25 Issued Ck. No. 1834 in payment of voucher no. 1737, $6,134.80 ($6,260 less 2 percent cash discount).

31 Issued voucher no. 1739 for wages payable, $4,985, in favor of the payroll bank account. (Assume that the payroll entry was previously recorded in the general journal.)

31 Paid voucher no. 1739 by issuing Ck. No. 1835, $4,985, to Payroll Bank Account.

Check Figure

Voucher Register, Vouchers Payable Credit total, $20,673

Instructions

1. Using the voucher issue date, enter the unpaid invoices in the voucher register, beginning with voucher no. 1729. Then draw double lines across all columns to separate the vouchers of February from those of March.
2. Record the transactions for March in the voucher register (page 65). Also record the appropriate transactions in the check register (page 71).
3. Total and rule the voucher register and the check register.
4. Prove the equality of the debits and credits in the voucher register and the check register.

P.O. 2,3,4

Problem I-2 Sellers Company, which uses a voucher system, has the following unpaid vouchers on July 1. The firm follows the practice of recording vouchers at the **gross amount.**

Voucher Number	Company	For	Date of Voucher	Amount
4789	Dolan and Son	Store equipment	June 15	$ 4,996
4795	Pauley and Company	Merchandise, FOB destination	June 28	$ 8,571
4797	K. P. Warren Company	Merchandise, FOB destination	June 28	$10,710

The company completed the following transactions during July:

July 1 Issued voucher no. 4800 in favor of Puget Insurance Company for a premium on a twelve-month fire insurance policy, $890.

2 Paid voucher no. 4789 by issuing Ck. No. 8219, $4,996.

2 Issued Ck. No. 8220 in payment of voucher no. 4800, $890.

3 Issued voucher no. 4801 in favor of Quint Quick Freight for transportation charges on merchandise purchases, $223.

5 Paid voucher no. 4801 by issuing Ck. No. 8221, $223.

7 Issued Ck. No. 8222 in payment of voucher no. 4795, $8,485.29 ($8,571 less 1 percent cash discount).

8 Issued Ck. No. 8223 in payment of voucher no. 4797, $10,602.90 ($10,710 less 1 percent cash discount).

11 Established a petty cash fund of $250. Issued voucher no. 4802.

11 Paid voucher no. 4802 by issuing Ck. No. 8224, $250.

13 Issued voucher no. 4803 in favor of Molini Company for merchandise, $14,708; terms 2/10, n/30; FOB shipping point; freight prepaid and added to the invoice, $384 (total, $15,092).

15 Received bill for advertising in the *Weekly Ads*. Issued voucher no. 4804 in the amount of $410.

July 17 Received a credit memo for $764 from Molini Company for merchandise returned to them, credit memo no. 540 (pertaining to voucher no. 4803).

20 Issued voucher no. 4805 in favor of Watcom County for six months' property tax (Prepaid Property Taxes), $2,272.

20 Paid voucher no. 4805 by issuing Ck. No. 8225, $2,272.

21 Issued Ck. No. 8226 in payment of voucher no. 4803, $14,049.12 ($14,708 less $764 return, less cash discount, plus freight).

23 Bought merchandise on account from Lander and Company, $6,039; terms 1/10, n/30; FOB destination. Issued voucher no. 4806.

27 Received a credit memo for $984 from Lander and Company for damaged merchandise, credit memo no. 437 (pertaining to voucher no. 4806).

31 Issued voucher no. 4807 to reimburse petty cash fund. The charges were:

Supplies Expense	$110.43
L. Sellers, Drawing	75.00
Miscellaneous Expense	39.67

31 Issued Ck. No. 8227 in payment of voucher no. 4807, $225.10.

31 Issued voucher no. 4808 for wages payable, $8,448, in favor of the payroll bank account. (Assume that the payroll entry was recorded previously in the general journal.)

31 Paid voucher no. 4808 by issuing Ck. No. 8228, payable to Payroll Bank Account.

Check Figure

Check Register, Cash Credit total $50,441.41

Instructions

1. Using the voucher issue date, enter the unpaid invoices in the voucher register, beginning with voucher no. 4789. Then draw double lines across all columns to separate the vouchers of June from those of July.
2. Enter the transactions for July in the voucher register (page 75) at the **gross amount.** Also record the appropriate transactions in the check register (page 86) and the general journal (page 41).
3. Total and rule the voucher register and the check register for the transactions recorded during July.
4. Prove the equality of the debits and credits on the voucher register and the check register.

P.O. 2,3,4

Problem I-3 Belson Systems uses a voucher system in which it records invoices at the **gross amount.** During October, it completed the following transactions:

Oct. 2 Prepared voucher no. 2632 in favor of Jacob and Bowen for the purchase of merchandise with an invoice price of $5,831; terms 30 days; FOB shipping point; freight prepaid and added to the invoice, $192 (total, $6,023). Leave an extra line after this entry.

3 Prepared vouchers no. 2633 for $1,010, 2634 for $1,010, and 2635 for $1,010. The debt arose because Belson Systems bought a personal computer, laser printer, and monitor from Interface, Inc. The terms are $1,010 cash on delivery, $1,010 in thirty days, and $1,010 in sixty days. (Use three lines.)

5 Issued Ck. No. 2725 in payment of voucher no. 2633, $1,010.

9 Issued voucher no. 2636 in favor of Wiggins Company for the purchase of supplies, $360.50; terms 30 days.

Oct. 12 Prepared voucher no. 2637 in favor of Glass Realty for rent for the month, $1,650.

12 Issued Ck. No. 2726 in payment of voucher no. 2637, $1,650.

16 Prepared voucher no. 2638 in favor of Blunt Cargo for freight charges on merchandise purchased, $104.

16 Prepared voucher no. 2639 in favor of Groen Company for the purchase of merchandise having a list price of $6,512 with a 25 percent trade discount (record voucher for $4,884); terms 2/10, n/30; FOB shipping point. Leave an extra line after this entry.

16 Issued Ck. No. 2727 in payment of voucher no. 2638, $104.00.

16 Canceled voucher no. 2632 because the invoice will be paid in two installments as follows: voucher no. 2640, payable November 1, $3,011.50; voucher no. 2641, payable November 15, $3,011.50. Prepared vouchers no. 2640 and 2641.

17 Received a credit memo from Groen Company for merchandise returned, $352, credit memo no. 580, voucher no. 2639.

22 Prepared voucher no. 2642 in favor of Maxel Telephone Company for telephone bill, $164.90.

22 Issued Ck. No. 2728 in payment of voucher no. 2642, $164.90.

23 Issued Ck. No. 2729 in payment of voucher no. 2639, $4,441.36. ($4,884 less $352 return, less cash discount.)

31 Prepared voucher no. 2643 for wages payable, $4,550, in favor of Payroll Bank Account. (Assume that the payroll entry was recorded previously in the general journal.)

31 Issued Ck. No. 2730 in payment of voucher no. 2643, $4,550.

31 Prepared voucher no. 2644 in favor of G. L. Belson, the owner, for personal withdrawal, $1,400.

31 Issued Ck. No. 2731 for payment of voucher no. 2644.

Check Figure

Schedule of Vouchers Payable total, $8,403.50

Instructions

1. Record the transactions for October in the voucher register (page 32), the check register (page 34), and the general journal (page 18).
2. Total and rule the voucher register and the check register.
3. Prove the equality of the debits and credits on the voucher register and the check register.
4. Post the amounts from the registers and the general journal to the Vouchers Payable account, No. 212. Assume no previous balance in the account.
5. Prepare a schedule of vouchers payable. Compare this total with the balance of the Vouchers Payable account.

19 Partnerships

LINKS TO ACCOUNTING

The partnership form of business organization may be used by any company that has more than one owner. Service businesses, such as law firms, are frequently structured as partnerships. Even Deloitte Touche Tohmatsu, PricewaterhouseCoopers, and Ernst & Young, the largest of the U.S.-based international public accounting firms, are set up as partnerships. In particular, they are limited liability partnerships (LLPs). Every partnership should have a written agreement that states the rights and responsibilities of each partner. You can find information about what to include in a partnership agreement by visiting **http://www.nolo.com/**. In the Search box type "partnership agreement" and below the box select "Search Entire Site." Then, choose "Creating a Partnership Agreement."

Performance Objectives

After you have completed this chapter, you will be able to do the following:

1. (a) Define the various kinds of partnerships and list the main advantages and disadvantages of a partnership; (b) journalize initial investments.

2. Provide for the division of net income and loss on the basis of (a) fractional shares; (b) ratio of capital investments; and (c) salary and interest allowances.

3. Journalize the closing entries for a partnership on the basis of (a) fractional shares; (b) ratio of capital investments; and (c) salary and interest allowances.

4. Prepare a statement of partners' equity.

5. Journalize entries involving the sale of a partnership interest or withdrawal of a partner.

6. Journalize entries pertaining to the liquidation of a partnership involving the immediate sale of the assets for cash.

Up until now, we have been dealing entirely with sole proprietorships. In this chapter, we turn our attention to partnerships. In the professions and in firms that stress personal service, partnerships are widely used. Each professional practitioner can maintain his or her own clientele, yet share with colleagues the expenses of operating an office or clinic. Partnerships are also popular in manufacturing and trade because they afford a means of combining the capital and abilities of two or more persons.

TYPES OF PARTNERSHIPS

 OBJECTIVE 1a

Define the various kinds of partnerships and list the main advantages and disadvantages of a partnership.

There are three types of partnerships: general, limited, and limited liability partnerships.

General Partnership (GP)

A **general partnership (GP)** is an association of two or more people or firms to carry on, as co-owners, a business for profit. The partners are called general partners, and each partner is personally liable for all of the debts the partnership incurs during his or her membership in the firm. Because of the unlimited liability of the general partners, firms today are usually not set up as general partnerships.

Limited Partnership (LP)

A **limited partnership (LP)** is an organization with two or more people or firms with at least one general partner and one limited partner. The general partner (with unlimited liability) may have little or no investment, organizes the partnership, manages day-to-day operations, and controls the operation of the partnership. The limited partner or partners have the largest share of invested capital, are not involved in the day-to-day operations, and usually cannot lose more than their capital contribution. Limited partnerships used to be the preferred entity as vehicles for raising capital. They have generally been replaced by limited liability corporations (LLCs) or corporations, which are discussed in Chapter 20.

Limited Liability Partnership (LLP)

A **limited liability partnership (LLP)** is an organization similar to a limited partnership except that all partners may take an active role in the business of the partnership with only their invested capital at risk. Many law and accounting firms are now operated as LLPs.

CHARACTERISTICS OF A PARTNERSHIP

General, limited, and limited liability partnerships all share the following characteristics.

Co-ownership of Partnership Property

All partners are co-owners of the assets of the partnership. For example, Towne and Dillon formed a 50-50 partnership to run a fuel business. The partnership owns two tank trucks of equal value. According to the **co-ownership** concept, each partner owns half of each truck, as well as half of the other assets of the firm.

Limited Life

> **REMEMBER!**
>
> Just because a partnership ends does not necessarily mean that the business ends. It can continue under a new partnership agreement.

A partnership may be ended by the death or withdrawal of any partner. Other factors that may bring about the end of a partnership include the bankruptcy or incapacity of a partner, the expiration of the period of time specified in the partnership agreement, or the completion of the project for which the partnership was formed.

Mutual Agency

Each partner can enter into binding contracts in the name of the firm for the purchase or sale of goods or services within the normal scope of the firm's business and based upon the provisions of the partnership agreement.

Although accounting for partnerships is essentially the same as accounting for sole proprietorships, not all partnerships are small. All the major accounting firms, as well as many legal organizations, are limited liability partnerships (note the "LLP" after the firm name of Ernst & Young).

ADVANTAGES OF A PARTNERSHIP

> **REMEMBER!**
>
> Partnerships allow pooling of time, money, and talent. They can also have the same difficulties as any personal relationship. Therefore, a written agreement is extremely important.

Here are four advantages of a partnership:

1. Partnerships offer the opportunity to pool the abilities and capital of two or more persons or firms.
2. It is easy to form a partnership, the only requirement being an agreement or mutual understanding by the partners. If there is no written partnership agreement, then it is a general partnership.
3. Legal restrictions are minimal. Although a partnership must have a legal purpose, there are no other limitations on types of business activities.
4. Federal income taxes are not levied against a partnership as an entity, although a partnership must file an information return (Form 1065) containing an income statement, balance sheet, and report of the distributive shares of income (the shares of the year's net income allocated to each partner). A partner has to file an individual income tax return and has to pay taxes on his or her share of the net income, whether or not this share is actually taken out of the business.

DISADVANTAGES OF A PARTNERSHIP

Here are five disadvantages of a partnership:

1. General partners (those who actively and publicly participate in transactions of the firm) have unlimited liability.
2. A partnership has limited life.
3. The actions of one partner are binding on the other partners, unless limited by the partnership agreement; this relationship is known as **mutual agency**. (This could also be an advantage.)
4. It is hard to transfer a partial or entire partnership interest to another person, as the transfer must generally be agreed to by all partners.
5. There may be some strain in personal relationships among partners as they carry out their daily responsibilities.

PARTNERSHIP AGREEMENTS

Although a general partnership may be formed on the basis of an oral understanding, a limited partnership and a limited liability partnership must be based upon a written contract. The following provisions are usually included:

- Effective date of the agreement
- Names and addresses of the partners
- Name, location, and nature of the business
- Type of partnership
- Management structure
- Duration of the agreement
- Investment of each partner
- Procedure for sharing profits and losses
- Withdrawals to be allowed each partner
- Procedure for a partner's exit from the business
- Provision for division of assets upon liquidation

ACCOUNTING ENTRIES FOR PARTNERSHIPS

REMEMBER!

Accounting for a partnership is basically the same as accounting for other business entities. The major difference is that the partnership has a Capital account and a Drawing account for each partner.

The only difference between accounting for a sole proprietorship and accounting for a partnership is in the owners' equity accounts. The accountant uses the same types of asset, liability, revenue, and expense accounts that we discussed before. But, because there is more than one owner, each partner has a Capital account and a Drawing account. As in sole proprietorships, the Capital accounts are involved only when there is a change in investments or when the Income Summary account and the Drawing accounts are closed.

Recording Investments

OBJECTIVE 1b
Journalize initial investments.

The accountant makes a separate entry for the investment of each partner. All assets contributed by a given partner are debited to the appropriate asset accounts. If the partnership assumes liabilities, the accountant credits the proper liability accounts. When the value of a partner's contributed assets exceeds the value of the partner's assumed liabilities, the partner's Capital account is credited for the net amount.

Let's look at the recording of initial investments in a partnership: Ralph H. Fox and Rita L. Lang decide to form a partnership on February 2 for the operation of a jewelry store. Fox presently owns and operates Fox Jewelers. He is contributing the assets and liabilities of his store to the new firm. Lang's investment is $190,000 in cash; the entry on page 1 of the general journal to record this investment is as follows:

	GENERAL JOURNAL			PAGE 1
DATE	DESCRIPTION	POST. REF.	DEBIT	CREDIT
20–				
Feb. 2	Cash		190 000 00	
	Rita L. Lang, Capital			190 000 00
	To record the original			
	investment of Rita L. Lang.			

Both partners have to agree on the monetary amounts at which Fox's non-cash assets are to be recorded. Assume that Fox Jewelers has the following account balances:

Cash	$ 2,900
Accounts Receivable	18,000
Allowance for Doubtful Accounts	200
Merchandise Inventory	180,400
Equipment	16,000
Accumulated Depreciation, Equipment	4,500
Notes Payable	1,600
Accounts Payable	8,400

Furthermore, $400 of the accounts receivable has been determined to be uncollectible; the $400 should not be recorded on the books of the new partnership. Of the remaining $17,600 of accounts receivable, there is some doubt as to the collectibility of $500. Assume that these amounts have been determined by aging the accounts receivable. Since the values of the merchandise and equipment may be more or less than the amounts recorded on Fox's books, both parties agree to have an independent appraisal made. Assume that the present appraised value of Fox's merchandise is $181,000 and his equipment is $9,000. Therefore, the accountant records Fox's investment as shown on the following page.

DATE		DESCRIPTION	POST. REF.	DEBIT	CREDIT	
6						6
7	Feb.	2	Cash		2 9 0 0 00		7
8			Accounts Receivable		17 6 0 0 00		8
9			Merchandise Inventory		181 0 0 0 00		9
10			Equipment		9 0 0 0 00		10
11			Allowance for Doubtful				11
12			Accounts			5 0 0 00	12
13			Notes Payable			1 6 0 0 00	13
14			Accounts Payable			8 4 0 0 00	14
15			Ralph H. Fox, Capital			200 0 0 0 00	15
16			To record the original				16
17			investment of Ralph H. Fox.				17
18							18

The accountant debits Accounts Receivable for the face amount of the accounts taken over by the new partnership and credits Allowance for Doubtful Accounts for the amount estimated to be uncollectible, which in this case is $500. Any definitely uncollectible customer accounts are excluded from those being taken over by the new business (in this case, the $400 in uncollectible accounts is subtracted from the $18,000 in Accounts Receivable).

The accountant debits the new firm's Merchandise Inventory and Equipment accounts for the amounts of their present appraised values. The accumulated depreciation is not recorded because the appraised value of the equipment represents the new book value for the partnership.

Additional Investments

Now let's say that eight months have gone by, and the new partnership needs more cash. On October 1, each partner invests an additional $7,000. The entry is as follows:

REMEMBER!

An original investment by a partner may include liabilities as well as assets.

FYI

Additional investments appear in the same place on the statement of partners' equity as on the statement of owner's equity.

	GENERAL JOURNAL		PAGE	28

	DATE		DESCRIPTION	POST. REF.	DEBIT	CREDIT	
1	20–						1
2	Oct.	1	Cash		14 0 0 0 00		2
3			Ralph H. Fox, Capital			7 0 0 0 00	3
4			Rita L. Lang, Capital			7 0 0 0 00	4
5			To record additional				5
6			investments.				6
7							7

At the end of the year, before the books are closed, the Capital accounts of the partners appear as shown here:

GENERAL LEDGER

ACCOUNT   Ralph H. Fox, Capital   ACCOUNT NO.   301

	DATE		ITEM	POST. REF.	DEBIT	CREDIT	BALANCE DEBIT	BALANCE CREDIT	
1	20–								1
2	Feb.	2		J1		200 0 0 0 00		200 0 0 0 00	2
3	Oct.	1		J28		7 0 0 0 00		207 0 0 0 00	3

ACCOUNT   Rita L. Lang, Capital   ACCOUNT NO.   303

	DATE		ITEM	POST. REF.	DEBIT	CREDIT	BALANCE DEBIT	BALANCE CREDIT	
1	20–								1
2	Feb.	2		J1		190 0 0 0 00		190 0 0 0 00	2
3	Oct.	1		J28		7 0 0 0 00		197 0 0 0 00	3

Drawing Accounts

Drawing accounts of partners serve the same purpose as the Drawing account of the owner of a sole proprietorship. Debits to the Drawing accounts originate through transactions such as those listed here and illustrated in Figure 1.

- Withdrawal of cash by Ralph. H. Fox, $4,620, March 17.
- Withdrawal of merchandise by Rita. L. Lang, $3,742, May 4.

FIGURE 1

	DATE		DESCRIPTION	POST. REF.	DEBIT	CREDIT	
1	20–						1
2	Mar.	17	Ralph H. Fox, Drawing		4 6 2 0 00		2
3			Cash			4 6 2 0 00	3
4			To record a cash withdrawal.				4
5							5
6	May	4	Rita L. Lang, Drawing		3 7 4 2 00		6
7			Purchases			3 7 4 2 00	7
8			To record a merchandise				8
9			withdrawal at cost.				9
10							10

DIVISION OF NET INCOME OR NET LOSS

Recall that the closing entries for a sole proprietorship require the following steps:

1. Close the revenue accounts into the Income Summary account.
2. Close the expense accounts into the Income Summary account (the expense accounts do not include any payments to the owner).
3. Close the Income Summary account into the Capital account by the amount of the net income or loss.
4. Close the Drawing account into the Capital account.

The only differences between closing entries for a partnership and those for a sole proprietorship occur in steps 3 and 4. Instead of a single Capital account and a single Drawing account, in a partnership there are as many accounts of each type as there are partners. Income Summary is closed into the Capital accounts by the amount of the net income or loss to be distributed to each partner, and the Drawing accounts are closed into the respective Capital accounts.

Let's look at step 3. The partnership agreement should specify the arrangement for the division of net income or net loss. However, if the partnership agreement fails to do this, from a legal standpoint, the partners should share any net income or loss equally. This is true regardless of differences in amounts invested, in special skills provided, or in time devoted to the business. The share of net income (or net loss) allocated to each partner is known as his or her **distributive share**.

Partners may use any one of a number of alternative methods of sharing partnership earnings, or they may use a combination of methods. The variety of methods reflects the different values of the services or investments contributed by individual partners. We discuss four methods for sharing earnings:

1. Division of income based on fractional shares
2. Division of income based on the ratio of capital investments
3. Division of income based on salary allowances
4. Division of income based on interest allowances

We look at two examples of each method.

In our first example, the partnership of Bell & Campbell LLP has a net *income* of $248,000. In the second, the partnership of Bell & Campbell LLP has a net *loss* of $4,000. We use the same balances in the Capital and Drawing accounts for each example and consider that each method used for dividing net income represents a separate provision in the partnership agreement.

The balances of the Capital accounts represent the partners' individual investments at the beginning of the year. The balances of the Drawing accounts represent the total personal withdrawals during the year. These are shown by T accounts as follows:

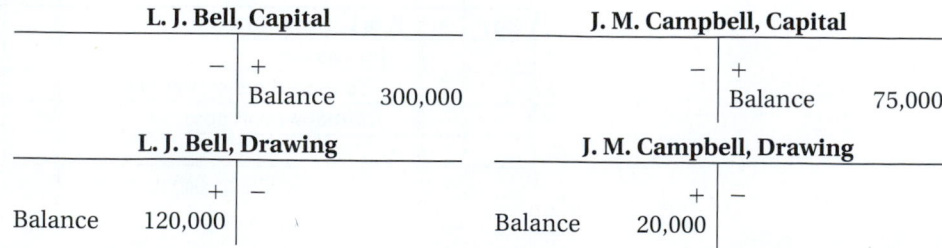

Closing entries for a partnership are similar to those of a sole proprietorship. The partnership agreement should detail the percentages of net income or net loss to attribute to each partner. In the case of Russ & Daughters, it would appear that there are at least three partners. They may divide the income based on fractional shares, the ratio of capital investments, salary allowances, or interest allowances.

Division of Income Based on Fractional Shares

OBJECTIVE 2a

Provide for the division of net income and loss on the basis of fractional shares.

The simplest way to divide net income or loss is to allot each partner a stated fraction of the total. You can establish the size of the fraction by taking into consideration (1) the amount of each partner's investment and (2) the value of the services rendered by each partner. Assume that the partnership agreement stipulates that profits and losses are to be divided this way: three-fourths to Bell and one-fourth to Campbell.

The accountant may present a report of the division of net income as a separate statement or record it on the income statement, immediately below Net Income.

REMEMBER!

Financial statements for a partnership are basically the same as those of other business entities except for one main difference—the section showing the division of net income.

Net Income of $248,000 If the accountant adopts the latter procedure, the division of net income appears as follows:

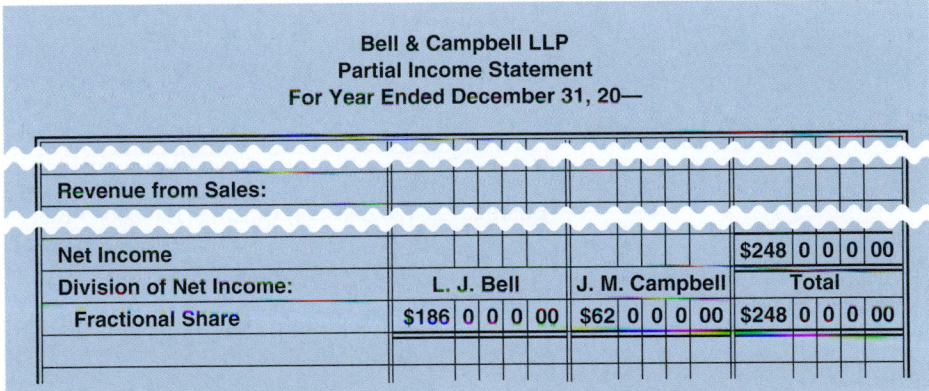

Bell & Campbell LLP
Partial Income Statement
For Year Ended December 31, 20—

	L. J. Bell	J. M. Campbell	Total
Revenue from Sales:			
Net Income			$248 0 0 0 00
Division of Net Income:	L. J. Bell	J. M. Campbell	Total
Fractional Share	$186 0 0 0 00	$62 0 0 0 00	$248 0 0 0 00

OBJECTIVE 3a

Journalize the closing entries for a partnership on the basis of fractional shares.

The division of net income is recorded as a closing entry in step 3 of the closing procedure, whether or not the partner has withdrawn his or her share. The entry is as follows:

	DATE		DESCRIPTION	POST. REF.	DEBIT	CREDIT	
1	20—		Closing Entry				1
2	Dec.	31	Income Summary		248 0 0 0 00		2
3			L. J. Bell, Capital			186 0 0 0 00	3
4			J. M. Campbell, Capital			62 0 0 0 00	4
5							5
6							6

The entries for step 4, closing the Drawing accounts into the Capital accounts, are as follows:

DATE		DESCRIPTION	POST. REF.	DEBIT	CREDIT	
20–		**Closing Entries**				1
Dec.	31	L. J. Bell, Capital		120 0 0 0 00		2
		L. J. Bell, Drawing			120 0 0 0 00	3
						4
	31	J. M. Campbell, Capital		20 0 0 0 00		5
		J. M. Campbell, Drawing			20 0 0 0 00	6
						7
						8

Now let's see what these entries look like in T accounts, with steps 3 and 4 labeled:

Income Summary	
(3) Closing 248,000	Balance 248,000

L. J. Bell, Capital	
− | +	
(4) 120,000	Balance 300,000
	(3) 186,000

J. M. Campbell, Capital	
− | +	
(4) 20,000	Balance 75,000
	(3) 62,000

L. J. Bell, Drawing	
+ | −	
Balance 120,000	**(4)** Closing 120,000

J. M. Campbell, Drawing	
+ | −	
Balance 20,000	**(4)** Closing 20,000

Note that step 4 is the same for partnerships as for sole proprietorships.

Net Loss of $4,000   The lower portion of the income statement reflects the net loss. (The parentheses around the totals indicate that the figures are negative numbers.)

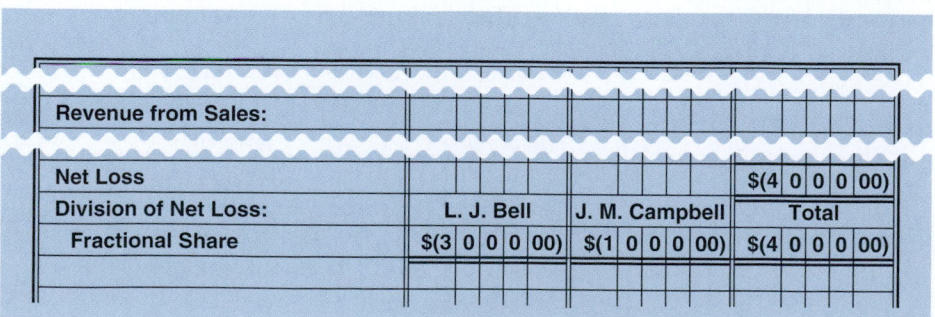

	L. J. Bell	J. M. Campbell	Total
Revenue from Sales:			
Net Loss			$(4 0 0 0 00)
Division of Net Loss:			
Fractional Share	$(3 0 0 0 00)	$(1 0 0 0 00)	$(4 0 0 0 00)

	DATE		DESCRIPTION	POST. REF.	DEBIT	CREDIT	
1	20–		**Closing Entries**				1
2	Dec.	31	L. J. Bell, Capital		3 0 0 0 00		2
3			J. M. Campbell, Capital		1 0 0 0 00		3
4			Income Summary			4 0 0 0 00	4
5							5
6		31	L. J. Bell, Capital		120 0 0 0 00		6
7			L. J. Bell, Drawing			120 0 0 0 00	7
8							8
9		31	J. M. Campbell, Capital		20 0 0 0 00		9
10			J. M. Campbell, Drawing			20 0 0 0 00	10
11							11

FIGURE 2

The closing entries and posting to the ledger accounts are shown in Figure 2 and the T accounts that follow:

Income Summary

Balance	4,000	(3) Closing	4,000

L. J. Bell, Capital

	–	+	
(3)	3,000	Balance	300,000
(4)	120,000		

J. M. Campbell, Capital

	–	+	
(3)	1,000	Balance	75,000
(4)	20,000		

L. J. Bell, Drawing

	+	–	
Balance	120,000	(4) Closing	120,000

J. M. Campbell, Drawing

	+	–	
Balance	20,000	(4) Closing	20,000

When partners share net income on a fractional basis, this basis is often expressed as a ratio. We can express Bell's three-fourths and Campbell's one-fourth as a 3 : 1 (3-to-1) ratio.

When you list the division of net income as a ratio and want to turn the ratio into a fraction, do it this way: First add the figures; then use the total as the denominator of the fraction.

$3 : 1$ $(3 + 1 = 4)$ $\frac{3}{4}$ and $\frac{1}{4}$

or (in the case of three partners):

$5 : 3 : 1$ $(5 + 3 + 1 = 9)$ $\frac{5}{9}$ and $\frac{3}{9}$ and $\frac{1}{9}$

or (in the case of four partners):

$3 : 2 : 1 : 1$ $(3 + 2 + 1 + 1 = 7)$ $\frac{3}{7}$ and $\frac{2}{7}$ and $\frac{1}{7}$ and $\frac{1}{7}$

Division of Income Based on Ratio of Capital Investments

OBJECTIVE 2b

Provide for the division of net income and loss on the basis of ratio of capital investments.

Allocating earnings to partners on the basis of the amounts of their investment often works well for enterprises whose earnings are closely related to the amount of money invested, such as real estate ventures, cattle feeding operations, and the like. Suppose that the partners of Bell & Campbell LLP have agreed to share earnings or losses according to the ratio of their investments at the beginning of the year. Let's say that Bell had $300,000 and Campbell had $75,000 in their Capital accounts. You can calculate their respective shares as follows:

Bell	$300,000
Campbell	75,000
Total	$375,000

Bell's share $= \dfrac{\$300,000}{\$375,000} = \dfrac{12}{15}$ or $\underline{0.80}$ (80%)

Campbell's share $= \dfrac{\$75,000}{\$375,000} = \dfrac{3}{15}$ or $\underline{0.20}$ (20%)

Net Income of $248,000 When the partnership has a net income of $248,000, the accountant determines the distribution like this:

Bell's share of earnings $\qquad$ $\$248,000 \times {}^{12}\!/_{15}$ (or $\$248,000 \times 0.80$) = $\underline{\$198,400}$

Campbell's share of earnings $\qquad$ $\$248,000 \times {}^{3}\!/_{15}$ (or $\$248,000 \times 0.20$) = $\underline{\$\ 49,600}$

The section of the income statement showing the division of net income looks like this:

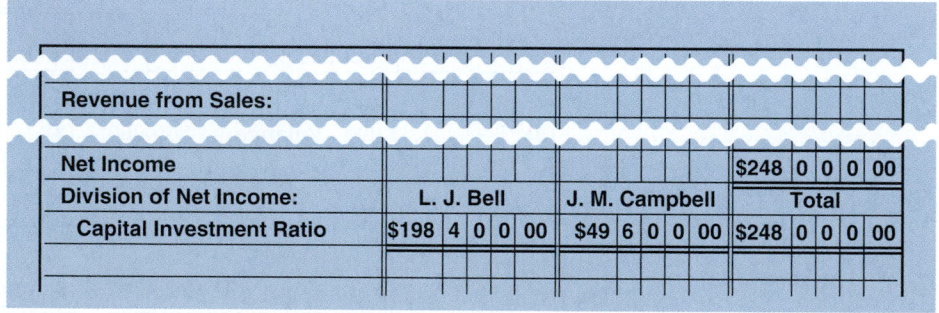

Revenue from Sales:			
Net Income			$248 0 0 0 00
Division of Net Income:	L. J. Bell	J. M. Campbell	Total
Capital Investment Ratio	$198 4 0 0 00	$49 6 0 0 00	$248 0 0 0 00

OBJECTIVE 3b

Journalize the closing entries for a partnership on the basis of ratio of capital investments.

The accompanying closing entries are as follows:

	DATE		DESCRIPTION	POST. REF.	DEBIT	CREDIT	
1	20–		**Closing Entries**				1
2	Dec.	31	Income Summary		248 0 0 0 00		2
3			L. J. Bell, Capital			198 4 0 0 00	3
4			J. M. Campbell, Capital			49 6 0 0 00	4
5							5
6		31	L. J. Bell, Capital		120 0 0 0 00		6
7			L. J. Bell, Drawing			120 0 0 0 00	7
8							8
9		31	J. M. Campbell, Capital		20 0 0 0 00		9
10			J. M. Campbell, Drawing			20 0 0 0 00	10
11							11

Net Loss of $4,000 When the partnership has a net loss of $4,000, the accountant calculates the sharing of the loss as follows:

Bell's share of the loss	$4,000 × 12⁄15 (or $4,000 × 0.80) = $3,200
Campbell's share of the loss	$4,000 × 3⁄15 (or $4,000 × 0.20) = $ 800

The section of the income statement showing the division of net loss and the accompanying closing entries look like this:

Revenue from Sales:			
Net Loss			$(4 0 0 0 00)
Division of Net Loss:	L. J. Bell	J. M. Campbell	Total
Capital Investment Ratio	$(3 2 0 0 00)	$(8 0 0 00)	$(4 0 0 0 00)

DATE		DESCRIPTION	POST. REF.	DEBIT	CREDIT	
20–		**Closing Entries**				1
Dec.	31	L. J. Bell, Capital		3 2 0 0 00		2
		J. M. Campbell, Capital		8 0 0 00		3
		Income Summary			4 0 0 0 00	4
						5
	31	L. J. Bell, Capital		120 0 0 0 00		6
		L. J. Bell, Drawing			120 0 0 0 00	7
						8
	31	J. M. Campbell, Capital		20 0 0 0 00		9
		J. M. Campbell, Drawing			20 0 0 0 00	10

Note that the entries for step 4—closing the Drawing accounts into the Capital accounts—are always the same, regardless of whether the firm finishes the year with a net income or a net loss.

Division of Income Based on Salary Allowances

OBJECTIVE 2c

Provide for the division of net income and loss on the basis of salary and interest allowances.

Salary allowances are purely allocations of net income. They are used as a means of recognizing and rewarding differences in ability and in the amount of time devoted to the business. **Salary allowances are different from payments to the partners, which are recorded in the Drawing accounts.** They are also different from payments to employees, which are recorded as Salary Expense or Wages Expense. For income tax purposes they are called guaranteed payments. The payments are determined without regard to the income of the partnership.

Suppose that Bell's and Campbell's partnership agreement provides for yearly salaries of $60,000 and $40,000, respectively, with the remainder of the net income to be divided equally. (It would also be possible to divide the remainder on the basis of the ratio of investments or any other ratio agreed to by the partners.)

Net Income of $248,000 When there is a net income of $248,000, the Division of Net Income section of the income statement is as follows:

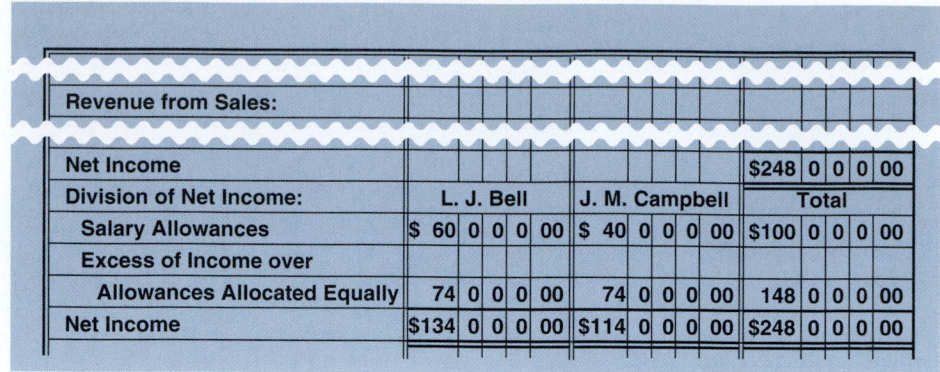

	L. J. Bell	J. M. Campbell	Total
Revenue from Sales:			
Net Income			$248 0 0 0 00
Division of Net Income:	L. J. Bell	J. M. Campbell	Total
Salary Allowances	$ 60 0 0 0 00	$ 40 0 0 0 00	$100 0 0 0 00
Excess of Income over Allowances Allocated Equally	74 0 0 0 00	74 0 0 0 00	148 0 0 0 00
Net Income	$134 0 0 0 00	$114 0 0 0 00	$248 0 0 0 00

REMEMBER!

If the partnership agreement does not stipulate the allocation of the net income or loss after allowances, it is assumed to be divided equally.

The accountant determines the allocation of the remainder as follows:

Net income	$248,000
Less amount allocated as salaries ($60,000 + $40,000)	100,000
Remainder	$148,000

$$\text{Remainder} \div 2 = \frac{\$148,000}{2} = \$74,000$$

OBJECTIVE 3c

Journalize the closing entries for a partnership on the basis of salary and interest allowances.

Now look at the closing entries:

	DATE		DESCRIPTION	POST. REF.	DEBIT	CREDIT	
1	20–		Closing Entries				1
2	Dec.	31	Income Summary		248 0 0 0 00		2
3			L. J. Bell, Capital			134 0 0 0 00	3
4			J. M. Campbell, Capital			114 0 0 0 00	4
5							5
6		31	L. J. Bell, Capital		120 0 0 0 00		6
7			L. J. Bell, Drawing			120 0 0 0 00	7
8							8
9		31	J. M. Campbell, Capital		20 0 0 0 00		9
10			J. M. Campbell, Drawing			20 0 0 0 00	10
11							11

Net Loss of $4,000 When salary allowances are stipulated in the partnership agreement, they must be allocated (not necessarily paid) regardless of whether there is enough net income to cover them.

The accountant determines the remainder as follows:

Net loss	$ (4,000)
Less amount allocated as salaries ($60,000 + $40,000)	100,000
Remainder	$(104,000)

$$\text{Remainder} \div 2 = \frac{\$(104,000)}{2} = \$(52,000)$$

The income statement and the closing entries appear as follows:

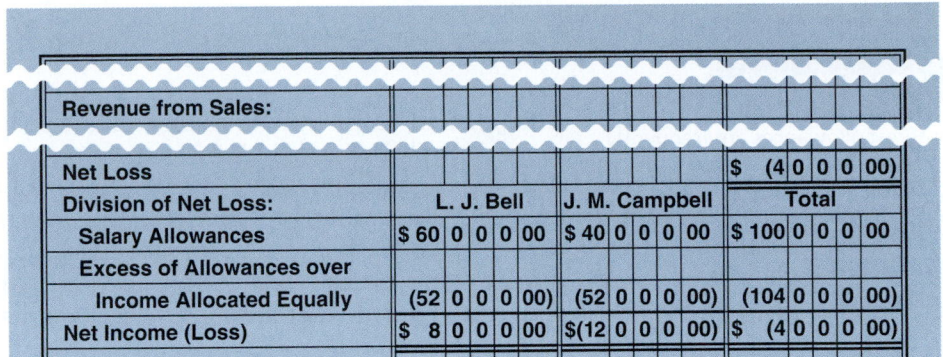

		Revenue from Sales:						

Net Loss					$ (4 0 0 0 00)
Division of Net Loss:	**L. J. Bell**	**J. M. Campbell**	**Total**
Salary Allowances	$ 60 0 0 0 00	$ 40 0 0 0 00	$ 100 0 0 0 00
Excess of Allowances over			
Income Allocated Equally	(52 0 0 0 00)	(52 0 0 0 00)	(104 0 0 0 00)
Net Income (Loss)	$ 8 0 0 0 00	$(12 0 0 0 00)	$ (4 0 0 0 00)

	DATE		DESCRIPTION	POST. REF.	DEBIT	CREDIT	
1	20–		**Closing Entries**				1
2	Dec.	31	J. M. Campbell, Capital		12 0 0 0 00		2
3			Income Summary			4 0 0 0 00	3
4			L. J. Bell, Capital			8 0 0 0 00	4
5							5
6		31	L. J. Bell, Capital		120 0 0 0 00		6
7			L. J. Bell, Drawing			120 0 0 0 00	7
8							8
9		31	J. M. Campbell, Capital		20 0 0 0 00		9
10			J. M. Campbell, Drawing			20 0 0 0 00	10
11							11

After posting, the partners' equity accounts look like this:

Income Summary

	Balance	4,000	(3) Closing 4,000

L. J. Bell, Capital

	–	+	
(4)	120,000	Balance	300,000
		(3)	8,000

J. M. Campbell, Capital

	–	+	
(3)	12,000	Balance	75,000
(4)	20,000		

L. J. Bell, Drawing

	+	–	
Balance	120,000	(4) Closing	120,000

J. M. Campbell, Drawing

	+	–	
Balance	20,000	(4) Closing	20,000

As a result of the $4,000 net loss for the year and the activity in the drawing accounts, Bell's Capital account decreased by $112,000 (credit $8,000 and debit $120,000), and Campbell's Capital account decreased by $32,000 (debit $12,000 and debit $20,000).

Division of Income Based on Interest Allowances

Sometimes a partnership agreement stipulates an allowance for interest on the partners' capital investments. This clause acts as an incentive for partners not only to leave their investments in the business, but even to increase them. For example, suppose that the partners at Bell & Campbell LLP are allowed, in addition to their salary allowances of $60,000 and $40,000, 6 percent interest on their Capital balances at the beginning of the fiscal year; the remainder is to be divided equally. Interest allowances, like salary allowances, are just allocations of net income.

Interest allowance for Bell $300,000 × 0.06 = $18,000

Interest allowance for Campbell $75,000 × 0.06 = $ 4,500

Net Income of $248,000 The section of the income statement relating to the division of a $248,000 net income appears as follows:

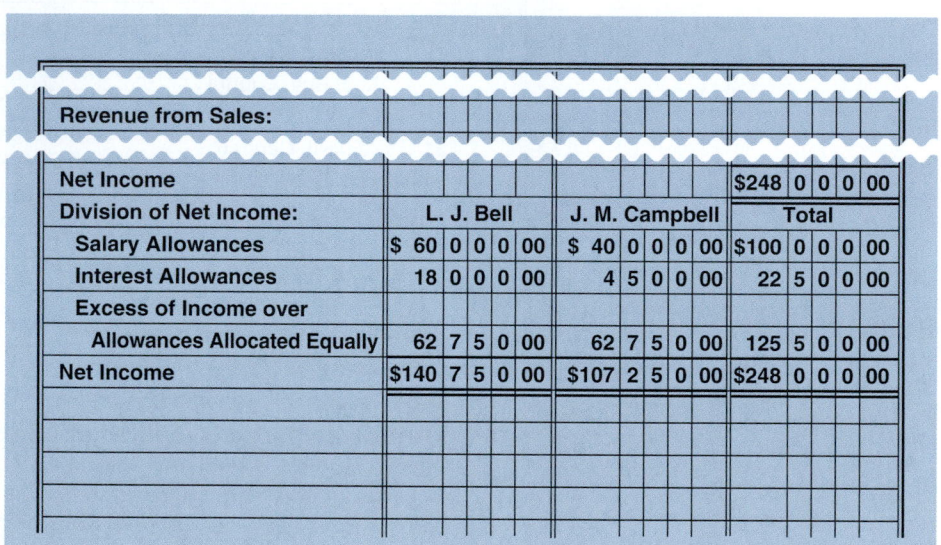

	L. J. Bell	J. M. Campbell	Total
Revenue from Sales:			
Net Income			$248 0 0 0 00
Division of Net Income:	L. J. Bell	J. M. Campbell	Total
Salary Allowances	$ 60 0 0 0 00	$ 40 0 0 0 00	$100 0 0 0 00
Interest Allowances	18 0 0 0 00	4 5 0 0 00	22 5 0 0 00
Excess of Income over			
Allowances Allocated Equally	62 7 5 0 00	62 7 5 0 00	125 5 0 0 00
Net Income	$140 7 5 0 00	$107 2 5 0 00	$248 0 0 0 00

The accountant calculates the remainder in the following way:

Net income		$248,000
Less:		
Amount allocated as salaries ($60,000 + $40,000)	$100,000	
Amount allocated as interest ($18,000 + $4,500)	22,500	122,500
Remainder		$125,500

$$\text{Remainder} \div 2 = \frac{\$125,500}{2} = \$62,750$$

And the closing entries look like the following:

	DATE		DESCRIPTION	POST. REF.	DEBIT	CREDIT	
1	20–		**Closing Entries**				1
2	Dec.	31	Income Summary		248 0 0 0 00		2
3			L. J. Bell, Capital			140 7 5 0 00	3
4			J. M. Campbell, Capital			107 2 5 0 00	4
5							5
6		31	L. J. Bell, Capital		120 0 0 0 00		6
7			L. J. Bell, Drawing			120 0 0 0 00	7
8							8
9		31	J. M. Campbell, Capital		20 0 0 0 00		9
10			J. M. Campbell, Drawing			20 0 0 0 00	10
11							11

Net Loss of $4,000   The accountant handles interest allowances the same way she or he handles salary allowances: Both must be allocated, whether or not there is enough net income to cover them. The section of the income statement relating to the division of a $4,000 net loss appears as follows:

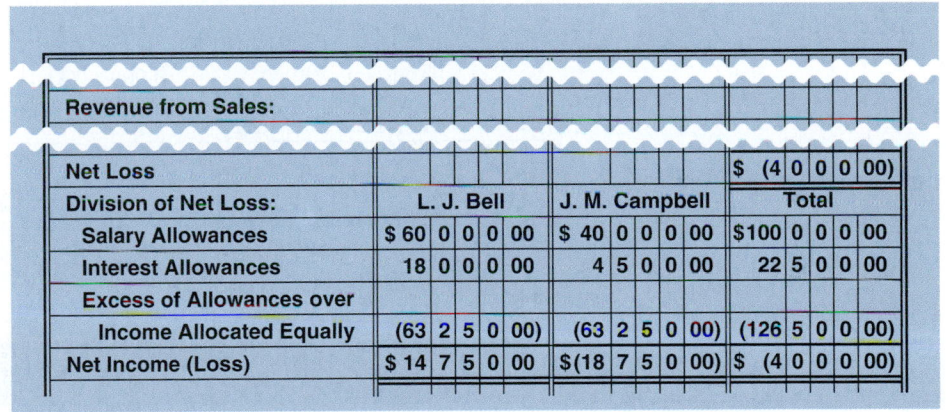

	L. J. Bell	J. M. Campbell	Total
Revenue from Sales:			
Net Loss			$ (4 0 0 0 00)
Division of Net Loss:	**L. J. Bell**	**J. M. Campbell**	**Total**
Salary Allowances	$ 60 0 0 0 00	$ 40 0 0 0 00	$100 0 0 0 00
Interest Allowances	18 0 0 0 00	4 5 0 0 00	22 5 0 0 00
Excess of Allowances over			
Income Allocated Equally	(63 2 5 0 00)	(63 2 5 0 00)	(126 5 0 0 00)
Net Income (Loss)	$ 14 7 5 0 00	$(18 7 5 0 00)	$ (4 0 0 0 00)

The accountant computes the remainder as follows:

Net loss		$(4,000)
Less:		
Amount allocated as salaries		
($60,000 + $40,000)	$100,000	
Amount allocated as interest		
($18,000 + $4,500)	22,500	122,500
Remainder		$(126,500)

$$\text{Remainder} \div 2 = \frac{\$(126,500)}{2} = \$(63,250)$$

And the closing entries look like those below.

	DATE		DESCRIPTION	POST. REF.	DEBIT	CREDIT	
1	20–		**Closing Entries**				1
2	Dec.	31	J. M. Campbell, Capital		18 7 5 0 00		2
3			Income Summary			4 0 0 0 00	3
4			L. J. Bell, Capital			14 7 5 0 00	4
5							5
6		31	L. J. Bell, Capital		120 0 0 0 00		6
7			L. J. Bell, Drawing			120 0 0 0 00	7
8							8
9		31	J. M. Campbell, Capital		20 0 0 0 00		9
10			J. M. Campbell, Drawing			20 0 0 0 00	10

After posting, the partners' equity accounts look like this:

Income Summary

	Balance	4,000	**(3)** Closing	4,000

L. J. Bell, Capital

	–	+	
(4)	120,000	Balance	300,000
		(3)	8,000

J. M. Campbell, Capital

	–	+	
(3)	12,000	Balance	75,000
(4)	20,000		

L. J. Bell, Drawing

	+	–	
Balance	120,000	**(4)** Closing	120,000

J. M. Campbell, Drawing

	+	–	
Balance	20,000	**(4)** Closing	20,000

FINANCIAL STATEMENTS FOR A PARTNERSHIP

OBJECTIVE 4

Prepare a statement of partners' equity

Changes in the balances of the partners' Capital accounts are recorded in the statement of partners' equity, which is just like a statement of owner's equity for a sole proprietorship, except that there is a separate column for each partner. The following statement of partners' equity presents the division of income based on the fractional shares method.

Bell & Campbell LLP
Statement of Partners' Equity
For Year Ended December 31, 20—

	L. J. Bell	J. M. Campbell	Total
Capital, January 1, 20—	$300 0 0 0 00	$ 75 0 0 0 00	$375 0 0 0 00
Net Income for the Year	186 0 0 0 00	62 0 0 0 00	248 0 0 0 00
Total	$486 0 0 0 00	$137 0 0 0 00	$623 0 0 0 00
Less Withdrawals for the Year	120 0 0 0 00	20 0 0 0 00	140 0 0 0 00
Capital, December 31, 20—	$366 0 0 0 00	$117 0 0 0 00	$483 0 0 0 00

REMEMBER!

A partner is taxed on the net income share, not on what the partner withdraws.

When a partner makes an additional permanent investment after the beginning of the fiscal period, the accountant records this amount right below the beginning balance of the Capital accounts.

Partners have to pay federal income taxes on the basis of each partner's distributive share (share of net income) in the business. For example, L. J. Bell's taxable income is $186,000, even though he withdrew only $120,000. He lists $186,000 on his personal income tax return. The Internal Revenue Code requires that details of the distributive share of each partner must be recorded on a U.S. Partnership Return of Income (Form 1065).

DISSOLUTION OF A PARTNERSHIP

One disadvantage of a partnership is its limited life. Any change in the personnel of the membership formally ends the partnership. When a partnership dissolves, the main visible result is a change in the names listed in the partnership agreement and a change in the division of net income; usually the routine transactions of the business continue. For example, suppose that a partnership originally consists of partners A, B, and C. Then C withdraws his or her investment from the firm, and a new partnership emerges: partners A and B. During the transition, business is continued. In other words, in a **dissolution**, the original partnership is dissolved by either the sale of one partner's interest in the firm to a new partner or the withdrawal of a partner. The firm continues to operate as before.

Sale of a Partnership Interest

OBJECTIVE 5

Journalize entries involving the sale of a partnership interest or withdrawal of a partner.

When a partner retires, that partner may sell his or her interest to a person outside the firm who is acceptable to the remaining partners. Let's say that, at the end of a given year, J. M. Campbell has a Capital balance of $163,520 and decides to sell his interest to D. N. Davis for $182,000. The accountant makes the following entry to account for the transfer of ownership:

	DATE		DESCRIPTION	POST. REF.	DEBIT	CREDIT	
1	20–						1
2	Dec.	31	J. M. Campbell, Capital		163 5 2 0 00		2
3			D. N. Davis, Capital			163 5 2 0 00	3
4			To transfer Campbell's equity				4
5			in the partnership to Davis.				5
6							6

The difference between $182,000 and $163,520 represents a personal profit to Campbell, not to the firm. The new partner, buyer D. N. Davis, paid the $182,000 directly to the old partner, seller J. M. Campbell, without affecting the partnership accounting records. *There has been no change in the partnership's assets or liabilities; consequently, there is no change in the total partners' equity.* However, if the firm is to continue, Bell (the other original partner) must be willing to accept Davis as a new partner.

Withdrawal of a Partner

The partnership agreement should outline a set procedure to follow if one of the partners withdraws. Such a procedure usually entails an examination of the books and a revaluation of the partnership's assets and liabilities to reflect current market values. Before the review, the partnership of Barbosa, Gant, and Hart LP had the following balance sheet:

Barbosa, Gant, and Hart LP
Balance Sheet
September 30, 20—

Assets				
Current Assets				
Cash			$ 68 0 0 0 00	
Accounts Receivable	$58 0 0 0 00			
Less Allowance for Doubtful Accounts	3 5 0 0 00		54 5 0 0 00	
Merchandise Inventory			197 5 0 0 00	
Total Current Assets				$320 0 0 0 00
Property and Equipment:				
Equipment			$ 20 0 0 0 00	
Less Accumulated Depreciation			11 0 0 0 00	9 0 0 0 00
Total Assets				$329 0 0 0 00
Liabilities				
Accounts Payable				$ 7 0 0 0 00
Partners' Equity				
K. L. Barbosa, Capital			$146 0 0 0 00	
N. B. Gant, Capital			54 0 0 0 00	
J. C. Hart, Capital			122 0 0 0 00	
Total Partners' Equity				322 0 0 0 00
Total Liabilities and Partners' Equity				$329 0 0 0 00

FIGURE 3

Partner Withdraws Book Value of His or Her Equity After Revaluation

Suppose that N. B. Gant is retiring from the partnership of Barbosa, Gant, and Hart LP. The partnership agreement stipulates that net income and net loss shall be shared on an equal basis; it also provides for an examination of the financial statements and revaluation of assets in the event that a partner retires. Figure 3 shows the firm's balance sheet immediately prior to the review and revaluation.

At this point, an accountant (usually someone from an outside firm) examines the books and the firm's assets are appraised. This review and appraisal indicate that Merchandise Inventory is undervalued by $9,600, that Allowance for Doubtful Accounts should be increased by $300, and that Equipment is overvalued by $2,100. The accountant allocates the net difference between debits and credits to the partners' Capital accounts, according to their basis for sharing profits and losses.

	DATE	DESCRIPTION	POST. REF.	DEBIT	CREDIT	
1	20–					1
2	Sept. 30	Merchandise Inventory		9 6 0 0 00		2
3		Allowance for Doubtful				3
4		Accounts			3 0 0 00	4
5		Equipment			2 1 0 0 00	5
6		K. L. Barbosa, Capital			2 4 0 0 00	6
7		N. B. Gant, Capital			2 4 0 0 00	7
8		J. C. Hart, Capital			2 4 0 0 00	8
9		To record the revaluation of				9
10		the assets; net increase in				10
11		partners' equity is $7,200.				11

After the entry has been posted, the partners' equity accounts look like this:

K. L. Barbosa, Capital				N. B. Gant, Capital				J. C. Hart, Capital	
−	+			−	+			−	+
	Balance	146,000			Balance	54,000			Balance	122,000
	Sept. 30	2,400			Sept. 30	2,400			Sept. 30	2,400

After the accountant has recorded the revaluation of the firm's assets, N. B. Gant withdraws cash from the partnership equal to her equity, which leads to the following entry:

	DATE	DESCRIPTION	POST. REF.	DEBIT	CREDIT	
12	20–					12
13	Sept. 30	N. B. Gant, Capital		56 4 0 0 00		13
14		Cash			56 4 0 0 00	14
15		To record the withdrawal of				15
16		N. B. Gant.				16
17						17

REMEMBER!

A partner has the right to leave a partnership. He or she may withdraw an amount equal to his or her equity or greater or less than the book value of his or her equity.

Partner Withdraws More than Book Value of His or Her Equity

Sometimes a partner withdraws more cash than the amount of his or her Capital account. There are two possible reasons for this.

1. The business is prosperous and shows excellent potential for growth.
2. The remaining partners are so anxious for the partner to retire that they are willing to buy out the partner.

When Gant announced that she was going to retire, for example, Barbosa and Hart agreed to pay her $57,400 for her interest in the partnership. Because the balance of her Capital account after the revaluation is $56,400, the excess of $1,000 must be deducted from the Capital accounts of the remaining partners, in accordance with their basis for sharing profits and losses. The general journal entry appears as follows:

DATE		DESCRIPTION	POST. REF.	DEBIT	CREDIT	
1	20–					1
2	Sept. 30	N. B. Gant, Capital		56 4 0 0 00		2
3		K. L. Barbosa, Capital		5 0 0 00		3
4		J. C. Hart, Capital		5 0 0 00		4
5		Cash			57 4 0 0 00	5
6		To record the withdrawal of				6
7		N. B. Gant.				7
8						8

Partner Withdraws Less than Book Value of His or Her Equity

Sometimes a partner may be so anxious to retire that he or she is willing to take less than the current value of his or her equity just to get out of the partnership or out of the business. In the firm of Barbosa, Gant, and Hart, let's say that Gant is willing to withdraw if she gets just $52,200 cash out of it. Because the balance of her Capital account after the revaluation is $56,400, the difference ($4,200) represents a bonus to the remaining partners. The entry to record this situation is as follows:

DATE		DESCRIPTION	POST. REF.	DEBIT	CREDIT	
6	Sept. 30	N. B. Gant, Capital		56 4 0 0 00		6
7		K. L. Barbosa, Capital			2 1 0 0 00	7
8		J. C. Hart, Capital			2 1 0 0 00	8
9		Cash			52 2 0 0 00	9
10		To record the withdrawal of				10
11		N. B. Gant.				11
12						12

Death of a Partner

The death of a partner automatically ends the partnership, and the partner's estate is entitled to receive the amount of his or her equity. The death of a partner makes it necessary to close the books immediately so that the accountant can determine the firm's net income for the current fiscal period. Partnership agreements usually provide for an examination and revaluation of the assets at this time. After the accountant has determined the current value of the deceased partner's Capital account, the remaining partners and the executor of the deceased partner's estate must agree on the method of payment. The journal entries are similar to those made for the withdrawal of a partner. To be certain that there is enough cash to meet such a demand, partners and partnerships often carry life insurance policies.

LIQUIDATION OF A PARTNERSHIP

 OBJECTIVE 6

Journalize entries pertaining to the liquidation of a partnership involving the immediate sale of the assets for cash.

A **liquidation** means an end, not only of the partnership, but of the business itself. This final winding-up process involves selling assets, paying off liabilities, and distributing the remaining cash to the partners. The closing entries are journalized and posted prior to the liquidation.

The accountant journalizes the entries for each step of the liquidation process as follows:

1. Sale of the assets, using the Loss or Gain from Realization account. The accountant debits this account for losses and credits it for gains. In this respect the account is comparable to the Cash Short and Over account. The word **realization** refers to the sale of the assets for cash.
2. Allocation of the loss or gain. The accountant closes the Loss or Gain from Realization account into the partners' Capital accounts according to the profit and loss ratio. It must be closed as a separate account because it came into being after the regular closing entries had been recorded.
3. Payment of the liabilities. The firm makes final settlement with all creditors.
4. Distribution of the remaining cash to the partners, in accordance with the balances of their Capital accounts.

REMEMBER!

Upon liquidation, creditors are first in line, before partners' interests.

Occasionally it takes a long time to convert merchandise inventory and other assets into cash; on the other hand, things can move quickly. It is impossible to predict how long liquidation operations may take. In the process, several things may happen. We will discuss two possibilities here.

Our first example concerns the partnership of Ryan, Shay, and Thom LLP. The partners share profits and losses as follows: Ryan one-half; Shay one-fourth; Thom one-fourth. Let's look at an abbreviated balance sheet for this firm (Figure 4).

FIGURE 4

Ryan, Shay, and Thom LLP
Balance Sheet
June 30, 20—

Assets		
Cash	$10 000 00	
Merchandise Inventory	80 000 00	
Other Assets	40 000 00	
Total Assets		$130 000 00
Liabilities		
Accounts Payable		$ 7 000 00
Partners' Equity		
G. P. Ryan, Capital	$47 000 00	
C. L. Shay, Capital	44 000 00	
R. H. Thom, Capital	32 000 00	123 000 00
Total Liabilities and Partners' Equity		$130 000 00

Assets Are Sold at a Profit

Assume that the firm sells its merchandise inventory for $86,000 and the other assets for $50,000. Figure 5 shows the journal entries to cover this transaction. (Amounts in parentheses are purely explanatory.)

The T accounts for the Cash and Capital accounts look like this:

Cash						C. L. Shay, Capital			
	+	–				–	+		
Balance	10,000	(3)	7,000		(4)	48,000	Balance	44,000
(1)	136,000	(4)	139,000				(2)	4,000

G. P. Ryan, Capital						R. H. Thom, Capital			
	–	+				–	+		
(4)	55,000	Balance	47,000		(4)	36,000	Balance	32,000
		(2)	8,000				(2)	4,000

FIGURE 5

	DATE		DESCRIPTION	POST. REF.	DEBIT	CREDIT	
1	20–						1
2	June	30	Cash ($86,000 + $50,000)		136 0 0 0 00		2
3			Merchandise Inventory			80 0 0 0 00	3
4	(1)		Other Assets			40 0 0 0 00	4
5			Loss or Gain from Realization			16 0 0 0 00	5
6			Sold the assets at a gain.				6
7							7
8		30	Loss or Gain from Realization		16 0 0 0 00		8
9			G. P. Ryan, Capital (1/2)			8 0 0 0 00	9
10	(2)		C. L. Shay, Capital (1/4)			4 0 0 0 00	10
11			R. H. Thom, Capital (1/4)			4 0 0 0 00	11
12			To allocate the net gain to the				12
13			partners' Capital accounts				13
14			according to the profit and				14
15			loss ratio.				15
16							16
17		30	Accounts Payable		7 0 0 0 00		17
18			Cash			7 0 0 0 00	18
19	(3)		To pay the claims of creditors.				19
20							20
21		30	G. P. Ryan, Capital		55 0 0 0 00		21
22			C. L. Shay, Capital		48 0 0 0 00		22
23	(4)		R. H. Thom, Capital		36 0 0 0 00		23
24			Cash			139 0 0 0 00	24
25			To distribute the remaining				25
26			cash to the partners				26
27			according to their account				27
28			balances.				28

REMEMBER!

The balance of Cash before the final distribution to the partners should equal the total of the balances of their Capital accounts.

Assets Are Sold at a Loss: Partners' Capital Accounts Sufficient to Absorb Loss

Now suppose that the partnership of Ryan, Shay, and Thom LLP sells its merchandise inventory for only $76,000 and its other assets for $32,000. The journal entries would look like those in Figure 6.

The T accounts for the Cash and Capital accounts look like this:

Cash						C. L. Shay, Capital			
	+	–					–	+	
Balance	10,000	(3)	7,000		(2)	3,000	Balance	44,000
(1)	108,000	(4)	111,000		(4)	41,000		

G. P. Ryan, Capital						R. H. Thom, Capital			
	–	+				–	+	
(2)	6,000	Balance	47,000		(2)	3,000	Balance	32,000
(4)	41,000				(4)	29,000		

FIGURE 6

	DATE		DESCRIPTION	POST. REF.	DEBIT	CREDIT	
1	20–						1
2	June	30	Cash ($76,000 + $32,000)		108 0 0 0 00		2
3			Loss or Gain from Realization		12 0 0 0 00		3
4	(1)		Merchandise Inventory			80 0 0 0 00	4
5			Other Assets			40 0 0 0 00	5
6			Sold the assets at a loss.				6
7							7
8		30	G. P. Ryan, Capital (¹/₂)		6 0 0 0 00		8
9			C. L. Shay, Capital (¹/₄)		3 0 0 0 00		9
10	(2)		R. H. Thom, Capital (¹/₄)		3 0 0 0 00		10
11			Loss or Gain from Realization			12 0 0 0 00	11
12			To allocate the net loss to the				12
13			partners' Capital accounts				13
14			according to the profit and				14
15			loss ratio.				15
16							16
17		30	Accounts Payable		7 0 0 0 00		17
18			Cash			7 0 0 0 00	18
19	(3)		To pay the claims of creditors.				19
20							20
21		30	G. P. Ryan, Capital		41 0 0 0 00		21
22			C. L. Shay, Capital		41 0 0 0 00		22
23	(4)		R. H. Thom, Capital		29 0 0 0 00		23
24			Cash			111 0 0 0 00	24
25			To distribute the remaining				25
26			cash to the partners				26
27			according to their account				27
28			balances.				28

REMEMBER!

As the last step in the liquidation process, cash remaining is distributed to the partners according to their Capital account balances.

CHAPTER REVIEW

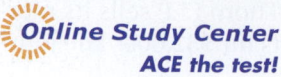

Review of Performance Objectives

1. (a) Define the various kinds of partnerships and list the main advantages and disadvantages of a partnership; (b) journalize initial investments.

   There are three types of partnerships: general, limited, and limited liability partnerships. A general partnership is an association of two or more people or firms to carry on, as co-owners, a business for profit. A limited partnership is an organization with two or more people or firms with at least one general partner and one limited partner. A limited liability partnership is an organization similar to a limited partnership except that all partners may take an active role in the business of the partnership with only their invested capital at risk. The main advantages of a partnership are the combining of people's abilities and investments to carry on a business, and its ease of formation. The main disadvantages of a partnership are the unlimited liability of a general partner and mutual agency. The accountant makes a separate journal entry for the investment of each partner. The investments may include cash and other assets, along with any related liabilities.

2. Provide for the division of net income and loss on the basis of (a) fractional shares; (b) ratio of capital investments; and (c) salary and interest allowances.

   The division of net income or loss may be reported as a separate statement or shown at the bottom of the income statement below Net Income. For division by fractional shares, multiply net income or loss by each partner's fraction. For ratio of capital investments, multiply net income or loss by a fraction with the partner's beginning Capital balance in the numerator and the total of partners' Capital balances in the denominator. To calculate the division on the basis of salary and interest allowances, deduct the amounts of salary or interest allowances from the net income (or add them to the net loss) and divide the remainder by specified shares (usually equally).

3. Journalize the closing entries for a partnership on the basis of (a) fractional shares; (b) ratio of capital investments; and (c) salary and interest allowances.

   Close the revenue and expense accounts into Income Summary, then close Income Summary into the partners' Capital accounts. For a net income, debit Income Summary and credit each partner's Capital account. For a net loss, debit each partner's Capital account and credit Income Summary. Close the Drawing accounts by crediting each partner's Drawing account and debiting each partner's Capital account.

4. Prepare a statement of partners' equity.

   The format of a statement of partners' equity is the same as that for a statement of owner's equity. One column per partner is used to record each partner's beginning capital, additional investment, share of net income, withdrawals, and ending capital. A Total column is used to record the combined total for each line.

5. Journalize entries involving the sale of a partnership interest or withdrawal of a partner.

   Any change in the composition of partners results in a dissolution of the partnership. For the sale of a partnership interest, debit the Capital account of the old partner and credit the Capital account of the new partner. When a partner withdraws, there is a revaluation of the assets. Next, an entry is made debiting the partner's Capital account and crediting Cash.

6. Journalize entries pertaining to the liquidation of a partnership involving the immediate sale of the assets for cash.

A liquidation requires four steps. First, for the sale of the assets, debit Cash, credit the assets, and debit or credit Loss or Gain from Realization. Next, close Loss or Gain from Realization into the partners' Capital accounts according to the partners' agreed-on profit and loss ratio. Next, pay off the liabilities. Last, distribute the remaining cash according to the partners' Capital account balances.

Glossary

Co-ownership A situation in which each party owns a fractional share of all the assets. (717)

Dissolution The ending of a partnership because of a change in the personnel of the membership and the forming of a new partnership. The transition results primarily in changes to the Capital accounts, with routine business being carried on as usual. (733)

Distributive share The share of the net income (or net loss) allocated to each partner. (722)

General partnership (GP) An association of two or more persons to carry on, as co-owners, a business for profit. The partners are general partners who actively and publicly participate in the transactions of the firm and have unlimited liability. (716)

Limited liability partnership (LLP) An organization similar to a limited partnership except that all partners may take an active role in the business of the partnership with only their invested capital at risk. (716)

Limited partnership (LP) A partnership with at least one general partner and one limited partner. The general partner normally manages the partnership and the limited partner or partners have the largest share of invested capital and usually cannot lose more than their capital contribution. (716)

Liquidation The ending of a partnership, involving the sale of the assets, payment of the liabilities, and distribution of the remaining cash to the partners. (737)

Mutual agency The ability of each partner to act as an agent of the firm, thereby committing the entire firm to a binding contract. (718)

Realization Conversion into cash, as happens in the case of the sale of assets. (737)

QUESTIONS, EXERCISES, AND CASES

Discussion Questions

1. List three advantages and three disadvantages of a partnership.
2. List six provisions that should be included in a partnership agreement.
3. What do accountants mean by co-ownership of partnership property?
4. Are partnerships required to pay federal income taxes? Why or why not?
5. Explain why a partner's distributive share in the division of partnership income does not involve cash.

6. Anton and Garcia are in the process of forming a partnership. Anton wishes to invest the assets and liabilities of his business, Anton's Upholstery. Is it possible to simply list these assets and liabilities at the same amounts on the new partnership books? Explain your answer.

7. How does the dissolution of a partnership differ from a liquidation?

8. What four steps are followed in a liquidation?

Exercises

P.O. 1b

Prepare an entry to record investment of a new partner.

Exercise 19-1 R. N. Mendoza, as his original investment in the firm of Mendoza and Glenco, contributes equipment that had been recorded in the books of his own business as costing $90,000, with accumulated depreciation of $62,000. The partners agree on a valuation of $40,000. They also agree to accept Mendoza's accounts receivable of $36,000, collectible to the extent of 85 percent. Give the journal entry to record Mendoza's investment in the partnership of Mendoza and Glenco on July 15.

P.O. 2b

Calculate the division of net income or loss based on a ratio of capital investments.

Exercise 19-2 L. Embuscado, G. Renaldo, and C. Thomas agreed to share earnings or losses according to the ratio of their investments at the beginning of the year ($30,000, $25,000, and $45,000, respectively). Calculate the partner shares under the following conditions: (a) $27,000 net income; (b) $24,000 net loss.

P.O. 2a,c

Calculate partner shares with salary allowance and fractional share of income.

Exercise 19-3 The partnership agreement of Laird and Bridger provides for salary allowances of $32,000 per year for Laird and $26,000 per year for Bridger. They share the remaining balance of net income on the basis of three-fifths for Laird and two-fifths for Bridger. The net income amounts to $60,000. Calculate the total share for each partner.

P.O. 2a,3a

Calculate fractional shares and journalize closing entries for a partnership.

Exercise 19-4 Fisk and Fulcer share profits and losses on a fractional-share basis with two-fifths for Fisk and three-fifths for Fulcer. This year the firm has a net income of $65,000. The beginning Capital balances for the year were $90,000 for Fisk and $130,000 for Fulcer. The balances of the Drawing accounts are $30,000 for Fisk and $24,000 for Fulcer. Journalize the entries to close Income Summary and the partners' Drawing accounts on December 31.

P.O. 2c

Calculate division of net income with salary allowances and interest allowances.

Exercise 19-5 The partners C. T. Wicks and J. L. Yates have agreed to salary allowances of $10,000 and $12,000, respectively. In addition, they are allowed 9 percent interest on their Capital balances at the beginning of the year. The remainder is to be divided equally. Wicks' Capital balance was $40,000, and Yates' Capital balance was $50,000. Complete the section of the income statement related to the division of a $42,000 net income.

P.O. 5

Journalize entries to record a partner's retirement.

Exercise 19-6 Griese is retiring from the partnership of Cochran, Karnes, and Griese. The profit and loss ratio is 2 : 2 : 1, respectively. After the accountant has posted the revaluation and closing entries, the credit balances in the Capital accounts are: Cochran, $53,000; Karnes, $43,000; and Griese, $21,000. Journalize the entries to record the retirement of Griese under each of the following unrelated assumptions:

a. Griese retires, taking $21,000 of partnership cash for her equity.
b. Griese retires, taking $27,000 of partnership cash for her equity.

P.O. 5

Journalize the entry to record revaluation of assets on the retirement of a partner.

Exercise 19-7 Brady is the senior member of the partnership of Brady, Bouchard, and Craswell. When Brady dies, the firm's accountant revalues the assets. The following assets are to be increased in value by these amounts: Merchandise Inventory, $28,000; Building, $56,000. The value of the asset, Equipment, is to be decreased by $9,000. Assuming that the partnership profit and loss ratio is 2 : 2 : 1, respectively, write the journal entry to show the revaluation of the assets on June 5 prior to dissolution of the firm.

P.O. 6

Calculate loss or gain on realization and the cash distribution to partners.

Exercise 19-8 Green and Wold are partners who share profits and losses equally. The credit balances of their Capital accounts before liquidation are $70,000 and $90,000, respectively. When they liquidate their partnership, they sell the noncash assets and pay all the partnership's liabilities, leaving a balance of $110,000 in cash. (a) What is the amount of loss or gain on realization? (b) How much cash should be distributed to each partner?

Let's go back to the **http://www.nolo.com/** website. In the Search box type in "partnership agreement" and below the box select "Search Entire Site." Then, choose "Creating a Partnership Agreement."

1. How can a partnership agreement help a business?
2. What major areas should be covered by a partnership agreement?
3. Which state does not have its own laws governing partnerships?

CONSIDER AND COMMUNICATE

A friend of yours is looking for a partner to begin a children's-wear boutique. She has fashion merchandising and sales education and experience, as well as cash and a good credit rating. She is enthusiastic and anxious to begin the new business. You have cash, a desire to own a business, and sales experience, and you feel you could get along well with this potential partner. Why would you hesitate? What should you discuss with your friend about partnerships?

CRITICAL THINKING

The following information concerns the partnership of Calderon and Small LLP.

The partnership agreement provides for salary allowances of $31,900 for Calderon and $29,350 for Small. The agreement also stipulates interest of 10 percent on invested capital at the beginning of the year (Calderon, $65,280; Small, $53,040). There were no changes in the partners' Capital accounts during the year. The remainder of the net income is to be divided equally. Using this information, fill in the missing numbers in the partial income statement from Net Income through Division of Net Income for Calderon and Small LLP and in the statement of partners' equity.

Calderon and Small LLP
Partial Income Statement
For Year Ended December 31, 20—

	J. V. Calderon	S. C. Small	Total
Net Income			$79 302 00
Division of Net Income:			
Salary Allowances	$	$	$
Interest Allowances			
Excess of Income over			
Allowances Allocated Equally			6 220 00
Net Income	$41 538 00	$37 764 00	$79 302 00

Calderon and Small LLP
Statement of Partners' Equity
For Year Ended December 31, 20—

	J. V. Calderon	S. C. Small	Total
Capital, January 1, 20—	$	$	$
Net Income for the Year			79 302 00
Total	$	$	$197 622 00
Less Withdrawals for the Year	30 192 00	29 376 00	
Capital, December 31, 20—	$	$	$

A QUESTION OF ETHICS

Joe and Sam are partners. Joe wanted to purchase a newer model computer. Sam said it was too expensive and had capabilities that they did not need. While Sam was on vacation, Joe bought the computer anyway. He believed that if Sam saw how much quicker the newer computer would be, he would be convinced of its benefits. Did Joe act appropriately under the rules of a partnership? Is what Joe did ethical?

PROBLEM SET A

For additional help, see the demonstration problem at the beginning of each chapter in your Working Papers.

P.O. 2,3

Problem 19-1A The partnership of T. L. Reglor, S. T. Garson, and B. C. Dunst has a net income of $90,000 for the current year. The balances in the partners' Capital accounts at the beginning of the year were $34,000, $38,000, and $45,000, respectively. At the end of the year, the balances of the Drawing accounts are $16,000, $19,300, and $17,000, respectively. The partnership agreement stipulates salary allowances as follows: Reglor, $18,000; Garson,

$23,000; Dunst, $20,000. The partnership agreement also allows interest of 10 percent on the balances of the partners' Capital accounts at the beginning of the year. The remainder of the net income, after salary and interest allowances, is divided equally.

Check Figure

Total Interest Allowances, $11,700

Instructions

1. Prepare the section of the income statement for the current year that deals with division of net income.
2. Prepare the entries to close the firm's Income Summary and Drawing accounts on December 31.
3. Assuming a net income of $43,000, prepare the section of the income statement that deals with division of net income.

P.O. 2,5

Problem 19-2A C. N. Bence and W. L. Rauch are forming a partnership for a beauty salon and plan to work full time in the firm. Bence will make an initial investment of $45,000 and Rauch, $35,000. They are considering the following plans for the division of net income:

a. Division in the same ratio as the balances of their Capital accounts.
b. Interest of 10 percent on the balances of their Capital accounts at the beginning of the year and the remainder of the net income to be divided equally.
c. Salary allowances of $17,500 to Bence and $15,500 to Rauch, based on the value of their services, interest of 10 percent on the balances of their Capital accounts at the beginning of the year, and the remainder of the net income to be divided equally.

Check Figure

With net income of $50,000, W. L. Rauch (B) interest allowance, $3,500

Instructions

1. Using the form in the Working Papers, record the distributive shares of net income for each of the partners, assuming (a) a net income of $50,000 (calculate ratio to 4 decimal places) and (b) a net income of $24,000.
2. Which plan is the fairest? Give reasons for your opinion.
3. Assume that three years later, on December 31, 2007, Bence's Capital balance is $38,000. With the approval of Rauch, Bence sells his interest to two new partners, S. G. Rhodes for $18,000 and J. M. Marks for $20,000. Journalize the entry to account for the transfer of ownership.
4. (a) Assume that W. L. Rauch, the remaining original partner, decides to withdraw from the partnership two years after Bence's sale of his partnership interest. The partnership agreement stipulates that net income and net loss be shared on a 2 : 1 : 1 ratio (Rauch, Rhodes, and Marks, respectively) and that an examination and revaluation of assets will take place upon retirement of a partner.

   The revaluation shows that Merchandise Inventory is undervalued by $10,000, that Equipment is overvalued by $1,800, and that Allowance for Doubtful Accounts should be increased by $500. As of December 31, journalize the allocation of the net difference between debits and credits to the partners' Capital accounts, according to the 2 : 1 : 1 ratio.

   (b) Assume W. L. Rauch's Capital balance is $42,150 before the revaluation. Journalize on December 31, 2009, the withdrawal of Rauch assuming he withdraws cash.

P.O. 2,4

Problem 19-3A Shown on the next page are the adjusted account balances of Arlen and Ward LLP as of December 31, the end of the current fiscal year.

Accounts Payable	$ 67,782
Accounts Receivable	54,507
Accumulated Depreciation, Equipment	46,287
Allowance for Doubtful Accounts	1,879
Cash	13,231
D. L. Arlen, Capital	61,200
D. L. Arlen, Drawing	32,640
Equipment	75,315
Freight In	22,488
General Expenses (control)	14,939
Interest Expense	3,500
Merchandise Inventory, December 31	132,042
Notes Payable	29,900
Prepaid Insurance	735
Purchases	540,716
Purchases Discounts	4,305
Purchases Returns and Allowances	25,960
P. W. Ward, Capital	49,960
P. W. Ward, Drawing	24,480
Sales	715,500
Sales Returns and Allowances	37,575
Selling Expenses (control)	38,588

There were no changes in the partners' Capital accounts during the year. The merchandise inventory at the beginning of the year was $144,059. The partnership agreement provides for salary allowances of $33,000 for Arlen and $29,000 for Ward. It also stipulates an interest allowance of 10 percent on invested capital at the beginning of the year, with the remainder of the net income to be divided equally.

Check Figure

Net Income, $75,942

Instructions

1. Prepare an income statement for the year.
2. Prepare a statement of partners' equity for the year.
3. Prepare a classified balance sheet for the partnership at the end of the year.

P.O. 6

Problem 19-4A The partnership of Hill, Cederblom, and Schultz is to be liquidated as of June 30 of this year. The partners share profits and losses in the ratio of 2 : 2 : 1, respectively. The firm's post-closing trial balance looks like this:

Hill, Cederblom, and Schultz
Post-Closing Trial Balance
June 30, 20—

ACCOUNT NAME	DEBIT	CREDIT
Cash	41 9 1 7 00	
Merchandise Inventory	61 2 3 0 00	
Other Assets	47 2 6 8 00	
Accounts Payable		13 1 3 5 00
A. L. Hill, Capital		56 1 6 0 00
L. S. Cederblom, Capital		43 6 8 0 00
S. R. Schultz, Capital		37 4 4 0 00
	150 4 1 5 00	150 4 1 5 00

The firm's realization and liquidation transactions are as follows:

June 30 The merchandise inventory sold for $58,280; the other assets sold for $55,090.

30 The accountant allocated the loss or gain from realization to the partners' Capital accounts according to the profit and loss ratio.

30 The firm paid its creditors in full.

30 The firm distributed the remaining cash to the partners in accordance with the balances in their Capital accounts.

Check Figure

Gain from realization, $4,872

Instructions

1. Record the balances in the selected ledger accounts.
2. Record the liquidating transactions in general journal form.
3. Post the entries to the ledger accounts.

PROBLEM SET B

For additional help, see the demonstration problem at the beginning of each chapter in your Working Papers.

P.O. 2,3

Problem 19-1B The partnership of H. G. Egger, L. V. Folgam, and R. M. Baylor has a net income of $115,300 for this year. The balances in the partners' Capital accounts at the beginning of the year were $46,000, $51,500, and $58,000, respectively. At the end of the year, the balances of the Drawing accounts are $25,000, $29,200, and $24,250, respectively. The partnership agreement stipulates salary allowances as follows: Egger, $24,500; Folgam, $27,500; Baylor, $28,400. It also allows 10 percent interest on the balances of the partners' Capital accounts at the beginning of the year. The remainder of the net income, after salary and interest allowances, is divided equally.

Check Figure

Assuming a net income of $49,000, H. G. Egger, Net Income, $13,450

Instructions

1. Prepare the section of the income statement for the current year that deals with the division of net income.
2. Prepare entries to close the firm's Income Summary and Drawing accounts on December 31.
3. Assuming a net income of $49,000, prepare the section of the income statement that deals with division of net income.

P.O. 2,5

Problem 19-2B S. L. Barkley and B. W. Caitlin, interior designers, are forming a partnership. Both plan to work in the firm on a full-time basis. Barkley's initial investment is $20,000; Caitlin's investment, $30,000. They are considering the following plans for the division of net income:

a. Division in the same ratio as the balances of their Capital accounts.
b. Interest of 10 percent on the balances of their Capital accounts at the beginning of the year and the remainder of the net income to be divided equally.
c. Salary allowances of $14,000 to Barkley and $17,000 to Caitlin, based on the value of their services, interest of 9 percent on the balances of their Capital accounts at the beginning of the year, and the remainder of the net income to be divided equally.

Instructions

1. Using the form provided in the Working Papers, record the distribution of net income for each of the partners, assuming (a) a net income of $32,000 and (b) a net income of $24,000.
2. Which plan is the fairest? Give reasons for your opinion.
3. Assume that three years later, on December 31, 2007, Barkley's Capital balance is $27,000. With the approval of Caitlin, Barkley sells his interest to two new partners, T. L. Milloy for $13,000 and W. H. Gray for $14,000. Journalize the entry to account for the transfer of ownership.
4. (a) Assume that B. W. Caitlin, the remaining original partner, decides to withdraw from the partnership two years after Barkley's sale of his partnership share. The partnership agreement stipulates that net income and net loss be shared on a 2 : 1 : 1 ratio (Caitlin, Milloy, and Gray, respectively) and that an examination and revaluation of assets will take place upon retirement of a partner.

   The revaluation shows that Merchandise Inventory is undervalued by $9,000, that Equipment is overvalued by $2,100, and that Allowance for Doubtful Accounts should be increased by $600. As of December 31, journalize the allocation of the net difference between debits and credits to the partners' Capital accounts, according to the 2 : 1 : 1 ratio.

   (b) Assume B. W. Caitlin's Capital balance is $45,000 before the revaluation. Journalize on December 31, 2009, the withdrawal of Caitlin assuming he withdraws cash.

P.O. 2,4

Problem 19-3B The following are the adjusted account balances of Aikens and Dominguez LLP of December 31, the end of the fiscal year:

Accounts Payable	$ 69,812
Accounts Receivable	60,143
Accumulated Depreciation, Equipment	47,756
Allowance for Doubtful Accounts	2,192
Cash	4,617
Equipment	80,710
Freight In	27,380
General Expenses (control)	14,495
Interest Expense	2,000
J. V. Aikens, Capital	65,280
J. V. Aikens, Drawing	30,192
Merchandise Inventory, December 31	128,760
Notes Payable	16,320
Prepaid Insurance	704
Purchases	522,043
Purchases Discounts	4,516
Purchases Returns and Allowances	26,204
Sales	701,332
Sales Returns and Allowances	36,590
S. C. Dominguez, Capital	53,040
S. C. Dominguez, Drawing	29,376
Selling Expenses (control)	36,273

The merchandise inventory at the beginning of the year was $141,929, and there were no changes in the partners' Capital accounts during the year. The partnership agreement provides for salary allowances of $31,900 for Aikens and $29,350 for Dominguez. The agreement also stipulates an interest allowance of 10 percent on invested capital at the beginning of the year. The remainder of the net income is to be divided equally.

Check Figure

Total assets, $224,986

Instructions

1. Prepare an income statement for the year.
2. Prepare a statement of partners' equity for the year.
3. Prepare a classified balance sheet for the partnership at the end of the year.

P.O. 6

Problem 19-4B The partnership of Hill, Cederblom, and Schultz is to be liquidated as of October 31 of this year. The partners share profits and losses in the ratio of 2 : 2 : 1, respectively. The firm's post-closing trial balance looks like this:

Hill, Cederblom, and Schultz
Post-Closing Trial Balance
October 31, 20—

ACCOUNT NAME	DEBIT	CREDIT
Cash	37 7 7 4 00	
Merchandise Inventory	67 9 1 2 00	
Other Assets	48 9 4 5 00	
Accounts Payable		15 8 7 7 00
A. L. Hill, Capital		54 3 8 8 00
L. S. Cederblom, Capital		43 8 1 4 00
S. R. Schultz, Capital		40 5 5 2 00
	154 6 3 1 00	154 6 3 1 00

The firm's realization and liquidation transactions are as follows:

Oct. 31 The merchandise inventory sold for $66,520; the other assets sold for $45,720.

31 The accountant allocated the loss or gain from realization to the partners' Capital accounts according to the profit and loss ratio.

31 The firm paid its creditors in full.

31 The firm distributed the remaining cash to the partners in accordance with the balances in their Capital accounts.

Check Figure

Loss from realization, $4,617

Instructions

1. Record the balances in the selected ledger accounts.
2. Record the liquidating transactions in general journal form.
3. Post the entries to the ledger accounts.

internet
LINKS TO ACCOUNTING

General Electric Company is one of the largest corporations in the world. How did it get where it is today? Have you ever wondered where GE and other large corporations get all the money needed to expand their operations? As you will learn in this chapter, one advantage of being or becoming a corporation is the ability to raise investment capital by selling stock. That is one way GE has been able to expand its operations. To find out how much of GE's capital was raised from common stock, examine GE's 2005 10-K report by going to **http://ge.com/en/company/investor/index.htm**, selecting Financial Reporting, then SEC Filing, and finally GE Company 2005 10K.

Performance Objectives

After you have completed this chapter, you will be able to do the following:

1. Define *corporation*.

2. Name at least two advantages and two disadvantages of the corporate form of business.

3. Describe the formation of a corporation.

4. Journalize entries for the issuance of par-value stock.

5. Journalize entries for the issuance of no-par stock.

6. Journalize entries for the sale of stock on the subscription basis.

7. Prepare a classified balance sheet for a corporation, including Subscriptions Receivable, Paid-in Capital, and Retained Earnings accounts.

REMEMBER!

Sole proprietorships and partnerships are generally limited to the wealth of their few owners.

Business organizations are usually classified as sole proprietorships, partnerships, or corporations. Corporations are fewest in number, but they account for more business transactions than the other two types of organizations combined. Frequently a firm that begins as a sole proprietorship or a partnership needs more investment capital as it grows and prospers. To raise additional investment capital, the firm incorporates. Other businesses are organized as corporations from the outset. Because of the predominance of corporations, everyone entering the business world should be familiar with the corporate form of organization and its financial structure. We consider corporations that issue stock and carry out business activities for the purpose of making profits and distributing the profits to their owners. Not-for-profit organizations generally do not issue stock or distribute profits, but carry out activities for charitable, educational, or other philanthropic purposes.

DEFINITION OF A CORPORATION

OBJECTIVE 1

Define *corporation*.

In 1818, Chief Justice John Marshall defined a **corporation** as "an artificial being, invisible, intangible, and existing only in contemplation of the law." A corporation does indeed act as an artificial legal being, deriving its existence from its charter. In every respect it is a separate legal entity, having a continuous existence apart from that of its owners, the stockholders. As an entity, a corporation may own property, enter into contracts, sue in the courts, be sued, and so forth.

ADVANTAGES OF THE CORPORATE FORM

OBJECTIVE 2

Name at least two advantages and two disadvantages of the corporate form of business.

1. **Limited liability** As a separate legal entity, a corporation is responsible for its own debts. All that a stockholder can lose is the amount of his or her investment.

2. **Ease of raising capital** A corporation can accumulate more investment capital than a sole proprietorship or partnership because a corporation can sell stock and issue corporate debt (bonds). Some corporations have more than 1 million stockholders.

3. **Ease of transferring ownership rights** Ownership rights in a corporation are represented by shares of stock, which can readily be transferred from one person to another without the permission of other stockholders, unless restricted by a shareholders agreement.

4. **Continuous existence** The length of life of a corporation is stipulated in its charter; when the charter expires, it may be renewed. The death, incapacity, or withdrawal of an owner does not affect the life of a corporation.

5. **No mutual agency** Stockholders who are not officers do not have the power to bind the corporation to contracts. Since owners need not participate in management, the corporation is free to employ the managerial talent it believes can best accomplish its objectives.

REMEMBER!

The owners of sole proprietorships and general partnerships are personally liable for the entire debt of the business.

DISADVANTAGES OF THE CORPORATE FORM

The corporate form also has a number of disadvantages.

1. **Additional taxation** In addition to the usual property and payroll taxes, corporations must pay income taxes. Since corporations are separate legal entities, they pay federal and state income taxes in their own names. Part of

the corporation's net income goes to the stockholders in the form of dividends; this money is personal income to the stockholders, and consequently the stockholders have to pay personal income taxes on it. This is known as **double taxation** to different entities (the corporation and the stockholders). It represents the corporate form's greatest disadvantage. The corporation may also have to pay charter fees to the state in return for the issuance of a charter.

2. **Government regulation** Since states create corporations by granting charters, states can exercise closer control and supervision over corporations than over sole proprietorships and partnerships. Corporations whose stock is traded on a stock exchange (publicly traded) are subject to extensive government regulations from the Securities and Exchange Commission and others.

3. **Lack of control by owners** The corporate ownership is separated from the control of operations. A minority shareholder (anyone who owns less than 50 percent of the company) has very limited, if any, say in how the corporation is managed.

S CORPORATIONS AND LIMITED LIABILITY COMPANIES

There are two important exceptions to the double taxation of corporations: S corporations and limited liability companies (LLCs).

An **S corporation** is a corporation that elects with the IRS to be treated as a pass-through entity for tax purposes. The income, gains, losses, and deductions are passed through in proportion to one's share of ownership in the S corporation. An S corporation can have no more than 100 shareholders, and there are other restrictions on who can own the stock (for example, no nonresident alien shareholders are allowed).

A **limited liability company (LLC)** is a relatively new type of business entity that is now allowed in all fifty states. The LLC can elect to be treated as a partnership for income tax purposes (a pass-through entity) and retain the corporate advantage of limited liability. The operating flexibility of the LLC, in combination with the freedom from corporate-level taxation, has made the LLC a very popular form of doing business for closely held and family-owned businesses. (Closely held corporations are discussed on the following page.)

FORMATION OF A CORPORATION

OBJECTIVE 3

Describe the formation of a corporation.

To organize a corporation, a person or persons must submit an application for a **charter**, which is a written permit for a corporation to exist. The charter is issued by the appropriate official (secretary of state or attorney general) of the state in which the company is to be incorporated. The corporation files a document called the **articles of incorporation**. Application requirements vary depending on the state in which the company incorporates. They generally include at least the following points of information:

- Name and legal address of the corporation
- Nature of the business to be conducted
- Amount and description of the capital stock to be issued
- Name and addresses of the first governing body of the corporation (directors and management team)

The articles of incorporation must be accompanied by a charter fee, which may be based on the dollar amount of maximum stock investment, or **authorized capital**.

When state officials approve the articles of incorporation, these articles become the charter or governing instrument of the corporation. Shortly after receiving the charter, the promoters or the sole promoter holds an initial meeting to elect an acting board of directors and formulate bylaws. The charter and the bylaws provide the basic rules for conducting the corporation's affairs. Next, the directors meet to appoint officers to serve as active managers of the business. Then the corporation issues **capital stock** to buyers of stock. The shares of stock are in the form of certificates. Since stockholders have come into existence at this point, they now elect a permanent board of directors.

The size of the corporation may vary in terms of number of stockholders and amount of investment. A corporation may be small, with only a few owners and a minimum investment of $1,000, or it may be a giant, with more than a million owners and an investment amounting to more than $1 billion. In a small corporation, the stockholders may also be the directors and officers. A corporation whose ownership is confined to a small group of stockholders is called a **closely held corporation**. A corporation whose ownership is widely distributed through a stock exchange or through over-the-counter markets to a large number of stockholders is called a **publicly traded corporation**.

Organization Costs

Let's suppose that a new corporation is being formed and the organizers call in an accountant to set up the books. The accountant debits the costs of organizing the corporation as they are incurred—such as fees paid to the state, attorneys' fees, promotional costs, travel outlays, costs of printing—to an account titled Organization Expense. This account will then appear on the income statement as an Operating Expense. Even though the organization costs benefit a corporation for many years, it is nearly impossible to match the benefits to the costs over the years of existence of the corporation. Therefore, corporations now expense the organization costs to Organization Expense rather than the prior method of amortizing the costs over a minimum of five years through a series of adjusting entries. For income tax purposes, organization costs must be capitalized and an election made to amortize the costs over sixty months.

Stock Certificate Book

One necessary element of organization costs is the printing of **stock certificates**. In a small corporation, the certificates often have stubs attached. The certificates and stubs are bound in a stock certificate book, rather like a checkbook. The corporation issues a stock certificate only when the stockholder has paid for the stock in full. On each blank certificate is written the name of the owner, the number of shares issued, and the date of issuance.

FIGURE 1

The stub must show the name and address of the stockholder, the number of shares listed on the stock certificate, and the date of issuance. Both certificates and stubs are numbered consecutively. Figure 1 is an example of a stock certificate.

When a transfer of ownership takes place, the stockholder surrenders the stock certificate to the corporation; the corporation cancels it and also cancels the matching stub; and the corporation then issues one or more new certificates to the new owner(s) in place of these documents. This procedure enables the corporation to maintain an up-to-date record of the names of all the stockholders and the number of shares owned by each. A corporation needs this information when it pays out dividends and when it sends out notices of annual meetings or other information.

The law requires large corporations whose stocks are listed on major stock exchanges to have independent registrars and transfer agents maintain their records of stock ownership. Banks and trust companies perform this service.

STRUCTURE OF A CORPORATION

FYI

Generally, the directors are also stockholders, although this is not always so.

The stockholders own the corporation; they delegate authority to the board of directors, which manages the corporation's affairs. The board of directors, in turn, delegates authority to the management team, which is responsible for the day-to-day operations of the business. The officers themselves may also be members of the board of directors. Figure 2 shows a typical organization chart for a corporation.

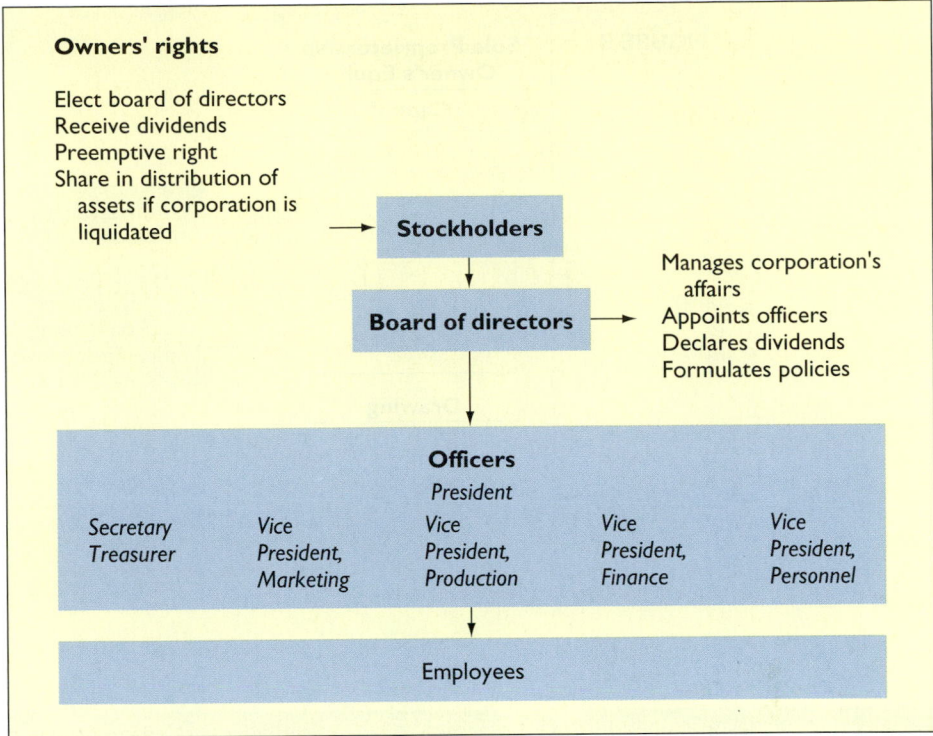

FIGURE 2

Owners' rights

Elect board of directors
Receive dividends
Preemptive right
Share in distribution of
assets if corporation is
liquidated

Stockholders

Board of directors

Manages corporation's
affairs
Appoints officers
Declares dividends
Formulates policies

Officers
President

| *Secretary Treasurer* | *Vice President, Marketing* | *Vice President, Production* | *Vice President, Finance* | *Vice President, Personnel* |

Employees

Dividends are the share of the corporation's earnings distributed to stockholders that can be paid in cash or with additional shares of stock. The sources of dividends are the current year's net income and the retained earnings of prior years.

Suppose the corporation issues some new stock. Each original stockholder then may have the right to subscribe to additional shares in proportion to her or his present holding. This feature is known as the **preemptive right**. For example, assume that the corporation's new issue consists of 1,000 shares. The present amount of stock outstanding is 10,000 shares, of which Ruth Allen owns 2,000 shares. Her proportion of stock held to stock outstanding is one-fifth (2,000/10,000). Therefore, she has the right to subscribe to 200 shares (one-fifth of 1,000 shares) of the new issue.

Stockholders' Equity

The owners' equity in a corporation is called **stockholders' equity**, or *capital*. Just as in sole proprietorships and partnerships, the equity of the owners represents the excess of assets over liabilities. Of the five major classifications of accounts, the main difference for a corporation occurs in the stockholders' equity classification, where capital stock accounts replace owners' Capital accounts. The **Retained Earnings** account is used to record earnings reinvested into the business. The T accounts in Figure 3 compare accounts for a sole proprietorship with those for a corporation.

FIGURE 3

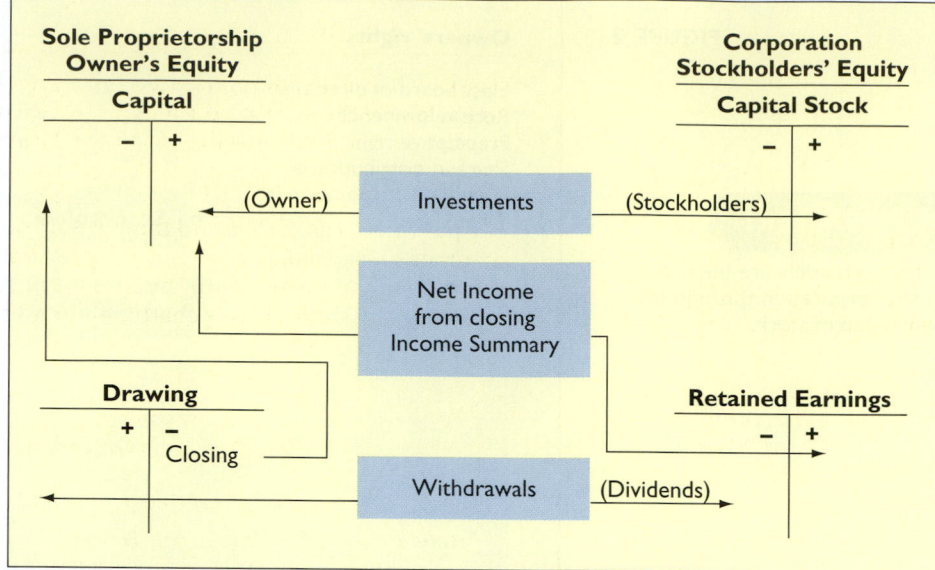

CAPITAL STOCK

Capital stock refers to shares of ownership in a corporation. *Authorized capital stock* is the maximum number of shares designated in the charter. **Issued stock** refers to the shares apportioned out to the stockholders. Stock that is actually in the hands of stockholders is called **outstanding stock**. Occasionally, a corporation may buy back its own stock or receive it as a donation; consequently, the number of shares that have been issued may differ from the number outstanding. Such reacquired stock is generally known as **treasury stock**.

A corporation may acquire treasury stock to:

1. Reissue shares to officers and employees under bonus and stock compensation plans
2. Rid the company of disgruntled investors
3. Increase trading of the company's stock in the securities market in the hopes of enhancing its market value

Classes of Capital Stock

To appeal to as many investors as possible, a corporation may issue more than one kind of stock, just as a refrigerator manufacturer, say, makes different models to please different groups of potential buyers. **The two main types of stock are *common* and *preferred*.** Each type may have a variety of characteristics. Some may be **par-value stock** (a value is printed on the stock certificate), and some may be **no-par stock** (no value is printed on the stock certificate). We will refer to these types of stock frequently. Following is a brief comparison of par-value and no-par stock:

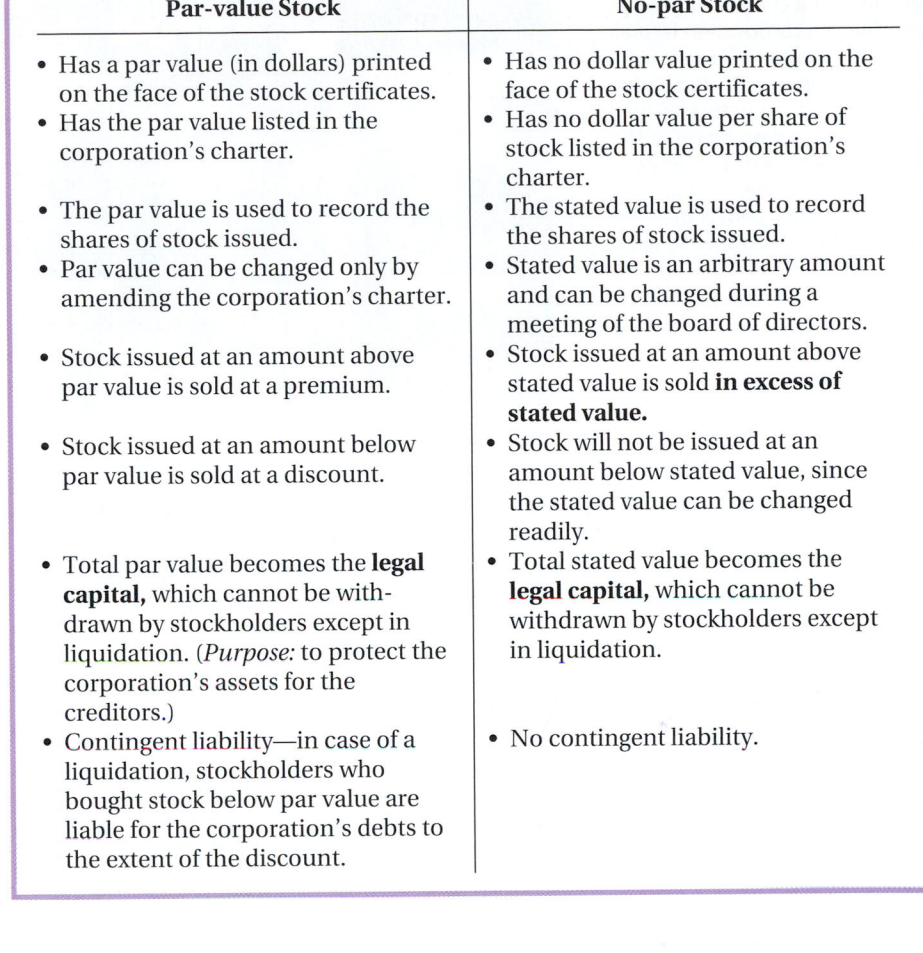

Par-value Stock	No-par Stock
• Has a par value (in dollars) printed on the face of the stock certificates.	• Has no dollar value printed on the face of the stock certificates.
• Has the par value listed in the corporation's charter.	• Has no dollar value per share of stock listed in the corporation's charter.
• The par value is used to record the shares of stock issued.	• The stated value is used to record the shares of stock issued.
• Par value can be changed only by amending the corporation's charter.	• Stated value is an arbitrary amount and can be changed during a meeting of the board of directors.
• Stock issued at an amount above par value is sold at a premium.	• Stock issued at an amount above stated value is sold **in excess of stated value.**
• Stock issued at an amount below par value is sold at a discount.	• Stock will not be issued at an amount below stated value, since the stated value can be changed readily.
• Total par value becomes the **legal capital,** which cannot be withdrawn by stockholders except in liquidation. (*Purpose:* to protect the corporation's assets for the creditors.)	• Total stated value becomes the **legal capital,** which cannot be withdrawn by stockholders except in liquidation.
• Contingent liability—in case of a liquidation, stockholders who bought stock below par value are liable for the corporation's debts to the extent of the discount.	• No contingent liability.

Some corporations are small, privately held family businesses.

Common Stock

When a corporation issues only one type of stock, it is called **common stock and may be either par-value or no-par stock.** Common stocks are shares that may yield dividends, but only after owners of preferred stock have been paid. Holders of common stock have the rights listed in Figure 2, with voting privileges of one vote for each share of stock.

Preferred Stock

Preferred stock, **which is generally par-value stock,** has two preferences. (1) A preference as to dividends: corporations pay dividends on preferred stock (if dividends are declared at all) before they pay dividends on common stock. They pay dividends on preferred stock at a uniform rate—a disadvantage if a corporation is very successful because the preferred shareholder is limited to the stated rate of dividends. The dividend on preferred stock consists of a percentage of the par value of the stock. (2) If the corporation is liquidated, holders of preferred stock are paid off before holders of common stock. In most circumstances, however, holders of preferred stock do not have voting privileges. There are several specific types of preferred stock.

Cumulative and Noncumulative Preferred Stock   Suppose that a corporation has a bad year and finds that it is not able to pay the dividend on its preferred stock. In this case, the dividend is said to be *passed.* Dividends on

All corporations begin life by applying for a charter or permit. Whether the corporation is small, medium, or large, its articles of incorporation must include information about the nature of the business and a description of the capital stock structure. Many corporations start small and grow over time, which allows them to raise additional capital and grow even more.

cumulative preferred stock may accrue to stockholders. The corporation has to pay these dividends in full before it can pay any dividends to common stockholders. However, for stockholders who own **noncumulative preferred stock**, dividends do not accumulate. In other words, if the corporation passes dividends, they are gone forever. Since preferred stockholders naturally want a regular dividend, most preferred stock is cumulative.

Participating and Nonparticipating Preferred Stock   The dividend on preferred stock consists of an established percentage of the par value of that stock. Some preferred stock, however, provides for the possibility of dividends in excess of this established amount; this kind of preferred stock is called **participating preferred stock.** Holders of participating preferred stock first get the regular dividend that is due them. Then the corporation allocates a stipulated amount to holders of its common stock. And *then* the stockholders who own participating preferred stock are allowed to participate or share in the extra earnings if they are distributed as cash dividends. The dividends of **nonparticipating preferred stock,** on the other hand, are limited to the regular rate. Most preferred stock is nonparticipating.

> **REMEMBER!**
>
> Since preferred stock can be cumulative or noncumulative, participating or nonparticipating, there are four possible combinations.

ISSUING STOCK

> **REMEMBER!**
>
> Authorized capital represents the maximum amount of stock that can be sold.

Stock is issued when the buyer has paid for it in full or when the corporation has received noncash assets in exchange for its stock. A corporation may issue par-value stock at an amount equal to, above, or below its par value.

Issuing Stock at Par for Cash

OBJECTIVE 4

Journalize entries for the issuance of par-value stock.

There is a separate ledger account for each class of stock. The accountant records investments of cash as debits to Cash and credits to the Stock accounts for the total amount of the par value. Remember that par value is the face value printed on each stock certificate. This designation of par value is a convenient means of dividing the corporation's capital into units, with the ownership of each unit known.

For example, Rocky Mountain Corporation is organized on July 16 with authorized capital of 4,000 shares of $100-par preferred 8 percent stock and

20,000 shares of $50-par common stock. On August 1, Rocky Mountain Corporation issues 2,000 shares of preferred 8 percent stock at par and 10,000 shares of common stock at par. In general journal form, the entry looks like this:

GENERAL JOURNAL   PAGE ___1___

	DATE		DESCRIPTION	POST. REF.	DEBIT	CREDIT	
1	20–						1
2	Aug.	1	Cash		700 0 0 0 00		2
3			Preferred 8 Percent Stock			200 0 0 0 00	3
4			Common Stock			500 0 0 0 00	4
5			Issued 2,000 shares of				5
6			preferred 8 percent stock at				6
7			par and 10,000 shares of				7
8			common stock at par.				8
9							9

In terms of T accounts, the situation looks like this:

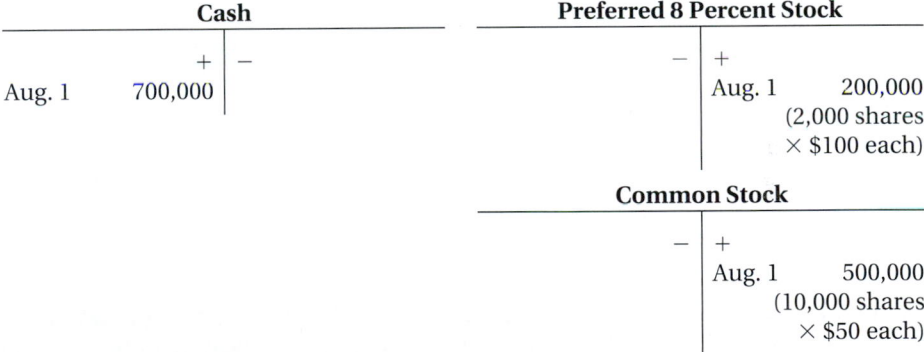

The capital stock accounts (Preferred 8 Percent Stock and Common Stock) are controlling accounts. The subsidiary ledger is known as the **stockholders' ledger**. The stockholders' ledger may consist of the stock certificate book or a supplementary record showing the name and address of each stockholder and the number of shares owned.

Issuing Stock at Par for Assets and Organization Expense

Corporations often accept assets other than cash in exchange for their stock. Rocky Mountain Corporation received equipment, a building, and land in exchange for 5,420 shares of common stock, as in the following journal entry.

REMEMBER!

Stock may be sold for cash or given in exchange for services or assets.

	DATE		DESCRIPTION	POST. REF.	DEBIT					CREDIT					
1	20–														1
2	Aug.	1	Equipment		11	0	0	0	00						2
3			Building		140	0	0	0	00						3
4			Land		120	0	0	0	00						4
5			Common Stock							271	0	0	0	00	5
6			Exchanged 5,420 shares of												6
7			common stock for equipment,												7
8			building, and land.												8
9															9

When a corporation accepts an asset other than cash, the accountant records the asset at its fair market value. The goal of the accountant is to have a realistic base on which to calculate future depreciation.

Now suppose that a corporation gives shares of its stock to its organizers in exchange for their services in organizing the corporation. Suppose that Rocky Mountain Corporation issues 100 shares of common stock to its organizers. The accountant handles it this way:

	DATE		DESCRIPTION	POST. REF.	DEBIT					CREDIT					
1	20–														1
2	Aug.	1	Organization Expense		5	0	0	0	00						2
3			Common Stock							5	0	0	0	00	3
4			Issued 100 shares of												4
5			common stock to the												5
6			promoters in exchange for												6
7			their services in organizing												7
8			the corporation.												8

If the fair market value of the asset or service is not determinable, as in the case of organization expense, then the current market price of the stock on the date the asset or service is acquired is used.

Issuing Stock at a Premium

A newly organized corporation, such as Larson Corporation, generally issues its stock at par. However, after the business has been operating for some time, the directors may realize that they need additional investment capital. Perhaps the business has been so successful that they want to expand it. Or perhaps they need to cover losses suffered during the early years of the business. So the directors decide to issue some new stock. The present market price of the original stock affects the price they can secure for the new shares. The market price of the stock of a corporation is usually influenced by the following factors:

1. The earnings record, financial condition, and dividend record of the corporation

2. The potential for growth in earnings of the corporation
3. The supply of and demand for money for investment purposes in the money market as a whole
4. General business conditions and prospects for the future

When a corporation issues stock at a price above par value, the stock is said to be issued at a **premium**; the premium is the amount by which the issuing price of the new stock exceeds the par value. The premium may exist because the corporation has performed successfully in the past and has good prospects for growth in earnings in the future. Conversely, when a corporation sells its stock at a price below par value, the stock is said to be issued at a **discount**; the discount is the amount by which the issuing price of the new stock falls below the par value. This discount may exist because the corporation incurred losses during its early period, or perhaps its prospects for the future are not too promising.

Premium on Stock

When a corporation issues stock at a price *above* its par value, the accountant debits Cash or other noncash assets for the amount received, credits the stock account for the par value, and credits a premium account, called **Paid-in Capital in Excess of Par Value**, for the difference between the amount received and the par value. Suppose McKay Corporation issues 900 shares of $100-par cumulative preferred 9 percent stock at $103 on July 1. In general journal form, the entry looks like this:

The major stock exchanges for publicly held corporations are hubs of activity. Buyers are trying to buy low and sellers are trying to sell high.

REMEMBER!

The recording of a premium may or may not reflect what is going on in the stock market, although the market may influence the price at which stock is issued.

DATE		DESCRIPTION	POST. REF.	DEBIT	CREDIT	
1	20–					1
2	July 1	Cash		92 7 0 0 00		2
3		Preferred 9 Percent Stock			90 0 0 0 00	3
4		Paid-in Capital in Excess of				4
5		Par Value			2 7 0 0 00	5
6		Issued 900 shares at $103				6
7		per share.				7
8						8

In terms of T accounts, the entry looks like this:

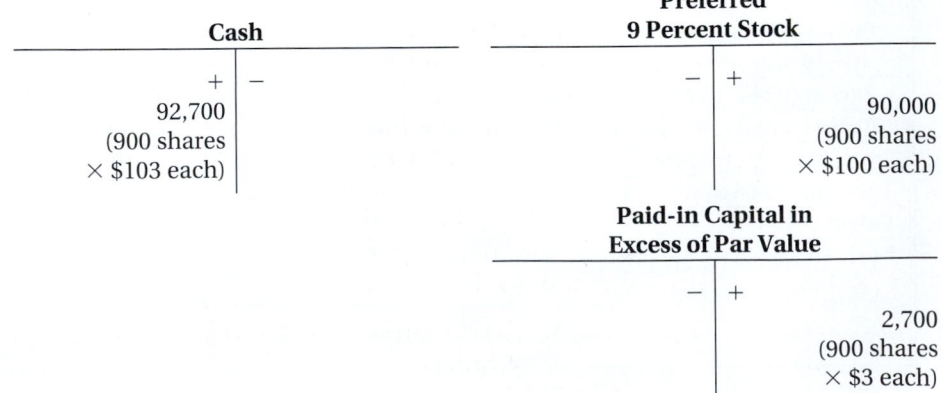

Cash			Preferred 9 Percent Stock	
+	–		–	+
92,700				90,000
(900 shares				(900 shares
× $103 each)				× $100 each)

	Paid-in Capital in Excess of Par Value
–	+
	2,700
	(900 shares
	× $3 each)

In the case of par-value stock, the stock account contains only the total par value of the stock. The Paid-in Capital in Excess of Par Value account is treated as an addition to stockholders' equity. Why would buyers be willing to pay a premium for McKay's 9 percent preferred stock? The 9 percent rate may be higher than the current market rate for this type of stock. For example, other companies in comparable financial condition may be paying only 8 percent dividends on their stock.

Let's review the placement of the major accounts presented thus far in the fundamental accounting equation:

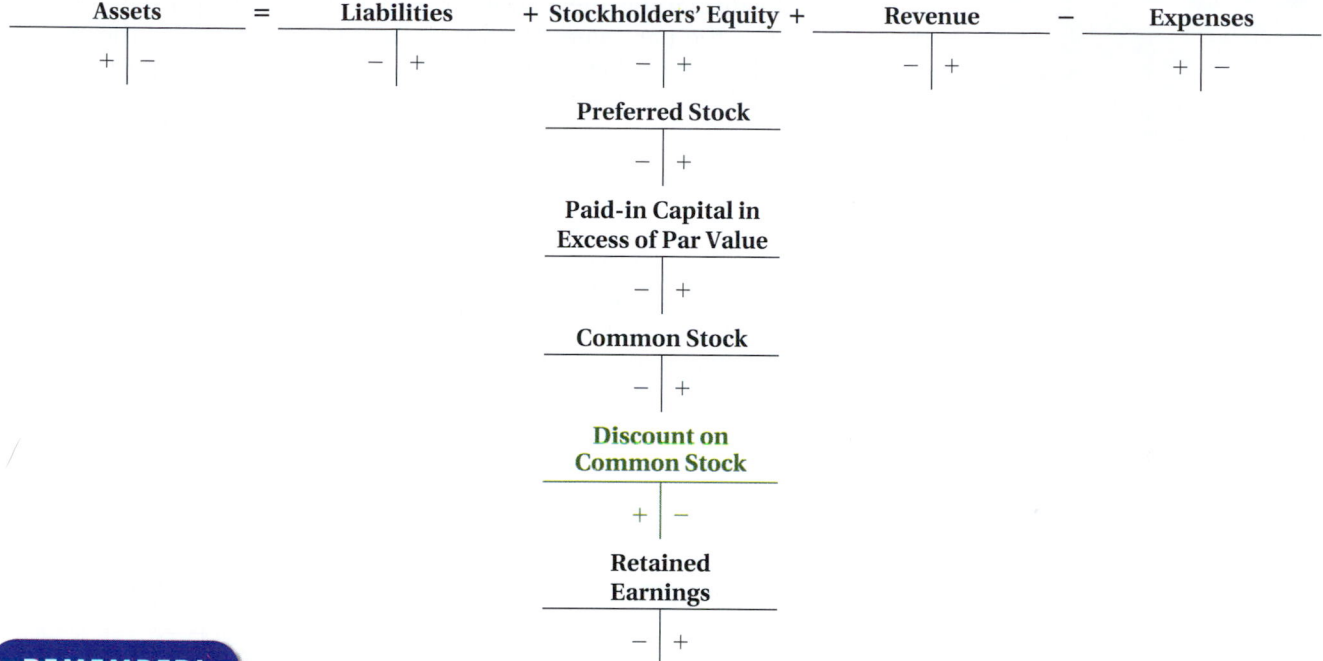

REMEMBER!

The Paid-in Capital in Excess of Par Value account is treated as an addition to stockholders' equity.

The Stockholders' Equity section of the balance sheet of McKay Corporation—showing the stock and premium accounts—looks like this:

Stockholders' Equity			
Paid-in Capital:			
Preferred 9 Percent Stock, cumulative, $100 par			
(2,000 shares authorized, 900 shares issued)	$90 0 0 0 00		
Paid-in Capital in Excess of Par Value	2 7 0 0 00	$ 92 7 0 0 00	
Common Stock, $20 par (20,000 shares authorized,			
10,000 shares issued)		200 0 0 0 00	
Total Paid-in Capital		$292 7 0 0 00	
Retained Earnings		45 0 0 0 00	
Total Stockholders' Equity			$337 7 0 0 00

Notice that the listing of the stock states the par value, the number of shares authorized, and the number of shares issued. The record also describes preferred stock as cumulative. If the preferred stock is noncumulative or nonparticipating, as in this case, the record does not mention it. Preferred stock is assumed to be noncumulative and nonparticipating unless otherwise stated.

Stockholders' Equity is divided into two major sections: **Paid-in Capital** and Retained Earnings. Paid-in or contributed capital includes the investments made by all the types of shareholders owning common and preferred stock in the corporation.

For the Retained Earnings account, note that the amount is not necessarily in the form of cash. Retained earnings represents accumulated net income (not necessarily cash) kept in the company and not paid to stockholders in the form of dividends.

No-Par Stock

Preferred stock generally has a par value. However, common stock may or may not have a par value. If it does not have a par value, it is referred to as *no-par stock*. Corporations in all fifty states can issue no-par stock, and some states only have no-par stock. The main advantages claimed for no-par stock are as follows:

1. Since it does not have a par value, no-par stock may be issued without a discount contingent liability.
2. No-par stock prevents any misconception on the part of naive stockholders as to the value of the stock. In the case of par stock, investors might believe that the stock is worth the amount printed on the face of the stock certificate. Actually, the market value of the stock may differ markedly from the par value, as a result of ups and downs in the corporation's past earnings and future prospects.

Stated Value and No-Par Stock

When all of a company's stock is of the par-value type, the par value of the shares represents the company's **legal capital**, which stockholders cannot withdraw. This law protects creditors. When various state legislatures passed laws permitting corporations to issue no-par stock, they tried to continue to protect creditors by stipulating that all or part of the amount the corporation receives for its no-par shares be exempt from withdrawal by stockholders. This amount is known as the stock's **stated value**. The minimum stated value per share of no-par stock varies from state to state. In some states the board of directors of the corporation, if it wishes, may choose a stated value for the company's no-par stock that is higher than the minimum required by the state law.

Established Amount of Stated Value

OBJECTIVE 5

Journalize entries for the issuance of no-par stock.

Total Security Corporation is located in a state that allows the board of directors of a corporation to designate a stated value for its stock. Accordingly, the board of directors of Total Security Corporation chooses a stated value of $50 per share for its common stock. On June 20, Total Security Corporation issues 1,400 shares at $56 per share, receiving cash. The accountant uses the account Paid-in Capital in Excess of Stated Value to record the amount received over and above the stated value.

The accountant's entry, in general journal form, is as follows:

	DATE		DESCRIPTION	POST. REF.	DEBIT	CREDIT	
1	20–						1
2	June	20	Cash		78 4 0 0 00		2
3			Common Stock			70 0 0 0 00	3
4			Paid-in Capital in Excess of				4
5			Stated Value			8 4 0 0 00	5
6			Issued 1,400 shares at $56				6
7			per share.				7

Next, on September 10, Total Security Corporation issues an additional 1,000 shares at $60 per share, receiving cash. The entry in general journal form is as follows:

	DATE		DESCRIPTION	POST. REF.	DEBIT	CREDIT	
1	20–						1
2	Sept.	10	Cash		60 0 0 0 00		2
3			Common Stock			50 0 0 0 00	3
4			Paid-in Capital in Excess of				4
5			Stated Value			10 0 0 0 00	5
6			Issued 1,000 shares at $60				6
7			per share.				7

In terms of T accounts, the entries look like this:

Cash		
	+	–
June 20	78,400	
Sept. 10	60,000	

Common Stock		
–	+	
	June 20	70,000
		(stated value)
	Sept. 10	50,000
		(stated value)

Paid-in Capital in Excess of Stated Value		
–	+	
	June 20	8,400 (excess)
	Sept. 10	10,000 (excess)

Subscriptions and Stock Issuance

We have been talking about corporations that issue stock for which investors pay in full, either by giving cash or by giving noncash assets or organizational services. However, a corporation often sells its stock directly to investors on

a subscription contract (installment) basis. This means that the investor enters into a contract with the corporation, promising to pay at a later date for a specified number of shares at an agreed-upon price. The corporation agrees to issue the shares when the investor has paid for them in full.

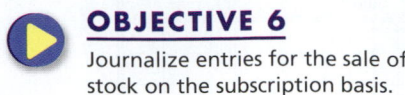

OBJECTIVE 6

Journalize entries for the sale of stock on the subscription basis.

The accountant records the amount of the subscription, which is an asset, in the Subscriptions Receivable account and credits the par or stated value of the stock to Stock Subscribed, a stockholders' equity account. The accountant then records the difference between the subscription price and the par value under Paid-in Capital in Excess of Par Value. In the case of no-par stock, the difference between the subscription price and the stated value is recorded under Paid-in Capital in Excess of Stated Value.

As the investor sends in payments, the accountant records them as debits to Cash and credits to Subscriptions Receivable. When the investor finishes paying for all the shares, the accountant records the issuance of the stock as a debit to Stock Subscribed and a credit to Common Stock or Preferred Stock. When investors want subscriptions to both common and preferred stock, the accountant uses separate accounts for each. We can best describe the procedure with some examples.

Subscription Transactions: No-Par Stock   Mariposa, Inc., a newly organized company, sets up its books with the following transactions involving its own stock:

May   1   Received subscriptions to 20,000 shares of common stock (stated value $10 per share) from various subscribers at $17 per share, with a down payment of 50 percent of the subscription price (20,000 × $17 × 0.50 = $170,000).

June   1   Received an additional 30 percent of the subscription price from all subscribers (20,000 × $17 × 0.30 = $102,000).

July   1   Received an additional 20 percent of the subscription price from all subscribers; then issued the stock (20,000 × $17 × 0.20 = $68,000).

The general journal entries are shown in Figure 4 on the following page. The items in parentheses are just explanations; they would not actually appear in the journal.

After the accountant has posted these transactions, the T accounts appear as follows:

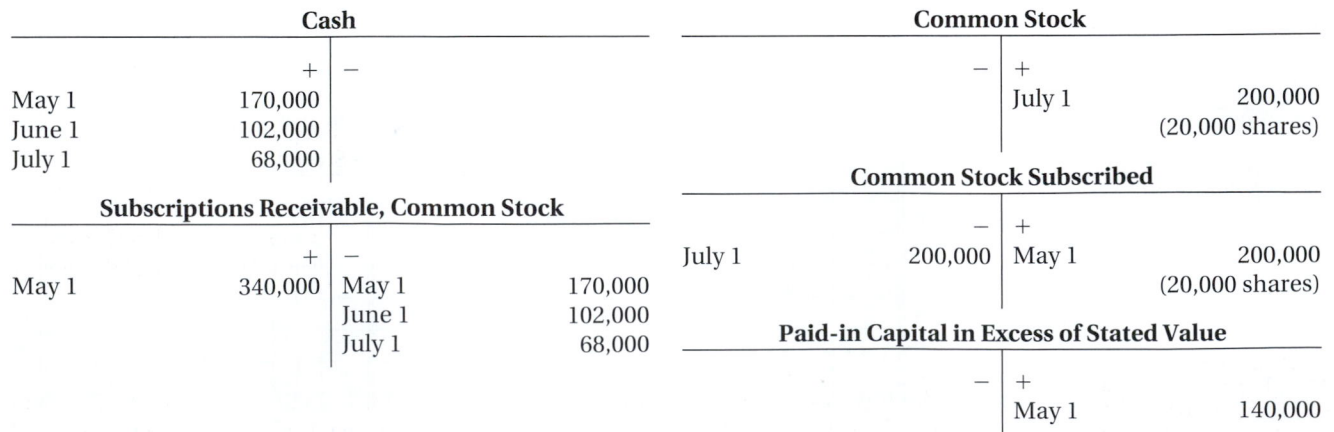

FIGURE 4

GENERAL JOURNAL   PAGE ___1___

	DATE		DESCRIPTION	POST. REF.	DEBIT	CREDIT	
1	20–						1
2	May	1	Subscriptions Receivable,				2
3			Common Stock (20,000 shares				3
4			at $17 per share)		340 0 0 0 00		4
5			Common Stock Subscribed				5
6			(20,000 shares at $10 per				6
7			share)			200 0 0 0 00	7
8			Paid-in Capital in Excess of				8
9			Stated Value (20,000 shares				9
10			× $7)			140 0 0 0 00	10
11			Received subscriptions to				11
12			20,000 shares at $17 per				12
13			share.				13
14							14
15		1	Cash (20,000 shares × $17 per				15
16			share × 0.50)		170 0 0 0 00		16
17			Subscriptions Receivable,				17
18			Common Stock			170 0 0 0 00	18
19			Received 50 percent of the				19
20			subscription of May 1 on				20
21			20,000 shares.				21
22							22
23	June	1	Cash (20,000 shares × $17 per				23
24			share × 0.30)		102 0 0 0 00		24
25			Subscriptions Receivable,				25
26			Common Stock			102 0 0 0 00	26
27			Received 30 percent of the				27
28			subscription of May 1 on				28
29			20,000 shares.				29
30							30
31	July	1	Cash (20,000 shares × $17 per				31
32			share × 0.20)		68 0 0 0 00		32
33			Subscriptions Receivable,				33
34			Common Stock			68 0 0 0 00	34
35			Received 20 percent of the				35
36			subscription of May 1 on				36
37			20,000 shares.				37
38							38
39		1	Common Stock Subscribed		200 0 0 0 00		39
40			Common Stock (20,000 shares				40
41			× $10 per share)			200 0 0 0 00	41
42			Issued 20,000 shares.				42
43							43
44							44
45							45
46							46
47							47

Common Stock Subscribed represents the total par value or stated value of the shares subscribed. It is a temporary account to handle subscribed shares that have not yet been paid for in full. When the investors finish paying for the shares, the accountant records the issuance of stock by debiting the Common Stock Subscribed account and crediting the Common Stock account.

In the ledger accounts for stock issued and subscribed, always list the number of shares in the Item column. Here is an example for Common Stock and Common Stock Subscribed:

ACCOUNT	Common Stock						ACCOUNT NO.	314	
							BALANCE		
DATE	ITEM	POST. REF.	DEBIT	CREDIT		DEBIT		CREDIT	
20–									
July 1	20,000								
	shares	J1		200 0 0 0 00				200 0 0 0 00	

ACCOUNT	Common Stock Subscribed						ACCOUNT NO.	316	
							BALANCE		
DATE	ITEM	POST. REF.	DEBIT	CREDIT		DEBIT		CREDIT	
20–									
May 1	20,000								
	shares	J1		200 0 0 0 00				200 0 0 0 00	
July 1		J1	200 0 0 0 00						

Subscription Transactions: Par-Value Stock   Reyes Masonry, Inc., a newly organized company, has the following transactions involving its own stock:

June   15   Received subscriptions to 4,000 shares of preferred 9 percent stock ($100 par value) from various subscribers at $104 per share, with a down payment of 40 percent of the subscription price.

July   1   Received 30 percent of the subscription price from all subscribers (4,000 shares).

15   Received 30 percent of the subscription price from subscribers to 500 shares, and issued 500 shares.

The general journal is shown in Figure 5 on the following page. The items in parentheses are explanations; they would not actually appear in the journal.

This illustrates that Preferred 9 Percent Stock Subscribed represents the total par value of the shares subscribed. **It also illustrates the fact that a firm does not issue stock until the investor has paid for it in full.** Since only 500 shares were paid for in full, the firm issued only 500 shares.

FIGURE 5

REMEMBER!

Stock accounts are always credited at par value or stated value when stock is issued.

	DATE		DESCRIPTION	POST. REF.	DEBIT	CREDIT	
1	20–						1
2	June	15	Subscriptions Receivable,				2
3			Preferred 9 Percent Stock (4,000				3
4			shares × $104 per share)		416 0 0 0 00		4
5			Preferred 9 Percent Stock				5
6			Subscribed (4,000 shares ×				6
7			$100 per share)			400 0 0 0 00	7
8			Paid-in Capital in Excess of				8
9			Par Value (4,000 shares				9
10			× $4 per share)			16 0 0 0 00	10
11			Received subscriptions to				11
12			4,000 shares at $104 per				12
13			share.				13
14							14
15		15	Cash (4,000 shares × $104 per				15
16			share × 0.40)		166 4 0 0 00		16
17			Subscriptions Receivable,				17
18			Preferred 9 Percent Stock			166 4 0 0 00	18
19			Received 40 percent of the				19
20			subscription of June 15 on				20
21			4,000 shares.				21
22							22
23	July	1	Cash (4,000 shares × $104 per				23
24			share × 0.30)		124 8 0 0 00		24
25			Subscriptions Receivable,				25
26			Preferred 9 Percent Stock			124 8 0 0 00	26
27			Received 30 percent of the				27
28			subscription of June 15 on				28
29			4,000 shares.				29
30							30
31		15	Cash (500 shares × $104 per				31
32			share × 0.30)		15 6 0 0 00		32
33			Subscriptions Receivable,				33
34			Preferred 9 Percent Stock			15 6 0 0 00	34
35			Received 30 percent, the				35
36			final installment of the				36
37			subscription of June 15, on				37
38			500 shares.				38
39							39
40		15	Preferred 9 Percent Stock				40
41			Subscribed		50 0 0 0 00		41
42			Preferred 9 Percent Stock (500				42
43			shares × $100 per share)			50 0 0 0 00	43
44			Issued 500 shares.				44

REMEMBER!

Get the number of shares issued from the ledger account for the stock.

Controlling Accounts and Subsidiary Ledgers

Investors may finish paying for subscriptions at different times, and the firm issues stock when the individual subscriber has paid in full. Therefore, the firm's accountant has to maintain an account for each individual subscriber.

As a result, the books exhibit the following relationships between controlling accounts and subsidiary ledgers:

Controlling Account	Subsidiary Ledger
Subscriptions Receivable, Preferred 9 Percent Stock	Preferred 9 percent stock subscribers' ledger
Subscriptions Receivable, Common Stock	Common stock subscribers' ledger

These records are similar to the Accounts Receivable controlling account and the accounts receivable ledger.

The firm's accountant also has to keep an accurate record of the number of shares owned by each stockholder. Consequently, each stock account is a controlling account:

Controlling Account	Subsidiary Ledger
Preferred 9 Percent Stock	Preferred 9 percent stockholders' ledger
Common Stock	Common stockholders' ledger

As we have said, a small corporation may use its stock certificate book as a subsidiary ledger. Naturally, the accountant must see to it that the information is complete, so that the company can declare and pay dividends correctly. Cash dividends are paid on outstanding stock only.

ILLUSTRATION OF A CORPORATE BALANCE SHEET

OBJECTIVE 7

Prepare a classified balance sheet for a corporation, including Subscriptions Receivable, Paid-in Capital, and Retained Earnings accounts.

REMEMBER!

The stockholders' equity items are each represented by a ledger account.

To reinforce your understanding of the accounts introduced in this chapter, examine the balance sheet shown in Figure 6 on page 770 to see where each account is placed. Because this balance sheet covers so many of the concepts just discussed, you will probably want to refer back to it in the future. Notice that Retained Earnings is added separately to Total Paid-in Capital. In this case, the Retained Earnings account has a $170,000 credit balance. **This credit balance represents a surplus, and it is the normal balance. However, if a company had big losses, its Retained Earnings account could have a debit balance, which is called a deficit.** On a balance sheet, a Retained Earnings account with a debit balance is subtracted from Total Paid-in Capital.

NEW ACCOUNTS AND THE FUNDAMENTAL ACCOUNTING EQUATION

The placement and use of the accounts we have introduced in this chapter with respect to the fundamental accounting equation are shown in Figure 7 on page 771.

Caitlin, Inc.
Balance Sheet
June 30, 20—

Assets				
Current Assets:				
Cash		$ 27 0 0 0 00		
Notes Receivable		50 0 0 0 00		
Accounts Receivable	$419 0 0 0 00			
Less Allowance for Doubtful Accounts	12 0 0 0 00	407 0 0 0 00		
Subscriptions Receivable, Preferred 9 Percent Stock		14 0 0 0 00		
Subscriptions Receivable, Common Stock		30 0 0 0 00		
Merchandise Inventory		279 0 0 0 00		
Prepaid Insurance		3 5 0 0 00		
Total Current Assets			$810 5 0 0 00	
Investments:				
Friedman Equipment Company 8 Percent Bonds			16 0 0 0 00	
Property and Equipment:				
Store Equipment	$ 82 0 0 0 00			
Less Accumulated Depreciation	19 0 0 0 00	$ 63 0 0 0 00		
Delivery Equipment	$ 60 0 0 0 00			
Less Accumulated Depreciation	40 0 0 0 00	20 0 0 0 00		
Total Property and Equipment			83 0 0 0 00	
Intangible Assets:				
Patents			8 0 0 0 00	
Total Assets			$917 5 0 0 00	
Liabilities				
Current Liabilities:				
Accounts Payable		$281 5 0 0 00		
Notes Payable		20 0 0 0 00		
Salaries Payable		3 0 0 0 00		
Interest Payable		1 0 0 0 00		
Total Liabilities			$305 5 0 0 00	
Stockholders' Equity				
Paid-in Capital:				
Preferred 7 Percent Stock, $50 par (2,000 shares				
authorized and issued)		$100 0 0 0 00		
Preferred 9 Percent Stock, $50 par (4,000 shares				
authorized, 1,500 shares issued)	$ 75 0 0 0 00			
Preferred 9 Percent Stock Subscribed (500 shares)	25 0 0 0 00			
Paid-in Capital in Excess of Par Value	2 0 0 0 00	102 0 0 0 00		
Common Stock, no-par, stated value $10 per share				
(20,000 shares authorized, 14,000 shares issued)	$140 0 0 0 00			
Common Stock Subscribed (2,000 shares)	20 0 0 0 00			
Paid-in Capital in Excess of Stated Value	80 0 0 0 00	240 0 0 0 00		
Total Paid-in Capital		$442 0 0 0 00		
Retained Earnings		170 0 0 0 00		
Total Stockholders' Equity			612 0 0 0 00	
Total Liabilities and Stockholders' Equity			$917 5 0 0 00	

FIGURE 6

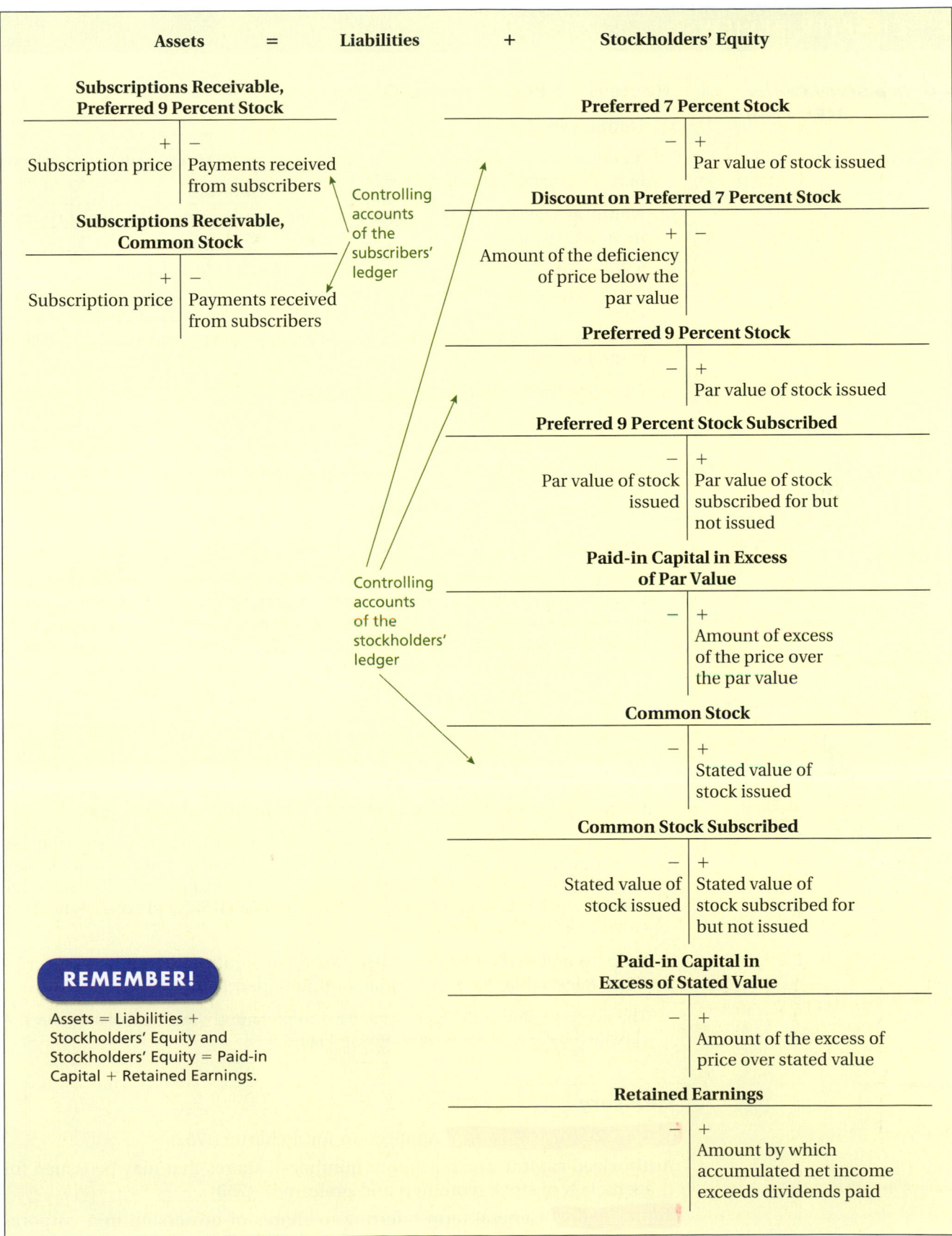

FIGURE 7

CHAPTER REVIEW

Online Study Center
ACE the test!

Review of Performance Objectives

1. Define *corporation*.

   A corporation is defined as "an artificial being, invisible, intangible, and existing only in contemplation of the law."

2. Name at least two advantages and two disadvantages of the corporate form of business.

   A corporation has the following advantages over a sole proprietorship or a general partnership: limited liability, ease of raising capital, ease of transferring ownership rights, continuous existence, and no mutual agency. Three disadvantages of a corporation are additional taxation, increased government regulation, and lack of control by owners.

3. Describe the formation of a corporation.

   To form a corporation, a person or persons must file articles of incorporation with the state. The corporation may be small (closely held) or large (publicly traded). Stock is sold to raise capital. Dividends (an amount per share owned) may be paid to stockholders. The capital stock accounts in a corporation replace owners' capital accounts in sole proprietorships.

4. Journalize entries for the issuance of par-value stock.

   The entry for the issuance of par-value stock for cash is a debit to Cash and credits to the Stock accounts. When stock is exchanged for assets other than cash, those asset accounts are debited. When stock is issued for more than its par value, the accountant must credit a Premium account. For stock issued at a discount, a Discount account is debited.

5. Journalize entries for the issuance of no-par stock.

   The entry for the issuance of no-par stock for cash is a debit to Cash and credit to the Stock account. When the stock is issued for more than its stated value, the accountant must credit a Premium account.

6. Journalize entries for the sale of stock on the subscription basis.

   The entry for the sale of stock on a subscription (installment) basis is a debit to a Subscriptions Receivable account (a current asset) and a credit to a Stock Subscribed account (a Paid-in Capital account). When the subscription is paid in full and the stock is issued, the entry is a debit to a Stock Subscribed account and a credit to a Stock account.

7. Prepare a classified balance sheet for a corporation, including Subscriptions Receivable, Paid-in Capital, and Retained Earnings accounts.

   The accounts shown in Figure 7 are used to prepare a classified balance sheet. A classified balance sheet is presented in Figure 6.

Glossary

Articles of incorporation Application for a charter. (752)

Authorized capital The maximum number of shares that may be issued for each class of stock (common and preferred). (753)

Capital stock General term referring to shares of ownership in a corporation. (753)

Charter Written permit, issued by a state government, for a corporation to exist; state approved articles of incorporation. (752)

Closely held corporation A corporation having a relatively small group of owners. (753)

Common stock Stock whose owners are paid dividends only after owners of preferred stock have been paid (residual share); holders of common stock have voting privileges. (757)

Corporation "An artificial being, invisible, intangible, and existing only in contemplation of the law." As such, it is a separate legal entity. (751)

Cumulative preferred stock Preferred stock whose holders must be paid accumulated dividends or dividends passed (dividends that the firm has failed to pay in prior years) before any dividends can be paid to holders of common stock. (758)

Deficit A debit or negative balance in the Retained Earnings account. (769)

Discount The amount by which the issuing price of the new stock falls below the par value. (761)

Dividends Distributions of earnings of a corporation, in the form of either cash or additional shares of stock. (755)

Double taxation Taxation of corporate income at two separate points. First, the net income of the corporation is taxed because the corporation is a separate entity. When the net income is distributed as dividends to stockholders, it becomes part of the personal income of the individual stockholder and is taxed a second time. (752)

Issued stock Stock issued by a corporation. (756)

Legal capital Minimum capital stock investment that a corporation must maintain; capital that is not subject to withdrawal by stockholders; usually equal to par or stated value. (763)

Limited liability company (LLC) A relatively new type of entity that can elect to be treated as a partnership for tax purposes and a corporation for legal purposes (limited liability); a very popular form of ownership for closely held and family-owned businesses. (752)

Noncumulative preferred stock Preferred stock in which dividends passed do not accumulate; once they are passed, they are gone forever. (758)

Nonparticipating preferred stock Stock in which the dividends are limited to the regular rate. (758)

No-par stock Stock that has no value printed on the stock certificates. (756)

Outstanding stock Stock actually in the possession of stockholders (issued stock less the number of shares reacquired by the company). (756)

Paid-in Capital A caption on the balance sheet listed immediately under Stockholders' Equity. The Paid-in Capital section includes the Stock accounts and their related Premium or Discount accounts. (763)

Paid-in Capital in Excess of Par Value The account name for amounts by which the issuing price of a stock exceeds the par value. (761)

Participating preferred stock Preferred stock whose holders share in any extra dividends distributed by the corporation after the regular dividend has been paid to holders of preferred stock and a stipulated dividend has been paid to holders of common stock. (758)

Par-value stock Stock for which a uniform face value, indicating the amount per share to be entered in the Capital Stock account, is printed on the stock certificates. (756)

Preemptive right A stockholder's right to maintain the same proportionate ownership in a corporation in the future as she or he does originally, through the privilege of subscribing to a new issue of stock in the same proportion as her or his present ownership. (755)

Preferred stock Stock whose holders are paid dividends at a uniform rate before any dividends are paid to holders of common stock. The holder of preferred stock also has preference in the distribution of assets in the event of a liquidation. (757)

Premium The amount by which the issuing price of a stock exceeds the par value. (761)

Publicly traded corporation A corporation having a large group of owners with shares traded on a stock exchange or in over-the-counter markets. (753)

Retained Earnings A stockholders' equity account representing capital generated by the corporation's earnings that remain in the firm; the amount by which net income exceeds dividends paid over the life of the corporation. (755)

S corporation A corporation that elects with the IRS to be treated as a pass-through entity for income tax purposes. There are restrictions on the number (currently there can be no more than 100 shareholders) and type of shareholders an S corporation may have. An S corporation enjoys the absence of double taxation while having limited liability. (752)

Stated value The amount per share of no-par stock that is recorded in the corporation's Stock accounts; an amount designated by law as not subject to withdrawal by stockholders. (763)

Stock certificates Documents giving evidence of ownership in shares of stock; issued only when the stockholder has paid for the shares in full. (753)

Stockholders' equity The owners' equity in a corporation. Also referred to as *capital*. (755)

Stockholders' ledger A record showing the name and address of each stockholder and the number of shares owned. (759)

Surplus A credit or positive balance in the Retained Earnings account. (769)

Treasury stock A corporation's own stock, which it has issued and which was at one time outstanding, that the firm reacquires. (756)

QUESTIONS, EXERCISES, AND CASES

Discussion Questions

1. If a corporation sells its stock at a premium, is the amount of the premium recorded as revenue to the firm?

2. Explain the difference between capital stock and retained earnings.

3. Identify five advantages and three disadvantages of the corporate form of business organization as compared to sole proprietorship and general

partnership forms. In your opinion, which is the greatest advantage and which is the greatest disadvantage?

4. What is the purpose of Common Stock Subscribed, and what happens to the account?

5. In what respect is a corporation a separate legal entity?

6. List the advantages preferred stockholders have over common stockholders. What are the disadvantages?

7. In regard to stock, what is the difference between par value and stated value?

8. Classify each of the following accounts as asset, liability, stockholders' equity, revenue, or expense, and indicate the normal balance of each account:

a. Common Stock
b. Common Stock Subscribed
c. Subscriptions Receivable, Common Stock
d. Retained Earnings
e. Preferred 8 Percent Stock
f. Organization Expense
g. Paid-in Capital in Excess of Par Value

Exercises

P.O. 3,4

Describe stock transactions from T accounts.

Exercise 20-1 Describe the transactions recorded in the following accounts of Chester Company:

Cash					Common Stock		
(1)	320,000	(2)	2,500			(1)	320,000
						(2)	1,500

Organization Expense	
(2)	4,000

P.O. 4

Journalize entries to sell common stock for cash and in exchange for other assets above par value.

Exercise 20-2 Horace Corporation is authorized to issue 40,000 shares of $85 par-value common stock. Record the following transactions in general journal form:

Feb. 10 Sold 7,500 shares of common stock at $86 per share; received cash.

27 Issued 2,150 shares of common stock in exchange for land with a fair market value of $92,000 and a building with a fair market value of $108,750.

Mar. 3 Sold 2,800 shares of common stock at $86.50 per share; received cash.

P.O. 4,5

Journalize entries to sell common and preferred stock for cash.

Exercise 20-3 On July 2, Estevez Corporation issued for cash 12,000 shares of no-par common stock (with a stated value of $13 per share) at $17. On July 17, it issued for cash 800 shares of $110-par preferred 10 percent stock at $112.

a. Write the entries in general journal form for July 2 and July 17.
b. What is the total amount invested by all stockholders as of July 17?

P.O. 4

Journalize entries to sell common and preferred stock for cash and in exchange for services and assets.

Exercise 20-4 Selden Corporation was organized on April 8 of this year. The corporation was authorized to issue 900 shares of cumulative preferred 9 percent stock, $100 par value, and 9,000 shares of common stock, $35 par value. Record in general journal form the following transactions, completed during the firm's first year of operations:

Apr.	8	Sold 3,200 shares of common stock at par for cash.
	8	Issued 90 shares of common stock to an attorney in return for legal services pertaining to incorporation. The stock is selling at par.
May	7	Sold 500 shares of preferred stock at $109; received cash.
Aug.	12	Issued 3,000 shares of common stock in exchange for land with a fair market value of $105,000.

P.O. 5

Journalize entries to sell common stock above stated value for cash.

Exercise 20-5 Venture Tours, Inc., is authorized to issue 220,000 shares of no-par common stock, $15 stated value. Record the following transactions in general journal form:

May	23	Sold 4,000 shares of common stock at $18 per share for cash.
June	19	Sold 12,500 shares of common stock at $17 per share for cash.

P.O. 6

Journalize entries to receive subscriptions for stock, receiving periodic payments.

Exercise 20-6 Best Bakery has authorized capital consisting of 25,000 shares of cumulative preferred 9 percent stock, $100 par value, and 25,000 shares of common stock, $30 par value. Record the following transactions in general journal form:

a. Received subscriptions to 12,000 shares of preferred 9 percent stock at $103 per share, with a down payment of 50 percent of the subscription price.
b. Received 30 percent of the subscription price from all subscribers.
c. Received 20 percent of the subscription price from all subscribers and issued the stock certificates.

P.O. 6

Describe stock transactions from T accounts.

Exercise 20-7 Describe the transactions recorded in the following ledger accounts of McCabe Corporation:

	Cash				Common Stock	
	+	−			−	+
(a)	25,000					(a) 22,000
(c)	34,500					(e) 45,000
(d)	25,500					

	Subscriptions Receivable, Common Stock				Common Stock Subscribed	
	+	−			−	+
(b)	60,000	(c) 34,500		(e) 45,000	(b) 45,000
		(d) 25,500				

Paid-in Capital in Excess of Stated Value

	−	+
		(a) 3,000
		(b) 15,000

P.O. 7

Prepare a Stockholders' Equity section of a balance sheet.

Exercise 20-8 Angelo's Deli, Inc., has a charter authorizing it to issue 3,000 shares of $50 par-value preferred 8 percent stock and 12,000 shares of no-par common stock (stated value $30). The following account balances are from the Balance Sheet columns of the work sheet:

Retained Earnings (debit balance)	$ 86,700
Common Stock Subscribed (2,500 shares)	75,000
Common Stock	150,000
Preferred 8 Percent Stock	60,000
Paid-in Capital in Excess of Stated Value	37,500

Prepare the Stockholders' Equity section of the balance sheet.

internet
LINKS TO ACCOUNTING

Now that you have learned about the issuance of stock, let's take another look at the General Electric Company. You should be able to use what you have learned and the information provided in a company's annual report to find the answers to certain questions regarding the company's capital stock. Look again at GE's 2005 10-K report by going to **http://ge.com/en/company/investor/index.htm**, selecting Financial Reporting, then SEC Filing, and finally GE Company 2005 10K. The consolidated statement of financial position (balance sheet) information is on page 180 (labeled page 66). Be careful to always look at the information for the consolidated company (General Electric Company).

1. What is the par value of GE's common stock shown in the 2005 10-K report? (*Hint:* Look on the first page of the 10-K report.)
2. What are the dollar amount of common stock and the number of common shares outstanding as reported on the statement of financial position as of December 31, 2005? (*Hint:* Look at the balance sheet.)
3. GE reports common stock and paid-in capital in excess of par as a combined amount on its statement of financial position. Using the information from the two questions above, calculate the amount of paid-in capital in excess of par.

CONSIDER AND COMMUNICATE

Marvin is planning to open a fabric dyeing business. He plans to do large-scale dyeing of both fabric bolts and ready-to-wear garments. The source of business will be garment makers and cleaners. He has worked in this part of the fashion industry and knows how much capital he will need to buy the equipment required for this specialized activity.

He has some cash, and he is trying to decide whether to incorporate or to form a sole proprietorship. What would you say to him about the major advantages and disadvantages of chartering a corporation rather than forming a sole proprietorship?

WHAT'S WRONG WITH THIS PICTURE?

After having been a partner in a personal services firm for five years, you decided to leave the partnership and form a corporation. After completing the necessary organization steps and forming a board of directors, you sold stock to raise the necessary capital. You have retained control of 51 percent of the stock. One day, one of your former partners (who owns 20 percent of the stock in your corporation) sends you a bill for $3,000 for a billboard campaign. He hired the public relations company to increase the visibility of the corporation in which he is a stockholder. Are you going to pay the $3,000 bill your former partner incurred? Why or why not?

CRITICAL THINKING

You asked your new assistant for the summer, a relative of your supervisor, to prepare the Stockholders' Equity section of the balance sheet. A copy of the result is reproduced below. Check your assistant's work and comment on its accuracy and logic. Prepare a corrected Stockholders' Equity section.

Total Liabilities				$ 786 1 7 5 00	
Stockholders' Equity					
Paid-in Capital:					
Preferred 9 Percent Stock, $100 par (3,500 shares authorized, 2,539 shares issued)	$ 603 9 0 0 00				
Preferred 9 Percent Stock Subscribed (520 shares)	52 0 0 0 00				
Paid-in Capital in Excess of Par Value	6 1 2 0 00	$ 662 0 2 0 00			
Common Stock, no-par, stated value $20 per share (35,000 shares authorized, 18,360 shares issued)	$1 067 2 0 0 00				
Common Stock Subscribed (4,590 shares)	91 8 0 0 00				
Paid-in Capital in Excess of Stated Value	114 7 5 0 00	1 273 7 5 0 00			
Total Paid-in Capital		$1 935 7 7 0 00			
Retained Earnings		284 5 8 0 00			
Total Stockholders' Equity				1 651 1 9 0 00	
Total Liabilities and Stockholders' Equity				$2 437 3 6 5 00	

PROBLEM SET A

For additional help, see the demonstration problem at the beginning of each chapter in your Working Papers.

P.O. 4,6

Problem 20-1A Kronenberg Caterers, Inc., was organized on May 4 of this year and has a charter that stipulates the following authorized capital:

a. 4,500 shares of preferred 9 percent stock, $110 par value
b. 42,000 shares of common stock, $30 par value

Kronenberg Caterers, Inc., completed the following transactions during its first year of operations:

May   8   Received subscriptions to 14,000 shares of common stock at $30 per share; collected 65 percent of the subscription price.

June   7   Subscribers to 14,000 shares of common stock paid an additional 20 percent of the subscription price.

July   6   Subscribers to 14,000 shares of common stock paid an additional 15 percent of the subscription price. Kronenberg Caterers, Inc., issued the 14,000 shares of stock.

Sept.   14   Received subscriptions to 4,300 shares of common stock at $32 per share; collected 60 percent of the subscription price.

Check Figure

June 7, Debit to Cash, $84,000

Instructions

Record the above transactions in general journal form.

P.O. 4,7

Problem 20-2A Three people—Elligan, Johnson, and Sharp—organized Ellsworth Book Shoppe, Inc. The charter of this corporation authorizes capital consisting of the following:

a. 2,600 shares of preferred 9 percent stock, $50 par value
b. 25,000 shares of common stock, $15 par value

During its first year of operations, Ellsworth Book Shoppe, Inc., completed the following transactions that affected stockholders' equity:

June   1   Issued to Elligan 4,000 shares of common stock, at par, for cash.

2   Bought equipment from Johnson for $45,000. Johnson accepted 3,000 shares of common stock in exchange for the equipment.

2   Bought land and a building from Sharp. The fair market value of the land was $20,000 and of the building, $60,000. There is an outstanding mortgage on the property of $46,250, held by Western Savings Bank. The corporation assumed responsibility for paying the mortgage. Sharp accepted 2,250 shares of common stock at par for her equity.

5   Paid an attorney $4,800 for reimbursement of state fees and for performing services related to incorporation.

7   Issued 150 shares of common stock to Elligan for organizational services. The stock is selling at par.

July   7   Issued 675 shares of preferred 9 percent stock at $53 per share to investors for cash.

Aug.   3   Issued 425 shares of preferred 9 percent stock at $54 per share to investors for cash.

Check Figure

August 3, Credit to Preferred 9 Percent Stock, $21,250

Instructions

1. Record the above transactions in general journal form on page 1.
2. Post the entries to the following accounts: Preferred 9 Percent Stock, Paid-in Capital in Excess of Par Value, and Common Stock.
3. Prepare the Stockholders' Equity section of the balance sheet as of December 31, the end of the first year of operations. Net income for the year was $56,000, and no dividends were declared during the year. As a result, Retained Earnings has a credit balance of $56,000.

P.O. 7

Problem 20-3A Bostwick Trucking Company, Inc., has authorized capital of 3,500 shares of preferred 9 percent stock, $100 par value, and 35,000 shares of no-par common stock, stated value $20. The following account balances are taken from the Balance Sheet columns of the work sheet for the fiscal year ended December 31 of this year. The accounts are listed in alphabetical order.

Accounts Payable	$589,723
Accounts Receivable	718,347
Accumulated Depreciation, Building	82,314
Accumulated Depreciation, Equipment	133,814
Allowance for Doubtful Accounts	22,705
Building	403,920
Cash	91,657
Common Stock	367,200
Common Stock Subscribed	91,800
Equipment	295,137
Land	104,040
Merchandise Inventory	491,314
Mortgage Payable (long-term liability)	140,760
Notes Payable	55,692
Paid-in Capital in Excess of Par Value	6,120
Paid-in Capital in Excess of Stated Value	114,750
Patents	21,787
Preferred 9 Percent Stock	253,900
Preferred 9 Percent Stock Subscribed	52,000
Retained Earnings (credit balance)	284,580
Subscriptions Receivable, Common Stock	49,572
Subscriptions Receivable, Preferred 9 Percent Stock	19,584

Check Figure

Total Liabilities and Stockholders' Equity, $1,956,525

Instructions

1. Determine the number of shares of preferred 9 percent stock subscribed and issued.
2. Determine the number of shares of common stock subscribed and issued.
3. Prepare a classified balance sheet.

P.O. 4,5,6

Problem 20-4A Temporary Services, Inc., was organized on October 1 of this year, with a charter providing for authorized capital as follows:

a. 4,000 shares of preferred 7 percent stock, $55 par value
b. 60,000 shares of no-par common stock, $12 stated value

During the first year of operations, Temporary Services, Inc., completed the following transactions:

Oct. 1 Received subscriptions to 7,200 shares of common stock at $14 per share, collecting 30 percent of the subscription price.

3 Bought equipment from Rigby, one of the promoters, for $27,000. In return for the equipment, Rigby accepted 2,000 shares of common stock. (Credit Paid-in Capital in Excess of Stated Value, $3,000.)

12 Subscribers to 7,200 shares of common stock paid an additional 30 percent of the subscription price.

14 Issued 125 shares of common stock to Rigby at $15 per share in return for promotional services valued at $1,875.

Oct.   25   Paid an attorney $3,865 for reimbursement of state fees and for performing services needed for incorporating the firm.

29   Subscribers to 7,200 shares of common stock paid the remaining 40 percent of the subscription price; Temporary Services, Inc., then issued the stock.

Nov.   4   Received subscriptions to 4,000 shares of common stock at $16 per share, collecting 55 percent of the subscription price.

30   Subscribers to 4,000 shares of common stock paid the remaining 45 percent of the subscription price; Temporary Services, Inc., then issued the stock.

Check Figure

Nov. 4, Debit to Cash, $35,200

Instructions

Record these transactions in general journal form.

Instructions for General Ledger Software

1. Journalize the transactions in the general journal.
2. Print the journal entries.

PROBLEM SET B

For additional help, see the demonstration problem at the beginning of each chapter in your Working Papers.

P.O. 4,6

Problem 20-1B Ferro Fabricating, Inc., was organized on June 4 of this year and has a charter that stipulates the following authorized capital:

a. 10,000 shares of preferred 9 percent stock, $60 par value
b. 35,000 shares of common stock, $22 par value

During the first year of its operations, Ferro Fabricating, Inc., completed the following transactions:

June   15   Received subscriptions to 8,000 shares of common stock at $22 per share; collected 60 percent of the subscription price.

Aug.   15   Subscribers to 8,000 shares of common stock paid an additional 25 percent of the subscription price.

Sept.   17   Subscribers to 8,000 shares of common stock paid an additional 15 percent of the subscription price. Ferro Fabricating, Inc., issued the 8,000 shares of stock.

Nov.   23   Received subscriptions to 1,800 shares of common stock at $25 per share; collected 25 percent of the subscription price.

Check Figure

Nov. 23, Debit to Cash, $11,250

Instructions

Record the above transactions in general journal form.

P.O. 4,7

Problem 20-2B Three people—Begley, Rice, and Silva—organized All-Purpose Rentals, Inc., with a charter providing for the following authorized capital:

a. 2,500 shares of preferred 9 percent stock, $60 par value
b. 25,000 shares of common stock, $20 par value

During its first year of operations, All-Purpose Rentals, Inc., completed the following transactions that affected stockholders' equity:

July   5   Issued to Begley 2,500 shares of common stock, at par, for cash.
6   Paid an attorney $5,250 for performing services related to incorporation as well as for reimbursement of state fees.
6   Bought equipment from Silva for $36,900. Silva accepted 1,845 shares of common stock in exchange for the equipment.
6   Bought land and a building from Rice. The fair market value of the land was $168,000 and of the building, $42,600. There is an outstanding mortgage on the property of $177,400, held by Westland Savings Bank. The corporation assumed responsibility for paying the mortgage. Rice accepted 1,660 shares of common stock at par for his equity.
8   Issued 55 shares of common stock to Begley for organizational services. The stock is selling at par.
Aug.   5   Issued 575 shares of preferred 9 percent stock at $64 per share to investors for cash.
31   Issued 400 shares of preferred 9 percent stock at $63 per share to investors for cash.

Check Figure

Total Stockholders' Equity, $230,295

Instructions

1. Record the above transactions in general journal form on page 1.
2. Post the entries to the following accounts: Preferred 9 Percent Stock, Paid-in Capital in Excess of Par Value, and Common Stock.
3. Prepare the Stockholders' Equity section of the balance sheet as of December 31, the end of the first year of operations. Net income for the year was $47,095, and no dividends were declared during the year. As a result, Retained Earnings has a credit balance of $47,095.

P.O. 7

Problem 20-3B Fleck Farms, Inc., has authorized capital of 5,000 shares of preferred 10 percent stock, $100 par value, and 30,000 shares of no-par common stock, stated value $20. The following account balances are taken from the Balance Sheet columns of the work sheet for the fiscal year ended December 31 of this year. The accounts are listed in alphabetical order.

Accounts Payable	$382,786
Accounts Receivable	452,554
Accumulated Depreciation, Building	42,024
Accumulated Depreciation, Equipment	84,966
Allowance for Doubtful Accounts	14,117
Building	261,120
Cash	56,304
Common Stock	244,800
Common Stock Subscribed	40,800
Equipment	187,680
Land	61,200
Merchandise Inventory	298,554
Mortgage Payable (long-term liability)	85,680
Notes Payable	33,456
Paid-in Capital in Excess of Par Value	3,672
Paid-in Capital in Excess of Stated Value	71,400
Patents	13,097
Preferred 10 Percent Stock	163,200
Preferred 10 Percent Stock Subscribed	20,400
Retained Earnings (credit balance)	171,360

Subscriptions Receivable, Common Stock	$17,748
Subscriptions Receivable, Preferred 10 Percent Stock	10,404

Check Figure

Total Liabilities and Stockholders' Equity, $1,217,554

Instructions

1. Determine the number of shares of preferred 10 percent stock subscribed and issued.
2. Determine the number of shares of common stock subscribed and issued.
3. Prepare a classified balance sheet.

P.O. 4,5,6

Problem 20-4B Berger Corporation was organized on April 1 of this year, with a charter providing for the following authorized capital:

a. 4,000 shares of preferred 10 percent stock, $50 par value
b. 25,000 shares of no-par common stock, $25 stated value

During the first year of operations, Berger Corporation completed the following transactions:

Apr.	2	Bought land from Berger for $142,900. Berger accepted 5,400 shares of common stock for the land. (Credit Paid-in Capital in Excess of Stated Value, $7,900.)
	4	Received subscriptions to 3,500 shares of common stock at $28 per share, collecting 45 percent of the subscription price.
	6	Issued 150 shares of common stock to Berger at $26 per share in return for organizational services.
	10	Subscribers to 3,500 shares of common stock paid an additional 35 percent of the subscription price.
	13	Paid an attorney $2,840 for performing services and for reimbursement of state fees needed for incorporating the firm.
	14	Received subscriptions to 950 shares of preferred 10 percent stock at $52 per share, collecting 20 percent of the subscription price.
	21	Subscribers to 3,500 shares of common stock paid the remaining 20 percent of the subscription price; Berger Corporation then issued the stock.
May	9	Received subscriptions to 4,000 shares of common stock at $28 per share, collecting 60 percent of the subscription price.
	17	Subscribers to 950 shares of preferred 10 percent stock paid an additional 50 percent of the subscription price.
	23	Sold 350 shares of preferred 10 percent stock at $52 per share for cash.

Check Figure

May 23, Debit to Cash, $18,200

Instructions

Record these transactions in general journal form.

Instructions for General Ledger Software

1. Journalize the transactions in the general journal.
2. Print the journal entries.

Sony Corporation is a huge Japanese company with U.S. subsidiaries that include Sony Corporation of America, Sony Electronics Inc., Sony Music Entertainment Inc., and Sony Pictures Entertainment Inc. (formerly Columbia Pictures Inc.). Sony Corporation's consolidated sales figures for its fiscal year ended March 31, 2005, exceeded $60 billion. As you learn about recording income taxes and dividends in this chapter, think about how much a large corporation such as Sony must pay in taxes and how much it might pay in dividends to its stockholders. You can find out now by going to **http://www.sony.net/SonyInfo/IR/library/sec.html** and then selecting Form 20F, Year Ended March 31, 2005. Note that Form 20F is for foreign companies whose stock trades on a U.S. stock exchange. The form is similar to the 10-K, which is for U.S. companies that are traded on a U.S. stock exchange.

Performance Objectives

After you have completed this chapter, you will be able to do the following:

1. Journalize entries for corporate income taxes.

2. Journalize closing entries for a corporation.

3. Complete a work sheet for a corporation.

4. Journalize entries for the appropriation of Retained Earnings.

5. Journalize entries for the declaration and issuance of cash dividends.

6. Journalize entries for the declaration and issuance of stock dividends.

7. Complete a corporate statement of retained earnings and a balance sheet, including the following types of accounts: Appropriated Retained Earnings, Stock Dividend Distributable, Dividends Payable, and Income Tax Payable.

8. Describe guidelines for accounting reports.

Let's assume that the corporation is an established, regular corporation (not a limited liability corporation or an S corporation). We now turn our attention to the year-to-year entries for taxes, dividends, and retained earnings.

PROCEDURE FOR RECORDING AND PAYING INCOME TAXES

Determining the net income of a corporation is simply a matter of

Revenue − Expenses = Net Income

You can compare most of the revenue and expense accounts of a corporation to those of sole proprietorships and partnerships. The net income of a sole proprietorship and the distributive shares of net income of a partnership are taxable as part of the owners' personal incomes. Since the corporation is a separate legal entity, however, it must pay income taxes in its own name. Corporations are subject to federal income taxes, and many states and cities also impose an income tax on them. We will talk about only the income tax levied by the federal government, but the same basic principles apply to state and city income taxes, if applicable.

To place corporations on a pay-as-you-go basis, the law requires most of them to estimate in advance the amount of their federal income taxes for the forthcoming fiscal year. The corporation then pays the estimated amount in four quarterly installments during the year. The firm's accountant records each entry as a debit to Income Tax Expense and a credit to Cash. The Income Tax Expense account is handled like any other expense account, except that the accountant usually makes a separate entry closing Income Tax Expense into Income Summary.

At the end of the fiscal year, after the corporation determines the exact amount of its income, it calculates how much income tax it owes. If the amount of income tax the corporation has paid in advance exceeds its tax liability for the year, the accountant debits the amount of the overpayment to Prepaid Income Tax, a current asset account, and credits it to Income Tax Expense. Usually, however, the amount of income tax paid in advance is less than the amount of the tax liability. In this case, the accountant debits the amount of the underpayment to Income Tax Expense and credits it to Income Tax Payable, a current liability account. The corporation is required to make full payment of its final tax with its income tax return. The entry is a debit to Income Tax Payable and a credit to Cash.

FYI

The tax return is due two and one-half months after the close of the fiscal year.

Corporate Income Tax Rates

Throughout this text, we assume that corporate income is subject to federal tax under a three-bracket, graduated-rate structure (the higher the income, the higher the tax rate), as follows:

Taxable Income	Tax Rate (%)
First $50,000	15%
Next $25,000 ($50,001 − $75,000)	25
Over $75,000	34

A 5 percent surtax (extra tax) is imposed on income between $100,000 and $335,000. In effect, corporations with taxable income from $335,000 to $10,000,000 pay a flat 34 percent rate on all taxable income. Following are three examples.

Taxable Income of $79,000

Tax on the first $50,000 ($50,000 × 0.15)	$ 7,500
Tax on the next $25,000 ($25,000 × 0.25)	6,250
Tax on the next $4,000 ($4,000 × 0.34)	1,360
Total tax	$15,110

Taxable Income of $200,000

Tax on the first $50,000 ($50,000 × 0.15)	$ 7,500
Tax on the next $25,000 ($25,000 × 0.25)	6,250
Tax on the next $125,000 ($125,000 × 0.34)	42,500
Surtax on amount between $100,000 and $200,000 ($100,000 × 0.05)	5,000
Total tax	$61,250

Taxable Income of $468,000

Tax on the first $50,000 ($50,000 × 0.15)	$ 7,500
Tax on the next $25,000 ($25,000 × 0.25)	6,250
Tax on the next $393,000 ($393,000 × 0.34)	133,620
Surtax on amount between $100,000 and $335,000 ($235,000 × 0.05)	11,750
Total tax	$159,120

Or: Since the taxable income is above $335,000, use the flat tax rate of 34 percent: $468,000 × 0.34 = $159,120.

Personal service corporations, such as attorneys, accountants, doctors, and consultants, are taxed at a flat rate of 35 percent. This is one reason why a professional group may be structured as a limited liability partnership rather than as a corporation.

Income Tax Entries for a Corporation: First Year

OBJECTIVE 1

Journalize entries for corporate income taxes.

Blue Mountain, Inc., began operations on January 5. The corporation's fiscal year is from January 1 through December 31. Its authorized capital consists of 200,000 shares of $20 par-value common stock. For the fiscal year, the corporation estimates that its taxable income will be $122,000 and its income tax will be $30,830.

Tax on the first $50,000 ($50,000 × 0.15)	$ 7,500
Tax on the next $25,000 ($25,000 × 0.25)	6,250
Tax on the next $47,000 ($47,000 × 0.34)	15,980
Surtax on amount between $100,000 and $122,000 ($22,000 × 0.05)	1,100
Total tax	$30,830

Blue Mountain, Inc., records the payment of this estimated tax in four equal installments of $7,707.50 ($30,830 ÷ 4), as required by the IRS.

	DATE		DESCRIPTION	POST. REF.	DEBIT	CREDIT	
1	Year 1						1
2	Apr.	15	Income Tax Expense		7 7 0 7 50		2
3			Cash			7 7 0 7 50	3
4			Paid first quarterly				4
5			installment of estimated				5
6			federal income tax for the				6
7			year (one-fourth of $30,830).				7

DATE		DESCRIPTION	POST. REF.	DEBIT	CREDIT	
Year 1						1
June	15	Income Tax Expense		7 7 0 7 50		2
		Cash			7 7 0 7 50	3
		Paid second quarterly				4
		installment of estimated				5
		federal income tax for the				6
		year.				7

DATE		DESCRIPTION	POST. REF.	DEBIT	CREDIT	
Year 1						1
Sept.	15	Income Tax Expense		7 7 0 7 50		2
		Cash			7 7 0 7 50	3
		Paid third quarterly install-				4
		ment of estimated federal				5
		income tax for the year.				6
						7

DATE		DESCRIPTION	POST. REF.	DEBIT	CREDIT	
Year 1						1
Dec.	15	Income Tax Expense		7 7 0 7 50		2
		Cash			7 7 0 7 50	3
		Paid fourth quarterly install-				4
		ment of estimated federal				5
		income tax for the year.				6
						7

At the end of the year, the accountant prepares a work sheet and determines that the taxable income of the corporation for the year was $128,000 ($996,000 in revenues minus $868,000 in costs and expenses). Since the estimated taxable income was $122,000, the additional amount of taxable income is $6,000 ($128,000 − $122,000). The additional tax owed is $2,340, and this amount first appears as an adjusting entry on the work sheet.

Tax on the first $50,000 ($50,000 × 0.15)	$ 7,500
Tax on the next $25,000 ($25,000 × 0.25)	6,250
Tax on the next $53,000 ($53,000 × 0.34)	18,020
Surtax on amount between $100,000 and $128,000 ($28,000 × 0.05)	1,400
Total tax	$33,170
Less estimated tax paid previously	30,830
Additional tax owed	$ 2,340

The adjusting entry is as follows:

DATE		DESCRIPTION	POST. REF.	DEBIT	CREDIT	
1	Year 1		**Adjusting Entry**				1
2	Dec.	31	**Income Tax Expense**		2 3 4 0 00		2
3			**Income Tax Payable**			2 3 4 0 00	3
4							4

OBJECTIVE 2

Journalize closing entries for a corporation.

The accountant now records the closing entries, assuming revenues of $996,000 and expenses of $868,000. In this example, to save time, "Revenues" represents all temporary-equity accounts having a credit balance and "Expenses" represents all temporary-equity accounts having a debit balance.

DATE		DESCRIPTION	POST. REF.	DEBIT	CREDIT	
1	Year 1		**Closing Entries**				1
2	Dec.	31	**Revenues**		996 0 0 0 00		2
3			**Income Summary**			996 0 0 0 00	3
4							4
5		31	**Income Summary**		868 0 0 0 00		5
6			**Expenses**			868 0 0 0 00	6
7							7
8		31	**Income Summary**		33 1 7 0 00		8
9			**Income Tax Expense**			33 1 7 0 00	9
10							10
11		31	**Income Summary**		94 8 3 0 00		11
12			**Retained Earnings**			94 8 3 0 00	12
13							13

REMEMBER!

Examine these closing entries. There are no individual drawing accounts in a corporation. The new closing entry is to close Income Tax Expense. The Income Summary account is closed into Retained Earnings.

Let's summarize the steps for journalizing the closing entries of a corporation:

1. Close revenue accounts into Income Summary.
2. Close expense accounts into Income Summary.
3. Close Income Tax Expense into Income Summary by the amount of the actual income tax for the year.
4. Close Income Summary into Retained Earnings by the amount of the net income (Revenues − Expenses − Income Tax Expense).

The Retained Earnings account is classified as a stockholders' equity account. It is a permanent or real account, as opposed to a temporary-equity or nominal account. After the accountant has finished posting to the Retained Earnings account, the account balance represents accumulated earnings if it is a credit balance. If the Retained Earnings account has a debit balance, it represents a deficit. In T account form, the entries for the year are as shown below.

Cash			
	+	−	
		Apr. 15	7,707.50
		June 15	7,707.50
		Sept. 15	7,707.50
		Dec. 15	7,707.50

Income Tax Expense			
	+	−	
Apr. 15	7,707.50	Dec. 31 Clos.	33,170.00
June 15	7,707.50		
Sept. 15	7,707.50		
Dec. 15	7,707.50		
Dec. 31 Adj.	2,340.00		

Revenues			
	−	+	
Dec. 31 Clos.	996,000	Balance	996,000

Expenses			
	+	−	
Balance	868,000	Dec. 31 Clos.	868,000

Income Tax Payable		
−	+	
	Dec. 31 Adj.	2,340

Income Summary			
Dec. 31 (Exp.)	868,000	Dec. 31 (Rev.)	996,000
Dec. 31 (Inc. Tax)	33,170		
Dec. 31 Clos.	94,830		

Retained Earnings		
−	+	
	Dec. 31	94,830

Although income taxes are considered a necessary expense of conducting business, most companies show income tax expense as a separate line item on the financial statements. It is common practice to make a separate entry closing Income Tax Expense into Income Summary rather than including the amount for income tax with the total amounts for all the other expenses. This procedure makes the amount of taxable income more evident from a quick analysis of Income Summary. Notice in the Income Summary T account that the balance of the account prior to transferring the Income Tax Expense balance is $128,000 ($996,000 − $868,000), the taxable income. If the amount of income tax were closed into Income Summary with all the other expenses, the amount of taxable income would not be as obvious.

Income Tax Entries for a Corporation: Second Year

The next year begins with a carryover of the income tax liability for the previous year payable March 15. The journal entry is shown below.

REMEMBER!

The corporation starts the next year with an income tax liability from the previous year.

	DATE		DESCRIPTION	POST. REF.	DEBIT	CREDIT	
1	Year 2						1
2	Mar.	15	Income Tax Payable		2 3 4 0 00		2
3			Cash			2 3 4 0 00	3
4			Paid tax liability for previous				4
5			year, due two and one-half				5
6			months after the close of the				6
7			fiscal year.				7
8							8

For the second year, Blue Mountain, Inc., estimates a net income of $132,000 with a related income tax of $34,730. The following is the calculation for the estimated tax.

Estimated Taxable Income $132,000

First $50,000 (15 percent)	$50,000 × 0.15 = $ 7,500
Next $25,000 (25 percent)	$25,000 × 0.25 = 6,250
Next $57,000 (34 percent)	$57,000 × 0.34 = 19,380
Surtax on amount over	
$100,000 (5 percent)	$32,000 × 0.05 = 1,600
Total estimated tax	$34,730

Each of the four installments will be $8,682.50 ($34,730 ÷ 4). Journal entries for payment of each installment are shown below.

One disadvantage of the regular corporate form is double taxation. Not only do the owners and employees pay income taxes based on their income, but the corporation itself, in this case Kinetic Concepts, has to pay taxes on its income as though it were a person. And like a person, the percentage of taxes is based on how much income it earns. If the corporation is a limited liability corporation or an S corporation, there is no double taxation. The taxable income passes through to the shareholders or members, so there is only one level of taxation.

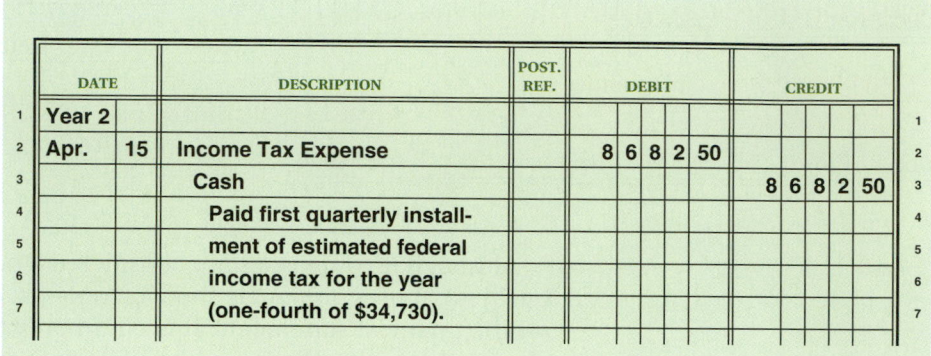

DATE		DESCRIPTION	POST. REF.	DEBIT	CREDIT
Year 2					
Apr.	15	Income Tax Expense		8 6 8 2 50	
		Cash			8 6 8 2 50
		Paid first quarterly install-			
		ment of estimated federal			
		income tax for the year			
		(one-fourth of $34,730).			

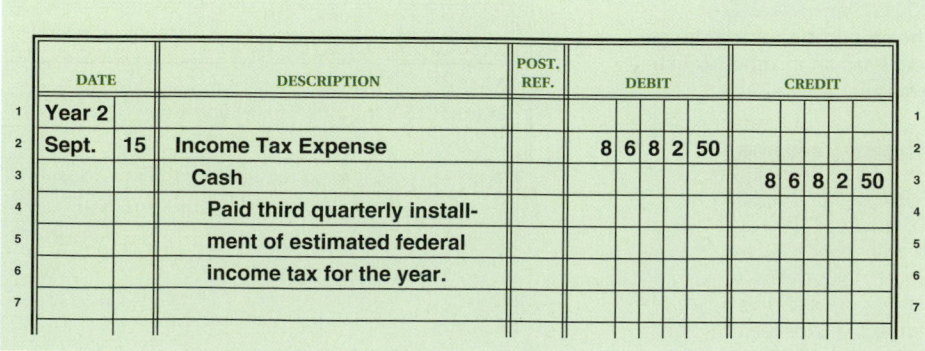

DATE		DESCRIPTION	POST. REF.	DEBIT	CREDIT
Year 2					
June	15	Income Tax Expense		8 6 8 2 50	
		Cash			8 6 8 2 50
		Paid second quarterly			
		installment of estimated			
		federal income tax for the			
		year.			

DATE		DESCRIPTION	POST. REF.	DEBIT	CREDIT
Year 2					
Sept.	15	Income Tax Expense		8 6 8 2 50	
		Cash			8 6 8 2 50
		Paid third quarterly install-			
		ment of estimated federal			
		income tax for the year.			

	DATE		DESCRIPTION	POST. REF.	DEBIT	CREDIT	
1	Year 2						1
2	Dec.	15	Income Tax Expense		8 6 8 2 50		2
3			Cash			8 6 8 2 50	3
4			Paid fourth quarterly install-				4
5			ment of estimated federal				5
6			income tax for the year.				6
7							7

WORK SHEET FOR A CORPORATION

OBJECTIVE 3

Complete a work sheet for a corporation.

FYI

The accountant's objective is to determine the taxable income as a basis for calculating the actual amount of income tax owed. Thus, the trial balance amount for Income Tax Expense must not be extended at this time.

REMEMBER!

At the end of the fiscal period, the adjustment for additional income taxes owed is recorded on the work sheet as a debit to Income Tax Expense and as a credit to Income Tax Payable.

The work sheet for the *second year* for Blue Mountain, Inc., is shown in Figure 1. When completing the work sheet, the accountant must give special treatment to the adjusting entry for the additional income tax. Before entering the adjustment for income tax, the accountant must do the following:

1. Enter and total the Trial Balance columns.
2. Enter all adjustments except the adjustment for income tax.
3. Extend account balances into the Income Statement columns and tentatively determine the income before income tax, as shown below. Here are the Income Statement columns taken from the work sheet in Figure 1 on pages 792–793 showing revenue and expenses. From here we can determine the amount of the income before income tax, $141,000 ($1,256,680 − $1,115,680). Note that $1,153,920 (total of Income Statement Debit columns) less $38,240 (Income Tax Expense) gives $1,115,680. These totals do not include Income Tax Expense, whereas the totals in Figure 1 do.

	ACCOUNT NAME	INCOME STATEMENT DEBIT	INCOME STATEMENT CREDIT
17	Sales		1,062 0 0 0 00
18	Purchases	729 2 3 4 00	
19	Purchases Discounts		4 8 0 0 00
20	Freight In	32 7 6 6 00	
21	Selling Expenses (control)	130 7 5 0 00	
22	General Expenses (control)	38 7 1 0 00	
26	Interest Expense	3 7 2 0 00	
29	Income Summary	180 5 0 0 00	189 8 8 0 00
32		1,115 6 8 0 00	1,256 6 8 0 00
33	Income Before Income Tax	141 0 0 0 00	
34		1,256 6 8 0 00	1,256 6 8 0 00
35			

FIGURE 1

Step 1: Record and total Trial Balance columns.

Step 2: Record all adjustments except income tax.

Step 3: Extend account balances into Income Statement columns.

Step 4: Determine taxable income and calculate tax.

Step 5: Record adjustment for income tax, and complete Adjustments columns totals.

Step 6: Record actual income tax in the Income Statement columns, and complete the section.

Step 7: Extend account balances into Balance Sheet columns, and total the columns.

	ACCOUNT NAME	TRIAL BALANCE	
		DEBIT	CREDIT
1	Cash	37 0 6 0 00	
2	Accounts Receivable	118 1 1 0 00	
3	Allowance for Doubtful Accounts		1 8 2 0 00
4	Merchandise Inventory	180 5 0 0 00	
5	Prepaid Insurance	1 2 2 0 00	
6	Store Equipment	104 7 2 0 00	
7	Accumulated Depreciation, Store Equipment		27 2 5 0 00
8	Office Equipment	28 9 2 0 00	
9	Accumulated Depreciation, Office Equipment		8 4 1 0 00
10	Patents	5 0 0 0 00	
11	Notes Payable		16 0 0 0 00
12	Accounts Payable		62 7 5 0 00
13	Common Stock		200 0 0 0 00
14	Common Stock Subscribed		20 0 0 0 00
15	Paid-in Capital in Excess of Par Value		2 4 0 0 00
16	Retained Earnings		29 6 3 0 00
17	Sales		1,062 0 0 0 00
18	Purchases	729 2 3 4 00	
19	Purchases Discounts		4 8 0 0 00
20	Freight In	32 7 6 6 00	
21	Selling Expenses (control)	126 4 5 0 00	
22	General Expenses (control)	32 7 5 0 00	
23			
24			
25			
26	Interest Expense	3 6 0 0 00	
27	Income Tax Expense	34 7 3 0 00	
28		1,435 0 6 0 00	1,435 0 6 0 00
29	Income Summary		
30	Interest Payable		Step 1
31	Income Tax Payable		
32			
33	Net Income		
34			
35			
36			
37			
38			
39			

4. Calculate the amount of the income tax. The accountant figures the additional income tax this way. Since both estimated ($132,000) and actual ($141,000) taxable incomes fall in the bracket between $100,000 and $335,000, the 5 percent surtax is involved.

Blue Mountain, Inc.
Work Sheet
For Year Ended December 31, Year 2

	ADJUSTMENTS DEBIT	ADJUSTMENTS CREDIT	INCOME STATEMENT DEBIT	INCOME STATEMENT CREDIT	BALANCE SHEET DEBIT	BALANCE SHEET CREDIT	
					37 0 6 0 00		1
					118 1 1 0 00		2
		(e) 1 6 8 0 00				3 5 0 0 00	3
	(b) 189 8 8 0 00	(a) 180 5 0 0 00			189 8 8 0 00		4
		(f) 5 2 0 00			7 0 0 0 00		5
					104 7 2 0 00		6
		(c) 4 3 0 0 00				31 5 5 0 00	7
					28 9 2 0 00		8
		(d) 2 7 6 0 00				11 1 7 0 00	9
		(g) 1 0 0 0 00			4 0 0 0 00		10
						16 0 0 0 00	11
						62 7 5 0 00	12
						200 0 0 0 00	13
						20 0 0 0 00	14
						2 4 0 0 00	15
						29 6 3 0 00	16
				1,062 0 0 0 00			17
			729 2 3 4 00				18
				4 8 0 0 00			19
			32 7 6 6 00				20
	(c) 4 3 0 0 00		130 7 5 0 00				21
	(d) 2 7 6 0 00						22
	(e) 1 6 8 0 00						23
	(f) 5 2 0 00						24
	(g) 1 0 0 0 00		38 7 1 0 00				25
	(h) 1 2 0 00		3 7 2 0 00				26
	(i) 3 5 1 0 00		38 2 4 0 00				27
							28
	(a) 180 5 0 0 00	(b) 189 8 8 0 00	180 5 0 0 00	189 8 8 0 00			29
		(h) 1 2 0 00				1 2 0 00	30
		(i) 3 5 1 0 00				3 5 1 0 00	31
	384 2 7 0 00	384 2 7 0 00	1,153 9 2 0 00	1,256 6 8 0 00	483 3 9 0 00	380 6 3 0 00	32
			102 7 6 0 00			102 7 6 0 00	33
			1,256 6 8 0 00	1,256 6 8 0 00	483 3 9 0 00	483 3 9 0 00	34
							35
		Step 2		Step 3		Step 7	36
		Step 5		Step 4			37
				Step 6			38
							39

Actual Taxable Income $141,000

First $50,000 (15 percent)	$50,000 × 0.15 = $ 7,500
Next $25,000 (25 percent)	$25,000 × 0.25 = 6,250
Next $66,000 (34 percent)	$66,000 × 0.34 = 22,440
Surtax on amount over $100,000 (5 percent)	$41,000 × 0.05 = 2,050
Total actual tax	$38,240

5. Enter the adjusting entry for the additional tax owed, $3,510. (Actual tax $38,240 − estimated tax of $34,730). Record $3,510 in the Adjustments columns of the work sheet, and add the column totals.
6. Enter the amount of the entire income tax ($38,240) in the Income Statement Debit column, and complete the Income Statement columns by determining the income after income tax: $102,760.
7. Extend all remaining figures, including Income Tax Payable and Net Income, into the Balance Sheet columns, and complete the Balance Sheet columns.

Financial Statements

Here is an abbreviated income statement for the second year:

Blue Mountain, Inc. Income Statement For Year Ended December 31, Year 2			
Revenue from Sales:			
Sales			$1 062 0 0 0 00
Income Before Income Tax			$ 141 0 0 0 00
Income Tax Expense			38 2 4 0 00
Net Income			$ 102 7 6 0 00

The order of presentation of financial statements is similar to that for a sole proprietorship:

1. Income statement
2. Statement of retained earnings (counterpart in most respects to the statement of owner's equity)—showing the net income
3. Balance sheet—listing the ending balance of Retained Earnings

We look at a complete statement of retained earnings and balance sheet later in this chapter. The balance sheet includes Income Tax Payable as a current liability.

Adjusting and Closing Entries

REMEMBER!

Income Tax Expense is closed separately into Income Summary.

The next step in the accounting cycle is to take the adjusting entries and closing entries directly from the Adjustments columns and the Income Statement columns of the work sheet and record them in the general journal (Figure 2 on page 795).

Income Statement Net Income Versus Taxable Income

In our example, we assume that the accountant for Blue Mountain, Inc., determined the income tax for the year by multiplying the corporation's income before income tax for the year (as shown on the income statement) by the tax rate. The accountant maintained that the corporation's income before income tax was its taxable income. In real life, things aren't quite that

	DATE		DESCRIPTION	POST. REF.	DEBIT	CREDIT	
1	Year 2		**Adjusting Entries**				1
2	Dec.	31	Income Summary		180 5 0 0 00		2
3	(a)		Merchandise Inventory			180 5 0 0 00	3
4							4
5	(b)	31	Merchandise Inventory		189 8 8 0 00		5
6			Income Summary			189 8 8 0 00	6
7							7
8	(c)	31	Selling Expenses (control)		4 3 0 0 00		8
9			Accumulated Depreciation, Store Equipment			4 3 0 0 00	9
10							10
11	(d)	31	General Expenses (control)		2 7 6 0 00		11
12			Accumulated Depreciation, Office Equipment			2 7 6 0 00	12
13							13
14	(e)	31	General Expenses (control)		1 6 8 0 00		14
15			Allowance for Doubtful Accounts			1 6 8 0 00	15
16							16
17	(f)	31	General Expenses (control)		5 2 0 00		17
18			Prepaid Insurance			5 2 0 00	18
19							19
20	(g)	31	General Expenses (control)		1 0 0 0 00		20
21			Patents			1 0 0 0 00	21
22							22
23	(h)	31	Interest Expense		1 2 0 00		23
24			Interest Payable			1 2 0 00	24
25							25
26	(i)	31	Income Tax Expense		3 5 1 0 00		26
27			Income Tax Payable			3 5 1 0 00	27
28							28
29			**Closing Entries**				29
30		31	Sales		1,062 0 0 0 00		30
31			Purchases Discounts		4 8 0 0 00		31
32			Income Summary			1,066 8 0 0 00	32
33							33
34		31	Income Summary		935 1 8 0 00		34
35			Purchases			729 2 3 4 00	35
36			Freight In			32 7 6 6 00	36
37			Selling Expenses (control)			130 7 5 0 00	37
38			General Expenses (control)			38 7 1 0 00	38
39			Interest Expense			3 7 2 0 00	39
40							40
41		31	Income Summary		38 2 4 0 00		41
42			Income Tax Expense			38 2 4 0 00	42
43							43
44		31	Income Summary		102 7 6 0 00		44
45			Retained Earnings			102 7 6 0 00	45

FIGURE 2

simple. The net income shown on the income statement may differ considerably from the income reported for tax purposes. Here are some of the reasons why:

1. The depreciation method used for income statement purposes may differ from the method used for tax purposes. For example, the firm might use the

CAREERS IN YOUR FUTURE

DAVID HEIBERG
President and Senior Consultant,
Heiberg Consulting, Inc.

Two things have provided the basis for David Heiberg's career: accounting and technology—a winning combination. Accounting grounded him in fundamental concepts like recording, reliability, accuracy, allocation, and accountability. But technology is his tool of choice for enabling and implementing these concepts to find solutions.

"Accounting is like algebra—it's basic business intelligence. No business decision is made without its influence."

David became interested in accounting as a college major while taking a bookkeeping class in high school. He built on this knowledge and added it to his arsenal of technological skills in order to best serve his clients—a combination his IT clients had not enjoyed in the past.

In northern Colorado, his company has two distinct roles and responsibilities—first as a technology consulting and service company and second as a software company. His company provides advice, strategy, and day-to-day support to small- and medium-sized companies. Heiberg serves larger companies as the architect of technology solutions while providing the cost justifications and sometimes assisting with financial arrangements on behalf of the client. This knowledge of accounting not only streamlines the process but also assures the client that David's company understands the client's position both in solving IT problems and in financing the solution. David has used accounting as a stepping-stone to becoming chief executive of a successful IT consulting firm.

straight-line method of depreciation for its income statement, but for tax purposes the business must use such IRS-prescribed methods as MACRS.
2. Some items listed on the income statement, such as interest on state and municipal bonds, are not taxable. Some expenses listed on the income statement, such as 50 percent of meals and entertainment expenses, club dues, penalties, and political contributions are not deductible for tax purposes.
3. A corporation may capitalize certain types of expenditures as assets on its financial statements, and these same expenditures may be listed on the tax return as expenses. For example, a company would include prepaid advertising on its balance sheet as an asset, whereas it may be able to deduct it as an expense on its tax return.

FYI

Research and development and the treatment of bad debts are other examples.

REASONS FOR APPROPRIATING RETAINED EARNINGS

OBJECTIVE 4

Journalize entries for the appropriation of Retained Earnings.

Since a corporation declares dividends out of its Retained Earnings, the *amount* of dividends is necessarily limited by the amount of Retained Earnings. However, rather than using the entire balance of Retained Earnings for cash or stock dividends, the board of directors may wish to earmark part of Retained Earnings for some specific purpose.

Such a restriction constitutes an **appropriation of Retained Earnings**. Let's say that the directors decide to provide for future expansion. The board passes a resolution, which is recorded in the minutes of a meeting, restricting or appropriating a certain amount of Retained Earnings for future expansion.

The minutes of the meeting are the source document for the accounting entry. For example, Blue Mountain, Inc., plans to erect its own building. To finance the project, it decides to restrict Retained Earnings for a total amount of $600,000 at the rate of $50,000 per year for twelve years. The accountant makes the entry to appropriate Retained Earnings at the end of each year, after the closing entries.

	DATE		DESCRIPTION	POST. REF.	DEBIT	CREDIT	
1	Year 2						1
2	Feb.	5	Retained Earnings		50 0 0 0 00		2
3			Retained Earnings				3
4			Appropriated for Building			50 0 0 0 00	4
5			To appropriate Retained				5
6			Earnings, as ordered by the				6
7			board of directors in the				7
8			meeting of February 5,				8
9			Year 2.				9

This appropriation of Retained Earnings does *not* represent a separate kitty or cash fund of $50,000. Consider cash dividends for a moment. If we think of the Retained Earnings account as a reservoir from which cash dividends are declared, then this reservoir has dried up by $50,000. **If the corporation does not declare and pay out these dividends, then the firm is preserving its net assets, particularly cash.** Of course, the $50,000 would not necessarily be in the form of cash. Perhaps the company can earn a higher return by putting the money into merchandise inventory or paying off its debts. By the term *net assets* we mean assets minus liabilities.

At the end of the twelve-year period, although the corporation does *not* have an actual $600,000 fund of cash, there is an additional $600,000 accumulated in net assets. The corporation can now formulate plans to convert the $600,000 increase in net assets into cash in order to put a down payment on the building.

When the objective—buying or erecting the building—has been accomplished, the corporation no longer needs to restrict Retained Earnings. The accountant may then reverse the twelve previous entries as follows:

	DATE		DESCRIPTION	POST. REF.	DEBIT	CREDIT	
1	Year 13						1
2	Mar.	18	Retained Earnings				2
3			Appropriated for Building		600 0 0 0 00		3
4			Retained Earnings			600 0 0 0 00	4
5			To return to Retained				5
6			Earnings the balance in				6
7			the Retained Earnings				7
8			Appropriated for Building				8
9			account, as ordered by the				9
10			board of directors in the				10
11			meeting of March 18,				11
12			Year 13.				12
13							13

Other examples of appropriated Retained Earnings accounts include:

- Retained Earnings Appropriated for Plant Expansion (no specific objective stated)
- Retained Earnings Appropriated for Bonded Indebtedness (an obligation imposed by contract)
- Retained Earnings Appropriated for Self-Insurance (workers' compensation or medical insurance for employees)
- Retained Earnings Appropriated for Inventory Losses (in the event of a price drop)
- Retained Earnings Appropriated for Contingencies (in the event of a "rainy day")

Each appropriated Retained Earnings is labeled "Retained Earnings Appropriated for ————." Therefore, the account Retained Earnings represents **unappropriated Retained Earnings**. Later in the chapter we'll show the placement of these accounts as they appear in the statement of retained earnings.

DECLARATION AND PAYMENT OF DIVIDENDS

A dividend is a distribution—of cash or other assets or shares of stock—that a corporation makes to its stockholders. Dividends are allocated to persons who own stock according to the number of shares they own and according to whether the stock is preferred or common. We discuss three types of dividends: cash dividends, stock dividends, and liquidating dividends. Cash dividends and stock dividends reduce Retained Earnings; liquidating dividends reduce Paid-in Capital.

Cash Dividends

A **cash dividend** is the most usual form of dividend. It ordinarily represents a share of the current earnings paid to stockholders as a reward for their investment. The board of directors declares dividends, generally paying up to a certain percentage of the firm's net income. The cash dividend is expressed as a specific amount per share—for example, $1.12 per share. A stockholder who owns 100 shares is thus entitled to $112.

Before a corporation can pay a cash dividend, three things are needed:

1. **Retained Earnings** The company must have a sufficient balance in the unappropriated Retained Earnings account.
2. **An adequate amount of cash** A corporation may have earned large profits, but not all profits are in cash. For example, the revenue may be in the form of charge accounts, such as Accounts Receivable. But this revenue becomes cash only when the company receives payments from charge customers.

Stockholders sometimes receive dividend checks. The amount they receive depends on the number of shares owned at the time the dividend is declared. Some stockholders choose to reinvest the amount of the dividend and get more shares.

3. **Formal declaration by the board of directors** The payment of dividends, although it may be a matter of policy, is not automatic. The board of directors must pass the declaration in the form of a motion and record it in the minute book—the source document for the accounting entry.

Dividend Dates

Three significant dates are involved in the declaration and payment of a dividend:

1. **Date of declaration** The date on which the board of directors votes to declare dividends. The entry recorded as of this date debits Retained Earnings and credits Dividends Payable.
2. **Date of record** The date as of which the ownership of shares is set. This date determines a person's eligibility for dividends and ordinarily is about three weeks after the date of declaration. No accounting entry is made; a memo entry is made in the minute book.
3. **Date of payment** The date on which payment is made; on this date, the accountant debits the amount to Dividends Payable and credits it to Cash.

For example, on January 20, the board of directors of Bell Athletic Supply declares a quarterly cash dividend of $0.91 per share (5,000 shares × $0.91 = $4,550) to stockholders of record as of February 11, payable on February 20. (Dividends Payable is classified as a current liability.) The entries are as follows:

REMEMBER!

The incentives for people to invest in a corporation's stock are the possibility of receiving cash dividends and/or the possibility of selling their stock at a gain.

OBJECTIVE 5

Journalize entries for the declaration and issuance of cash dividends.

DATE		DESCRIPTION	POST. REF.	DEBIT	CREDIT	
Year 2						1
Jan.	20	Retained Earnings		4 5 5 0 00		2
		Dividends Payable			4 5 5 0 00	3
		To record declaration of				4
		quarterly cash dividend on				5
		common stock at the rate				6
		of $0.91 per share to				7
		stockholders of record as				8
		of February 11, payable				9
		February 20, as ordered by				10
		the board of directors in				11
		the meeting of January 20.				12

DATE		DESCRIPTION	POST. REF.	DEBIT	CREDIT	
Year 2						1
Feb.	20	Dividends Payable		4 5 5 0 00		2
		Cash			4 5 5 0 00	3
		Payment of quarterly				4
		dividend declared on				5
		January 20 to stockholders				6
		of record as of February 11.				7
						8

REMEMBER!

Dividends Payable is a current liability (it must be paid in cash).

The Retained Earnings account before closing entries in Year 2 appears here. During the year, an appropriation was made for a building, and regular cash dividends were declared and paid. To make the entries more understandable, we have included explanations in the Item column:

		ACCOUNT Retained Earnings												ACCOUNT NO. 316	
														BALANCE	
	DATE		ITEM	POST. REF.		DEBIT			CREDIT			DEBIT		CREDIT	
1	Year 1														1
2	Dec.	31	Net income						124 8 3 0 00					124 8 3 0 00	2
3	Year 2														3
4	Jan.	20	Cash dividend			4 5 5 0 00								120 2 8 0 00	4
5	Feb.	5	Appropriation			50 0 0 0 00								70 2 8 0 00	5
6	Apr.	20	Cash dividend			4 5 5 0 00								65 7 3 0 00	6
7	July	20	Cash dividend			4 5 5 0 00								61 1 8 0 00	7
8	Oct.	20	Cash dividend			4 5 5 0 00								56 6 3 0 00	8
9															9

The balance of $56,630 would appear in the Trial Balance columns of the work sheet for the year ended December 31, Year 2.

Stock Dividends

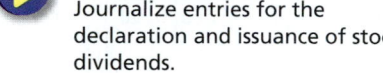

OBJECTIVE 6

Journalize entries for the declaration and issuance of stock dividends.

A **stock dividend** is a distribution, on a pro rata (proportional) basis, of additional shares of a company's stock to the stockholders. In other words, the dividend consists of shares of stock rather than cash. You could describe it as a dividend payable in stock. Generally, stock dividends consist of common stock distributed to holders of common stock. Stock dividends are usually issued by corporations that retain cash in order to finance future expansion.

Suppose that the board of directors of Bell Athletic Supply, Inc., declared a 10 percent stock dividend on October 11 of Year 3 to stockholders of record as of November 1, distributable on November 16. The ledger account for Common Stock on October 11 looks like this in T account form:

Common Stock

Balance	200,000
	$40 par value
	per share
	(5,000 shares)

Number of shares in the stock dividend:

10 percent of 5,000 shares = 500 shares

The current market value of the shares is $47 per share (par value $40). The entries, in general journal form, are as follows:

FYI

The calculations appear here just by way of explanation.

	DATE		DESCRIPTION	POST. REF.	DEBIT					CREDIT					
1	Year 3														1
2	Oct.	11	Retained Earnings (500 shares												2
3			× $47 each)		23	5	0	0	00						3
4			Stock Dividend Distributable												4
5			(500 shares × $40 each)							20	0	0	0	00	5
6			Paid-in Capital in Excess of												6
7			Par Value							3	5	0	0	00	7
8			To record the declaration of												8
9			a 10 percent stock dividend												9
10			to stockholders of record												10
11			as of November 1;												11
12			distributable November 16,												12
13			as ordered by the board of												13
14			directors in the meeting of												14
15			October 11.												15

	DATE		DESCRIPTION	POST. REF.	DEBIT					CREDIT					
1	Year 3														1
2	Nov.	16	Stock Dividend Distributable		20	0	0	0	00						2
3			Common Stock							20	0	0	0	00	3
4			Issuance of a stock												4
5			dividend (500 shares)												5
6			declared on October 11 to												6
7			stockholders of record as												7
8			of November 1.												8

Stock Dividend Distributable is a stockholders' equity account representing the total par value of the shares of stock to be issued. If the account is on the books at the time of the preparation of a balance sheet, the accountant lists it in the Paid-in Capital section, just below Common Stock.

A stock dividend—unlike a cash dividend—does *not* result in a reduction of assets. It transfers amounts among the stockholders' equity accounts. The stock dividend increases the Capital Stock accounts and decreases the Retained Earnings account without making any change in the total stockholders' equity.

The stock dividend has no effect on the proportionate share of ownership held by an individual stockholder. For example, Scott James owns 500 shares of the corporation's stock, which represents a one-tenth share in the corporation, since the total

Some companies issue stock certificates indicating the number of shares bought and par or stated value. Selling shares of stock is one way a corporation raises capital.

number of shares issued was 5,000. The corporation declares a 10 percent stock dividend. As his part of this dividend, James receives 50 shares (10 percent of 500 shares). His total stock now amounts to 550 shares; the corporation's total issued stock is now at 5,500 shares. Consequently, Scott James still has a one-tenth share in the ownership (550 shares ÷ 5,500 shares).

For accounting purposes, corporations make a distinction between a stock dividend of 25 percent or less (small) and a stock dividend of 26 percent or more (large). The preceding example represented a 10 percent stock dividend, in which the accountant debited Retained Earnings for the fair market value of the shares issued. If the stock dividend had been over 25 percent, the accountant would have debited Retained Earnings for the par or stated value of the shares to be issued instead of for the fair market value.

Reasons for Issuing Stock Dividends

Since a stockholder's proportionate share of equity in a company does not change when the company issues a stock dividend, why does a corporation bother with stock dividends? Here are a few reasons:

1. Stock dividends appease stockholders by giving them paper to hold onto. The corporation can conserve its cash, and the stockholders feel partially rewarded. They didn't get cash, but at least they got something.
2. Stock dividends tend to increase the marketability of the company's stock by increasing the number of shares outstanding and thereby decreasing the market price per share. Stock with a lower price per share is more easily sold to the public.
3. Stock dividends enable stockholders to postpone any income tax liability until they sell the shares. Stock dividends are not considered to be income to the recipients. Therefore, the recipients do not have to pay any income tax on stock dividends.

Liquidating Dividends

A corporation pays a **liquidating dividend** when it is (1) going out of existence or (2) permanently reducing the size of its operations. It returns to the stockholders all or a part of their investment. For example, in the situation shown below, Coast Motors, Inc., has returned all stockholders' investments:

> **REMEMBER!**
>
> The Stock Dividend Distributable account is used to record the par or stated value of a stock dividend that has been declared but not yet issued to stockholders.

> **REMEMBER!**
>
> A stock dividend does not reduce total stockholders' equity; it is simply an exchange of Retained Earnings for stock.

	DATE		DESCRIPTION	POST. REF.	DEBIT	CREDIT	
1	20–						1
2	Aug.	12	Common Stock		240 0 0 0 00		2
3			Paid-in Capital in Excess of				3
4			Par Value		10 0 0 0 00		4
5			Cash			250 0 0 0 00	5
6			To end the business affairs				6
7			of the corporation, the board				7
8			of directors during the				8
9			meeting of August 12				9
10			authorized a 100 percent				10
			liquidating dividend.				

STOCK SPLIT

When there is a **stock split**, a corporation splits or subdivides its stock, on the basis of its par or stated value, and issues a proportionate number of additional shares. For example, a corporation with 10,000 shares of $50 par-value stock outstanding may reduce the par value to $25 and increase the number of shares to 20,000 through a 2-for-1 stock split. If you own 200 shares before the split, you will own 400 shares after it. The company may call in all the old shares and issue certificates for new ones (either in paper or electronic form) on a 2-for-1 basis, or it may issue an additional share for each old share. The accountant records a stock split by making the following entry:

REMEMBER!

A stock split does not change Retained Earnings because total paid-in capital remains the same after a split.

FYI

Par values are listed by way of explanation.

	DATE		DESCRIPTION	POST. REF.	DEBIT	CREDIT	
1	20–						1
2	Oct.	15	Common Stock ($50 par value)		500 0 0 0 00		2
3			Common Stock ($25 par value)			500 0 0 0 00	3
4			The board of directors have				4
5			this day ordered a 2-for-1				5
6			stock split, increasing the				6
7			outstanding shares from				7
8			10,000 to 20,000, and				8
9			reducing the par value from				9
10			$50 to $25.				10
11							11
12							12
13							13

FYI

Some accountants record stock splits with a memorandum entry.

This 2-for-1 stock split reduces the market price per share by approximately half, thereby increasing the stock's salability. Since each share now costs less, more investors are able to afford the stock.

There is no change in Retained Earnings. The accountant changes the headings of the Capital Stock accounts in the ledger to show the new par or stated value per share and revises the stockholders' ledger to show the new distribution of shares.

Minute Book

The **minute book** is an important source document for any accounting entries involving the declaration of dividends and the appropriation of Retained Earnings. The minute book is just like the minute book of a club: It is a written (either manual or electronic) narrative of all actions taken at official meetings of the board of directors. A corporation's minute book may also contain details relating to purchasing property and equipment, obtaining bank loans, establishing officers' compensation, and so on.

STATEMENT OF RETAINED EARNINGS AND BALANCE SHEET FOR A CORPORATION

OBJECTIVE 7

Complete a corporate statement of retained earnings and a balance sheet, including the following types of accounts: Appropriated Retained Earnings, Stock Dividend Distributable, Dividends Payable, and Income Tax Payable.

REMEMBER!

The ending balances of unappropriated Retained Earnings and each appropriation account will appear in the Stockholders' Equity section of the corporation's balance sheet.

We have discussed a number of possible situations that would affect the status of retained earnings within a given period of time. These changes are reported on a separate financial statement called a *statement of retained earnings*. Generally, this statement lists only those items that represent significant changes. For example, the statement of retained earnings of Garcia, Inc. (Figure 3), lists specific appropriations for property expansion and possible price declines. The statement of retained earnings for a corporation may be compared, in some respects, to a statement of owner's equity for a sole proprietorship or partnership, with the ending balances appearing in the stockholders' or owner's equity section of a balance sheet.

To better visualize the relationship of the statement of retained earnings to the balance sheet, Figure 4 presents the balance sheet for Garcia, Inc. The accountant may use the account Paid-in Capital from Donation to record a situation in which the corporation receives a material gift. For example, the city of Ainley gave Garcia, Inc., an acre of land valued at $11,650 as an incentive to locate a manufacturing plant there. The accountant for Garcia, Inc., debited Land and credited Paid-in Capital from Donation for $11,650 each at that time.

FIGURE 3

Garcia, Inc.
Statement of Retained Earnings
For Year Ended December 31, 20—

Unappropriated Retained Earnings:			
Unappropriated Retained Earnings, Jan. 1, 20—	$112 7 0 0 00		
Net Income for the Year	73 0 0 0 00	$185 7 0 0 00	
Less: Cash Dividends Declared	$ 20 0 0 0 00		
Stock Dividends Declared	39 5 0 0 00		
Transfer to Appropriation for Property			
Expansion (see below)	4 0 0 0 00		
Transfer to Appropriation for			
Possible Price Declines (see below)	3 0 0 0 00	66 5 0 0 00	
Unappropriated Retained Earnings, Dec. 31, 20—			$119 2 0 0 00
Appropriated Retained Earnings:			
Appropriated for Property Expansion, Jan. 1, 20—	$ 16 0 0 0 00		
Add Appropriation for the Year (see above)	4 0 0 0 00		
Appropriated for Property Expansion, Dec. 31, 20—		$ 20 0 0 0 00	
Appropriated for Possible Price Declines,			
Jan. 1, 20—	$ 15 0 0 0 00		
Add Appropriation for the Year (see above)	3 0 0 0 00		
Appropriated for Possible Price Declines,			
Dec. 31, 20—		18 0 0 0 00	
Retained Earnings Appropriated, Dec. 31, 20—			38 0 0 0 00
Total Retained Earnings, Dec. 31, 20—			$157 2 0 0 00

Garcia, Inc.
Balance Sheet
December 31, 20—

Assets			
Current Assets:			
Cash		$ 11 170 00	
Accounts Receivable	$163 390 00		
Less Allowance for Doubtful Accounts	4 290 00	159 100 00	
Merchandise Inventory		320 220 00	
Total Current Assets			$490 490 00
Property and Equipment:			
Land		$ 40 000 00	
Building	$160 000 00		
Less Accumulated Depreciation	78 000 00	82 000 00	
Equipment	$ 80 760 00		
Less Accumulated Depreciation	26 750 00	54 010 00	
Total Property and Equipment			176 010 00
Intangible Assets:			
Copyrights		$ 7 200 00	
Patents		7 000 00	
Total Intangible Assets			14 200 00
Total Assets			$680 700 00
Liabilities			
Current Liabilities:			
Accounts Payable	$ 85 690 00		
Notes Payable	16 000 00		
Income Tax Payable	9 200 00		
Dividends Payable	4 000 00		
Interest Payable	960 00		
Total Current Liabilities		$115 850 00	
Long-Term Liabilities:			
Mortgage Payable (due July 1, 20—)		54 000 00	
Total Liabilities			$169 850 00
Stockholders' Equity			
Paid-in Capital:			
Preferred 7 Percent Stock, $25 par (4,600 shares authorized and issued)		$115 000 00	
Common Stock, no par, stated value $10 per share (20,000 shares authorized, 16,000 shares issued)	$160 000 00		
Stock Dividend Distributable (3,950 shares)	39 500 00		
Common Stock Subscribed (500 shares)	5 000 00		
Paid-in Capital in Excess of Stated Value	22 500 00	227 000 00	
Paid-in Capital from Donation		11 650 00	
Total Paid-in Capital		$353 650 00	
Retained Earnings:			
Unappropriated Retained Earnings	$119 200 00		
Appropriated:			
For Property Expansion $20,000.00			
For Possible Price Declines 18,000.00	38 000 00		
Total Retained Earnings		157 200 00	
Total Stockholders' Equity			510 850 00
Total Liabilities and Stockholders' Equity			$680 700 00

FIGURE 4

GUIDELINES FOR ACCOUNTING REPORTS

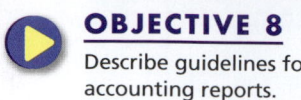

OBJECTIVE 8

Describe guidelines for accounting reports.

We have called accounting the "language of business." This language is used in accounting reports or statements. Accountants want to make sure that their reports are clear and consistent. To make their reports consistent, accountants follow certain guidelines. Three of these fundamental guidelines are full disclosure, materiality, and conservatism.

Full Disclosure

To disclose means "to uncover or make known." The guideline of **full disclosure** requires that anyone preparing a financial statement include enough information so that the statement is complete. Leaving relevant information out of a report or including half-truths is not acceptable. Information included in the report must not lead the reader to wrong conclusions.

Example: At the end of its report, a business includes a note about a lawsuit in which it is involved. The note also states that the case has not been settled and that no financial claim has yet been made against the company. This note prepares the readers to expect a possible financial claim that the company may have to pay. The report would not meet the requirement of full disclosure if it failed to mention the lawsuit and the possible claim.

Materiality

If something is "material," it is important and carries weight. The guideline of **materiality** states that relatively important data are included in financial reports. Important data are material; unimportant data are immaterial. Accounting staffs deal with many different kinds of financial transactions involving small dollar amounts. These transactions may have very little effect on the results shown in financial statements and would not be likely to influence decisions made by users of the financial statements.

Example: In an annual report of a business reporting a profit of $14 million a year, the understatement of profit by $6,000 may be immaterial. The same understatement of profit for a business reporting profit of $122,000 would be material.

Conservatism

To be conservative means to take the safe route. When faced with a decision about which accounting procedures to apply, accountants generally follow the "safer" principle. According to the guideline of **conservatism**, they use the alternative that is the least likely to result in an overstatement of income or asset value.

Example: An accountant is estimating an amount of money to be received in the future. The accountant must choose between $12,000 and $22,000. Conservatism requires the accountant to choose the smaller amount.

CHAPTER REVIEW

Review of Performance Objectives

1. Journalize entries for corporate income taxes.

   A corporation has to estimate the federal income tax that it will have to pay for the forthcoming year. The amount of the estimate is to be paid in four quarterly installments. The entry when each installment is paid is a debit to Income Tax Expense and a credit to Cash. At the end of the year, when the exact amount of taxable income is known, an adjusting entry is made for the amount either underpaid or overpaid. If the tax is underpaid, the entry is a debit to Income Tax Expense and a credit to Income Tax Payable. The liability must be paid within two and one-half months. If the tax is overpaid, the entry is a debit to Prepaid Income Tax and a credit to Income Tax Expense.

2. Journalize closing entries for a corporation.

   The steps in the closing process for a corporation are as follows:
   (1) Close revenue accounts into Income Summary.
   (2) Close expense accounts into Income Summary.
   (3) Close Income Tax Expense into Income Summary.
   (4) Close Income Summary into Retained Earnings.

3. Complete a work sheet for a corporation.

   The Trial Balance and Adjustments columns are handled in the same manner as for all other businesses. After those columns are completed, the accountant first determines the amount of taxable income in the Income Statement columns. Next, the accountant backtracks to record the adjusting entry for income tax. Finally, the accountant extends all remaining current figures into the appropriate columns and completes the work sheet.

4. Journalize entries for the appropriation of Retained Earnings.

   An appropriation of Retained Earnings is a restriction of a portion of the Retained Earnings account, making the amount unavailable for dividends. The entry in each case is a debit to Retained Earnings and a credit to Retained Earnings Appropriated for ————— (some specific purpose). The Retained Earnings account by itself is unappropriated.

5. Journalize entries for the declaration and issuance of cash dividends.

   The entry for the declaration of a cash dividend is a debit to Retained Earnings and a credit to Dividends Payable. The entry for the payment of a cash dividend is a debit to Dividends Payable and a credit to Cash.

6. Journalize entries for the declaration and issuance of stock dividends.

   The entry for the declaration of a small stock dividend is a debit to Retained Earnings for the amount of the number of shares multiplied by the market value per share, a credit to Stock Dividend Distributable for the amount of the number of shares multiplied by the par or stated value per share, and a credit to Paid-in Capital in Excess of Par (or Stated) Value. The entry for the issuance of stock is a debit to Stock Dividend Distributable and a credit to Common Stock.

7. Complete a corporate statement of retained earnings and a balance sheet, including the following types of accounts: Appropriated Retained Earnings, Stock Dividend Distributable, Dividends Payable, and Income Tax Payable.

   A statement of retained earnings consists of two sections: Unappropriated Retained Earnings and Appropriated Retained Earnings. Unappropriated Retained Earnings reflects the increases and decreases in the Retained Earnings account, consisting of net income, dividends, and transfers to Appropriated Retained Earnings accounts. The Appropriated Retained Earnings section consists of a listing of each Appropriated Retained Earnings account, including additions or deductions affecting each account.

On a corporate balance sheet, Stock Dividend Distributable is listed under Paid-in Capital. Dividends Payable and Income Tax Payable are listed under Current Liabilities.

8. Describe guidelines for accounting reports.

Three of the guidelines used to make accounting reports consistent are:

Full disclosure—to include enough information to make the statement complete, being sure not to leave out relevant information.

Materiality—to include important data or information.

Conservatism—to use accounting procedures that will result in a safer outcome by avoiding gross overstatements of revenues and assets or understatements of expenses and liabilities.

Glossary

Appropriation of Retained Earnings Designation of a portion of Retained Earnings for a specific purpose; the amount appropriated may not be used for cash or stock dividends. (796)

Cash dividend Distribution of a corporation's earnings to stockholders in the form of cash. (798)

Conservatism An accounting rule that means that, when accountants are faced with major uncertainties as to which alternative accounting procedure to apply, they should choose the procedure that is least likely to overstate a firm's revenues and assets or understate its expenses and liabilities. (806)

Date of declaration The date on which the board of directors votes to declare dividends. (799)

Date of payment The date on which dividends are paid. (799)

Date of record The date as of which the ownership of shares is set, determining a person's eligibility for dividends. (799)

Full disclosure An accounting rule requiring that financial statements and their accompanying notes contain all information that would influence a user's understanding of a firm's financial position. (806)

Liquidating dividend Distribution of assets to stockholders when a corporation is going out of existence or is permanently reducing the size of its operations. (802)

Materiality An accounting rule that refers to the inclusion in financial statements of important items that significantly affect a firm's financial position. (806)

Minute book A written narrative of all actions taken at official meetings of the board of directors; source document for dividend accounting entries. (803)

Stock dividend Distribution of a corporation's Retained Earnings to stockholders in the form of shares of the corporation's own stock. (800)

Stock split A deliberate reduction of the par value or stated value of a corporation's stock and the issuing of a proportionate number of additional shares. (803)

Unappropriated Retained Earnings The portion of Retained Earnings available for distribution as dividends to the stockholders. (798)

QUESTIONS, EXERCISES, AND CASES

Discussion Questions

1. How does a corporation account for federal income taxes? What are the related journal entries?

2. Name and explain the three dates that are involved in processing a cash dividend.

3. What effect does a cash dividend have on stockholders' equity? What effect does a stock dividend have?

4. Describe the difference between a small stock dividend and a stock split.

5. Classify each of the following accounts as asset, liability, stockholders' equity, revenue, or expense, and indicate the normal balance of each account:

   a. Paid-in Capital in Excess of Par Value
   b. Preferred 7 Percent Stock
   c. Stock Dividend Distributable
   d. Appropriated Retained Earnings
   e. Organization Expense
   f. Paid-in Capital from Donation
   g. Retained Earnings
   h. Common Stock Subscribed
   i. Subscriptions Receivable, Common Stock
   j. Common Stock

6. Explain why an appropriation of Retained Earnings is not the same thing as setting aside cash. How does a corporation dispose of a Retained Earnings Appropriated account, such as Retained Earnings Appropriated for Building?

7. How do the closing entries for a corporation differ from the closing entries for a sole proprietorship?

8. What are some possible reasons why a corporation's net income shown on its income statement may differ from the amount of its taxable income?

Exercises

P.O. 1

Compute corporation income taxes.

Exercise 21-1 Assuming 15 percent tax on the first $50,000; 25 percent on the next $25,000 ($50,001–$75,000), 34 percent over $75,000, and a 5 percent surtax on amounts over $100,000, compute Adel Corporation's first-year total tax on a taxable income of $235,000.

P.O. 1,2

Describe entries from T accounts.

Exercise 21-2 Describe the entries recorded by letters in the T accounts below.

Income Tax Expense		Cash		Revenues		Retained Earnings	
+	−	+	−	−	+	−	+
(a)	(e)		(a)	(c)			(f)
(b)							

Income Summary		Income Tax Payable		Expenses	
		−	+	+	−
(d)	(c)		(b)		(d)
(e)					
(f)					

P.O. 4

Journalize entries to appropriate Retained Earnings, purchase a building, and release the appropriation.

Exercise 21-3 On January 3, the board of directors of Tinsley Company, Inc., voted to appropriate $90,000 of the corporation's unappropriated Retained Earnings to Retained Earnings Appropriated for Property Expansion. This is the fourth such appropriation; it gives a balance of $298,000 in Retained Earnings Appropriated for Property Expansion. On September 1, the corporation buys a warehouse for $320,000 (building, $190,000; land, $130,000), paying $135,000 down and financing the remainder on a mortgage note. Write the entries to record the following:

a. The appropriation of Retained Earnings on January 3.
b. The purchase of the building and land on September 1.
c. The release of $298,000 of the Retained Earnings Appropriated for Property Expansion on September 2.

P.O. 5

Journalize entries to declare and pay a cash dividend.

P.O. 6

Journalize entries to record the declaration and issuance of a stock dividend.

Exercise 21-4 The dates connected with a cash dividend of $115,000 on a corporation's common stock are April 12, April 29, and May 8. Present the entries in general journal form pertaining to the declaration and payment of the dividend.

Exercise 21-5 On December 31, the stockholders' equity of Hernandez Auto Body Repair, Inc., is as follows:

Paid-in Capital:			
Common Stock, no par, stated value $20 per share			
(30,000 shares authorized, 18,000 shares issued)	$360 0 0 0 00		
Paid-in Capital in Excess of Stated Value	54 0 0 0 00		
Total Paid-in Capital		$414 0 0 0 00	
Retained Earnings:			
Unappropriated	$205 0 2 0 00		
Appropriated for Contingencies	91 8 0 0 00		
Total Retained Earnings		296 8 2 0 00	
Total Stockholders' Equity			$710 8 2 0 00

On March 6 of the following year, when the stock was selling at $38 per share, the board of directors voted a 20 percent stock dividend, distributable on March 28 to stockholders of record on March 22. Give the entries to record the declaration and distribution of the stock dividend.

P.O. 7

Calculate paid-in capital and total stockholders' equity.

Exercise 21-6 A corporation's balance sheet includes the following:

Preferred 9 Percent Stock, $100 par	$135,800
Preferred 9 Percent Stock Subscribed	45,900
Common Stock, no-par, stated value $10 per share	229,500
Paid-in Capital in Excess of Stated Value	61,200
Retained Earnings (credit balance)	84,250

a. How much of the corporation's capital is the result of the preferred 9 percent stock?

b. How much of the paid-in capital is the result of the common stock?
c. What is the total stockholders' equity?

P.O. 7

Indicate the effect of transactions on total Retained Earnings.

Exercise 21-7 Indicate the effect, if any, of each of the following transactions on total Retained Earnings of Company, Inc.:

a. Paid accounts payable.
b. Wrote off Accounts Receivable against Allowance for Doubtful Accounts.
c. Bought equipment on account, $58,000.
d. The board of directors declared a 20 percent stock dividend to be issued thirty days from the present date.
e. The board of directors voted to appropriate $98,000 for future expansion.
f. Issued 2,500 shares of $25 par-value common stock, receiving $34 per share.
g. Issued the stock dividend declared in transaction **d.**

P.O. 7

Prepare the Stockholders' Equity section of a balance sheet.

Exercise 21-8 Prepare the Stockholders' Equity section of the balance sheet from the following account balances:

Retained Earnings	$143,000
Common Stock, $40 par (30,000 shares authorized, 10,000 shares issued)	400,000
Preferred 10 Percent Stock, $50 par (2,000 shares authorized, 500 shares issued)	25,000
Paid-in Capital in Excess of Par Value—Common	40,000
Preferred 10 Percent Stock Subscribed (400 shares)	20,000

internet
LINKS TO ACCOUNTING

So how much did Sony Corporation pay in income taxes for the year ended March 31, 2005? Did it pay any dividends? You can find out now by going to **http://www.sony.net/SonyInfo/IR/library/sec.html** and then selecting Form 20F, Year Ended March 31, 2005. When reviewing Sony's financial information, **note that the amounts are shown in Japanese yen (¥), not in U.S. dollars ($). To determine the U.S. dollars, you must divide the amount in yen by the international exchange rate.** For ease of understanding, first state your answer in Japanese yen and then convert the amount to dollars using the average exchange rate for fiscal 2005. That rate was 107.49 yen = 1 U.S. dollar.

1. For fiscal year 2005, how much was reported in net sales on Sony's consolidated income statement?
2. What was the company's current income tax expense, in yen, for fiscal year 2005? (*Hint:* Look at Sony's consolidated income statement.)
3. How much did the company pay in cash for income tax expenses during fiscal year 2005? (*Hint:* Look near the end of the consolidated statement of cash flows found on page F-9.)
4. What is one reason that a company's income tax expense and the amount it paid in cash for income taxes might differ? From what you have learned in this chapter, you should be able to come up with one explanation.
5. How much cash, if any, did Sony Corporation pay in dividends during its fiscal year ended March 31, 2005? (*Hint:* Look in the consolidated statement of cash flows found on page F-9.)

WHAT'S WRONG WITH THIS PICTURE?

Suppose that a stockholder who received notice of a 2-for-1 stock split told you that he had just doubled his money. Is the stockholder correct? If not, what has actually happened?

CRITICAL THINKING

You have just received the following note dated November 30 from one of your corporation's stockholders:

"Help! Please explain why I haven't received my dividend check. I own 100 shares that I bought at $30 and they are now selling for $35. I read in the annual report that the board of directors declared a 10 percent stock dividend, but I haven't received a dime yet. What is going on? Where is my dividend check? I was a stockholder of record on the declaration date of the dividend."

Assume that he was a stockholder of record for both of the following dividends. The following selected journal entries may help you answer his questions.

		GENERAL JOURNAL				PAGE 78
	DATE	DESCRIPTION	POST. REF.	DEBIT	CREDIT	
1	20–					1
2	Sept. 15	Retained Earnings		98 0 0 0 00		2
3		Stock Dividend Distributable			65 0 0 0 00	3
4		Paid-in Capital in Excess of				4
5		Par Value			33 0 0 0 00	5
6		To record the declaration of				6
7		a 10 percent stock dividend				7
8		to stockholders as of				8
9		September 30, distributable				9
10		October 9.				10

16	Oct. 9	Stock Dividend Distributable		65 0 0 0 00		16
17		Common Stock			65 0 0 0 00	17
18		Issuance of stock dividend				18
19		declared on September 15 to				19
20		stockholders as of				20
21		September 30.				21
22						22
23	Nov. 17	Retained Earnings		74 8 0 0 00		23
24		Dividends Payable			74 8 0 0 00	24
25		Declared dividend of $6.80				25
26		per share to stockholders of				26
27		record on November 30,				27
28		payable December 9.				28
29						29
30	Dec. 9	Dividends Payable		74 8 0 0 00		30
31		Cash			74 8 0 0 00	31
32		Paid cash dividend declared				32
33		on November 17.				33

A QUESTION OF ETHICS

Your friend has been telling you that she knows someone in a publicly traded corporation who gives her information that lets her know when to buy and sell stock in that corporation. Consequently, your friend has made quite a bit of money. She has offered to share these inside tips with you for a small percentage of any gain you may make as a result. Her offer is very tempting to you. Are these friendly tips ethical?

PROBLEM SET A

For additional help, see the demonstration problem at the beginning of each chapter in your Working Papers.

P.O. 1,4,5,6

Problem 21-1A Some of the transactions of Island Car Rental, Inc., during this fiscal year are as follows:

Mar.	15	Paid balance due on previous year's federal income tax, $23,750.
Apr.	15	Paid $39,780 for the first quarterly installment of estimated federal income tax for this year.
June	15	Paid $39,780 for the second quarterly installment of estimated federal income tax for this year.
July	12	Declared a cash dividend of $40,836 ($4.98 per share on 8,200 shares, $50 par value) to stockholders of record as of July 22, payable on August 7.
Aug.	7	Paid the cash dividend.
Sept.	15	Paid $39,780 for the third quarterly installment of estimated federal income tax for this year.
	18	Declared a 10 percent stock dividend on common stock outstanding to stockholders of record as of September 28, distributable on October 6. Current market value of stock: $64 per share (8,200 shares outstanding before stock dividend).
Oct.	6	Issued stock comprising the stock dividend.
Nov.	14	Declared a cash dividend of $44,920 ($4.98 per share on 9,020 shares) to stockholders of record as of November 30, payable on December 8.
Dec.	8	Paid the cash dividend.
	15	Paid $39,780 for the fourth quarterly installment of estimated federal income tax for this year.
	31	The board of directors authorized the appropriation of Retained Earnings for contingencies, $14,688.
	31	Recorded $43,042 additional federal income tax allocable to taxable income for the year in an adjusting entry.

Check Figure

Nov. 14, Retained Earnings Debit, $44,920

P.O. 3,7

Instructions

Record these transactions in general journal form.

Problem 21-2A The trial balance of Crandal Products, Inc., dated December 31 of this year, is shown on the next page.

To reduce the number of accounts in the trial balance, Selling Expenses (control) is used in place of all selling expenses. Likewise, General Expenses (control) is used in place of all general expenses.

Crandal Products, Inc.
Trial Balance
December 31, 20—

ACCOUNT NAME	DEBIT	CREDIT
Cash	40 1 4 2 00	
Notes Receivable	30 0 0 0 00	
Accounts Receivable	321 3 4 9 00	
Allowance for Doubtful Accounts		5 4 9 0 00
Merchandise Inventory	571 4 2 3 00	
Prepaid Insurance	2 6 4 4 00	
Equipment	173 6 2 3 00	
Accumulated Depreciation, Equipment		32 8 3 4 00
Patents	19 5 8 4 00	
Accounts Payable		149 2 2 4 00
Preferred 9 Percent Stock ($100 par)		153 0 0 0 00
Preferred 9 Percent Stock Subscribed		30 6 0 0 00
Paid-in Capital in Excess of Par Value		6 7 3 2 00
Common Stock ($20 stated value)		306 0 0 0 00
Paid-in Capital in Excess of Stated Value		36 7 2 0 00
Retained Earnings		159 1 2 0 00
Sales		3 605 9 0 0 00
Purchases	2 630 1 5 2 00	
Purchases Discounts		15 9 2 0 00
Freight In	109 5 8 7 00	
Selling Expenses (control)	405 8 4 8 00	
General Expenses (control)	114 4 4 4 00	
Income Tax Expense	86 2 3 0 00	
Interest Income		3 4 8 6 00
	4 505 0 2 6 00	4 505 0 2 6 00

The charter states that authorized preferred 9 percent stock amounts to 2,000 shares and authorized common stock amounts to 20,000 shares.

Data for the adjustments are as follows:

a.–b. Merchandise Inventory, December 31 (ending inventory), $592,100.
  c. Additional depreciation of equipment for the year amounts to $14,327; record depreciation expense under Selling Expenses (control).
  d. Insurance expired during the year, $1,589; record insurance expired under General Expenses (control).
  e. Analysis of accounts receivable indicates $10,771 is uncollectible; record estimated bad debt losses under General Expenses (control).
  f. Accrued interest on notes receivable, $390.
  g. Additional income tax due for this year, $26,357.
  h. No dividends were declared during the year.

Check Figure

Total Stockholders' Equity, $944,730

Instructions

1. Record the trial balance on the work sheet (leave two lines for General Expenses control), and complete the work sheet for the year.
2. Prepare an income statement.
3. Prepare a statement of retained earnings.
4. Prepare a classified balance sheet.

P.O. 7

Problem 21-3A The account balances taken from the general ledger for Burr Windows, Inc., are as follows:

a. Preferred 8 percent stock: 3,000 shares authorized, 2,500 shares issued
b. Common stock: 30,000 shares authorized, 21,500 shares issued

Accounts Payable	$285,940
Accounts Receivable	386,660
Accumulated Depreciation, Building	72,700
Accumulated Depreciation, Equipment	76,100
Allowance for Doubtful Accounts	14,137
Building	270,865
Cash	48,890
Common Stock, $15 stated value	322,500
Dividends Payable	14,680
Equipment	142,500
Income Tax Payable	44,680
Land	38,000
Merchandise Inventory	727,882
Mortgage Payable (due in 8 years)	124,500
Notes Receivable	37,000
Paid-in Capital from Donation	36,000
Paid-in Capital in Excess of Par Value	5,000
Paid-in Capital in Excess of Stated Value	55,640
Patents	18,400
Preferred 8 Percent Stock, $100 par value	250,000
Preferred 8 Percent Stock Subscribed (700 shares)	70,000
Prepaid Insurance	2,630
Retained Earnings	235,300
Retained Earnings Appropriated for Inventory Losses	13,800
Retained Earnings Appropriated for Property Expansion	23,500
Stock Dividend Distributable (1,890 shares)	28,350

Check Figure

Total Liabilities and Stockholders' Equity, $1,509,890

Instructions

Prepare a classified balance sheet dated December 31.

P.O. 2,4,5,6,7

Problem 21-4A The Stockholders' Equity section of the balance sheet of Leblanc Wholesale, Inc., as of January 1 is as follows:

Stockholders' Equity					
Paid-in Capital:					
Preferred 9 Percent Stock, $100 par (4,000 shares authorized, 2,300 shares issued)	$ 230 0 0 0 00				
Paid-in Capital in Excess of Par Value	9 2 0 0 00	$ 239 2 0 0 00			
Common Stock, no par, stated value $20 per share (23,000 shares authorized, 19,000 shares issued)	$ 380 0 0 0 00				
Paid-in Capital in Excess of Stated Value	152 0 0 0 00	532 0 0 0 00			
Total Paid-in Capital		$ 771 2 0 0 00			
Retained Earnings:					
Unappropriated Retained Earnings	$ 195 0 7 5 00				
Appropriated for Expansion	41 3 1 0 00				
Total Retained Earnings		236 3 8 5 00			
Total Stockholders' Equity		$ 1 007 5 8 5 00			

Some of the transactions that took place during the year are:

Feb. 24 Declared the regular semiannual $4.75 per share dividend on the preferred stock and a $1.50 per share dividend on the common stock to stockholders of record on March 15, payable March 23.

Mar. 23 Paid cash dividends declared on February 24.

27 Received subscriptions to 1,200 shares of common stock at $31 per share, collecting 60 percent of the subscription price.

Apr. 19 Subscribers to 1,200 shares of common stock paid the remaining 40 percent of the subscription price; Leblanc Wholesale, Inc., then issued the 1,200 shares.

Aug. 24 Declared the regular semiannual $4.75 per share dividend on the preferred stock and $1.30 per share dividend on the common stock to stockholders of record on September 15, payable on September 23.

Sept. 23 Paid cash dividends declared on August 24.

Dec. 20 Declared a 10 percent stock dividend on common stock outstanding to stockholders of record on January 15, distributable on January 23. Current market value of the stock is $32 per share.

31 Increased the appropriation for expansion by $30,000.

31 After the accountant has closed all revenue, expense, and Income Tax Expense accounts, the Income Summary account has a credit balance of $165,500. Closed the Income Summary account.

Check Figure

Total Stockholders' Equity, $1,133,675

Instructions

1. Enter in the ledger accounts the balances appearing in the Stockholders' Equity section of the balance sheet as of January 1. In the Item column of the stock accounts, record the word *Balance* on the first line and the number of shares on the second line.

2. Journalize entries in general journal form on pages 54 and 55 to record the transactions that occurred during the year, and post to the stockholders' equity accounts.

3. Prepare the Stockholders' Equity section of the balance sheet as of December 31.

PROBLEM SET B

P.O. 1,4,5,6

For additional help, see the demonstration problem at the beginning of each chapter in your Working Papers.

Problem 21-1B Some of the transactions of Baldwin Video Corporation during this fiscal year are as follows:

Mar. 15 Paid balance due on previous year's federal income tax, $47,230.

Apr. 15 Paid $63,860 for the first quarterly installment of estimated federal income tax for this year.

June 15 Paid $63,860 for the second quarterly installment of estimated federal income tax for this year.

July 16 Declared a cash dividend of $76,800 ($6.40 per share on 12,000 shares, $65 par value) to stockholders of record as of July 31, payable on August 10.

Aug. 10 Paid the cash dividend.

Sept. 15 Declared a 10 percent stock dividend on common stock outstanding to stockholders of record as of September 30, distributable on October 9. Current market value of stock: $99 per share (12,000 shares outstanding before stock dividend).

15 Paid $63,860 for the third quarterly installment of estimated federal income tax for this year.

Oct. 9 Issued stock comprising the stock dividend.

Nov. 17 Declared a cash dividend of $91,080 ($6.90 per share on 13,200 shares) to stockholders of record as of November 30, payable on December 9.

Dec. 9 Paid the cash dividend.

15 Paid $63,860 for the fourth quarterly installment of estimated federal income tax for this year.

31 The board of directors authorized the appropriation of Retained Earnings for property expansion, $33,750.

31 Recorded $42,850 additional federal income tax allocable to taxable income for the year in an adjusting entry.

Check Figure

Nov. 17, Retained Earnings Debit, $91,080

P.O. 3,7

Instructions

Record these transactions in general journal form.

Problem 21-2B The trial balance for Eng Fabrics, Inc., dated May 31 of this year, is shown below.

Eng Fabrics, Inc.
Trial Balance
May 31, 20—

ACCOUNT NAME	DEBIT	CREDIT
Cash	93 5 4 2 00	
Accounts Receivable	353 1 5 5 00	
Allowance for Doubtful Accounts		5 7 1 0 00
Merchandise Inventory	580 3 9 0 00	
Store Supplies	1 9 2 8 00	
Store Equipment	220 4 0 0 00	
Accumulated Depreciation, Store Equipment		35 5 5 7 00
Patents	16 5 8 5 00	
Notes Payable		32 0 0 0 00
Accounts Payable		154 7 8 2 00
Preferred 8 Percent Stock ($100 par)		120 0 0 0 00
Paid-in Capital in Excess of Par Value		6 0 0 0 00
Common Stock ($20 stated value)		330 0 0 0 00
Common Stock Subscribed		90 0 0 0 00
Paid-in Capital in Excess of Stated Value		42 0 0 0 00
Retained Earnings		157 8 9 6 00
Sales		3 121 6 3 8 00
Purchases	2 146 2 6 7 00	
Purchases Discounts		16 2 7 9 00
Freight In	84 7 8 0 00	
Selling Expenses (control)	410 9 7 0 00	
General Expenses (control)	117 0 9 4 00	
Interest Expense	4 7 1 2 00	
Income Tax Expense	82 0 3 9 00	
	4 111 8 6 2 00	4 111 8 6 2 00

To reduce the number of accounts in the trial balance, Selling Expenses (control) is used in place of all selling expenses. Likewise, General Expenses (control) is used in place of all general expenses.

The charter states that authorized preferred 8 percent stock amounts to 1,400 shares and authorized common stock amounts to 20,000 shares.

Data for the adjustments are as follows:

a.–b. Merchandise Inventory, May 31 (ending inventory), $594,313.
   c. Additional depreciation of store equipment for the year amounts to $12,638; record depreciation expense under Selling Expenses (control).
   d. Prepaid insurance expired, $600. Use General Expenses (control).
   e. Analysis of accounts receivable indicates $10,680 is uncollectible; record estimated bad debt losses under General Expenses (control).
   f. Accrued interest on notes payable, $430.
   g. Additional income tax due for this year, $28,820.
   h. No dividends were declared during the year.

Check Figure

Total Stockholders' Equity, $1,004,416

Instructions

1. Record the trial balance on the work sheet (leave two lines for Selling Expenses control), and complete the work sheet for the year.
2. Prepare an income statement.
3. Prepare a statement of retained earnings.
4. Prepare a classified balance sheet.

P.O. 7

Problem 21-3B The account balances taken from the general ledger for Maldonado, Inc., are as follows:

a. Preferred 8 percent stock: 3,000 shares authorized, 2,320 shares issued
b. Common stock: 40,000 shares authorized, 36,720 shares issued

Accounts Payable	$ 345,046
Accounts Receivable	497,036
Accumulated Depreciation, Building	190,945
Accumulated Depreciation, Equipment	104,650
Allowance for Doubtful Accounts	17,260
Building	367,000
Cash	63,545
Common Stock, $15 stated value	550,800
Dividends Payable	25,092
Equipment	223,075
Income Tax Payable	63,036
Land	76,500
Merchandise Inventory	1,048,080
Mortgage Payable (due in 7 years)	149,000
Notes Receivable	38,560
Paid-in Capital from Donation	22,000
Paid-in Capital in Excess of Par Value	6,120
Paid-in Capital in Excess of Stated Value	110,160
Patents	25,000
Preferred 8 Percent Stock, $100 par value	232,000
Preferred 8 Percent Stock Subscribed (735 shares)	73,500
Prepaid Insurance	2,938
Retained Earnings	326,500
Retained Earnings Appropriated for Inventory Losses	25,700
Retained Earnings Appropriated for Property Expansion	49,000
Stock Dividend Distributable (3,395 shares)	50,925

Check Figure

Total Paid-in Capital, $1,045,505

Instructions

Prepare a classified balance sheet dated December 31.

P.O. 2,4,5,6,7

Problem 21-4B The Stockholders' Equity section of the balance sheet of Pratt's Video, Inc., as of January 1 is as follows:

Stockholders' Equity				
Paid-in Capital:				
Preferred 9 Percent Stock, $100 par (8,000 shares authorized, 6,900 shares issued)	$ 690 0 0 0 00			
Paid-in Capital in Excess of Par Value	27 6 0 0 00	$ 717 6 0 0 00		
Common Stock, no par, stated value $20 per share (90,000 shares authorized, 55,080 shares issued)	$1 101 6 0 0 00			
Paid-in Capital in Excess of Stated Value	330 4 8 0 00	1 432 0 8 0 00		
Total Paid-in Capital		$2 149 6 8 0 00		
Retained Earnings:				
Unappropriated Retained Earnings	$ 642 6 0 0 00			
Appropriated for Expansion	129 4 0 0 00			
Total Retained Earnings		772 0 0 0 00		
Total Stockholders' Equity		$2 921 6 8 0 00		

Some of the transactions that took place during the year are:

May 10 Declared the regular semiannual $4.80 per share dividend on the preferred stock and a $1.40 per share dividend on the common stock to stockholders of record on June 1, payable on June 10.

June 2 Received subscriptions to 11,000 shares of common stock at $27 per share, collecting 60 percent of the subscription price.

10 Paid cash dividends declared on May 10.

26 Subscribers to 11,000 shares of common stock paid the remaining 40 percent of the subscription price; Pratt's Video, Inc., then issued the 11,000 shares.

Nov. 10 Declared the regular semiannual $4.80 per share dividend on the preferred stock and $1.60 per share dividend on the common stock to stockholders of record on December 1, payable on December 10.

Dec. 10 Paid cash dividends declared on November 10.

27 Declared a 5 percent stock dividend on common stock outstanding to stockholders of record on January 14, distributable on January 30. Current market value of the stock is $27 per share.

31 Increased the appropriation for expansion by $53,000.

31 After the accountant has closed all revenue, expense, and Income Tax Expense accounts, the Income Summary account has a credit balance of $340,000. Closed the Income Summary account.

Check Figure

Total Stockholders' Equity, $3,309,600

Instructions

1. Enter in the ledger accounts the balances appearing in the Stockholders' Equity section of the balance sheet as of January 1. In the Item column of the stock accounts, record the word *Balance* on the first line and the number of shares on the second line.
2. Journalize entries in general journal form on pages 54 and 55 to record the transactions that occurred during the year, and post to the stockholders' equity accounts.
3. Prepare the Stockholders' Equity section of the balance sheet as of December 31.

Corporate Bonds

internet
LINKS TO ACCOUNTING

In Chapter 21, you learned that corporations finance capital investments by issuing stock. In this chapter, you will learn about issuing bonds, which is another method corporations use to finance capital investments. Bonds represent long-term liabilities that provide capital. Companies such as GMAC, Wal-Mart, Verizon Communications, and DaimlerChrysler issue bonds. You can learn about investing in bonds at **http://www.investinginbonds.com**. Click on Corporate Market At-A-Glance under Bond Markets & Prices to find information on bond issues by companies registered with the Securities and Exchange Commission. The bonds on this site can be traded without the physical transfer of a certificate. The list of bonds provides information on the issue date, name of the company, coupon, maturity, yield, price, and size. You will learn about these terms in this chapter and will then have a much better understanding of bonds.

Performance Objectives

After you have completed this chapter, you will be able to do the following:

1. Journalize transactions involving the issuance of bonds at a premium or discount.

2. Journalize adjusting entries for amortization of bond premiums and discounts and accrued interest payable.

3. Journalize entries pertaining to the establishment of a bond sinking fund, the receipt of income from sinking fund investments, and the eventual payment of the principal of the bonds.

4. Journalize transactions involving the redemption of bonds.

In our discussions of corporations, we have assumed that the company got the money it needed for building and expansion by selling stock and from retaining earnings. There is another possibility: A corporation can borrow money for a long period (5 to 100 years) by issuing bonds. A **bond** is a long-term obligation that provides capital. For all practical purposes, a bond is a long-term promissory note. A **bond issue** refers to the total number of bonds that a corporation issues at the same time. Bonds are issued in denominations of $1,000 or $5,000 each, with $1,000 being more common. You can get a better picture of bonds by comparing them with capital stock.

	Bonds	Capital Stock
	Bondholders are creditors; they receive interest and are eventually repaid the principal.	Stockholders are owners; they receive dividends.
	Bonds Payable is classified as a long-term liability account.	Capital stock is subdivided into Common Stock and Preferred Stock accounts, which are stockholders' equity accounts.
	Interest paid on bonds is an expense that must be paid year after year. Otherwise, bondholders may initiate bankruptcy proceedings against the debtor corporation.	Dividends are not expenses; they are distributions of net income.
	Interest expense is deducted to arrive at net income.	Dividends are not deducted to arrive at net income. They are deducted

REMEMBER!

A bondholder is a creditor of a corporation; a stockholder is an owner.

CLASSIFICATION OF BONDS

Just as car manufacturers offer different models with various combinations of accessories, corporations have created a wide variety of bonds, each with a slightly different combination of characteristics, to appeal to different investors.

Bondholders may hold the bonds themselves, or the bonds may be held in the bondholders' brokerage accounts. Bond investments are also made through mutual funds. For example, the Vanguard High-Yield Corporate Fund invests in approximately 400 different corporate bonds.

Bonds Classified as to Time of Payment

- **Term bonds** All term bonds of a particular issue have the same term, or time period to maturity. Thus, the entire issue of bonds comes due at the same time. For example, $1,000,000 worth of 10-year bonds issued January 1, 2001, all mature January 1, 2011.
- **Serial bonds** Serial bonds of a particular issue have a series of maturity dates. For example, $1,000,000 worth of bonds issued March 1, 2002, may mature as follows:

$100,000 on March 1, 2007
$100,000 on March 1, 2008
$100,000 on March 1, 2009
$100,000 on March 1, 2010
$100,000 on March 1, 2011
$100,000 on March 1, 2012
$100,000 on March 1, 2013
$100,000 on March 1, 2014
$100,000 on March 1, 2015
$100,000 on March 1, 2016

Bonds Classified as to Security

- **Secured bonds** When bonds are secured, they are covered or collateralized by mortgages on real estate or by titles to personal property. In case the corporation defaults in its payment of principal or interest, the bondholders, acting through a trustee, may take over the pledged assets.
- **Unsecured bonds** Unsecured bonds, also called *debenture bonds*, are backed only by the corporation's credit standing, or good name. Such bonds usually succeed only when issued by financially strong firms.

A bond can have characteristics of both classifications. For example, if a corporation issues twenty-year mortgage bonds, the bonds are term bonds and secured bonds.

WHY A CORPORATION ISSUES BONDS

A corporation that needs money on a long-term basis has the choice of raising the necessary funds by issuing (1) common stock, (2) preferred stock, or (3) bonds. Each choice has advantages and disadvantages. Since the holders of common stock control the corporation through their voting power, they choose the means of financing. Corporate boards of directors calculate the pros and cons of bonds as follows.

Advantages of Issuing Bonds

1. The bond-issuing corporation has the prospect of earning a greater return on the money it raises than it has to pay out in interest. This is known as **leverage**. For example, if a firm can borrow money at an interest rate of 8 percent and use this cash in the business to earn a net income of 15 percent (after taxes), then the additional earnings of 7 percent (15 percent − 8 percent) are available to pay dividends to the holders of common stock. Thus, debt is used as a *lever* to raise the owners' rate of return.
2. Interest payments are tax-deductible expenses.
3. Bondholders cannot vote; therefore, the existing common stockholders retain control of the company's affairs.

Disadvantages of Issuing Bonds

1. Bondholders are creditors of the corporation, so interest payments must be made to bondholders each year. In contrast, a corporation pays dividends to stockholders only when it has enough money to do so and when the board of directors declares a dividend.
2. The corporation must eventually pay back the principal of the bonds it issues, but it does not have to repay the money it receives from issuing stock.

When a corporation is trying to decide whether to issue additional stock or to issue bonds, an important factor is estimated future earnings and the probable stability of these earnings. The advantages and disadvantages of issuing bonds become apparent in the following example.

Southern Development Corp., which has 160,000 shares of $50-par-value common stock outstanding ($8,000,000), wishes to raise an additional $4,000,000 for expansion. Southern Development Corp. is considering three alternatives for raising the money:

- **Plan 1**   Issue an additional $4,000,000 of common stock, thereby increasing the total stock outstanding from 160,000 to 240,000 shares.
- **Plan 2**   Issue $4,000,000 of 8 percent cumulative preferred stock.
- **Plan 3**   Issue $4,000,000 of 7 percent bonds.

Figure 1 shows how Southern Development Corp. comes out if it has a yearly income from operations of (1) $1,680,000 and (2) $300,000. (We assume that the combined federal and state income taxes amount to 40 percent.)

FIGURE 1

	Income from Operations $1,680,000			Income from Operations $300,000		
	Plan 1	**Plan 2**	**Plan 3**	**Plan 1**	**Plan 2**	**Plan 3**
Common stock now outstanding (160,000 shares)	$ 8,000,000	$ 8,000,000	$ 8,000,000	$ 8,000,000	$ 8,000,000	$ 8,000,000
Additional common stock, $50 par (80,000 shares)	4,000,000			4,000,000		
Preferred stock, 8% cumulative		4,000,000			4,000,000	
Bonds, 7%			4,000,000			4,000,000
Total capitalization	$12,000,000	$12,000,000	$12,000,000	$12,000,000	$12,000,000	$12,000,000
Income from operations (before income taxes)	$ 1,680,000	$ 1,680,000	$ 1,680,000	$ 300,000	$ 300,000	$ 300,000
Deduct bond interest expense	0	0	280,000	0	0	280,000
Income before income taxes	$ 1,680,000	$ 1,680,000	$ 1,400,000	$ 300,000	$ 300,000	$ 20,000
Deduct federal and state income taxes (40%)	672,000	672,000	560,000	120,000	120,000	8,000
Net income	$ 1,008,000	$ 1,008,000	$ 840,000	$ 180,000	$ 180,000	$ 12,000
Deduct preferred dividends		320,000			320,000	
Earnings (loss) available to common shareholders	$ 1,008,000	$ 688,000	$ 840,000	$ 180,000	$ (140,000)	$ 12,000
Earnings (loss) available to common shareholders	$ 1,008,000	$ 688,000	$ 840,000	$ 180,000	$ (140,000)	$ 12,000
Common shares outstanding	240,000	160,000	160,000	240,000	160,000	160,000
Earnings (loss) per share of common stock	$4.20	$4.30	$5.25	$0.75	$(0.875)	$0.075

Money from the sale of bonds may finance a large project, like building construction.

You can see that plan 3 offers the greatest advantage to the original holders of common stock, provided that the company's earnings are large enough to pay the bondholders and still leave a sizable share for the holders of common stock. When the company has a *low* level of earnings, plan 1 is most advantageous to the holders of common stock because there are no prior claims of bondholders or preferred stockholders. The firm can use a combination of the three, but this entails larger financing costs.

ACCOUNTING FOR THE ISSUANCE OF BONDS

 OBJECTIVE 1

Journalize transactions involving the issuance of bonds at a premium or discount.

When a corporation issues bonds at face value, it records the transaction as a debit to Cash and a credit to Bonds Payable. Bonds Payable is a long-term liability account. If there is more than one bond issue, the company keeps a separate account for each issue. The listing on the balance sheet should identify the issue by stipulating its interest rate and due date.

Bonds Sold at a Premium

REMEMBER!

Bonds Payable is a long-term liability. Its normal balance is a credit.

The corporation may receive a price for its bonds that is above or below their face value, depending on the rate of interest offered and the general credit standing of the company. If a corporation offers a rate of interest that is higher than the market rate for similar securities, investors may be willing to pay a **premium** for the bonds.

For example, on January 1, Cooper Construction Corporation issues $750,000 of 9 percent, 10-year bonds at 103, with interest payable semiannually, on June 30 and December 31. The term "103" refers to the price of the bonds; it is a percentage of the face value of the bonds, with the percent symbol omitted. This is how the securities exchanges record bond prices. In this example, $750,000 of bonds at 103 means 103 percent of $750,000 ($750,000 × 1.03 = $772,500). Cooper Construction Corporation's entry to record the sale of the bonds, in general journal form, is as follows:

	DATE		DESCRIPTION	POST. REF.	DEBIT	CREDIT	
1	20—						1
2	Jan.	1	Cash		772 5 0 0 00		2
3			Bonds Payable			750 0 0 0 00	3
4			Premium on Bonds Payable			22 5 0 0 00	4
5			Sold 10-year, 9 percent				5
6			bonds, dated January 1, at				6
7			103.				7
8							8

Premium on Bonds Payable represents the amount received over and above the face value of the bonds. The accountant lists Premium on Bonds Payable right below the bond account in the Long-Term Liabilities section of the balance sheet. To illustrate the placement of Bonds Payable and Premium on Bonds Payable, a partial balance sheet on January 1 is shown here.

Cooper Construction Corporation
Balance Sheet
January 1, 20—

Long-Term Liabilities:		
9 Percent Bonds Payable, due January 1, 20—	$750 0 0 0 00	
Add Premium on Bonds Payable	22 5 0 0 00	$772 5 0 0 00

The corporation will write off or amortize Premium on Bonds Payable over the remaining life of the bond issue. The entries for each year to pay the interest on the bonds, in general journal form, are

	DATE		DESCRIPTION	POST. REF.	DEBIT	CREDIT	
1	20—						1
2	June	30	Interest Expense		33 7 5 0 00		2
3			Cash			33 7 5 0 00	3
4			Semiannual interest				4
5			payment on bonds, face				5
6			value of $750,000, 9 percent.				6
7			($750,000 × 0.09 × $^{6}/_{12}$)				7
8							8
9							9
10							10

	DATE		DESCRIPTION	POST. REF.	DEBIT		CREDIT	
1	20–							1
2	Dec.	31	Interest Expense		33 7 5 0 00			2
3			Cash				33 7 5 0 00	3
4			Semiannual interest					4
5			payment on bonds, face					5
6			value of $750,000, 9 percent.					6
7								7

Adjusting Entry for Bonds Sold at a Premium

OBJECTIVE 2

Journalize adjusting entries for amortization of bond premiums and discounts and accrued interest payable.

What is **amortization**? A company writes off, or *amortizes,* the Premium on Bonds Payable account over the remaining life of the bonds by debiting the account and using Interest Expense as the offsetting credit. The entry appears as an adjusting entry at the end of the fiscal period. It is first recorded in the Adjustments columns of the work sheet, like any other adjusting entry. Here is the entry to amortize or write off one year of the $22,500 premium on the 10-year bonds issued by Cooper Construction Corporation.

	DATE		DESCRIPTION	POST. REF.	DEBIT		CREDIT	
1	20–		Adjusting Entry					1
2	Dec.	31	Premium on Bonds Payable		2 2 5 0 00			2
3			Interest Expense				2 2 5 0 00	3
4			($22,500 ÷ 10 years)					4
5								5

FYI

The calculation is recorded here purely as a demonstration.

By T accounts, the entries for the year look like this:

Cash			
	+	–	
Jan. 1	772,500	June 30	33,750
		Dec. 31	33,750

Bonds Payable		
–	+	
	Jan. 1	750,000

Interest Expense			
	+	–	
June 30	33,750	Dec. 31 Adj.	2,250
Dec. 31	33,750		

Premium on Bonds Payable		
–	+	
Dec. 31 Adj. 2,250	Jan. 1	22,500

The adjusting entry reduces the balance of the Interest Expense account from $67,500 to $65,250. The accountant then closes Interest Expense into Income Summary in the amount of $65,250. The adjusting entry also has the effect of reducing the Premium on Bonds Payable account at the rate of $2,250 per year until it reaches zero, when the bonds come due.

In this illustration, we showed the amortization of the bond premium calculated by the straight-line method on an annual basis, which will also be used in the problems. This is like calculating depreciation by the straight-line method. (One can also record the amortization of the bond premium, just as one can record depreciation, on a monthly basis.) Many corporations, however, amortize premiums and discounts on bonds using the effective interest rate method, as required by the IRS.

Returning to our illustration, after the accountant records the adjusting entry, the balance of Interest Expense is $65,250. This amount represents the annual interest expense on the books. Here is another way of looking at it:

Cash to Be Paid

Face value of the bonds	$750,000	
Interest (20 payments of $33,750 each)	675,000	$1,425,000

Less Cash Received

Face value of the bonds	$750,000	
Premium on the bonds	22,500	772,500

Excess of Cash to Be Paid over Cash Received

(Interest expense for 10 years)	$ 652,500

$$\text{Interest Expense per Year} = \frac{\$652,500}{10 \text{ years}} = \$65,250$$

Example: Bonds Sold at a Premium, with Interest Payment Dates That Do Not Coincide with the End of the Fiscal Year   On March 1, Nunez Electronics issues $6,000,000 worth of 20-year, 9 percent bonds, at 104, dated March 1, with interest payable semiannually, on September 1 and March 1. The corporation's fiscal year ends on December 31. A diagram of the dates looks like this:

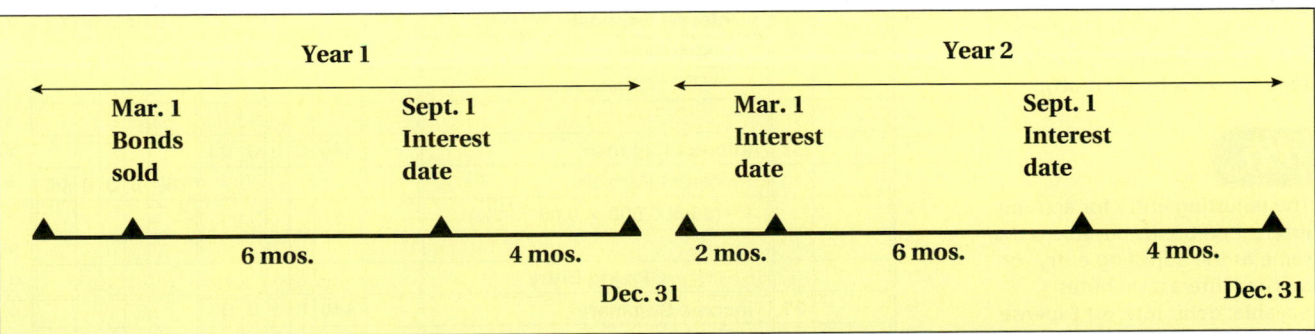

Since the date on which the interest has to be paid does not coincide with the end of the fiscal year, Nunez Electronics has to make an adjusting entry for the accrued interest for the period from September 1 to December 31. The entries for the first year, in general journal form, are as shown on the following page.

	DATE		DESCRIPTION	POST. REF.	DEBIT	CREDIT	
1	Year 1						1
2	Mar.	1	Cash ($6,000,000 × 1.04)		6,240 0 0 0 00		2
3			Bonds Payable			6,000 0 0 0 00	3
4			Prem. on Bonds Payable			240 0 0 0 00	4
5			Sold 20-year bonds,				5
6			9 percent, dated March 1,				6
7			at 104.				7
8							8

	DATE		DESCRIPTION	POST. REF.	DEBIT	CREDIT	
1	Year 1						1
2	Sept.	1	Interest Expense		270 0 0 0 00		2
3			Cash			270 0 0 0 00	3
4			Semiannual interest on				4
5			bonds, face value of				5
6			$6,000,000, 9 percent.				6
7			($6,000,000 × 0.09 × $^{6}/_{12}$)				7
8							8

	DATE		DESCRIPTION	POST. REF.	DEBIT	CREDIT	
1	Year 1		Adjusting Entries				1
2	Dec.	31	Premium on Bonds Payable		10 0 0 0 00		2
3			Interest Expense			10 0 0 0 00	3
4			($240,000 ×				4
5			10 months/240 months)				5
6							6
7		31	Interest Expense		180 0 0 0 00		7
8			Interest Payable			180 0 0 0 00	8
9			($6,000,000 × 0.09 × $^{4}/_{12}$)				9
10							10
11			Closing Entry				11
12		31	Income Summary		440 0 0 0 00		12
13			Interest Expense			440 0 0 0 00	13
14							14

REMEMBER!

Since Premium on Bonds Payable has a credit balance, we debit it to amortize it (write it off).

FYI

The adjusting entry for accrued interest on bonds payable is the same as the adjusting entry for accrued interest on notes payable: debit Interest Expense and credit Interest Payable.

REMEMBER!

The premium or discount on a bond payable is spread over the life of the bond.

The amortization of the premium on December 31 is for only part of a year. The next year, amortization will be for a full year. The adjusting entry for accrued interest on a bond is like the one for accrued interest on an interest-bearing note payable. In T account form, the first-year entries look like those on the following page.

Cash

	+		−	
Year 1		Year 1		
Mar. 1	6,240,000	Sept. 1		270,000

Interest Expense

	+		−	
Year 1		Year 1		
Sept. 1	270,000	Dec. 31 Adj.		10,000
Dec. 31 Adj.	180,000	Dec. 31 Clos.		440,000

Income Summary

Year 1		Year 1		
(Int. Exp.)	440,000	Closed		xxxx

Bonds Payable

	−	+	
		Year 1	
		Mar. 1	6,000,000

Premium on Bonds Payable

		−	+	
Year 1			Year 1	
Dec. 31 Adj.	10,000		Mar. 1	240,000

Interest Payable

−	+	
	Year 1	
	Dec. 31 Adj.	180,000

Because the adjusting entry for accrued interest opened a new balance sheet account, Interest Payable, Nunez Electronics' accountant should make a reversing entry as of the first day of the next fiscal year. The reversing entry enables the accountant to follow the regular routine for the payment of six months' interest on March 1 without having to split up the interest for the period between September 1 of one year and March 1 of the following year.

DATE		DESCRIPTION	POST. REF.	DEBIT	CREDIT	
Year 2		Reversing Entry				1
Jan.	1	Interest Payable		180 000 00		2
		Interest Expense			180 000 00	3
						4

The entries for the rest of the second year are

DATE		DESCRIPTION	POST. REF.	DEBIT	CREDIT	
Year 2						1
Mar.	1	Interest Expense		270 000 00		2
		Cash			270 000 00	3
		Semiannual interest on				4
		bonds, face value of				5
		$6,000,000, 9 percent.				6
		($6,000,000 × 0.09 × $^{6}/_{12}$)				7
						8

DATE		DESCRIPTION	POST. REF.	DEBIT	CREDIT	
1	Year 2					1
2	Sept.	1	Interest Expense		270 0 0 0 00		2
3			Cash			270 0 0 0 00	3
4			Semiannual interest on				4
5			bonds, face value of				5
6			$6,000,000, 9 percent.				6
7			($6,000,000 × 0.09 × $^{6}/_{12}$)				7
8							8

DATE		DESCRIPTION	POST. REF.	DEBIT	CREDIT	
1	Year 2		Adjusting Entries				1
2	Dec.	31	Premium on Bonds Payable		12 0 0 0 00		2
3			Interest Expense			12 0 0 0 00	3
4			($240,000 ×				4
5			12 months/240 months)				5
6							6
7		31	Interest Expense		180 0 0 0 00		7
8			Interest Payable			180 0 0 0 00	8
9			($6,000,000 × 0.09 × $^{4}/_{12}$)				9
10							10
11			Closing Entry				11
12		31	Income Summary		528 0 0 0 00		12
13			Interest Expense			528 0 0 0 00	13
14							14

REMEMBER!

If the interest payment date does not happen to be the same date as the end of a corporation's fiscal period, an adjusting entry must be made at the end of the fiscal period to record the accrued bond interest expense.

Here are the relevant T accounts from the previous year posted up to date:

Interest Expense

	+		–	
Year 1		Year 1		
Sept. 1	270,000	Dec. 31 Adj.	10,000	
Dec. 31 Adj.	180,000	Dec. 31 Clos.	440,000	
Year 2		Year 2		
Mar. 1	270,000	Jan. 1 Rev.	180,000	
Sept. 1	270,000	Dec. 31 Adj.	12,000	
Dec. 31 Adj.	180,000	Dec. 31 Clos.	528,000	

Income Summary

Year 1		Year 1		
(Int. Exp.)	440,000	Closed	xxxx	
Year 2		Year 2		
(Int. Exp.)	528,000	Closed	xxxx	

Bonds Payable

	–		+	
		Year 1		
		Mar. 1	6,000,000	

Premium on Bonds Payable

	–		+	
Year 1		Year 1		
Dec. 31 Adj.	10,000	Mar. 1	240,000	
Year 2				
Dec. 31 Adj.	12,000			

Interest Payable

	–		+	
		Year 1		
		Dec. 31 Adj.	180,000	
Year 2		Year 2		
Jan. 1 Rev.	180,000	Dec. 31 Adj.	180,000	

Bonds Sold at a Discount

When a corporation issues bonds that will pay a rate of interest that is less than the prevailing market rate of interest for comparable bonds, it sells its bonds at less than face value—or at a **discount**.

To demonstrate this, assume that on January 1, Mullen, Inc., issues 6 percent, 20-year bonds with a face value of $700,000, at 96, with interest to be paid semiannually, on June 30 and December 31.

> **REMEMBER!**
>
> Contra accounts have their signs reversed. Since the signs for Bonds Payable are debit minus and credit plus, the signs for Discount on Bonds Payable are the opposite.

	DATE		DESCRIPTION	POST. REF.	DEBIT	CREDIT	
1	20–						1
2	Jan.	1	Cash ($700,000 × 0.96)		672 0 0 0 00		2
3			Discount on Bonds Payable		28 0 0 0 00		3
4			Bonds Payable			700 0 0 0 00	4
5			Sold 20-year bonds, 6 percent,				5
6			dated January 1, at 96.				6
7							7
8							8

Discount on Bonds Payable is a **contra-liability account**; it is listed on a classified balance sheet as a deduction from Bonds Payable. A partial balance sheet on January 1 is shown here.

Mullen, Inc.
Balance Sheet
January 1, 20—

Long-Term Liabilities:			
6 Percent Bonds Payable, due January 1, 20–	$700 0 0 0 00		
Less Discount on Bonds Payable	28 0 0 0 00	$672 0 0 0 00	

The journal entries for the payment of interest semiannually, each year are

	DATE		DESCRIPTION	POST. REF.	DEBIT	CREDIT	
1	20–						1
2	June	30	Interest Expense		21 0 0 0 00		2
3			Cash			21 0 0 0 00	3
4			Semiannual interest on				4
5			bonds, face value of				5
6			$700,000, 6 percent.				6
7			($700,000 × 0.06 × $^{6}/_{12}$)				7
8							8

	DATE		DESCRIPTION	POST. REF.	DEBIT	CREDIT	
1	20–						1
2	Dec.	31	Interest Expense		21 0 0 0 00		2
3			Cash			21 0 0 0 00	3
4			Semiannual interest on				4
5			bonds, face value of				5
6			$700,000, 6 percent.				6
7			($700,000 × .06 × $^{6}/_{12}$)				7
8							8

Adjusting Entry for Bonds Sold at a Discount

The corporation amortizes the Discount on Bonds Payable account, as it does the Premium on Bonds Payable account, over the remaining life of the bond issue. The write-off consists of an adjusting entry at the end of the fiscal period. Again, the accountant uses Interest Expense as the offsetting account in the adjusting entry. Here is the adjusting entry to amortize one year of the $28,000 discount on the 20-year bonds issued by Mullen, Inc.

	DATE		DESCRIPTION	POST. REF.	DEBIT	CREDIT	
1	20–		Adjusting Entry				1
2	Dec.	31	Interest Expense		1 4 0 0 00		2
3			Discount on Bonds Payable			1 4 0 0 00	3
4			($28,000 ÷ 20 years)				4

By T accounts, the entries for the year look like this:

Cash			
	+	–	
Jan. 1	672,000	June 30	21,000
		Dec. 31	21,000

Interest Expense	
+	–
June 30	21,000
Dec. 31	21,000
Dec. 31 Adj.	1,400

Bonds Payable		
–	+	
	Jan. 1	700,000

Discount on Bonds Payable		
+	–	
Jan. 1 28,000	Dec. 31 Adj.	1,400

The adjusting entry increases the balance of Interest Expense from $42,000 to $43,400. The accountant then closes Interest Expense into Income Summary in the amount of $43,400. The adjusting entry also has the effect of reducing the Discount on Bonds Payable account at the rate of $1,400 per year until it reaches zero, when the bonds come due.

Here is another way of looking at interest expense:

Cash to Be Paid

Face value of the bonds	$700,000	
Interest (40 payments of $21,000 each)	840,000	$1,540,000

Less Cash Received

Face value of the bonds	$700,000	
Less discount on the bonds	28,000	672,000

Excess of Cash to Be Paid over Cash Received

(Interest expense for 20 years) $ 868,000

$$\text{Interest Expense per Year} = \frac{\$868,000}{20 \text{ years}} = \$43,400$$

BOND SINKING FUND

To provide greater security for bondholders, the bond agreement may specify that the issuing corporation make annual deposits of cash into a special fund—called a **sinking fund**—to be used to pay off the bond issue when it comes due. The company keeps the sinking fund separate from its other assets and puts the cash deposited in the sinking fund to work by investing it in income-producing securities. When the bonds mature, the total of the annual deposits plus the earnings on the investments should add up to approximately the face value of the bonds. The sinking fund may be controlled by either the corporation or a trustee—usually a bank.

Like a large corporation, the government may want to sell bonds to raise additional money for projects. The government may, at the same time, set up a bond sinking fund to provide reassurance to bondholders that the bonds will be paid when due. A sinking fund is similar to putting money aside for a specific future purchase.

OBJECTIVE 3

Journalize entries pertaining to the establishment of a bond sinking fund, the receipt of income from sinking fund investments, and the eventual payment of the principal of the bonds.

When the corporation deposits cash in its sinking fund, it records the transaction as a debit to Sinking Fund Cash and a credit to Cash. When the corporation or the trustee invests the sinking fund cash, the transaction is recorded as a debit to Sinking Fund Investments and a credit to Sinking Fund Cash. **Both Sinking Fund Cash and Sinking Fund Investments are classified as investment accounts.** These accounts are classified as long-term assets because their use is restricted to paying off the bond issue—long-term liabilities. When the corporation receives interest or dividend income on the investments, it debits Sinking Fund Cash and credits Sinking Fund Income. Sinking Fund Income is classified as an Other Income account on the income statement.

For example, Links Development issues $800,000 worth of 10-year bonds dated January 1, with the provision that at the end of each of the ten years, it will make an equal deposit into a sinking fund. Links Development, which manages its own sinking fund, intends to invest this money in securities that will yield approximately 6 percent per year. Let's assume that, according to compound interest tables, an annual deposit of $60,693 will accumulate to approximately $800,000 in ten years, given the 6 percent annual interest rate.

The following are a few of the many routine transactions that affect the sinking fund during the ten-year period:

- **Annual deposits of cash in bond sinking fund**

DATE	DESCRIPTION	POST. REF.	DEBIT	CREDIT	
	Sinking Fund Cash		60 6 9 3 00		1
	Cash			60 6 9 3 00	2
	Annual deposit in bond				3
	sinking fund, according to				4
	bond agreement.				5
					6
					7

- **Purchase of investments** Time of purchase and amount invested may vary.

DATE	DESCRIPTION	POST. REF.	DEBIT	CREDIT	
	Sinking Fund Investments		59 7 3 0 00		1
	Sinking Fund Cash			59 7 3 0 00	2
	Bought $60,000 of Consoli-				3
	dated Steel 7 percent bonds				4
	at 99$^1/_2$, plus $30 brokerage				5
	commission.				6
	($60,000 × 0.995 = $59,700)				7
	($59,700 + $30 = $59,730)				8

- **Receipt of income from investments** Interest and dividends are received at different times during the year.

	DATE	DESCRIPTION	POST. REF.	DEBIT	CREDIT	
1		Sinking Fund Cash		6 5 7 0 00		1
2		Sinking Fund Income			6 5 7 0 00	2
3		Received interest and				3
4		dividends on sinking fund				4
5		investments.				5
6						6

- **Sale of investments** Investments may be sold and the proceeds reinvested.

	DATE	DESCRIPTION	POST. REF.	DEBIT	CREDIT	
1		Sinking Fund Cash		148 9 6 0 00		1
2		Sinking Fund Investments			147 2 0 0 00	2
3		Gain on Sale of Sinking Fund				3
4		Investments			1 7 6 0 00	4
5		Sold sinking fund investments,				5
6		yielding a profit of $1,760.				6
7						7
8						8
9						9
10						10
11						11

- **Payment of bonds** Cash available consists of the sinking fund after the sale of the investments plus the last annual deposit, which should bring the sinking fund up to approximately $800,000.

	DATE	DESCRIPTION	POST. REF.	DEBIT	CREDIT	
1		Bonds Payable		800 0 0 0 00		1
2		Sinking Fund Cash			800 0 0 0 00	2
3		Paid bond obligation with				3
4		sinking fund cash.				4
5						5
6						6

REDEMPTION OF BONDS

OBJECTIVE 4

Journalize transactions involving the redemption of bonds.

To protect itself against a decline in market interest rates, a corporation may issue **callable bonds**. Callable bonds give the corporation the right—as stipulated in the bond **indenture**, or agreement—to **redeem** or buy back the bonds at a specified figure—the *call price*—that is ordinarily higher than the face value.

Harold, Inc., issues $2,000,000 worth of 9 percent, 20-year, callable bonds, with a call price of 104. Later, interest rates in general fall. Under the new market conditions, Harold, Inc., could sell $2,000,000 worth of bonds at face value, with an interest rate of 6 percent. It would pay Harold, Inc., to buy back the bonds, even though it would have to pay $2,080,000 for them ($2,000,000 × 1.04), then turn around and issue new bonds at 6 percent. The annual savings in interest would amount to $60,000 (3 percent of $2,000,000). Even if a corporation's bonds are not callable, it may still buy its own bonds on the open market, if it can find any for sale.

When a corporation redeems its bonds at a price that is less than their book value, it realizes a gain. Conversely, if it redeems its bonds at a price that is more than their book value, it incurs a loss. The book value is the sum of the Bonds Payable account and the Premium on Bonds Payable account (or the Bonds Payable account less the Discount on Bonds Payable account).

For example, Sound, Inc., a different corporation, has $500,000 worth of callable bonds outstanding on December 31, with a call price of 105; there is an unamortized discount of $2,000. Sound, Inc., pays the interest up to date on December 31 and exercises its option of calling in or redeeming the bonds on the same date, December 31. The entry is shown below in general journal form. The loss represents the difference between the book value and the price paid (also determined by the difference between debits and credits).

	DATE		DESCRIPTION	POST. REF.	DEBIT	CREDIT	
1	20–						1
2	Dec.	31	Bonds Payable		500 0 0 0 00		2
3			Loss on Redemption of Bonds		27 0 0 0 00		3
4			Cash			525 0 0 0 00	4
5			Discount on Bonds Payable			2 0 0 0 00	5
6			To record redemption of				6
7			bonds at 105.				7
8							8

Recall that, even if a corporation's bonds are not callable, the firm can buy back the bonds—all of them, or as many as it can find on the open market. For example, Erwin Fabrics, another corporation, has $1,000,000 worth of 7 percent bonds outstanding, on which there is an unamortized premium of $30,000. On July 15, Erwin Fabrics buys $100,000 of bonds (one-tenth of the original issue) in the open market at 97, plus fifteen days' accrued interest. The entry, in general journal form, is as follows:

The phone company invests huge amounts of money in an effort to keep its cables well maintained and state-of-the-art. Such a company may issue bonds to produce the needed capital. To protect itself against market fluctuations, it may issue callable bonds, which allow the corporation to buy back the bonds at a certain price.

	DATE		DESCRIPTION	POST. REF.	DEBIT					CREDIT					
1	20–														1
2	July	15	Bonds Payable		100	0	0	0	00						2
3			Premium on Bonds Payable		3	0	0	0	00						3
4			Interest Expense ($100,000,												4
5			7 percent, 15 days)			2	9	1	67						5
6			Cash							97	2	9	1	67	6
7			Gain on Redemption of Bonds							6	0	0	0	00	7
8			To record redemption of bonds												8
9			at 97 plus accrued interest.												9
10			($100,000 × 0.07 × $^{15}/_{360}$ =												10
11			$291.67)												11

Redemption in effect cancels all or a portion of the Bonds Payable account, as well as the accompanying premium or discount. **We list Gain (or Loss) on Redemption of Bonds on the income statement under the heading Other Income or Other Expense.** If the gain or loss is significant, unusual, and an infrequent event, it is listed (net of any related income tax effect) under the heading **Extraordinary Items**, a classification of accounts appearing at the bottom of an income statement. Extraordinary items are unusual in nature and do not occur with any regularity. They may include a disposition of a segment of a business.

BALANCE SHEET

The balance sheet of Bayshore Electronics, Inc., shown in Figure 2 on page 838, shows how to place the accounts introduced in this chapter.

Bayshore Electronics, Inc.
Balance Sheet
December 31, 20—

Assets															
Current Assets:															
Cash							$	14	0	0	0	00			
Notes Receivable								30	0	0	0	00			
Accounts Receivable	$	220	0	0	0	00									
Less Allowance for Doubtful Accounts		4	0	0	0	00		216	0	0	0	00			
Merchandise Inventory								647	0	0	0	00			
Total Current Assets													$	907	0 0 0	00
Investments:															
Sinking Fund Cash							$	5	0	0	0	00			
Sinking Fund Investments								84	0	0	0	00			
Total Investments														89	0 0 0	00
Property and Equipment:															
Land							$	70	0	0	0	00			
Building	$	180	0	0	0	00									
Less Accumulated Depreciation		45	0	0	0	00		135	0	0	0	00			
Equipment	$	222	0	0	0	00									
Less Accumulated Depreciation		32	0	0	0	00		190	0	0	0	00			
Total Property and Equipment														395	0 0 0	00
Intangible Assets:															
Goodwill							$	20	0	0	0	00			
Patents								8	0	0	0	00			
Total Intangible Assets														28	0 0 0	00
Total Assets													$1	419	0 0 0	00
Liabilities															
Current Liabilities:															
Accounts Payable							$	70	0	0	0	00			
Income Tax Payable								8	0	0	0	00			
Dividends Payable								12	0	0	0	00			
Total Current Liabilities													$	90	0 0 0	00
Long-Term Liabilities:															
6 percent Bonds Payable, due December 31, 20–	$	100	0	0	0	00									
Less Discount on Bonds Payable		3	0	0	0	00	$	97	0	0	0	00			
8 percent Bonds Payable, due March 31, 20–	$	200	0	0	0	00									
Add Premium on Bonds Payable		2	0	0	0	00		202	0	0	0	00			
Total Long-Term Liabilities														299	0 0 0	00
Total Liabilities													$	389	0 0 0	00
Stockholders' Equity															
Paid-in Capital:															
Common Stock, $10 par (100,000 shares authorized,															
40,000 shares issued)	$	400	0	0	0	00									
Paid-in Capital in Excess of Par Value		220	0	0	0	00									
Total Paid-in Capital							$	620	0	0	0	00			
Retained Earnings:															
Unappropriated Retained Earnings	$	310	0	0	0	00									
Appropriated for Property Expansion		100	0	0	0	00									
Total Retained Earnings								410	0	0	0	00			
Total Stockholders' Equity													1	030	0 0 0	00
Total Liabilities and Stockholders' Equity													$1	419	0 0 0	00

FIGURE 2

CHAPTER REVIEW

Online Study Center
ACE the test!

Review of Performance Objectives

1. Journalize transactions involving the issuance of bonds at a premium or discount.

   A bond is sold at a premium when the stated rate of interest is higher than the market rate of interest. The entry for selling a bond at a premium is a debit to Cash, a credit to Bonds Payable, and a credit to Premium on Bonds Payable. A bond is sold at a discount when the stated rate of interest is less than the market rate of interest. The entry for selling a bond at a discount is a debit to Cash, a debit to Discount on Bonds Payable, and a credit to Bonds Payable.

2. Journalize adjusting entries for amortization of bond premiums and discounts and accrued interest payable.

   Premiums and discounts are written off, or amortized, over the remaining life of the bond from the time of the sale. The entry to write off a premium is a debit to Premium on Bonds Payable and a credit to Interest Expense. The entry to write off a discount is a debit to Interest Expense and a credit to Discount on Bonds Payable. Accrued interest represents the amount of interest incurred between the last interest-payment date and the end of the fiscal period. The entry to record accrued interest is a debit to Interest Expense and a credit to Interest Payable.

3. Journalize entries pertaining to the establishment of a bond sinking fund, the receipt of income from sinking fund investments, and the eventual payment of the principal of the bonds.

   The entry to establish a bond sinking fund is a debit to Sinking Fund Cash and a credit to Cash. The entry for the receipt of income from sinking fund investments is a debit to Sinking Fund Cash and a credit to Sinking Fund Income. The entry for the payment of the principal of the bonds is a debit to Bonds Payable and a credit to Sinking Fund Cash.

4. Journalize transactions involving the redemption of bonds.

   Assuming interest is paid up to date, the entry for the redemption of bonds is a debit to Bonds Payable, either a debit to Premium on Bonds Payable or a credit to Discount on Bonds Payable, either a debit to Loss on Redemption of Bonds or a credit to Gain on Redemption of Bonds, and a credit to Cash. If there is accrued interest on the bonds, the entry would also include a debit to Interest Expense.

Glossary

Amortization The systematic writing off of costs, discounts, or premiums over a period of years. (826)

Bond A long-term obligation that provides capital. (820)

Bond issue The total number of bonds that a corporation issues at one time, in denominations of $1,000 or $5,000 each. (820)

Callable bonds Bonds that give the corporation the right to redeem or buy back the bonds, prior to the date of maturity, at a specified figure, known as the *call price*. (836)

Contra-liability account A deduction from a liability, such as Discount on Bonds Payable, which is a deduction from the balance of Bonds Payable. (831)

Discount The amount by which the issue price is less than the face value of a bond. (831)

Extraordinary Items Significant transactions that appear at the bottom of an income statement (net of any related income tax effect) because they are unusual in nature and do not recur with any regularity. (837)

Indenture A bond agreement, or contract, between the corporation and its bondholders. (836)

Leverage The use of debt as a lever to raise the owners' rate of return by earning income on borrowed money at a higher rate than that paid to borrow the money (as, for example, borrowing money at 8 percent and using it to earn a 15 percent rate of return). (822)

Premium The excess of the price received over the face value of a bond. (824)

Redeem Buy back or repurchase bonds from bondholders. (836)

Secured bonds Bonds that are covered or backed by mortgages on real estate or by titles to personal property that may be claimed by the bondholders in the event that the issuing corporation defaults on its payment of principal or interest. (822)

Serial bonds Bonds of a particular issue that have a series of maturity dates. (821)

Sinking fund A special fund of cash accumulated over the life of a bond issue to enable the issuing corporation to pay off the bonds when they mature (come due). The fund is kept separate from other assets, and the cash is invested in income-producing securities. (833)

Term bonds Bonds of a particular issue that all have the same maturity date. (821)

Unsecured bonds Bonds backed only by the credit standing (good name) of the issuing corporation; also called *debenture bonds*. (822)

QUESTIONS, EXERCISES, AND CASES

Discussion Questions

1. What is a bond discount, and how is it reported on a balance sheet?
2. What are two definite obligations a corporation incurs when it issues bonds?
3. Distinguish between the following: secured bonds and unsecured bonds; term bonds and serial bonds.
4. What is meant by amortization? What accounts are debited and credited in the amortization of a bond premium?
5. If the market rate of interest is lower than the rate of interest stated in the bond agreement, will the bonds be sold at a premium or a discount? Why?
6. What is a bond sinking fund? What is the title of the account involved, and how is it classified on a balance sheet?
7. What do accountants mean by the redemption of callable bonds? What is involved in the journal entry?
8. Why would a corporation want to exercise the callable provision of a bond when it could wait longer to pay off the debt?

Exercises

P.O. 1

Journalize issuance of bonds.

Exercise 22-1 Journalize the following transactions for Ayler Corporation:

July   10 Issued $800,000, 8 percent, 20-year bonds at 102.
Oct.   5 Issued $600,000, 9 percent, 10-year bonds at 103.

P.O. 2

Journalize adjusting entry for bonds sold at a premium.

Exercise 22-2 Journalize the adjusting entry on December 31, the company's year end, to amortize the premium resulting from the issuance on January 5 of $200,000, 10-year bonds at 104.

P.O. 2

Journalize adjustment for interest expense.

Exercise 22-3 Max, Inc., issued $900,000 of 30-year, 9 percent bonds dated March 1. Interest is payable on March 1 and September 1. The fiscal year extends from January 1 through December 31. Journalize entries for the following:

Sept.   1 Payment of semiannual interest
Dec.   31 Adjustment for accrued interest expense

P.O. 1,2

Journalize bond issue and adjusting entry.

Exercise 22-4 On January 1, Reba, Inc., issues 7 percent, 20-year bonds with a face value of $800,000 at 96. Journalize the following entries:

a. Issuance of the bonds
b. Adjusting entry to amortize the discount on December 31, the company's year end

P.O. 1,2

Journalize bond issue, interest payment, and adjusting entries for discount and for accrued interest.

Exercise 22-5 On April 1, Anson Corporation issues $1,000,000 of 10-year, 9 percent bonds at 98, dated April 1 with interest payable semiannually on October 1 and April 1. The corporation's fiscal year ends on December 31. Journalize the issuance of the bonds, the payment of the semiannual interest on October 1, and the adjusting entries to amortize the Discount on Bonds Payable and record the accrued interest as of December 31.

P.O. 1,2

Describe transactions from T accounts.

Exercise 22-6 Describe the entries in the following T accounts:

	Cash					Bonds Payable					Interest Expense			
	+	**−**				**−**	**+**				**+**	**−**		
(1)	1,040,000	(2)	80,000				(1)	1,000,000		(2)	80,000	(4)	2,000
										(3)	20,000	(5)	98,000

	Premium on Bonds Payable		
	−	**+**	
(4)	2,000	(1)	40,000

		(6)	20,000

	Interest Payable		
	−	**+**	
(6)	20,000	(3)	20,000

	Income Summary	
(5)	98,000	

P.O. 3

Journalize sale of investments, sinking fund deposit, and payment of bonds.

Exercise 22-7 Parsons, Inc., has outstanding $650,000 of 10-year sinking fund bonds. At the end of the ninth year after it had issued the bonds, the balance of Parsons Inc.'s Sinking Fund Investments account is $598,600. List the entries to record the transactions given on the following page.

a. The sale of the investments for $611,000
b. The final deposit in the sinking fund, bringing the balance of the account up to $650,000
c. The payment of the bonds

P.O. 4

Journalize bond redemption.

Exercise 22-8 Olivo Corporation has the following account balances: Bonds Payable, $1,300,000; Premium on Bonds Payable, $40,000. As a step in redeeming the bond issue, Olivo Corporation buys $130,000 worth of its bonds on the open market at 97. Give the entry to record the redemption.

internet
LINKS TO ACCOUNTING

Learning about bonds may seem overwhelming at first. Let's go back to InvestinginBonds.com at **http://www.investinginbonds.com** and look at some examples. Click on Corporate Market At-A-Glance under Bond Markets & Prices. Then, under Show Me Corporate Price Data, click on Most active bonds during the last trading day to find information on corporate bond issues. Hopefully, after working through the following problems, understanding bonds might not seem quite so complicated!

1. Can you tell from the information provided whether the bonds are selling at a premium or a discount? If yes, how can you tell?
2. Assume the following fictional bond is listed at InvestinginBonds.com and that interest is paid semiannually:

Trade Date	Company	CUSIP	Coupon	Maturity	Yield	Price	Size
12/31/2006	XL Corporation	11234XL3	6.2	12/31/2016	5.443	101.772	1K

- CUSIP is a unique number used to identify a specific bond. The acronym stands for the "Committee on Uniform Security Identification Procedures."
- Coupon is the rate of interest payable annually.
- Yield is the annual return you earn on the bond, based on the price you paid and the interest payment you receive.
- Size is the amount in millions of dollars of a given wholesale transaction. Since "K" represents 1,000, the 1K size means $1 million × 1,000 = $1,000,000,000, or $1 billion.

What is the journal entry to record the issue of this bond on December 31, 2006?

3. Show XL Corporation's journal entry to record the first semiannual interest payment on June 30, 2007.
4. Show XL Corporation's adjusting journal entry to record amortization of the bond premium on December 31, 2007. (Use the straight-line method.)
5. How do semiannual interest payments and amortization of the bond premium affect the Interest Expense account? (*Hint:* Look at the journal entries you prepared above.)

CONSIDER AND COMMUNICATE

A fellow student states that bond premium and bond discount are the same, because (a) they are reduced by amortization; (b) both occur because the cash received differs from the face value of the bond; and (c) both affect interest expense. Respond to the accuracy of this statement.

CRITICAL THINKING

Below is a partial Stockholders' Equity section of a corporate balance sheet. The preparer has carelessly left out several numbers. Please fill in the missing information.

Stockholders' Equity			
Paid-in Capital:			
1. Preferred 9 Percent Stock, $50 par (40,000 shares authorized, _____ shares issued)	$ 400,000		
2. Preferred 9 Percent Stock Subscribed (1,600 shares)	80,000	$	
3. Common Stock, $_____ par (250,000 shares authorized, 58,000 shares issued)	$1,160,000		
4. Paid-in Capital in Excess of Par Value	40,000		
Paid-in Capital from Donation		16,000	
5. Total Paid-in Capital		$	
Retained Earnings		189,000	
6. Total Stockholders' Equity			$

A QUESTION OF ETHICS

You walk into an unoccupied office to put something in the person's in-basket. As you do so, you cannot help noticing an open folder in which you see a list of names of people marked for outplacement—a polite way of saying, "You are fired." You see that your name isn't on it and breathe a sigh of relief, but you also see the names of several people you know. What should you do? Should you keep quiet or give your friends a heads-up?

For additional help, see the demonstration problem at the beginning of each chapter in your Working Papers.

P.O. 1,2

Problem 22-1A During two consecutive years, Pedroza Company, Inc., completed the following transactions:

Year 1

Jan.	2	Issued $2,000,000 face value, 30-year, 8 percent bonds, dated January 1 of this year, at 97. Interest is payable semiannually on June 30 and December 31.
June	30	Paid semiannual interest on bonds.
Dec.	31	Paid semiannual interest on bonds.
	31	Recorded an adjusting entry for amortization of discount on bonds.
	31	Closed the Interest Expense account.

Year 2

June	30	Paid semiannual interest on bonds.
Dec.	31	Paid semiannual interest on bonds.
	31	Recorded an adjusting entry for amortization of discount on bonds.
	31	Closed the Interest Expense account.

Check Figure

Adjustment, Year 1, Discount on Bonds Payable, $2,000 Credit

Instructions

Record the transactions in general journal form.

P.O. 1,2

Problem 22-2A Becker Hotel, Inc., completed the following selected transactions:

Year 1

Apr.	1	Issued $1,500,000 worth of 30-year, 9 percent bonds, dated April 1 of this year, at 103. Interest is payable semiannually on October 1 and April 1.
Oct.	1	Paid semiannual interest on bonds.
Dec.	31	Recorded an adjusting entry for amortization of premium on bonds.
	31	Recorded an adjusting entry for accrued interest payable.
	31	Closed the Interest Expense account.

Year 2

Jan.	1	Reversed the adjusting entry for accrued interest payable.
Apr.	1	Paid semiannual interest on bonds.
Oct.	1	Paid semiannual interest on bonds.
Dec.	31	Made an adjusting entry to record amortization of premium on bonds.
	31	Made an adjusting entry to record accrued interest payable.
	31	Closed the Interest Expense account.

Check Figure

Adjustment, Year 2, Premium on Bonds Payable, $1,500 Debit

P.O. 1,2,3

Instructions

1. Record the transactions in general journal form.
2. Post entries to the Interest Expense account, No. 581. Label the adjusting, closing, and reversing entries.

Problem 22-3A During two consecutive years, Stateline Freight Line Corporation completed the following transactions relating to its $15,000,000 issue of 25-year, 7 percent bonds, dated May 1 of the first year. Interest is payable on May 1 and November 1. The corporation's fiscal year extends from January 1 through December 31.

Year 1

May	1	Sold the bond issue at 97¾.
Nov.	1	Paid semiannual interest on bonds.
Dec.	31	Deposited $216,560 in a bond sinking fund.
	31	Made an adjusting entry to record amortization of bond discount.
	31	Made an adjusting entry to record accrued interest payable.
	31	Closed the Interest Expense account.

Year 2

Jan.	1	Reversed the adjustment for accrued interest payable.
	9	Bought various securities with sinking fund cash; cost, $216,560.
May	1	Paid semiannual interest on bonds.
Nov.	1	Paid semiannual interest on bonds.
Dec.	31	Recorded receipt of $16,245 of income derived from sinking fund investments, depositing cash in the sinking fund.
	31	Deposited $322,500 in bond sinking fund.
	31	Made an adjusting entry to record amortization of bond discount.
	31	Made an adjusting entry to record accrued interest payable.
	31	Closed the Interest Expense account.

Check Figure

Year 2, Balance of Discount on Bonds Payable, $315,000 Debit

P.O. 1,2,3

Instructions

1. Record the transactions in general journal form.
2. Post entries to the Discount on Bonds Payable account, No. 242, and the Interest Expense account, No. 581. Label the adjusting, closing, and reversing entries.

Problem 22-4A On May 1, Vargas Recreation Corporation issued $4,500,000 worth of 10-year, 8 percent bonds, dated May 1, with interest payable on May 1 and November 1. The corporation's fiscal year is the calendar year. The following transactions pertain to the bond issue for the first two years:

Year 1

May	1	Sold the bond issue at 102.
Nov.	1	Paid semiannual interest on bonds.
Dec.	31	Deposited $80,250 in a bond sinking fund.
	31	Recorded an adjusting entry for amortization of bond premium.
	31	Recorded an adjusting entry for accrued interest payable.
	31	Closed the Interest Expense account.

Year 2

Jan.	1	Reversed the adjusting entry for accrued interest payable.
	12	Bought various securities with sinking fund cash; cost, $80,250.

May	1	Paid semiannual interest on bonds.
July	1	Recorded receipt of $2,907 of income derived from sinking fund investments, depositing cash in sinking fund.
	2	Bought various securities with sinking fund cash; cost, $3,750.
Nov.	1	Paid semiannual interest on bonds.
Dec.	31	Recorded receipt of $3,249 of income derived from sinking fund investments, depositing the cash in the sinking fund.
	31	Deposited $101,500 in the bond sinking fund.
	31	Recorded an adjusting entry for amortization of bond premium.
	31	Recorded an adjusting entry for accrued interest payable.
	31	Closed the Sinking Fund Income account.
	31	Closed the Interest Expense account.

Check Figure

Adjustment, Year 2, Interest Payable, $60,000 Credit

Instructions

1. Record the transactions in general journal form.
2. Post entries to the Premium on Bonds Payable account, No. 243, and the Interest Expense account, No. 581. Label the appropriate entries in the ledger accounts as adjusting, closing, or reversing.

PROBLEM SET B

For additional help, see the demonstration problem at the beginning of each chapter in your Working Papers.

P.O. 1,2

Problem 22-1B During two consecutive years, Carter Corporation completed the following transactions:

Year 1

Jan.	2	Issued $3,000,000 face value, 10-year, 8 percent bonds, dated January 1 of this year, at 104. Interest is payable semiannually on June 30 and December 31.
June	30	Paid semiannual interest on bonds.
Dec.	31	Paid semiannual interest on bonds.
	31	Recorded an adjusting entry for amortization of premium on bonds.
	31	Closed the Interest Expense account.

Year 2

June	30	Paid semiannual interest on bonds.
Dec.	31	Paid semiannual interest on bonds.
	31	Recorded an adjusting entry for amortization of premium on bonds.
	31	Closed the Interest Expense account.

Check Figure

Year 2, June 30 Interest Expense Debit, $120,000

Instructions

Record the transactions in general journal form.

P.O. 1,2

Problem 22-2B Payson Bakers, Inc., completed the following selected transactions:

Year 1

Mar.	1	Issued $600,000 worth of 20-year, 8 percent bonds, dated March 1 of this year, at 103. Interest is payable semiannually on September 1 and March 1.
Sept.	1	Paid semiannual interest on bonds.
Dec.	31	Recorded an adjusting entry for amortization of premium on bonds.
	31	Recorded an adjusting entry for accrued interest payable.
	31	Closed the Interest Expense account.

Year 2

Jan.	1	Reversed the adjusting entry for accrued interest payable.
Mar.	1	Paid semiannual interest on bonds.
Sept.	1	Paid semiannual interest on bonds.
Dec.	31	Made an adjusting entry to record amortization of premium on bonds.
	31	Made an adjusting entry to record accrued interest payable.
	31	Closed the Interest Expense account.

Check Figure

Year 2, December 31 Closing Entry, Income Summary Debit, $47,100

P.O. 1,2,3

Instructions

1. Record the transactions in general journal form.
2. Post entries to the Interest Expense account, No. 581. Label the adjusting, closing, and reversing entries.

Problem 22-3B During two consecutive years, Cardor Medical Clinic completed the following transactions relating to its $6,750,000 issue of 30-year, 7 percent bonds, dated April 1 of the first year. Interest is payable April 1 and October 1. The corporation's fiscal year extends from January 1 through December 31.

Year 1

Apr.	1	Sold the bond issue at 98.
Oct.	1	Paid semiannual interest on bonds.
Dec.	31	Deposited $59,625 in a bond sinking fund.
	31	Made an adjusting entry to record amortization of bond discount.
	31	Made an adjusting entry to record accrued interest payable.
	31	Closed the Interest Expense account.

Year 2

Jan.	1	Reversed the adjusting entry for accrued interest payable.
	4	Bought various securities with sinking fund cash; cost, $59,625.
Apr.	1	Paid semiannual interest on bonds.
Oct.	1	Paid semiannual interest on bonds.
Dec.	31	Recorded receipt of $4,629 of income derived from sinking fund investments, depositing the cash in the sinking fund.
	31	Deposited $82,950 in bond sinking fund.
	31	Made an adjusting entry to record amortization of bond discount.
	31	Made an adjusting entry to record accrued interest payable.
	31	Closed the Interest Expense account.

Check Figure

Year 2, Balance of Discount on Bonds Payable, $127,125 Debit

Instructions

1. Record the transactions in general journal form.
2. Post entries to the Discount on Bonds Payable account, No. 242, and the Interest Expense account, No. 581. Label the adjusting, closing, and reversing entries.

P.O. 1,2,3

Problem 22-4B On June 1, Wood Design Products, Inc., whose fiscal year is the calendar year, issued $14,400,000 worth of 20-year, 8 percent bonds, dated June 1, with interest payable on June 1 and December 1. The following transactions pertain to the bond issue for the first two years:

Year 1

June	1	Sold the bond issue at 101.
Dec.	1	Paid semiannual interest on bonds.
	31	Deposited $284,400 in a bond sinking fund.
	31	Recorded an adjusting entry for amortization of bond premium.
	31	Recorded an adjusting entry for accrued interest payable.
	31	Closed the Interest Expense account.

Year 2

Jan.	1	Reversed the adjusting entry for accrued interest payable.
	9	Bought various securities with sinking fund cash; cost, $284,400.
June	1	Paid semiannual interest on bonds.
July	1	Recorded receipt of $9,737 of income derived from sinking fund investments, depositing the cash in the sinking fund.
	8	Bought various securities with sinking fund cash; cost, $9,737.
Dec.	1	Paid semiannual interest on bonds.
	31	Recorded receipt of $19,190 of income derived from sinking fund investments, depositing the cash in the sinking fund.
	31	Deposited $402,000 in the bond sinking fund.
	31	Recorded an adjusting entry for amortization of bond premium.
	31	Recorded an adjusting entry for accrued interest payable.
	31	Closed the Sinking Fund Income account.
	31	Closed the Interest Expense account.

Check Figure

Year 2, Balance of Premium on Bonds Payable, $132,600 Credit

Instructions

1. Record the transactions in general journal form.
2. Post entries to the Premium on Bonds Payable account, No. 243, and the Interest Expense account, No. 581. Label the appropriate entries in the ledger accounts as adjusting, closing, or reversing.

PART I: True/False Questions

T   F   1. A salary allowance represents a withdrawal by a partner for personal use when allocating partnership net income to partners.

T   F   2. Mutual agency means that each partner can enter into contracts in the name of the firm.

T   F   3. The primary difference between accounting for a sole proprietorship and accounting for a partnership is in the owners' equity accounts.

T   F   4. Stockholders' equity in a corporation can also be referred to as capital.

T   F   5. The Organization Expense account for a corporation is classified as an expense account.

T   F   6. Double taxation means that corporate income is taxed first at the corporate level and then again as dividends to stockholders.

T   F   7. The issuance of a stock dividend results in a decrease in the assets of a corporation.

T   F   8. When retained earnings are appropriated for property expansion, cash is set aside to pay for the expansion.

T   F   9. Dividends are declared only by a vote of the board of directors that is recorded in the minute book.

T   F   10. The limit of liability is the same for partners in a general partnership as for stockholders in a corporation.

T   F   11. A premium on bonds payable is amortized over the period from the date of issue until the maturity date.

T   F   12. Discount on Bonds Payable is classified as a contra-liability account.

PART II: Completion

1. _____ occurs when a partnership ends, the assets are sold, creditors are paid, and the remaining cash is distributed among the partners.

2. The ability of each partner to act as an agent of the firm, thereby committing the entire firm to a binding contract, is called _____.

3. A corporation's stock that is in the hands of its stockholders is called _____.

4. The owners of a corporation are referred to as _____.

5. A distribution of earnings of a corporation in the form of cash is called a(n) _____.

Note: Answers to Before a Test Check begin on page A-1.

6. A distribution of a corporation's retained earnings to stockholders in the form of shares of corporate stock is called a(n) _____.

7. A restriction of a portion of retained earnings designated for a specific purpose is called a(n) _____.

8. The systematic writing off of a bond premium or discount over the remaining life of the bond is called _____.

9. The _____ is the excess of the price received over the face value of a bond.

10. An account such as Discount on Bonds Payable, which represents a deduction from a liability, is called a(n) _____ account.

PART III: Application

A. PARTNERSHIPS

Calculations Involving Division of Net Income

Lopez and Rell are partners in the Cruise Line Shop. Balances in the Capital accounts of Lopez and Rell at the beginning of the year are $90,000 and $70,000, respectively. The net income of the firm for the year is $80,000. Calculate each partner's share of net income under the specified conditions. The first answer is given as an example.

0. Equally.
1. Ratio of 3:1.
2. In the ratio of the balances of their Capital accounts at the beginning of the year.
3. Salary allowances of $30,000 to Lopez and $35,000 to Rell; the remainder divided equally.
4. Interest allowances of 9 percent on the balances of their Capital accounts at the beginning of the year; the remainder divided equally.
5. Salary allowances of $25,000 to Lopez and $30,000 to Rell and interest allowances of 10 percent on the balances of their Capital accounts at the beginning of the year; the remainder divided equally.

	Lopez's Share	Rell's Share
0.	$40,000	$40,000
1.		
2.		
3.		
4.		
5.		

B. CORPORATIONS

Stockholders' Equity

The charter of the Warder Corporation authorized the issuance of 20,000 shares of cumulative preferred 8 percent stock, $50 par, and 160,000 shares of common stock, $10 par. At the end of this year, the balances of the stockholders' equity accounts are as follows:

Common Stock	$750,000
Paid-in Capital from Donation	6,500
Preferred 8 Percent Stock	240,000
Preferred 8 Percent Stock Subscribed	30,000
Retained Earnings (credit balance)	240,000

Prepare the Stockholders' Equity section of the balance sheet, including descriptive details of stock accounts, for the end of this year.

Stockholders' Equity			
Paid-in Capital:			

Skechers USA, Inc., a company that designs and markets a collection of contemporary footwear for men, women, and children, reported a net increase in cash flow for 2005 of more than $61 million. But the net increase in cash flow for 2004 was just under $23 million. Why were the two years so different? So far, you have learned about the income statement, the balance sheet, and the statement of retained earnings. But, if you want to know the reasons for cash inflows and outflows, you'll need to look at a company's statement of cash flows. The statement of cash flows has three sections and reports on cash flows from operating activities, investing activities, and financing activities. To look at Skechers' 2005 and 2004 statements of cash flows, go to **http://www.sec.gov,** select Search for Company Filings, and then, under General-Purpose Searches, click on Companies & Other Filers. In the Company Name box, type Skechers. In the list of forms, select the 10-K that was filed on 2006-03-16. The statement of cash flows is on page 46 of the 10-K report.

Performance Objectives

After you have completed this chapter, you will be able to do the following:

1. Describe the statement of cash flows, and define *cash* and *cash equivalents.*

2. State the purpose of the statement of cash flows.

3. State the uses of the statement of cash flows by management, investors, and creditors.

4. Identify cash inflows and outflows as operating, investing, or financing activities.

5. Calculate amounts of cash inflows and outflows involving operating, investing, and financing activities.

6. Prepare a statement of cash flows using the direct method.

Certainly the financial statements presented in earlier chapters are important. Each statement serves a specific purpose. The income statement shows the results of operations. The statement of retained earnings shows additional investments by owners and payments to owners. The balance sheet portrays a company's financial condition. However, there are important questions that these statements do not answer. For example, what new assets did the firm invest in (buy) during the year? If liabilities increased during the year, where were the proceeds spent? Or, if liabilities decreased, how were they reduced? Did a corporation's operations for the year generate enough cash to pay dividends? If a corporation issued common stock during the year, where were the proceeds spent?

You may wonder why these questions can't be answered by the existing financial statements. When the income statement is prepared on the accrual basis, it does not show the amounts of cash either generated or paid. The amounts of cash involved in changes in the balances of assets and liabilities during the year are not shown on the balance sheet. The statement of retained earnings shows only transactions that affect equity accounts. The statement of cash flows was developed to explain the reasons for the inflows and outflows of cash.

A BROAD LOOK AT THE STATEMENT OF CASH FLOWS

Definition

OBJECTIVE 1
Describe the statement of cash flows, and define *cash* and *cash equivalents*.

The **statement of cash flows** is a financial statement that explains in detail how the balance of cash and cash equivalents has changed between the beginning and the end of a fiscal period. Some accountants refer to the statement of cash flows as the "where got, where gone" statement of cash. The Financial Accounting Standards Board, in its Statement of Financial Accounting Standards No. 95, requires a statement of cash flows as part of a full set of financial statements.

On the statement of cash flows, cash is defined to include both cash as you think of it and cash equivalents. **Cash equivalents** are short-term, highly liquid investments, including money market accounts, U.S. Treasury bills, and commercial paper, that mature within ninety days from the date acquired. When a company has more cash on hand than it needs immediately, it seems logical to put the excess cash to work earning interest. Money market accounts are interest-bearing accounts available at banks. U.S. Treasury bills may be considered short-term government bonds. Commercial paper is another corporation's short-term, interest-bearing notes.

Cash, checking accounts, and CDs, as well as U.S. Treasury bills and commercial paper with a 90-day or less maturity, are all considered cash and cash equivalents.

CAREERS IN YOUR FUTURE

JAMES NEWKIRK

CFO, TeraCloud Corporation
Formerly director of finance, then vice president
of finance and administration

At the core of Jim's advancement at TeraCloud has been his many years in accounting. And now he is at the top of the ladder as Chief Financial Officer. Jim is responsible for:

- Financial accounting/reporting
- Corporate taxes
- Audit/review
- Financial planning and analysis
- Strategic planning
- Insurance selection
- Treasury/cash management
- Human resources/benefits
- Legal liaison with law firms
- Banking/cash flow
- Board of directors monthly reporting
- Shareholder/investor relations
- Business modeling
- Internal controls
- Intellectual property protection (trademark filings, etc.)
- Staff management
- Leadership team

Jim brings to his position years of experience as well as an innate ability to deal with the people around him to keep the various parts of the organization pointed in a positive and profitable direction. His is an extremely complex assignment with his duties including far more than is usually required of a Chief Financial Officer of a corporation.

How did Jim find himself in this highly professional and pressure-filled career? He credits his accounting education, which taught him to organize and maintain control over controllable areas of the business so that he can focus more attention on areas that are not controllable. Financial statements are the principal means of communicating business performance. Accounting's functions are at the core of Jim's career, and its basics are integrated into his daily practices. Accounting is the language of business, and Jim speaks it with expertise.

"The statement of cash flows condenses the activity of a business to a statement that communicates how cash is being used by or generated by a business. Over time, the statement of cash flows indicates the health and vitality of a business."

Jim's advice to accounting students is to be disciplined in their studies. Practice the mechanics of accounting, but focus on the concepts and the theory behind the mechanics. Know where to find relevant professional standards to solve accounting problems.

Purpose

> **OBJECTIVE 2**
> State the purpose of the statement of cash flows.

The main purpose of the statement of cash flows is to provide a summary of information concerning a company's cash receipts and payments during a fiscal period. A secondary purpose is to provide information about a firm's investing and financing activities during a fiscal period.

Uses of the Statement of Cash Flows

> **OBJECTIVE 3**
> State the uses of the statement of cash flows by management, investors, and creditors.

Management's Use of the Statement of Cash Flows Management uses the statement of cash flows to assess or determine the liquidity of the business, to determine dividend policy, and to evaluate possible investments and means of financing. Management asks the following questions:

Liquidity Is enough cash being generated to enable the company to pay its bills?

Dividend policy Is enough cash being generated to enable the corporation to establish a regular cash dividend policy?

Investment and financing If the firm borrows to buy an asset, is enough cash being generated to make the payments?

Investors' and Creditors' Use of the Statement of Cash Flows   Investors (stockholders) are interested in a corporation's ability to pay dividends and increase the value of the company. Creditors are concerned with a company's ability to pay its liabilities. Both investors and creditors are interested in the firm's ability to generate future cash flows as well as its need for additional financing.

CLASSIFICATIONS OF CASH FLOWS

OBJECTIVE 4

Identify cash inflows and outflows as operating, investing, or financing activities.

The statement of cash flows classifies cash receipts and payments into three categories: operating activities, investing activities, and financing activities.

Operating Activities

Operating activities is the first category on the statement of cash flows, and this category lists and classifies cash inflows and outflows from a variety of sources. *Cash inflows* include cash receipts from customers for the sale of merchandise and services and cash receipts in the form of interest and dividend income. Think of the items listed on an income statement; include the Revenue from Sales section, and then refer to the Other Income section to include interest income and dividend income.

Cash outflows include cash payments for merchandise purchases and operating expenses, such as Wages Expense and Rent Expense. Cash outflows for operating activities also include cash payments in the form of interest and income taxes expense. Think of the items listed on an income statement; include merchandise purchases and the Operating Expenses (Selling and General) section, then refer to the Other Expenses section to include interest expense.

Financing activities include cash inflows from the sale of common or preferred stock or from the issuance of debt. Cash outflows from financing activities may be used to reacquire stock, to repay debt, or to pay dividends.

Incidentally, when you think about the income statement, you find the account Gain on Disposal of Property and Equipment listed in the Other Income section and the account Loss on Disposal of Property and Equipment listed in the Other Expenses section. These items generally arise because of investing activities; consequently, they are included with the sale or purchase of property and equipment in the Investing Activities section.

Investing Activities

Investing activities include (1) buying and selling property and equipment (long-term assets); (2) acquiring and selling investments other than cash equivalents; and (3) making and collecting loans. *Cash inflows* include the cash received from selling property and equipment, from selling investments, and from collecting loans. *Cash outflows* include cash paid to purchase property and equipment, cash invested in another corporation's stocks or bonds, and cash loaned to borrowers.

Financing Activities

Financing activities include cash transactions that involve borrowing from or repaying creditors, as well as additional cash investments from owners and transactions that reduce owners' investments. *Cash inflows* include proceeds received from short- or long-term borrowing (issuing notes or bonds) and those from issuing stock for cash. *Cash outflows* include repayments of loans (notes and bonds) and payments to owners, including personal withdrawals and cash dividends.

FORM OF THE STATEMENT OF CASH FLOWS

OBJECTIVE 5

Calculate amounts of cash inflows and outflows involving operating, investing, and financing activities.

The statement of cash flows is divided into these three categories: operating activities, followed by investing activities, followed by financing activities. Within each activity, cash inflows and outflows are shown separately. For example, suppose that a company sells its used equipment for $5,000 in cash. Next, the company turns around and buys new equipment for $30,000, paying cash. Under investing activities, the sale of equipment, $5,000, is listed as an inflow of cash. The purchase of equipment, $30,000, is listed as an outflow of cash.

First, we present an example of a complete statement of cash flows so you can see the entire picture. Then we provide four other companies as illustrations, starting with a one-owner business and working up to a corporation.

Actually, the statement of cash flows may be presented using either of two methods: the direct method or the indirect method. The FASB recommends the direct method, although the indirect method is also acceptable. **The direct method primarily involves converting each amount recorded on the income statement from the accrual basis to the cash basis.** The direct method shows the specific sources and uses of cash during a fiscal period.

A statement of cash flows using the indirect method is illustrated in Appendix J, following this chapter.

Ferguson Corporation
Statement of Cash Flows
For Year Ended December 31, 2009

Cash Flows from (used by) Operating Activities:				
Cash Receipts from:				
Customers		$1 412 000 00		
Interest and Dividends		6 000 00		
Total Cash Receipts			$1 418 000 00	
Cash Payments for:				
Merchandise Purchases		$ (520 000 00)		
Operating Expenses:				
Employees	$ (190 000 00)			
Supplies	(14 000 00)			
Insurance	(3 000 00)			
Total Operating Expenses		(207 000 00)		
Interest		(20 000 00)		
Income Taxes		(93 000 00)		
Total Cash Payments			(840 000 00)	
Net Cash Flows from Operating Activities			$ 578 000 00	
Cash Flows from (used by) Investing Activities:				
Purchase of Investments		$ (10 000 00)		
Sale of Investments		20 000 00		
Purchase of Property and Equipment		(530 000 00)		
Sale of Property and Equipment		5 000 00		
Net Cash Flows used by Investing Activities			(515 000 00)	
Cash Flows from (used by) Financing Activities:				
Issuance of Note		$ 10 000 00		
Issuance of Bonds		210 000 00		
Repayment of Bonds		(60 000 00)		
Issuance of Common Stock		140 000 00		
Payment of Dividends		(50 000 00)		
Net Cash Flows from Financing Activities			250 000 00	
Net Increase (Decrease) in Cash			$ 313 000 00	
Cash and Cash Equivalents, January 1, 2009			50 000 00	
Cash Balance and Cash Equivalents, December 31, 2009			$ 363 000 00	

DEVELOPING THE STATEMENT OF CASH FLOWS

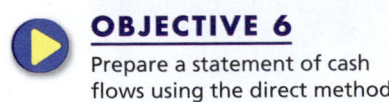

OBJECTIVE 6

Prepare a statement of cash flows using the direct method.

To describe the development of the statement of cash flows, we need the company's three basic financial statements for the present fiscal period, and its balance sheet at the end of the previous fiscal period (which is the same as the balance sheet at the beginning of the present fiscal period). From the balance sheets at the beginning and end of the fiscal period, we can compile a comparative balance sheet listing the increases and decreases in all accounts for each of our illustrations.

Illustration 1

Our first illustration shows conversions of Incomes from Services, Wages Expense, Supplies Expense, Insurance Expense, Depreciation Expense, Equipment, and Drawing into cash flows. Hank's Welding operates on a cash basis, in which revenue is counted only when it is received in cash and expenses are counted only when they are paid in cash. However, even on the cash basis, the firm makes adjusting entries for insurance expired and depreciation. The financial statements for Hank's Welding are presented here.

Hank's Welding
Income Statement
For Year Ended December 31, 2008

Revenue:		
Income from Services		$99 0 8 0 00
Expenses:		
Wages Expense	$24 0 0 0 00	
Supplies Expense	3 2 0 0 00	
Insurance Expense	4 8 0 00	
Depreciation Expense, Equipment	26 4 0 0 00	
Total Expenses		54 0 8 0 00
Net Income		$45 0 0 0 00

Hank's Welding
Statement of Owner's Equity
For Year Ended December 31, 2008

H. A. Bain, Capital, January 1, 2008		$82 4 0 0 00
Net Income	$45 0 0 0 00	
Less Withdrawals	40 0 0 0 00	
Increase in Capital		5 0 0 0 00
H. A. Bain, Capital, December 31, 2008		$87 4 0 0 00

Hank's Welding
Comparative Balance Sheet
December 31, 2008 and December 31, 2007

	2008	2007	INCREASE OR (DECREASE)
Assets			
Cash	$ 32 9 0 0 00	$ 1 5 6 0 00	$ 31 3 4 0 00
Prepaid Insurance	1 1 0 0 00	1 0 4 0 00	6 0 00
Equipment	101 4 0 0 00	101 4 0 0 00	0 00
Less Accumulated Depreciation	(48 0 0 0 00)	(21 6 0 0 00)	(26 4 0 0 00)
Total Assets	$ 87 4 0 0 00	$ 82 4 0 0 00	$ 5 0 0 0 00
Owner's Equity			
H. A. Bain, Capital	$ 87 4 0 0 00	$ 82 4 0 0 00	$ 5 0 0 0 00
Total Owner's Equity	$ 87 4 0 0 00	$ 82 4 0 0 00	$ 5 0 0 0 00

Note the $31,340 increase in Cash on the comparative balance sheet ($32,900 − $1,560). The purpose of the statement of cash flows is to show how this increase in Cash came about ("where got, where gone"). In essence, the company's income statement must be converted to a cash basis.

Cash Flows from Operating Activities: Convert Revenue and Expenses to Cash Basis

1. **Convert Income from Services to Cash Receipts from Customers.** Since Hank's Welding records revenue only when it is received in cash, the $99,080 listed as Income from Services on the income statement is the exact amount of cash received.
2. **Convert Wages Expense to Cash Payments to Employees.** Since Hank's Welding records wages expense only when employees are paid, the $24,000 listed as Wages Expense on the income statement is the exact amount of cash paid.
3. **Convert Supplies Expense to Cash Payments for Supplies.** Since the company uses the cash basis of accounting, we can conclude that the $3,200 listed as Supplies Expense on the income statement was indeed paid in cash.
4. **Convert Insurance Expense to Cash Payments for Insurance.** During 2008, Prepaid Insurance increased from $1,040 to $1,100. We calculate the cash payment like this:

Operating activities include cash inflows from selling goods and services to customers. This income has to be converted to a cash basis. Employee wages also have to be converted from Wages Expense to Cash Payments to Employees.

Insurance Expense	$ 480
+ Ending Prepaid Insurance	1,100
= Total	$1,580
− Beginning Prepaid Insurance	1,040
= Cash Payments for Insurance	$ 540

5. **Convert Depreciation Expense, Equipment to Cash Payments for Depreciation.** Because the $26,400 listed on the income statement as Depreciation Expense, Equipment was not paid to anyone, it does not involve cash. Consequently, it is eliminated as an expense; depreciation is not recorded on a statement of cash flows prepared on a direct method basis.

Cash Flows from Investing Activities   Investing activities are concerned with changes in property and equipment. The balance of the Equipment account has not changed during the year. However, the balance of Accumulated Depreciation has increased from $21,600 to $48,000. This $26,400 change is accounted for by recording $26,400 as Depreciation Expense, Equipment on the income statement. This amount is not paid to anyone. Since this is the only change we have, we can say that there have been no cash transactions involving investing activities.

Cash Flows from Financing Activities   Financing activities include additions to or reductions in owner's equity. On the statement of owner's equity, we note $40,000 in personal withdrawals, which we assume are in the form of cash. The withdrawals result in a decrease in cash. We can easily check our assumption that the withdrawals involved cash by reviewing the transactions affecting the H. A. Bain, Drawing, account. Because there were no additional changes reported on the statement of owner's equity, we have gathered all the information we need to prepare our statement of cash flows for Hank's Welding. It is shown on the following page.

Hank's Welding
Statement of Cash Flows
For Year Ended December 31, 2008

Cash Flows from (used by) Operating Activities:		
Cash Receipts from Customers		$99 0 8 0 00
Cash Payments for Operating Expenses:		
Employees	$(24 0 0 0 00)	
Supplies	(3 2 0 0 00)	
Insurance	(5 4 0 00)	
Total Cash Payments		(27 7 4 0 00)
Net Cash Flows from Operating Activities		$71 3 4 0 00
Cash Flows from (used by) Financing Activities:		
Payment of Personal Withdrawals	$(40 0 0 0 00)	
Net Cash Flows used by Financing Activities		(40 0 0 0 00)
Net Increase (Decrease) in Cash		$31 3 4 0 00
Cash, January 1, 2008		1 5 6 0 00
Cash, December 31, 2008		$32 9 0 0 00

Summary of the Conversions in Illustration 1

- **For Prepaid Expenses** Prepaid expenses include items such as Prepaid Insurance.

  Amount of the Expense Listed on the Income Statement + Ending Balance of the Prepaid Expense Account − Beginning Balance of the Prepaid Expense Account

- Each expense is listed individually in the operating expenses section under Cash Flows from (used by) Operating Activities.
- **For Depreciation** The amount of depreciation expense listed on the income statement is eliminated.
- **For Personal Cash Withdrawals** The amount taken from the statement of owner's equity is listed as a negative amount (used by) under Cash Flows from (used by) Financing Activities.

Illustration 2

REMEMBER!

The accrual basis means that revenue is recognized when it is earned and expenses are recognized when they are incurred.

Our second illustration shows the conversions of Income from Services, Wages Expense, Supplies Expense, Insurance Expense, Depreciation Expense, Equipment, purchase of equipment, and Drawing into cash flows. McMann Company is a one-owner service business operating on the accrual basis. The financial statements for McMann Company are presented on the following page.

Note the $24,370 increase in Cash shown on the comparative balance sheet ($37,370 − $13,000). To explain this increase, we must first convert the income statement of McMann Company from the accrual basis to the cash basis. Then we look over the statement of owner's equity and the comparative balance sheet to note any possible cash received or paid out that has not shown up in the conversion of the income statement.

McMann Company
Income Statement
For Year Ended December 31, 2009

Revenue:		
Income from Services		$280 0 0 0 00
Expenses:		
Wages Expense	$96 0 0 0 00	
Supplies Expense	4 0 0 0 00	
Insurance Expense	3 0 0 0 00	
Depreciation Expense, Equipment	5 0 0 0 00	
Total Expenses		108 0 0 0 00
Net Income		$172 0 0 0 00

McMann Company
Statement of Owner's Equity
For Year Ended December 31, 2009

J. B. McMann, Capital, January 1, 2009		$71 0 0 0 00
Net Income	$172 0 0 0 00	
Less Withdrawals	150 0 0 0 00	
Increase in Capital		22 0 0 0 00
J. B. McMann, Capital, December 31, 2009		$93 0 0 0 00

McMann Company
Comparative Balance Sheet
December 31, 2009 and December 31, 2008

	2009	2008	INCREASE OR (DECREASE)
Assets			
Cash	$37 3 7 0 00	$13 0 0 0 00	$24 3 7 0 00
Accounts Receivable	10 4 0 0 00	8 4 0 0 00	2 0 0 0 00
Prepaid Insurance	9 3 0 00	1 0 0 0 00	(7 0 00)
Equipment	63 8 5 0 00	63 2 5 0 00	6 0 0 00
Less Accumulated Depreciation	(15 0 0 0 00)	(10 0 0 0 00)	(5 0 0 0 00)
Total Assets	$97 5 5 0 00	$75 6 5 0 00	$21 9 0 0 00
Liabilities			
Accounts Payable	$ 2 7 0 0 00	$ 2 7 0 0 00	$ 0 00
Wages Payable	1 8 5 0 00	1 9 5 0 00	(1 0 0 00)
Total Liabilities	$ 4 5 5 0 00	$ 4 6 5 0 00	$ (1 0 0 00)
Owner's Equity			
J. B. McMann, Capital	93 0 0 0 00	71 0 0 0 00	22 0 0 0 00
Total Liabilities and Owner's Equity	$97 5 5 0 00	$75 6 5 0 00	$21 9 0 0 00

Cash Flows from Operating Activities

1. **Convert Income from Services to Cash Receipts from Customers.** Income from Services is in the form of cash and customer charge accounts. During 2009, Accounts Receivable increased from $8,400 to $10,400. Evidently, $2,000 more was recorded in the charge accounts than was collected in cash. Starting with the $280,000 listed as Income from Services on the income statement, we say that we collected the beginning balance of Accounts Receivable ($8,400) and did not collect the ending balance of Accounts Receivable ($10,400). The amount of cash received from customers is calculated as

Income from Services	$280,000
+ Beginning Accounts Receivable	8,400
= Total	$288,400
− Ending Accounts Receivable	10,400
= Cash Receipts from Customers	$278,000

Here's another way to picture the situation. Assume the company collects its beginning Accounts Receivable first. Next, of the $280,000 listed on the income statement as Income from Services, all but $10,400 (the ending balance of Accounts Receivable) was collected. The calculation is:

		or		
Beginning Accounts Receivable	$ 8,400		Beginning Accounts Receivable	$ 8,400
+ Income from Services	280,000		+ Cash Income from Services ($280,000 − $10,400)	269,600
= Total	$288,400		= Cash Receipts from Customers	$278,000
− Ending Accounts Receivable	10,400			
= Cash Receipts from Customers	$278,000			

REMEMBER!

You need the other three financial statements in order to prepare a statement of cash flows.

2. **Convert Wages Expense to Cash Payments to Employees.** Start with the amount shown on the income statement as Wages Expense, $96,000. During the first part of the year, McMann Company also paid out to its employees the amount shown as the beginning balance of Wages Payable, $1,950. We add this amount to the $96,000. However, of the $96,000 listed as Wages Expense, $1,850 was not paid to the employees. The calculation for the amount paid in cash to employees looks like this:

Wages Expense	$96,000
+ Beginning Wages Payable	1,950
= Total	$97,950
− Ending Wages Payable	1,850
= Cash Payments to Employees	$96,100

Here's another way to picture the situation. Assume the company pays its beginning Wages Payable first. Next, of the $96,000 listed on the income statement as Wages Expense, all but $1,850 (the ending balance of Wages Payable) was paid. The calculation looks like this:

		or		
Beginning Wages Payable	$ 1,950		Beginning Wages Payable	$ 1,950
+ Wages Expense	96,000		+ Cash Wages Expense ($96,000 − $1,850)	94,150
= Total	$97,950		= Cash Payments to Employees	$96,100
− Ending Wages Payable	1,850			
= Cash Payments to Employees	$96,100			

3. **Convert Supplies Expense to Cash Payments for Supplies.** Since there is no amount included in Accounts Payable for supplies, we can conclude that the $4,000 listed as Supplies Expense on the income statement was indeed paid in cash.
4. **Convert Insurance Expense to Cash Payments for Insurance.** During 2009, Prepaid Insurance decreased from $1,000 to $930. The calculation looks like this:

Insurance Expense	$3,000
+ Ending Prepaid Insurance	930
= Total	$3,930
− Beginning Prepaid Insurance	1,000
= Cash Payments for Insurance	$2,930

5. **Convert Depreciation Expense, Equipment to Cash Payments for Depreciation.** Since no cash is involved in Depreciation Expense, Equipment, it is eliminated.

Cash Flows from Investing Activities Look for clues to identify investment activities by examining changes in property and equipment accounts. The comparative balance sheet shows that the balance of the Equipment account has increased from $63,250 to $63,850. When we review the Equipment ledger account, we see the posting reference for the one entry recorded this period. When we trace the entry to the journal page, we find a debit to Equipment for $600 and a credit to Cash for $600. Since this was a cash purchase, we list the purchase of equipment for $600 on the statement of cash flows as an outflow of cash.

Cash Flows from Financing Activities On the statement of owner's equity, we note a $150,000 personal withdrawal. After reviewing the journal entries affecting the J. B. McMann, Drawing account, we see that the $150,000 was paid in cash. On the statement of cash flows, $150,000 is listed as an outflow of cash. Here's the statement of cash flows for McMann Company:

McMann Company
Statement of Cash Flows
For Year Ended December 31, 2009

Cash Flows from (used by) Operating Activities:			
Cash Receipts from Customers			$ 278 000 00
Cash Payments for Operating Expenses:			
Employees	$ (96 100 00)		
Supplies	(4 000 00)		
Insurance	(2 930 00)		
Total Cash Payments		(103 030 00)	
Net Cash Flows from Operating Activities			$ 174 970 00
Cash Flows from (used by) Investing Activities:			
Purchase of Equipment	$ (600 00)		
Net Cash Flows used by Investing Activities		(600 00)	
Cash Flows from (used by) Financing Activities:			
Payment of Personal Withdrawals	$(150 000 00)		
Net Cash Flows used by Financing Activities		(150 000 00)	
Net Increase (Decrease) in Cash			$ 24 370 00
Cash, January 1, 2009			13 000 00
Cash, December 31, 2009			$ 37 370 00

Summary of the Additional Conversions in Illustration 2

- **For Revenue Involving Accounts Receivable—like Income from Services**

    Amount of Revenue Listed on the Income Statement + Beginning Accounts Receivable − Ending Accounts Receivable

- **For Accrued Expenses and Their Respective Liabilities—like Wages Expense and Wages Payable**

    Amount of Expense Listed on the Income Statement + Beginning Wages Payable − Ending Wages Payable

- **For Purchases of Equipment for Cash** The amount credited to the Cash account in the journal entry for the transaction is listed as a negative amount (used by) under Cash Flows from (used by) Investing Activities.

Illustration 3

Our third example shows conversion of Net Sales, Delivered Cost of Purchases, Salary Expense, Rent Expense, Depreciation Expense, Equipment, Supplies Expense, Insurance Expense, and Drawing into cash flows. File Company is a one-owner merchandising business operating on the accrual basis. The financial statements for File Company are presented here.

File Company
Income Statement
For Year Ended December 31, 2009

Net Sales			$800 0 0 0 00
Cost of Goods Sold:			
Merchandise Inventory, January 1, 2009	$126 0 0 0 00		
Delivered Cost of Purchases	514 0 0 0 00		
Cost of Goods Available for Sale	$640 0 0 0 00		
Less Merchandise Inventory, December 31, 2009	130 0 0 0 00		
Cost of Goods Sold		510 0 0 0 00	
Gross Profit		$290 0 0 0 00	
Operating Expenses:			
Salary Expense	$100 0 0 0 00		
Rent Expense	20 0 0 0 00		
Depreciation Expense, Equipment	22 0 0 0 00		
Supplies Expense	1 6 0 0 00		
Insurance Expense	4 0 0 00		
Total Operating Expenses		144 0 0 0 00	
Net Income		$146 0 0 0 00	

File Company
Statement of Owner's Equity
For Year Ended December 31, 2009

S. D. File, Capital, January 1, 2009		$233 2 0 0 00
Net Income	$146 0 0 0 00	
Less Withdrawals	150 0 0 0 00	
Decrease in Capital		(4 0 0 0 00)
S. D. File, Capital, December 31, 2009		$229 2 0 0 00

File Company
Comparative Balance Sheet
December 31, 2009 and December 31, 2008

	2009	2008	INCREASE OR (DECREASE)
Assets			
Cash	$ 31 4 0 0 00	$ 35 0 0 0 00	$ (3 6 0 0 00)
Accounts Receivable	45 6 0 0 00	33 0 0 0 00	12 6 0 0 00
Merchandise Inventory	130 0 0 0 00	126 0 0 0 00	4 0 0 0 00
Prepaid Insurance	2 3 0 0 00	1 4 0 0 00	9 0 0 00
Equipment	136 6 0 0 00	136 6 0 0 00	0 00
Less Accumulated Depreciation	(62 0 0 0 00)	(40 0 0 0 00)	(22 0 0 0 00)
Total Assets	$283 9 0 0 00	$292 0 0 0 00	$ (8 1 0 0 00)
Liabilities			
Accounts Payable	$ 51 5 0 0 00	$ 56 0 0 0 00	$ (4 5 0 0 00)
Salaries Payable	3 2 0 0 00	2 8 0 0 00	4 0 0 00
Total Liabilities	$ 54 7 0 0 00	$ 58 8 0 0 00	$ (4 1 0 0 00)
Owner's Equity			
S. D. File, Capital	229 2 0 0 00	233 2 0 0 00	(4 0 0 0 00)
Total Liabilities and Owner's Equity	$283 9 0 0 00	$292 0 0 0 00	$ (8 1 0 0 00)

Note the $3,600 decrease in cash. Let's start from the top.

Cash Flows from Operating Activities

1. **Convert Net Sales to Cash Receipts from Customers.** During 2009, Accounts Receivable increased from $33,000 to $45,600. Evidently, $12,600 more was recorded in the customer charge accounts than was collected in cash. The amount of cash received from customers is calculated like this:

Net Sales	$800,000
+ Beginning Accounts Receivable	33,000
= Total	$833,000
− Ending Accounts Receivable	45,600
= Cash Receipts from Customers	$787,400

REMEMBER!

If Accounts Receivable has *increased* between the beginning and the end of the fiscal period, cash receipts from customers will be *less* than the revenue listed on the income statement. If Accounts Receivable has *decreased* between the beginning and the end of the fiscal period, cash receipts from customers will be *more* than the revenue listed on the income statement.

2. **Convert Delivered Cost of Purchases to Cash Payments for Merchandise Purchases.** During 2009, Accounts Payable decreased from $56,000 to $51,500. Evidently, $4,500 more was paid in cash than was recorded as amounts owed to creditors. Starting with the $514,000 listed as Delivered Cost of Purchases on the income statement, we'll say that we paid the beginning Accounts Payable ($56,000) and did not pay the ending Accounts Payable ($51,500). The amount of cash paid to creditors is calculated in the following manner:

Delivered Cost of Purchases	$514,000
+ Beginning Accounts Payable	56,000
= Total	$570,000
− Ending Accounts Payable	51,500
= Cash Payments for Merchandise Purchases	$518,500

Here's another way to analyze the situation. Assume the company pays its beginning balance of Accounts Payable first. Next, of the $514,000 listed on the income statement as Delivered Cost of Purchases, all but $51,500 (the ending balance of Accounts Payable) was paid out. The calculation looks like this:

Beginning Accounts Payable	$ 56,000	or Beginning Accounts Payable	$ 56,000
+ Delivered Cost of Purchases	514,000	+ Delivered Cost of Purchases Paid in Cash ($514,000 − $51,500)	462,500
= Total	$570,000	= Cash Payments for Merchandise Purchases	$518,500
− Ending Accounts Payable	51,500		
= Cash Payments for Merchandise Purchases	$518,500		

Operating Expenses In this section of the statement of cash flows, each expense is listed in the same order as it appears on the income statement.

1. **Convert Salary Expense to Cash Payments to Employees.** On the income statement, Salary Expense is $100,000. On the comparative balance sheet, Salaries Payable increased from $2,800 to $3,200. Evidently, $400 less than the $100,000 listed on the income statement was paid out in cash to employees. The calculation looks like this:

Salary Expense	$100,000
+ Beginning Salaries Payable	2,800
= Total	$102,800
− Ending Salaries Payable	3,200
= Cash Payments to Employees	$ 99,600

2. **Convert Rent Expense to Cash Payments for Rent.** Since there is no amount listed on the balance sheet as Prepaid Rent or Rent Payable, we can conclude that the $20,000 listed on the income statement was indeed paid in cash.

3. **Convert Depreciation Expense, Equipment to Cash Payments for Depreciation.** Because the amount listed as Depreciation Expense, Equipment is not paid to anyone, no cash is involved. Depreciation expense is a non-cash expense—ignore it.

4. **Convert Supplies Expense to Cash Payments for Supplies.** Since there is no amount included in Accounts Payable for supplies, we can conclude that the $1,600 listed as Supplies Expense on the income statement was indeed paid in cash.

REMEMBER!

If a prepaid expense (like Prepaid Rent or Prepaid Insurance) has *increased* between the beginning and the end of the fiscal period, cash payments for the item(s) are *more* than the amount listed as expense (Rent Expense or Insurance Expense). If a prepaid expense (like Prepaid Rent or Prepaid Insurance) has *decreased* between the beginning and the end of the fiscal period, cash payments for the item(s) are *less* than the amount listed as expense (Rent Expense or Insurance Expense).

5. **Convert Insurance Expense to Cash Payments for Insurance.** During 2009, Prepaid Insurance increased from $1,400 to $2,300. Evidently, File Company bought more insurance than was used up (expired) during the year. So $900 more in cash than the $400 listed as Insurance Expense on the income statement was paid out. The calculation looks like this:

Insurance Expense	$ 400
+ Ending Prepaid Insurance	2,300
= Total	$2,700
− Beginning Prepaid Insurance	1,400
= Cash Payments for Insurance	$1,300

Cash Flows from Investing Activities There were no changes in the Equipment account balance between the beginning and end of the fiscal period. However, the Accumulated Depreciation account balance increased by the amount of the year's depreciation expense. No equipment was bought or sold, so no cash is involved.

Cash Flows from Financing Activities On the statement of owner's equity, we note personal withdrawals of $150,000. We trace through the entries involving the Drawing account and note entries debiting S. D. File, Drawing, and crediting Cash for a total of $150,000 in each account. We record $150,000 as an outflow of cash. Putting these cash conversions all together, we have the statement of cash flows for File Company.

File Company
Statement of Cash Flows
For Year Ended December 31, 2009

Cash Flows from (used by) Operating Activities:			
Cash Receipts from Customers			$ 787 400 00
Cash Payments for:			
Merchandise Purchases		$(518 500 00)	
Operating Expenses:			
Employees	$(99 600 00)		
Rent	(20 000 00)		
Supplies	(1 600 00)		
Insurance	(1 300 00)		
Total Operating Expenses		(122 500 00)	
Total Cash Payments			(641 000 00)
Net Cash Flows from Operating Activities			$ 146 400 00
Cash Flows from (used by) Financing Activities:			
Payment of Personal Withdrawals		$(150 000 00)	
Net Cash Flows used by Financing Activities			(150 000 00)
Net Increase (Decrease) in Cash			$ (3 600 00)
Cash, January 1, 2009			35 000 00
Cash, December 31, 2009			$ 31 400 00

Summary of Additional Conversions in Illustration 3

- **Handling Delivered Cost of Purchases Involving Accounts Payable** This is figured as:

  Delivered Cost of Purchases Listed on the Income Statement + Beginning Accounts Payable − Ending Accounts Payable

Illustration 4

Our final example shows the conversion of Net Sales, Delivered Cost of Purchases, Wages Expense, Rent Expense, Depreciation Expense, Equipment, Supplies Expense, Property Tax Expense, Insurance Expense, Interest Expense, sale of equipment, issuance of note payable, issuance of stock, and payment of dividends into cash flows. Gale Corporation is a merchandising business operating on an accrual basis.

Gale Corporation
Income Statement
For Year Ended December 31, 2009

Revenue from Sales:			
Sales		$620 000 00	
Less Sales Returns and Allowances		6 000 00	
Net Sales			$614 000 00
Cost of Goods Sold:			
Merchandise Inventory, January 1, 2009		$224 000 00	
Purchases	$426 000 00		
Less Purchases Returns and Allowances	3 000 00		
Net Purchases	$423 000 00		
Add Freight In	47 000 00		
Delivered Cost of Purchases		470 000 00	
Cost of Goods Available for Sale		$694 000 00	
Less Merchandise Inventory, December 31, 2009		260 000 00	
Cost of Goods Sold			434 000 00
Gross Profit			$180 000 00
Operating Expenses:			
Wages Expense		$123 000 00	
Rent Expense		20 000 00	
Depreciation Expense, Equipment		24 000 00	
Supplies Expense		2 000 00	
Property Tax Expense		2 000 00	
Insurance Expense		1 000 00	
Total Operating Expenses			172 000 00
Income from Operations			$ 8 000 00
Other Income:			
Gain on Disposal of Property and Equipment		$ 5 000 00	
Other Expenses:			
Interest Expense		26 000 00	(21 000 00)
Net Loss			$ (13 000 00)

Gale Corporation
Statement of Retained Earnings
For Year Ended December 31, 2009

Retained Earnings, January 1, 2009		$94 600 00
Less: Net Loss for the Year	$13 000 00	
Cash Dividends Declared	16 000 00	
Decrease in Retained Earnings		(29 000 00)
Retained Earnings, December 31, 2009		$65 600 00

Gale Corporation
Comparative Balance Sheet
December 31, 2009 and December 31, 2008

	2009	2008	INCREASE OR (DECREASE)
Assets			
Cash	$ 41 3 0 0 00	$ 33 4 0 0 00	$ 7 9 0 0 00
Accounts Receivable	58 4 0 0 00	69 0 0 0 00	(10 6 0 0 00)
Merchandise Inventory	260 0 0 0 00	224 0 0 0 00	36 0 0 0 00
Prepaid Rent	3 0 0 0 00	3 0 0 0 00	0 00
Prepaid Insurance	1 0 0 0 00	9 0 0 00	1 0 0 00
Equipment	114 0 0 0 00	143 0 0 0 00	(29 0 0 0 00)
Less Accumulated Depreciation	(47 0 0 0 00)	(35 0 0 0 00)	(12 0 0 0 00)
Total Assets	$430 7 0 0 00	$438 3 0 0 00	$ (7 6 0 0 00)
Liabilities			
Accounts Payable	$ 28 6 0 0 00	$ 39 7 0 0 00	$(11 1 0 0 00)
Notes Payable	24 0 0 0 00	0 00	24 0 0 0 00
Wages Payable	2 1 0 0 00	2 4 0 0 00	(3 0 0 00)
Dividends Payable	2 0 0 0 00	3 0 0 0 00	(1 0 0 0 00)
Property Tax Payable	1 3 0 0 00	1 1 0 0 00	2 0 0 00
Interest Payable	6 0 0 00	0 00	6 0 0 00
Total Liabilities	$ 58 6 0 0 00	$ 46 2 0 0 00	$ 12 4 0 0 00
Stockholders' Equity			
Common Stock	$306 5 0 0 00	$297 5 0 0 00	$ 9 0 0 0 00
Retained Earnings	65 6 0 0 00	94 6 0 0 00	(29 0 0 0 00)
Total Stockholders' Equity	$372 1 0 0 00	$392 1 0 0 00	$(20 0 0 0 00)
Total Liabilities and Stockholders' Equity	$430 7 0 0 00	$438 3 0 0 00	$ (7 6 0 0 00)

Note the $7,900 increase in Cash. In spite of having a $13,000 net loss for the year, Gale Corporation winds up with a positive cash flow. Let's find out how this situation came about.

Cash Flows from Operating Activities

1. **Convert Net Sales to Cash Receipts from Customers.** During 2009, Accounts Receivable decreased from $69,000 to $58,400. Evidently, $10,600 more was collected in cash than was recorded as net sales. The calculation looks like this:

Net Sales	$614,000
+ Beginning Accounts Receivable	69,000
= Total	$683,000
− Ending Accounts Receivable	58,400
= Cash Receipts from Customers	$624,600

2. **Convert Delivered Cost of Purchases to Cash Payments for Merchandise Purchases.** During 2009, Accounts Payable decreased from $39,700 to $28,600. Evidently, $11,100 more in cash was paid for merchandise purchases than the amount listed as delivered cost of purchases on the income statement. The amount of cash paid to creditors is calculated like this:

Delivered Cost of Purchases	$470,000
+ Beginning Accounts Payable	39,700
= Total	$509,700
− Ending Accounts Payable	28,600
= Cash Payments for Merchandise Purchases	$481,100

Operating and Other Expenses In preparing this section of the statement of cash flows, list each expense in its order shown on the income statement.

1. **Convert Wages Expense to Cash Payments to Employees.** During 2009, Wages Payable decreased from $2,400 to $2,100. Evidently, $300 more in cash was paid to employees than is recorded as Wages Expense. The calculation looks like this:

Wages Expense	$123,000
+ Beginning Wages Payable	2,400
= Total	$125,400
− Ending Wages Payable	2,100
= Cash Payments to Employees	$123,300

2. **Convert Rent Expense to Cash Payments for Rent.** Since the balance of the Prepaid Rent account has not changed during the year, the $20,000 recorded as Rent Expense on the income statement was paid in cash.
3. **Convert Depreciation Expense, Equipment, to Cash Payments for Depreciation.** Depreciation expense is a noncash expense, so it is eliminated.
4. **Convert Supplies Expense to Cash Payments for Supplies.** Since there is no amount included in Accounts Payable for supplies, we can conclude that the $2,000 listed as Supplies Expense on the income statement was indeed paid in cash.
5. **Convert Property Tax Expense to Cash Payments for Property Taxes.** During 2009, Property Tax Payable increased from $1,100 to $1,300. Evidently, $200 less was paid out in cash than is recorded as Property Tax Expense. The calculation looks like this:

Property Tax Expense	$2,000
+ Beginning Property Tax Payable	1,100
= Total	$3,100
− Ending Property Tax Payable	1,300
= Cash Payments for Property Taxes	$1,800

6. **Convert Insurance Expense to Cash Payments for Insurance.** During 2009, Prepaid Insurance increased from $900 to $1,000. Evidently, $100 more was paid in cash than is recorded as Insurance Expense. The calculation looks like this:

Insurance Expense
+ Ending Prepaid Insurance

= Total
− Beginning Prepaid Insurance ⟶ 90~

= Cash Payments for Insurance $1,100

7. **Convert Interest Expense to Cash Payments for Inte~**
Interest Payable increased from $0 to $600. Evidently, $600 ~
in cash than is recorded as Interest Expense on the income state~.
calculation looks like this:

Interest Expense	$26,000
+ Beginning Interest Payable	0
= Total	$26,000
− Ending Interest Payable	600
= Cash Payments for Interest	$25,400

Before we continue, we should mention that if Gale Corporation had reported income tax expense on its income statement, we would need to convert that amount using the process we've just described. The cash payments for income taxes would be listed below the cash payments for interest on the statement of cash flows.

Cash Flows from Investing Activities

1. **Record Cash Receipts from the Sale of Equipment.** During 2009, Equipment decreased from $143,000 to $114,000. On the income statement, a Gain on Disposal of Property and Equipment of $5,000 is listed in the Other Income section. In addition, the Accumulated Depreciation account increased only $12,000 even though there was $24,000 of depreciation expense. Examine the general ledger accounts and journals to reconstruct the transactions. The following entry is found in the general journal:

DATE		DESCRIPTION	POST. REF.	DEBIT	CREDIT	
2009						1
Jan.	3	Cash		22 0 0 0 00		2
		Accumulated Depreciation,				3
		Equipment		12 0 0 0 00		4
		Equipment			29 0 0 0 00	5
		Gain on Disposal of Property				6
		and Equipment			5 0 0 0 00	7
		To record the sale of				8
		equipment.				9

By reconstructing the entries, we spot the debit to Cash of $22,000. We list sale of equipment, $22,000, as a positive cash flow under Investing Activities.

Cash Flows from Financing Activities

1. **Convert Notes Payable to Cash Receipts from the Issuance of a Note.** During 2009, Notes Payable increased from $0 to $24,000. We must examine the general ledger account and journals to reconstruct the transaction(s). The following entry is found in the general journal:

GENERAL JOURNAL　　PAGE _____

	DATE		DESCRIPTION	POST. REF.	DEBIT	CREDIT	
1	2009						1
2	Oct.	2	Cash		24 0 0 0 00		2
3			Notes Payable			24 0 0 0 00	3
4			Borrowed from County Bank.				4
5			Issued 120-day, 10 percent				5
6			note dated October 2.				6

We list the issuance of the note for $24,000 as a positive cash flow under Financing Activities.

2. **Convert Common Stock to Cash Receipts from the Issuance of Common Stock.** During 2009, Common Stock increased from $297,500 to $306,500. Examine the general ledger account and journals to reconstruct the transaction(s). The following entry is found in the general journal:

GENERAL JOURNAL　　PAGE _____

	DATE		DESCRIPTION	POST. REF.	DEBIT	CREDIT	
1	2009						1
2	June	16	Cash		9 0 0 0 00		2
3			Common Stock			9 0 0 0 00	3
4			To record the sale of 900				4
5			shares of $10 par-value				5
6			common stock at par.				6

We list the sale of common stock as a positive cash flow under Financing Activities.

3. **Convert Dividends to Cash Payments of Dividends.** On the statement of retained earnings, we note $16,000 listed as cash dividends. During 2009, Dividends Payable decreased from $3,000 to $2,000. Evidently, $1,000 more was paid in cash than is recorded as cash dividends. The calculation looks like this:

Cash Dividends Declared	$16,000
+ Beginning Dividends Payable	3,000
= Total	$19,000
− Ending Dividends Payable	2,000
= Cash Payments of Dividends	$17,000

Let's put all these conversions together in the correct format to make up the statement of cash flows for Gale Corporation.

Gale Corporation
Statement of Cash Flows
For Year Ended December 31, 2009

Cash Flows from (used by) Operating Activities:					
Cash Receipts from Customers				$ 624 600 00	
Cash Payments for:					
Merchandise Purchases		$(481 100 00)			
Operating Expenses:					
Employees	$(123 300 00)				
Rent	(20 000 00)				
Supplies	(2 000 00)				
Property Taxes	(1 800 00)				
Insurance	(1 100 00)				
Total Operating Expenses		(148 200 00)			
Interest		(25 400 00)			
Total Cash Payments				(654 700 00)	
Net Cash Flows used by Operating Activities				$ (30 100 00)	
Cash Flows from (used by) Investing Activities:					
Sale of Equipment		$ 22 000 00			
Net Cash Flows from Investing Activities				22 000 00	
Cash Flows from (used by) Financing Activities:					
Issuance of Note		$ 24 000 00			
Issuance of Common Stock		9 000 00			
Payment of Dividends		(17 000 00)			
Net Cash Flows from Financing Activities				16 000 00	
Net Increase (Decrease) in Cash				$ 7 900 00	
Cash, January 1, 2009				33 400 00	
Cash, December 31, 2009				$ 41 300 00	

Summary of Conversions in Illustration 4

- **For Sale of Equipment for Cash** The amount debited to the Cash account in the journal entry for the transaction is listed as a positive amount under Cash Flows from (used by) Investing Activities.
- **For Accrued Liabilities—like Interest Expense and Interest Payable** This is figured like accrued wages:

  Amount of Interest Expense Listed on the Income Statement + Beginning Balance of Interest Payable − Ending Balance of Interest Payable

- **For Issuance of a Note** The amount debited to the Cash account in the journal entry for the transaction is listed as a positive amount under Cash Flows from (used by) Financing Activities.
- **For Issuance of Common Stock** The amount debited to the Cash account in the journal entry for the transaction is listed as a positive amount under Cash Flows from (used by) Financing Activities.
- **For Cash Dividend Payments** This is also similar to accrued wages:

  Amount Taken from the Statement of Retained Earnings Listed as Cash Dividends Declared + Beginning Balance of Dividends Payable − Ending Balance of Dividends Payable

INTERPRETING THE STATEMENT OF CASH FLOWS

Interpretation of the statement of cash flows begins with the net cash flows from operating activities. Is the net cash flow a positive amount, and how does it compare with net income on the income statement? It is useful to note the net cash flows from operating activities to see if the company is covering its cash outflows for dividends listed in the Financing Activities section. It is also useful to examine the Investing and Financing Activities sections to determine if the company is expanding and how the expansion is being financed. If the expansion is being financed primarily by long-term debt, we can be certain that, unless the expansion produces more cash revenue or a reduction in cash expenses, cash flows from operating activities will decline in the future as interest payments are made.

Anyone who uses financial statements can gather a great deal of information from the statement of cash flows. Let's take a closer look at Gale Corporation's statement of cash flows to see what we can find out.

Benefits to Users

Managers, investors, and creditors all use the statement of cash flows to judge how a company is doing. What kinds of conclusions could they draw about Gale Corporation from studying its financial statements?

Evidently, Gale Corporation is in a shaky financial position. The $7,900 increase in cash is not consistent with the $13,000 net loss. Users of the statement of cash flows are interested in the company's ability to generate enough cash to pay its bills and pay dividends.

Because of limited information, we will simply cite observations and pose questions. The negative $30,100 Net Cash Flows used by Operating Activities is bad news indeed. The $624,600 of cash receipts from customers is more than offset by the $654,700 of cash payments for operating activities. Evidently, a note payable with a principal of $24,000 was issued. However, the interest rates were quite high, resulting in an excessive amount of interest payments. Is the merchandise inventory salable? If so, can it be worked down to generate more cash? The $22,000 generated from the sale of equipment is a one-shot transaction. Will the equipment have to be replaced? If so, how will it be financed?

Although the company had a comfortable beginning credit balance of $94,600 in Retained Earnings ($81,600 after closing the net loss into Retained Earnings), the declaration and payment of cash dividends were simply not feasible under the circumstances. Actually, Gale Corporation had to borrow funds to pay its dividends. Although dividends resulted in a cash outflow of $17,000, this is well below the $25,400 cash outflow for interest payments. Despite the fact that interest payments are tax-deductible, whereas dividends are not, will Gale Corporation be better off selling stock in the future to finance expansion?

By using additional analytical tools, some interesting facts are discovered. Gale Corporation's working capital is $305,100 ($363,700 − $58,600); its current ratio is 6.21:1 ($363,700 ÷ $58,600); and its quick ratio is 1.70:1 ($99,700 ÷ $58,600). However, the firm is still not generating enough cash to pay its bills. Incidentally, the return on stockholders' equity is a dismal negative.

SCHEDULE OF NONCASH INVESTING AND FINANCING TRANSACTIONS

A company occasionally engages in significant transactions that do not affect cash directly. For example, a corporation may issue a long-term mortgage for the purchase of land and building. Or it may issue common stock for the land and building. These transactions represent important investing and financing activities, but they would not show up on a statement of cash flows because they do not involve either cash receipts or cash payments. However, since these transactions will affect future cash flows, the Financial Accounting Standards Board has determined that they should be presented in a separate schedule at the bottom of the statement of cash flows. An example of such a schedule is shown here.

Schedule of Noncash Investing and Financing Transactions					
Issue of Mortgage Payable for Building		$900	0	0	0	00

In this way, readers of the statement of cash flows will have a complete picture of a company's investing and financing activities.

CHAPTER REVIEW

Online Study Center
ACE the test!

Review of Performance Objectives

1. Describe the statement of cash flows, and define *cash* and *cash equivalents*.

   The statement of cash flows explains the changes in cash and cash equivalents between the beginning and the end of a fiscal period. Cash equivalents are short-term (mature ninety days or less from the date acquired) investments in money market accounts, U.S. Treasury bills, and commercial paper. Commercial paper consists of promissory notes issued by corporations.

2. State the purpose of the statement of cash flows.

   The statement of cash flows provides a summary of information concerning a company's cash receipts and payments during a fiscal period. A secondary purpose is to provide information about a firm's investing and financing activities during a fiscal period.

3. State the uses of the statement of cash flows by management, investors, and creditors.

   The statement of cash flows is useful to management, and also to investors and creditors, in assessing or evaluating the liquidity of a business, including the ability of the business to generate future cash flows and to pay its debts and dividends.

4. Identify cash inflows and outflows as operating, investing, or financing activities.

Cash flows are classified as operating activities, investing activities, or financing activities. Operating activities include the cash effects of transactions that enter into the determination of net income. Investing activities include cash flows involving the making and collecting of loans, the buying and selling of investments, and the buying and selling of property and equipment. Financing activities include cash flows involving the selling or retiring of bonds, the issuing or paying of notes, the issuing of stock, and payments of personal withdrawals or dividends.

5. Calculate amounts of cash inflows and outflows involving operating, investing, and financing activities.

To calculate cash flows from operating activities:

- Cash Receipts from Customers

  Net Sales + Beginning Accounts Receivable − Ending Accounts Receivable

- Cash Payments for Merchandise Purchases

Delivered Cost of Purchases + Beginning Accounts Payable − Ending Accounts Payable

To determine cash payments for operating expenses:

- Cash Payments to Employees

  Wages Expense + Beginning Wages Payable − Ending Wages Payable

- Cash Payments for Prepaid Expenses (e.g., Prepaid Insurance)

  Insurance Expense + Ending Prepaid Insurance − Beginning Prepaid Insurance

- Cash Payments for Interest

  Interest Expense + Beginning Interest Payable − Ending Interest Payable

- Cash Payments for Income Taxes

Income Tax Expense + Beginning Income Tax Payable − Ending Income Tax Payable

- Depreciation

  Depreciation Expense does not require an outlay of cash—it is eliminated.

To calculate cash flows from investing activities or financing activities:

Changes in the balances of property and equipment, investments, long-term liabilities, and owner's or stockholders' equity accounts may indicate possible cash inflows or outflows. The amounts of cash involved are determined by exposing the related journal entries.

- Cash Payments of Dividends

Cash Dividends Declared + Beginning Dividends Payable − Ending Dividends Payable

6. Prepare a statement of cash flows using the direct method.

   Preparing the statement of cash flows involves converting a company's financial statements from an accrual to a cash basis. Starting with a company's balance sheet at the beginning and end of the accounting period, along with the income statement and statement of owner's equity or retained earnings for the period ended, we compile a comparative balance sheet listing the increases and decreases in all accounts. Then we convert changes in account balances to cash flows using the calculations presented in the chapter.

Glossary

Cash equivalents Items included in the broad definition of cash. Included are short-term, highly liquid investments, such as money market accounts, U.S. Treasury bills, and commercial paper, having maturities with a maximum of ninety days from the date acquired. (853)

Financing activities A category on the statement of cash flows (involving inflows and outflows) that includes borrowing money or repaying loans and additional cash investments or reductions of owners' investments through cash dividends or personal withdrawals. (856)

Investing activities A category on the statement of cash flows (involving inflows and outflows) that includes the buying and selling of property and equipment, the acquiring and selling of investments other than cash equivalents, and the making and collecting of loans. (856)

Operating activities A category on the statement of cash flows (involving inflows and outflows) that includes cash receipts from customers for the sale of merchandise and services, cash receipts from interest and dividends, cash payments for merchandise purchases, cash payments for operating expenses, cash payments for interest, and cash payments for income taxes. (855)

Statement of cash flows A financial statement that explains in detail how the balance of cash and cash equivalents has changed between the beginning and the end of a fiscal period. A schedule on the statement presents important noncash investing and financing activities that occurred during the same period. (853)

QUESTIONS, EXERCISES, AND CASES

Discussion Questions

1. What are the three categories listed on the statement of cash flows? Give two examples of each category.
2. What is included in *cash* as the term is used on a statement of cash flows?
3. What are the purposes of the statement of cash flows?
4. What are the effects of the following items on cash flows from operating activities?
   a. an increase in Accounts Receivable, $15,000
   b. an increase in Interest Payable, $400
   c. Depreciation Expense, Equipment, $92,000

5. In which of the three categories listed on a statement of cash flows would each of the following appear? Also, state for each item whether it represents a cash inflow or outflow.
   a. Cash purchase of land
   b. Cash payment of wages
   c. Cash payment of dividends
   d. Cash sale of investments
   e. Cash proceeds from issuing stock
   f. Cash payment of interest

6. Kelley Company sold equipment at a gain of $1,000. The equipment cost $47,000 and had accumulated depreciation of $40,000. Describe how this event is handled in the statement of cash flows.

7. As a means of gaining a greater return on its cash balance, Viking Company transferred $20,000 from its checking account to a money market account, purchased an $11,000 three-month U.S. Treasury bill, and bought $13,000 of another company's stock. How will each of these transactions affect the statement of cash flows?

8. Victors, Inc., has a net loss of $110,000 for the fiscal year but a positive cash flow of $10,000. What are some conditions that might have caused this situation?

Exercises

P.O. 4

Classify operating, investing, and financing activities.

Exercise 23-1 C. Wickman, Inc., had the following transactions during the year. Classify each transaction as (O) an Operating activity, (I) an Investing activity, (F) a Financing activity, or (X) a noncash transaction. Also note each transaction as a plus (+) for inflow, a minus (−) for outflow, or zero (0) if neither inflow nor outflow.

1. Paid $9,000 for rent.
2. Purchased a bond for $10,000.
3. Paid $3,000 interest.
4. Sold equipment for $5,000.
5. Repaid the principal of a mortgage of $24,000.
6. Received cash from customers of $73,000.
7. Paid $4,000 of federal income taxes.
8. Paid $7,800 for computer equipment.
9. Extended a customer's note of $1,600.

P.O. 5

Determine cash payments for insurance.

Exercise 23-2 The income statement of Shroud, Inc., for 2008 includes Insurance Expense of $12,280. The beginning balance of Prepaid Insurance amounted to $5,410, and the ending balance of Prepaid Insurance amounted to $6,420. Determine the cash payments for insurance by Shroud, Inc., for the year 2008.

P.O. 5

Determine cash receipts from customers.

Exercise 23-3 During 2008, Masters Company had net sales of $450,000. During the same year, the beginning balance of Accounts Receivable was $96,400, and the ending balance of Accounts Receivable was $92,680. Determine the amount of cash receipts from customers during the year 2008.

P.O. 5

Determine cash payments for merchandise purchases.

Exercise 23-4 During 2008, Paydar Optical had Delivered Cost of Purchases of $217,000. The beginning balance of Accounts Payable (trade) amounted to $62,000, and the ending balance of Accounts Payable (trade) amounted to $66,500. Determine the cash payments for merchandise purchases for 2008.

P.O. 5

Determine cash payments for income taxes.

Exercise 23-5 Income Tax Expense for Logger Corporation was $83,100 for the year 2008. During the year, the beginning balance of Income Tax Payable was $5,600, and the ending balance of Income Tax Payable was $12,400. Determine the amount of cash payments for income taxes during 2008.

P.O. 5

Determine the cash payments for operating expenses.

Exercise 23-6 During 2008, Watani and Company had operating expenses of $196,300, including depreciation on equipment of $45,800. Also during 2008, the beginning balance of Prepaid Insurance was $5,130, and the ending balance of Prepaid Insurance was $5,980. The beginning balance of Wages Payable was $2,630, and the ending balance of Wages Payable was $2,250. Assume that operating expenses consisted only of Depreciation Expense, Equipment; Insurance Expense; and Wages Expense. Determine the total cash payments for operating expenses during the year 2008.

P.O. 4,5

Determine how transactions are to be recorded on the statement of cash flows.

Exercise 23-7 All transactions involving Notes Payable and Interest Payable for Nishke Company during the year 2008 are presented in the general journal.

GENERAL JOURNAL   PAGE _____

	DATE		DESCRIPTION	POST. REF.	DEBIT	CREDIT	
1	2008		Reversing Entry				1
2	Jan.	1	Interest Payable		6 6 0 00		2
3			Interest Expense			6 6 0 00	3
4							4
5	Feb.	3	Notes Payable		28 0 5 0 00		5
6			Interest Expense		2 2 5 5 00		6
7			Cash			30 3 0 5 00	7
8			Repayment of note at				8
9			maturity.				9
10							10
11	Dec.	1	Cash		19 2 5 0 00		11
12			Notes Payable			19 2 5 0 00	12
13			Bank loan, receiving the full				13
14			principal.				14
15							15
16			Adjusting Entry				16
17		31	Interest Expense		4 1 2 50		17
18			Interest Payable			4 1 2 50	18

Determine the amounts and describe how these transactions are to be recorded on the statement of cash flows.

P.O. 5,6

Compute amounts to be included in the statement of cash flows and indicate where they should be shown.

Exercise 23-8 On page 880 are the T accounts for Equipment; Accumulated Depreciation, Equipment; and Loss on Disposal of Property and Equipment for Roley Company at the end of 2008.

Equipment			
	+	−	
Beg. Balance	75,600	Disposal	16,200
Purchases	24,300		
End. Balance	83,700		

Accumulated Depreciation, Equipment			
−		+	
Disposal	8,100	Beg. Balance	55,800
		Adjusting	12,600
		End. Balance	60,300

**Loss on Disposal of
Property and Equipment**

	+	−
Disposal	5,400	

New equipment was bought for cash, and the used equipment was sold for cash. Compute the amounts to be included on the statement of cash flows, and indicate where these amounts should be shown.

internet
LINKS TO ACCOUNTING

Now that you have a better understanding of the statement of cash flows and how it is prepared using the direct method, let's take another look at the 2005 and 2004 financial information for Skechers USA, Inc. Go to **http://www.sec.gov**, select Search for Company Filings, and then, under General-Purpose Searches, click on Companies & Other Filers. In the Company Name box, type Skechers. In the list of forms, select the 10-K that was filed on 2006-03-16. The statement of cash flows is on page 46 of the 10-K report.

1. Does Skechers use the direct method for its statement of cash flows? How can you tell?
2. What were Skechers USA, Inc.'s net income (net earnings) amounts reported for 2005 and 2004?
3. What were Skechers USA, Inc.'s net cash flows from operating activities, investing activities, and financing activities for 2005 and 2004? What are the main reasons for any significant differences in those three categories between the two years?

CONSIDER AND COMMUNICATE

Your manager feels strongly that all he needs from the accountant are the income statement, statement of owner's equity, and balance sheet. He does not want to pay the additional fees for preparation of a statement of cash flows. Explain to your manager why this additional statement is important.

WHAT'S WRONG WITH THIS PICTURE?

The new accountant can't understand why there is a need for a statement of cash flows. She says that a comparative balance sheet will show the change in the Cash account, and that that should be enough information. What is your response to this opinion?

CRITICAL THINKING

On page 882 is a partially completed statement of cash flows for Cedrel Company. Selected line amounts have been left out because the accounting intern was not sure what to do. Fill in the missing amounts. The following information may be helpful:

Cash Receipts from Customers	
Net Sales	$656,780
Beginning Accounts Receivable	45,820
Ending Accounts Receivable	49,000

Insurance	
Beginning Prepaid Insurance	$ 400
Ending Prepaid Insurance	1,600
Insurance Expense	320

Property Taxes	
Beginning Property Tax Payable	$ 545
Ending Property Tax Payable	850
Property Tax Expense	1,540

Employees	
Beginning Salaries Payable	$ 3,010
Ending Salaries Payable	2,890
Salary Expense	94,500

Cedrel Company
Statement of Cash Flows
For Year Ended December 31, 2007

Cash Flows from (used by) Operating Activities:			
Cash Receipts from Customers			
Cash Payments for:			
Merchandise Purchases		$492 575 00	
Operating Expenses:			
Employees			
Rent	19 000 00		
Property Taxes			
Insurance			
Total Operating Expenses			
Total Cash Payments			608 950 00
Net Cash Flows from Operating Activities			$ 44 650 00
Cash Flows from (used by) Financing Activities:			
Payment of Personal Withdrawals		$ (47 500 00)	
Net Cash Flows used by Financing Activities			(47 500 00)
Net Increase (Decrease) in Cash			$ (2 850 00)
Cash, January 1, 2007			38 600 00
Cash, December 31, 2007			$ 35 750 00

PROBLEM SET A

For additional help, see the demonstration problem at the beginning of each chapter in your Working Papers.

P.O. 6

Problem 23-1A The financial statements of Bubar Realty are presented below and on the following page.

Bubar Realty
Income Statement
For Year Ended December 31, 2008

Revenue:			
Income from Services			$96 107 00
Expenses:			
Commissions Expense	$27 864 00		
Advertising Expense	7 560 00		
Repairs Expense	1 688 00		
Rent Expense	4 860 00		
Telephone Expense	1 242 00		
Depreciation Expense, Automobile	3 078 00		
Depreciation Expense, Office Equipment	1 647 00		
Insurance Expense	5 54 00		
Utilities Expense	2 201 00		
Total Expenses		50 694 00	
Net Income		$45 413 00	

Bubar Realty
Statement of Owner's Equity
For Year Ended December 31, 2008

F. N. Bubar, Capital, January 1, 2008			$30 9 1 5 00
Net Income	$45 4 1 3 00		
Less Withdrawals	40 5 0 0 00		
Increase in Capital			4 9 1 3 00
F. N. Bubar, Capital, December 31, 2008			$35 8 2 8 00

Bubar Realty
Comparative Balance Sheet
December 31, 2008 and December 31, 2007

	2008	2007	INCREASE OR (DECREASE)
Assets			
Cash	$22 8 9 6 00	$13 8 9 2 00	$9 0 0 4 00
Prepaid Rent	1 2 1 5 00	4 0 5 00	8 1 0 00
Prepaid Insurance	8 3 7 00	1 0 1 3 00	(1 7 6 00)
Automobile	15 3 9 0 00	15 3 9 0 00	0 00
Less Accumulated Depreciation	(6 1 5 6 00)	(3 0 7 8 00)	(3 0 7 8 00)
Office Equipment	8 2 3 5 00	8 2 3 5 00	0 00
Less Accumulated Depreciation	(6 5 8 9 00)	(4 9 4 2 00)	(1 6 4 7 00)
Total Assets	$35 8 2 8 00	$30 9 1 5 00	$4 9 1 3 00
Owner's Equity			
F. N. Bubar, Capital	$35 8 2 8 00	$30 9 1 5 00	$4 9 1 3 00
Total Liabilities and Owner's Equity	$35 8 2 8 00	$30 9 1 5 00	$4 9 1 3 00

Check Figure

Net Increase in Cash, $9,004

Instructions

Prepare a statement of cash flows for the year 2008.

P.O. 6

Problem 23-2A Sanchez Van and Storage's financial statements for the current year are presented on page 884.

Check Figure

Net Increase in Cash, $31,428

Instructions

Prepare a statement of cash flows for the year 2008.

Sanchez Van and Storage
Income Statement
For Year Ended December 31, 2008

Revenue:														
Revenue from Moving Services	$149	7	6	0	00									
Revenue from Storage Rentals	87	2	6	4	00									
Total Revenue							$237	0	2	4	00			
Expenses:														
Wages Expense	$140	5	2	0	00									
Truck Repair Expense	5	5	6	8	00									
Gas and Oil Expense	4	3	5	6	00									
Insurance Expense	3	4	2	0	00									
Supplies Expense	1	4	8	8	00									
Depreciation Expense, Building	11	5	4	4	00									
Depreciation Expense, Trucks	22	5	6	0	00									
Interest Expense	12	1	2	0	00									
Total Expenses							201	5	7	6	00			
Net Income							$ 35	4	4	8	00			

Sanchez Van and Storage
Statement of Owner's Equity
For Year Ended December 31, 2008

G. A. Sanchez, Capital, January 1, 2008						$273	6	4	8	00
Net Income	$35	4	4	8	00					
Less Withdrawals	32	4	0	0	00					
Increase in Capital						3	0	4	8	00
G. A. Sanchez, Capital, December 31, 2008						$276	6	9	6	00

Sanchez Van and Storage
Comparative Balance Sheet
December 31, 2008 and December 31, 2007

	2008					2007					INCREASE OR (DECREASE)				
Assets															
Cash	$ 44	1	6	0	00	$ 12	7	3	2	00	$31	4	2	8	00
Prepaid Insurance	4	5	7	2	00	1	4	8	8	00	3	0	8	4	00
Land	38	6	4	0	00	38	6	4	0	00				0	00
Building	376	8	0	0	00	376	8	0	0	00				0	00
Less Accumulated Depreciation	(130	5	6	0	00)	(119	0	1	6	00)	(11	5	4	4	00)
Trucks	112	8	0	0	00	112	8	0	0	00				0	00
Less Accumulated Depreciation	(45	1	2	0	00)	(22	5	6	0	00)	(22	5	6	0	00)
Total Assets	$401	2	9	2	00	$ 400	8	8	4	00	$	4	0	8	00
Liabilities															
Mortgage Payable	$124	5	9	6	00	$ 127	2	3	6	00	$ (2	6	4	0	00)
Owner's Equity															
G. A. Sanchez, Capital	276	6	9	6	00	273	6	4	8	00	3	0	4	8	00
Total Liabilities and Owner's Equity	$401	2	9	2	00	$ 400	8	8	4	00	$	4	0	8	00

P.O. 6

Problem 23-3A Financial statements for Will's Marine Sales are presented below and on page 886.

Will's Marine Sales
Income Statement
For Year Ended December 31, 2008

Revenue from Sales:								
Net Sales					$891	1	2	0	00
Cost of Goods Sold:								
Merchandise Inventory, Jan. 1, 2008	$160	4	0	4	00			
Delivered Cost of Purchases	654	3	3	6	00			
Cost of Goods Available for Sale	$814	7	4	0	00			
Less Merchandise Inventory,								
December 31, 2008	165	3	0	0	00			
Cost of Goods Sold						649	4	4	0	00
Gross Profit						$241	6	8	0	00
Operating Expenses:								
Salary Expense	$131	8	5	6	00			
Rent Expense	28	8	0	0	00			
Depreciation Expense, Equipment	35	5	2	0	00			
Supplies Expense	3	3	0	0	00			
Insurance Expense	1	4	4	0	00			
Total Operating Expenses						200	9	1	6	00
Net Income						$ 40	7	6	4	00

Will's Marine Sales
Statement of Owner's Equity
For Year Ended December 31, 2008

W. A. Mack, Capital, January 1, 2008						$296	6	0	4	00
Net Income	$40	7	6	4	00				
Less Withdrawals	48	0	0	0	00				
Decrease in Capital						(7	2	3	6	00)
W. A. Mack, Capital, December 31, 2008						$289	3	6	8	00

Will's Marine Sales
Comparative Balance Sheet
December 31, 2008 and December 31, 2007

	2008	2007	INCREASE OR (DECREASE)
Assets			
Cash	$ 45 1 6 8 00	$ 46 0 9 2 00	$ (9 2 4 00)
Accounts Receivable	61 3 5 6 00	50 5 9 2 00	10 7 6 4 00
Merchandise Inventory	165 3 0 0 00	160 4 0 4 00	4 8 9 6 00
Prepaid Insurance	2 6 0 4 00	1 8 2 4 00	7 8 0 00
Equipment	185 8 8 0 00	185 8 8 0 00	0 00
Less Accumulated Depreciation	(142 0 8 0 00)	(106 5 6 0 00)	(35 5 2 0 00)
Total Assets	$318 2 2 8 00	$338 2 3 2 00	$ (20 0 0 4 00)
Liabilities			
Accounts Payable	$ 24 6 7 2 00	$ 38 3 4 0 00	$ (13 6 6 8 00)
Salaries Payable	4 1 8 8 00	3 2 8 8 00	9 0 0 00
Total Liabilities	$ 28 8 6 0 00	$ 41 6 2 8 00	$ (12 7 6 8 00)
Owner's Equity			
W. A. Mack, Capital	289 3 6 8 00	296 6 0 4 00	(7 2 3 6 00)
Total Liabilities and Owner's Equity	$318 2 2 8 00	$338 2 3 2 00	$ (20 0 0 4 00)

Check Figure

Net (Decrease) in Cash, ($924)

P.O. 6

Instructions

Prepare a statement of cash flows for the year 2008.

Problem 23-4A Financial statements for Mariano Corporation are presented on pages 887 and 888.

Additional information contained in the records revealed that equipment, having a cost of $37,600 and accumulated depreciation of $28,480, was sold for $14,400 cash. Also, 3,760 shares of common stock having a par value of $10 per share were sold for $43,200 cash.

Mariano Corporation
Income Statement
For Year Ended December 31, 2008

Revenue from Sales:				
Sales		$709 5 1 2 00		
Less Sales Returns and Allowances		8 6 2 4 00		
Net Sales			$700 8 8 8 00	
Cost of Goods Sold:				
Merchandise Inventory, January 1, 2008		$282 0 9 6 00		
Delivered Cost of Purchases		500 6 0 8 00		
Cost of Goods Available for Sale		$782 7 0 4 00		
Less Merchandise Inventory, December 31, 2008		300 0 7 2 00		
Cost of Goods Sold			482 6 3 2 00	
Gross Profit			$218 2 5 6 00	
Operating Expenses:				
Salary Expense		$ 81 9 9 2 00		
Rent Expense		14 4 0 0 00		
Advertising Expense		5 1 2 0 00		
Depreciation Expense, Equipment		17 7 2 8 00		
Insurance Expense		2 1 6 8 00		
Miscellaneous Expense		7 3 6 00		
Total Operating Expenses			122 1 4 4 00	
Income from Operations			$ 96 1 1 2 00	
Other Income:				
Interest Income	$ 3 7 6 00			
Gain on Disposal of Property and Equipment	5 2 8 0 00			
Total Other Income		$ 5 6 5 6 00		
Other Expenses:				
Interest Expense		2 5 6 00	5 4 0 0 00	
Income Before Income Taxes			$101 5 1 2 00	
Income Tax Expense			30 9 3 6 00	
Net Income			$ 70 5 7 6 00	

Mariano Corporation
Statement of Retained Earnings
For Year Ended December 31, 2008

Retained Earnings, January 1, 2008		$ 82 7 9 2 00
Net Income	$70 5 7 6 00	
Less Cash Dividends Declared	42 4 0 0 00	
Increase in Retained Earnings		28 1 7 6 00
Retained Earnings, December 31, 2008		$110 9 6 8 00

Mariano Corporation
Comparative Balance Sheet
December 31, 2008 and December 31, 2007

	2008	2007	INCREASE OR (DECREASE)
Assets			
Cash	$ 19 840 00	$ 5 392 00	$ 14 448 00
Notes Receivable	0 00	2 296 00	(2 296 00)
Accounts Receivable	70 936 00	50 888 00	20 048 00
Merchandise Inventory	300 072 00	282 096 00	17 976 00
Prepaid Advertising	992 00	768 00	224 00
Prepaid Insurance	344 00	168 00	176 00
Equipment	176 296 00	213 896 00	(37 600 00)
Less Accumulated Depreciation	(62 024 00)	(72 776 00)	10 752 00
Total Assets	$506 456 00	$482 728 00	$ 23 728 00
Liabilities			
Notes Payable	$ 2 080 00	$ 7 360 00	$ (5 280 00)
Accounts Payable	22 584 00	63 456 00	(40 872 00)
Salaries Payable	1 760 00	2 320 00	(560 00)
Income Tax Payable	3 864 00	4 208 00	(344 00)
Dividends Payable	3 160 00	3 576 00	(416 00)
Interest Payable	32 00	208 00	(176 00)
Total Liabilities	$ 33 480 00	$ 81 128 00	$(47 648 00)
Stockholders' Equity			
Common Stock	$343 608 00	$306 008 00	$ 37 600 00
Paid-in Capital in Excess of Par Value	18 400 00	12 800 00	5 600 00
Retained Earnings	110 968 00	82 792 00	28 176 00
Total Stockholders' Equity	$472 976 00	$401 600 00	$ 71 376 00
Total Liabilities and Stockholders' Equity	$506 456 00	$482 728 00	$ 23 728 00

Check Figure

Net Increase in Cash, $14,448

Instructions

Prepare a statement of cash flows for the year 2008.

PROBLEM SET B

For additional help, see the demonstration problem at the beginning of each chapter in your Working Papers.

P.O. 6

Problem 23-1B The financial statements of Razo and Company are presented on the following page.

Razo and Company
Income Statement
For Year Ended December 31, 2008

Revenue:		
Income from Services		$82 7 0 7 00
Expenses:		
Wages Expense	$38 2 3 3 00	
Rent Expense	7 8 0 00	
Advertising Expense	5 4 6 00	
Utilities Expense	9 9 3 00	
Depreciation Expense, Equipment	10 6 7 3 00	
Supplies Expense	6 1 1 00	
Insurance Expense	3 1 2 00	
Miscellaneous Expense	4 1 9 00	
Total Expenses		52 5 6 7 00
Net Income		$30 1 4 0 00

Razo and Company
Statement of Owner's Equity
For Year Ended December 31, 2008

J. Z. Razo, Capital, January 1, 2008		$84 5 2 3 00
Net Income	$30 1 4 0 00	
Less Withdrawals	46 8 0 0 00	
Decrease in Capital		(16 6 6 0 00)
J. Z. Razo, Capital, December 31, 2008		$67 8 6 3 00

Razo and Company
Comparative Balance Sheet
December 31, 2008 and December 31, 2007

	2008	2007	INCREASE OR (DECREASE)
Assets			
Cash	$ 8 8 3 5 00	$14 9 7 2 00	$ (6 1 3 7 00)
Prepaid Insurance	8 2 7 00	6 7 7 00	1 5 0 00
Equipment	90 2 2 0 00	90 2 2 0 00	0 00
Less Accumulated Depreciation	(32 0 1 9 00)	(21 3 4 6 00)	(10 6 7 3 00)
Total Assets	$67 8 6 3 00	$84 5 2 3 00	$(16 6 6 0 00)
Owner's Equity			
J. Z. Razo, Capital	$67 8 6 3 00	$84 5 2 3 00	$(16 6 6 0 00)
Total Liabilities and Owner's Equity	$67 8 6 3 00	$84 5 2 3 00	$(16 6 6 0 00)

Check Figure

Net (Decrease) in Cash, ($6,137)

P.O. 6

Instructions

Prepare a statement of cash flows for the year 2008.

Problem 23-2B Hairlines Beauty Salon uses the cash basis. The financial statements for Hairlines Beauty Salon are shown on page 890.

Hairlines Beauty Salon
Income Statement
For Year Ended December 31, 2008

Revenue:			
Income from Services			$111 2 7 4 00
Expenses:			
Salary Expense	$62 1 5 0 00		
Rent Expense	11 4 0 0 00		
Supplies Expense	2 0 8 1 00		
Insurance Expense	4 3 7 00		
Utilities Expense	1 5 9 6 00		
Depreciation Expense, Equipment	1 8 2 4 00		
Depreciation Expense, Furniture	7 8 9 00		
Interest Expense	3 5 2 00		
Miscellaneous Expense	1 0 5 00		
Total Expenses			80 7 3 4 00
Net Income			$ 30 5 4 0 00

Hairlines Beauty Salon
Statement of Owner's Equity
For Year Ended December 31, 2008

C. L. Herron, Capital, January 1, 2008		$20 0 6 4 00
Net Income	$30 5 4 0 00	
Less Withdrawals	35 3 4 0 00	
Decrease in Capital		(4 8 0 0 00)
C. L. Herron, Capital, December 31, 2008		$15 2 6 4 00

Hairlines Beauty Salon
Comparative Balance Sheet
December 31, 2008 and December 31, 2007

	2008	2007	INCREASE OR (DECREASE)
Assets			
Cash	$ 9 1 9 5 00	$13 0 8 2 00	$(3 8 8 7 00)
Prepaid Insurance	1 4 2 5 00	1 0 5 5 00	3 7 0 00
Equipment	9 1 2 0 00	9 1 2 0 00	0 00
Less Accumulated Depreciation	(5 4 7 1 00)	(3 6 4 7 00)	(1 8 2 4 00)
Furniture	5 5 4 8 00	5 5 4 8 00	0 00
Less Accumulated Depreciation	(2 3 6 8 00)	(1 5 7 9 00)	(7 8 9 00)
Total Assets	$17 4 4 9 00	$23 5 7 9 00	$(6 1 3 0 00)
Liabilities			
Notes Payable	$ 2 1 8 5 00	$ 3 5 1 5 00	$(1 3 3 0 00)
Owner's Equity			
C. L. Herron, Capital	15 2 6 4 00	20 0 6 4 00	(4 8 0 0 00)
Total Liabilities and Owner's Equity	$17 4 4 9 00	$23 5 7 9 00	$(6 1 3 0 00)

Check Figure

Net (Decrease) in Cash, ($3,887)

P.O. 6

Instructions

Prepare a statement of cash flows for the year 2008.

Problem 23-3B Financial statements for Rowe Fine Clothes are presented below and on page 892.

Rowe Fine Clothes
Income Statement
For Year Ended December 31, 2008

Revenue from Sales:			
Net Sales			$769 1 4 0 00
Cost of Goods Sold:			
Merchandise Inventory, Jan. 1, 2008	$146 3 1 3 00		
Delivered Cost of Purchases	552 7 0 8 00		
Cost of Goods Available for Sale	$699 0 2 1 00		
Less Merchandise Inventory,			
December 31, 2008	110 3 8 5 00		
Cost of Goods Sold		588 6 3 6 00	
Gross Profit		$180 5 0 4 00	
Operating Expenses:			
Salary Expense	$124 1 5 5 00		
Rent Expense	24 3 0 0 00		
Depreciation Expense, Equipment	28 0 2 6 00		
Supplies Expense	2 8 8 9 00		
Insurance Expense	1 3 5 0 00		
Miscellaneous Expense	6 4 8 00		
Total Operating Expenses		181 3 6 8 00	
Net Loss		$ (8 6 4 00)	

Rowe Fine Clothes
Statement of Owner's Equity
For Year Ended December 31, 2008

A. S. Rowe, Capital, January 1, 2008		$262 9 2 6 00
Less: Net Loss	$ 8 6 4 00	
Withdrawals	13 5 0 0 00	
Decrease in Capital		(14 3 6 4 00)
A. S. Rowe, Capital, December 31, 2008		$248 5 6 2 00

Rowe Fine Clothes
Comparative Balance Sheet
December 31, 2008 and December 31, 2007

	2008	2007	INCREASE OR (DECREASE)
Assets			
Cash	$ 39 393 00	$ 28 404 00	$ 10 989 00
Accounts Receivable	56 556 00	43 011 00	13 545 00
Merchandise Inventory	110 385 00	146 313 00	(35 928 00)
Prepaid Insurance	2 799 00	1 341 00	1 458 00
Equipment	164 034 00	164 034 00	0 00
Less Accumulated Depreciation	(84 078 00)	(56 052 00)	(28 026 00)
Total Assets	$289 089 00	$327 051 00	$(37 962 00)
Liabilities			
Accounts Payable	$ 37 872 00	$ 61 101 00	$(23 229 00)
Salaries Payable	2 655 00	3 024 00	(369 00)
Total Liabilities	$ 40 527 00	$ 64 125 00	$(23 598 00)
Owner's Equity			
A. S. Rowe, Capital	248 562 00	262 926 00	(14 364 00)
Total Liabilities and Owner's Equity	$289 089 00	$327 051 00	$(37 962 00)

Check Figure

Net Increase in Cash, $10,989

P.O. 6

Instructions

Prepare a statement of cash flows for the year 2008.

Problem 23-4B Lee Corporation's financial statements are presented on pages 893 and 894.

    Additional information contained in the records revealed that equipment, having a cost of $52,500 and accumulated depreciation of $46,200, was sold for $12,842 cash. Also, 5,250 shares of common stock having a par value of $10 per share were sold for $63,000.

Lee Corporation
Income Statement
For Year Ended December 31, 2008

Revenue from Sales:															
Sales	$1	043	9	7	3	00									
Less Sales Returns and Allowances		12	7	2	6	00									
Net Sales							$1	031	2	4	7	00			
Cost of Goods Sold:															
Merchandise Inventory, Jan. 1, 2008	$	416	5	3	5	00									
Delivered Cost of Purchases		738	2	5	5	00									
Cost of Goods Available for Sale	$1	154	7	9	0	00									
Less Merchandise Inventory,															
December 31, 2008		442	5	2	3	00									
Cost of Goods Sold								712	2	6	7	00			
Gross Profit							$	318	9	8	0	00			
Operating Expenses:															
Wages Expense	$	132	7	2	0	00									
Rent Expense		21	0	0	0	00									
Depreciation Expense, Equipment		27	3	0	0	00									
Supplies Expense		3	0	9	8	00									
Insurance Expense		1	2	6	0	00									
Total Operating Expenses								185	3	7	8	00			
Income from Operations							$	133	6	0	2	00			
Other Income:															
Gain on Disposal of Property and															
Equipment	$		6	5	4	2	00								
Other Expenses:															
Interest Expense			8	3	0	00			5	7	1	2	00		
Income Before Income Taxes							$	139	3	1	4	00			
Income Tax Expense								47	3	6	7	00			
Net Income							$	91	9	4	7	00			

Lee Corporation
Statement of Retained Earnings
For Year Ended December 31, 2008

Retained Earnings, January 1, 2008						$122	1	0	5	00
Net Income	$91	9	4	7	00					
Less Cash Dividends Declared and Paid	63	0	0	0	00					
Increase in Retained Earnings						28	9	4	7	00
Retained Earnings, December 31, 2008						$151	0	5	2	00

Lee Corporation
Comparative Balance Sheet
December 31, 2008 and December 31, 2007

	2008	2007	INCREASE OR (DECREASE)
Assets			
Cash	$ 38 7 6 5 00	$ 11 4 9 8 00	$ 27 2 6 7 00
Accounts Receivable	104 6 2 2 00	77 3 9 6 00	27 2 2 6 00
Merchandise Inventory	442 5 2 3 00	416 5 3 5 00	25 9 8 8 00
Prepaid Rent	6 3 0 0 00	6 3 0 0 00	0 00
Prepaid Insurance	1 3 8 6 00	1 3 5 5 00	3 1 00
Equipment	263 5 2 9 00	316 0 2 9 00	(52 5 0 0 00)
Less Accumulated Depreciation	(93 1 3 5 00)	(112 0 3 5 00)	18 9 0 0 00
Total Assets	$763 9 9 0 00	$717 0 7 8 00	$ 46 9 1 2 00
Liabilities			
Notes Payable	$ 10 9 2 0 00	$ 25 4 1 0 00	$(14 4 9 0 00)
Accounts Payable	33 3 0 6 00	62 6 2 2 00	(29 3 1 6 00)
Wages Payable	1 0 9 2 00	2 0 9 0 00	(9 9 8 00)
Income Tax Payable	11 8 4 4 00	10 9 8 3 00	8 6 1 00
Dividends Payable	12 6 0 0 00	12 6 0 0 00	0 00
Interest Payable	1 2 6 00	1 2 1 8 00	(1 0 9 2 00)
Total Liabilities	$ 69 8 8 8 00	$114 9 2 3 00	$(45 0 3 5 00)
Stockholders' Equity			
Common Stock	$532 5 5 0 00	$480 0 5 0 00	$ 52 5 0 0 00
Paid-in Capital in Excess of Par Value	10 5 0 0 00	0 00	10 5 0 0 00
Retained Earnings	151 0 5 2 00	122 1 0 5 00	28 9 4 7 00
Total Stockholders' Equity	$694 1 0 2 00	$602 1 5 5 00	$ 91 9 4 7 00
Total Liabilities and Stockholders' Equity	$763 9 9 0 00	$717 0 7 8 00	$ 46 9 1 2 00

Check Figure

Net Increase in Cash, $27,267

Instructions

Prepare a statement of cash flows for the year 2008.

Statement of Cash Flows—Indirect Method

Performance Objectives

1. Classify cash flows as operating, investing, and financing activities.

2. Prepare a comparative balance sheet for a business over a two-year period.

3. Convert the effects of the changes in balance sheet accounts into increases or decreases in cash flows.

4. Prepare a statement of cash flows.

The purpose of the statement of cash flows (alias "where got, where gone" statement of cash) is to convert an income statement for a business from an accrual basis to a cash basis. Two methods are available. Under the direct method, which was presented in Chapter 23, each item in a firm's income statement is adjusted from the accrual basis to the cash basis. The indirect method, on the other hand, lists only the adjustments necessary to convert net income to cash flows from operations as determined by changes in balance sheet accounts (assets, liabilities, and capital).

Both methods are presently in use. Many accountants prefer the indirect method because it is easier to organize and less expensive to prepare. Of course, under both methods, the amount of increase or decrease in cash over a two-year period should be the same.

GUIDELINES FOR CONVERSION

Each method uses the same three classifications: operating activities, investing activities, and financing activities. Remember that under the accrual system, income is counted when it is earned, *not* when cash is received. The same holds true for expenses. To convert from the accrual to the cash basis, we must add to or deduct from net income to get to the correct amount for cash. Here are the guidelines for converting an income statement from the accrual basis (revenue minus expenses) to the amount of cash actually received or paid out.

From the Income Statement

Net income is treated as an addition to cash flows.
Net loss is treated as a deduction from cash flows.

Depreciation expense is treated as an addition to cash flows.

Gain on disposal of property and equipment is treated as a deduction from cash flows.

Loss on disposal of property and equipment is treated as an addition to cash flows.

From the Balance Sheet

When converting net income derived on the accrual basis to net income derived on the cash basis and calculating cash flows from investing and financing activities, we must consider changes in the balance sheet accounts.

Current Assets

Accounts Receivable (net)	Increase—Deduction from Net Income
Accounts Receivable (net)	Decrease—Addition to Net Income
Merchandise Inventory	Increase—Deduction from Net Income
Merchandise Inventory	Decrease—Addition to Net Income
Prepaid Expenses	Increase—Deduction from Net Income
Prepaid Expenses	Decrease—Addition to Net Income

Current Liabilities

Accounts Payable	Increase—Addition to Net Income
Accounts Payable	Decrease—Deduction from Net Income
Income Tax Payable	Increase—Addition to Net Income
Income Tax Payable	Decrease—Deduction from Net Income

Investing Activities

Property and Equipment (Purchase)	Deduction from Net Income
Property and Equipment (Sell)	Addition to Net Income
Investments (Purchase)	Deduction from Net Income
Investments (Sell)	Addition to Net Income

Financing Activities

Cash Investments by Owners	Addition to Net Income
Cash Withdrawals by Owners	Deduction from Net Income

Let's now ask ourselves why and how the changes affect each account involved.

When Accounts Receivable (net) increases, more was recorded as revenue than was received in cash, so we reduce net income.

When Merchandise Inventory increases, more goods were purchased than were actually sold, so we reduce net income.

When Prepaid Expenses (for example, insurance) increase, more insurance was paid for than actually used or expired, so we reduce net income.

When Accounts Payable increase, more goods were purchased than were actually paid for, so we increase net income.

When Property and Equipment increase, cash is paid now rather than being written off or depreciated in the future, so we reduce net income.

When Investments increase, cash is paid out now for the investments, so we reduce net income.

When owner's(s') cash withdrawals increase, cash is paid out now for the owner's(s') personal use, so we reduce net income.

To illustrate the formulation of statements of cash flows using the indirect method, we'll return to two of the examples that were presented in Chapter 23 (illustration 3, File Company, and illustration 4, Gale Corporation). First, we present the financial statements for File Company. Using the indirect method, prepare a statement of cash flows for the year 2009.

File Company
Income Statement
For Year Ended December 31, 2009

Net Sales			$800 0 0 0 00
Cost of Goods Sold:			
Merchandise Inventory, January 1, 2009	$126 0 0 0 00		
Delivered Cost of Purchases	514 0 0 0 00		
Cost of Goods Available for Sale	$640 0 0 0 00		
Less Merchandise Inventory, December 31, 2009	130 0 0 0 00		
Cost of Goods Sold		510 0 0 0 00	
Gross Profit		$290 0 0 0 00	
Operating Expenses:			
Salary Expense	$100 0 0 0 00		
Rent Expense	20 0 0 0 00		
Depreciation Expense, Equipment	22 0 0 0 00		
Supplies Expense	1 6 0 0 00		
Insurance Expense	4 0 0 00		
Total Operating Expenses		144 0 0 0 00	
Net Income		$146 0 0 0 00	

File Company
Statement of Owner's Equity
For Year Ended December 31, 2009

S. D. File, Capital, January 1, 2009		$233 2 0 0 00
Net Income	$146 0 0 0 00	
Less Withdrawals	150 0 0 0 00	
Decrease in Capital		(4 0 0 0 00)
S. D. File, Capital, December 31, 2009		$229 2 0 0 00

File Company
Comparative Balance Sheet
December 31, 2009 and December 31, 2008

	2009	2008	INCREASE OR (DECREASE)
Assets			
Cash	$ 31 4 0 0 00	$ 35 0 0 0 00	$(3 6 0 0 00)
Accounts Receivable	45 6 0 0 00	33 0 0 0 00	12 6 0 0 00
Merchandise Inventory	130 0 0 0 00	126 0 0 0 00	4 0 0 0 00
Prepaid Insurance	2 3 0 0 00	1 4 0 0 00	9 0 0 00
Equipment	136 6 0 0 00	136 6 0 0 00	0 00
Less Accumulated Depreciation	(62 0 0 0 00)	(40 0 0 0 00)	(22 0 0 0 00)
Total Assets	$283 9 0 0 00	$292 0 0 0 00	$(8 1 0 0 00)
Liabilities			
Accounts Payable	$ 51 5 0 0 00	$ 56 0 0 0 00	$(4 5 0 0 00)
Salaries Payable	3 2 0 0 00	2 8 0 0 00	4 0 0 00
Total Liabilities	$ 54 7 0 0 00	$ 58 8 0 0 00	$(4 1 0 0 00)
Owner's Equity			
S. D. File, Capital	229 2 0 0 00	233 2 0 0 00	(4 0 0 0 00)
Total Liabilities and Owner's Equity	$283 9 0 0 00	$292 0 0 0 00	$(8 1 0 0 00)

File Company
Statement of Cash Flows
For Year Ended December 31, 2009

Cash Flows from (used by) Operating Activities:			
Net Income			$146 0 0 0 00
Add (Deduct) Items to Convert Net Income			
from Accrual Basis to Cash Basis:			
Depreciation Expense, Equipment	$ 22 0 0 0 00		
Increase in Accounts Receivable	(12 6 0 0 00)		
Increase in Merchandise Inventory	(4 0 0 0 00)		
Increase in Prepaid Insurance	(9 0 0 00)		
Decrease in Accounts Payable	(4 5 0 0 00)		
Increase in Salaries Payable	4 0 0 00	4 0 0 00	
Net Cash Flows from Operating Activities			$146 4 0 0 00
Cash Flows from (used by) Financing Activities:			
Payment of Personal Withdrawals	$(150 0 0 0 00)		
Net Cash Flows used by Financing Activities		(150 0 0 0 00)	
Net Increase (Decrease) in Cash			$ (3 6 0 0 00)
Cash, January 1, 2009			35 0 0 0 00
Cash, December 31, 2009			$ 31 4 0 0 00

As an additional illustration, here are the financial statements for Gale Corporation. By the use of the indirect method, prepare a statement of cash flows for the year 2009.

Gale Corporation
Income Statement
For Year Ended December 31, 2009

Revenue from Sales:			
Sales		$620 0 0 0 00	
Less Sales Returns and Allowances		6 0 0 0 00	
Net Sales			$614 0 0 0 00
Cost of Goods Sold:			
Merchandise Inventory, January 1, 2009		$224 0 0 0 00	
Purchases	$426 0 0 0 00		
Less Purchases Returns and Allowances	3 0 0 0 00		
Net Purchases	$423 0 0 0 00		
Add Freight In	47 0 0 0 00		
Delivered Cost of Purchases		470 0 0 0 00	
Cost of Goods Available for Sale		$694 0 0 0 00	
Less Merchandise Inventory, December 31, 2009		260 0 0 0 00	
Cost of Goods Sold			434 0 0 0 00
Gross Profit			$180 0 0 0 00
Operating Expenses:			
Wages Expense		$123 0 0 0 00	
Rent Expense		20 0 0 0 00	
Depreciation Expense, Equipment		24 0 0 0 00	
Supplies Expense		2 0 0 0 00	
Property Tax Expense		2 0 0 0 00	
Insurance Expense		1 0 0 0 00	
Total Operating Expenses			172 0 0 0 00
Income from Operations			$ 8 0 0 0 00
Other Income:			
Gain on Disposal of Property and Equipment		$ 5 0 0 0 00	
Other Expenses:			
Interest Expense		26 0 0 0 00	(21 0 0 0 00)
Net Loss			$ (13 0 0 0 00)

Gale Corporation
Statement of Retained Earnings
For Year Ended December 31, 2009

Retained Earnings, January 1, 2009		$94 6 0 0 00
Less: Net Loss	$13 0 0 0 00	
Cash Dividends Declared	16 0 0 0 00	
Decrease in Retained Earnings		(29 0 0 0 00)
Retained Earnings, December 31, 2009		$65 6 0 0 00

Gale Corporation
Comparative Balance Sheet
December 31, 2009 and December 31, 2008

	2009					2008					INCREASE OR (DECREASE)				
Assets															
Cash	$ 41	3	0	0	00	$ 33	4	0	0	00	$ 7	9	0	0	00
Accounts Receivable	58	4	0	0	00	69	0	0	0	00	(10	6	0	0	00)
Merchandise Inventory	260	0	0	0	00	224	0	0	0	00	36	0	0	0	00
Prepaid Rent	3	0	0	0	00	3	0	0	0	00				0	00
Prepaid Insurance	1	0	0	0	00		9	0	0	00		1	0	0	00
Equipment	114	0	0	0	00	143	0	0	0	00	(29	0	0	0	00)
Less Accumulated Depreciation	(47	0	0	0	00)	(35	0	0	0	00)	(12	0	0	0	00)
Total Assets	$430	7	0	0	00	$438	3	0	0	00	$ (7	6	0	0	00)
Liabilities															
Accounts Payable	$ 28	6	0	0	00	$ 39	7	0	0	00	$ (11	1	0	0	00)
Notes Payable	24	0	0	0	00				0	00	24	0	0	0	00
Wages Payable	2	1	0	0	00	2	4	0	0	00	(	3	0	0	00)
Dividends Payable	2	0	0	0	00	3	0	0	0	00	(1	0	0	0	00)
Property Tax Payable	1	3	0	0	00	1	1	0	0	00		2	0	0	00
Interest Payable		6	0	0	00				0	00		6	0	0	00
Total Liabilities	$ 58	6	0	0	00	$ 46	2	0	0	00	$ 12	4	0	0	00
Stockholders' Equity															
Common Stock	$306	5	0	0	00	$297	5	0	0	00	$ 9	0	0	0	00
Retained Earnings	65	6	0	0	00	94	6	0	0	00	(29	0	0	0	00)
Total Stockholders' Equity	$372	1	0	0	00	$392	1	0	0	00	$ (20	0	0	0	00)
Total Liabilities and Stockholders' Equity	$430	7	0	0	00	$438	3	0	0	00	$ (7	6	0	0	00)

Note the $7,900 increase in Cash. In spite of having a $13,000 net loss for the year, Gale Corporation winds up with a positive cash flow. Let's find out how this situation came about.

Gale Corporation
Statement of Cash Flows
For Year Ended December 31, 2009

Cash Flows from (used by) Operating Activities:										
Net Income (Loss)						$(13	0	0	0	00)
Add (Deduct) Items to Convert Net Income										
from Accrual Basis to Cash Basis:										
Depreciation Expense, Equipment	$24	0	0	0	00					
Decrease in Accounts Receivable	10	6	0	0	00					
Increase in Merchandise Inventory	(36	0	0	0	00)					
Increase in Prepaid Insurance		(1	0	0	00)					
Decrease in Accounts Payable	(11	1	0	0	00)					
Decrease in Wages Payable		(3	0	0	00)					
Increase in Property Tax Payable		2	0	0	00					
Increase in Interest Payable		6	0	0	00					
Gain on Disposal of Property and Equipment	(5	0	0	0	00)	(17	1	0	0	00)
Net Cash Flows used by Operating Activities						$(30	1	0	0	00)
Cash Flows from (used by) Investing Activities:										
Sale of Equipment	$22	0	0	0	00					
Net Cash Flows from Investing Activities						22	0	0	0	00
Cash Flows from (used by) Financing Activities:										
Issuance of Note	$24	0	0	0	00					
Issuance of Common Stock	9	0	0	0	00					
Payment of Dividends	(17	0	0	0	00)					
Net Cash Flows from Financing Activities						16	0	0	0	00
Net Increase (Decrease) in Cash						$ 7	9	0	0	00
Cash, January 1, 2009						33	4	0	0	00
Cash, December 31, 2009						$41	3	0	0	00

PROBLEMS

P.O. 4

Problem J-1 Financial statements for Trevino Company are presented below and on the following page.

Trevino Company
Income Statement
For Year Ended December 31, 2008

Revenue:			
Net Sales			$740 0 0 0 00
Cost of Goods Sold:			
Merchandise Inventory, January 1, 2008	$124 0 0 0 00		
Delivered Cost of Purchases	499 0 0 0 00		
Cost of Goods Available for Sale	$623 0 0 0 00		
Less Merchandise Inventory, December 31, 2008	127 0 0 0 00		
Cost of Goods Sold			496 0 0 0 00
Gross Profit			$244 0 0 0 00
Operating Expenses:			
Salary Expense	$104 0 0 0 00		
Rent Expense	18 0 0 0 00		
Advertising Expense	12 0 0 0 00		
Supplies Expense	8 4 5 00		
Depreciation Expense, Equipment	12 0 0 0 00		
Utilities Expense	1 7 9 0 00		
Insurance Expense	2 4 0 0 00		
Miscellaneous Expense	3 6 0 00		
Total Operating Expenses			151 3 9 5 00
Net Income			$ 92 6 0 5 00

Trevino Company
Statement of Owner's Equity
For Year Ended December 31, 2008

R. B. Trevino, Capital, January 1, 2008		$220 3 0 0 00
Net Income	$92 6 0 5 00	
Less Withdrawals	54 0 0 0 00	
Increase in Capital		38 6 0 5 00
R. B. Trevino, Capital, December 31, 2008		$258 9 0 5 00

Trevino Company
Comparative Balance Sheet
December 31, 2008 and December 31, 2007

Assets	2008	2007	INCREASE OR (DECREASE)
Cash	$ 42 4 6 5 00	$ 42 5 0 0 00	$ (3 5 00)
Accounts Receivable	41 0 0 0 00	32 0 0 0 00	9 0 0 0 00
Merchandise Inventory	137 0 0 0 00	103 0 0 0 00	34 0 0 0 00
Prepaid Insurance	3 5 4 0 00	2 5 6 0 00	9 8 0 00
Equipment:	128 0 0 0 00	128 0 0 0 00	0 00
Less Accumulated Depreciation	(34 0 0 0 00)	(22 0 0 0 00)	(12 0 0 0 00)
Total Assets	$318 0 0 5 00	$286 0 6 0 00	$31 9 4 5 00
Liabilities			
Accounts Payable	$ 56 0 0 0 00	$ 62 8 6 0 00	$ (6 8 6 0 00)
Salaries Payable	3 1 0 0 00	2 9 0 0 00	2 0 0 00
Total Liabilities	$ 59 1 0 0 00	$ 65 7 6 0 00	$ (6 6 6 0 00)
Owner's Equity			
R. B. Trevino, Capital	258 9 0 5 00	220 3 0 0 00	38 6 0 5 00
Total Liabilities and Owner's Equity	$318 0 0 5 00	$286 0 6 0 00	$31 9 4 5 00

Check Figure

Net (Decrease) in Cash, ($35)

Instructions

Using the statements of Trevino Company, construct a statement of cash flows, using the indirect method, for the year ended December 31, 2008.

P.O. 4

Problem J-2 Financial statements for Miracle Company are presented below and on the following page.

Miracle Company
Income Statement
For Year Ended December 31, 2008

Revenue from Sales:		
Net Sales		$630 0 0 0 00
Cost of Goods Sold:		
Merchandise Inventory, January 1, 2008	$110 0 0 0 00	
Delivered Cost of Purchases	360 0 0 0 00	
Cost of Goods Available for Sale	$470 0 0 0 00	
Less Merchandise Inventory, December 31, 2008	135 0 0 0 00	
Cost of Goods Sold		335 0 0 0 00
Gross Profit		$295 0 0 0 00
Operating Expenses:		
Salary Expense	$110 0 0 0 00	
Rent Expense	20 0 0 0 00	
Advertising Expense	14 0 0 0 00	
Supplies Expense	7 9 0 00	
Depreciation Expense, Equipment	12 0 0 0 00	
Utilities Expense	1 8 7 0 00	
Insurance Expense	2 6 0 0 00	
Miscellaneous Expense	5 1 0 00	
Total Operating Expenses		161 7 7 0 00
Net Income		$133 2 3 0 00

Miracle Company
Statement of Owner's Equity
For Year Ended December 31, 2008

J. Miracle, Capital, January 1, 2008		$218 0 0 0 00
Net Income	$133 2 3 0 00	
Less Withdrawals	20 0 0 0 00	
Increase in Capital		113 2 3 0 00
J. Miracle, Capital, December 31, 2008		$331 2 3 0 00

Miracle Company
Comparative Balance Sheet
December 31, 2008 and December 31, 2007

	2008	2007	INCREASE OR (DECREASE)
Assets			
Cash	$137 4 5 0 00	$ 36 3 4 0 00	$101 1 1 0 00
Accounts Receivable	35 0 0 0 00	20 0 0 0 00	15 0 0 0 00
Merchandise Inventory	127 0 0 0 00	118 0 0 0 00	9 0 0 0 00
Prepaid Insurance	2 5 4 0 00	2 5 6 0 00	(2 0 00)
Equipment	132 0 0 0 00	132 0 0 0 00	0 00
Less Accumulated Depreciation	(45 0 0 0 00)	(33 0 0 0 00)	(12 0 0 0 00)
Total Assets	$388 9 9 0 00	$275 9 0 0 00	$113 0 9 0 00
Liabilities			
Accounts Payable	$ 54 6 6 0 00	$ 55 0 0 0 00	$ (3 4 0 00)
Salaries Payable	3 1 0 0 00	2 9 0 0 00	2 0 0 00
Total Liabilities	$ 57 7 6 0 00	$ 57 9 0 0 00	$ (1 4 0 00)
Owner's Equity			
J. Miracle, Capital	331 2 3 0 00	218 0 0 0 00	113 2 3 0 00
Total Liabilities and Owner's Equity	$388 9 9 0 00	$275 9 0 0 00	$113 0 9 0 00

Check Figure

Net Increase in Cash, $101,110

Instructions

Using the statements of Miracle Company, construct a statement of cash flows, using the indirect method, for the year ended December 31, 2008.

P.O. 4

Problem J-3 Financial statements for Gilbertson Corporation are presented below and on the following page.

Gilbertson Corporation
Income Statement
For Year Ended December 31, 2008

Revenue from Sales:			
Sales		$718 0 0 0 00	
Less: Sales Returns and Allowances	$ 4 3 0 0 00		
Sales Discounts	2 3 0 0 00	6 6 0 0 00	
Net Sales			$711 4 0 0 00
Cost of Goods Sold:			
Merchandise Inventory, January 1, 2008		$236 0 0 0 00	
Purchases	$360 0 0 0 00		
Less: Purchases Returns and Allowances	2 8 0 0 00		
Purchases Discounts	7 0 0 0 00		
Net Purchases	$350 2 0 0 00		
Add Freight In	37 0 0 0 00		
Delivered Cost of Purchases		387 2 0 0 00	
Cost of Goods Available for Sale		$623 2 0 0 00	
Less Merchandise Inventory, December 31, 2008		240 0 0 0 00	
Cost of Goods Sold			383 2 0 0 00
Gross Profit			$328 2 0 0 00
Operating Expenses:			
Wages and Salary Expense		$136 0 0 0 00	
Delivery Expense		2 3 0 0 00	
Advertising Expense		14 0 0 0 00	
Credit Card Expense		3 6 0 0 00	
Supplies Expense		9 0 0 00	
Depreciation Expense, Equipment		11 0 0 0 00	
Insurance Expense		3 8 0 0 00	
Utilities Expense		2 6 0 0 00	
Miscellaneous Expense		8 0 0 00	
Total Operating Expenses			175 0 0 0 00
Income from Operations			$153 2 0 0 00
Other Income:			
Rental Income		$ 4 5 0 0 00	
Other Expenses:			
Interest Expense		1 2 0 0 00	3 3 0 0 00
Income Before Income Taxes			$156 5 0 0 00
Income Tax Expense			2 0 0 0 00
Net Income			$154 5 0 0 00

Gilbertson Corporation
Statement of Retained Earnings
For Year Ended December 31, 2008

Retained Earnings, January 1, 2008		$220 0 0 0 00
Net Income	$154 5 0 0 00	
Less Cash Dividends Declared	120 0 0 0 00	
Increase in Retained Earnings		34 5 0 0 00
Retained Earnings, December 31, 2008		$254 5 0 0 00

Gilbertson Corporation
Comparative Balance Sheet
December 31, 2008 and December 31, 2007

	2008	2007	INCREASE OR (DECREASE)
Assets			
Cash	$ 94 3 7 0 00	$ 45 0 0 0 00	$49 3 7 0 00
Accounts Receivable	33 8 9 0 00	31 5 0 0 00	2 3 9 0 00
Merchandise Inventory	115 0 0 0 00	102 0 0 0 00	13 0 0 0 00
Prepaid Rent	18 0 0 0 00	18 0 0 0 00	0 00
Prepaid Insurance	6 6 4 0 00	6 5 0 0 00	1 4 0 00
Equipment	130 0 0 0 00	130 0 0 0 00	0 00
Less Accumulated Depreciation	(32 0 0 0 00)	(21 0 0 0 00)	(11 0 0 0 00)
Total Assets	$365 9 0 0 00	$312 0 0 0 00	$53 9 0 0 00
Liabilities			
Notes Payable	$ 25 0 0 0 00	0 00	$25 0 0 0 00
Accounts Payable	36 0 0 0 00	$ 39 5 0 0 00	(3 5 0 0 00)
Wages and Salaries Payable	3 1 0 0 00	3 9 0 0 00	(8 0 0 00)
Dividends Payable	2 5 0 0 00	4 5 0 0 00	(2 0 0 0 00)
Property Tax Payable	3 6 0 0 00	3 4 0 0 00	2 0 0 00
Interest Payable	1 2 0 0 00	1 7 0 0 00	(5 0 0 00)
Total Liabilities	$ 71 4 0 0 00	$ 53 0 0 0 00	$18 4 0 0 00
Stockholders' Equity			
Common Stock	$ 40 0 0 0 00	$ 39 0 0 0 00	$ 1 0 0 0 00
Retained Earnings	254 5 0 0 00	220 0 0 0 00	34 5 0 0 00
Total Stockholders' Equity	$294 5 0 0 00	$259 0 0 0 00	$35 5 0 0 00
Total Liabilities and Stockholders' Equity	$365 9 0 0 00	$312 0 0 0 00	$53 9 0 0 00

Check Figure

Net Increase in Cash, $49,370

Instructions

Using the statements of Gilbertson Corporation, construct a statement of cash flows, using the indirect method, for the year ended December 31, 2008.

Comparative Financial Statements

24

LINKS TO ACCOUNTING

The airline industry has had its share of financial ups and downs, but the impact of the September 11, 2001, terrorist attack, which was devastating to the industry overall, has left some major airlines still struggling years later just to survive. One company that seems to continuously survive, however, is Southwest Airlines. How does this company compare with others in the airline industry? And how has its performance changed in recent years? These questions can be answered by evaluating comparative financial statements and using industry comparisons. What are comparative financial statements? Basically, they are financial statements that compare items within a statement to the final figure in that statement (vertical analysis) or compare the same items for two or more periods (horizontal analysis). Why would you want this type of information? It helps you determine whether a company is performing better or worse over time or better or worse than other companies in the same industry. How does Southwest Airlines present its comparative financial statements? Go to **http://www.southwest.com** and take a look at its 2005 annual report to find out.

Performance Objectives

After you have completed this chapter, you will be able to do the following:

1. Prepare a comparative income statement and balance sheet involving horizontal analysis.

2. Prepare a comparative income statement and balance sheet involving vertical analysis.

3. Express income statement data in trend percentages.

4. Compute (a) working capital, (b) current ratio, (c) quick ratio, (d) accounts receivable turnover, (e) merchandise inventory turnover, (f) ratio of stockholders' equity to liabilities, and (g) ratio of property and equipment to long-term liabilities.

5. Calculate (a) equity per share, (b) rate of return on common stockholders' equity, (c) earnings per share of common stock, and (d) price-earnings ratio.

Accounting is the process of analyzing, classifying, recording, summarizing, and *interpreting* business transactions. We are now ready to interpret the information. How do you draw conclusions from financial data that have been summarized in financial statements?

The financial condition of a company and the results of operations of business enterprises are of interest not only to owners, employers, and managers, but also to creditors and to prospective owners and creditors. Everybody is interested in two aspects of an enterprise:

1. Its **solvency**, or its ability to pay its debts
2. Its **profitability**, or its ability to earn a reasonable profit on the owners' investment

This chapter explains the techniques used to determine solvency and profitability.

TYPES OF COMPARISON

To interpret a set of facts, you have to have similar data with which to compare it. In other words, a given set of facts by itself is not significant. If you are told that a certain corporation earned a net income of $156,000 during the past year, this figure by itself is not meaningful. Does this net income indicate a successful year or a poor year? Does it compare favorably or unfavorably with other years? Does it represent a reasonable return on sales and investment or not? How does it compare with the net income of other firms in the same industry?

A company's financial statements are meaningful only if you analyze them on a comparative basis. There are three useful bases for making such a comparison:

1. Statements of the same company for the current year and one or more prior years
2. Financial data for other companies in the same industry
3. Previously established financial standards or objectives

COMPARATIVE STATEMENTS

One technique for analyzing and interpreting financial data is the preparation of comparative statements. Two types of analysis—horizontal and vertical—are commonly used.

Horizontal Analysis

OBJECTIVE 1

Prepare a comparative income statement and balance sheet involving horizontal analysis.

Income Statement **Horizontal analysis** is the comparison of the same item in a company's financial statements for two or more periods. Let's look at the comparative income statement (Figure 1) for Bill's Bike Shop, Inc., for 2008 and 2007.

Note that for each item on the income statement, the accountant expressed the difference—that is, the increase or decrease in 2008 over 2007—first in dollars and then in percentages. Look at the increase in Sales, on the second line, for example. Subtract Sales in 2007 from Sales in 2008.

$982,100	Sales for 2008
− 861,700	Sales for 2007
$120,400	Increase of 2008 over 2007

Bill's Bike Shop, Inc.
Comparative Income Statement
For Years Ended December 31, 2008 and December 31, 2007

	2008	2007	INCREASE OR (DECREASE) AMOUNT	PERCENT
Revenue from Sales:				
Sales	$ 982 1 0 0 00	$ 861 7 0 0 00	$ 120 4 0 0 00	14.0
Less Sales Returns and Allowances	15 2 0 0 00	13 1 0 0 00	2 1 0 0 00	16.0
Net Sales	$ 966 9 0 0 00	$ 848 6 0 0 00	$ 118 3 0 0 00	13.9
Cost of Goods Sold:				
Merchandise Inventory, January 1	$ 206 5 0 0 00	$ 138 7 0 0 00	$ 67 8 0 0 00	48.9
Delivered Cost of Purchases	804 8 0 0 00	636 6 0 0 00	168 2 0 0 00	26.4
Cost of Goods Available for Sale	$1 011 3 0 0 00	$ 775 3 0 0 00	$ 236 0 0 0 00	30.4
Less Merchandise Inventory, December 31	348 4 0 0 00	206 5 0 0 00	141 9 0 0 00	68.7
Cost of Goods Sold	$ 662 9 0 0 00	$ 568 8 0 0 00	$ 94 1 0 0 00	16.5
Gross Profit	$ 304 0 0 0 00	$ 279 8 0 0 00	$ 24 2 0 0 00	8.6
Operating Expenses:				
Selling Expenses:				
Sales Salary Expense	$ 114 6 5 0 00	$ 102 4 0 0 00	$ 12 2 5 0 00	12.0
Delivery Expense	14 7 0 0 00	13 7 0 0 00	1 0 0 0 00	7.3
Advertising Expense	7 9 0 0 00	6 9 0 0 00	1 0 0 0 00	14.5
Depreciation Expense, Equipment	6 8 0 0 00	6 6 0 0 00	2 0 0 00	3.0
Store Supplies Expense	7 5 0 00	6 0 0 00	1 5 0 00	25.0
Total Selling Expenses	$ 144 8 0 0 00	$ 130 2 0 0 00	$ 14 6 0 0 00	11.2
General Expenses:				
Office Salary Expense	$ 33 4 4 0 00	$ 27 6 8 0 00	$ 5 7 6 0 00	20.8
Depreciation Expense, Building	14 2 0 0 00	14 2 0 0 00	0 00	0.0
Bad Debts Expense	6 2 0 0 00	5 4 0 0 00	8 0 0 00	14.8
Taxes Expense	6 1 0 0 00	5 2 0 0 00	9 0 0 00	17.3
Insurance Expense	1 1 0 0 00	1 0 0 0 00	1 0 0 00	10.0
Miscellaneous General Expense	8 6 0 00	7 2 0 00	1 4 0 00	19.4
Total General Expenses	$ 61 9 0 0 00	$ 54 2 0 0 00	$ 7 7 0 0 00	14.2
Total Operating Expenses	$ 206 7 0 0 00	$ 184 4 0 0 00	$ 22 3 0 0 00	12.1
Income from Operations	$ 97 3 0 0 00	$ 95 4 0 0 00	$ 1 9 0 0 00	2.0
Other Expenses:				
Interest Expense	7 9 2 0 00	7 8 6 0 00	6 0 00	0.8
Income Before Income Tax	$ 89 3 8 0 00	$ 87 5 4 0 00	$ 1 8 4 0 00	2.1
Income Tax Expense	18 4 2 0 00	18 0 1 0 00	4 1 0 00	2.3
Net Income	$ 70 9 6 0 00	$ 69 5 3 0 00	$ 1 4 3 0 00	2.1

FIGURE 1

To calculate the *percentage* increase in Sales in 2008 over 2007, divide the dollar increase by the amount of Sales during the base year. Then round the answer to three decimal places and multiply by 100 to change the decimal to a percentage.

$$\frac{\$120,400}{\$861,700} = 861,700\overline{)120,400}^{.1397} = 0.140 \times 100 = \underline{14.0\%}$$

Note: The expression **base year** means the year you are using as a basis for comparison, which is the earlier year.

Now look at the change in Sales Returns and Allowances:

$15,200	Sales Returns and Allowances for 2008
− 13,100	Sales Returns and Allowances for 2007
$ 2,100	Increase of 2008 over 2007

The percentage rate of increase is

$$\frac{\$2,100}{\$13,100} = 13,100\overline{)2,100}^{.1603} = 0.160 \times 100 = \underline{16.0\%}$$

People appraising an income statement often use the percentage change in net sales as a basis for comparison. In other words, they compare all other percentage changes with the percentage change in net sales to determine reasonably whether the other percentage changes are out of line. If net sales increased 14 percent from 2007 to 2008, other percentage changes should also amount to approximately 14 percent. If they vary considerably from 14 percent, they may be out of line, and you should investigate to find the reasons for the difference. Let's look at the main items on the income statement.

Item	Percentage Change
Net Sales	14.0
Cost of Goods Sold	16.5
Gross Profit	8.6
Total Operating Expenses	12.1
Net Income	2.1

You can see that the percentage changes in Gross Profit and Net Income are considerably less than the percentage change in Net Sales. Since Gross Profit is determined by subtracting Cost of Goods Sold from Net Sales, you should investigate the entire Cost of Goods Sold section of the income statement. This is a starting point in accounting for the comparatively small percentage increase in Net Income. The percentage changes in items in the Cost of Goods Sold section are

Horizontal analysis of an income statement lets management see the percentage of increase and decrease for each component of the income statement.

Item	Percentage Change
Merchandise Inventory, January 1	48.9
Delivered Cost of Purchases	26.4
Merchandise Inventory, December 31	68.7

The merchandise inventory of January 1 was a carryover from the previous year, but why the large increase in Delivered Cost of Purchases? And look at the large increase in Merchandise Inventory at the end of the year. Buying all those goods required a large cash investment, which either increased debt and related interest expense or decreased investments and related interest income. In addition, carrying the larger inventory increased handling and storage expense plus the risk of an inventory loss write-off due to obsolescence. Also, with such a large increase in Merchandise Inventory, we would expect a larger increase in sales. Is the increase in sales large enough?

Incidentally, a percentage change can be calculated only when a positive amount is reported in the base year. For example, let's say a company had a net loss of $3,500 in Year 1 (base year) and a net income of $2,000 in Year 2. Because the $3,500 is not a positive amount, it is not possible to state the amount of the change as a percentage.

Balance Sheet   Now look at the balance sheet in Figure 2 on page 913, which shows the comparison between 2008 and 2007. Again you see why changes are expressed in both dollars and percentages. Items showing either a large dollar change or a large percentage change really stand out. This time, some negative totals show up in the Increase or (Decrease) Amount column.

The following items are based on data from the comparative balance sheet:

Item	Increase or (Decrease) Amount	Increase or (Decrease) Percentage
Cash	$(16,900)	(43.7)
Merchandise Inventory	141,900	68.7
Accounts Payable	41,100	141.7

Recall that the comparative income statement already exposed the increase in the Merchandise Inventory account. You should also consider the effects of changes in the balances of other related accounts. The fact that Cash is down by 43.7 percent while Accounts Payable is up by 141.7 percent may indicate a pending financial crisis. To pay its bills, the firm may be forced to liquidate that large stock of goods by selling it at cost, or even less. The other current liabilities also show significant unfavorable increases. Note the 128.6 percent increase in Income Tax Payable, the 200 percent increase in Dividends Payable, and the 42.5 percent increase in Salaries Payable. One point in the company's favor, though, is the decrease in Accounts Receivable. The increase in Allowance for Doubtful Accounts, although relatively small in amount, could be considered unreasonable when expressed as a percentage (on the other hand, the increase may involve just one account).

Vertical Analysis

OBJECTIVE 2

Prepare a comparative income statement and balance sheet involving vertical analysis.

Income Statement   Another tool accountants can use to analyze financial statements is **vertical analysis**. Using this method, you can see in a single statement the relationship of each part to the whole. For an income statement, *the whole is net sales*. Although each percentage applies to a single item only, you can quickly see the relative importance of each item on the statement. Let's look first at the comparative income statement (Figure 3 on page 914) and then at the comparative balance sheet (Figure 4 on page 915) for Bill's Bike Shop, Inc.—this time, arranged for vertical analysis.

Bill's Bike Shop, Inc.
Comparative Balance Sheet
December 31, 2008 and December 31, 2007

	2008	2007	INCREASE OR (DECREASE) AMOUNT	PERCENT
Assets				
Current Assets:				
Cash	$ 21 800 00	$ 38 700 00	$ (16 900 00)	(43.7)
Accounts Receivable	79 700 00	81 400 00	(1 700 00)	(2.1)
Less Allowance for Doubtful Accounts	(3 300 00)	(2 600 00)	700 00	26.9
Merchandise Inventory	348 400 00	206 500 00	141 900 00	68.7
Prepaid Insurance	2 000 00	2 100 00	(100 00)	(4.8)
Total Current Assets	$448 600 00	$326 100 00	$122 500 00	37.6
Investments:				
Sinking Fund Cash	$ 4 100 00	$ 5 800 00	$ (1 700 00)	(29.3)
Sinking Fund Investments	61 700 00	59 400 00	2 300 00	3.9
Total Investments	$ 65 800 00	$ 65 200 00	$ 600 00	0.9
Property and Equipment:				
Land	$ 40 000 00	$ 40 000 00	$ 0 00	0.0
Building	160 000 00	160 000 00	0 00	0.0
Less Accumulated Depreciation	(56 800 00)	(42 600 00)	14 200 00	33.3
Equipment	88 600 00	86 000 00	2 600 00	3.0
Less Accumulated Depreciation	(41 000 00)	(34 200 00)	6 800 00	19.9
Total Property and Equipment	$190 800 00	$209 200 00	$ (18 400 00)	(8.8)
Intangible Assets:				
Patents	$ 3 000 00	$ 4 000 00	$ (1 000 00)	(25.0)
Total Assets	$708 200 00	$604 500 00	$103 700 00	17.2
Liabilities				
Current Liabilities:				
Accounts Payable	$ 70 100 00	$ 29 000 00	$ 41 100 00	141.7
Income Tax Payable	12 800 00	5 600 00	7 200 00	128.6
Dividends Payable	12 000 00	4 000 00	8 000 00	200.0
Salaries Payable	5 700 00	4 000 00	1 700 00	42.5
Total Current Liabilities	$100 600 00	$ 42 600 00	$ 58 000 00	136.2
Long-Term Liabilities:				
Bonds Payable, 6%, due Dec. 31, 2015	$100 000 00	$100 000 00	$ 0 00	0.0
Less Discount on Bonds Payable	(2 200 00)	(2 400 00)	(200 00)	(8.3)
Total Long-Term Liabilities	$ 97 800 00	$ 97 600 00	$ (200 00)	(0.2)
Total Liabilities	$198 400 00	$140 200 00	$ 58 200 00	41.5
Stockholders' Equity				
Paid-in Capital:				
Common Stock, $100 par value (4,000 shares authorized, 3,000 shares issued)	$300 000 00	$300 000 00	$ 0 00	0.0
Paid-in Capital in Excess of Par Value	86 000 00	86 000 00	0 00	0.0
Total Paid-in Capital	$386 000 00	$386 000 00	$ 0 00	0.0
Retained Earnings:				
Unappropriated	$103 800 00	$ 66 300 00	$ 37 500 00	56.6
Appropriated for Property Expansion	20 000 00	12 000 00	8 000 00	66.7
Total Retained Earnings	$123 800 00	$ 78 300 00	$ 45 500 00	58.1
Total Stockholders' Equity	$509 800 00	$464 300 00	$ 45 500 00	9.8
Total Liabilities and Stockholders' Equity	$708 200 00	$604 500 00	$103 700 00	17.2

FIGURE 2

Bill's Bike Shop, Inc.
Comparative Income Statement
For Years Ended December 31, 2008 and December 31, 2007

	2008		2007	
	AMOUNT	PERCENT*	AMOUNT	PERCENT*
Revenue from Sales:				
Sales	$ 982 1 0 0 00	101.6	$ 861 7 0 0 00	101.5
Less Sales Returns and Allowances	15 2 0 0 00	1.6	13 1 0 0 00	1.5
Net Sales	$ 966 9 0 0 00	100.0	$ 848 6 0 0 00	100.0
Cost of Goods Sold:				
Merchandise Inventory, January 1	$ 206 5 0 0 00	21.4	$ 138 7 0 0 00	16.3
Delivered Cost of Purchases	804 8 0 0 00	83.2	636 6 0 0 00	75.0
Cost of Goods Available for Sale	$1 011 3 0 0 00	104.6	$ 775 3 0 0 00	91.4
Less Merchandise Inventory, December 31	348 4 0 0 00	36.0	206 5 0 0 00	24.3
Cost of Goods Sold	$ 662 9 0 0 00	68.6	$ 568 8 0 0 00	67.0
Gross Profit	$ 304 0 0 0 00	31.4	$ 279 8 0 0 00	33.0
Operating Expenses:				
Selling Expenses:				
Sales Salary Expense	$ 114 6 5 0 00	11.9	$ 102 4 0 0 00	12.1
Delivery Expense	14 7 0 0 00	1.5	13 7 0 0 00	1.6
Advertising Expense	7 9 0 0 00	0.8	6 9 0 0 00	0.8
Depreciation Expense, Equipment	6 8 0 0 00	0.7	6 6 0 0 00	0.8
Store Supplies Expense	7 5 0 00	0.1	6 0 0 00	0.1
Total Selling Expenses	$ 144 8 0 0 00	15.0	$ 130 2 0 0 00	15.3
General Expenses:				
Office Salary Expense	$ 33 4 4 0 00	3.5	$ 27 6 8 0 00	3.3
Depreciation Expense, Building	14 2 0 0 00	1.5	14 2 0 0 00	1.7
Bad Debts Expense	6 2 0 0 00	0.6	5 4 0 0 00	0.6
Taxes Expense	6 1 0 0 00	0.6	5 2 0 0 00	0.6
Insurance Expense	1 1 0 0 00	0.1	1 0 0 0 00	0.1
Miscellaneous General Expense	8 6 0 00	0.1	7 2 0 00	0.1
Total General Expenses	$ 61 9 0 0 00	6.4	$ 54 2 0 0 00	6.4
Total Operating Expenses	$ 206 7 0 0 00	21.4	$ 184 4 0 0 00	21.7
Income from Operations	$ 97 3 0 0 00	10.0	$ 95 4 0 0 00	11.2
Other Expenses:				
Interest Expense	7 9 2 0 00	0.8	7 8 6 0 00	0.9
Income Before Income Tax	$ 89 3 8 0 00	9.2	$ 87 5 4 0 00	10.3
Income Tax Expense	18 4 2 0 00	1.9	18 0 1 0 00	2.1
Net Income	$ 70 9 6 0 00	7.3	$ 69 5 3 0 00	8.2

*There may be slight differences in the tenth's place due to the rounding methods of various calculators and computers. For the same reason, percentages may not add up exactly.

FIGURE 3

Bill's Bike Shop, Inc.
Comparative Balance Sheet
December 31, 2008 and December 31, 2007

	2008 AMOUNT	2008 PERCENT*	2007 AMOUNT	2007 PERCENT*
Assets				
Current Assets:				
Cash	$ 21 800 00	3.1	$ 38 700 00	6.4
Accounts Receivable	79 700 00	11.3	81 400 00	13.5
Less Allowance for Doubtful Accounts	(3 300 00)	0.5	(2 600 00)	0.4
Merchandise Inventory	348 400 00	49.2	206 500 00	34.2
Prepaid Insurance	2 000 00	0.3	2 100 00	0.3
Total Current Assets	$448 600 00	63.3	$326 100 00	53.9
Investments:				
Sinking Fund Cash	$ 4 100 00	0.6	$ 5 800 00	1.0
Sinking Fund Investments	61 700 00	8.7	59 400 00	9.8
Total Investments	$ 65 800 00	9.3	$ 65 200 00	10.8
Property and Equipment:				
Land	$ 40 000 00	5.6	$ 40 000 00	6.6
Building	160 000 00	22.6	160 000 00	26.5
Less Accumulated Depreciation	(56 800 00)	8.0	(42 600 00)	7.0
Equipment	88 600 00	12.5	86 000 00	14.2
Less Accumulated Depreciation	(41 000 00)	5.8	(34 200 00)	5.7
Total Property and Equipment	$190 800 00	26.9	$209 200 00	34.6
Intangible Assets:				
Patents	$ 3 000 00	0.4	$ 4 000 00	0.7
Total Assets	$708 200 00	100.0	$604 500 00	100.0
Liabilities				
Current Liabilities:				
Accounts Payable	$ 70 100 00	9.9	$ 29 000 00	4.8
Income Tax Payable	12 800 00	1.8	5 600 00	0.9
Dividends Payable	12 000 00	1.7	4 000 00	0.7
Salaries Payable	5 700 00	0.8	4 000 00	0.7
Total Current Liabilities	$100 600 00	14.2	$ 42 600 00	7.0
Long-Term Liabilities:				
Bonds Payable, 6%, due Dec. 31, 2015	$100 000 00	14.1	$100 000 00	16.5
Less Discount on Bonds Payable	(2 200 00)	0.3	(2 400 00)	0.4
Total Long-Term Liabilities	$ 97 800 00	13.8	$ 97 600 00	16.1
Total Liabilities	$198 400 00	28.0	$140 200 00	23.2
Stockholders' Equity				
Paid-in Capital:				
Common Stock, $100 par value (4,000 shares authorized, 3,000 shares issued)	$300 000 00	42.4	$300 000 00	49.6
Paid-in Capital in Excess of Par Value	86 000 00	12.1	86 000 00	14.2
Total Paid-in Capital	$386 000 00	54.5	$386 000 00	63.9
Retained Earnings:				
Unappropriated	$103 800 00	14.7	$ 66 300 00	11.0
Appropriated for Property Expansion	20 000 00	2.8	12 000 00	2.0
Total Retained Earnings	$123 800 00	17.5	$ 78 300 00	13.0
Total Stockholders' Equity	$509 800 00	72.0	$464 300 00	76.8
Total Liabilities and Stockholders' Equity	$708 200 00	100.0	$604 500 00	100.0

*Percentages may not add up exactly due to rounding.

FIGURE 4

When you arrange an income statement for vertical analysis, you express each item as a *percentage of net sales.* In other words, you divide each item by net sales. Below is an illustration:

$$\text{Gross Profit \%} = \text{Gross Profit} \div \text{Net Sales}$$

$$\textbf{Gross Profit \% (2008)} = \frac{\$304,000}{\$966,900} = 0.3144 = \underline{\underline{31.4\%}}$$

$$\textbf{Gross Profit \% (2007)} = \frac{\$279,800}{\$848,600} = 0.3297 = \underline{\underline{33.0\%}}$$

$$\text{Income from Operations \%} = \text{Income from Operations} \div \text{Net Sales}$$

$$\textbf{Income from Operations \% (2008)} = \frac{\$97,300}{\$966,900} = 0.1006 = \underline{\underline{10.1\%}}$$

$$\textbf{Income from Operations \% (2007)} = \frac{\$95,400}{\$848,600} = 0.1124 = \underline{\underline{11.2\%}}$$

$$\text{Net Income \%} = \text{Net Income} \div \text{Net Sales}$$

$$\textbf{Net Income \% (2008)} = \frac{\$70,960}{\$966,900} = 0.0734 = \underline{\underline{7.3\%}}$$

$$\textbf{Net Income \% (2007)} = \frac{\$69,530}{\$848,600} = 0.0819 = \underline{\underline{8.2\%}}$$

You could also interpret the percentages as shown here:

2008

- For every $100 in net sales, gross profit was $31.40.
- For every $100 in net sales, income from operations was $10.10.
- For every $100 in net sales, net income was $7.30.

2007

- For every $100 in net sales, gross profit was $33.00.
- For every $100 in net sales, income from operations was $11.20.
- For every $100 in net sales, net income was $8.20.

Again we see the relative importance in 2008 of Delivered Cost of Purchases (83.2 percent of Net Sales) and ending Merchandise Inventory (36.0 percent of Net Sales). In the area of Selling Expenses, the percentage of Sales Salary Expense declined slightly from that of 2007. Advertising Expense as a percentage of Net Sales remained the same. (Is that necessarily a good sign?)

Major corporate advertisers reevaluate their advertising expense at least annually. By performing vertical analysis (and thus relating its advertising expense directly to net sales), a company is in a better position to assess the impact of one element on another.

Balance Sheet   **When you perform a vertical analysis of a comparative balance sheet, you express the figure for each item as a *percentage of total assets*, or as a percentage of the total of liabilities and stockholders' equity, which is the same figure.** (See Figure 4.) For example, suppose you want to find the percentage of total assets represented by Cash, Accounts Receivable, and Merchandise Inventory. (In referring to Accounts Receivable, we mean net Accounts Receivable [Accounts Receivable less Allowance for Doubtful Accounts].)

$$\text{Cash \%} = \text{Cash} \div \text{Total Assets}$$

$$\text{Cash \% (2008)} = \frac{\$21,800}{\$708,200} = 0.0308 = \underline{\underline{3.1\%}}$$

$$\text{Cash \% (2007)} = \frac{\$38,700}{\$604,500} = 0.0640 = \underline{\underline{6.4\%}}$$

$$\text{Accounts Receivable \%} = \text{Net Accounts Receivable} \div \text{Total Assets}$$

$$\text{Accounts Receivable, net \% (2008)} = \frac{\$76,400}{\$708,200} = 0.1079 = \underline{\underline{10.8\%}}$$

$$\text{Accounts Receivable, net \% (2007)} = \frac{\$78,800}{\$604,500} = 0.1304 = \underline{\underline{13.0\%}}$$

$$\text{Merchandise Inventory \%} = \text{Merchandise Inventory} \div \text{Total Assets}$$

$$\text{Merchandise Inventory \% (2008)} = \frac{\$348,400}{\$708,200} = 0.4920 = \underline{\underline{49.2\%}}$$

$$\text{Merchandise Inventory \% (2007)} = \frac{\$206,500}{\$604,500} = 0.3416 = \underline{\underline{34.2\%}}$$

One could also interpret the above percentages as follows:

2008

- Of every $100 in total assets, $3.10 was in cash.
- Of every $100 in total assets, $10.80 was net accounts receivable.
- Of every $100 in total assets, $49.20 was merchandise inventory.

2007

- Of every $100 in total assets, $6.40 was in cash.
- Of every $100 in total assets, $13.00 was net accounts receivable.
- Of every $100 in total assets, $34.20 was merchandise inventory.

These percentages accentuate Bill's Bike Shop's poor status with respect to Cash and Merchandise Inventory, as well as its favorable status with respect to Accounts Receivable. Also striking a warning note is that the

- Percentage of Accounts Payable more than doubled during 2008.

Our illustrations show full income statements and balance sheets. But sometimes accountants prepare financial statements in condensed form and put the details in supporting schedules. In this case, the figures are taken from the supporting schedules, and the percentages are calculated in the same way. Since the percentages are rounded, the Percent column may not always add to exactly 100 in vertical analysis. (The Percent column is never added in horizontal analysis because it does not involve a common base.)

FYI

On an income statement arranged for vertical analysis, each dollar amount is expressed as a percentage of net sales. On a balance sheet arranged for vertical analysis, each dollar amount is expressed as a percentage of total assets or total liabilities and stockholders' equity.

TREND PERCENTAGES

OBJECTIVE 3

Express income statement data in trend percentages.

You may also use percentages to determine trends, or general directions that become evident only when you make a comparison covering a period of years. **Trend percentages** are calculated by dividing a specific item on an income statement by the corresponding item on the base year income statement. Here is the way to calculate the percentages:

1. Select a representative year as the base year.
2. Label the base year 100 percent.
3. Express all other years as percentages of the base year.

Let's say that you have been able to pull the following figures from the income statements for Bill's Bike Shop, Inc., for 2004 through 2008.

Item	Year				
	2004	**2005**	**2006**	**2007**	**2008**
Net Sales	$714,200	$782,380	$806,400	$848,600	$966,900
Cost of Goods Sold	466,150	519,180	540,300	568,800	662,900
Gross Profit	248,050	263,200	266,100	279,800	304,000

You establish 2004 as the base year and calculate the trend percentages for Net Sales by dividing the Net Sales for each year by the Net Sales for 2004.

For 2005: $\dfrac{\$782,380}{\$714,200} = 714,200\overline{)782,380}^{\,1.095} = 1.095 \times 100 = \underline{\underline{109.5\%}}$

For 2006: $\dfrac{\$806,400}{\$714,200} = 714,200\overline{)806,400}^{\,1.129} = 1.129 \times 100 = \underline{\underline{112.9\%}}$

For 2007: $\dfrac{\$848,600}{\$714,200} = 714,200\overline{)848,600}^{\,1.188} = 1.188 \times 100 = \underline{\underline{118.8\%}}$

For 2008: $\dfrac{\$966,900}{\$714,200} = 714,200\overline{)966,900}^{\,1.354} = 1.354 \times 100 = \underline{\underline{135.4\%}}$

You determine trend percentages for Cost of Goods Sold and Gross Profit the same way. Here are the results, with the percentages rounded off as before.

Trend percentages, a form of horizontal analysis, use a particular year as a base from which to compare previous or subsequent years. Rising college tuition and fees are easier to compare using this method.

Item	Year				
	2004	**2005**	**2006**	**2007**	**2008**
Net Sales	100.0%	109.5%	112.9%	118.8%	135.4%
Cost of Goods Sold	100.0	111.4	115.9	122.0	142.2
Gross Profit	100.0	106.1	107.3	112.8	122.6

Observe that, over the five-year period, the trend of Net Sales is upward. However, Cost of Goods Sold is going up at a more rapid rate. In other words, over the five years, Cost of Goods Sold increased faster than Net Sales, resulting in smaller increases in Gross Profit. This is fine if the company's plan is to achieve a greater volume of sales accompanied by more moderate profits. But if this shrinking Gross Profit is *not* consistent with company policy, then it may be a sign that the company is not passing along its increased costs to its customers.

INDUSTRY COMPARISONS

Vertical analysis, using percentage figures, is very useful when you wish to compare the figures for one company with the average figures for the given industry. The format of the financial statement defines it as a **common-size statement**. You express all items as percentages of a common base. Common-size statements can be used to compare one company with another as well as with industry averages. For the income statement, the common base is again net sales. Net sales is set at 100 percent, and all other items are expressed as a percentage of net sales. Trade and marketing associations often gather information and publish common-size statements.

ANALYSIS BY CREDITORS AND MANAGEMENT

Because management is vitally interested in increasing the company's solvency and profitability, managers are concerned with all types of analytical tools and techniques. Because creditors want assurance of being repaid, they are concerned first with the company's solvency and second with its profitability.

How Do Short-Term Creditors and Management Analyze an Enterprise?

FYI

Current means within one year or the operating cycle, whichever is longer.

OBJECTIVE 4a

Compute working capital.

REMEMBER!

Working capital equals current assets minus current liabilities.

Bankers and other short-term creditors are primarily interested in the *current* position of a given firm: Does the firm have enough money coming in to meet its current operating needs and to pay its current debts promptly? Let's use as an example some calculations derived from the comparative financial statements of Bill's Bike Shop, Inc., for 2008 and 2007.

Working Capital   **Working capital** is the excess of current assets over current liabilities. One determines the working capital for Bill's Bike Shop, Inc., as shown in the following equations:

Working Capital = Current Assets − Current Liabilities

Working Capital (2008) = $448,600 − $100,600 = **$348,000**

Working Capital (2007) = $326,100 − $42,600 = **$283,500**

Bill's Bike Shop has $348,000 of capital available to work with during 2008 compared with $283,500 of capital available to work with during 2007.

OBJECTIVE 4b
Compute current ratio.

Current Ratio   The relationship of a company's current assets to its current liabilities is its **current ratio**. You arrive at this figure by dividing current assets by current liabilities.

$$\text{Current Ratio} = \frac{\text{Current Assets}}{\text{Current Liabilities}}$$

$$\text{Current Ratio (2008)} = \frac{\$448,600}{\$100,600} = 4.46$$

$$\text{Current Ratio (2007)} = \frac{\$326,100}{\$42,600} = 7.65$$

> **REMEMBER!**
>
> To compute the current ratio, divide current assets by current liabilities.

A firm's current ratio reveals its current debt-paying ability. Bill's Bike Shop's current ratio of 4.46 in 2008 indicates that there is $4.46 of cash coming in within a year from now for every dollar Bill's Bike Shop has to pay out within a year. But the firm was better off in 2007, because in that year, it had $7.65 coming in within a year for every dollar to be paid out within the year.

From the point of view of bankers and other creditors, the adequacy of a company's current ratio depends on what type of business the firm is in. A favorable ratio for a merchandising business is generally 2—higher if the type of merchandise the firm sells is subject to abrupt changes in design or technology that create higher risk. But a public utility, which has no inventories other than supplies, is considered solvent even if its current ratio is less than 1. But notice that a current ratio of 4.46 for Bill's Bike Shop only indicates that current assets (not cash inflows) at one point in time (year-end date, for example) exceed current liabilities (not cash outflows). (*Note:* If the company has changed inventory valuation methods from one year to another—for example, if it has switched from FIFO to LIFO—a restatement should be made in the costs of merchandise inventories; otherwise, there is no common base for making a comparison.)

OBJECTIVE 4c
Compute quick ratio.

Quick Ratio   The relationship of a company's current assets that can be quickly converted into cash to its current liabilities is known as its **quick ratio** or *acid-test ratio*. **Quick assets** are Cash, current Notes Receivable, net Accounts Receivable (that is, Accounts Receivable less Allowance for Doubtful Accounts), Interest Receivable, and Marketable Securities. They do not include inventories and prepaid expenses because these are less easily converted into cash than are other current assets. Determine the quick ratio by dividing quick assets by current liabilities.

$$\text{Quick Ratio} = \frac{\text{Quick Assets}}{\text{Current Liabilities}}$$

$$\text{Quick Ratio (2008)} = \frac{\$21,800 + (\$79,700 - \$3,300)}{\$100,600} = \frac{\$98,200}{\$100,600} = 0.98$$

$$\text{Quick Ratio (2007)} = \frac{\$38,700 + (\$81,400 - \$2,600)}{\$42,600} = \frac{\$117,500}{\$42,600} = 2.76$$

> **REMEMBER!**
>
> Quick assets do not include inventories or prepaid expenses—only assets quickly convertible to cash.

Bill's Bike Shop's quick ratio of 0.98 in 2008 indicates that there are 98 cents in cash coming in quickly—without involving the liquidation of inventory—for every dollar it has to pay out on a given date. For 2007, there was $2.76 that the firm could realize quickly for every dollar it had to pay out on a given date.

A quick ratio of 1 is normally considered satisfactory. However, the quick ratio for Bill's Bike Shop exposes a precarious short-term financial position. Consider this quick ratio in conjunction with the company's working capital and its current ratio. Although working capital and current ratio are two indicators of a firm's ability to meet its current obligations, they don't reveal the *composition of its current assets*—a very important factor.

Relationship of Each Current Asset to Total Current Assets Suppose that you are asked to find out the proportionate position of each item in the list of current assets of Bill's Bike Shop. Your first step is to compile a schedule of each current asset as it relates to total current assets, as shown in the following illustration:

	DECEMBER 31, 2008		DECEMBER 31, 2007	
	AMOUNT	PERCENT	AMOUNT	PERCENT
Current Assets:				
Cash	$ 21 800 00	4.9	$ 38 700 00	11.9
Accounts Receivable (net)	76 400 00	17.0	78 800 00	24.2
Merchandise Inventory	348 400 00	77.7	206 500 00	63.3
Prepaid Insurance	2 000 00	0.4	2 100 00	0.6
Total Current Assets	$448 600 00	100.0	$326 100 00	100.0

As an example, cash as a percentage of total current assets is calculated like this:

$$\frac{\$21,800}{\$448,600} = 0.0486 = \underline{\underline{4.9\%}}$$

We have already commented on the large increase in the proportion of merchandise inventory (it was 63.3 percent of current assets in 2007 but amounts to 77.7 percent of current assets in 2008). This change, coupled with the decline in the cash position (11.9 percent of current assets for 2007; only 4.9 percent of current assets for 2008), reinforces the message we got from the decline in the quick ratio: The firm may have a hard time paying its current debts.

OBJECTIVE 4d

Compute accounts receivable turnover.

Accounts Receivable Turnover Since money tied up in accounts receivable does not yield any revenue, any firm tries to collect accounts receivable promptly and to keep them at a minimum. It can use the cash it gets from collection of accounts receivable to reduce bank loans or to take advantage of cash discounts. This action reduces the amount of interest it has to pay and the cost of the merchandise it buys. It also reduces the risk of loss from bad debts.

Accounts receivable turnover is the number of times charge accounts are turned over (or paid off) per year. A turnover implies a sale on account followed by payment of the debt in cash. Compute this by *dividing net sales on* *account by average net accounts receivable.* If possible, use the average of the monthly balances of Accounts Receivable because this allows for seasonal fluctuations. If you don't have figures for monthly balances, use the average of the balances at the beginning and the end of the year. Here is how accounts receivable turnover looks for Bill's Bike Shop. (You have to take the beginning balance of net Accounts Receivable for 2007, which was $61,460, from the 2006 balance sheet. Net sales on account (charge sales, not cash sales), taken from the sales journal, were $773,020 for 2008 and $678,880 for 2007.)

$$\text{Accounts Receivable Turnover} = \frac{\text{Net Sales on Account}}{\text{Average Accounts Receivable (Net)}}$$

$$\text{Average Accounts Receivable} = \frac{\text{Beginning Accounts Receivable (Net)} + \text{Ending Accounts Receivable (Net)}}{2}$$

$$\text{Accounts Receivable Turnover (2008)} = \frac{\$773,020}{\dfrac{\$78,800 + \$76,400}{2}} = \frac{\$773,020}{\$77,600} = \underline{\underline{9.96}} \text{ times per year}$$

$$\text{Accounts Receivable Turnover (2007)} = \frac{\$678,880}{\dfrac{\$61,460 + \$78,800}{2}} = \frac{\$678,880}{\$70,130} = \underline{\underline{9.68}} \text{ times per year}$$

You can use the accounts receivable turnover to determine the number of days that the receivables were on the books. Calculate this by dividing 365 days by the turnover figure:

$$\text{Year (2008)} = \frac{365 \text{ days}}{9.96 \text{ times per year}} = 36.65 \text{ or } \underline{\underline{37}} \text{ days}$$

$$\text{Year (2007)} = \frac{365 \text{ days}}{9.68 \text{ times per year}} = 37.71 \text{ or } \underline{\underline{38}} \text{ days}$$

It took an average of one day less to collect accounts receivable in 2008 than it did in 2007. This reduction represents a slight improvement in collections for Bill's Bike Shop. Since the company's credit terms are net 30 days, 37 or 38 days is reasonable.

OBJECTIVE 4e

Compute merchandise inventory turnover.

Merchandise Inventory Turnover   **Merchandise inventory turnover** is the number of times a company's average inventory is sold during a given year. Calculate this by *dividing Cost of Goods Sold by average Merchandise Inventory.* Here is the calculation for Bill's Bike Shop (beginning Merchandise Inventory for 2007, taken from the 2006 balance sheet, was $138,700):

$$\text{Merchandise Inventory Turnover} = \frac{\text{Cost of Goods Sold}}{\text{Average Merchandise Inventory}}$$

$$\text{Average Merchandise Inventory} = \frac{\text{Beginning Merchandise Inventory} + \text{Ending Merchandise Inventory}}{2}$$

$$\text{Merchandise Inventory Turnover (2008)} = \frac{\$662,900}{\dfrac{\$206,500 + \$348,400}{2}} = \frac{\$662,900}{\$277,450} = \underline{\underline{2.39}} \text{ times per year}$$

$$\text{Merchandise Inventory Turnover (2007)} = \frac{\$568,800}{\dfrac{\$138,700 + \$206,500}{2}} = \frac{\$568,800}{\$172,600} = \underline{\underline{3.30}} \text{ times per year}$$

If possible, you should use the average of the monthly balances of Merchandise Inventory (add them and divide by 12). The figure for merchandise inventory turnover varies depending on the type of product involved. You can compare the figure for merchandise inventory turnover for one company with figures for the rest of the industry as a test of merchandising efficiency. Each turnover yields a gross profit or markup to the company. Note that there has been a serious decline in the rate of merchandise inventory turnover for Bill's Bike Shop. This is something to investigate further with management and monitor for future corrective action.

You may also use the figure for merchandise inventory turnover to determine the number of days that the merchandise was kept in stock. Calculate this the same way you calculate the number of days that the receivables were collectible: divide 365 days by the turnover figure.

$$\text{Year (2008)} = \frac{365 \text{ days}}{2.39 \text{ times per year}} = 152.72 = \underline{\underline{153}} \text{ days}$$

$$\text{Year (2007)} = \frac{365 \text{ days}}{3.30 \text{ times per year}} = 110.61 = \underline{\underline{111}} \text{ days}$$

Note that Bill's Bike Shop's merchandise remained in stock 42 days longer in 2008 than it did in 2007. This fact surely calls for an investigation of the company's sales and purchasing practices.

In addition to yielding a higher gross profit, rapid merchandise inventory turnover has other advantages. The money invested in the inventory is tied up for a shorter period of time; storage costs are lower; there is less risk of spoilage (if the merchandise is perishable); there is less risk of change in demand (if the merchandise is affected by changes in style or in business conditions).

How Do Long-Term Creditors and Management Analyze an Enterprise?

REMEMBER!

A corporation's bonds are classified as long-term liabilities.

Long-term creditors include secured creditors (such as banks) and bondholders. Whenever specific property has been pledged, secured creditors have first claim on the property in the event that the company cannot keep up its payments. Even in the case of debentures (unsecured bonds), the bondholders have a prior claim to the general assets of the company, a claim that takes precedence over that of the stockholders. Management is concerned with taking care of the company's present obligations, as well as preserving its credit standing, and hence its ability to borrow in the future.

Two ratios are particularly useful from the standpoint of long-term creditors:

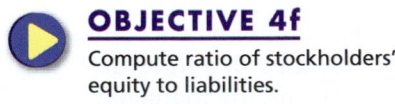

OBJECTIVE 4f

Compute ratio of stockholders' equity to liabilities.

Ratio of Stockholders' Equity to Liabilities   The ratio of stockholders' equity to liabilities is the ratio of the stockholders' investment to the creditors' claims.
   In calculating any ratio, we mean the ratio *of* one thing *to* something else. When we write the ratio as a fraction, we put the *of* part in the numerator and the *to* part in the denominator. Look at this calculation for Bill's Bike Shop.

$$\text{Ratio of Stockholders' Equity to Liabilities} = \frac{\text{Stockholders' Equity}}{\text{Liabilities}}$$

$$\text{Ratio of Stockholders' Equity to Liabilities (2008)} = \frac{\$509,800}{\$198,400} = \underline{\underline{2.57}}$$

$$\text{Ratio of Stockholders' Equity to Liabilities (2007)} = \frac{\$464,300}{\$140,200} = \underline{\underline{3.31}}$$

In 2008 for every $2.57 of stockholders' investment, the creditors have loaned $1. Bill's Bike Shop's ratio of stockholders' equity to liabilities shows a decline since 2007, from 3.31 to 2.57. Creditors like to see a high proportion of stockholders' equity because stockholders' equity, or owners' equity, acts as a buffer in case the company has to absorb losses. Also, owners often prefer a high proportion of equity to liabilities.

OBJECTIVE 4g

Compute ratio of property and equipment to long-term liabilities.

Ratio of Property and Equipment to Long-Term Liabilities There is another factor that provides a margin of safety to mortgage holders and bondholders—the ratio of the value of a firm's total property and equipment to its long-term liabilities. This ratio also indicates the potential ability of the enterprise to borrow more money on a long-term basis. Let's look at the calculation for Bill's Bike Shop.

$$\text{Ratio of Property and Equipment to Long-Term Liabilities} = \frac{\text{Property and Equipment}}{\text{Long-Term Liabilities}}$$

$$\text{Ratio of Property and Equipment to Long-Term Liabilities (2008)} = \frac{\$190,800}{\$97,800} = \underline{\underline{1.95}}$$

$$\text{Ratio of Property and Equipment to Long-Term Liabilities (2007)} = \frac{\$209,200}{\$97,600} = \underline{\underline{2.14}}$$

In 2007, there was $2.14 book value of property and equipment for every dollar of long-term liabilities. In 2008, there is $1.95 book value of property and equipment for every dollar of long-term liabilities. This ratio, too, has deteriorated.

As we have seen, a firm's creditors and managers may use any of eight devices to determine the financial position of a firm:

REMEMBER!

To find the ratio of . . . to . . . , divide the "of . . ." amount by the "to . . ." amount.

- Working capital
- Current ratio
- Quick ratio
- Relationship of each current asset to total current assets
- Accounts receivable turnover
- Merchandise inventory turnover
- Ratio of stockholders' equity to liabilities
- Ratio of property and equipment to long-term liabilities

ANALYSIS BY OWNERS AND MANAGEMENT

In addition to being concerned about the solvency and profitability of a company, owners and managers are vitally interested in the value of and return on investment in the company. In many cases, the owners are the managers. In other situations, managers are employed by the owners. What diagnostic tools do owners and managers use to determine the financial health of their company?

Equity per Share

OBJECTIVE 5a

Calculate equity per share.

When you examine the annual report of a corporation, you encounter the term *book value per share,* also referred to as *equity per share.* If a corporation has only one class of common stock outstanding, equity per share is determined by dividing the total stockholders' equity by the number of shares of stock issued and outstanding. Here are the calculations for Bill's Bike Shop.

$$\text{Equity per Share} = \frac{\text{Total Stockholders' Equity Available to a Class of Stock}}{\text{Number of Shares Issued and Outstanding}}$$

$$\text{Equity per Share (2008)} = \frac{\$509,800}{3,000 \text{ shares}} = \$169.93 \text{ per share}$$

$$\text{Equity per Share (2007)} = \frac{\$464,300}{3,000 \text{ shares}} = \$154.77 \text{ per share}$$

When there are shares of preferred stock outstanding, you must deduct the liquidation value of the preferred stockholders' equity, including any dividends in arrears on cumulative preferred stock, to arrive at the stockholders' equity available to holders of common stock.

The term *equity per share* does *not* mean the cash value or market value of a share; it means the amount that would be distributed per share of stock on a book basis *if* the corporation were to **liquidate** (wind up its affairs by paying off its creditors and selling its assets for cash) without incurring any expenses, gains, or losses in selling its assets and paying its liabilities. The equity per share increases as a firm retains net income. This concept of equity per share is important in contracts involving the sale of stock. For example, a large stockholder might obtain an option to buy the shares of small stockholders at the value of the equity per share as of a certain future date.

Rate of Return on Common Stockholders' Equity

A corporation exists first and foremost to earn a net income for its stockholders. Therefore, the rate of return on the common stockholders' equity is important as a means of measuring how good or bad the investment is. This rate is calculated by dividing the net income available to holders of common stock by the *average value* of their equity. Here is the calculation for Bill's Bike Shop (beginning common stockholders' equity for 2007 was $422,100):

Rate of Return on Common Stockholders' Equity

$$= \frac{\text{Net Income Available to Common Stock}}{\dfrac{\text{Beginning Common Stockholders' Equity} + \text{Ending Common Stockholders' Equity}}{2}}$$

Rate of Return on Common Stockholders' Equity (2008)

$$= \frac{\$70,960}{\dfrac{\$464,300 + \$509,800}{2}} = \frac{\$70,960}{\$487,050} = 0.1457 = 14.6\%$$

Rate of Return on Common Stockholders' Equity (2007)

$$= \frac{\$69,530}{\dfrac{\$422,100 + \$464,300}{2}} = \frac{\$69,530}{\$443,200} = 0.1569 = 15.7\%$$

The rate of return on common stockholders' equity declined 1.1 percent. Management should look into the matter to uncover the possible causes. Again, begin by investigating the large increase in merchandise inventory because it represents 49.2 percent of total assets in 2008.

OBJECTIVE 5c

Calculate earnings per share of common stock.

REMEMBER!

Dividends on preferred stock are paid before those on common stock.

Earnings per Share of Common Stock

You often see **earnings per share** of stock listed in the financial columns of newspapers. If a corporation has no preferred stock outstanding, compute the earnings per share of common stock by dividing net income by the average number of shares of common stock outstanding during the year. When there is preferred stock, you must first deduct any dividends on preferred stock to arrive at the amount available to common stock. Here is the calculation of earnings per share of common stock for Bill's Bike Shop:

$$\text{Earnings per Share of Common Stock} = \frac{\text{Net Income Available to Common Stock}}{\text{Average Number of Shares of Common Stock Outstanding}}$$

$$\text{Earnings per Share of Common Stock (2008)} = \frac{\$70,960}{3,000 \text{ shares}} = \underline{\$23.65} \text{ per share}$$

$$\text{Earnings per Share of Common Stock (2007)} = \frac{\$69,530}{3,000 \text{ shares}} = \underline{\$23.18} \text{ per share}$$

Any big change during the year in the *number* of shares outstanding naturally has a significant impact on the amount of earnings per share. That's why a company must disclose (or show) the average number of shares outstanding and disclose any information relating to stock dividends and stock splits. If the company has stock options or stock awards outstanding, the earnings per share must also be computed taking into account the additional shares of stock that could potentially be outstanding. This calculation is called *diluted earnings per share*.

OBJECTIVE 5d

Calculate price-earnings ratio.

Price-Earnings Ratio

The **price-earnings ratio** is a measure commonly used to determine whether the market price of a corporation's stock is reasonable. You calculate the price-earnings ratio of a company's stock by dividing the market price per share by the annual earnings per share. Suppose that the market price of a share of common stock of Bill's Bike Shop at the end of 2008 is $141, and that at the end of 2007 it was $137. Here is how you calculate the price-earnings ratio:

$$\text{Price-Earnings Ratio} = \frac{\text{Market Price per Share}}{\text{Earnings per Share}}$$

$$\text{Price-Earnings Ratio (2008)} = \frac{\$141}{\$23.65} = 5.962 = \underline{5.96}$$

$$\text{Price-Earnings Ratio (2007)} = \frac{\$137}{\$23.18} = 5.910 = \underline{5.91}$$

What constitutes a reasonable price-earnings ratio varies from one industry to another and with the state of the economy. Stocks quoted in the Dow Jones Average usually have about a 16:1 to 30:1 price-earnings ratio. Corporations that have shown a large continued growth in earnings over a period of years may have a ratio of more than 30:1.

You may also use the price-earnings ratio in this manner: If the acceptable price-earnings ratio for a given stock is 16:1 and the earnings per share equal $2.50, it follows that the maximum reasonable price you ought to pay for the stock is $40 (that is, $2.50 × 16). But what if the stock is selling for only $20? You may well consider it to be undervalued.

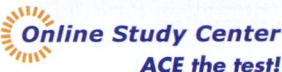

CHAPTER REVIEW

Review of Performance Objectives

1. **Prepare a comparative income statement and balance sheet involving horizontal analysis.**

   Horizontal analysis involves the comparison of the same item on an income statement or balance sheet for two or more periods. First, determine the difference between the two periods. Next, express the difference as a percentage of the base period (usually the earliest period).

2. **Prepare a comparative income statement and balance sheet involving vertical analysis.**

   In vertical analysis, each item in a financial statement is expressed as a percentage of a base amount. For an income statement, the base amount is net sales. For a balance sheet, the base amount is total assets or total liabilities and stockholders' equity.

3. **Express income statement data in trend percentages.**

   Income statement data shown in trend percentages involve a comparison of the same item over a number of periods. One period or year (usually the earliest) is designated as the base period and the amount for this period is set at 100 percent. Each amount in later years is expressed as a percentage of the amount for the base period.

4. **Compute (a) working capital, (b) current ratio, (c) quick ratio, (d) accounts receivable turnover, (e) merchandise inventory turnover, (f) ratio of stockholders' equity to liabilities, and (g) ratio of property and equipment to long-term liabilities.**

   Short-term creditors and management use the following techniques:

   $$\text{Working Capital} = \text{Current Assets} - \text{Current Liabilities}$$

   $$\text{Current Ratio} = \frac{\text{Current Assets}}{\text{Current Liabilities}}$$

   $$\text{Quick Ratio} = \frac{\text{Quick Assets}}{\text{Current Liabilities}}$$

   $$\text{Accounts Receivable Turnover} = \frac{\text{Net Sales on Account}}{\text{Average Accounts Receivable (Net)}}$$

   $$\text{Merchandise Inventory Turnover} = \frac{\text{Cost of Goods Sold}}{\text{Average Merchandise Inventory}}$$

   Long-term creditors and management use the following ratios:

   $$\text{Ratio of Stockholders' Equity to Liabilities} = \frac{\text{Stockholders' Equity}}{\text{Liabilities}}$$

   $$\text{Ratio of Property and Equipment to Long-Term Liabilities} = \frac{\text{Property and Equipment}}{\text{Long-Term Liabilities}}$$

5. **Calculate (a) equity per share, (b) rate of return on common stockholders' equity, (c) earnings per share of common stock, and (d) price-earnings ratio.**

Owners and managers use the following measures:

$$\text{Equity per Share} = \frac{\text{Total Stockholders' Equity Available to a Class of Stock}}{\text{Number of Shares Issued and Outstanding}}$$

$$\text{Rate of Return on Common Stockholders' Equity} = \frac{\text{Net Income Available to Common Stock}}{\text{Average Common Stockholders' Equity}}$$

$$\text{Earnings per Share of Common Stock} = \frac{\text{Net Income Available to Common Stock}}{\text{Average Number of Shares of Common Stock Outstanding}}$$

$$\text{Price-Earnings Ratio} = \frac{\text{Market Price per Share}}{\text{Earnings per Share}}$$

Glossary

Accounts receivable turnover The number of times charge accounts are paid off per year; a turnover is a sale on account and subsequent repayment. (921)

Base year The year used as a basis for comparison. (911)

Common-size statement A financial statement using vertical analysis with all items expressed as percentages; allows comparison of one company with another as well as with industry averages. (919)

Current ratio Current assets divided by current liabilities. (920)

Earnings per share The proportionate amount of a company's net earnings for each outstanding share of common stock. (926)

Horizontal analysis Comparing the same item in the financial statements of an enterprise for two or more periods. (909)

Liquidate To wind up the affairs of a business by paying off the creditors and selling the assets for cash. (925)

Merchandise inventory turnover The number of times a company's average inventory is sold during a given year. (922)

Price-earnings ratio A common measure for deciding whether a stock's market price is reasonable; calculated by dividing the market price per share by the annual earnings per share. (926)

Profitability An enterprise's ability to earn a reasonable profit on the owners' investment. (909)

Quick assets Cash, current Notes Receivable, net Accounts Receivable, Interest Receivable, and Marketable Securities. (920)

Quick ratio Quick assets divided by current liabilities. Also called *acid-test ratio.* (920)

Solvency An enterprise's ability to pay its debts. (909)

Trend percentages Percentages calculated by dividing a specific item on an income statement by the corresponding item on the base year income statement. (918)

Vertical analysis Portraying items in financial statements as percentages (or proportional parts) of a given item on the same financial statement. (912)

Working capital The excess of current assets over current liabilities. (919)

QUESTIONS, EXERCISES, AND CASES

Discussion Questions

1. A company has a net income percentage of 10 percent. What does this mean?

2. What does an increase in the accounts receivable turnover indicate as far as a company is concerned?

3. What is the difference between a firm's solvency and its profitability?

4. How does a company's current ratio differ from its quick ratio?

5. Why is a high merchandise inventory turnover more desirable than a low turnover?

6. Describe the difference between horizontal analysis and vertical analysis with regard to comparative balance sheets.

7. Which of the following types of business firms would you expect to have a high merchandise inventory turnover?
   a. Furniture store
   b. Women's clothing boutique
   c. Jeweler
   d. Gift shop
   e. Grocery
   f. Florist

8. Why are creditors interested in the ratio of stockholders' equity to liabilities? Is it more desirable to have a high ratio or a low ratio?

Exercises

P.O. 1

Calculate the percentage of increase and decrease—horizontal analysis.

Exercise 24-1 Calculate the amount and percentage of increase and decrease for the following items (horizontal analysis). Round off to three decimal places.

	2008	2007
Cash	$ 73,400	$ 80,000
Notes Receivable	52,000	40,000
Equipment (net)	180,500	182,500
Retained Earnings	120,200	115,000

P.O. 2

Prepare a comparative income statement—vertical analysis.

Exercise 24-2 Using the following revenue and expense data, prepare a comparative income statement, expressing each item for both 2008 and 2007 as a percentage of net sales (vertical analysis). Round off to three decimal places. Comment on the results.

	2008	2007
Sales (net)	$703,000	$650,000
Cost of Goods Sold	501,000	448,145
Selling Expenses	40,500	38,000
General Expenses	21,850	19,500
Income Tax Expense	48,125	44,340

P.O. 3

Calculate trend percentages and comment on the trends.

Exercise 24-3 Calculate trend percentages for the following items, and comment on the trends. Use 2005 as the base year. Round off to three decimal places. Comment on the results.

	2005	2006	2007	2008
Net Sales	$688,000	$665,000	$632,000	$605,000
Cost of Goods Sold	370,000	365,000	392,000	362,000
Merchandise Inventory	75,000	72,000	65,000	62,000

P.O. 4a,b,c

Calculate working capital, current ratio, and quick ratio.

Exercise 24-4 The following items are from the balance sheets of C. C. Rister Company as of December 31, 2008 and 2007.

	2008	2007
Current Assets:		
Cash	$ 98 000 00	$ 89 000 00
Notes Receivable	15 000 00	13 000 00
Accounts Receivable (net)	67 000 00	58 000 00
Merchandise Inventory	273 000 00	236 000 00
Total Current Assets	$453 000 00	$396 000 00
Current Liabilities	$228 000 00	$182 000 00

Calculate the following for each year (round to two decimals):

a. Working capital
b. Current ratio
c. Quick ratio

P.O. 4a,b,c

Compute working capital, current ratio, and quick ratio.

Exercise 24-5 The following items are taken from the balance sheet of Morrisey Company:

Cash	$126,000
Accounts Receivable (net)	378,000
Merchandise Inventory	123,000
Prepaid Expenses	3,850
Accounts Payable	175,700
Notes Payable (current)	18,500
Salaries Payable	3,800

Compute the following:

a. Working capital
b. Current ratio
c. Quick ratio

P.O. 2,4d,e

Calculate the gross profit percentage, accounts receivable turnover, and merchandise inventory turnover.

Exercise 24-6 The data on the following page are taken from the financial statements of the Westin Company. For 2008, calculate the gross profit percentage, the accounts receivable turnover, and the merchandise inventory turnover. Round off to two decimal places.

	2008	2007
Sales (net on account)	$825,000	$700,000
Cost of Goods Sold	616,000	520,000
Merchandise Inventory (at end of year)	138,400	131,000
Accounts Receivable (at end of year)	100,600	103,500

P.O. 4d,e,g;5b

Compute turnovers, ratios, and rate of return.

Exercise 24-7 The following items are taken from the financial statements of Vargas Company. All sales are made on account. Common stock is the only stock issued by Vargas Company.

	2008	2007
Accounts Receivable	$ 421,000	$ 392,000
Merchandise Inventory	312,000	285,000
Property and Equipment (net)	2,504,000	2,200,000
Long-Term Liabilities	1,012,000	1,000,000
Stockholders' Equity	3,985,000	3,645,000
Sales (net)	1,852,000	1,688,000
Gross Profit	563,000	515,000
Net Income	197,000	185,000

Compute the following:

a. Accounts receivable turnover
b. Merchandise inventory turnover
c. Ratio of property and equipment to long-term liabilities
d. Rate of return on common stockholders' equity

P.O. 5a,b,c,d

Calculate equity per share, rate of return on common stockholders' equity, earnings per share, and price-earnings ratio.

Exercise 24-8 The Stockholders' Equity section of the balance sheet of Forks Corporation is as follows:

Stockholders' Equity		
Paid-in Capital:		
Common Stock, $5 par value (100,000		
shares authorized, 80,000 shares		
issued and outstanding)	$400 0 0 0 00	
Paid-in Capital in Excess of Par Value	140 0 0 0 00	
Total Paid-in Capital	$540 0 0 0 00	
Retained Earnings	290 0 0 0 00	
Total Stockholders' Equity		$830 0 0 0 00

Net income for the year is $123,000. Stockholders' equity was $879,000 at the beginning of the year. The present market price of the stock is $44 per share. Determine the following, rounding to two decimal places:

a. Equity per share
b. Rate of return on common stockholders' equity.
c. Earnings per share
d. Price-earnings ratio

So, how has Southwest Airlines fared over the past few years? Let's take a look at Southwest Airlines' 2005 annual report by going to **http://www .southwest.com** and, under the Inside southwest.com heading at the bottom of the screen, clicking on Investor Relations. Then click Annual Reports and then the 2005 Annual Report. Scroll down until you reach the consolidated statement of income on page 29 of the 10-K report. (*Hint:* This is on page 48 of the pdf file.) Now that you have an understanding of comparative financial statements, you can decide for yourself.

1. Does Southwest Airlines present its comparative financial statements horizontally or vertically in its 10-K report?
2. What was Southwest Airlines' net income for each of the three years: 2005, 2004, and 2003? What does that information tell you about how Southwest did over those three years?
3. JetBlue Airways Corporation reported net income (loss) of ($20,000,000), $46,000,000, and $103,000,000 for the years 2005, 2004, and 2003, respectively. Compare these two airlines by using the net income (loss) data for the three years. What trends do you see? Which airline would you consider the better investment based on the information provided? Explain your reasoning.
4. Is it reasonable to compare JetBlue, a much smaller airline, to Southwest? Why or why not?

WHAT'S WRONG WITH THIS PICTURE?

What if you see that purchases discounts for this year are 5 percent lower than for last year? Who would you talk to about it? What is happening? How has it affected your "bottom line"?

CRITICAL THINKING

The following data were analyzed by the new accounting assistant:

Gross sales	$102,000
Sales returns and allowances	4,804
Sales discounts	1,040
Cost of goods sold	54,540
Operating expenses	36,890

The accounting assistant concluded the following:

The gross profit percentage for the year is 40.8 percent.
The income from operations percentage for the year is 4.6 percent.

You are suspicious of the percentages reported. Check the numbers. If there are errors, do you have any suggestions for the next step?

A QUESTION OF ETHICS

A manager of a company is evaluated on the gross profit percentage of his department. To boost sales, in spite of potential higher uncollectible accounts expense, he unduly extends more credit. Comment on this tactic as well as the board of directors' buying back significant blocks of stock at the end of the year so that stock is not outstanding when earnings per share is calculated.

PROBLEM SET A

For additional help, see the demonstration problem at the beginning of each chapter in your Working Papers.

P.O. 1

Problem 24-1A During 2007, Yomoto's Jewelry Store, Inc., put on a sales promotion campaign that cost $9,672 more than it usually spent on advertising. A condensed partial comparative income statement for the fiscal years ended December 31, 2007, and December 31, 2006, is shown below.

Yomoto's Jewelry Store, Inc.
Comparative Income Statement
For Years Ended December 31, 2007 and December 31, 2006

	2007	2006
Revenue from Sales:		
Sales	$476 760 00	$376 000 00
Less Sales Returns and Allowances	26 000 00	20 000 00
Net Sales	$450 760 00	$356 000 00
Cost of Goods Sold	205 140 00	156 000 00
Gross Profit	$245 620 00	$200 000 00
Operating Expenses:		
Selling Expenses	$ 66 925 00	$ 55 300 00
General Expenses	18 104 00	16 310 00
Total Operating Expenses	$ 85 029 00	$ 71 610 00
Income from Operations	$160 591 00	$128 390 00
Other Expenses	397 00	305 00
Income Before Income Tax	$160 194 00	$128 085 00
Income Tax Expense	33 000 00	26 386 00
Net Income	$127 194 00	$101 699 00

Check Figure

Increase in Income Before Income Tax, 25.1 percent

Check Figure

2007 percentage of Income Before Income Tax to Net Sales, 35.5

Instructions

1. Using horizontal analysis, prepare a comparative income statement for the two-year period. Round off percentages to three decimal places.
2. Comment on the percentages of increase or decrease.

P.O. 2

Problem 24-2A Use the comparative income statement for Yomoto's Jewelry Store, Inc., presented in Problem 24-1A.

Instructions

1. Using vertical analysis, prepare a comparative income statement for the two-year period. Round off percentages to three decimal places.
2. Comment on the percentage figures.

P.O. 3

Problem 24-3A The condensed comparative income statement of Alonso Manufacturing Corporation is shown below.

Alonso Manufacturing Corporation
Comparative Income Statement
For Years Ended December 31, 2006, 2007, 2008 (in thousands)

	2006	2007	2008
Sales (net)	$15 0 0 0 00	$16 3 5 0 00	$17 1 0 1 00
Cost of Goods Sold	10 6 0 0 00	11 7 6 9 00	12 0 4 0 00
Gross Profit	$ 4 4 0 0 00	$ 4 5 8 1 00	$ 5 0 6 1 00
Operating Expenses:			
Selling Expenses	$ 2 1 4 2 00	$ 2 2 8 8 00	$ 2 4 3 7 00
General Expenses	1 3 9 0 00	1 3 9 2 00	1 3 9 7 00
Total Operating Expenses	$ 3 5 3 2 00	$ 3 6 8 0 00	$ 3 8 3 4 00
Income Before Income Tax	$ 8 6 8 00	$ 9 0 1 00	$ 1 2 2 7 00
Income Tax Expense	2 9 5 00	3 0 6 00	4 1 7 00
Net Income	$ 5 7 3 00	$ 5 9 5 00	$ 8 1 0 00

Check Figure

2008 percentage of Net Income, 141.4

Instructions

1. Express the income statement data in trend percentages. Round off to the nearest tenth of a percent (three decimal places).
2. Comment on any significant relationships revealed by the percentages.

P.O. 4a,b,c,e;5b,c,d

Problem 24-4A Here are the year-end financial statements of Scott's Music Store (see balance sheet on the following page).

Scott's Music Store
Income Statement
For Year Ended December 31, 2007

Revenue from Sales:			
Sales			$567 0 0 0 00
Cost of Goods Sold:			
Merchandise Inventory, Jan. 1, 2007	$ 84 0 0 0 00		
Delivered Cost of Purchases	353 2 0 0 00		
Cost of Goods Available for Sale	$437 2 0 0 00		
Less Merchandise Inventory,			
Dec. 31, 2007	93 0 3 0 00		
Cost of Goods Sold			344 1 7 0 00
Gross Profit			$222 8 3 0 00
Operating Expenses:			
Selling Expenses (control)	$118 1 2 5 00		
General Expenses (control)	58 0 6 5 00		
Total Operating Expenses			176 1 9 0 00
Income from Operations			$ 46 6 4 0 00
Other Expenses:			
Interest Expense			7 2 0 0 00
Income Before Income Tax			$ 39 4 4 0 00
Income Tax Expense			8 7 0 0 00
Net Income			$ 30 7 4 0 00

Scott's Music Store
Balance Sheet
December 31, 2007

Assets						
Current Assets:					
Cash		$ 23 4 3 0 00			
Notes Receivable		6 6 0 0 00			
Accounts Receivable (net)		85 4 7 0 00			
Merchandise Inventory		93 0 3 0 00			
Prepaid Expenses		1 9 8 0 00			
Total Current Assets				$210 5 1 0 00	
Property and Equipment:					
Store Equipment (net)		$ 50 9 8 5 00			
Office Equipment (net)		15 5 1 0 00			
Delivery Equipment (net)		82 0 0 5 00			
Total Property and Equipment				148 5 0 0 00	
Total Assets				$359 0 1 0 00	
Liabilities					
Current Liabilities:					
Notes Payable	$ 3 9 6 0 00				
Accounts Payable	59 0 0 0 00				
Total Current Liabilities		$ 62 9 6 0 00			
Long-Term Liabilities:					
Mortgage Payable (due June 30, 2012)		89 8 1 0 00			
Total Liabilities				$152 7 7 0 00	
Stockholders' Equity					
Common Stock, $7 par value (20,000 shares authorized					
and issued)		$140 0 0 0 00			
Retained Earnings		66 2 4 0 00			
Total Stockholders' Equity				206 2 4 0 00	
Total Liabilities and Stockholders' Equity				$359 0 1 0 00	

The current market price of common stock is $29.50 per share. At the beginning of the year, stockholders' equity was $192,000.

Check Figure

Price-earnings ratio, 19.16

Instructions

Determine the following, showing the figures you used in your calculations (round off to two decimal places):

1. Working capital
2. Current ratio
3. Quick ratio
4. Merchandise inventory turnover
5. Number of days merchandise inventory kept in stock
6. Rate of return on common stockholders' equity
7. Earnings per share of common stock
8. Price-earnings ratio

PROBLEM SET B

For additional help, see the demonstration problem at the beginning of each chapter in your Working Papers.

P.O. 1

Problem 24-1B During 2007, Broder Design, Inc., put on a sales promotion campaign that cost $4,831 more than it usually spent for advertising. The condensed partial comparative income statement for the fiscal years ended December 31, 2007, and December 31, 2006, is shown below.

Broder Design, Inc.
Comparative Income Statement
For Years Ended December 31, 2007 and December 31, 2006

	2007	2006
Revenue from Sales:		
Sales	$320 5 0 0 00	$258 4 6 8 00
Less Sales Returns and Allowances	26 1 9 0 00	19 4 0 0 00
Net Sales	$294 3 1 0 00	$239 0 6 8 00
Cost of Goods Sold	167 1 0 5 00	139 2 5 4 00
Gross Profit	$127 2 0 5 00	$ 99 8 1 4 00
Operating Expenses:		
Selling Expenses	$ 57 8 9 1 00	$ 49 0 6 0 00
General Expenses	17 0 0 6 00	15 3 2 1 00
Total Operating Expenses	$ 74 8 9 7 00	$ 64 3 8 1 00
Income from Operations	$ 52 3 0 8 00	$ 35 4 3 3 00
Other Expenses	7 0 7 00	5 9 5 00
Income Before Income Tax	$ 51 6 0 1 00	$ 34 8 3 8 00
Income Tax Expense	10 6 3 0 00	7 1 7 7 00
Net Income	$ 40 9 7 1 00	$ 27 6 6 1 00

Check Figure

Increase in Income Before Income Tax, 48.1 percent

Instructions

1. Using horizontal analysis, prepare a comparative income statement for the two-year period. Round off percentages to three decimal places.
2. Comment on the percentages of increase or decrease.

P.O. 2

Problem 24-2B Use the comparative income statement for Broder Design, Inc., presented in Problem 24-1B.

Check Figure

2006 percentage of Income Before Income Tax to Net Sales, 14.6

Instructions

1. Using vertical analysis, prepare a comparative income statement for the two-year period. Round off percentages to three decimal places.
2. Comment on the percentage figures.

P.O. 3

Problem 24-3B Following is the condensed comparative income statement of Pacific Electric Corporation:

Pacific Electric Corporation
Comparative Income Statement
For Years Ended December 31, 2006, 2007, 2008 (in thousands)

	2006	2007	2008
Sales (net)	$8 9 0 0 00	$9 6 7 4 00	$10 3 0 1 00
Cost of Goods Sold	5 7 0 0 00	6 2 6 4 00	6 7 9 1 00
Gross Profit	$3 2 0 0 00	$3 4 1 0 00	$ 3 5 1 0 00
Operating Expenses:			
Selling Expenses	$1 2 3 5 00	$1 2 4 9 00	$ 1 2 6 3 00
General Expenses	7 9 0 00	8 0 2 00	8 1 7 00
Total Operating Expenses	$2 0 2 5 00	$2 0 5 1 00	$ 2 0 8 0 00
Income Before Income Tax	$1 1 7 5 00	$1 3 5 9 00	$ 1 4 3 0 00
Income Tax Expense	4 0 0 00	4 6 2 00	4 8 6 00
Net Income	$ 7 7 5 00	$ 8 9 7 00	$ 9 4 4 00

Check Figure

2008 percentage of Net Income, 121.8

P.O. 4a,b,c,e;5b,c,d

Instructions

1. Express the income statement data in trend percentages. Round off to the nearest tenth of a percent (three decimal places).
2. Comment on any significant relationships revealed by the percentages.

Problem 24-4B Here is the income statement of Ortiz Corporation. The balance sheet is shown on page 938.

Ortiz Corporation
Income Statement
For Year Ended December 31, 2007

Revenue from Sales:		
Sales		$635 0 0 0 00
Cost of Goods Sold:		
Merchandise Inventory, Jan. 1, 2007	$102 0 0 0 00	
Delivered Cost of Purchases	414 0 0 0 00	
Cost of Goods Available for Sale	$516 0 0 0 00	
Less Merchandise Inventory,		
Dec. 31, 2007	109 0 0 0 00	
Cost of Goods Sold		407 0 0 0 00
Gross Profit		$228 0 0 0 00
Operating Expenses:		
Selling Expenses (control)	$125 1 0 0 00	
General Expenses (control)	62 7 0 0 00	
Total Operating Expenses		187 8 0 0 00
Income from Operations		$ 40 2 0 0 00
Other Expenses:		
Interest Expense		5 7 4 0 00
Income Before Income Tax		$ 34 4 6 0 00
Income Tax Expense		7 0 0 0 00
Net Income		$ 27 4 6 0 00

Ortiz Corporation
Balance Sheet
December 31, 2007

Assets			
Current Assets:			
Cash		$ 15 5 2 5 00	
Notes Receivable		5 4 0 0 00	
Accounts Receivable (net)		72 5 0 0 00	
Merchandise Inventory		109 0 0 0 00	
Prepaid Expenses		1 8 9 0 00	
Total Current Assets			$204 3 1 5 00
Property and Equipment:			
Store Equipment (net)		$ 42 1 2 0 00	
Office Equipment (net)		12 2 9 0 00	
Delivery Equipment (net)		69 4 0 0 00	
Total Property and Equipment			123 8 1 0 00
Total Assets			$328 1 2 5 00
Liabilities			
Current Liabilities:			
Notes Payable	$2 7 0 0 00		
Accounts Payable	29 0 2 5 00		
Total Current Liabilities		$ 31 7 2 5 00	
Long-Term Liabilities:			
Mortgage Payable (due June 30, 2010)		92 4 0 0 00	
Total Liabilities			$124 1 2 5 00
Stockholders' Equity			
Common Stock, $15 par value (10,000 shares authorized			
and issued)		$150 0 0 0 00	
Retained Earnings		54 0 0 0 00	
Total Stockholders' Equity			204 0 0 0 00
Total Liabilities and Stockholders' Equity			$328 1 2 5 00

The current market price of common stock is $43 per share. At the beginning of the year, stockholders' equity was $174,000.

Check Figure

Price-earnings ratio, 15.64

Instructions

Determine the following, showing the figures you used in your calculations (round off to two decimal places):

1. Working capital
2. Current ratio
3. Quick ratio
4. Merchandise inventory turnover
5. Number of days merchandise inventory kept in stock
6. Rate of return on common stockholders' equity
7. Earnings per share of common stock
8. Price-earnings ratio

Departmental Accounting

25

In September 1907, Neiman Marcus first opened its doors in Dallas, Texas, with the goal of selling exclusive lines of women's clothing. In the century that followed, the company expanded its merchandise to include clothing for men and children as well as fine home furnishings and unique his-and-hers gifts. It also developed a very high-end catalog that showcases many expensive products. The Nieman Marcus Group, Inc., is recognized around the world as a premier luxury retailer offering distinctive merchandise and superior service.

Certainly, for a company to operate successfully for a century, it must manage its resources carefully and maintain a close watch on its operations. Companies like The Neiman Marcus Group, Inc., often use a divisional or departmental approach to run the business. Departmental accounting helps a company separately track the performance of each department and make informed management decisions, such as which departments to expand and which to reduce or, possibly, close. You can view information about The Neiman Marcus Group, Inc., by going to **http://www .neimanmarcusgroup.com** and selecting Financial Information and then SEC Filings.

Performance Objectives

After you have completed this chapter, you will be able to do the following:

1. Compile a departmental income statement extended through Gross Profit.

2. Compile a departmental work sheet.

3. Compile a departmental income statement extended through Income from Operations.

4. Apportion operating expenses among various operating departments.

5. Compile a departmental income statement extended through Departmental Margin.

A company that carries on several different business activities should be divided into a number of subdivisions or departments. This enables the company's management to delegate authority to departmental managers, who are responsible for their respective departments, and to measure the profitability of each department. It is the element of profitability that we discuss in this chapter.

Large companies have greater opportunities to use departmental accounting than small ones. However, even a small business—if it carries on more than one type of business activity—may benefit from departmental accounting. For example, Lee Enterprises operates a real estate and insurance firm and accounts separately for real estate and insurance commissions. At the end of the fiscal year, Lee Enterprises can compare the profitability of each activity with the amount of time and attention it had to devote to that activity. With these comparisons, it may decide to spend more time on one activity and less on the other.

For large business firms—those that engage in service, merchandising, or manufacturing—departmental accounting is a must. The accounting reports consist of several levels of income statements recorded on a departmental basis and extended from sales through gross profit or income from operations or departmental margin.

GROSS PROFIT BY DEPARTMENTS

A department's gross profit depends on its sales volume and its markup on the goods sold:

Net Sales − Cost of Goods Sold = Gross Profit

Gross profit, in the same context, consists of the items listed on the income statement shown in Figure 1. To determine the gross profit of a given department, you need a separate set of figures for the department for each element entering into the gross profit. There are two ways to obtain these figures:

1. Keep separate general ledger accounts for each item affecting gross profit, such as a Sales account for each department, a Sales Returns and

FIGURE 1

INCOME STATEMENT

Revenue from Sales:					
Sales					$220 0 0 0 00
Less: Sales Returns and Allowances			$ 6 0 0 0 00		
Sales Discounts			3 0 0 0 00	9 0 0 0 00	
Net Sales					$211 0 0 0 00
Cost of Goods Sold:					
Merchandise Inventory (beginning)			$ 48 0 0 0 00		
Purchases		$76 4 0 0 00			
Less: Purchases Returns					
and Allowances	$4 0 0 0 00				
Purchases Discounts	2 0 0 0 00	6 0 0 0 00			
Net Purchases		$70 4 0 0 00			
Add Freight In		4 6 0 0 00			
Delivered Cost of Purchases			75 0 0 0 00		
Cost of Goods Available for Sale			$123 0 0 0 00		
Less Merchandise Inventory (ending)			52 0 0 0 00		
Cost of Goods Sold				71 0 0 0 00	
Gross Profit					$140 0 0 0 00

	DATE	INV. NO.	CUSTOMER'S NAME	POST. REF.	ACCOUNTS RECEIVABLE DEBIT	SALES CREDIT					
						DEPT. A	DEPT. B	DEPT. C	DEPT. D	DEPT. E	
1	20–										1
2	Sept. 1	1698	Elsa Batista	✓	1 6 5 00	1 6 5 00					2
3	3	1702	Rob Carler	✓	3 7 6 00			3 7 6 00			3
4	3	1704	Steve Krane	✓	7 1 6 00		7 1 6 00				4
16	30				14 9 3 3 00	2 6 8 1 00	8 6 4 00	4 7 9 4 00	3 7 1 6 00	2 8 7 8 00	16
17					(1 1 4)	(4 1 1)	(4 1 2)	(4 1 3)	(4 1 4)	(4 1 5)	17

FIGURE 2

Allowances account for each department, and so on. Then record the balances of these accounts on the income statement, OR
2. Keep only one general ledger account for each item affecting gross profit, and apportion the balance to the various departments. For example, maintain one Sales account and one Sales Returns and Allowances account for the company, and in addition keep a breakdown of sales and sales returns for each department. Then record the figures for each department on the income statement.

Keeping Separate Accounts by Department

Keeping separate accounts by department yields the most accurate accounting data. You need separate accounts for each department for Sales, Sales Returns and Allowances, Sales Discounts, Purchases, Purchases Returns and Allowances, Purchases Discounts, Freight In, and Merchandise Inventory. For example, Boag Hardware has five departments and uses five Sales accounts, five Sales Returns and Allowances accounts, five Sales Discounts accounts, five Merchandise Inventory accounts, and so forth. The special journals contain columns for each departmental account, as shown in the sales journal in Figure 2.

The accountant posts each total to a separate account, as indicated by the ledger account numbers. A company that has many departments and keeps a separate journal column for each may find that the journal becomes quite cumbersome. In a situation like this, it is better to post from the sales invoices directly to the departmental sales accounts. Another alternative is to establish a controlling account in the general ledger and to record each department in a subsidiary ledger.

Maintaining One General Ledger Account

When a company keeps only one general ledger account for each item involved in gross profit, the accountant has to distribute the total amount among the various departments at the end of the accounting period. To do so, the accountant has to accumulate departmental information on supplementary records. Winn's Pharmacy, for example, has pharmacy, cosmetics, gifts, and cards departments. Winn's Pharmacy uses a counter scanner that reads bar codes on products to record sales by department electronically. Products without bar codes may be entered by key pad. At the end of each day, the

Not only big corporations, but also entities such as hospitals, are best divided into departments to track revenues and expenses. Operating expenses are divided among departments so that revenue can be matched against expenses.

FYI

Computerized systems are well suited to departmental accounting.

sales are recorded in a journal, with the totals taken from the cash register tapes. Sales are also recorded on a departmental analysis sheet.

Businesses use separate analysis sheets for sales returns, purchases, purchases returns and allowances, purchases discounts, and so forth. At the end of the accounting period, these analysis sheets give departmental breakdowns for each item.

Gross Profit by Departments

OBJECTIVE 1

Compile a departmental income statement extended through Gross Profit.

Jones & Co., Inc., has two departments, A and B, and keeps separate accounts for each. The income statement for the fiscal year ended December 31, showing departmental reporting only through Gross Profit, appears in Figure 3 on pages 944–945. An outline of this process is as follows:

From Sales Through Gross Profit

Revenue from Sales
Less Cost of Goods Sold   } Based on separate departmental accounts or supplementary analysis sheets

Gross Profit
Less Operating Expenses

Income from Operations
Add Other Income
Less Other Expenses

Income Before Income Tax
Less Income Tax Expense

Net Income

INCOME FROM OPERATIONS BY DEPARTMENTS

A company may extend departmental reporting of income through Income from Operations. Jones & Co., Inc., keeps separate accounts for each item that enters into gross profit and apportions the operating expenses between Gross Profit and Income from Operations to Department A or Department B on a logical basis. Let's look at the outline of the income statement:

From Sales Through Income from Operations

Departmentalized

Revenue from Sales
Less Cost of Goods Sold   } Separate departmental accounts or supplementary analysis sheets

Gross Profit
Less Selling Expenses
Less General Expenses   } Account balances are apportioned

Income from Operations

Nondepartmentalized

Add Other Income
Less Other Expenses

Income Before Income Tax
Less Income Tax Expense

Net Income

Jones & Co., Inc.
Income Statement
For Year Ended December 31, 20—

		DEPARTMENT A		
1	Revenue from Sales:			
2	Sales		$560 0 0 0 00	
3	Less Sales Returns and Allowances		14 2 0 0 00	
4	Net Sales			$545 8 0 0 00
5	Cost of Goods Sold:			
6	Merchandise Inventory, Jan. 1, 20—		$ 96 4 0 0 00	
7	Purchases	$312 1 1 5 00		
8	Less: Purchases Returns and Allowances	9 5 8 0 00		
9	Purchases Discounts	5 7 4 0 00		
10	Net Purchases	$296 7 9 5 00		
11	Add Freight In	13 0 0 5 00		
12	Delivered Cost of Purchases		309 8 0 0 00	
13	Cost of Goods Available for Sale		$406 2 0 0 00	
14	Less Merchandise Inventory, Dec. 31, 20—		110 0 0 0 00	
15	Cost of Goods Sold			296 2 0 0 00
16	Gross Profit			$249 6 0 0 00
17				
18	Operating Expenses:			
19	Selling Expenses:			
20	Sales Salary Expense			
21	Advertising Expense			
22	Depreciation Expense, Store Equipment			
23	Miscellaneous Selling Expense			
24	Total Selling Expenses			
25	General Expenses:			
26	Office Salary Expense			
27	Rent Expense			
28	Utilities Expense			
29	Insurance Expense			
30	Bad Debts Expense			
31	Miscellaneous General Expense			
32	Total General Expenses			
33	Total Operating Expenses			
34	Income from Operations			
35				
36	Other Income:			
37	Interest Income			
38	Other Expenses:			
39	Interest Expense			
40	Income Before Income Tax			
41	Income Tax Expense			
42	Net Income			
43				

FIGURE 3

	DEPARTMENT B		TOTAL	
1				
2	$240 0 0 0 00		$800 0 0 0 00	
3	5 8 0 0 00		20 0 0 0 00	
4		$234 2 0 0 00		$780 0 0 0 00
5				
6	$ 82 7 4 0 00		$179 1 4 0 00	
7	$161 1 7 5 00		$473 2 9 0 00	
8	4 7 5 6 00		14 3 3 6 00	
9	3 2 7 4 00		9 0 1 4 00	
10	$153 1 4 5 00		$449 9 4 0 00	
11	6 7 1 5 00		19 7 2 0 00	
12		159 8 6 0 00		469 6 6 0 00
13		$242 6 0 0 00		$648 8 0 0 00
14	90 0 0 0 00		200 0 0 0 00	
15		152 6 0 0 00		448 8 0 0 00
16		$ 81 6 0 0 00		$331 2 0 0 00
17				
18				
19				
20			$140 8 2 5 00	
21			17 6 0 0 00	
22			3 3 0 0 00	
23			4 2 7 0 00	
24				$165 9 9 5 00
25				
26			$ 32 1 0 0 00	
27			16 4 0 0 00	
28			4 8 4 0 00	
29			4 4 0 0 00	
30			2 5 7 0 00	
31			9 2 0 00	
32			61 2 3 0 00	
33				227 2 2 5 00
34				$103 9 7 5 00
35				
36				
37			$ 3 6 2 4 00	
38				
39			2 4 0 0 00	1 2 2 4 00
40				$105 1 9 9 00
41				24 2 7 8 00
42				$ 80 9 2 1 00
43				

OBJECTIVE 2
Compile a departmental work sheet.

Work Sheet for Departmental Accounting

Each department assumes its share of overhead expenses. Recall once again the sequential steps of the accounting cycle: Record the trial balance in the first columns of the work sheet, formulate and record the adjustments, complete the work sheet, and then use the work sheet to prepare the income statement. The Income Statement columns of the work sheet for a company that keeps track of income by departments contain debit and credit columns for each department, as well as debit and credit columns titled Nondepartmental. These last two columns include Other Income and Other Expenses accounts that are not directly assigned to a department. By the time the accountant gets to the income statement, she or he has already performed the calculations apportioning the expenses, which are accordingly subdivided on the work sheet. A sample portion of the work sheet for Jones & Co., Inc., is shown in Figure 4 on pages 948–951. Various asset, liability, and owners' equity accounts are not shown, but they are included in the totals.

OBJECTIVE 3
Compile a departmental income statement extended through Income from Operations.

Income Statement for Departmental Accounting

The income statement contains a set of columns for each department, as well as a set of columns for the combined total of all departments. The income statement in Figure 5 on pages 952–953, which is extended through Income from Operations, is a more representative example than the one in Figure 3. A discussion of the apportionment of operating expenses between the two departments follows.

OBJECTIVE 4
Apportion operating expenses among various operating departments.

Apportionment of Operating Expenses

Apportionment of expenses is a crucial element of departmental accounting. It consists of allocating operating expenses among operating departments. You can readily identify some operating expenses as belonging to a given department. For example, if a salesperson makes sales in one department only, the accountant assigns that salesperson's salary or commission directly to that department. However, other operating expenses, such as Miscellaneous Selling Expense or Utilities Expense, cannot be restricted to one department and must be divided on some equitable basis. Let's look at the operating expenses of Jones & Co. and see how they are apportioned.

Sales Salary Expense   Jones & Co. allocates the salespersons' salaries to Department A or Department B according to the payroll register, which lists each employee by department. Department A's share is $88,625; Department B's is $52,200.

Advertising Expense   Jones & Co. advertises in three media: billboards, newspapers, and radio. The cost breakdown is as follows:

Billboard advertising	$ 1,600
Newspaper advertising	9,600
Radio advertising	6,400
Total	$17,600

The billboard advertising displays the name of the company and tells where it is, but it doesn't advertise the products of Department A or

Although Volkswagen markets several products, this billboard is solely advertising its New Beetle. The expense for this advertising piece may be billed to that department alone. If it had shown more than one model, the expense would have been allocated to more than one department, either equally or based on gross sales. Compare this to newspaper advertising, which is generally billed to each department based on column inches, or to radio, which is based on air time.

Department B. Since no specific department is featured, Jones & Co.'s accountant apportions the cost of these billboard ads according to gross sales, as follows:

Sales for Department A	$560,000
Sales for Department B	240,000
Total Sales	$800,000

Dept. A's sales as percentage of total: $\dfrac{\$560,000}{\$800,000} = 70\%$

Dept. B's sales as percentage of total: $\dfrac{\$240,000}{\$800,000} = 30\%$

Dept. A's share of cost of billboard advertising: 70% of $1,600 = $1,600 × 0.7 = $1,120

Dept. B's share of cost of billboard advertising: 30% of $1,600 = $1,600 × 0.3 = $480

Jones & Co. allocates the cost of its newspaper advertising according to the number of column inches each department uses. In a year, Jones & Co. buys 3,200 inches of newspaper advertising, divided according to departments as follows:

Advertising for Dept. A: 1,920 column inches or $\dfrac{1,920}{3,200} = 60\%$

Advertising for Dept. B: 1,280 column inches or $\dfrac{1,280}{3,200} = 40\%$

Dept. A's share of cost of newspaper advertising: 60% of $9,600 = $9,600 × 0.6 = $5,760

Dept. B's share of cost of newspaper advertising: 40% of $9,600 = $9,600 × 0.4 = $3,840

Jones & Co., Inc.
Work Sheet
For Year Ended December 31, 20—

#	ACCOUNT NAME	TRIAL BALANCE DEBIT	TRIAL BALANCE CREDIT	ADJUSTMENTS DEBIT	ADJUSTMENTS CREDIT	DEPARTMENT A INCOME STATEMENT DEBIT	DEPARTMENT A INCOME STATEMENT CREDIT
3	Accounts Receivable	82 0 4 0 00					
4	Allowance for						
5	Doubtful Accounts		8 6 2 00		(f) 2 5 7 0 00		
6	Merchandise						
7	Inventory						
8	Department A	96 4 0 0 00		(b)110 0 0 0 00	(a) 96 4 0 0 00		
9	Department B	82 7 4 0 00		(d) 90 0 0 0 00	(c) 82 7 4 0 00		
10	Prepaid Insurance	5 5 4 0 00			(e) 4 4 0 0 00		
11	Store Equipment	32 4 0 0 00					
12	Accumulated Depre-						
13	ciation, Store						
14	Equipment		21 6 0 0 00		(g) 3 3 0 0 00		
27	Sales						
28	Department A		560 0 0 0 00				560 0 0 0 00
29	Department B		240 0 0 0 00				
30	Sales Returns and						
31	Allowances						
32	Department A	14 2 0 0 00				14 2 0 0 00	
33	Department B	5 8 0 0 00					
34	Purchases						
35	Department A	312 1 1 5 00				312 1 1 5 00	
36	Department B	161 1 7 5 00					
37	Purchases Returns						
38	and Allowances						
39	Department A		9 5 8 0 00				9 5 8 0 00
40	Department B		4 7 5 6 00				
41	Purchases Discounts						
42	Department A		5 7 4 0 00				5 7 4 0 00
43	Department B		3 2 7 4 00				
44	Freight In						
45	Department A	13 0 0 5 00				13 0 0 5 00	
46	Department B	6 7 1 5 00					
47	Sales Salary						
48	Expense	140 8 2 5 00				88 6 2 5 00	
49	Advertising Expense	17 6 0 0 00				10 3 3 6 00	
50	Misc. Selling						
51	Expense	4 2 7 0 00				2 9 8 9 00	
52	Office Salary						
53	Expense	32 1 0 0 00				22 4 7 0 00	
54	Rent Expense	16 4 0 0 00				10 2 5 0 00	
55	Utilities Expense	4 8 4 0 00				3 0 2 5 00	
56	Totals carried forward	1,468 5 4 4 00	1,490 4 9 0 00	200 0 0 0 00	189 4 1 0 00	477 0 1 5 00	575 3 2 0 00

FIGURE 4

	DEPARTMENT B INCOME STATEMENT		NONDEPARTMENTAL INCOME STATEMENT		BALANCE SHEET		
	DEBIT	CREDIT	DEBIT	CREDIT	DEBIT	CREDIT	
					82 0 4 0 00		3
							4
						3 4 3 2 00	5
							6
							7
					110 0 0 0 00		8
					90 0 0 0 00		9
					1 1 4 0 00		10
					32 4 0 0 00		11
							12
							13
						24 9 0 0 00	14
							27
							28
		240 0 0 0 00					29
							30
							31
							32
	5 8 0 0 00						33
							34
							35
	161 1 7 5 00						36
							37
							38
							39
			4 7 5 6 00				40
							41
							42
			3 2 7 4 00				43
							44
							45
	6 7 1 5 00						46
							47
	52 2 0 0 00						48
	7 2 6 4 00						49
							50
	1 2 8 1 00						51
							52
	9 6 3 0 00						53
	6 1 5 0 00						54
	1 8 1 5 00						55
	252 0 3 0 00	248 0 3 0 00			1,118 7 6 1 00	1,035 8 1 2 00	56

(continued)

	ACCOUNT NAME	TRIAL BALANCE DEBIT	TRIAL BALANCE CREDIT	ADJUSTMENTS DEBIT	ADJUSTMENTS CREDIT	DEPARTMENT A INCOME STATEMENT DEBIT	DEPARTMENT A INCOME STATEMENT CREDIT
1	Totals brought forward	1,468 5 4 4 00	1,490 4 9 0 00	200 0 0 0 00	189 4 1 0 00	477 0 1 5 00	575 3 2 0 00
2	Misc. General						
3	Expense		9 2 0 00			6 4 4 00	
4	Income Tax Expense	22 2 5 0 00		(h) 2 0 2 8 00			
5	Interest Income		3 6 2 4 00				
6	Interest Expense	2 4 0 0 00					
7		1,494 1 1 4 00	1,494 1 1 4 00				
8	Inc. Summary, A			(a) 96 4 0 0 00	(b)110 0 0 0 00	96 4 0 0 00	110 0 0 0 00
9	Inc. Summary, B			(c) 82 7 4 0 00	(d) 90 0 0 0 00		
10	Insurance Expense			(e) 4 4 0 0 00		2 5 4 0 00	
11	Bad Debts Expense			(f) 2 5 7 0 00		1 7 9 9 00	
12	Depreciation						
13	Expense, Store						
14	Equipment			(g) 3 3 0 0 00		1 8 4 0 00	
15	Income Tax Payable				(h) 2 0 2 8 00		
16				391 4 3 8 00	391 4 3 8 00	580 2 3 8 00	685 3 2 0 00
17	Income (Loss)						
18	from Operations					105 0 8 2 00	
19						685 3 2 0 00	685 3 2 0 00
20	Net Income						

FIGURE 4 (continued)

Jones & Co. allocates cost of radio advertising to the two departments according to the amount of air time each department uses. In a year, Jones & Co. buys 1,250 minutes of radio time, divided according to departments as shown here:

Advertising for Dept. A: 675 minutes or $\frac{675}{1,250}$ = 54%

Advertising for Dept. B: 575 minutes or $\frac{575}{1,250}$ = 46%

Dept. A's share of cost of radio advertising: 54% of $6,400 = $6,400 \times 0.54$ = $3,456

Dept. B's share of cost of radio advertising: 46% of $6,400 = $6,400 \times 0.46$ = $2,944

Here is a summary of Jones & Co.'s allocation of advertising expense:

Expense	Department A	Department B	Total
Billboard advertising	$ 1,120	$ 480	$ 1,600
Newspaper advertising	5,760	3,840	9,600
Radio advertising	3,456	2,944	6,400
	$10,336	$7,264	$17,600

| DEPARTMENT B INCOME STATEMENT | | NONDEPARTMENTAL INCOME STATEMENT | | BALANCE SHEET | | |
DEBIT	CREDIT	DEBIT	CREDIT	DEBIT	CREDIT	
252 0 3 0 00	248 0 3 0 00			1,118 7 6 1 00	1,035 8 1 2 00	1
						2
	2 7 6 00					3
		24 2 7 8 00				4
			3 6 2 4 00			5
		2 4 0 0 00				6
						7
						8
82 7 4 0 00	90 0 0 0 00					9
1 8 6 0 00						10
7 7 1 00						11
						12
						13
1 4 6 0 00						14
					2 0 2 8 00	15
339 1 3 7 00	338 0 3 0 00					16
						17
	1 1 0 7 00		103 9 7 5 00			18
339 1 3 7 00	339 1 3 7 00	26 6 7 8 00	107 5 9 9 00	1,118 7 6 1 00	1,037 8 4 0 00	19
		80 9 2 1 00			80 9 2 1 00	20
		107 5 9 9 00	107 5 9 9 00	1,118 7 6 1 00	1,118 7 6 1 00	21
						22
						23
						24

Depreciation Expense, Store Equipment Jones & Co. keeps a property and equipment ledger that notes the department in which each piece of equipment is located. The total year's depreciation of the equipment used in Department A is $1,840; the total year's depreciation of the equipment used in Department B is $1,460.

Office Salary Expense People who work in the office of the company get paid a total of $32,100 per year. Jones & Co. apportions the amount of money that is paid in salaries to office workers on the basis of the amount of time the office personnel have to spend on each department. Management estimates that 70 percent of the office force's time is devoted to Department A and 30 percent to Department B:

Dept. A's share: 70% of $32,100 = $32,100 $\times$ 0.7 = <u>$22,470</u>

Dept. B's share: 30% of $32,100 = $32,100 $\times$ 0.3 = <u>$9,630</u>

REMEMBER!

To apportion or to allocate means to divide up.

Rent Expense and Utilities Expense Jones & Co. rents 40,000 square feet of floor space and allocates the expenses of rent and utilities on the basis of floor space occupied by each department, as follows. (Yearly expense for rent is $16,400; yearly expense for utilities is $4,840.)

Jones & Co., Inc.
Income Statement
For Year Ended December 31, 20—

	DEPARTMENT A		
1 Revenue from Sales:			
2 Sales		$560 0 0 0 00	
3 Less Sales Returns and Allowances		14 2 0 0 00	
4 Net Sales			$545 8 0 0 00
5 Cost of Goods Sold:			
6 Merchandise Inventory, Jan. 1, 20—		$ 96 4 0 0 00	
7 Purchases	$312 1 1 5 00		
8 Less: Purchases Returns and Allowances	9 5 8 0 00		
9 Purchases Discounts	5 7 4 0 00		
10 Net Purchases	$296 7 9 5 00		
11 Add Freight In	13 0 0 5 00		
12 Delivered Cost of Purchases		309 8 0 0 00	
13 Cost of Goods Available for Sale		$406 2 0 0 00	
14 Less Merchandise Inventory, Dec. 31, 20—		110 0 0 0 00	
15 Cost of Goods Sold			296 2 0 0 00
16 Gross Profit			$249 6 0 0 00
17			
18 Operating Expenses:			
19 Selling Expenses:			
20 Sales Salary Expense	$ 88 6 2 5 00		
21 Advertising Expense	10 3 3 6 00		
22 Depreciation Expense, Store Equipment	1 8 4 0 00		
23 Miscellaneous Selling Expense	2 9 8 9 00		
24 Total Selling Expenses		$103 7 9 0 00	
25 General Expenses:			
26 Office Salary Expense	$ 22 4 7 0 00		
27 Rent Expense	10 2 5 0 00		
28 Utilities Expense	3 0 2 5 00		
29 Insurance Expense	2 5 4 0 00		
30 Bad Debts Expense	1 7 9 9 00		
31 Miscellaneous General Expense	6 4 4 00		
32 Total General Expenses		40 7 2 8 00	
33 Total Operating Expenses			144 5 1 8 00
34 Income (Loss) from Operations			$105 0 8 2 00
35			
36 Other Income:			
37 Interest Income			
38 Other Expenses:			
39 Interest Expense			
40 Income Before Income Tax			
41 Income Tax Expense			
42 Net Income			
43			

FIGURE 5

Line	DEPARTMENT B			TOTAL		
2	$240 0 0 0 00			$800 0 0 0 00		
3	5 8 0 0 00			20 0 0 0 00		
4		$234 2 0 0 00				$780 0 0 0 00
5						
6		$ 82 7 4 0 00		$179 1 4 0 00		
7	$161 1 7 5 00			$473 2 9 0 00		
8	4 7 5 6 00			14 3 3 6 00		
9	3 2 7 4 00			9 0 1 4 00		
10	$153 1 4 5 00			$449 9 4 0 00		
11	6 7 1 5 00			19 7 2 0 00		
12		159 8 6 0 00			469 6 6 0 00	
13		$242 6 0 0 00			$648 8 0 0 00	
14		90 0 0 0 00			200 0 0 0 00	
15			152 6 0 0 00			448 8 0 0 00
16			$ 81 6 0 0 00			$331 2 0 0 00
20	$ 52 2 0 0 00			$140 8 2 5 00		
21	7 2 6 4 00			17 6 0 0 00		
22	1 4 6 0 00			3 3 0 0 00		
23	1 2 8 1 00			4 2 7 0 00		
24		$ 62 2 0 5 00			$165 9 9 5 00	
26	$ 9 6 3 0 00			$ 32 1 0 0 00		
27	6 1 5 0 00			16 4 0 0 00		
28	1 8 1 5 00			4 8 4 0 00		
29	1 8 6 0 00			4 4 0 0 00		
30	7 7 1 00			2 5 7 0 00		
31	2 7 6 00			9 2 0 00		
32		20 5 0 2 00			61 2 3 0 00	
33			82 7 0 7 00			227 2 2 5 00
34			$ (1 1 0 7 00)			$103 9 7 5 00
37					$ 3 6 2 4 00	
39					2 4 0 0 00	1 2 2 4 00
40						$105 1 9 9 00
41						24 2 7 8 00
42						$ 80 9 2 1 00

Rent and utilities expenses are often allocated on the basis of square feet of floor space occupied by a department or production area.

Dept. A occupies 25,000 square feet or $\frac{25,000}{40,000} = 62.5\%$

Dept. B occupies 15,000 square feet or $\frac{15,000}{40,000} = 37.5\%$

Dept. A's share of rent: 62.5% of $16,400 = $10,250

Dept. B's share of rent: 37.5% of $16,400 = $6,150

Dept. A's share of utilities: 62.5% of $4,840 = $3,025

Dept. B's share of utilities: 37.5% of $4,840 = $1,815

In this case, for simplicity, we assume that all floor space is of equal value. However, when apportioning the rent expense in a multistory building, you have to take into account differences in the value of the various floors and locations.

Insurance Expense Jones & Co. carries insurance policies to cover losses that might result from (1) damage to merchandise or equipment (annual cost, $3,600) and (2) injury incurred by customers while on the premises (annual cost, $800). The allocation of the cost of the insurance on merchandise and equipment is based on the average cost of the assets held by each department. The average is equal to the cost of assets on hand at the beginning of the year plus the cost of assets on hand at the end of the year, divided by 2. Following are the computations presented in tabular form:

Computations for Insurance Expense					
Item	**Department A**		**Department B**		**Total**
Merchandise Inventory					
Balance, Jan. 1	$ 96,400		$ 82,740		
Balance, Dec. 31	110,000		90,000		
Total	2)$206,400		2)$172,740		
Average (Total ÷ 2)	$103,200	$103,200	$ 86,370	$86,370	
Store Equipment					
Balance, Jan. 1	$ 19,440		$ 12,960		
Balance, Dec. 31	19,440		12,960		
Total	2)$ 38,880		2)$ 25,920		
Average (Total ÷ 2)	$ 19,440	19,440	$ 12,960	12,960	
Total		$122,640		$99,330	$221,970

REMEMBER!

The allocation of insurance for damage to merchandise or inventory is based on the average cost of assets held by a department. But the allocation of liability insurance due to injury to customers is based on gross sales.

The balances for the Store Equipment in the two departments are contained in the property and equipment ledger.

Dept. A's percentage: $\frac{\$122,640}{\$221,970} = 55\%$

Dept. B's percentage: $\frac{\$99,330}{\$221,970} = 45\%$

Dept. A's share of property insurance: 55% of $3,600 = $1,980

Dept. B's share of property insurance: 45% of $3,600 = $1,620

The allocation of the cost of liability insurance (in case of personal injury to customers) is based on sales. Using the same percentages as for billboard advertising, Jones & Co. apportions the cost of liability insurance as follows:

Dept. A's share of liability insurance: 70% of $800 = $560

Dept. B's share of liability insurance: 30% of $800 = $240

A summary of the way Jones & Co. allocates its insurance expense is shown here.

Type of Insurance	Department A	Department B	Total
Property Insurance	$1,980	$1,620	$3,600
Liability Insurance	560	240	800
	$2,540	$1,860	$4,400

Bad Debts Expense, Miscellaneous Selling Expense, and Miscellaneous General Expense

Bad Debts Expense and the miscellaneous expense accounts vary according to the volume of sales. Accordingly, Jones & Co. apportions them on this basis: 70% for Department A and 30% for Department B. Division of these expense accounts by department is as follows:

Dept. A's share of Bad Debts Expense: 70% of $2,570 = $1,799

Dept. B's share of Bad Debts Expense: 30% of $2,570 = $771

Dept. A's share of Miscellaneous Selling Expense: 70% of $4,270 = $2,989

Dept. B's share of Miscellaneous Selling Expense: 30% of $4,270 = $1,281

Dept. A's share of Miscellaneous General Expense: 70% of $920 = $644

Dept. B's share of Miscellaneous General Expense: 30% of $920 = $276

Item	Department A	Department B	Total
Bad Debts Expense	$1,799	$ 771	$2,570
Miscellaneous Selling Expense	2,989	1,281	4,270
Miscellaneous General Expense	644	276	920
	$5,432	$2,328	$7,760

DEPARTMENTAL MARGIN

OBJECTIVE 5

Compile a departmental income statement extended through Departmental Margin.

Departmental margin is a measurement of the contribution that a given department makes to the income of the firm—gross profit of a department minus the department's direct expenses. When a company breaks down its expense figures on a departmental-margin basis, its income statement indicates the contribution each department makes toward the overhead expenses incurred on behalf of the business as a whole. You can divide operating expenses into two classes: (1) **direct expenses**, which are incurred for the sole benefit of a given department and are under the control of the department head but not necessarily under the department being considered; and (2) **indirect expenses**, which are incurred as overhead expenses of the entire business and thus are not under the control of one department head. For example, Sales Salary Expense is a direct expense because it is incurred purely for the benefit of one department. Officers' Salary Expense, on the other hand, is an overhead expense incurred for the business as a whole; it is not directly chargeable to one department.

Some operating expenses may be partially direct and partially indirect. For example, Jones & Co.'s Advertising Expense consisted partially of billboard advertising, which stresses the name and location of the company, and partially of newspaper and radio advertising, which directly benefits separate departments of the company. So the part of the advertising budget that went to billboard advertising is an indirect expense, and the part that went to newspaper and radio advertising is a direct expense. Costs of insurance on merchandise inventories and store equipment are a direct expense; costs of liability insurance are an indirect or overhead expense. When you classify an expense as direct or indirect, use this rule of thumb to identify direct expenses: **The expense would not have been incurred if the department were not in existence.** The expense must be directly related to the department.

Here is an outline of an income statement that emphasizes departmental margin:

> **REMEMBER!**
>
> In any departmental accounting system, it is necessary to keep separate accounts or supplementary records by department for each account involved in determining gross profit on sales.

From Sales Through Departmental Margin

Revenue from Sales
Less Cost of Goods Sold   } Based on separate departmental accounts or supplementary analysis sheets

Gross Profit
Less Direct Departmental Expenses   } Expenses that are directly related to the department

Departmental Margin
Less Indirect Expenses

Income from Operations
Add Other Income
Less Other Expenses

Income Before Income Tax
Less Income Tax Expense

Net Income

The income statement shown in Figure 6 on pages 958–959 presents the same figures that we saw in Figure 5 for Jones & Co. This time, however, they are in the departmental-margin format. It is interesting to compare the two.

The Meaning of Departmental Margin

Departmental margin is the most realistic portrayal of the profitability of a department. **If the company closes the department, the company's income before income tax will decrease or increase by the amount of the departmental margin.** For example, in the case of Jones & Co., Department B had a positive departmental margin of $18,765; if Jones & Co. eliminated the department, its income before income tax would be reduced by $18,765 (assuming that Jones & Co. didn't create a new department to take the place of Department B or expand Department A to occupy the void).

In the company's work sheet (Figure 4), in which operating expenses were apportioned to departments, Department B showed a loss from operations of $1,107. Department B sustained this loss because it was assigned a number of indirect expenses. If Jones & Co. eliminates Department B, these indirect expenses, or overhead, will still exist and will therefore be assigned entirely to Department A, thereby accounting in part for the reduction in income before income tax of $18,765 for the company as a whole (the amount of the departmental margin). Based on this limited analysis, Department B should continue to operate because it has a positive departmental (or contribution) margin whereby incremental Department B sales exceed incremental (direct) Department B expenses by $18,765.

The Usefulness of Departmental Margin

Income statements that show departmental margin are extremely useful when it comes to controlling a company's direct expenses, because the company can hold the head of a given department accountable for expenses directly chargeable to that department. If a department head reduces direct expenses, this action will have a favorable effect on the departmental margin.

A company that manufactures a number of different products can also use the concept of departmental margin to determine the profitability of a particular product. This is clearly one of the most important uses of departmental margin.

Management can use an income statement showing departmental margin as a tool for making future plans and analyzing future operations. Sometimes such an income statement may even lead to the elimination of a department. For example, Rivera Company, Inc., has five departments. Its income from operations for last year was $120,000, which is about the same as it has been for the past four years. Rivera's partial income statement, in which all operating expenses are apportioned to the various departments, shows that Department E has a loss from operations of $9,000. In an abbreviated departmental-margin format, the results of the fiscal year are shown in the following table.

Item	Department E (only)	Departments A to D (only)	Total, Departments A to E	Total, Departments A to D (with E eliminated)
Sales	$120,000	$1,480,000	$1,600,000	$1,480,000
Cost of Goods Sold	72,000	880,000	952,000	880,000
Gross Profit	$ 48,000	$ 600,000	$ 648,000	$ 600,000
Direct Departmental Expenses	32,000	336,000	368,000	336,000
Departmental Margin	$ 16,000	$ 264,000	$ 280,000	$ 264,000
Indirect Expenses	25,000	135,000	160,000	160,000
Income (Loss) from Operations	$ (9,000)	$ 129,000	$ 120,000	$ 104,000

Jones & Co., Inc.
Income Statement
For Year Ended December 31, 20—

		DEPARTMENT A		
1	**Revenue from Sales:**			
2	Sales		$560 0 0 0 00	
3	Less Sales Returns and Allowances		14 2 0 0 00	
4	Net Sales			$545 8 0 0 00
5	**Cost of Goods Sold:**			
6	Merchandise Inventory, Jan. 1, 20–		$ 96 4 0 0 00	
7	Purchases	$312 1 1 5 00		
8	Less: Purchases Returns and Allowances	9 5 8 0 00		
9	Purchases Discounts	5 7 4 0 00		
10	Net Purchases	$296 7 9 5 00		
11	Add Freight In	13 0 0 5 00		
12	Delivered Cost of Purchases		309 8 0 0 00	
13	Cost of Goods Available for Sale		$406 2 0 0 00	
14	Less Merchandise Inventory, Dec. 31, 20–		110 0 0 0 00	
15	Cost of Goods Sold			296 2 0 0 00
16	**Gross Profit**			$249 6 0 0 00
17				
18	**Direct Departmental Expenses:**			
19	Sales Salary Expense		$ 88 6 2 5 00	
20	Advertising Expense		9 2 1 6 00	
21	Insurance Expense		1 9 8 0 00	
22	Depreciation Expense, Store Equipment		1 8 4 0 00	
23	Bad Debts Expense		1 7 9 9 00	
24	Total Direct Departmental Expenses			103 4 6 0 00
25	**Departmental Margin**			$146 1 4 0 00
26				
27	**Indirect Expenses:**			
28	Office Salary Expense			
29	Rent Expense			
30	Utilities Expense			
31	Advertising Expense (billboard)			
32	Insurance Expense (liability)			
33	Miscellaneous Selling Expense			
34	Miscellaneous General Expense			
35	Total Indirect Expenses			
36	**Income from Operations**			
37				
38	**Other Income:**			
39	Interest Income			
40	**Other Expenses:**			
41	Interest Expense			
42	**Income Before Income Tax**			
43	**Income Tax Expense**			
44	**Net Income**			
45				

FIGURE 6

Line	DEPARTMENT B (1)	DEPARTMENT B (2)	DEPARTMENT B (3)	TOTAL (1)	TOTAL (2)	TOTAL (3)
1						
2		$240 0 0 0 00			$800 0 0 0 00	
3		5 8 0 0 00			20 0 0 0 00	
4			$234 2 0 0 00			$780 0 0 0 00
5						
6		$ 82 7 4 0 00			$179 1 4 0 00	
7	$161 1 7 5 00			$473 2 9 0 00		
8	4 7 5 6 00			14 3 3 6 00		
9	3 2 7 4 00			9 0 1 4 00		
10	$153 1 4 5 00			$449 9 4 0 00		
11	6 7 1 5 00			19 7 2 0 00		
12		159 8 6 0 00			469 6 6 0 00	
13		$242 6 0 0 00			$648 8 0 0 00	
14		90 0 0 0 00			200 0 0 0 00	
15			152 6 0 0 00			448 8 0 0 00
16			$ 81 6 0 0 00			$331 2 0 0 00
17						
18						
19		$ 52 2 0 0 00			$140 8 2 5 00	
20		6 7 8 4 00			16 0 0 0 00	
21		1 6 2 0 00			3 6 0 0 00	
22		1 4 6 0 00			3 3 0 0 00	
23		7 7 1 00			2 5 7 0 00	
24			62 8 3 5 00			166 2 9 5 00
25			$ 18 7 6 5 00			$164 9 0 5 00
26						
27						
28					$ 32 1 0 0 00	
29					16 4 0 0 00	
30					4 8 4 0 00	
31					1 6 0 0 00	
32					8 0 0 00	
33					4 2 7 0 00	
34					9 2 0 00	
35						60 9 3 0 00
36						$103 9 7 5 00
37						
38						
39					$ 3 6 2 4 00	
40						
41					2 4 0 0 00	1 2 2 4 00
42						$105 1 9 9 00
43						24 2 7 8 00
44						$ 80 9 2 1 00
45						

Now suppose that Rivera Company eliminates Department E. Because Department E's departmental margin amounts to $16,000, the Income from Operations of the entire firm will decrease by $16,000 ($120,000 − $104,000 = $16,000). Another factor Rivera Company has to consider is possible "spillover sales" of Department E; that is, customers of Department E may buy things in other departments. Also, any change in income will cause a change in the amount of income taxes paid by Rivera Company. However, to simplify our analysis, we have omitted income taxes from our discussion.

CHAPTER REVIEW

Review of Performance Objectives

1. Compile a departmental income statement extended through Gross Profit.

From Sales Through Gross Profit

Based on separate departmental accounts or supplementary analysis sheets {

   Revenue from Sales
− Cost of Goods Sold
_____

= Gross Profit
− Operating Expenses
_____

= Income from Operations
+ Other Income
− Other Expenses
_____

= Income Before Income Tax
− Income Tax Expense
_____

= Net Income

2. Compile a departmental work sheet.

Accountants use work sheets with separate Income Statement columns for each department to facilitate the correct apportionment of revenues and expenses.

3. Compile a departmental income statement extended through Income from Operations.

From Sales Through Income from Operations

Based on separate departmental accounts or supplementary analysis sheets {

   Revenue from Sales
− Cost of Goods Sold
_____

= Gross Profit
− Operating Expenses
_____

= Income from Operations
+ Other Income
− Other Expenses
_____

= Income Before Income Tax
− Income Tax Expense
_____

= Net Income

} One ledger account for each expense apportioned to various departments

4. Apportion operating expenses among various operating departments.

   Operating expenses may be apportioned or subdivided on a variety of bases, such as gross sales, advertising space, floor space, amounts in the payroll register, amounts in the equipment ledger, and so on.

5. Compile a departmental income statement extended through Departmental Margin.

From Sales Through Departmental Margin

Based on separate departmental accounts or supplementary analysis sheets {

   Revenue from Sales
− Cost of Goods Sold

= Gross Profit
− Direct Departmental Expenses } Expenses that are directly related to the department

= Departmental Margin
− Indirect Expenses

= Income from Operations
+ Other Income
− Other Expenses

= Income Before Income Tax
− Income Tax Expense

= Net Income

Glossary

Apportionment of expenses Allocating operating expenses among operating departments. (946)

Departmental margin The contribution that a given department makes to the income of the firm—gross profit of a department minus the department's direct expenses. (955)

Direct expenses Expenses that benefit only one department and are controlled by the head of the department. (956)

Indirect expenses Overhead expenses that benefit several departments or the business as a whole and are not under the control of any one department head. (956)

QUESTIONS, EXERCISES, AND CASES

Discussion Questions

1. Explain two ways in which Purchases Returns and Allowances may be recorded in a departmentalized company.

2. Explain the three types of departmentalized income statements illustrated in the chapter.

3. Describe the difference between a direct and an indirect operating expense.

4. For a retail store, what is the logical basis for allocating advertising expense?

5. In what ways may departmental accounting information be useful?

6. What is departmental margin, and why is a positive departmental margin important?

7. How does a departmentalized income statement differ from one that is not departmentalized?

8. You have been hired as the new manager of an athletic supply store. Previously, the income statement listed total revenue and operating expenses only. The company can be divided into two departments: clothing and shoes. You want to know the gross profit for each department. Describe the changes in the accounting system that will be required.

Exercises

P.O. 1

Determine amount of gross profit.

Exercise 25-1 The ski department of B and I Sports buys all its products FOB destination and has the following account balances:

Sales	$ 410,000
Purchases	218,800
Purchases Discounts	4,900
Sales Returns and Allowances	9,600
Merchandise Inventory (beginning)	69,600
Purchases Returns and Allowances	7,200
Merchandise Inventory (ending)	61,300

Determine the amount of the gross profit.

P.O. 4

Allocate office salaries expense over three operating departments.

Exercise 25-2 McKabe Electronics has annual expenses for salaries of office staff of $136,380, which it allocates to the various departments on the basis of gross sales for each department. Sales by department are as follows:

Department	Gross Sales
Cellular phones	$490,000
MP3 players	436,000
DVD players	47,000
Total	$973,000

Determine what share of the office salaries expense each of the three operating departments should bear. (On a calculator, select the floating decimal setting or the maximum number of decimal places.)

P.O. 4

Apportion rent expense to five departments.

Exercise 25-3 B and I Sports occupies an area of 22,580 square feet. The departments and the floor space each department occupies are as follows:

Department	Floor Space
Basketball	980 square feet
Skiing	12,075 square feet
Skating	3,700 square feet
Baseball	2,800 square feet
Receiving and Storage	3,025 square feet
Total	22,580 square feet

B and I Sports leases the building for $45,000 per year. Apportion the rent expense to the five departments based upon square footage.

P.O. 4

Allocate insurance costs over three operating departments.

Exercise 25-4 The premium for public liability insurance for the electronics company in Exercise 25-2 is $2,920, and the premium for fire and theft insurance on the inventory is $2,360. The balances of the inventories at the end of the fiscal period are as follows:

Department	Inventories
Cellular phones	$180,000
MP3 players	150,000
DVD players	43,000
Total	$373,000

How much of the insurance costs should be allocated to each department, given that public liability insurance is apportioned on the basis of gross sales and that property insurance is allocated on the basis of the values of the ending inventories?

P.O. 4

Determine the apportionment of depreciation expense and insurance over three operating departments.

Exercise 25-5 Traeger Company apportions depreciation on equipment on the basis of the average cost of equipment. Insurance expense is apportioned on the basis of average cost of the inventory. Depreciation expense on equipment amounted to $28,500. Insurance expense amounted to $12,600. Determine the apportionment of the depreciation expense and the insurance expense based on the information below. Round to the nearest dollar amount.

	Average Cost	
Department	Equipment	Inventory
A	$134,000	$ 460,000
B	269,000	541,000
C	136,000	271,000
Total	$539,000	$1,272,000

P.O. 5

Determine the amount of the departmental margin.

Exercise 25-6 The following figures apply to Pinion and Shay's hardware department:

Sales	$712,200
Direct Departmental Expenses	150,300
Purchases	492,260
Purchases Returns and Allowances	8,780
Freight In	32,293
Interest Expense	6,700
Sales Returns and Allowances	10,300
Merchandise Inventory (ending)	218,400
Indirect Expenses	89,250
Merchandise Inventory (beginning)	189,100

Determine the amount of the departmental margin.

P.O. 5

Determine the departmental margin on a department considered for closing.

Exercise 25-7 Marsoli, Inc., is considering eliminating its Drapery Department. Management does not believe that the indirect expenses and the level of operations in the other departments will be affected if the Drapery Department closes. Information from Marsoli's income statement for the fiscal year ended December 31, which is considered a typical year, is shown below.

	Drapery Department	All Other Departments	Total of All Departments (including Drapery)
Sales	$75,000	$563,000	$638,000
Cost of Goods Sold	49,000	395,000	444,000
Gross Profit	$26,000	$168,000	$194,000
Operating Expenses	32,000	112,000	144,000
Income (Loss) from Operations	$(6,000)	$ 56,000	$ 50,000

Marsoli considers that $19,000 of the operating expenses of the Drapery Department are direct expenses. What is the departmental margin of the Drapery Department?

P.O. 3

Prepare an income statement assuming the Drapery Department in Exercise 25-7 is closed.

Exercise 25-8 For Marsoli, Inc., in Exercise 25-7, prepare an income statement for the forthcoming year, assuming that Marsoli discontinues the Drapery Department.

Departmental accounting can be applied at many different levels within a company. Let's go back to The Neiman Marcus Group, Inc. Look at its 2005 financial report by going to **http://www.neimanmarcusgroup.com** and selecting Financial Information and then SEC Filings. Select the 10-K with the 09/16/2005 filing date. The 10-K is an annual filing.

1. How many segments does the company have? What are they called? (*Hint*: Look under Note 13. Segment Reporting on page F-36.)
2. Within each segment there are seven merchandising departments. What are they? Do these categories make sense for a company like Neiman Marcus? Why or why not? (*Hint*: Look in the Merchandise section on page 7.)
3. Look at the Overview in the Management's Discussion and Analysis of Financial Condition and Results of Operations. From the information given in that section, what is another way the segments could be departmentalized?
4. How might an individual store apportion nondepartmental operating expenses such as utilities expense?

CONSIDER AND COMMUNICATE

You work for a sports equipment company that has three departments: the Swim Shop, the Climbing Corner, and the Pedal Room. This company is continuing to grow, but it has not set up departmentalized accounting procedures. The owner is not sure that the benefits of departmentalized information will outweigh the additional paperwork and potential employee retraining. Briefly describe the benefits of changing to departmentalized accounting and producing departmentalized income statements through departmental margin.

WHAT'S WRONG WITH THIS PICTURE?

As a result of company-wide remodeling, several hundred square feet that had been a part of Department A became a part of Department B. This detail, however, escaped the new accountant, who allocated the rent expense (based on the floor space) the same way it had been allocated in the prior year. Comment on this situation.

CRITICAL THINKING

The following is a table that your company is using to analyze the possibility of eliminating Department A. Some of the numbers are missing. Complete the table and give an analysis of the impact of eliminating Department A.

Item	Department A (only)	Departments B to D (only)	Total, Departments A to D	Total, Departments B to D (A gone)
Sales	$121,800	$	$1,624,000	$
Cost of Goods Sold		875,500	958,300	
Gross Profit	$ 39,000	$626,700	$	$
Direct Departmental Expenses		302,000	327,200	
Departmental Margin	$ 13,800	$	$ 338,500	$
Indirect Expenses	18,750	101,250		
Income (Loss) from Operations	$	$223,450	$	$204,700

PROBLEM SET A

For additional help, see the demonstration problem at the beginning of each chapter in your Working Papers.

P.O. 1

Problem 25-1A Carrera Lumber has two sales departments: lumber and hardware. Carrera Lumber's accountant prepared the adjusted trial balance shown on page 966 at the end of the fiscal year, after all adjustments, including adjustments for merchandise inventory, had been recorded and posted.

Check Figure

Net Income, $212,932

Instructions

Prepare an income statement to show gross profit for each department and income from operations, as well as net income, for the entire business. Beginning balances of merchandise inventory are as follows: lumber, $284,280; hardware, $263,826.

Carrera Lumber
Adjusted Trial Balance
December 31, 20—

ACCOUNT NAME	DEBIT	CREDIT
Cash	11 5 4 9 00	
Accounts Receivable	162 6 8 0 00	
Allowance for Doubtful Accounts		5 8 3 2 00
Merchandise Inventory, Lumber Dept.	310 0 2 8 00	
Merchandise Inventory, Hardware Dept.	245 5 0 2 00	
Store Equipment	72 6 6 2 00	
Accumulated Depreciation, Store Equipment		45 9 6 5 00
Accounts Payable		184 7 4 6 00
E. Carrera, Capital		422 2 3 3 00
E. Carrera, Drawing	73 4 4 0 00	
Income Summary	283 0 1 8 00	310 0 2 8 00
	260 9 3 5 00	245 5 0 2 00
Sales, Lumber Department		1,344 8 1 2 00
Sales, Hardware Department		1,134 8 6 4 00
Sales Returns and Allowances, Lumber Department	25 7 0 8 00	
Sales Returns and Allowances, Hardware Department	23 3 1 4 00	
Purchases, Lumber Department	1,214 1 1 2 00	
Purchases, Hardware Department	836 8 8 5 00	
Purchases Returns and Allowances, Lumber Department		19 0 2 2 00
Purchases Returns and Allowances, Hardware Department		15 7 8 2 00
Purchases Discounts, Lumber Department		24 6 2 8 00
Purchases Discounts, Hardware Department		17 8 5 6 00
Freight In, Lumber Department	37 5 5 0 00	
Freight In, Hardware Department	40 3 5 2 00	
Sales Salary Expense	103 6 4 4 00	
Depreciation Expense, Store Equipment	15 7 7 5 00	
Miscellaneous Selling Expense	6 3 4 00	
Office Salary Expense	21 1 6 8 00	
Rent Expense	17 2 8 0 00	
Utilities Expense	10 3 9 0 00	
Bad Debts Expense	8 7 1 00	
Miscellaneous General Expense	4 3 2 00	
Interest Expense	3 3 4 1 00	
	3,771 2 7 0 00	3,771 2 7 0 00

P.O. 2

Problem 25-2A Cycle City has two departments: bicycle and clothing. The trial balance, as of October 31, the end of the fiscal year, is shown on the following page.

The data for the adjustments are as follows:

a.–d. Merchandise inventories, October 31, the end of the fiscal period: bicycle department, $43,000; clothing department, $26,300

e. Depreciation of store equipment for the year, $6,070
f. Estimated uncollectible customer charge accounts (based on a percentage of charge sales), $1,640
g. Insurance expired, $420
h. Accrued wages, $490
i. Accrued interest payable, $182 (interest expense is nondepartmental)

Cycle City
Trial Balance
October 31, 20—

ACCOUNT NAME	DEBIT	CREDIT
Cash	6 5 1 0 00	
Accounts Receivable	41 5 8 0 00	
Allowance for Doubtful Accounts		1 0 9 2 00
Merchandise Inventory, Bicycle Department	44 1 0 0 00	
Merchandise Inventory, Clothing Department	29 4 0 0 00	
Prepaid Insurance	6 3 0 00	
Store Equipment	19 1 1 0 00	
Accumulated Depreciation, Store Equipment		8 5 4 9 00
Accounts Payable		40 6 5 6 00
R. M. Potts, Capital		69 5 9 5 00
R. M. Potts, Drawing	14 7 0 0 00	
Sales, Bicycle Department		126 0 0 0 00
Sales, Clothing Department		84 0 0 0 00
Purchases, Bicycle Department	60 4 8 0 00	
Purchases, Clothing Department	46 3 6 8 00	
Freight In, Bicycle Department	2 5 2 0 00	
Freight In, Clothing Department	1 9 3 2 00	
Wages and Commissions Expense	45 1 5 0 00	
Advertising Expense	6 7 2 0 00	
Rent Expense	7 5 6 0 00	
Utilities Expense	1 5 2 5 00	
Miscellaneous Expense	1 1 4 5 00	
Interest Expense	4 6 2 00	
	329 8 9 2 00	329 8 9 2 00

The bases for apportioning expenses to the two departments are as follows:

- Wages and Commissions Expense (time sheets): bicycle department, $31,878; clothing department, $13,762
- Advertising Expense (column inches of space): bicycle department, $5,376; clothing department, $1,344
- Depreciation Expense (equipment ledger): bicycle department, $3,543; clothing department, $2,527
- Rent Expense, Utilities Expense, Miscellaneous Expense, Bad Debts Expense, Insurance Expense (sales): bicycle department, 60 percent; clothing department, 40 percent

Check Figure

Net Income, $23,136

Instructions

Complete the work sheet.

P.O. 3

Problem 25-3A Harbor Book and Software has two sales departments: book and software. After recording and posting all adjustments, including the adjustments for merchandise inventory, the accountant prepared the adjusted trial balance (shown below) at the end of the fiscal year.

Harbor Book and Software
Adjusted Trial Balance
December 31, 20—

ACCOUNT NAME	DEBIT	CREDIT
Cash	31 2 6 8 00	
Accounts Receivable	34 8 8 0 00	
Allowance for Doubtful Accounts		1 8 9 3 00
Merchandise Inventory, Book Department	53 5 5 7 00	
Merchandise Inventory, Software Department	24 9 8 7 00	
Prepaid Insurance	6 5 6 00	
Store Supplies	5 3 2 00	
Store Equipment	42 8 1 3 00	
Accumulated Depreciation, Store Equipment		32 6 1 9 00
Accounts Payable		32 2 8 0 00
Sales Tax Payable		8 9 5 00
Income Tax Payable		1 1 6 6 00
Common Stock		74 6 3 0 00
Retained Earnings		18 3 0 0 00
Income Summary	52 6 1 9 00	53 5 5 7 00
	24 1 4 9 00	24 9 8 7 00
Sales, Book Department		317 4 0 0 00
Sales, Software Department		136 0 0 0 00
Sales Returns and Allowances, Book Department	8 1 6 1 00	
Sales Returns and Allowances, Software Department	5 5 1 00	
Purchases, Book Department	199 8 9 5 00	
Purchases, Software Department	96 2 7 3 00	
Purchases Returns and Allowances, Book Department		2 8 1 7 00
Purchases Returns and Allowances, Software Department		8 6 4 00
Purchases Discounts, Book Department		3 9 2 3 00
Purchases Discounts, Software Department		2 8 5 3 00
Freight In, Book Department	7 2 5 0 00	
Freight In, Software Department	2 8 7 5 00	
Sales Salary Expense	81 1 8 8 00	
Advertising Expense	10 6 7 0 00	
Depreciation Expense, Store Equipment	10 5 3 3 00	
Store Supplies Expense	4 0 4 00	
Miscellaneous Selling Expense	3 5 0 00	
Rent Expense	6 4 0 0 00	
Utilities Expense	2 4 0 0 00	
Insurance Expense	5 6 0 00	
Bad Debts Expense	1 4 7 0 00	
Miscellaneous General Expense	5 2 0 00	
Interest Expense	1 2 0 8 00	
Income Tax Expense	8 0 1 5 00	
	704 1 8 4 00	704 1 8 4 00

Merchandise inventories at the beginning of the year were as follows: book department, $53,410; software department, $23,839. The bases (and sources of figures) for apportioning expenses to the two departments are as follows (rounded to the nearest dollar):

- Sales Salary Expense (payroll register): book department, $45,559; software department, $35,629
- Advertising Expense (newspaper column inches): book department, 550 inches; software department, 450 inches
- Depreciation Expense, Store Equipment (property and equipment ledger): book department, $7,851; software department, $2,682
- Store Supplies Expense (requisitions): book department, $205; software department, $199
- Miscellaneous Selling Expense (volume of gross sales): book department, $240; software department, $110
- Rent Expense and Utilities Expense (floor space): book department, 9,000 square feet; software department, 7,000 square feet
- Insurance Expense (average cost of merchandise inventory, rounded off in dollars): book department, $384; software department, $176
- Bad Debts Expense (volume of gross sales): book department, $1,029; software department, $441
- Miscellaneous General Expense (volume of gross sales): book department, $364; software department, $156

Check Figure

Net Income, $26,429

Instructions

Prepare an income statement by department to show income from operations, as well as a nondepartmentalized income statement (using the Total columns) to show net income for the entire company.

P.O. 5

Problem 25-4A Deco Decorators is a sole proprietorship. After the firm has recorded adjustments, it has the balances, shown in the work sheet on page 970, for revenue and expense accounts and merchandise inventories for its two departments on December 31, the end of the fiscal year. The store has two departments: carpets and draperies. The values of merchandise inventory on January 1 (beginning) are: carpets, $220,205; draperies, $109,730.

Essential data for direct expenses (and sources of figures) are as follows:

a. Sales Salary Expense (sales personnel work in one department only) is allocated as follows: carpets, $146,430; draperies, $63,790.
b. Advertising Expense: Newspaper advertising is allocated as follows: carpets, $16,182; draperies, $3,840.
c. Depreciation: Depreciation of store equipment is apportioned on the basis of the average cost of equipment in each department. The average cost of store equipment is carpets, $22,500; draperies, $7,500.
d. Bad Debts Expense: Department managers are responsible for granting credit on sales made by their respective departments. Bad Debts Expense is allocated as follows: carpets, $6,156; draperies, $2,394.

Check Figure

Net Income, $143,618

Instructions

Prepare an income statement to show each department's departmental margin.

Deco Decorators
Partial Work Sheet
For Year Ended December 31, 20—

ACCOUNT NAME	ADJUSTED TRIAL BALANCE	
	DEBIT	CREDIT
Merchandise Inventory, Carpets	236 9 7 0 00	
Merchandise Inventory, Draperies	103 4 1 0 00	
Sales, Carpets		854 3 5 2 00
Sales, Draperies		333 6 4 8 00
Sales Returns and Allowances, Carpets	21 6 7 2 00	
Sales Returns and Allowances, Draperies	9 8 2 8 00	
Purchases, Carpets	474 3 5 3 00	
Purchases, Draperies	187 4 0 3 00	
Purchases Returns and Allowances, Carpets		7 4 1 6 00
Purchases Returns and Allowances, Draperies		3 0 1 5 00
Purchases Discounts, Carpets		5 3 1 9 00
Purchases Discounts, Draperies		3 3 3 0 00
Freight In, Carpets	30 2 7 8 00	
Freight In, Draperies	7 4 0 3 00	
Sales Salary Expense	210 2 2 0 00	
Advertising Expense	20 0 2 2 00	
Depreciation Expense, Store Equipment	14 4 0 0 00	
Bad Debts Expense	8 5 5 0 00	
Office Salary Expense	38 3 4 0 00	
Rent Expense	37 8 0 0 00	
Utilities Expense	5 6 7 0 00	
Insurance Expense	1 8 9 0 00	
Miscellaneous Selling Expense	1 7 5 5 00	
Miscellaneous General Expense	1 5 3 0 00	
Interest Expense	2 7 9 3 00	

PROBLEM SET B

For additional help, see the demonstration problem at the beginning of each chapter in your Working Papers.

P.O. 1

Problem 25-1B Randi's Floral Shop has two sales departments: plants and gifts. After recording and posting all departments, including the adjustments for merchandise inventory, the accountant presented the adjusted trial balance shown on the following page at the end of the fiscal year.

Check Figure

Net Income, $62,968

Instructions

Prepare an income statement to show gross profit for each department and income from operations, as well as net income, for the entire business. Beginning balances of merchandise inventory are as follows: plants, $72,400; gifts, $39,140.

Randi's Floral Shop
Adjusted Trial Balance
December 31, 20—

ACCOUNT NAME	DEBIT	CREDIT
Cash	5 8 2 0 00	
Accounts Receivable	58 5 5 5 00	
Allowance for Doubtful Accounts		2 8 5 3 00
Merchandise Inventory, Plants	62 8 7 8 00	
Merchandise Inventory, Gifts	44 4 2 4 00	
Store Equipment	30 0 8 1 00	
Accumulated Depreciation, Store Equipment		18 8 5 3 00
Accounts Payable		38 6 9 9 00
R. B. Roy, Capital		106 9 2 8 00
R. B. Roy, Drawing	28 6 5 0 00	
Income Summary	71 3 0 0 00	62 8 7 8 00
	40 1 3 3 00	44 4 2 4 00
Sales, Plants		462 6 7 0 00
Sales, Gifts		321 8 2 8 00
Sales Returns and Allowances, Plants	8 9 2 8 00	
Sales Returns and Allowances, Gifts	7 6 4 8 00	
Purchases, Plants	378 3 5 6 00	
Purchases, Gifts	260 8 2 9 00	
Purchases Returns and Allowances, Plants		8 8 0 3 00
Purchases Returns and Allowances, Gifts		6 4 2 0 00
Purchases Discounts, Plants		6 4 3 8 00
Purchases Discounts, Gifts		5 3 8 8 00
Freight In, Plants	11 7 0 1 00	
Freight In, Gifts	8 0 7 0 00	
Sales Salary Expense	33 9 5 3 00	
Depreciation Expense, Store Equipment	5 3 8 3 00	
Miscellaneous Selling Expense	6 8 5 00	
Office Salary Expense	15 4 0 3 00	
Rent Expense	7 4 0 3 00	
Utilities Expense	3 0 1 8 00	
Bad Debts Expense	7 9 8 00	
Miscellaneous General Expense	6 3 3 00	
Interest Expense	1 5 3 3 00	
	1,086 1 8 2 00	1,086 1 8 2 00

P.O. 2

Problem 25-2B The Hiker Station has two departments: equipment and clothing. The trial balance, as of April 30, the end of the fiscal year, is shown on page 972.

The data for the adjustments are as follows:

a.–d. Merchandise inventories, April 30, the end of the fiscal period: equipment department, $21,387; clothing department, $14,358

e. Depreciation of store equipment for the year, $2,430

f. Estimated uncollectible customer charge accounts (based on an analysis of accounts), $1,989

g. Insurance expired, $256
h. Accrued wages and commissions, $171
i. Accrued interest payable, $69 (interest expense is nondepartmental)

The Hiker Station
Trial Balance
April 30, 20—

ACCOUNT NAME	DEBIT	CREDIT
Cash	3 4 0 3 00	
Accounts Receivable	20 0 6 0 00	
Allowance for Doubtful Accounts		5 2 1 00
Merchandise Inventory, Equipment Department	22 0 3 3 00	
Merchandise Inventory, Clothing Department	15 7 6 7 00	
Prepaid Insurance	2 9 0 00	
Store Equipment	8 9 8 1 00	
Accumulated Depreciation, Store Equipment		4 0 5 5 00
Accounts Payable		19 3 7 0 00
J. E. Pry, Capital		33 0 4 0 00
J. E. Pry, Drawing	7 7 5 0 00	
Sales, Equipment Department		64 0 0 0 00
Sales, Clothing Department		42 6 6 7 00
Purchases, Equipment Department	28 6 0 8 00	
Purchases, Clothing Department	21 9 8 4 00	
Freight In, Equipment Department	1 1 9 2 00	
Freight In, Clothing Department	9 1 6 00	
Wages and Commissions Expense	24 3 8 3 00	
Advertising Expense	3 3 0 0 00	
Rent Expense	3 6 0 0 00	
Utilities Expense	7 1 0 00	
Miscellaneous Expense	4 4 5 00	
Interest Expense	2 3 1 00	
	163 6 5 3 00	163 6 5 3 00

The bases for apportioning expenses to the two departments are as follows:

- Advertising Expense (column inches of space): equipment department, $2,640; clothing department, $660
- Depreciation Expense (equipment ledger): equipment department, $1,675; clothing department, $755
- Wages and Commissions Expense (time sheets): equipment department, $15,894; clothing department, $8,660
- Rent Expense, Utilities Expense, Miscellaneous Expense, Bad Debts Expense, Insurance Expense (sales): equipment department, 60 percent; clothing department, 40 percent

Check Figure

Net Income, $14,849

Instructions

Complete the work sheet.

P.O. 3

Problem 25-3B Cecil Franco, Inc., has two departments: furniture and lighting. Cecil Franco's accountant prepares an adjusted trial balance (shown below) at the end of the fiscal year.

Cecil Franco, Inc.
Adjusted Trial Balance
January 31, 20—

ACCOUNT NAME	DEBIT	CREDIT
Cash	4 8 2 6 00	
Accounts Receivable	68 8 9 0 00	
Allowance for Doubtful Accounts		2 6 2 0 00
Merchandise Inventory, Furniture Department	84 1 4 2 00	
Merchandise Inventory, Lighting Department	41 1 3 8 00	
Prepaid Insurance	8 4 0 00	
Store Supplies	7 6 2 00	
Store Equipment	53 6 8 2 00	
Accumulated Depreciation, Store Equipment		41 8 1 0 00
Accounts Payable		38 6 8 0 00
Sales Tax Payable		1 2 8 4 00
Income Tax Payable		1 7 3 3 00
Common Stock		69 4 4 4 00
Retained Earnings		41 8 7 5 00
Income Summary	82 7 6 0 00	84 1 4 2 00
	40 7 2 0 00	41 1 3 8 00
Sales, Furniture Department		409 8 0 0 00
Sales, Lighting Department		273 2 0 0 00
Sales Returns and Allowances, Furniture Department	11 6 8 5 00	
Sales Returns and Allowances, Lighting Department	1 7 1 6 00	
Purchases, Furniture Department	251 8 4 7 00	
Purchases, Lighting Department	165 2 4 2 00	
Purchases Returns and Allowances, Furniture Department		4 6 1 8 00
Purchases Returns and Allowances, Lighting Department		1 7 9 2 00
Purchases Discounts, Furniture Department		5 4 9 6 00
Purchases Discounts, Lighting Department		2 9 6 4 00
Freight In, Furniture Department	13 2 5 5 00	
Freight In, Lighting Department	6 8 8 5 00	
Sales Salary Expense	123 2 2 0 00	
Advertising Expense	14 0 0 0 00	
Depreciation Expense, Store Equipment	13 4 3 6 00	
Store Supplies Expense	7 4 2 00	
Miscellaneous Selling Expense	6 8 0 00	
Rent Expense	8 0 0 0 00	
Utilities Expense	3 2 0 0 00	
Insurance Expense	9 0 0 00	
Bad Debts Expense	1 8 0 0 00	
Miscellaneous General Expense	8 2 0 00	
Interest Expense	2 8 0 0 00	
Income Tax Expense	22 6 0 8 00	
	1,020 5 9 6 00	1,020 5 9 6 00

The trial balance is prepared after all adjustments, including the adjustments for merchandise inventory, have been recorded and posted.

Merchandise inventories at the beginning of the year were as follows: furniture department, $83,850; lighting department, $42,630. The bases (and sources of figures) for apportioning expenses to the two departments are as follows (rounded to the nearest dollar):

- Sales Salary Expense (payroll register): furniture department, $74,800; lighting department, $48,420
- Advertising Expense (newspaper column inches): furniture department, 600 inches; lighting department, 400 inches
- Depreciation Expense, Store Equipment (property and equipment ledger): furniture department, $9,616; lighting department, $3,820
- Store Supplies Expense (requisitions): furniture department, $418; lighting department, $324
- Rent Expense and Utilities Expense (floor space): furniture department, 2,500 square feet; lighting department, 1,500 square feet
- Insurance Expense (average cost of merchandise inventory, rounded off in dollars): furniture department, $600; lighting department, $300
- Miscellaneous Selling Expense (volume of gross sales): furniture department, $408; lighting department, $272
- Bad Debts Expense (volume of gross sales): furniture department, $1,080; lighting department, $720
- Miscellaneous General Expense (volume of gross sales): furniture department, $492; lighting department, $328

Check Figure

Net Income, $53,834

Instructions

Prepare an income statement by department to show income from operations, as well as a nondepartmentalized income statement (using the Total columns) to show net income for the entire company.

P.O. 5

Problem 25-4B On December 31, the end of the fiscal year, Wilder RV Stop, a sole proprietorship, has the revenue and expense account and merchandise inventory balances, after adjustments have been recorded, shown in the partial work sheet on the following page. The store has two departments: parts and accessories. The values of merchandise inventory on January 1 (beginning) are: parts, $48,960; accessories, $24,872.

Essential data for direct expenses (and sources of the figures) are as follows:

a. Sales Salary Expense (sales personnel work in one department only) is allocated as follows: parts, $31,860; accessories, $13,640.
b. Advertising Expense: Newspaper advertising is allocated as follows: parts, $3,280; accessories $830.
c. Depreciation: Depreciation of store equipment is apportioned on the basis of the average cost of equipment in each department. The average cost of store equipment is parts, $7,500; accessories, $2,500.
d. Bad Debts Expense: Department managers are responsible for granting credit on sales made by their respective departments. Bad Debts Expense is allocated as follows: parts, $1,296; accessories, $524.

Check Figure

Net Income, $29,534

Instructions

Prepare an income statement to show each department's departmental margin.

Wilder RV Stop
Partial Work Sheet
For Year Ended December 31, 20—

ACCOUNT NAME	ADJUSTED TRIAL BALANCE									
	DEBIT					CREDIT				
Merchandise Inventory, Parts	51	0	3	0	00					
Merchandise Inventory, Accessories	21	7	8	2	00					
Sales, Parts						187	4	1	6	00
Sales, Accessories						73	9	2	8	00
Sales Returns and Allowances, Parts	4	7	8	2	00					
Sales Returns and Allowances, Accessories	2	0	0	6	00					
Purchases, Parts	105	2	5	6	00					
Purchases, Accessories	41	6	6	8	00					
Purchases Returns and Allowances, Parts						2	6	4	0	00
Purchases Returns and Allowances, Accessories							6	8	4	00
Purchases Discounts, Parts						1	9	8	0	00
Purchases Discounts, Accessories							7	2	0	00
Freight In, Parts	6	7	1	8	00					
Freight In, Accessories	1	6	4	6	00					
Sales Salary Expense	45	5	0	0	00					
Advertising Expense	4	1	1	0	00					
Depreciation Expense, Store Equipment	3	2	0	0	00					
Bad Debts Expense	1	8	2	0	00					
Office Salary Expense	8	6	0	0	00					
Rent Expense	8	4	0	0	00					
Utilities Expense	1	2	4	0	00					
Insurance Expense		3	9	0	00					
Miscellaneous Selling Expense		3	7	4	00					
Miscellaneous General Expense		3	5	6	00					
Interest Expense		7	4	8	00					

LINKS TO ACCOUNTING

Did you know that the first motorcycle to ascend Pike's Peak was a Harley-Davidson? And according to legend, the first carburetor on a Harley-Davidson motorcycle was made from a tomato soup can! The Harley-Davidson Motor Company celebrated its one-hundredth anniversary in 2003. The company reported over twenty consecutive years of record revenues and earnings through 2005! What is the company's profit margin? Over the years, this company has produced a lot of motorcycles (as well as golf carts!). How much do you think it costs to build a Harley? As you learn about job-order and process cost accounting systems in this chapter, think about which system Harley-Davidson would use. You can find Harley-Davidson Motor Company's financial statements at **http://investor.harley-davidson.com.** Click on SEC Filings, search for 10-K, and select the 10-K annual report filed 03-03-06.

Performance Objectives

After you have completed this chapter, you will be able to do the following:

1. Prepare a statement of cost of goods manufactured.

2. Complete a work sheet for a manufacturing enterprise and journalize the closing entries.

3. Define a *job-order cost accounting system* and make the related entries.

4. Define a *process cost accounting system* and make the related entries.

Now let's turn to another type of business operation: manufacturing. The accounting principles we have already discussed pertain to manufacturing concerns, but manufacturers also have special procedures to account for manufacturing costs. In this chapter, we describe how manufacturers determine the total cost of goods manufactured during each accounting period. To acquaint you with the end results, early in the chapter we present a statement of cost of goods manufactured. This statement will enable you to understand the function of the work sheet and its relationship to the financial statements. This chapter is only an introduction to accounting for manufacturing operations. As you continue your accounting education, you will have the opportunity to deal with more advanced systems and procedures.

COMPARISON OF INCOME STATEMENTS FOR MERCHANDISING AND MANUFACTURING ENTERPRISES

FYI

The main difference between accounting for a merchandising business and for a manufacturing business is in determining the cost of goods sold.

Manufacturing and merchandising companies have the same type of revenue accounts. However, a merchant buys goods in a finished condition and later sells them at a higher price in the same condition. A manufacturer, on the other hand, buys raw materials, transforms them into finished goods, and later sells the finished goods.

To compare the two types of companies, study the portions of the income statements for a merchandising firm and for a manufacturing firm shown in Figure 1.

Merchandising Firm	**Manufacturing Firm**
Beginning Merchandise Inventory	Beginning Finished Goods Inventory
Plus Delivered Cost of Purchases	Plus Cost of Goods Manufactured
Cost of Goods Available for Sale	Cost of Goods Available for Sale
Less Ending Merchandise Inventory	Less Ending Finished Goods Inventory
Cost of Goods Sold	Cost of Goods Sold

Cost of Goods Manufactured for a manufacturer is the equivalent of Delivered Cost of Purchases for a merchandiser.

FIGURE 1

A Merchandising Company, Inc.
Income Statement
For Year Ended December 31, 20—

Sales (net)			$2 500 0 0 0 00	
Cost of Goods Sold:				
Merchandise Inventory, Jan. 1, 20—	$ 390 0 0 0 00			
Delivered Cost of Purchases	1 200 0 0 0 00			
Cost of Goods Available for Sale	$1 590 0 0 0 00			
Less Merchandise Inventory,				
December 31, 20—	250 0 0 0 00			
Cost of Goods Sold		1 340 0 0 0 00		
Gross Profit			$1 160 0 0 0 00	

A Manufacturing Company, Inc.
Income Statement
For Year Ended December 31, 20—

Sales (net)			$2 500 0 0 0 00	
Cost of Goods Sold:				
Finished Goods Inv., Jan. 1, 20—	$ 390 0 0 0 00			
Cost of Goods Manufactured	1 200 0 0 0 00			
Cost of Goods Available for Sale	$1 590 0 0 0 00			
Less Finished Goods Inventory,				
December 31, 20—	250 0 0 0 00			
Cost of Goods Sold		1 340 0 0 0 00		
Gross Profit			$1 160 0 0 0 00	

Park Manufacturing Company, Inc.
Statement of Cost of Goods Manufactured
For Year Ended December 31, 20—

Work-in-Process Inventory, January 1, 20—			$ 140 000 00
Raw Materials:			
Raw Materials Inventory, January 1, 20—	$ 90 000 00		
Raw Materials Purchases (net)	230 000 00		
Cost of Raw Materials Available for Use	$ 320 000 00		
Less Raw Materials Inventory, December 31, 20—	100 000 00		
Cost of Raw Materials Used		$ 220 000 00	
Direct Labor		565 000 00	
Factory Overhead:			
Indirect Labor	$ 120 000 00		
Supervisory Salaries	110 000 00		
Heat, Light, and Power	42 000 00		
Depreciation Expense, Factory Equipment	32 000 00		
Depreciation Expense, Factory Building	25 000 00		
Repairs and Maintenance	24 000 00		
Factory Insurance Expired	22 000 00		
Factory Supplies Used	14 000 00		
Miscellaneous Factory Costs	16 000 00		
Total Factory Overhead		405 000 00	
Total Manufacturing Costs			1 190 000 00
Total Cost of Work-in-Process During Period			$1 330 000 00
Less Work-in-Process Inventory, December 31, 20—			130 000 00
Cost of Goods Manufactured			$1 200 000 00

FIGURE 2

STATEMENT OF COST OF GOODS MANUFACTURED

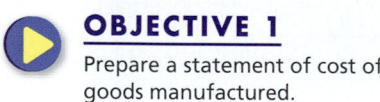

OBJECTIVE 1

Prepare a statement of cost of goods manufactured.

As an illustration, we'll use the statement of cost of goods manufactured for Park Manufacturing Company, Inc., shown in Figure 2 above. **Because Cost of Goods Manufactured is included on the income statement, the accountant naturally prepares the statement of cost of goods manufactured first.**

ELEMENTS OF MANUFACTURING COSTS

No matter what type of product a manufacturer produces, the three elements that make up the cost of the goods manufactured are *raw materials used, direct labor,* and *factory overhead.*

Raw Materials Used

Raw materials are the materials that enter directly into—and become a part of—the finished product. The delivered cost of these materials is Cost of Raw Materials Used. For example, if you are manufacturing tables, you need

Manufacturing plants maintain more than one inventory—they have raw materials, work-in-process, and finished goods inventories. Raw materials are also called direct materials because they directly become a part of the finished product.

REMEMBER!

The cost of manufacturing any product consists of direct (raw) materials, direct labor, and factory overhead.

wood, glue, hardware, finishing materials, etc. Raw materials are also called *direct materials*.

Direct Labor

Direct labor consists of the wages paid to factory employees who work—with machines or hand tools—directly on the materials to convert them into finished products. The manufacturer debits the Direct Labor account for the gross wages of those who work directly on the raw materials. The cost of direct labor varies directly with the level of production.

Factory Overhead

Factory overhead consists of manufacturing costs (other than raw materials used and direct labor) that cannot be traced directly to products being manufactured. A manufacturer uses Factory Overhead as a control account. The specific titles of accounts in the factory overhead subsidiary ledger vary from company to company. In Figure 2, the accounts in the factory overhead ledger are Indirect Labor; Supervisory Salaries; Heat, Light, and Power; Depreciation Expense, Factory Equipment; Depreciation Expense, Factory Building; Repairs and Maintenance; Factory Insurance Expired; Factory Supplies Used; and Miscellaneous Factory Costs.

Indirect labor is the wages paid to those people who keep the plant in operation, rather than directly working on production. Examples are operations personnel, maintenance workers, and timekeepers.

The balance of Factory Supplies Used reveals the cost of materials used to keep the plant in operation (oil, grease, and so on). These items are also called **indirect materials**.

Other items that may be included in Factory Overhead are workers' compensation insurance, payroll taxes on wages of factory employees, pension contributions for factory employees, taxes on factory building and equipment, taxes on raw materials and work-in-process inventories, patents written off, and small tools written off.

WORK SHEET FOR A MANUFACTURING FIRM

OBJECTIVE 2

Complete a work sheet for a manufacturing enterprise and journalize the closing entries.

A manufacturer's work sheet must include two extra columns headed Statement of Cost of Goods Manufactured.

Let's examine the work sheet for Park Manufacturing Company, Inc., shown in Figure 3 (pages 980–983). First, notice that all accounts in the Trial Balance columns representing manufacturing costs have debit balances, just as expense accounts have debit balances. Next, look at the adjusting entries for inventories. (We are assuming that Park Manufacturing Company uses a periodic inventory system.) A manufacturer, like a merchandiser, takes two steps to adjust inventory: The accountant (1) takes off (or closes off) the beginning inventory and (2) adds on the ending inventory. However, in manufacturing accounting, three inventories are involved: Raw Materials, Work-in-Process, and Finished Goods.

	ACCOUNT NAME	TRIAL BALANCE DEBIT	TRIAL BALANCE CREDIT	ADJUSTMENTS DEBIT	ADJUSTMENTS CREDIT	
1	Cash	124 0 0 0 00				
2	Notes Receivable	50 0 0 0 00				
3	Accounts Receivable	180 0 0 0 00				
4	Allowance for Doubtful Accounts		2 5 0 0 00		(k) 3 5 0 0 00	
5	Raw Materials Inventory	90 0 0 0 00		(b) 100 0 0 0 00	(a) 90 0 0 0 00	
6	Work-in-Process Inventory	140 0 0 0 00		(d) 130 0 0 0 00	(c) 140 0 0 0 00	
7	Finished Goods Inventory	390 0 0 0 00		(f) 250 0 0 0 00	(e) 390 0 0 0 00	
8	Prepaid Insurance	25 0 0 0 00			(i) 22 0 0 0 00	
9	Land	316 0 0 0 00				
10	Factory Building	700 0 0 0 00				
11	Accumulated Deprec., Factory Building		250 0 0 0 00		(g) 25 0 0 0 00	
12	Factory Equipment	360 0 0 0 00				
13	Accumulated Deprec., Factory Equipment		218 0 0 0 00		(h) 46 0 0 0 00	
14	Office Equipment	62 0 0 0 00				
15	Accumulated Deprec., Office Equipment		40 0 0 0 00		(j) 5 0 0 0 00	
16	Notes Payable		40 0 0 0 00			
17	Accounts Payable		55 5 5 0 00			
18	Dividends Payable		12 0 0 0 00			
19	Bonds Payable		280 0 0 0 00			
20	Common Stock		310 0 0 0 00			
21	Paid-in Capital in Excess of Par Value		100 0 0 0 00			
22	Retained Earnings		314 9 0 0 00			
23	Sales (net)		2,500 0 0 0 00			
24	Raw Materials Purchases	230 0 0 0 00				
25	Direct Labor	565 0 0 0 00				
26	Indirect Labor	120 0 0 0 00				
27	Supervisory Salaries	110 0 0 0 00				
28	Heat, Light, and Power	42 0 0 0 00				
29	Repairs and Maintenance	24 0 0 0 00				
30	Miscellaneous Factory Costs	16 0 0 0 00				
31	Selling Expenses (control)	300 0 0 0 00				
32	General Expenses (control)	123 5 0 0 00		(j) 5 0 0 0 00		
33				(k) 3 5 0 0 00		
34	Interest Expense	18 0 0 0 00				
35	Income Tax Expense	137 4 5 0 00		(l) 103 9 5 0 00		
36		4,122 9 5 0 00	4,122 9 5 0 00			
37	Totals carried forward			592 4 5 0 00	721 5 0 0 00	
38						
39						
40						

FIGURE 3

Park Manufacturing Company, Inc.
Work Sheet
For Year Ended December 31, 20—

	STATEMENT OF COST OF GOODS MANUFACTURED		INCOME STATEMENT		BALANCE SHEET		
	DEBIT	CREDIT	DEBIT	CREDIT	DEBIT	CREDIT	
					124 0 0 0 00		1
					50 0 0 0 00		2
					180 0 0 0 00		3
						6 0 0 0 00	4
					100 0 0 0 00		5
					130 0 0 0 00		6
					250 0 0 0 00		7
					3 0 0 0 00		8
					316 0 0 0 00		9
					700 0 0 0 00		10
						275 0 0 0 00	11
					360 0 0 0 00		12
						264 0 0 0 00	13
					62 0 0 0 00		14
						45 0 0 0 00	15
						40 0 0 0 00	16
						55 5 5 0 00	17
						12 0 0 0 00	18
						280 0 0 0 00	19
						310 0 0 0 00	20
						100 0 0 0 00	21
						314 9 0 0 00	22
				2,500 0 0 0 00			23
	230 0 0 0 00						24
	565 0 0 0 00						25
	120 0 0 0 00						26
	110 0 0 0 00						27
	42 0 0 0 00						28
	24 0 0 0 00						29
	16 0 0 0 00						30
			300 0 0 0 00				31
							32
			132 0 0 0 00				33
			18 0 0 0 00				34
			241 4 0 0 00				35
							36
	1,107 0 0 0 00		691 4 0 0 00	2,500 0 0 0 00	2,261 0 0 0 00	1,688 4 5 0 00	37
							38
							39
							40

(continued)

	ACCOUNT NAME	TRIAL BALANCE		ADJUSTMENTS		
		DEBIT	CREDIT	DEBIT	CREDIT	
1	Totals brought forward			592 4 5 0 00	721 5 0 0 00	
2	Manufacturing Summary			(a) 90 0 0 0 00	(b) 100 0 0 0 00	
3				(c)140 0 0 0 00	(d) 130 0 0 0 00	
4	Income Summary			(e)390 0 0 0 00	(f) 250 0 0 0 00	
5	Depreciation Expense, Factory Building			(g) 25 0 0 0 00		
6	Depreciation Expense, Factory Equipment			(h) 46 0 0 0 00		
7	Factory Insurance Expired			(i) 22 0 0 0 00		
8	Income Tax Payable				(l) 103 9 5 0 00	
9				1,305 4 5 0 00	1,305 4 5 0 00	
10	Cost of Goods Manufactured					
11						
12	Net Income					
13						
14						

FIGURE 3 (continued)

Since Raw Materials Inventory and Work-in-Process Inventory appear in the statement of cost of goods manufactured, the accountant adjusts them using the **Manufacturing Summary** account, an account similar to Income Summary used to make adjustments to Raw Materials and Work-in-Process Inventory accounts and to close out all other manufacturing accounts. Since Finished Goods Inventory appears on the income statement, the accountant adjusts it using the Income Summary account. Finished Goods Inventory for a manufacturing firm is equivalent to Merchandise Inventory for a merchandising firm.

Data for the adjustments are as follows:

a.–b. Raw materials inventory at December 31, $100,000
c.–d. Work-in-process inventory at December 31, $130,000
e.–f. Finished goods inventory at December 31, $250,000

In T account form, the adjusting entries for the inventory accounts are:

REMEMBER!

The raw materials inventory and the work-in-process inventory are adjusted using the Manufacturing Summary account.

Raw Materials Inventory		Work-in-Process Inventory		Manufacturing Summary	
+	−	+	−	(a) 90,000	(b) 100,000
Bal. 90,000	(a) 90,000	Bal. 140,000	(c) 140,000	(c) 140,000	(d) 130,000
(b) 100,000		(d) 130,000			

Finished Goods Inventory		Income Summary	
+	−	(e) 390,000	(f) 250,000
Bal. 390,000	(e) 390,000		
(f) 250,000			

g. Depreciation of factory building, $25,000
h. Depreciation of factory equipment, $32,000

Statement of Cost of Goods Manufactured		Income Statement		Balance Sheet		
DEBIT	CREDIT	DEBIT	CREDIT	DEBIT	CREDIT	
1,107 000 00		691 400 00	2,500 000 00	2,275 000 00	1,702 450 00	1
90 000 00	100 000 00					2
140 000 00	130 000 00					3
		390 000 00	250 000 00			4
25 000 00						5
46 000 00						6
22 000 00						7
					103 950 00	8
1,430 000 00	230 000 00					9
	1,200 000 00	1,200 000 00				10
1,430 000 00	1,430 000 00	2,281 400 00	2,750 000 00	2,275 000 00	1,806 000 00	11
		468 600 00			468 600 00	12
		2,750 000 00	2,750 000 00	2,275 000 00	2,275 000 00	13
						14

FYI

The adjustments other than those for the inventory accounts are like the ones we have already seen.

i. Expired factory insurance, $22,000 (assuming the unexpired portion had already been calculated)
j. Depreciation of office equipment, $5,000
k. Estimated uncollectible accounts, $6,000 (determined by an aging analysis)
l. Income tax, $241,400 (based on a taxable income before income tax of $710,000; the accountant determined this by completing the Income Statement columns of the work sheet without including income tax)

REMEMBER!

Cost of Goods Manufactured is the equivalent of Delivered Cost of Purchases for a merchandising firm.

Notice how the figures in the Adjustments columns are transferred to the remaining columns of the work sheet. Just as the accountant transfers the figures on the Income Summary line into the Income Statement columns as separate figures, he or she also transfers the four figures on the Manufacturing Summary lines into the Statement of Cost of Goods Manufactured columns as separate figures, like this:

ACCOUNT NAME	ADJUSTMENTS		Statement of Cost of Goods Manufactured		Income Statement	
	DEBIT	CREDIT	DEBIT	CREDIT	DEBIT	CREDIT
22 Manufacturing						
23 Summary	(a) 90 000 00	(b) 100 000 00	90 000 00	100 000 00		
24	(c) 140 000 00	(d) 130 000 00	140 000 00	130 000 00		
25 Income						
26 Summary	(e) 390 000 00	(f) 250 000 00			390 000 00	250 000 00
27						

On the work sheet, the accountant transfers the cost of goods manufactured ($1,200,000, the difference between the debit and credit totals in the Statement of Cost of Goods Manufactured columns) to the Income Statement Debit column as shown in the following section of Park Manufacturing Company's work sheet.

	ACCOUNT NAME	STATEMENT OF COST OF GOODS MANUFACTURED		INCOME STATEMENT	
		DEBIT	CREDIT	DEBIT	CREDIT
10		1,430 0 0 0 00	230 0 0 0 00		
11	Cost of Goods Manufactured		1,200 0 0 0 00	1,200 0 0 0 00	
12		1,430 0 0 0 00	1,430 0 0 0 00	2,281 4 0 0 00	2,750 0 0 0 00
13	Net Income			468 6 0 0 00	
14				2,750 0 0 0 00	2,750 0 0 0 00

Closing Entries

Here are the steps to take in making the closing entries for a manufacturer:

1. Close the costs that appear on the statement of cost of goods manufactured into the Manufacturing Summary account.
2. Close the Manufacturing Summary account into the Income Summary account (by the amount of the cost of goods manufactured).
3. Close the revenue accounts into the Income Summary account.
4. Close the expense accounts into the Income Summary account.
5. Close the Income Tax Expense account into the Income Summary account.
6. Close the Income Summary account into the Retained Earnings account (by the amount of the net income).

Following are T accounts for Manufacturing Summary and Income Summary, labeled so that you can readily identify the manufacturing accounts recorded. The end-of-month entries are shown in Figure 4 (pages 985–986).

REMEMBER!

Manufacturing Summary is closed into Income Summary by the amount of the Cost of Goods Manufactured.

Manufacturing Summary

Raw Materials Inventory, Jan. 1	90,000	Raw Materials Inventory, Dec. 31	100,000
Work-in-Process Inventory, Jan. 1	140,000	Work-in-Process Inventory, Dec. 31	130,000
Raw Materials Purchases	230,000	Closing	1,200,000
Direct Labor	565,000	(To Income Summary)	
Indirect Labor	120,000		
Supervisory Salaries	110,000		
Heat, Light, and Power	42,000		
Repairs and Maintenance	24,000		
Miscellaneous Factory Costs	16,000		
Depr. Expense, Factory Equipment	46,000		
Depr. Expense, Factory Building	25,000		
Factory Insurance Expired	22,000		
	1,430,000		**1,430,000**

Income Summary

Finished Goods Inventory, Jan. 1	390,000	Finished Goods Inventory, Dec. 31	250,000
(From Manufacturing Summary)	1,200,000		

FIGURE 4

<table>
<tr><td colspan="2"></td><td></td><td></td><td colspan="5" align="center">GENERAL JOURNAL</td><td colspan="5" align="right">PAGE _____</td></tr>
<tr>
<td colspan="2" align="center">DATE</td>
<td align="center">DESCRIPTION</td>
<td align="center">POST. REF.</td>
<td colspan="5" align="center">DEBIT</td>
<td colspan="5" align="center">CREDIT</td>
<td></td>
</tr>
<tr><td>20–</td><td></td><td>**Adjusting Entries**</td><td></td><td></td><td></td><td></td><td></td><td></td><td></td><td></td><td></td><td></td><td></td><td>1</td></tr>
<tr><td>Dec.</td><td>31</td><td>Manufacturing Summary</td><td></td><td>90</td><td>0</td><td>0</td><td>0</td><td>00</td><td></td><td></td><td></td><td></td><td></td><td>2</td></tr>
<tr><td></td><td></td><td>Raw Materials Inventory</td><td></td><td></td><td></td><td></td><td></td><td></td><td>90</td><td>0</td><td>0</td><td>0</td><td>00</td><td>3</td></tr>
<tr><td></td><td></td><td></td><td></td><td></td><td></td><td></td><td></td><td></td><td></td><td></td><td></td><td></td><td></td><td>4</td></tr>
<tr><td></td><td>31</td><td>Raw Materials Inventory</td><td></td><td>100</td><td>0</td><td>0</td><td>0</td><td>00</td><td></td><td></td><td></td><td></td><td></td><td>5</td></tr>
<tr><td></td><td></td><td>Manufacturing Summary</td><td></td><td></td><td></td><td></td><td></td><td></td><td>100</td><td>0</td><td>0</td><td>0</td><td>00</td><td>6</td></tr>
<tr><td></td><td></td><td></td><td></td><td></td><td></td><td></td><td></td><td></td><td></td><td></td><td></td><td></td><td></td><td>7</td></tr>
<tr><td></td><td>31</td><td>Manufacturing Summary</td><td></td><td>140</td><td>0</td><td>0</td><td>0</td><td>00</td><td></td><td></td><td></td><td></td><td></td><td>8</td></tr>
<tr><td></td><td></td><td>Work-in-Process Inventory</td><td></td><td></td><td></td><td></td><td></td><td></td><td>140</td><td>0</td><td>0</td><td>0</td><td>00</td><td>9</td></tr>
<tr><td></td><td></td><td></td><td></td><td></td><td></td><td></td><td></td><td></td><td></td><td></td><td></td><td></td><td></td><td>10</td></tr>
<tr><td></td><td>31</td><td>Work-in-Process Inventory</td><td></td><td>130</td><td>0</td><td>0</td><td>0</td><td>00</td><td></td><td></td><td></td><td></td><td></td><td>11</td></tr>
<tr><td></td><td></td><td>Manufacturing Summary</td><td></td><td></td><td></td><td></td><td></td><td></td><td>130</td><td>0</td><td>0</td><td>0</td><td>00</td><td>12</td></tr>
<tr><td></td><td></td><td></td><td></td><td></td><td></td><td></td><td></td><td></td><td></td><td></td><td></td><td></td><td></td><td>13</td></tr>
<tr><td></td><td>31</td><td>Income Summary</td><td></td><td>390</td><td>0</td><td>0</td><td>0</td><td>00</td><td></td><td></td><td></td><td></td><td></td><td>14</td></tr>
<tr><td></td><td></td><td>Finished Goods Inventory</td><td></td><td></td><td></td><td></td><td></td><td></td><td>390</td><td>0</td><td>0</td><td>0</td><td>00</td><td>15</td></tr>
<tr><td></td><td></td><td></td><td></td><td></td><td></td><td></td><td></td><td></td><td></td><td></td><td></td><td></td><td></td><td>16</td></tr>
<tr><td></td><td>31</td><td>Finished Goods Inventory</td><td></td><td>250</td><td>0</td><td>0</td><td>0</td><td>00</td><td></td><td></td><td></td><td></td><td></td><td>17</td></tr>
<tr><td></td><td></td><td>Income Summary</td><td></td><td></td><td></td><td></td><td></td><td></td><td>250</td><td>0</td><td>0</td><td>0</td><td>00</td><td>18</td></tr>
<tr><td></td><td></td><td></td><td></td><td></td><td></td><td></td><td></td><td></td><td></td><td></td><td></td><td></td><td></td><td>19</td></tr>
<tr><td></td><td>31</td><td>Depreciation Expense, Factory</td><td></td><td></td><td></td><td></td><td></td><td></td><td></td><td></td><td></td><td></td><td></td><td>20</td></tr>
<tr><td></td><td></td><td>Building</td><td></td><td>25</td><td>0</td><td>0</td><td>0</td><td>00</td><td></td><td></td><td></td><td></td><td></td><td>21</td></tr>
<tr><td></td><td></td><td>Accumulated Depreciation,</td><td></td><td></td><td></td><td></td><td></td><td></td><td></td><td></td><td></td><td></td><td></td><td>22</td></tr>
<tr><td></td><td></td><td>Factory Building</td><td></td><td></td><td></td><td></td><td></td><td></td><td>25</td><td>0</td><td>0</td><td>0</td><td>00</td><td>23</td></tr>
<tr><td></td><td></td><td></td><td></td><td></td><td></td><td></td><td></td><td></td><td></td><td></td><td></td><td></td><td></td><td>24</td></tr>
<tr><td></td><td>31</td><td>Depreciation Expense, Factory</td><td></td><td></td><td></td><td></td><td></td><td></td><td></td><td></td><td></td><td></td><td></td><td>25</td></tr>
<tr><td></td><td></td><td>Equipment</td><td></td><td>46</td><td>0</td><td>0</td><td>0</td><td>00</td><td></td><td></td><td></td><td></td><td></td><td>26</td></tr>
<tr><td></td><td></td><td>Accumulated Depreciation,</td><td></td><td></td><td></td><td></td><td></td><td></td><td></td><td></td><td></td><td></td><td></td><td>27</td></tr>
<tr><td></td><td></td><td>Factory Equipment</td><td></td><td></td><td></td><td></td><td></td><td></td><td>46</td><td>0</td><td>0</td><td>0</td><td>00</td><td>28</td></tr>
<tr><td></td><td></td><td></td><td></td><td></td><td></td><td></td><td></td><td></td><td></td><td></td><td></td><td></td><td></td><td>29</td></tr>
<tr><td></td><td>31</td><td>Factory Insurance Expired</td><td></td><td>22</td><td>0</td><td>0</td><td>0</td><td>00</td><td></td><td></td><td></td><td></td><td></td><td>30</td></tr>
<tr><td></td><td></td><td>Prepaid Insurance</td><td></td><td></td><td></td><td></td><td></td><td></td><td>22</td><td>0</td><td>0</td><td>0</td><td>00</td><td>31</td></tr>
<tr><td></td><td></td><td></td><td></td><td></td><td></td><td></td><td></td><td></td><td></td><td></td><td></td><td></td><td></td><td>32</td></tr>
<tr><td></td><td>31</td><td>General Expenses (control)</td><td></td><td>5</td><td>0</td><td>0</td><td>0</td><td>00</td><td></td><td></td><td></td><td></td><td></td><td>33</td></tr>
<tr><td></td><td></td><td>Accumulated Depreciation,</td><td></td><td></td><td></td><td></td><td></td><td></td><td></td><td></td><td></td><td></td><td></td><td>34</td></tr>
<tr><td></td><td></td><td>Office Equipment</td><td></td><td></td><td></td><td></td><td></td><td></td><td>5</td><td>0</td><td>0</td><td>0</td><td>00</td><td>35</td></tr>
<tr><td></td><td>31</td><td></td><td></td><td></td><td></td><td></td><td></td><td></td><td></td><td></td><td></td><td></td><td></td><td>36</td></tr>
<tr><td></td><td></td><td>General Expenses (control)</td><td></td><td>3</td><td>5</td><td>0</td><td>0</td><td>00</td><td></td><td></td><td></td><td></td><td></td><td>37</td></tr>
<tr><td></td><td></td><td>Allowance for Doubtful Accts.</td><td></td><td></td><td></td><td></td><td></td><td></td><td>3</td><td>5</td><td>0</td><td>0</td><td>00</td><td>38</td></tr>
<tr><td></td><td></td><td></td><td></td><td></td><td></td><td></td><td></td><td></td><td></td><td></td><td></td><td></td><td></td><td>39</td></tr>
<tr><td></td><td>31</td><td>Income Tax Expense</td><td></td><td>103</td><td>9</td><td>5</td><td>0</td><td>00</td><td></td><td></td><td></td><td></td><td></td><td>40</td></tr>
<tr><td></td><td></td><td>Income Tax Payable</td><td></td><td></td><td></td><td></td><td></td><td></td><td>103</td><td>9</td><td>5</td><td>0</td><td>00</td><td>41</td></tr>
<tr><td></td><td></td><td></td><td></td><td></td><td></td><td></td><td></td><td></td><td></td><td></td><td></td><td></td><td></td><td>42</td></tr>
<tr><td></td><td></td><td></td><td></td><td></td><td></td><td></td><td></td><td></td><td></td><td></td><td></td><td></td><td></td><td>43</td></tr>
</table>

(continued)

FIGURE 4
(continued)

		GENERAL JOURNAL				PAGE _____			

	DATE		DESCRIPTION	POST. REF.	DEBIT	CREDIT	
1	20–		**Closing Entries**				1
2	Dec.	31	**Manufacturing Summary**		1,200 0 0 0 00		2
3			Raw Materials Purchases			230 0 0 0 00	3
4			Direct Labor			565 0 0 0 00	4
5			Indirect Labor			120 0 0 0 00	5
6			Supervisory Salaries			110 0 0 0 00	6
7			Heat, Light, and Power			42 0 0 0 00	7
8			Repairs and Maintenance			24 0 0 0 00	8
9			Misc. Factory Costs			16 0 0 0 00	9
10			Depreciation Expense,				10
11			Factory Building			25 0 0 0 00	11
12			Depreciation Expense,				12
13			Factory Equipment			46 0 0 0 00	13
14			Factory Insurance Expired			22 0 0 0 00	14
15							15
16		31	**Income Summary**		1,200 0 0 0 00		16
17			Manufacturing Summary			1,200 0 0 0 00	17
18							18
19		31	**Sales (net)**		2,500 0 0 0 00		19
20			Income Summary			2,500 0 0 0 00	20
21							21
22		31	**Income Summary**		450 0 0 0 00		22
23			Selling Expenses (control)			300 0 0 0 00	23
24			General Expenses (control)			132 0 0 0 00	24
25			Interest Expense			18 0 0 0 00	25
26							26
27		31	**Income Summary**		241 4 0 0 00		27
28			Income Tax Expense			241 4 0 0 00	28
29							29
30		31	**Income Summary**		468 6 0 0 00		30
31			Retained Earnings			468 6 0 0 00	31
32							32
33							33
34							34

DETERMINING THE VALUE OF ENDING INVENTORIES

A manufacturer has to record the costs of the ending inventories for (1) raw materials, (2) work-in-process, and (3) finished goods. The manufacturer first lists these costs in the Adjustments columns of the work sheet and then carries the figures forward into the financial statement columns. Now let's consider raw materials inventory and work-in-process inventory separately, because each poses a slightly different set of problems.

Computers have become essential in compiling the data needed to compute the cost of goods manufactured.

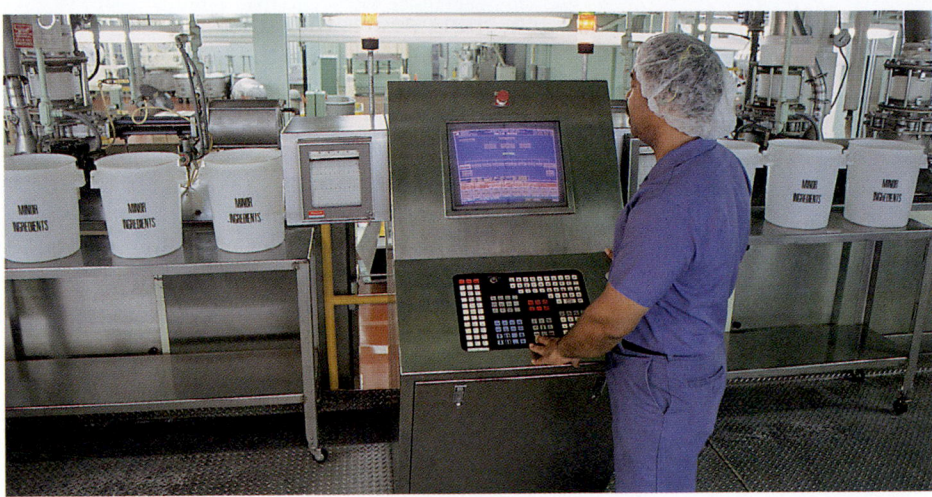

Raw Materials Inventory

The items that make up the raw materials inventory are in the same form they were in when the manufacturer bought them; nothing has been done to them yet. So the accountant first determines the quantities on hand and the unit costs and then figures the value of the inventory. The value of the ending inventory may be calculated by either FIFO, LIFO, or weighted-average method. You may also use the lower-of-cost-or-market rule. These alternatives involve periodic and perpetual inventory systems.

A manufacturer may choose to use a *perpetual inventory system,* which provides a continuous or running balance of the firm's inventory. When a firm that uses a perpetual inventory system buys raw materials, it immediately debits Raw Materials Inventory for the cost of these materials. When the materials are put into production, the manufacturer credits Raw Materials Inventory for the cost of the materials used and debits Work-in-Process Inventory. The same debiting and crediting process goes on in the Work-in-Process Inventory and the Finished Goods Inventory accounts as the materials go through the manufacturing process. If a company keeps a perpetual inventory, it verifies the balance of the account periodically by physically counting the goods on hand. Any discrepancy that exists can be handled by an adjusting entry either debiting or crediting the Inventory account and either debiting or crediting the Cost of Goods Sold account.

Work-in-Process Inventory

How do you calculate the cost of the work-in-process inventory? We have seen that the cost of manufacturing any product consists of (1) *raw materials used,* (2) *direct labor expended,* and (3) *factory overhead.* Therefore, the manufacturer keeps a record of the amount and cost of raw materials placed in production. The manufacturer also records the cost of direct labor expended on the ending work-in-process inventory.

The third item, factory overhead, consists of a group of accounts such as Heat, Light, and Power; Repairs and Maintenance; and Miscellaneous Factory Costs; to name a few. The manufacturer cannot calculate the *exact* cost of factory overhead included in the ending work-in-process inventory and must therefore estimate this cost. One way the firm does this is by using a percentage of the direct labor cost involved in the ending inventory. The reasoning here is that since factory overhead is closely related to the level of production, and since the level of production varies directly with the amount of direct labor, the cost of factory overhead should be regarded as a percentage of direct labor. For example, Heat, Light, and Power is part of factory overhead and varies directly with the level of production.

You may determine the percentage for factory overhead from the most recent statement of cost of goods manufactured. The factory overhead rate for Park Manufacturing Company, Inc., is as follows:

$$\text{Factory Overhead Rate} = \frac{\text{Factory Overhead}}{\text{Direct Labor}} = \frac{\$405,000}{\$565,000} = 0.72 = \underline{\underline{72\%}}$$

In heavily computerized factories, machine time used or some other appropriate measure may be more accurate than direct labor in apportioning factory overhead.

COST ACCOUNTING SYSTEMS FOR MANUFACTURING OPERATIONS

There are two principal cost accounting systems: (1) the job-order cost accounting system and (2) the process cost accounting system.

Job-Order Cost Accounting System

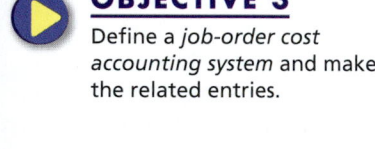

OBJECTIVE 3

Define a *job-order cost accounting system* and make the related entries.

In a **job-order cost accounting system**, materials, labor, and overhead costs are accumulated *by the job* or batch on a job order cost sheet as the batch is transferred through the various production departments. The job order may originate from a customer's request or be initiated by the company itself to increase its inventory of finished products. After the job is completed and included in the finished goods inventory, the cost per unit can be calculated by dividing the total costs of materials, labor, and overhead accumulated from each department by the total units completed in the job or batch. For each job order, there is a definite beginning and, when the objective has been achieved, a definite ending.

For example, one of the products made by Ace Manufacturing Company is bicycle pumps. The company has an order for 5,000 pumps. Ace Manufacturing sets up a subsidiary Work-in-Process Inventory account in the work-in-process subsidiary ledger and titles it Work in Process—Job Order 72. Work-in-Process Inventory is a control account, and the subsidiary ledger contains an account for each job order number. Below are typical entries pertaining to Job Order 72. These entries relate to a perpetual inventory system.

a. Purchased raw materials, $100,000, paying cash. (For simplicity, assume that all payments are made in cash.)

			GENERAL JOURNAL				PAGE _____	
	DATE		DESCRIPTION	POST. REF.		DEBIT		CREDIT
1			Raw Materials Inventory		100 0 0 0 00				1
2			Cash				100 0 0 0 00		2

b. Placed $80,000 of raw materials into production.

	DATE	DESCRIPTION	POST. REF.	DEBIT	CREDIT	
1		Work-in-Process Inventory		80 0 0 0 00		1
2		Raw Materials Inventory			80 0 0 0 00	2

c. Issued checks for direct labor, $40,000.

	DATE	DESCRIPTION	POST. REF.	DEBIT	CREDIT	
1		Work-in-Process Inventory		40 0 0 0 00		1
2		Cash			40 0 0 0 00	2

REMEMBER!

We pay for factory overhead (debit Factory Overhead and credit Cash), and then we distribute (apply) the factory overhead.

d. Applied factory overhead at the rate of 70 percent of direct labor.

	DATE	DESCRIPTION	POST. REF.	DEBIT	CREDIT	
1		Work-in-Process Inventory		28 0 0 0 00		1
2		Factory Overhead			28 0 0 0 00	2

e. Transferred completed production to Finished Goods Inventory.

	DATE	DESCRIPTION	POST. REF.	DEBIT	CREDIT	
1		Finished Goods Inventory		148 0 0 0 00		1
2		Work-in-Process Inventory			148 0 0 0 00	2

To carry on its production, Ace Manufacturing must keep a variety of raw materials. Consequently, Raw Materials Inventory (sometimes called Materials) is a control account, and the materials ledger contains a separate account for each type of material. As mentioned before, since Ace Manufacturing may be working on a number of job orders at the same time, Work-in-Process Inventory is also a control account. Finally, Finished Goods Inventory is a control account, and the finished goods ledger contains a separate account for bicycle pumps as well as a separate account for each other product manufactured.

The entries involving the inventories in T account form are shown below.

General Ledger

Raw Materials Inventory		Work-in-Process Inventory		Finished Goods Inventory		Factory Overhead		Cash	
Bal. xxx	**(b)** 80,000	Bal. xxx	**(e)**	Bal. xxx		Bal. xxx	**(d)** 28,000	Bal. xxx	**(a)**
(a)		**(b)** 80,000	148,000	**(e)**					100,000
100,000		**(c)** 40,000		148,000					**(c)** 40,000
		(d) 28,000							

Materials Ledger		Work-in-Process Ledger		Finished Goods Ledger	

Material A

Bal. xx	**(b)** 60,000
(a) 100,000	

Material B

Bal. xx	**(b)** 10,000

Material C

Bal. xx	**(b)** 10,000

Job Order 72

Bal. xx	**(e)** 148,000
(b) 80,000	
(c) 40,000	
(d) 28,000	

Job Order 73

Bal. xx	

Job Order 74

Bal. xx	

Product No. 1

Bal. xx	
(e) 148,000	

Product No. 2

Bal. xx	

Product No. 3

Bal. xx	

Since the Factory Overhead account is a control account, it will be debited when actual expenses are paid. Note that a variety of materials are used for Job Order 72. Note the output of Job Order 72 is Product No. 1.

Process Cost Accounting System

OBJECTIVE 4

Define a *process cost accounting system* and make the related entries.

Companies whose product is homogeneous, such as this wheat processing plant, use a process cost accounting system. In this plant, one bag of grain is indistinguishable from the next.

A **process cost accounting system** is used by manufacturers of homogeneous units (items that are exactly the same and are not distinguishable from one another) in a continuous production process. For example, the production of cement or flour is the result of a continuous process. Also,

in the case of cement, one 90-pound bag of cement is the same as another 90-pound bag of cement.

Production of such goods is continuous and is completed in stages, with one department completing one stage and another department completing the next stage. Each department accumulates the costs of materials, labor, and overhead. As a result, in a process cost accounting system, costs are accumulated by department, in contrast to the job-order cost system, where costs are accumulated by the job or batch. The cost per unit of output in a process cost accounting system is calculated by dividing each department's costs of materials, labor, and overhead by the equivalent units of output processed in each department. The calculations of equivalent units and equivalent unit costs are complex calculations covered in a more advanced managerial or cost accounting text.

There is a Work-in-Process Inventory account for each department that is debited for the costs of materials, labor, and overhead used by that department. In the continuous process, the production of the first department is passed on to the second department. The first department's total cost is debited to the second department's Work-in-Process Inventory account. For example, assume that the production of rolled roofing takes place in two departments. The flow of production from Department 1 to Department 2 and ending up in Finished Goods Inventory is illustrated in T accounts using symbolic amounts. Note that additional raw materials have been added in Department 2.

FYI

Other industries using process cost accounting systems are producers of paper, aluminum, cola, and beer.

Work-in-Process Inventory—Department 1			
Raw Materials	100	To Department 2	200
Direct Labor	50		
Factory Overhead	50		

Work-in-Process Inventory—Department 2			
From Department 1	200	To Finished Goods	270
Raw Materials	10		
Direct Labor	20		
Factory Overhead	40		

Finished Goods Inventory		
From Department 2	270	

CHAPTER REVIEW

Online Study Center
ACE the test!

Review of Performance Objectives

1. **Prepare a statement of cost of goods manufactured.**

   The statement of cost of goods manufactured includes the beginning work-in-process inventory, plus the cost of raw materials used, plus direct labor, plus factory overhead, less the ending work-in-process inventory.

2. **Complete a work sheet for a manufacturing enterprise and journalize the closing entries.**

   A work sheet for a manufacturing company contains an extra pair of columns entitled "Statement of Cost of Goods Manufactured." Manufacturing costs—Raw Materials Purchases, Direct Labor, and Factory Overhead account balances—are recorded in the Debit column. Debit amounts recorded in the Manufacturing Summary account (representing the beginning balances of Raw Materials Inventory and Work-in-Process Inventory) are listed in the Statement of Cost of Goods Manufactured Debit column. Credit amounts recorded in the Manufacturing Summary account (representing the ending balances of Raw Materials Inventory and Work-in-Process Inventory) are listed in the Statement of Cost of Goods Manufactured Credit column. The difference between the Statement of Cost of Goods Manufactured Debit and Credit columns is the amount of the cost of goods manufactured, and this amount is recorded as a credit to balance off the columns. The amount of the cost of goods manufactured is also recorded in the Income Statement Debit column.

3. Define a *job-order cost accounting system* and make the related entries.

   A job-order cost accounting system is used by manufacturers producing distinct products in batches of a specified number of units. Each batch of units is given a job-order number. The costs of production (raw materials, direct labor, and factory overhead) are debited to the account for that job-order number in the work-in-process subsidiary ledger. When the job is completed, the Finished Goods Inventory account is debited and the Work-in-Process Inventory account is credited.

4. Define a *process cost accounting system* and make the related entries.

   A process cost accounting system is used by manufacturers whose production involves a continuous process. The output consists of homogeneous units. The production flows from one department to another department. A Work-in-Process Inventory account is set up for each department to record the costs of production. The entry to record the passing on of production from one department to another is a debit to the second department's Work-in-Process Inventory account and a credit to the first department's Work-in-Process Inventory account. Upon completion of the last stage of production, the entry is a debit to Finished Goods Inventory and a credit to the last department's Work-in-Process Inventory account.

Glossary

Direct labor Wages paid to factory employees who work—with machines or hand tools—directly on raw materials to convert them into finished products. (979)

Factory overhead All manufacturing costs that cannot be traced directly to products being manufactured. Examples: heat, light, and power; repairs and maintenance; indirect labor; indirect materials. (979)

Indirect labor The cost of work performed by workers who keep the plant in operation—such as operations personnel, factory maintenance workers, and timekeepers—rather than by workers who are directly occupied with production; considered part of factory overhead. (979)

Indirect materials Factory supplies, such as oil, grease, and cleaning fluids, used to keep the plant in operation; considered part of factory overhead. (979)

Job-order cost accounting system A product costing system used by companies making products in batches. Raw materials, direct labor, and factory overhead costs are assigned to specific job orders. (988)

Manufacturing Summary An account used to make adjustments to Raw Materials Inventory and Work-in-Process Inventory accounts and to close all other manufacturing accounts. (982)

Process cost accounting system A product costing system used by companies that maintain a continuous production flow. Manufacturing costs are assigned to departments that complete successive stages of production. (990)

Raw materials The materials (also called *direct materials*) that enter directly into and become a part of the finished product. (978)

QUESTIONS, EXERCISES, AND CASES

Discussion Questions

1. In manufacturing operations, how do direct materials differ from indirect materials?

2. Which inventory accounts appear on a company's statement of cost of goods manufactured, and which appear on its income statement?

3. Compare the Manufacturing Summary account with the Income Summary account.

4. Why is cost of goods manufactured entered in the Statement of Cost of Goods Manufactured Credit and the Income Statement Debit columns on a work sheet?

5. Compare cost of goods manufactured for a manufacturing business with cost of goods sold for a merchandising business.

6. List six examples of factory overhead accounts.

7. Is it possible for paint to be considered an indirect material for one company and a direct material for another company?

8. Does the Manufacturing Summary account have a balance during the fiscal period? Explain your answer.

Exercises

P.O. 1

Determine cost of goods manufactured.

Exercise 26-1 From the following balances, determine the cost of goods manufactured:

Cost of Goods Sold	$3,640,000
Finished Goods Inventory, March 1	850,000
Finished Goods Inventory, March 31	682,000

P.O. 1

Prepare a statement of cost of goods manufactured.

Exercise 26-2 Prepare a statement of cost of goods manufactured, using any of the following balances that you need:

Raw Materials Purchases	$632,000
Raw Materials Inventory, June 30	74,000
Raw Materials Inventory, June 1	43,000
Work-in-Process Inventory, June 1	230,000
Work-in-Process Inventory, June 30	302,000
Finished Goods Inventory, June 30	122,000
Direct Labor	901,000
Factory Overhead	676,000
Finished Goods Inventory, June 1	134,000

P.O. 1

Prepare a statement of cost of goods manufactured.

Exercise 26-3 The Statement of Cost of Goods Manufactured columns and the Income Statement columns of the work sheet for Ryan Manufacturing Company for the year ended December 31 are as shown on page 994. Ryan Manufacturing Company's beginning inventory of raw materials is $8,000; its beginning inventory of work-in-process is $38,400. Prepare a statement of cost of goods manufactured.

	ACCOUNT NAME	STATEMENT OF COST OF GOODS MANUFACTURED		INCOME STATEMENT		
		DEBIT	CREDIT	DEBIT	CREDIT	
1	Sales				360 0 0 0 00	1
2	Raw Materials Purchases	64 0 0 0 00				2
3	Direct Labor	160 0 0 0 00				3
4	Indirect Labor	3 2 0 0 00				4
5	Heat, Light, and Power	1 6 0 0 00				5
6	Miscellaneous Factory Costs	8 0 0 00				6
7	Selling Expenses (control)			34 0 0 0 00		7
8	General Expenses (control)			14 0 0 0 00		8
9	Income Tax Expense			22 4 8 0 00		9
10	Manufacturing Summary	8 0 0 0 00	12 0 0 0 00			10
11		38 4 0 0 00	40 0 0 0 00			11
12	Income Summary			32 0 0 0 00	36 0 0 0 00	12
13		276 0 0 0 00	52 0 0 0 00			13
14	Cost of Goods Manufactured		224 0 0 0 00	224 0 0 0 00		14
15		276 0 0 0 00	276 0 0 0 00	326 4 8 0 00	396 0 0 0 00	15
16	Net Income			69 5 2 0 00		16
17				396 0 0 0 00	396 0 0 0 00	17
18						18
19						19

P.O. 2

Journalize the closing entries.

Exercise 26-4 From the information in Exercise 26-3, journalize the closing entries for Ryan Manufacturing Company.

P.O. 1

Determine cost of raw materials used.

Exercise 26-5 From the following balances, determine the cost of the raw materials used:

Raw Materials Purchases	$1,801,000
Raw Materials Inventory, August 31	479,000
Raw Materials Inventory, August 1	356,000

P.O. 2

Calculate total manufacturing costs.

Exercise 26-6 From the following balances, calculate the total manufacturing costs, which contain the following three elements:

Raw Materials Used	$241,000
Direct Labor	274,000
Factory Overhead (60% of direct labor cost)	

P.O. 1

Compute factory overhead amount and the percentage of factory overhead to direct labor.

Exercise 26-7 Assume that the cost of work-in-process during the period is $298,500, comprising raw materials of $92,000 and direct labor of $122,000. How much is the factory overhead? Verify the figure by means of the percentage of factory overhead to direct labor.

P.O. 1

Prepare an income statement.

Exercise 26-8 From the information in Exercise 26-3, prepare an income statement for Ryan Manufacturing Company. Beginning inventory of finished goods is $32,000.

internet
LINKS TO ACCOUNTING

You should now have an understanding of the materials, labor, and overhead costs involved in manufacturing a product and how these costs are determined. So how much does Harley-Davidson clear in profit after covering all its costs? Let's go back to Harley-Davidson, Inc., and examine the company's financial statements, which can be found at **http://investor .harley-davidson.com.** Click on SEC Filings, search for 10-K, and select the 10-K annual report filed 03-03-06.

1. What was the company's net income for the year ended December 31, 2005?
2. Can you tell what Harley-Davidson's cost of goods sold was for 2005 by looking at its income statement?
3. What was the value of ending inventory as of December 31, 2005?
4. Is Harley-Davidson, Inc., a manufacturing firm or a merchandising firm?
5. Now that you have learned about job-order and process cost accounting systems, which system do you think Harley-Davidson uses for its motorcycles?

WHAT'S WRONG WITH THIS PICTURE?

The Tender Loving Toy Company manufactures plush animals that move and talk. The accountant is trying to set up the accounting records. These animals need to be kept dust-free until they are sold so that they will look crisp and clean. To accomplish this, the animals are put into boxes with cellophane windows. They are boxed by hand because they need to be attached to the inside of the boxes. The accountant is not certain whether this boxing work is direct labor or indirect labor because the animals are completely finished before they are boxed. How would you classify it?

A QUESTION OF ETHICS

The accountant at Gomez Manufacturing is afraid that he will be fired if he is not able to show management what they want to see—higher profits. Part of the raw materials inventory is stored off the property, and he is considering inflating its value. If he does so, the cost of goods manufactured will be lower and the gross profit higher. Comment on this practice.

CRITICAL THINKING

On the following page is a statement of cost of goods manufactured for Pabrucy Manufacturing, Inc. Since the records that support this statement were destroyed by water damage caused by a collapsed roof, fill in the missing amounts.

Pabrucy Manufacturing, Inc.
Statement of Cost of Goods Manufactured
For Year Ended December 31, 20—

Work-in-Process Inventory, January 1, 20—				$
Raw Materials:				
Raw Materials Inventory, January 1, 20—	$ 135 000 00			
Raw Materials Purchases (net)				
Cost of Raw Materials Available for Use	$ 399 500 00			
Less Raw Materials Inventory, December 31, 20—				
Cost of Raw Materials Used		$ 253 000 00		
Direct Labor		553 700 00		
Factory Overhead:				
Indirect Labor	$			
Supervisory Salaries	112 000 00			
Heat, Light, and Power	45 300 00			
Depreciation Expense, Factory Building	27 400 00			
Depreciation Expense, Factory Equipment	30 700 00			
Repairs and Maintenance	18 430 00			
Factory Supplies Used	11 200 00			
Factory Insurance Expired	24 800 00			
Miscellaneous Factory Costs	12 520 00			
Total Factory Overhead		414 350 00		
Total Manufacturing Costs				
Total Cost of Work-in-Process During Period				$1 364 050 00
Less Work-in-Process Inventory, December 31, 20—				
Cost of Goods Manufactured				$1 239 050 00

PROBLEM SET A

For additional help, see the demonstration problem at the beginning of each chapter in your Working Papers.

P.O. 2

Problem 26-1A On the following page is the statement of cost of goods manufactured for Valley Manufacturing Company.

Check Figure

Amount to close Manufacturing Summary into Income Summary, $2,263,660

Instructions

1. Journalize the adjusting entries for Raw Materials Inventory and Work-in-Process Inventory.
2. Journalize the closing entries for manufacturing costs.
3. Post the entries to the Manufacturing Summary account, No. 511.
4. Journalize and post the entry to close the Manufacturing Summary account.

Valley Manufacturing Company
Statement of Cost of Goods Manufactured
For Year Ended December 31, 20—

Work-in-Process Inventory, January 1, 20—			$ 228 000 00
Raw Materials:			
Raw Materials Inventory, January 1, 20—	$ 475 000 00		
Raw Materials Purchases (net)	741 000 00		
Cost of Raw Materials Available for Use	$1 216 000 00		
Less Raw Materials Inventory, December 31, 20—	503 500 00		
Cost of Raw Materials Used		$ 712 500 00	
Direct Labor		1 140 000 00	
Factory Overhead:			
Indirect Labor	$ 209 000 00		
Supervisory Salaries	180 500 00		
Depreciation Expense, Factory Equipment	123 500 00		
Heat, Light, and Power	36 100 00		
Depreciation Expense, Factory Building	35 720 00		
Repairs and Maintenance	26 980 00		
Factory Supplies Used	22 800 00		
Factory Insurance Expired	16 720 00		
Property Tax on Factory Building	13 680 00		
Miscellaneous Factory Costs	12 160 00		
Total Factory Overhead		677 160 00	
Total Manufacturing Costs			2 529 660 00
Total Cost of Work-in-Process During Period			$2 757 660 00
Less Work-in-Process Inventory, December 31, 20—			494 000 00
Cost of Goods Manufactured			$2 263 660 00

P.O. 1,2

Problem 26-2A The trial balance of Ronde Products Company, Inc., as of December 31 of this year, is shown below.

Ronde Products Company, Inc.
Trial Balance
December 31, 20—

ACCOUNT NAME	DEBIT	CREDIT
Cash	4 6 2 0 00	
Accounts Receivable	39 3 8 0 00	
Allowance for Doubtful Accounts		1 5 9 5 00
Raw Materials Inventory	49 5 0 0 00	
Work-in-Process Inventory	78 4 3 0 00	
Finished Goods Inventory	75 0 2 0 00	
Prepaid Factory Insurance	1 9 8 0 00	
Machinery	145 7 0 0 00	
Accumulated Depreciation, Machinery		46 2 0 0 00
Accounts Payable		32 2 3 0 00
Common Stock		110 0 0 0 00
Paid-in Capital in Excess of Stated Value		22 0 0 0 00
Retained Earnings		77 0 0 0 00
Sales		702 6 2 5 00
Raw Materials Purchases	77 0 0 0 00	
Direct Labor	180 6 7 0 00	
Indirect Labor	87 8 9 0 00	
Heat, Light, and Power	17 6 0 0 00	
Machinery Repairs	9 9 0 0 00	
Selling Expenses (control)	153 9 4 5 00	
General Expenses (control)	66 0 5 5 00	
Income Tax Expense	3 9 6 0 00	
	991 6 5 0 00	991 6 5 0 00

You are given the following information for the adjustments:

a.–f. Year-end inventories: raw materials, $46,300; work-in-process, $68,740; finished goods, $75,175.

g. Allowance for Doubtful Accounts to be increased by $890 (debit General Expenses (control)).

h. Estimated depreciation of factory machinery, $11,625.

i. A study of the company's insurance policies shows that $1,430 of factory insurance expired during the year.

j. Accrued direct labor, $350; accrued indirect labor, $180; accrued sales commissions, $190 (credit Wages and Commissions Payable).

k. Additional income tax, $1,429.

Check Figure

Net Income, $76,776

Instructions

1. Prepare a work sheet.
2. Prepare a statement of cost of goods manufactured.
3. Prepare an income statement.

P.O. 1,2

Problem 26-3A The columns reflecting the statement of cost of goods manufactured and the income statement from the work sheet of Northwest Container Company, Inc., as of December 31, the end of the fiscal year, are shown below. Beginning inventory of raw materials is $131,328; beginning inventory of work in process is $236,360.

ACCOUNT NAME	STATEMENT OF COST OF GOODS MANUFACTURED DEBIT	CREDIT	INCOME STATEMENT DEBIT	CREDIT
Sales				2,849 9 2 4 00
Sales Returns and Allowances			23 5 6 0 00	
Sales Discounts			22 4 2 0 00	
Selling Expenses (control)			341 0 3 1 00	
General Expenses (control)			138 4 3 4 00	
Raw Materials Purchases	730 5 5 0 00			
Direct Labor	917 5 1 0 00			
Indirect Labor	210 1 7 8 00			
Heat, Light, and Power	51 2 6 2 00			
Factory Supervision	51 2 0 5 00			
Rent, Factory	30 4 0 0 00			
Machinery Repairs	30 2 1 0 00			
Depreciation Expense, Machinery	30 0 9 6 00			
Factory Supplies Used	11 7 8 0 00			
Factory Insurance Expired	7 2 2 0 00			
Small Tools Expense	2 3 9 4 00			
Miscellaneous Factory Costs	1 2 9 2 00			
Loss on Disposal of Equipment			16 3 4 0 00	
Interest Expense			12 9 2 0 00	
Income Tax Expense			81 7 0 0 00	
Manufacturing Summary	131 3 2 8 00	136 0 4 0 00		
	236 3 6 0 00	240 3 3 1 00		
Income Summary			344 6 6 0 00	354 7 6 8 00
	2,441 7 8 5 00	376 3 7 1 00		
Cost of Goods Manufactured		2,065 4 1 4 00	2,065 4 1 4 00	
	2,441 7 8 5 00	2,441 7 8 5 00	3,046 4 7 9 00	3,204 6 9 2 00
Net Income			158 2 1 3 00	
			3,204 6 9 2 00	3,204 6 9 2 00

Check Figure

Income from Operations, $269,173

Instructions

1. Prepare a statement of cost of goods manufactured.
2. Prepare an income statement.
3. Journalize the adjusting entries for the inventories.
4. Journalize the closing entries.

P.O. 1

Problem 26-4A Here are adjusting and closing entries that appear on the books of Sharp Tool Company at the end of the fiscal year, May 31.

	DATE		DESCRIPTION	POST. REF.	DEBIT	CREDIT	
1	20–		**Adjusting Entries**				1
2	May	31	Manufacturing Summary		52 0 2 0 00		2
3			Raw Materials Inventory			52 0 2 0 00	3
4							4
5		31	Raw Materials Inventory		47 0 9 4 00		5
6			Manufacturing Summary			47 0 9 4 00	6
7							7
8		31	Manufacturing Summary		66 4 4 4 00		8
9			Work-in-Process Inventory			66 4 4 4 00	9
10							10
11		31	Work-in-Process Inventory		63 8 5 2 00		11
12			Manufacturing Summary			63 8 5 2 00	12
13							13
14			**Closing Entries**				14
15		31	Purchases Discounts		2 3 0 4 00		15
16			Manufacturing Summary			2 3 0 4 00	16
17							17
18		31	Manufacturing Summary		572 7 1 8 00		18
19			Raw Materials Purchases			142 0 2 0 00	19
20			Direct Labor			293 3 6 4 00	20
21			Indirect Labor			29 2 4 4 00	21
22			Supervision			41 6 8 8 00	22
23			Depreciation of Machinery			30 0 0 0 00	23
24			Depreciation of Factory Bldg.			12 0 0 0 00	24
25			Heat, Light, and Power			8 5 2 0 00	25
26			Repairs and Maintenance			7 6 7 4 00	26
27			Property Tax, Machinery			1 1 1 0 00	27
28			Property Tax, Factory Bldg.			1 3 2 0 00	28
29			Factory Supplies Used			4 1 2 2 00	29
30			Factory Insurance Expired			1 0 8 0 00	30
31			Miscellaneous Factory Costs			5 7 6 00	31
32							32
33		31	Income Summary		577 9 3 2 00		33
34			Manufacturing Summary			577 9 3 2 00	34
35							35
36							36
37							37
38							38
39							39

Check Figure

Cost of Goods Manufactured, $577,932

Instructions

Prepare a statement of cost of goods manufactured for the year.

PROBLEM SET B

P.O. 2

For additional help, see the demonstration problem at the beginning of each chapter in your Working Papers.

Problem 26-1B Below is the statement of cost of goods manufactured for Bane Manufacturing Company.

Bane Manufacturing Company
Statement of Cost of Goods Manufactured
For Year Ended June 30, 20—

Work-in-Process Inventory, July 1, 20—			$ 88 0 0 0 00
Raw Materials:			
Raw Materials Inventory, July 1, 20—	$149 6 0 0 00		
Raw Materials Purchases (net)	217 2 5 0 00		
Cost of Raw Materials Available for Use	$366 8 5 0 00		
Less Raw Materials Inventory, June 30, 20—	143 0 0 0 00		
Cost of Raw Materials Used		$223 8 5 0 00	
Direct Labor		320 1 0 0 00	
Factory Overhead:			
Indirect Labor	$ 59 6 2 0 00		
Supervisory Salaries	41 8 5 5 00		
Depreciation Expense, Factory Equipment	39 6 0 0 00		
Depreciation Expense, Factory Building	11 9 9 0 00		
Heat, Light, and Power	10 2 3 0 00		
Repairs and Maintenance	7 9 2 0 00		
Factory Supplies Used	7 6 4 5 00		
Factory Insurance Expired	4 1 8 0 00		
Property Tax on Factory Building	4 1 2 5 00		
Miscellaneous Factory Costs	3 9 0 5 00		
Total Factory Overhead		191 0 7 0 00	
Total Manufacturing Costs			735 0 2 0 00
Total Cost of Work-in-Process for Period			$823 0 2 0 00
Less Work-in-Process Inventory, June 30, 20—			96 2 5 0 00
Cost of Goods Manufactured			$726 7 7 0 00

Check Figure

Amount to close Manufacturing Summary into Income Summary, $726,770

Instructions

1. Journalize the adjusting entries for Raw Materials Inventory and Work-in-Process Inventory.
2. Journalize the closing entries for manufacturing costs.
3. Post the entries to the Manufacturing Summary account, No. 511.
4. Journalize and post the entry to close the Manufacturing Summary account.

P.O. 1,2

Problem 26-2B The trial balance of Seabird Manufacturing Corporation as of December 31 of this year is shown below.

Seabird Manufacturing Corporation
Trial Balance
December 31, 20—

ACCOUNT NAME	DEBIT	CREDIT
Cash	3 0 4 5 00	
Accounts Receivable	24 2 9 0 00	
Allowance for Doubtful Accounts		9 4 5 00
Raw Materials Inventory	32 0 6 0 00	
Work-in-Process Inventory	49 7 3 5 00	
Finished Goods Inventory	48 4 4 0 00	
Prepaid Factory Insurance	1 4 7 0 00	
Machinery	111 9 5 0 00	
Accumulated Depreciation, Machinery		30 2 4 0 00
Accounts Payable		19 2 1 5 00
Common Stock		70 0 0 0 00
Paid-in Capital in Excess of Stated Value		17 5 0 0 00
Retained Earnings		45 7 8 4 00
Sales		451 9 9 0 00
Raw Materials Purchases	48 9 6 5 00	
Direct Labor	97 4 4 8 00	
Indirect Labor	56 5 1 1 00	
Heat, Light, and Power	11 3 4 0 00	
Machinery Repairs	6 8 6 0 00	
Selling Expenses (control)	99 1 9 7 00	
General Expenses (control)	41 5 6 3 00	
Income Tax Expense	2 8 0 0 00	
	635 6 7 4 00	635 6 7 4 00

You are given the following information for the adjustments:

a.–f. Year-end inventories: raw materials, $28,750; work-in-process, $45,830; finished goods, $48,118.

g. Estimated depreciation of factory machinery, $7,980.

h. A study of the company's insurance policies shows that $1,085 of factory insurance expired during the year.

i. Allowance for Doubtful Accounts to be increased by $543 (debit General Expenses (control)).

j. Accrued direct labor, $252; accrued indirect labor, $84; accrued sales commissions, $98 (credit Wages and Commissions Payable).

k. Additional income tax, $800.

Check Figure

Cost of Goods Manufactured, $237,740

Instructions

1. Prepare a work sheet.
2. Prepare a statement of cost of goods manufactured.
3. Prepare an income statement.

P.O. 1,2

Problem 26-3B The columns reflecting the statement of cost of goods manufactured and the income statement from the work sheet of Lohr Motor Corporation as of December 31, the end of the fiscal year, are shown below. Beginning inventory of raw materials is $85,752; beginning inventory of work in process is $152,040.

ACCOUNT NAME	STATEMENT OF COST OF GOODS MANUFACTURED DEBIT	STATEMENT OF COST OF GOODS MANUFACTURED CREDIT	INCOME STATEMENT DEBIT	INCOME STATEMENT CREDIT
Sales				1,809 8 8 8 00
Sales Returns and Allowances			15 1 2 0 00	
Sales Discounts			14 4 0 0 00	
Selling Expenses (control)			224 3 4 0 00	
General Expenses (control)			88 3 3 2 00	
Raw Materials Purchases	458 4 0 0 00			
Direct Labor	584 2 8 0 00			
Indirect Labor	133 0 0 8 00			
Heat, Light, and Power	33 1 4 4 00			
Factory Supervision	32 3 1 6 00			
Rent, Factory	21 6 0 0 00			
Machinery Repairs	21 5 0 4 00			
Depreciation Expense, Machinery	20 8 5 6 00			
Factory Supplies Used	5 8 8 0 00			
Factory Insurance Expired	4 3 2 0 00			
Small Tools Expense	1 4 8 8 00			
Miscellaneous Factory Costs	7 8 0 00			
Loss on Disposal of Equipment			9 6 0 0 00	
Interest Expense			9 1 2 0 00	
Income Tax Expense			49 8 0 0 00	
Manufacturing Summary	85 7 5 2 00	88 5 8 4 00		
	152 0 4 0 00	159 4 0 8 00		
Income Summary			221 5 2 0 00	231 3 6 0 00
	1,555 3 6 8 00	247 9 9 2 00		
Cost of Goods Manufactured		1,307 3 7 6 00	1,307 3 7 6 00	
	1,555 3 6 8 00	1,555 3 6 8 00	1,939 6 0 8 00	2,041 2 4 8 00
Net Income			101 6 4 0 00	
			2,041 2 4 8 00	2,041 2 4 8 00

Check Figure

Gross Profit, $482,832

Instructions

1. Prepare a statement of cost of goods manufactured.
2. Prepare an income statement.
3. Journalize the adjusting entries for the inventories.
4. Journalize the closing entries.

P.O. 1

Problem 26-4B Here are adjusting and closing entries that appear on the books of Howe Belt Company at the end of the fiscal year, December 31.

	DATE		DESCRIPTION	POST. REF.	DEBIT	CREDIT	
1	20–		**Adjusting Entries**				1
2	Dec.	31	Manufacturing Summary		97 6 4 7 00		2
3			Raw Materials Inventory			97 6 4 7 00	3
4							4
5		31	Raw Materials Inventory		99 6 8 0 00		5
6			Manufacturing Summary			99 6 8 0 00	6
7							7
8		31	Manufacturing Summary		124 1 0 2 00		8
9			Work-in-Process Inventory			124 1 0 2 00	9
10							10
11		31	Work-in-Process Inventory		128 5 2 4 00		11
12			Manufacturing Summary			128 5 2 4 00	12
13							13
14			**Closing Entries**				14
15		31	Purchases Discounts		4 6 3 1 00		15
16			Manufacturing Summary			4 6 3 1 00	16
17							17
18		31	Manufacturing Summary		874 3 5 7 00		18
19			Raw Materials Purchases			280 4 5 6 00	19
20			Direct Labor			373 4 0 6 00	20
21			Indirect Labor			42 3 2 8 00	21
22			Supervision			64 5 0 4 00	22
23			Depreciation of Machinery			46 2 0 0 00	23
24			Depreciation of Factory Bldg.			26 4 0 0 00	24
25			Heat, Light, and Power			14 1 0 2 00	25
26			Repairs and Maintenance			10 6 4 8 00	26
27			Property Tax, Machinery			1 3 9 7 00	27
28			Property Tax, Factory Bldg.			2 0 2 4 00	28
29			Factory Supplies Used			10 4 1 7 00	29
30			Factory Insurance Expired			1 3 2 0 00	30
31			Miscellaneous Factory Costs			1 1 5 5 00	31
32							32
33		31	Income Summary		863 2 7 1 00		33
34			Manufacturing Summary			863 2 7 1 00	34
35							35
36							36
37							37

Check Figure

Cost of Goods Manufactured, $863,271

Instructions

Prepare a statement of cost of goods manufactured for the year.

PART I: True/False

T   F   1. A company acquired a long-lived asset by issuing $480,000 par-value common stock. This event is listed under Financing Activities in a statement of cash flows.

T   F   2. It is possible for a business to have a net loss and still have a positive cash flow.

T   F   3. Money market accounts are listed as a part of cash on a statement of cash flows.

T   F   4. Generally, the lower the current ratio, the lower the risk to creditors.

T   F   5. Presenting each asset as a percentage of total assets is an example of horizontal analysis.

T   F   6. When percentage analysis is applied to the income statement, net sales is used as the base.

T   F   7. The only accounts that companies must keep departmentalized to compute gross profit by department are Sales and Purchases.

T   F   8. If a department covers its direct expenses, but not all of its indirect expenses, the business can increase its operating income if it discontinues the department.

T   F   9. Departmental margin equals gross profit minus direct expenses.

T   F   10. The statement of costs of goods manufactured supports the income statement by providing the figure for cost of goods sold.

T   F   11. The Manufacturing Summary account is closed by an entry debiting the Income Summary account and crediting the Manufacturing Summary account.

T   F   12. Supervisory salaries are part of factory overhead.

PART II: Completion

1. If a company's income statement lists Delivered Cost of Purchases as $440,000, beginning Accounts Payable (trade) as $54,000, and ending Accounts Payable (trade) as $51,500, the amount of cash paid for merchandise purchased is _____.

2. If a company's income statement lists Income from Services as $85,300, beginning Accounts Receivable as $8,400, and ending Accounts Receivable as $9,700, the amount of cash received from customers is _____.

3. If Income Tax Expense is listed on a corporation's income statement as $36,800 and the balance of Income Tax Payable increased by $2,800

Note: Answers to Before a Test Check begin on page A-1.

between the beginning and the end of the year, the amount of cash paid for income taxes is _____.

4. Merchandise Inventory Turnover = $\dfrac{(\underline{\hspace{3cm}})}{\text{Average Merchandise Inventory}}$.

5. Quick Ratio = $\dfrac{(\underline{\hspace{2.5cm}})}{\text{Current Liabilities}}$.

6. Accounts Receivable Turnover = $\dfrac{(\underline{\hspace{3cm}})}{\text{Average Accounts Receivable}}$.

7. Those expenses that benefit only one department and are controlled by the head of that department are called _____ expenses.

8. The gross profit of a department minus the department's direct expenses is known as _____.

9. _____ consists of all manufacturing costs that cannot be traced directly to products being manufactured.

10. Raw materials and work-in-process inventories are adjusted using the _____ account.

PART III: Application

A. Statement of Cash Flows

1. Compute the amount of cash paid for insurance if a company's income statement lists Insurance Expense as $640, and its balance sheet lists beginning Prepaid Insurance as $820 and ending Prepaid Insurance as $920.

2. Compute the amount of cash paid for rent expense if a company's income statement lists Rent Expense as $24,000 and the balance of Prepaid Rent decreased by $1,800 between the beginning and the end of the year.

B. Financial Statement Analysis

1. Compute the current ratio if current assets are $210,000 and current liabilities are $202,000.

2. Compute working capital if total liabilities equal $400,000, long-term liabilities are $200,000, and current assets are $500,000.

C. Departmental Accounting

If a company's property taxes of $4,000 are apportioned on the basis of floor space, and Department X has 4,000 square feet, Department Y has 5,000 square feet, and Department Z has 6,000 square feet, what would be the amount of property taxes per department?

Before a Test Check Solutions

CHAPTERS 1–3

Part I: 1. d; 2. e; 3. d; 4. b; 5. e; 6. a

Part II: 1.

GENERAL JOURNAL   PAGE __31__

	DATE		DESCRIPTION	POST. REF.	DEBIT	CREDIT	
1	20–						1
2	Dec.	1	Cash	111	9 5 0 0 00		2
3			Service Income	411		9 5 0 0 00	3
4			Sold services for cash.				4
5							5
6		4	Rent Expense	513	1 0 0 0 00		6
7			Cash	111		1 0 0 0 00	7
8			Ck. No. 2331.				8
9							9
10		11	Cash	111	1 7 5 0 00		10
11			Accounts Receivable	113		1 7 5 0 00	11
12			Cash on account from				12
13			customers, Cash Receipt				13
14			Nos. 1430-1438.				14
15							15
16		19	Accounts Receivable	113	2 0 7 5 00		16
17			Service Income	411		2 0 7 5 00	17
18			Sales Inv. No. 2591.				18
19							19
20		22	Utilities Expense	512	2 5 5 00		20
21			Cash	111		2 5 5 00	21
22			Ck. No. 2332.				22
23							23
24		23	Supplies Expense	514	2 9 2 00		24
25			Accounts Payable	221		2 9 2 00	25
26			Office Works, Inv. No. 2606.				26
27							27
28		31	Wages Expense	511	1 7 7 5 00		28
29			Cash	111		1 7 7 5 00	29
30			Paid month's wages, Ck. No.				30
31			2333.				31
32							32
33		31	J. Dunn, Drawing	312	1 5 0 0 00		33
34			Cash	111		1 5 0 0 00	34
35			Ck. No. 2334.				35

2, 3, 4.

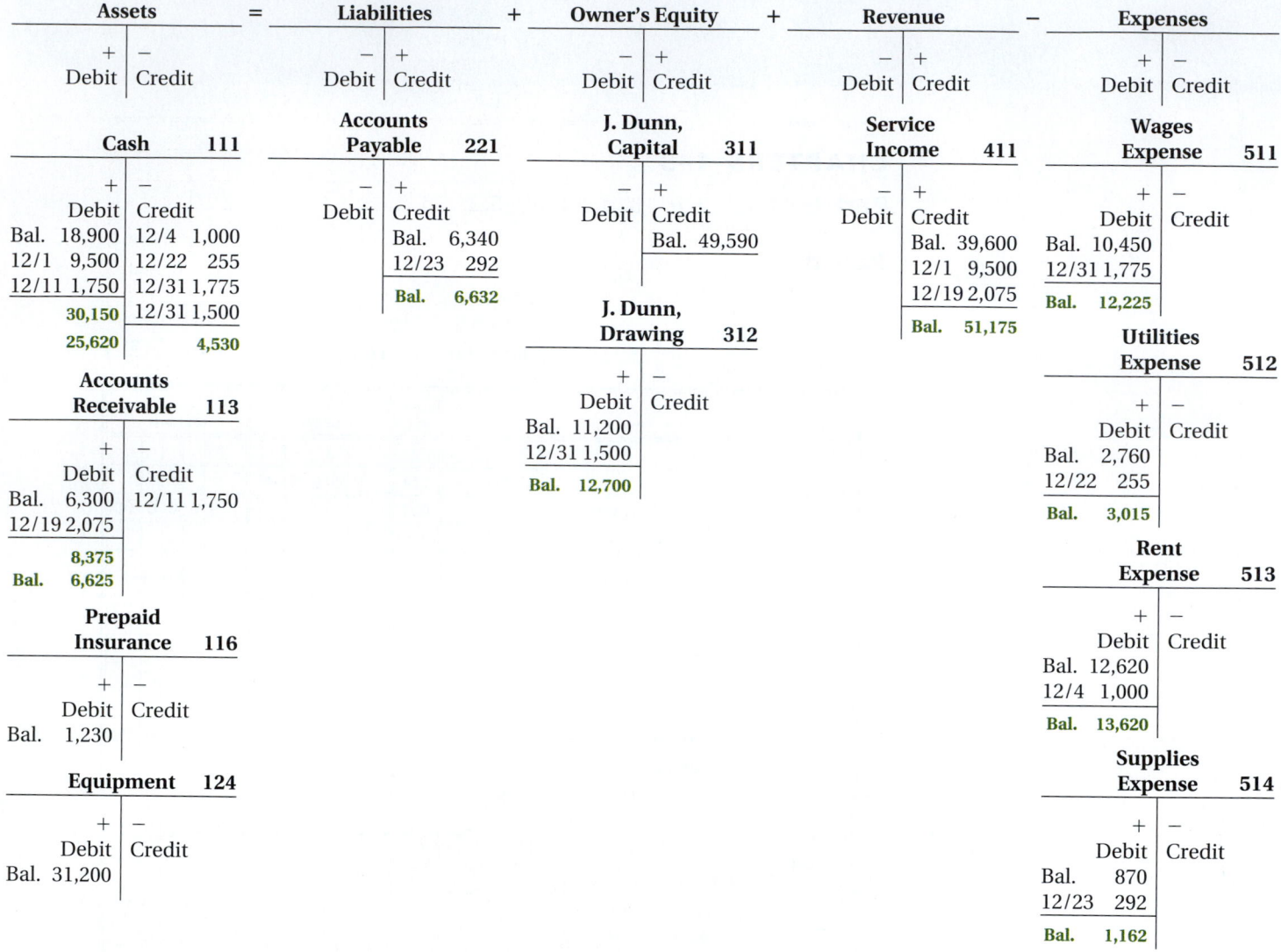

	Assets		=		Liabilities		+		Owner's Equity		+		Revenue		−		Expenses	
	+	−			−	+			−	+			−	+			+	−
	Debit	Credit			Debit	Credit			Debit	Credit			Debit	Credit			Debit	Credit

Cash   111

+	−
Debit	Credit
Bal. 18,900	12/4 1,000
12/1 9,500	12/22 255
12/11 1,750	12/31 1,775
30,150	12/31 1,500
25,620	**4,530**

Accounts Receivable   113

+	−
Debit	Credit
Bal. 6,300	12/11 1,750
12/19 2,075	
8,375	
Bal. 6,625	

Prepaid Insurance   116

+	−
Debit	Credit
Bal. 1,230	

Equipment   124

+	−
Debit	Credit
Bal. 31,200	

Accounts Payable   221

−	+
Debit	Credit
	Bal. 6,340
	12/23 292
	Bal. 6,632

J. Dunn, Capital   311

−	+
Debit	Credit
	Bal. 49,590

J. Dunn, Drawing   312

+	−
Debit	Credit
Bal. 11,200	
12/31 1,500	
Bal. 12,700	

Service Income   411

−	+
Debit	Credit
	Bal. 39,600
	12/1 9,500
	12/19 2,075
	Bal. 51,175

Wages Expense   511

+	−
Debit	Credit
Bal. 10,450	
12/31 1,775	
Bal. 12,225	

Utilities Expense   512

+	−
Debit	Credit
Bal. 2,760	
12/22 255	
Bal. 3,015	

Rent Expense   513

+	−
Debit	Credit
Bal. 12,620	
12/4 1,000	
Bal. 13,620	

Supplies Expense   514

+	−
Debit	Credit
Bal. 870	
12/23 292	
Bal. 1,162	

5.

Antec Services
Trial Balance
December 31, 20—

ACCOUNT NAME	DEBIT	CREDIT
Cash	25 6 2 0 00	
Accounts Receivable	6 6 2 5 00	
Prepaid Insurance	1 2 3 0 00	
Equipment	31 2 0 0 00	
Accounts Payable		6 6 3 2 00
J. Dunn, Capital		49 5 9 0 00
J. Dunn, Drawing	12 7 0 0 00	
Service Income		51 1 7 5 00
Wages Expense	12 2 2 5 00	
Utilities Expense	3 0 1 5 00	
Rent Expense	13 6 2 0 00	
Supplies Expense	1 1 6 2 00	
	107 3 9 7 00	107 3 9 7 00

6.

Antec Services
Income Statement
For Year Ended December 31, 20—

Revenue:		
Service Income		$51 1 7 5 00
Expenses:		
Wages Expense	$12 2 2 5 00	
Utilities Expense	3 0 1 5 00	
Rent Expense	13 6 2 0 00	
Supplies Expense	1 1 6 2 00	
Total Expenses		30 0 2 2 00
Net Income		$21 1 5 3 00

7.

Antec Services
Statement of Owner's Equity
For Year Ended December 31, 20—

J. Dunn, Capital, January 1, 20—						$49	5	9	0	00
Net Income for Year	$21	1	5	3	00					
Less Withdrawals for Year	12	7	0	0	00					
Increase in Capital						8	4	5	3	00
J. Dunn, Capital, December 31, 20—						$58	0	4	3	00

8.

Antec Services
Balance Sheet
December 31, 20—

Assets										
Cash	$25	6	2	0	00					
Accounts Receivable	6	6	2	5	00					
Prepaid Insurance	1	2	3	0	00					
Equipment	31	2	0	0	00					
Total Assets						$64	6	7	5	00
Liabilities										
Accounts Payable						$ 6	6	3	2	00
Owner's Equity										
J. Dunn, Capital						58	0	4	3	00
Total Liabilities and Owner's Equity						$64	6	7	5	00

CHAPTERS 4–5

Part I

1. b;   2. d;   3. d;   4. a;   5. a;   6. b;   7. c;   8. c

Part II

		GENERAL JOURNAL			PAGE ___4___	
	DATE	DESCRIPTION	POST. REF.	DEBIT	CREDIT	
1	20–	**Closing Entries**				1
2	Dec. 31	Income from Services		35 9 0 0 00		2
3		Income Summary			35 9 0 0 00	3
4						4
5	31	Income Summary		20 4 0 0 00		5
6		Wages Expense			11 5 0 0 00	6
7		Rent Expense			2 4 0 0 00	7
8		Utilities Expense			1 0 0 0 00	8
9		Depreciation Expense,				9
10		Equipment			5 0 0 00	10
11		Supplies Expense			4 1 0 0 00	11
12		Miscellaneous Expense			9 0 0 00	12
13						13
14	31	Income Summary		15 5 0 0 00		14
15		K. Payton, Capital			15 5 0 0 00	15
16						16
17	31	K. Payton, Capital		16 4 0 0 00		17
18		K. Payton, Drawing			16 4 0 0 00	18

Part III

1. b;   2. h;   3. m;   4. q;   5. d;   6. k;   7. u;   8. w;   9. o;   10. s;   11. e;
12. f;   13. i;   14. n;   15. a;   16. t;   17. x;   18. p;   19. y;   20. v;   21. j;   22. c;
23. r;   24. l;   25. g

CHAPTERS 7–9

Part I

1. canceled; 2. deposit in transit or late deposit; 3. endorsement; 4. payee; 5. petty cash fund.

Part II

1. $1,775 per month × 12 months = $21,300 per year
$21,300 per year ÷ 52 weeks = $409.62 per week
$409.62 per week ÷ 40 hours = $10.24 per regular hour
$10.24 per regular hour × 1.5 = $15.36 per overtime hour

Earnings for 45 hours:

Forty hours at straight time = 40 × $10.24 = $409.60
Five hours overtime = 5 × $15.36 =   76.80

Total gross pay $486.40

2.

	DATE		DESCRIPTION	POST. REF.	DEBIT	CREDIT	
1	20–						1
2	June	30	Cleaning Salary Expense		9 0 0 0 00		2
3			Office Salary Expense		3 0 0 0 00		3
4			Employees' Federal Income Tax Payable			1 5 0 0 00	4
5			FICA Tax Payable ($12,000 × 0.062) + ($12,000 × 0.0145)			9 1 8 00	5
6			Savings Bonds Payable			5 0 0 00	6
7			Medical Insurance Payable			9 6 2 00	7
8			Salaries Payable			8 1 2 0 00	8

GENERAL JOURNAL   PAGE _____

3.

	DATE		DESCRIPTION	POST. REF.	DEBIT	CREDIT	
1	20–						1
2	Dec.	31	Payroll Tax Expense		12 4 7 7 50		2
3			FICA Tax Payable ($143,000 × 0.062) + ($155,000 × 0.0145)			11 1 1 3 50	3
4			State Unemployment Tax Payable ($22,000 × 0.054)			1 1 8 8 00	4
5			Federal Unemployment Tax Payable ($22,000 × 0.008)			1 7 6 00	5

GENERAL JOURNAL   PAGE _____

Part III

1. T; 2. F; 3. F; 4. T; 5. F

CHAPTERS 10–11

Part I

1. credit; 2. accounts payable ledger; 3. cash discount; 4. purchase order; 5. Purchases; 6. buyer; 7. credit period; 8. debit; 9. sales of merchandise on account; 10. charge customers.

Part II

1. CP; 2. J; 3. J; 4. CP; 5. S; 6. J; 7. CP; 8. P; 9. CR; 10. CP

Part III

1. F; 2. T; 3. F; 4. F; 5. F

CHAPTERS 12–13

Part I

1. physical inventory; 2. perpetual inventory; 3. current liability; 4. Income Summary; 5. Cost of Goods Sold, Merchandise Inventory; 6. decrease; 7. Cost of Goods Sold; 8. working capital; 9. Income from Operations; 10. Freight In.

Part II

1. F;   2. F;   3. T;   4. T;   5. T;   6. F;   7. F;   8. T;   9. F;   10. T

Part III

1.

	DATE		DESCRIPTION	POST. REF.	DEBIT	CREDIT	
1	20–		**Adjusting Entries**				1
2	Dec.	31	Income Summary		132 0 0 0 00		2
3			Merchandise Inventory			132 0 0 0 00	3
4							4
5		31	Merchandise Inventory		136 0 0 0 00		5
6			Income Summary			136 0 0 0 00	6

GENERAL JOURNAL   PAGE _____

2.

	DATE		DESCRIPTION	POST. REF.	DEBIT	CREDIT	
1	20–		**Adjusting Entries**				1
2	Dec.	31	Cost of Goods Sold		2 0 0 0 00		2
3			Merchandise Inventory			2 0 0 0 00	3

GENERAL JOURNAL   PAGE _____

3.

	DATE		DESCRIPTION	POST. REF.	DEBIT	CREDIT	
1	20–						1
2	Dec.	1	Cash		20 0 0 0 00		2
3			Unearned Revenue			20 0 0 0 00	3
4			To record collection of cash				4
5			for a four-month job.				5
6							6
7			Adjusting Entry				7
8		31	Unearned Revenue		5 0 0 0 00		8
9			Remodeling Revenue			5 0 0 0 00	9
10			To record one month's				10
11			revenue earned.				11

GENERAL JOURNAL   PAGE _____

4. a. $250,000 total assets − $140,000 noncurrent assets = $110,000 current assets
   $130,000 total liabilities − $80,000 long-term liabilities = $50,000 current liabilities
   $110,000 current assets − $50,000 current liabilities = $60,000 working capital

   b. $\dfrac{\$110,000 \text{ current assets}}{\$50,000 \text{ current liabilities}} = 2.2$ current ratio

CHAPTERS 14–15

Part I

A. 1. January 18 of the next year; 2. $12,000; 3. $360; 4. $12,360; 5. $306

B. 1. January 18 of the next year; 2. $8,000; 3. $160; 4. Discount on Notes Payable, $160; 5. $8,160; 6. $128; 7. Debit Interest Expense, credit Discount on Notes Payable; 8. Debit Interest Expense, $32.00; credit Discount on Notes Payable, $32.00

Part II

A. 1. Debit Notes Receivable, $9,000; credit Accounts Receivable, Fryer Company, $9,000; 2. Debit Interest Receivable, $59.50; credit Interest Income, $59.50; 3. February 1 of the next year; 4. $9,127.50; 5. Debit Cash, $9,127.50; credit Notes Receivable, $9,000; credit Interest Income, $127.50

B. 1. 20 days; 2. 70 days; 3. $6,500; 4. $6,630; 5. $109.58; 6. $6,520.42; 7. Interest Income; 8. $20.42

CHAPTERS 16–18

Part I

1. F; 2. T; 3. F; 4. F; 5. T; 6. T; 7. F; 8. F; 9. F; 10. T

Part II

1. book value or net realizable value; 2. specific charge-off; 3. bankruptcy; 4. LIFO; 5. specific identification; 6. perpetual inventory; 7. Land Improvements; 8. accelerated; 9. revenue expenditures; 10. periodic

Part III

1. E; 2. O; 3. I; 4. N; 5. F; 6. B; 7. C; 8. J; 9. K; 10. L

CHAPTERS 19–22

Part I

1. F; 2. T; 3. T; 4. T; 5. T; 6. T; 7. F; 8. F; 9. T; 10. F; 11. T; 12. T

Part II

1. Liquidation; 2. mutual agency; 3. outstanding stock; 4. stockholders; 5. cash dividend; 6. stock dividend; 7. appropriation of retained earnings; 8. amortization; 9. premium; 10. contra-liability

Part III

A. Partnerships

	Lopez's Share	Rell's Share
0.	$40,000	$40,000
1.	60,000	20,000
2.	45,000	35,000
3.	37,500	42,500
4.	40,900	39,100
5.	38,500	41,500

B. Corporations

Stockholders' Equity			
Paid-in Capital:			
1. Preferred 8 Percent Stock, $50 par, cumulative (20,000 shares authorized, 4,800 shares issued)	$240,000		
2. Preferred 8 Percent Stock Subscribed (600 shares)	30,000	$ 270,000	
3. Common Stock, $10 par (160,000 shares authorized, 75,000 shares issued)		750,000	
4. Paid-in Capital from Donation		6,500	
5. Total Paid-in Capital		$1,026,500	
6. Retained Earnings		240,000	
7. Total Stockholders' Equity			$1,266,500

CHAPTERS 23–26

Part I

1. F; 2. T; 3. T; 4. F; 5. F; 6. T; 7. F; 8. F; 9. T; 10. F; 11. T; 12. T

Part II

1. $442,500; 2. $84,000; 3. $34,000; 4. Cost of Goods Sold; 5. Quick Assets; 6. Net Sales on Account; 7. direct; 8. departmental margin; 9. Factory overhead; 10. Manufacturing Summary

Part III

A. 1. $740; 2. $22,200

B. 1. 1:04; 2. $300,000

C. Department X = $1,067, Y = $1,333, Z = $1,600

Photo Credits

Introduction

p. 2, Tony Freeman/PhotoEdit, Inc.; p. 4, Michael Newman/PhotoEdit, Inc.; p. 5, © Syracuse Newspaper/Gary Walts/The Image Works.

Chapter 1

p. 8, AP Photo/Paul Vathis; p. 10, Tony Freeman/PhotoEdit, Inc; p. 16, Bob Daemmrich/Stock, Boston.

Chapter 2

p. 39, Digital Vision/Getty Images; p. 49, Terry Huseby/Getty Images; p. 52, Myrleen Ferguson Cate/PhotoEdit, Inc.

Chapter 3

p. 76, John Elk/Stock Boston; p. 92, Chris Fredrikson/Alamy.

Chapter 4

p. 126, Rudi Von Vriel/PhotoEdit, Inc.

Chapter 5

p. 157, Jeff Greenberg/PhotoEdit, Inc; p. 164, David Young Wolff/PhotoEdit, Inc.

Chapter 6

p. 200, R. P. Kingston/Index Stock; p. 202, Richard Pasley/Stock Boston; p. 204, Brian Hainer/PhotoEdit, Inc.

Chapter 7

p. 232, Courtesy, JP Morgan Chase Corporation; p. 242, Tony Freeman/PhotoEdit, Inc; p. 246, Chris Salvo/Taxi/Getty Images.

Chapter 8

p. 270, Bruce Forester/Getty Images; p. 271 (left), C. Greenlar/The Image Works; p. 271 (right), Bilderbox/INSADCO Photography/Alamay; p. 278, Courtesy of United Way.

Chapter 9

p. 296, Stephen Perry/Getty Images; p. 302, B. Roland/The Image Works; p. 313, Alan Thornton/Getty Images; p. 315, Gregg Mancuso/Stock Boston.

Chapter 10

p. 358, Check Pefley/Alamy.

Chapter 11

p. 392, AFP/Getty Images; p. 397, Bill Aaron/PhotoEdit, Inc.

Chapter 12

p. 444, Bob Mahoney.

Chapter 13

p. 482, Joe Sohm/Stock Boston; p. 486, Bob Daemmrich/Stock Boston.

Chapter 14

p. 537, © Novastock/PhotoEdit, Inc; p. 543, Mark Richards/PhotoEdit, Inc.

Chapter 15

p. 568, David Young Wolff/PhotoEdit, Inc; p. 573, Bob Daemmrich/Stock Boston; p. 576, Swerve/Alamy.

Chapter 16

p. 597, David Young Wolff/PhotoEdit, Inc; p. 603, Mark Burnett/Stock Boston; p. 611, Tony Freeman/PhotoEdit, Inc.

Chapter 17

p. 633, Robert Llewellyn/Image State/Alamy; p. 635, Richard Pasley/Stock Boston; p. 641, Monika Graff/The Image Works.

Chapter 18

p. 670, Al Bello/Getty Images.

Chapter 19

p. 717, Bill Aaron/PhotoEdit, Inc; p. 723, Mark Antman/The Image Works.

Chapter 20

p. 757, Kayte M. Deioma/PhotoEdit, Inc; p. 758, Paul Hellstern/Bloomberg News/Landov; p. 761, C. Savino/The Image Works.

Chapter 21

p. 790, Bob Daemmrich/The Image Works; p. 798, Ziggy Kaluzny/Stone/Getty Images; p. 801, B.D. Lanphere/Stock Boston.

Chapter 22

p. 824, Joe Sohm/The Image Works; p. 833, © Ed Quinn/Corbis; p. 837, James Nubile/The Image Works.

Chapter 23

p. 853, Joel Rifkin/PhotoEdit, Inc.; p. 855, Rhoda Sidney/PhotoEdit, Inc; p. 859, Michael Newman/PhotoEdit, Inc.

Chapter 24

p. 911, Susan Van Etten/PhotoEdit, Inc.; p. 916, Jonathan Nourok/PhotoEdit, Inc; p. 918, Lee Snider/The Image Bank.

Chapter 25

p. 942, Billy Barnes/PhotoEdit, Inc; p. 947, David Young Wolff/PhotoEdit, Inc; p. 954, Jon Feingersh/Stock Boston.

Chapter 26

p. 979, John Zoiner/Workbook Stock/Getty Images; p. 987, C. Crandall/The Image Works; p. 990, Cary Wolinsky/Stock Boston.

Index

Note: Boldface type indicates key terms and the pages on which they are defined.